THE LAW OF PUBLIC EDUCATION

FOURTH EDITION

By

E. EDMUND REUTTER, JR.
Professor of Education, Teachers College
Columbia University

Westbury, New York
THE FOUNDATION PRESS, INC.
1994

Library of Congress Cataloging-in-Publication Data

Reutter, E. Edmund, 1924–
    The law of public education / by E. Edmund Reutter, Jr. — 4th ed.
        p. cm.
    Includes index.
    ISBN 1–56662–154–2
    1. Educational law and legislation—United States—Cases.
I. Title.
KF4118.R4   1994
344.73'071—dc20
[347.30471]   94–15897

To Bettie
 —still a constant inspiration

*

PREFACE

This textbook-casebook is designed to provide basic knowledge of the law directly affecting public education in the United States. The textual material covers principles and patterns of law applied to problems of education. In the Fourth Edition important recent developments are woven into the conceptual framework that has been used since the First Edition in 1970. The substantially increased textual portion includes significant points of law decided or clarified since the Third Edition, expanded treatment of some subjects, and addition of some topics.

The more than 2300 judicial decisions selected for specific citation on concrete points in the footnotes and notes-on-cases were chosen as being among the most authoritative and clear illustrations of the applicable law. The screening should enhance usefulness of the book as a reference volume and starting point for further exploration and research.

Except for Chapter 1, which is intended for those unfamiliar with the general operation of the law, each chapter focuses on the legal aspects of an area in education. As obviously there is overlapping among these areas, extensive use of the Table of Contents and the Index is recommended.

The 145 principal cases, 28 newly presented, provide opportunity to examine firsthand the reasoning of the courts in deciding important issues. The cases were edited to improve readability by deleting material unimportant to themes of education law, yet to preserve flavor as well as continuity. (Omissions, except of citations, are marked. Citations left in opinions are given by name for cases listed in the Table of Cases and in complete form for others.) The cases were selected individually for their value as precedents on substantive points decided, and collectively to illustrate judicial processes applied to educational matters. Notes appended to the cases are intended to enhance understanding of issues and principles.

I should like to take this occasion to articulate my deep gratitude to Robert R. Hamilton (long-time Dean, College of Law, University of Wyoming), teacher and friend for 35 years. Among our many collaborations are the first two editions and supplements of this book. A pioneer in the field of education law, his writing and teaching significantly helped to shape an area of specialization at the intersection of two professions.

Effort has been made to analyze and synthesize the judicial interpretations of constitutions, statutes, rules and regulations, and the common law in an objective manner. Personal value judgments, legal or educational, have been avoided. It is hoped, however, that readers will concern themselves ultimately not only with what the law is, but with what it should be. Intelligent decisions concerning the latter, however, are dependent on a knowledge of the former. To help supply such knowledge to students and practitioners of education and of law is the purpose of this volume.

E. EDMUND REUTTER, JR.

April 1994

SUMMARY OF CONTENTS

*

TABLE OF CONTENTS

*

TABLE OF LEGAL TOPICS
ILLUSTRATED BY CASES

*

TABLE OF CASES

Principal cases are in italic type. Non-principal cases are in roman type. References are to Pages.

TABLE OF CASES

xlix

lii

THE LAW OF PUBLIC EDUCATION

*

Chapter 1

LEGAL FRAMEWORK FOR
PUBLIC EDUCATION

The public education system in the United States is an instrumentality for carrying out a function that society has determined to be a desirable one—the education of all the children of all the people. At the outset of any discussion of the law as it relates to public education, it must be understood that although there is much law which relates specifically to education, there is an infinitely greater body which relates to the operation of government generally and affects education by the fact that the educational system is a part of government. Thus it becomes important to understand the origins and types of law under which our society, including the public school system, operates.

The Common Law

Much attention was given in medieval England to the "discovery" of law under the spur of a belief that there were always laws of nature to deal with problems if those laws could but be found.[1] Much effort was given to the study of court decisions in all parts of the realm with the purpose of finding what was the widely held view of the natural law. Professional committees, which Churchill described as "half colleges, half law schools," produced annual "yearbooks," whose authority was recognized by the judges.[2] Thus, common law is "discovered" law in contrast to the enacted law of constitutions and statutes. Common law is the law that emerges from the case decisions—"case law."

The original law in the United States was founded on the common law of England. Certain customs became the accepted bases of proper conduct. These customs became crystalized into principles that in specific cases were enunciated by the courts. These judicial pronouncements formed American common law. The courts then tended to follow their earlier decisions and there came into being the doctrine of "stare decisis," "let the decision stand." The greater part of the law today is still basically common law. The principles of land ownership, the rights and responsibilities of parents relative to minor children, the elements of a contract, the essentials of torts, and a myriad of other legal concepts are based on common law doctrines. Thus, the fundamental principles governing many aspects of public school operation are not the result of

1. Blackstone embraced this belief in his famous commentaries (circa 1760). It is reflected in the Declaration of Independence. Today some such concept as "widespread agreement" would more likely be invoked as a basis for the values underlying law.

2. Churchill, Winston S., *History of the English Speaking Peoples* (New York: Dodd, Mead, 1956–58), Vol. 1, p. 224.

statutory or constitutional provisions, but rather exist by virtue of the common law.

The Federal Constitution

The Constitution of the United States is the basic law of the land. All statutes passed by Congress, state constitutions, state legislation, ordinances of local government units, and rules and regulations of boards of education are subject to the provisions of the Constitution of the United States. The Constitution covers a wide area of powers, duties, and limitations, but at no point does it refer expressly to education.

Tenth Amendment

Because of the preceding fact, education becomes a state function under the Tenth Amendment, which provides:

> The powers not delegated to the United States by the Constitution, nor prohibited by it to the States, are reserved to the States respectively, or to the people.

However, it should not be concluded from this fact that the federal Constitution does not affect education. The number of education cases in which the Constitution is directly involved has been increasing at a very rapid rate in recent years.

There are relatively few sections of the original Constitution that with any frequency find their way into the legal problems arising in the operation of the schools. The sections that bear most intimately on the schools are the amendments which protect the rights of individuals. The restrictions on the power of Congress and the states that most frequently come before the courts for interpretation in education settings are Article I, Section 10, and the First, Fourth, Fifth, and Fourteenth Amendments.

Contracts Clause

Early in our national history the importance of preserving the integrity of contracts became apparent to our forebears. It was recognized that unless contractual agreements between parties may be relied upon without possible subsequent modification or abrogation by the law of the states, the economy of the country could not progress and develop. Thus, Article I, Section 10, provides in part that "no State shall * * * pass any * * * law impairing the obligation of contracts." As illustrated subsequently, this provision of the Constitution can be involved when, for example, the legislature of a state seeks to change a teacher tenure, salary, or retirement statute to the possible detriment of teachers who acquired a particular status under the law. One of the important considerations will be whether the relationship between the state and the teachers is in fact a contractual one. If it is held to be so, it may not be changed without violating Article I, Section 10, of the Constitution of the United States.

First Amendment

Following the establishment of the Constitution, it became apparent to our political leaders that perhaps the Constitution had created a federal government which, unless its powers were restricted, might ride roughshod over the civil rights of individual citizens. Consequently, ten amendments comprising the so-called Bill of Rights were adopted in 1791.

The First Amendment was designed to insure certain basic personal freedoms or civil rights. It is as follows:

Congress shall make no law respecting an establishment of religion, or prohibiting the free exercise thereof; or abridging the freedom of speech, or of the press; or the right of the people peaceably to assemble, and to petition the Government for a redress of grievances.

The first portion of the Amendment ("Congress shall make no law respecting an establishment of religion, or prohibiting the free exercise thereof") through the years has much affected education matters. The right of every individual to worship according to the dictates of personal conscience and free of government intervention is a right which, from the beginning of the country, has been considered a fundamental one. It will be observed that the restrictions concerning religion relate solely to the power of Congress in this regard. However, by interpretation of the Fourteenth Amendment, the Supreme Court has held that this restriction applies to the states as well as to Congress.

This clause of the First Amendment is involved in two categories of school cases: those involving use of public funds for parochial schools or students, and those involving regulations or procedures in public schools which are objected to on religious grounds. Chapter 2 is devoted to consideration of these church-state-education cases.

The "freedom of speech" provision in recent years has become the part of the First Amendment most often invoked in education cases. Most of the large number of judicial decisions regarding so-called civil rights of students and teachers have substantially involved the area of expression—spoken, written, or symbolic. Increasing attention is being brought to bear on the rights of assembly and petition as employee organizations engage in concerted actions to influence educational policies, especially those affecting working conditions. Over the years a derivative right of "association" has evolved through Supreme Court decisions interpreting the First Amendment.

Fourth and Fifth Amendments

The Fourth Amendment forbids "unreasonable searches and seizures" and provides that warrants "describing the place to be searched, and the persons or things to be seized" can be issued only "upon probable cause." The amendment may be germane in school situations when there develops a criminal prosecution based on evidence obtained on school premises with the involvement of school authorities. In addition, the amendment is sometimes mentioned in connection with the concept of a right of "privacy," which right is also associated with the concept of liberty in the Fourteenth Amendment.

The Fifth Amendment, which provides certain protections for persons accused of crimes, includes the following:

> No person * * * shall be compelled in any criminal case to be a witness against himself, nor be deprived of life, liberty, or property, without due process of law; nor shall private property be taken for public use, without just compensation.

The last clause is relevant in cases where states or local school boards attempt to acquire property for school building sites. The next to the last clause provides "due process" as regards acts of the federal government. The remainder of the quoted part of the amendment is implicated in matters encompassing possible crimes, such as connections which teachers or other public officials or employees may have with subversive organizations or illegal dealings involving school funds or property. It should be observed that school operations essentially involve civil matters, as distinguished from criminal.

Fourteenth Amendment

Section 1 of the Fourteenth Amendment defines citizenship and specifies certain privileges which citizens of the United States and other persons have. Its provisions are as follows:

> All persons born or naturalized in the United States, and subject to the jurisdiction thereof, are citizens of the United States and of the State wherein they reside. No State shall make or enforce any law which shall abridge the privileges or immunities of citizens of the United States; nor shall any State deprive any person of life, liberty, or property, without due process of law; nor deny to any person within its jurisdiction the equal protection of the laws.

The parts of this Amendment having most application to public education are the last two clauses. The next to last clause is the well-known "due process" clause, which, possibly, has been construed more frequently than any other provision of the Constitution; the last is the "equal protection" clause. Both have had wide interpretation in cases involving the administration of the public school system.

It is important to observe that "due process" includes two distinct aspects. "Substantive" due process pertains to legislation itself. A law must have a purpose within the power of government to pursue, and it must be rationally related to the accomplishment of that purpose. Substantive due process protects against grossly unfair acts of government. "Procedural" due process pertains to the decision-making process followed in determining whether the law has been violated. A basic fairness in adjudication is required of those purporting to implement the law. The party who may suffer the deprivation must be told what he is accused of having done, and be offered an opportunity to defend his actions before an impartial tribunal.

The core thrust of "equal protection" is that individuals or groups that are similar must be treated in similar fashion. All within a classification must be accorded the same rights and privileges and be subjected to the same duties. Classifications per se also are subject to examination. They must be based on differences relevant to the subject and not prohibited by law. Failure of government to follow these principles can constitute forbidden "discrimination".

The general constitutional test for acceptability of a criterion for classification is whether it is somehow rationally related to a legitimate governmental objective. The very strong presumption is that a criterion established through the legislative process is constitutional. If, however, the classification is based on a constitutionally "suspect" factor (such as race) or a legislatively "protected" factor (such as age in some situations) the courts will require a compelling justification. Some classification bases (such as illegitimacy) fall in-between.

In the discussion of the First Amendment it was pointed out that, by interpretation of the Supreme Court, the Fourteenth Amendment makes the provisions of the First applicable to the states. Thus, restrictions of the First and Fourteenth Amendments must be considered along with restrictions of the state constitution when examining the validity of a state statute or a local school board rule.

In the area of funding nonpublic schools both the Fourteenth and First Amendments must be examined. The Fourteenth Amendment proscription is against public funds being used for private purposes. The First Amendment's relevant bar is against public funds being used for religious purposes, a subcategory of private purposes.

A wide variety of types of education cases have seen the Fourteenth Amendment invoked. Among them are flag salute, rights of parents, racial segregation, teacher dismissal, uses of school funds, and student discipline.

Federal Statutes

As previously observed, pursuant to the Tenth Amendment Congress is not empowered to enact legislation controlling educational matters. However, Congress has the power to implement provisions of the Constitution throughout the nation. Thus, for example, public education systems are subject to the antidiscrimination-in-employment portions of the Civil Rights Act of 1964[3] and the Americans with Disabilities Act of 1990,[4] which were enacted under authority of the equal protection clause of the Fourteenth Amendment.

3. 42 U.S.C.A. § 2000e [popularly known as "Title VII," its designation in the Civil Rights Act of 1964, made applicable to public schools in 1972].

4. 42 U.S.C.A. § 12101.

The vast majority of the federal statutes directly and substantially affecting education policies, however, offer federal funds to the states conditioned upon the states' observing certain prescriptions for the use of the money. Congress acts under the "general welfare" clause when it offers funds for purposes it deems to serve the public good. If a state elects to accept the money, it is bound by the conditions attached. A condition, of course, must not be unconstitutional, which determination is made by the federal courts in a properly presented case. Also, what a condition means in a specific operational situation is in the province of the federal courts in their role of interpreters of federal legislation. Rights created by federal legislation of the "funding" type are completely enforceable where the funds are involved.

Beginning in the 1960's Congress has passed several statutes that require or prohibit certain conduct by state and local authorities in connection with any "program or activity receiving Federal financial assistance." (In 1987 Congress defined "program or activity" to encompass "all of the operations of [an entity] any part of which is extended Federal financial assistance.") The broad general prohibitions cover "race, color or national origin," [5] "sex," [6] and "otherwise qualified handicapped individuals." [7] In 1975 Congress passed the Education for All Handicapped Children Act,[8] which mandates that states accepting federal financial assistance provide for handicapped children a "free appropriate public education which emphasizes special education and related services designed to meet their unique needs." The Act requires states as a condition of qualification for funds to establish detailed procedures for identifying such children, for developing "individualized education programs" for them, for involving parents in the process, and for various related matters. In 1990 the name of the Act was changed to Individuals with Disabilities Education Act.

IDEA

State Constitutions

Subject to the supremacy of the federal Constitution (and federal statutes enacted within Congress's powers), state constitutions form the basic law of the individual states. The primary function of state constitutions is to restrict the powers of state legislatures, which have complete legislative authority except as restricted by federal law or state constitutions. State constitutions may require legislatures to perform certain acts (such as establishing public education systems) and may forbid certain acts (such as using the state's credit to support private ventures).

Very frequently state constitutions deal with the same matters which have been treated in the federal Constitution. This is most

5. 42 U.S.C.A. § 2000d [popularly known as "Title VI," its designation in the Civil Rights Act of 1964].

6. 20 U.S.C.A. § 1681 [popularly known as "Title IX," its designation in the Education Amendments of 1972].

7. 29 U.S.C.A. § 794 [popularly known as "Section 504," its designation in the Rehabilitation Act of 1973].

8. 20 U.S.C.A. § 1401 [popularly known as "P.L. 94–142," its designation when passed as a federal statute].

common in the areas of church-state relations and individual freedoms. States may provide more, but not fewer, bars to governmental relations with religious bodies than are mandated by the federal Constitution. States may provide more, but not fewer, rights to teachers and students than are required by the federal Constitution.

Because the state constitution is a direct product of the people themselves, no legislature, although it represents the people, has sole authority to amend a state constitution. Indeed, the legislature itself is a creature of the constitution. Thus, it follows that it would have no authority to amend the document which gives it existence. Procedures for amending state constitutions are found within those documents. Normally the amendment of a constitution is a rather slow process because of the importance of deliberation before changes are made in such a fundamental legal document.

It should be noted that a specific state statute may violate both the federal Constitution and the constitution of the state involved, may violate neither, or may violate one and not the other. For example, in the single area of church-state-education relations, all four possibilities come to the fore.

State Statutes and Local Regulations

The most abundant source of law affecting public schools is found in the statutes enacted by state legislatures, which have vast power in this area. The courts consistently say that the power of the state legislatures over the public school systems of the respective states is plenary. This, of course, is true only in a relative sense. As indicated above, a state legislature is always subject to the limitations of federal law and of the state constitution in its actions as they apply to education, just as is the case with legislation applying to other agencies and segments of society.

Obviously public school systems, as well as many other governmental agencies, have become so complex that it is impossible, or even undesirable, to attempt to control their administration in detail by specific legislative enactments. In recognition of this fact, the law is well settled that state and local boards of education, school administrators, and classroom teachers have the authority to adopt and enforce reasonable rules and regulations for the operation and management of the public school system. Such rules and regulations are, within the area in which they are authorized to operate, as truly "law" as is an enactment of Congress or of a state legislature. It follows that they are subject to the same constitutional limitations as specific statutes passed by duly constituted legislative bodies. It is as possible for a teacher, through the promulgation of a rule or regulation for classroom management, to violate the civil rights of students as it is for the legislature to do so. For example, if it is unconstitutional for Congress or a state legislature to enact a law violating a child's freedom of religion, it is equally unconstitutional for a teacher to do so by a regulation applicable only to one classroom.

It is important to observe that "legislation" or "rule-making" on any level within the state cannot be in conflict with higher authority. For instance, a local school board cannot require payment of fees if such is prohibited on the state level. On the other hand, a local school board cannot be required to perform an act not mandated by higher authority.

The Courts

In General

The common law, constitutional provisions, statutes, and rules and regulations of the various levels of school administration are not self-executing. They merely permit or require the respective agencies of government, including the educational system, to take or not to take certain actions pursuant to their provisions. If an individual or a body affected by a provision believes it is being improperly implemented, resort to the courts is available to settle the controversy. Courts do not act on their own initiatives. They can assume jurisdiction only of disputes properly referred to them for decision.

The technical responsibility of the various courts is to interpret the law within the scope of their respective jurisdictions. If there is no codified law, a court applies common law. Because common law is created by courts, however, courts may adjust it to changing conditions. Where there is legislation it becomes the task of the court to determine, as far as possible, what it deems was the "intent" of the legislative body when it enacted the law in question. In many cases the conclusion is almost impossible to escape that the court is obliged to impute to the legislature the intent which the court thinks the legislature would have had in a particular case had the matter been called specifically to its attention. The courts cannot avoid taking some account in their decisions of the economic, political, social, educational, and perhaps other implications of the cases before them. The extent to which this should be done is a subject of disagreement among legal scholars.

Although in some respects the judicial system in the United States is a rather complicated one, it may be described very broadly in terms of the federal system and the state system.

Federal System

The matter of federal jurisdiction is an area in which many learned treatises have been written, but for purposes of this volume it may be said that recourse usually may be had to the federal courts when a federal constitutional question or a federal statute is involved, or when there is diversity of state residence between litigants.

Federal jurisdiction is created by acts of Congress. Since the 1960's one such provision has profoundly affected public education, along with other governmental functions, by serving as a basis for suits in federal courts. The statute goes back to the Civil Rights Act of 1871, but it has been revitalized and utilized as a vehicle for federal court scrutiny of many rules of school authorities pertaining to students or teachers. The provision, popularly known as "Section 1983," reads:

> Every person who, under color of any statute, ordinance, regulation, custom, or usage, of any State or Territory, subjects, or causes to be subjected, any citizen of the United States or other person within the jurisdiction thereof to the deprivation of any rights, privileges, or immunities secured by the Constitution and laws, shall be liable to the party injured in an action at law, suit in equity, or other proper proceeding for redress.[9]

By invoking this section a student or teacher who claims the deprivation of a federal constitutional or statutory right by the act of a school authority or by operation of a regulation often can invoke federal jurisdiction and in effect have the federal courts rule on the regulation in the process of adjudicating his complaint against school officials in situations where federal jurisdiction might be difficult to establish otherwise. However, Section 1983 does not require federal courts to hear and decide all suits in which unconstitutional deprivations are asserted. A federal constitutional or statutory question must exist in substance, not in mere assertion. The federal courts on the whole, however, have become very receptive to such suits in recent years.

The federal trial court of general jurisdiction is named the United States District Court. Each state contains one or more districts, for a total of 89 federal districts. In addition, separate districts exist in the District of Columbia, Puerto Rico, and certain territories. From 1910 to 1976 if it was sought to enjoin the enforcement of a state statute on the ground that it violated the federal Constitution, a special three-judge District Court was required. Appeals from such courts went directly to the Supreme Court. In 1976 Congress sharply curtailed the types of cases that were to be handled in this manner.

For appeals of all but special types of cases in the federal judicial system, the country is divided into 12 "circuits." There is a United States Court of Appeals for each circuit.[10] (See chart on page 15.) Rulings of each Court of Appeals are binding on federal trial courts in the states within its circuit and persuasive on other courts. Cases in Courts of Appeals usually are heard and decided by three-judge panels. Under special circumstances all judges in a circuit will hear a case. This is called "en banc." Appeals from circuit court decisions are to the Supreme Court of the United States.

State Systems

Each state has its own judicial system established by its constitution and legislature. The various state systems vary in organization and

9. 42 U.S.C.A. § 1983.

10. With general appellate jurisdiction, there are 11 "numbered" circuits, plus the District of Columbia Circuit. (In 1981 the states now in the Eleventh Circuit were detached from the Fifth Circuit.) In 1982 the United States Court of Appeals for the Federal Circuit was established to assume appellate jurisdiction over patents, federal government contracts, federal merit system protection, trademarks, and international trade.

degree of complexity. The judicial system generally includes a number of inferior courts, each having limited jurisdiction expressly indicated in the law creating it. There is an appropriate trial court for each type of controversy. There is no consistency in names given such courts from state to state. In each state there are one or two levels of appellate courts. Names of these, too, vary and must be checked for each state to determine a court's status in the judicial hierarchy. The highest court in any state is referred to generically as the "court of last resort." In those states having two levels of appeal, the court of first appeal is known as the "intermediate appellate court." In these states the absolute right of appeal for some cases is only to the intermediate appellate court.

Of course, state courts are bound by the United States Constitution and are obliged to apply it in their decisions, which are reviewable under certain conditions by the Supreme Court of the United States. State courts, however, are considered to be parallel to federal district and circuit courts. They are not subordinate to them. Thus, state courts are not bound by decisions of such courts as to the meaning of the federal Constitution or federal statutes. State courts' interpretations of federal law are subject to review only by the Supreme Court.

Because education is a state function and federal courts exist for federal matters, most education controversies are handled by state courts. Unless there is a substantial federal question the case must be tried in a state court. If a substantial federal question is involved along with state questions, either state or federal courts can be utilized. The increased emphasis in more recent years on civil rights and liberties and the increased use of "Section 1983" for federal jurisdiction has led to increasing numbers of education cases being decided in federal courts. When a federal court decides a case involving both state and federal law, it must follow any interpretations of state law made by the state's courts, for the meaning of state law is for state courts to enunciate.

The Supreme Court

Established by the Constitution and superior to all courts, state and federal, on federal matters is the Supreme Court of the United States. This nine-member body is required to consider appeals in a limited number of situations, but can summarily affirm lower court holdings or dismiss the appeals "for want of a substantial federal question," rather than deciding the cases with full opinions after examining the complete record of lower court proceedings, studying briefs, and hearing oral arguments. In addition, the Court is empowered at its discretion to reexamine the holdings of federal Courts of Appeals and those of final courts in state systems when federal constitutional or statutory issues have been ruled on. Such a proceeding is known as "certiorari." If four Justices so vote, a case is accepted for review. When the case is decided, the "opinion of the Court" authoritatively enunciates the federal law on

ivil - preponderance of the evidence

lawsuit
file a complaint / petition
- certain facts are alleged
- show that law has been violated
* injunction against illegal
acts / maintain legal status quo
* mandamus - perform a
non-discretionary duty
ie - required by law
statute or regulation challenged
in court
- on its face - completely
invalid & incapable of any
legal application

the matter and explains the reasoning behind the decision.[11]

Operational Aspects

The procedures of federal and state courts are complex in many respects, being an amalgam of statutes, rules, and common law. Some basic items, however, are generally consistent and must be understood by those working with education law.

A lawsuit is started by the filing of a complaint or, as it is called in some states, a petition, in which certain facts are alleged. These facts are designed to show that some law is being or has been violated, or that some individual or agency is not performing or has not performed a duty imposed upon it by law. The party who initiates the action, usually called the "plaintiff," requests that the court grant specific relief. One, for example, may ask that the court find that a contract with the board of education has been broken and that plaintiff receive from the district such damages as flowed from the breach of the contract. Or, it may be requested that certain actions of a board of education be declared illegal. If the plaintiff is seeking to require a public officer or agency to perform a nondiscretionary duty, the action is called "mandamus." If an agency or an individual allegedly is indulging in certain illegal activity, the plaintiff may ask that the court grant an "injunction" ordering the party to discontinue the illegal acts.

Injunctions also may be sought to maintain the legal status quo by preventing an action that is being contemplated. Permanent injunctions are issued after trials on "the merits" (the substance of the controversy). Preliminary or temporary injunctions are put into effect temporarily, pending full adjudication of the matter. Temporary injunctions are issued when the plaintiff can show he will suffer irreparable harm if relief is not granted at once, that there is a reasonable probability or substantial likelihood he will prevail on the merits, that the threatened injury to the plaintiff outweighs the potential harm an injunction would do to the defendant, and that the public interest will not suffer. The court's reasoning on a motion for a preliminary injunction is instructive on the law, but the court cannot ultimately apply the law to the facts until they are fully adduced at a trial.

Courts do not decide hypothetical cases. Not only must there be a genuine controversy, but the plaintiff must have an individualized legal interest in the resolution of the disputed point. Common law precedents grant a "standing to sue" to taxpayers wishing to challenge local school board expenditures. Merely being a taxpayer, however, under the common law generally does not accord standing to sue state-level agencies, and taxpayer status definitely does not give standing to sue federal-level agencies. In the absence of a statute, an individual bringing an action

---

11. Opinions of the Supreme Court in cases directly involving education matters or having substantial impact thereon are analyzed and synthesized in Reutter, E. Edmund, Jr., *The Supreme Court's Impact on* *Public Education* (Bloomington, Ind., and Topeka, Kan.: Phi Delta Kappa and National Organization on Legal Problems of Education, 1982).

solely to contest a state or federal expenditure must allege some individualized harm, not simply an injury that would be suffered by all citizens or taxpayers.

When a statute or a regulation is being challenged in court, the attack may be either "on its face" or "as applied." A facial challenge involves a claim that the provision is completely invalid and incapable of any legal application. In such a situation the court is not required to examine the facts of any actual instances of alleged unlawfulness.

In most situations the ultimate burden of proof in a lawsuit lies with the plaintiff. In civil cases, as distinguished from criminal cases, the general standard of proof is "preponderance of the evidence." Sometimes, however, after the plaintiff has established an initial point, the burden may be shifted to the defendant to counter inferences by proving another point. As illustration, if a teacher who is contesting the nonrenewal of an employment contract can prove that an activity protected by the First Amendment was a substantial factor in the decision by the school board, the board then must bear the burden of demonstrating that the teacher's contract would not have been renewed even if the protected activity had not occurred.

Also, when a piece of legislation or an act of a government official is shown to infringe a "fundamental constitutional right" or disadvantage a "suspect class," courts apply so-called "strict scrutiny", and the burden shifts to the government to show a compelling need for the arrangement. Fundamental rights in this sense are those mentioned explicitly in the Constitution or those implicitly there as declared by the Supreme Court. Suspect classes are clearly defined groups that require extraordinary protection from the majoritarian political process because they suffer severe disabilities, have been subjected purposefully to grossly unequal treatment, or are relegated to a position of virtual political powerlessness.

A complaint may be dismissed before trial when the court determines that, beyond doubt, the allegations (if eventually proved) would not legally entitle the plaintiff to the relief requested. Also, a case may be terminated at trial if, after the plaintiff has presented its evidence, the court believes that the evidence, accepted as true, does not show a violation of law. If these two hurdles are passed by the plaintiff, the defendant must present its version of the situation.

The trial court then makes findings of fact (determinations of what events did occur) and applies to them the law, reaching conclusions that culminate in a judgment and decree specifying the outcome of the litigation. Federal District Courts and some state trial courts issue opinions explaining in detail the reasoning used. Although technically only the parties to a given case are bound by the court's ruling,[12] the

---

12. A "class action" case involves one or more representatives of a "class" bringing suit on behalf of all members of the class. If the court approves a suit as being a class action, the outcome is binding on all members of the class. To maintain a class action, the plaintiff(s) must assert claims typical of the class, the question(s) of law must be common to all members of the class, getting all members of the class into the

opinion becomes part of the common law, indicating what the outcome of a similar case likely would be unless there are material differences between the cases.

Appeals from trial court decisions may be taken to appellate courts. At least one level of appeal is available for all cases. The party bringing the appeal is known as the "appellant," the other party as the "appellee." The appellant attempts to demonstrate that the lower court erred either in its findings of fact, conclusions of law, or both. As to facts, the claim may be that the court admitted improper evidence, misinterpreted testimony and exhibits, or otherwise incorrectly conducted the trial. As to law, the claim may be that the judge applied the wrong law or misconstrued the law in some fashion in reaching the judgment.

The appellate court does not hear witnesses. Nor does it consider issues not raised in the trial court. It reviews the written record of the lower court proceedings, including the testimony of the witnesses, examines briefs, and usually hears oral arguments of both parties. It can affirm, reverse, or modify the judgment of the lower court, or it can order the case to be tried over. The case may be "remanded," that is, sent back to the lower court, with instructions to modify its decision or to retry the case. On questions of fact, the appellate court must accept the trial court's findings unless they are "clearly erroneous." This is because the trial court was "on the scene" to observe the parties and witnesses, whereas the appellate court has before it only a written record.[13] On conclusions of law, however, the appellate court owes no deference to the trial court's reasoning. It may simply disagree on what the law provides.

The "opinion of the court" is that of a majority of the judges deciding a case. This becomes the law of the case and is controlling within the court's jurisdiction. Judges who agree with the ultimate outcome but who do not support all of the reasoning as it is stated in the opinion of the majority may file concurring opinions. Dissenting opinions may also be recorded. It is, however, the opinion of the court, irrespective of the margin of the vote, that becomes the precedent.

The opinion of the appellate court indicates the point or points of contested law on which the lower court erred and those which it interpreted correctly. The higher the court in the judicial hierarchy, the more authoritative its opinions are. Lower courts within a jurisdiction are bound by the orders and opinions of higher courts of that jurisdiction. Under the common-law system, opinions of courts in one state, although not binding on courts in another state, are considered persuasive on points not differently treated by the respective legislatures. Decisions of a federal Court of Appeals are binding on lower federal

suit must be impracticable, and the plaintiff(s) must adequately protect the interests of the class.

13. If a trial court's factual findings are held to be clearly erroneous, the appellate court may not reach an outcome by independently considering the totality of circumstances as it sees them. Instead the case is to be remanded to the lower court.

courts within the circuit and persuasive elsewhere. As there is ultimately only one federal answer to a question of federal law, the Supreme Court usually grants certiorari to resolve disagreements among the circuits. Each time a judicial point of view is cited with approval by another court, the weight of the holding on the point is increased.

After a case has been decided by the highest court having jurisdiction, it becomes "res judicata" ("a matter judged"), and it may not subsequently be brought into court for further litigation. This is true not only for a specific court system, but also between state and federal courts when one system has decided the point. Furthermore, the doctrine bars any attempt to relitigate the same claim under a different theory of recovery.

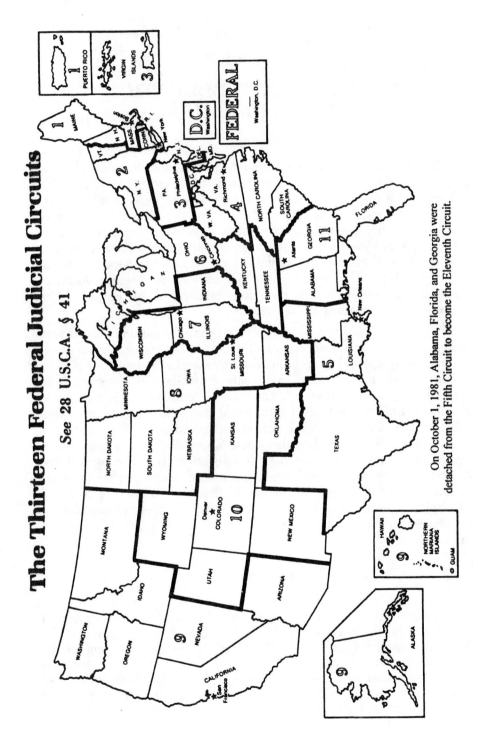

The Thirteen Federal Judicial Circuits

See 28 U.S.C.A. § 41

On October 1, 1981, Alabama, Florida, and Georgia were detached from the Fifth Circuit to become the Eleventh Circuit.

Chapter 2

CHURCH–STATE–EDUCATION
RELATIONSHIPS

In General

One of the most persistent areas of constitutional litigation affecting public education is that involving church-state-education relationships. Numerous cases on the subject have been decided by high state courts and federal courts. The Supreme Court of the United States since World War II has decided a score of cases squarely in the area of graded schools. It has declined to review or has affirmed without opinion a large number of other cases during the period and has decided some in other church-state areas that have implications for public education. Major church-state-education cases are collected in this chapter. The index should be checked for other cases.

One part of the First Amendment to the Constitution of the United States provides that "Congress shall make no law respecting an establishment of religion, or prohibiting the free exercise thereof." It is to be observed that this provision specifically prohibits only Congress from making such laws. However, United States Supreme Court interpretations beginning in 1940 [1] have established that this prohibition is applicable to the states, the legal link being provided by the Fourteenth Amendment. It follows then that citizens are afforded the same rights against state government as regards religion as they are against the federal government. State constitutions can place further bars on actions by the governments of specific states. While the so-called principle of "separation of church and state" is rarely philosophically challenged, applications of it in practice have led to an abundance of lawsuits.

The Oregon Case

What have turned out to be two key cases in the area were decided on bases other than the First Amendment. These two cases were argued before the Supreme Court of the United States on the basis of the Fourteenth Amendment alone. The first, and more important of the two, was decided in 1925 basically not as a case of civil or personal rights, but rather as a case of property rights.[2] An initiative act had been passed by the voters of Oregon requiring attendance in public schools by normal children between ages of 8 and 16 who had not

1. Cantwell v. Connecticut, 310 U.S. 296, 60 S.Ct. 900, 84 L.Ed. 1213 (1940).

2. Pierce v. Society of Sisters of the Holy Names of Jesus and Mary, 268 U.S. 510, 45 S.Ct. 571, 69 L.Ed. 1070 (1925).

completed the eighth grade. An injunction against enforcement was sought by a Catholic parochial school and a secular military academy.

The Supreme Court noted that enforcement of the statute would seriously impair, perhaps destroy, the profitable features of the schools' business and greatly diminish the value of their property. The Court based its unanimous decision essentially on the point that the schools had asked protection against unreasonable interference with their patrons and the consequent destruction of their business and property. Included in the decision, however, were several paragraphs which have become of great importance because of the doctrine set forth. These portions recognized the fundamental liberty of parents and guardians to direct the upbringing and education of the children under their control. The Court emphasized that the state had the power reasonably to regulate all schools, set up qualifications for teachers, and require that certain studies plainly essential to good citizenship be taught to all. But even though the state could regulate nonpublic schools, it was not empowered to eliminate them indirectly or directly.

Textbooks for Parochial School Students

The other "early" case, decided in 1930, involved a Louisiana statute which provided free textbooks for children regardless of the school they attended.[3] The law had been attacked on the grounds that it violated the Fourteenth Amendment by taking private property (through taxation) for a nonpublic purpose. The Supreme Court unanimously rejected the argument by accepting verbatim the reasoning of the Supreme Court of Louisiana that the beneficiaries of the act were the children, rather than the schools, and therefore a public purpose was served. Thus was born the "child benefit" doctrine that benefits which accrue to the child, rather than to the school, are not barred by the federal Constitution. It should be noted that in this case, even though the statute did not so specify, the Supreme Court of Louisiana stated in its opinion quoted by the Supreme Court of the United States that the same textbooks were to be furnished children in nonpublic schools as were furnished to children in public schools and that none of the books would be adapted to religious instruction. Again, it must be emphasized that the First Amendment question did not come before the Supreme Court of the United States in this case.

The question of free textbooks for children in nonpublic schools has been decided differently by state courts interpreting state constitutions, with several of the courts rejecting the "child benefit" reasoning and barring the practice under state constitutional provisions.[4] The Su-

---

3. Cochran v. Louisiana State Bd. of Educ., 281 U.S. 370, 50 S.Ct. 335, 74 L.Ed. 913 (1930).

4. E.g., Gaffney v. State Dep't of Educ., 192 Neb. 358, 220 N.W.2d 550 (1974); Paster v. Tussey, 512 S.W.2d 97 (Mo.1974), cert. den. 419 U.S. 1111, 95 S.Ct. 785, 42 L.Ed.2d 807 (1975); In re Advisory Opinion re Constitutionality of 1974 PA 242, 394 Mich. 41, 228 N.W.2d 772 (1975); Fannin v. Williams, 655 S.W.2d 480 (Ky.1983); Matter of Certification of a Question of Law from U.S. Dist. Court, Dist. of South Dakota, 372 N.W.2d 113 (S.D.1985).

preme Court of the United States in a six-to-three decision in 1968 found constitutional a statute which required local boards of education to loan books to children in grades 7 to 12 who attended nonpublic schools.[5] The statute did not require that the books be the same as those used in the public schools, but that they be approved by a board of education. The nub of the reasoning was the "child benefit" theory. The Court found that the purpose of the statute was not to aid religion or private schools, and that its primary effect would be to improve the quality of education for all. The Court stated that parents had a right to send their children to nonpublic schools, that the state had a right to regulate nonpublic schools, and that the state of New York relied heavily upon such schools for fulfillment of compulsory education requirements.

In 1974 the Court affirmed the decision of a three-judge federal District Court invalidating a New Jersey arrangement whereby parents of nonpublic school students were reimbursed for purchases of secular textbooks whereas public school students were lent textbooks.[6] That the reimbursement provision was directed exclusively to parents whose children were enrolled in private, primarily religious schools, constituted the violation of the clause prohibiting laws respecting an establishment of religion.

An Illinois statute provided that textbooks selected from a list maintained by the state superintendent of public instruction were to be furnished to nonpublic school students on the same basis as to public school students, with the state paying for costs of the service to nonpublic school students. Because the textbooks for public school students were purchased from local funds while those for nonpublic school students were paid for by state funds, the Supreme Court of Illinois invalidated the plan as one affording a special economic benefit to a single class of citizen.[7]

Transportation of Parochial School Students

In 1947 the Supreme Court answered the question whether a state can furnish transportation to children attending parochial schools.[8] The Everson, or New Jersey bus, case marked the first time the Court considered the application of the establishment of religion clause of the First Amendment in an educational context.

New Jersey had enacted a statute which permitted boards of education to arrange at public expense for the transportation of children to public or nonprofit schools. A school board authorized reimbursement to parents of money spent by them for bus fares to send their children to parochial schools. The statute was attacked by a taxpayer on the

---

5. Board of Educ. v. Allen, 392 U.S. 236, 88 S.Ct. 1923, 20 L.Ed.2d 1060 (1968). [Case No. 5]

6. Public Funds for Public Schools v. Marburger, 358 F.Supp. 29 (D.N.J.1973), aff. 417 U.S. 961, 94 S.Ct. 3163, 41 L.Ed.2d 1134 (1974).

7. People ex rel. Klinger v. Howlett, 56 Ill.2d 1, 305 N.E.2d 129 (1973).

8. Everson v. Board of Educ., 330 U.S. 1, 67 S.Ct. 504, 91 L.Ed. 711 (1947). [Case No. 1]

ground that it violated the federal Constitution in two respects: first, it authorized the state to take by taxation money of some citizens, and bestow it upon others to be used for private purposes, namely, the support of private schools, in contravention of the Fourteenth Amendment; second, it was one "respecting an establishment of religion" in that it forced him to contribute to the support of church schools, thus contravening the First Amendment.

By a five-to-four vote the Court sustained the constitutionality of the legislation. The Fourteenth Amendment contention was flatly rejected, because facilitating secular education is clearly a public purpose. As to the First Amendment, the opinion of the Court stated that neither a state nor the federal government could aid one religion, aid all religions, or prefer one religion over another; further, no tax, large or small, could be levied to support any religious activity or institution. However, the First Amendment did not prohibit a state from extending its general benefits to all its citizens without regard to their religious beliefs. The Court placed the furnishing of transportation of all pupils in the category of other public services for all, such as police, fire, and health protection. The transportation law was viewed as establishing a general program to help parents get their children, regardless of their religion, safely and expeditiously to and from their schools.

The decision in the Everson case left the issue to each state to decide for itself, and much litigation has ensued. About two years after Everson, the first case involving the same issue reached a state court of last resort, the Supreme Court of Washington.[9] That state had a statute which entitled all children attending school in accordance with the laws relating to compulsory attendance to use the transportation facilities provided by the school district in which they resided. The state constitution provided that no public money or property shall be appropriated for the support of any religious establishment. A board of education declined to furnish transportation to children attending a school owned and operated by the Sumas Christian School Society, Inc. The Society sued to require the board to furnish such transportation. The Everson case was relied upon as authority for sustaining the law. However, the court pointed out that the Everson case did nothing more than settle the parochial pupil transportation question in favor of the permissibility of such transportation as far as the First Amendment is concerned. In the opinion of the court, the state constitution was violated by the statute. The child-benefit, general-welfare reasoning of the United States Supreme Court was not persuasive to the majority of the Washington court.

In subsequent years the highest courts of many states have considered the issue and have reached contrary conclusions based on their respective state constitutions. Frequently the claim has been raised that not to furnish transportation to children attending nonpublic schools

9. Visser v. Nooksack Valley School Dist. No. 506, 33 Wash.2d 699, 207 P.2d 198 (1949).

denies them the equal protection required by the Fourteenth Amendment. This argument uniformly has been rejected.[10]

A different aspect of equal protection in relation to transportation arose in New Jersey under a statute which provided that children attending nonpublic schools had the same right (except for a dollar limitation) to transportation as children attending public schools.[11] Thus, if a child attending nonpublic school lived in a district which transported any public school children, he would be transported; otherwise he would not be eligible. Overruling a trial court decision that this arrangement violated the equal protection clause, the Supreme Court of New Jersey stated that the legislature does not have to choose between attacking every aspect of a problem or not attacking the problem at all. Likewise, a claim of unequal protection by parents of nonpublic school students was rejected by the Supreme Court of Appeals of West Virginia when it upheld the paying of transportation stipends to parents of parochial school students and the permitting of parochial school students to ride on buses on established public school bus routes, rather than the providing of direct school transportation.[12]

The constitutionality of giving transportation advantages to parochial school students has led to judicial results that appear not entirely consistent. A three-judge federal District Court in Iowa enjoined execution of a statutory provision that children attending nonpublic schools could be transported across district lines at public expense, whereas children attending public schools in districts other than those of their residences were charged for such service.[13] The court emphasized that the program was not one available to all children, as was the situation in the Everson case, but rather was a benefit available only to nonpublic school enrollees, thus advancing religious interests. However, a federal District Court that had cited the Iowa decision with approval in invalidating a Rhode Island statute was reversed by the First Circuit Court of Appeals.[14] The higher court, while recognizing that disparities favoring parochial school students are limited by the Constitution, ruled that strict equality in treatment is not constitutionally required, and allowing nonpublic school students transportation to any school within a given region of the state while restricting public school students to transportation within their school district was not an impermissible aid to religion.[15] The court based its holding on the fact that the Supreme Court,

---

10. Epeldi v. Engelking, 94 Idaho 390, 488 P.2d 860 (1971), cert. den. 406 U.S. 957, 92 S.Ct. 2058, 32 L.Ed.2d 343 (1972); Luetkemeyer v. Kaufmann, 364 F.Supp. 376 (W.D.Mo.1973), aff. 419 U.S. 888, 95 S.Ct. 167, 42 L.Ed.2d 134 (1974).

11. West Morris Regional Bd. of Educ. v. Sills, 58 N.J. 464, 279 A.2d 609 (1971), cert. den. 404 U.S. 986, 92 S.Ct. 450, 30 L.Ed.2d 370 (1971).

12. Janasiewicz v. Board of Educ. of County of Kanawha, 171 W.Va. 423, 299 S.E.2d 34 (1982).

13. Americans United for Separation of Church and State v. Benton, 413 F.Supp. 955 (S.D.Iowa 1975).

14. Members of Jamestown School Committee v. Schmidt, 699 F.2d 1 (1 Cir. 1983), cert. den. 464 U.S. 851, 104 S.Ct. 162, 78 L.Ed.2d 148 (1983).

15. The court invalidated a provision in the statute for variances to be granted by the State Commissioner of Education for transportation of nonpublic school students outside of their regions. The basis was that the plan fostered "excessive entanglement"

subsequent to the District Court's opinion, had dismissed "for want of a substantial federal question" several cases in which the Supreme Court of Pennsylvania had upheld a statute providing for transportation of nonpublic school students for up to ten miles beyond district lines.[16] Both the Supreme Court of Pennsylvania and the First Circuit, however, cautioned that the Constitution limits the permissible degree of disparity, including cost considerations, between transportation arrangements for public and nonpublic school students.

The Supreme Court of the United States in 1977 decided the question of use of publicly financed transportation for field trips by children enrolled in parochial schools. It held that such was prohibited by the Constitution.[17] That field trips are curricularly oriented places them in the category of instruction, rather than that of nonideological secular services like transportation to and from school.

Parochiaid

Beginning in 1971 the Supreme Court has issued a series of opinions covering many specific legislative provisions involving public funds and religious graded schools.

Secular Services and Salary Supplements

With only one dissent the Court in 1971 declared unconstitutional a "purchase of secular services" statute in Pennsylvania and a "salary supplement" statute in Rhode Island.[18] These two forms of parochiaid were held to violate the establishment of religion clause of the First Amendment. The primary basis of the decision was a criterion which had first been formulated in a 1970 case involving tax exemption of religious property.[19] The criterion was that there must not be excessive entanglement between government and religion. To determine whether the government entanglement with religion is excessive, it is necessary to examine the character and purposes of the institutions which are benefited, the nature of the aid that is provided, and the resulting relationship between the government and religious authority. The Court reviewed its prior holdings in the church-state-education area and concluded that they did not call for total separation. Here, however, it found that the parochial schools constituted an integral part of the religious mission of the Catholic Church and involved substantial religious activity and purpose. (Schools of the Catholic Church were the sole beneficiaries in Rhode Island to the date of the case, and virtually so in Pennsylvania.)

between government and religion. See Lemon v. Kurtzman, infra.

16. Pequea Valley School Dist. v. Commonwealth of Pennsylvania, Dep't of Educ., 483 Pa. 539, 397 A.2d 1154 (1979), app. dism. for want of a sub. fed. ques. 443 U.S. 901, 99 S.Ct. 3091, 61 L.Ed.2d 869 (1979).

17. Wolman v. Walter, 433 U.S. 229, 97 S.Ct. 2593, 53 L.Ed.2d 714 (1977). [Case No. 7]

18. Lemon v. Kurtzman, 403 U.S. 602, 91 S.Ct. 2105, 29 L.Ed.2d 745 (1971). [Case No. 6]

19. Walz v. Tax Comm'n, 397 U.S. 664, 90 S.Ct. 1409, 25 L.Ed.2d 697 (1970).

The Pennsylvania statute authorized the state superintendent of education to "purchase" specified "secular educational services" from nonpublic schools. The state then directly reimbursed the nonpublic schools for their actual expenditures for teachers' salaries, textbooks, and instructional materials. The textbooks and materials, which were restricted to the areas of mathematics, modern foreign languages, physical science, and physical education, had to be approved by the state superintendent. In Rhode Island the state officials were authorized to supplement the salaries of teachers of secular subjects in nonpublic elementary schools by paying directly to the teacher an amount not in excess of fifteen percent of his current annual salary. Recipients were required to be teachers in nonpublic schools at which the average per pupil expenditure on secular education was less than the average in the state's public schools. The salary could not exceed the maximum paid to teachers in the public schools and recipients were to be certificated in substantially the same manner as public school teachers. Eligible teachers were required to teach only those subjects offered in the public schools and to use only materials which were used in the public schools.

The Court distinguished aid for teachers' salaries from "secular, neutral, or non-ideological services, facilities, or materials." Recalling the 1968 New York textbook case (Case No. 5), the Court here said that teachers have a "substantially different ideological character than books." In terms of potential for involving some aspect of faith or morals in secular subjects, a textbook's content is ascertainable, but a teacher's handling of a subject is not. The Court took notice of the inherent conflict in functions when a teacher under religious control and discipline is faced with separating religious from secular aspects of pre-college education. Furthermore, the restrictions and surveillance necessary to ensure that teachers play a non-ideological role give rise to the kind of entanglement which the Constitution does not permit. The Court observed that the history of government grants on a continuing basis indicates that such programs have almost always been accompanied by varying measures of control. Determining which expenditures of church-related schools are religious and which are secular creates an intimate and continuing relationship between church and state. Additionally, the Court discussed the divisive political potential of such programs. It observed that although political debate and division generally are normal and healthy manifestations of our way of government, protection against political division along religious lines was one of the principal purposes of the religion clauses of the First Amendment.

The criterion of "excessive entanglement" has been the basis for invalidation of statutes in several states providing various forms of financial aid to parochial schools. "Its emergence as an independent test is significant in that its co-equal combination with the 'primary effect' test * * * creates a constitutional Scylla and Charybdis which causes any state program designed to aid its parochial schools to find hazardous sailing." [20]

The Court took the occasion of this case to summarize past decisions and to enunciate, in a form that has been followed in subsequent establishment clause cases, three tests "gleaned" from prior opinions. To be constitutional, a statute must have a "secular legislative purpose," have a "principal or primary effect * * * that neither advances nor inhibits religion," and not "foster 'an excessive government entanglement with religion.' "

Tuition Reimbursements to Parents

Two months after the Supreme Court invalidated the Pennsylvania "purchase of secular services" statute the legislature enacted a "parent reimbursement" statute. The act provided for reimbursement of tuition payments to parents whose children attended a nonpublic school in the state if the school fulfilled state compulsory education requirements and did not discriminate on the ground of race, color, or national origin. Suit was brought by the same parent who had brought the successful challenge to the other statute. A three-judge federal District Court held that the arrangement had a primary effect of advancing religion and thus was unconstitutional. [21]

By a vote of six-to-three the Supreme Court in 1973 affirmed. [22] Looking to the substance of the effects of the legislation rather than to its characterization by supporters, the Court stated that the state had singled out a class of its citizens for a special economic benefit. Whether that benefit was to be viewed as "a simple tuition subsidy, as an incentive to parents to send their children to sectarian schools, or as a reward for having done so," its basic intended consequence was to preserve and support religion-oriented institutions. The Court said it was plain that this was quite unlike the sort of "indirect" and "incidental" benefits that flowed to sectarian schools from programs aiding *all* parents by supplying bus transportation and secular textbooks for their children. It observed that those benefits had been carefully restricted to the purely secular side of church-affiliated institutions and provided no special aid for those who had chosen to support religious schools.

In a companion case from New York the Court expanded its reasoning. [23] There it said that the mere fact the grants were delivered to parents rather than to schools was not of such significance as to compel a result contrary to that of the 1971 cases. Since the money would be used by parents for tuition, with no attempt made to separate secular from sectarian uses, the effect of the aid would be "unmistakably to provide desired financial support for nonpublic, sectarian institutions." The argument was advanced by defenders of the legislation that the

20. Americans United for Separation of Church and State v. Oakey, 339 F.Supp. 545 (D.Vt.1972).

21. Lemon v. Sloan, 340 F.Supp. 1356 (E.D.Pa.1972).

22. Sloan v. Lemon, 413 U.S. 825, 93 S.Ct. 2982, 37 L.Ed.2d 939 (1973).

23. Committee for Public Educ. and Religious Liberty v. Nyquist, 413 U.S. 756, 93 S.Ct. 2955, 37 L.Ed.2d 948 (1973).

parent was not simply a conduit because he was free to spend the money he received from the state in any manner, the tuition having been paid by the parent and the statute providing for a reimbursement. The Court rejected this view, stating that if the grants were offered as an incentive to parents to send their children to sectarian schools by making unrestricted cash payments to the parents, the establishment clause would be violated whether or not the payments eventually found their way into the sectarian institutions. Other unsuccessful arguments were: because the amount of money paid for reimbursement would cover a percentage of cost less than the percentage of parochial school time devoted to teaching secular courses, the arrangement would not be advancing religion; and because the New York statute provided the subsidy only to low income parents, it had the result of aiding them in the free exercise of their religion.

Income Tax Benefits

Another section of the same New York statute provided for aid through the device of income tax benefits. Parents of children attending nonpublic schools were permitted to subtract from their adjusted gross income a specified amount (provided they did not receive a tuition reimbursement under the other part of the statute). The Court by a six-to-three vote invalidated this procedure. It said that in practical terms there was little difference, for purposes of determining whether such aid had the effect of advancing religion, between the tax benefit and the tuition grant. The qualifying parent under either program received the same form of encouragement and reward for sending his children to nonpublic schools.

Defenders of this provision of the statute argued that there was an analogy to tax exemptions for church property, which previously had been approved by the Court.[24] But an important element of that decision had been a recognition that the concept of exempting church property was deeply embedded in the fabric of our national life predating the American Revolution. As to tax benefits to parents of nonpublic school students, there was no "historical precedent for New York's recently promulgated tax relief program." The Court added, however, that historical acceptance alone would not suffice to support a legislative scheme, and furthermore, that such had not sufficed in the church property tax exemption case.[25]

By a one-vote margin the Court in 1983 sustained the constitutionality of a Minnesota statute that provided for deductions on one's state income tax of actual expenses incurred for tuition, textbooks, and transportation of dependents attending any elementary or secondary schools.[26] Maximum deductions per dependent were specified ($500 for grades K through 6 and $700 for grades 7 through 12). The case was

24. Walz v. Tax Comm'n, 397 U.S. 664, 90 S.Ct. 1409, 25 L.Ed.2d 697 (1970).

25. See Note 2 on Case No. 6.

26. Mueller v. Allen, 463 U.S. 388, 103 S.Ct. 3062, 77 L.Ed.2d 721 (1983). [Case No. 8]

distinguished from the preceding one primarily on the bases that here the tax benefit was available to every parent (not only to those whose children were in nonpublic schools) and that here the deduction was one among many (not a single, favored type of taxpayer expenditure).

The Court observed that state legislatures have traditionally been given broad latitude in creating classifications and distinctions in tax statutes, and that the state could be considered to benefit from the present scheme in that it would promote the education of the citizenry and reduce costs of public education. Thus the "secular purpose" test was met. The "primary effect" test is addressed by the conclusion that, because parents receive the direct benefits and are afforded personal choices before any benefits accrue to parochial schools, the aid to those schools is "attenuated." This factor, in combination with the aforementioned factors of "availability to all parents" and "one of many deductible items," satisfied the "primary effect" test. The "entanglement" test was met because state surveillance would be no greater than that required for such approved programs as those involving textbooks. The Court declined to attach constitutional significance to the facts that Minnesota's public schools are essentially free and thus expenses of parents are at most minimal, and that probably 96 percent of children in private schools there are in religiously-affiliated institutions.

Reimbursements to Parochial Schools

By an eight-to-one vote the Court found unconstitutional a "maintenance and repair" provision for private schools in New York.[27] This statute offered funds for these purposes without a guarantee of secular use of the aid. Almost no restrictions were placed on the use of the funds. The Court stated that it was clear government may not erect buildings in which religious activities are conducted. It may not, therefore, maintain such buildings or renovate them when they fall into disrepair.

In a different case from New York decided the same day also by an eight-to-one vote, the Court used essentially the same reasoning to invalidate a statute providing that nonpublic schools be reimbursed for expenses incurred while complying with state requirements pertaining to the administration and reporting of results of tests and compilation of other records.[28] As the use of the funds was not restricted (even teacher-prepared tests with religious indoctrination potential were apparently reimbursable), the inquiry by the Court was not whether the state could pay for any mandated activity, but whether the challenged state aid had the primary effect of advancing religious education. The Court found that it had such effect. It rejected the view that the state could pay for whatever it required a private school to do. Such a position would not square with the establishment clause.

27. Committee for Public Educ. and Religious Liberty v. Nyquist, 413 U.S. 756, 93 S.Ct. 2955, 37 L.Ed.2d 948 (1973).

28. Levitt v. Committee for Public Educ. and Religious Liberty, 413 U.S. 472, 93 S.Ct. 2814, 37 L.Ed.2d 736 (1973).

Wolman

Four years later, however, by a vote of six-to-three the Court found permissible the provision in Ohio of "such standardized tests and scoring services as are in use in the public schools of the state." [29]   The Court distinguished these tests from those not permitted in that these tests were to be neither drafted nor scored by nonpublic school personnel. Furthermore, no payments to the church-sponsored schools for costs of administering the tests were authorized.

In 1980 the Court by a vote of five-to-four upheld the constitutionality of a New York statute providing for reimbursements to private schools for the actual costs of complying with state requirements for reporting on students and for administering both mandatory and optional state-prepared examinations.[30]   Unlike the testing procedure in Ohio, however, the New York procedure provided that the tests be graded by personnel employed by the nonpublic schools, which were to be reimbursed for the services performed.   Accounting procedures were established to monitor reimbursements.   The majority found the differences "not of constitutional dimension."   The scoring of the essentially objective tests and the recording of the results and of attendance data offered no significant opportunity for religious indoctrination and served secular state educational purposes.   The accounting method was not such as to require "excessive entanglement" in insuring that the reimbursements equalled actual costs.

Instructional Materials and Equipment

Meek

In 1975 the Supreme Court considered the constitutionality of direct loans of instructional materials and equipment to nonpublic religious schools.[31]   It found six-to-three that Pennsylvania's supplying of periodicals, films, recordings, laboratory equipment, and equipment for recording and projecting had the unconstitutional primary effect of advancing religion because of "the predominantly religious character of the schools benefiting from the Act."   The only requirement imposed on nonpublic schools to qualify for the loans of instructional material and equipment was that they provide for the subjects and activities prescribed by the state board of education.   There were no bars against a school's having a religious purpose, imposing religious restrictions on student admissions or faculty selection, or even requiring attendance at religious services. More than 75 percent of the state's nonpublic schools were church-related, and about 95 percent of nonpublic elementary and secondary school students were in the religiously affiliated institutions.   The Court said that the church-related schools were the primary beneficiaries of the loans, and that the "massive" aid to the educational function of such schools necessarily results in aid to the sectarian school enterprise as a

---

29. Wolman v. Walter, 433 U.S. 229, 97 S.Ct. 2593, 53 L.Ed.2d 714 (1977). [Case No. 7]

30. Committee for Public Educ. and Religious Liberty v. Regan, 444 U.S. 646, 100 S.Ct. 840, 63 L.Ed.2d 94 (1980).

31. Meek v. Pittenger, 421 U.S. 349, 95 S.Ct. 1753, 44 L.Ed.2d 217 (1975).

whole. Two years later the Court reached the same conclusion as to an Ohio provision that specified the loans were to be made to pupils or parents, rather than directly to the nonpublic schools.[32]

Auxiliary Services

The Supreme Court in 1975 by a six-to-three vote struck down a provision for "auxiliary services" to be performed on parochial school property by public school teachers.[33] These included remedial and accelerated instruction, guidance counseling and testing, and services to aid the educationally disadvantaged. The Court cited as precedent its 1971 decision (Case No. 6), which included the reasoning that it is not constitutionally sufficient to rely on good faith and professionalism of secular teachers functioning in church-related schools to ensure the absence of ideological stances. That the students here affected would be receiving remedial or advanced work, rather than normal, was held to be immaterial. The surveillance required to ensure the absence of ideology would "necessarily give rise to a constitutionally intolerable degree of entanglement between church and state."

The Court in an eight-to-one decision in 1977 upheld the furnishing in the school attended of speech, hearing, and psychological diagnostic services.[34] Such services, unlike prohibited teaching or counseling services, have little or no educational content and are not closely associated with the educational mission of the school. Nor does the diagnostician have more than limited contact with the student. Therapeutic services for religious school students were approved by seven Justices when conducted in "public schools, public centers, or mobile units." The distinction between diagnostic services and therapeutic services is crucial, for the latter afford the opportunity for transmission of ideological views. For the provision of "remedial, therapeutic, and guidance services" to meet constitutional muster, the services are "to be offered under circumstances that reflect their religious neutrality," thus not in parochial schools.

Other cases involving public funds for parochial education are treated at the end of this chapter under "Shared Facilities and Shared Time."

In 1993 the Supreme Court answered a narrow question in a case that reached it in an unusual legal posture.[35] A school district refused to continue to provide a sign-language interpreter for a deaf student when he transferred to a sectarian school. The sole reason offered was that such would violate the establishment clause. A five-Justice majority of the Supreme Court disagreed, holding that such a service neutrally aided the child without financial benefit to the parent or the school and there was no governmental participation in the instruction because the inter-

32. Wolman v. Walter, 433 U.S. 229, 97 S.Ct. 2593, 53 L.Ed.2d 714 (1977). [Case No. 7]

33. Meek v. Pittenger, 421 U.S. 349, 95 S.Ct. 1753, 44 L.Ed.2d 217 (1975).

34. Wolman v. Walter, 433 U.S. 229, 97 S.Ct. 2593, 53 L.Ed.2d 714 (1977). [Case No. 7]

35. Zobrest v. Catalina Foothills School Dist., ___ U.S. ___, 113 S.Ct. 2462, 125 L.Ed.2d 1 (1993).

preter was only a conduit to effectuate the child's communications. Cited was a case decided in 1986 that upheld the federal constitutionality of extending a general vocational assistance program in Washington state to a blind person studying at a religious college to become a clergyman.[36] (The Supreme Court of Washington subsequently ruled that the state constitution forbade such use of public funds, and the Supreme Court denied certiorari.[37]) Four Justices dissented, believing that the constitutional question should not have been decided when federal statutory and regulatory issues with IDEA had not been briefed or argued. (Two of the four dissented on the merits; two did not comment on the merits.)

Released Time for Religious Instruction

The concept of public schools' releasing children during the school day in order that they may receive religious instruction has taken several forms in practice. One such program was challenged before the Supreme Court of the United States in 1948.[38] In Champaign, Illinois, interested members of Jewish, Roman Catholic, and Protestant faiths formed a voluntary association and obtained board of education approval of a cooperative plan to offer religious classes. The classes were taught in three separate religious groups by Protestant teachers, Catholic priests, and a Jewish rabbi. Classes were conducted in the regular classrooms of the school buildings. Pupils whose parents so requested were released from their regular studies to attend the religious courses. They were required to be present at these sessions, and reports of absence were made to their regular teachers. Students who did not take religious instruction were required to leave their classrooms and go to some other place in the school building for pursuit of their secular studies.

The Supreme Court by a vote of eight-to-one invalidated the program. The Court pointed out that not only were the tax-supported public school buildings being used for the dissemination of religious doctrine, but that the state also afforded sectarian groups an invaluable aid in that it helped to provide pupils for their religious classes through use of the state's compulsory education machinery. "This is not separation of Church and State."

Four years later the constitutionality of a different type of "released time" program was considered by the Supreme Court.[39] A New York statute, as implemented by regulations of the state commissioner of education, expressly provided for the release of public school pupils from public school attendance to attend religious classes off school premises.

36. Witters v. Washington Dept. of Services for the Blind, 474 U.S. 481, 106 S.Ct. 748, 88 L.Ed.2d 846 (1986).

37. Witters v. State Com'n for the Blind, 112 Wash.2d 363, 771 P.2d 1119 (1989), cert. den. 493 U.S. 850, 110 S.Ct. 147, 107 L.Ed.2d 106 (1989).

38. People of State of Illinois ex rel. McCollum v. Board of Educ. of School Dist. No. 71, Champaign County, 333 U.S. 203, 68 S.Ct. 461, 92 L.Ed. 649 (1948). [Case No. 2]

39. Zorach v. Clauson, 343 U.S. 306, 72 S.Ct. 679, 96 L.Ed. 954 (1952). [Case No. 3]

Those who contested the New York plan contended that it was not basically different from the Champaign plan. Their key argument was that the weight and influence of the school was used to support a program of religious instruction because records were kept of attendance of pupils released to attend religious classes, regular classes were halted during the period of "released time," and pupils not attending such classes were required to remain in school.

By a vote of six-to-three the validity of the plan was sustained. The majority reasoned that the state can "accommodate" the religious wishes of parents to the extent of releasing pupils at parental request at a specified time. That school buildings were not used for the religious instruction was a crucial difference from the Champaign case. The majority commented that the problem, like many in constitutional law, was one of degree, here degree of "separation of Church and State." Analogy was made between this arrangement and excuses accepted for student absences for religious reasons.

Use of the Bible

Through the years before 1963 much litigation had arisen regarding the use of the Bible in public schools. A majority of the state courts that had ruled on the question upheld the legality of Bible reading as part of opening exercises if two conditions were met: the reading was without comment (that is, without any intent to indoctrinate), and those whose parents objected must be excused. In 1963, however, in an eight-to-one decision, the Court found the practice to be in violation of the establishment clause of the First Amendment (made applicable to the states by the Fourteenth Amendment).[40] The Court took the occasion to extensively document the point that in barring this exercise as part of the school program it was not deviating from its established precedents in the area of church-state-education relationships. It ruled that the Bible was a sectarian document, a point which had been the subject of considerable litigation in state courts over the years with varying holdings. The Court stated that the First Amendment and its subsequent interpretations indicated that there should be a neutrality of the state in regard to religious matters. This neutrality was based on the premises that the government could not aid any or all religions and that every person has a right to choose a personal course with reference to religion free of any compulsion from the state. The Court observed that it had consistently held that the clause of the First Amendment regarding religion withdrew from government all legislative power respecting religious belief or the expression thereof. It set forth the following test for distinguishing permitted from forbidden governmental involvements with religion: "What are the purpose and the primary effect of the enactment? If either is the advancement or inhibition of religion then the enactment exceeds the scope of legislative power as circumscribed by

40. School Dist. of Abington Tp., Pa. v.   L.Ed.2d 844 (1963). [Case No. 4]
Schempp, 374 U.S. 203, 83 S.Ct. 1560, 10

the Constitution. That is to say that to withstand the strictures of the Establishment Clause there must be a secular legislative purpose and a primary effect that neither advances nor inhibits religion." Because the reading of the Bible as part of opening exercises was religious in character and was conducted in school buildings under the supervision and participation of teachers, the two-pronged test was not met. The Court was careful to emphasize that religion had an exalted place in American society and that it was not saying that the Bible was unworthy of study for its literary and historic qualities. It observed that nothing in the opinion indicated that the First Amendment barred study of the Bible or of religion when presented objectively as part of a program of education.

Lower courts have had to examine in detail how the Bible was used in order to decide whether a curricular element was constitutional. For example, the Fifth Circuit Court of Appeals disapproved a "Bible Literature" course because of the viewpoint from which the course was taught—essentially "a Christian religious perspective and within that a fundamentalist and/or evangelical doctrine." [41] The state-approved textbook revealed this approach and contained no discussion of the Bible's literary qualities. Although the teacher was fully certificated (in addition to being an active minister) and testified that he used a recognized secular teaching guide, the court found that his approach and examinations were not consistent with the guide. The course and the textbook were ordered out of the school.

In an Arkansas school district classes to learn about the Bible were conducted during regular school hours for those students who wished to attend. They were taught by volunteers (not employees) who were not acting on behalf of any church. No course credit was given. Students taking the instruction left their regular classrooms to receive it. There was a dispute as to whether the purpose of the classes was primarily religious or secular. The court, however, did not have to determine the nature of the purpose because it found the principal effect of the content to be the advancement of Christianity. [42]

Guidelines under which the Bible may be studied in public schools have been suggested by several courts. These include use of fully certificated teachers employed in the same manner as other teachers, complete control of course content and materials by the school board, supervision of the course to assure objectivity in teaching, and no part of the course to be a required activity of students. [43]

---

41. Hall v. Board of School Commissioners of Conecuh County, 656 F.2d 999 (5 Cir.1981).

42. Doe v. Human, 725 F.Supp. 1503 (W.D.Ark.1989), aff. 923 F.2d 857 (8 Cir.

1990), cert. den. 499 U.S. 922, 111 S.Ct. 1315, 113 L.Ed.2d 248 (1991).

43. Wiley v. Franklin, 497 F.Supp. 390 (E.D.Tenn.1980); Crockett v. Sorenson, 568 F.Supp. 1422 (W.D.Va.1983).

Prayers

The Supreme Court Decisions

The legality of prayers in the public schools was argued in many courts with differing results before the Supreme Court decided a case on the subject in 1962. Most of the cases involved prayers as part of a school's opening exercises, often in combination with Bible reading. The first prayer case to be accepted by the Supreme Court was from New York and involved use of a specially written prayer designed to inculcate "moral and spiritual" values and purported to be nonsectarian.[44] The prayer was composed by state educational authorities (the Board of Regents) and suggested for use by local school boards. A local school board then required that the so-called Regents' prayer be said in its classrooms; however, any pupil could be excused on his parent's objection. The prayer was:

> Almighty God, we acknowledge our dependence upon Thee, and we beg Thy blessings upon us, our parents, our teachers and our country.

In a six-to-one decision the Supreme Court held that the First Amendment prohibited the arrangement. The religious nature of the prayer had not been denied, and the Court found that recitation of the prayer was a state-sponsored religious activity, which was unconstitutional. The Court stated that it was no part of the business of government to compose official prayers for any group to recite as part of a religious program carried on by the government. That the prayer using the word "God" may be denominationally neutral was not a relevant consideration. The Court further noted that violations of the establishment clause did not depend upon a showing of direct governmental compulsion. Precluded are laws related to establishing an official religion whether or not those laws operate directly to coerce non-observing individuals. The Court pointed out (regrettably in a footnote which was missed by many observers) that there was nothing in the decision inconsistent with the fact that school children and others are officially encouraged to express love for the United States by reciting historical documents which contain references to a deity or by singing official anthems which include the composer's professions of faith in a supreme being or with other manifestations in public life of a belief in God. Ruled out were references to a supreme being in religious exercises, as distinguished from such references on patriotic or ceremonial occasions.

Use of the Lord's Prayer in opening exercises in public schools was specifically barred in the Supreme Court's 1963 Bible reading decision (Case No. 4), discussed in the preceding section.

In 1992 the Supreme Court declared unconstitutional an arrangement for the inclusion of invocation and benediction prayers at graduation ceremonies.[45] In the words of the Court, the question was "whether including clerical members who offer prayers as part of the official school graduation ceremony is consistent with the Religion Clauses of

---

44. Engel v. Vitale, 370 U.S. 421, 82 S.Ct. 1261, 8 L.Ed.2d 601 (1962).

45. Lee v. Weisman, __ U.S. __, 112 S.Ct. 2649, 120 L.Ed.2d 467 (1992). [Case No. 12]

the First Amendment." School policy in Providence, Rhode Island, allowed principals to invite members of the clergy to offer nonsectarian prayers. Guidelines for prayers on civic occasions prepared by an interfaith group were given to the rabbi in the present case. Attendance of a student at the graduation ceremony was not required to receive the diploma.

The five-Justice opinion of the Court was grounded in the prayer cases of 1962 and 1963. It said that the government was involved in a "state-sponsored and state-directed religious exercise in a public school." That the school endeavored to exclude sectarianism from the prayers did not diminish its participation. The argument that the prayer should be permitted when attendance at the ceremony is voluntary "lacks all persuasion" and "is formalistic in the extreme." The graduation event is one of singular importance in a young person's life. "The principle that government may accommodate the free exercise of religion does not supersede the fundamental limitations imposed by the Establishment Clause."

School-Encouraged Prayers

Decisions in federal Courts of Appeals have dealt with the question of other types of prayers. Upheld in one was the rule of a principal prohibiting the recitation of prayers by pupils before eating a mid-morning snack.[46] One of the prayers was:

Thank you for the world so sweet.

Thank you for the food we eat.

Thank you for the birds that sing.

Thank you, God, for everything.

In another case, arising in another circuit, the Court of Appeals barred use of this prayer without the word "God."[47] That school assemblies were voluntary and that the student council had requested permission to begin them with a prayer did not form a basis for the principal's permitting the practice, according to a case in a third circuit.[48]

The question of "voluntary" prayer on school premises has been raised in several forms. The Supreme Judicial Court of Massachusetts ordered an end to a local board's scheme for so-called voluntary prayer that had been instituted in accordance with a state statute permitting boards to allow students to participate in such activity before the beginning of the school day if their parents approved.[49] The court stated

46. Stein v. Oshinsky, 348 F.2d 999 (2 Cir.1965), cert. den. 382 U.S. 957, 86 S.Ct. 435, 15 L.Ed.2d 361 (1965).

47. DeSpain v. DeKalb County Community School Dist., 384 F.2d 836 (7 Cir.1967), cert. den. 390 U.S. 906, 88 S.Ct. 815, 19 L.Ed.2d 873 (1968).

48. Collins v. Chandler Unified School Dist., 644 F.2d 759 (9 Cir.1981), cert. den.

454 U.S. 863, 102 S.Ct. 322, 70 L.Ed.2d 163 (1981).

49. Commissioner of Educ. v. School Committee of Leyden, 358 Mass. 776, 267 N.E.2d 226 (1971), cert. den. 404 U.S. 849, 92 S.Ct. 85, 30 L.Ed.2d 88 (1971). See also Kent v. Commissioner of Educ., 380 Mass. 235, 402 N.E.2d 1340 (1980).

that Supreme Court decisions barred the conducting of prayers on school property even though there was no requirement of teacher or student participation, the exercises were under student control, and there was no prescription as to form of exercise. A decade later a very similar statute in Louisiana was declared unconstitutional by the Fifth Circuit Court of Appeals, and the Supreme Court affirmed without dissent.[50]

The Supreme Court of New Jersey held unconstitutional a plan in a local school district whereby, immediately prior to the formal opening of school, students who wished to join in a religious exercise could come to the gymnasium, where a student volunteer would read from the Congressional Record the "remarks" of the chaplain to that body.[51] The selection of the material would be made by the volunteer reader. Constitutionally this procedure was held to be no different from reading prayers directly from a religious source.

It is important to observe that state action that initiates a pattern of conduct is the equivalent for Fourteenth Amendment purposes of state action that mandates a pattern of conduct. The Court of Appeals, Third Circuit, ruled unconstitutional a program to permit voluntary nondenominational mass prayer, which had been adopted after some urging by students and parents.[52] The board had passed a motion that the district "install Bible reading and some non-denominational mass prayer." No procedure was specified by the school board. However, a program was inaugurated and conducted by teachers, parents, and students in which a student, acting without direction or command, would read a passage of his choosing from his personal Bible over the school's public address system. No student was compelled to remain within hearing of any such program. It was held that a motion in a school board session is legislative action, and that the program which was brought about by reason of such action was prohibited.

The Eleventh Circuit Court of Appeals rejected the contention that it was constitutional for teachers to engage in prayer activities if there was no board policy or state statute that motivated the activities.[53] The court said that, as the school board members were aware of the activities and took no steps to stop them, the board had in effect ratified the teachers' conduct. "If a statute authorizing the teachers' activities would be unconstitutional, then the activities, in the absence of a statute, are also unconstitutional."

When a school board knowingly permitted a band teacher to conduct prayer and religious activities at school functions, the Eighth Circuit held the board liable for attorney fees incurred in obtaining an injunc-

50. Karen B. v. Treen, 653 F.2d 897 (5 Cir.1981), aff. 455 U.S. 913, 102 S.Ct. 1267, 71 L.Ed.2d 455 (1982).

51. State Bd. of Educ. v. Board of Educ. of Netcong, 57 N.J. 172, 270 A.2d 412 (1970), cert. den. 401 U.S. 1013, 91 S.Ct. 1253, 28 L.Ed.2d 550 (1971).

52. Mangold v. Albert Gallatin Area School Dist., 438 F.2d 1194 (3 Cir.1971).

53. Jaffree v. Wallace, 705 F.2d 1526 (11 Cir.1983), aff. as to this issue, 466 U.S.

tion to stop the practice.[54]   The Eleventh Circuit barred a plan for allowing the student government to randomly select invocation speakers from nonclergy volunteers proposed by various school clubs and organizations.[55]   The plan was to replace a judicially invalidated custom of having clergy open school-sponsored football games with prayers.

Student-Initiated Prayer Groups

In 1981 the Supreme Court without dissent declined to review a holding of the Second Circuit Court of Appeals that had upheld a school board's refusal to allow a group of students called "Students for Voluntary Prayer" to conduct communal prayer meetings in the public school immediately before the school day started.[56]   The circuit court ruled that the prohibition did not infringe the students' free exercise of religion rights, their freedom of speech rights, or their equal protection rights. It observed that there was a compelling interest of the state in removing from the public schools any indication of sponsorship of religious activity.

A week before the Supreme Court's denial of certiorari on the preceding case, the high court had held that a state university that makes its facilities generally available for activities of registered student groups cannot close them to such groups desiring use for religious activities.[57]   The Court decided the case in the framework of freedom of speech.   Over one hundred registered student groups used the facilities. The university had created a forum for exchange of ideas, and thus it could not bar access to it solely because of content of the speech.   The Court expressly distinguished the case from those involving religious activities in public graded schools by observing that facilities in the latter are not generally used as open forums and that university students are less impressionable than younger students.

In 1983 the Supreme Court without dissent let stand a decision of the Court of Appeals, Fifth Circuit, that had held to be unconstitutional a school board policy allowing students to gather at school with supervision for voluntary religious meetings close to the beginning or end of the school day.[58]   The circuit court said that the policy implied recognition of religious activities and meetings as an integral part of the district's extracurricular program and carried an implicit approval by school authorities of those programs.   Because students are drawn to the school by the compulsory education machinery, the court gave no weight to the fact that the meetings were not during the official school day.

924, 104 S.Ct. 1704, 80 L.Ed.2d 178 (1984).

54. Steele v. Van Buren Public School Dist., 845 F.2d 1492 (8 Cir.1988).

55. Jager v. Douglas County School Dist., 862 F.2d 824 (11 Cir.1989), cert. den. 490 U.S. 1090, 109 S.Ct. 2431, 104 L.Ed.2d 988 (1989).

56. Brandon v. Board of Educ. of Guilderland Central School Dist., 635 F.2d 971 (2 Cir.1980), cert. den. 454 U.S. 1123, 102 S.Ct. 970, 71 L.Ed.2d 109 (1981).

57. Widmar v. Vincent, 454 U.S. 263, 102 S.Ct. 269, 70 L.Ed.2d 440 (1981).

58. Lubbock Civil Liberties Union v. Lubbock Independent School Dist., 669 F.2d 1038 (5 Cir.1982), cert. den. 459 U.S. 1155, 103 S.Ct. 800, 74 L.Ed.2d 1003 (1983).

Subsequent to the judicial developments in the preceding three paragraphs Congress passed the Equal Access Act,[59] which in essence provided that any "public secondary school which receives Federal financial assistance" and which permits "one or more noncurriculum related student groups to meet on school premises during noninstructional time" must not withhold such privilege "on the basis of the religious, political, philosophical, or other content of the speech at such meetings." The Act, in effect, made the Widmar holding applicable to secondary schools receiving federal funds.

In 1990 the Supreme Court upheld the Act against an establishment clause challenge.[60] The question of the maturity of secondary school students to recognize that allowing a religious club to function alongside other clubs does not imply endorsement of religion was decided in the affirmative by Congress, a legislative determination that the Court found to be rational. But Congress did not define "noncurriculum related," and the Court was required to do so in order to ascertain the status of some student groups in the case at hand. The Court ruled that the term covered any group that failed to meet any of the following criteria: the subject matter of the group is actually being, or soon to be, taught in a regularly offered course (e.g., French club); the subject matter of the group concerns the body of courses as a whole (e.g., student government); participation in the group is required for a course; participation results in academic credit. Band or orchestra activity was cited for both of the last two categories. In the school in the case several existing clubs were found not to meet the criteria (scuba club, chess club, service club related to nonschool organization), and thus the student religious group was entitled to meet on school premises. The Court said it was expressing no opinion on whether the First Amendment required the same result.

Unsuccessful was an attempt to justify on the basis of the Mergens case the encouragement of prayers by a basketball coach in connection with games and practice sessions. The Fifth Circuit pointed out that Mergens involved noncurriculum-related activities (not extracurricular ones), that the prayers here were not student-initiated as required by the Equal Access Act, and the teacher participated whereas the Act permitted teacher presence only in a custodial capacity.[61]

The Equal Access Act expressly does not protect speech that is "otherwise unlawful." The Ninth Circuit held that this provision did not encompass a violation of a state constitutional church-state restriction greater than that in the federal establishment clause.[62] The court emphasized the Supreme Court's determination that the Act must be read to effectuate a broad Congressional purpose. Thus, for those covered by the Act, it preempts state law.

59. 20 U.S.C.A. § 4071.

60. Board of Educ. of Westside Community Schools v. Mergens, 496 U.S. 226, 110 S.Ct. 2356, 110 L.Ed.2d 191 (1990). [Case No. 11]

61. Doe v. Duncanville Independent School Dist., 994 F.2d 160 (5 Cir.1993).

62. Garnett v. Renton School Dist. No. 403, 987 F.2d 641 (9 Cir.1993), cert. den. ___ U.S. ___, 114 S.Ct. 72, 126 L.Ed.2d 41 (1993).

Periods of Silence

Having a brief period of silence before the start of the school day in and of itself obviously would be uninvolved with religion. In many places, however, such a period was introduced in an atmosphere that indicated the practice was intended by many supporters as a way to avoid the impact of the constitutional ban on beginning the school day with a prayer. Although a state statute authorizing a period of silence for "meditation" or "contemplation" would be unnecessary and might be considered by some an intrusion into methodology for conducting the schools, it would be within the power of the state to enact unless courts found that it was a pretext for reintroducing the notion of prayer, albeit silent prayer. Early challenges to silence statutes on their faces were rejected by courts.[63] However, within the period of a year in 1982–3 three federal District Courts invalidated such statutes, concluding in their reviews of circumstances surrounding the adoptions of the provisions, as well as some actual provisions suggesting prayer, that the purposes and effects were not secular and neutral.[64]

The Supreme Court reviewed an Alabama statute that authorized a period of silence at the start of the school day for "meditation or voluntary prayer" and found it to be unconstitutional.[65] Based on the legislative history of the provision (including the purpose of the sponsors "to return voluntary prayer to the public schools" and the preamble to the bill) were the conclusions that there was a clear sectarian purpose in the enactment and that the statute "had no secular purpose." (An older statute already provided for a period of silence for "meditation" and implicitly protected a student's right to engage in voluntary prayer during that period.) Thus, the first of the three establishment-clause criteria for a constitutional enactment in the church-state area was not met.

Other Religious Influences

Garb of Teachers

Many older cases dealt with the issue of the wearing of distinctive religious garb by teachers in public schools. Cases arose either to require that boards permit Catholic nuns to wear their habiliments while teaching or to force boards to cease allowing the practice. More recent cases have involved dress of other religions.

In an early case on the subject the Supreme Court of Pennsylvania sustained the authority of a local board of education to hire nuns as teachers and to permit them to appear in the school room in the habit of

---

63. Opinion of the Justices, 108 N.H. 97, 228 A.2d 161 (1967); Gaines v. Anderson, 421 F.Supp. 337 (D.Mass.1976).

64. Beck v. McElrath, 548 F.Supp. 1161 (M.D.Tenn.1982); Duffy v. Las Cruces Public Schools, 557 F.Supp. 1013 (D.N.M.1983);

May v. Cooperman, 572 F.Supp. 1561 (D.N.J.1983), aff. 780 F.2d 240 (3 Cir.1985).

65. Wallace v. Jaffree, 472 U.S. 38, 105 S.Ct. 2479, 86 L.Ed.2d 29 (1985).

their order.[66] A few months after the Pennsylvania decision had been rendered the legislature of that state enacted a statute specifically designed to prevent the wearing by teachers in the public schools of any dress or insignia indicating membership in any religious order. The constitutionality of that act was upheld by the Supreme Court of Pennsylvania.[67] The court noted that the legislation was aimed against acts, not beliefs, and only against acts of the teachers while they were performing duties as teachers.

The prohibition of the wearing of religious garb by a regulation of the state commissioner of education was sustained by the highest court of New York.[68] That court held that the commissioner's general power to supervise the schools of the state included the implied power so to restrict teachers' appearance.

The Supreme Court of Oregon, in a case involving a teacher who had become a Sikh and thereafter wore white clothes and a white turban while teaching, held that the teacher was subject to a state legislative ban on religious dress while performing teaching duties.[69] The court said that the prohibition would not apply to incidental elements such as a cross or Star of David, nor to ethnic or cultural dress. The United States Supreme Court in 1987 dismissed her appeal "for want of a substantial federal question," thereby enhancing the precedential stature of the case.

The Third Circuit Court of Appeals relied heavily on the preceding case in ruling against a female Muslim teacher who adhered to the religious conviction that she should, when in public, cover her entire body except face and hands.[70] She filed an unsuccessful discrimination in employment suit when the Philadelphia school district applied the old Pennsylvania statute on the subject that had been upheld eight decades before.

Where there are no state-level proscriptions, whether local boards can permit the wearing of extensive religious apparel by teachers is not settled. The highest courts of New Mexico [71] and Kentucky,[72] for example, have taken diametrically opposed views. It should be further observed that the fact that nuns may turn their earnings over to a religious society is not a basis for barring them as public school teachers.[73]

66. Hysong v. Gallitzin Borough School Dist., 164 Pa. 629, 30 A. 482 (1894).

67. Commonwealth v. Herr, 229 Pa. 132, 78 A. 68 (1910).

68. O'Connor v. Hendrick, 184 N.Y. 421, 77 N.E. 612 (1906).

69. Cooper v. Eugene School Dist. No. 4J, 301 Or. 358, 723 P.2d 298 (1986), app. dism. 480 U.S. 942, 107 S.Ct. 1597, 94 L.Ed.2d 784 (1987).

70. United States v. Board of Educ. for School Dist. of Philadelphia, 911 F.2d 882 (3 Cir.1990).

71. Zellers v. Huff, 55 N.M. 501, 236 P.2d 949 (1951).

72. Rawlings v. Butler, 290 S.W.2d 801 (Ky.1956).

73. Gerhardt v. Heid, 66 N.D. 444, 267 N.W. 127 (1936).

Distribution of Literature

Another persistent problem area is that of dissemination of religious literature through mechanisms of the public schools. In a leading case the highest court in New Jersey struck down an attempt by Gideons International to distribute the Gideon Bible through the public schools.[74] This Bible contains the New Testament and the Book of Psalms and the Book of Proverbs from the Old Testament. Distribution of the Bible was with the express consent of the board of education. It was proposed to distribute the Bibles only to those pupils whose parents requested that their children receive copies. The court made a determination that the Gideon Bible was sectarian, based upon testimony of representatives of some faiths which did not accept part or all of the Gideon Bible. It also gave weight to the testimony of psychologists and educators, who asserted that the distribution of the slips to be signed by the parents requesting that their children be given copies would create a subtle pressure on all children to accept them, that the distribution of the Bible through the schools would leave the impression that school authorities had given the Bible a stamp of approval, and that tensions among religious groups would be increased. The court found the arrangement to constitute a preference of one religion over others, and thus to be unconstitutional.

In a unanimous fourteen-judge en banc decision in 1978, the Fifth Circuit Court of Appeals agreed with this holding.[75] In 1993 the Supreme Court without dissent denied certiorari on a similar Seventh Circuit decision.[76] The circuit court observed that Supreme Court decisions over the years had not eroded the bases of the bar. It here rejected a free speech claim because the schools were being used in essence to furnish a captive audience of impressionable children to religious presenters.

In that 1978 case, however, the Fifth Circuit split seven-to-seven in affirming the constitutionality of guidelines that a local board had established related to distribution on a voluntary basis of religious literature. Literature could be made available only at one place in a school; all faiths could utilize the location; no school employee could comment about the literature, but the fact that literature was available at the designated location could be periodically announced.

No reference was made in the case to a decision of the Supreme Court of New Mexico that had enjoined a practice whereby a Presbyterian church furnished religious pamphlets to a school.[77] The materials were not handed to the pupils by the teachers, nor did the teachers instruct the pupils to take or to read them. However, the pamphlets were kept in sight and were readily available, and the supply was replenished as required.

74. Tudor v. Board of Educ. of Borough of Rutherford, 14 N.J. 31, 100 A.2d 857 (1953), cert. den. 348 U.S. 816, 75 S.Ct. 25, 99 L.Ed. 644 (1954).

75. Meltzer v. Board of Public Instr. of Orange County, Florida, 577 F.2d 311 (5 Cir.1978), cert. den. 439 U.S. 1089, 99 S.Ct. 872, 59 L.Ed.2d 56 (1979).

76. Berger v. Rensselaer Central School Corp., 982 F.2d 1160 (7 Cir.1993), cert. den. ___ U.S. ___, 113 S.Ct. 2344, 124 L.Ed.2d 254 (1993).

77. Miller v. Cooper, 56 N.M. 355, 244 P.2d 520 (1952).

Curricular Elements

Another issue in the Fifth Circuit case was the constitutionality on its face of a Florida statute providing that teachers "embrace every opportunity to inculcate * * * the practice of every Christian virtue." The state argued successfully in the lower court, whose decision was affirmed by a seven-to-seven vote, that the word "Christian" was "a mere adjective with little or no import," a shorthand for "virtue in a general philosophical sense."

The Supreme Court of New Hampshire considered not offensive to the Constitution the displaying on the wall of each classroom a plaque which would be visible from any place in the room including the words "In God we trust." [78] It found that because this was a national motto (appearing on coins and currency, on public buildings, and in the national anthem), its appearance in this fashion would not be barred by the establishment clause of the First Amendment.

The United States Supreme Court held in 1980, however, that the posting in classrooms of "The Ten Commandments" violated the first prong of the establishment clause test in that the purpose of a Kentucky statute requiring the posting was not a secular one.[79] The Court decided the case with a per curiam opinion and without oral argument. Two Justices dissented from this treatment of the case. The vote on the merits was five-to-two.

Citing its opinion in the 1963 Bible reading case (Case No. 4), the Court emphasized that the Ten Commandments were not "integrated into the school curriculum, where the Bible may constitutionally be used in an appropriate study of history, civilization, ethics, comparative religion, or the like." It found no secular purpose in the posting, being unpersuaded by a notation "in small print" to the effect that the Commandments were part of "the fundamental legal code of Western Civilization and the Common Law of the United States." The Commandments, said the Court, constitute a sacred text in Jewish and Christian faiths, and some of them set forth solely religion-based duties.

The Third Circuit Court of Appeals enjoined the teaching in public schools of the "Science of Creative Intelligence," also known as "Transcendental Meditation" or "TM".[80] The course was an elective taught at five New Jersey high schools in different school districts using the same textbook and techniques of instruction, with special teachers paid by an organization seeking to disseminate the experience throughout the United States. The finding that the offering of this course violated the establishment clause was based largely upon the trial court's detailed analysis of the ceremony of receiving one's mantra, a sound aid essential to practicing TM. Invocations and chants in the complex ceremony led to the conclusion that the activity was religious in nature.

78. Opinion of the Justices, 108 N.H. 97, 228 A.2d 161 (1967).

79. Stone v. Graham, 449 U.S. 39, 101 S.Ct. 192, 66 L.Ed.2d 199 (1980).

80. Malnak v. Yogi, 592 F.2d 197 (3 Cir.1979).

A set of guidelines for handling religious observances and holidays in public schools was upheld on its face by the Eighth Circuit Court of Appeals.[81] The guidelines permitted objective discussion in the schools of holidays having both religious and secular bases. There could be explanations of historical and contemporary values related to the holiday, short term use of religious symbols as examples of the heritage, and integration into the curriculum of music, art, literature, and drama having religious themes if presented "in a prudent and objective manner and as a traditional part of the cultural and religious heritage of the particular holiday." The trial court that had approved the rules also had held that segments of a Christmas program presented before the rules were adopted were impermissible because the activities were predominantly religious in character.

Shared Facilities and Shared Time

Many problems arise when there is "cooperation" between public and parochial schools. Precisely what arrangements run afoul of constitutional restrictions is an open question in most jurisdictions. Only a careful study of the facts of the many decided cases can give any degree of guidance, and not all courts interpret similar facts in like fashion. Focal points have been the sharing of facilities and, more recently, variations of "shared time" or "dual enrollment". Issues are whether public funds are being used for sectarian purposes and whether sectarian influences are being exercised in public schools.

Regarding public funds for sectarian purposes, problems occur when a school district leases part or all of a building from a church. In one situation a church used portions of the building for its own purposes while renting other portions to the public school district. The building was situated on land belonging to the local Roman Catholic church. Religious emblems and manifestations were prevalent throughout the building, including the classrooms. The Supreme Court of Nebraska held that the school was not a public school, and denied it a share of state school funds.[82] The court emphasized that the garb and devotional attitude of the sisters, the instructions and services of the church priest in the chapel and classrooms, and the insignia around the building created an environment that reflected the belief of the Catholic religion in the school itself.

Forty years later the same court by a divided vote held that it is not unconstitutional for a public school district to use or lease classrooms in a church or other sectarian building for public school purposes if the property is under the control of public school authorities and the instruction offered is secular.[83] Both students enrolled in the public

81. Florey v. Sioux Falls School Dist. 49–5, 619 F.2d 1311 (8 Cir.1980), cert. den. 449 U.S. 987, 101 S.Ct. 409, 66 L.Ed.2d 251 (1980).

82. State ex rel. Public School Dist. No. 6, Cedar County v. Taylor, 122 Neb. 454, 240 N.W. 573 (1932).

83. State ex rel. School Dist. of Hartington v. Nebraska State Bd. of Educ., 188 Neb. 1, 195 N.W.2d 161 (1972), cert. den.

schools and students enrolled in nonpublic schools would be included in the classes held in the leased classrooms. Where only parochial school students were taught by publicly paid teachers in rooms in a parochial school, the Court of Appeals of Oregon found the denoting of these rooms as "annexes" to be meaningless, and the arrangement to violate the state constitution.[84]

Judicially disapproved by several federal courts have been dual enrollment plans that have essentially provided for the leasing by a public school district of space in a parochial school and having teachers selected by public school authorities teach certain secular subjects to the nonpublic school students in the leased rooms.[85]

Tangled relationships between parochial and public schools were discussed and enjoined by the Supreme Court of New Mexico in a complicated fact situation in 1951.[86] Many direct and indirect religious influences were involved. The court found that, "in short, New Mexico had a Roman Catholic school system supported by public funds within its public school system."

The Supreme Court of Montana has held that the state constitution prevented a public school board from making a levy for, or expending funds for, the employment of teachers to teach in a parochial school.[87] There had been a vote to employ eight additional high school teachers as full time employees to provide the standard course of instruction to students currently enrolled in the local parochial high school. The court found the whole procedure invalid in that the school board was without authority to call for a special levy in the first place, because statutes limited the power to call for levies to the purpose of benefitting public schools of the district. Furthermore, the state constitution prevented the expenditure of funds for teachers in parochial schools. The court rejected the contention that free exercise of religion would be denied parochial school students if they were not permitted to have the educational benefits, which the school board had resolved to provide and which the voters had approved, solely on account of their being enrolled in a parochial school.

Current questions involving "shared time" or "dual enrollment" would appear to depend to a large extent on the wording of the compulsory education statute in each state, as well as on separation of church and state. In a somewhat narrow holding involving a Pennsylvania statute, the Supreme Court of Pennsylvania in 1913 held that a pupil attending a parochial school could not be refused the opportunity to

409 U.S. 921, 93 S.Ct. 220, 34 L.Ed.2d 182 (1972).

84. Fisher v. Clackamas County School Dist. 12, 13 Or.App. 56, 507 P.2d 839 (1973).

85. Americans United for Separation of Church and State v. Paire, 359 F.Supp. 505

(D.N.H.1973); Americans United for Separation of Church and State v. Board of Educ., 369 F.Supp. 1059 (E.D.Ky.1974).

86. Zellers v. Huff, 55 N.M. 501, 236 P.2d 949 (1951).

87. State ex rel. Chambers v. School Dist. No. 10, 155 Mont. 422, 472 P.2d 1013 (1970).

enroll in a manual training course in a local public school.[88]

An appellate court in Illinois upheld an experimental program through which students who would otherwise be eligible for full-time enrollment at a public high school could attend the public high school on a part-time basis and take some courses in a parochial school.[89] The experiment when challenged involved one high school in Chicago and one Roman Catholic school. Students affected took at the public high school all courses except English, social studies, music, and art. The court rested its holding, not on the church-state issue, but on the points that the board of education had the power to experiment in its educational programs and that the program applied to all nonpublic school educational institutions, not specifically to any religious group or groups. Furthermore, reasoned the court, the Illinois compulsory education law did not specify that all of the education had to be taken in one place.

Very shortly thereafter the Supreme Court of Missouri took a contrary position in regard to the compulsory education law in Missouri.[90] But that court's opinion covered more points. Questioned were procedures whereby public moneys were used to send speech teachers into parochial schools for speech therapy, and also whereby parochial school children came into the public schools for the sole purpose of achieving instruction in speech therapy during the regular school day. The court made a point of the fact that it was not considering a third possible situation in which parochial school children might come into public school buildings for speech therapy in addition to their regular school day. The court held that the practice of sending public school personnel into parochial schools was in violation of the Constitution of Missouri, which provided that public funds could be used only for establishing and maintaining free public schools. The second procedure the court found invalid because it interpreted the compulsory education law as stipulating that the school day be of a certain length and that it be spent entirely in one type of school.

The Supreme Court of Michigan discussed at length the issue of shared time in relation to a newly adopted state constitutional amendment prohibiting financial aid to students attending nonpublic schools as well as to the schools directly.[91] Shared time programs at public schools were held not to be prohibited. If, however, the teaching arrangements were conducted on leased premises or on nonpublic school premises, services must be provided only under conditions appropriate for a public school. Ultimate and immediate control of subject matter, personnel, and premises must be under public school authorities and the courses open to all eligible to attend the public school. The court added that incidental or casual occasions of shared time instruction upon nonpublic school premises were not barred even if not all the controls existed.

88. Commonwealth ex rel. Wehrle v. School Dist., 241 Pa. 224, 88 A. 481 (1913).

89. Morton v. Board of Educ., 69 Ill. App.2d 38, 216 N.E.2d 305 (1966).

90. Special Dist. for Educ. and Training of Handicapped Children v. Wheeler, 408 S.W.2d 60 (Mo.1966).

91. In re Proposal C, 384 Mich. 390, 185 N.W.2d 9 (1971).

Examples given were special limited courses by experts employed by the public school system and instruction at a planetarium or art collection of a nonpublic school.

Subsequent to this decision an extensive shared time program was instituted in Grand Rapids. The program increased to the point where publicly paid teachers were conducting in the religious schools ten percent of the classes, and the total expenditure of public funds was six million dollars. A substantial number of the teachers employed in the program had previously been employed in the parochial schools concerned. The Sixth Circuit Court of Appeals held that the plan violated the federal Constitution.[92]

This holding was affirmed by the Supreme Court.[93] Religion was found to be promoted in three ways. The state-paid instructors in these pervasively religious schools might "subtly or overtly" indoctrinate the students in specific religious tenets; the provision of state-funded instruction in religious school buildings might convey a symbolic message to students and general public of state support for religion; the funding of the program subsidizes the religious functions of the parochial schools by assuming a substantial portion of their responsibility for teaching secular subjects. Another program in Grand Rapids was invalidated by the same Supreme Court decision. This was an after-school program of "community education" in which parochial school instructors were employed part-time by the public school system to teach in the same parochial school buildings that were used by those parochial students who elected to enroll.

The Supreme Court in a case from Missouri considered the question whether federal funds provided under the Elementary and Secondary Education Act of 1965 (ESEA) for "educationally deprived children" in private as well as in public schools must be used to supply publicly employed teachers to give remedial instruction on the premises of private schools.[94] The Court concluded that such was not required. What was required was that comparable, not identical, services be provided. (The word "comparable" was not included in the Act.) The Court said that state law governed uses of federal funds under the Act. If it were eventually determined that Missouri law prohibited the use of federal funds for on-the-premises private school instruction, the federal statute would require "not that that law be preempted, but, rather, that it be accommodated by the use of services not proscribed under state law."

A three-judge federal District Court refused to issue a preliminary injunction against using federal funds under ESEA to pay teachers assigned to perform education services for disadvantaged youth in reli-

---

92. Americans United for Separation of Church and State v. School Dist. of City of Grand Rapids, 718 F.2d 1389 (6 Cir.1983).

93. School Dist. of City of Grand Rapids v. Ball, 473 U.S. 373, 105 S.Ct. 3216, 87 L.Ed.2d 267 (1985). [Case No. 9]

94. Wheeler v. Barrera, 417 U.S. 402, 94 S.Ct. 2274, 41 L.Ed.2d 159 (1974).

gious schools during regular school hours.[95] The court instead ordered that the question be considered at a trial where the evidence could be carefully evaluated. It said such was necessary because the attack was on only one aspect of the statute as applied. Eventually the Court of Appeals, Second Circuit, found that the system used in New York City to provide the services was unconstitutional.[96]

The Supreme Court affirmed this holding.[97] It found the program as conducted to be very similar to that it invalidated in the Grand Rapids case. Publicly funded instructors taught classes composed exclusively of private school students in private school buildings. An "overwhelming" number of the participating private schools were religiously affiliated. The federal funds provided not only instructors, but all materials and supplies for the program. The one major difference was that New York City had adopted a system for monitoring the religious content of the ESEA classes in the religious schools. This was not constitutionally significant, however, because such a system "inevitably results in the excessive entanglement of church and state" that violates the establishment clause.

After the preceding decision the Department of Education required each local school board administering the federal funds to deduct as part of "administrative costs" the expenses of implementing the decision (e.g., transporting the private school students to public schools, obtaining mobile classrooms, insuring the new property). "Administrative costs" were to be taken from the total allotment to the school district before dividing the funds between public and private schools. The regulation was challenged as an aid to parochial schools because it had the effect of reducing funds available for public school students and directing more money to services for students in parochial schools. The argument that parochial school students were unconstitutionally favored was rejected by several circuits, the Seventh consolidating their opinions.[98]

[Case No. 1] Constitutionality of Providing Transportation to Parochial School Students

appelant → EVERSON v. BOARD OF EDUC. OF EWING TP. ←

Supreme Court of the United States, 1947.

330 U.S. 1, 67 S.Ct. 504, 91 L.Ed. 711.

appelee

Mr. Justice Black delivered the opinion of the Court.

A New Jersey statute authorizes its local school districts to make rules and contracts for the transportation of children to and from schools. The appellee, a township board of education, acting pursuant to

---

95. National Coalition for Public Educ. and Religious Liberty v. Califano, 446 F.Supp. 193 (S.D.N.Y.1978).

96. Felton v. Secretary, United States Dep't of Educ., 739 F.2d 48 (2 Cir.1984).

97. Aguilar v. Felton, 473 U.S. 402, 105 S.Ct. 3232, 87 L.Ed.2d 290 (1985). [Case No. 10]

98. Board of Educ. of City of Chicago v. Alexander, 983 F.2d 745 (7 Cir.1992).

this statute authorized reimbursement to parents of money expended by them for the bus transportation of their children on regular busses operated by the public transportation system. Part of this money was for the payment of transportation of some children in the community to Catholic parochial schools. These church schools give their students, in addition to secular education, regular religious instruction conforming to the religious tenets and modes of worship of the Catholic Faith. The superintendent of these schools is a Catholic priest.

* * *

The only contention here is that the State statute and the resolution, in so far as they authorized reimbursement to parents of children attending parochial schools, violate the Federal Constitution in these two respects, which to some extent, overlap. First. They authorize the State to take by taxation the private property of some and bestow it upon others, to be used for their own private purposes. This, it is alleged, violates the due process clause of the Fourteenth Amendment. Second. The statute and the resolution forced inhabitants to pay taxes to help support and maintain schools which are dedicated to, and which regularly teach, the Catholic Faith. This is alleged to be a use of State power to support church schools contrary to the prohibition of the First Amendment which the Fourteenth Amendment made applicable to the states.

First. The due process argument that the State law taxes some people to help others carry out their private purposes is framed in two phases. The first phase is that a state cannot tax A to reimburse B for the cost of transporting his children to church schools. This is said to violate the due process clause because the children are sent to these church schools to satisfy the personal desires of their parents, rather than the public's interest in the general education of all children. This argument, if valid, would apply equally to prohibit state payment for the transportation of children to any non-public school, whether operated by a church, or any other non-government individual or group. But, the New Jersey legislature has decided that a public purpose will be served by using tax-raised funds to pay the bus fares of all school children, including those who attend parochial schools. The New Jersey Court of Errors and Appeals has reached the same conclusion. The fact that a state law, passed to satisfy a public need, coincides with the personal desires of the individuals most directly affected is certainly an inadequate reason for us to say that a legislature has erroneously appraised the public need.

* * *

It is much too late to argue that legislation intended to facilitate the opportunity of children to get a secular education serves no public purpose. The same thing is no less true of legislation to reimburse needy parents, or all parents, for payment of the fares of their children so that they can ride in public busses to and from schools rather than run the risk of traffic and other hazards incident to walking or "hitchhiking." Nor does it follow that a law has a private rather than a public purpose because it provides that tax-raised funds will be paid to reimburse individuals on account of money spent by them in a way which furthers a public program. Subsidies and loans to individuals such as farmers and home owners, and to privately owned transportation systems, as well as many other kinds of businesses, have been commonplace practices in our state and national history.

* * *

Second. The New Jersey statute is challenged as a "law respecting an establishment of religion." The First Amendment, as made applicable to the states by the Fourteenth, commands that a state "shall make no law respecting an establishment of religion, or prohibiting the free exercise thereof." These words of the First Amendment reflected in the minds of early Americans a vivid mental picture of conditions and practices which they fervently wished to stamp out in order to preserve liberty for themselves and for their posterity. Doubtless their goal has not been entirely reached; but so far has the Nation moved toward it that the expression "law respecting an establishment of religion," probably does not so vividly remind present-day Americans of the evils, fears, and political problems that caused that expression to be written into our Bill of Rights. Whether this New Jersey law is one respecting the "establishment of religion" requires an understanding of the meaning of that language, particularly with respect to the imposition of taxes. Once again, therefore, it is not inappropriate briefly to review the background and environment of the period in which that constitutional language was fashioned and adopted.

* * *

The "establishment of religion" clause of the First Amendment means at least this: Neither a state nor the Federal Government can set up a church. Neither can pass laws which aid one religion, aid all religions, or prefer one religion over another. Neither can force nor influence a person to go to or to remain away from church against his will or force him to profess a belief or disbelief in any religion. No person can be punished for entertaining or professing religious beliefs or disbeliefs, for church attendance or non-attendance. No tax in any amount, large or small, can be levied to support any religious activities or institutions, whatever they may be called, or whatever form they may adopt to teach or practice religion. Neither a state nor the Federal Government can, openly or secretly, participate in the affairs of any religious organizations or groups and vice versa. In the words of Jefferson, the clause against establishment of religion by law was intended to erect "a wall of separation between Church and State."

* * * New Jersey cannot consistently with the "establishment of religion" clause of the First Amendment contribute tax-raised funds to the support of an institution which teaches the tenets and faith of any church. On the other hand, other language of the amendment commands that New Jersey cannot hamper its citizens in the free exercise of their own religion. Consequently, it cannot exclude individual Catholics, Lutherans, Mohammedans, Baptists, Jews, Methodists, Nonbelievers, Presbyterians, or the members of any other faith, *because of their faith, or lack of it,* from receiving the benefits of public welfare legislation. While we do not mean to intimate that a state could not provide transportation only to children attending public schools, we must be careful, in protecting the citizens of New Jersey against state-established churches, to be sure that we do not inadvertently prohibit New Jersey from extending its general State law benefits to all its citizens without regard to their religious belief.

Measured by these standards, we cannot say that the First Amendment prohibits New Jersey from spending tax-raised funds to pay the bus fares of parochial school pupils as a part of a general program under which it pays the fares of pupils attending public and other schools. It is undoubtedly true that children are helped to get to church schools. There is even a possibility that some of the children might not be sent to the church schools if the parents were compelled to pay their children's bus fares out of their own pockets when transportation to a public school would have been paid for by the State. * * * Similarly, parents might be reluctant to permit their children to attend schools which the state had cut off from such general government services as ordinary police and fire protection, connections for sewage disposal, public highways and sidewalks. Of course, cutting off church schools from these services, so separate and so indisputably marked off from the religious function, would make it far more difficult for the schools to operate. But such is obviously not the purpose of the First Amendment. That Amendment requires the state to be a neutral in its relations with groups of religious believers and non-believers; it does not require the state to be their adversary. State power is no more to be used so as to handicap religions, than it is to favor them.

This Court has said that parents may, in the discharge of their duty under state compulsory education laws, send their children to a religious rather than a public school if the school meets the secular educational requirements which the state has power to impose. It appears that these parochial schools meet New Jersey's requirements. The State contributes no money to the schools. It does not support them. Its legislation, as applied, does no more than provide a general program to help parents get their children, regardless of their religion, safely and expeditiously to and from accredited schools.

The First Amendment has erected a wall between church and state. That wall must be kept high and impregnable. We could not approve the slightest breach. New Jersey has not breached it here.

Affirmed.

Notes

1. The Court of Appeals of New York declared unconstitutional a statute permitting the use of public funds to transport pupils to church-sponsored schools. Judd v. Board of Education, 278 N.Y. 200, 15 N.E.2d 576 (1938). Following this decision, the people of New York approved a constitutional

amendment approving such transportation. The same sequence occurred in Wisconsin. State ex rel. Reynolds v. Nusbaum, 17 Wis.2d 148, 115 N.W.2d 761 (1962).

2. The last paragraph of the majority opinion upset many of those who applauded the holding of the Court because it seemed to say that transportation aid for parochial school children was as far as the state could go in this area. Do you agree? Justice Jackson was disturbed along other lines. In his dissent he said that the last sentence reminded him of Byron's Julia, who "whispering I will ne'er consent, consented." Was his point well taken?

3. This case laid to rest the contention that the First Amendment barred only official preference of one or more religions over others. The statement that "neither a state nor the Federal Government can * * * aid all religions * * * has been repeated many times by the Supreme Court since 1947.

4. Justice Rutledge, in the minority opinion signed by all four dissenters, stated that it is impossible to select the cost of transportation from among other costs of education and characterize it as not aiding the private schools, because where needed it is "as essential to education as any other element" of the total cost burden. Is this point answered by the majority? If so, how?

5. Fifteen years later in a concurring opinion in Engel v. Vitale, 370 U.S. 421, 82 S.Ct. 1261, 8 L.Ed.2d 601 (1962), Justice Douglas (the "fifth man" in the present case) stated that in retrospect he agreed with the dissenters. He repeated this thought in a concurring opinion in 1963 in School District of Abington Tp., Pa. v. Schempp [Case No. 4].

[Case No. 2] Constitutionality of Voluntary Religious Instruction in Public Schools   *as represented by*

PEOPLE OF STATE OF ILLINOIS EX REL. McCOLLUM v. BOARD OF EDUC. OF SCHOOL DIST. NO. 71, CHAMPAIGN COUNTY

Supreme Court of the United States, 1948.
333 U.S. 203, 68 S.Ct. 461, 92 L.Ed. 649.

Mr. Justice Black delivered the opinion of the Court.

* * *

* * * In 1940 interested members of the Jewish, Roman Catholic, and a few of the Protestant faiths formed a voluntary association called the Champaign Council on Religious Education. They obtained permission from the Board of Education to offer classes in religious instruction to public school pupils in grades four to nine inclusive. Classes were made up of pupils whose parents signed printed cards requesting that their children be permitted to attend; they were held weekly, thirty minutes for the lower grades, forty-five minutes for the higher. The council employed the religious teachers at no expense to the school authorities, but the instructors were subject to the approval and supervision of the superintendent of schools. The classes were taught in three separate religious groups by Protestant teachers, Catholic priests, and a Jewish rabbi, although for the past several years there have apparently been no classes instructed in the Jewish religion. Classes were conduct-

ed in the regular classrooms of the school building. Students who did not choose to take the religious instruction were not released from public school duties; they were required to leave their classrooms and go to some other place in the school building for pursuit of their secular studies. On the other hand, students who were released from secular study for the religious instructions were required to be present at the religious classes. Reports of their presence or absence were to be made to their secular teachers.

The foregoing facts, without reference to others that appear in the record, show the use of tax-supported property for religious instruction and the close cooperation between the school authorities and the religious council in promoting religious education. The operation of the state's compulsory education system thus assists and is integrated with the program of religious instruction carried on by separate religious sects. Pupils compelled by law to go to school for secular education are released in part from their legal duty upon the condition that they attend the religious classes. This is beyond all question a utilization of the tax-established and tax-supported public school system to aid religious groups to spread their faith. And it falls squarely under the ban of the First Amendment (made applicable to the States by the Fourteenth) as we interpreted it in Everson v. Board of Education. There we said: "Neither a state nor the Federal Government can set up a church. Neither can pass laws which aid one religion, aid all religions, or prefer one religion over another. Neither can force or influence a person to go to or to remain away from church against his will or force him to profess a belief or disbelief in any religion. No person can be punished for entertaining or professing religious beliefs or disbeliefs, for church attendance or nonattendance. No tax in any amount, large or small, can be levied to support any religious activities or institutions, whatever they may be called, or whatever form they may adopt to teach or practice religion. Neither a state nor the Federal Government can, openly or secretly, participate in the affairs of any religious organizations or groups, and vice versa. In the words of Jefferson, the clause against establishment of religion by law was intended to erect 'a wall of separation between Church and State.' " The majority in the Everson case, and the minority as shown by quotations from the dissenting views, * * * agreed that the First Amendment's language, properly interpreted, had erected a wall of separation between Church and State. They disagreed as to the facts shown by the record and as to the proper application of the First Amendment's language to those facts.

* * *

To hold that a state cannot consistently with the First and Fourteenth Amendments utilize its public school system to aid any or all religious faiths or sects in the dissemination of their doctrines and ideals does not, as counsel urge, manifest a governmental hostility to religion or religious teachings. A manifestation of such hostility would be at war with our national tradition as embodied in the First Amendment's guaranty of the free exercise of religion. For the First Amendment rests upon the premise that both religion and government can best work to achieve their lofty aims if each is left free from the other within its respective sphere. Or, as we said in the Everson case, the First Amendment has erected a wall between Church and State which must be kept high and impregnable.

Here not only are the state's tax-supported public school buildings used for the dissemination of religious doctrines. The State also affords sectarian groups an invaluable aid in that it helps to provide pupils for their religious classes through use of the state's compulsory public school machinery. This is not separation of Church and State.

* * *

Notes

1. Observe that the Court in this eight-Justice opinion quotes with approval from *Everson* on the point of the unconstitutionality of government aid to *all* religions.

2. Do you think the same result would be reached by the Court (1) if the children not attending classes in religion were dismissed; (2) if the classes in religion were held after school hours; (3) if the classes were held on Saturdays?

3. It has been suggested that a child not instructed in religion is not fully educated and that the public schools, as the special agency established to provide education, should assume responsibility for religious education as part of the school's program. What are the pros and cons of this suggestion?

4. Is the method of operation here, which was found to be constitutionally forbidden, sound in terms of general educational principles when applied to education in religion?

5. Counsel for the board of education argued that to bar the plan in Champaign would manifest a governmental hostility to religion and religious teachings. The Court expressly rejected this view of its holding. Can failure to aid an item ever be the same as opposition to it?

[Case No. 3] Constitutionality of "Released Time" Program for Religious Instruction

ZORACH v. CLAUSON

Supreme Court of the United States, 1952.
343 U.S. 306, 72 S.Ct. 679, 96 L.Ed. 954.

Mr. Justice Douglas delivered the opinion of the Court.

New York City has a program which permits its public schools to release students during the school day so that they may leave the school buildings and school grounds and go to religious centers for religious instruction or devotional exercises. A student is released on written request of his parents. Those not released stay in the classrooms. The churches make weekly reports to the schools, sending a list of children who have been released from public school but who have not reported for religious instruction.

This "released time" program involves neither religious instruction in public school classrooms nor the expenditure of public funds. All costs, including the application blanks, are paid by the religious organizations. The case is therefore unlike McCollum v. Board of Education * * *.

* * *

It takes obtuse reasoning to inject any issue of the "free exercise" of religion into the present case. No one is forced to go to the religious classroom and no religious exercise or instruction is brought to the classrooms of the public schools. A student need not take religious instruction. He is left to his own desires as to the manner or time of his religious devotions, if any.

There is a suggestion that the system involves the use of coercion to get public school students into religious classrooms. There is no evidence in the record before us that supports that conclusion. The present record indeed tells us that the school authorities are neutral in this regard and do no more than release students whose parents so request. If in fact coercion were used, if it were established that any one or more teachers were using their office to persuade or force students to take the religious instruction, a wholly different case would be presented. * * *

Moreover, apart from that claim of coercion, we do not see how New York by this type of "released time" program has made a law respecting an establishment of religion within the meaning of the First Amendment. There is much talk of the separation of Church and State in the history of the Bill of Rights and in the decisions clustering around the First Amendment. There cannot be the slightest doubt that the First Amendment reflects the philosophy that Church and State should be separated. And so far as interference with the "free exercise" of religion and an "establishment" of religion are concerned, the separation must be complete and unequivocal. The First Amendment within the scope of its coverage permits no exception; the prohibition is absolute. The First Amendment, however, does not say that in every and all respects there shall be a separation of Church and State. Rather, it studiously defines the manner, the specific ways, in which there shall be no concert or union or dependency one on the other. That is the common sense of the matter. Otherwise the state and religion would be aliens to each other—hostile, suspicious, and even unfriendly. Churches could not be required to pay even property taxes. Municipalities would not be permitted to render police or fire protection to religious groups. * * *

We would have to press the concept of separation of Church and State to these extremes to condemn the present law on constitutional grounds. The nullification of this law would have wide and profound effects. A Catholic student applies to his teacher for permission to leave the school during hours on a Holy Day of Obligation to attend a mass. A Jewish student asks his teacher for permission to be excused for Yom Kippur. A Protestant wants the afternoon off for a family baptismal ceremony. In each case the teacher requires parental consent in writing. In each case the teacher, in order to make sure the student is not a truant, goes further and requires a report from the priest, rabbi, or the minister. The teacher in other words cooperates in a religious program to the extent of making it possible for her students to participate in it. Whether she does it occasionally for a few students, regularly for one, or pursuant to a systematized program designed to further the religious needs of all the students does not alter the character of the act.

We are a religious people whose institutions presuppose a Supreme Being. We guarantee the freedom to worship as one chooses. We make room for as wide a variety of beliefs and creeds as the spiritual needs of man deem necessary. We sponsor an attitude on the part of government that shows no partiality to any one group and that lets each flourish according to the zeal of its adherents and the appeal of its dogma. When the state encourages religious instruction or cooperates with religious authorities by adjusting the schedule of public events to sectarian needs, it follows the best of our traditions. For it then respects the religious nature of our people and accommodates the public service to their spiritual needs. To hold that it may not would be to find in the Constitution a requirement that the government show a callous indifference to religious groups. That would be preferring those who believe in no religion over those who do believe. Government may not finance religious groups nor undertake religious instruction nor blend secular and sectarian education nor use secular institutions to force one or some religion on any person. But we find no constitutional requirement which makes it necessary for government to be hostile to religion and to throw its weight against efforts to widen the effective scope of religious influence. The government must be neutral when it comes to competition between sects. It may not thrust any sect on any person. It may not make a religious observance compulsory. It may not coerce anyone to attend church, to observe a religious holiday, or to take religious instruction. But it can close its doors or suspend its operations as to those who want to repair to their religious sanctuary for worship or instruction. No more than that is undertaken here.

This program may be unwise and improvident from an educational or a community viewpoint. That appeal is made to us on a theory, previously advanced, that each case must be decided on the basis of "our own prepossessions." Our individual preferences, however, are not the constitutional standard. The constitutional standard is the separation of Church and State. The problem, like many problems in constitutional law, is one of degree.

In the McCollum case the classrooms were used for religious instruction and the force of the public school was used to promote that instruction. Here, as we have said, the public schools do no more than accommodate their schedules to a program of outside religious instruction. We follow the McCollum case. But we cannot expand it to cover the present released program unless separation of Church and State means that public institutions can make no adjustments of their schedules to accommodate the religious needs of the people. We cannot read into the Bill of Rights such a philosophy of hostility to religion.

* * *

Notes

1. This is the only case decided by the Supreme Court in the church-state-education area in which Justices Black and Douglas were in disagreement. In his dissent Justice Black saw "no significant difference" between the invalid Champaign plan (*McCollum*) and the New York plan because in both "school authorities release some of the children on the condition that they attend the religious classes, get reports on whether they attend, and hold the other children in the school building until the religious hour is over."

2. Justice Frankfurter in dissent suggested that "dismissed time" would be constitutional. Why do you think that religious leaders have not advocated that plan as they have "released time?"

3. Justice Douglas for the six-Justice majority comments that the "released time" program may be unwise from an educational viewpoint. What is your opinion?

4. A released time program was upheld in 1975 by the Supreme Court of Wisconsin, which found *Zorach* to be controlling. The court rejected a claim that *Zorach* had been superseded by subsequent United States Supreme Court opinions. The Wisconsin constitution had been amended to permit the practice. State ex rel. Holt v. Thompson, 66 Wis.2d 659, 225 N.W.2d 678 (1975). The Fourth Circuit reached a similar conclusion about the continued viability of *Zorach*. Smith v. Smith, 523 F.2d 121 (4 Cir.1975), cert. den. 423 U.S. 1073, 96 S.Ct. 856, 47 L.Ed.2d 83 (1976).

[Case No. 4] Constitutionality of the Bible and the Lord's Prayer in Public Schools

SCHOOL DIST. OF ABINGTON TP., PENNSYLVANIA v. SCHEMPP

MURRAY v. CURLETT

Supreme Court of the United States, 1963.
374 U.S. 203, 83 S.Ct. 1560, 10 L.Ed.2d 844.

Mr. Justice Clark delivered the opinion of the Court.

* * * These companion cases present the issues in the context of state action requiring that schools begin each day with readings from the Bible. While raising the basic questions under slightly different factual situations, the cases permit of joint treatment. In light of the history of the First Amendment and of our cases interpreting and applying its requirements, we hold that the practices at issue and the laws requiring them are unconstitutional under the Establishment Clause, as applied to the States through the Fourteenth Amendment.

* * * The Commonwealth of Pennsylvania by law, * * * requires that "At least ten verses from the Holy Bible shall be read, without comment, at the opening of each public school on each school day. Any child shall be excused from such Bible reading, or attending such Bible reading, upon the written request of his parent or guardian." The Schempp family, husband and wife and two of their three children, brought suit to enjoin enforcement of the statute * * *.

The appellees Edward Lewis Schempp, his wife Sidney, and their children, Roger and Donna, are of the Unitarian faith and are members of the Unitarian Church in Germantown, Philadelphia, Pennsylvania, where they * * * regularly attend religious services. * * *

On each school day at the Abington Senior High School between 8:15 and 8:30 a.m., while the pupils are attending their home rooms or advisory sections, opening exercises are conducted pursuant to the statute. The exercises are broadcast into each room in the school building through an intercommunications system and are conducted under the supervision of a teacher by students attending the school's radio and television workshop. Selected students from this course gather each morning in the school's workshop studio for the exercises, which include readings by one of the students of 10 verses of the Holy Bible, broadcast to each room in the building. This is followed by the recitation of the Lord's Prayer, likewise over the intercommunications system, but also by the students in the various classrooms, who are asked to stand and join in repeating the prayer in unison. The exercises are closed with the flag salute and such pertinent announcements as are of interest to the students. Participation in the opening exercises, as directed by the statute, is voluntary. The student reading the verses from the Bible may select the passages and read from any version he chooses, although the only copies furnished by the school are the King James version, copies of which were circulated to each teacher by the school district. During the period in which the exercises have been conducted the King James, the Douay and the Revised Standard versions of the Bible have been used, as well as the Jewish Holy Scriptures. There are no prefatory statements, no questions asked or solicited, no comments or explanations made and no interpretations given at or during the exercises. The students and parents are advised that the student may absent himself from the classroom or, should he elect to remain, not participate in the exercises.

* * *

At the first trial Edward Schempp and the children testified as to specific religious doctrines purveyed by a literal reading of the Bible "which were contrary to the religious beliefs which they held and to their familial teaching." The children testified that all of the doctrines to which they referred were read to them at various times as part of the exercises. Edward Schempp testified at the second trial that he had considered having Roger and Donna excused from attendance at the exercises but decided against it for several reasons, including his belief that the children's relationships with their teachers and classmates would be adversely affected.

* * *

* * * [In the Baltimore, Maryland, case of Murray, the] petition particularized the petitioners' atheistic beliefs and stated that the rule, as practiced, violated their rights

"in that it threatens their religious liberty by placing a premium on belief as against non-belief and subjects their freedom of conscience to the rule of the majority; it pronounces belief in

God as the source of all moral and spiritual values, equating these values with religious values, and thereby renders sinister, alien and suspect the beliefs and ideals of your Petitioners, promoting doubt and question of their morality, good citizenship and good faith."

* * *

The wholesome "neutrality" of which this Court's cases speak * * * stems from a recognition of the teachings of history that powerful sects or groups might bring about a fusion of governmental and religious functions or a concert or dependency of one upon the other to the end that official support of the State or Federal Government would be placed behind the tenets of one or of all orthodoxies. This the Establishment Clause prohibits. And a further reason for neutrality is found in the Free Exercise Clause, which recognizes the value of religious training, teaching and observance and, more particularly, the right of every person to freely choose his own course with reference thereto, free of any compulsion from the state. This the Free Exercise Clause guarantees. Thus, as we have seen, the two clauses may overlap. As we have indicated, the Establishment Clause has been directly considered by this Court eight times in the past score of years and, with only one Justice dissenting on the point, it has consistently held that the clause withdrew all legislative power respecting religious belief or the expression thereof. The test may be stated as follows: what are the purpose and the primary effect of the enactment? If either is the advancement or inhibition of religion then the enactment exceeds the scope of legislative power as circumscribed by the Constitution. That is to say that to withstand the strictures of the Establishment Clause there must be a secular legislative purpose and a primary effect that neither advances nor inhibits religion.
* * *

Applying the Establishment Clause principles to the cases at bar we find that the States are requiring the selection and reading at the opening of the school day of verses from the Holy Bible and the recitation of the Lord's Prayer by the students in unison. These exercises are prescribed as part of the curricular activities of students who are required by law to attend school. They are held in the school buildings under the supervision and with the participation of teachers employed in those schools. * * *

* * *

* * * Nor are these required exercises mitigated by the fact that individual students may absent themselves upon parental request, for that fact furnishes no defense to a claim of unconstitutionality under the Establishment Clause. Further, it is no defense to urge that the religious practices here may be relatively minor encroachments on the First Amendment. * * *

It is insisted that unless these religious exercises are permitted a "religion of secularism" is established in the schools. We agree of course that the State may not establish a "religion of secularism" in the sense of affirmatively opposing or showing hostility to religion, thus "preferring those who believe in no religion over those who do believe." We do not agree, however, that this decision in any sense has that effect. In addition, it might well be said that one's education is not complete without a study of comparative religion or the history of religion and its relationship to the advancement of civilization. It certainly may be said that the Bible is worthy of study for its literary and historic qualities. Nothing we have said here indicates that such study of the Bible or of religion, when presented objectively as part of a secular program of education, may not be effected consistent with the First Amendment. But the exercises here do not fall into those categories. They are religious exercises, required by the States in violation of the command of the First Amendment that the Government maintain strict neutrality, neither aiding nor opposing religion.

* * *

The place of religion in our society is an exalted one, achieved through a long tradition of reliance on the home, the church and the inviolable citadel of the individual heart and mind. We have come to recognize through bitter experience that it is not within the power of government to invade that citadel, whether its purpose or effect be to aid or oppose, to advance or retard. In the relationship between man and religion, the State is firmly committed to a position of neutrality. Though the application of that rule requires interpretation of a delicate sort, the rule itself is clearly and concisely stated in the words of the First Amendment. * * *

* * *

Notes

1. In the trial court, the father of the Schempp children testified that he declined to request that the children be excused from the morning exercises because he thought they would be labeled "odd balls." Was this concern of the father justified?

2. In the case of Engel v. Vitale (Regent's Prayer), cited in the text, the Supreme Court struck down as unconstitutional a requirement by school authorities that a prescribed "non-denominational" prayer be said aloud at the beginning of each school day. Is there a different constitutional issue raised when the prescribed prayer is formulated by school authorities, rather than their requiring the Lord's Prayer? What issues arise with "silent" prayer?

3. In *Engel* the Supreme Court distinguished patriotic and ceremonial references to the Deity from religious exercises, the latter being constitutionally forbidden in public schools. How would "under God" in the phrase "one nation under God" in the official Pledge of Allegiance since 1954 be characterized?

4. In the present case, in addition to the opinion of the Court and the one-Justice dissent, there were three concurring opinions. Do concurring opinions, expressing the writer's legal points of view, clarify or blur the opinion of the Court as a precedent for the future?

[Case No. 5] Constitutionality of Providing Textbooks to Parochial School Students

BOARD OF EDUC. OF CENTRAL SCHOOL DIST. NO. 1 v. ALLEN

Supreme Court of the United States, 1968.
392 U.S. 236, 88 S.Ct. 1923, 20 L.Ed.2d 1060.

Mr. Justice White delivered the opinion of the Court.

A law of the State of New York requires local public school authorities to lend textbooks free of charge to all students in grades seven through 12; students attending private schools are included. This case presents the question whether this statute is a "law respecting the establishment of religion or prohibiting the free exercise thereof," and so in conflict with the First and Fourteenth Amendments to the Constitution, because it authorizes the loan of textbooks to students attending parochial schools. We hold that the law is not in violation of the Constitution.

Until 1965, § 701 of the Education Law of the State of New York, McKinney's Consol. Laws, c. 16, authorized public school boards to designate textbooks for use in the public schools, to purchase such books with public funds, and to rent or sell the books to public school students. In 1965 the Legislature amended § 701, basing the amendments on findings that the "public welfare and safety require that the state and local communities give assistance to educational programs which are important to our national defense and the general welfare of the state." Beginning with the 1966–1967 school year, local school boards were required to purchase textbooks and lend them without charge "to all children residing in such district who are enrolled in grades seven to twelve of a public or private school which complies with the compulsory education law." The books now loaned are "textbooks which are designated for use in any public, elementary or secondary schools of the state or are approved by any boards of education," and which—according to a 1966 amendment—"a pupil is required to use as a text for a semester or more in a particular class in the school he legally attends."

* * *

Everson v. Board of Education is the case decided by this Court that is most nearly in point for today's problem.   * * *

* * *

Of course books are different from buses. Most bus rides have no inherent religious significance, while religious books are common. However, the language of § 701 does not authorize the loan of religious books, and the State claims no right to distribute religious literature. Although the books loaned are those required by the parochial school for use in specific courses, each book loaned must be approved by the public school authorities; only secular books may receive approval. The law was construed by the Court of Appeals of New York as "merely making available secular textbooks at the request of the individual student," supra, and the record contains no suggestion that religious books have been loaned. Absent evidence we cannot assume that school authorities, who constantly face the same problem in selecting textbooks for use in the public schools, are unable to distinguish between secular and religious books or that they will not honestly discharge their duties under the law. In judging the validity of the statute on this record we must proceed on the assumption that books loaned to students are books that are not unsuitable for use in the public schools because of religious content.

The major reason offered by appellants for distinguishing free textbooks from free bus fares is that books, but not buses, are critical to the teaching process, and in a sectarian school that process is employed to teach religion. However, this Court has long recognized that religious schools pursue two goals, religious instruction and secular education. In the leading case of Pierce v. Society of Sisters, the Court held that although it would not question Oregon's power to compel school attendance or require that the attendance be at an institution meeting State-imposed requirements as to quality and nature of curriculum, Oregon had not shown that its interest in secular education required that all children attend publicly operated schools. A premise of this holding was the view that the State's interest in education would be served sufficiently by reliance on the secular teaching that accompanied religious training in the schools maintained by the Society of Sisters. Since *Pierce,* a substantial body of case law has confirmed the power of the States to insist that attendance at private schools, if it is to satisfy state compulsory-attendance laws, be at institutions which provide minimum hours of instruction, employ teachers of specified training, and cover prescribed subjects of instruction. Indeed, the State's interest in assuring that these standards are being met has been considered a sufficient reason for refusing to accept instruction at home as compliance with compulsory education statutes. * * *

Underlying these cases, and underlying also the legislative judgments that have preceded the court decisions, has been a recognition that private education has played and is playing a significant and valuable role in raising national levels of knowledge, competence, and experience. Americans care about the quality of the secular education available to their children. They have considered high quality education to be an indispensable ingredient for achieving the kind of nation, and the kind of citizenry, that they have desired to create. Considering this attitude, the continued willingness to rely on private school systems, including parochial systems, strongly suggests that a wide segment of informed opinion, legislative and otherwise, has found that those schools do an acceptable job of providing secular education to their students. This judgment is further evidence that parochial schools are performing, in addition to their sectarian function, the task of secular education.

Against this background of judgment and experience, unchallenged in the meager record before us in this case, we cannot agree with appellants either that all teaching in a sectarian school is religious or that the processes of secular and religious training are so intertwined that secular textbooks furnished to students by the public are in fact instrumental in the teaching of religion. This case comes to us after summary judgment entered on the pleadings. Nothing in this record supports the proposition that all textbooks, whether they deal with mathematics, physics, foreign languages, history, or literature, are used by the parochial schools to teach religion. No evidence has been offered about particular schools, particular courses, particular teachers, or particular books. We are unable to hold, based solely on judicial notice, that this statute results in unconstitutional involvement of the State with religious instruction or that § 701, for this or the other reasons urged, is a law respecting the establishment of religion within the meaning of the First Amendment.

* * *

The judgment is affirmed.

Notes

1. In this case the Court of Appeals of New York, in upholding the statute by a vote of four-to-three, expressly rejected thinking on the same New York constitutional provision by the same court three decades earlier. See Note 1 on Case No. 1. That amendment covered only transportation.

2. Justice Douglas said in dissent that there is nothing ideological about a bus, school lunch, public nurse, or scholarship. But, in his opinion, the textbook "goes to the very heart of education in a parochial school." Is this distinction valid? He also rhetorically asked, "Can there be the slightest doubt that the head of the parochial school will select the book or books that best promote its sectarian creed?" He further pointed out problems of distinguishing sectarian from secular books by citing examples of history, science, economics, and other texts giving dramatically different treatments of the same subject. Can local boards properly "check on" all proposed texts for all pupils in private schools? Should they be expected to do so?

3. Justice Black in dissent feared that the present textbook law could be a "foot in the door" to obtain public funds to buy real property for parochial schools, pay the salaries of their teachers, etc. How real is this fear? It has been argued that more extensive support should be sustained since the State has a vital interest in the quality of parochial school education. Is this argument persuasive?

4. The Supreme Court has invalidated the furnishing of textbooks to students attending private schools having racially discriminatory policies. (Mississippi had furnished textbooks to private school students long before desegregation of public schools was ordered; so no ruse was involved in the practice.) Norwood v. Harrison, 413 U.S. 455, 93 S.Ct. 2804, 37 L.Ed.2d 723 (1973).

[Case No. 6] Constitutionality of Reimbursements to Parochial Schools

LEMON v. KURTZMAN

EARLEY v. DiCENSO

Supreme Court of the United States, 1971.
403 U.S. 602, 91 S.Ct. 2105, 29 L.Ed.2d 745.

MR. CHIEF JUSTICE BURGER delivered the opinion of the Court.

These two appeals raise questions as to Pennsylvania and Rhode Island statutes providing state aid to church-related elementary and secondary schools. Both statutes are challenged as violative of the Establishment and Free Exercise Clauses of the First Amendment and the Due Process Clause of the Fourteenth Amendment.

Pennsylvania has adopted a statutory program that provides financial support to nonpublic elementary and secondary schools by way of reimbursement for the cost of teachers' salaries, textbooks, and instructional materials in specified secular subjects. Rhode Island has adopted a statute under which the State pays directly to teachers in nonpublic elementary schools a supplement of 15% of their annual salary. Under each statute state aid has been given to church-related educational institutions as well as other private schools. We hold that both statutes are unconstitutional.

I

The Rhode Island Statute

The Rhode Island Salary Supplement Act was enacted in 1969. It rests on the legislative finding that the quality of education available in nonpublic elementary schools has been jeopardized by the rapidly rising salaries needed to attract competent and dedicated teachers. The Act authorizes state officials to supplement the salaries of teachers of secular subjects in nonpublic elementary schools by paying directly to a teacher an amount not in excess of 15% of his current annual salary. As supplemented, however, a nonpublic school teacher's salary cannot exceed the maximum paid to teachers in the State's public schools, and the recipient must be certified by the state board of education in substantially the same manner as public school teachers.

In order to be eligible for the Rhode Island salary supplement, the recipient must teach in a nonpublic school at which the average per-pupil expenditure on secular education is less than the average in the State's public schools during a specified period. Appellant state Commissioner of Education also requires eligible schools to submit financial data. If this information indicates a per-pupil expenditure in excess of the statutory limitation, the records of the school in question must be examined in order to assess how much of the expenditure is attributable to secular education and how much to religious activity.

The Act also requires that teachers eligible for salary supplement must teach only those subjects that are offered in the State's public schools. They must use "only teaching materials which are used in the public schools." Finally, any teacher applying for a salary supplement must first agree in writing "not to teach a course in religion for so long as or during such time as he or she receives any salary supplements" under the Act.

* * *

The District Court concluded that the Act violated the Establishment Clause, holding that it fostered "excessive entanglement" between government and religion. In addition two judges thought that the Act had the impermissible effect of giving "significant aid to a religious enterprise." We affirm.

The Pennsylvania Statute

* * *

The statute authorizes appellee state Superintendent of Public Instruction to "purchase" specified "secular educational services" from nonpublic schools. Under the "contracts" authorized by the statute, the State directly reimburses nonpublic schools solely for their actual expenditures for teachers' salaries, textbooks, and instructional materials. A school seeking reimbursement must maintain prescribed accounting procedures that identify the "separate" cost of the "secular educational service." These accounts are subject to state audit. The funds for this program were originally derived from a new tax on horse and harness racing, but the Act is now financed by a portion of the state tax on cigarettes.

There are several significant statutory restrictions on state aid. Reimbursement is limited to courses "presented in the curricula of the public schools." It is further limited "solely" to courses in the following "secular" subjects: mathematics, modern foreign languages, physical science, and physical education. Textbooks and instructional materials included in the program must be approved by the state Superintendent of Public Instruction. Finally, the statute prohibits reimbursement for any course that contains "any subject matter expressing religious teaching, or the morals or forms of worship of any sect."

* * *

The court granted [Pennsylvania's] motion to dismiss the complaint for failure to state a claim for relief. It held that the Act violated neither the Establishment nor the Free Exercise Clauses, Chief Judge Hastie dissenting. We reverse.

II

In Everson v. Board of Education this Court upheld a state statute which reimbursed the parents of parochial school children for bus transportation expenses. There Mr. Justice Black, writing for the majority, suggested that the decision carried to "the verge" of forbidden territory under the Religion Clauses. Candor compels acknowledgement, moreover, that we can only dimly perceive the lines of demarcation in this extraordinarily sensitive area of constitutional law.

The language of the Religion Clauses of the First Amendment is at best opaque, particularly when compared with other portions of the Amendment. Its authors did not simply prohibit the establishment of a state church or a state religion, an area history shows they regarded as very important and fraught with great dangers. Instead they commanded that there should be "no law *respecting* an establishment of religion." A law may be one "respecting" the forbidden objective while falling short of its total realization. A law "respecting" the proscribed result, that is, the establishment of religion, is not always easily identifiable as one violative of the Clause. A given law might not *establish* a state religion but nevertheless be one "respecting" that end in the sense of being a step that could lead to such establishment and hence offend the First Amendment.

In the absence of precisely stated constitutional prohibitions, we must draw lines with reference to the three main evils against which the Establishment Clause was intended to afford protection: "sponsorship, financial support, and active involvement of the sovereign in religious activity." Walz v. Tax Commission.

Every analysis in this area must begin with consideration of the cumulative criteria developed by the Court over many years. Three such tests may be gleaned from our cases. First, the statute must have a secular legislative purpose; second, its principal or primary effect must be one that neither advances nor inhibits religion, Board of Education v. Allen; finally, the statute must not foster "an excessive government entanglement with religion." *Walz.*

* * *

III

* * *

Our prior holdings do not call for total separation between church and state; total separation is not possible in an absolute sense. Some relationship between government and religious organizations is inevitable. Fire inspections, building and zoning regulations, and state requirements under compulsory school attendance laws are examples of necessary and permissible contacts. * * *

* * *

In order to determine whether the government entanglement with religion is excessive, we must examine the character and purposes of the institutions which are benefited, the nature of the aid that the State provides, and the resulting relationship between the government and the religious authority. * * * Here we find that both statutes foster an impermissible degree of entanglement.

(a) Rhode Island program

* * *

The church schools involved in the program are located close to parish churches. This understandably permits convenient access for religious exercises since instruction in faith and morals is part of the total educational process. The school buildings contain identifying religious symbols such as crosses on the exterior and crucifixes, religious paintings and statues either in the classrooms or hallways. Although only approximately 30 minutes a day are devoted to direct religious instruction, there are religiously oriented extracurricular activities. Approximately two-thirds of the teachers in these schools are nuns of various religious orders. Their dedicated efforts provide an atmosphere in which religious instruction and religious vocations are natural and proper parts of life in such schools. Indeed, as the District Court found, the role of teaching nuns in enhancing the religious atmosphere has led the parochial school authorities to attempt to maintain a one-to-one ratio between nuns and lay teachers in all schools rather than permitting some to be staffed almost entirely by lay teachers.

On the basis of these findings the District Court concluded that the parochial schools constituted "an integral part of the religious mission of the Catholic Church." The various characteristics of the schools make them "a powerful vehicle for transmitting the Catholic faith to the next generation." This process of inculcating religious doctrine is, of course, enhanced by the impressionable age of the pupils, in primary schools particularly. In short, parochial schools involve substantial religious activity and purpose.

The substantial religious character of these church-related schools gives rise to entangling church-state relationships of the kind the Religion Clauses sought to avoid. Although the District Court found that concern for religious values did not inevitably or necessarily intrude into the content of secular subjects, the considerable religious activities of these schools led the legislature to provide for careful governmental controls and surveillance by state authorities in order to ensure that state aid supports only secular education.

The dangers and corresponding entanglements are enhanced by the particular form of aid that the Rhode Island Act provides. Our decisions from *Everson* to *Allen* have permitted the States to provide church-related schools with secular, neutral, or non-ideological services, facilities, or materials. But transportation, school lunches, public health services, and secular textbooks supplied in common to all students were not thought to offend the Establishment Clause. We note that the dissenters in *Allen* seemed chiefly concerned with the pragmatic difficulties involved in ensuring the truly secular content of the textbooks provided at state expense.

In *Allen* the Court refused to make assumptions, on a meager record, about the religious content of the textbooks that the State would be asked to provide. We cannot, however, refuse here to recognize that teachers have a substantially different ideological character than books. In terms of potential for involving some aspect of faith or morals in secular subjects, a textbook's content is ascertainable, but a teacher's handling of a subject is not. We cannot ignore the dangers that a teacher under religious control and discipline poses to the separation of the religious from the purely secular aspects of precollege education. The conflict of functions inheres in the situation.

* * *

We do not assume, however, that parochial school teachers will be unsuccessful in their attempts to segregate their religious beliefs from their secular educational responsibilities. But the potential for impermissible fostering of religion is present. The Rhode Island Legislature has not, and could not, provide state aid on the basis of a mere assumption that secular teachers under religious discipline can avoid conflicts. The State must be certain, given the Religion Clauses, that subsidized teachers do not inculcate religion—indeed the State here has undertaken to do so. To ensure that no trespass occurs, the State has therefore carefully conditioned its aid with pervasive restrictions. An eligible recipient must teach only those courses that are offered in the public schools and use only those texts and materials that are found in the public schools. In addition the teacher must not engage in teaching any course in religion.

A comprehensive, discriminating, and continuing state surveillance will inevitably be required to ensure that these restrictions are obeyed and the First Amendment otherwise respected. Unlike a book, a teacher cannot be inspected once so as to determine the extent and intent of his or her personal beliefs and subjective acceptance of the limitations imposed by the First Amendment. These prophylactic contacts will involve excessive and enduring entanglement between state and church.

* * *

(b) Pennsylvania program

The Pennsylvania statute also provides state aid to church-related schools for teachers' salaries. The complaint describes an educational system that is very similar to the one existing in Rhode Island. According to the allegations, the church-related elementary and secondary schools are controlled by religious organizations, have the purpose of propagating and promoting a particular religious faith, and conduct their operations to fulfill that purpose. Since this complaint was dismissed for failure to state a claim for relief, we must accept these allegations as true for purposes of our review.

As we noted earlier, the very restrictions and surveillance necessary to ensure that teachers play a strictly non-ideological role give rise to entanglements between church and state. The Pennsylvania statute, like that of Rhode Island, fosters this kind of relationship. Reimbursement is not only limited to courses offered in the public schools and materials approved by state officials, but the statute excludes "any subject matter expressing religious teaching, or the morals or forms of worship of any sect." In addition schools seeking reimbursement must maintain accounting procedures that require the State to establish the cost of the secular as distinguished from the religious instruction.

The Pennsylvania statute, moreover, has the further defect of providing state financial aid directly to the church-related schools. This factor distinguishes both *Everson* and *Allen,* for in both those cases the Court was careful to point out that state aid was provided to the student and his parents—not to the church-related school. * * * The history of government grants of a continuing cash subsidy indicates that such programs have almost always been accompanied by varying measures of control and surveillance. The government cash grants before us now provide no basis for predicting that comprehensive measures of surveillance and controls will not follow. In particular the government's post-audit power to inspect and evaluate a church-related school's financial records and to determine which expenditures are religious and which are secular creates an intimate and continuing relationship between church and state.

IV

A broader base of entanglement of yet a different character is presented by the divisive political potential of these state programs. In a community where such a large number of pupils are served by church-related schools, it can be assumed that state assistance will entail considerable political activity. Partisans of parochial schools, understandably concerned with rising costs and sincerely dedicated to both the religious and secular educational missions of their schools, will inevitably champion this cause and promote political action to achieve their goals. Those who oppose state aid, whether for constitutional, religious, or fiscal reasons, will inevitably respond and employ all of the usual political campaign techniques to prevail. Candidates will be forced to declare and voters to choose. It would be unrealistic to ignore the fact that many people confronted with issues of this kind will find their votes aligned with their faith.

Ordinarily political debate and division, however vigorous or even partisan, are normal and healthy manifestations of our democratic system of government, but political division along religious lines was one of the principal evils against which the First Amendment was intended to protect. The potential divisiveness of such conflict is a threat to the normal political process. To have States or communities divide on the issues presented by state aid to parochial schools would tend to confuse and obscure other issues of great urgency. We have an expanding array of vexing issues, local and national, domestic and international, to debate and divide on. It conflicts with our whole history and tradition to permit questions of the Religion Clauses to assume such importance in our legislatures and in our elections that they could divert attention from the myriad issues and problems which confront every level of government. The highways of church and state relationships are not likely to be one-way streets, and the Constitution's authors sought to protect religious worship from the pervasive power of government. The history of many countries attests to the hazards of religion intruding into the political arena or of political power intruding into the legitimate and free exercise of religious belief.

* * *

The potential for political divisiveness related to religious belief and practice is aggravated in these two statutory programs by the need for continuing annual appropriations and the likelihood of larger and larger demands as costs and populations grow. * * *

V

* * *

Finally, nothing we have said can be construed to disparage the role of church-related elementary and secondary schools in our national life. Their contribution has been and is enormous. Nor do we ignore their economic plight in a period of rising costs and expanding need. Taxpayers generally have been spared vast sums by the maintenance of these educational institutions by religious organizations, largely by the gifts of faithful adherents.

The merit and benefits of these schools, however, are not the issue before us in these cases. The sole question is whether state aid to these schools can be squared with the dictates of the Religion Clauses. Under our system the choice has been made that government is to be entirely excluded from the area of religious instruction and churches excluded from the affairs of government. The Constitution decrees that religion must be a private matter for the individual, the family, and the institutions of private choice, and that while some involvement and entanglement is inevitable, lines must be drawn.

* * *

Notes

1. Only Justice White dissented from this decision. Recall that he wrote the six-Justice majority opinion in *Allen* [Case No. 5]. Between *Allen* and *Lemon,* Justices Warren and Fortas (who were not in agreement in *Allen)* had been replaced by Burger and Blackmun.

2. The issue in Walz v. Tax Commission, 397 U.S. 664, 90 S.Ct. 1409, 25 L.Ed.2d 697 (1970) was the constitutionality of tax exemptions for property "used solely for religious worship." It was held that such exemptions are permitted. "Few concepts are more deeply embedded in the fabric of our national life" as manifested by affirmative state action in this regard from colonial times. There is no sponsorship because the government in granting the exemption "does not transfer part of its revenue to churches but simply abstains from demanding that the church support the state." There is no "entanglement" because there is no supervision of the activities of any church. Churches may be considered in a permissible tax-exempt category embracing such organizations as nonprofit hospitals, libraries, and scientific groups.

3. Note the distinction made here between a law "respecting an establishment" of religion and one "establishing" a religion.

4. Consider the discussion in Part IV of the opinion. The "entanglement test" was first articulated as such by Chief Justice Burger in his first church-state case, *Walz.* Observe that here he expands its scope.

5. On the same day that it delivered the opinion in *Lemon,* the Supreme Court by a five-to-four vote upheld the constitutionality of the Higher Education Facilities Act of 1963, except for the provision that after twenty years restrictions against sectarian use of facilities would be removed. Tilton v. Richardson, 403 U.S. 672, 91 S.Ct. 2091, 29 L.Ed.2d 790 (1971). The act provided construction grants to "institutions of higher education" for construction of "academic facilities." Grants to church-related colleges were challenged. The major differences between *Tilton* and *Lemon* as perceived by the Justices who distinguished the cases were that indoctrination was not a substantial purpose or activity of church-related colleges which would not be attended by impressionable children, the aid was of a nonideological nature, and excessive entanglement was absent because the grants were one-time and single-purpose. The fact that religion was not pervasive in the institution led the Court to conclude in 1973 that it was constitutional for South Carolina to issue revenue bonds that benefited a church-related college. The state did not guarantee the bonds with state funds. Hunt v. McNair, 413 U.S. 734, 93 S.Ct. 2868, 37 L.Ed.2d 923 (1973).

6. A federal suit in Missouri sought to have declared unconstitutional a provision in the Missouri Constitution which barred use of state funds directly or indirectly to aid religion or religious institutions. The attack was based on the free exercise of religion clause of the First Amendment and the equal protection clause of the Fourteenth Amendment. Plaintiffs lost, and the Supreme Court affirmed the holding. Brusca v. State of Missouri ex rel. State Board of Education, 332 F.Supp. 275 (E.D.Mo.1971), aff. 405 U.S. 1050, 92 S.Ct. 1493, 31 L.Ed.2d 786 (1972).

[Case No. 7] Constitutionality of Providing Certain Services to Parochial School Students

WOLMAN v. WALTER

Supreme Court of the United States, 1977.
433 U.S. 229, 97 S.Ct. 2593, 53 L.Ed.2d 714.

MR. JUSTICE BLACKMUN delivered the opinion of the Court (Parts I, V, VI, VII, and VIII), together with an opinion (Parts II, III, and IV), in which THE CHIEF JUSTICE, MR. JUSTICE STEWART, and MR. JUSTICE POWELL joined.

This is still another case presenting the recurrent issue of the limitations imposed by the Establishment Clause of the First Amendment, made applicable to the States by the Fourteenth Amendment, Meek v. Pittenger, on state aid to pupils in church-related elementary and secondary schools.   * * *

I

Section 3317.06 was enacted after this Court's May 1975 decision in Meek v. Pittenger, supra, and obviously is an attempt to conform to the teachings of that decision.   * * * In broad outline, the statute authorizes the State to provide nonpublic school pupils with books, instructional materials and equipment, standardized testing and scoring, diagnostic services, therapeutic services, and field trip transportation.

The initial biennial appropriation by the Ohio Legislature for implementation of the statute was the sum of $88,800,000. Funds so appropriated are paid to the State's public school districts and are then expended by them. All disbursements made with respect to nonpublic schools have their equivalents in disbursements for public schools, and the amount expended per pupil in nonpublic schools may not exceed the amount expended per pupil in the public schools.

The parties stipulated that during the 1974–1975 school year there were 720 chartered nonpublic schools in Ohio. Of these, all but 29 were sectarian. More than 96% of the nonpublic enrollment attended sectarian schools, and more than 92% attended Catholic schools. It was also stipulated that, if they were called, officials of representative Catholic schools would testify that such schools operate under the general supervision of the Bishop of their Diocese; that most principals are members of a religious order within the Catholic Church; that a little less than one-third of the teachers are members of such religious orders; that "in all probability a majority of the teachers are members of the Catholic faith"; and that many of the rooms and hallways in these schools are decorated with a Christian symbol. All such schools teach the secular subjects required to meet the State's minimum standards. The state-mandated five-hour day is expanded to include, usually, one-half hour of religious instruction. Pupils who are not members of the Catholic faith are not required to attend religion classes or to participate in religious exercises or activities, and no teacher is required to teach religious doctrine as a part of the secular courses taught in the schools.

The parties also stipulated that nonpublic school officials, if called, would testify that none of the schools covered by the statute discriminate in the admission of pupils or in the hiring of teachers on the basis of race, creed, color, or national origin. * * *

II

The mode of analysis for Establishment Clause questions is defined by the three-part test that has emerged from the Court's decisions. In order to pass muster, a statute must have a secular legislative purpose, must have a principal or primary effect that neither advances nor inhibits religion, and must not foster an excessive government entanglement with religion.

In the present case we have no difficulty with the first prong of this three-part test. We are satisfied that the challenged statute reflects Ohio's legitimate interest in protecting the health of its youth and in providing a fertile educational environment for all the school children of the State. As is usual in our cases, the analytical difficulty has to do with the effect and entanglement criteria.

We have acknowledged before, and we do so again here, that the wall of separation that must be maintained between church and state "is a blurred, indistinct, and variable barrier depending on all the circumstances of a particular relationship." Nonetheless, the Court's numerous precedents "have become firmly rooted," and now provide substantial guidance. We therefore turn to the task of applying the rules derived from our decisions to the respective provisions of the statute at issue.

III

Textbooks

Section 3317.06 authorizes the expenditure of funds:

> "(A) To purchase such secular textbooks as have been approved by the superintendent of public instruction for use in public schools in the state and to loan such textbooks to pupils attending nonpublic schools within the district or to their parents. * * * As used in this section, 'textbook' means any book or book substitute which a pupil uses as a text or text substitute in a particular class or program in the school he regularly attends."

The parties' stipulations reflect operation of the textbook program in accord with the dictates of the statute. In addition, it was stipulated:

> "The secular textbooks used in nonpublic schools will be the same as the textbooks used in the public schools of the state. Common suppliers will be used to supply books to both public and nonpublic school pupils.

> "Textbooks, including book substitutes, provided under this Act shall be limited to books, reusable workbooks, or manuals, whether bound or in looseleaf form, intended for use as a principal source of study material for a given class or a group of students, a copy of which is expected to be available for the individual use of each pupil in such class or group."

This system for the loan of textbooks to individual students bears a striking resemblance to the systems approved in Board of Education v. Allen, and in Meek v. Pittenger. Indeed, the only distinction offered by appellants is that the challenged statute defines "textbook" as "any book or book substitute." Appellants argue that a "book substitute" might include auxiliary equipment and materials that, they assert, may not constitutionally be loaned. See Part VII, infra. We find this argument untenable in light of the statute's separate treatment of instructional materials and equipment in its subsections (B) and (C), and in light of the stipulation defining textbooks as "limited to books, reusable workbooks, or manuals." * * * We find no grounds * * * to doubt the Board of Education's reading of the statute, or to fear that the Board is using the stipulations as a subterfuge. As read, the statute provides the same protections against abuse as were provided in the textbook programs under consideration in *Allen* and in *Meek*.

In the alternative, appellants urge that we overrule *Allen* and *Meek*. This we decline to do. Accordingly, we conclude that § 3317.06(A) is constitutional.

IV

Testing and Scoring

Section 3317.06 authorizes expenditure of funds:

"(J) To supply for use by pupils attending nonpublic schools within the district such standardized tests and scoring services as are in use in the public schools of the state."

These tests "are used to measure the progress of students in secular subjects." Nonpublic school personnel are not involved in either the drafting or scoring of the tests. The statute does not authorize any payment to nonpublic school personnel for the costs of administering the tests.

In Levitt v. Committee for Public Education this Court invalidated a New York statutory scheme for reimbursement of church-sponsored schools for the expenses of teacher-prepared testing. The reasoning behind that decision was straight-forward. The system was held unconstitutional because "no means are available, to assure that internally prepared tests are free of religious instruction."

There is no question that the State has a substantial and legitimate interest in insuring that its youth receive an adequate secular education. The State may require that schools that are utilized to fulfill the State's compulsory education requirement meet certain standards of instruction, and may examine both teachers and pupils to ensure that the State's legitimate interest is being fulfilled. Under the section at issue, the State provides both the schools and the school district with the means of ensuring that the minimum standards are met. The nonpublic school does not control the content of the test or its result. This serves to prevent the use of the test as a part of religious teaching, and thus avoids that kind of direct aid to religion found present in Levitt. Similarly, the inability of the school to control the test eliminates the need for the supervision that gives rise to excessive entanglement. We therefore agree with the District Court's conclusion that § 3317.06(J) is constitutional.

V

Diagnostic Services

Section 3317.06 authorizes expenditures of funds:

"(D) To provide speech and hearing diagnostic services to pupils attending nonpublic schools within the district. Such service shall be provided in the nonpublic school attended by the pupil receiving the service.

* * *

"(F) To provide diagnostic psychological services to pupils attending nonpublic schools within the district. Such services shall be provided in the school attended by the pupil receiving the service."

It will be observed that these speech and hearing and psychological diagnostic services are to be provided within the nonpublic school. It is stipulated, however, that the personnel (with the exception of physicians) who perform the services are employees of the local board of education; that physicians may be hired on a contract basis; that the purpose of these services is to determine the pupil's deficiency or need of assistance; and that treatment of any defect so found would take place off the nonpublic school premises. See Part VI, infra.

Appellants assert that the funding of these services is constitutionally impermissible. They argue that the speech and hearing staff might engage in unrestricted conversation with the pupil and, on occasion, might fail to separate religious instruction from secular responsibilities. They further assert that the communication between the psychological diagnostician and the pupil will provide an impermissible opportunity for the intrusion of religious influence.

The District Court found these dangers so insubstantial as not to render the statute unconstitutional. We agree. This Court's decisions contain a common thread to the effect that the provision of health services to all school children—public and nonpublic—does not have the primary effect of aiding religion. * * * Indeed, appellants recognize this fact in not challenging subsection (E) of the statute that authorizes publicly funded physician, nursing, dental, and optometric services in nonpublic schools. We perceive no basis for drawing a different conclusion with respect to diagnostic speech and hearing services and diagnostic psychological services.

In *Meek* the Court did hold unconstitutional a portion of a Pennsylvania statute at issue there that authorized certain auxiliary services— "remedial and accelerated instruction, guidance counseling and testing, speech and hearing services"—on nonpublic school premises. The Court noted that the teacher or guidance counselor might "fail on occasion to separate religious instruction and the advancement of religious beliefs from his secular educational responsibilities." The Court was of the view that the publicly employed teacher or guidance counselor might depart from religious neutrality because he was "performing important educational services in schools in which education is an integral part of the dominant sectarian mission and in which an atmosphere dedicated to the advancement of religious belief is constantly maintained." The statute was held unconstitutional on entanglement grounds, namely, that in order to insure that the auxiliary teachers and guidance counselors remained neutral, the State would have to engage in continuing surveillance on the school premises. The Court in *Meek* explicitly stated, however, that the provision of diagnostic speech and hearing services by Pennsylvania seemed "to fall within that class of general welfare services for children that may be provided by the State regardless of the incidental benefit that accrues to church-related schools." The provision of such services was invalidated only because it was found unseverable from the unconstitutional portions of the statute.

The reason for considering diagnostic services to be different from teaching or counseling is readily apparent. First, diagnostic services, unlike teaching or counseling, have little or no educational content and are not closely associated with the educational mission of the nonpublic school. Accordingly, any pressure on the public diagnostician to allow the intrusion of sectarian views is greatly reduced. Second, the diagnostician has only limited contact with the child, and that contact involves chiefly the use of objective and professional testing methods to detect students in need of treatment. The nature of the relationship between the diagnostician and the pupil does not provide the same opportunity for the transmission of sectarian views as attends the relationship between teacher and student or that between counselor and student.

We conclude that providing diagnostic services on the nonpublic school premises will not create an impermissible risk of the fostering of ideological views. It follows that there is no need for excessive surveillance, and there will not be impermissible entanglement. We therefore hold that §§ 3317.06(D) and (F) are constitutional.

VI

Therapeutic Services

Sections 3317.06(G), (H), (I), and (K) authorize expenditures of funds for certain therapeutic, guidance, and remedial services for students who have been identified as having a need for specialized attention. Personnel providing the services must be employees of the local board of education or under contract with the State Department of Health. The services are to be performed only in public schools, in public centers, or in mobile units located off the nonpublic school premises. The parties have stipulated: "The determination as to whether these programs would be offered in the public school, public center, or mobile unit will depend on the distance between the public and nonpublic school, the safety factors involved in travel, and the adequacy of accommodations in public schools and public centers."

Appellants concede that the provision of remedial, therapeutic, and guidance services in public schools, public centers, or mobile units is constitutional if both public and nonpublic school students are served simultaneously. Their challenge is limited to the situation where a facility is used to service only nonpublic school students. They argue that any program that isolates the sectarian pupils is impermissible because the public employee providing the service might tailor his approach to reflect and reinforce the ideological view of the sectarian school attended by the children. Such action by the employee, it is claimed, renders direct aid to the sectarian institution. Appellants express particular concern over mobile units because they perceive a danger that such a unit might operate merely as an annex of the school or schools it services.

At the outset, we note that in its present posture the case does not properly present any issue concerning the use of a public facility as an adjunct of a sectarian educational enterprise. The District Court construed the statute, as do we, to authorize services only on sites that are "neither physically nor educationally identified with the functions of the nonpublic school." Thus, the services are to be offered under circumstances that reflect their religious neutrality.

We recognize that, unlike the diagnostician, the therapist may establish a relationship with the pupil in which there might be opportunities to transmit ideological views. In *Meek* the Court acknowledged the danger that publicly employed personnel who provide services analogous to those at issue here might transmit religious instruction and advance religious beliefs in their activities. But, as discussed in Part V, supra, the Court emphasized that this danger arose from the fact that the services were performed in the pervasively sectarian atmosphere of the church-related school. The danger existed there not because the public employee was likely deliberately to subvert his task to the service of religion, but rather because the pressures of the environment might alter his behavior from its normal course. So long as these types of services are offered at truly religiously neutral locations, the danger perceived in *Meek* does not arise.

The fact that a unit on a neutral site on occasion may serve only sectarian pupils does not provoke the same concerns that troubled the Court in *Meek*. The influence on a therapist's behavior that is exerted by the fact that he serves a sectarian pupil is qualitatively different from the influence of the pervasive atmosphere of a religious institution. The dangers perceived in *Meek* arose from the nature of the institution, not from the nature of the pupils.

Accordingly, we hold that providing therapeutic and remedial services at a neutral site off the premises of the nonpublic schools will not have the impermissible effect of advancing religion. Neither will there be any excessive entanglement arising from supervision of public employees to insure that they maintain a neutral stance. It can hardly be said that the supervision of public employees performing public functions on public property creates an excessive entanglement between church and state. Sections 3317.06(G), (H), (I), and (K) are constitutional.

VII

Instructional Materials and Equipment

Sections 3317.06(B) and (C) authorize expenditures of funds for the purchase and loan to pupils or their parents upon individual request of instructional materials and instructional equipment of the kind in use in the public schools within the district and which is "incapable of diversion to religious use." Section 3717.06 also provides that the materials and equipment may be stored on the premises of a nonpublic school and that publicly hired personnel who administer the lending program may perform their services upon the nonpublic school premises when necessary "for efficient implementation of the lending program."

Although the exact nature of the material and equipment is not clearly revealed, the parties have stipulated: "It is expected that materials and equipment loaned to pupils or parents under the new law will be similar to such former materials and equipment except that to the extent that the law requires that materials and equipment capable of diversion to religious issues will not be supplied." Equipment provided under the predecessor statute * * * included projectors, tape recorders, record players, maps and globes, science kits, weather forecasting charts, and the like. * * *

In *Meek,* * * * the Court considered the constitutional validity of a direct loan to nonpublic schools of instructional material and equipment, and, despite the apparent secular nature of the goods, held the loan impermissible. Mr. Justice Stewart, in writing for the Court, stated:

> "The very purpose of many of those schools is to provide an integrated secular and religious education; the teaching process is, to a large extent, devoted to the inculcation of religious values and belief. See Lemon v. Kurtzman. Substantial aid to the educational function of such schools, accordingly, necessarily results in aid to the sectarian school enterprise as a whole. '[T]he secular education those schools provide goes hand in hand with the religious mission that is the only reason for the schools' existence. Within the institution, the two are inextricably intertwined.' "

Thus, even though the loan ostensibly was limited to neutral and secular instructional material and equipment, it inescapably had the primary effect of providing a direct and substantial advancement of the sectarian enterprise.

Appellees seek to avoid *Meek* by emphasizing that it involved a program of direct loans to nonpublic schools. In contrast, the material and equipment at issue under the Ohio statute are loaned to the pupil or his parent. In our view, however, it would exalt form over substance if this distinction were found to justify a result different from that in *Meek.* Before *Meek* was decided by this Court, Ohio authorized the loan of material and equipment directly to the nonpublic schools. Then, in light of *Meek,* the state legislature decided to channel the goods through the parents and pupils. Despite the technical change in legal bailee, the program in substance is the same as before: the equipment is substantially the same; it will receive the same use by the students; and it may still be stored and distributed on the nonpublic school premises. In view of the impossibility of separating the secular education function from the sectarian, the state aid inevitably flows in part in support of the religious role of the schools.

Indeed, this conclusion is compelled by the Court's prior consideration of an analogous issue in Committee for Public Education v. Nyquist. There the Court considered, among others, a tuition reimbursement program whereby New York gave low income parents who sent their children to nonpublic schools a direct and unrestricted cash grant of $50 to $100 per child (but no more than 50% of tuition actually paid). The State attempted to justify the program, as Ohio does here, on the basis that the aid flowed to the parents rather than to the church-related schools. The Court observed, however, that, unlike the bus program in Everson v. Board of Education, and the book program in *Allen,* there "has been no endeavor 'to guarantee the separation between secular and religious educational functions and to insure that State financial aid supports only the former.' " The Court thus found that the grant program served to establish religion. If a grant in cash to parents is impermissible, we fail to see how a grant in kind of goods furthering the religious enterprise can fare any better. Accordingly, we hold §§ 3317.06(B) and (C) to be unconstitutional.

VIII

Field Trips

Section 3317.06 also authorizes expenditures of funds:

"(L) To provide such field trip transportation and services to nonpublic school students as are provided to public school students in the district. School districts may contract with commercial transportation companies for such transportation service if school district buses are unavailable."

There is no restriction on the timing of field trips; the only restriction on number lies in the parallel the statute draws to field trips provided to public school students in the district. The parties have stipulated that the trips "would consist of visits to governmental, industrial, cultural, and scientific centers designed to enrich the secular studies of students." The choice of destination, however, will be made by the nonpublic school teacher from a wide range of locations.

The District Court held this feature to be constitutionally indistinguishable from that with which the Court was concerned in Everson v. Board of Education. We do not agree. In *Everson* the Court approved a system under which a New Jersey board of education reimbursed parents for the cost of sending their children to and from school, public or parochial, by public carrier. The Court analogized the reimbursement to situations where a municipal common carrier is ordered to carry all school children at a reduced rate, or where the police force is ordered to protect all children on their way to and from school. * * * The critical factors in these examples, as in the *Everson* reimbursement system, are that the school has no control over the expenditure of the funds and the effect of the expenditure is unrelated to the content of the education provided. Thus, the bus fare program in *Everson* passed constitutional muster because the school did not determine how often the pupil traveled between home and school—every child must make one round trip every day—and because the travel was unrelated to any aspect of the curriculum.

The Ohio situation is in sharp contrast. First, the nonpublic school controls the timing of the trips and, within a certain range, their frequency and destinations. Thus, the schools, rather than the children, truly are the recipients of the service and, as this Court has recognized, this fact alone may be sufficient to invalidate the program as impermissible direct aid. Second, although a trip may be to a location that would be of interest to those in public schools, it is the individual teacher who makes a field trip meaningful. The experience begins with the study and discussion of the place to be visited; it continues on location with the teacher pointing out items of interest and stimulating the imagination; and it ends with a discussion of the experience. The field trips are an integral part of the educational experience, and where the teacher works within and for a sectarian institution, an unacceptable risk of fostering of religion is an inevitable by-product. * * * Funding of field trips, therefore, must be treated as was the funding of maps and charts in Meek v. Pittenger, the funding of buildings and tuition in Committee for Public Education v. Nyquist, and the funding of teacher-prepared tests in Levitt v. Committee for Public Education; it must be declared an impermissible direct aid to sectarian education.

Moreover, the public school authorities will be unable adequately to insure secular use of the field trip funds without close supervision of the nonpublic teachers. This would create excessive entanglement * * *.

We hold § 3317.06(L) to be unconstitutional.

IX

In summary, we hold constitutional those portions of the Ohio statute authorizing the State to provide nonpublic school pupils with books, standardized testing and scoring, diagnostic services, and therapeutic and remedial services. We hold unconstitutional those portions relating to instructional materials and equipment and field trip services.

* * *

Notes

1. Observe that although a majority of the Justices voted with Justice Blackmun on each of the six issues, his reasoning was not accepted as the Opinion of the Court on the points of books and tests (Parts III and IV). There was no opinion accepted by a majority on these two points despite a vote of six-to-three on the conclusion regarding each of them. (The votes on each of the six points are given in the textual treatment of this case.)

2. Justice Brennan, who would have found all aspects of the statute unconstitutional, said that the statute's provision of a "subsidy" to sectarian schools of $88,800,000 by its enormity offends the First Amendment's prohibition against laws "respecting an establishment of religion." To what extent, if any, should the amount of such a "subsidy" enter the determination of the constitutionality of such a statute?

3. Justices Brennan and Marshall have indicated that they believe *Allen* (Case No. 5) should be overruled. (They were two of the six in that 1968 six-to-three decision. Compare Note 5 on Case No. 1). Justice Marshall emphasized that belief in his opinion here. He would have sustained only the diagnostic health services (Part V). He said he agreed with Justice Brennan that in *Allen* the court did not consider "the significance of the potential for political divisiveness inherent in programs of aid to sectarian schools." This consideration was enunciated in 1971 in *Lemon* (Case No. 6) in the opinion written by Chief Justice Burger and endorsed by all Justices except White. (Justice White wrote the *Allen* opinion.)

4. In this case Justices Burger, White, and Rehnquist would have found no aspect of the Ohio statute unconstitutional. Chief Justice Burger gave no hint as to his reasoning. Justices White and Rehnquist tersely referred to other expressions of their views essentially rejecting the test of "excessive entanglement" set forth in *Lemon*. Justice Rehnquist, however, subsequently applied the test in *Mueller* (Case No. 8), and Justice White signed that opinion.

5. The distinction made between acceptable sites for diagnostic and therapeutic services affects the practice in many states of simply assigning teachers of various types of "special education" to parochial schools.

[Case No. 8] Constitutionality of Income Tax Deduction for Certain Educational Expenses in Public or Parochial Schools

MUELLER v. ALLEN

Supreme Court of the United States, 1983.
463 U.S. 388, 103 S.Ct. 3062, 77 L.Ed.2d 721.

Justice Rehnquist delivered the opinion of the Court.

* * *

Minnesota, by a law originally enacted in 1955 and revised in 1976 and again in 1978, permits state taxpayers to claim a deduction from gross income for certain expenses incurred in educating their children. The deduction is limited to actual expenses incurred for the "tuition, textbooks and transportation" of dependents attending elementary or secondary schools. A deduction may not exceed $500 per dependent in grades K through six and $700 per dependent in grades seven through twelve. Minn.Stat. § 290.09.

* * *

Today's case is no exception to our oft-repeated statement that the Establishment Clause presents especially difficult questions of interpretation and application. * * *

One fixed principle in this field is our consistent rejection of the argument that "any program which in some manner aids an institution with a religious affiliation" violates the Establishment Clause. For example, it is now well-established that a state may reimburse parents for expenses incurred in transporting their children to school, Everson v. Board of Education, and that it may loan secular textbooks to all schoolchildren within the state, Board of Education v. Allen.

Notwithstanding the repeated approval given programs such as those in *Allen* and *Everson*, our decisions also have struck down arrangements resembling, in many respects, these forms of assistance. See, e.g., Lemon v. Kurtzman; Levitt v. Committee for Public Education; Meek v. Pittenger; Wolman v. Walter. In this case we are asked to decide whether Minnesota's tax deduction bears greater resemblance to those types of assistance to parochial schools we have approved, or to those we have struck down. Petitioners place particular reliance on our decision in Committee for Public Education v. Nyquist, where we held invalid a

New York statute providing public funds for the maintenance and repair of the physical facilities of private schools and granting thinly disguised "tax benefits," actually amounting to tuition grants, to the parents of children attending private schools. As explained below, we conclude that § 290.09(22) bears less resemblance to the arrangement struck down in *Nyquist* than it does to assistance programs upheld in our prior decisions and those discussed with approval in *Nyquist*.

The general nature of our inquiry in this area has been guided, since the decision in Lemon v. Kurtzman, by the "three-part" test laid down in that case:

> "First, the statute must have a secular legislative purpose; second, its principle or primary effect must be one that neither advances nor inhibits religion * * *; finally, the statute must not foster 'an excessive government entanglement with religion.' "

While this principle is well settled, our cases have also emphasized that it provides "no more than [a] helpful signpost" in dealing with Establishment Clause challenges. With this *caveat* in mind, we turn to the specific challenges raised against § 290.09(22) under the *Lemon* framework.

Little time need be spent on the question of whether the Minnesota tax deduction has a secular purpose. Under our prior decisions, governmental assistance programs have consistently survived this inquiry even when they have run afoul of other aspects of the *Lemon* framework. This reflects, at least in part, our reluctance to attribute unconstitutional motives to the states, particularly when a plausible secular purpose for the state's program may be discerned from the face of the statute.

A state's decision to defray the cost of educational expenses incurred by parents—regardless of the type of schools their children attend—evidences a purpose that is both secular and understandable. An educated populace is essential to the political and economic health of any community, and a state's efforts to assist parents in meeting the rising cost of educational expenses plainly serves this secular purpose of ensuring that the state's citizenry is well-educated. Similarly, Minnesota, like other states, could conclude that there is a strong public interest in assuring the continued financial health of private schools, both sectarian and non-sectarian. By educating a substantial number of students such schools relieve public schools of a correspondingly great burden—to the benefit of all taxpayers. * * * All these justifications are readily available to support § 290.09(22), and each is sufficient to satisfy the secular purpose inquiry of *Lemon*.

We turn therefore to the more difficult but related question whether the Minnesota statute has "the primary effect of advancing the sectarian aims of the nonpublic schools." In concluding that it does not, we find several features of the Minnesota tax deduction particularly significant. First, an essential feature of Minnesota's arrangement is the fact that § 290.09(22) is only one among many deductions—such as those for medical expenses and charitable contributions—available under the

Minnesota tax laws. Our decisions consistently have recognized that traditionally "[l]egislatures have especially broad latitude in creating classifications and distinctions in tax statutes," in part because the "familiarity with local conditions" enjoyed by legislators especially enables them to "achieve an equitable distribution of the tax burden." Under our prior decisions, the Minnesota legislature's judgment that a deduction for educational expenses fairly equalizes the tax burden of its citizens and encourages desirable expenditures for educational purposes is entitled to substantial deference.

Other characteristics of § 290.09(22) argue equally strongly for the provision's constitutionality. Most importantly, the deduction is available for educational expenses incurred by *all* parents, including those whose children attend public schools and those whose children attend non-sectarian private schools or sectarian private schools. * * * "[T]he provision of benefits to so broad a spectrum of groups is an important index of secular effect."

In this respect, as well as others, this case is vitally different from the scheme struck down in *Nyquist*. There, public assistance amounting to tuition grants, was provided only to parents of children in *nonpublic* schools. This fact had considerable bearing on our decision striking down the New York statute at issue; we explicitly distinguished both *Allen* and *Everson* on the grounds that "In both cases the class of beneficiaries included *all* schoolchildren, those in public as well as those in private schools." Moreover, we intimated that "public assistance (*e.g.*, scholarships) made available generally without regard to the sectarian-nonsectarian or public-nonpublic nature of the institution benefited," might not offend the Establishment Clause. We think the tax deduction adopted by Minnesota is more similar to this latter type of program than it is to the arrangement struck down in *Nyquist*. Unlike the assistance at issue in *Nyquist*, § 290.09(22) permits *all* parents— whether their children attend public school or private—to deduct their children's educational expenses. * * * [A] program, like § 290.09(22), that neutrally provides state assistance to a broad spectrum of citizens is not readily subject to challenge under the Establishment Clause.

We also agree with the Court of Appeals that, by channeling whatever assistance it may provide to parochial schools through individual parents, Minnesota has reduced the Establishment Clause objections to which its action is subject. It is true, of course, that financial assistance provided to parents ultimately has an economic effect comparable to that of aid given directly to the schools attended by their children. It is also true, however, that under Minnesota's arrangement public funds become available only as a result of numerous, private choices of individual parents of school-age children. For these reasons, we recognized in *Nyquist* that the means by which state assistance flows to private schools is of some importance: we said that "the fact that aid is disbursed to parents rather than to * * * schools" is a material consideration in Establishment Clause analysis, albeit "only one among many to be considered." It is noteworthy that all but one of our recent cases invalidating state aid to parochial schools have involved the direct transmission of assistance from the state to the schools themselves. The exception, of course, was *Nyquist,* which, as discussed previously, is distinguishable from this case on other grounds. Where, as here, aid to parochial schools is available only as a result of decisions of individual parents no "imprimatur of State approval" can be deemed to have been conferred on any particular religion, or on religion generally.

* * * The Establishment Clause of course extends beyond prohibition of a state church or payment of state funds to one or more churches. We do not think, however, that its prohibition extends to the type of tax deduction established by Minnesota. The historic purposes of the clause simply do not encompass the sort of attenuated financial benefit, ultimately controlled by the private choices of individual parents, that eventually flows to parochial schools from the neutrally available tax benefit at issue in this case.

Petitioners argue that, notwithstanding the facial neutrality of § 290.09(22), in application the statute primarily benefits religious institutions. Petitioners rely * * * on a statistical analysis of the type of persons claiming the tax deduction. They contend that most parents of public school children incur no tuition expenses, and that other expenses deductible under § 290.09(22) are negligible in value; moreover, they claim that 96% of the children in private schools in 1978–1979 attended religiously-affiliated institutions. Because of all this, they reason, the bulk of deductions taken under § 290.09(22) will be claimed by parents of children in sectarian schools. Respondents reply that petitioners have failed to consider the impact of deductions for items such as transportation, summer school tuition, tuition paid by parents whose children attended schools outside the school districts in which they resided, rental or purchase costs for a variety of equipment, and tuition for certain types of instruction not ordinarily provided in public schools.

We need not consider these contentions in detail. We would be loath to adopt a rule grounding the constitutionality of a facially neutral law on annual reports reciting the extent to which various classes of private citizens claimed benefits under the law. Such an approach would scarcely provide the certainty that this field stands in need of, nor can we perceive principled standards by which such statistical evidence might be evaluated. * * *

* * *

Thus, we hold that the Minnesota tax deduction for educational expenses satisfies the primary effect inquiry of our Establishment Clause cases.

Turning to the third part of the *Lemon* inquiry, we have no difficulty in concluding that the Minnesota statute does not "excessively entangle" the state in religion. The only plausible source of the "comprehensive, discriminating, and continuing state surveillance" necessary to run afoul of this standard would lie in the fact that state officials must determine whether particular textbooks qualify for a deduction. Making decisions such as this does not differ substantially from making the types of decisions approved in earlier opinions of this Court. In Board of Education v. Allen, for example, the Court upheld the loan of secular textbooks to parents or children attending nonpublic schools; though state officials were required to determine whether particular books were or were not secular, the system was held not to violate the Establishment Clause. * * *

For the foregoing reasons, the judgment of the Court of Appeals is Affirmed.

Notes

1. The vote was five-to-four. In *Nyquist* it was six-to-three against the constitutionality of the New York tax benefit plan. The five comprised the three dissenters in *Nyquist* (Justices Burger, White, and Rehnquist), Powell (who wrote the *Nyquist* opinion), and O'Connor (who was not on the Court in 1973). The present dissenters were three of the majority in *Nyquist* (Brennan, Marshall, and Blackmun) and Stevens (who was not on the Court in 1973). Justices Douglas and Stewart (both of whom had voted against the New York plan) left the Court before 1983.

2. It is important to recognize the distinct features of the Minnesota plan that enabled it to pass constitutional muster.

3. How do you react to the Court's handling of the fact that 96 percent of the children in nonpublic schools in Minnesota were in sectarian schools?

4. Evaluate the tax deduction from the points of view of (1) public policy, (2) economics, (3) fairness to various groups.

5. What changes in concepts of financing public schools might the case encourage? Would they be desirable?

6. In Massachusetts, where the state constitution barred use of public money to aid any institution not publicly owned and under the exclusive control and supervision of public officers or agents, the highest court opined that a statute similar to the one in Minnesota would violate the state constitution. The court had previously ruled that furnishing transportation to nonpublic schools was only a remote, not a substantial, aid and was not unconstitutional in the state. Here, however, the court said the aid would underwrite the school's "essential enterprise." Opinion of the Justices to the Senate, 401 Mass. 1201, 514 N.E.2d 353 (1987).

[Case No. 9] Constitutionality of Shared Time Program

SCHOOL DIST. OF CITY OF GRAND RAPIDS v. BALL

Supreme Court of the United States, 1985.
473 U.S. 373, 105 S.Ct. 3216, 87 L.Ed.2d 267.

JUSTICE BRENNAN delivered the opinion of the Court.

The School District of Grand Rapids, Michigan, adopted two programs in which classes for nonpublic school students are financed by the public school system, taught by teachers hired by the public school system, and conducted in "leased" classrooms in the nonpublic schools. Most of the nonpublic schools involved in the programs are sectarian religious schools. This case raises the question whether these programs impermissibly involve the government in the support of sectarian religious activities and thus violate the Establishment Clause of the First Amendment.

I

* * *

The Shared Time program offers classes during the regular school day that are intended to be supplementary to the "core curriculum" courses that the State of Michigan requires as a part of an accredited school program. Among the subjects offered are "remedial" and "enrichment" mathematics, "remedial" and "enrichment" reading, art, music, and physical education. A typical nonpublic school student attends these classes for one or two class periods per week; approximately "ten percent of any given nonpublic school student's time during the academic year would consist of Shared Time instruction." Although Shared Time itself is a program offered only in the nonpublic schools, there was testimony that the courses included in that program are offered, albeit perhaps in a somewhat different form, in the public schools as well. All of the classes that are the subject of this case are taught in elementary schools, with the exception of Math Topics, a remedial math course taught in the secondary schools.

The Shared Time teachers are full-time employees of the public schools, who often move from classroom to classroom during the course of the school day. A "significant portion" of the teachers (approximately 10%) "previously taught in nonpublic schools, and many of those had been assigned to the same nonpublic school where they were previously employed." * * *

The Community Education Program is offered throughout the Grand Rapids community in schools and on other sites, for children as well as adults. The classes at issue here are taught in the nonpublic elementary schools and commence at the conclusion of the regular school day. * * * The District Court found that "[a]lthough certain Community Education courses offered at nonpublic school sites are not offered at the public schools on a Community Education basis, all Community Education programs are otherwise available at the public schools, usually as a part of their more extensive regular curriculum."

Community Education teachers are part-time public school employees. Community Education courses are completely voluntary and are offered only if 12 or more students enroll. Because a well-known teacher is necessary to attract the requisite number of students, the School District accords a preference in hiring to instructors already teaching within the school. Thus, "virtually every Community Education course conducted on facilities leased from nonpublic schools has an instructor otherwise employed full time by the same nonpublic school."

* * *

* * * Each room used in the programs has to be free of any crucifix, religious symbol, or artifact, although such religious symbols can be present in the adjoining hallways, corridors, and other facilities used in connection with the program. * * *

Although petitioners label the Shared Time and Community Education students as "part-time public school students," the students attending Shared Time and Community Education courses in facilities leased from a nonpublic school are the same students who attend that particular school otherwise. There is no evidence that any public school student has ever attended a Shared Time or Community Education class in a nonpublic school. * * * Thus, "beneficiaries are wholly designated on the basis of religion" and these "public school" classes, in contrast to ordinary public school classes which are largely neighborhood-based, are as segregated by religion as are the schools at which they are offered.

Forty of the forty-one schools at which the programs operate are sectarian in character. * * *

* * *

II

A

The First Amendment's guarantee that "Congress shall make no law respecting an establishment of religion," as our cases demonstrate, is more than a pledge that no single religion will be designated as a state religion. It is also more than a mere injunction that governmental programs discriminating among religions are unconstitutional. The Establishment Clause instead primarily proscribes "sponsorship, financial support, and active involvement of the sovereign in religious activity." "Neither [a State nor the Federal Government] can pass laws which aid one religion, aid all religions, or prefer one religion over another." * * *

* * *

We have noted that the three-part test first articulated in *Lemon v. Kurtzman* guides "[t]he general nature of our inquiry in this area" * * *. * * * We have particularly relied on *Lemon* in every case involving the sensitive relationship between government and religion in the education of our children. * * * The *Lemon* test concentrates attention on the issues—purposes, effect, entanglement—that determine whether a particular state action is an improper "law respecting an establishment of religion." We therefore reaffirm that state action alleged to violate the Establishment Clause should be measured against the *Lemon* criteria.

As has often been true in school aid cases, there is no dispute as to the first test. * * *

B

Our inquiry [for the second test] must begin with a consideration of the nature of the institutions in which the programs operate. Of the 41 private schools where these "part-time public schools" have operated, 40 are identifiably religious schools. * * * The District Court found * * * that "[b]ased upon the massive testimony and exhibits, the conclusion is inescapable that the religious institutions receiving instructional services from the public schools are sectarian in the sense that a substantial portion of their functions are subsumed in the religious mission." At the religious schools here—as at the sectarian schools that have been the subject of our past cases—"the secular education those schools provide goes hand in hand with the religious mission that is the only reason for the schools' existence. Within that institution, the two are inextricably intertwined."

* * *

(1)

Although Establishment Clause jurisprudence is characterized by few absolutes, the Clause does absolutely prohibit government-financed or government-sponsored indoctrination into the beliefs of a particular religious faith. * * *

In *Meek v. Pittenger* the Court invalidated a statute providing for the loan of state-paid professional staff—including teachers—to nonpublic schools to provide remedial and accelerated instruction, guidance counseling and testing, and other services on the premises of the nonpublic schools. Such a program, if not subjected to a "comprehensive, discriminating, and continuing state surveillance," would entail an unacceptable risk that the state-sponsored instructional personnel would "advance the religious mission of the church-related schools in which they serve." * * *

The programs before us today share the defect that we identified in *Meek*. With respect to the Community Education Program, the District Court found that "virtually every Community Education course conducted on facilities leased from nonpublic schools has an instructor otherwise employed full time by the same nonpublic school." * * * Nonetheless, as petitioners themselves asserted, Community Education classes are not specifically monitored for religious content.

We do not question that the dedicated and professional religious school teachers employed by the Community Education program will attempt in good faith to perform their secular mission conscientiously. Nonetheless, there is a substantial risk that, overtly or subtly, the religious message they are expected to convey during the regular school day will infuse the supposedly secular classes they teach after school. The danger arises "not because the public employee [is] likely deliberately to subvert his task to the service of religion, but rather because the pressures of the environment might alter his behavior from its normal course." "The conflict of functions inheres in the situation."

The Shared Time program, though structured somewhat differently, nonetheless also poses a substantial risk of state-sponsored indoctrination. The most important difference between the programs is that most of the instructors in the Shared Time program are full-time teachers hired by the public schools.   Moreover, although "virtually every" Community Education instructor is a full-time religious school teacher, only "[a] significant portion" of the Shared Time instructors previously worked in the religious schools.   Nonetheless, as with the Community Education program, no attempt is made to monitor the Shared Time courses for religious content.

Thus, despite these differences between the two programs, our holding in *Meek* controls the inquiry with respect to Shared Time, as well as Community Education.   Shared Time instructors are teaching academic subjects in religious schools in courses virtually indistinguishable from the other courses offered during the regular religious-school day.   The teachers in this program, even more than their Community Education colleagues, are "performing important educational services in schools in which education is an integral part of the dominant sectarian mission and in which an atmosphere dedicated to the advancement of religious belief is constantly maintained."   * * *

* * *

(2)

Our cases have recognized that the Establishment Clause guards against more than direct, state-funded efforts to indoctrinate youngsters in specific religious beliefs.   Government promotes religion as effectively when it fosters a close identification of its powers and responsibilities with those of any—or all—religious denominations as when it attempts to inculcate specific religious doctrines.   If this identification conveys a message of government endorsement or disapproval of religion, a core purpose of the Establishment Clause is violated.   * * *

It follows that an important concern of the effects test is whether the symbolic union of church and state effected by the challenged governmental action is sufficiently likely to be perceived by adherents of the controlling denominations as an endorsement, and by the nonadherents as a disapproval, of their individual religious choices.   * * *   The symbolism of a union between church and state is most likely to influence children of tender years, whose experience is limited and whose beliefs consequently are the function of environment as much as of free and voluntary choice.

* * *

In the programs challenged in this case, the religious school students spend their typical school day moving between religious-school and "public-school" classes.   Both types of classes take place in the same religious-school building and both are largely composed of students who are adherents of the same denomination.   In this environment, the students would be unlikely to discern the crucial difference between the religious-school classes and the "public-school" classes, even if the latter were successfully kept free of religious indoctrination.   * * *

* * *

(3)

* * *

We have noted in the past that the religious school has dual functions, providing its students with a secular education while it promotes a particular religious perspective. * * * The programs challenged here, which provide teachers in addition to the instructional equipment and materials, have a * * * forbidden effect of advancing religion. This kind of direct aid to the educational function of the religious school is indistinguishable from the provision of a direct cash subsidy to the religious school that is most clearly prohibited under the Establishment Clause.

* * *

III

We conclude that the challenged programs have the effect of promoting religion in three ways. The state-paid instructors, influenced by the pervasively sectarian nature of the religious schools in which they work, may subtly or overtly indoctrinate the students in particular religious tenets at public expense. The symbolic union of church and state inherent in the provision of secular, state-provided instruction in the religious school buildings threatens to convey a message of state support for religion to students and to the general public. Finally, the programs in effect subsidize the religious functions of the parochial schools by taking over a substantial portion of their responsibility for teaching secular subjects. For these reasons, the conclusion is inescapable that the Community Education and Shared Time programs have the "primary or principal" effect of advancing religion, and therefore violate the dictates of the Establishment Clause of the First Amendment.

* * *

[Affirmed.]

Notes

1. The vote on Community Education was seven-to-two. On Shared Time it was five-to-four.

2. Note those characteristics of Shared Time that resulted in the holding of unconstitutionality. As amplified in the textual portion of this chapter, the concept of "shared time" can embrace widely differing features that could affect constitutionality.

3. Bear in mind that "pervasively sectarian" is practically a given description of precollegiate parochial school education. In higher education "religion connected" institutions vary widely as to religiosity. Also, of course, maturity of students markedly reduces the indoctrination factor.

4. In Meek v. Pittenger, cited in the case, the Court had said, "Whether the subject is 'remedial reading,' 'advanced reading,' or simply 'reading,' a teacher remains a teacher, and the danger that religious doctrine will become intertwined with secular instruction persists."

[Case No. 10] Constitutionality of Use of Federal Funds for Educationally Deprived Children in Parochial Schools

AGUILAR v. FELTON

Supreme Court of the United States, 1985.
473 U.S. 402, 105 S.Ct. 3232, 87 L.Ed.2d 290.

JUSTICE BRENNAN delivered the opinion of the Court.

The City of New York uses federal funds to pay the salaries of public employees who teach in parochial schools. In this companion case to *School District of Grand Rapids v. Ball,* we determine whether this practice violates the Establishment Clause of the First Amendment.

I

A

The program at issue in this case, originally enacted as Title I of the Elementary and Secondary Education Act of 1965, authorizes the Secretary of Education to distribute financial assistance to local educational institutions to meet the needs of educationally deprived children from low-income families. The funds are to be appropriated in accordance with programs proposed by local educational agencies and approved by state educational agencies. "To the extent consistent with the number of educationally deprived children in the school district of the local educational agency who are enrolled in private elementary and secondary schools, such agency shall make provisions for including special educational services and arrangements * * * in which such children can participate." The proposed programs must also meet the following statutory requirements: the children involved in the program must be educationally deprived, the children must reside in areas comprising a high concentration of low-income families, and the programs must supplement, not supplant, programs that would exist absent funding under Title I.

Since 1966, the City of New York has provided instructional services funded by Title I to parochial school students on the premises of parochial schools. Of those students eligible to receive funds in 1981–1982, 13.2% were enrolled in private schools. Of that group, 84% were enrolled in schools affiliated with the Roman Catholic Archdiocese of New York and the Diocese of Brooklyn and 8% were enrolled in Hebrew day schools. With respect to the religious atmosphere of these schools, the Court of Appeals concluded that "the picture that emerges is of a system in which religious considerations play a key role in the selection of students and teachers, and which has as its substantial purpose the inculcation of religious values."

The programs conducted at these schools include remedial reading, reading skills, remedial mathematics, English as a second language, and guidance services. These programs are carried out by regular employees of the public schools (teachers, guidance counselors, psychologists, psychiatrists and social workers) who have volunteered to teach in the parochial schools. The amount of time that each professional spends in the parochial school is determined by the number of students in the particular program and the needs of these students.

* * * The professionals involved in the program are directed to avoid involvement with religious activities that are conducted within the private schools and to bar religious materials in their classrooms. All material and equipment used in the programs funded under Title I are supplied by the Government and are used only in those programs. The professional personnel are solely responsible for the selection of the students. Additionally, the professionals are informed that contact with private school personnel should be kept to a minimum. Finally, the administrators of the parochial schools are required to clear the classrooms used by the public school personnel of all religious symbols.

* * *

II

* * * The New York programs challenged in this case are very similar to the programs we examined in *Ball*. In both cases, publicly funded instructors teach classes composed exclusively of private school students in private school buildings. In both cases, an overwhelming number of the participating private schools are religiously affiliated. In both cases, the publicly funded programs provide not only professional personnel, but also all materials and supplies necessary for the operation of the programs. Finally, the instructors in both cases are told that they are public school employees under the sole control of the public school system.

The appellants attempt to distinguish this case on the ground that the City of New York, unlike the Grand Rapids Public School District, has adopted a system for monitoring the religious content of publicly funded Title I classes in the religious schools. At best, the supervision in this case would assist in preventing the Title I program from being used, intentionally or unwittingly, to inculcate the religious beliefs of the surrounding parochial school. But appellants' argument fails in any event, because the supervisory system established by the City of New York inevitably results in the excessive entanglement of church and state, an Establishment Clause concern distinct from that addressed by the effects doctrine. Even where state aid to parochial institutions does not have the primary effect of advancing religion, the provision of such aid may nonetheless violate the Establishment Clause owing to the nature of the interaction of church and state in the administration of that aid.

The principle that the state should not become too closely entangled with the church in the administration of assistance is rooted in two concerns. When the state becomes enmeshed with a given denomination in matters of religious significance, the freedom of religious belief of those who are not adherents of that denomination suffers, even when the governmental purpose underlying the involvement is largely secular. In addition, the freedom of even the adherents of the denomination is limited by the governmental intrusion into sacred matters. "[T]he First Amendment rests upon the premise that both religion and government can best work to achieve their lofty aims if each is left free from the other within its respective sphere."

* * *

The critical elements of the entanglement proscribed in *Lemon* and *Meek* are thus present in this case. First, as noted above, the aid is provided in a pervasively sectarian environment. Second, because assistance is provided in the form of teachers, ongoing inspection is required to ensure the absence of a religious message. In short, the scope and duration of New York's Title I program would require a permanent and pervasive State presence in the sectarian schools receiving aid.

This pervasive monitoring by public authorities in the sectarian schools infringes precisely those Establishment Clause values at the root of the prohibition of excessive entanglement. Agents of the State must visit and inspect the religious school regularly, alert for the subtle or overt presence of religious matter in Title I classes. In addition, the religious school must obey these same agents when they make determinations as to what is and what is not a "religious symbol" and thus off limits in a Title I classroom. In short, the religious school, which has as a primary purpose the advancement and preservation of a particular religion must endure the ongoing presence of state personnel whose primary purpose is to monitor teachers and students in an attempt to guard against the infiltration of religious thought.

The administrative cooperation that is required to maintain the educational program at issue here entangles church and state in still another way that infringes interests at the heart of the Establishment Clause. Administrative personnel of the public and parochial school systems must work together in resolving matters related to schedules, classroom assignments, problems that arise in the implementation of the program, requests for additional services, and the dissemination of information regarding the program. Furthermore, the program necessitates "frequent contacts between the regular and the remedial teachers (or other professionals), in which each side reports on individual student needs, problems encountered, and results achieved."

* * *

III

Despite the well-intentioned efforts taken by the City of New York, the program remains constitutionally flawed owing to the nature of the aid, to the institution receiving the aid, and to the constitutional principles that they implicate—that neither the State nor Federal Government shall promote or hinder a particular faith or faith generally through the advancement of benefits or through the excessive entanglement of church and state in the administration of those benefits.

Affirmed.

Reutter,Law of Pub.Educ.4th--4

Notes

1. The vote was five-to-four. Each of the dissenters wrote an opinion that somewhere therein alluded to the Act's having "done so much good" without much "detectable harm". To what extent should a perceived good effect be taken into account in evaluating a constitutional challenge?

2. Be sure to understand the rationale behind the excessive entanglement criterion. Note the aspect of protecting religion against government, which concern is also present in the "inhibit" portion of the effects test.

3. The appropriate degree of monitoring can be a major source of contention. How much should government simply trust human beings to behave according to the law? What factors affect your answer?

[Case No. 11]   Interpretation of Federal Equal Access Act

BOARD OF EDUC. OF WESTSIDE COMMUNITY SCHOOLS v. MERGENS

Supreme Court of the United States, 1990.
496 U.S. 226, 110 S.Ct. 2356, 110 L.Ed.2d 191.

JUSTICE O'CONNOR delivered the opinion of the Court, except as to Part III.

This case requires us to decide whether the Equal Access Act, 98 Stat. 1302, 20 U.S.C. §§ 4071–4074, prohibits Westside High School from denying a student religious group permission to meet on school premises during noninstructional time, and if so, whether the Act, so construed, violates the Establishment Clause of the First Amendment.

I

* * *

Students at Westside High School are permitted to join various student groups and clubs, all of which meet after school hours on school premises. The students may choose from approximately 30 recognized groups on a voluntary basis. * * *

* * *

There is no written school board policy concerning the formation of student clubs. Rather, students wishing to form a club present their request to a school official who determines whether the proposed club's goals and objectives are consistent with school board policies and with the school district's "Mission and Goals"—a broadly worded "blueprint" that expresses the district's commitment to teaching academic, physical, civic, and personal skills and values.

In January 1985, respondent Bridget Mergens * * * requested permission to form a Christian club at the school. The proposed club would have the same privileges and meet on the same terms and conditions as other Westside student groups, except that the proposed club would not have a faculty sponsor. According to the students' testimony at trial, the club's purpose would have been, among other things, to permit the students to read and discuss the Bible, to have fellowship, and to pray together.   Membership would have been voluntary and open to all students regardless of religious affiliation.

* * * The school officials explained that school policy required all student clubs to have a faculty sponsor, which the proposed religious club would not or could not have, and that a religious club at the school would violate the Establishment Clause.   In March 1985, Mergens appealed the denial of her request to the Board of Education, but the Board voted to uphold the denial.

* * *

II

A

In *Widmar v. Vincent,* we invalidated, on free speech grounds, a state university regulation that prohibited student use of school facilities " 'for purposes of religious worship or religious teaching.' "   In doing so, we held that an "equal access" policy would not violate the Establishment Clause under our decision in *Lemon v. Kurtzman.*   In particular, we held that such a policy would have a secular purpose, would not have the primary effect of advancing religion, and would not result in excessive entanglement between government and religion.   We noted, however, that "[u]niversity students are, of course, young adults.   They are less impressionable than younger students and should be able to appreciate that the University's policy is one of neutrality toward religion."

In 1984, Congress extended the reasoning of *Widmar* to public secondary schools.   Under the Equal Access Act, a public secondary school with a "limited open forum" is prohibited from discriminating against students who wish to conduct a meeting within that forum on the basis of the "religious, political, philosophical, or other content of the speech at such meetings."   Specifically, the Act provides:

> "It shall be unlawful for any public secondary school which receives Federal financial assistance and which has a limited open forum to deny equal access or a fair opportunity to, or discriminate against, any students who wish to conduct a meeting within that limited open forum on the basis of the religious, political, philosophical, or other content of the speech at such meetings."

A "limited open forum" exists whenever a public secondary school "grants an offering to or opportunity for one or more noncurriculum related student groups to meet on school premises during noninstructional time."   "Meeting" is defined to include "those activities of student groups which are permitted under a school's limited open forum and are not directly related to the school curriculum."   "Noninstructional time" is defined to mean "time set aside by the school before actual classroom instruction begins or after actual classroom instruction ends."   Thus, even if a public secondary school allows only one "noncurriculum related student group" to meet, the Act's obligations are triggered and the school may not deny other clubs, on the basis of the content of their speech, equal access to meet on school premises during noninstructional time.

The Act further specifies that "[s]chools shall be deemed to offer a fair opportunity to students who wish to conduct a meeting within its limited open forum" if the school uniformly provides that the meetings are voluntary and student-initiated; are not sponsored by the school, the government, or its agents or employees; do not materially and substantially interfere with the orderly conduct of educational activities within the school; and are not directed, controlled, conducted, or regularly attended by "nonschool persons." "Sponsorship" is defined to mean "the act of promoting, leading, or participating in a meeting. The assignment of a teacher, administrator, or other school employee to a meeting for custodial purposes does not constitute sponsorship of the meeting." If the meetings are religious, employees or agents of the school or government may attend only in a "nonparticipatory capacity." Moreover, a State may not influence the form of any religious activity, require any person to participate in such activity, or compel any school agent or employee to attend a meeting if the content of the speech at the meeting is contrary to that person's beliefs.

Finally, the Act does not "authorize the United States to deny or withhold Federal financial assistance to any school" or "limit the authority of the school, its agents or employees, to maintain order and discipline on school premises, to protect the well-being of students and faculty, and to assure that attendance of students at the meetings is voluntary".

B

The parties agree that Westside High School receives federal financial assistance and is a public secondary school within the meaning of the Act. The Act's obligation to grant equal access to student groups is therefore triggered if Westside maintains a "limited open forum"—*i.e.*, if it permits one or more "noncurriculum related student groups" to meet on campus before or after classes.

Unfortunately, the Act does not define the crucial phrase "noncurriculum related student group." Our immediate task is therefore one of statutory interpretation. We begin, of course, with the language of the statute. The common meaning of the term "curriculum" is "the whole body of courses offered by an educational institution or one of its branches." Webster's Third New International Dictionary 557 (1976); see also Black's Law Dictionary 345 (5th ed. 1979) ("The set of studies or courses for a particular period, designated by a school or branch of a school"). Any sensible interpretation of "noncurriculum related student group" must therefore be anchored in the notion that such student groups are those that are not related to the body of courses offered by the school. The difficult question is the degree of "unrelatedness to the curriculum" required for a group to be considered "noncurriculum related."

The Act's definition of the sort of "meeting[s]" that must be accommodated under the statute sheds some light on this question. "[T]he term 'meeting' includes those activities of student groups which are * * * not *directly related* to the school curriculum." (emphasis added). Congress' use of the phrase "directly related" implies that student groups directly related to the subject matter of courses offered by the school do not fall within the "noncurriculum related" category and would therefore be considered "curriculum related."

The logic of the Act also supports this view, namely, that a curriculum-related student group is one that has more than just a tangential or attenuated relationship to courses offered by the school. Because the purpose of granting equal access is to prohibit discrimination between religious or political clubs on the one hand and other noncurriculum-related student groups on the other, the Act is premised on the notion that a religious or political club is itself likely to be a noncurriculum-related student group. It follows, then, that a student group that is "curriculum related" must at least have a more direct relationship to the curriculum than a religious or political club would have.

Although the phrase "noncurriculum related student group" nevertheless remains sufficiently ambiguous that we might normally resort to legislative history, we find the legislative history on this issue less than helpful. Because the bill that led to the Act was extensively rewritten in a series of multilateral negotiations after it was passed by the House and reported out of committee by the Senate, the committee reports shed no light on the language actually adopted. During congressional debate on the subject, legislators referred to a number of different definitions, and thus both petitioners and respondents can cite to legislative history favoring their interpretation of the phrase. * * *

We think it significant, however, that the Act, which was passed by wide, bipartisan majorities in both the House and the Senate, reflects at least some consensus on a broad legislative purpose. The committee reports indicate that the Act was intended to address perceived widespread discrimination against religious speech in public schools, and, as the language of the Act indicates, its sponsors contemplated that the Act would do more than merely validate the status quo. The committee reports also show that the Act was enacted in part in response to two federal appellate court decisions holding that student religious groups could not, consistent with the Establishment Clause, meet on school premises during noninstructional time. A broad reading of the Act would be consistent with the views of those who sought to end discrimination by allowing students to meet and discuss religion before and after classes.

In light of this legislative purpose, we think that the term "noncurriculum related student group" is best interpreted broadly to mean any student group that does not *directly* relate to the body of courses offered by the school. In our view, a student group directly relates to a school's curriculum if the subject matter of the group is actually taught, or will soon be taught, in a regularly offered course; if the subject matter of the group concerns the body of courses as a whole; if participation in the group is required for a particular course; or if participation in the group results in academic credit. We think this limited definition of groups that directly relate to the curriculum is a commonsense interpretation of the Act that is consistent with Congress' intent to provide a low threshold for triggering the Act's requirements.

For example, a French club would directly relate to the curriculum if a school taught French in a regularly offered course or planned to teach the subject in the near future. A school's student government would generally relate directly to the curriculum to the extent that it addresses concerns, solicits opinions, and formulates proposals pertaining to the body of courses offered by the school. If participation in a school's band or orchestra were required for the band or orchestra classes, or resulted in academic credit, then those groups would also directly relate to the curriculum. The existence of such groups at a school would not trigger the Act's obligations.

On the other hand, unless a school could show that groups such as a chess club, a stamp collecting club, or a community service club fell within our description of groups that directly relate to the curriculum, such groups would be "noncurriculum related student groups" for purposes of the Act. The existence of such groups would create a "limited open forum" under the Act and would prohibit the school from denying equal access to any other student group on the basis of the content of that group's speech. Whether a specific student group is a "noncurriculum related student group" will therefore depend on a particular school's curriculum, but such determinations would be subject to factual findings well within the competence of trial courts to make.

Petitioners contend that our reading of the Act unduly hinders local control over schools and school activities, but we think that schools and school districts nevertheless retain a significant measure of authority over the type of officially recognized activities in which their students participate. First, schools and school districts maintain their traditional latitude to determine appropriate subjects of instruction. To the extent that a school chooses to structure its course offerings and existing student groups to avoid the Act's obligations, that result is not prohibited by the Act. On matters of statutory interpretation, "[o]ur task is to apply the text, not to improve on it." Second, the Act expressly does not limit a school's authority to prohibit meetings that would "materially and substantially interfere with the orderly conduct of educational activities within the school." The Act also preserves "the authority of the school, its agents or employees, to maintain order and discipline on school premises, to protect the well-being of students and faculty, and to assure that attendance of students at meetings is voluntary." Finally, because the Act applies only to public secondary schools that receive federal financial assistance, a school district seeking to escape the statute's obligations could simply forego federal funding. Although we do not doubt that in some cases this may be an unrealistic option, Congress clearly sought to prohibit schools from discriminating on the basis of the content of a student group's speech, and that obligation is the price a federally funded school must pay if it opens its facilities to noncurriculum-related student groups.

* * *

C

* * * Petitioners contend that all of these student activities [cited as being noncurriculum-related] are curriculum-related because they further the goals of particular aspects of the school's curriculum. * * * Subsurfers [scuba diving] furthers "one of the essential goals of the Physical Education Department—enabling students to develop lifelong recreational interests." Chess "supplement[s] math and science courses because it enhances students' ability to engage in critical thought processes." * * *

To the extent that petitioners contend that "curriculum related" means anything remotely related to abstract educational goals, however, we reject that argument. To define "curriculum related" in a way that results in almost no schools having limited open fora, or in a way that permits schools to evade the Act by strategically describing existing student groups, would render the Act merely hortatory. * * *

Rather, we think it clear that Westside's existing student groups include one or more "noncurriculum related student groups." Although Westside's physical education classes apparently include swimming, counsel stated at oral argument that scuba diving is not taught in any regularly offered course at the school. Based on Westside's own description of the group, Subsurfers does not directly relate to the curriculum as a whole in the same way that a student government or similar group might. Moreover, participation in Subsurfers is not required by any course at the school and does not result in extra academic credit. Thus, Subsurfers is a "noncurriculum related student group" for purposes of the Act. Similarly, although math teachers at Westside have encouraged their students to play chess, chess is not taught in any regularly offered course at the school, and participation in the chess club is not required for any class and does not result in extra credit for any class. The chess club is therefore another "noncurriculum related student group" at Westside. * * * The record therefore supports a finding that Westside has maintained a limited open forum under the Act.

* * *

The remaining statutory question is whether petitioners' denial of respondents' request to form a religious group constitutes a denial of "equal access" to the school's limited open forum. Although the school apparently permits respondents to meet informally after school, respondents seek equal access in the form of official recognition by the school. Official recognition allows student clubs to be part of the student activities program and carries with it access to the school newspaper, bulletin boards, the public address system, and the annual Club Fair. Given that the Act explicitly prohibits denial of "equal access * * * to * * * any students who wish to conduct a meeting within [the school's] limited open forum" on the basis of the religious content of the speech at such meetings, we hold that Westside's denial of respondents' request to form a Christian club denies them "equal access" under the Act.

Because we rest our conclusion on statutory grounds, we need not decide—and therefore express no opinion on—whether the First Amendment requires the same result.

III

Petitioners contend that even if Westside has created a limited open forum within the meaning of the Act, its denial of official recognition to the proposed Christian club must nevertheless stand because the Act violates the Establishment Clause of the First Amendment, as applied to the States through the Fourteenth Amendment. Specifically, petitioners maintain that because the school's recognized student activities are an integral part of its educational mission, official recognition of respondents' proposed club would effectively incorporate religious activities into the school's official program, endorse participation in the religious club, and provide the club with an official platform to proselytize other students.

We disagree. * * *

[Eight Justices concluded that the Act did not violate the Establishment Clause, but there was no Opinion of the Court on the point. Three opinions expressed the views of four, two, and two Justices.]

Notes

1. The vote of the Court was eight-to-one. Notice the process followed by the Court to ascertain the intent of Congress.

2. Essential provisions of the Act are given in IIA. While including much specificity, the Act conspicuously failed to define "noncurriculum related student group." Why do you suppose this happened?

3. How does the Court's view of curriculum square with those found in curriculum development textbooks? Note the sources of the Court's definition.

4. If the Act were to be repealed, could the school district reestablish its bar to the Christian club? Would it be obliged to do so? See the last paragraph of IIC.

5. In the plurality opinion accompanying the upholding of the constitutionality of the Act (Part III) four Justices said that it was rational for Congress to make the determination left open by the Court in Widmar v. Vincent: secondary school students are "capable of distinguishing between State-initiated, school-sponsored, or teacher-led religious speech on the one hand and student-initiated, student-led religious speech on the other."

[Case No. 12] Constitutionality of Invocation and Benediction at Graduation Ceremony

LEE v. WEISMAN

Supreme Court of the United States, 1992.
___ U.S. ___, 112 S.Ct. 2649, 120 L.Ed.2d 467.

JUSTICE KENNEDY delivered the opinion of the Court.

School principals in the public school system of the city of Providence, Rhode Island, are permitted to invite members of the clergy to offer invocation and benediction prayers as part of the formal graduation ceremonies for middle schools and for high schools. The question before us is whether including clerical members who offer prayers as part of the official school graduation ceremony is consistent with the Religion Clauses of the First Amendment, provisions the Fourteenth Amendment makes applicable with full force to the States and their school districts.

I

A

Deborah Weisman graduated from Nathan Bishop Middle School, a public school in Providence, at a formal ceremony in June 1989. She was about 14 years old. * * * Acting for himself and his daughter, Deborah's father, Daniel Weisman, objected to any prayers at Deborah's middle school graduation, but to no avail. The school principal, petitioner Robert E. Lee, invited a rabbi to deliver prayers at the graduation exercises for Deborah's class. * * *

It has been the custom of Providence school officials to provide invited clergy with a pamphlet entitled "Guidelines for Civic Occasions," prepared by the National Conference of Christians and Jews. The Guidelines recommend that public prayers at nonsectarian civic ceremonies be composed with "inclusiveness and sensitivity," though they acknowledge that "[p]rayer of any kind may be inappropriate on some civic occasions." The principal gave Rabbi Gutterman the pamphlet before the graduation and advised him the invocation and benediction should be nonsectarian.

* * *

The school board (and the United States, which supports it as *amicus curiae*) argued that these short prayers and others like them at graduation exercises are of profound meaning to many students and parents throughout this country who consider that due respect and acknowledgement for divine guidance and for the deepest spiritual aspirations of our people ought to be expressed at an event as important in life as a graduation. We assume this to be so in addressing the difficult case now before us, for the significance of the prayers lies also at the heart of Daniel and Deborah Weisman's case.

* * *

II

These dominant facts mark and control the confines of our decision: State officials direct the performance of a formal religious exercise at promotional and graduation ceremonies for secondary schools. Even for those students who object to the religious exercise, their attendance and participation in the state-sponsored religious activity are in a fair and real sense obligatory, though the school district does not require attendance as a condition for receipt of the diploma.

This case does not require us to revisit the difficult questions dividing us in recent cases, questions of the definition and full scope of the principles governing the extent of permitted accommodation by the State for the religious beliefs and practices of many of its citizens. For without reference to those principles in other contexts, the controlling precedents as they relate to prayer and religious exercise in primary and secondary public schools compel the holding here that the policy of the city of Providence is an unconstitutional one. We can decide the case without reconsidering the general constitutional framework by which public schools' efforts to accommodate religion are measured. Thus we do not accept the invitation of petitioners and *amicus* the United States to reconsider our decision in *Lemon v. Kurtzman.* The government involvement with religious activity in this case is pervasive, to the point of creating a state-sponsored and state-directed religious exercise in a public school. Conducting this formal religious observance conflicts with settled rules pertaining to prayer exercises for students, and that suffices to determine the question before us.

The principle that government may accommodate the free exercise of religion does not supersede the fundamental limitations imposed by the Establishment Clause. It is beyond dispute that, at a minimum, the Constitution guarantees that government may not coerce anyone to support or participate in religion or its exercise, or otherwise act in a way which "establishes a [state] religion or religious faith, or tends to do so." The State's involvement in the school prayers challenged today violates these central principles.

That involvement is as troubling as it is undenied. A school official, the principal, decided that an invocation and a benediction should be given; this is a choice attributable to the State, and from a constitutional perspective it is as if a state statute decreed that the prayers must occur. The principal chose the religious participant, here a rabbi, and that choice is also attributable to the State. The reason for the choice of a rabbi is not disclosed by the record, but the potential for divisiveness over the choice of a particular member of the clergy to conduct the ceremony is apparent.

Divisiveness, of course, can attend any state decision respecting religions, and neither its existence nor its potential necessarily invalidates the State's attempts to accommodate religion in all cases. The potential for divisiveness is of particular relevance here though, because it centers around an overt religious exercise in a secondary school environment where, as we discuss below, subtle coercive pressures exist and where the student had no real alternative which would have allowed her to avoid the fact or appearance of participation.

The State's role did not end with the decision to include a prayer and with the choice of clergyman.   Principal Lee provided Rabbi Gutterman with a copy of the "Guidelines for Civic Occasions," and advised him that his prayers should be nonsectarian.   Through these means the principal directed and controlled the content of the prayer.   Even if the only sanction for ignoring the instructions were that the rabbi would not be invited back, we think no religious representative who valued his or her continued reputation and effectiveness in the community would incur the State's displeasure in this regard.   It is a cornerstone principle of our Establishment Clause jurisprudence that "it is no part of the business of government to compose official prayers for any group of the American people to recite as a part of a religious program carried on by government," *Engel v. Vitale,* and that is what the school officials attempted to do.

Petitioners argue, and we find nothing in the case to refute it, that the directions for the content of the prayers were a good-faith attempt by the school to ensure that the sectarianism which is so often the flashpoint for religious animosity be removed from the graduation ceremony.   The concern is understandable, as a prayer which uses ideas or images identified with a particular religion may foster a different sort of sectarian rivalry than an invocation or benediction in terms more neutral.   The school's explanation, however, does not resolve the dilemma caused by its participation.   The question is not the good faith of the school in attempting to make the prayer acceptable to most persons, but the legitimacy of its undertaking that enterprise at all when the object is to produce a prayer to be used in a formal religious exercise which students, for all practical purposes, are obliged to attend.

* * *

The First Amendment's Religion Clauses mean that religious beliefs and religious expression are too precious to be either proscribed or prescribed by the State.   The design of the Constitution is that preservation and transmission of religious beliefs and worship is a responsibility and a choice committed to the private sphere, which itself is promised freedom to pursue that mission.   * * *

These concerns have particular application in the case of school officials, whose effort to monitor prayer will be perceived by the students as inducing a participation they might otherwise reject.   Though the efforts of the school officials in this case to find common ground appear to have been a good-faith attempt to recognize the common aspects of religions and not the divisive ones, our precedents do not permit school officials to assist in composing prayers as an incident to a formal exercise for their students.   *Engel v. Vitale.*   And these same precedents caution us to measure the idea of a civic religion against the central meaning of the Religion Clauses of the First Amendment, which is that all creeds must be tolerated and none favored.   The suggestion that government may establish an official or civic religion as a means of avoiding the establishment of a religion with more specific creeds strikes us as a contradiction that cannot be accepted.

The degree of school involvement here made it clear that the graduation prayers bore the imprint of the State and thus put school-age children who objected in an untenable position. We turn our attention now to consider the position of the students, both those who desired the prayer and she who did not.

To endure the speech of false ideas or offensive content and then to counter it is part of learning how to live in a pluralistic society, a society which insists upon open discourse towards the end of a tolerant citizenry. And tolerance presupposes some mutuality of obligation. It is argued that our constitutional vision of a free society requires confidence in our own ability to accept or reject ideas of which we do not approve, and that prayer at a high school graduation does nothing more than offer a choice. * * * This argument cannot prevail, however. It overlooks a fundamental dynamic of the Constitution.

The First Amendment protects speech and religion by quite different mechanisms. Speech is protected by insuring its full expression even when the government participates, for the very object of some of our most important speech is to persuade the government to adopt an idea as its own. The method for protecting freedom of worship and freedom of conscience in religious matters is quite the reverse. In religious debate or expression the government is not a prime participant, for the Framers deemed religious establishment antithetical to the freedom of all. The Free Exercise Clause embraces a freedom of conscience and worship that has close parallels in the speech provisions of the First Amendment, but the Establishment Clause is a specific prohibition on forms of state intervention in religious affairs with no precise counterpart in the speech provisions. The explanation lies in the lesson of history that was and is the inspiration for the Establishment Clause, the lesson that in the hands of government what might begin as a tolerant expression of religious views may end in a policy to indoctrinate and coerce. A state-created orthodoxy puts at grave risk that freedom of belief and conscience which are the sole assurance that religious faith is real, not imposed.

* * *

As we have observed before, there are heightened concerns with protecting freedom of conscience from subtle coercive pressure in the elementary and secondary public schools. Our decisions in *Engel v. Vitale* and *School District of Abington Tp. v. Schempp* recognize, among other things, that prayer exercises in public schools carry a particular risk of indirect coercion. * * * What to most believers may seem nothing more than a reasonable request that the nonbeliever respect their religious practices, in a school context may appear to the nonbeliever or dissenter to be an attempt to employ the machinery of the State to enforce a religious orthodoxy.

* * *

* * * Research in psychology supports the common assumption that adolescents are often susceptible to pressure from their peers towards conformity, and that the influence is strongest in matters of social convention. * * * [T]he government may no more use social pressure to enforce orthodoxy than it may use more direct means.

* * *

There was a stipulation in the District Court that attendance at graduation and promotional ceremonies is voluntary. Petitioners and the United States, as *amicus,* made this a center point of the case, arguing that the option of not attending the graduation excuses any inducement or coercion in the ceremony itself. The argument lacks all persuasion. Law reaches past formalism. And to say a teenage student has a real choice not to attend her high school graduation is formalistic in the extreme. True, Deborah could elect not to attend commencement without renouncing her diploma; but we shall not allow the case to turn on this point. Everyone knows that in our society and in our culture high school graduation is one of life's most significant occasions. A school rule which excuses attendance is beside the point. Attendance may not be required by official decree, yet it is apparent that a student is not free to absent herself from the graduation exercise in any real sense of the term "voluntary," for absence would require forfeiture of those intangible benefits which have motivated the student through youth and all her high school years. Graduation is a time for family and those closest to the student to celebrate success and express mutual wishes of gratitude and respect, all to the end of impressing upon the young person the role that it is his or her right and duty to assume in the community and all of its diverse parts.

The importance of the event is the point the school district and the United States rely upon to argue that a formal prayer ought to be permitted, but it becomes one of the principal reasons why their argument must fail. Their contention, one of considerable force were it not for the constitutional constraints applied to state action, is that the prayers are an essential part of these ceremonies because for many persons an occasion of this significance lacks meaning if there is no recognition, however brief, that human achievements cannot be understood apart from their spiritual essence. We think the Government's position that this interest suffices to force students to choose between compliance or forfeiture demonstrates fundamental inconsistency in its argumentation. It fails to acknowledge that what for many of Deborah's classmates and their parents was a spiritual imperative was for Daniel and Deborah Weisman religious conformance compelled by the State. While in some societies the wishes of the majority might prevail, the Establishment Clause of the First Amendment is addressed to this contingency and rejects the balance urged upon us. The Constitution forbids the State to exact religious conformity from a student as the price of attending her own high school graduation. This is the calculus the Constitution commands.

The Government's argument gives insufficient recognition to the real conflict of conscience faced by the young student. The essence of the Government's position is that with regard to a civic, social occasion of this importance it is the objector, not the majority, who must take unilateral and private action to avoid compromising religious scruples, here by electing to miss the graduation exercise. This turns conventional First Amendment analysis on its head. It is a tenet of the First Amendment that the State cannot require one of its citizens to forfeit his or her rights and benefits as the price of resisting conformance to state-sponsored religious practice. To say that a student must remain apart from the ceremony at the opening invocation and closing benediction is to risk compelling conformity in an environment analogous to the classroom setting, where we have said the risk of compulsion is especially high. Just as in *Engel v. Vitale* and *School District of Abington Tp. v. Schempp,* we found that provisions within the challenged legislation permitting a student to be voluntarily excused from attendance or participation in the daily prayers did not shield those practices from invalidation, the fact that attendance at the graduation ceremonies is voluntary in a legal sense does not save the religious exercise.

* * *

We do not hold that every state action implicating religion is invalid if one or a few citizens find it offensive. People may take offense at all manner of religious as well as nonreligious messages, but offense alone does not in every case show a violation. We know too that sometimes to endure social isolation or even anger may be the price of conscience or nonconformity. But, by any reading of our cases, the conformity required of the student in this case was too high an exaction to withstand the test of the Establishment Clause. The prayer exercises in this case are especially improper because the State has in every practical sense compelled attendance and participation in an explicit religious exercise at an event of singular importance to every student, one the objecting student had no real alternative to avoid.

* * *

For the reasons we have stated, the judgment of the Court of Appeals is

Affirmed.

Notes

1. The vote was five-to-four. For the first time since 1971 in a school establishment clause case the Court did not use the analytic approach of the Lemon v. Kurtzman tests. The majority, however, expressly rejected the urging of the school district (and the United States as amicus curiae) to reconsider the Lemon decision. The basic prayer cases of Engel v. Vitale and School Dist. of Abington Tp. v. Schempp were decided in 1962 and 1963.

2. To what extent did the efforts of the school authorities to make the prayers widely acceptable affect the legal outcome of the case? To what extent is the religious significance of a prayer diminished by generalizing the supplication and the divine entity to which it is directed?

3. Observe the legal discussion of the constitutional differences between freedom of speech and freedom of religion.

4. Notice the Court's reference to psychological research regarding peer pressure and to its treatment of the voluntary attendance argument.

5. Five days after issuing this opinion the Supreme Court vacated and remanded for further consideration in light of this case a Fifth Circuit opinion that had upheld a school board policy on the same subject. That court reconsidered and again upheld on its face the policy that differed from the Providence one primarily in its leaving the decision whether to have an invocation and/or benediction to the discretion of the graduating class and providing that, if used, it shall be given by a student volunteer. Jones v. Clear Creek Independent School Dist., 977 F.2d 963 (5 Cir.1992) The Supreme Court without comment denied certiorari, ___ U.S. ___, 113 S.Ct. 2950, 124 L.Ed.2d 697 (1993).

Chapter 3

STATE–LEVEL ENTITIES

Powers of the Legislature in General

Because education is a state function,[1] the only restrictions on the state's power over education are to be found in the United States Constitution and its implementation by Congress. The legislature of the state has plenary power to carry out the education function of the state subject only to any affirmative directives and additional restrictions imposed by the state constitution. Literally hundreds of citations to holdings of courts could be given to sustain the point that the legislature has complete control over the public schools within the state. The legislature can organize the state for the purpose of education and distribute duties and responsibilities among central agencies, intermediate agencies, and local agencies as it sees fit. Since the power over public education is legislative and plenary, it is not exhausted by exercise, and the legislature may change the educational system in any manner and as often as it deems necessary or expedient if thereby no federal or state constitutional provisions are violated.

Establishment and Alteration of School Districts

In General

School districts are governmental agencies of the state created by the state as instrumentalities through which the legislature carries out the state constitutional mandate to provide for a system of public education. At any time the legislature may abolish all local school units and redistrict the state irrespective of the boundaries of the old districts.[2] Unless the constitution of the state requires it, it is not necessary to procure the consent of the inhabitants of the territory as a condition to redistricting.[3] Indeed, even though local inhabitants have voted against a boundary alteration, the legislature can still proceed to effect the consolidation of districts.[4] Further, if the legislature authorizes a local school board to petition for a boundary change, it may do so despite the wishes of local voters.[5] The legislature may not, of course,

1. See Chapter 1.

2. Moore v. Board of Educ. of Iredell County, 212 N.C. 499, 193 S.E. 732 (1937); Opinion of the Justices, 246 A.2d 90 (Del. 1968); Rose v. Council for Better Educ., Inc., 790 S.W.2d 186 (Ky.1989).

3. Fisher v. Fay, 288 Ill. 11, 122 N.E. 811 (1919).

4. Fruit v. Metropolitan School Dist. of Winchester, 241 Ind. 621, 172 N.E.2d 864 (1961).

5. Kosmicki v. Kowalski, 184 Neb. 639, 171 N.W.2d 172 (1969).

change boundaries in a way which would violate the federal Constitution, as, for examples, deliberately to affect adversely racial balance of students [6], or innocently to impede the process of correction of de jure segregation [7], or intentionally to aid a religious sect. [8]

Although a school district is a legal body that may sue or be sued, the Supreme Court of Kansas has held that a district has no authority to maintain an action questioning the boundaries or the validity of the organization of another school district. [9] Such a suit can be brought only in the name of the state by the duly authorized officers of the state. The case involved a school district's attempt to challenge the validity of orders made by the state superintendent of public instruction transferring certain territory from the district to other school districts.

The same conclusion was reached by the Supreme Court of Minnesota. [10] In that case the court held that the statewide association of school boards lacked standing to contest the constitutionality of a school district consolidation statute because its interests were those of its members and they could not bring such a suit. Further, the association could not assert interests of children because its interest in good schools was not dissimilar to that of any other member of the general public.

Unsuccessful in Nebraska was an attempt by local school board members to sue as individuals rather than officially as a board in order to avoid the established case law. The Supreme Court of Nebraska disapproved of the "facade." [11]

Because the state creates political subdivisions for the purpose of better ordering of government, a subdivision has no substantive federal constitutional rights it may invoke against its creator. This is true for municipal corporations, [12] as well as for school districts. [13] Challenges by school districts may be considered by courts, however, upon a substantial allegation that the legislature has used unconstitutional means to effect a boundary change. [14] Such an unusual claim in reality would not be to the basic power of the legislature to create, alter, or abolish school districts, and therefore courts could rule upon the merits of the contention.

Delegation of Legislative Power

Clearly the state legislature, in its discretion, can enact legislation which of itself creates or abolishes school districts. However, since the

6. Akron Bd. of Educ. v. State Bd. of Educ. of Ohio, 490 F.2d 1285 (6 Cir.1974).

7. Wright v. Council of City of Emporia, 407 U.S. 451, 92 S.Ct. 2196, 33 L.Ed.2d 51 (1972).

8. Grumet v. Board of Educ. of Kiryas Joel Village School Dist., 81 N.Y.2d 518, 601 N.Y.S.2d 61, 618 N.E.2d 94 (1993).

9. Unified School Dist. No. 335 v. State Bd. of Educ., 206 Kan. 229, 478 P.2d 201 (1970).

10. Minnesota Ass'n of Public Schools v. Hanson, 287 Minn. 415, 178 N.W.2d 846 (1970).

11. In re Plummer Freeholder Petition, 229 Neb. 520, 428 N.W.2d 163 (1988).

12. Williams v. Mayor and City Council of Baltimore, 289 U.S. 36, 53 S.Ct. 431, 77 L.Ed. 1015 (1933).

13. Triplett v. Tiemann, 302 F.Supp. 1239 (D.Neb.1969).

14. Hall v. City of Taft, 47 Cal.2d 177, 302 P.2d 574 (1956).

legislature is seldom in the position to make the necessary surveys of the state to determine the most effective plan for the formation of districts, the usual procedure is to enact general legislation setting out the legislative policy for districting, and to delegate to some lower official or body the responsibility for the execution of the plan.

The legislature may "delegate to others the authority to do those things which the legislature might properly do, but cannot do as understandingly or advantageously." [15]   Thus, a county board of education may be empowered to act as the agent of the legislature with power circumscribed by the enabling statute. The interpretation of the statute under which the agency acts is a judicial question. It is the courts that determine whether the agency exceeds or misinterprets its authority.[16] The courts, however, will not determine whether the decision of the agency is for the best interests of the territory, for such is properly a legislative decision.[17]

The legislature cannot avoid its constitutional responsibilities by the act of delegation to local authorities.[18] The Supreme Court of California, for example, ordered the state to take action to prevent the planned closing of a local school district six weeks early due to financial difficulties.

One of the fundamental principles of government in the United States, however, is that of the separation of powers among the executive, legislative, and judicial branches. Put another way, the principle is that there shall be no encroachment by one branch upon the prerogatives of another. Since each branch is charged with the exercise of certain powers, it may not divest itself thereof or delegate the powers to any other branch. An unconstitutional delegation of power occurs "when the Legislature confers upon an administrative agency the unrestricted authority to make fundamental policy determinations." [19] The division of powers among the branches of the government of a state, however, does not present a question of federal constitutional law.[20]

All courts purport to adhere to the principle of separation of powers, but they differ in degree on how far the legislature can go in delegating the formation and alteration of districts to subordinate agencies or officials. That the state legislature can do so in general is almost universally held. The basic inquiry is how much detail the legislature has placed in the statute to guide the administrative action. State high courts seem to vary in the amount of attention to guidelines and standards which they require the legislation to contain in order for it to be sustained as not constituting an unconstitutional delegation of legisla-

15. Hill v. Relyea, 34 Ill.2d 552, 216 N.E.2d 795 (1966).

16. Brandon Valley Independent School Dist. No. 150 v. Minnehaha County Bd. of Educ., 85 S.D. 255, 181 N.W.2d 96 (1970).

17. Thorland v. Independent Consolidated School Dist., 246 Minn. 96, 74 N.W.2d 410 (1956).

18. Butt v. State, 4 Cal.4th 668, 15 Cal. Rptr.2d 480, 842 P.2d 1240 (1992).

19. Clean Air Constituency v. California State Air Resources Bd., 11 Cal.3d 801, 114 Cal.Rptr. 577, 523 P.2d 617 (1974).

20. Highland Farms Dairy, Inc. v. Agnew, 300 U.S. 608, 57 S.Ct. 549, 81 L.Ed. 835 (1937).

tive authority. "Adequate standards which will guide and restrain the exercise of the delegated administrative functions" is the abstract standard in school district reorganization situations, according to the Supreme Court of Pennsylvania.[21] Most states subscribe to such a statement. The Supreme Court of Kansas has interpreted the Constitution of Kansas as permitting the legislature to go so far as to authorize the state superintendent to establish unified school districts and disorganize other districts either if an election has been held approving the establishment or if certain local school boards have petitioned for the establishment.[22]

Where the formation of high school districts was left to county superintendents of schools without any guidelines as to requisites for the formation of satisfactory and efficient high school districts on such points as area, assessed valuation, number of pupils, or form and size of districts, the Supreme Court of Illinois struck down the statute as an unconstitutional delegation of legislative power.[23] The court found it not to be a uniform law applicable alike to similar situations and territory throughout the state because it was subject to varying opinions of the county superintendents in the several counties and to variations within the same county if a superintendent left office and was replaced.

It should be noted at this point that uniformity does not necessarily mean sameness; it simply means that the bases of classification should be clear and reasonable in relation to the subject matter and purposes of the statute. The Supreme Court of Iowa was called upon to rule on the constitutionality of a statute providing for the reorganization of school districts based on whether there was or was not a resident average daily attendance of at least 300.[24] In upholding the classification, the court observed that if there were any reasonable grounds for a classification and if it operated equally on all within the same class, constitutional uniformity was achieved. Classifications by population almost always meet this generally accepted standard.

Impairment of Obligations of Contracts

The universally acknowledged right of the legislature to create, alter, or abolish districts as it may deem to be in the best educational interests of the state is subject to the limitation that such legislative action must not conflict with Article I, Section 10, of the Constitution of the United States, which provides that no state shall enact any law which impairs the obligation of contracts.

It should be noted that subdivisions of a state do not have any contract between them and the legislature which can be impaired by adjustment of boundaries. That the legislature of a state has the power

---

21. Chartiers Valley Joint Schools v. County Bd. of School Directors, 418 Pa. 520, 211 A.2d 487 (1965).

22. Tecumseh School Dist. v. Throckmorton, 195 Kan. 144, 403 P.2d 102 (1965).

23. Kenyon v. Moore, 287 Ill. 233, 122 N.E. 548 (1919).

24. Becker v. Board of Educ., 258 Iowa 277, 138 N.W.2d 909 (1965).

to create and alter local government units and divide and apportion the property of such districts is firmly rooted in American jurisprudence. There is no reciprocity of stipulation between the state and subordinate agencies, and their objects and duties are incompatible with the nature of a compact. Thus no contract can arise. The Supreme Court of the United States restated that view in 1905 in a case involving a contested school redistricting in the State of Michigan.[25] The reorganization act had been upheld as not violative of the Michigan Constitution, and the Supreme Court of the United States found no violation of the federal Constitution.

Another Michigan case illustrates the way in which the federal Constitution's bar against obligation of contract impairment is raised.[26] A statute provided that where territory of a school district was annexed to another district, the remaining portion would remain liable for bonds issued for lands and buildings located in the remaining portion. It seems that as a result of a change of district boundaries the amount of property upon which a tax could be levied to meet bond obligations was lessened. The act was held unconstitutional as impairing the obligations of a contract of the bondholders in that it relieved a considerable part of the territory, which was in the district when the bonds were issued, from payment without making any provision for payment from any other source.

Providing that the towns detached from a school district having outstanding bonds would be liable only in the event the reorganized district could not pay after levy on all its assets was held unconstitutional by the highest court in Maine.[27]

Pre-existing Assets and Debts

The distribution of assets and liabilities when districts are reorganized can be effected by the legislature in any manner that does not affect any contracts. In the absence of a statute making other disposition of property, the rule followed by a majority of courts is that the property is that of the district in which it is located after the changes in boundaries have been met. As discussed before, school property is not that of the district in the sense that it may not be transferred to other districts through legislative act. Rather it is state property held in trust for the state and used by the district to carry out the state function of providing educational opportunities for the children of the state living in the district. Furthermore, the fact that property becomes located in another district after district boundary changes does not relieve the original district from liability for the payment of an indebtedness incurred in connection therewith because the original district remains an

---

25. Attorney General of State of Mich. v. Lowrey, 199 U.S. 233, 26 S.Ct. 27, 50 L.Ed. 167 (1905). [Case No. 13]

26. Board of Educ. of City of Lincoln Park v. Board of Educ. of City of Detroit, 245 Mich. 411, 222 N.W. 763 (1929).

27. Canal Nat. Bank v. School Administrative Dist. No. 3, 160 Me. 309, 203 A.2d 734 (1964).

entity regardless of the fact that it may have territory added to or detached from it.[28] The doctrine is based upon the theory that no district owns property in the true sense of the word and when it binds itself to pay for such property it incurs liability for state and not local purposes. Inhabitants of a district are legally bound to know that the legislature may change district boundaries and that the school building, or other property, may finally be located in another district.

The United States Supreme Court without dissent has dismissed "for want of a substantial federal question" an appeal from a Supreme Court of Washington decision upholding the constitutionality of a statute which transferred to the State Board of Community College Education property financed by bonds issued by local school districts.[29] The legislature expressly reaffirmed all contracts between local school districts and their bondholders.

Approaching the issue from another perspective, it can be said that, although the legislature may provide for the division of the property of a school district and the apportionment of its debts when a portion of its territory and property are transferred to the jurisdiction of another district, the failure of the legislature to so provide does not invalidate a district reorganization statute. In the absence of such a provision, the common law rule observed by a majority of courts leaves the property where it is found and the debt on the original debtor.[30]

This rule can result in hardships. For example, in People v. Bartlett (footnote 28, supra) it was held that the county clerk could not be required to extend a tax for the payment of bonded indebtedness incurred before the district was divided against territory which had been detached. Thus a much larger burden of taxation than was contemplated at the time the debts were incurred was placed on the shoulders of the remaining district. But in that case the bondholders were not parties to the suit and were not contending that their security had been impaired, nor that the district as reconstituted after the detachment of the territory was unable to pay the full amount of the indebtedness.

Financial difficulties which may arise when changes are made in district boundaries have been treated by statutes in most states. Legislatures have made various attempts to provide for an equitable division of debts. Such legislation has been attacked on various grounds, but has been uniformly upheld. For example, a statute requiring a district to which territory of another district has been attached to pay debts of the latter in proportion to the value of the property detached was held not to violate the constitutional inhibition against taking property without due process of law.[31]

28. People ex rel. Raymond Community High School Dist. v. Bartlett, 304 Ill. 283, 136 N.E. 654 (1922).

29. Moses Lake School Dist. No. 161 v. Big Bend Community College, 81 Wash.2d 551, 503 P.2d 86 (1972), app. dism. 412 U.S. 934, 93 S.Ct. 2776, 37 L.Ed.2d 393 (1973).

30. Pass School Dist. v. Hollywood City School Dist., 156 Cal. 416, 105 P. 122 (1909).

31. School Dist. No. 3 of Bloomfield Tp. v. School Dist. of City of Pontiac, 261 Mich. 352, 246 N.W. 145 (1933).

However, the state constitution may provide that no indebtedness shall be imposed upon a district without a vote of the electors. Under such a provision, the legislature may not require one district to pay any portion of the bonded or other indebtedness of a district or part of a district attached to it.[32] Where a portion of a district is detached, however, this type of provision is not violated by the original district's being allocated a proportional share of the bonded indebtedness that had been incurred before the detachment.[33]

But unless there are controlling constitutional provisions, the legislature has almost unlimited authority to provide for the payment of the debts in the old district. Typical statutes on this point provide that a designated agency, frequently the county board of education, shall make an equitable distribution of the assets and debts of the old district. Such statutes have been upheld as not violating either state or federal constitutions.[34] What constitutes an equitable distribution would be a question of fact to be decided in each case.

A Wyoming statute provided that in a reorganization of school districts a county committee had the power to allocate equitably the assets and debts affected by the plan of reorganization. It was contended that this statute was in violation of a state constitutional provision that no new debts could be created without a vote of the people affected. The Supreme Court of Wyoming held that the statute was constitutional because it concerned division of existing debts rather than creation of new ones.[35] It further construed the statute, however, to mean that there must be a bona fide allocation of debts to any area according to benefits received by that area from additional assets accrued in the reorganization.

Various other aspects of the distribution of financial assets and liabilities have been before the courts. It has been held that no provision of either the state or federal constitution was violated by consolidating a district which had a surplus in its treasury with another district without the consent of the voters of the first district.[36] Also upheld has been the arrangement whereby taxpayers of a district to which a district having bonded indebtedness was attached were taxed on their property for payment of the indebtedness of the old district.[37]

In another type of situation, a new district was created out of another, and an agreement was made by the districts to divide the assets of the old with the new, the old district having had no debts at the time of the division. A statute provided that where a county was to be divided the new county would be liable for a just and equitable portion of

32. Protest of Missouri-Kansas-Texas Railroad Co., 181 Okl. 229, 73 P.2d 173 (1937).

33. Fullerton Joint Union High School Dist. v. State Bd. of Educ., 32 Cal.3d 779, 187 Cal.Rptr. 398, 654 P.2d 168 (1982).

34. Rapp v. Bethel-Tate Consolidated School Dist., 58 Ohio App. 126, 16 N.E.2d 224 (1937).

35. Lund v. Schrader, 492 P.2d 202 (Wyo.1971).

36. State ex rel. Bilby v. Brooks, 249 S.W. 73 (Mo.1923).

37. Rapp v. Bethel-Tate Consolidated School Dist., 58 Ohio App. 126, 16 N.E.2d 224 (1937).

the indebtedness of the old unit. (The statute was held to apply to school districts.) Since there was no legislative provision for the apportionment of assets, any agreement relating thereto was held void.[38] Also unenforceable, according to another court, was an arrangement whereby it was agreed by a board that so long as ten students were in an area a school would be maintained there.[39] The agreement had been made when the area in question had been consolidated with a larger district. The principle is that local school districts can contract only as provided by the state.

Exercise of Discretion

While it is recognized that the agency designated to pass upon the matter of alteration or consolidation of districts must exercise discretion, it is also well settled that the exercise of this discretion must not be arbitrary or unreasonable, a matter ultimately for the determination of the courts. Thus, the Supreme Court of South Dakota reviewed the refusal of a legislatively designated body to allow some property owners to have their land detached from an independent district and added to a common school district.[40] The plaintiffs alleged that the taxes in the independent district were so great that difficulty was had in meeting them. The court considered the adverse effects on the independent school district. It found the property to be needed in the independent district as a source of revenue, a fact sufficient to justify the refusal of the statutory committee to detach the property from the district.

In a later case the same court held that taxpayers had the right to seek judicial review of an order of a state agency having power to alter school districts.[41] The court found that the state commission had exceeded its authority under a statute, and the territorial change ordered by the commission was annulled.

The power of courts to invalidate an administrative act that is arbitrary or unreasonable does not include the power to direct a specific course of action. Thus the Supreme Court of Minnesota affirmed a trial court's annulling the chief state school officer's rejection of an application to consolidate school districts, but held that the court was without authority to order approval of the proposed plan for consolidation.[42]

Apparently the legislature must designate some body to examine district boundaries and cannot leave the matter completely to the desires of individual residents. A Kansas statute which permitted certain landowners to exclude their land from a school district by exercise of their own will was held unconstitutional on the ground that it was a

---

38. School Dist. No. 14 in Fremont County v. School Dist. No. 21 in Fremont County, 51 Wyo. 370, 67 P.2d 192 (1937).

39. Brown v. Gardner, 232 Ark. 197, 334 S.W.2d 889 (1960).

40. Snow v. South Shore Independent School Dist., 66 S.D. 379, 283 N.W. 530 (1939).

41. Elk Point Independent School Dist. No. 3 v. State Commission on Elementary and Secondary Educ., 85 S.D. 600, 187 N.W.2d 666 (1971).

42. Granada Independent School Dist. No. 455 v. Mattheis, 284 Minn. 174, 170 N.W.2d 88 (1969).

delegation of legislative power.[43]   However, it has been held that, "all things being equal," the personal desires of the residents may be considered. Thus, petitions may be given weight provided statutory and constitutional procedures and safeguards are observed.[44]

The Supreme Court of Nebraska invalidated a statute which conferred upon the county superintendent of schools, county clerk, and county board of education authority to change district boundaries without notice or opportunity for hearing to property owners. It held that the arrangement violated the due process clause of the United States Constitution.[45] Some statutes mandate hearings before school districts may be altered. It already has been observed that decision-making agencies are not bound to follow sentiments expressed thereat. However, courts will examine the conduct of such hearings to assure that basic facts have been presented and that viewpoints have not been suppressed.

Although the courts are inclined to overlook technical irregularities in reorganization proceedings, proposals may be so inadequately presented as to be judicially disapproved. An example from Illinois is illustrative.[46] A statute provided that prior to a hearing on a proposed reorganization a map showing the districts involved should be submitted to the county board and there should be information as to the probable effects of the proposed changes. In a proceeding invalidated by the court the secretary's map consisted merely of a drawing of rectangles and his report of financial conditions merely showed assessed valuations, amounts levied and expended, and the amount of state aid claims. There was no information regarding tax rate or indebtedness, there was no testimony to supplement the scanty information in the report, and there was unsatisfactory testimony on some questions of educational conditions in one of the districts. Such circumstances the court found to be inadequate for the proper implementation of the statute.

The New York legislature enacted a scheme for the decentralization of the New York City school system. Certain general criteria were established, including one that each of the subdistricts should contain 20,000 students. The board of education of the city issued a tentative decentralization plan for Manhattan containing six districts, with some districts having far less than the statutorily prescribed number of pupils. The board conducted the prescribed hearing on the plan. Subsequently it adopted a plan which provided for five districts. The Court of Appeals of New York, however, held that the plan was invalidly adopted and ordered further hearings.[47] The court said that the final plan was substantially different from the one on which the hearing had been held.

43. State ex rel. Jackson v. School Dist. No. 2, 140 Kan. 171, 34 P.2d 102 (1934).

44. Burnidge v. County Bd. of School Trustees of Kane County, 25 Ill.App.2d 503, 167 N.E.2d 21 (1960).

45. Ruwe v. School Dist. No. 85 of Dodge County, 120 Neb. 668, 234 N.W. 789 (1931).

46. Crainville School Dist. v. County Bd. of School Trustees, 32 Ill.App.2d 143, 177 N.E.2d 248 (1961).

47. Tinsley v. Monserrat, 26 N.Y.2d 110, 308 N.Y.S.2d 843, 257 N.E.2d 28 (1970).

Furthermore, the districts proposed at the hearing did not meet the legislative mandate for number of pupils.

Where statutes provide for alteration of districts by a process of election, courts will strictly enforce procedural matters before the election is held, but after the election the courts will intervene only upon a showing of fraud or that the alleged procedural violations prevented the electors from giving a full expression of their will.[48]

Powers of the State Education Agency

In General

To control the education function on a state-wide basis each of the fifty states has a central education agency. The limits of the authority and responsibility of these departments are to be found in the respective state constitutions and statutes. In all but one state there is a state board of education having general authority over the public schools. Each state has a chief state school officer, usually called the state superintendent of schools or the state commissioner of education. Also in each state is a staff consisting of various specialists and officials who actually perform the functions of the state-level education agency. In general, the state boards are charged with policy making for education, one level below the legislature in the hierarchy. The execution of legislation and state board policy is under the direction of the chief state school officer. In most states there are some "intermediate" educational agencies operating between the state agency and the local boards of education. Frequently the unit is the county. The duties and powers of the intermediate educational units vary widely among the states. They are, however, generally considered agencies of the state with specified responsibilities for operation within their geographical boundaries.

The most common methods of selection of state board of education members are appointment by the governor and popular election. A few state board members get their posts ex officio, that is, they are placed on the state board of education because they have been elected to some other post in the state government. The method of selection of the members of the state board of education generally is not critical as regards its legal powers.

Chief state school officers are appointed by the state board of education, popularly elected, or appointed by the governor. Where chief state school officers are elected, there frequently are statutes (and occasionally constitutional provisions) giving certain powers specifically to that office. A considerable number of problems arise in the general area of responsibility and authority when the chief administrator is selected by the voters rather than by the state board of education or the governor.

The Oregon constitution authorized the legislature to provide by law for the election of a state superintendent of public instruction. A statute

48. Eriksen v. Ray, 212 Neb. 8, 321 N.W.2d 59 (1982).

was enacted providing that the state board of education elect the state superintendent to serve as executive head of the state department and as administrative officer of the state board of education. The Supreme Court of Oregon was asked whether it was constitutional for the state board to select the chief administrator under the circumstances. The court answered in the negative.[49] It was argued that the selection of a professional person by the state board of education was a more desirable method of obtaining the superintendent than election by popular vote. The court observed that this argument could well be sound from the political science viewpoint, and the legislature apparently thought so or it would not have enacted the statute. But the constitutional provision was held to be overriding, and the word "election" in the constitution was construed to mean election by the voters, not election by the state board of education.

The Idaho Constitution provides for a state board of education to be created by the legislature to have general supervision over all state educational institutions and the public school system of the state. The state's highest court in 1993 declared unconstitutional a legislative act dividing jurisdiction among three bodies: a "council" governing higher education, a "council" governing public schools, and a "board" comprising both councils for the governance of public educational endeavors not falling directly under either of the councils. The court said that the constitution of the state plainly required a single board and the legislature and governor were powerless to change that basic structure.[50]

There arose a conflict in Oregon as to the powers of the state superintendent in relation to the powers of the state board. Involved was the area of rule-making powers with respect to public education. The rule at issue had to do with the minimum standard covering average class load per teacher. The state board wished to raise the class load per teacher. The superintendent contended that because he was mentioned in the constitution, the legislature could delegate this authority only to him and not to an appointed board. The court disagreed, holding that the legislature had authority to create and empower the state board of education to make such rules and to place the superintendent in the position of executive officer charged with implementing and enforcing them.[51]

The Supreme Court of Wyoming held that where a statute empowered the state board of education to adopt rules governing the certification of teachers and administrators and to grant exceptions, it was the board, rather than the chief state school officer, that had final say when a dispute over the rules arose.[52] The issue involved an exception not granted by the board for a person whom a local board wanted to employ as superintendent.

49. State of Oregon ex rel. Musa v. Minear, 240 Or. 315, 401 P.2d 36 (1965).

50. Evans v. Andrus, 124 Idaho 6, 855 P.2d 467 (1993).

51. State Bd. of Educ. v. Fasold, 251 Or. 274, 445 P.2d 489 (1968).

52. Wyoming State Dept. of Educ. v. Barber, 649 P.2d 681 (Wyo.1982).

Not infrequently conflicts develop because of lack of clarity or specificity in constitutional or statutory language. In the Virgin Islands power to determine the school calendar was held to reside in the territorial board of education, rather than the department of education, even though the department was designated as the collective bargaining agency for the territory. The Third Circuit Court of Appeals relied on the more expansive general powers of the board to resolve the issue but suggested that a legislative response would be desirable.[53]

In New Jersey the state's highest court emphasized that the commissioner and the state board do not share equal status as administrative decision makers.[54] The court said that the "ultimate administrative decision maker in school matters" is the state board. An intermediate appellate court, here reversed, had relied on a difference of opinion between the commissioner and the board as grounds for affording the board less deference than it would ordinarily be accorded.

Delegation of Legislative Power to the State Education Agency

The problem of delegation of legislative authority was discussed under "Establishment and Alteration of School Districts." Also, the general principle of separation of powers frequently is evoked in attempts to strike down rules and regulations of state agencies and officials. Where a legislative power cannot be delegated, the issue of the reasonableness of the administrative regulation is not reached.

An application of the preceding principle is found in a decision of the Supreme Court of Nebraska.[55] Involved was a statute expressly conferring upon the state superintendent the authority to "formulate rules and regulations for the approval of all high schools for the collection of free high school tuition money." A successful action was brought to enjoin the superintendent from enforcing a rule covering teacher-pupil ratio. The court was of the opinion that the legislature had not provided with sufficient definiteness a framework of policy within which the superintendent might establish rules for the approval of high schools. In other words, the legislature had delegated its legislative authority to the superintendent in violation of the constitutional principle of separation of powers.

The courts, however, are aware of the fact that the increasing complexity of society requires that guidelines not be too specific. The court that decided the preceding case has stated that the delegation of authority to a specialized department under more generalized standards has been the natural trend as the need for regulation has become more complex.[56] It is self-evident that the constitutional doctrine of separa-

53. Virgin Islands Joint Bd. of Educ. v. Farrelly, 984 F.2d 97 (3 Cir.1993).

54. Probst v. Board of Educ. of Borough of Haddonfield, Camden County, 127 N.J. 518, 606 A.2d 345 (1992).

55. School Dist. No. 39 of Washington County v. Decker, 159 Neb. 693, 68 N.W.2d 354 (1955). [Case No. 16]

56. School Dist. No. 8 of Sherman County v. State Bd. of Educ., 176 Neb. 722, 127 N.W.2d 458 (1964).

tion of powers was not intended to confine the legislature to the alternatives of virtual inaction or the imposition of rigidly inflexible laws which would distort rather than promote its objectives. Broad guidelines consistent with a legislative plan will generally suffice to meet constitutional standards.[57] But a statute delegating power must not be so vague that its operational meaning is almost totally dependent on the subjective discretion of administrative boards or officers. Such was found to be the situation in Connecticut where that state's highest court invalidated a grant to local school boards of power to expel students for "conduct inimical to the best interests of the school." [58]

The issue of delegation of authority to a state superintendent of education developed in an unusual way in Illinois, at the time a state not having a state board of education. The Illinois legislature had directed the state superintendent of public instruction to specify minimum requirements for the health and safety of pupils. The superintendent prepared a lengthy set of regulations on the subject. A local district contested the necessity of complying with the standards, alleging that the law was unconstitutional as an illegal delegation of legislative power. The reply was that the legislation included guides as to the kinds of standards to be formulated by the superintendent, namely, minimum standards for such matters as lighting, heating, ventilation, seating, and plumbing for the purpose of conserving the health and safety of pupils, and therefore the delegation was one of purely administrative, as opposed to legislative, power. The Supreme Court of Illinois noted that the judicial yardsticks to be applied to the problem of delegation of powers must necessarily vary according to the nature of the ultimate objective of the particular legislation.[59] In the case at bar, technical complexity and diversity were clearly present. The court upheld the delegation of the authority to the superintendent. Having so ruled, however, the court then examined the standards set by the superintendent and found that he had gone beyond the intent of the legislature, which had been the establishment of minimum standards. The court found the standards of the superintendent to be considerably more stringent than other well-recognized norms for school construction. Undisputed also was the fact that the public schools of the plaintiff district were reasonably safe from a health and fire standpoint, although they did not meet all of the prescriptions in the contested regulations. The court indicated that the legislature had not given the superintendent unfettered power to prescribe his own standards of excellence.

Ramifications of the question of delegation of authority to the state board of education constitute less of a problem than delegation of authority to the state superintendent of education. In Ohio, for example, a challenge was made to the power of the state board of education to revoke a high school charter. The local board involved had been warned

57. Schreiber v. County Bd. of School Trustees, 31 Ill.2d 121, 198 N.E.2d 848 (1964).

58. Mitchell v. King, 169 Conn. 140, 363 A.2d 68 (1975). [Case No. 15]

59. Board of Educ. of City of Rockford v. Page, 33 Ill.2d 372, 211 N.E.2d 361 (1965).

that the high school had not met minimum standards in a number of specific instances. After a hearing the state board revoked the charter, and the local board appealed to the courts. The trial court concluded that the school substantially met the minimum standards and was in no worse condition than many other schools throughout the state. The Court of Appeals of Ohio, in reversing this decision, indicated that although its sympathies lay with the local board, the law had to be enforced, and local high schools must meet the minimum requirements of the state.[60] The fact that lack of money was apparently the reason for the deficiencies, and the fact that lack of financial help from state-level sources could well be involved, were not relevant to the power of the state board to revoke the charter of the high school. The court found that the doctrines of substantial compliance and comparative compliance did not apply. The point of improper delegation of authority to the state board of education was raised, but the court indicated that it was not a "real question" because the legislature was clothed with almost unlimited power which could be delegated to any agency the legislature created as long as the legislature retained the power to withdraw that authority.

Whether in fact certain authority had been delegated to the state board of education arose in Illinois in connection with rules promulgated to enforce, ultimately through fund cut-offs, a statute requiring steps to be taken to correct de facto segregation in local school districts. The state's highest court concluded that the rules were beyond the power of state education authorities to issue because a statute specifically treating the matter placed responsibility in the hands of local school boards and provided a procedure for ultimate enforcement by the state attorney general.[61] The court said that the legislative provision empowering the state board generally to promulgate rules for establishing and maintaining free schools was limited by the specific legislation pertaining to de facto segregation and means to correct it.

A few years later the state board sought to withhold funds for educating the gifted from a school district because the state board believed there was racial segregation in that program, over which the board had specific supervisory power. Here, too, the authority to withhold money was found not to exist for the same reasons, and no federal law gave the board the power.[62]

The authority of the state board of education of Hawaii was questioned when that body adopted a curriculum dealing with family life and sex education. It was unsuccessfully argued before the state's highest court that a specific authorization from the legislature was needed before the board could take such action.[63] The assertion that the plan was

60. Board of Educ. of Aberdeen-Huntington Local School Dist. v. State Bd. of Educ., 116 Ohio App. 515, 189 N.E.2d 81 (1962).

61. Aurora East Public School Dist. No. 131 v. Cronin, 92 Ill.2d 313, 66 Ill.Dec. 85, 442 N.E.2d 511 (1982).

62. Board of Educ. of City of Peoria, School Dist. No. 150, v. Sanders, 150 Ill. App.3d 755, 104 Ill.Dec. 233, 502 N.E.2d 730 (1986), cert. den. 484 U.S. 926, 108 S.Ct. 290, 98 L.Ed.2d 250 (1987).

63. Medeiros v. Kiyosaki, 52 Hawaii 436, 478 P.2d 314 (1970). [Case No. 14]

adopted through an improper delegation of authority by the state board to the administrative staff of the state department of education was also rejected. The court found that the actions of the administrative staff were merely recommendatory.

It was argued in a North Carolina case that the state board of education was exercising powers regarding teacher certification without standards or guidelines from the legislature.[64] The Supreme Court of North Carolina ruled, however, that the state constitution conferred powers in this area on the state board, subject to limitation and revision by the legislature. As the legislature had not acted, the board retained the broad power to regulate qualifications of teachers. It stated that the issue of delegation of powers comes into play in relation to legislative powers, not to constitutional powers.

Twenty years later the same court decided a case involving the effect of an act of the legislature upon a policy of the state board. The state board had enacted a rule that sought to prevent local boards from contracting with a private company to provide each day a twelve-minute television news program that contained two minutes of commercial advertising. The state board long had held the statutory power to adopt textbooks, and statutes directed local boards to adopt written procedures used in selecting supplementary materials not inconsistent with the textbooks. Shortly after the state board enacted the new rule the legislature amended the supplementary materials statute to give complete control thereover to local boards. The court held that this legislative act abrogated the state board rule.[65] Public policy, it said, was in the province of the legislature, and no constitutional rights of students or others were violated.

The separation principle is not restricted to the powers of agencies exercising state-wide powers. An illustration is a case which involved the power of county boards to fix the boundaries of reorganized school districts. Iowa law vested this power in the county boards, which were to act after they had made studies of educational conditions in the area and after they had held hearings on petitions filed for district reorganization. A board's power was challenged on the ground that the legislature had reposed absolute, unregulated, and undefined discretionary powers of a legislative nature in the county boards of education. The constitutionality of the statute was sustained against this attack.[66] In the opinion of the court, the fact that certain standards for the action of county boards were prescribed in the statute (that educational conditions in the areas should be studied and that hearings were to be held on petitions for district reorganization) was a sufficient statement of the legislative policy under which the boards were authorized to act. The court emphasized the fact that the mode of life has become so complex that for the legislature to enact laws in detail covering many governmen-

64. Guthrie v. Taylor, 279 N.C. 703, 185 S.E.2d 193 (1971).

65. State v. Whittle Communications, 328 N.C. 456, 402 S.E.2d 556 (1991).

66. Wall v. County Bd. of Educ., 249 Iowa 209, 86 N.W.2d 231 (1957).

tal services would not only be impractical, but impossible. Thus, reasoned the court, many matters must be left to administrative agencies.

It is well established that the legislature may confer powers of local regulation on municipal corporations without violating the separation-of-powers principle. Under this theory local school boards are recognized as quasi municipal corporations, and proper powers of "local self-government" may be delegated to them.[67] Any power that is delegated, however, must not be in conflict with overarching state legislation. For example, a provision in the city charter of San Francisco relating to tenure for school administrators and supervisors was held to be invalid because it conflicted with state statutes on the subject.[68] The court also stated that the fact the charter enactment preceded enactment of the conflicting statutes was of no consequence.

That the state legislature must be deemed to have ultimate control over education in the state in the absence of some clear constitutional provision to be contrary was held by the Supreme Court of Louisiana.[69] The case involved the power of the legislature to require a balanced treatment in the curriculum of "creation science" and "evolution science." The court rejected arguments that certain provisions in the Louisiana constitution allocated decisions regarding course content and methodology exclusively to the state board. The board's powers of supervision and control of public education "must yield to the legislative will as expressed by the elected representatives of the people," said the court. That the state board members also were elected did not influence the court to detach ultimate authority from the legislature. The constitutionality of the particular statute that precipitated the decision was not at issue in the case. Eventually the statute was declared unconstitutional by the United States Supreme Court.[70] (See footnote 52 in Chapter 4.)

The different legal effect of a legislature's enacting a prescription and a state board's doing so under legislatively delegated powers is well illustrated in connection with changing teacher certification requirements. As amplified in Chapter 9, it is well settled that one holding a certificate does not have a contract, and requirements for retention or renewal are subject to change. However, when the state board of education attempted to reduce the length of already issued five-year certificates, the Supreme Court of Rhode Island enjoined the action.[71] It expressly distinguished the case from one decided differently shortly before in Connecticut [72] on the basis of the source of the changes, state board rather than legislature.

67. American Federation of Teachers v. Yakima School Dist. No. 7, 74 Wash.2d 865, 447 P.2d 593 (1968).

68. Whisman v. San Francisco Unified School Dist., 86 Cal.App.3d 782, 150 Cal. Rptr. 548 (1978).

69. Aguillard v. Treen, 440 So.2d 704 (La.1983).

70. Edwards v. Aguillard, 482 U.S. 578, 107 S.Ct. 2573, 96 L.Ed.2d 510 (1987).

71. Reback v. Rhode Island Bd. of Regents for Elementary and Secondary Educ., 560 A.2d 357 (R.I.1989).

72. Connecticut Educ. Ass'n, Inc. v. Tirozzi, 210 Conn. 286, 554 A.2d 1065 (1989).

Administrative Powers

The generality of many statutes related to the powers of the state education agency has given rise to a large volume of litigation involving the extent of these powers. Statutes commonly provide that the state superintendent, state board of education, or both shall have general supervision and control of the school system of the state. Whether a particular power is within those legally conferred by general statutes must be decided by the courts in a properly presented case. Also, although it is uniformly held that, within their powers, state administrative officials can make reasonable rules and take reasonable actions for the operation of the state school system, whether a specific rule or action is reasonable is also a judicial question to be determined in each case as it arises.

Interpreting the state constitutional provisions related to powers of the state board and of local boards, the highest court in Virginia has held that the state board lacked the power to require local boards to submit to binding arbitration certain disputes between local boards and nonsupervisory employees.[73] The court distinguished the power of "general supervision" (vested in the state board) from "supervision of schools" (vested in local school boards). It said that to give to the state board the authority it claimed would render meaningless the grant of power by the constitution to local boards for "supervision of schools." It should be emphasized that the mention of local boards in the constitution is uncommon.

If legislation is specific, state boards are not empowered to deviate from the prescriptions. Thus, when a Wyoming statute provided for a minimum of 175 days each school year, the state supreme court held that the state board lacked the authority to approve an experimental four-day week for a school district. By increasing hours per day there would have been 144 days in the school year.[74] (The state attorney general had incorrectly advised that the schedule was legal for the experiment.) The court commented that the alternative schedule, which had been in operation for about seven months "may have jeopardized" state-aid entitlements in that the number of days required was fixed.

The state board of education in Pennsylvania promulgated regulations of statewide application covering a wide range of aspects of student discipline—rights, punishments, procedural requirements. As these were mandatory, rather than advisory, the effect was to establish a statewide code. The action was challenged on the ground it exceeded the state board's power and interfered with some powers delegated by the legislature to local boards. Overruling lower courts, the Supreme Court of Pennsylvania upheld the state board's power to establish such

73. School Bd. of City of Richmond v. Parham, 218 Va. 950, 243 S.E.2d 468 (1978).

74. Johnston v. Board of Trustees, School Dist. No. 1 West, Sheridan County, 661 P.2d 1045 (Wyo.1983).

rules.[75] The legislature had granted the state board authority to make regulations to carry out the board's mandate to set standards governing "educational programs," and the court held that student discipline was an essential element of the education process. The court said that it was not ruling on the validity of any of the regulations, but that to invalidate a rule it would be necessary to show that it was not the result of a reasonable exercise of judgment. Some disciplinary powers legislatively granted to local authorities were to be considered complementary to powers granted the state board.

In Kansas, where the constitution granted general supervisory powers over education to the state board, the highest state court found that the provision empowered the board to require each local board to adopt policies regulating student and employee conduct, which policies were to be reviewed by the attorney of the local board and filed with the state board.[76] The content of the policies was not circumscribed. When the issue was school district organization, however, the Supreme Court of Kansas has held that the state board of education must follow legislative guidelines and that its failure to do so was arbitrary as a matter of law.[77]

The extent of a general grant of power was interpreted by the Court of Appeals of Maryland in a situation in which a local school board had passed a resolution requiring that fingerprint cards of school system employees be sent to the local police for review.[78] The state board of education set aside the resolution and the county board challenged the state board's authority to overrule it. The court, in sustaining the authority of the state board, relied upon the general statutes giving control and supervision of public schools to the state board and held that this general statutory mandate gave the state board the final word on matters concerning educational policy or administration. The contested action the court held to be in the category of educational policy. It said that the problem of screening employees was administrative and thus lay within the power of the state board's review. The court expressly declined to comment on the wisdom of the state board's action, saying that its province was only to determine whether the board had the power to act and had a rational basis for the action. The latter was here linked to the problem of staffing the schools.

In New York the highest state court upheld a decision by the state commissioner of education invalidating a local school board regulation on the ground that it was unsound educational policy.[79] The provision in question required teachers who formerly had been members of the Communist Party to identify colleagues whom they knew to be Party members in order to show their good faith withdrawal from the Party.

75. Girard School Dist. v. Pittenger, 481 Pa. 91, 392 A.2d 261 (1978).

76. State ex rel. Miller v. Board of Educ. of Unified School Dist. No. 398, Marion County (Peabody), 212 Kan. 482, 511 P.2d 705 (1973).

77. State ex rel. Dix v. Board of Educ., 224 Kan. 38, 578 P.2d 692 (1978).

78. Wilson v. Board of Educ. of Montgomery County, 234 Md. 561, 200 A.2d 67 (1964).

79. Board of Educ. of City of New York v. Allen, 6 N.Y.2d 127, 188 N.Y.S.2d 515, 160 N.E.2d 60 (1959).

The commissioner's determination that such a situation would be educationally upsetting to the school system was reasonable enough for the court to sustain his opinion.

Power of the state commissioner of education of Massachusetts to require a local school board to conduct a racial census was examined by the Supreme Judicial Court of Massachusetts.[80] The commissioner was given general statutory authority to supervise educational activities in the schools of the state and to require annual reports from the school districts. The court held that the statutes were sufficiently broad to serve as a basis for requiring the submission of the racial information requested.

Also involved in this case was the legality of the punishment of withholding state aid from the recalcitrant district. A statute empowered the commissioner to withhold state funds from districts which failed to file certain reports. These reports contain information which the district superintendent was required to swear to the accuracy of. The commissioner threatened to withhold state aid in the instant case to force compliance. On this question the court said that the commissioner would be exceeding his power if he withheld state aid because the information he desired regarding race was not to be submitted under oath. So it was held that the commissioner had the power to require the report, but did not have the power to enforce the mandate by withholding state aid.

Where state education authorities have adopted policies of promoting better balance of the races in the schools, the courts have sustained actions to implement this state-level policy.[81] New York has gone further than perhaps any other state in establishing as a state-wide educational policy the elimination of de facto segregation in public schools. The rationale of the policy is that de facto segregation results in a poorer quality of education than takes place in settings where the races are better balanced. A formidable number of cases have arisen in which citizens or local school boards have challenged various aspects of the implementation by state-level agencies of this policy. In one local school district the commissioner ultimately ordered a particular plan to be put into effect to effectuate better racial balance. A challenge of his power to do so reached the highest court in New York.[82] The court indicated that, since the legislature had made the commissioner administrative head of the state system of education and the final authority on questions of administration of the system, the courts would not interfere except in cases of "pure arbitrariness." Here the commissioner's decision rested squarely on his finding of educational inadequacy in de facto segregated schools. Since the commissioner could substitute his judgment for that of local school boards, his action could not be judicially

80. School Committee of New Bedford v. Commissioner of Educ., 349 Mass. 410, 208 N.E.2d 814 (1965).

81. The Illinois case in footnote 61 can be distinguished on the ground that Illinois had an uncommon statute specifically creating an affirmative duty to correct de facto segregation and providing details on how it was to be done.

82. Vetere v. Allen, 15 N.Y.2d 259, 258 N.Y.S.2d 77, 206 N.E.2d 174 (1965).

overturned on the ground of educational disagreement. The court expressly indicated that its function did not include evaluating the sociological, psychological, or educational implications relied on by the commissioner. The remedy for plaintiffs, suggested the court, would be through the state board of education (in New York called Board of Regents) or through the legislature.

The increasing complexity of legal matters developing in the field of education has prompted some courts to construe very broadly the powers of state administrative officers so that educational aspects will be fully considered. These would then be in the record of the case if it should eventually be brought to them for judicial determination. The Supreme Court of New Jersey, for example, has indicated that the powers of the state commissioner of education are more extensive than incumbents had interpreted them to be, and has required that officer to make some decisions which some commissioners apparently preferred not to make on their own initiatives. Expressly in one case the court indicated the commissioner had a responsibility to make independent determinations on some matters concerning nonretention of an administrator, not merely to decide whether the actions of local school boards were arbitrary, capricious, or the result of prejudice.[83] The court pointed out that its view did not interfere with the commissioner's policy of allowing local boards the choice among various solutions in the first instance, but that on an appeal to him he would have to substitute his own judgment in certain circumstances rather than simply disapprove a local board's decision and remand the case to the local board for further action. The point was reaffirmed and extended further in a case involving de facto segregation.[84] Here the court expressly ordered the commissioner to take whatever action appeared appropriate to him to correct the problem the local board was not alleviating. The state board of education had approved the actions of the commissioner and thus also was encompassed by the court order.

In another case involving racial balance six years later, at issue was the quasi-judicial finding of the commissioner that the proposed establishment of a new high school in a virtually all-white community which had been sending its students to a high school in a district with a mixed racial population would result in an increased racial imbalance in the one school and the creation of a virtually all-white school in the neighboring community.[85] The one school district completely encircled the other and the two districts were very closely interrelated by commercial and transportation patterns. There was also considerable interdependency in municipal public services. The commissioner had concluded that he had no power to act in the situation, but the Supreme Court of New Jersey took a strongly-worded contrary view. Citing the cases previously discussed, the court said that the legislature had granted broad powers to the commissioner and that the court would not "permit

---

83. In re Masiello, 25 N.J. 590, 138 A.2d 393 (1958).

84. Booker v. Board of Educ., Plainfield, 45 N.J. 161, 212 A.2d 1 (1965).

85. Jenkins v. Township of Morris School Dist., 58 N.J. 483, 279 A.2d 619 (1971).

their administrative narrowing which in effect represents not only a disavowal of power but also a disavowal of responsibility." The court noted that the state had pursued a vigorous policy in favor of a thorough and efficient public school system and against racial discrimination and segregation in the public schools. It ruled that the commissioner had power to direct the continuance of the sending-receiving relationship between the two school districts after the expiration of the present contract, to order the boards of education to proceed with suitable steps toward regionalization, and to direct a merger on his own if he found such course ultimately necessary for the fulfillment of the state's educational and desegregation policies in the public schools. (De facto segregation is treated in Chapter 13.)

State officials and agencies, however, as an administrative policy cannot simply retrospectively approve local board actions where important rights of individuals are implicated. An example involves teacher tenure in New York. Areas of teaching in which tenure may be earned were not specified by statute or regents rules. Over the years administrative rules of the commissioner and state department had become judicially recognized. These provided for "horizontal" tenure (kindergarten, elementary, secondary, with some specified special subjects), rather than "vertical" tenure (English, mathematics, social studies, etc.). At a particular point in time the commissioner in an unreviewed quasi-judicial ruling stated that tenure areas could be created by administrative action at the school district level, subject only to his ad hoc retrospective approval. Five years later the Court of Appeals held such a view to be erroneous in that the state-level authorities furnished no standards for the local boards, thus undermining the purposes of the tenure statute in that it could easily be manipulated by boards seeking to withhold or withdraw tenure from a teacher and by a teacher seeking to avoid an assignment outside his area.[86] The court observed that vertical tenure areas were not prohibited by the statute, but held that before such could be put into effect the arrangement must be prospectively clarified by the legislature or the regents.

Where a state administrative official or board has construed a statute such interpretation is entitled to consideration by courts, but it is not binding despite the facts it may be reasonable in the abstract, have been consistently applied, and been so applied for a long period. Thus, even though the Teachers' Retirement Board of Montana had interpreted a 1949 statute to preclude purchase of retirement credits for out-of-state teaching service in private schools (because those who taught in private schools within the state could not purchase credit if they became public school employees), the highest court of that state in 1977 found that the legislation as written did not so provide.[87] The court said that the statute covering out-of-state teaching service clearly did not restrict the site of that teaching and that where legislation was unambiguous neither administrators nor courts could change the meaning. Further,

86. Baer v. Nyquist, 34 N.Y.2d 291, 357 N.Y.S.2d 442, 313 N.E.2d 751 (1974).

87. State ex rel. Sullivan v. State Teachers' Retirement Board, 174 Mont. 482, 571 P.2d 793 (1977).

the distinction between in-state and out-of-state service in private schools was justifiable on a ground of the legislature's desiring to attract out-of-state teacher candidates for public school employment.

A New York statute provided that state funds for construction of school buildings would not be paid to any district scheduled for reorganization under a state plan unless the state commissioner of education certified that such allocation of funds would not impede reorganization. Voters in two school districts which were to be merged under a state developed master plan had voted down consolidation by decisive margins. One of the districts then applied for a certificate of non-impedance and for an apportionment of state aid for the construction of a new music room. The commissioner declined to furnish the money, and the board sued to require him to do so. It contended that since the improvement could be utilized after the reorganization the commissioner should approve it. The court, however, did not agree that that was the test the legislature had intended.[88] The question was not whether the addition would be usable upon reorganization, but whether reorganization would be impeded by the use of state funds to improve existing facilities that happened to be scheduled to become part of the reorganized district. The court upheld the statute which left the decision on whether such aid would impede reorganization to the discretion of the education commissioner. It found this arrangement to be a valid delegation of authority and, further, that the petitioners had not shown that the commissioner abused his discretion in the instant case.

A statute in Maine provided for a state subsidy to a certain type of school district for "capital outlay" purposes. One such district purchased some land adjacent to a school lot and developed it into an athletic field with bleachers, parking lot, and several other improvements. The state commissioner of education refused to grant the state aid on the ground that the project was not one covered by the statute. A lawsuit to collect the subsidy was successful.[89] The Supreme Judicial Court of Maine issued a ruling that the project was covered by the statute. The court said that the statute invited broad interpretation, and that there was a traditional liberal policy toward the concept of educational purposes and needs.

A statutory provision that the chief state school officer shall be "the legal adviser" of all school officers and when requested shall give his opinion upon "any question arising under the school laws" has been judicially upheld.[90] The court said the legislation did not encroach on the judicial branch's power to regulate the practice of law and it did not take away common law powers of the attorney general, which did not extend beyond acting as adviser to executive officers, boards, and departments of the state government.

---

88. Siegel v. Allen, 23 A.D.2d 520, 255 N.Y.S.2d 336 (1965).

89. City of Westbrook v. Logan, 227 A.2d 793 (Me.1967).

90. Board of Educ., School Dist. No. 142, Cook County v. Bakalis, 54 Ill.2d 448, 299 N.E.2d 737 (1973).

The question of whether the state board of education can deny accreditation to a proposed high school when the local board controlling that school has complied with all of the formal requirements established by the state board was considered by the Supreme Court of Washington.[91] The state board denied accreditation, concluding that no imperative need existed for the high school. It appeared that there were adequate high school facilities in the neighboring district, and that additional facilities and programs could be more economically and reasonably provided in the neighboring district than through the proposed new high school. The court held that the legislature did not intend accreditation to be granted automatically to every district which met the minimum standards established by the state board. In other words, the court did not find that accreditation was a purely ministerial determination.

Several years later the state board of education again denied accreditation to the high school program of the district on substantially the same grounds.[92] The district brought another suit, this time contending that there had been a report and recommendations by the state superintendent's staff which were not properly considered by the board. The court disagreed, pointing out that the staff recommendations were advisory only, and also that a review of the board's minutes indicated the staff report was not ignored. Not only did the report contain some caveats, but the staff's findings of fiscal responsibility were seriously questioned and found wanting by the state board. Observing that accreditation was a qualification for participation in certain state funds in addition to a recognition of academic proficiency, the court emphasized that the state board must exercise fiscal as well as academic responsibility.

An Ohio statute provided that any school district not operating schools encompassing all twelve grades would be dissolved as of a given date. Exceptions could be authorized by the state board of education under special conditions. A few weeks before the deadline a local district requested a two-year exception at the end of which time the district would be joined to another. The state board granted the request, specifically resolving to the effect requested. About five months before the agreed date of dissolution the local district requested a further postponement. The request was denied without a hearing. The procedure was approved by the Supreme Court of Ohio.[93] The court held that the failure of the state board to change its position was not an adjudication requiring notice and hearing. The prior decision, which was not appealed, was determinative of any rights of the district to remain in existence.

91. State ex rel. DuPont-Fort Lewis School Dist. No. 7 v. Bruno, 62 Wash.2d 790, 384 P.2d 608 (1963).

92. Dupont-Fort Lewis School Dist. No. 7 v. Bruno, 79 Wash.2d 736, 489 P.2d 171 (1971).

93. State ex rel. Bd. of Educ. of Bratenahl Local School Dist. v. State Bd. of Educ., 53 Ohio St.2d 173, 373 N.E.2d 1238 (1978). Federal claims were subsequently rejected in Wilt v. State Bd. of Educ., 608 F.2d 1126 (6 Cir.1979).

Frequently discretion must be exercised by state authorities in relation to issuance or revocation of teaching certificates. Powers in this area are discussed in Chapter 9.

Enforcement of Administrative Powers

The enforcement of administrative powers and the penalties the state-level agency may invoke against those who do not comply with its orders lead frequently to litigation. Withdrawing the accreditation of schools and revoking the certificates of teachers are sanctions that already have been mentioned. In some circumstances, to a large extent dependent on statutes, state officials can remove local board members from office. A condition to taking such an extreme measure, however, is substantial proof that derelictions have been very serious. This is particularly true where, as in the overwhelming majority of local districts, local board members are popularly elected. The Court of Appeals of Kentucky gave consideration to a situation in which the state board attempted to remove a local board for failure to follow the recommendations of the state board.[94] The attempted removal was based on the allegation that the local board members had been guilty of bad faith, misconduct, and neglect of duty in the conduct of district affairs. According to the evidence, the University of Kentucky had made a comprehensive survey of the school system of the district in question, the study including school plant needs and possible relocation and consolidation of facilities. A similar survey was made by the state department of education at the request of the state board of education. The state board, however, was never able to reach agreement with the local board on how the recommendations of the surveys should be implemented. The court, noting that the statutes granted each board some discretion in the matter of the construction of school buildings, held that there were to be negotiations and that the local board was not bound to carry out all state board directions in this area without question. It concluded that the evidence fell short of establishing such bad faith, misconduct, or neglect of duty of the local members as would warrant their removal.

In regard to removal of local school board members it should be observed that the legislature is not under the same restrictions as are subordinate agencies such as the state board of education. The point arose regarding a challenge to the constitutionality of a statute under which the legislature of the state of New York abolished the incumbent board of education in New York City and ordered that a new board be appointed by the mayor under a different system. The statute had been enacted in an extraordinary session of the legislature called by the governor to deal with a crisis in the educational affairs of the New York City Board of Education. The statute terminated the offices of those who constituted the board of education on the date of the law. The Court of Appeals of New York upheld the action of the legislature, stating that the legislature had the power to abolish an office of its

---

94. Kentucky State Bd. of Educ. v. Isenberg, 421 S.W.2d 81 (Ky.1967).

creation or to modify its term or other incidents attending it in the public interest even though the effect was to curtail an incumbent's unexpired term.[95]

In New York the state commissioner of education has statutory authority to remove local school board members for violations of law or neglect of duty. It has been held, however, that this express power does not include imposing on a board an overseer invested with veto power.[96] But when a local school system falls into chaos, it can be considered an implied power of the state education authorities to take steps to correct the situation. Hence, the highest court of New Jersey upheld the appointment of a "monitor general" to supervise all activities within a school district where the educational system was "in an abysmal state due almost entirely to the mismanagement and incompetence of the members of the local board of education."[97] The Supreme Court of California ruled that the state had a duty to intervene financially and administratively when a school district planned to close down because of financial problems.[98] No statutory authority was needed for a state "takeover" of operations. In this case the state was resisting taking action, but the court held that the state's ultimate responsibility cannot be avoided.

Many of the challenges to the authority of central agencies arise from the attempts of the agencies to control the actions and policies of local boards by withholding state funds from the districts concerned. Several such cases were discussed earlier in this chapter. Another leading case on the point arose in Texas.[99] In that state the law provided that the salary and expenses of the county superintendent shall be paid from funds of the local school districts of the county. Also, a statute provided that the state superintendent was responsible for the general superintendency of the business relating to the public schools of the state. One district refused to contribute its prescribed share, and the state superintendent sought to impound the district's allocation of state funds to compel payment of the amount assessed against the district. It was held that the superintendent had no power to interfere with the legally prescribed course of state funds from the state to the district treasury.

Another case concerning the right of the state superintendent to withhold funds in order to enforce state regulations arose in Wisconsin.[100] It involved an attempt by the state department to require a local board to abandon an antiquated school building and replace it with a satisfactory one. The law provided for the appointment of a building inspector and permitted the withholding of state funds to enforce his orders. Suit was brought to require the state superintendent to allot the

95. Lanza v. Wagner, 11 N.Y.2d 317, 229 N.Y.S.2d 380, 183 N.E.2d 670 (1962).

96. Verbanic v. Nyquist, 41 A.D.2d 466, 344 N.Y.S.2d 406 (1973).

97. In re Board of Educ. of Trenton, 86 N.J. 327, 431 A.2d 808 (1981).

98. Butt v. State, 4 Cal.4th 668, 15 Cal. Rptr.2d 480, 842 P.2d 1240 (1992).

99. Austin Independent School Dist. v. Marrs, 121 Tex. 72, 41 S.W.2d 9 (1931).

100. State ex rel. School Dist. No. 8, Town of Wauwatosa v. Cary, 166 Wis. 103, 163 N.W. 645 (1917).

district's share of state funds to it despite the failure of the local board to comply with the order of the building inspector. The suit was successful. The court emphasized the point that other sections of the statutes placed the power of building school houses in the local district. This power, according to the court, may not be assumed by the state superintendent by the device of withholding state funds to enforce the regulations of his office.

A case supporting the withholding of state aid by the chief state school officer was decided in New Jersey.[101] A statute provided that state funds could be withheld until a district provided suitable facilities "convenient of access" to the students. The phrase "convenient of access" was interpreted to impose a duty to provide transportation to students living more than two miles from school. More recently appellate courts in Illinois and Ohio have approved withholding funds from districts not in compliance with statutes prescribing certain transportation requirements.[102] But the Supreme Court of Ohio ordered the state superintendent to grant a waiver of one day of required instruction to the Cleveland school system when it would have cost $750,000 to add the day to make up for a midwinter closure occasioned by a strike of personnel who operated the boilers.[103]

It may be said that in general the courts are rather reluctant to approve the cutting off of funds as a weapon to bring about the execution of a state approved policy. This is particularly true if the state-level authority does not afford an offending district an opportunity to be heard and/or an opportunity to correct objectionable practices before denying it state aid. But if a financing statute clearly is being violated a court may order that state funds be withheld until there is compliance. The Supreme Court of Arkansas so ruled where a statute as to teacher salaries was unambiguous. The state department of education had permitted a school district not to comply.[104]

Quasi-Judicial Powers

Normally, disputes involving the rights of citizens or organizations are decided by courts. In many jurisdictions, however, certain controversies may be, or shall be, heard and decided by tribunals other than courts. Such tribunals include various boards and agencies of the national and state governments. Some states provide that education controversies be decided by the chief state school officer or the state board of education. Even in those states in which special tribunals are provided for the determination of school controversies, not all such conflicts necessarily must be referred to them. It thus becomes of great

101. Board of Educ. of West Amwell Tp. v. State Bd. of Educ., 5 N.J.Misc. 152, 135 A. 664 (1927).

102. Board of Educ., School Dist. No. 142, Cook County v. Bakalis, 54 Ill.2d 448, 299 N.E.2d 737 (1973); In re Resolution, 57 Ohio App.2d 59, 385 N.E.2d 295 (1978).

103. State ex rel. Cleveland Bd. of Educ. v. State Bd. of Educ. of Ohio, 11 Ohio St.3d 89, 464 N.E.2d 137 (1984). [Case No. 17]

104. Junction City School Dist. v. Alphin, 313 Ark. 456, 855 S.W.2d 316 (1993).

importance to examine what disputes may, or must, be referred to designated tribunals prior to petitioners' having recourse to the courts. There also is the question of what kind of review is possible in the courts: trial de novo or review on the record, and, if the latter, the standard of review to be applied.

In some states the problem has not been dealt with legislatively. In these states it would seem that aggrieved persons not only may have recourse directly to the courts, but have no other forum for redress. In others, parties are statutorily required to exhaust their remedies within the education hierarchy before their cases may be carried to the courts. Illustrations of some state provisions for quasi-judicial functioning within the state-level education agency follow.

In New York one has a choice of appealing an educational decision to the state commissioner of education or directly to the courts. If the appeal is to the commissioner, the decision of that officer is final, court review being limited to determining whether, on the record, the commissioner's determination is arbitrary or lacks a rational basis.[105] The commissioner is empowered to substitute his judgment for that of other education authorities, including local school boards and statutory hearing panels.[106] If the matter involves primarily the meaning of constitutional or statutory provisions, the courts, of course, examine the commissioner's decision especially closely.[107] But if an educational policy issue is linked with a constitutional one (as in academic freedom matters) the scope of judicial review remains limited.[108] That the regulations governing appeal to the commissioner do not provide for an evidentiary hearing, but rather for affidavits and exhibits, has been held not to be violative of constitutional due process rights.[109] However, where the commissioner's determination failed to conform to prior administrative precedent, it was annulled because the rationale of the deviation was inadequately explained.[110] That substantial evidence supported the conclusion was not relevant.

In Rhode Island, by contrast, the state commissioner of education holds evidentiary hearings on complaints and must make a decision de novo.[111] Also, unlike New York, Rhode Island law provides for appeal of most decisions of the commissioner to the state board before courts will assume jurisdiction. The courts review a case on the facts found by the commissioner and affirmed by the board, unless they are unsupported by

105. Gundrum v. Ambach, 55 N.Y.2d 872, 448 N.Y.S.2d 466, 433 N.E.2d 531 (1982). For 102 years prior to legislation in 1976, the standard of review was the unusual and more limited *"purely* arbitrary" one.

106. Board of Educ. of City of New York v. Allen, 6 N.Y.2d 127, 188 N.Y.S.2d 515, 160 N.E.2d 60 (1959); Conley v. Ambach, 61 N.Y.2d 685, 472 N.Y.S.2d 598, 460 N.E.2d 1083 (1984). [Case No. 18]

107. Ross v. Wilson, 308 N.Y. 605, 127 N.E.2d 697 (1955). [Case No. 50]

108. Malverne Union Free School Dist. v. Sobol, 181 A.D.2d 371, 586 N.Y.S.2d 673 (1992).

109. Forrest v. Ambach, 93 A.D.2d 965, 463 N.Y.S.2d 84 (1983).

110. Engel v. Sobol, 161 A.D.2d 873, 556 N.Y.S.2d 179 (1990).

111. Slattery v. Cranston School Committee, 116 R.I. 252, 354 A.2d 741 (1976).

the evidence in the record.[112] That the record may also contain evidence to support contrary conclusions is irrelevant.[113] When a statute expressly vests a power in a local board in Rhode Island, the commissioner is not empowered to substitute his judgment for that of the board.[114]

In New Jersey appeals in educational controversies are decided by the state commissioner, with a further appeal possible to the state board of education. Evidentiary hearings are held. Although the law provides for the exhaustion of statutory remedies prior to appealing to the courts, this requirement is not absolute. The highest court of the state has said that the requirement is a policy of convenience and discretion rather than of law. Apparently the New Jersey courts will assume the responsibility for deciding a school controversy if, in their discretion, they conclude that courts are at least as competent as the central education agency to render a proper decision. The Supreme Court of New Jersey indicated that in a proper case the courts definitely would intervene without waiting for other tribunals to act.[115] However, it stated that the courts generally leave decisions on educational matters to the disposition of the state education authorities.

The court set up no test to distinguish between educational and legal matters. Its opinion was in a case in which it declined to consider the petition of a principal, who had been dismissed by a school board, because he had not first appealed to the state board of education. It appears that the timing of judicial intervention was dependent upon the statutory provisions and the desire of the judiciary to get into the record a review on educational grounds of the local board action. More recently, particularly where federal or state constitutional rights are involved, the courts of New Jersey have become more active in deciding educational matters. The attitude of the Supreme Court of New Jersey regarding the power of the commissioner and state board to substitute their judgments for those of local boards in educational matters has been noted earlier in this chapter.

The legislature of Texas has provided for review of school disputes through appeals to the state commissioner and the state board of education. The courts of that state appear to have been quite insistent that a party exhaust administrative remedies before resorting to the courts,[116] but they have made a major exception regarding tax matters. These can be taken directly to the courts without recourse to the central agency.[117] Also, initial resort to the courts is permitted where there are undisputed facts and there remains for decision only a pure question of law.[118]

112. Campbell v. School Committee of Coventry, 67 R.I. 276, 21 A.2d 727 (1941).

113. Brown v. Elston, 445 A.2d 279 (R.I.1982).

114. Exeter–West Greenwich Regional School Dist. v. Pontarelli, 460 A.2d 934 (R.I.1983).

115. Redcay v. State Bd. of Educ., 128 N.J.L. 281, 25 A.2d 632 (1942).

116. Ball v. Kerrville Independent School Dist., 504 S.W.2d 791 (Tex.Civ.App. 1973).

117. City of Dallas v. Mosely, 286 S.W. 497 (Tex.Civ.App.1926). [Case No. 19]

118. Alvin Independent School Dist. v. Cooper, 404 S.W.2d 76 (Tex.Civ.App.1966).

In reviewing a state board decision Texas courts apply the common rule that the decision be upheld if it is supported by substantial evidence.[119] They do not determine whether they would have reached the same conclusion that the board reached on the evidence. The rule is applied to the order of the state board, not to those of the local board or the commissioner, because the latter are subordinate in the administrative area.[120] This process of review is widely used. Not so common is the Texas courts' requirement that the trial court accept testimony from the parties in addition to examining the record of the testimony considered by the state-level administrative bodies.[121]

A challenge to the pattern of the legislature's authorizing the chief state school officer to hear and determine controversies was rejected by the Supreme Court of Illinois.[122] The court said that an officer charged with administrative duties may be granted quasi-judicial powers incidental to those duties. Such an arrangement is not an unconstitutional grant of judicial power as long as ultimate review lies with the courts.

In Maryland arose the question whether the state board of education was required to hear appeals from decisions of county boards. (In that state the chief state school officer has no quasi-judicial role.) A statute provides for appeals from decisions of county boards, which operate the schools, to the state board, but the latter board took the position that it had something approaching certiorari jurisdiction and was not mandated to decide such appeals. The state's highest court said that the language of the statute would not support the state board's interpretation.[123] It added that arguments of the board regarding fiscal implications and workload of the board must be addressed to the legislature.

It should be noted that there is a trend for the courts in many jurisdictions to accept cases without first obtaining a decision of central agencies unless the statutes rather clearly intend otherwise. This is especially true for matters involving expenditures or civil liberties.

Judicial Review of Actions of State-Level Agencies

In General

It may be generalized that the courts are inclined to allow state education authorities wide discretion in the formulation and enforcement of rules. But, as illustrated by material in the preceding portions of the chapter, this does not lead to the conclusion that courts will not examine rules and actions of central agencies. Courts will look into these matters on allegations that the rules or actions violate a substan-

---

119. Board of Trustees of Crystal City Independent School' Dist. v. Briggs, 486 S.W.2d 829 (Tex.Civ.App.1972).

120. Temple Independent School Dist. v. State Bd. of Educ., 493 S.W.2d 543 (Tex. Civ.App.1973).

121. Wylie Independent School Dist. v. Central Educ. Agency, 488 S.W.2d 166 (Tex. Civ.App.1972).

122. Board of Educ., School Dist. No. 142, Cook County v. Bakalis, 54 Ill.2d 448, 299 N.E.2d 737 (1973).

123. Board of Educ. of Garrett County v. Lendo, 295 Md. 55, 453 A.2d 1185 (1982).

tive constitutional right, are contrary to a specific law, exceed general powers, or are unreasonable. Also, proper procedures for rule making and enforcing must be observed.

The judiciary seems more inclined to examine actions of a quasi-judicial nature than those of a purely administrative nature. That the judiciary is ill-equipped to act as a "super-school-board" in evaluating complex factors affecting education of children is frequently expressly recorded in opinions of courts. But, as has been stated by the Supreme Court of Wyoming, "the courts are always open to correct arbitrary, capricious, or fraudulent action taken by an administrative official or board." [124] So long, however, as important rights are not extinguished, the legislature can provide for review of different decisions by different paths to the courts.[125]

Rules and Their Enforcement

The extent of rule-making authority possessed by administrative agencies under general grants of power has been the subject of much litigation. Generalizations are difficult, but have been attempted by several courts. The Supreme Court of Montana has stated two criteria for determining whether administrative regulations are "out of harmony" with legislation. Regulations are unauthorized if they "engraft additional and contradictory requirements on the statute" or if they "engraft additional, noncontradictory requirements on the statute which were not envisioned by the legislature." [126] The highest court of Washington has said that rules may fill in gaps in legislation if they are "necessary to the effectuation of a general statutory scheme." [127] That court added that administrative rules adopted pursuant to a legislative grant of authority are to be upheld by courts if they are "reasonably consistent with the statute being implemented."

As demonstrated in the earlier parts of this chapter, administrative rulings of state officials on specific matters have been a prolific source of litigation. In general, courts say that a state agency has the authority to decide those matters which fall within its jurisdiction. However, considerable difficulty ensues when the power exercised is claimed to be based upon a generalized type of statute. When passing upon the authority of state education officials it is often stated by courts that the powers of their offices extend only to educational matters, as distinguished from legal matters. Constitutional rights as to person and property and statutory interpretation clearly are basically legal matters. Yet they are often inextricably intertwined with educational considerations. The more cases one reads relative to the distinction between legal and educational matters the more involved the differentiation becomes. As the courts have the final word as to whether a matter is educational or

124. School Dists. Nos. 2, 3, 6, 9, and 10 v. Cook, 424 P.2d 751 (Wyo.1967).

125. Board of Educ. of Armstrong High School Dist. No. 225 v. Ellis, 60 Ill.2d 413, 328 N.E.2d 294 (1975).

126. Bell v. Department of Licensing, 182 Mont. 21, 594 P.2d 331 (1979).

127. Green River Community College, Dist. No. 10 v. Higher Educ. Personnel Bd., 95 Wash.2d 108, 622 P.2d 826 (1980).

legal, their decisions thereon are frequently as influential on the course of education as are their decisions on the substantive issues should they take jurisdiction.

There is a presumption that an administrative officer or body has exercised its power properly, and the burden of proof generally is on one contesting the reasonableness of an action by legally constituted authorities.[128] The courts consistently say that they will not pass on the wisdom of a discretionary act of competent officials, but will confine themselves to legal considerations.

Another pertinent generalization is that if there is a provision in a statute outlining procedures for solving a problem or gaining redress within the executive branch, the courts usually will require that the administrative remedies be exhausted before they will assume jurisdiction. If, however, a federal constitutional or statutory right is involved, "Section 1983" has been held by the Supreme Court to provide "immediate access to the federal courts notwithstanding any provision of state law to the contrary." [129]

It should be observed that where a court invalidates an administrative action, the court does not substitute its judgment for that of the administrative agency. Rather, the court requires further administrative action in conformity with its holding. Also of import here is the observation that courts can review the application of a reasonable regulation if it is alleged that the application was unreasonable or arbitrary. Of importance in this connection is the penalty to be placed on a party not conforming to a rule of the central agency.

Occasionally a state board or chief state school officer will not act when there is a duty to do so. If the duty is ministerial (e.g., apportioning state funds), a writ of mandamus will be issued by a court to require performance.[130] Where the duty involves elements of discretion, it is up to the judiciary in a proper case to fix liabilities for harm flowing from the nonperformance. An example of the latter is to be found in the ruling of the United States Court of Appeals, Sixth Circuit, that the state board of education in Ohio did not discharge its responsibilities to act to halt intentional segregative practices, of which it was aware, in the Cleveland school district between 1956 and 1980.[131] The state board had continued to support financially the practices. Eventually the state was assessed a share of the costs of desegregating the district's schools.

Hearings

Where statutes require that administrative bodies hold hearings before taking certain actions, courts will examine the conduct of the hearings to assure that statutory procedures were followed and general

128. Steubenville v. Culp, 38 Ohio St. 18 (1882).

129. Patsy v. Board of Regents of the State of Florida, 457 U.S. 496, 102 S.Ct. 2557, 73 L.Ed.2d 172 (1982).

130. Board of Educ. of Iron Mt. v. Voelker, 271 Mich. 207, 259 N.W. 891 (1935).

131. Reed v. Rhodes, 662 F.2d 1219 (6 Cir.1981).

due process was observed. In this connection it is vital to distinguish two basic types of hearings: legislative or rule-making, and quasi-judicial or adversarial.

The purpose of the legislative hearing is to convey information and opinions to the decision making body. There is no constitutional requirement that a rule making agency must hold hearings before adopting a rule, but frequently statutes so provide. Also, of course, there is no legal compulsion for the body to do any more than listen to the views expressed, because the body has been granted the power in the legislative scheme to make the decision.

Quasi-judicial hearings are required where precise determinations of fact and law must be made. It is in this type of hearing that constitutional due process is implicated because liberty or property rights are involved. Cases of teacher dismissal and student discipline are the most common in this category. As will be illustrated in connection with those topics, the courts require certain minimal procedures, but do not hold administrative bodies to the same procedural strictness as they do trial courts.

State boards may utilize hearing officers to conduct quasi-judicial hearings and make recommendations. Although when acting in an adjudicatory posture a state board can reject the findings or conclusions of its hearing officer, it is required that the board review the transcript of the hearing before voting to do so.[132] Constitutional due process requirements are satisfied if deciding officials understand and consider the evidence before rendering a decision. It is not necessary that officials whose responsibility it is to make the ultimate decision be present when the evidence is received. That contention was rejected by the Supreme Court in 1936.[133]

If there is no statutory specification as how a hearing is to be conducted, and if the subject is essentially one of policy formulation or application, rather than of individual rights, the presumption is that a legislative-type hearing is intended.[134] For example, a judicial-type hearing was held not to be necessary where a district boundary board created by the legislature had conducted a hearing on proposed changes after giving required notice.[135] The chairman of the board at the hearing reviewed the stipulations which governed boundary boards in acting on petitions for annexation, after which members of the audience were invited to express their support or opposition. Both points of view were expressed and recorded in the board's minutes. Following the hearing the board made the requested changes in the boundaries. The action was unsuccessfully challenged on the ground that the board did not make formal findings on required points such as that the proposed

---

132. Board of Educ. of Melrose Municipal Schools v. New Mexico State Bd. of Educ., 106 N.M. 129, 740 P.2d 123 (App. 1987).

133. Morgan v. United States, 298 U.S. 468, 56 S.Ct. 906, 80 L.Ed. 1288 (1936).

134. Johnson v. Schrader, 507 P.2d 814 (Wyo.1973).

135. School Dist. No. 7 of Wallowa County v. Weissenfluh, 236 Or. 165, 387 P.2d 567 (1963).

changes would have no effect upon the ability of the districts to provide mandated educational programs.

The Supreme Court of Wisconsin has said that for hearings not judicial in nature the only issues to be brought before the courts are whether the board acted within its jurisdiction and whether its order was "arbitrary and capricious." [136] A decision of a board fits the latter category when the action has no rational base, is unreasonable when all facts and opinions are considered, or when it is the result of an "unconsidered, wilful and irrational choice of conduct" rather than the result of a "winnowing and sifting" process. That court stated that the board was not limited to considering facts within the record. It may utilize other information within its knowledge and expertise in the field of educational policy. Furthermore, the fact that a board member has already expressed a general view on a controversial matter like school district reorganization does not bar him from participating in the board's decision following a hearing on a particular reorganization question.

Treatment of other aspects of hearings can be found through use of the index.

[Case No. 13] Power of State Legislature to Change District Boundaries

ATTORNEY GENERAL OF STATE OF MICHIGAN EX REL. KIES v. LOWREY

Supreme Court of the United States, 1905.
199 U.S. 233, 26 S.Ct. 27, 50 L.Ed. 167.

Mr. Justice McKenna delivered the opinion of the court: The Constitution of the state of Michigan requires the legislature to establish and provide a system of public schools, whereby a school shall be kept open at least three months in each year in every school district in the state. In fulfillment of this requirement legislation was enacted from time to time providing for the formation of school districts. Under this legislation (1881) four school districts were organized in the townships of Somerset and Moscow, county of Hillsdale. In 1901 the legislature passed an act * * *. By this act one of the districts formed in the townships of Somerset and Moscow in which the village of Jerome is situated, and portions of other districts, were set off and incorporated in one school district to be known as "the public schools of the village of Jerome." The act appointed defendants in error trustees of the new district, to continue in office until their successors should be elected, as provided in the act. The act gave to the new district the property within its limits which had belonged to the districts from which it was created, and required the new district to assume and pay the debts and obligations of the old districts. The new district did not include all of the lands of the old districts.

* * *

136. Joint School Dist. No. 2 v. State (1978).
Appeal Bd., 83 Wis.2d 711, 266 N.W.2d 374

The grounds of attack upon the validity of the act creating the new district in the supreme court of the state were as follows:

First. It deprives this school district or municipality of the right of local self-government, guaranteed to all municipalities by the Constitution.

* * *

Fourth. The act as passed impairs the obligation of contracts, within the meaning of the Constitution of the United States and the Constitution of the state of Michigan.

With the first three grounds we have no concern. They present strictly local questions. We are concerned with the fourth ground only in so far as it invokes the Constitution of the United States. The supreme court disposed of this ground as follows: "We have already shown that the obligation of contracts is not impaired. The districts did not hold this property under any contract with the state, but as a public agency." In other words, the nonexistence of a contract was rested on the construction of the Constitution and the laws of the state, and hence defendant in error contends that the decision of the court did not involve a Federal question. This, however, overlooks the power and duty of this court to determine for itself the existence or nonexistence of a contract. Other grounds in support of the motion to dismiss are urged which, we think, are also untenable. The motion is therefore denied.

Plaintiff in error broadened in this court his objection to the act, based on the Constitution of the United States. He urges, besides the contract clause of the Constitution, that provision of the 14th Amendment which protects private property from deprivation without due process of law, and section 4, article 4, which provides: "The United States shall guarantee to every state in this Union a republican form of government." But the grounds all depend ultimately upon the same arguments. If the legislature of the state has the power to create and alter school districts, and divide and apportion the property of such district, no contract can arise, no property of a district can be said to be taken, and the action of the legislature is compatible with a republican form of government even if it be admitted that section 4, article 4, of the Constitution, applies to the creation of, or the powers or rights of property of, the subordinate municipalities of the state. We may omit, therefore, that section and article from further consideration. The decision of the other grounds urged we may rest upon the opinion of the supreme court of the state and the case of Laramie County v. Albany County, 92 U.S. 307, 23 L.Ed. 552 [1875]. It is there said in many ways, with citation of many supporting cases, that the legislature of the state has absolute power to make and change subordinate municipalities. The following quotation meets exactly the contentions of plaintiff in error:

"Institutions of the kind, whether called counties or towns, are the auxiliaries of the state in the important business of municipal rule and cannot have the least pretension to sustain their privileges or their existence upon anything like a contract between them and the legislature of the state, because there is not, and cannot be, any reciprocity of stipulation, and their objects and duties are utterly incompatible with everything of the nature of compact. Instead of that, the constant practice is to divide large counties and towns, and to consolidate small ones, to meet the wishes of the residents, or to promote the public interests as understood by those who control the action of the legislature. Opposition is sometimes manifested, but it is everywhere acknowledged that the legislature possesses the power to divide counties and towns at their pleasure, and to apportion the common property and the common burdens in such manner as to them may seem reasonable and equitable." * * *

* * *

Notes

1.   Consider this Supreme Court holding in terms both of consolidating small districts and of breaking up large districts. How should a state proceed to organize school districts for the present and future? If you were writing a state constitution would you include any limitations on the power of the legislature to redistrict the state?

2.   In Hunter v. City of Pittsburgh, 207 U.S. 161, 28 S.Ct. 40, 52 L.Ed. 151 (1907), the Supreme Court held that a state may take without compensation property paid for by a political subdivision and may hold it itself or vest it in other agencies.

3.   "There is no contract relation existing between the state and the school districts provided for by the Legislature. Such a relation, however, does exist between the plaintiff district and the purchasers of the bonds issued by it." Citing the instant case, it was held that although the legislature possessed the power to detach a part of the territory from one school district and attach it to another, "it may not impair the obligation in the bondholders' contract by taking such action without making provision for the payment thereof." Board of Educ. of City of Lincoln Park v. Board of Educ. of Detroit, 245 Mich. 411, 222 N.W. 763 (1929).

4.   Observe that for purposes of this case no distinction is made between school districts and municipal corporations.

[Case No. 14]   Constitutionality of Curriculum for Family Life and Sex Education—Delegation of Legislative Powers

MEDEIROS v. KIYOSAKI

Supreme Court of Hawaii, 1970.
52 Hawaii 436, 478 P.2d 314.

RICHARDSON, CHIEF JUSTICE.   Plaintiffs-appellants, residents of the City and County of Honolulu and parents of 5th and 6th grade children in the public school system, sought to enjoin the defendants-appellees, Ralph H. Kiyosaki, the State Superintendent of Education, the members of the State Board of Education, and Alice M. Doyle, Program Specialist of the Department of Education, from continuing with a film series entitled "A Time of Your Life." The film series was being shown in the 5th and 6th grade levels of the public school system as part of a newly adopted curriculum for family life and sex education. The plaintiffs based their action on the constitutional grounds that the program is an invasion of privacy and a violation of their religious freedom. Plaintiffs further alleged that the program was illegal because it was adopted by an improper delegation of authority by the State Board of Education to the administrative staff of the State Department of Education. The trial court dismissed the complaint and denied the request for injunctive relief.

* * *

I. Constitutional Issues.

Plaintiffs contend that the basic and underlying issue of this case is whether parents are free to educate their offspring in the intimacies of sexual matters according to their own moral and religious beliefs without undue interference by the State. More specifically, they argue that the sex education program (hereinafter referred to as "Program") adopted by the State is unconstitutional because it unduly interferes with their right of privacy and freedom of religion.

A. Right of Privacy.

* * *

The question we now face is this: Can this State through its proper agencies adopt and initiate a curriculum of family life and sex education for use in the fifth and sixth grades without invading its citizens' constitutional right to privacy? We must not look to see if there has been a possible or technical invasion of privacy but instead whether the government has by "unnecessarily broad means" contravened the plaintiffs' right of privacy.

The State in formulating policies for the adoption of the Program anticipated possible objections by parents and guardians of fifth and sixth grade children to the context of the film series, especially the treatment of the subject matter in lessons numbered 11 through 15. The State therefore, established an "excusal system" whereby parents and guardians had the option of withholding or withdrawing their children from the Program by submitting a written excuse to the school. Furthermore, in order to allow parents and guardians an opportunity to view the 15 lessons of the film series before they were shown to their children at school, the lessons were shown each Monday evening at 10 p.m. on Educational Television. The Monday night telecasts enabled the parents to consider the content of the lesson and then submit a written excuse if they found it objectionable. We view this "excusal system" as an effort by the defendants to allow those parents or guardians who might object to the Program or parts thereof on moral or religious grounds to have their children excused. The Program was in no way compulsory, and, therefore, we cannot see how the State by "unnecessarily broad means" contravened plaintiffs' right of privacy.

* * *

B.   Freedom of Religion.

* * *

It has been argued that *requiring* attendance at sex education courses would burden the free exercise of religion of those who honestly believe that exposure to certain subjects covered within those courses is sinful or that sex education must be accompanied by moral instruction. However, in view of the fact that the program to which the plaintiffs now seek a permanent injunction is not compulsory, we fail to find any direct or substantial burden on their "free exercise" of religion.

* * *

* * * [P]ertinent to our discussion is the Supreme Court's holding in Epperson v. Arkansas, in which an Arkansas statute prohibiting the teaching of the Darwinian theory of evolution because such theory was contrary to the religious views of some of its citizens was held unconstitutional. * * * If we were to hold that the "family life and sex education" program adopted by the State is contrary to certain religious beliefs of some of our citizens and therefore unconstitutional on the grounds that it prevents the free exercise of their religion, we would come dangerously close to approving that which is prohibited by *Epperson*. We must be equally protective of the freedoms of speech, inquiry and belief as we are of the freedom of religion.

Inasmuch as we have found no compulsion or coercion related to the educational Program in question, we find no violation of the First Amendment's Free Exercise of Religion Clause.

II.   Improper Delegation of Authority.

Plaintiffs also seek reversal on the argument that the Program in question is illegal because it was adopted by an improper delegation of authority by the State Board of Education to the administrative staff of the State Department of Education. They argue that the Board of Education's power is based upon law and since no legislative authority was granted for such a program, either the Board's action, or lack thereof, or defendant Ralph Kiyosaki's action in accepting and adopting this program was an unlawful delegation of power. In other words, plaintiffs contend that in order for curriculum dealing with family life and sex education to be used in the public school system, the State Board of Education must have specific authorization from the legislature before it can establish policies or adopt programs. We do not agree.

There is no question that the Board of Education, as the executive head of the State Department of Education, is granted broad discretionary powers in formulating and enacting educational programs for the State's public schools. Section 3 of Article IX of our constitution (as amended) provides:

> The board of education shall have power, in accordance
> with law, to formulate policy, and to exercise control over the

public school system through its executive officer, the superintendent of education * * *.

* * *

The Program in question was adopted in response to the appropriation for the operating budget of the Department of Education for the fiscal year ending June 30, 1969, as set forth in a lump sum in Act 74, Session Laws of Hawaii 1968. With reference to such appropriation, House Conf.Comm.Rep. No. 3 (1968 Budget Session, Hawaii State Legislature) contains, *inter alia,* the following, on page 8:

> 10. *Program for instruction of social problems.* The rapidly expanding population, expanding and changing economy, and a change in social mores, are conditions which call for a program of instruction related to social problems. These problems include, but are not limited to, family living and sex education. * * * The department presently has a program offering courses in the area of social problems. However, this program is spotty and it has not been planned in a comprehensive fashion or programmed in a manner which would allow articulation of levels of expectation from the beginning to the terminal point of instruction. The Committee approves of the department's intent to devote resources toward the planning and programming of instruction in the area of social problems.

As the trial court correctly ruled, the cited passage indicates the legislative intent as to what direction sex education programs in the schools should take. Pursuant to such expressed intent, the Department of Education recommended for adoption the Program in question.

However, plaintiffs argue that even if such a program is deemed to be within the discretionary powers of the Board of Education or that there was a sufficient mandate by the legislature for the adoption of such program, there was, nevertheless, a clear abuse of such discretionary powers. Reference is again made by plaintiffs to HRS § 296–11, which states in relevant part: "Under policies established by the board of education, the superintendent of education shall administer programs of education and public instruction throughout the State * * *." The plaintiffs contend that the Program was formally adopted before any policies were established by the Board of Education. There is no validity to such a contention since the actions of the administrative staff were merely recommendatory, the actual adoption being made by Superintendent Kiyosaki as executive officer of the Board. The Board meeting of January 9, 1969, reaffirmed the policy which Mr. Kiyosaki understood to be in effect at the time he adopted the program.

Affirmed.

Notes

1. On the issue of improper delegation of authority, compare this holding with that of Case No. 16.

2. On the constitutional effect of excusing a student from a "required" curricular element which has been objected to, compare this holding with that in Case No. 25 (flag salute) and Case No. 4 (Bible-reading).

3. Why might counsel for plaintiffs have decided to put major emphasis on freedom of religion and "right of privacy" rather than on "parents' rights"?

4. Do you believe parents have a right to determine whether their children will be taught anything about sex in public schools?

5. A three-judge federal District Court refused to declare invalid on its face a statute that forbade giving instruction in birth control in public schools. The Supreme Court summarily affirmed. Mercer v. Michigan State Bd. of Educ., 379 F.Supp. 580 (E.D.Mich.1974), aff. 419 U.S. 1081, 95 S.Ct. 673, 42 L.Ed.2d 678 (1974).

[Case No. 15] Constitutionality of Statute Covering Student Expulsions—Delegation of Legislative Powers

MITCHELL v. KING

Supreme Court of Connecticut, 1975.
169 Conn. 140, 363 A.2d 68.

Loiselle, Associate Justice. The named plaintiff, a minor, hereinafter designated the plaintiff, was permanently expelled from high school as a result of his alleged participation in a gang assault upon a student. The alleged attack occurred on September 28, 1972, on the grounds of Central High School in Bridgeport prior to the commencement of the school day. * * * In an action brought to the Court of Common Pleas, judgment was rendered in favor of the plaintiff enjoining the defendant board of education from continuing the expulsion * * *.

In rendering judgment for the plaintiff, the court based its decision solely on the ground that § 10–234 of the General Statutes, which authorizes a school board to expel any student found guilty of "conduct inimical to the best interests of the school" and under which the plaintiff was expelled, was invalid as an illegal delegation of legislative power. (General Statutes § 10–234 provides in pertinent part: "The board of education of any town may expel from school any pupil regardless of age who after a full hearing is found guilty of conduct inimical to the best interests of the school.") The legislative power to delegate is not unlimited. To be constitutionally sustained, "it is necessary that the statute declare a legislative policy, establish primary standards for carrying it out, or lay down an intelligible principle to which the administrative officer or body must conform, with a proper regard for the protection of the public interests and with such degree of certainty as the nature of the case permits, and enjoin a procedure under which, by appeal or otherwise, both public interests and private rights shall have due consideration." No declaration of legislative policy is contained in § 10–234; however, title 10 of the General Statutes, of which § 10–234 is a part, declares the state's special interest in the education of children. It can hardly be doubted that the statute in question was enacted pursuant to the policies and aims expressed in title 10 * * *.

It is true that the modern tendency is liberal in approving delegation under broad regulatory standards so as to facilitate the operational functions of administrative boards or commissions, and it is unrealistic to demand detailed standards which are impracticable. A statute, however, which forbids or requires conduct in terms so vague that persons of common intelligence must necessarily guess at its meaning and differ as to its application violates the first essential of due process. Laws must give a person of ordinary intelligence a reasonable opportunity to know what is prohibited so that he may act accordingly. Also, if arbitrary and discriminatory enforcement is to be prevented, laws must provide adequately delineated standards for those who apply them. It is a basic principle of due process that a statute is void for vagueness if its prohibitions are not clearly defined. A vague statute may inhibit the exercise of constitutionally protected freedoms by having persons " 'steer far wider of the unlawful zone' * * * than if the boundaries of the forbidden areas were clearly marked."

Distinct from, but often congruent with, the defect of vagueness is that of statutory overbreadth, that is, where the reach of the statutory language, no matter how precise, prohibits conduct protected by the constitution. The claim of the plaintiffs that the statutory language of § 10–234 is overbroad need not be discussed in view of the disposition made on the issue of vagueness.

The court's decision as to the unconstitutionality of § 10–234 was not based on its application to the defendant. Rather, the court found the statute to be invalid as an illegal delegation because the language, "conduct inimical to the best interests of the school," was too vague and indefinite to be regarded as a standard for expulsion of students. A statute must be construed as a whole since particular words or sections of the statute, considered separately, may be "lacking in precision of meaning to afford a standard sufficient to sustain" it. The "best-interest" standard has been widely used and well understood in our law; however, when juxtaposed with "inimical" the standard must be examined to determine if it conveys sufficiently definite warning as to the proscribed conduct when measured by common understanding and practice. What the phrase "inimical to the best interests" may mean to different persons is virtually unlimited. The descriptions and illustrations used in Webster's New International Dictionary (3d Ed.) to indicate the meaning of "inimical" and its synonym "adverse" are numerous and varied. Its meaning may range from unsympathetic in tendency to having the disposition of an enemy. A term so varied in meaning is not sufficient to constitute definition, inclusive or exclusive.

This court is mindful of the comprehensive authority of school officials to prescribe and control conduct in schools and the need for flexibility and reasonable breadth in statutes which guide them in their duties and which authorize them to accomplish educational ends. That authority, however, must be consistent with constitutional safeguards. Section 10–234, when read in the light of the legal principles enunciated, is unconstitutionally vague on its face. It does not give fair notice that certain conduct is proscribed; it makes no distinction between student conduct on or off school property, during school hours or while school is not in session. It fails to provide any meaningful indication as to what range of behavior would legitimately subject a student to expulsion. Thus, the time, the place, and the nature of student conduct that might be deemed "inimical to the best interests of the school" would lie entirely within the subjective discretion of the board of education. A more specific legislative standard is required. "[T]he vice to be guarded against is arbitrary action by officials. The fact that a particular instance or action appears not arbitrary does not save the validity of the authority under which the action was taken." The court was not in error in concluding that General Statutes § 10–234 was invalid as an illegal delegation of legislative power.

* * *

Notes

1. Increased clarity is required in statutes (or regulations) as they encroach upon important rights or provide for substantial penalties. Consider the penalty in this case. What was the source of the right involved?

2. Does this case require that expulsions be handled only through a state-level agency? If not, how could the power to expel be constitutionally delegated to local boards?

3. Why did the court not consider the actual offense of the student and/or whether he received a fair hearing?

4. Is it possible that conduct could be so clearly outrageous that "persons of common intelligence" would be aware that it was prohibited regardless of vague wording such as "inimical to the best interests of the school"?

[Case No. 16] Delegation of Legislative Powers to Chief State School Officer

SCHOOL DIST. NO. 39 OF WASHINGTON COUNTY v. DECKER

Supreme Court of Nebraska, 1955.
159 Neb. 693, 68 N.W.2d 354.

CHAPPELL, JUSTICE.   Plaintiff, School District No. 39 of Washington County, generally known as Rose Hill School District, is a rural Class II school district conducting both elementary and ninth and tenth high school grades in Washington County. It brought this action in equity to enjoin the enforcement of Rule III–3 of Section B, "Criteria for Approved Schools" promulgated as of July 1, 1952, by defendant Freeman Decker, then Superintendent of Public Instruction, under purported authority granted him by the last sentence of section 79–307, R.R.S.1943. Such section provides: "The Superintendent of Public Instruction shall prescribe forms for making all reports and regulations for all proceedings under the general school laws of the state. *He shall also formulate rules and regulations for the approval of all high schools for the collection of free high school tuition money.*" (Italics supplied.)

Rule III–3 also provides: "The teacher-pupil ratio for high school (grades 9–12) shall not be less than 1–5."

On May 12, 1953, defendant had removed plaintiff's high school from the list of approved schools for the school year 1953–1954 because its teacher-pupil ratio was "1–4 which is less than the minimum standards" required by Rule III–3. Concededly, such removal made plaintiff ineligible for collection of free high school tuition for nonresident pupils, deprived it of exemption from the free high school tax levy together with the right to be considered for accreditation status, and, as stated by defendant, "so far as our records are concerned, there is no high school in Rose Hill."

Insofar as important here, plaintiff sought injunctive relief primarily upon the ground that the last sentence of section 79–307, R.R.S.1943, was an unconstitutional and invalid delegation of legislative authority and power to an executive or administrative officer of the state. In other words, plaintiff contended that Rule III–3 was invalid and unenforceable because such statute granted defendant authority to "formulate rules and regulations for the approval of all high schools for the collection of free high school tuition money" without therein or otherwise in any statute in pari materia therewith providing any legislative numerical limitations, standards, rules, or criteria for the guidance of defendant in so doing.

* * *

As disclosed by the record, defendant admitted that there is no magic in the ratio of 1–5 required by Rule III–3, and that it could as well have been higher or lower, but should be higher. As a matter of fact, defendant also admitted that there are only eight ninth and tenth grade high schools left in Nebraska, but that in the recent past he had waived the ratio of 1–5 for two or three other like high schools in Washington County because they had prospects for more students in the future, or had suggested the possibility of reorganization.

Thus the Superintendent of Public Instruction has been delegated a free hand without legislative limitations or standards to make or change at will any numerical ratio or standard required for approval of high schools for the collection of free high school tuition money when it would have been a simple matter for the Legislature, which had the power and authority, to have incorporated limits and standards in the statute. As a consequence, without questioning the motives or ability of the Superintendent of Public Instruction, there might well be approval of some high schools upon one standard and a withholding of approval from others by a qualification of such standard or by virtue of another. Thus, defendant had arbitrary power over the life or death of all high schools in this state and the preservation or destruction of their property and the grant or denial of free high school revenue, dependent upon the granting or refusal of approval.

Article II, section 1, Constitution of Nebraska provides: "The powers of the government of this state are divided into three distinct departments, the legislative, executive and judicial, and no person or collection of persons being one of these departments, shall exercise any power properly belonging to either of the others, except as hereinafter expressly directed or permitted."

* * *

As said in 42 Am.Jur., Public Administrative Law, § 45, p. 342, citing authorities from many states: "It is a fundamental principle of our system of government that the rights of men are to be determined by the law itself, and not by the let or leave of administrative officers or bureaus. This principle ought not to be surrendered for convenience, or in effect nullified for the sake of expediency. However, it is impossible for the legislature to deal directly with the host of details in the complex conditions on which it legislates, and when the legislature states the purpose of the law and sets up standards to guide the agency which is to administer it, there is no constitutional objection to vesting discretion as to its execution in the administrators. * * * A statute which in effect reposes an absolute, unregulated, and undefined discretion in an administrative body bestows arbitrary powers and is an unlawful delegation of legislative powers. The presumption that an officer will not act arbitrarily but will exercise sound judgment and good faith cannot sustain a delegation of unregulated discretion." * * *

* * *

* * * We have considered the question of constitutionality in the light of the presumption of validity to which a legislative act is entitled. Nevertheless, we conclude that the last sentence of section 79–307, R.R.S. 1943, * * * [unconstitutionally] delegates legislative authority to the Superintendent of Public Instruction.

* * *

Notes

1. The line of demarcation between a chief state school officer's legislating, which is unconstitutional, and his authority to formulate reasonable rules and regulations is very indistinct. Do you agree with the court's placing the power to classify districts on the legislative side of the line?

2. From an educational view, was the regulation promulgated by the superintendent of public instruction a sound one?

3. Do you think it likely the regulation that precipitated the case would stand if the legislature had indicated that one of the items that the superintendent could take into account was pupil-teacher ratio?

4. The chief state school officer has no implied authority to adopt a regulation providing that no new public high school will be recommended for registration if the establishment of the school would conflict with an approved plan for district reorganization. Carter v. Allen, 25 N.Y.2d 7, 302 N.Y.S.2d 525, 250 N.E.2d 30 (1969).

[Case No. 17] Mandamus against Chief State School Officer

STATE EX REL. CLEVELAND BD. OF EDUC.
v. STATE BD. OF EDUC. OF OHIO

Supreme Court of Ohio, 1984.
11 Ohio St.3d 89, 464 N.E.2d 137.

This action in mandamus was brought by the Cleveland Board of Education to compel respondent, the State Board of Education of Ohio and its superintendent, Dr. Franklin B. Walter, to waive one day of required instruction in the Cleveland Public School System for the 1983–1984 school year.

On January 11, 1984 and January 12, 1984, members of the Unity Unions employed by the Cleveland Board of Education engaged in a work stoppage. These were primarily custodial employees whose duties included operating the boilers in the schools and other maintenance functions. On the days in question, the temperature in Cleveland ranged from 5° F to 18° F. Considering the lack of personnel to operate the heating systems and maintain the buildings, relator's superintendent closed the schools for those two days.

As a result of the closing of school on these two days, the Cleveland Public Schools will have been open for instruction one day less than required by R.C. 3313.48 if the regularly scheduled school year is not extended. The make-up day of instruction is currently scheduled for June 19, 1984, which Relator alleges will cost $750,000.

Relator initially sought a waiver of two days of instruction from respondent which was denied. Relator's request for an adjudication hearing pursuant to R.C. 119.07 and 119.09 was granted. A hearing was held and on May 24, 1984, the state superintendent issued his final order denying the requested waiver.

On May 25, 1984, this action in mandamus was filed seeking the issuance of a writ to compel respondent to waive the one day of instruction. (It is conceded that relator has available an appeal to the court of common pleas from its R.C. Chapter 119 appeal. However, in view of the fact that this dispute concerns whether the schools will be open on June 19, 1984, it would be impossible for relator to obtain the relief requested through that appeal process.)

* * *

PER CURIAM. The sole issue presented is whether relator is entitled to the waiver of one day of required instruction as requested. The waiver of the minimum school year requirements is governed by R.C. 3317.01(B) which provides in relevant part:

" * * * This requirement shall be waived by the superintendent of public instruction if it had been necessary for a school to be closed because of disease epidemic, hazardous weather conditions, damage to a school building, or other temporary circumstances due to utility failure rendering the school building unfit for school use, * * *."

For the reasons that follow, we conclude that relator is entitled to the waiver of one day of instruction due to "other temporary circumstances due to utility failure rendering the school building unfit for school use" under R.C. 3317.01(B). We note first that no argument was made nor evidence presented to suggest that relator's superintendent acted imprudently in closing the schools. The utilities were inoperable, creating a genuine concern for the welfare of the students if classes were held. We sympathize with respondent's concern that too lenient enforcement of minimum school year requirements will erode the protections they afford to Ohio's public school students. However, the purpose of the minimum school year is to provide guidelines to insure that public schools offer quality education. We cannot conclude that one day of instruction will improve the quality of education offered in the Cleveland Public Schools this year, particularly when the one day will cost relator $750,000.

In so holding, we expressly reject relator's contention that the reason for the utility failure is irrelevant in determining whether a waiver is appropriate under R.C. 3317.01(B). We find simply that the reasons for the utility failure herein do not justify requiring relator to schedule a make-up day of instruction at a cost of $750,000. This expenditure can only adversely affect relator's students in the long run, with no practical benefit in return.

Accordingly, the writ is allowed.

Notes

1. The common-law writ of mandamus is designed to compel performance of a non-discretionary duty. Was the superintendent's decision not to grant the waiver clearly in that category (see statute quoted in the opinion)?

2. Why was this case decided by the state's highest court without its having gone through the lower courts first?

3. At the time of the case, the school district of Cleveland was experiencing a severe financial crisis, compounded by federal-court-ordered desegregation to correct a situation for which the state education agency bore some responsibility. (See footnote 131 in this Chapter).

4. Which decision would you have made—the superintendent's or the court's?

[Case No. 18] Judicial Review of Decision of Chief State School Officer

CONLEY v. AMBACH

Court of Appeals of New York, 1984.
61 N.Y.2d 685, 472 N.Y.S.2d 598, 460 N.E.2d 1083.

MEMORANDUM. * * *

The authority of the Commissioner of Education to review the findings of a hearing panel * * * [in connection with charges against a tenure teacher] includes the right to annul the decision of the panel on the ground of bias or partiality of the panel chairman. The standard by which the determination of the commissioner in the exercise of such authority is to be judged on judicial review is whether his determination "was made in violation of lawful procedure, was affected by an error of law or was arbitrary and capricious or an abuse of discretion". The operative test in this instance is whether the commissioner's determination to annul the decision of the hearing panel was arbitrary and capricious.

His determination was made on the ground that, during the course of the proceedings before the panel, its chairman accepted a remunerative position with the New York State United Teachers (NYSUT) as one of eight arbitrators available to hear disputes between NYSUT and its professional employees, without disclosure thereof to the board of education until subsequent to the close of the hearings. This employment, coupled with the circumstance that counsel for NYSUT represented the teacher at the hearings, was found to raise a sufficient question as to the impartiality of the chairman (or the appearance thereof) as to warrant vacatur of the decision of the panel. Although no direct relationship between the chairman and one of the parties to the proceeding was revealed, there was shown to have been an undisclosed connection between the chairman and counsel for the teacher. This connection alone, without any showing of actual partiality or impropriety on the part of the chairman (of neither of which is there any suggestion in this record), constituted a rational basis for the commissioner's action. Accordingly, his determination of annulment was not arbitrary or capricious and must be sustained.

The commissioner had no authority, however, to impose the prescriptions that he did on the further conduct of the hearings. Specifically, he had no authority to direct the selection of the new chairman of the panel by the parties; the statute mandates that the third member of the panel shall be chosen by mutual agreement of the other two panel members.

Additionally, inasmuch as portions of the evidence at the hearings consisted of conflicting testimony of live witnesses, the credibility and persuasive force of which testimony might not be susceptible to adequate evaluation on the basis of a reading of the transcript only, it was an abuse of discretion, in view of the key role played by the chairman of the hearing panel as its only impartial member, to order the determination of the reconstituted panel to be based only "upon the record already established". This is not to say that portions or all of the transcript of the first hearings cannot be employed by the new panel in making its determination; it is to say only that, absent agreement of the parties and the new chairman, the commissioner cannot order that the consideration of the new panel be confined to the record already established.

* * *

Notes

1. The hearing panel found the teacher guilty of two of thirteen charged specifications and recommended a $300 fine. On appeal by the school board, the commissioner annulled the panel's decision. The trial court overturned the commissioner's annulment. The Appellate Division reinstated it, saying that "the commissioner, as chief educational officer of the State, certainly may adopt higher ethical standards for disclosure than might exist in commercial or other arbitration situations."

2. The Appellate Division did not address the commissioner's remedy, thereby implicitly accepting it. Observe that here the Court of Appeals struck down two parts of that remedy, one on statutory grounds and one on common-law grounds.

3. An arbitration decision made by the person who chaired the panel in this case was subsequently set aside by the Appellate Division because of his failure to disclose his relationship to NYSUT, which was "substantial enough to create an inference of bias." City School Dist. of Oswego v. Oswego Classroom Teachers Ass'n, 100 A.D.2d 13, 473 N.Y.S.2d 284 (1984). However, when this person's biographical data card, which was submitted to the parties before he was selected as arbitrator, contained information about a relationship with NYSUT, a school board could not raise a claim of bias to vacate an award against it. Canajoharie Central School Dist. v. Canajoharie United School Employees, 108 A.D.2d 1087, 485 N.Y.S.2d 866 (1985).

4. "To us it seems utter sophistry to suggest that the appearance of bias does not exist" in a case where the board's appointee to the hearing panel sought and obtained from the board an additional $100 per-diem fee, an arrangement unknown to the teacher, her attorney or the other panel members. So said a unanimous five-judge court in upholding the annulment of the panel's split decision recommending the teacher's dismissal and the board's acceptance thereof. (The panel had held 46 days of hearings, after which the chair and the board's appointee voted for dismissal, with the teacher's appointee disagreeing on guilt as to the major charges and recommending only a letter of reprimand and caution.) An entirely new hearing panel would have to consider the charges. Syquia v. Board of Educ. of Harpursville Central School Dist., 180 A.D.2d 883, 579 N.Y.S.2d 487 (1992), aff. 80 N.Y.2d 531, 591 N.Y.S.2d 996, 606 N.E.2d 1387 (1992).

[Case No. 19] Necessity of Appeal to Chief State School Officer— Power of Local Board to Maintain a Department of Health

CITY OF DALLAS v. MOSELY

Court of Civil Appeals of Texas, 1926.
286 S.W. 497.

JONES, C.J. Appellees prevailed in the trial of an injunction suit in the district court of Dallas County, Tex., and a judgment was entered restraining the board of education of the city of Dallas, and each individual member thereof, from maintaining in the public free schools of the city of Dallas the department of health in connection with said schools, and restraining the city of Dallas, its auditor and treasurer, from the payment of any money for such purpose. * * *

The allegations of the petition for injunction charge that said health department is being maintained in said public schools without lawful

authority and by the illegal expenditure of large sums of money thus diverted from the legitimate purpose for which it was collected by the levy of taxes for the support of public free schools in the city of Dallas. The answer of appellant challenged the jurisdiction of the court to entertain said suit, because of the failure of appellees to seek relief by an appeal to the superintendent of public instruction, and, if necessary, to the state board of education, before filing the suit. Appellants also contend that the establishment and maintenance of said health department in the public free schools of said city in the manner and for the purpose same was maintained is legal and clearly within the discretionary powers of the board of education; that such health department is necessary for the proper discharge of the duty resting on said board to establish and maintain an efficient system of public free schools. These respective contentions present the controlling issues on this appeal.
* * *

After a careful investigation of the working of health departments in other cities by the school authorities of the city of Dallas, and believing that the efficiency of the city's free schools would thereby be increased, the board of education, by resolution duly adopted, established this department, and it was in force for the school year 1925–26. An appropriation of $30,000, or so much thereof as necessary, was duly made from the funds derived from the special taxes levied by the city of Dallas for maintaining its public schools, for the establishment and maintenance of said health department. A competent physician was employed as superintendent of this department at a salary of $4,000 per year, and such physician is required to devote his entire time to the work. Six women nurses were employed for the school year of nine months, each at a salary of $125 per month. During a portion of the year a dentist was employed at a salary of $2,000 * * *.

* * *

Appellants have duly assigned error on the action of the trial court in overruling their plea in abatement. The specific ground on which the plea in abatement was urged is that, as the petition of appellees discloses that no appeal was prosecuted by them from the action of the board of education in overruling their protest to the establishment of said department of health and in making the appropriation of school money for that purpose, to the state superintendent of public instruction, and, if necessary, to the state board of education, this suit cannot be maintained. This contention is based on a provision in article 2656, which reads as follows:

> "The state superintendent shall be charged with the administration of the school laws and a general superintendency of the business relating to the public schools of the state, and he shall have printed for general distribution such number of copies of school laws as the state board of education may determine. He shall hear and determine all appeals from the rulings and decisions of subordinate school officers, and all such officers and

teachers shall conform to his decisions. Appeal shall always be from his rulings to the state board. * * * "

If the allegations in appellees' petition are susceptible to the construction that the board of education only abused its discretion either in establishing the said health department or in the manner in which it is maintained, then we think appellants' position would be well taken. We cannot agree with appellees that, because section 1 of article 5 of the charter of the city of Dallas provides that the board of education created by said section "shall have exclusive control of the public schools of the city of Dallas," that the state superintendent is thereby divested by this special legislative act of all power of supervision of the public free schools within said city. Such has not been the construction of our higher courts in reference to similar provisions in city charters.

The petition in the instant case does not charge an abuse of discretion that could be legally exercised by the board of education, but charges the doing of acts beyond its power and concerning which it had no discretion, and that, in furtherance of such unlawful acts, it is diverting public money, coming into its possession for a special purpose. We do not believe it was the intention of the Legislature in the above-quoted enactment to close the door of the courts to taxpayers in cases of misapplication of public school money by public officers, charged with its proper expenditure, until the slow processes of appeal have been perfected to the state superintendent of public instruction and the state board of education, who are not vested with judicial powers. We think the appeal authorized by the said statute is from purely administrative matters in the conduct of the schools by boards of education. * * *

* * * We therefore hold that the court did not err in overruling appellants' plea in abatement. * * *

It is apparent, therefore, that the correct solution of the question under inquiry is dependent largely on whether the said health department, as it is maintained by the said board of education, has for its primary purpose improving the efficiency of the system of public schools for the city of Dallas. As shown by the rules governing said department, by means of the records made of the physical examination made of the pupils, the teachers are informed of the physical condition of the children under their instruction and said teachers are thereby enabled intelligently to diagnose the mental aptitude and powers of such pupils and to direct their teaching in the light of such knowledge. The parents are informed of the physical defects, in many instances curable, that may hinder the mental process of their children, and thereby given opportunity to have such defects as will yield to treatment corrected. Those in charge of the health department are also required to instruct the teachers and pupils in reference to the laws of health and hygiene, and the children are thereby enabled to pursue their education under more favorable conditions than would otherwise obtain. The directors of the playground activities, where the children are given the necessary healthful exercise, are enabled to judge the amount of exercise and character of play in which those children who are physically deficient can engage without endangering their health.

As shown by this record, the work of the health department in the public free schools of the city of Dallas is within itself educational and instructive on matters directly related to the efficiency of such schools, and tends to their betterment. This being true, its establishment and maintenance as a part of the public free school system of Dallas are within the lawful discretion of the board of education.

* * *

Notes

1. The rule set out in the instant case, that it is not necessary to appeal "legal" matters to the state superintendent of public instruction as a condition precedent to having recourse to the courts, represents the decided weight of authority.

2. Note the breadth of the language used in the statute set out in the case. Observe that the state superintendent is given general superintendency of the "business" relating to the schools of the state. Could not the spending of money in this case be considered "business"? Note that in the last analysis, the court decides that the work of the health department is educational. Who is better qualified to decide such a matter, the state superintendent or the court?

3. Examine the statutes in your state to determine the rights of aggrieved persons in connection with educational matters. How, if at all, are the chief state school officer and the state board of education involved?

4. "Decisions of local boards involving the exercise of their discretion must ordinarily be appealed to the county superintendent and the state board. However, where jurisdiction and power of a board of directors of a local school district are placed in question, or in cases involving construction of statutes conferring authority upon school officers, the courts of the state are the sole arbiters." Board of Directors of Independent School Dist. of Waterloo v. Green, 259 Iowa 1260, 147 N.W.2d 854 (1967).

Chapter 4

LOCAL SCHOOL BOARDS

Powers in General

The evolution of the public school system has been characterized by broad judicial interpretation of implied powers of local school authorities in most states. This attitude of the courts has encouraged freedom and experimentation out of proportion to that suggested by the legal structure itself. Typically, creative local school districts lead off with the introduction of a new practice. In legal parlance, this is the exercise of a latent implied power. If the practice is not challenged judicially, it may spread until it becomes generally accepted even though its legal foundation may be insecure. If, of course, it is challenged and sustained, its status is as if the legislature had expressly given permission for the activity to be provided locally. In an overwhelming number of the instances of legal challenge to a new educational practice, the local school district has been upheld. The usual legal basis offered is that the activity in question is a desirable educational method of achieving broad educational goals enunciated in general legislation. Perhaps the most dramatic example of this process is that of the extension of the Michigan common school system to include high schools. Acceptance of the legality of such action of the Kalamazoo school board by the Supreme Court of Michigan [1] and general acceptance of the idea by the American people meant that challenge in other states was not vigorously pursued. But, largely because many extensions of the powers of local school boards have an impact on the public purse, the issue has been a fruitful source of litigation.

Regardless of the manner in which school board members are appointed or elected they are state, not local, officers.[2] It should be reemphasized that the education function is classified as one of statewide responsibility. This legal fact does not change even though certain aspects of the education function may be delegated to local authorities. Local school board members are selected as the legislature prescribes, they hold office by virtue of legislative enactment, and their powers as a board may be extended or limited in the discretion of the legislature. Even though local school board members may be appointed by a mayor, they are not considered municipal officials.[3] The method of selection of board members may be changed by the legislature even though an

---

1. Stuart v. School Dist. No. 1 of Village of Kalamazoo, 30 Mich. 69 (1874).

2. State ex rel. Walsh v. Hine, 59 Conn. 50, 21 A. 1024 (1890); Landis v. Ashworth, 57 N.J.L. 509, 31 A. 1017 (1895).

3. Ham v. The Mayor, Aldermen, and Commonality of the City of New York, 70 N.Y. 459 (1877).

incumbent is removed in the process.[4] If the legislature provides for recall elections it may do so as it sees fit. Courts will function as they do in connection with regular elections [5] unless the recall provisions specify additional duties, such as determining sufficiency or specificity of grounds for holding the recall election.[6]

Because in any geographic location there exists both a school government and a general local government, relations between the two are frequently before the courts. Instances will appear in subsequent sections. It is essential, however, to stress here the basic separateness of the two entities. Even where boundaries of a municipal unit and a school district are coterminous, there is no merger of city affairs and school district affairs.[7] So-called "home rule" charters for cities do not diminish the state's power to deal with the subject of education.[8]

Because obviously it is not possible to foresee, and legislate with particularity on, every problem which may arise in school administration, the courts have agreed that in addition to express powers, local boards may exercise powers necessarily implied to enable them to carry out the express powers granted. This doctrine of "necessity" in relation to implied powers applies also to municipal corporations. It is important to emphasize, however, that in legal contemplation, school boards can have implied powers related only to education, not to general government concerns. Thus, although an expenditure of funds to help combat juvenile delinquency in the city could be proper for a municipal governing body, such was held not to be implied by the local school board's education powers.[9]

When in doubt, the courts, under common law, are inclined to find against an implied power. There are no inherent powers in school boards. A study of the great number of cases in the area, however, indicates that, although they do not deviate from the aforementioned principle, most courts have construed implied powers broadly, seeming to have become even more liberal in modern times. But in no instance can a board enlarge its powers so as to conflict with a state-level prescription. Where state law provided for annual contracts for teachers, a local board could not give to a teacher a term of employment beyond that authorized by the statute providing for an annual contract.[10] Nor, where a statute permitted corporal punishment only if the parent agreed in writing, could a school board establish a "fundamental" school

4. Lanza v. Wagner, 11 N.Y.2d 317, 229 N.Y.S.2d 380, 183 N.E.2d 670 (1962), app. dism. 371 U.S. 74, 83 S.Ct. 177, 9 L.Ed.2d 163 (1962).

5. Johnson v. Maehling, 123 Ariz. 15, 597 P.2d 1 (1979). See Chapter 14.

6. State ex rel. Citizens against Mandatory Bussing v. Brooks, 80 Wash.2d 121, 492 P.2d 536 (1972); CAPS v. Board Members, 113 N.M. 729, 832 P.2d 790 (1992).

7. State ex rel. Harbach v. Mayor of City of Milwaukee, 189 Wis. 84, 206 N.W. 210 (1925).

8. School Committee of the Town of Winslow v. Inhabitants of the Town of Winslow, 404 A.2d 988 (Me.1979).

9. Barth v. School Dist. of Philadelphia, 393 Pa. 557, 143 A.2d 909 (1958).

10. Nethercutt v. Pulaski County Special School Dist., 251 Ark. 836, 475 S.W.2d 517 (1972).

with an admission requirement that the parent so agree.[11]

Furthermore, it should not be concluded that school boards have an unfettered control of public money for purposes which they deem to be for the good of the education of children. For example, the Supreme Court of Washington has held that the maintenance of a so-called "clinic" equipped with appliances for rendering medical, surgical, and dental services in the treatment for physical ailments of pupils of the school is beyond the authority of the local board under implied powers.[12] The Supreme Court of Georgia decided one of the few cases concerned with the question of whether a school lunch program impliedly may be tax supported.[13] Although the court was in full accord with a broad construction to allow educators the greatest possible leeway in providing an education for the children of the state, it ruled that "educational purposes" cannot be expanded to include the feeding of children.

The rule that local boards possess not only express, but also implied, powers essentially is a rule of expediency developed by the courts as a legal basis for sustaining board actions which to the judges appear educationally sound. Obviously a court by strict interpretation of what school board powers are implied may limit educational experimentation. If this should occur, the empowering statute can be changed to bring the power in question within the scope of the board's express statutory powers. By the same token, if extension by court interpretation of the implied powers of boards results in judicial approval of programs not deemed desirable by the legislature, the specific powers can be restricted or withdrawn.

As will be observed subsequently the general powers of boards to manage the school system are called into question in some matters not involving expenditure of funds, even indirectly. Major examples would be rules and regulations governing admission, attendance, and conduct of pupils and regulations pertaining to staff personnel policies. If, however, it is found that a board possesses a particular power, the courts are limited to an examination of whether the board has exercised it in an arbitrary or unreasonable manner.[14]

The powers of school boards must be exercised by the boards themselves in accordance with statutory and common law procedures. (See Chapter 14.) It is a principle of the common law that a delegated power may not be further delegated by the person or body to whom it is originally delegated. Because local boards function with powers delegated by the legislature, they alone must exercise the powers. Even if not required to do so, boards may seek advice and recommendations from board committees, regular employees, consultants, students, the public— anyone at all. But final decisions must be made by the boards. Boards have no power to diminish their powers by any device even though they

11. Burton v. Pasadena City Bd. of Educ., 71 Cal.App.3d 52, 139 Cal.Rptr. 383 (1977).

12. McGilvra v. Seattle School Dist. No. 1, 113 Wash. 619, 194 P. 817 (1921).

13. Wright v. Absalom, 224 Ga. 6, 159 S.E.2d 413 (1968).

14. Pell v. Board of Educ. of Union Free School Dist. No. 1, etc., 34 N.Y.2d 222, 356 N.Y.S.2d 833, 313 N.E.2d 321 (1974).

may so desire. Statutes, however, may reduce the common law restrictions on exercise by boards of authority delegated to them by the legislature.[15]

Frequently it is not clear whether the power to execute some matter is nondelegable, or even whether certain acts constitute an improper delegation. The latter problem is similar to that of delegation of legislative power discussed in Chapter 3. Delegation by local school boards, however, can be substantially clarified by the legislature through specific statutes pertaining to board powers, whereas only the courts can enunciate the boundaries of delegation of legislative power. The principle of nondelegability by local school boards will be examined in many cases treated in later chapters, but some examples will be presented here.

Questions of delegation of school board authority to administrators frequently arise through arguments of plaintiffs seeking to have decisions nullified. Where a teacher whose transfer had been approved by the superintendent but denied by the board attempted to use a provision of the collective bargaining contract to preclude such board action, the Supreme Court of Wyoming stated that if the provision placed final authority over transfers in the superintendent, it would be forced to declare that portion of the contract invalid.[16] Teacher assignment is a discretionary function, which boards cannot delegate. The Supreme Court of Washington invalidated a board policy authorizing the superintendent to place a teacher on probation and to impose a monetary sanction.[17] The court stated that even if the policy is negotiated with a professional organization the result is a nullity because only school boards can set working conditions. Nor may a board grant a teachers association the right to allocate at least $339,600 as increased economic benefits among the board's professional employees.[18]

Boards can delegate, however, the ministerial functions employed to execute a board decision. Thus, where a statute prescribed that a teacher be "notified in writing by the board" of intent not to renew the teacher's contract, the fact that the letter conveying the message was signed only by the superintendent was held not to constitute a violation of the statute.[19] The court said that only a strained construction would suggest that the board was precluded from having the information transmitted by the superintendent.

Nondelegable powers must be retained by boards even where collective bargaining contracts per se are enforceable.[20] A board can no more bargain away such a power than it unilaterally can delegate it. Where

15. School Bd. of Collier County v. Florida Teaching Profession National Educ. Ass'n, 559 So.2d 1197 (Fla.App.1990).

16. Diefenderfer v. Budd, 563 P.2d 1355 (Wyo.1977).

17. Noe v. Edmonds School Dist. No. 15 of Snohomish County, 83 Wash.2d 97, 515 P.2d 977 (1973).

18. Chatham Ass'n of Educators, Teacher Unit v. Board of Public Educ., 231 Ga. 806, 204 S.E.2d 138 (1974).

19. Cutshaw v. Karim, 256 N.W.2d 566 (S.D.1977).

20. Dayton Classroom Teachers Ass'n v. Dayton Bd. of Educ., 41 Ohio St.2d 127, 323 N.E.2d 714 (1975).

collective bargaining statutes specifically cover a matter in relation to other statutes applicable to school board functioning, the question of delegability may be answered implicitly, if not explicitly.

Giving substantial weight to the principle of nondelegability of school board powers, the Court of Appeals of New York has held that where questions of arbitrability arise in collective bargaining contracts, it must be taken, in the absence of "clear, unequivocal agreement to the contrary," that the board of education did not intend to refer differences to the forum of arbitration.[21]

In a different case the same court held that a school board could not bargain away its right to inspect teacher personnel files.[22] The court cited several statutory charges to boards of education (e.g., employing teachers who are qualified) that could not be carried out without access to personnel files. The invalid provision in the contract limited access to the faculty member and specified administrators. The teachers association asserted that the provision was merely to prevent lay board members from randomly perusing teacher files and making judgments concerning teacher performance without one of the professional administrators laying a proper foundation. The court found both a right and a duty in the board to examine certain materials. It added the caveat, however, that any inspection must be related to legitimate board purposes and functions.

Boards generally are empowered to adopt policies, collectively bargained or unilaterally determined, establishing procedures for exercising their nondelegable powers. Such procedures may have the effect of curtailing the exercise of a power for a period, but courts generally do not consider agreeing to procedural parameters to constitute illegal delegation. For example, it has been held that a board is authorized to bind itself for a limited period in time to observe certain criteria in disapproving transfers of personnel that had been approved by the superintendent.[23]

The question of illegal delegation of school board powers has been unsuccessfully raised in some cases in which it has been sought to invalidate rules of state athletic or activities associations. The Supreme Court of South Dakota, in upholding a statute that expressly permitted boards to join such an association and to have the association regulate interscholastic activities on a year to year basis, emphasized that a school board was not required to join.[24] If it became a member, the board, in effect, ratified the association's rules and made them the board's rules. Nothing prevented a board from withdrawing from the association should a rule undesirable to the board be adopted.

21. Acting Superintendent of Schools of Liverpool Central School Dist. v. United Liverpool Faculty Ass'n, 42 N.Y.2d 509, 399 N.Y.S.2d 189, 369 N.E.2d 746 (1977). [Case No. 93]

22. Board of Educ., Great Neck Union Free School Dist. v. Areman, 41 N.Y.2d 527, 394 N.Y.S.2d 143, 362 N.E.2d 943 (1977).

23. Bradley v. School Committee of Boston, 373 Mass. 53, 364 N.E.2d 1229 (1977).

24. Anderson v. South Dakota High School Activities Ass'n, 247 N.W.2d 481 (S.D.1976).

Through contracts a board may limit certain of its powers for the period of the contract. (See Chapters 8 and 9 for discussion of authority of boards to enter into contracts.) Unless bound by contract (or the common law doctrine of promissory estoppel) a board can change policies as it sees fit in the interests of carrying out its responsibilities.[25]

Rules and Regulations in General

It is well settled that a board of education has the implied power to make and enforce reasonable rules and regulations for the efficient conduct of the schools. The question of what is reasonable is often a difficult one. Since rules and regulations pertain to such a wide range of subjects, the scope of cases in which reasonableness of board action has been considered by courts is vast. It is generally presumed that a board has acted reasonably. The burden of proof is placed upon the party contesting the rule.[26] The strong presumption in favor of legality of regulations rests on the premise that the role of the courts is not to make policy, but is to assure that the discretion is not exercised arbitrarily or unreasonably. A court cannot substitute its judgment for the reasonable judgment of the responsible body. Legality and wisdom are not synonymous. The courts examine legality.

A substantial part of the "common law of education" derives from situations in which courts have been asked to review actions of local school authorities. It is clear that most of the matters that require the attention of educational authorities cannot be dealt with definitively on levels above the local. In many areas they could be dealt with more specifically, but they are not, either by intent or by omission. For example, a statute may specify that a child is eligible to enter school at age six, but literally this could mean on the day he reaches six, at the beginning of the school year in which he reaches six, or at various other points in time. Thus raised is the question of the reasonableness of entrance "cut off" dates.

One such situation was considered by the Supreme Court of Montana.[27] A statute provided that the schools shall be open to all between the ages of six and twenty-one. The local board had a rule that only children who had reached the age of six prior to November 15 would be admitted to first grade at the commencement of the fall term in September of that year. Parents sought admission at the beginning of the September term for a child whose birthday was November 18. The court stated the question before it to be: "Does a school board have power under our Constitution and statutes to set an arbitrary date, after the beginning of a school term, after which a child who reaches his sixth birthday may not be admitted for that particular term?" The question was answered in the affirmative. The court, taking judicial notice of the

---

25. Michie v. Board of Trustees of Carbon County School Dist. No. 1, 847 P.2d 1006 (Wyo.1993). [Case No. 20]

26. An exception is found where a fundamental constitutional right of the plaintiff is involved or if the plaintiff is a member of a suspect class. See Chapter 1.

27. State ex rel. Ronish v. School Dist. No. 1 of Fergus County, 136 Mont. 453, 348 P.2d 797 (1960).

practical difficulties which would arise if children had to be admitted immediately after their sixth birthdays, found that the school board made a reasonable rule not in conflict with the purpose of the state statute.

That locally adopted regulations cannot be contrary to a statute is a fundamental principle. But whether certain regulations conflict with state legislation is not always clear. The problem is illustrated by a Connecticut case. One statute there provided that, after a probationary period, teachers could be discharged only for specified reasons. Another provided that retirement was compulsory at age seventy. Two local school boards adopted regulations setting the retirement age for teachers therein at sixty-five and sixty-eight years of age, respectively. Legal action was brought by teachers in each district to have these regulations invalidated. The Supreme Court of Errors of Connecticut consolidated the cases and ruled in favor of the teachers. It held that, under certain general authority conferred upon them by statutes, the boards could not adopt policies which altered state-level policies.[28] The local boards could not change the retirement age and in effect prescribe grounds for removal of employees beyond those enumerated in the relevant statute. Without referring to this case the Supreme Court of Vermont reached the same conclusion on similar facts.[29] (The legal principles of these cases are not affected by the 1986 Amendments to the federal Age Discrimination in Employment Act, which generally forbid involuntary retirements based on age.)

The offering of incentives by local boards to encourage "early" retirement has been struck down by the Supreme Court of New Jersey largely because of the financial effect on the state retirement system.[30] The Supreme Court of Ohio had emphasized this aspect 40 years before.[31]

Also, provisions in board policies that are out of line with state-level prescriptions for teacher tenure are not enforceable. For examples, boards cannot bind themselves to reemploy probationary teachers who have received favorable evaluations[32] or to submit to arbitration the merits of a decision not to reemploy a probationary teacher.[33] The Supreme Court of Illinois held that a statutory provision of full-time service during the probationary period cannot be avoided by local board actions even if shortage of funds caused the deviation.[34] The Appellate Court of Illinois applied the principle despite the fact that a local board had formally approved "tenure status" for some teachers six years

28. Herzig v. Board of Educ. of Town of West Hartford, 152 Conn. 144, 204 A.2d 827 (1964).

29. Cole v. Town of Hartford School Dist., 131 Vt. 464, 306 A.2d 101 (1973).

30. Fair Lawn Educ. Ass'n v. Fair Lawn Bd. of Educ., 79 N.J. 574, 401 A.2d 681 (1979). [Case No. 21]

31. Verberg v. Board of Educ. of Cleveland, 135 Ohio St. 246, 20 N.E.2d 368 (1939).

32. Leonard v. Converse County School Dist. No. 2, 788 P.2d 1119 (Wyo.1990).

33. Mindemann v. Independent School Dist. No. 6 of Caddo County, 771 P.2d 996 (Okl.1989).

34. Johnson v. Board of Educ. of Decatur School Dist., 85 Ill.2d 338, 53 Ill.Dec. 234, 423 N.E.2d 903 (1981).

before a case involving the issue arose.[35] Where a state-level system of conducting disciplinary hearings for tenure teachers included a pay scale for the members of the hearing panel, a local board was held not to have the authority to augment the per diem stipend of its appointee.[36]

In Utah the state board policy on fees for certain elements of school-sponsored activities provided for fee waivers to ensure that no student was denied the opportunity to participate in an activity because of financial inability to pay. A local board implementation of the policy limited the waiver of fees to families receiving public assistance. It also provided for partial waivers. Both of these features were declared invalid.[37] The first was more restrictive than the state regulation. The second was not provided for in the state regulation, which spoke only of "waivers." The court said that local rules "may not abridge, enlarge, extend, or modify" the statute or state-level regulation creating the right or imposing the duty.

In matters where the state has not set up prescriptions, however, a school board may have implied power to act. For example, a board has been held to have the implied power to determine by physical examination whether an applicant for a teaching position is afflicted with any communicable disease or is incapable of discharging his duties.[38] A teacher already employed can be required to submit to an examination to check on fitness to continue.[39] Also, before a teacher is permitted to return from medical leave, the teacher can be required to present medical records and pass a physical examination.[40] In this connection, of course, a board cannot set up rules regarding physical qualifications unrelated to the performance of the duties of a teacher.[41] A school board rule requiring all probationary teachers to submit to urinalysis to detect potential drug abuse was struck down by the Court of Appeals of New York as violative of the constitutional bar to unreasonable searches and seizures.[42] The court said that a reasonable suspicion of drug use could be basis for an individualized requirement for teachers. School bus drivers, however, said the Court of Appeals of Oklahoma, because of the safety factor can be required to submit to such tests on an annual basis.[43]

35. Evans v. Benjamin School Dist. No. 25, 134 Ill.App.3d 875, 89 Ill.Dec. 637, 480 N.E.2d 1380 (1985).

36. Syquia v. Board of Educ. of Harpursville Central School Dist., 80 N.Y.2d 531, 591 N.Y.S.2d 996, 606 N.E.2d 1387 (1992).

37. Lorenc v. Call, 789 P.2d 46 (Utah App.1990).

38. School Dist. No. 1, Multnomah County v. Teachers' Retirement Fund Ass'n, 163 Or. 103, 95 P.2d 720 (1939).

39. Dusanek v. Hannon, 677 F.2d 538 (7 Cir.1982), cert. den. 459 U.S. 1017, 103 S.Ct. 379, 74 L.Ed.2d 512 (1982).

40. Strong v. Board of Educ. of Uniondale Union Free School Dist., 902 F.2d 208 (2 Cir.1990). [Case No. 22]

41. Chavich v. Board of Examiners, 23 A.D.2d 57, 258 N.Y.S.2d 677 (1965). See also Sontag v. Bronstein, 33 N.Y.2d 197, 351 N.Y.S.2d 389, 306 N.E.2d 405 (1973). Application of federal antidiscrimination in employment statutes to public schools began in 1972. See Chapter 9.

42. Patchogue–Medford Congress of Teachers v. Board of Educ. of Patchogue–Medford Union Free School Dist., 70 N.Y.2d 57, 514 N.Y.S.2d 456, 510 N.E.2d 325 (1987).

43. Independent School Dist. No. 1 of Tulsa County v. Logan, 789 P.2d 636 (Okl. App.1989).

If statutes enumerate powers of local boards in relation to a specific subject, implied powers do not extend to the point of handling the subject differently. Hence, where procedures for erecting and paying for school buildings are spelled out, it has been held that a local board has no power to enter an agreement to lease a building with an arrangement for future purchase.[44] Neither may a local board discharge all attendance personnel where only such employees are statutorily authorized to enforce compulsory education requirements.[45]

Failure of boards to adopt rules and regulations also can lead to litigation. In some situations boards can be in violation of a state mandate to adopt rules in an area, and in other situations the absence of any rules can be considered evidence of negligence or of civil rights violations.

Any rules adopted by a board must be administered with an even hand. Thus, the United States Court of Appeals, First Circuit, held that if a board allows the use of the internal distribution system of its schools to disseminate notices opposing the use of busing to achieve school integration, it must permit the use to groups having other views.[46] An appellate court in Illinois stated that if a school board uses a mailing list to communicate with parents relative to a referendum, that list must be made available to others wishing to express their opinions on the matter.[47] If a board sponsors a career day for students, it cannot allow speakers to point out advantages of a particular career and concurrently ban any speaker from supplying factual information about disadvantages of that career. So held the United States Court of Appeals, Eleventh Circuit, in a case involving military recruiting.[48]

The United States Court of Appeals, Sixth Circuit, however, held that a parent group had no right to have certain materials carried home by pupils.[49] The material presented the group's views on some school matters. The parents claimed that a public forum had been created by the sending home of other materials and that the First Amendment mandated free access to it. The court ruled against the group. The materials which had been distributed through the students were essentially informational in nature. Materials sought to be distributed were not in response to any item previously given out. The fact that once before the school had allowed the plaintiff to distribute an item was insufficient to establish that a public forum for expression of ideas or dissemination of information had been established.

Curriculum

Establishment of the Elements

Every state has certain statutory prescriptions related to the curriculum of the public schools. These laws cover certain things that must

44. Haschke v. School Dist. of Humphrey in County of Platte, 184 Neb. 298, 167 N.W.2d 79 (1969).

45. Geduldig v. Board of Educ. of City of New York, 43 A.D.2d 840, 351 N.Y.S.2d 167 (1974).

46. Bonner-Lyons v. School Committee of City of Boston, 480 F.2d 442 (1 Cir.1973).

47. Wood v. School Dist. No. 65, 18 Ill. App.3d 33, 309 N.E.2d 408 (1974).

48. Searcey v. Harris, 888 F.2d 1314 (11 Cir.1989).

49. Buckel v. Prentice, 572 F.2d 141 (6 Cir.1978).

be taught in the schools and in some instances directions as to how they should be taught. Also, there may be prohibitions against teaching certain matters. Except for constitutional restraints the legislature has plenary power over the curriculum of the public schools. It is well established that the legislature can require children to submit to education and can require to be studied in public and private schools those subjects which are "plainly essential to good citizenship." Prohibited can be that which is "manifestly inimical to the public welfare." These expressions are those enunciated by the Supreme Court in 1925.[50]

States may, and to differing degrees do, delegate curriculum powers to local school boards. Local boards are directly involved in the operational aspects of state policies, and they must deal with the innumerable minutiae of the school program that are not specifically covered by state pronouncements.

In 1968 the Supreme Court of the United States considered an attack on a statute prohibiting the teaching of evolution in the state-supported schools of Arkansas and found that the statute was unconstitutional on the ground that the establishment of religion clause of the Constitution was breached.[51] The Court observed that the proscription against the teaching of evolution was derived from certain religious conceptions of the Bible and of creation. It held that the law attempted to blot out a particular theory because of its supposed conflict with the biblical account literally read.

A Louisiana statute which forbade the teaching of "evolution-science" in public elementary and secondary schools unless accompanied by a balanced treatment of "creation-science" was declared unconstitutional by the Supreme Court in 1987.[52] The Court found that the first prong of the three establishment clause criteria for a constitutional enactment in the church-state area was not met because the purpose of the statute was a religious one. The legislation affected the science curriculum in a way that reflected a religion-based view, namely, either the banishment of the theory of evolution from the classroom or the presentation of a religious viewpoint that rejects evolution in its entirety.

In 1923 the United States Supreme Court invalidated a statutory prohibition against teaching a foreign language in grades lower than the ninth.[53] There, however, it was a teacher in a private school who was convicted of teaching German as a distinct subject. The Court did not accept as a valid defense of such a statute that its purpose was to promote civic development by inhibiting training of the immature in foreign tongues and ideals before they could learn English and acquire

---

50. Pierce v. Society of the Sisters of the Holy Names of Jesus and Mary, 268 U.S. 510, 45 S.Ct. 571, 69 L.Ed. 1070 (1925).

51. Epperson v. Arkansas, 393 U.S. 97, 89 S.Ct. 266, 21 L.Ed.2d 228 (1968). [Case No. 23]

52. Edwards v. Aguillard, 482 U.S. 578, 107 S.Ct. 2573, 96 L.Ed.2d 510 (1987).

53. Meyer v. Nebraska, 262 U.S. 390, 43 S.Ct. 625, 67 L.Ed. 1042 (1923).

American ideals. It found the statute limited the rights of modern language teachers to teach, of pupils to gain knowledge, and of parents to control the education of their children. The Court emphasized that there was no showing of harm which the state had the right to prevent and that no emergency had arisen which rendered the knowledge by a child of some language other than English so clearly harmful as to warrant its being prohibited. The Court made clear that the power of the state over the curriculum in general in its tax-supported public schools was not questioned. The main pillar of the reasoning was the constitutional right of one to pursue an occupation not contrary to the public interest.

The Supreme Court decision barring the recitation of the Lord's Prayer and the reading of the Bible as a religious exercise invalidated statutes in many states which theretofore had prescribed or expressly permitted such practices.[54] The courts within the various states in the years before 1963 had been in marked disagreement as to the constitutionality of Bible reading. Religious influences in the curriculum are treated in Chapter 2.

The authority of local boards to offer courses beyond those mandated by the state rests on the legal basis of implied delegated powers, rather than either plenary or inherent powers. That local boards have implied powers in this area is very well established. Reference has been made to the 1874 Kalamazoo case, in which the Supreme Court of Michigan, in the absence of express legislative authority, held that a local board had the power to maintain a high school.[55] An analysis of the scores of pertinent decisions in appellate state courts warrants a generalization that local boards have a vast amount of discretion to supplement courses required by the state-level authorities.[56] Probably in no sphere of school operation have the courts been more liberal in interpreting implied powers of local boards than in curricular matters. This statement applies not only to addition of specific curricular elements, but to determination of methods of carrying out both specific and general mandates.

Whether family life and sex education may be introduced into the public school curriculum without violating any rights of parents or pupils was decided affirmatively by the Supreme Court of Hawaii and by the United States Court of Appeals, Fourth Circuit.[57] Both general rights of parents and rights of religious freedom are not violated, according to the Supreme Court of Hawaii, so long as the parents have the right to have their children excused from the instruction. The Fourth Circuit analogized the program to public health measures with which the state may go far without violating the religion clauses of the

54. School Dist. of Abington Tp., Pa. v. Schempp, 374 U.S. 203, 83 S.Ct. 1560, 10 L.Ed.2d 844 (1963). [Case No. 4]

55. Stuart v. School Dist. No. 1 of Village of Kalamazoo, 30 Mich. 69 (1874).

56. E.g., State ex rel. Andrews v. Webber, 108 Ind. 31, 8 N.E. 708 (1886); State

Tax Comm'n v. Board of Educ. of Holton, 146 Kan. 722, 73 P.2d 49 (1937).

57. Medeiros v. Kiyosaki, 52 Hawaii 436, 478 P.2d 314 (1970) [Case No. 14]; Cornwell v. State Bd. of Educ., 428 F.2d 471 (4 Cir.1970), cert. den. 400 U.S. 942, 91 S.Ct. 240, 27 L.Ed.2d 246 (1970).

First Amendment. The United States Supreme Court in 1982 dismissed for want of a substantial federal question a challenge to the offering of family life education to students whose parents did not object.[58]

Additions challenged by taxpayers unsurprisingly often have been those which involve substantial expenditures. But programs of physical education, including the building of gymnasiums and stadiums for competitive games, have been uniformly sustained.[59] It has been frequently stated by the courts that more than academics are involved in an education. Also upheld against frequent attack have been health programs established by local boards for inspectorial, as distinguished from therapeutic, purposes.[60] It has been held a proper function of school authorities to check the physical condition of pupils so that they can profit from schooling. Also boards must be sure that those with health problems which might harm others are not admitted. However, authority is not implied to pay for actual treatment except in emergency situations.[61]

In Ohio a taxpayer objected to the imposition of a local tax to help finance a state-required vocational education program in a joint vocational school district. He urged that vocational schools offering job training courses were not included in the state constitutional provision for publicly supported education. The Court of Appeals of Ohio disagreed, holding that the purpose of public schools was "to initiate and to enlarge the knowledge" of pupils in areas "pertinent to present day living" and that the vocational education program constituted one such area of knowledge.[62]

When an offering is required by the state, financial resources to support it properly must be made available by the local board.[63] Nonmandated programs must be curtailed if necessary to maintain the required program. The Appellate Court of Illinois rejected the suit of a school district for a declaratory judgment finding some statutory provisions illegal because of incapability of performance.[64] The statutes required local school districts to establish special educational facilities for handicapped children and permitted reimbursement only after the facilities were provided. The court stated that there was no justiciable question because legislative acts may not be reviewed judicially on allegations that they are "unwise, unjust, oppressive or unworkable."

58. Smith v. Ricci, 89 N.J. 514, 446 A.2d 501 (1982), app. dism. 459 U.S. 962, 103 S.Ct. 286, 74 L.Ed.2d 272 (1982).

59. McNair v. School Dist. No. 1, 87 Mont. 423, 288 P. 188 (1930); Concerned School Patrons and Taxpayers v. Ware County Bd. of Educ., 245 Ga. 202, 263 S.E.2d 925 (1980). [Case No. 40]

60. City of Dallas v. Mosely, 286 S.W. 497 (Tex.Civ.App.1926). [Case No. 19]

61. Jarrett v. Goodall, 113 W.Va. 478, 168 S.E. 763 (1933).

62. Mercure v. Board of Educ. of Columbiana School Dist., 49 Ohio App.2d 409, 361 N.E.2d 273 (1976).

63. Talbot v. Board of Educ. of New York, 171 Misc. 974, 14 N.Y.S.2d 340 (1939).

64. Board of Educ., School Dist. No. 150, Peoria v. Cronin, 51 Ill.App.3d 838, 10 Ill.Dec. 113, 367 N.E.2d 501 (1977).

Although a course or element prescribed by the state must not be eliminated,[65] local boards have the implied power to drop a nonmandated course or element from the curriculum even if it has been offered over a long period of time.[66] The courts recognize that it is an administrative function of school boards and administrators to meet changing educational conditions through the creation of new courses, reassignment of teachers, and rearrangement of curriculum. A local district cannot be required to offer a course because it is offered in some other districts. No constitutional rights of the district's students are violated by its not offering a non-state-required course.[67]

Methods and Materials

Although almost all states have some statutes impinging on methodology, most of the prescriptions are general and suggestive, rather than specific and exclusive. Thus, in general, the determination of methods is essentially a local, rather than a state, decision. Generally the courts accept the authority of the school boards and the expertise of the school personnel as to pedagogical techniques.[68]

The establishment and operation of a nongraded school program in elementary school was legally contested in Michigan. The Court of Appeals held that the discretionary authority of school boards was sufficiently broad to encompass the establishment of such a program.[69] The court said that general supervision over public education was vested in the state board of education and that there had been no action by that board prohibiting the establishment of nongraded schools. It cited a Supreme Court of Michigan decision upholding the discretionary authority of local boards to establish one-half day sessions and to offer certain subjects on a compressed schedule because of lack of funds. In that case the highest state court held that there was no legal duty imposed upon local boards by the state board to operate a minimum number of hours per day.[70]

When the board of education of New York City as part of a collective bargaining contract agreed to shorten by two 45-minute periods per week the hours of instruction the act was challenged in both state and federal courts. The Court of Appeals of New York held that in the absence of state regulations specifying minimum length of school day or week the local board was within its authority.[71] That most of the community school boards set up by a legislatively mandated decentrali-

65. Jones v. Board of Trustees of Culver City School Dist., 8 Cal.App.2d 146, 47 P.2d 804 (1935).

66. Jones v. Holes, 334 Pa. 538, 6 A.2d 102 (1939).

67. Board of Educ. of Okay Independent School Dist. v. Carroll, 513 P.2d 872 (Okl. 1973); Zykan v. Warsaw Community School Corp., 631 F.2d 1300 (7 Cir.1980).

68. State ex rel. Williams v. Avoyelles Parish School Bd., 147 So.2d 729 (La.App. 1962).

69. Schwan v. Board of Educ. of Lansing School Dist., 27 Mich.App. 391, 183 N.W.2d 594 (1970).

70. Welling v. Board of Educ. for Livonia School Dist., 382 Mich. 620, 171 N.W.2d 545 (1969).

71. New York City School Boards Ass'n v. Board of Educ. of City School Dist. of City of New York, 39 N.Y.2d 111, 383 N.Y.S.2d 208, 347 N.E.2d 568 (1976).

zation scheme disapproved was of no legal import because the matter was in the province of the central board. There was no requirement that public hearings precede the issuance of the board's directive to reduce the hours. The federal court found no federal constitutional violation.[72] The directive, it said, did not operate to curtail a student's right to an education granted under laws of New York significantly enough to be violative of due process.

There is no question as to the legal right of the state to prescribe textbooks.[73] The statutory trend, however, has been increasingly to delegate more and more power to local authorities to make selections of textbooks. Supplementary books and instructional materials generally have been held to be within the discretion of local boards to purchase if it can be shown that the items are appropriate for the proper conduct of a course. In modern times the courts have become more liberal in holding that boards have implied powers to purchase instructional materials and equipment.

Selection of materials by local boards is a power that can be exercised independent of wishes of teachers. Recommendations of faculty committees need not be accepted by boards.[74] Courts will not review such educational decisions in the absence of very unusual circumstances, such as a clear attempt completely to suppress a point of view on a basis solely of personal tastes of board members. The courts are increasingly likely to scrutinize decisions about books as the continuum is traversed from textbooks to supplementary materials to library materials. Furthermore, courts tend to look more closely at removals of items than at failures to add items.[75] It is to be noted that the constitutional rights basically involved are those of students and parents, not those of teachers.[76] However, because it is the school board that has authority over the curriculum, there is no constitutional violation for a board to refuse to permit to be produced as a school play a particular musical show that was urged by students.[77]

Although a book used in a humanities course had been approved by the state department of education, a local school board in Florida voted to discontinue its use after parental complaints about vulgarity and sexual subject matter in two of the readings. Other parents then sought to prevent the removal, claiming violation of First Amendment speech rights and emphasizing that the course was elective rather than required. (As a matter of fact, the offending selections in the book never had been required reading.) The Eleventh Circuit held that the book was part of the curriculum and that the board could control the materi-

72. Zoll v. Anker, 414 F.Supp. 1024 (S.D.N.Y.1976).

73. Leeper v. State of Tennessee, 103 Tenn. 500, 53 S.W. 962 (1899).

74. Minarcini v. Strongsville City School Dist., 541 F.2d 577 (6 Cir.1976).

75. Pratt v. Independent School Dist. No. 831, Forest Lake, Minnesota, 670 F.2d 771 (8 Cir.1982).

76. Johnson v. Stuart, 702 F.2d 193 (9 Cir.1983).

77. Seyfried v. Walton, 668 F.2d 214 (3 Cir.1981). [Case No. 24]

als used therein. The book remained in the library.[78]

The Tenth Circuit has held that school authorities acted properly in restricting indirect use of the Bible in a fifth-grade teacher's classroom.[79] The teacher maintained an in-class library containing the Bible, he would frequently silently read the Bible while the students were silently reading books of their choice, the Bible was always on his desk, and he displayed a poster with the message "You have only to open your eyes to see the hand of God." These practices constituted a violation of the establishment clause. Putting the Bible in the school library did not.

In 1982 the Supreme Court decided a case brought by students against a school board that had removed from the school library some books it described as "anti-American, anti-Christian, anti-Semitic, and just plain filthy."[80] By a vote of five-to-four, but with no opinion accepted by a majority of the Justices, the Court remanded the case to the district court to determine with more specificity why the board removed the books. Five Justices believed that when the district court granted summary judgment for the board, the circumstances surrounding the removal had not been clearly enough established to enable them to assess fully the First Amendment freedom of speech implications of the action. The other four Justices, in separate dissenting opinions, would have upheld the board without further judicial inquiry.

Four of the five Justices voting for remand subscribed to the view that the removal of the books would be unconstitutional if denying the students access to ideas with which the board disagreed had been a decisive factor. These Justices said, however, that the board could remove books if they were "pervasively vulgar" or did not meet standards of "educational suitability." The fifth Justice declined to make any statements about the First Amendment's relation to the case pending a "factual refinement."

Citizens of the community cannot through court action require a board of education to offer particular instruction[81] or use a specific book in a particular way.[82] Such a decision is within the discretion of the board if there is no state mandate to the contrary and no constitutional deprivation can be shown. Likewise, in the absence of proof that a book is sectarian, "subversive," or "maliciously written," citizens cannot require a board to remove a book from use in the curriculum.[83]

---

78. Virgil v. School Bd. of Columbia County, Fla., 862 F.2d 1517 (11 Cir.1989).

79. Roberts v. Madigan, 921 F.2d 1047 (10 Cir.1990), cert. den. ___ U.S. ___, 112 S.Ct. 3025, 120 L.Ed.2d 896 (1992).

80. Board of Educ., Island Trees Union Free School Dist. No. 26 v. Pico, 457 U.S. 853, 102 S.Ct. 2799, 73 L.Ed.2d 435 (1982).

81. Wright v. Houston Independent School Dist., 486 F.2d 137 (5 Cir.1973); Mercer v. Michigan State Bd. of Educ., 379 F.Supp. 580 (E.D.Mich.1974), aff. 419 U.S. 1081, 95 S.Ct. 673, 42 L.Ed.2d 678 (1974).

82. Presidents Council, Dist. 25 v. Community School Bd. No. 25, 457 F.2d 289 (2 Cir.1972), cert. den. 409 U.S. 998, 93 S.Ct. 308, 34 L.Ed.2d 260 (1972).

83. Rosenberg v. Board of Educ. of City of New York, 196 Misc. 542, 92 N.Y.S.2d 344 (1949); Todd v. Rochester Community Schools, 41 Mich.App. 320, 200 N.W.2d 90 (1972); Williams v. Board of Educ. of County of Kanawha, 388 F.Supp. 93 (S.D.W.Va. 1975), aff. 530 F.2d 972 (4 Cir.1975); Grove v. Mead School Dist. No. 354, 753 F.2d 1528 (9 Cir.1985), cert. den. 474 U.S. 826, 106 S.Ct. 85, 88 L.Ed.2d 70 (1985).

Perhaps the most extensive judicial attack on books used in public schools came in Mobile, Alabama, where a federal District Judge upheld a claim that through the use of forty-four state approved books in history, social studies, and home economics the religion of secular humanism was being taught. The Eleventh Circuit Court of Appeals disagreed.[84] "Even assuming that secular humanism is a religion for purposes of the establishment clause," the court ruled that the books had the primary effect of conveying information essentially neutral in religious content and that none conveyed a message of governmental approval of secular humanism or governmental disapproval of theism. That certain facts or views might not be included in some books is inevitable, and there was no basis for the lower court's concluding that there was antagonism towards theistic religion or the place of religion in culture and values.

In New York City there were assertions that a planned city-wide examination had been compromised. On a complaint by some parents and teachers a trial court issued a temporary injunction against administering the test, and the intermediate appellate court affirmed. The order was reversed by the highest state court, however, on the ground that such matters as the selection and use of a test are peculiarly in the province of the discretion of school authorities and are inappropriate for judicial resolution.[85] Interference at this point would place the courts in the role of displacing, or at least overseeing, the school officials charged with management of the school system. The same reasoning was applied by a Washington appellate court in holding that there was no cause of action against school district personnel for alleged failure to meet criteria established by a state basic education statute.[86]

Bilingual-Bicultural Studies

The Supreme Court of the United States in 1974 held that non-English speaking Chinese students in the San Francisco school district were entitled to relief as a class from the district's policy of providing special English instruction for only about 1,000 of over 2,800 Chinese students who needed it in order to profit from their studies.[87] The district had asserted a lack of funds. The Court observed that a student who does not understand the English language and is not provided with special instruction is effectively precluded from any meaningful education. The Court, however, did not decide the case on Fourteenth Amendment equal protection grounds. Rather, it found the practice to be barred by Title VI of the Civil Rights Act of 1964, which bars discrimination under federally assisted programs on a ground of "race, color, or national origin." [88] The guidelines of the Department of

---

84. Smith v. Board of School Com'rs of Mobile County, 827 F.2d 684 (11 Cir.1987).

85. James v. Board of Educ. of City of New York, 42 N.Y.2d 357, 397 N.Y.S.2d 934, 366 N.E.2d 1291 (1977).

86. Camer v. Seattle School Dist. No. 1, 52 Wash.App. 531, 762 P.2d 356 (1988).

87. Lau v. Nichols, 414 U.S. 563, 94 S.Ct. 786, 39 L.Ed.2d 1 (1974).

88. See Appendix.

Health, Education, and Welfare required instruction for correction of language deficiencies, and the district had contractually agreed to abide by the statute and guidelines in order to receive federal funds. The Court expressly took no position on what educational techniques should be applied to the situation.

A similar holding on the same legal grounds affecting Spanish-surnamed students in Portales, New Mexico, was made by the Court of Appeals, Tenth Circuit.[89] It had been shown that many such students spoke Spanish at home and were growing up "in a Spanish culture totally alien to the environment thrust upon them in the Portales school system" with resultant lower achievement and higher dropout rates. A type of bilingual program was ordered.

The question of a constitutional right to bilingual-bicultural education was squarely answered in the negative by the same court a year later.[90] As one aspect of the Denver case (Case No. 131) the trial court on remand ordered a bilingual-bicultural program to be instituted for Hispano students. The Court of Appeals reversed, holding that (even though urged by some Hispano groups) bilingual education is not a substitute for desegregation. Hispano students were constitutionally entitled to a nonsegregated education and to "the opportunity to acquire proficiency in the English language."

Subsequently, the Ninth Circuit Court of Appeals ruled[91] that no right to bilingual-bicultural education was conferred by Title VI or by the Equal Educational Opportunities Act of 1974.[92] The program to cure language deficiencies of non-English-speaking students met legal requirements, although there was no bar to the board's instituting the bilingual-bicultural program advocated by the plaintiffs.

The Fifth Circuit Court of Appeals has said that a school district's program that would constitute "appropriate action to overcome language barriers that impede equal participation by its students in its instructional programs" (the language of the 1974 federal statute) must be evaluated on such criteria as whether it is based on an arguably sound educational theory, is reasonably calculated to implement the theory, is proving out after a legitimate test, and is a good faith effort consistent with local circumstances and resources.[93] The Seventh Circuit Court of Appeals has held that the statute can be enforced by a class action suit against the state board of education brought by Spanish-speaking students of limited English proficiency.[94]

The Court of Appeals of North Carolina held that parents cannot keep their children out of school because the district does not provide

89. Serna v. Portales Municipal Schools, 499 F.2d 1147 (10 Cir.1974).

90. Keyes v. School Dist. No. 1, Denver, Colorado, 521 F.2d 465 (10 Cir.1975).

91. Guadalupe Organization, Inc. v. Tempe Elementary School Dist., 587 F.2d 1022 (9 Cir.1978).

92. 20 U.S.C.A. § 1703(f).

93. United States v. State of Texas, 680 F.2d 356 (5 Cir.1982).

94. Gomez v. Illinois State Bd. of Educ., 811 F.2d 1030 (7 Cir.1987), on remand 117 F.R.D. 394 (N.D.Ill.1987).

instruction in the heritage and culture of the child's parents.[95] The court did not accept the argument that a deep-rooted conviction for Indian heritage was on a constitutional plane equal to religious beliefs. The rationale of Yoder (Case No. 110) did not apply.

In a New York case, a mother who "had a Blackfoot [Indian] in her ancestral line" withdrew her child from school because of objection to some remarks made about Indians by her seventh-grade daughter's teacher. The court held to be insufficient reason for not complying with the compulsory education law the fact that the school would not accede to the mother's demands that curricular programs be instituted on the problems of Indians and that a steering committee be set up to implement a policy against racism in any form.[96]

Federal Statutes re Handicapped Students

As the constitutional rights of handicapped students were beginning to be refined judicially in line with emerging theories of "special education," Congress passed the Rehabilitation Act of 1973 and the Education for All Handicapped Children Act of 1975 (renamed in 1990 the Individuals with Disabilities Education Act). The regulations promulgated by the Department of Health, Education and Welfare in 1977 to implement "Section 504" of the Rehabilitation Act [97] and the Education for All Handicapped Children Act ("P.L. 94–142") [98] must be considered by courts in future litigation affecting rights of handicapped students. Where rights and duties are set out in statutes by the legislature, constitutional rights will not be delineated by the courts. The Supreme Court in 1977 applied this general principle when it vacated and remanded for consideration under Section 504 a three-judge federal District Court judgment that had held unconstitutional a Virginia statute pertaining to special education.[99]

Section 504 prohibits discrimination against an "otherwise qualified handicapped individual * * * solely by reason of his handicap * * * under any program or activity receiving Federal financial assistance." The factual context for the Supreme Court's first opinion construing the statute was that a person who was aurally impaired, to the extent of having to read lips of those speaking to her, sought admission to a community college program leading to state certification as a registered nurse and was rejected because of this condition. She argued that the statute required admittance if she met academic standards and, further, that the statute required affirmative action on the part of the college to provide her with aids (in the form of persons, equipment, or modified curriculum) that would presumably render her handicap irrelevant. Substantial reliance was placed on an HEW regulation requiring post-

95. Matter of McMillan, 30 N.C.App. 235, 226 S.E.2d 693 (1976).

96. Matter of Baum, 61 A.D.2d 123, 401 N.Y.S.2d 514 (1978).

97. 29 U.S.C.A. § 794. The regulations (45 CFR 84) were effective June 3, 1977.

98. 20 U.S.C.A. § 1401 et seq. The regulations (45 CFR 121a) were effective October 1, 1977.

99. Kruse v. Campbell, 431 F.Supp. 180 (E.D.Va.1977), vac. 434 U.S. 808, 98 S.Ct. 38, 54 L.Ed.2d 65 (1977).

secondary institutions to make "modifications" in their programs to accommodate handicapped persons and to provide "auxiliary aids," such as sign-language interpreters.

The Court unanimously held that the statute did not require the college to admit the candidate.[100] It defined an "otherwise qualified" person as one "who is able to meet all of a program's requirements in spite of his handicap" (*not* one who would be able to meet the requirements in every respect except as to limitations imposed by the handicap). The Court said that Section 504 did not compel educational institutions to disregard the disabilities of handicapped individuals or to make substantial modifications in their programs to allow disabled persons to participate. Mere possession of a handicap, however, is not a permissible ground for assuming an inability to function in a particular context.

In addressing the question whether the physical qualifications required of students in the nursing program were necessary to functioning as a registered nurse, the Court concluded that the ability to understand speech without reliance on lipreading is essential for patient safety both in the clinical phase of the program and in practice after certification as a registered nurse. On the point of modifications that might be required by HEW, the Court observed that if the HEW regulations were interpreted to require substantial adjustments in existing programs beyond those necessary to eliminate discrimination against otherwise qualified individuals, they would be invalid as constituting an unauthorized extension of the obligations imposed by Section 504.

The Court's holding that "affirmative action" of the nature sought here is beyond the scope of Section 504 (and thus beyond any HEW mandate under authority of the section) must be interpreted with an emphasis on the facts that the program was a professional one, it involved clinical work where that particular handicap related to patient safety, and only a very substantial change in program would accommodate the plaintiff.

The Supreme Court issued its first opinion on P.L. 94–142 in a case in which it held the act does not require a school district to furnish a sign-language interpreter for a deaf elementary school student "who is receiving substantial specialized instruction and related services, and who is performing above average in the regular classrooms of a public school system." [101] The Court said that the act did not require a state "to maximize the potential of each handicapped child commensurate with the opportunity provided nonhandicapped children. * * * Rather, Congress sought primarily to identify and evaluate handicapped children and to provide them with access to a free public education." The Court held that the requirement of a "free appropriate public education" is satisfied by providing "personalized instruction with sufficient support services to permit the child to benefit educationally from that instruction." If the child is being educated in the regular classrooms of the

100. Southeastern Community College v. Davis, 442 U.S. 397, 99 S.Ct. 2361, 60 L.Ed.2d 980 (1979).

101. Board of Educ. of Hendrick Hudson Central School Dist. v. Rowley, 458 U.S. 176, 102 S.Ct. 3034, 73 L.Ed.2d 690 (1982).

public education system, the child's "individualized educational program" (IEP) should be "reasonably calculated to enable the child to achieve passing marks and advance from grade to grade."

The second Supreme Court decision on P.L. 94–142 was an interpretation of the meaning of "related services" to which handicapped children are entitled. The case involved an eight-year-old who suffered spina bifida and required catheterization every three or four hours to avoid injury to her kidneys. The procedure can be performed in a few minutes by a lay-person with less than an hour's training. The Court unanimously held that the school district must provide the service.[102] The Court found to be reasonable the distinction in the rules of the Department of Education [103] between "medical services" (which must be performed by a physician, and are required only for diagnosis or evaluation) and "school health services" (which may be performed by a school nurse or other qualified person, and are required if necessary to aid a handicapped child to benefit from special education).

The Supreme Court also has held that under P.L. 94–142 a parent, who while challenging a child's IEP in administrative or court proceedings places the child at his own expense in a state-approved private school for special education, can obtain reimbursement if it is ultimately determined that such placement, rather than a proposed IEP, is proper.[104] If, however, the ultimate determination is that the proposed IEP was appropriate, no reimbursement at all can be obtained. The Court recognized that "the review process is ponderous" and that a final judicial decision on the merits of an IEP "will in most instances come a year or more after the school term covered by that IEP has passed."

In 1993 the Supreme Court held that under special circumstances courts could order reimbursement to parents who unilaterally placed their children with disabilities in private schools that were not fully approved by the state.[105] The court stressed that there had been judicial findings that the school district's proposal for educating the child was not adequate, that the program of the private school was appropriate to her needs, and that the private school's lack of compliance with certain standards was not substantial.

Discipline of handicapped children is discussed in Chapter 12 under "Specific Punishments." Graduation requirements are discussed later in this chapter.

The procedural provisions of P.L. 94–142, the terminology of substantive rights (e.g., "individualized educational program," "free appropriate public education," "related services"), the large number of children who might be covered by the act, and the large sums of money potentially involved make the statute by far the most litigation-prone

102. Irving Independent. School Dist. v. Tatro, 468 U.S. 883, 104 S.Ct. 3371, 82 L.Ed.2d 664 (1984).

103. A separate Department of Education was established in 1980.

104. School Committee of Town of Burlington, Mass. v. Department of Educ. of Mass., 471 U.S. 359, 105 S.Ct. 1996, 85 L.Ed.2d 385 (1985).

105. Florence County School Dist. Four v. Carter, ___ U.S. ___, 114 S.Ct. 361, 126 L.Ed.2d 284 (1993).

education measure ever to be enacted. At the same time, the cases tend to be fact-bound, with generalizations beyond those contained in the statute and regulations quite elusive.

Required Elements

A persistently controversial question is whether a subject or activity can be required. Also involved, of course, is what action may be taken if a pupil does not accede to the requirement. Here it is important to examine both the nature of the activity and the nature of the punishment, if any. The fundamental right of parents to guide the upbringing of their children has been referred to previously, as has the right of the state to require the study of subjects essential to citizenship. The judicial problem is to establish a reasonable working balance between these concepts. The courts under the common law have tended to give the parents the benefit of the doubt as against the state in matters not likely to affect adversely the child or the state.

It appears to have been established by an 1878 case that a pupil cannot be compelled by physical punishment to take a course against the wish of the parent. The case involved the whipping of a child because of her refusal to study algebra at her father's direction. The evidence showed that the child's health was somewhat delicate, and for this reason her father had requested that she be excused from attending school in the afternoon, when the algebra class met. The Supreme Court of Iowa held that this action of the father was reasonable, but it cautioned that, normally, if a pupil attends school it must be presumed that he will submit to school regulations.[106] But the court refused to sanction the view that a teacher may punish a pupil for not doing something the parent has instructed the pupil not to do.

If a constitutional right of a student or parent is violated by a requirement that the child take a particular subject or course, the board has no legal power to compel him to do so. It follows, in such cases, that the pupil cannot be expelled or suspended because of the refusal. In a California case, the board had prescribed dancing as part of the physical education curriculum. The father of two pupils objected to their participation in dancing and requested the board to substitute some other game or exercise for those opposed to dancing. The board refused to do so, the children persisted in their refusal to participate, and they were expelled. In an action to compel reinstatement, the California Court of Appeal held that if a regulation is unduly burdensome on, or violative of, any of the fundamental rights of a person or set of persons, it will be set aside as unconstitutional.[107] In this case the parent had claimed a religious reason, although he was not affiliated with a religious organization opposed to the activity of dancing.

106. State v. Mizner, 50 Iowa 145 (1878).

107. Hardwick v. Board of School Trustees of Fruitridge, 54 Cal.App. 696, 205 P. 49 (1921).

A case from Alabama dealt both with the requirement of attendance at physical education classes and the wearing of gymnasium uniforms. A high school girl was suspended for refusing to participate in the physical education program because the costume prescribed was deemed immodest and sinful according to the religious beliefs of her and her parents. She also refused to attend the physical education class because such attendance would require her to be in the presence of other girls and the teacher who wore the costume and performed the exercises. The school authorities had made certain adjustments for the religious beliefs of the family in that they offered to allow the girl to wear clothing that she would consider modest and suitable and to excuse her from performing any exercises that seemed immodest for the girl when clad in ordinary clothing. Despite the concessions, the parents declined to permit the girl to attend the classes and brought the action against the board to compel it to readmit the girl and excuse her completely from attending the classes. The court held that, when the concessions made by the school authorities were considered, the legislative policy overrode the parents' objections.[108] No constitutional right was found to be abridged by the requirement that the girl be present when other girls were engaged in the physical exercises.

The general principle is that a parent has a right to make a reasonable selection for his children from among the subjects offered by the school district. When a selection has been made, the local authorities must excuse a pupil from taking the courses to which the parent objects unless the subjects are essential to citizenship. In a leading case on the point, a parent first objected to his daughter's studying rhetoric. His desire to have her study grammar instead was granted. Later he ordered her not to study grammar. The board expelled her. The Supreme Court of Nebraska in 1891 ruled in favor of the parent and ordered the girl readmitted without being required to study grammar.[109] In another case parents had instructed their daughter not to attend a class in domestic science which was required of all girls of her grade. The parents felt that the time consumed in travel to the domestic science class could be used more profitably in private music lessons. She was expelled from school for refusing to take the domestic science course. The court ordered her reinstatement, holding that the parents' request was reasonable under the circumstances.[110] It stated that if the parents desired to have their daughter study music, they had the unquestionable right to have her do so. According to the court it was reasonable for them to select the course in domestic science as a course to be dropped in order that she might continue her music.

Both old and modern courts, however, recognize limits to the power of parents idiosyncratically to determine what their children will study

108. Mitchell v. McCall, 273 Ala. 604, 143 So.2d 629 (1962).

109. State ex rel. Sheibley v. School-Dist. No. 1, 31 Neb. 552, 48 N.W. 393 (1891).

110. State ex rel. Kelley v. Ferguson, 95 Neb. 63, 144 N.W. 1039 (1914).

in school.[111]   This is especially true where religious claims are tenuous, where secular reasons are weak, or where the parents or children pressure others to follow their lead in trying to get excused.[112]

Although schools must try to accommodate minor requests of parents, they are not required to make major curriculum adjustments.   The issue was treated extensively by the Sixth Circuit Court of Appeals in a case where parents unsuccessfully sought to have their children placed in a core reading program other than the one used by the school system for grades 1–8.[113]   The reading program, which was coordinated with other subjects, contained books with ideas objected to by the parents largely on religious grounds.   The court said that there was no right not to be exposed to ideas by the government so long as the views are not promoted and the recipient is not required to affirm or disaffirm agreement with them.

Flag Salute Situation

During the 1930's courts were divided on the constitutionality of the requirement that students salute the flag of the United States and repeat the Oath of Allegiance.   The Supreme Court of the United States, after declining to review several cases, in 1940 accepted one on the subject and held, eight-to-one, that the flag salute could be required.[114]   The case involved a group of Jehovah's Witnesses, who claimed that saluting the flag was equivalent to worshipping an image contrary to a fundamental of their belief.

The decision of the Supreme Court that being required to participate in the flag ceremony was not a deprivation of the individual's constitutional right to religious freedom was widely and severely criticized.   Two years later, in another case involving Jehovah's Witnesses but not involving the schools, three of the justices in the flag salute case majority indicated that they believed that the flag case had been wrongly decided.[115]   The stage was thus set for a reconsideration of the issue, particularly since another justice who had voted with the majority had been replaced.   The "new" case involved the constitutionality of a regulation of the state board of education of West Virginia rather than a local board rule.   Also, under this regulation legal action could be taken against parents of children who were unlawfully absent in consequence of their dismissal for refusing to salute the flag.   Basically, however, the issue was the same, and the Court in 1943, by a six-to-three margin, overruled its prior decision.[116]   The majority indicated that the sole conflict was between "authority and rights of the individual."   It noted

111. Kidder v. Chellis, 59 N.H. 473 (1879); Muka v. Cornell, 48 A.D.2d 944, 368 N.Y.S.2d 874 (1975).

112. Davis v. Page, 385 F.Supp. 395 (D.N.H.1974).

113. Mozert v. Hawkins County Bd. of Educ., 827 F.2d 1058 (6 Cir.1987), cert. den. 484 U.S. 1066, 108 S.Ct. 1029, 98 L.Ed.2d 993 (1988).

114. Minersville School Dist. v. Gobitis, 310 U.S. 586, 60 S.Ct. 1010, 84 L.Ed. 1375 (1940).

115. Jones v. City of Opelika, 316 U.S. 584, 62 S.Ct. 1231, 86 L.Ed. 1691 (1942).

116. West Virginia State Bd. of Educ. v. Barnette, 319 U.S. 624, 63 S.Ct. 1178, 87 L.Ed. 1628 (1943).

that the freedom asserted by Jehovah's Witnesses to refuse to participate in the ceremony did not interfere with or deny rights of others to participate, nor was there any question that their behavior was peaceable and orderly. It struck down the flag salute requirement as transcending constitutional limitations on governmental power because it invaded the individual's "sphere of intellect and spirit" that is protected by the First Amendment.

Almost a quarter-century later the Supreme Court of New Jersey was faced with the issue whether children who refused to pledge allegiance to the flag could be excluded from the public schools when they claimed that the ceremony violated a religion known as "Islam," adherents thereto being commonly called "black Muslims." [117] The school board that excluded the pupils because they refused to pledge allegiance contended that the beliefs of the students were "as much politically as religiously motivated." The board did not accept the objections of the students as "conscientious scruples" because they were "closely intertwined with their racial aspirations." The officials were ordered by the court to admit the students. The court did not decide whether the reason for refusal to salute the flag was religious or basically political. It took the view that the United States Supreme Court decision had a broader base than that of organized religion. Especially noted was that the students stood respectfully at attention during the ceremony and did not cause any disruption.

The highest court of Maryland and federal courts in Florida ruled invalid requirements that students who objected to participation in the flag salute and pledge of allegiance must stand while the rest of the class recited the pledge.[118] In these cases provision for leaving the room was not offered as an alternative.

Even where an option of either leaving the room or standing silently during the pledge ceremony was offered, school authorities were barred from disciplining a student who remained quietly seated. The Court of Appeals, Second Circuit, held that forcing one to stand could no more be required than the pledge itself, and leaving the room during the pledge might reasonably be viewed as a punishment for not participating. The court emphasized the lack of evidence of disruption or of interference with the rights of others in the case at bar.[119]

The constitutionality of including the phrase "under God" in the pledge came before the Seventh Circuit Court of Appeals in 1992.[120] The court held that the use of the phrase in the context of the secular vow of allegiance was as a "patriotic or ceremonial" expression, not a religious one.

117. Holden v. Board of Educ., Elizabeth, 46 N.J. 281, 216 A.2d 387 (1966).

118. State v. Lundquist, 262 Md. 534, 278 A.2d 263 (1971); Banks v. Board of Public Instr. of Dade County, 314 F.Supp. 285 (S.D.Fla.1970), aff. 450 F.2d 1103 (5 Cir.1971).

119. Goetz v. Ansell, 477 F.2d 636 (2 Cir.1973). [Case No. 25]

120. Sherman v. Community Consolidated School Dist. 21 of Wheeling Tp., 980 F.2d 437 (7 Cir.1992).

Graduation Requirements

The establishment of requirements for graduation from a public school program lies within the powers of the state education agency and, to the extent expressly or impliedly delegated, the local school board. The legal principles previously discussed in connection with curricular elements apply to graduation requirements. If the requirements are reasonable in relation to that to which the diploma attests, students who for any reason fail or refuse to meet them may be denied graduation.

Although the rule is that school authorities are vested with sound discretion in the determination of whether a pupil has completed the requisite courses and possesses the necessary qualifications to entitle him to a diploma, when it has been determined that the prescribed requisites have been met, the issuance of a diploma is a ministerial act which is mandatory. The Supreme Court of Iowa has held that a pupil may not have his diploma withheld for refusal to wear a cap and gown at graduation exercises, although he may legally be denied the privilege of participation in the exercises.[121] In a Kansas case, a pupil who was accused of cheating in the final examination was denied a diploma. The court found that the cheating had not been proved satisfactorily and ordered the diploma issued.[122] In a Missouri case it was held that a pupil may not be refused a certificate of attainment for failure to pay a fee assessed by the board of education for the support of the high school, there being no funds to maintain it otherwise. The court was of the opinion that the rule which required the payment of the fee was outside the authority of the board to make or enforce.[123] (See "Fees," infra.) In Pennsylvania it was held that a student could not be denied a high school diploma after he had successfully completed all coursework and examinations.[124] The student was expelled on the morning of graduation day because he had sold a controlled substance.

In Memphis, Tennessee, all male students at all high schools except one were required to take an ROTC (Reserve Officers Training Corps) course in order to be graduated. A student who was conscientiously opposed to participation in war in any form and to being subjected to combat training for the purpose of being prepared to enter into war requested through his father that he be allowed to participate in a physical education course instead of the required ROTC course. School authorities denied his request. He was allowed to continue his other courses, but on the sole ground that he did not complete the ROTC course, he was not given a diploma. The Sixth Circuit Court of Appeals held that the school authorities wrongfully withheld the diploma, for the withholding was a direct result of the student's practice of his religious

121. Valentine v. Independent School Dist., 191 Iowa 1100, 183 N.W. 434 (1921).

122. Ryan v. Board of Educ., 124 Kan. 89, 257 P. 945 (1927).

123. State ex rel. Roberts v. Wilson, 221 Mo.App. 9, 297 S.W. 419 (1927).

124. Shuman v. Cumberland Valley School Dist. Bd. of Directors, 113 Pa. Cmwlth. 63, 536 A.2d 490 (1988).

beliefs, the sincerity of which were not questioned.[125]

In a case of first impression for an appellate court, the Third Circuit Court of Appeals held that a school board could require students to complete sixty hours of community service before graduation.[126] The options were broad, and thus the claim of forced expression was not of constitutional consequence. The service was an educational method of accomplishing the important purpose of developing good citizens who have a sense of community responsibility. The claim of "involuntary servitude" outlawed by the Thirteenth Amendment also was unavailing for plaintiffs.

In Missouri a local school board required eight semesters of attendance to qualify for a high school diploma. A student who had left school following a disciplinary incident eight weeks before the end of his third year (whether he left completely voluntarily was not clear) reentered at the start of the next year and with previous credits earned the units of credit needed for graduation. He was denied a diploma, however, under the aforementioned eight-semester rule. When requested to waive the rule in this situation the school authorities said that the diploma could be obtained only if he enrolled for eight additional weeks to make up for the weeks lost. The Court of Appeals of Missouri held that the application of the rule in the present case was unreasonable, especially since the superintendent's testimony showed clearly that it would not be necessary for the student to earn any additional credits, pass any courses, or even attend any number of classes.[127] The court said that the eight-week enrollment would "do no more than work an exercise in futility" that would benefit neither the school district nor the student. It ordered the diploma to be issued.

In a Colorado case the issue was whether a school board was required to credit toward a high school diploma certain academic work completed by a former student while he was in a correctional institution to which he had been committed. A statute provided that full credit shall be given by school districts for work completed in such institutions. The school board refused to grant the diploma because three local requirements for the diploma were not met: (1) clock hours of instruction were fewer per credit in the institutional facility than in the school district (and the regional accrediting association required the number of hours provided by the district); (2) eight semesters of instruction (or equivalent) were not attended by the young man; (3) the final school semester was not completed in the district. The Supreme Court of Colorado upheld the school district because the first two requirements were deemed reasonable and the statute was construed to require only

125. Spence v. Bailey, 465 F.2d 797 (6 Cir.1972).

126. Steirer v. Bethlehem Area School Dist., 987 F.2d 989 (3 Cir.1993), cert. den. __ U.S. __, 114 S.Ct. 85, 126 L.Ed.2d 53 (1993).

127. State ex rel. Sageser v. Ledbetter, 559 S.W.2d 230 (Mo.App.1977). [Case No. 24]

that bona fide equivalencies must be accepted.[128] The court said, however, that the third requirement was not reasonable.

The requirement to pass a competency test as a prerequisite to receiving a diploma is within the power of education authorities to adopt provided that the students have a fair opportunity to learn the material on the test. The Court of Appeals, Fifth Circuit, stated this principle in a case in which it prohibited use of a statewide test until the state of Florida demonstrated that the test met the standard and also showed that the discrepancy in passing rates of white and black students was not due to educational deprivations suffered by the blacks before the schools were effectively integrated.[129] Florida met the burdens, and the test was judicially approved.[130]

Whether a handicapped student who is unable to pass a minimum competency test nevertheless has a right to a diploma has been answered in the negative by the Seventh Circuit Court of Appeals [131] and the highest state court of New York.[132] These courts delineated circumstances under which diplomas could be withheld without violation of the Constitution or of P.L. 94–142. A crucial one is adequacy of notice that the test must be taken so that there is time for preparation. The federal court found a year and a half to be insufficient time in light of the students' lack of prior exposure to the objectives of the test. It said that the notice requirement could be met by ensuring that a handicapped student was sufficiently exposed to most of the material on the test, or by presenting evidence of a well-informed decision by parents and teacher that a particular student would be better off concentrating on educational objectives other than preparing for the test. The New York court found a three-year notice to be sufficient time for the incorporation in IEPs of the material to be tested.

In 1978 the Supreme Court, in deciding a case concerning graduation requirements from a medical school, made several pronouncements directly applicable to graded schools.[133] The basic issue was whether a medical school student could be dismissed during her final year of study for failure to meet academic standards. All nine Justices agreed that under the facts she had received procedural due process through warnings and chances to demonstrate improvement. Four saw no need to discuss what due process requirements must be met. Five Justices, however, citing several cases including a public school case decided by the Supreme Judicial Court of Massachusetts in 1913,[134] stated that

128. Department of Institutions v. Bushnell, 195 Colo. 566, 579 P.2d 1168 (1978).

129. Debra P. v. Turlington, 644 F.2d 397 (5 Cir.1981).

130. Debra P. v. Turlington, 730 F.2d 1405 (11 Cir.1984). [The Eleventh Circuit was created in 1981.]

131. Brookhart v. Illinois State Bd. of Educ., 697 F.2d 179 (7 Cir.1983).

132. Board of Educ. of Northport-East Northport Union Free School Dist. v. Ambach, 60 N.Y.2d 758, 469 N.Y.S.2d 669, 457 N.E.2d 775 (1983).

133. Board of Curators of University of Missouri v. Horowitz, 435 U.S. 78, 98 S.Ct. 948, 55 L.Ed.2d 124 (1978).

134. Barnard v. Inhabitants of Shelburne, 216 Mass. 19, 102 N.E. 1095 (1913).

there were distinct differences between excluding a student for disciplinary reasons and for academic reasons. In the former a hearing definitely would be required, the degree of formality depending on the circumstances (see Case No. 127). In the latter no hearing would be required because "the educational process is not by nature adversary; instead it centers around a continuing relationship between faculty and students, 'one in which the teacher must occupy many roles—educator, adviser, friend, and, at times, parent-substitute.' " The five Justices, noting that several lower courts had said as dicta that academic dismissals could be enjoined if shown to be clearly arbitrary or capricious, avoided making a pronouncement on the point because "even assuming that the courts can review under such a standard," no showing of such a situation had been made in the case.

The Supreme Court reinforced its position regarding the judiciary and academic determinations with a unanimous decision upholding the dismissal from a medical degree program of a student who had a generally poor record and who failed a written test administered by the National Board of Medical Examiners.[135] Passing the test was a requirement for entering the final two years of the program. The student failed five of the seven subjects on the examination and received an exceptionally low total score. A faculty board of nine members reviewed the student's record and unanimously voted to drop him without allowing him to retake the examination. The student was allowed to appear before the board to explain why he believed his score did not fairly reflect his academic progress or potential, but the board reaffirmed its position. There were other unsuccessful appeals by the student within the university. Eventually, the Sixth Circuit Court of Appeals ordered that the student be allowed to retake the examination (largely because for seven years all who failed the examination had been given that opportunity) and to be reinstated if he passed it.

The Supreme Court reversed and held that "even if [the student's] assumed property interest gave rise to a substantive right under the Due Process Clause to continued enrollment free from arbitrary state action, the facts of record disclose no such action." Courts "may not override [a faculty's academic decision] unless it is such a substantial departure from accepted academic norms as to demonstrate that the person or committee responsible did not actually exercise professional judgment."

"Malpractice"

Beginning in the 1970's there have been attempts to hold school districts liable for perceived failures in educational results allegedly due to pedagogical errors committed during the plaintiff's stay in the schools. To date, all efforts to have courts recognize a tort of "educational malpractice" ultimately have failed. ("Malpractice" is a term of art for negligence of professional personnel, usually those who work in a one-to-one relationship with clients, such as physicians or lawyers.)

135. Regents of Univ. of Michigan v. Ewing, 474 U.S. 214, 106 S.Ct. 507, 88   L.Ed.2d 523 (1985).

In the leading case, the suit charged that the school district wrongly allowed to be graduated one who could read only at the eighth grade level.[136]   Peter W. sought redress for having attended the schools of the district for twelve years and being qualified at the end only for employment requiring little or no ability to read or write.   The court discussed at length the "duty of care" concept as it exists in negligence law and found in this situation no cause of action.   There was no workable rule of care against which to measure the alleged conduct of the defendant school district, no injury within the meaning of the law of negligence, and no perceptible connection between the conduct of the school district and the injury alleged to have been suffered.   In other words, the claims were too amorphous to be justiciable under a theory of negligence.   The charge of intentional misrepresentation was dismissed because no facts were alleged to show the requisite element of reliance upon the asserted misrepresentation.   (It is interesting that the plaintiff was given opportunity to submit such facts, but declined.)

In addition to the reasons cited above, courts of last resort in several states have cited the difficulties of measuring damages and the public policy consideration that the acceptance of such cases would in effect position the courts as overseers of day-to-day operation of the schools.[137] Parents who may be aggrieved by educational decisions have recourse through the administrative channels of local boards and state-level education agencies, and thus are not helpless bystanders as decisions are made affecting the education of their children.   Of course, if a specific act by a school employee directly causes an injury to a student, the ordinary doctrines of tort liability would be activated.   (See Chapter 7.)

Classification and Assignment of Students

Although school boards have the general power to classify pupils, sometimes a procedure may seem arbitrary, and it is left to the courts to decide the legality of the method.   Involved here is the recurring question of whether the issue is educational or legal.   For example, the Supreme Court of Ohio considered a case where a parent sought to have his son placed in the seventh grade rather than the sixth on the ground that he had been tutored during the summer and had made such satisfactory progress that he was qualified for the higher grade.[138]   He had been in the fifth grade the previous year.   The trial court had supported the parent, but the higher court indicated that the lower court had been mistaken in believing that the question whether the pupil was fit to enter the seventh grade was rightfully to be determined by the court.   It was held to be within the power of school authorities to decide on a reasonable basis.

136. Peter W. v. San Francisco Unified School Dist., 60 Cal.App.3d 814, 131 Cal. Rptr. 854 (1976).

137. E.g., Donohue v. Copiague Union Free School Dist., 47 N.Y.2d 440, 418 N.Y.S.2d 375, 391 N.E.2d 1352 (1979); Hunter v. Board of Educ. of Montgomery County, 292 Md. 481, 439 A.2d 582 (1982). [Case No. 59]

138. Board of Educ. of Sycamore v. State ex rel. Wickham, 80 Ohio St. 133, 88 N.E. 412 (1909).

In a New York case a parent contended that because the maintenance of kindergartens in public schools was optional under state law, and because a five-year-old under state law had a right to attend public schools, his child who was five should be placed in first grade, not in kindergarten. The court held that once a kindergarten was established it became a part of the school system.[139] It reemphasized that, although a child may have a right to attend school, the grade assignment is in the discretion of the board. Also, the court made the point that after the child had been admitted on the criterion of age, the board had the power to establish regulations for promotion based not on age but on training, knowledge, and ability. The constitutionality of statutes basing admission to public schools solely on age have been consistently upheld.[140]

A Pennsylvania appellate court held that where maintenance of a kindergarten was optional, there was no constitutionally protected right of a child below the minimum age for elementary school to attend kindergarten.[141] Therefore, there was no constitutional right to a formal and complete hearing before a decision to deny admission to the kindergarten. In the case the school board had offered homebound instruction, which fact the court cited as evidence that the board's decision was not arbitrary.

Rules, however, must not have a discriminatory effect. For example, where seven-year-olds who did not attend the kindergarten in the district were automatically registered in first grade, a court invalidated the requirement to pass a "readiness" test imposed on those who had attended the kindergarten.[142] The Supreme Court of Kansas, however, decided that a board did have the implied authority to require an examination as an entrance provision for the public high schools for graduates of private and parochial elementary schools.[143] Three quarters of a century later the United States Court of Appeals, Sixth Circuit, upheld a similar provision for those transferring from home study situations.[144] In a similar decision a New York court approved use of a test for placement of a pupil who had attended a private kindergarten.[145] Where a statute permitted local school boards to assess a child's readiness to attend school and to allow him to attend prior to the date established for his right to attend, it was held that a board that had conducted such assessments for two years could cease to do so.[146] The court also decided that the fact the board in the present case (under lower court order) did assess the child and permit his enrollment failed to render the legal issue moot.

139. Isquith v. Levitt, 285 App.Div. 833, 137 N.Y.S.2d 497 (1955).

140. Hammond v. Marx, 406 F.Supp. 853 (D.Me.1975).

141. Goldsmith v. Lower Moreland School Dist., 75 Pa.Cmwlth. 288, 461 A.2d 1341 (1983).

142. Morgan v. Board of Educ., Trico Community Unit School Dist. # 176, 22 Ill. App.3d 241, 317 N.E.2d 393 (1974).

143. Creyhon v. Board of Educ., 99 Kan. 824, 163 P. 145 (1917).

144. Vandiver v. Hardin County Bd. of Educ., 925 F.2d 927 (6 Cir.1991).

145. Silverberg v. Board of Educ. of Union Free School Dist. No. 18, 60 Misc.2d 701, 303 N.Y.S.2d 816 (1969).

146. Morrison v. Chicago Bd. of Educ., 188 Ill.App.3d 588, 136 Ill.Dec. 324, 544 N.E.2d 1099 (1989).

Requirements for progress from grade to grade generally are not judicially reviewable except on a substantial claim of unreasonableness. The Fourth Circuit Court of Appeals refused to intervene in the failure of a school system to promote to the third grade students who failed to pass a test of reading-level.[147]   The court accepted the educational judgment that even though the students' intelligence was such that they were capable of reading at the third-grade level, they should not be promoted until they had mastered the requisite reading skill.   The Eleventh Circuit Court of Appeals permitted the institution of a new policy whereby promotions of those performing at an unsatisfactory level would be discontinued.[148]

The Fifth Circuit Court of Appeals held that for a federal claim to be stated based on one's not being allowed to enroll in a particular course of study, there must be a specific state mandate that is violated.[149]   The court hypothesized that a claim might arise if a state statute or regulation required local school boards to provide special education for students who were gifted musically, and there was an allegation that a board failed to do so for such a student.

In an Eighth Circuit case a student sought reinstatement to a special program in automobile mechanics that was conducted at an area vocational-technical school.[150]   He had been dropped after being involved in a theft of automobile parts from a different location.   The school district said that participation in all school-supported off-campus programs was conditional on good citizenship in the community.   The student claimed that the rule as applied to him served no legitimate purpose.   The court, finding the rule to be related to protecting the integrity of off-campus programs and community support for them, ruled against the student.

Evaluation of academic progress of students has led to increasing amounts of litigation.   One specific issue is whether attendance can be a factor affecting final course grades.   The courts seem agreed that the answer is affirmative.   The Supreme Court of Connecticut issued an extensive opinion (Case No. 27) that responded to a wide array of constitutional and other arguments raised in precollegiate cases.[151]   The basic educational consideration that courts accept is that presence in class adds a dimension to subject matter learning and affords many less tangible benefits such as interactions with teachers and fellow students. The Court of Appeals of Michigan did not believe that the matter was of constitutional dimension, but said that assuming it was, the Connecticut case was persuasive.[152]

Broad discretion is conferred upon boards of education to assign pupils to specific schools, and the courts will not substitute their judg-

---

147. Sandlin v. Johnson, 643 F.2d 1027 (4 Cir.1981).

148. Bester v. Tuscaloosa City Bd. of Educ., 722 F.2d 1514 (11 Cir.1984).

149. Arundar v. DeKalb County School Dist., 620 F.2d 493 (5 Cir.1980).

150. Felton v. Fayette School Dist., 875 F.2d 191 (8 Cir.1989).

151. Campbell v. Board of Educ. of Town of New Milford, 193 Conn. 93, 475 A.2d 289 (1984). [Case No. 27]

152. Slocum v. Holton Bd. of Educ., 171 Mich.App. 92, 429 N.W.2d 607 (1988).

ment for that of the boards.[153] The fact that a certain school is more conveniently located for the pupil is not determinative of his right to attend that school.[154] In a typical situation parents in a Michigan school district wished to have their children continue to attend the school nearest their homes when a rearrangement of pupils was adopted by the board of education. The board gave as the reason for the transfer action overcrowded conditions at a high school and the need for additional classroom space to take care of the high school overflow. The additional classroom space was to be obtained in the elementary school from which plaintiffs' children were to be moved. The parents pointed out that the building housing the elementary school was particularly adapted for young children rather than for high school youth. The Supreme Court of Michigan, however, supported the board's position and indicated that the allegations merely presented alternative proposals for dealing with the space problem, and that, even assuming all of the facts to be true, the court could not substitute its judgment for that of the school board.[155]

Challenged before the highest court in New York state was a decision of a school board to revise district school attendance zones and to reassign some students.[156] No issue of race was involved. The main substantive objection was based on a consideration of safety and particularly on the point that, even though a certain proposed walkway had not been constructed by the village, the board did not change its determination to reassign the students. The court found that the board had a rational basis for its determination and that its action was not arbitrary. The fact that a citizens advisory committee had been convened and submitted a detailed report was evidence that the board had information, and the fact that the report was largely followed did not support the plaintiff's contention that the board relied solely upon it. Members of the board had personally visited classrooms, held safety discussions with certain village officials, walked the proposed routes, and made some modifications in the advisory committee's plans. The court stated that to require a quasi-judicial hearing every time the school board revised school attendance lines would pose serious problems for the administration of the schools.

With similar reasoning as to board powers to assign students to schools, the Supreme Court of Washington supported the Seattle school board's plan for busing to correct de facto segregation.[157] The court found the purpose a proper one and the deliberation of the board prior to adopting the plan sufficient. No hearing was necessary for this type of pupil assignment decision. The court flatly asserted that there was no substance to the parents' claim that they had a right to send their

153. State ex rel. Lewis v. Board of Educ. of Wilmington School Dist., 137 Ohio St. 145, 28 N.E.2d 496 (1940).

154. Bernstein v. Board of Educ. of Prince George's County, 245 Md. 464, 226 A.2d 243 (1967).

155. Hiers v. Brownell, 376 Mich. 225, 136 N.W.2d 10 (1965).

156. Older v. Board of Educ. of Union Free School Dist. No. 1, 27 N.Y.2d 333, 318 N.Y.S.2d 129, 266 N.E.2d 812 (1971). [Case No. 28]

157. Citizens Against Mandatory Bussing v. Palmason, 80 Wash.2d 445, 495 P.2d 657 (1972).

children to neighborhood schools. A decade later in a case arising from the Seattle situation the United States Supreme Court held to be unconstitutional a statute adopted by statewide referendum to prevent assignments of students to correct de facto segregation.[158] The key reasoning was that the state had continued to allow local boards to make all assignment decisions except those for a race-connected purpose, thus violating the equal protection clause.

In Indiana, when a school board decided to close an elementary school, some citizens brought suit claiming that the decision was arbitrary in that the board had acted without sufficient information and study. Stating that the burden is on the party seeking to upset an administrative order to show that there are no substantial facts to support the action taken, the court noted that the school board had acted after recommendations of a survey team of a teachers college, an oral report of an architect, and a report from the administrative building council.[159]

An example of success in overturning through the judiciary a school board decision to close a school is provided by a Nevada case. A county school board decided by a vote of four-to-three to close a small school and transport the students 40 miles to a larger school. A key claim by plaintiffs was that the information before the board that prompted the majority to vote for closing the school was erroneous. The board member who had presented the resolution to close the school had stated that his reason (a bona fide belief) was that the move would assist in meeting a financial crisis. But "his belief rested upon misinformation and was grossly in error." Further, a comparison of achievement test scores between the students of the two schools was not accurate and "of no value for educational comparison purposes." It was correct, however, that the per pupil cost was approximately twice as great at the smaller school. But the highest court of the state held that persuasive force could not be given this particular statistic.[160] The court said that the per pupil cost is always much greater at a rural school than at an urban one. To predicate the closing on this fact "would place the continued existence of rural high schools in extreme jeopardy." As to the point of educational quality, which the court said was the central issue, the board had been advised by an expert that the 80 mile per day busing would have a negative effect on students' achievement and reduce their participation in school activities. The only evidence produced by the board to support educational advantages of the closing was a study prepared by some consultants 15 years before the vote to close the school. Use of that study, the court concluded, was as "an excuse rather than a reason" for its action.

The general discretionary power of school boards to close individual schools does not permit closing useful buildings in a black neighborhood

---

158. Washington v. Seattle School Dist. No. 1, 458 U.S. 457, 102 S.Ct. 3187, 73 L.Ed.2d 896 (1982). [Case No. 136]

159. Kinzel v. Rettinger, 151 Ind.App. 119, 277 N.E.2d 913 (1972).

160. Bartlett v. Board of Trustees of White Pine County School Dist., 92 Nev. 347, 550 P.2d 416 (1976).

on the ground that whites would probably refuse to attend.[161] In the instant case the other schools in the formerly de jure segregated district would be forced to operate on split sessions.

Because school boards have the authority to assign pupils, and because no pupil has a vested right to attend a particular school, it does not follow that in all circumstances the assignment of a particular pupil to a particular school will not be examined by the courts. For example, a North Carolina school board attempted to transfer a high school girl who had taken Latin during her freshman year, was a member of the school band, and generally received high grades. She expected to go to a college which required for entrance a minimum of two units in two foreign languages or three units in Latin. The school to which the girl was assigned for her sophomore year had no course in Latin, nor did it have a band. A statute provided that after a certain procedure for assigning students was completed, reassignment could be made by the board after a hearing at which it was found that the best interests of the child would be served by the reassignment and that reassignment would not interfere with the proper administration of the school. When the board, after the hearing, refused to reassign the girl to the original school, the parents sought relief in the courts. The state supreme court, observing that the statute placed all emphasis on the welfare of the child and the effect upon the school to which reassignment was requested, ordered her reassigned.[162]

Judicially contested at an increasing rate have been testing procedures for grouping pupils in public schools, the allegation being that the procedures violate federal constitutional rights of certain students. The issue was first posed within the context of a broad assault on policies and practices in the Washington, D.C., public school system. The practices as a whole, it was successfully charged, unconstitutionally deprived black and poor public school children of their rights to equal educational opportunity with white and more affluent public school children. It seems that on the basis of examinations given relatively early in their school careers, children were assigned to curricular "tracks." The "tracks" were designed to prepare students for different types of jobs. The absence of compensatory education made it almost impossible for a child originally on one track to move to a higher one. The United States District Court found the concept of the system "undemocratic and discriminatory." Raising general questions about the tests as a measure of ability, the court barred any system of ability grouping which, through failure to include and implement the concept of compensatory education, failed in fact to bring the great majority of children into the mainstream of public education.[163] The United States Court of Appeals, D.C. Circuit,

161. Bell v. West Point Municipal Separate School Dist., 446 F.2d 1362 (5 Cir. 1971).

162. In re Reassignment of Hayes, 261 N.C. 616, 135 S.E.2d 645 (1964).

163. Hobson v. Hansen, 269 F.Supp. 401 (D.D.C.1967).

upheld the order requiring that the track system of pupil classification be abandoned.[164]

In several cases involving the elimination of dual school systems the courts have refused to permit groupings based on achievement test scores, the primary reason being that because white students in these systems performed better on such tests than black students, desegregation would be impeded if assignments were made on the basis of such tests.[165] But neither achievement nor ability grouping per se is unconstitutional.[166] They may be permissible even if their use causes some segregation in an otherwise unitary system when overall segregation will be remedied through better educational opportunities as a result of testing and grouping.[167] The courts remain alert to possible resegregation of classes or schools in recently desegregated systems.[168] Also permissible, even in desegregation situations, is the offering of elective high school courses that are especially attractive to college-bound students.[169]

To prevail on a disparate impact claim based on use of achievement tests for grouping, the plaintiff must first show by a preponderance of the evidence that the facially neutral practice does have a disproportional effect. The burden then shifts to the defendant school system to provide a substantial legitimate justification for its practice. The plaintiff then has an opportunity to show that the practice is a pretext for discrimination or to proffer an equally effective practice that results in less racial disproportionality in achieving the legitimate goal of the school system.[170]

The use of I.Q. tests as a primary determinant for placement in classes for the educable mentally retarded has been challenged with differing results on the claim of cultural bias. A federal District Court in San Francisco [171] and one in Chicago [172] came to opposite conclusions as to whether certain tests were culturally biased.

A classification of students as gifted is within the power of the state or a local board to create. Use of I.Q. tests as a criterion has been upheld as rational for assigning such students to special curricula.[173] If

164. Smuck v. Hobson, 408 F.2d 175 (D.C.Cir.1969).

165. United States v. Tunica County School Dist., 421 F.2d 1236 (5 Cir.1970); United States v. Gadsden County School Dist., 572 F.2d 1049 (5 Cir.1978).

166. McNeal v. Tate County School Dist., 508 F.2d 1017 (5 Cir.1975); Castaneda v. Pickard, 648 F.2d 989 (5 Cir.1981), 781 F.2d 456 (5 Cir.1986); Georgia State Conference of Branches of NAACP v. State of Georgia, 775 F.2d 1403 (11 Cir.1985).

167. United States v. Gadsden County School Dist. 572 F.2d 1049 (5 Cir.1978); Montgomery v. Starkville Mun. Separate School Dist., 854 F.2d 127 (5 Cir.1988).

168. Bester v. Tuscaloosa City Bd. of Educ., 722 F.2d 1514 (11 Cir.1984).

169. Andrews v. City of Monroe, 730 F.2d 1050 (5 Cir.1984).

170. Quarles v. Oxford Mun. Separate School Dist., 868 F.2d 750 (5 Cir.1989).

171. Larry P. v. Riles, 495 F.Supp. 926 (N.D.Cal.1979), aff. 793 F.2d 969 (9 Cir. 1984, amended 1986).

172. Parents in Action on Special Educ. (PASE) v. Hannon, 506 F.Supp. 831 (N.D.Ill.1980).

173. Student Roe v. Commonwealth of Pennsylvania, 638 F.Supp. 929 (E.D.Pa. 1986), aff. 813 F.2d 398 (3 Cir.1987), cert. den. 483 U.S. 1021, 107 S.Ct. 3265, 97 L.Ed.2d 764 (1987).

the program for the gifted can accommodate only a limited number of students, a lottery can be employed to select from those qualified.[174]

The Supreme Court of Illinois has held that records of standardized test scores of groups of students must be made available under the state freedom of information act provided that individually identifiable scores are not released.[175] The court said that scrambled scores grouped by such factors as school, grade, race, or sex are subject to disclosure. Although school authorities are not required to create new records upon request, to delete or mask material from an existing record is not creating a new record.

Sex discrimination in assignment of students is being charged with increasing frequency. Four cases are illustrative. The school district of Boston maintained a Boys Latin School and a Girls Latin School. The building housing the girls school was smaller. Admissions were by scores on a competitive examination, with the cut off score for each sex determined by the number of seats in the assigned building. The result was that some girls who were not admitted scored higher than some boys who were admitted. This situation was held to violate equal protection, and the school district was ordered to use the same standard for admission of boys and girls.[176]

The San Francisco school district maintained a prestigious academic high school to which admissions were based on grade point averages in junior high school. To get equal numbers of boys and girls in the school the district required girls to present higher averages than boys. The Ninth Circuit Court of Appeals ordered the practice stopped.[177] The court noted that the board presented no evidence that a balance of the sexes furthered the goal of better academic education. In this case the admissions procedures were attacked also on the ground that there was an underrepresentation in the school of black students, Spanish-American students, and students from low-income families. The court upheld the admission standards against these contentions.

In Philadelphia the school district maintained among its high schools one solely for boys (founded in 1836) and one solely for girls (founded in 1848 and made an academic school in 1893). Enrollment at either of these schools was voluntary, and standards at both were very high. Only these two academic high schools had such high scholastic requirements for admission. They were similar in size and in prestige. A female brought suit seeking admission to the male-only school. After reviewing the evidence as to substantial academic equality and testimony from some educators indicating that education in a separate-sex school was widely accepted as a reasonable approach with a long history and worldwide acceptance, the Court of Appeals, Third Circuit, found in

---

174. Bennett v. City School Dist. of New Rochelle, 114 A.D.2d 58, 497 N.Y.S.2d 72 (1985).

175. Bowie v. Evanston Community Consol. School Dist. No. 65, 128 Ill.2d 373, 131 Ill.Dec. 182, 538 N.E.2d 557 (1989).

176. Bray v. Lee, 337 F.Supp. 934 (D.Mass.1972).

177. Berkelman v. San Francisco Unified School Dist., 501 F.2d 1264 (9 Cir. 1974). [Case No. 29]

favor of the school district.[178]   This judgment was affirmed by an equally divided Supreme Court.

A school district in Massachusetts sought a legislative exception to an anti-discrimination statute for its "Girl Officers Regiment," members of which served as ushers at social events and as honor guards at civic ceremonies, marched in parades, and sponsored their own social events. The statute barred exclusion from or discrimination in any school sponsored activity on basis of race, color, sex, religion, or national origin. As permitted by Massachusetts law an advisory opinion was requested by the Senate of the Supreme Judicial Court of Massachusetts.   That court stated that the proposal would violate the state constitution's provision against sex discrimination because the purpose was to exclude male students in a coeducational public high school from participation in a program in order to perpetuate a sex-restrictive membership require- ment completely unrelated to any legitimate governmental purpose.[179] The court expressed doubts that any proper purpose could be shown should the legislation be enacted and then challenged in court.

Cases involving student honor societies have reached the courts. Grades and faculty recommendations are judicially acceptable criteria for membership.   That the latter are subjective does not constitute a basis for court involvement.   There is no constitutional right to be selected even if one meets the academic requirements.[180]   However, if a claim of use of an unconstitutional or statutorily barred standard is made, the courts may intervene.   The Third Circuit Court of Appeals examined the case of a female dismissed from the honor society after she became pregnant out-of-wedlock.[181]   The court said that an honor society that emphasized leadership and character could consider conduct of unmar- ried high school student members.   However, the case was remanded to the trial court to take testimony regarding whether the school authori- ties had not dismissed from the society a male who had fathered a child out-of-wedlock.   The testimony had been excluded and could be critical in determining whether there had been sex discrimination.

Fees

The great majority of state constitutions provide that the legislature shall establish a system of "free" public schools.   Whether under such a provision schools can charge any type of fee has been given much judicial attention.

It has been held that school pupils may not be charged a registration fee in order to enable the school to be maintained for the full school

---

178. Vorchheimer v. School Dist. of Philadelphia, 532 F.2d 880 (3 Cir.1976), aff. 430 U.S. 703, 97 S.Ct. 1671, 51 L.Ed.2d 750 (1977).

179. Opinion of the Justices to the Sen- ate, 373 Mass. 883, 366 N.E.2d 733 (1977).

180. Karntein v. Pewaukee School Bd., 557 F.Supp. 565 (E.D.Wis.1983).

term.[182] The courts have also said that a school district may not, by indirection violate the spirit of the constitutional provision that the state shall maintain a system of free public schools. The charging of athletic, library, literary, and other such fees as a condition to being admitted to school has been declared violative of the constitutional provision that schools shall be free.[183] The court in the case sustaining the proposition just stated indicated that the school trustees had the authority to charge the students for the use of the facilities provided. It distinguished between the right to make the special charges complained of, and the right to deny pupils admission to the school if the charges were not paid. The distinction between curricular and extracurricular activities has been perpetuated and amplified in modern cases.

That needy children must be provided textbooks for instruction covered by the state constitutional mandate seems settled.[184] State courts are in disagreement, however, on the question whether free textbooks must be furnished to all students.

The leading case for one view was decided by the Supreme Court of Idaho.[185] That court found textbooks to be necessary elements of the school's activity, to represent a fixed expense peculiar to education, and to be outside the choice of the student as to quality or quantity. The test adopted in Idaho for items to be furnished free—"necessary elements of any school's activity"—was adopted a few months later by the Supreme Court of Michigan.[186]

Differing in approach and result, the Supreme Court of Illinois examined the meaning of "free schools" as used at the state constitutional convention of 1869–70.[187] It emphasized that in determining the intention and purpose of a constitutional provision courts should look to the natural and popular meaning of language as it was understood at the time the constitution was adopted. It determined that free books for all were not included in the concept. It noted that there was no allegation that the plaintiff could not afford to pay the rental, in which circumstance books would be furnished free under a statute. It also observed that the Idaho decision was given without any citation of authority and that the Michigan decision was decided with only the Idaho decision as authority. Subsequently upheld were charges for clean towels where the use of the service was optional,[188] a mandatory fee for a wide variety of

181. Pfeiffer v. Marion Center Area School Dist., 917 F.2d 779 (3 Cir.1990).

182. Dowell v. School Dist. No. 1, Boone County, 220 Ark. 828, 250 S.W.2d 127 (1952).

183. Morris v. Vandiver, 164 Miss. 476, 145 So. 228 (1933).

184. For a narrow interpretation of constitutional coverage, see Carpio v. Tucson High School Dist. No. 1 of Pima County, 111 Ariz. 127, 524 P.2d 948 (1974), cert. den. 420 U.S. 982, 95 S.Ct. 1412, 43 L.Ed.2d 664 (1975).

185. Paulson v. Minidoka County School Dist. No. 331, 93 Idaho 469, 463 P.2d 935 (1970). [Case No. 30]

186. Bond v. Public Schools of Ann Arbor School Dist., 383 Mich. 693, 178 N.W.2d 484 (1970).

187. Hamer v. Board of Educ. of School Dist. No. 109, 47 Ill.2d 480, 265 N.E.2d 616 (1970).

188. Hamer v. Board of Educ. of School Dist. No. 109, Lake County, 9 Ill.App.3d 663, 292 N.E.2d 569 (1973).

supplies and materials that would be consumed by or retained by the student,[189] and a lunchroom supervision fee for students who lived near the school but elected to eat their lunches in the school lunchroom.[190]

In 1978 the Supreme Court of North Dakota examined and summarized the holdings of the 11 appellate state courts that had adjudicated questions of fees in public schools over the preceding eight years.[191] The court had been asked to decide whether fees for textbooks could be charged. It concluded that the courts had consistently construed language related to "tuition-free" to mean that no fee may be charged for school attendance but that a fee may be charged for textbooks. A majority of courts construed language related to "free public schools" to contemplate furnishing textbooks at no charge, at least in elementary schools. Exceptions to the latter view relied upon extrinsic material such as history as well as the language itself. The present court found the state constitutional debates in North Dakota to be of no help in determining the intent of the framers of the constitution as to the meaning of the words "uniform system of free public schools throughout the state." The court then observed the different wording used in the constitutions of the three other states which gained statehood under the Enabling Act covering North Dakota. It ultimately concluded that the term "free public schools" did include textbooks (but only in the elementary schools as that level alone was covered by the suit). The court made no comment about fees for other items.

Two years later the Supreme Court of North Carolina upheld the charging of "modest, reasonable fees" for the purchase of supplementary supplies and materials for use by or on behalf of students whose parents are "financially able to pay." [192] The court required that local boards give notice of procedures by which parents may confidentially apply for waivers or reductions of the fees.

The Supreme Court of Montana has established the test that fees may not be charged in connection with those activities that are "reasonably related to a recognized academic and educational goal of the particular school system." [193] The court thought this formulation provided for flexibility in that the school district may define its goals and those courses and activities which will carry credit toward graduation and the individual student can pursue courses within the framework without regard to financial ability.

The question of fees for course offerings was addressed by the Supreme Court of New Mexico, which held that courses required of every student must be without charge but that reasonable fees were permitted

189. Beck v. Board of Educ. of Harlem Consolidated School Dist. No. 122, 63 Ill.2d 10, 344 N.E.2d 440 (1976).

190. Ambroiggio v. Board of Educ. of School Dist. No. 44, 101 Ill.App.3d 187, 56 Ill.Dec. 622, 427 N.E.2d 1027 (1981).

191. Cardiff v. Bismarck Public School Dist., 263 N.W.2d 105 (N.D.1978).

192. Sneed v. Greensboro City Bd. of Educ., 299 N.C. 609, 264 S.E.2d 106 (1980).

193. Granger v. Cascade County School Dist. No. 1, 159 Mont. 516, 499 P.2d 780 (1972).

for "elective" courses.[194] The court added the judicial pronouncement that the state board of education "shall define what are 'required' or 'elective' courses."

One item at issue in the case was whether fees could be charged for driver education. The trial court had upheld the charge. The higher court affirmed, adding that the state board of education could declare the course "required." The Supreme Judicial Court of Massachusetts took a contrary view, holding that where driver education is offered it had to be completely free of charge.[195] The school board had attempted to provide free only classroom instruction, with on-the-road training offered separately outside of regular school hours for a fee.

Appellate courts in California and South Carolina have reached differing results on whether a summer program offered by a school board must be free of charge. The former held that the board had no power to charge a fee unless such was authorized by the legislature.[196] The latter found the summer program not to be encompassed by the state constitutional provision for free public schools even though courses completed in the summer could be credited toward graduation.[197]

The Supreme Court of California in 1984 held that "the imposition of fees for educational activities offered by public high school districts violates the free school guarantee" of the California constitution.[198] The court said that any *educational* activity offered must be free to all, regardless of its characterization as noncredit or extracurricular. In 1992, however, the court held that fees for transporting children to school could be charged.[199] A statute authorizing such charges (except for handicapped or indigent children) had been challenged on its face. The court said that "transportation is not an essential element of school activity."

Statutes authorizing specific fees are to be strictly construed, according to the Supreme Court of Ohio. That court invalidated as not covered by the phrase "any materials used in a course of instruction" a fee assessed for paper products, copier materials, and "other necessary consumable educational supply items which directly affect all students in their classrooms/buildings."[200]

Interscholastic Activities

It has been noted that boards of education can join state or regional associations for interscholastic activities and can agree to be bound by

194. Norton v. Board of Educ. of School Dist. No. 16, Hobbs Municipal Schools, 89 N.M. 470, 553 P.2d 1277 (1976).

195. Johnson v. School Committee of Brockton, 371 Mass. 896, 358 N.E.2d 820 (1977).

196. California Teachers Ass'n v. Board of Educ. of Glendale, 109 Cal.App.3d 738, 167 Cal.Rptr. 429 (1980).

197. Washington v. Salisbury, 279 S.C. 306, 306 S.E.2d 600 (1983).

198. Hartzell v. Connell, 35 Cal.3d 899, 201 Cal.Rptr. 601, 679 P.2d 35 (1984).

199. Arcadia Unified School Dist. v. State Dept. of Educ., 2 Cal.4th 251, 5 Cal. Rptr.2d 545, 825 P.2d 438 (1992).

200. Association for the Defense of Washington Local School Dist. v. Kiger, 42 Ohio St.3d 116, 537 N.E.2d 1292 (1989).

the rules of the associations. Even though technically the associations may be voluntary, privately governed bodies, courts generally do not apply the law of such associations to their actions. Rather, because most associations are so intertwined with the state, courts consider an association action to be "state action" [201] (although some precollegiate interscholastic associations that include private schools may not technically be operating "under the color of state law" for federal constitutional purposes).[202] Thus, courts will inquire into matters such as equal protection and due process, which would not be applicable to private associations. In an operational sense the acts of such bodies are akin to acts of state or local educational authorities and subject to the same legal parameters.

There seems to be general agreement that interscholastic associations can enforce rules against individual schools or school districts. The Supreme Court of Ohio declined to interfere in the suspension from competition of a school district that had violated a rule governing recruitment of football players, even though the offending district could not carry out its contract to play football with certain other high schools.[203] The contracts, it said, were made with full knowledge of, and subject to, the rules of the association.

The Supreme Court of Pennsylvania, citing this case, refused relief where a high school was placed on probation by the state interscholastic athletic association because of incidents of fighting among spectators following a football game.[204] The Third Circuit Court of Appeals rejected a claim by a student that it was unconstitutional to deprive him of opportunity to play in postseason games because his team had been suspended for rules violations.[205]

The association rules, however, must meet constitutional standards both on their face and as applied. Thus, a rule which operated to disadvantage small-school debating teams in reaching the national tournament did not pass constitutional muster.[206] A rule valid on its face as being designed for the legitimate end of minimizing athletic recruitment and school "jumping" was struck down as unreasonably applied to a student who had moved from his parents' home to become a ward of his brother because of "demoralizing" conditions at home.[207] Also, of course, if a rule regulating eligibility of students who transfer schools

201. Clark v. Arizona Interscholastic Ass'n, 695 F.2d 1126 (9 Cir.1982), cert. den. 464 U.S. 818, 104 S.Ct. 79, 78 L.Ed.2d 90 (1983). See Crane v. Indiana High School Athletic Ass'n, 975 F.2d 1315 (7 Cir.1992).

202. Burrows v. Ohio High School Athletic Ass'n, 891 F.2d 122 (6 Cir.1989). See also National Collegiate Athletic Ass'n v. Tarkanian, 488 U.S. 179, 109 S.Ct. 454, 102 L.Ed.2d 469 (1988).

203. State ex rel. Ohio High School Athletic Ass'n v. Judges of Court of Common Pleas of Stark County, 173 Ohio St. 239, 181 N.E.2d 261 (1962).

204. School Dist. of Harrisburg v. Pennsylvania Interscholastic Athletic Ass'n, 453 Pa. 495, 309 A.2d 353 (1973).

205. Moreland v. Western Pennsylvania Interscholastic Athletic League, 572 F.2d 121 (3 Cir.1978).

206. Baltic Independent School Dist. v. South Dakota High School Activities Ass'n, 362 F.Supp. 780 (D.S.D.1973).

207. Sturrup v. Mahan, 261 Ind. 463, 305 N.E.2d 877 (1974).

will add to the reluctance to transfer of black students in formerly segregated school districts, it will be struck down as applied.[208]

It seems settled that participation in interscholastic activities is not per se a constitutionally protected civil right. Only where a regulation denies a constitutionally protected right or makes a classification on a constitutionally suspect basis will federal courts intervene. The Tenth Circuit Court of Appeals has said that although a public education is an interest constitutionally protected, as the Supreme Court said expressly in Goss (Case No. 127), there is no constitutional protection for each component of the "educational process."[209] This view applies to procedures for enforcing rules as well as to the rules themselves.[210]

There is a strong presumption in favor of rules designed to protect the educational value and integrity of interscholastic sports and the health and welfare of the student participants. Although some lower courts have set aside rules or applications that the judges found unreasonable, both state and federal appellate courts have upheld virtually all such rules that could possibly be supported on any rational basis. The number of cases has become very substantial, and the arguments have become somewhat attenuated.

Upheld against claims of burdens on right to travel and freedom of family association was a rule requiring in essence that a student be a resident of the school district for a year before participating in interscholastic events.[211] Sustained against claims of infringement of parent rights was a rule suspending for one year thereafter the eligibility of a student who attended a special athletic training camp designed for football or basketball.[212] The Supreme Court of Florida supported a rule for post-season play that reduced each team's player limit below that allowed for regular season play.[213] The Supreme Court of New Hampshire refused to overrule a decision of the athletic association that a student not be allowed to run in a special event because he did not qualify in the preliminary, the student having claimed that he did not qualify because he had been fouled.[214] The last three cases were reversals of lower court decisions.

There is no constitutional requirement that rules provide for exceptions. As long as a rule is reasonable it is not the function of the courts to rewrite or administer it so as to care for exceptions. This view was expressed by the Supreme Court of North Dakota in a case in which no

208. Rogers v. Board of Educ., 281 F.Supp. 39 (E.D.Ark.1968).

209. Albach v. Odle, 531 F.2d 983 (10 Cir.1976). [Case No. 31]

210. Hamilton v. Tennessee Secondary School Athletic Ass'n, 552 F.2d 681 (6 Cir. 1976). See also Braesch v. DePasquale, 200 Neb. 726, 265 N.W.2d 842 (1978). [Case No. 122]

211. Niles v. University Interscholastic League, 715 F.2d 1027 (5 Cir.1983), cert. den. 465 U.S. 1028, 104 S.Ct. 1289, 79 L.Ed.2d 691 (1984).

212. Kite v. Marshall, 661 F.2d 1027 (5 Cir.1981), cert. den. 457 U.S. 1120, 102 S.Ct. 2934, 73 L.Ed.2d 1333 (1982). [Case No. 32]

213. The Florida High School Activities Ass'n, Inc. v. Thomas, 434 So.2d 306 (Fla. 1983).

214. Snow v. New Hampshire Interscholastic Athletic Ass'n, 122 N.H. 735, 449 A.2d 1223 (1982).

exception to transfer rules was made for those changing schools primarily for academic reasons.[215] Although commenting that "the rule appears harsh in this case," the Supreme Court of Georgia upheld a rule specifying that eligibility would be for only eight consecutive semesters or four consecutive years from date of first entrance into ninth grade.[216] The plaintiff had dropped out of school for a little over a year because he had been forced to work due to his mother's illness.

Academic requirements for eligibility to participate in extracurricular activities have been uniformly upheld. This has been true regardless of the legal source of the regulation—the legislature,[217] the state board of education,[218] or a local board of education.[219] Any or all extracurricular activities can be covered.[220]

Many legal attacks on rules have been based on charges of sex discrimination. A leading holding that eligibility to participate in a noncontact sport cannot be based on sex is one of the United States Court of Appeals, Eighth Circuit. The court ruled that where there were no teams for females in tennis, skiing, and running, and where females were qualified to compete with males in those noncontact sports, a rule of the state interscholastic athletic league barring mixed athletics was unenforceable.[221] The first appellate court not to limit to noncontact sports its holding in favor of women plaintiffs was the Commonwealth Court of Pennsylvania. It declared unconstitutional on its face a bylaw of the state interscholastic athletic association barring girls from competing or practicing with boys in any athletic activity.[222] The equal rights amendment to the state constitution was cited. Referring to this case and a similar provision in the Washington Constitution, that state's highest court struck down sex barriers to contact sports.[223]

The state equal rights amendment was held by the highest court of Massachusetts to require overturning the blanket barring of boys from girls teams.[224] The court applied a strict scrutiny standard. But in Rhode Island, where there was no equal rights amendment, that state's highest court said that a lower standard of scrutiny should be applied to determine whether a similar state association rule violated the state constitution.[225] In remanding the case the court observed that promotion of safety and preservation of interscholastic competition for both boys and girls constituted important government interests.

215. Crandall v. North Dakota High School Activities Ass'n, 261 N.W.2d 921 (N.D.1978).

216. Smith v. Crim, 240 Ga. 390, 240 S.E.2d 884 (1977).

217. Spring Branch I.S.D. v. Stamos, 695 S.W.2d 556 (Tex.1985). [Case No. 33]

218. Bailey v. Truby, 174 W.Va. 8, 321 S.E.2d 302 (1984).

219. Thompson v. Fayette County Public Schools, 786 S.W.2d 879 (Ky.App.1990).

220. State ex rel. Bartmess v. Board of Trustees of School Dist. No. 1, 223 Mont. 269, 726 P.2d 801 (1986).

221. Brenden v. Independent School Dist. 742, 477 F.2d 1292 (8 Cir.1973).

222. Commonwealth by Packel v. Pennsylvania Interscholastic Athletic Ass'n, 18 Pa.Cmwlth. 45, 334 A.2d 839 (1975).

223. Darrin v. Gould, 85 Wash.2d 859, 540 P.2d 882 (1975).

224. Attorney General v. Massachusetts Interscholastic Athletic Ass'n, 378 Mass. 342, 393 N.E.2d 284 (1979).

225. Kleczek v. Rhode Island Interscholastic League, Inc., 612 A.2d 734 (R.I.1992).

Where there is no girls team in a sport that is offered for boys only, the school authorities have three choices: discontinue the sport; field separate teams by sex (with "substantial equality in funding, coaching, officiating and opportunity to play"); permit both sexes to compete for positions on the same team.[226] The sport in the case setting forth the preceding was soccer. Citing this case with approval, another federal District Court held that exclusion of females from all contact sports in order to protect them from an unreasonable risk of injury is not substantially related to an important governmental objective in the context of the Fourteenth Amendment as applied to gender-based classifications.[227] The court suggested separate female teams in contact sports as an alternative.[228] Where only one girl expressed a desire to play football, a different federal District Court ordered that she be allowed to compete for team membership.[229] That court cited a 1982 Supreme Court decision requiring the admission of a qualified male to a public college's school of nursing.[230] The Supreme Court had found that the female-only policy was not defensible on the asserted ground that it aided in compensating for discrimination against women. Women did not suffer under the classification. Instead the classification reinforced a gender stereotype regarding the profession of nursing, and a practice of allowing males to attend classes as auditors undermined any claim of adverse effect on women in the program.

If a school has two basketball teams, however, it appears not necessary to allow a particular girl to try out for the boys team.[231] There is disagreement among the courts on the issue of whether a school may maintain only a female volleyball team and exclude males therefrom.[232] The major competing interests are those of males to try out for the only team in a specific sport and of females to have equal overall opportunities to participate in athletics.

Title IX and implementing regulations must be considered in relation to nondiscrimination in athletic activities on the basis of sex. Constitutional questions will not be treated by courts if Title IX validly covers a matter.[233] The gender equity goal of Title IX applies to reduction in options due to financial considerations as well as to addition

---

226. Hoover v. Meiklejohn, 430 F.Supp. 164 (D.Colo.1977).

227. Leffel v. Wisconsin Interscholastic Athletic Ass'n, 444 F.Supp. 1117 (E.D.Wis. 1978).

228. This alternative for contact sports is acceptable under federal regulations for a district receiving federal funds under Title IX of the Education Amendments of 1972. 45 CFR 86.41(b).

229. Force v. Pierce City R–VI School Dist., 570 F.Supp. 1020 (W.D.Mo.1983).

230. Mississippi Univ. for Women v. Hogan, 458 U.S. 718, 102 S.Ct. 3331, 73 L.Ed.2d 1090 (1982).

231. O'Connor v. Board of Educ. of School Dist. No. 23, 645 F.2d 578 (7 Cir. 1981), cert. den. 454 U.S. 1084, 102 S.Ct. 641, 70 L.Ed.2d 619 (1981), on remand 545 F.Supp. 376 (N.D.Ill.1982).

232. Compare Gomes v. Rhode Island Interscholastic League, 469 F.Supp. 659 (D.R.I.1979), vac. as moot 604 F.2d 733 (1 Cir.1979), and Clark v. Arizona Interscholastic Ass'n, 695 F.2d 1126 (9 Cir.1982), cert. den. 464 U.S. 818, 104 S.Ct. 79, 78 L.Ed.2d 90 (1983).

233. Williams v. School Dist. of Bethlehem, Pa., 998 F.2d 168 (3 Cir.1993), cert. den. __ U.S. __, 114 S.Ct. 689, 126 L.Ed.2d 656 (1994).

of opportunities for the underrepresented sex.[234]

The Appellate Court of Illinois rejected a claim that, because a school board required as a prerequisite to participation in the school's interscholastic athletic program the payment of a fee for a premium on an insurance policy covering medical treatment for injuries sustained in the athletic program, the board had assumed a duty to provide protection adequate to cover the injury suffered by the plaintiff student (an alleged permanent disability set at one million dollars in the complaint).[235] The court observed that legislation permitted, rather than required, such an arrangement for insurance and that there was no allegation that the student had been misled as to coverage. There was no obligation on the board to explain, without request, the meaning of the policy to the senior-class student.

Interest in interscholastic games has led some broadcasting stations to desire to broadcast them. When boards have sought to control the broadcasting of school athletic events, it has been claimed that the power did not exist in the absence of a specific statute. The courts, however, have taken the opposite view. It has been judicially stated that the right to broadcast a description of school athletic events is a valuable property right which boards have the power to exercise and protect.[236]

School Building Sites and Standards

Provided that any statutory limitations or procedures are observed, the implied power of local boards of education to select and purchase sites on which school buildings are to be placed is well settled. Taxpayer challenges to board actions in regard to locations of buildings, however, are frequently litigated. The general charge is that a school board has abused its discretion. Illustrative is a case decided by the Supreme Court of Errors of Connecticut.[237] There the taxpayers did not claim that action of the board was in any way tainted by fraud or corruption or that it was not legal in the sense that it was procedurally irregular. The only contention was that the action should be enjoined because it constituted a gross abuse of discretionary power. The taxpayers sought to require a reexamination of the decision more fully before it was implemented. The court refused to consider the arguments that other sites were more desirable, and commented that it is not for the courts to say how many alternative methods of accomplishing a desired result must be investigated or considered before proper authorities may decide on a particular method of proceeding. The court recognized that at some point a definite decision had to be made. The board's discretionary decision was upheld.

234. Cohen v. Brown Univ., 991 F.2d 888 (1 Cir.1993).

235. Friederich v. Board of Educ. of Community Unit School Dist. No. 304, Carroll County, 59 Ill.App.3d 79, 16 Ill.Dec. 510, 375 N.E.2d 141 (1978).

236. Southwestern Broadcasting Co. v. Oil Center Broadcasting Co., 210 S.W.2d 230 (Tex.Civ.App.1947); Colorado High School Activities Ass'n v. Uncompahgre Broadcasting Co., 134 Colo. 131, 300 P.2d 968 (1956).

237. McAdam v. Sheldon, 153 Conn. 278, 216 A.2d 193 (1965).

A charge of abuse of discretion heard by the Supreme Court of Indiana involved the complaint that board members had been unduly influenced by recommendations following a survey of the building situation by a group of experts from a university.[238] One or more of the board members who were originally opposed to the establishment of a single senior high school apparently became convinced after the survey that a recommendation to that effect should be followed. The court commented favorably on the board's seeking the services of the university and sustained the action of the board.

The Supreme Court of Nebraska declined to enjoin a school board's selecting a site different from the one on which it was indicated the school would be built when the bond issue to finance it passed.[239] A survey of the land showed there would be serious drainage problems. The board wrote to the district's residents about preferences for another site and selected the one favored by a majority of respondents.

In New Mexico, where recall of school board members was constitutionally permitted on grounds of malfeasance or misfeasance in office or violation of the oath of office, the state's highest court halted a recall election based on a choice of site for a new high school.[240] The site had a number of disadvantages that were listed in the petition. The court, however, held that malfeasance in connection with recall must evince an improper or corrupt motive.

Administrative agencies which have fiscal relationships with school authorities cannot dispute the location of a school building in the absence of specific authority to do so. Authority invested in nonschool bodies for general fiscal approval of school expenditures does not extend to location of buildings.[241]

The Commonwealth Court of Pennsylvania decided a case in which the question was whether city officials could withhold approval under a zoning code for an addition to a school because they believed the school board was overbuilding.[242] The school board complied with all zoning and building requirements except obtaining conditional use approval. The court ordered the approval granted. It said that a municipality may not interfere with a school board's power to locate a school facility anywhere in the district. Style of building, size of building, assignment patterns, and transportation arrangements are beyond the power of the municipality to regulate. The court added, however, that it was making part of its holding the requirement that school districts make properly documented applications for permits as required of all other developers in the municipality.

238. Cooper v. Huntington County Community School Corp., 249 Ind. 653, 232 N.E.2d 887 (1968).

239. Christian v. Geis, 193 Neb. 146, 225 N.W.2d 868 (1975).

240. CAPS v. Board Members, 113 N.M. 729, 832 P.2d 790 (1992).

241. Mosier v. J.C. Thompson, 216 Tenn. 655, 393 S.W.2d 734 (1965).

242. School Dist. of Pittsburgh v. City of Pittsburgh, 23 Pa.Cmwlth. 405, 352 A.2d 223 (1976).

To what extent, if any, school boards must comply with local building and zoning codes varies from state to state. The considerations which are crucial in deciding whether a school district is bound by a municipal building code have been discussed by the Supreme Court of Washington.[243] The major point is whether the state, by legislation and delegation to administrative agencies, has preempted the field of regulating school construction. This would be the situation if there were detailed and comprehensive standards for school construction and state governmental machinery for their enforcement by an agency other than the city in which a school district lies. In the present case the court found that the state had not deprived the municipality of jurisdiction over certain aspects of school construction although it could do so. The court said that fixing minimum offsets for streets, alleys, and front, side and back yards would fit more relevantly into a city building code than into the general rules for the operation and maintenance of a high school. It found illusory the contention that making a school conform to the municipal building code in such regards would lead ultimately to permitting municipalities to interfere with the operation, management, and control of the public schools. A similar decision by the Supreme Court of Pennsylvania held that a school board must comply with a local zoning ordinance requiring provision for off street parking when a new building was erected.[244] By contrast an appellate court in New Jersey held that a school board is not subject to municipal regulations covering such matters as height, setbacks, and parking.[245]

Rather than dealing with specific items of codes, the Supreme Court of Kansas has held that the existence of comprehensive state building codes for school buildings absolutely precludes local municipalities from enforcing local building codes "which are or may be" in conflict therewith.[246] The court urged cooperation between educational and municipal authorities and indicated that it might intervene in a concrete dispute where there was evidence of exercise of the state's power "to arbitrarily override all important legitimate local interests." This phraseology was quoted from a decision of the Supreme Court of New Jersey that had invalidated a local zoning regulation having the effect of blocking the erection of dormitories for married students attending the state university.[247]

Where board selection of a site is subject to voter approval in a referendum, the question of how much information the board must voluntarily give the public arises. Indicted in New Jersey for alleged failure to disclose conditions of subsurface soil were the members of a school board, an architect, and a school building consultant. The

243. Edmonds School Dist. No. 15 v. City of Mountlake Terrace, 77 Wash.2d 609, 465 P.2d 177 (1970).

244. School Dist. of Philadelphia v. Zoning Bd. of Adjustment, 417 Pa. 277, 207 A.2d 864 (1965).

245. Murnick v. Board of Educ. of City of Asbury Park, 235 N.J.Super. 225, 561 A.2d 1193 (1989).

246. State ex rel. Schneider v. City of Kansas City, 228 Kan. 25, 612 P.2d 578 (1980).

247. Rutgers, State Univ. v. Piluso, 60 N.J. 142, 286 A.2d 697 (1972).

indictment was dismissed by the court, which found that the misconduct in office charge was not supported by sufficient specifics.[248] No corrupt activity was charged. The court found that the board had made a policy decision to build the school after it considered the facts and had no legal duty to give all details to the public.

The power to take private property for public use under certain conditions is known as eminent domain or condemnation. The power resides in the state, and municipal corporations and school districts do not possess it unless it is provided by statute. Usually the statutes specify procedures to be followed. Clear need for the land must always be shown, and just compensation must be awarded the owner. The latter is in accordance with a specific provision in the Fifth Amendment. The question of just compensation is a judicial one.

[Case No. 20] Power of Board to Change Policy—Promissory Estoppel

MICHIE v. BOARD OF TRUSTEES

Supreme Court of Wyoming, 1993.
847 P.2d 1006.

MACY, CHIEF JUSTICE.

* * *

Dr. Michie served as an elected member of the Board of Trustees from 1981 to December 1988. In the fall of 1984, the Board of Trustees requested the school superintendent to investigate whether the board members could legally participate in the school district's insurance plan. The superintendent contacted the school attorney for a legal opinion.

At a Board of Trustees meeting held on October 11, 1984, the school attorney opined that the board members could participate in the insurance plan without violating [a Wyoming statute barring compensation for school trustees] as long as each participant paid his own premium. The superintendent also informed the board members that participation in the insurance plan would not be limited to their terms on the Board of Trustees. The minutes reflect that the Board of Trustees took the following action:

> Smith then moved to allow board members to be put on the group insurance program at their own expense. Motion seconded by Michie and carried.

Dr. Michie canceled his family's health insurance policy shortly after the aforestated action was taken and enrolled under the school district's insurance plan effective December 1, 1984. John Smith enrolled sometime later.

Dr. Michie and Mr. Smith did not serve on the Board of Trustees after 1988. On March 23, 1989, the then-elected Board of Trustees

---

248. State v. Lally, 80 N.J.Super. 502, 194 A.2d 252 (1963).

voted unanimously to disallow participation by all board members, past or present, in the school district's insurance plan.   * * *

The Michies filed a complaint against the Board of Trustees in the United States District Court for the District of Wyoming on April 3, 1991.   * * *

* * *

The federal district court ruled in its summary judgment order that the Michies could not maintain their 42 U.S.C. § 1983 action because they possessed no property right, under either contract law or equity, to continue to participate in the school district's insurance plan. The court made this ruling upon determining: (1) that the 1989 Board of Trustees effectively voided the alleged contract because the Michies failed to demonstrate that it was either "reasonably necessary or of a definable advantage" to the school district; and (2) that equitable remedies, being discretionary in nature, do not give rise to legal rights cognizable under 42 U.S.C. § 1983. The court accordingly granted a summary judgment in favor of the Board of Trustees on the Michies' breach-of-contract and 42 U.S.C. § 1983 claims. It also dismissed the Michies' promissory estoppel * * * [claim], without prejudice, for lack of subject matter jurisdiction.

The Michies renewed their promissory estoppel claim against the Board of Trustees by filing a complaint in state district court on January 13, 1992.   * * *

The Michies concede on appeal that the federal district court determined that they did not have an enforceable contract with the school district because any contract which might have existed was effectively voided by the 1989 Board of Trustees. They contend, however, that the state district court erred as a matter of law by granting a summary judgment on their promissory estoppel claim, apparently on this basis. The Michies argue that an enforceable contractual obligation is not an element of a promissory estoppel claim.

We agree that a claim for promissory estoppel is not dependent upon the existence of a promise which is enforceable under traditional contract principles. By definition, promissory estoppel is an equitable remedy for detrimental reliance upon a promise which does not rise to the level of a formal contract. As explained in Restatement (Second) of Contracts § 90(1) (1981):

> A promise which the promisor should reasonably expect to induce action or forbearance on the part of the promisee or a third person and which does induce such action or forbearance is binding if injustice can be avoided only by enforcement of the promise. The remedy granted for breach may be limited as justice requires.

This Court has recognized that promissory estoppel may be used as an affirmative cause of action. The elements which must be proved in a promissory estoppel action are:

"(1) a clear and definite agreement; (2) proof that the party urging the doctrine acted to its detriment in reasonable reliance on the agreement; and (3) a finding that the equities support the enforcement of the agreement."

Whether elements one and two exist are questions for the finder of fact. Whether element three is satisfied is decided as a matter of law by the court.

In the instant case, the Michies contend that they presented evidence to satisfy each promissory estoppel element. We agree, however, with the state district court that the Michies failed to demonstrate "the existence of a contract or enforceable promise." * * * [W]e understand the court's summary judgment order to be founded upon simple deductive reasoning: If it is against public policy to enforce an extended-term governmental contract, it is also against public policy to enforce an extended-term governmental promise embodied in the contract.

In [a prior case] this Court directly addressed the issue of whether extended-term governmental contracts are voidable as a matter of public policy. * * * On appeal, this Court stated:

[A]n agreement extending beyond the term of the contracting authority * * * may be voidable by the government or void upon attack by a third party if, under the facts and circumstances, the agreement is not reasonably necessary or of a definable advantage to the city or governmental body. The issue when raised is decided as a matter of law, and the burden of evidence of the actual facts defining convenience and necessity devolve either upon the non-governmental contracting party when attacked by the government or upon the third party who separately might attack the validity of the contract.

* * *

The public policy underlying the rule * * * is straightforward: A governing body should not be able to deprive its successor in interest of discretion to act for the public good. We believe that this policy applies not only to extended-term governmental contracts but also to extended-term governmental promises which do not constitute formal contracts. Accordingly, both are voidable absent a showing of reasonable necessity or definable advantage. The Michies were not able to satisfy this requirement in federal court and are collaterally estopped from attempting to do so now. The equities of this case do not support the application of the doctrine of promissory estoppel against the Board of Trustees. The Board of Trustees was entitled to a summary judgment as a matter of law.

Affirmed.

Notes

1. This case illustrates well the interrelations of federal and state courts.

2. Although a board of education as a corporate body is not affected by changes in membership, successor boards (with new members or with old

members who change their minds) are not powerless to change course. Observe the court's articulation of the common-law principle as it relates to contracts.

3. Do you agree with the school board attorney's initial advice that the arrangement would not violate the statutory provision that board members "shall serve without compensation"?

4. The Court of Appeals of Ohio held that even though the superintendent, based on conversations with individual board members, promised that two nonresident students would be able to attend the schools of the district upon payment of tuition until their graduation, the arrangement was unenforceable. Only the board could enter into a binding contract. The fact that the girls attended for four years did not create a basis for promissory estoppel against the board. Walker v. Lockland City School Dist. Bd. of Educ., 69 Ohio App.2d 27, 429 N.E.2d 1179 (1980).

[Case No. 21] Power of Board to Offer Retirement Incentive

FAIR LAWN EDUC. ASS'N v. FAIR LAWN BD. OF EDUC.

Supreme Court of New Jersey, 1979.
79 N.J. 574, 401 A.2d 681.

PASHMAN, J. In this case we are called upon to assess the validity of an Early Retirement Remuneration Plan (ERR) agreed to by the Fair Lawn Board of Education (Board) and the Fair Lawn Education Association (Association)—the majority representative of the Board's teaching employees. For the reasons to be given below, we conclude that the particular plan here at issue: (1) lacks statutory authorization; (2) contravenes this Court's holdings in [2 cases]; and (3) is preempted by the comprehensive statutory scheme relating to the operation of retirement benefits. Consequently, that plan cannot be implemented.

On July 1, 1976, the Association and the Board entered into a collective agreement covering the 1976–1977 and 1977–1978 school years. Article VI of that agreement set forth the provisions of the ERR plan whose legality is here in dispute. Under the terms of the contract, teachers between the ages of 55 and 64 who retired prior to September 1, 1977 would receive an additional payment in the amount of $6,000 upon leaving the Board's employ. Instructors retiring after the start of the 1977–1978 school year were also entitled to remuneration over and above their normal pension. The value of their benefit, however, was dependent upon age, with those relinquishing their positions at an earlier age receiving a larger bonus. The sums to be paid ranged from $500 for a 64-year-old teacher to $6,000 for retiring instructors aged 55 to 57. Four payment options—including lump sum and various installment alternatives—were provided. The goals underlying the adoption of this plan were twofold: (1) to "reward loyalty and long years of service," and (2) to encourage early retirements in order that tenured teachers could be replaced by younger, less experienced instructors whose salary levels would be much lower.

* * *

On June 24, 1977, the Association filed suit in the Chancery Division seeking both a declaration that the ERR plan was valid and specific performance of its terms. The Board—named as sole defendant—joined the Teachers' Pension and Annuity Fund (TPAF) as third-party defendant. The pleadings and arguments below demonstrate that of these parties, the Board and the Association are in fact aligned in interest, and that TPAF is the only opponent of the plan.

* * *

I

Local boards of education are creations of the State and, as such, may exercise only those powers granted to them by the Legislature—either expressly or by necessary or fair implication. We must therefore determine whether local boards have been delegated the authority to make payments to employees which are unrelated to services rendered for the sole purpose of inducing early retirement.

The trial court held that authorization for the plan could be found in two statutory provisions: N.J.S.A. 18A:27–4 (a local board may set the "terms and tenure of employment, * * * salaries and time and mode of payment thereof * * * ") and N.J.S.A. 34:13A–5.3 (public employers and their employees may negotiate concerning "terms and conditions of employment"). We disagree.

N.J.S.A. 18A:27–4 does not confer upon local boards an unlimited power to negotiate all types of financial benefits for their teaching employees. Rather, the statute's use of the word "salaries" indicates that the Legislature intended to grant boards the power to set the "time and mode of payment" only of compensation which bears some relation to the rendition of past or present services. Under the ERR plan here at issue, payments are geared to age, not service. Moreover, the sums to which instructors are entitled decrease as length of service increases. It is thus clear that the parties to this contract intended to reward early retirement rather than the amount and quality of the work that a particular teacher had performed. As such, these payments are not authorized by N.J.S.A. 18A:27–4.

Nor are the payments called for by the ERR plan authorized by the Employer-Employee Relations Act, N.J.S.A. 34:13A–1 et seq. That statute does not enlarge the areas in which the Board has been delegated the responsibility to act. Rather, it merely recognizes the right of public employee representatives to negotiate with the Board over matters which, in the absence of negotiation, could have been set unilaterally by the Board. As such, the provisions of the Employer-Employee Relations Act do not operate to confer authority upon the Board to agree to compensation schemes which bear no relation to the amount and quality of the services which its teaching employees have rendered.

We therefore conclude that the Board has not been delegated the power to agree to or make the payments called for by the ERR plan here at issue. These payments, being unrelated to service, do not constitute "compensation" or "customary fringe benefits" with respect to which negotiation is permissible. Consequently, Article VI of the parties' collective agreement is *ultra vires* and unenforceable.

II

* * *

[The court reviewed two prior decisions (involving nonschool public employees) in which it had enunciated the principle that "actions taken by a state agency which may substantially affect retirement age and thus the actuarial assumptions of a statutory pension system are impermissible unless clearly and unequivocally authorized by the legislature."]

III

It is axiomatic that a municipality may not act in an area which the Legislature has preempted. In deciding whether a particular municipal activity has been preempted, the Court must determine whether the Legislature intended its action to preclude the exercise of local authority. * * *

In assessing the legislative intent, the primary factor to be considered is whether the municipal action adversely affects the legislative scheme. * * * [ERR's] adverse effect upon the comprehensive legislative scheme has been fully documented * * *. Hence, its existence stands " 'as an obstacle to the accomplishment and execution of the full purposes and objectives' of the Legislature[.]"

* * *

Conclusion

* * *

Although we are not unsympathetic to the desire of local boards of education to reduce their expenses, sanction for plans such as the one at issue must come from the Legislature. That branch of government has determined that preservation of the TPAF's fiscal integrity is presently to be accorded paramount concern. We are not at liberty to reassess the policy judgment which it has made. Absent clear and unequivocal statutory authority, ERR plans such as Fair Lawn's may not be established.

* * *

Notes

1. From an educational viewpoint, do you think the invalidated plan had merit?

2. The court lists three bases for invalidating the plan (first paragraph). Are they independent of each other?

3. Could a New Jersey local school board pay teachers upon their retirement a lump sum for unused sick leave days? Could the state legislature permit local boards to offer financial incentives for early retirement?

4. Concern for the financial stability of retirement plans has been expressed by many courts over the years. The Supreme Court of Ohio four decades before had said that if the mandatory retirement age were allowed to be set by local boards, "varying ages may be established by various boards throughout the state which, of course, would materially increase the demand upon the state employees' retirement fund." Verberg v. Board of Educ. of Cleveland, 135 Ohio St. 246, 20 N.E.2d 368 (1939).

5. Retirement is treated in Chapter 11.

[Case No. 22] Power of Board to Require Physical Examination of Teacher

STRONG v. BOARD OF EDUC. OF UNIONDALE UNION FREE SCHOOL DIST.

United States Court of Appeals, Second Circuit, 1990.
902 F.2d 208.

IRVING R. KAUFMAN, CIRCUIT JUDGE: The primary issue presented is whether a local school board denied a tenured public school teacher due process by refusing to allow her to return from an extended medical absence before she provided medical records and submitted to a physical examination by the school board doctor. In affirming the grant of summary judgment below, we hold that procedural due process is satisfied when a teacher in such circumstances is provided notice and an opportunity to respond to the adverse action of the school board, and when the state also affords a mechanism for obtaining judicial review of the board's decision on a subsequent petition for reinstatement. In addition, we find no constitutional violation of appellant's interest in privacy.

BACKGROUND

Appellant Marilyn Strong has been employed since 1980 by the Uniondale Union Free School District, in Nassau County, New York (School District). She has taught sixth grade at Northern Parkway Elementary School since 1981, and was awarded tenure in 1984.

From May 17, 1988 through the end of the academic year in late June, Strong was absent from the classroom because of illness. On June 8, after the School District inquired into the condition of its employee's health, it received a terse note from Strong's personal physician describing her as suffering from "severe nosebleed, vertigo, [and] arthritis."

In addition, Strong signed an insurance form (The form was a request by Strong to her insurance company to have certain premiums waived because of her disability.) and forwarded it to the School District in July, indicating she was currently "disabled" and that the date of her return to work was "unknown." Significantly, the form contained an "Authorization to Obtain Information" clause directly above Strong's signature which explicitly authorized any doctor who had treated her to release "any and all information" concerning her medical history to the insurance company.

During the ensuing summer months, the School District sought in vain to communicate with Strong. Registered letters to her home address went unclaimed; repeated efforts to reach her by telephone proved futile. Moreover, Strong's mother purportedly refused to provide the School District with her daughter's current address. Strong explains by alleging that she was under doctor's orders not to contact her employers because it made her ill to do so.

Unsuccessful in its efforts to contact Strong directly, the School District sent a letter dated August 17, 1988 to Strong's counsel, who had been retained pursuant to an unrelated discrimination claim against it. The letter directed Strong to produce an evaluation by her treating physician of her medical condition indicating whether she would be capable of resuming her teaching post. The communication specifically required Strong to provide "the names of all doctors she has seen since the commencement of her illness, along with releases permitting such doctors to provide the District with her medical records."

In response, Strong's lawyers stated that she would be returning to work at the start of the 1988–89 school year, but omitted any discussion of their client's health or medical records. Accordingly, on August 29 the School District asserted that Strong needed to provide "her medical records and history" to the School District's physician and be examined by him before returning to the classroom. Strong did not comply.

When Strong attempted to resume teaching on the first day of the new school year, September 6, 1988, School District Superintendent Alan Hernandez informed her (both orally and in subsequent letters summarizing their conversation) that she could not return until she submitted to a medical examination and produced her records. Strong indicated her willingness to be examined by the School District's doctor, but steadfastly refused to provide her medical records, except for a doctor's note stating that she has been treated "for chest pains, arthritis, palpitations, [and] headaches" and asserting her ability to return to teaching. The School District's doctor, however, maintained that he could not certify a teacher as fit to return from an extended illness without medical reports from that teacher's treating physician and that the conclusory assertions of Strong's personal physician fell far short of the information necessary to render an informed medical opinion.

On November 22, 1988, the Board of Education passed a resolution * * * instructing Strong to appear at the office of the School District's doctor for a physical examination. The resolution directed Strong to bring any and all medical records relating to her absence from school commencing May 16, 1988, to her examination so that the School District's physician could properly evaluate the status of her health. To date, Strong has neither submitted to an examination nor proffered her medical records. Since she has exhausted her accrued sick leave, Strong no longer receives a salary.

Strong initiated this suit in December 1988, alleging that the School District's actions violated her constitutional rights to privacy and due process * * *. * * *

DISCUSSION

I. *Due Process*

Strong urges that before the School District acted to bar her from the classroom she should have been notified of the "charges" against her, given an explanation of the School District's evidence, and provided an opportunity to present her side of the story.

Strong's procedural due process claim triggers analysis under a familiar framework. The threshold issue is whether Strong asserts a property interest protected by the Constitution. *See Board of Regents v. Roth.* If a protected interest exists, we must then determine whether the School District deprived Strong of that interest without due process. The constitutional contours of due process turn on the specific circumstances of the case, including the governmental and private interests at issue. Due process is a flexible concept requiring only such procedural protection as the particular situation demands.

Strong's position as a tenured teacher is indisputably a property interest protected by the fourteenth amendment. Whether the School District deprived her of that interest without affording adequate procedural safeguards thus depends on what process was due.

Under New York law a tenured teacher may be removed only pursuant to certain substantive and procedural safeguards, including notice and a full-blown adversarial hearing. On the other hand, the New York Court of Appeals has held that a prior hearing is not necessary before placing a tenured teacher on involuntary sick leave, *i.e.,* inactive status without pay due to illness. *Brown v. Bd. of Educ.,* 16 N.Y.2d 1021, 265 N.Y.S.2d 903, 213 N.E.2d 314 (1965). The *Brown* court's decision rested on the fact that the plaintiff, unlike a teacher who had been suspended or removed, retained all of her rights as a tenured teacher and could apply at anytime to be returned to active status. The court noted, moreover, that an adverse decision on Brown's application for reinstatement could be reviewed * * * in state court.

In the instant appeal, Strong has neither been "removed" from her teaching position, nor has she been involuntarily placed on sick leave. Under New York law, a teacher who is not permitted to return from an extended voluntary sick leave because of a failure to supply medical records is not considered suspended or terminated. Rather, we face the mirror image of the situation confronted in *Brown.* Here, we have a tenured teacher who has been barred against her will from resuming teaching after a hiatus taken on her own initiative. Yet the result is the same. By refusing to automatically reinstate her following her voluntary sick leave, the School District has barred her from working and effectively cut off her salary. As in *Brown,* Strong retains the right to petition for reinstatement and to challenge the denial of that petition in state court.

We recognize that, ordinarily, procedural due process requires notice and an opportunity to be heard. But an important government interest, accompanied by a substantial assurance that the deprivation is not baseless or unwarranted may justify postponing the opportunity to be heard until after the initial deprivation. In cases where a pretermination hearing is required, "an initial check" to determine whether there are reasonable grounds to support the proposed action is sufficient. *Cleveland Bd. of Educ. v. Loudermill.* Accordingly, deciding whether the procedures followed by the School District meet the constitutional minimum requires a balancing of the private and governmental interests at stake.

The private interest affected—the right of a tenured teacher to continue practicing her profession and receiving her salary—is substantial indeed. On the other hand, the School District had a strong interest in safeguarding the health and welfare of the students in the teacher's class and the other children attending the school; also, it had ample reason to question Strong's physical fitness to teach and to require more than conclusory assertions that she had regained her health.

Moreover, Strong received adequate notice in the August letters to her counsel that she was required to provide her medical records to the School District's doctor prior to returning to work. Contrary to Strong's assertions, the letters could not have provided details as to the "charges" against her, since there are no pending charges. The letters were not disciplinary; they merely sought information from which the School District's doctor could make a reasoned professional judgment about her fitness to teach.

Although Strong urges that there should have been some type of hearing before she was barred from the classroom, it is difficult to envision what would have transpired at such a hearing. She was adequately notified that the School District needed her medical records to assess her fitness to teach. The parties were well aware of each other's assertions and any further hearing would have amounted to an empty formality.

Moreover, as we have noted, adequate "post-deprivation" procedures are available to protect Strong's property interest in her tenured teaching position. All the process that was due in this case has been provided.

II. *Right to Privacy*

Strong also contends that even if the procedures for barring her from automatically returning to work were fair, compelling her to disclose her medical records amounts to an unconstitutional invasion of privacy.

Legitimate requests for medical information by those responsible for the health of the community do not rise to an impermissible invasion of privacy. The Sixth Circuit recently upheld a city ordinance requiring employees returning from extended absences to divulge certain medical information. *Gutierrez v. Lynch,* 826 F.2d 1534, 1539 (6th Cir.1987). We find persuasive the position of the Sixth Circuit in this similar setting. As we have noted, the School District has a strong interest in protecting the children under its care. Its request for Strong's medical records, limited to the period of her absence from school, was reasonably tailored in scope and does not violate her privacy rights.

* * *

Notes

1. Board of Regents v. Roth is Case No. 77. Cleveland Bd. of Educ. v. Loudermill is Case No. 105.

2. A school board's refusal to allow a female teacher to be examined at her own expense by any female physician selected by the board (rather than by the male school physician) was held to be arbitrary. Gargiul v. Tompkins, 704 F.2d 661 (2 Cir.1983), vacated on other grounds, 465 U.S. 1016, 104 S.Ct. 1263, 79 L.Ed.2d 670 (1984).

3. Requiring a second medical opinion attesting to fitness to return to duty for a driver education teacher was within the power of a school board. There was no need for a hearing before the imposition of the condition. Scheideman v. West Des Moines Community School Dist., 989 F.2d 286 (8 Cir.1993).

[Case No. 23] Constitutionality of Statute Forbidding Teaching of Evolution

EPPERSON v. STATE OF ARKANSAS

Supreme Court of the United States, 1968.
393 U.S. 97, 89 S.Ct. 266, 21 L.Ed.2d 228.

Mr. Justice Fortas delivered the opinion of the Court.

I.

This appeal challenges the constitutionality of the "anti-evolution" statute which the State of Arkansas adopted in 1928 to prohibit the teaching in its public schools and universities of the theory that man evolved from other species of life. * * *

The Arkansas law makes it unlawful for a teacher in any state-supported school or university "to teach the theory or doctrine that mankind ascended or descended from a lower order of animals," or "to adopt or use in any such institution a textbook that teaches" this theory. Violation is a misdemeanor and subjects the violator to dismissal from his position.

The present case concerns the teaching of biology in a high school in Little Rock. According to the testimony, until the events here in litigation, the official textbook furnished for the high school biology course "did not have a section on the Darwinian Theory." Then, for the academic year 1965–1966, the school administration, on recommendation of the teachers of biology in the school system, adopted and prescribed a textbook which contained a chapter setting forth "the theory about the origin * * * of man from a lower form of animal."

Susan Epperson, a young woman who graduated from Arkansas' school system and then obtained her master's degree in zoology at the University of Illinois, was employed by the Little Rock school system in the fall of 1964 to teach 10th grade biology at Central High School. At the start of the next academic year, 1965, she was confronted by the new textbook (which one surmises from the record was not unwelcome to her). She faced at least a literal dilemma because she was supposed to use the new textbook for classroom instruction and presumably to teach the statutorily condemned chapter; but to do so would be a criminal offense and subject her to dismissal.

* * *

* * * Only Arkansas, Mississippi, and Tennessee have such "anti-evolution" or "monkey" laws on their books. There is no record of any prosecutions in Arkansas under its statute. It is possible that the statute is presently more of a curiosity than a vital fact of life in these States. Nevertheless, the present case was brought, the appeal as of right is properly here, and it is our duty to decide the issues presented.

II.

At the outset, it is urged upon us that the challenged statute is vague and uncertain and therefore within the condemnation of the Due Process Clause of the Fourteenth Amendment. The contention that the Act is vague and uncertain is supported by language in the brief opinion of Arkansas' Supreme Court. That court, perhaps reflecting the discomfort which the statute's quixotic prohibition necessarily engenders in the modern mind, stated that it "expresses no opinion" as to whether the Act prohibits "explanation" of the theory of evolution or merely forbids "teaching that the theory is true." Regardless of this uncertainty, the court held that the statute is constitutional.

On the other hand, counsel for the State, in oral argument in this Court, candidly stated that, despite the State Supreme Court's equivocation, Arkansas would interpret the statute "to mean that to make a student aware of the theory * * * just to teach that there was such a theory" would be grounds for dismissal and for prosecution under the statute; and he said "that the Supreme Court of Arkansas' opinion should be interpreted in that manner." He said "If Mrs. Epperson would tell her students that 'Here is Darwin's theory, that man ascended or descended from a lower form of being,' then I think she would be under this statute liable for prosecution."

In any event, we do not rest our decision upon the asserted vagueness of the statute. On either interpretation of its language, Arkansas' statute cannot stand. It is of no moment whether the law is deemed to prohibit mention of Darwin's theory, or to forbid any or all of the infinite varieties of communication embraced within the term "teaching." Under either interpretation, the law must be stricken because of its conflict with the constitutional prohibition of state laws respecting an establishment of religion or prohibiting the free exercise thereof. The overriding fact is that Arkansas' law selects from the body of knowledge a particular segment which it proscribes for the sole reason that it is deemed to conflict with a particular religious doctrine; that is, with a particular interpretation of the Book of Genesis by a particular religious group.

* * *

Judicial interposition in the operation of the public school system of the Nation raises problems requiring care and restraint. Our courts, however, have not failed to apply the First Amendment's mandate in our educational system where essential to safeguard the fundamental values of freedom of speech and inquiry and of belief. By and large, public education in our Nation is committed to the control of state and local authorities. Courts do not and cannot intervene in the resolution of conflicts which arise in the daily operation of school systems and which do not directly and sharply implicate basic constitutional values. On the other hand, "The vigilant protection of constitutional freedoms is nowhere more vital than in the community of American schools," Shelton v. Tucker, and "This Court will be alert against invasions of academic freedom * * *." Barenblatt v. United States, 360 U.S. 109, 112, 79 S.Ct. 1081, 3 L.Ed.2d 1115 (1959). As this Court said in Keyishian v. Board of Regents, the First Amendment "does not tolerate laws that cast a pall of orthodoxy over the classroom."

* * *

There is and can be no doubt that the First Amendment does not permit the State to require that teaching and learning must be tailored to the principles or prohibitions of any religious sect or dogma. In Everson v. Board of Education, this Court, in upholding a state law to provide free bus service to school children, including those attending parochial schools, said: "Neither [a State nor the Federal Government] can pass laws which aid one religion, aid all religions, or prefer one religion over another."

* * *

In the present case, there can be no doubt that Arkansas has sought to prevent its teachers from discussing the theory of evolution because it is contrary to the belief of some that the Book of Genesis must be the exclusive source of doctrine as to the origin of man. No suggestion has been made that Arkansas' law may be justified by considerations of state policy other than the religious views of some of its citizens. It is clear that fundamentalist sectarian conviction was and is the law's reason for existence. Its antecedent, Tennessee's "monkey law," candidly stated its purpose: to make it unlawful "to teach any theory that denies the story of the Divine Creation of man, as taught in the Bible, and to teach instead, that man has descended from a lower order of animals." Perhaps the sensational publicity attendant upon the *Scopes* trial induced Arkansas to adopt less explicit language. It eliminated Tennessee's reference to "the story of the Divine Creation of man" as taught in the Bible, but there is no doubt that the motivation for the law was the same: to suppress the teaching of a theory which, it was thought, "denied" the divine creation of man.

* * *

The judgment of the Supreme Court of Arkansas is reversed.

Notes

1. The vote was unanimous. Three Justices wrote concurring opinions. Justices Black and Harlan individually expressed displeasure with the treatment of the case by Arkansas enforcement officials and by the Supreme Court of Arkansas. Each also criticized some of Justice Fortas's dicta. Justice Stewart distinguished between a state's clear right to determine whether an item should be in the curriculum and the present situation where a criminal sanction was placed on a teacher's mentioning the existence "of an entire system of respected human thought."

2. Was this case a significant one for "academic freedom"? Was it worth the time of the Supreme Court?

3. Do you think Mrs. Epperson's job was in danger? Why do you believe counsel for the state implied a strict enforcement of the statute when no one had ever been prosecuted under it?

4. In the famous Scopes "monkey trial" in 1927 in Tennessee, Scopes was convicted of violating a similar statute and fined one hundred dollars by the trial judge. However, the Supreme Court of Tennessee reversed the conviction on the ground that the jury, and not the judge, should have assessed the fine. It directed that no further action be taken against Scopes because "nothing [was] to be gained by prolonging the life of this bizarre case." Scopes v. State of Tennessee, 154 Tenn. 105, 289 S.W. 363 (1927).

5. The Tennessee legislature repealed its anti-evolution statute, and the Supreme Court of Mississippi struck down the last of such statutes in Smith v. State, 242 So.2d 692 (Miss.1970). Subsequently Tennessee enacted a statute prohibiting the use of any textbook that discussed evolution unless there were a disclaimer that the doctrine was only a theory and not scientific fact as to the origin of man. The statute further required the inclusion of the Genesis version of creation (if any version at all was included) while permitting that version alone to be printed without the disclaimer. Also the statute declared "the Holy Bible shall not be defined as a textbook, but is hereby declared to be a reference work, and shall not be required to carry the disclaimer." The United States Court of Appeals, Sixth Circuit, declared the statute unconstitutional because it gave a preferential position to the Biblical version of creation. Daniel v. Waters, 515 F.2d 485 (6 Cir.1975).

6. See text discussion accompanying footnote 52 for another Supreme Court case involving evolution.

[Case No. 24] Power of School Authorities to Choose Spring Play

SEYFRIED v. WALTON

United States Court of Appeals, Third Circuit, 1981.
668 F.2d 214.

ALDISERT, CIRCUIT JUDGE. The question presented is whether a public school superintendent's decision to cancel a high school dramatic production because of its sexual theme violated the students' first amendment right of expression. Plaintiffs, parents of three students in the play, sued the school district, the school board, and the district superintendent, seeking compensatory and equitable relief under 42 U.S.C. § 1983. The district court, sitting without a jury, held that the school superintendent's decision to cancel the production as inappropriate for school sponsorship was no different from other administrative decisions involving allocation of educational resources and that the cancellation did not offend the students' first amendment rights. We accept the reasoning given by the district court and we will affirm * * *.

I.

* * * Caesar Rodney High School, located in Dover, Delaware, sponsors autumn and spring theatrical productions each year. In December 1980, the director of the spring production, an English teacher at the school, selected the musical "Pippin" for presentation the following spring. Because the play contained certain sexually explicit scenes, the director consulted the assistant principal before reaching a final decision. After the director edited the script, she and the assistant principal agreed that the revised scenes, although still sexually suggestive, were appropriate for a high school production.

In March 1981, shortly after rehearsals for the spring production had begun, the father of a "Pippin" cast member complained to his brother, the president of the school board, that the play mocked religion. The board president directed the district superintendent to look into the matter. After reviewing the edited script, the superintendent determined that the play did not mock religion, but that it was inappropriate for a public high school because of its sexual content. He directed the principal to stop production of the play. After hearing the views of interested parents, the school board refused to overturn the superintendent's decision. As a result, the school did not present a spring play in 1981.

Parents of three members of the "Pippin" cast and crew then filed a civil rights action under 42 U.S.C. § 1983, claiming that the students' first amendment rights of expression had been unconstitutionally abridged. After a two-day trial, the district court entered judgment in favor of the defendants. Plaintiffs appeal.

II.

Appellants' principal contention is that the students of the "Pippin" cast and crew had a first amendment right to produce the play. Although we agree that, in general, dramatic expression is "speech" for purposes of the first amendment, we also agree with the district court that the decision to cancel the production of "Pippin" in these circumstances did not infringe on the students' constitutional rights.

In his well reasoned opinion, Judge Stapleton noted that a school community "exists for a specialized purpose—the education of young people," including the communication of both knowledge and social values. The first amendment, he concluded, must therefore be "applied in light of the special characteristics of the school environment * * *."

We believe that the district court properly distinguished student newspapers and other "non-program related expressions of student opinion" from school-sponsored theatrical productions. The critical factor in this case is the relationship of the play to the school curriculum. As found by the district court, both the staff and the administration view the spring production at Caesar Rodney as "an integral part of the school's educational program." Participation in the play, though voluntary, was considered a part of the curriculum in the theater arts. * * * Viewed in this light,

> the selection of the artistic work to be given as the spring production does not differ in principle from the selection of course curriculum, a process which courts have traditionally left to the expertise of educators. Just as a student has no First Amendment right to study a particular aspect or period of history in his or her senior history course, he or she has no First Amendment right to participate in the production of a particular dramatic work or version thereof.

The district court also noted the likelihood that the school's sponsorship of a play would be viewed as an endorsement of the ideas it contained. A school has an important interest in avoiding the impression that it has endorsed a viewpoint at variance with its educational program. The district court cautioned that administrators may not so chill the school's atmosphere for student and teacher expression that they cast "a pall of orthodoxy" over the school community, but it found no such danger here. The court found that no student was prohibited from expressing his views on any subject; no student was prohibited from reading the script, an unedited version of which remains in the school library; and no one was punished or reprimanded for any expression of ideas. In light of these facts, the court could find no reasonable threat of a chilling effect on the free exchange of ideas within the school community. These findings are amply supported by the record.

We agree with the district court that those responsible for directing a school's educational program must be allowed to decide how its limited resources can be best used to achieve the goals of educating and socializing its students. "Limitations of time and resources * * * dictate that choices be made * * *. [S]ince the objective of the process is the 'inculcation of both knowledge and social values' in young people, these decisions as to what will be taught will necessarily involve an acceptance or preference of some values over others."

Because of the burden of responsibility given to school administrators, courts are reluctant to interfere with the operation of our school systems. * * * We agree with the district court that the conflict here does not "directly and sharply implicate" the first amendment rights of the students. We hold, therefore, that the court properly entered judgment for the defendants.

* * *

Notes

1. The superintendent overruled the dramatic arts teacher's decision to produce "Pippin." The teacher did not legally challenge the action. Could she have? If so, on what grounds?

2. Note how the superintendent got involved. Could this be fairly characterized as censorship? Would your answer differ if the superintendent, rather than the teacher, was the one who was to select the spring play in the first place?

3. No play was produced during the spring session. Who gained and who lost in this situation?

4. How can this case be reconciled with those upholding student rights of expression? (See "Rules of Conduct" in Chapter 12.)

[Case No. 25] Constitutionality of Requirement That Students Stand During Flag Salute

GOETZ v. ANSELL

United States Court of Appeals, Second Circuit, 1973.
477 F.2d 636.

FEINBERG, CIRCUIT JUDGE: Plaintiff Theodore Goetz, a senior at Shaker High School in Latham, New York, an honor student and the president of his class, refuses to participate in the Pledge of Allegiance because he believes "that there [isn't] liberty and justice for all in the United States." Defendants [school authorities] have offered plaintiff the option of either leaving the room or standing silently during the pledge ceremony. But plaintiff maintains that he has a first amendment right to remain quietly seated, even though if he adheres to that position, he faces suspension from school. * * *

* * * [T]he State Commissioner of Education had ruled on the issue in 1970, holding that requiring a student "either to stand silently or to leave the classroom" did not infringe his rights. The Commissioner cited that decision with implicit approval the following year, and thereafter issued guidelines that indicated no subsequent change of heart. * * * [The United States District Court found no constitutional violation.]

This brings us to the merits of plaintiff's case. In West Virginia State Board of Education v. Barnette the Court made clear, in Mr. Justice Jackson's memorable words, that

> no official, high or petty, can prescribe what shall be orthodox
> in politics, nationalism, religion, or other matters of opinion or
> force citizens to confess by word or act their faith therein.

It is true that the Court dealt in that case with the compulsion of saluting the flag and reciting the pledge, whereas here plaintiff is given the option of standing silently * * *. In this case, the act of standing is itself part of the pledge. New York State Regulations so provide; and standing "is no less a gesture of acceptance and respect than is the salute or the utterance of the words of allegiance." Therefore, the alternative offered plaintiff of standing in silence is an act that cannot be compelled over his deeply held convictions. It can no more be required than the pledge itself.

Defendants point out, however, that plaintiff has the option of leaving the classroom; he is not, as in *Barnette,* excluded from the school. While we agree that the effect upon plaintiff of adhering to his convictions is far less drastic than in *Barnette,* we do not believe that this disposes of the case. If the state cannot compel participation in the pledge, it cannot punish non-participation. And being required to leave the classroom during the pledge may reasonably be viewed by some as having that effect, however benign defendants' motives may be. See Abington School District v. Schempp (Brennan, J., concurring) ("[T]he excluded pupil loses caste with his fellows, and is liable to be regarded with aversion, and subjected to reproach and insult.").

Recognizing the force of *Barnette* and of Tinker v. Des Moines Independent Community School District (upholding right of students to wear black arm band), defendants concede that plaintiff has a protected first amendment right not to participate in the pledge. They argue, however, that the other students also have rights and that *Tinker* does not protect conduct that

> materially disrupts classwork or involves substantial disorder or invasion of the rights of others * * *.

The argument is sound, but the facts of this case do not justify applying it. There is no evidence here of disruption of classwork or disorder or invasion of the rights of others. The record is just to the contrary: Plaintiff took a poll of his approximately 30 classmates; 25 said that it did not disturb them that plaintiff had remained seated during the pledge earlier in the year and the other five he "could not contact or else they did not see" him. Defendants ask where, if plaintiff prevails, the line is to be drawn. May plaintiff "kneel, lie down, stand on his hands? May he make derisive motions?" Those situations are not before us, and we doubt that they will occur in the North Colonie Central School District, any more than they have occurred in the New York City school system after [a United States District Court decision] which wholly accepted plaintiff's position. Of course, if such disruptive acts should occur, we would have no hesitancy in holding them unprotected. But we do not believe that a silent, non-disruptive expression of belief by sitting down may similarly be prohibited. While we do not share plaintiff's resistance to pledging allegiance to this nation, his reservations of belief must be protected. In time, perhaps, he will recognize that such protection is sound ground for a firmer trust in his country.

Judgment reversed.

Notes

1. Observe that the court found the act of standing to be part of the pledge.

2. Do you agree that leaving the room during the pledge may be considered a punishment?

3. Suppose a teacher refused to engage in the pledge ceremony. Would the reasoning of this court apply? See Case No. 98 and Note 2 thereon.

4. Suppose a student in the choir remained seated on the stage when the remainder of the choir stood to sing a selection which he disapproved. Would he be protected by this case? Would the particular selection make a difference?

5. The quotation in the third paragraph is a famous one. Notice that, although the plaintiffs in that 1943 case were Jehovah's Witnesses, the statement acknowledges a range of rights beyond those that may be religion-based.

[Case No. 26] Power of Board to Establish Graduation Requirements

STATE EX REL. SAGESER v. LEDBETTER

Missouri Court of Appeals, 1977.
559 S.W.2d 230.

STONE, PRESIDING JUDGE. In this proceeding * * * relator Ronnie Sageser (hereinafter Ronnie) sought a writ of mandamus to compel * * * the members of the board of education of the Sarcoxie R–2 School District (hereinafter collectively referred to as the board), W.D. Ledbetter, the superintendent of schools for that district, and Jess Bair, the principal of Sarcoxie High School at the time of suit, to execute and deliver to relator Ronnie a diploma evidencing his graduation from that school. * * *

* * *

[For "showing disrespect" to a teacher, Ronnie had been suspended by the former principal Smith during his junior year.]

Either the next day by relator Ronnie's account, or "about five days later" according to principal Smith, the latter called Ronnie's home and requested that he report to the principal's office. Upon trial, principal Smith recalled that, when Ronnie did report, "his attitude [was] that of indifference toward returning to school and behaving"—in short, that "his attitude hadn't improved," so Smith told Ronnie "to go home until his attitude improved." Ronnie's recollection was that, in the course of this meeting, principal Smith had exclaimed, "You don't even know what you are doing here, do you" and, when Ronnie agreed and answered "No," the principal "just said, '[w]hy don't you just check out your books and go home.'" Although the principal declared that Ronnie's check-out and withdrawal were voluntary and without compulsion by any school official, certain portions of the principal's testimony cast doubt upon that characterization of Ronnie's withdrawal. (E.g., when asked on cross-examination "[d]id you instruct Ronald Sageser to check out of school," principal Smith responded "I don't remember whether I did or didn't"; and, in one entry book, Ronnie's name was listed with the comment "dropped 4/1/74.") But, regardless of whether the principal's above-quoted utterances to Ronnie constituted a mere suggestion, an admonition or a command, Ronnie did "go home" after having completed a "checkout form" obtainable only from the principal or upon his authorization. This "checkout form" was dated April 1, 1974, which was approximately eight weeks prior to the last day of the 1973–74 school year.

Ronnie reentered Sarcoxie High School in September 1974, was listed as a senior, continued in school through the 1974–75 academic year, and (with his academic credits from the three previous years) earned the twenty units of credit required for graduation. However, he was denied a diploma (so superintendent Ledbetter declared) because he had not completed "eight semesters of attending" as prescribed "in the policy that is made by the Board of Education" (hereinafter the eight-semester requirement).

When Ronnie's parents learned that he would not graduate with his class, one of the parents attended a meeting of the board of education and requested that the board waive the eight-semester requirement and give Ronnie's diploma to him, but the board refused to do so. However, acknowledging that Ronnie had satisfied all other requirements for graduation, superintendent Ledbetter declared that, if Ronnie would *enroll* for "[e]xactly the amount of time that was lacking from the time he dropped out [April 1, 1974] until the end of school which, I believe, [was] eight weeks, give or take a day or two," he would receive his diploma.

Since the Sarcoxie eight-semester requirement hatched this controversy, it becomes both appropriate and necessary to note the evidence concerning its origin, meaning and prior enforcement. We observe initially that the eight-semester requirement was *not* imposed or ordained by statute, but was a requirement for graduation formulated and prescribed by the Sarcoxie Board of Education (so superintendent Ledbetter declared) pursuant to a *recommendation* nestling in a footnote to the last sentence of paragraph 17, "High School Graduation Requirements," in the *Handbook for Classification and Accreditation of Public School Districts in Missouri* (1973) published by the Missouri State Board of Education, that sentence and footnote reading as follows:

> "The local board of education may require more than 20 units, adopt specific course requirements, and/or specify the number of semesters of attendance **
>
> " * * Eight semesters of attendance after grade eight are *recommended*."
> (All emphasis herein is ours.)
>
> required for graduation from their local school district."

Inasmuch as the proper disposition of this appeal does not involve or depend upon the wisdom vel non of this recommendation, the acceptance of which mandatorily herded all high school students, without regard to ability, aptitude, ambition, intellect, motivation, performance or prior scholastic record, onto the same conveyor belt geared to the pace of the mediocre or average student, we eschew comment concerning its adoption by the Sarcoxie board.

* * *

Respondents' position in this proceeding (as *initially* stated by superintendent Ledbetter) was that, by reason of Ronnie's absence during approximately the last eight weeks of his Junior school year, he did not satisfy the four-year requirement and will not be entitled to receive a diploma until he does. Thus, Ledbetter initially declared that relator Ronnie would be required to attend Sarcoxie High School for "exactly" the additional number of school days that he missed in his

Junior year from his suspension or "checkout" on April 1, 1974, to the end of that school year. However, Ledbetter subsequently conceded not only that the eight-semester requirement did *not* demand or necessitate any *attendance* but also that relator Ronnie already had earned the twenty units of credit which constituted and satisfied the "measure of academic achievement" required for graduation, from which it followed that it would not be necessary for Ronnie to earn any additional units of credit, pass any courses in which he might be enrolled, or for that matter even attend any classes. Thus, it becomes plain that the additional requirement of *enrollment* for eight weeks imposed by the school authorities would do no more than work an exercise in futility which would benefit neither the school district nor relator Ronnie and thus would fly in the teeth of the commonsense maxim that the law does not require the doing of a useless thing.

Although the foregoing is dispositive of this appeal, the earnest presentations of counsel move us to note other record evidence pointing to and supporting the same conclusion. * * * Supt. Ledbetter conceded that, during the three years prior to trial of this proceeding, four girls, identified by name in the transcript, had been graduated with a diploma although they had not *attended* eight semesters. One of those four girls who had become pregnant, had missed the last few weeks of the 1973–74 school year, but had graduated with her class in 1975. Relator Ronnie likewise had missed the last few weeks of the 1973–74 school year, but contrawise had been denied graduation with the 1975 class.

Although respondents assert that mandamus is inappropriate, the transcript establishes that relator had satisfied all academic requirements for graduation and that respondents rely solely, albeit mistakenly, on the eight-semester requirement to justify and support their denial of a diploma to relator Ronnie. Within reasonable limits a school board may determine graduation requirements but where, as here, a rule is applied or enforced unreasonably, capriciously, arbitrarily or inequitably to deny a diploma to a qualified candidate, mandamus is an appropriate remedy. * * *

Notes

1. Is this decision based on a finding of (1) an unauthorized rule, (2) an unreasonable rule, (3) an unreasonable application of an authorized and reasonable rule, or (4) an unreasonable application of a rule the reasonableness of which was not here determined?

2. Evaluate the professional performance in dealing with the educational situation presented here of Superintendent Ledbetter; of former principal Smith.

3. Should there be a required minimum period of attendance for high school graduation; should graduation be based on completion of a fixed number of courses; should graduation be based on passing tests regardless of either or both of the preceding? What should be the roles of the state and the local board in setting graduation requirements?

[Case No. 27] Power of Board to Include Attendance in Determining Course Grades

CAMPBELL v. BOARD OF EDUC. OF TOWN OF NEW MILFORD

Supreme Court of Connecticut, 1984.
193 Conn. 93, 475 A.2d 289.

PETERS, ASSOCIATE JUSTICE. This case concerns the validity of the policy of a local school board that imposes academic sanctions for nonattendance upon high school students. In a class action brought by the named plaintiff, John A. Campbell, for himself and others similarly situated, the plaintiff class sought injunctive and declaratory relief, mandamus, and compensatory damages from the named defendant, the New Milford board of education, and others. The plaintiff claimed that the defendants' policy was ultra vires in light of governing state statutes, and unconstitutional in light of operative provisions of the Connecticut constitution and the United States constitution. The trial court rendered judgment for the defendants and the plaintiff has appealed.

The underlying facts are undisputed. The New Milford attendance policy, set out in an annually distributed student handbook, provides two sets of academic sanctions for students who are absent from school. Course credit is withheld from any student who, without receiving an administrative waiver, is absent from any year-long course for more than twenty-four class periods. In the calculation of the twenty-four maximum absences, all class absences are included except absences on school-sponsored activities or essential administrative business. In addition to the twenty-four absence limit, the course grade of any student whose absence from school is unapproved is subject to a five-point reduction for each unapproved absence after the first. In any one marking period, the grade may not, however, be reduced to a grade lower than 50, which is a failing grade. The grade reduction for unexcused absences is, like the twenty-four maximum absence policy, subject to administrative waiver. The policy of the school board entails extensive opportunities for counseling after a student's first confirmed unapproved absence from a class and thereafter.

The stated purpose of the attendance policy is educational rather than disciplinary. A student's disciplinary suspension from school, for reasons unrelated to attendance, is considered an approved rather than an unapproved absence. Such an absence cannot result in the diminution of a class grade although it may be counted, unless waived, as part of the twenty-four maximum absences for class credit. A student's absence from school, whether approved or unapproved, is not a ground for suspension or expulsion.

A student's report card lists, for each course, grades for each marking period, a final examination grade, a final grade, the amount of credit awarded, and the number of approved and unapproved absences. The report card conspicuously bears the following legend: "A circled grade indicates that the grade was reduced due to unapproved absences." In the case of the named plaintiff, his report card indicated grade reductions by the circling of grades in each of his academic courses, with the result that in three of the courses his final grade was lowered from passing to failing. In a fourth course, Architectural Drafting II, where the plaintiff's final grade was passing despite an indicated reduction for unapproved absences, the report card assigned him no credit because of a total of thirty-eight absences, thirty-one of which were approved and seven of which were unapproved. Any report card thus discloses, on its face, those grades which are affected by the enforcement of the attendance policy.

* * *

I

The plaintiff's first argument on appeal is that the defendant school board's policy is invalid because it conflicts with a number of state statutes. This argument is twofold, that the attendance policy is ultra vires because it exceeds the authority conferred upon local school boards by state law and that the policy is preempted by state statutes with which it is inconsistent. We find neither argument persuasive.

The authority of local boards of education derives from their role as agents of the state. "[T]he furnishing of education for the general public, required by article eighth, § 1, of the Connecticut constitution, is by its very nature a state function and duty." This responsibility has been delegated to local boards which, as "agencies of the state in charge of education in the town * * * possess only such powers as are granted to them by the General Statutes expressly or by necessary implication."

* * *

* * * The authority to adopt uniform rules concerning irregularity of attendance is necessarily implied in the conjunction of statutory provisions authorizing local implementation of the educational mission of the state. Significantly, § 10–220 expressly charges local boards with responsibility for the oversight of the school attendance of children from the ages of seven to sixteen made mandatory by § 10–184. Furthermore, the plaintiff's concession that school teachers, upon the instruction of local school boards, may properly consider class participation in the assignment of grades, logically implies the existence of an educational nexus between classroom presence and grading. If local school boards can delegate to others the authority to impose academic sanctions for nonattendance, the decision to adopt uniform school-wide rules for such sanctions can hardly be deemed ultra vires.

None of the out-of-state cases upon which the plaintiff relies compels the conclusion that school-wide academic sanctions for nonattendance should generally be adjudged to be ultra vires. It may well be improper to reduce a student's grade for nonattendance as an additional punishment for unrelated conduct leading to a suspension from class; but this school board's program does not permit such double punishment. It would indubitably be unlawful to apply a nonattendance program in an unreasonable, capricious, arbitrary or inequitable manner; but no such allegation has been factually demonstrated. It would finally be troublesome to bar a truant student from further class attendance and from taking a final examination; but the defendant board's program neither removes such a student from class nor excuses further compliance with the state's compulsory education law. In short, the plaintiff has cited no authority for his claim that attendance rules promulgated by local school boards, if carefully drafted and fairly applied, are to be deemed per se ultra vires. Our own research has likewise revealed no such caselaw. We agree that such regulations fall within the authority granted to local school boards by the statutes of this state.

In the alternative, the plaintiff maintains that the defendant school board's attendance policy is preempted by state statutes governing school attendance. * * *

The defendant school board's reply * * * calls upon us to recognize a distinction between sanctions which are disciplinary in nature and sanctions which relate to academic requirements. The question is not whether we concur in the judgment of the defendant board of education that "[l]earning experiences that occur in the classroom are ... essential components of the learning process" or that "[t]ime lost from class tends to be irretrievable in terms of opportunity for instructional interaction." The policy decision that academic credentials should reflect more than the product of quizzes, examinations, papers and classroom participation nonetheless constitutes an academic judgment about academic requirements. We agree with the defendants' characterization of their policy.

* * *

II

Even if the defendant school board's attendance policy is authorized by the relevant state statutes, the plaintiff class asserts that the policy cannot pass constitutional muster. The plaintiff relies on provisions of our state and federal constitutions to raise three different constitutional claims: a right to substantive due process, a right to procedural due process, and a right to equal protection of the laws. The trial court, upon consideration of these claims, found no infringement of the plaintiff's constitutional rights. We agree.

A

The plaintiff's challenge to the New Milford attendance policy as violative of the requirements of substantive due process claims infringement of students' fundamental rights to public education, of students' liberty interests in their academic reputation and of students' property interests in grades reflecting academic achievement. * * *

Of these substantive due process claims, the most serious is the charge of impairment of a fundamental right, because, if such an impairment were properly before us, the validity of the questioned governmental regulation would require strict scrutiny to determine whether the regulation was compellingly justified and narrowly drafted. We must therefore decide the applicability of the fundamental rights guaranteed by article eighth, § 1, to a school board's policy of imposing uniform school-wide academic sanctions for nonattendance. In *Horton v. Meskill* we held, in the context of state-wide disparities in the financing of public school education, that "elementary and secondary education is a fundamental right, [and] that pupils in the public schools are entitled to the equal enjoyment of that right." The plaintiff argues that *Horton v. Meskill* implies that strict scrutiny must be the test for any and all governmental regulations affecting public school education. We disagree. The underlying issue in *Horton v. Meskill* was the provision of "a substantially equal educational opportunity" for Connecticut students in the state's "free public elementary and secondary schools." This school board policy, which is neither disciplinary nor an infringement of equal educational opportunity, does not jeopardize any fundamental rights under our state constitution.

The standard by which the plaintiff's remaining substantive due process claims must be measured is therefore the more usual rational basis test. In order to succeed on these claims, the plaintiff bears the heavy burden of proving that the challenged policy has no reasonable relationship to any legitimate state purpose and that the plaintiff class has suffered a specific injury as a result of the policy's enforcement. The plaintiff has established neither the legal nor the factual predicate for meeting this burden of proof.

The plaintiff argues that it is unconstitutionally arbitrary and capricious for the defendant school board to require student grades to reflect more than academic achievement. With respect to the plaintiff's liberty interest, we can find no factual impairment of whatever rights the plaintiff might possibly assert. Inspection of the report card of the named plaintiff discloses the relationship between his academic performance and the reduction in his grades and class credit that resulted from application of the attendance policy. The plaintiff has failed to show how a student's reputation could be injured by a report card in this form. With respect to the plaintiff's property interest, we find it difficult to understand how a uniform school-wide policy that links class grades with attendance can be on its face more arbitrary, as a constitutional matter, than are similar judgments by individual teachers who may justifiably, according to the plaintiff, adjust classroom grades to reflect classroom participation. Furthermore, the trial court made no findings of fact that application of the attendance policy was arbitrary or capricious in the only two specific cases about which evidence was adduced at trial. On this record, the plaintiff class has not proven infringement of its liberty or property interest in a fair grading system.

The plaintiff argues finally that impermissible vagueness in the waiver provisions that ameliorate the potential rigor of the defendant board's attendance policy requires the conclusion that the policy is substantively unconstitutional. The policy of grade reduction is subject to waiver for "outstanding performance," and denial of class credit may be waived in extenuating circumstances calling for "special consideration." These provisions for waiver are unconstitutional, according to the plaintiff, because they permit school administrators to exercise unbridled discretion and hence invite arbitrary action. It is, however, by no means clear that provisions for waiver, which necessarily depend upon the equities of particular circumstances, require the same degree of precision as must accompany the imposition of sanctions in the first instance. Significantly, the plaintiff's challenge for vagueness does not contest any part of the attendance policy other than its provisions of waiver. In any case, the plaintiff class has again failed to make the factual showing necessary to prove that it has suffered a constitutional injury. The record contains no findings that any member of the class in fact misunderstood the waiver policy or was deprived of a waiver because of ambiguity in its statement. The plaintiff's claim of unconstitutional vagueness therefore cannot succeed.

B

The plaintiff also claims a deprivation of procedural due process. The plaintiff maintains that the New Milford attendance policy fails to provide constitutionally mandated basic procedural safeguards because students are not given notice of the dates of their alleged absences and are not afforded the opportunity to contest the imposition of an academic penalty, either at an internal hearing or before the board of education. These omissions, according to the plaintiff, jeopardize accurate and fair application of the defendants' policy.

Before we can consider this claim on its merits, we must clarify the standards that govern procedural fairness in a school setting. We have already held that the defendants' policy is academic rather than disciplinary in intent and effect, and that the policy impairs no fundamental rights. The Supreme Court of the United States has recently determined that flexible standards of procedural due process call for "far less stringent procedural requirements in the case of an academic dismissal" than for a dismissal based on disciplinary reasons. *Board of Curators of the University of Missouri v. Horowitz.* That court found it compelling that academic evaluations of a student necessarily depend upon professional judgments that are "more subjective and evaluative than the typical factual questions presented in the average disciplinary decision." For similar reasons, it is appropriate for this court to defer to the policy judgments of the academic administrators who formulated the defendant school board's attendance program. Such deferral does not of course obviate the fundamental requirements of procedural due process that a student must be given adequate notice of the program, and a meaningful timely opportunity to be heard. It does, however, mean that notice and hearings need not take any one particular form in order to pass constitutional muster.

In this case, the plaintiff does not argue that students at New Milford High School were not provided with sufficient notice of the existent attendance policy or of the academic sanctions that would ensue from recurrent class absences. The plaintiff asserts only that students had inadequate opportunities to contest whether absences had occurred, whether they were excused or unexcused, or whether they should be waived. The defendants introduced evidence to the contrary. In the absence of express findings by the trial court, we must conclude that the plaintiff class has not met the requirement that the challenged attendance program must be shown to have adversely affected a constitutionally protected right under the facts of this particular case rather than of some possible or hypothetical facts not proven to exist.

C

The plaintiff's final constitutional claim invokes the equal protection provisions of article first, § 20, of the Connecticut constitution and the fourteenth amendment to the United States constitution. The plaintiff urges us to hold that because the defendant board's attendance policy permits waiver of grade reductions for unexcused absences, the policy creates two unequal classes of students: students who are denied a waiver and students who are granted a waiver. In part the plaintiff's argument depends upon the assertion that the defendants' classification, because it allegedly affects a fundamental right to education, must meet the test of strict scrutiny. That assertion we have rejected, supra. Even if the applicable test is whether the waiver provision bears a reasonable relationship to legitimate governmental ends, the plaintiff argues that the waiver provision is constitutionally flawed because it ties eligibility for waiver to a student's "outstanding performance for the latter portion of the marking period." It is irrational, and a violation of equal protection, according to the plaintiff, to waive grade reduction for students who do "outstanding" work and to impose such sanctions on students whose work is, because of academic difficulties unrelated to class absence, only average.

The defendants offer several answers to this argument. Factually, they deny the premise that the waiver provision favors students on account of their ability rather than on account of their effort, since work may be considered "outstanding" in light of a particular student's past performance. Legally, they note that the waiver provision imports a reasonable element of flexibility into the assessment of a student's total classroom performance. Finally, they remind us that a district-wide policy is more likely to assure equality of treatment for all students than is a policy administered on an ad-hoc basis by individual classroom teachers. We find the defendants' arguments persuasive and therefore reject the plaintiff's equal protection claim.

There is no error.

Notes

1. Are you impressed by (1) the quantity of arguments advanced by the plaintiff, (2) the evidence put in the record to support the claims, (3) the educational quality of the claims?

2. Observe the court's emphasis on the distinction between disciplinary and academic rules. Also note its ruling that the policy here is an academic one.

3. How, if at all, should "approved" and "unapproved" absences be handled differently as regards academics? Where should absences caused by suspension fit?

4. In Colorado the compulsory attendance statute required that students attend during a school year at least 172 days including days of illness or suspension. This statute was held to void enforcement of a local attendance policy that denied academic credit to students with more than seven absences for any reasons. The court said that this rule was inconsistent with the legislative intent that non-attendance sanctions not be imposed for absences due to illness or suspension. Gutierrez v. School Dist. R–1, 41 Colo.App. 411, 585 P.2d 935 (1978).

5. The argument that denial of credit after a number of cuts is equivalent to dropping a student from enrollment contrary to the compulsory education law was rejected in Bitting v. Lee, 168 A.D.2d 836, 564 N.Y.S.2d 791 (1990).

[Case No. 28] Power of Board to Assign Students to Schools

OLDER v. BOARD OF EDUC. OF UNION FREE SCHOOL DIST. NO. 1, TOWN OF MAMARONECK

Court of Appeals of New York, 1971.
27 N.Y.2d 333, 318 N.Y.S.2d 129, 266 N.E.2d 812.

JASEN, JUDGE. On this appeal we are asked to review the actions of the Board of Education of the Town of Mamaroneck in revising district school attendance zones, resulting in the reassignment of petitioners' children from the Murray Avenue School to the Mamaroneck School.

The pre-existing school attendance zones had produced a heavy concentration of students in two of the four elementary schools in the Larchmont-Mamaroneck area, while the other two schools in the district had extra classroom space. As a result, a citizens advisory committee, appointed to study the educational needs of the community, recommended, among other things, a redrawing of the school attendance lines in order to cope with the problem of overcrowding by utilizing existing school facilities more efficiently. The board, after further study, submitted its own report, relying largely upon the report of the committee.

One of the considerations in drawing new school attendance lines was the safety of the pupils who would be shifted to new schools. Indeed, the board in its report mentioned the safety factor and that it had requested the village to construct certain sidewalks to alleviate the worst hazards. In addition, the board stated that after safety considerations had been raised, some members of the board personally inspected the available routes and determined that the routes to the redistricted schools were no more hazardous than those currently traveled. The board also received assurances from police and governmental authorities that safety precautions, such as stop signs and traffic guards, would be provided to ameliorate any safety hazards.

The court at Special Term, without hearing any testimony, annulled the board's redistricting plan and remitted the proceeding to the board "to take further proceedings in order to provide a record of its findings and the facts upon which they are based, which are susceptible of judicial review." The court was also of the opinion that the board had adopted the redistricting plan without any independent investigation or consideration of its own. The Appellate Division affirmed, without opinion.

The threshold issue in this proceeding is whether the Board of Education had before it sufficient data upon which a discretionary determination could be made and which the court could review for arbitrariness or capriciousness. We conclude that the board, acting in an administrative capacity, had a rational basis for its determination and that its action was neither arbitrary nor capricious.

There can be no question that the Board of Education, by statute, has the power and responsibility to manage and administer the affairs of the school district, including the assignment of pupils to school therein. The Education Law specifically grants district school boards power "To have in all respects the superintendence, management and control of the educational affairs of the district, and * * * all the powers reasonably necessary to exercise powers granted expressly or by implication and to discharge duties imposed expressly or by implication by this chapter or other statutes."

It cannot be denied that the power to assign pupils to schools within the district is a power that is "reasonably necessary" to the management and control of the educational affairs of the district. Moreover, it has been consistently held that, in the assignment of pupils to schools, the Board of Education has broad discretion.

In exercising its discretion, the board was not acting in a quasi-judicial capacity necessitating formal hearings and a record of its findings supported by substantial evidence, but, rather, was acting in an administrative capacity requiring only that the determination have a rational basis. To require a quasi-judicial hearing every time the school board revised school attendance lines would pose serious problems for the administration of our schools.

The record before us is clearly sufficient to demonstrate a rational basis existed for the board's determination. The fact that a citizens advisory committee was convened and submitted a detailed report, which was largely followed, indicates that the board had a rational basis for its discretionary action and that it had met the requirement that its decision must be an informed one. Moreover, the contention that the board relied solely upon the citizens committee report simply is inaccurate. It is uncontroverted that members of the board personally visited the classrooms, held safety discussions with certain village officials, walked the proposed routes, and then made certain modifications in the advisory committee's plans.

Petitioners' greatest expressed concern is the safety aspect. In particular, they now contend that since a certain proposed walkway was not constructed by the village, the board should have reconsidered its determination, and having failed to do so, its actions were arbitrary.

To be sure, the board had considered safety factors in arriving at its redistricting plans. The record is replete with uncontroverted evidence that the board devoted much thought to safety problems and adopted the redistricting plan only after concluding that the safety of pupils transferred to new schools would not be impaired. The subsequent failure of the village to construct the proposed walkway does not mandate reconsideration by the board of its determination to revise school attendance lines, since the acceptance of this plan was not solely predicated upon the proposed construction of the walkway. The record reveals that this was just one of many factors considered by the board and that, in any event, the board was of the opinion that the proposed routes to the schools were no more hazardous than the existing paths. Moreover, the failure to construct this walkway can in no way be said to make the board's action arbitrary or capricious, so as to require further hearings, since we are dealing with a discretionary administrative matter. Even if we assume that a traffic hazard has been created, it is a matter to be handled administratively without voiding the entire plan. Any other conclusion would put serious doubt upon the finality of any administrative action.

Thus, the school board, in adopting new school boundary lines and revising school attendance lines, was acting in an administrative capacity in a matter committed by law to its discretion, and its action was neither arbitrary nor capricious.

The order of the Appellate Division should be reversed and the petition dismissed.

Notes

1. In assigning pupils to schools, the board acts in an administrative rather than in a quasi-judicial capacity. How distinct a line can be drawn between types of acts?

2. Courts will sustain administrative acts of boards if the acts have a "rational basis." Quasi-judicial acts must be supported by "substantial evidence." How significant is this difference in school administration?

3. Observe that quasi-judicial acts require "formal hearings and a record of * * * findings." Why are such hearings not required for administrative acts?

4. Consider implications of the facts that the Appellate Division of five judges unanimously had affirmed the trial judge and here the Court of Appeals, with six of seven judges sitting, unanimously reversed.

5. In Illinois it has been held that parents have no standing to sue a board of education in relation to the location of attendance centers within a district. An injunction had been sought to prevent a board's consolidating two schools. Potter v. School Directors of Dist. No. 87, County of McLean, 17 Ill.App.3d 781, 309 N.E.2d 58 (1974).

6. "We find no authority in law for the proposition that parents have a vested right to send their children to, or that children have a vested right to attend, any particular public school." Citizens Against Mandatory Bussing v. Palmason, 80 Wash.2d 445, 495 P.2d 657 (1972).

[Case No. 29]   Power of Board to Use Academic and Sex Admission Standards

BERKELMAN v. SAN FRANCISCO UNIFIED SCHOOL DIST.

United States Court of Appeals, Ninth Circuit, 1974.
501 F.2d 1264.

ALFRED T. GOODWIN, CIRCUIT JUDGE: * * *

Lowell High School is an academic, or college-preparatory, public high school which accepts each year those applicants for admission whose prior academic achievement places them within approximately the top 15 per cent of the junior-high-school graduates in the district.

The issues on appeal, phrased broadly, are: (1) whether a school district may admit students to a preferred high school on the basis of past academic achievement if the percentage of black, Spanish-American, and low-income students who qualify for admission is substantially disproportionate to the percentage of black, Spanish-American, and low-income students in the school district at large; (2) whether a school district, in order to maintain equal numbers of boys and girls in the school, may apply higher admission requirements to girls than to boys.

I

The district operates eleven high schools. Seven are "comprehensive" high schools, to which students are assigned substantially on the basis of residence. The other four high schools have special educational objectives and accept qualified students from anywhere in the district. Lowell, one of these special schools, offers advanced, college-preparatory courses. Others serve students who need special help because of language or other problems, who work part-time, or who desire vocational training.

Except for students admitted under a pilot minority-admissions program, or under the balancing-of-the-sexes policy at issue in this case, admission to Lowell is based solely upon a student's junior-high-school grade-point average in four college-preparatory subjects. All applicants in the district are ranked numerically by their junior-high-school grade-point averages, and students are admitted in their numerical order until their class is filled. Grade averages are not weighted according to schools in which they were earned. All junior-high grades are accepted at face value, regardless of neighborhood or demographic factors that might produce nonuniformity of grading among junior-high schools.

The statistical data stipulated into this record indicate a lower proportion of low-income students at Lowell than in the high school population city-wide. The data also show that 7.5% of Lowell's students are black, while 25.9% of the district's high school students are black; 5.2% of Lowell's students are Spanish-American, and 13% of the district's high-school students are Spanish-American. The minority percentages in Lowell's student body would be even lower than they are but for the minority-admissions program instituted in 1970.

However, the district-court record reveals that Lowell has not become an exclusive province of the affluent and white. Chinese students contribute 29.8% of Lowell's student body, while they make up only 17.9% of the district's high-school population. Further, 3.2% of Lowell's students are Japanese, and 3.8% are Filipino, while the respective city-wide percentages are 1.9% and 4.5%.

There was no evidence that the Board's actions in connection with its administration of Lowell were racially motivated. The admission standard is neither an intentionally discriminatory standard, nor a neutral standard applied in an intentionally discriminatory manner.

* * *

However, if an admission standard operates in fact to exclude a disproportionate number of black and Spanish-American students from Lowell, the court has a duty to test the constitutionality of that standard. Where a nonsuspect classification (past academic achievement) is alleged to operate to the detriment of a disadvantaged class or classes (black and Spanish-American students), neither "strict" nor "minimal" scrutiny provides useful guidance as a standard of review. The task is to examine the school district's assertion that the standard of past academic achievement substantially furthers the purpose of providing the best education possible for the public-school students in the district. If the past-achievement standard does substantially further that purpose, then the district has not unconstitutionally discriminated in its Lowell admission policy.

The advantages of an "academic" high school offering advanced courses to students who have excelled in a traditional curriculum are obvious. Lowell provides in one school a program which cannot be duplicated in ten other schools any more than special courses for students with specific educational needs can be economically taken from the other special high schools in the city and spread among all eleven schools. The student whose past performance has demonstrated ability to move at an advanced rate in an advanced program will receive a "better" education than he or she would receive if required to work in subject matter and at a pace which does not provide as great an educational challenge. Likewise, a student with an interest in vocational training receives a "better" education if permitted to take vocational courses than if required to continue against his wishes with the "traditional" high-school program. The school district has determined that it is educationally "better" to consolidate special offerings for the benefit of those who can meet the performance standards than to dispense with the effort entirely because budget considerations make is impossible to offer every program at every school.

Conditioning admission to Lowell upon the level of past academic achievement substantially furthers the district's purpose of operating an academic high school. Those students who have best mastered their junior-high-school courses are well prepared for more advanced courses at the high-school level. Of course, it does not necessarily follow that all applicants who fall below the cutoff line are educationally disqualified for

Lowell's program. The cutoff is the result of space and budget limitations, not the result of a perfect determination of who can and who cannot benefit from the program.

Those students not admitted to Lowell are neither denied a quality education nor relegated to an inadequate school. Rather, they attend one of San Francisco's seven "comprehensive" high schools. Unlike a "tracking" system in which the challenged classifications are "predictive" and isolate students of "less promising" ability, the classification here is based upon past achievement impartially measured. There is slight potential for psychic injury to a student from attending a comprehensive high school with the majority of the city's high-school students. We conclude that the district's legitimate interest in establishing an academic high school, admission to which is based upon past achievement, outweighs any harm imagined or suffered by students whose achievement had not qualified them for admission to that school.

Our decision does not mean that we are not troubled by the underrepresentation of some racial and ethnic groups at Lowell. Uncertainty on this score, however, does not mean that the maintenance of Lowell High is itself unconstitutional or that conditioning admission on the basis of past academic achievement is unconstitutional.

Nor does the alleged underrepresentation at Lowell of students of low-income families render the admission policy unconstitutional. Low-income persons have no greater status under the equal-protection clause of the Fourteenth Amendment than members of racial minorities. It follows that since the admission policy is not made unconstitutional by its impact upon black students, it is likewise not made unconstitutional by a similar impact upon low-income students.

II

Appellants also attack as discrimination on the basis of sex the school district's policy of requiring higher admission standards for girls than for boys. The school district asserts that the standards were designed to produce an equal number of boys and girls at Lowell. * * *

* * *

* * * No actual proof that a balance of the sexes furthers the goal of better academic education was offered by the school district.

We note that had the advanced courses been offered in each high school, rather than in a separate high school, and had the school authorities applied the same or similar admission standards to such courses, the admission standards would have been an illegal discrimination on the basis of sex under Title IX of the Education Amendments of 1972. Although Congress condemned discrimination on the basis of sex in any education program, the prohibition with regard to sex discrimination in admissions to educational institutions was not extended to public secondary schools. This omission, however, indicates nothing more than that Congress did not know the manner, extent, or rationale of separate education below the college level, and could not anticipate the effect of a prohibition upon such single-sex schools. On the other hand, its reasons for prohibiting sex discrimination in educational programs in general bears directly upon this case. Congress recognized that, because education provides access to jobs, sex discrimination in education is potentially destructive to the disfavored sex. Lowell High, as a conduit to better university education and hence to better jobs, is exactly that type of educational program with regard to which Congress intended to eliminate sex discrimination when it passed Title IX.

On the basis of the foregoing, we hold that the use of higher admission standards for female than for male applicants to Lowell High School violates the Equal Protection Clause of the Fourteenth Amendment.

* * *

Notes

1. Why do you think the school district offered no proof that a balance of the sexes was educationally desirable? Is there any? What educational rationale is offered by those who favor single sex private schools (and colleges)?

2. Observe the court's statements about Title IX. If it does not apply to secondary schools, why was it so emphasized by this court?

3. Note that the maintenance of a separate school for the academically gifted was not challenged here. That issue was abandoned by appellants at oral argument.

4. Would admission standards other than grade averages be more valid? If so, what would you suggest?

[Case No. 30] Power of Board to Charge Fees to Students

PAULSON v. MINIDOKA COUNTY SCHOOL DIST. NO. 331

Supreme Court of Idaho, 1970.
93 Idaho 469, 463 P.2d 935.

McQUADE, JUSTICE. This action was instituted by Jack Paulson, and his sons Dan and Kirk Paulson, * * *. They sought to compel the defendants Minidoka County School District, its trustees and superintendent, hereinafter referred to collectively as the "school," to furnish a transcript of grades to Dan Paulson who graduated from Minidoka County High School in June, 1968. Dan and Kirk both attended the high school during the school year 1967–1968. Dan graduated that school year, and Kirk attended school during the 1968–1969 term. The issues in the present case arose from the adoption in 1967 by the Board of Trustees of the Minidoka County School District of * * * [a] schedule of fees to be charged each student attending the high school. * * * In July, 1968, the fee schedule was amended so that although the same total of $25.00 per student was charged, the fees were itemized only as "Text Book Fees"—$12.50 and "School Activity Fees"—$12.50, total $25.00.

Dan and Kirk Paulson have each year refused to pay these fees. The school would not accept partial payment allocated to any one particular item, but insisted that the fees be paid in their entirety. Failure to pay the fees, however, did not in any way affect the student's right to attend classes. Not only were non-paying students allowed to attend classes, but they were also furnished textbooks free of charge. Until 1968–1969 all students were regularly given a student activity card and thereby allowed to attend social and athletic events even though the fees were not paid. Yearbooks were not furnished, nor were non-paying students allowed to purchase a yearbook since the school's policy was that the entire $25.00 fee be paid. Upon graduation Dan Paulson was furnished a cap and gown and presented a diploma.

Although a student could thus accumulate an "education" without payment of the fees, the impediment is that the school refuses to furnish a transcript of courses studied and grades achieved. When Dan applied to Idaho State University for admission, the school would not furnish a University required transcript. Dan was, however, provisionally admitted and this action was instituted to compel the high school to furnish a transcript.

* * *

Our task in this case is to determine the application of art. 9, sec. 1 of the Constitution of the State of Idaho to this particular factual situation. That section is:

> "The stability of a republican form of government depending mainly upon the intelligence of the people, it shall be the duty of the legislature of Idaho, to establish and maintain a general, uniform and thorough system of public, free common schools."

Because of the delicacy and difficulty in resolving constitutional problems we settle such questions on a case-by-case basis. We, today, affirm the judgment of the lower court; and we hold that public high schools in Idaho are "common schools" within the meaning of art. 9, sec. 1; that the $25.00 fee *as it was charged in this case* offended the requirement that the "common schools" be "free;" and that the appellants were under a clear legal duty to furnish transcripts to eligible graduates of Minidoka County High School. * * *

* * *

The appellants, however, argue at some length that the high school in this case was "free" despite the mandatory $25.00 fee. One half of the $25.00 fee is assigned as payment for what appellants themselves call extra-curricular activities. If a student of Minidoka County High School wishes a transcript of his scholastic achievement he must pay the entire $25.00, one-half of which is expressly consigned to fund extra-curricular activities. Items which are "extra-curricular" are, by definition, outside of or in addition to the regular academic courses or curriculum of a school. A levy for such purposes, imposed generally on all students whether they participate in extra-curricular activities or not, becomes a charge on attendance at the school. Such a charge contravenes the constitutional mandate that the school be free. But it should be noted that, because social and extra-curricular activities are not necessary elements of a high school career, the constitution does not prohibit appellants from setting fees to cover costs of such activities to be paid by students who wish to exercise an option to participate in them.

The other half of the $25.00 fee, the $12.50 "textbook fee," stands on different ground. Textbooks are necessary elements of any school's activity. They represent a fixed expense peculiar to education, the benefits from which inure to every student in equal proportion (ignoring differences in ability and motivation) solely as a function of his being a student. Unlike pencils and paper, the student has no choice in the quality or quantity of textbooks he will use if he is to earn his education. He will use exactly the books, prescribed by the school authorities, that his classmates use; and no voluntary act of his can obviate the need for books nor lessen their expense. School books are, thus, indistinguishable from other fixed educational expense items such as school building maintenance or teachers' salaries. The appellants may not charge students for such items because the common schools are to be "free" as our constitution requires. (Appellants argue that if books must be provided free of charge then it becomes impossible to draw a line and even school clothing must be given away. This contention is answered by pointing out that clothing is not an item peculiarly necessary for the use of free schools—everyone must be clothed if he walks the streets— and it is an item of expense which is especially subject to personal taste in terms of the cost, quality and quantity of it used by any individual student.)

Appellants contend, however, that they are giving and have given the respondents "free high school educations," which is all that is required by the constitution. The appellants would separate the transcript from the educational experience it evidences and they argue that they are merely making availability of a transcript contingent upon payment of the fees. They also reason that they are under no clear legal duty to furnish a transcript and are not subject to mandamus. This argument evidences a serious misapprehension of the constitutional requirement of free schools. If the constitution said that all that was necessary was a "free common school education" the case might be different, but the constitution instead demands "free common schools." The *school* and the entire product to be received from it by the student must be "free."

The appellants failed to provide "free common schools" when they made access to the official reports of the students' records contingent on the $25.00 fee charged in this case. This fee bears no apparent relationship to the actual costs of printing and distributing the transcripts. It instead serves an enforcement purpose only. The appellants have withheld Dan's transcript to coerce payment of the lump-sum $25.00 fee. Because they may not charge the fee it follows that they may not penalize nonpayment of the fee by withholding an incidental but necessary transcript.

The legal duty to make available a transcript arises from the practicality that, in our society, the ability to obtain a transcript without cost is a necessary incident of a high school education. A reasonable fee, after the first free transcript, representing actual average costs, would be proper and may be charged for the duplication and issuance of subsequent transcripts.

* * *

Notes

1. Was it necessary for the court to cover so many specifics to decide the basic question presented?

2. The court says boards in Idaho may set fees "to cover costs of such [extra-curricular] activities to be paid by * * * [participating] students." Consider the following:

(a) May football players or students participating in drama be charged the cost of such activities?

(b) How would cost be determined? If it includes salaries, maintenance and depreciation of facilities, debt service, utilities, etc., would not the cost be prohibitive for many students?

(c) What would constitute "participation" in such activities? Do spectators "participate?"

(d) What are the "necessary elements of a high school career?"

3. The court says "the *school* (emphasis by the court) and the entire product to be received from it by the student must be 'free'." How does this statement square with the dichotomy made between curricular and extra-curricular activities?

4. Are there cogent objections to a holding (1) that all undertakings supported wholly or partially by public funds must be free? (2) that all undertakings required or permitted by school authorities must be free? (3) that certain undertakings be free only to "needy" students?

5. "The suspension of a student from school for a parent's failure to pay textbook fees amounts to a denial of equal protection." (The legality of imposing the fees was not questioned by plaintiffs in the case). Carder v. Michigan City School Corp., 552 F.Supp. 869 (N.D.Ind.1982).

6. This was the first modern appellate court textbook-fee case. Within ten years, there had been twelve. In states that by statute require free textbooks, the issue, of course, would not arise.

[Case No. 31] Constitutionality of Eligibility Requirement for Interscholastic Athletics—General Considerations

ALBACH v. ODLE

United States Court of Appeals, Tenth Circuit, 1976.
531 F.2d 983.

PER CURIAM. This appeal seeks to test the application of transfer rules adopted by the New Mexico Activities Association. The rules automatically bar from interscholastic high school athletic competition for one year any student who transfers from his home district to a boarding school or from a boarding school to his home district. * * *

The trial court dismissed the complaint on various grounds, one of which was that it failed to raise a substantial federal question. We affirm.

Controlling precedent is found in Oklahoma High School Athletic Ass'n v. Bray, 321 F.2d 269 (10th Cir.), where this court stated:

" * * * In the case at bar, once the pleadings were pierced at pre-trial, it became apparent that Bray's grievance with the Athletic Association lay only with the application of its residence rule, the Board's refusal to grant an exception for hardship, and a general attack upon the amount of power delegated by the high schools to the Association. Such complaints are not within federal cognizance, * * *."

The court held that if Bray had not voluntarily dismissed the action, the trial court would have been compelled to dismiss for lack of a substantial federal question. Appellant's allegations are virtually identical with those noted above.

Appellant cites numerous cases in support of the contention that high school athletic regulations must survive constitutional scrutiny. The cases are distinguished by the fact that, in the context of athletic regulations, clearly defined constitutional principles are at issue. See Brenden v. Independent School District 742, 477 F.2d 1292 (8th Cir.), Gilpin v. Kansas State High School Activities Ass'n, Inc., 377 F.Supp. 1233 (D.Kan.), and Reed v. Nebraska School Activities Ass'n, 341 F.Supp. 258 (D.Neb.)—sexual discrimination; Davis v. Meek, 344 F.Supp. 298 (N.D.Ohio)—invasion of marital privacy. See also Howard University v. National Collegiate Athletic Ass'n, 166 U.S.App.D.C. 260, 510 F.2d 213—alienage discrimination; Louisiana High School Athletic Ass'n v. St. Augustine High School, 396 F.2d 224 (5th Cir.)—racial discrimination. That is not the case here. Participation in interscholastic athletics is not a constitutionally protected civil right. Oklahoma High School Athletic Ass'n v. Bray, supra; Mitchell v. Louisiana High School Athletic Ass'n, 430 F.2d 1155 (5th Cir.). The supervision and regulation of high school athletic programs remain within the discretion of appropriate state boards, and are not within federal cognizance under 42 U.S.C.A. § 1983 unless the regulations deny an athlete a constitutionally protected right or classify him or her on a suspect basis.

Appellant also argues that Goss v. Lopez somehow negates our decision in *Bray*. We disagree. *Goss* recognizes a student's entitlement to a public education as a property interest which is constitutionally protected. A ten-day suspension from school without a hearing was found to violate a student's right to due process under the Fourteenth Amendment. But it is necessary to note that in framing the property interest the Court in *Goss* speaks in terms of the "educational process." The educational process is a broad and comprehensive concept with a variable and indefinite meaning. It is not limited to classroom attendance but includes innumerable separate components, such as participation in athletic activity and membership in school clubs and social groups, which combine to provide an atmosphere of intellectual and moral advancement. We do not read *Goss* to establish a property interest subject to constitutional protection in each of these separate components.

Affirmed.

Notes

1. How do you account for the rash of cases attacking rules covering eligibility for participation in interscholastic athletics that started in the late 1960's? The present opinion succinctly covers many established constitutional principles relevant to the area.

2. The mere fact that there may be reason to oppose a rule or that the rule may appear unfair when applied to a particular student does not permit courts to intervene and substitute their judgment for that of school authorities when there is a rational basis for the rule. In re United States ex rel. Missouri State High School Activities Ass'n, 682 F.2d 147 (8 Cir.1982).

3. In a few states girls basketball may operate under rules different from boys basketball. It has been held not to violate constitutional rights of girls that the rules are not the same. Jones v. Oklahoma Secondary School Activities Ass'n, 453 F.Supp. 150 (W.D.Okl.1977); Cape v. Tennessee Secondary School Athletic Ass'n, 563 F.2d 793 (6 Cir.1977). For an opposing view, see Dodson v. Arkansas Activities Ass'n, 468 F.Supp. 394 (E.D.Ark.1979).

4. A college student has no constitutional property right to play intercollegiate football in anticipation of a career in professional football. National Collegiate Athletic Ass'n v. Gillard, 352 So.2d 1072 (Miss.1977). Neither does a high school student have a constitutional property right to be on the wrestling team in expectation of earning a college scholarship. Brands v. Sheldon Community School, 671 F.Supp. 627 (N.D.Iowa 1987).

5. A rule setting the number of players that a school can use in play-off games below the number it can use in regular season play does not deny equal protection to those players eliminated. The Florida High School Activities Ass'n, Inc. v. Thomas, 434 So.2d 306 (Fla.1983).

[Case No. 32] Constitutionality of Eligibility Requirement for Interscholastic Athletics—Parent Rights

KITE v. MARSHALL

United States Court of Appeals, Fifth Circuit, 1981.
661 F.2d 1027.

POLITZ, CIRCUIT JUDGE: These consolidated actions challenge the validity of Section 21 of Article VIII of the Constitution and Contest Rules of the University Interscholastic League (UIL) of Texas. The challenged section suspends for one year the varsity athletics eligibility of any high school student who attends certain training camps. The district court enjoined the enforcement of section 21 and subsequently declared the rule unconstitutional as applied. We reverse.

UIL is a voluntary, non-profit association of public schools below collegiate rank in the State of Texas. * * * Its stated objective is "to foster among the public schools of Texas interschool competitions as an aid in the preparation for citizenship." In pursuit of this goal, UIL promulgates rules and regulations governing various aspects of competition in speech, journalism, literary and academic contests, drama, music and athletics. Although a private organization, UIL's functioning constitutes state action subject to the limitations of the fourteenth amendment to the Constitution. We must determine whether section 21 violates either the due process or equal protection clause of that amendment.

The district court found section 21 to be constitutionally infirm because it infringed protected parental authority in the child-rearing arena. Appellees exhort us to affirm the trial court's conclusions, principally relying on the "family choice doctrine" which has its genesis in Prince v. Massachusetts, Pierce v. Society of Sisters, and Meyer v. Nebraska. We cannot accept the invitation.

The *Meyer* and *Pierce* decisions are based on the premise that the state has no power to "standardize its children," or to "foster a homogeneous people," by foreclosing the opportunity of individuals "to heed the music of different drummers." * * *

Appellees cite as controlling precedent a line of Supreme Court decisions which purportedly recognize the existence of a "private realm of family life which the state cannot enter," absent compelling reasons. Uncertainty abounds, not only as to the constitutional spring from which this family privacy right flows, but also as to its definition and character.

Recent decisions by the Supreme Court declaring that parents have no constitutional right to educate their children in private segregated academies, Runyon v. McCrary, or to demand approval before the administration of corporal punishment in school, Ingraham v. Wright, * * * clearly signal that parental authority falls short of being constitutionally absolute. Confronted with these situations which, at first blush, appear to rest at the heart of parental decision making, the Supreme Court refrained from clothing parental judgment with a constitutional mantle.

The instant case presents a similar inquiry. Reduced to essentials, the legal questions posed are: (1) whether parents possess a fundamental right to send their children to summer athletic camps; and (2) whether the children have a constitutional right to attend such activities. As is frequently the case, in the very postulation of the questions the answer lies. A negative response to both questions is mandated. This case implicates no fundamental constitutional right.

The determination that no fundamental right to participate in summer athletic camp exists establishes the level of scrutiny to which we must subject section 21. The regulation will pass constitutional muster if it is found to have a rational basis.

Due Process

The UIL contends that its rules are designed to make competition among its 1,142 member schools as fair and equitable as possible. The UIL program, including the athletics component, is only a part of the overall educational process. Several reasons are advanced in support of section 21, including the need to control over-zealous coaches, parents and communities, the achieving of a competitive balance between those who can afford to attend summer camp and those who cannot, the avoidance of various excessive pressures on students, and the abrogation of the use of camps as recruiting mechanisms.

It cannot be argued seriously that section 21 is wholly arbitrary and totally without value in the promotion of a legitimate state objective. We do not evaluate the ultimate wisdom, *vel non,* of section 21, or the sagacity of its methodology. The school authorities have concluded that section 21 serves the purpose of making interscholastic athletics fairer and more competitive. We are not prepared to say that section 21 bears no meaningful relationship to the achievement of that ideal. The due process clause of the fourteenth amendment has not been offended.

Equal Protection

Traditionally, the equal protection analysis has been performed against the backdrop of the standards of strict scrutiny and minimum rationality. To withstand strict scrutiny, a statute must necessarily relate to a compelling state interest. The rational basis test requires only that the legislation or regulation under challenge rationally promote a legitimate governmental objective.

A state action viewed under the rational basis banner is presumed to be valid. In such a situation, "the burden is not upon the state to establish the rationality of its restriction, but is upon the challenger to show that the restriction is wholly arbitrary." Accordingly, only when a demonstration is made that the classification contained in the regulation is wholly arbitrary or does not teleologically relate to a permissible governmental objective is the equal protection clause violated. When "the classification created by the regulatory scheme neither trammels fundamental rights or interests nor burdens an inherently suspect class, equal protection analysis requires that the classification be rationally related to a legitimate state interest."

In view of the Supreme Court's prevailing opinions * * * we believe that the minimum rationality test provides the guide for our equal protection evaluation.

Admittedly section 21 operates to treat student-athletes who attend summer athletic camps differently from those students who do not. The former lose eligibility in all varsity sports for the next year. But the categorization is not premised on impermissible, suspect grounds. Nor does the classification impinge upon the exercise of fundamental rights. The rule seeks to achieve a balance in interscholastic athletics. It is not unconstitutional.

The judgment of the district court, in these consolidated cases, is reversed.

Notes

1. The Supreme Court without dissent denied certiorari, 457 U.S. 1120, 102 S.Ct. 2934, 73 L.Ed.2d 1333 (1982).

2. The emphasis by the plaintiff on the parent rights argument apparently was to try to avoid the precedential effect of the numerous cases decided as was Case No. 31 and the cases in the Notes thereto.

3. Suppose the parents sent their son to a summer drama school. Could education authorities enforce a ban on his trying out for the school play?

4. The drinking party in Case No. 122 was held at the home of the parents of one of the students. That the parents may have approved of the activity was not relevant in that case either.

5. Runyon v. McCrary, 427 U.S. 160, 96 S.Ct. 2586, 49 L.Ed.2d 415 (1976), presented "only two basic questions: whether § 1981 prohibits private, commercially operated, nonsectarian schools from denying admission to prospective students because they are Negroes, and, if so, whether that federal law is constitutional as so applied." The answer to each, by a vote of seven-to-two, was "yes." The Court said, "It is clear that the present application of § 1981 infringes no parental right recognized in *Meyer, Pierce,* [Wisconsin v.] *Yoder,* or *Norwood.*" (§ 1981 is in the Appendix and the cases are in the Table of Cases.)

[Case No. 33] Power of State to Set Academic Requirements for Participants in Extracurricular Activities

SPRING BRANCH I.S.D. v. STAMOS

Supreme Court of Texas, 1985.
695 S.W.2d 556.

RAY, JUSTICE. This is a direct appeal brought by the Attorney General, representing the Texas Education Agency, and others, seeking immediate appellate review of an order of the trial court which held unconstitutional, and enjoined enforcement of, a provision of the Texas Education Code.   * * * We hold that the statutory provision is not unconstitutional and reverse the judgment of the trial court.

Chris Stamos and others brought this suit on behalf of Nicky Stamos and others, seeking a permanent injunction against enforcement of the Texas "no pass, no play" rule by the Spring Branch and Alief Independent School Districts. The Texas Education Agency and the University Interscholastic League intervened. The district court issued a temporary restraining order and later, after a hearing, a temporary injunction enjoining all parties from enforcing the rule. This court issued an order staying the district court's order and setting the cause for expedited review.

THE "NO PASS, NO PLAY" RULE

The Second Called Session of the 68th Legislature adopted a package of educational reforms known as "H.B. 72." A major provision of these educational reforms was the so-called "no pass, no play" rule, which generally requires that students maintain a "70" average in all classes to be eligible for participation in extracurricular activities. The rule is incorporated in section 21.920 of the Texas Education Code and provides as follows:

§ 21.920.   Extracurricular Activities

(a) The State Board of Education by rule shall limit participation in and practice for extracurricular activities during the school day and the school week. The rules shall, to the extent possible, preserve the school day for academic activities without interruption for extracurricular activities. In scheduling those activities and practices, a district must comply with the rules of the board.

(b) A student, other than a mentally retarded student, enrolled in a school district in this state shall be suspended from participation in any extracurricular activity sponsored or sanctioned by the school district during the grade reporting period after a grade reporting period in which the student received a grade lower than the equivalent of 70 on a scale of 100 in any academic class. The campus principal may remove this suspension if the class is an identified honors or advanced class. A student may not be suspended under this subsection during the period in which school is recessed for the summer or during the initial grade reporting period of a regular school term on the basis of grades received in the final grade reporting period of the preceding regular school term.

* * *

ISSUES RAISED

The sole issue before this court is the constitutionality of the no pass, no play rule. The district court held the rule unconstitutional on the grounds that it violated equal protection and due process guarantees. The burden is on the party attacking the constitutionality of an act of the legislature. There is a presumption in favor of the constitutionality of an act of the legislature.

This court has long recognized the important role education plays in the maintenance of our democratic society. Article VII of the Texas Constitution "discloses a well-considered purpose on the part of those who framed it to bring about the establishment and maintenance of a comprehensive system of public education, consisting of a general public free school system and a system of higher education." Section 1 of article VII of the Constitution establishes a mandatory duty upon the legislature to make suitable provision for the support and maintenance of public free schools. The Constitution leaves to the legislature alone the determination of which methods, restrictions, and regulations are necessary and appropriate to carry out this duty, so long as that determination is not so arbitrary as to violate the constitutional rights of Texas' citizens.

Equal Protection

Stamos challenges the constitutionality of the "no pass, no play" rule on the ground that it violates the equal protection clause of the Texas Constitution. The first determination this court must make in the context of equal protection analysis is the appropriate standard of review. When the classification created by a state regulatory scheme neither infringes upon fundamental rights or interests nor burdens an inherently suspect class, equal protection analysis requires that the classification be rationally related to a legitimate state interest. Therefore, we must first determine whether the rule burdens an inherently suspect class or infringes upon fundamental rights or interests.

The no pass, no play rule classifies students based upon their achievement levels in their academic courses. We hold that those students who fail to maintain a minimum level of proficiency in all of their courses do not constitute the type of discrete, insular minority necessary to constitute a "suspect" class. Thus, the rule does not burden an inherently "suspect" class.

* * *

Stamos also argues that the rule is subject to strict scrutiny under equal protection analysis because it impinges upon a fundamental right, i.e., the right to participate in extracurricular activities. We note that the overwhelming majority of jurisdictions have held that a student's right to participation in extracurricular activities does *not* constitute a fundamental right.

Stamos cites the case of *Bell v. Lone Oak Independent School District* for the proposition that students have a fundamental right to participate in extracurricular activities. In *Bell,* a school regulation prohibited married students from participating in extracurricular activities. Because the regulation impinged upon the fundamental right of marriage, the court of appeals held the regulation subject to strict scrutiny and struck it down because the school district had shown no compelling interest to support its enforcement. The presence of a fundamental right (marriage) distinguishes *Bell* from the present cause.

Fundamental rights have their genesis in the express and implied protections of personal liberty recognized in federal and state constitutions. A student's "right" to participate in extracurricular activities does not rise to the same level as the right to free speech or free exercise of religion, both of which have long been recognized as fundamental rights under our state and federal constitutions. We adopt the majority rule and hold that a student's right to participate in extracurricular activities *per se* does *not* rise to the level of a fundamental right under our constitution.

Because the no pass, no play rule neither infringes upon fundamental rights nor burdens an inherently suspect class, we hold that it is *not* subject to "strict" or heightened equal protection scrutiny. * * *

The no pass, no play rule distinguishes students based upon whether they maintain a satisfactory minimum level of performance in each of their classes. Students who fail to maintain a minimum proficiency in all of their classes are ineligible for participation in school-sponsored extracurricular activities for the following six-week period, with no carry over from one school year to the next. The rule provides a strong incentive for students wishing to participate in extracurricular activities to maintain minimum levels of performance in all of their classes. In view of the rule's objective to promote improved classroom performance by students, we find the rule rationally related to the legitimate state interest in providing a quality education to Texas' public school students. * * *

The distinctions recognized in the rule for mentally retarded students and students enrolled in honors or advanced courses likewise do not render the rule violative of the equal protection guarantees of the Texas Constitution. While the statute itself does not deprive students of their right to equal protection of the law, we recognize that the discretion given to school principals in the rule's provision dealing with honors or advanced courses may well give rise to arbitrary or discriminatory application violative of equal protection principles. *See Yick Wo v. Hopkins,* 118 U.S. 356, 6 S.Ct. 1064, 30 L.Ed. 220 (1886). We are faced with no allegations of discriminatory application of the rule's honors exception in the present case.

Procedural Due Process

We begin our analysis of the due process arguments in this cause by recognizing that the strictures of due process apply only to the threatened deprivation of liberty and property interests deserving the protection of the federal and state constitutions. The federal courts have made it clear that the federal constitution's due process guarantees do not protect a student's interest in participating in extracurricular activities. We must, then, examine our state constitution to determine whether its due process guarantees extend to a student's desire to participate in school-sponsored extracurricular activities.

A property or liberty interest must find its origin in some aspect of state law. Nothing in either our state constitution or statutes entitles students to an absolute right to participation in extracurricular activities. We are in agreement, therefore, with the overwhelming majority of jurisdictions that students do not possess a constitutionally protected interest in their participation in extracurricular activities. Therefore, the strictures of procedural due process do *not* apply to the determination by a campus principal, pursuant to section 21.920(b) of the Texas Education Code, as to whether a student who fails an identified honors or advanced course shall be permitted to participate in extracurricular activities.

Substantive Due Process

Stamos cites *Spann v. City of Dallas,* 111 Tex. 350, 235 S.W. 513 (1921), to support his argument that the rule violates principles of fundamental fairness and notions of substantive due process by giving school principals discretion to determine whether students who fail honors or advanced courses may participate in extracurricular activities. In *Spann,* this court declared void a city ordinance that required persons seeking to construct commercial buildings within residential areas to first obtain the consent of both neighboring residents and the city building inspector. There, we found that the ordinance provided no standards for builders or building inspectors with regard to the proper design for such buildings. By leaving the approval for such buildings "subject to the arbitrary discretion of the inspector," the ordinance violated the would-be builders' property right to use their property as they saw fit. This court emphasized that the ordinance in *Spann* infringed upon well-recognized property rights by permitting wholly arbitrary limitations upon the uses which owners could make of their property.

In the present case, appellees liken the school principals' unfettered discretion in determining both which classes shall constitute "advanced" or "honors" courses and whether students failing such classes may participate in extracurricular activities to the building inspectors' unfettered discretion over approving commercial building plans. *Spann* is distinguishable for the obvious reason that a recognized property interest was affected by the Dallas ordinance. As stated previously, students have no constitutionally protected interest in participation in extracurricular activities. Because no constitutionally protected interest is implicated by this delegation of authority to school principals, no violation of due process, substantive or procedural, results therefrom.

We do not agree with Stamos' argument that a school principal's exercise of discretion pursuant to the "honors" exception to the rule is shielded from all review. Arbitrary, capricious, or discriminatory exercise of a school principal's discretion pursuant to subsection 21.920(b) of the Texas Education Code may well give rise to claims based upon equal protection grounds. See Yick Wo v. Hopkins, 118 U.S. 356, 6 S.Ct. 1064, 30 L.Ed. 220 (1886). Accreditation audits of schools and school districts may also afford relief against improper utilization of the "honors" exception. We also note there are no findings of fact before us that any of the student-plaintiffs received failing grades in honors or advanced courses.

* * *

Accordingly, we reverse the district court's judgment with regard to the constitutionality of section 21.920 of the Texas Education Code and dissolve the temporary injunction ordered by the district court.

Notes

1. Legal aspects of the school program are a focus of Chapter 4. Also see the Index.

2. Bear in mind that this detailed "rule" was adopted at the highest state functional level, the legislature. The opinion of the court is structured along the basic Fourteenth Amendment thrusts outlined in Chapter 1.

3. A similar rule promulgated under its general supervisory powers by the West Virginia state board of education was upheld in Bailey v. Truby, 174 W.Va. 8, 321 S.E.2d 302 (1984). The highest court of the state rejected an argument that powers of county boards were infringed. County boards could not act to diminish the state board's constitutional power to pursue academic excellence. But, said the court, a county board could set a higher standard than the state board requirement.

4. A policy adopted locally that required a 2.0 grade point average in five of six classes to remain eligible to participate in extracurricular activities was upheld by the Court of Appeals of Kentucky. The policy was found to be reasonably designed "to minimize outside activities which distract from academic endeavors while providing incentive to make acceptable grades so the eligibility may again be retained." Thompson v. Fayette County Public Schools, 786 S.W.2d 879 (Ky.App.1990).

5. In Yick Wo v. Hopkins, cited in the case, the Supreme Court in 1886 found an equal protection violation in a situation where a municipal ordinance for licensing wooden laundries had been administered so as to refuse licenses to Chinese applicants while granting licenses to others. The Court inferred purposeful discrimination from the statistics of almost 300 applications.

Chapter 5

FINANCING EDUCATION

In General

In forty-nine states the financing of the schools is a joint enterprise of the state as a whole and the local school districts. Some funds come from state-level sources and some from local-level sources. While there are many judicial decisions involving local districts because of the limitations on the power under which they operate, the cases affecting the state are comparatively few and deal primarily with constitutional mandates and limitations placed on the legislature with respect to the manner of raising or allocating state funds. Problems related to church-state separation are discussed in Chapter 2. Chapter 3 gives some attention to financial considerations involved in the alteration of school districts and to the device of withholding state aid as a means of enforcing state-level regulations. Also, there are often important financial implications of elements discussed under curriculum, school property, and contracts. In this chapter the focus will be on raising and distributing funds for public schools.

The School Tax

Power to Levy

As has been emphasized previously, the courts are uniform in holding that school districts are instrumentalities of the state created by the legislature to carry out the state constitutional mandates relative to providing educational opportunities for the children of the state. It has been noted that school districts are not agencies with broad powers, but are limited to those powers that are expressly or by necessary implication conferred upon them by the legislature. Further, the legislature may classify districts and delegate different financial powers to different classes of districts.[1]

It is well settled that there is no inherent power in school districts to levy taxes.[2] This view is applied both to kinds of taxes and to rates of taxes. Taxation is a special power which must be specifically conferred upon a subordinate governmental agency by the legislature if the power is to exist there. The power to establish and maintain schools does not carry with it any implied power to levy taxes therefor.

The legislature may delegate its power to tax, both as to kinds and rates, to subordinate bodies. It may or may not set limits as long as the

1. Pirrone v. City of Boston, 364 Mass. 403, 305 N.E.2d 96 (1973).

2. Marion and McPherson Railway Co. v. Alexander, 63 Kan. 72, 64 P. 978 (1901). [Case No. 34]

248

taxing authorities comprise elected officials. State constitutional tax limitations, of course, must be observed.[3] The courts will not permit even indirect exceptions.[4] The power to levy taxes, however, cannot be delegated to appointed bodies unless there are clear limitations put on the extent of the transferred power.[5] If purposes and maximum amounts or rates are specified, the delegation is proper.[6] Under such an arrangement it is deemed that the legislature has in fact set the tax and merely left leeway for local administrative discretion. It has been held a violation of the separation of powers doctrine, however, for the legislature to provide that legislators from a county must approve any increase in the tax rate imposed by the county school board.[7]

Judicially examined was the authority in tax matters of the board of education in Chicago, which was appointed by the mayor.[8] The school budget was prepared by the board of education, but taxes therefor were levied by the city. It was alleged that by levying taxes for its educational system the city was unlawfully exercising the power to tax under the constitution of Illinois. The court pointed out that the statutory language authorizing the levy was framed in the conjunctive, joining the board and the city authorities. Even though all preliminary steps had to be taken by the board and a final budget adopted by the board, no school taxes would be forthcoming without the adoption by the city council of an ordinance levying the tax. It followed that no tax was levied in this situation by the board.

It has been held that if the legislature sets the rate of the tax by which the amount is mathematically deduced from the facts and events occurring within the year, then there is no delegation of the taxing power but rather a direct exercise of it.[9] Similar reasoning has been applied to uphold the granting of power to a state board of education to impose on reorganized school districts a tax to cover bonded indebtedness payments.[10]

It has also been held that due process of law is not violated by a statute which allows the voters of a larger municipal unit to outvote those in a smaller municipality in regard to a tax matter. A case in point arose in Alaska. In an area where school district and municipal boundaries were not coterminous, validity of a sales tax levied by a school district was contested. The statute in question empowered a

3. Hurd v. City of Buffalo, 41 A.D.2d 402, 343 N.Y.S.2d 950 (1973), aff. 34 N.Y.2d 628, 355 N.Y.S.2d 369, 311 N.E.2d 504 (1974).

4. Bethlehem Steel Corp. v. Board of Educ. of City School Dist. of Lackawanna, 44 N.Y.2d 831, 406 N.Y.S.2d 752, 378 N.E.2d 115 (1978), app. dism. 439 U.S. 922, 99 S.Ct. 303, 58 L.Ed.2d 315 (1978).

5. Wilson v. School Dist. of Philadelphia, 328 Pa. 225, 195 A. 90 (1937); Crow v. McAlpine, 277 S.C. 240, 285 S.E.2d 355 (1981).

6. Minsinger v. Rau, 236 Pa. 327, 84 A. 902 (1912); Village of West Milwaukee v. Area Bd. of Vocational, Technical and Adult Educ., 51 Wis.2d 356, 187 N.W.2d 387 (1971).

7. Gunter v. Blanton, 259 S.C. 436, 192 S.E.2d 473 (1972).

8. Latham v. Board of Educ. of the City of Chicago, 31 Ill.2d 178, 201 N.E.2d 111 (1964).

9. Kee v. Parks, 153 Tenn. 306, 283 S.W. 751 (1926).

10. Opinion of the Justices, 246 A.2d 90 (Del.1968).

school district to levy a tax not exceeding two percent on sales and services within the district provided fifty-five percent of the voters within the district consented thereto. The statute further provided that no such sales tax could be levied upon sales or services within an incorporated municipality which is part of a school district if the municipality levied a sales tax upon sales and services within the municipality. A tax levy for schools had been approved in the school district which included the city of Fairbanks. An analysis of election results showed that fewer than fifty-five percent of the voters within the school district outside the city of Fairbanks approved the tax. Since the city of Fairbanks had its own sales tax, the residents within the municipality were not subject to the school district tax under provisions of the challenged statute. The Supreme Court of Alaska found the statute to be constitutional.[11]

School taxes are state, not local, in nature, even though they are levied by the local district. This result follows from the concept that education is a state, rather than a local, function. It further follows that a district may be compelled by the state to establish and maintain schools of a given standard, and the burden of financing them may be imposed upon the local district without the consent of its inhabitants.[12] Also, the district may be required to issue bonds for the purpose of raising funds for the erection of a school building despite the fact that no consent has been obtained from the voters.[13]

Where a tax is levied for a special purpose, the funds raised must be used only for that purpose.[14] Any funds remaining after the purpose is achieved may be distributed as the legislature determines.[15]

In the absence of a statute to the contrary, where a municipal body collects the taxes levied by a board of education, the entire proceeds must be turned over to the board.[16] Neither a collection fee or retention of any accrued interest by the municipality is permitted.

Whether land developers can be assessed impact fees to be used for facilities needed to accommodate changes in civic services occasioned by the developments has been the subject of litigation in which generally the provision has been upheld. Schools frequently have been one or the sole beneficiary. Where the latter was the situation and the fee was locally imposed the Supreme Court of California found no equal protection breach [17] and the Supreme Court of Florida held that the state constitutional mandate for a uniform system of free schools was not

---

11. Bailey v. Fairbanks Independent School Dist., 370 P.2d 526 (Alaska 1962).

12. State v. Freeman, 61 Kan. 90, 58 P. 959 (1899).

13. Revell v. Mayor, etc., of Annapolis, 81 Md. 1, 31 A. 695 (1895). [Case No. 35]

14. Thomas v. Board of Educ., County of McDowell, 161 W.Va. 84, 261 S.E.2d 66 (1979).

15. Douglas Independent School Dist. No. 3 of Meade and Pennington Counties v. Bell, 272 N.W.2d 825 (S.D.1978).

16. New Orleans v. Fisher, 180 U.S. 185, 21 S.Ct. 347, 45 L.Ed. 485 (1901).

17. Candid Enterprises, Inc. v. Grossmont Union High School Dist., 39 Cal.3d 878, 218 Cal.Rptr. 303, 705 P.2d 876 (1985).

violated.[18]

Irregular Levies

Despite the fact that the law lays down the procedures to be followed by local agencies in levying taxes, failure to follow the indicated procedures is very frequent. The question of the validity of the tax then arises. The answer depends upon whether the courts construe the statutory provisions as mandatory or directory.

The courts purport to determine whether the legislature intended the statutory steps to be conditions precedent to the validity of the tax. If so, the provisions are held to be mandatory. Courts are faced with the alternatives of declaring an irregularly levied tax invalid and perhaps crippling the schools, or declaring it valid and working a hardship on the taxpayers. In general the courts tend to hold such taxes valid if the irregularity is of minor importance and the taxpayers are not deprived of some substantial right through the irregularity.

However, it appears that if the irregularity is one which deprives the taxpayer of a voice in determining whether a particular tax should be levied, the courts are disposed to hold the statutory provision mandatory. This situation arises most frequently in connection with giving notice of elections at which a tax is to be voted on, especially if the election is not a general one, the time and place of which are fixed by law, but one which is set by proclamation of a local board. In the former case, the electorate is bound to take cognizance of elections set by statute, and the notice required of the local agency is considered merely as a reminder. In the latter case, since the voters have no notice of the election except that given by the local agency, it is generally held that the statutory notice is mandatory.[19] But if the evidence shows that the electors in fact knew of the election and had an opportunity to vote, or that the giving of the statutory notice would not have changed the result, the election usually will be held valid.[20]

Rate of Levy

After a body of competent jurisdiction has determined the budget for a school district, it becomes necessary to levy the taxes to raise the money. To establish a tax rate, an estimate of revenues must be made. Thus, it may come about that more money is raised than was anticipated. However, generally speaking, a school board cannot use its taxing power to establish a surplus fund. The Supreme Court of Illinois ruled unconstitutional an action whereby a local board of education levied a tax with a view to accumulating a fund which would be used at some

18. St. Johns County v. Northeast Florida Builders Ass'n, Inc., 583 So.2d 635 (Fla. 1991).

19. Roberts v. Murphy, 144 Ga. 177, 86 S.E. 545 (1915).

20. Shelton v. School Bd., 43 Okl. 239, 142 P. 1034 (1914).

time in the future to build a schoolhouse.[21] In that case it was shown that the board of directors did not intend to use the levy for building purposes during the year, but rather intended in the future to decide on a building and apply surpluses accrued to that venture.

The Supreme Court of Nebraska, however, has specifically recognized the authority to levy a tax rate which would produce a relatively small surplus should all of the funds be collected.[22] A taxpayer had challenged the validity of a levy for school purposes on the ground that the levy was in excess of the needs of the district. It was charged that an excess was budgeted resulting from a failure to take into account a balance on hand at the end of the school year. The court upheld a levy which it was anticipated would produce an excess for all purposes of about eight hundred thousand dollars in a budget of thirteen million dollars. The court pointed out that possible, if not even probable, fluctuations in expenses of operation and of revenue from various sources made necessary adequate estimates of the sums required.

The Supreme Court of Illinois decided a case in which it was contended that a tax levy by a school district was illegal because it was excessive.[23] The levy for the district's retirement fund was for $166,000. The three preceding years the levies were $118,174; $121,666; $114,102. The state's highest court refused to invalidate the levy. It stated that although taxing bodies may not levy taxes beyond their needs and thereby unnecessarily accumulate money in the public treasury, they need not wait until the money is actually required to pay outstanding obligations before levying the tax.

When a county school board in Georgia increased the tax rate to almost twice that of the previous year, some taxpayers sought an injunction on the ground that this was an abuse of discretion warranting judicial intervention. The reason offered by the board was that there was considerable uncertainty over the continued availability of federal funds for aid to federally impacted areas. One persuasive element of evidence was a letter to this effect to one of the defendants from a United States Senator. The Supreme Court of Georgia, observing that the funds to be raised by the increase in the rate were approximately equivalent to the money ordinarily expected from the federal source, refused to enjoin the board.[24]

In New Jersey a municipality coterminous with a school district sought to compel the board of education to spend an accumulated surplus before the municipality paid to the board taxes it was required to collect for the board. The court held that the board was entitled to maintain "a reasonable surplus" in order to meet unforeseen contingencies.[25] There was a procedure for review of the board's budget by the

---

21. Cleveland, C., C. & St. L. Ry. Co. v. People, 208 Ill. 9, 69 N.E. 832 (1904).

22. C. R. T. Corp. v. Board of Equalization, 172 Neb. 540, 110 N.W.2d 194 (1961).

23. People ex rel. Sweet v. Central Illinois Public Service Co., 48 Ill.2d 145, 268 N.E.2d 404 (1971).

24. Watkins v. Jackson, 227 Ga. 213, 179 S.E.2d 747 (1971).

25. Board of Educ. of Borough of Fair

state commissioner of education. Furthermore, the board would have to account for all funds, including investment income derived from the surplus. These were sufficient restrictions on the board, and the municipality could place no others.

In a case which had become moot the Supreme Court of South Dakota observed that although it had previously approved a transfer by a school board of one year's surplus general funds to capital outlay funds,[26] there was a substantial difference where this was done for three years.[27] The latter could be a circumvention of the requirement of voter approval for funding large building programs.

Remedies of Taxpayer against Illegal Taxation

It sometimes happens that a taxpayer pays taxes under a law later held unconstitutional, his property is improperly assessed, or payment is made through other mistake of law. The question then arises as to the right of the taxpayer to recover the taxes illegally paid. That a tax paid voluntarily cannot be recovered is the general rule.[28] This position is based upon the theory that every person is presumed to know the law, and since he has paid the tax knowing of its invalidity, he may not subsequently set up ignorance as a ground upon which to recover payments made.[29]

The general rule on recovery of taxes improperly collected is not applicable when payment is made under duress or compulsion, such as an imminent threat of seizure of the property. Payment after mere protest is made is not sufficient to make the payment an involuntary one and to establish payment under duress according to the majority of cases.[30] Payment under protest, however, is recognized by statute in some jurisdictions for purposes of possible recovery.[31] Also, by liberally construing duress or compulsion, courts can permit recovery. In addition, some courts distinguish between conduct of the taxing authority that is erroneous and conduct that is illegal, making recovery possible in the latter circumstance.[32]

It appears that many decisions turn upon whether the courts believe that the public interest should be protected to the extent of requiring individual taxpayers to bear the loss. Since commitments are made by

Lawn v. Mayor and Council of Borough of Fair Lawn, 143 N.J.Super. 259, 362 A.2d 1270 (1976), aff. 153 N.J.Super. 480, 380 A.2d 290 (1977).

26. Blumer v. School Bd. of Beresford Independent School Dist., 89 S.D. 623, 237 N.W.2d 655 (1975).

27. Anderson v. Kennedy, 264 N.W.2d 714 (S.D.1978).

28. American Can Co. v. Gill, 364 Ill. 254, 4 N.E.2d 370 (1936).

29. Cornell v. Board of Educ. for Dist. No. 99, 286 Ill.App. 398, 3 N.E.2d 717 (1936).

30. Wilson v. School Dist. of Philadelphia, 328 Pa. 225, 195 A. 90 (1937).

31. McDonough v. Aylward, 500 S.W.2d 721 (Mo.1973); Jenkins by Agyei v. State of Missouri, 967 F.2d 1248 (8 Cir.1992), cert. den. ___ U.S. ___, 113 S.Ct. 811, 121 L.Ed.2d 684 (1992).

32. Niagara Mohawk Power Corp. v. City School Dist. of City of Troy, 59 N.Y.2d 262, 464 N.Y.S.2d 449, 451 N.E.2d 207 (1983).

public tax spending agencies on the assumption that funds paid into their treasuries will remain available, it is evident that great hardship to the public could result if such agencies subsequently find their funds depleted through being required to make repayments. While there is some conflict among the cases, the rule of nonrecovery is still generally applied, especially where the failure of the taxing authority was due to error or to an exceeding of power that was not clear beforehand.[33] However, it seems well settled that the collection of an illegal tax may be enjoined.[34]

Even though the collection of an illegal tax may be enjoined, the fact the tax is illegal is not necessarily a defense in an action against a taxpayer for delinquent taxes. The Court of Civil Appeals of Texas considered a situation in which the city of Houston and the Houston Independent School District were found to have employed an illegal scheme of taxation.[35] The taxpayers in question had done nothing, not even the suggestion of a protest, when the plan was instituted. Subsequently they refused to pay the tax, and then attempted to defend their position by attacking the illegality of the system when they were sued. This the court would not permit. It noted that the issue was not that of enjoining an illegal tax; nor was it an attack on the illegality of the system. Thus, it stated that the burden was on the taxpayers to show that they had suffered substantial financial loss as a result of the failure of the city and school district to assess the property legally. It was not enough to show that an illegal system of rendering and assessing taxes was employed. The taxpayers here failed to prove by sufficient evidence that their taxes were substantially higher because of the illegal taxing procedure, and their suit was dismissed.

Failure of school taxing authorities to include personal property on the tax roll has been held not to be a basis for enjoining the assessment of real property. The assertion was made in another Texas case that the omission of personal property from the tax rolls required higher taxes to be levied on real property in order to raise the revenue for school operation. The contention was rejected by the court where there was no showing that the omission was more than a theretofore unchallenged custom, and the complaining taxpayers failed to show that substantial changes in their taxes resulted from the practice.[36]

It is axiomatic that a taxpayer cannot claim a tax adjustment simply because the person does not receive an equal share of benefits.[37] The Supreme Court of New Hampshire in 1992 applied this principle in interpreting a century-and-a-half-old statute permitting town governments to abate taxes of those "aggrieved by the assessment of a tax." [38] The court held that a taxpayer must be personally aggrieved to activate

33. Gulesian v. Dade County School Bd., 281 So.2d 325 (Fla.1973).

34. Shaffer v. Carter, 252 U.S. 37, 40 S.Ct. 221, 64 L.Ed. 445 (1920).

35. City of Houston v. McCarthy, 371 S.W.2d 587 (Tex.Civ.App.1963).

36. Kirkpatrick v. Parker, 406 S.W.2d 81 (Tex.Civ.App.1966).

37. Union Refrigerator Transit Co. v. Kentucky, 199 U.S. 194, 26 S.Ct. 36, 50 L.Ed. 150 (1905).

38. Barksdale v. Town of Epsom, 136 N.H. 511, 618 A.2d 814 (1992).

the statute and that such was not the situation where a town allowed a limited real estate tax abatement to those who paid for the education of their high school children outside of the school system. The town's invalidated plan for rebates had been prompted by "an escalating education budget and a perceived need for expanded choice and competition in education."

Apportionment of State School Funds

Funds collected in local districts are state funds and may be expended in any manner the legislature determines to be for the best interest of the whole state, subject only to constitutional restrictions. Thus, a statewide tax to raise money for school purposes is constitutional even if the proceeds are distributed so that less wealthy districts get more state aid than wealthier ones. It has been urged that such legislation deprives some citizens of property without due process of law, that it violates the constitutional inhibition against unequal taxation, and that it constitutes taxation for a private purpose. These contentions consistently have been judicially rejected, and the validity of statutes designed to equalize educational opportunity on a financial base within a state has been firmly established.[39]

While it is settled that taxes need not be spent in the district in which they are collected, the manner of apportionment of state funds among districts has caused considerable legal difficulty. In some states the plan of distribution of certain funds is specified in the state constitution. In other states only goals or purposes are to be found in the constitution. It has been held that the constitutional expression "the state has the primary responsibility for financing the system of public education" is to be considered a purpose and does not mean the state must supply more than half of needed funds.[40]

The constitutional plan of apportionment, if any, comprehends only those funds set out in the constitution. If it is constitutionally possible to create a fund separate and distinct from the funds covered by the constitution, it may be distributed as the legislature desires. Thus, the Supreme Court of Errors of Connecticut has held that, although constitutional funds could not be used to transport children to nonpublic schools, non-constitutional funds could be so used.[41] On the other hand, if all money coming into the hands of the state for school purposes automatically becomes part of the constitutional fund, it cannot be distributed except in accordance with the constitutional plan. The Michigan constitution once provided for distribution according to school population. When the legislature set up a plan of distribution according to a measure of need, the statute was declared unconstitutional by the

39. Sawyer v. Gilmore, 109 Me. 169, 83 A. 673 (1912). [Case No. 36]; State ex rel. Woodahl v. Straub, 164 Mont. 141, 520 P.2d 776 (1974).

40. Blase v. State, 55 Ill.2d 94, 302 N.E.2d 46 (1973).

41. Snyder v. Town of Newtown, 147 Conn. 374, 161 A.2d 770 (1960).

Supreme Court of Michigan.[42]

The Supreme Court of Idaho considered the validity of a county school tax to be levied on all taxable property within the county and distributed among the schools in the county according to their needs.[43] The constitution provided that "all taxes shall be uniform upon the same class of subjects within the territorial limits of the authority levying the tax." The court held that since the levy was on all taxable property in the county there was no lack of uniformity of taxation. The fact that the proceeds were not distributed equally throughout the county did not destroy the uniformity of the tax so long as receipts were apportioned reasonably in an effort to equalize educational standards throughout the county. Financial need of districts was found to be a reasonable basis for distribution.

Under a Georgia statute a certain type of school district received its state financial aid based on a calculation of property values one-third higher than they actually were. This had the effect of reducing the state contribution to such systems and increasing the state contribution proportionally to other types of districts which were less wealthy. The court held the statute valid when it was contested by the school district of Atlanta.[44] The court stated that one feature of the law stood out: through it the state sought to help all schools, but required that each school district do its best before receiving a supplement from the state to secure the minimum level. The court commented that, although the system was imperfect, the idea was commendable and could not be "shackled by legalistic theories and hair splitting." So-called independent school systems did constitute a reasonable class, and uniformity required simply that all in a class be treated alike.

In Michigan, where the constitution prevented the state's "reducing the state financed proportion of the necessary costs of any existing activity or service required of units of local government by state law," the state's highest court held that the provision covered categorical aid for specific courses required by state-level authorities (e.g., driver education, special education) but did not cover general aid to education.[45] Subsequently that court held that the employer's share of social security coverage for school district employees was not encompassed by the provision.[46]

Beginning in the late 1960's there developed a massive legal assault on state education financing systems that tolerated markedly uneven per pupil expenditures among local school districts. In 1971 the Supreme Court of California issued an opinion that in the year and a half before its federal constitutional theory was rejected by the Supreme Court of the United States possibly generated more reaction than any other

---

42. Board of Educ. of City of Detroit v. Fuller, 242 Mich. 186, 218 N.W. 764 (1928).

43. Board of Trustees of Joint Class A School Dist. No. 151 v. Board of County Commissioners of Cassia County, 83 Idaho 172, 359 P.2d 635 (1961).

44. Rice v. Cook, 222 Ga. 499, 150 S.E.2d 822 (1966).

45. Durant v. State Bd. of Educ., 424 Mich. 364, 381 N.W.2d 662 (1985).

46. Schmidt v. Department of Educ., 441 Mich. 236, 490 N.W.2d 584 (1992).

decision of a single state court.[47] The core of the decision was that a funding scheme which makes the quality of a child's education dependent upon the wealth of his school district invidiously discriminates against the poor in contravention of the equal protection clause of the Fourteenth Amendment and parallel clauses in the California constitution. (The ruling was binding in California, of course, despite the court's misconstruction of the Fourteenth Amendment. It was reaffirmed in 1976 solely on state constitutional grounds by a vote of four-to-three.[48])

The court observed that wealth of districts was the basis for substantially different per pupil expenditures. This was demonstrated by examples of districts with high property values which with low tax rates spent much more per pupil than other districts with high tax rates and lower valuations of property. The state financial aid program in California fell far short of equalizing these discrepancies. Indeed, of the $355 per child guaranteed by the state for elementary pupils, $125 was distributed on a flat basis irrespective of a district's wealth, thus actually widening the gap in some instances between rich and poor districts. The court discussed the concept of education as a fundamental interest to both the individual and to society. It applied the "strict scrutiny" test and found that the present financing system was not necessary to serve a compelling state interest.

Later in 1971 a three-judge federal District Court in Texas embraced this reasoning and concluded that the Texas system of financing schools was in violation of the equal protection clause of the Fourteenth Amendment.[49] It ordered that the taxing and financing system for schools in Texas be altered, but stayed its mandate for two years to give the legislature time to act so that the educational opportunities afforded were not made "a function of wealth other than the wealth of the State as a whole."

The Supreme Court reversed the lower court.[50] Its first conclusion was that the proper Fourteenth Amendment test to be applied was the usual "rational basis" test, not the exceptional "strict scrutiny" test. The opinion stated that the form of wealth discrimination involved was unlike any of the forms of wealth discrimination it had heretofore reviewed. In prior cases in which wealth classifications had been declared unconstitutional the individuals or groups of individuals constituting a class discriminated against had two distinguishing characteristics: "because of their impecunity they were completely unable to pay for some desired benefit, and as a consequence, they sustained an absolute deprivation of a meaningful opportunity to enjoy that benefit." In the Texas situation no one was completely deprived of educational

---

47. Serrano v. Priest, 5 Cal.3d 584, 96 Cal.Rptr. 601, 487 P.2d 1241 (1971).

48. Serrano v. Priest, 18 Cal.3d 728, 135 Cal.Rptr. 345, 557 P.2d 929 (1976), cert. den. 432 U.S. 907, 97 S.Ct. 2951, 53 L.Ed.2d 1079 (1977).

49. Rodriguez v. San Antonio Independent School Dist., 337 F.Supp. 280 (W.D.Tex.1971), rev. 411 U.S. 1, 93 S.Ct. 1278, 36 L.Ed.2d 16 (1973).

50. San Antonio Independent School Dist. v. Rodriguez, 411 U.S. 1, 93 S.Ct. 1278, 36 L.Ed.2d 16 (1973). [Case No. 38]

opportunity because of the existence of a statewide minimum foundation program financed by state and local revenue. (The amount of the contribution of a local school district to the program reflected the relative taxpaying ability of the district measured by assessable property. Local districts could supplement the foundation program by additionally levied local property taxes.)

Plaintiffs alleged that the system was discriminatory because expenditures per child showed an inverse variation with the wealth of the child's family. The evidence, however, did not support the conclusion that the poorest families were clustered in the poorest-property districts. The Court commented that the suit involved "a large, diverse, and amorphous class, unified only by the common factor of residence in districts that happen to have less taxable wealth than other districts."

On the question whether education is a fundamental right in the constitutional sense, the Court stated that the key to "fundamental" is not to be found in "comparisons of the relative societal significance of education as opposed to subsistence or housing" or "by weighing whether education is as important as the right to travel." The answer lies "in assessing whether there is a right to education explicitly or implicitly guaranteed by the Constitution." It found there was no such right.

The Court held to be rational the state's desire to maintain a degree of local autonomy in connection with education. Although recognizing that reliance on local property taxation for school revenues provides less freedom of choice with respect to expenditures for some districts than for others, the Court said the existence of some inequalities in the manner in which a state's rationale is achieved is not alone a sufficient basis for striking down an entire system. In a "cautionary postscript" the Court referred to the need for expertise and deliberation in deciding matters of educational finance and expressed concern about the consequences of a court-ordered change at the present time. It emphasized, however, that its action was not to be viewed as approval of the status quo. "But the ultimate solutions must come from the lawmakers and from the democratic pressures of those who elect them."

Thus, the basic decisions regarding financing the public schools remain with the individual states under their respective constitutions. State-level judicial action has continued with reference to methods of distribution of state funds in relation to equality of educational opportunity as measured by expenditures. The key arguments remain the same as in the California and Texas cases presented above. State-level equal protection provisions are considered, as are the particular state constitutional provisions for education. The detailed effect of the financing plan in operation in a state, however, seems most crucial to the ultimate decisions by that state's judiciary. Where the discrepancies among districts were very great, where the lower end was very low, where the plan of distributing state financial aid did little to help poor districts or increased the variations between richer and poorer districts, where state mandates impeded local districts in providing education of reasonable quality, where state funds were small compared to local funds—these have been some factors that have compelled some state courts of last resort to order changes in financing systems. Typically these courts have given the legislatures a period of time in which to redesign the plans.

The highest court of New Jersey, for example, found the method of finance in that state to be in violation of an 1875 constitutional provision for a "thorough and efficient system of free public schools" on the basis of discrepancies in dollar input per pupil.[51] State aid covered only 28 percent of operating expenses, and some of this was distributed regardless of local taxpaying ability. The Supreme Court of Errors of Connecticut invalidated a similar state aid plan under general state constitutional provisions, which it decided mandated a strict scrutiny approach.[52]

The Supreme Court of Washington, emphasizing the unique words "paramount duty" and "ample provision" used in that state's constitutional mandate for education, held that these words necessitated the legislature's making available dependable and regular tax sources for a "basic education" program, that program to be defined by the legislature.[53] The Supreme Court of Arkansas found to be completely irrational as regards any state objective that state's system of distributing state funds, an arrangement that actually increased the inequities among districts.[54] There was a provision that districts not have state aid reduced regardless of enrollment declines; half of funds remaining after that distribution were disbursed on a flat grant per student basis, regardless of local differences in resources; the remaining funds, which were distributed on a true equalization basis, amounted to less than seven percent of the state aid.

On the other hand, as one of the final state courts that have considered and sustained financing systems, the Supreme Court of Oregon, following the reasoning of the United States Supreme Court,[55] found the interest of Oregon in local control, the fact that a minimum educational program was provided in all districts, and the fact that several "important" services other than education are largely reliant on local property taxes to be sufficient to support the constitutionality of the system. It observed that the New Jersey court, unlike the California court, did not base its decision that a new financing method was needed on the state constitution's equal protection clause, but rather on the education clause of the state constitution. The New Jersey court used a "balancing" approach, not a "fundamental interest" approach. The Supreme Court of Oregon used that approach to reach the conclusion for Oregon which was contrary to the New Jersey conclusion.

51. Robinson v. Cahill, 62 N.J. 473, 303 A.2d 273 (1973), cert. den. 414 U.S. 976, 94 S.Ct. 292, 38 L.Ed.2d 219 (1973).

52. Horton v. Meskill, 172 Conn. 615, 376 A.2d 359 (1977).

53. Seattle School Dist. No. 1 of King County v. State, 90 Wash.2d 476, 585 P.2d 71 (1978).

54. Dupree v. Alma School Dist. No. 30 of Crawford County, 279 Ark. 340, 651 S.W.2d 90 (1983).

55. Olsen v. State, 276 Or. 9, 554 P.2d 139 (1976).

Commenting that the test for a fundamental right under the federal Constitution (which is one of delegated powers) was not appropriate under a state constitution that mentions many areas for statutory enactment, the Supreme Court of Ohio upheld that state's financing system as being a rational one for meeting the constitutional mandate for a "thorough and efficient system of common schools." [56] The highest court of Maryland reached the same conclusion as to a similarly worded constitutional education provision.[57] That court added the dictum that even under a test of "heightened scrutiny," the finance plan would be constitutional because the means "do bear a fair and substantial relationship to the legitimate goal of providing an adequate education for all children, while at the same time maintaining the viability of local control."

A new argument was presented as one aspect of the challenge to the system of finance of New York: the pattern discriminated against large city school systems for a variety of reasons, including special noneducation demands on the property tax in large cities, diminished purchasing power of the municipal education dollar, and larger concentrations of pupils with special needs. In upholding the system, the state's highest court observed that the state long had been regarded as a leader in public education, that it was third in the nation in per pupil expenditures, and that it was a legislative function to allocate funds among services, certainly in the absence of "gross and glaring inadequacy," which had not been shown to exist in consequence of the financing system.[58]

A three-judge federal District Court upheld against a Fourteenth Amendment equal protection challenge a financing plan in Pennsylvania whereby certain districts received "modified sparsity payments" while other districts similar in most respects did not.[59] The court found to be reasonable the aim of the provision, which was to encourage mergers of small, sparsely-populated school districts with other districts to develop a more efficient system of education. If one district had been receiving a "sparsity" payment, the modified payment would go to the reorganized district regardless of its characteristics.

A school finance plan adopted in Wisconsin attempted to remove property wealth as a factor in school district expenditures. It embodied the notion of establishing a ratio for each school district between equalized value of real estate per student within the district and a statewide amount. Under the plan districts would be equalized in power to finance education because the formula purported to get equal tax dollars for educational purposes from equal tax effort regardless of the disparity in tax base. Some property-wealthy districts would receive no

56. Board of Educ. of City School Dist. of Cincinnati v. Walter, 58 Ohio St.2d 368, 390 N.E.2d 813 (1979).

57. Hornbeck v. Somerset County Bd. of Educ., 295 Md. 597, 458 A.2d 758 (1983).

58. Board of Educ., Levittown Union Free School Dist. v. Nyquist, 57 N.Y.2d 27, 453 N.Y.S.2d 643, 439 N.E.2d 359 (1982), app. dism. 459 U.S. 1139, 103 S.Ct. 775, 74 L.Ed.2d 986 (1983).

59. Northwestern School Dist. v. Pittenger, 397 F.Supp. 975 (W.D.Pa.1975).

state aid as a result of their raising by a given tax rate more than the state-guaranteed amount. The overage would go into the general state fund ultimately to be distributed to property-poor districts. The state's highest court found the arrangement to be unconstitutional.[60] It said that the state cannot compel one school district to tax itself for the direct benefit of other districts or for the sole benefit of the state. A concurring opinion said that if the tax were viewed as a state tax, rather than a local tax, the result would be the same because it would not be uniform throughout the state.

Similar reasoning by the Supreme Court of Texas led to its disapproval of a legislative plan that was created to comply with that court's order for a change in the state's method of financing public schools.[61] The court said that property tax revenues raised locally for educational purposes are not subject to takeover and redistribution by the state. The state, however, could redistrict and thereby alter the local tax bases of school districts. The original decision required "a direct and close correlation between a district's tax effort and the educational resources available to it." [62]

The New Jersey Supreme Court reentered the school finance area seventeen years after its original decision (supra). It held that the legislative response, found constitutional on its face fourteen years before,[63] was unconstitutional as applied to poorer urban school districts.[64] It ordered that the legislature revamp the financing system in the state to assure that "poorer urban districts' educational funding is substantially equal to that of property-rich districts." Further, the level must be adequate to provide for the special educational needs of the disadvantaged districts.

The emphasis on quality of education, in addition to more parity in access to funds by local school districts, was carried further by the highest courts of Kentucky [65] and Massachusetts.[66] The most expansive outcome of a financing case probably was the ruling that "Kentucky's *entire system* of common schools is unconstitutional * * *. This decision applies to the statutes creating, implementing and financing the *system* and to all regulations, etc., pertaining thereto." The court ordered no specific acts nor deadlines, but it articulated a list of child-centered goals that characterize an "efficient" (the adjective in the Kentucky Constitution) system of common schools. The Supreme Judicial Court of Massachusetts utilized the Kentucky goals in broadly outlining what the Massachusetts constitutional duty towards education entailed. That provision, first adopted while a colony in 1780, mandated that the legislature "cherish * * * public schools * * * in the towns."

60. Buse v. Smith, 74 Wis.2d 550, 247 N.W.2d 141 (1976).

61. Edgewood Independent School Dist. v. Kirby, 804 S.W.2d 491 (Tex.1991).

62. Edgewood Independent School Dist. v. Kirby, 777 S.W.2d 391 (Tex.1989).

63. Robinson v. Cahill, 69 N.J. 449, 355 A.2d 129 (1976).

64. Abbott v. Burke, 119 N.J. 287, 575 A.2d 359 (1990).

65. Rose v. Council for Better Educ., 790 S.W.2d 186 (Ky.1989).

66. McDuffy v. Secretary of Executive Office of Educ., 415 Mass. 545, 615 N.E.2d 516 (1993).

School Bonds

In General

In the absence of express statutory authorization, it is presumed that school districts will operate on a "pay as you go" basis. That is, no authority to borrow money is implied from the fact that the board is charged with the operation and management of the schools. It follows that there is no implied power to issue bonds or other negotiable instruments.[67] Even when the right to borrow is granted, it is strictly construed. For example, if power is granted to borrow money or issue bonds for a specific purpose, the funds so borrowed must be applied to that purpose and no other.

When authority to issue bonds is conferred by statute, the procedure and prerequisites are set out in detail. The question then arises as to the validity of the bonds when the exact procedure has not been followed. The rule, as generally stated, is that if it appears from the statute that it was the legislative intent for the prescribed procedure to be a condition precedent to the validity of the issue, failure to follow it would render the bonds invalid. On the other hand, there is a strong judicial disposition to uphold the validity of a bond issue if it appears that mere irregularities which may have occurred did not deprive the taxpayers of some substantial right which they would have enjoyed had the irregularity not occurred [68] or did not affect the outcome of the election.[69] This problem occurs very frequently in connection with the requirement that notice of the election shall be published a given number of days before the election is held. If the electors had adequate notice so that a majority of them appeared and voted, and the result of the election could not have been affected by the shorter notice, the election will be held valid.[70] (Elections are treated in Chapter 14.)

In a case before the Supreme Court of New Hampshire, the validity of a school bond issue was sustained against the charge that there were some defects in the report required to be submitted to certain state authorities by the school district.[71] The court indicated that the acts of town meetings should be liberally construed, and if they fell within the authorized power of the town, minor distinctions would not be allowed to defeat the plain intent of the voters. Since the information required in the report had been given wide publicity otherwise, and had been discussed in public meetings, the court concluded that the statute had been substantially complied with.

Problems can develop when school boards publish statements in connection with bond elections and later wish to deviate somewhat from

---

67. Hewitt v. Board of Educ., 94 Ill. 528 (1880).

68. Ganske v. Independent School Dist., 271 Minn. 531, 136 N.W.2d 405 (1965).

69. Abts v. Board of Educ. of School Dist. Re–1 Valley in Logan County, 622 P.2d 518 (Colo.1980).

70. State ex rel. School Dist. No. 2 v. March, 108 Neb. 749, 189 N.W. 283 (1922).

71. Hecker v. McKernan, 105 N.H. 195, 196 A.2d 38 (1963).

the statements. The issue was discussed by the Supreme Court of Utah in a case where suit was brought by taxpayers to prevent a board from proceeding with a school building program. The board had published a notice of a school bond election and had printed an explanatory brochure. Copies were distributed to the public, and parts were published in the newspapers in connection with, but not as part of, the statutory notice. The brochure indicated that in general the funds would be spent under the two main categories of high schools and elementary schools. The bond issue passed, but subsequently it developed that the building costs projected in the preliminary estimate for the construction of the high school were too low. The board then proposed to use a much greater proportion of the total bond fund for the construction of that school. This left a relatively small amount of money for the elementary school needs mentioned in the brochure. The contention of plaintiffs was that if the board did this it would constitute a breach of faith. The court, however, sustained the board's action, indicating that the board had to have latitude in order to carry out its goal of providing the best possible school system in the most efficient and economic way.[72] In the absence of any deceit, fraud, or corruption or of evidence that the board was so completely failing to follow the course of its duties that its actions could be classified as arbitrary, the court declined to interfere.

A Kansas statute raised the maximum rate of interest which could be paid on school bonds. The question arose as to whether this new rate was applicable to bonds that had been authorized by an election held prior to the passage of the statute. The Supreme Court of Kansas held in the affirmative.[73] It stated that bonds are not considered to be issued until they are actually delivered or put into circulation. The law in effect at the time of the issuance becomes part of the contract. Thus, the statute was not being made retroactive when applied to bonds which had not been issued as of the effective date of the statute.

Liability on Illegal Bonds

If bonds are issued contrary to law they are, of course, void and no recovery may be had thereon. However, such illegality is often not discovered until after the funds derived from the sale of the bonds have been received and spent by the district. The issue then is presented as to whether the bondholders must bear the loss or may recover from the district on some theory despite the invalidity of the bonds.

In the discussion of contract liability of districts it is pointed out that some courts permit recovery in quasi-contract for the value of the benefit conferred upon the district. The same rule is frequently applied in bond cases subject to the same exception, namely, that there must have been authority to issue valid bonds in the first instance.[74] In other

---

72. Ricker v. Board of Educ. of Millard County School Dist., 16 Utah 2d 106, 396 P.2d 416 (1964). [Case No. 39]

73. Baker v. Unified School Dist. No. 346, County of Linn, 206 Kan. 581, 480 P.2d 409 (1971).

74. Geer v. School Dist. No. 11, 111 Fed. 682 (8 Cir.1901).

words, if the bonds are invalid due to the lack of power to issue them, there can be no recovery for the benefit conferred, although the bond-holder may recover any unexpended money received from him remaining in the hands of the district. He may also recover property purchased with the money received if he is able to trace it into specific property and the recovery will not seriously injure other district property or disrupt the orderly management of the schools. If there is no power to issue the bonds, no implied contract will be raised in favor of the bondholder, since to do so would deprive the district of the very protection the statute was designed to afford it.

School District Warrants

School warrants are orders drawn against district funds, or, if the statute specifically permits it, against funds to be collected within a period stated in the law. They are not designed to run for a number of years as are bonds. They are not negotiable instruments in the sense that an innocent purchaser may be protected against the district if it appears that the district had a defense when they were issued. Any purchaser is charged with notice of any illegality in the issuance of the instrument and purchases it at his own risk.[75] The reason is clear. If innocent purchasers were afforded protection, boards of education would thereby be enabled to expend district funds illegally through the device of issuing negotiable warrants, and the district taxpayer would have no recourse. It is considered the more sound public policy to require individuals dealing with district boards to assume responsibility for the legality of warrants rather than open the way to possible depletion of school funds through the issue of illegal warrants.

Limitations on District Indebtedness

In General

In many states the amount of indebtedness which may be incurred by school districts is limited by constitutional provision or statutory enactment. The question of what constitutes indebtedness under such provisions and enactments is one upon which the cases are in conflict. The majority hold that net, not gross, indebtedness is the measure to be applied when it is sought to determine whether a district may become further indebted.[76] Net indebtedness is that which remains after deducting from the total of all outstanding debts the assets of the district which are available for the payment of existing debts. This includes sinking funds, cash on hand, taxes levied and other assets which may be made available. It should be noticed that the assets need not actually be applied to the payment of the indebtedness, but only that they be available.

75. Kellogg v. School Dist. No. 10, 13 Okl. 285, 74 P. 110 (1903).

76. Rettinger v. School Bd. of City of Pittsburgh, 266 Pa.St. 67, 109 A. 782 (1920).

Contracts for current expenses are not considered indebtedness, nor funds on hand to meet them, assets. That is to say, even though the legal limit of indebtedness has been reached, taxes may still be levied for current operating expenses.[77]

Some courts refuse to apply the net indebtedness test. They hold that even though assets may be on hand which may be used to pay the district debts, the fact is that the debts remain until they are paid.[78] This view may appear more logical and more nearly in accord with the commonly accepted understanding of what constitutes a debt, but in application it would greatly restrict the district in financing its operations.

Borrowed money is not considered a debt if the funding is through revenue bonds rather than general obligation bonds. Holders of revenue bonds must depend entirely on income produced by the venture that is financed by the bond money. Generally school districts may not issue revenue bonds, but states may. The Supreme Court of Michigan was asked whether the state constitutional debt limit applied to bonds the state proposed to issue to raise money to loan to school districts having large operating deficits.[79] Under the plan the payments of principal and interest would be made by the local districts, and, if they defaulted, by the state from state aid payments due the district. The court disapproved the plan. It stated that the borrower is the state regardless of the fact that repayment would be primarily by residents of some individual school districts and that the bonds were in effect general obligation bonds subject to the constitutional debt limit.

If it appears to the district board that it is advantageous to the district to enter into contracts for a period of years for supplies or services, the majority of cases hold that such contracts are legal even though the amount extends the district indebtedness beyond the legal limit. In such cases it is usually provided that payment shall be made from year to year from funds accruing to the district. Then only the amount falling due each year is the amount of indebtedness incurred, not the total stated in the contract.[80] The application of this rule is restricted to contracts for goods or services and is not extended to those for the construction of buildings. It has been applied, however, to a lease agreement between a school board and a public corporation set up for school construction.[81]

In a New Hampshire case, it was claimed that a contested bond issue would exceed constitutional debt limits.[82] Pertinent to this ques-

77. Grant v. City of Davenport, 36 Iowa 396 (1873).

78. Angola Brick and Tile Co. v. Millgrove School Tp., 73 Ind.App. 557, 127 N.E. 855 (1920).

79. In re Advisory Opinion, Constitutionality of P.A. 1 & 2, 390 Mich. 166, 211 N.W.2d 28 (1973).

80. La Porte v. Gamewell Fire-Alarm Telegraph Co., 146 Ind. 466, 45 N.E. 588 (1896).

81. Teperich v. North Judson-San Pierre High School Bldg. Corp., 257 Ind. 516, 275 N.E.2d 814 (1971), cert. den. 407 U.S. 921, 92 S.Ct. 2462, 32 L.Ed.2d 806 (1972).

82. Hecker v. McKernan, 105 N.H. 195, 196 A.2d 38 (1963).

tion was the fact that at the time of the bond vote the district had on hand ten thousand dollars in cash, which was set aside solely for payment on the principal of the outstanding debt. If this sum were subtracted from the outstanding authorized indebtedness, the amount of the bond issue would be within the legal debt limit. The court held that the subtraction was proper.

Special problems can occur when school districts are reorganized. In a South Carolina case, the highest court of that state was asked to determine the validity of bonds issued by a consolidated school district.[83] The district had succeeded to the property, rights, and obligations of the districts that comprised it, and the existence of the latter as separate entities was terminated. The basic question was whether the consolidated district could incur an indebtedness in excess of the constitutional limitation of eight percent of property value placed upon each of the constituent districts. The court held that the new district formed from the several old ones was also bound by the maximum of eight percent.

Where school districts and counties or cities are coterminous and each unit has a debt limit, the relationship of the debt limits arises. In South Carolina a school district coterminous with a county could raise only about three hundred thousand dollars of a needed eight hundred thousand because of its constitutional debt limit. In order to provide the remaining funds the county sold county bonds in the amount of five hundred thousand dollars and turned the proceeds over to the school district. The state constitution permitted the sale of bonds for a corporate purpose of a county. It was argued that the sale of the bonds was not for such a purpose because the duty of operating the school system devolved upon the school district rather than the county. Further argument was that, since the area of the school district was coterminous with that of the county, the effect of turning over the county bond sale to the district was indirectly to permit the district to incur a debt beyond what was permitted by the applicable constitutional debt limitation. However, a section of the state constitution provided that the legislature shall not have the power to authorize any county to levy a tax or issue bonds except for specified purposes, one of which was an educational purpose. The court construed this to be express constitutional authority for the authorization.[84] Further, it held that the arrangement did not exceed the debt limit, because although the county and school district were coterminous in area, they were separate and distinct corporate entities subject to separate constitutional debt limitations.

Short Term Borrowing

Short term borrowing is usually made necessary by the happening of some emergency, the failure to collect anticipated revenue, or the desire of the district to carry out some program deemed immediately necessary

83. Boatwright v. McElmurray, 247 S.C. 199, 146 S.E.2d 716 (1966).

84. Grey v. Vaigneur, 243 S.C. 604, 135 S.E.2d 229 (1964).

or desirable for the welfare of the schools for which funds are not presently available. As in the case of individuals or business organizations, occasions may arise in which it is advisable to borrow money for short periods rather than operate on a strictly cash basis. In recognition of this fact, short term borrowing, subject to various restrictions, is generally permitted by statute. It would not in most situations be considered an implied power of boards.[85]

The constitutional or statutory debt limits are applicable equally to short and long time borrowings. Anticipation of revenues is limited since it would be poor business and educational practice to permit present boards to obligate the revenues of the district for an unreasonable time in advance. It is conceivable that, in the absence of limitations, the operation of the schools in subsequent years would be rendered impossible. The most common restriction is that there shall be no anticipation of revenue in excess of the revenue of the fiscal year in which the anticipation is made. The purpose is, of course, to prevent the district from continuing to pile up nonbonded indebtedness.

When authority to borrow is granted, the procedure is usually contained in the statute and must be followed strictly. Authority to borrow does not ordinarily carry with it authority to issue negotiable instruments of indebtedness, but there are cases to the contrary. For example, it has been held that when the statute permits borrowing but does not specify the procedure to be followed, there is implied authority to execute such evidence of indebtedness as would be in accord with usual business practices.[86]

In the conduct of the schools, a combination or variety of circumstances may have caused the district to accumulate indebtedness over a period of years. To pay off the indebtedness in a single year would put too great a strain on the budget for that year. The question then arises as to the power of the board of education to fund the indebtedness and arrange for its payment over a relatively short period of time. Some statutes permit the issuance of bonds in such cases, but this procedure necessitates a vote of the people of the district and involves considerable expense. If, then, existing indebtedness may be funded by short time borrowings, much expense and inconvenience will be avoided. In recognition of this fact, statutory authorization to fund obligations by this device is granted in a number of states.

The question most frequently faced in connection with attempts at funding obligations is whether the funding constitutes the creation of new indebtedness, which extends the total indebtedness beyond the statutory or constitutional limit or beyond that permitted to be incurred during a single year. It is usually held that funding of present obligations does not create a new debt. The validity of the obligation must

85. An exception is found in Logan v. Board of Public Instr. for Polk County, 118 Fla. 184, 158 So. 720 (1935).

86. Board of Public Instr. for Bay County v. Barefoot, 141 Fla. 522, 193 So. 823 (1939).

be determined by the financial status of the district at the time the original obligation was incurred, not as of the date of the funding.[87]

Budgetary Procedures

In order that school expenditures may be more intelligently planned and to some extent controlled, states require school officials to prepare budgets of proposed expenditures. Detailed provisions vary, but they include such requirements as itemization of the budget, publication of the budget, public hearings on the budget, submission of the budget to a reviewing agency, and procedures for transferring funds from some budgetary items to others.

When some measure of control is sought to be exercised over school expenditures by a reviewing agency, or when the budget is attacked by a taxpayer, budgetary legislation comes before the courts for interpretation. In general, attempts to modify expenditures of school districts by reviewing agencies or by taxpayers have not been successful in the courts unless pertinent statutes are clear that such control can be exercised. The judicial attitude has generally been that, since boards of education are charged with the responsibility of operating the schools, they must have a free hand in determining how and where expenditures are to be made, subject only to limitations on total amount by the constitution or statute. The major exception seems to arise in cases in which the schools are fiscally dependent on the municipal government. In most such situations the school board presents a total budget to municipal authorities, who may reduce the total or eliminate items not required by state law and not placed in the province of school boards to determine. Courts in general construe board powers in such instances liberally.[88] Under this form of organization it has been held that the school board is not restricted to adherence to particular items in the budget as long as there is no attempt to spend more than the total amount appropriated for the support of the schools.[89] The courts have treated similarly powers of boards where approval of budgets is by popular vote.[90]

In a school district in New Hampshire the voters had rejected an item in the proposed budget which would have specifically provided for four teacher aides. Subsequently the board rehired the one aide it had previously employed and paid her under an appropriation "for the salaries of school district officials and agents." The state's highest court held that this procedure was not improper.[91] It stated that the board had the power to transfer funds that had voter approval and that the

---

87. Citizens Bank v. Rowan County Bd. of Educ., 274 Ky. 481, 118 S.W.2d 704 (1938).

88. Ring v. Woburn, 311 Mass. 679, 43 N.E.2d 8 (1942); Carroll v. City of Malden, 2 Mass.App. 735, 320 N.E.2d 843 (1974).

89. Leonard v. School Committee of Springfield, 241 Mass. 325, 135 N.E. 459 (1922). See also Lynch v. City of Fall River, 336 Mass. 558, 147 N.E.2d 152 (1958); Warwick School Committee v. Gibbons, 122 R.I. 670, 410 A.2d 1354 (1980).

90. Board of Selectmen of Pittsfield v. School Bd., 113 N.H. 598, 311 A.2d 124 (1973).

91. Ashley v. Rye School Dist., 111 N.H. 54, 274 A.2d 795 (1971).

action of the voters could not be interpreted as a retroactive disapproval of the employment of an aide.

The Supreme Court of Georgia, in upholding a school board's contracting for a field house for athletics, construed the requirement that no funds shall be disbursed by a local board except in accordance with a budget filed with the state board of education.[92] The court said that the meaning was not that every expenditure must be a line item in the budget submitted. The local board had a balance of unobligated funds in excess of the amount of the proposed expenditure, and the purpose of the expenditure was one within the board's power.

Contentions that there has not been sufficient budget itemization have not generally prevailed in the courts. An illustrative case was decided by the Supreme Court of Utah.[93] A statute of that state required that the budget be itemized. As prepared and published the contested budget consisted of ten classifications of accounts, such as, administration, operation of buildings, and instruction. Each of these classifications had been broken down, and the whole budget contained sixty items. After the budget was approved, it was further divided for administrative purposes into more than fifteen hundred accounts. It was held that the budget as published was sufficiently itemized to comply with the statute.

The Supreme Court of Arizona was confronted with a case in which the question was whether broad classifications constituted sufficient itemization to state the "purposes" for which expenditures were to be made.[94] A total of forty-one sub-items in six categories was held sufficient. The question then arose as to the legal authority of the board to transfer funds from one sub-item to another, and from one general category to another. It was ruled that the board had the power to transfer funds among the various sub-items in each of the six general categories, but it could not transfer funds among the general categories.

Courts adhere to the rule that a fund raised by taxation for one purpose cannot be diverted to another.[95] Contested in South Dakota was a budgetary transfer from the general fund to the capital outlay fund. The transfer was upheld by the state's highest court on the grounds that there was no evidence the proceeds transferred were raised by local tax levies and the amount of the transfer was less than the amount derived from sources other than local taxes.[96]

Current tax revenues cannot be used to pay obligations accrued during a previous school year (unless the budget so provides), and such

92. Concerned School Patrons and Taxpayers v. Ware County Bd. of Educ., 245 Ga. 202, 263 S.E.2d 925 (1980). [Case No. 40]

93. Tuttle v. Board of Educ. of Salt Lake City, 77 Utah 270, 294 P. 294 (1930).

94. Isley v. School Dist., 81 Ariz. 280, 305 P.2d 432 (1956).

95. School Dist. No. 2 v. Jackson-Wilson High School Dist., 49 Wyo. 115, 52 P.2d 673 (1935).

96. Stene v. School Bd. of Beresford Independent School Dist., No. 68, 87 S.D. 234, 206 N.W.2d 69 (1973).

payment can be enjoined.[97] If, however, the debts have been paid, an injunction suit is moot.[98]

Where a board of education by statute could not incur a contractual liability without an appropriation therefor, and appropriations were made annually, a two-year collective bargaining contract was held not enforceable as to the second year's salary provisions.[99]

In Massachusetts the towns comprising a regional school district had voted substantial sums for architectural services for a new building, but had rejected a supplemental appropriation to continue the architect's work. The regional school board then decided to use its "surplus revenue" account, and made payments until it abandoned the project because of high bids on the projected construction. Pursuant to its contract the architect demanded arbitration, and was granted an award that was to be paid from the surplus revenue account. The award was held to be in excess of the authority of the arbitrator because the school committee was not authorized to use that account under the above facts.[100]

School Finance and Municipal Authorities

Many problems concerning financial matters develop between school boards and general local government agencies such as city councils. Some have been referred to previously. Since the state legislature grants powers both to school districts and to municipalities, the legislature may establish methods of finance in which the two operations are kept completely separate or in which they are intertwined.

The power of the state legislature to require city authorities to issue bonds to raise money to be used for erecting school buildings was challenged in a leading old Maryland case. The highest court of Maryland found that the legislature indeed had the power to direct the city authorities to create a debt for a public school building.[101] Likewise the legislature can fix a minimum sum to be raised by a city for school purposes and can require that the sum be raised without discretion on the part of municipal officials.[102] Furthermore, the legislature can require a city to allocate no less than a specified percent of its total expense budget to the fiscally-dependent board of education.[103]

In Pennsylvania a municipality sought to enjoin construction of a high school planned by the school district until the indebtedness neces-

97. Warren v. Sanger Independent School Dist., 116 Tex. 183, 288 S.W. 159 (1926).

98. Rawson v. Brownsboro Independent School Dist., 263 S.W.2d 578 (Tex.Civ.App. 1953).

99. Board of Educ. v. Chicago Teachers Union, Local 1, American Federation of Teachers, 26 Ill.App.3d 806, 326 N.E.2d 158 (1975).

100. Plymouth-Carver Regional School Dist. v. David M. Crawley Associates, Inc., 17 Mass.App. 901, 455 N.E.2d 990 (1983).

101. Revell v. Mayor, etc., of Annapolis, 81 Md. 1, 31 A. 695 (1895). [Case No. 35]

102. City of Louisville v. Commonwealth, 134 Ky. 488, 121 S.W. 411 (1909).

103. Board of Educ. of City School Dist. of City of New York v. City of New York, 41 N.Y.2d 535, 394 N.Y.S.2d 148, 362 N.E.2d 948 (1977).

sary was approved by a referendum. The highest state court held that to grant one governmental unit standing to sue because of a hypothetical threat to property tax revenues by an action of the other would mean that neither could effectively function, for each could challenge the other's actions and have the other's decisions reviewed.[104] The court also rejected the argument that the city could sue on behalf of its taxpayers, who do have a recognized standing to sue.

A different aspect of municipal and school board power was decided by the Supreme Court of Alaska.[105] A home rule borough sought to require the coterminous school system to participate in centralized accounting without the statutorily required approval of the school board. Thus, the issue was the validity of a home rule borough ordinance conflicting with a state statute. The court stated that it had previously adopted a "local activity rule" as a method for resolving impasses between state statutes seeking to further a specific policy and municipal ordinances which either directly or collaterally impeded the implementation. The determination would depend upon whether the matter regulated was of statewide or local concern. That the state constitution vested in the legislature the mandate for establishing and maintaining a system of public schools was considered decisive. Further, it was held that this state control was not diminished by the fact that certain educational functions had been delegated to local school boards to meet varying conditions of different localities. It was held, therefore, that the school board could not be required to participate in centralized accounting.

The preceding should not be construed to mean that it is not possible through statutes to require that appropriations for educational purposes be approved by a municipal body. Generally, however, in the absence of a statute clearly giving this power to a municipal body, the courts hold that the school board has the independent authority to determine the amount of money needed for schools, and the council must levy, collect, and turn over the proceeds of the tax without question.[106] Also, generally the municipal or county unit collecting the tax cannot retain a share for expenses of administration unless permitted by statute to do so.[107] Nor can it keep any interest that has accrued on collected school taxes.[108] Even if funds improperly diverted by municipal agencies for expenses of tax collection have been expended, the funds may be recovered by the school board.[109]

Occasionally a municipal or county tax collector may receive more money from a given tax for schools than had been requested by the board of education. This situation can develop because of the impossi-

104. City of Hazleton v. Hazleton Area School Dist., 442 Pa. 477, 276 A.2d 545 (1971).

105. Macauley v. Hildebrand, 491 P.2d 120 (Alaska 1971).

106. Board of Educ. of Town of Stamford v. Board of Finance of Town of Stamford, 127 Conn. 345, 16 A.2d 601 (1940).

107. Coleman v. Kiley, 236 Ga. 751, 225 S.E.2d 273 (1976).

108. State ex rel. School Dist. of Springfield R-12 v. Wickliffe, 650 S.W.2d 623 (Mo. 1983).

109. Venhaus v. Board of Educ. of Pulaski County, 280 Ark. 441, 659 S.W.2d 179 (1983).

bility of predicting at the time of the levy the exact amount of money a given tax will produce during the fiscal year. Where such a surplus was accrued, the Court of Appeals of Maryland held that the school board was entitled to it.[110] Under Maryland law a county board of education submits its proposed budget to county authorities, who levy the taxes and distribute school tax proceeds to the school board.

The Supreme Court of New Hampshire discussed relations between a city council and a coterminous board of education when the council refused to appropriate the money the school board said it needed.[111] The court held that the council must appropriate funds necessary to meet obligations imposed by the state board of education. If the council reduces the budget, the school may determine the areas to be reduced. Optional educational programs may be dropped because of insufficient appropriations. If, however, the board believes services and programs would be diminished below requirements, it may present evidence to substantiate the claim and to establish an entitlement to the funds needed.

A provision of a collective bargaining agreement between a school district and a teachers union was challenged by the city coterminous with the school district. The contract set up a procedure for payments to a health and welfare fund which was to be administered by five members of the school board and five persons appointed by the union. The trustees of the fund voted to adopt an insurance program and secured an insurance carrier to issue a policy to carry it out. The city claimed that the school board's power to fix compensation of teachers did not include any payments to third persons for their benefit. The court disagreed, observing that the agreed payments to the fund were modest in amount and intelligent in purpose, and had no different impact on the city than direct payments to teachers.[112]

It should be observed that courts may require municipal governing boards, school boards, or both to expend funds to implement court orders. The Second Circuit Court of Appeals, although pointing out that it would be better practice to order a fiscally dependent school board under a desegregation order to supply details regarding expenditures to be made and uses for additional funds needed from the city, nevertheless upheld an order that a particular sum be additionally appropriated to the school board by the city council of Buffalo, New York.[113]

Alimentation of School Funds

The procedure for distributing funds to the districts of the state by the agencies into whose hands they come is provided by statute in all states. The statutes vary widely as to the degree of particularity of their

110. Board of Educ. of Montgomery County v. Montgomery County, 237 Md. 191, 205 A.2d 202 (1964).

111. Laconia Bd. of Educ. v. City of Laconia, 111 N.H. 389, 285 A.2d 793 (1971).

112. Kerrigan v. City of Boston, 361 Mass. 24, 278 N.E.2d 387 (1972).

113. Arthur v. Nyquist, 712 F.2d 809 (2 Cir.1983), cert. den. 466 U.S. 936, 104 S.Ct. 1907, 80 L.Ed.2d 456 (1984).

provisions. Some provide the manner of distribution and the amount to be received by each district in the state. That is, if a district is found to fall within a certain classification, the amount it will receive is definitely set. Others place the distribution within the discretion of indicated boards or officers with only broad restrictions. In the latter event the courts will not interfere with the exercise of the discretion in the absence of bad faith or unreasonable actions.[114] In the former, no discretion is vested in the agencies, and their duties are purely ministerial.

Problems occur when officials or boards either fail to, or refuse to, make payments to the districts, or the determination of the amounts is brought into question. In Michigan, for example, the superintendent of public instruction was required by statute to apportion the state equalization funds among the districts of the state by a specified date. A city board of education was successful in a mandamus action to compel the apportionment to be made.[115]

The legal right of the apportioning agency to change or rescind apportionments made was contested in a Texas case. The statute required the state board of education to meet and fix the apportionment on or before August 1 of each year. This it did, but it did not certify its final action to the several school units. The board met after August 1 and made revisions in its previous apportionment. The contention that the board could not make the revisions after August 1 was overruled. It was held that the board retains the power of control over the apportionment until its final action is certified to the school districts.[116]

Another aspect of the alimentation problem arises when one district receives funds to which it is not entitled from the state through the mistake of the officers involved. Frequently the error does not appear until the funds have been spent. In such cases a writ of mandamus obviously will not lie since there are no longer funds in the officer's hands which he may be compelled to pay a complainant district. The remedy in such cases is a suit by the district receiving less than its share against the one receiving more than its share.[117]

In many states there are provisions that the proceeds from fines, forfeitures and stated other sources, shall become part of the school fund. The Constitution of North Carolina, for example, provided that "Clear proceeds of all penalties and forfeitures and all fines collected in the several counties for any breach of penal or military laws of the state shall be faithfully appropriated for establishing and maintaining the free public schools in the several counties of the state." A statute provided that 5 percent commissions shall be allowed the clerk on all fines, penalties, and taxes paid him by virtue of his office. In a case contesting the right of the clerk to make the deduction, it was held that the term

114. State ex rel. King v. Board of Educ. of Russell County, 214 Ala. 620, 108 So. 588 (1926).

115. Board of Educ. of Iron Mountain v. Voelker, 271 Mich. 207, 259 N.W. 891 (1935).

116. San Antonio Independent School Dist. v. State Bd. of Educ., 108 S.W.2d 445 (Tex.Civ.App.1937).

117. Independent School Dist. No. 1 v. Common School Dist. No. 1, 56 Idaho 426, 55 P.2d 144 (1936).

"clear proceeds" means "total sums collected," and there can be no subtractions.[118]

Throughout the alimentation cases, the disposition of the courts to insist that there be no interference with the orderly course of school funds from the source to the spending agency is very apparent. Attempts by any agency or officer to hold up the funds in the absence of express authority have been defeated. The courts recognize that the conduct of the schools could be rendered impossible if funds may be held up pending the determination of every question with reference to the funds which might be raised by various officials who play a part in the alimentation process.

The Supreme Court of Wisconsin held that the disbursement of aid to schools in that state was a ministerial function once certain facts were ascertained and it was determined that school districts were in compliance with program standards. The initial discretionary authority of the state-level education officials did not transform the mandatory aid payments into "departmental expenditures incurred in the execution or administration of a program responsibility," which expenditures would have been subject to reductions by the state's chief fiscal officer.[119]

It is important to distinguish between a legislative authorization of funds for some purpose and an appropriation of funds. Appropriations allocate funds to be expended for authorized programs. Thus, if there is only an authorization, there is no money to be sought by a school district through a mandamus action against the state.[120] In Michigan it developed that insufficient funds had been appropriated to pay all intermediate school districts the amounts to which they were entitled under the formula included in certain legislation. The state board of education decided to reduce each district's allowance by the percent needed to conform to the appropriation. This procedure was upheld by the state supreme court.[121]

In Pennsylvania the statutory definition of "exceptional children" included gifted and talented students. The statute made it an obligation of the state to reimburse school districts for costs of special education. A school district declined to establish a program for the gifted until it received money from the state. The court held that the receipt of state money was not a condition precedent and that the board was required to establish the program on its own.[122] It then could apply and obtain a writ of mandamus if the ministerial duty of allocating the reimbursement was not fulfilled.

The board of education of Chicago operated schools during one year for fewer than the state-mandated minimum number of days because of

118. Board of Educ. of Guilford County v. City of High Point, 213 N.C. 636, 197 S.E. 191 (1938).

119. School Dist. of LaFarge v. Lindner, 100 Wis.2d 111, 301 N.W.2d 196 (1981).

120. Board of Educ. of Oakland Schools v. Porter, 392 Mich. 613, 221 N.W.2d 345 (1974).

121. Board of Educ. of Oakland Schools v. Superintendent of Public Instr., 401 Mich. 37, 257 N.W.2d 73 (1977).

122. Central York School Dist. v. Commonwealth, Dept. of Educ., 41 Pa.Cmwlth. 383, 399 A.2d 167 (1979).

a teacher strike and a shortage of funds. The state then made a deduction from the amount of financial aid which was due the city district. The Chicago board unsuccessfully argued that the teacher strike was "an act of God" rendering impossible its compliance and therefore the shortened school year should be excused. The Supreme Court of Illinois said that the argument was not valid legally and that the plea for forgiveness should be addressed to the legislature.[123] The state superintendent of education had decided to apportion the reduction over a three-year period, but the state comptroller insisted that the reduction be made entirely in the first year. The court ruled that the superintendent was empowered to prorate the reduction.

The Supreme Court of Pennsylvania also has upheld the reducing of state aid to districts that operated fewer than the required number of days due to teacher strikes.[124] The Supreme Court of Montana, however, reached a contrary conclusion regarding such reductions for a certain classification of districts.[125] It said that various relevant statutes were so vague and uncertain that the imposition of penalties under them for not operating the specified number of days could not be permitted. (Withholding of state aid to enforce a regulation is treated in Chapter 3.)

The power of governors to reduce state aid to education formulas of various kinds is partly a statutory question and partly a constitutional one involving the separation of powers concept. The highest court of Massachusetts, finding that statutes authorizing reductions by the governor did not cover education aid because it was not administered by an agency "under the control of the governor or one of his secretaries," stated that constitutional issues of significance would be "worthy of attention" if the case could not have been decided on the basis of the statutory wording.[126]

Federal Funds

Congress is authorized under the "general welfare" clause of the Constitution to spend money for the educational benefit of the people of the United States as long as the primary purpose is not that of regulation or control.[127] If it offers money to the states primarily for educational purposes, it may attach conditions to the grants. These conditions become contractual when the money is accepted.[128] Also, the receipt of funds may be dependent on the execution of an "assurance of compliance" form.[129] Furthermore, if funds are misspent, they may be

123. Cronin v. Lindberg, 66 Ill.2d 47, 4 Ill.Dec. 424, 360 N.E.2d 360 (1976).

124. School Dist. of Pittsburgh v. Commonwealth, Dept. of Educ., 492 Pa. 140, 422 A.2d 1054 (1980).

125. Missoula High School Legal Defense Ass'n v. Superintendent of Public Instr., 196 Mont. 106, 637 P.2d 1188 (1981).

126. Town of Brookline v. Governor, 407 Mass. 377, 553 N.E.2d 1277 (1990).

127. U.S. Const. art. I, § 8. See United States v. Butler, 297 U.S. 1, 56 S.Ct. 312, 80 L.Ed. 477 (1936) and Helvering v. Davis, 301 U.S. 619, 57 S.Ct. 904, 81 L.Ed. 1307 (1937).

128. Lau v. Nichols, 414 U.S. 563, 94 S.Ct. 786, 39 L.Ed.2d 1 (1974).

129. Grove City College v. Bell, 465 U.S. 555, 104 S.Ct. 1211, 79 L.Ed.2d 516 (1984).

recovered by the federal government from the states.[130]   However, before a state that accepts federal money will be bound to comply with a particular condition, it is required that Congress express clearly its intent to impose the condition so that the state knowingly can decide whether to accept the funds.[131]

Any condition, of course, must not be unconstitutional. Nor, if it is in the form of an administrative regulation, may it be beyond the power of the administrative agency to promulgate. The discussion in Chapter 3 regarding powers of state-level agencies under state statutes would generally apply to federal agencies under federal statutes. Thus, it was held by the Court of Appeals, District of Columbia Circuit, that the Secretary of Agriculture exceeded the department's rule making authority by barring the sale of foods competitive to those provided in the federally subsidized school breakfast and lunch program throughout the school and until after the last service of the day.[132]   Restrictions on "junk food" sales at the time and place of meal service, however, were found to have been authorized by Congress for the purpose of promoting consumption of nutritious foods.

Under an act of Congress, "impacted" school areas (those whose populations had been substantially enlarged by the attendance of children of federal employees, but which at the same time were losing school tax revenues because of the immunity from property taxes of the United States Government) were provided funds according to a formula. Virginia, in applying a formula for state assistance to local school districts, deducted from the share otherwise allocable to a district a sum equal to a substantial percentage of any federal "impact" funds received by the district. A three-judge federal District Court held this procedure to be violative of the supremacy clause of the Constitution [133] because the financial relief did not go to the local taxpayers to the extent Congress contemplated.[134]   The purpose of the federal legislation was determined to be to aid local districts, not to provide compensation for the state.

It will not be presumed, however, that the supremacy clause makes federal legislation supersede the power of a state in the absence of Congressional intent to do so. Applying this rule, the Court of Appeals, Tenth Circuit, upheld a New Mexico state finance plan that treated the Los Alamos school district differently from others in the state as long as it received special federal funds connected with the community's having been established as a federally owned and managed installation for atomic research and development.[135]   The federal government had transferred without cost the public schools it had built to a newly created school district and was continuing to provide financial grants.   The

---

130. Bell v. New Jersey and Pennsylvania, 461 U.S. 773, 103 S.Ct. 2187, 76 L.Ed.2d 312 (1983).

131. Pennhurst State School and Hospital v. Halderman, 451 U.S. 1, 101 S.Ct. 1531, 67 L.Ed.2d 694 (1981).

132. National Soft Drink Ass'n v. Block, 721 F.2d 1348 (D.C.Cir.1983).

133. U.S. Const. art. VI, cl. 2.

134. Shepheard v. Godwin, 280 F.Supp. 869 (E.D.Va.1968). [Case No. 37]

135. Los Alamos School Bd. v. Wugalter, 557 F.2d 709 (10 Cir.1977), cert. den. 434 U.S. 968, 98 S.Ct. 512, 54 L.Ed.2d 455 (1977).

Court of Appeals distinguished this situation from that in impact aid cases, where the aid was to be supplementary. The court found no such intent in the atomic-energy-community legislation, remarking that when the federal plan to finance Los Alamos was originated, there was nothing to supplement.

Substantial cutbacks in federal impact aid prompted a North Carolina school district, which enrolled large numbers of children whose parents were connected with the federal government in or out of the military services, to charge tuition for all nondomiciliary enrollees. The Court of Appeals, Fourth Circuit, found the plan invalid both on contractual and constitutional grounds.[136] The contractual bar was premised on the board's having accepted over the years federal aid for constructing school buildings, which aid was available only to districts that experienced substantial increases in enrollments of federally connected children and that promised to make the facilities (which were still in service) equally available to federally connected children and domiciliary children. Constitutional violations were found as to the supremacy clause. The tuition charges were, in effect, a tax that discriminated against federally-connected persons and, therefore, against the federal government. That eight percent of those charged tuition were not federally-connected was of questionable import, especially since no nondomiciliary persons could vote. Also implicated was the war powers authority of Congress.

The Supreme Court applied the supremacy clause to invalidate a South Dakota statute that required local governments to distribute federal payments "in lieu of taxes" (to compensate for loss of tax revenues from federally administered national parks and wilderness areas) in the same way they distributed general tax revenues.[137] The Court said that the intent of Congress was to allow units of local government to make the decisions as to how to use the money unfettered by state intervention.

[Case No. 34] Power of Board to Levy Taxes

MARION & McPHERSON RAILWAY CO. v. ALEXANDER

Supreme Court of Kansas, 1901.
63 Kan. 72, 64 P. 978.

CUNNINGHAM, J. The plaintiff in error in this action seeks to enjoin the collection of all taxes levied for school purposes in school district No. 79, Marion county, Kan., in excess of 2 per cent. on the taxable property owned by it in said district. A graded school district, No. 79, had been organized, identical in boundaries and inhabitants with school district No. 79; such organization being authorized by article 7, c. 92, of the General Statutes of 1889. That article generally provided for the organization of union or graded schools, its principal sections being as

---

136. United States v. Onslow County Bd. of Educ., 728 F.2d 628 (4 Cir.1984).

137. Lawrence County v. Lead–Deadwood School Dist. No. 40–1, 469 U.S. 256, 105 S.Ct. 695, 83 L.Ed.2d 635 (1985).

follows: Section 107 provides for the selection of a board of directors by the graded school district, and that such board shall consist of a director, clerk, and treasurer. Section 108 directs that such board of directors shall, in all matters relating to the graded school, possess all the powers and discharge all the like duties of boards of directors in other districts. Section 109 provides that the union districts thus formed shall be entitled to an equitable share of the school funds, to be drawn from the treasurer of each district so uniting, in proportion to the number of children attending the said graded school for each district. Section 110: "The said union district may levy taxes for the purpose of purchasing a building or furnishing proper buildings for the accommodation of the school or for the purpose of defraying necessary expenses and paying teachers, but shall be governed in all respects by the law herein provided for levying and collecting district taxes." Section 111 provides certain duties for the clerk of the union district in relation to reports, and that the district treasurer shall apportion the amount of school moneys due the union district, and pay the same over to the treasurer of the union district on order of the clerk and director thereof. Section 112, that the clerk of the union district shall make report to the county superintendent, and discharge all the duties of clerk in like manner as the clerk of the district. Section 113, that the treasurer of the district shall perform all the duties of treasurer as prescribed in the act in like manner as the district treasurer. Section 115, that any single district shall possess power to establish graded schools in like manner and subject to the same provisions as two or more districts united. Section 28 of the same chapter (being the section which gives the general power for levying district taxes) provides: "The inhabitants qualified to vote at a school meeting, lawfully assembled, shall have power: * * * To vote a tax annually not exceeding two per cent. on the taxable property in the district, as the meeting shall deem sufficient for the various school purposes, and distribute the amount as the meeting shall deem proper in the payment of teachers' wages, and to purchase or lease a site."

These are all the sections which afford light for the solution of the question involved. From these, it is contended by plaintiff in error that while the inhabitants of one or more school districts may form a union or graded district, and create machinery to run the same and to maintain any and all schools therein, the total levy "for the various school purposes" cannot exceed 2 per cent. on the taxable property in any one district annually. It is contended by the defendants in error that the various sections quoted, conferring as they do upon the various members of the graded school district board all the powers of like officers of ordinary district boards, and erecting a separate entity for the purpose of managing a separate school, and conferring upon that entity the power to levy taxes as found in section 110, give the power to such graded school district to make within its bounds an additional levy not to exceed 2 per cent.; that is, that it may levy as much as the original school district may, and this in addition to what the original district levies, and not that the total of both levies must be the limit fixed in section 28. The court below took this view of the question. In this we do not agree.

We think that by section 28 the entire levy may not exceed 2 per cent.; and we are strengthened in this conclusion by the language of section 109, which says that a union district shall be entitled to "an equitable share of the school funds," and also by that in section 111,—"the district treasurer shall apportion the amount of school money due the union district and pay the same over to the union district." The law fixes the time for holding the annual meetings of the union or graded districts in June, while the annual meetings of school districts occur in July. All these provisions, taken together, indicate that it was the purpose of the legislature that, while the first meeting—that of the graded district— could suggest the levy desired for graded school purposes, the last one only possessed the power to vote the tax which for "the various school purposes" could not in any one year exceed 2 per cent. Or, at least, there must be such harmony in the action of both bodies that the aggregate levy may not exceed the limit found in section 28. We may say that the question is not one entirely free from doubt, but can hardly believe that the legislature would have left it in that condition, had its purpose been to confer the right to so largely increase the burden of taxation. The authority to levy taxes is an extraordinary one. It is never left to implication, unless it is a necessary implication. Its warrant must be clearly found in the act of the legislature. Any other rule might lead to great wrong and oppression, and when there is a reasonable doubt as to its existence the right must be denied. Therefore to say that the right is in doubt is to deny its existence.

The levies sought to be enjoined are those for the years 1894 and 1895, and our conclusion is that the judgment of the district court must be reversed, and it be directed to make the injunction perpetual, enjoining all of the defendants from collecting all of said school taxes in excess of 2 per cent. All the justices concurring.

Notes

1. "The power of the board of education of a non-high school district to levy taxes is statutory. The language granting that power is to be strictly construed and will not be extended beyond the plain import of the words used." People ex rel. Smith, County Collector v. Wabash Railway Co., 374 Ill. 165, 28 N.E.2d 119 (1940).

2. How do you account for such tax limitations? How are they justified?

3. Generally a school district may not levy taxes so as to build up surpluses beyond their current expenses. Although a contingency fund of a reasonable amount may be permissible, a tax levy creating a surplus of some fifty percent of the school district budget was excessive. Kissinger v. School Dist. No. 49 of Clay County, 163 Neb. 33, 77 N.W.2d 767 (1956).

4. A state may tax the income earned by a resident of another state within the borders of the first state. Oklahoma had enacted a state income tax which was imposed upon a citizen of Illinois engaged in the oil business in Oklahoma. Shaffer v. Carter, 252 U.S. 37, 40 S.Ct. 221, 64 L.Ed. 445 (1920).

[Case No. 35]   Power of State to Require Local Issue of Bonds

REVELL v. MAYOR, ETC., OF ANNAPOLIS

Court of Appeals of Maryland, 1895.
81 Md. 1, 31 A. 695.

ROBINSON, C.J.   The act of 1894, c. 620, provides for the erection of a public school building in the city of Annapolis, and, to pay for the same, it authorizes and directs the school commissioners of Anne Arundel county to borrow money, not exceeding the sum of $20,000, on bonds to be indorsed by the county commissioners; and for the same purpose it directs that the city of Annapolis shall issue bonds to the amount of $10,000, and that said bonds shall be issued without submitting the question of their issue to the voters of said city.   The city of Annapolis has refused to issue the bonds as thus directed by the act, and the question is whether the legislature has the power to direct that the city authorities shall issue bonds to raise money to be applied to the erection of a public school building in said city.   This power is denied, on the broad ground that it is not competent for the legislature to compel a municipal corporation to create a debt or levy a tax for a local purpose, in which the state has no concern, or to assume a debt not within the corporate powers of a municipal government.   If the correctness of this general proposition be conceded for the purposes of this case, we do not see how it affects in any manner the validity of the act now in question. We cannot agree that the erection of buildings necessary for the public schools is a matter of merely local concern, in which the state has no interest.   In this country the people are not only in theory, but in practice, the source of all governmental power, and the stability of free institutions mainly rests upon an enlightened public opinion.   Fully recognizing this, the constitution declares that it shall be the duty of the legislature "to establish throughout the state a thorough and efficient system of free public schools, and to provide, by taxation or otherwise," for their maintenance and support.   * * * And the legislature has accordingly established a public school system, and has provided for its support by state and local taxation.   It cannot be said, therefore, that the erection of buildings for public school purposes is a matter in which the state has no concern; nor can we agree that the creation of a debt for such purposes is not within the ordinary functions of municipal government.   What is a municipal corporation?   It is but a subordinate part of the state government, incorporated for public purposes, and clothed with special and limited powers of legislation in regard to its own local affairs.   It has no inherent legislative power, and can exercise such powers only as have been expressly or by fair implication delegated to it by the legislature.   * * * The legislature may, at its pleasure, alter, amend, and enlarge its powers.   It may authorize the city authorities to establish public schools within the corporate limits, and direct that bonds shall be issued to raise money for their support, payable at intervals during a series of years.   There is no difference in principle between issuing bonds and the levying of a tax in one year sufficient to meet the necessary expenditure. It would be less burdensome to the taxpayers to issue bonds payable at intervals than to levy a tax to raise $10,000 in any one year. This, however, is a matter of detail, within the discretion of the legislature, and over which the courts have no control.

If the legislature has the power to direct the city authorities to create a debt for a public school building, the exercise of this power in no manner depends upon their consent or upon the consent of the qualified voters of the city. We recognize the force of the argument that the question whether a municipal debt is to be created ought to be left to the discretion and judgment of the people who are to bear the burden. We recognize the fact that the exercise of this power by the legislature may be liable to abuse. But this abuse of a power is no argument against its exercise. The remedy, however, in such cases, is with the people to whom the members of the legislature are responsible for the discharge of the trust committed to them. It is a matter over which the courts have no control. * * *

* * *

Notes

1. When a school board fails to carry out its functions to the satisfaction of the community, are the community members justified in appealing to the legislature for special action in lieu of school board action?

2. To what extent is "special" legislation justified to cope with problems not generally present throughout a state?

3. This case is frequently cited in opinions involving legislative powers, status of local political entities, and the role of the judiciary.

[Case No. 36] Power of State to Raise and Distribute School Funds

SAWYER v. GILMORE

Supreme Judicial Court of Maine, 1912.
109 Me. 169, 83 A. 673.

CORNISH, J. This bill in equity is brought to enjoin the Treasurer of State and his successors in office from collecting a tax assessed under the provisions of chapter 177 of the Public Laws of 1909 * * *.

The case comes up on report, and by stipulation the only question raised and to be considered is the constitutionality of the chapter above referred to under the state and federal Constitutions.

Chapter 177 of the Public Laws of 1909, the statute in question, reads as follows:

"Section 1. A tax of one and a half mills on a dollar shall annually be assessed upon all of the property in the state according to the valuation thereof and shall be known as the tax for the support of common schools.

* * *

"Sec. 3. One-third of this fund shall be distributed by the Treasurer of State on the first day of January, annually, to the several cities, towns and plantations according to the number of scholars therein, as the same shall appear from the official returns made to the state superintendent of public schools for the preceding year, and the remaining two-thirds of said fund shall be distributed by the Treasurer of State on the first day of January, annually, to the several cities, towns and plantations, according to the valuation thereof as the same shall be fixed by the state assessors for the preceding year."

* * *

Objections * * * are raised to the manner of distribution * * *.

The first objection is that this act imposes an unequal burden of taxation upon the unorganized townships of the state, because, while the fund is created by the taxation of all the property in such townships as well as upon the property in the cities, towns, and plantations, no provision is made for the distribution of any part thereof to such townships, but it is all apportioned among the cities, towns, and plantations. The townships are omitted. In other words, while four subdivisions of the state are made to contribute to the fund, only three are permitted to share in the financial benefits.

This objection, however, is without legal foundation. The Legislature has the right under the Constitution to impose an equal rate of taxation upon all the property in the state, including the property in unorganized townships, for the purpose of distributing the proceeds thereof among the cities, towns, and plantations for common school purposes, and the mere fact that the tax is assessed upon the property in four municipal subdivisions and distributed among three is not in itself fatal.

* * *

* * * The fundamental question is this: Is the purpose for which the tax is assessed a public purpose, not whether any portion of it may find its way back again to the pocket of the taxpayer or to the direct advantage of himself or family. Were the latter the test, the childless man would be exempt from the support of schools and the sane and well from the support of hospitals. In order that taxation may be equal and uniform in the constitutional sense, it is not necessary that the benefits arising therefrom should be enjoyed by all the people in equal degree, nor that each one of the people should participate in each particular benefit. Laws must be general in their character, and the benefits must affect different people differently. This is due to difference in situation. * * * In a Republic like ours each must contribute for the common good, and the benefits are received not directly in dollars and cents, but indirectly in a wider diffusion of knowledge, in better homes, saner laws, more efficient administration of justice, higher social order, and deeper civic righteousness.

* * *

But the plaintiff further attacks the method of distribution as unconstitutional because it is made, not according to the number of scholars, as is the school mill fund, but one-third according to the number of scholars and two-thirds according to valuation, thus benefiting the cities, and richer towns more than the poorer.

But that result is not the test of constitutionality. Inequality of assessment is necessarily fatal, inequality of distribution is not, provided the purpose be the public welfare. The method of distributing the proceeds of such a tax rests in the wise discretion and sound judgment of the Legislature. If this discretion is unwisely exercised, the remedy is with the people, and not with the court. Such distribution might be according to population, or according to the number of scholars of school age, or according to school attendance, or according to valuation, or partly on one basis and partly on another. The Constitution prescribes no regulation in regard to this matter, and it is not for the court to say that one method should be adopted in preference to another. We are not to substitute our judgment for that of a co-ordinate branch of the government working within its constitutional limits. The distribution of the school mill fund of 1872 has resulted in inequality. That distribution has been, and continues to be, based on the number of scholars, thereby benefiting the poorer towns more than the richer, because they receive more than they pay, and in the opinion of the justices before cited that method is deemed constitutional. The act under consideration apportions the newly created common school fund one-third according to the number of scholars and two-thirds according to the valuation as fixed by the state assessors, thereby benefiting the richer towns more than the poorer, producing inequality in the other direction, but we are unable to see why this method is not equally constitutional with the other. Both taxes are assessed for the same admittedly public purpose, both promote the common welfare, and the fact that the Legislature has seen fit to distribute the two on different bases is not fatal to the validity of either. It may be that the two methods taken together produce a more equal distribution than either operating alone. In any event, the Legislature has adopted both methods, and both must stand or fall together. * * *

Our conclusion therefore is that chapter 177 of the Public Laws of 1909 violates neither the state nor the federal Constitution * * *.

* * *

Notes

1. In 1876 this court found constitutional the School Mill Act of 1872, which was the first in the state to impose a state tax on property and devote the proceeds to the maintenance of common schools. Opinion of the Justices, 68 Me. 582 (1876).

2. How do you reconcile the requirement of "equal protection of the laws" with the holding in this case.

3. How sound do you consider the court's appraisal of the benefits of public education? To what extent, if at all, should public services be supported by those who use them? Does your answer depend on the particular service?

[Case No. 37] Relation between Congress and the States Regarding Financial Aid to Local School Districts

SHEPHEARD v. GODWIN

United States District Court, Eastern District of Virginia, 1968.
280 F.Supp. 869.

ALBERT V. BRYAN, CIRCUIT JUDGE: "Impacted" school areas are those whose school populations have been substantially enlarged by the attendance of Federal employees' children, but at the same time are losing school tax revenues because of the United States government's immunity from land taxes, both factors arising from increased Federal activities in the area. These conditions prompted Congress to provide financial aid for operation of the local educational facilities, P.L. 874.

In applying a State formula for State assistance to local school districts, Virginia has deducted from the share otherwise allocable to the district a sum equal to a substantial percentage of any Federal "impact" funds receivable by the district.

Residents, real estate owners and taxpayers of the City of Norfolk, later joined by those of the County of Fairfax, Virginia, in behalf of themselves and others similarly situated, here attack this deduction and an alternative provision as violative of the purpose and intent of the act of Congress and as transgressing the Fourteenth Amendment. We uphold their contention.

* * *

Commencing at the 1948–49 school term Virginia established the Minimum Education Program. As the title indicates, it represents a program which was determined necessary to provide each child in the State a minimum education. To take care of the program's cost a Basic State School Aid Fund was created. It fixed a minimum program cost for every political subdivision of the State, i.e. counties and cities.

* * *

A contribution to be made by the State to the cost in every political subdivision is spelled out also. It is comprised of (1) a basic State share and (2) a supplementary State share. The *basic* State share amounts to 60% of the instructional salaries. The *supplementary* State share is reached by subtracting from the minimum program cost (the gross instructional salaries plus the total of the $100 per pupil ADA) the following items: (1) the basic State share; (2) an amount equivalent to a uniform tax levy of 60 cents per $100 of true values of local taxable real estate and public service corporation property in the subdivision; and (3) 50% (in 1966–68) of the impact funds receivable by the subdivision from the Federal government for operating costs. A maximum is fixed for the supplementary State share. Administration of this allocation of State money is put in the hands of the State Board of Education.

* * *

The grievance of the plaintiffs is obvious: any deduction whatsoever of the Federal supplement in apportioning State aid, pro tanto burdens them as taxpayers, for they and the other property owners in Norfolk and Fairfax have to make up the unindemnified portion of the impact costs. They contend that any deduction is prohibited by the purpose and plan of the Federal act.

The rejoinder of the defendant officials is, first, that the impact pupils are counted by the State in computing the minimum program cost in the district, and in accounting with the district for the State's supplementary aid it is not inequitable to insist upon a deduction of a commensurate amount of the impact moneys. At first appealing, this argument ignores the fact that the Federal children are to a large extent paying their own way so far as the *State* is concerned. Quite soundly, the Congressional Committee on Education and Labor in recommending passage of P.L. 874, observed that the influx of Federal employees, and the withdrawal of real estate from taxes, did not diminish the tax sources of the State or otherwise burden the State. Its revenues are obtained from taxation to which the additional Federal employees are subject along with the other residents of the area.   * * *

Secondly, say the defendant State officials, the calculation of the district's share—the equivalent of 60-cent tax—in computing the supplementary aid, omits consideration of the value of the Federal occupied property and hence, in place of this omitted deduction, it is only fair to subtract the amount of the impact funds which are intended to substitute for the Federal-occupied land taxes. But this argument is based on misconception of the Federal aid as *substituting for* rather than *supplementing* local revenues. As will appear when we later scrutinize the act, this is a mistaken understanding of the Federal act.

Our conclusion is that the State formula wrenches from the impacted localities the very benefaction the act was intended to bestow. The State plan must fall as violative of the supremacy clause of the Constitution. Our decision rests entirely on the terms, pattern and policy of the act.

The act makes these propositions clear: (1) the Federal funds are exclusively for supplementation of the local sources of revenues for school purposes; and (2) the act was not intended to lessen the efforts of the State. Those postulates are manifested in the statute by these provisions, especially: that the Federal contribution be paid directly to the local school agency on reports of the local agency, and that the contribution be computed by reference to the expenditures "made from revenues derived from local sources" in comparable school districts.

But the State formula at once sets these precepts at naught. It uses the impact funds to account in part for fulfillment of the State's pledge of supplementary aid to the community; and the State moneys thus saved are available for State retention or such use as Virginia determines. Without the inclusion of the Federal sums the State's annual payments towards supplementary aid would be increased, it is estimated, by more than $10,000,000.

This commandeering of credit for the Federal moneys severely injures both the community and the pupil. First and foremost, it does not relieve the local taxpayers to the extent Congress contemplated. Next, without the exclusive application of the funds to the areas where the need arose and remains, the result may be to lower the standard of education provided in an impacted district. Instead of maintaining the previous standards for the additional pupils, the impact money when thinned by the State would obviously be inadequate to continue that level for the increased school attendance, a result certainly thwarting the aim of the Federal law.

The construction and the implications we put upon the act find confirmation in its legislative history. * * *

* * * Necessarily, then, the upshot is that the defendants must be enjoined from hereafter in any way denying to the impacted area the exclusive use and enjoyment of the impact funds.

* * *

The Norfolk plaintiffs have also prayed for an order directing the defendants to restore to the Norfolk schools the amounts of State aid which in prior years have been withheld by the State on account of the Federal impact funds. To accomplish this restitution would require an appropriation by the legislature of Virginia. A decree to that effect would be an order to the State to take affirmative political action, and would convert this into a suit against the Commonwealth of Virginia, prohibited by the Eleventh Amendment. * * *

* * *

Notes

1. Within a year this became a leading case. Two additional three-judge federal District Courts in other circuits cited it in coming to the same conclusions regarding congressional intent and invalidating state finance plans which provided for diminutions in state aid where federal aid was granted to "impacted" school districts. Douglas Independent School Dist. No. 3 v. Jorgenson, 293 F.Supp. 849 (D.S.D.1968); and Hergenreter v. Hayden, 295 F.Supp. 251 (D.Kan. 1968).

2. Consider the last paragraph of the opinion in light of (1) our federal system of government; (2) power of the federal courts; (3) justice.

3. Observe how this case differs from the one involving federal funds in the Los Alamos schools (footnote 135, this chapter).

[Case No. 38] Constitutionality of State Finance Plan in Relation to Equality of Educational Opportunity

SAN ANTONIO INDEPENDENT SCHOOL DIST. v. RODRIGUEZ

Supreme Court of the United States, 1973.
411 U.S. 1, 93 S.Ct. 1278, 36 L.Ed.2d 16.

MR. JUSTICE POWELL delivered the opinion of the Court.

This suit attacking the Texas system of financing public education was initiated by Mexican-American parents whose children attend the elementary and secondary schools in the Edgewood Independent School District, an urban school district in San Antonio, Texas. They brought a class action on behalf of schoolchildren throughout the State who are members of minority groups or who are poor and reside in school districts having a low property tax base. * * * The complaint was filed in the summer of 1968 and a three-judge court was impaneled in January 1969. In December 1971 the panel rendered its judgment in a *per curiam* opinion holding the Texas school finance system unconstitutional under the Equal Protection Clause of the Fourteenth Amendment. * * * For the reasons stated in this opinion, we reverse the decision of the District Court.

I

The first Texas State Constitution, promulgated upon Texas' entry into the Union in 1845, provided for the establishment of a system of free schools. Early in its history, Texas adopted a dual approach to the financing of its schools, relying on mutual participation by the local school districts and the State. * * *

* * *

Recognizing the need for increased state funding to help offset disparities in local spending and to meet Texas' changing educational requirements, the state legislature in the late 1940's undertook a thorough evaluation of public education with an eye toward major reform. In 1947, an 18-member committee, composed of educators and legislators, was appointed to explore alternative systems in other States and to propose a funding scheme that would guarantee a minimum or basic educational offering to each child and that would help overcome interdistrict disparities in taxable resources. The Committee's efforts led to the passage of the Gilmer-Aikin bills, named for the Committee's co-chairmen, establishing the Texas Minimum Foundation School Program. Today, this Program accounts for approximately half of the total educational expenditures in Texas.

The Program calls for state and local contributions to a fund earmarked specifically for teacher salaries, operating expenses, and transportation costs. The State, supplying funds from its general revenues, finances approximately 80% of the Program, and the school districts are responsible—as a unit—for providing the remaining 20%. The districts' share, known as the Local Fund Assignment, is apportioned among the school districts under a formula designed to reflect each district's relative taxpaying ability. The Assignment is first divided among Texas' 254 counties pursuant to a complicated economic index that takes into account the relative value of each county's contribution to the State's total income from manufacturing, mining, and agricultural activities. It also considers each county's relative share of all payrolls paid within the State and, to a lesser extent, considers each county's share of all property in the State. Each county's assignment is then divided among its school districts on the basis of each district's share of assessable property within the county. The district, in turn, finances its share of the Assignment out of revenues from local property taxation.

The design of this complex system was twofold. First, it was an attempt to assure that the Foundation Program would have an equalizing influence on expenditure levels between school districts by placing the heaviest burden on the school districts most capable of paying. Second, the Program's architects sought to establish a Local Fund Assignment that would force every school district to contribute to the education of its children but that would not by itself exhaust any district's resources. Today every school district does impose a property tax from which it derives locally expendable funds in excess of the amount necessary to satisfy its Local Fund Assignment under the Foundation Program.

* * *

The school district in which appellees reside, the Edgewood Independent School District, has been compared throughout this litigation with the Alamo Heights Independent School District. This comparison between the least and most affluent districts in the San Antonio area serves to illustrate the manner in which the dual system of finance operates and to indicate the extent to which substantial disparities exist despite the State's impressive progress in recent years. Edgewood is one of seven public school districts in the metropolitan area. Approximately 22,000 students are enrolled in its 25 elementary and secondary schools. The district is situated in the core-city sector of San Antonio in a residential neighborhood that has little commercial or industrial property. The residents are predominantly of Mexican-American descent: approximately 90% of the student population is Mexican-American and over 6% is Negro. The average assessed property value per pupil is $5,960—the lowest in the metropolitan area—and the median family income ($4,686) is also the lowest. At an equalized tax rate of $1.05 per $100 of assessed property—the highest in the metropolitan area—the district contributed $26 to the education of each child for the 1967–1968 school year above its Local Fund Assignment for the Minimum Foundation Program. The Foundation Program contributed $222 per pupil for a state-local total of $248. Federal funds added another $108 for a total of $356 per pupil.

Alamo Heights is the most affluent school district in San Antonio. Its six schools, housing approximately 5,000 students, are situated in a residential community quite unlike the Edgewood District. The school population is predominantly "Anglo," having only 18% Mexican-Americans and less than 1% Negroes. The assessed property value per pupil exceeds $49,000, and the median family income is $8,001. In 1967–1968 the local tax rate of $.85 per $100 of valuation yielded $333 per pupil over and above its contribution to the Foundation Program. Coupled with the $225 provided from that Program, the district was able to supply $558 per student. Supplemented by a $36 per-pupil grant from federal sources, Alamo Heights spent $594 per pupil.

Although the 1967–1968 school year figures provide the only complete statistical breakdown for each category of aid, more recent partial statistics indicate that the previously noted trend of increasing state aid has been significant. For the 1970–1971 school year, the Foundation School Program allotment for Edgewood was $356 per pupil, a 62% increase over the 1967–68 school year. Indeed, state aid alone in 1970–1971 equaled Edgewood's entire 1967–1968 school budget from local, state, and federal sources. Alamo Heights enjoyed a similar increase under the Foundation Program, netting $491 per pupil in 1970–1971. These recent figures also reveal the extent to which these two districts' allotments were funded from their own required contributions to the Local Fund Assignment. Alamo Heights, because of its relative wealth, was required to contribute out of its local property tax collections approximately $100 per pupil, or about 20% of its Foundation grant. Edgewood, on the other hand, paid only $8.46 per pupil, which is about 2.4% of its grant. It appears then that, at least as to these two districts, the Local Fund Assignment does reflect a rough approximation of the relative taxpaying potential of each.

Despite these recent increases, substantial interdistrict disparities in school expenditures found by the District Court to prevail in San Antonio and in varying degrees throughout the State still exist. And it was these disparities, largely attributable to differences in the amounts of money collected through local property taxation, that led the District Court to conclude that Texas' dual system of public school financing violated the Equal Protection Clause. The District Court held that the Texas system discriminates on the basis of wealth in the manner in which education is provided for its people. Finding that wealth is a "suspect" classification and that education is a "fundamental" interest, the District Court held that the Texas system could be sustained only if the State could show that it was premised upon some compelling state interest. On this issue the court concluded that "[n]ot only are defendants unable to demonstrate compelling state interests * * * they fail even to establish a reasonable basis for these classifications."

* * *

This, then, establishes the framework for our analysis. We must decide, first, whether the Texas system of financing public education operates to the disadvantage of some suspect class or impinges upon a fundamental right explicitly or implicitly protected by the Constitution, thereby requiring strict judicial scrutiny. If so, the judgment of the District Court should be affirmed. If not, the Texas scheme must still be examined to determine whether it rationally furthers some legitimate, articulated state purpose and therefore does not constitute an invidious discrimination in violation of the Equal Protection Clause of the Fourteenth Amendment.

II

* * *

A

The wealth discrimination discovered by the District Court in this case, and by several other courts that have recently struck down school-financing laws in other States, is quite unlike any of the forms of wealth discrimination heretofore reviewed by this Court. Rather than focusing on the unique features of the alleged discrimination, the courts in these cases have virtually assumed their findings of a suspect classification through a simplistic process of analysis: since, under the traditional systems of financing public schools, some poorer people receive less expensive educations than other more affluent people, these systems discriminate on the basis of wealth. This approach largely ignores the hard threshold questions, including whether it makes a difference for purposes of consideration under the Constitution that the class of disadvantaged "poor" cannot be identified or defined in customary equal protection terms, and whether the relative—rather than absolute—nature of the asserted deprivation is of significant consequence. Before a State's laws and the justifications for the classifications they create are subjected to strict judicial scrutiny, we think these threshold considerations must be analyzed more closely than they were in the court below.

The case comes to us with no definitive description of the classifying facts or delineation of the disfavored class. Examination of the District Court's opinion and of appellees' complaint, briefs and contentions at oral argument suggests, however, at least three ways in which the discrimination claimed here might be described. The Texas system of school financing might be regarded as discriminating (1) against "poor" persons whose incomes fall below some identifiable level of poverty or who might be characterized as functionally "indigent," or (2) against those who are relatively poorer than others, or (3) against all those who, irrespective of their personal incomes, happen to reside in relatively poorer school districts. Our task must be to ascertain whether, in fact, the Texas system has been shown to discriminate on any of these possible bases and, if so, whether the resulting classification may be regarded as suspect.

The precedents of this Court provide the proper starting point. The individuals, or groups of individuals, who constituted the class discriminated against in our prior cases shared two distinguishing characteristics: because of their impecunity they were completely unable to pay for some desired benefit, and as a consequence, they sustained an absolute deprivation of a meaningful opportunity to enjoy that benefit. In Griffin v. Illinois, 351 U.S. 12, 76 S.Ct. 585, 100 L.Ed. 891 (1956), and its progeny, the Court invalidated state laws that prevented an indigent criminal defendant from acquiring a transcript, or an adequate substitute for a transcript, for use at several stages of the trial and appeal process. The payment requirements in each case were found to occasion *de facto* discrimination against those who, because of their indigency, were totally unable to pay for transcripts. And the Court in each case emphasized that no constitutional violation would have been shown if the State had provided some "adequate substitute" for a full stenographic transcript.

Likewise, in Douglas v. California, 372 U.S. 353, 83 S.Ct. 814, 9 L.Ed.2d 811 (1963), a decision establishing an indigent defendant's right to court-appointed counsel on direct appeal, the Court dealt only with defendants who could not pay for counsel from their own resources and who had no other way of gaining representation. *Douglas* provides no relief for those on whom the burdens of paying for a criminal defense are relatively speaking, great but not insurmountable. Nor does it deal with relative differences in the quality of counsel acquired by the less wealthy.

* * *

Only appellees' first possible basis for describing the class disadvantaged by the Texas school-financing system—discrimination against a class of definably "poor" persons—might arguably meet the criteria established in these prior cases. Even a cursory examination, however, demonstrates that neither of the two distinguishing characteristics of wealth classifications can be found here. First, in support of their charge that the system discriminates against the "poor," appellees have made no effort to demonstrate that it operates to the peculiar disadvantage of any class fairly definable as indigent, or as composed of persons whose incomes are beneath any designated poverty level. Indeed, there is reason to believe that the poorest families are not necessarily clustered in the poorest property districts. A recent and exhaustive study of school districts in Connecticut concluded that "[i]t is clearly incorrect * * * to contend that the 'poor' live in 'poor' districts * * *. Thus, the major factual assumption of *Serrano*—that the educational financing system discriminates against the 'poor'—is simply false in Connecticut." Defining "poor" families as those below the Bureau of the Census "poverty level," the Connecticut study found, not surprisingly, that the poor were clustered around commercial and industrial areas—those same areas that provide the most attractive sources of property tax income for school districts. Whether a similar pattern would be discovered in Texas is not known, but there is no basis on the record in this case for assuming that the poorest people—defined by reference to any level of absolute impecunity—are concentrated in the poorest districts.

Second, neither appellees nor the District Court addressed the fact that, unlike each of the foregoing cases, lack of personal resources has not occasioned an absolute deprivation of the desired benefit. The argument here is not that the children in districts having relatively low assessable property values are receiving no public education; rather, it is that they are receiving a poorer quality education than that available to children in districts having more assessable wealth. Apart from the unsettled and disputed question whether the quality of education may be determined by the amount of money expended for it, a sufficient answer to appellees' argument is that, at least where wealth is involved, the Equal Protection Clause does not require absolute equality or precisely equal advantages. Nor indeed, in view of the infinite variables affecting the educational process, can any system assure equal quality of education except in the most relative sense. * * *

For these two reasons—the absence of any evidence that the financing system discriminates against any definable category of "poor" people or that it results in the absolute deprivation of education—the disadvantaged class is not susceptible of identification in traditional terms.

As suggested above, appellees and the District Court may have embraced a second or third approach, the second of which might be characterized as a theory of relative or comparative discrimination based on family income. Appellees sought to prove that a direct correlation exists between the wealth of families within each district and the expenditures therein for education. That is, along a continuum, the poorer the family the lower the dollar amount of education received by the family's children.

The principal evidence adduced in support of this comparative-discrimination claim is an affidavit submitted by Professor Joel S. Berke of Syracuse University's Educational Finance Policy Institute. * * *

* * *

Professor Berke's affidavit is based on a survey of approximately 10% of the school districts in Texas. His findings * * * show only that the wealthiest few districts in the sample have the highest median family incomes and spend the most on education, and that the several poorest districts have the lowest family incomes and devote the least amount of money to education. For the remainder of the districts—96 districts composing almost 90% of the sample—the correlation is inverted, i.e., the districts that spend next to the most money on education are populated by families having next to the lowest median family incomes while the districts spending the least have the highest median family incomes. It is evident that, even if the conceptual questions were answered favorably to appellees, no factual basis exists upon which to found a claim of comparative wealth discrimination.

This brings us, then, to the third way in which the classification scheme might be defined—*district* wealth discrimination. Since the only correlation indicated by the evidence is between district property wealth and expenditures, it may be argued that discrimination might be found without regard to the individual income characteristics of district residents. Assuming a perfect correlation between district property wealth and expenditures from top to bottom, the disadvantaged class might be viewed as encompassing every child in every district except the district that has the most assessable wealth and spends the most on education. Alternatively * * * the class might be defined more restrictively to include children in districts with assessable property which falls below the statewide average, or median, or below some other artificially defined level.

However described, it is clear that appellees' suit asks this Court to extend its most exacting scrutiny to review a system that allegedly discriminates against a large, diverse, and amorphous class, unified only by the common factor of residence in districts that happen to have less taxable wealth than other districts. The system of alleged discrimination and the class it defines have none of the traditional indicia of suspectness: the class is not saddled with such disabilities, or subjected to such a history of purposeful unequal treatment, or relegated to such a position of political powerlessness as to command extraordinary protection from the majoritarian political process.

We thus conclude that the Texas system does not operate to the peculiar disadvantage of any suspect class. But in recognition of the fact that this Court has never heretofore held that wealth discrimination alone provides an adequate basis for invoking strict scrutiny, appellees have not relied solely on this contention. They also assert that the State's system impermissible interferes with the exercise of a "fundamental" right and that accordingly the prior decisions of this Court require the application of the strict standard of judicial review. It is this question—whether education is a fundamental right, in the sense that it is among the rights and liberties protected by the Constitution—which has so consumed the attention of courts and commentators in recent years.

B

In Brown v. Board of Education, a unanimous Court recognized that "education is perhaps the most important function of state and local governments." What was said there in the context of racial discrimination has lost none of its vitality with the passage of time. * * * This theme, expressing an abiding respect for the vital role of education in a free society, may be found in numerous opinions of Justices of this Court writing both before and after *Brown* was decided.

Nothing this Court holds today in any way detracts from our historic dedication to public education. We are in complete agreement with the conclusion of the three-judge panel below that "the grave significance of education both to the individual and to our society" cannot be doubted. But the importance of a service performed by the State does not determine whether it must be regarded as fundamental for purposes of examination under the Equal Protection Clause. * * *

* * *

* * * It is not the province of this Court to create substantive constitutional rights in the name of guaranteeing equal protection of the laws. Thus, the key to discovering whether education is "fundamental" is not to be found in comparisons of the relative societal significance of education as opposed to subsistence or housing. Nor is it to be found by weighing whether education is as important as the right to travel. Rather, the answer lies in assessing whether there is a right to education explicitly or implicitly guaranteed by the Constitution.

Education, of course, is not among the rights afforded explicit protection under our Federal Constitution. Nor do we find any basis for saying it is implicitly so protected. As we have said, the undisputed importance of education will not alone cause this Court to depart from the usual standard for reviewing a State's social and economic legislation. It is appellees' contention, however, that education is distinguishable from other services and benefits provided by the State because it bears a peculiarly close relationship to other rights and liberties accorded protection under the Constitution. Specifically, they insist that education is itself a fundamental personal right because it is essential to the effective exercise of First Amendment freedoms and to intelligent utilization of the right to vote. * * *

* * *

We need not dispute any of these propositions. The Court has long afforded zealous protection against unjustifiable governmental interference with the individual's rights to speak and to vote. Yet we have never presumed to possess either the ability or the authority to guarantee to the citizenry the most *effective* speech or the most *informed* electoral choice. That these may be desirable goals of a system of freedom of expression and of a representative form of government is not to be doubted. These are indeed goals to be pursued by a people whose thoughts and beliefs are freed from governmental interference. But they are not values to be implemented by judicial intrusion into otherwise legitimate state activities.

Even if it were conceded that some identifiable quantum of education is a constitutionally protected prerequisite to the meaningful exercise of either right, we have no indication that the present levels of educational expenditures in Texas provide an education that falls short. Whatever merit appellees' argument might have if a State's financing system occasioned an absolute denial of educational opportunities to any of its children, that argument provides no basis for finding an interference with fundamental rights where only relative differences in spending levels are involved and where—as is true in the present case—no charge fairly could be made that the system fails to provide each child with an opportunity to acquire the basic minimal skills necessary for the enjoyment of the rights of speech and of full participation in the political process.

Furthermore, the logical limitations on appellees' nexus theory are difficult to perceive. How, for instance, is education to be distinguished from the significant personal interests in the basics of decent food and shelter? Empirical examination might well buttress an assumption that the ill-fed, ill-clothed and ill-housed are among the most ineffective participants in the political process, and that they derive the least enjoyment from the benefits of the First Amendment. * * *

* * *

C

It should be clear, for the reasons stated above and in accord with the prior decisions of this Court, that this is not a case in which the challenged state action must be subjected to the searching judicial scrutiny reserved for laws that create suspect classifications or impinge upon constitutionally protected rights.

We need not rest our decision, however, solely on the inappropriateness of the strict-scrutiny test. A century of Supreme Court adjudication under the Equal Protection Clause affirmatively supports the application of the traditional standard of review, which requires only that the State's system be shown to bear some rational relationship to legitimate state purposes. This case represents far more than a challenge to the manner in which Texas provides for the education of its children. We have here nothing less than a direct attack on the way in which Texas has chosen to raise and disburse state and local tax revenues. We are asked to condemn the State's judgment in conferring on political subdivisions the power to tax local property to supply revenues for local interests. In so doing, appellees would have the Court intrude in an area in which it has traditionally deferred to state legislatures. * * *

Thus, we stand on familiar grounds when we continue to acknowledge that the Justices of this Court lack both the expertise and the familiarity with local problems so necessary to the making of wise decisions with respect to the raising and disposition of public revenues. * * *

In addition to matters of fiscal policy, this case also involves the most persistent and difficult questions of educational policy, another area in which this Court's lack of specialized knowledge and experience counsels against premature interference with the informed judgments made at the state and local levels. * * * On even the most basic questions in this area the scholars and educational experts are divided. Indeed, one of the major sources of controversy concerns the extent to which there is a demonstrable correlation between educational expenditures and the quality of education—an assumed correlation underlying virtually every legal conclusion drawn by the District Court in this case. Related to the questioned relationship between cost and quality is the equally unsettled controversy as to the proper goals of a system of public education. And the question regarding the most effective relationship between state boards of education and local school boards, in terms of their respective responsibilities and degrees of control, is now undergoing searching re-examination. The ultimate wisdom as to these and related problems of education is not likely to be divined for all time even by the scholars who now so earnestly debate the issues. In such circumstances, the judiciary is well advised to refrain from imposing on the States inflexible constitutional restraints that could circumscribe or handicap the continued research and experimentation so vital to finding even partial solutions to educational problems and to keeping abreast of ever-changing conditions.

* * *

III

* * *

In its reliance on state as well as local resources, the Texas system is comparable to the systems employed in virtually every other State. * * *

* * *

* * * While assuring a basic education for every child in the State, it permits and encourages a large measure of participation in and control of each district's schools at the local level. In an era that has witnessed a consistent trend toward centralization of the functions of government, local sharing of responsibility for public education has survived. * * *

The persistence of attachment to government at the lowest level where education is concerned reflects the depth of commitment of its supporters. * * *

Appellees do not question the propriety of Texas' dedication to local control of education. To the contrary, they attack the school-financing system precisely because, in their view, it does not provide the same level of local control and fiscal flexibility in all districts. Appellees suggest that local control could be preserved and promoted under other financing systems that resulted in more equality in educational expenditures. While it is no doubt true that reliance on local property taxation for school revenues provides less freedom of choice with respect to expenditures for some districts than for others, the existence of "some inequality" in the manner in which the State's rationale is achieved is not alone a sufficient basis for striking down the entire system. It may not be condemned simply because it imperfectly effectuates the State's goals. Nor must the financing system fail because, as appellees suggest, other methods of satisfying the State's interest, which occasion "less drastic" disparities in expenditures, might be conceived. Only where state action impinges on the exercise of fundamental constitutional rights or liberties must it be found to have chosen the least restrictive alternative. * * *

* * *

IV

In light of the considerable attention that has focused on the District Court opinion in this case and on its California predecessor, Serrano v. Priest, a cautionary postscript seems appropriate. It cannot be questioned that the constitutional judgment reached by the District Court and approved by our dissenting Brothers today would occasion in Texas and elsewhere an unprecedented upheaval in public education. Some commentators have concluded that, whatever the contours of the alternative financing programs that might be devised and approved, the result could not avoid being a beneficial one. But, just as there is nothing simple about the constitutional issues involved in these cases, there is nothing simple or certain about predicting the consequences of massive change in the financing and control of public education. Those who have devoted the most thoughtful attention to the practical ramifications of these cases have found no clear or dependable answers and their scholarship reflects no such unqualified confidence in the desirability of completely uprooting the existing system.

The complexity of these problems is demonstrated by the lack of consensus with respect to whether it may be said with any assurance that the poor, the racial minorities, or the children in overburdened core-city school districts would be benefited by abrogation of traditional modes of financing education. * * *

* * * We hardly need add that this Court's action today is not to be viewed as placing its judicial imprimatur on the status quo. The need is apparent for reform in tax systems which may well have relied too long and too heavily on the local property tax. And certainly innovative thinking as to public education, its methods, and its funding is necessary to assure both a higher level of quality and greater uniformity of opportunity. These matters merit the continued attention of the scholars who already have contributed much by their challenges. But the ultimate solutions must come from the lawmakers and from the democratic pressures of those who elect them.

Reversed.

* * *

Notes

1. Justices Douglas, Brennan, White, and Marshall dissented. Justice Stewart wrote a concurring opinion in which he said that although the method of financing education in Texas and almost every other state has resulted in a system of public education that can "fairly be described as chaotic and unjust," the method does not violate the Constitution. What is the relationship between the Constitution and "justice"?

2. To what extent is this type of case an attempt to use the judicial branch to accomplish essentially a legislative function? Discuss the ramifications of this question in terms of education, politics, and social policy.

3. Contemplate the ramifications of what the original plaintiffs sought. Might the Court have reacted differently (1) if the data had better supported the claims of the "class"; (2) if specialists in school finance could have pointed to successful alternate plans of financing schools?

4. Observe the legal meaning of "fundamental" when used in connection with rights. Why is the designation of a right as fundamental of such legal importance?

5. What is really meant by "equality of educational opportunity"? Is it to be measured by expenditures? Are there judicially manageable standards for assessing it? Must a state endeavor to provide it under the Constitution?

[Case No. 39] Power of Board to Change Building Plans after Approval of Bonds

RICKER v. BOARD OF EDUC. OF MILLARD COUNTY SCHOOL DIST.

Supreme Court of Utah, 1964.
16 Utah 2d 106, 396 P.2d 416.

CROCKETT, JUSTICE: Plaintiffs as taxpayers sued to prevent the Board of Education of Millard County School District from going forward with a planned school-building program, particularly from proceeding with a new junior and senior high school at Delta projected to cost about $1,786,000.

Acting pursuant to Section 53–10–7, U.C.A.1953, the defendant Board published in two local newspapers notice of a school bond election and a copy of the official ballot. It also had printed an explanatory brochure concerning the election and its purpose. Copies were distributed to the public and parts of it were published in the newspapers "in conjunction with," but not as a part of, the statutory notice. The explanation included the purpose of the bonding program, the amount of money to be raised and the effect on the tax levy. It indicated generally that the funds would be spent under two main categories: high schools and elementary schools; that the main item in high schools would be a new combined junior and senior high school at Delta at a cost of about $1,250,000; that about $75,000 would be spent in building a new farm shop at the Millard High School at Fillmore; and at the latter school about $80,000 would be spent on a remodeling project. It also mentioned several proposals under consideration for construction and remodeling of grade schools in the district, for which no cost estimates were given.

The bond election carried, and the Board then proceeded to get a definite estimate from an architect as to the cost of the junior-senior high school at Delta. As is not uncommon in regard to building costs, particularly in recent years, it was found that the preliminary estimate of $1,250,000 for that project was too low; that its actual cost would be between $1,645,000 and $1,786,000. This increase is the main cause of the instant difficulty. Based on the 1964 assessed valuation, the maximum amount of bonds that could be issued is $1,935,000. Consequently, if the Board proceeds with its expressed intention to construct the junior-senior high school at Delta and carries out the project of building the farm shop and remodeling program at the Millard High School at Fillmore, only a comparatively small amount of money will be left for elementary school needs mentioned in the brochure.

Plaintiffs contend that the defendant Board should not be allowed to use substantially all of the money for the high-school projects, but should allocate a proper portion to the elementary school needs as was represented in the brochure. They insist that to do otherwise is a violation of the condition upon which the public voted for the bonds and a breach of faith by defendants in the performance of their duties.   * * *

* * *

* * * [F]or the purposes of meeting the principal issue in this case forthrightly, we proceed upon the assumption that plaintiffs are correct in asserting that the public reasonably could and did regard the statements as to the various school needs as part of the notice of the election.

It is undoubted that Sections 53–10–9 and 7, relating to the purpose and requiring publication of the notice of the school bond election, are designed to give notice of the essential facts to the public. But it will be noted that the requirement concerning the use of funds refers only to the general purpose.   * * *

* * * The duties of the board include that of purchasing school-house sites and erecting and remodeling school buildings. Also in harmony with the import of the statutes * * * is the fact that it is inherent in the nature of the board's function in managing school district business that it have a broad latitude of discretion in order to carry out its objective of providing the best possible school system in the most efficient and economical way. Indeed it should be said that the board not only has this prerogative, but it could not divest itself of this duty. It is the policy of the law not to favor limitations on the powers of the administrative body, but rather to give it a free hand to function within the sphere of its responsibilities. For that reason, it is to be assumed that the board has and retains its prerogative of using its best judgment as to what course will prove to be of greatest advantage in serving the interests of the district in the long run. And any representations made by it or its members should not be regarded as restricting that prerogative unless it clearly and unequivocally appears that the Board has made a binding commitment or so acted that justice and equity would require it to follow some predetermined course of action. There is no basis to compel any such conclusion here.

As is the case in other areas in our system of government, it is the citizen's right to vote for and elect officials he thinks best qualified to represent his interests. Having so elected the school board, he then must trust them to administer the school program. But it is not his privilege to intrude directly into the management of school affairs. This principle carries over into the bond election. The taxpayers may give or withhold their consent to the issuance of bonds and the creation of the indebtedness. But if the consent is given, the disposition of the money raised then becomes the responsibility of the board. This is not to say that the voters are entirely without remedy. If they believe an unwise course is being followed, there is nothing to prevent them from petitioning the board for further hearings on the matter and bringing to bear whatever force of argument or persuasion is available. Moreover, the power of the future ballot always exists which may influence policies of the board. It is also true that if it were shown that there existed some actual deceit, fraud or corruption; or if the board was acting outside the scope of its authority, or was so completely failing to follow the course of its duties that its actions could be classified as capricious and arbitrary, redress might be had in the courts. But under the facts shown here, the conduct of the Board cannot be so classified. Accordingly, the proposed building program, involving its judgment and discretion, cannot properly be interfered with.

Finally, the conclusion we have arrived at here is in conformity with what we regard as the sound and well-advised policy of reluctance of courts to intrude into the functions of other branches of government. * * *

* * *

Notes

1. Do you see any substantial danger of fraud or misrepresentation by bond proponents under the rule of this court? Aside from the duty of boards to act in good faith, should there be other limitations on the authority to change building programs after bond approval?

2. The court refers to the "sound and well-advised policy of reluctance of courts to intrude into the functions of other branches of government." How consistent are the courts in adhering to such a policy?

3. Observe that the court "assumed" the statements in the brochure to be part of the notice of the election. The usual rule is that it is the notice published pursuant to statute which binds the board, not collateral statements or explanatory materials.

4. The Supreme Court of South Carolina has held that failure to issue bonds for several years after they have been authorized by vote does not render them void. "The only limitation which should affect the right to issue bonds under these circumstances is where the purposes for which the bonds were originally voted have ceased to be necessary, or where the conditions have so changed that it would be inequitable to allow the bonds to be issued, and, unless one of these conditions clearly appears to the satisfaction of the court, the exercise of their discretion by the trustees should not be interfered with." Covington v. McInnis, 144 S.C. 391, 142 S.E. 650 (1928).

5. Elections in general are covered in Chapter 14.

[Case No. 40] Power of Board to Use Unobligated Funds

CONCERNED SCHOOL PATRONS AND TAXPAYERS v. WARE COUNTY BD. OF EDUC.

Supreme Court of Georgia, 1980.
245 Ga. 202, 263 S.E.2d 925.

BOWLES, JUSTICE. This controversy arose when the Board of Education of Ware County adopted a resolution authorizing a contract to construct a field house/physical education/athletic facility for a school. Plaintiffs, as taxpayers and patrons of the school system, brought a suit in the superior court of that county seeking to enjoin the action of the board. * * *

* * * A permanent injunction was denied. Plaintiffs appeal to this court. We affirm.

* * *

Art. VII, Sec. I, Par. I of the State Constitution (Code Ann. § 2-4901) provides for a system of common schools in the state. Art. VIII, Sec. VII, Par. I (Code Ann. § 2-5501) providing for local taxation for education reads in part as follows: "The fiscal authority of each county shall annually levy a school tax for the support and maintenance of education, not greater than twenty mills per dollar as certified to it by the county board of education, upon the assessed value of all taxable property within the county located outside any independent school system or area school district therein * * *. School tax funds shall be expended only for the support and maintenance of public schools, public education, and activities necessary or incidental thereto, including school lunch purposes * * *." The legislature in keeping with constitutional provisions adopted an Act known as "Adequate Program for Education in Georgia Act." The Act specifically recognizes the development of good physical and mental health as a part of the educational process. Additionally, [a section] provides for a course in health and physical education. [Another section] provides: "The county boards of education shall have the power to purchase, lease, or rent school sites, build, repair or rent schoolhouses, purchase maps, globes, and school furniture and make all arrangements necessary to the efficient operation of the school * * *. In respect to the building of schoolhouses, the said board of education may provide for the same by a tax on all property located in the county and outside the territorial limits of any independent school system." Plaintiffs have made no constitutional attack on any pertinent statute.

We conclude that boards of education do have lawful authority to provide for and construct physical education facilities which may incidentally include a field house or related athletic facility.

Although no funds of a county board of education can be disbursed except in accordance with a budget filed with the State Board of Education, this does not mean that every expenditure must be a line item in the budget submitted. With respect to the year in question, the Ware County Board of Education had a beginning balance of unobligated or uncommitted funds in excess of the amount of the proposed expenditure for the athletic facility. Unobligated funds included in the budget may be used by a board of education for any purpose provided by statute, within the constitutional parameters of our state educational system. The unobligated funds on hand may have been accumulated as a result of thrift practiced by the board with respect to any prior year's budget. There is no contention on the part of the plaintiffs that any millage has been determined or levied by county authorities with respect to any year in excess of the 20 mills limitation included in the Georgia Constitution (Code Ann. § 2–5501). * * *

Plaintiffs' petition was filed after the millage for the year had been determined and assessed. (And we suspect by December largely paid.) The issue involved is one of authority by the board of education to spend tax money already collected, not the power to levy a tax for a designated purpose.

The obligation incurred by the board of education regarding the expenditure of accumulated funds on hand at the time of the execution of the contract, which were sufficient for the purpose, was not an attempt to bind a succeeding board of education to a future obligation. A board of education may incur a lawful obligation to pay for the purchase or construction of a facility where sufficient funds are on hand for that purpose, even though the construction contract may not be fully completed before the end of the term of some or all of the members of that body.

The trial court did not err in finding in favor of the defendants.

Judgment affirmed.

Notes

1. What do you think was the major reason this case was brought? The building of athletic facilities, as an implied power of local boards, seemed well settled a half century before (e.g., McNair v. School Dist. No. 1, 87 Mont. 423, 288 P. 188 (1930).

2. Note "the issue," as delineated by the court in the next to last full paragraph. What is the difference in theory; in practice?

3. In connection with the last full paragraph, see "Actions Extending beyond the Term of the Board" in Chapter 14.

4. Do you believe a board should be allowed to spend "unobligated funds" with fewer restraints than those imposed on other funds?

5. The express provision authorizing use of tax funds for "school lunch purposes" (second paragraph) was enacted in response to a holding of the Supreme Court of Georgia (see footnote 13 in Chapter 4).

Chapter 6

USE OF SCHOOL MONEY AND PROPERTY

In General

Uses of school funds and school property have furnished the bases of many lawsuits through the years. Because constitutions and statutes cannot specifically cover all "proper" uses, it becomes the function of the courts to construe general grants of power and apply them to concrete circumstances. The implied powers of local school boards in spending money have been very frequently challenged directly. Analysis will reveal also that many cases classified under other headings contain very substantial financial considerations. Many issues related to curriculum, pupil personnel, construction, staff personnel, and other problem areas are adjudicated in a framework of expenditures or property use.

Decisions often depend on what the courts consider desirable public policy under the facts of particular cases. What may be considered a proper use of school funds or property in one state may be held to be an improper use in another. Furthermore, what may be held to be improper in a given state at one time may be considered to be a proper use at another. With the passage of time courts have been increasingly liberal in construing board powers to determine uses.

Legal attacks made upon expenditures are based on several grounds. The most common is the broad one that the expenditure or use is not for an educational purpose. Other contentions include considerations of church-state separation, subversive activity, disruptive activity, vagueness of rules, discriminatory application of rules, and aid or harm to private persons or businesses.

Transportation of Students

In the absence of express legislative authority most courts have not permitted boards to transport children.[1] Furthermore, there has been a tendency to interpret transportation statutes narrowly. Courts have adopted the view that the basic responsibility for getting children to school lies with the parent. Also possibly affecting the general judicial attitude is the fact that furnishing transportation is a relatively expensive venture and one not contributing to education per se. For example, in Michigan it was held that even under a statute which provided that boards of education had the power "to do all things needful and necessary for the maintenance, prosperity and success of the schools of the district and the promotion of the thorough education of the children

---

1. Ex parte Perry County Bd. of Educ.,
278 Ala. 646, 180 So.2d 246 (1965).

thereof," the board did not have authority to expend school funds for transportation purposes.[2]

Over the years legislatures have permitted or required transportation for public school students and sometimes for nonpublic school students. Even when such legislative authority is granted, however, the courts have construed it very strictly. The construction placed on the transportation statute of Iowa by the highest court of that state is typical.[3] The statute provided that the board furnish suitable transportation for certain pupils "to and from" school. It was the practice of the board of the defendant district to transport pupils to basketball games outside the district, to spelling contests, to school picnics, and other functions sponsored by the school. The court said that the statutory provision that boards transport children "to and from school" conferred upon the board no discretion to expand the power.

The Supreme Court of Rhode Island held that, under statutes requiring school boards to furnish transportation for public school students "to and from school" and to afford private school students the same rights and privileges, there was no mandate for transportation to be provided as far as the town line for students attending a private school outside the boundaries of the school district.[4] The court held that the legislature contemplated schools, public or private, located within the district. The Supreme Court of North Dakota, without reaching any constitutional question, held that local school boards were not entitled to reimbursement for transporting children to nonpublic schools under a statute providing such state money for each "pupil" transported.[5] The court found that, in the context of North Dakota statutes, "pupil" meant "public school enrollee" and "school" meant "public school."

The Supreme Court of Utah permitted students to be transported at district expense if their presence was required in activities after school hours.[6] The court differentiated between those who were participating in the extracurricular functions and those who were spectators. Students who attended at their option were considered spectators because their attendance was not required. The court further indicated that the board could not at district expense furnish transportation to patrons of entertainments, games, or other activities. In another case on the point the Supreme Court of North Carolina found that boards of education controlling school activities had the power to contract for transportation necessary to transport their athletic teams and bands to and from events scheduled under their supervision.[7]

Problems often develop under statutes which authorize transportation but do not specify the distance beyond which transportation must be

2. Township School Dist. of Bates v. Elliott, 276 Mich. 575, 268 N.W. 744 (1936).

3. Schmidt v. Blair, 203 Iowa 1016, 213 N.W. 593 (1927).

4. Chaves v. School Committee of Town of Middletown, 100 R.I. 140, 211 A.2d 639 (1965).

5. Dickinson Public School Dist. No. 1 v. Scott, 252 N.W.2d 216 (N.D.1977).

6. Beard v. Board of Educ. of North Summit School Dist., 81 Utah 51, 16 P.2d 900 (1932).

7. State ex rel. North Carolina Util. Comm. v. McKinnon, 254 N.C. 1, 118 S.E.2d 134 (1961).

supplied for students. For example, a Connecticut statute required local boards to provide for the transportation of school children wherever that was "reasonable and desirable." Parents of some students sought transportation because of hazards between their homes and the school. The local board was required to furnish transportation under order of the state board following an appeal to that agency on the ground that the transportation was demanded by considerations of safety. The court sustained the state board's order.[8] Two decades later the same scenario was followed in Rhode Island where the statute required transportation of students who live "so far" from school as to make regular attendance "impractical."[9]

In California the highest court decided that the refusal of a school board to provide transportation for certain pupils was an abuse of discretion.[10] The board had successfully claimed in lower courts that furnishing transportation to eight children situated in a rather inaccessible part of the district was too costly, that it would lead to requests from families in other areas, and that the bus would have trouble operating on the narrow roads in the area. The Supreme Court of California examined these contentions in relation to the situation of the eight children, who would be deprived of a way to get to school without the bus because the family was very poor. It reviewed the financial circumstances of the district and found that the district could afford to buy a new smaller bus if that should be warranted. The district was ordered to provide the transportation. The same result was reached in a very similar fact situation by the Supreme Court of Appeals of West Virginia, which rested the decision on federal equal protection grounds.[11] An appellate court in Illinois, however, sustained a board rule that school buses would not traverse dead-end roads less than one and one-half miles in length.[12]

The option of paying a mileage rate to parents residing in "out of the way" locations, rather than providing bus transportation, has been upheld as meeting a statutory obligation to "provide or furnish transportation."[13] The reason of the board and the rate of reimbursement are subject to judicial review. Parents have been held not entitled to compensation for their time, depreciation of the vehicle, and actual fuel costs where the rate was reasonable.[14]

It may be said that generally discretion of boards regarding the furnishing of transportation for purposes within their powers will not be disturbed by the courts in the absence of arbitrariness. For example, the Supreme Court of Tennessee decided a case in which parents

8. Town of Waterford v. Connecticut State Bd. of Educ., 148 Conn. 238, 169 A.2d 891 (1961).

9. Brown v. Elston, 445 A.2d 279 (R.I. 1982).

10. Manjares v. Newton, 64 Cal.2d 365, 49 Cal.Rptr. 805, 411 P.2d 901 (1966).

11. Shrewsbury v. Board of Educ., County of Wyoming, 164 W.Va. 698, 265 S.E.2d 767 (1980).

12. Randolph v. School Unit 201, 132 Ill.App.2d 936, 270 N.E.2d 50 (1971).

13. State ex rel. Stephan v. Board of Educ. of Unified School Dist. 428, Barton County, Kansas, 231 Kan. 579, 647 P.2d 329 (1982).

14. State ex rel. Rosenberg v. Grand Coulee Dam School Dist., 85 Wash.2d 556, 536 P.2d 614 (1975).

maintained that their child should be transported to a school nearer their home when the board had provided transportation for him to a more distant school.[15] The board would not provide it to the nearer school, the child being assigned to the more distant school. The parent claimed that the board could have furnished transportation to the nearer school without changing the present bus routes. The board agreed to allow the child to attend the nearer school but without transportation. The court upheld the board's discretionary decision.

A Pennsylvania statute mandated transportation for nonpublic school students up to ten miles beyond district boundaries if public school students received transportation to district schools. The state's highest court held that a school board was not required to furnish transportation to resident students who attended public schools in other districts on a tuition basis.[16]

An appellate court in Florida upheld the power of a school board to permit students under certain conditions to attend schools outside their attendance zones but to furnish no transportation.[17] As the board could decide to furnish an option, it had the discretionary authority to condition the manner in which the option was exercised.

Where legislation does not require that transportation be afforded, boards that have offered it can withdraw it. Thus, when there developed a shortage of funds, a local board was held empowered to halt transportation.[18] Also, the furnishing of transportation only one-way for children attending kindergarten, has been sustained. As neither kindergarten nor transportation of public school students was mandated by state law, and the board's decision was rationally based on not employing drivers or engaging buses at midday, the Court of Appeals, Third Circuit, held that there was no federal constitutional violation.[19] (Attempting to exercise pendent jurisdiction on remand, the federal District Court ruled that the state's grant of power to the board was for transportation "to and from," and that the general purposes of transportation would not be served by providing it only one-way. This holding was reversed on jurisdictional grounds.)

Also upheld was the temporary withdrawal of transportation on routes plagued by vandalism and disruptive conduct on buses. The First Circuit Court of Appeals held that the disciplinary program was not unconstitutional.[20]

It should be noted that where a statute specifically uses distance as a yardstick the courts generally retain that measure and do not consider

15. Davis v. Fentress County Bd. of Educ., 218 Tenn. 280, 402 S.W.2d 873 (1966).

16. Babcock School Dist. v. Potocki, 502 Pa. 349, 466 A.2d 616 (1983).

17. School Bd. of Leon County v. Ehrlich, 421 So.2d 18 (Fla.App.1982).

18. Sutton v. Cadillac Area Public Schools, 117 Mich.App. 38, 323 N.W.2d 582 (1982).

19. Shaffer v. Board of School Directors of Albert Gallatin Area School Dist., 687 F.2d 718 (3 Cir.1982), cert. den. 459 U.S. 1212, 103 S.Ct. 1209, 75 L.Ed.2d 449 (1983), on remand 570 F.Supp. 698 (W.D.Pa.1983), rev. 730 F.2d 910 (3 Cir. 1984).

20. Rose v. Nashua Bd. of Educ., 679 F.2d 279 (1 Cir.1982). [Case No. 41]

hazard.[21] Measurement of distance can create a number of problems, but usually these are settled before they reach appellate courts. An exception was a question which "borders on the ridiculous" according to the Supreme Court of Mississippi in 1964.[22] The board of education maintained that the distance travelled was from the center point of the end of the home's driveway to the point at the school where the children were discharged. The parents asserted that the distance was from a point in front of the door of the home where the children lived to the point where they were discharged. The court held that the legislature intended that no pupil be required to walk more than one mile and that children lived in the house, not at the end of the driveway.

In Wisconsin mileage was measured "along the usually traveled route." A statute requiring local school boards to furnish transportation for private school students provided that such schools shall not be more than five miles beyond the boundaries of the school district. No matter what point of the private high school property was utilized, the school was beyond the five mile limit, although barely so. The supreme court stated that there was no leeway for it to construe the limit because it was precisely set out by the legislature.[23] The court, however, remanded the case for additional testimony as to the application of another provision that where local boards provide transportation it must be on a "reasonably uniform basis to children attending either public or private schools."

Generally boards may determine the route and the times and places for bus stops. So long as distances are reasonable children can be required to walk to the stops.[24] But, at least in some jurisdictions, students cannot be required to walk to pick-up points that are located at a distance from their homes equal to the distance beyond which transportation must be furnished.[25]

The Supreme Court of Nebraska upheld a statute providing that the state must supply allowances for transportation of students living more than four miles from school to travel up to the four mile perimeter of the school.[26] Furthermore, the court ruled that there was no constitutional violation where some local boards furnished transportation within the four mile radius and some did not.

The state or local boards may treat different categories of students differently as regards transportation. Thus handicapped children and children attending vocational schools constitute rational classes for transportation purposes.[27] So also may transportation be furnished

21. Studley v. Allen, 24 A.D.2d 678, 261 N.Y.S.2d 138 (1965).

22. Madison County Bd. of Educ. v. Grantham, 250 Miss. 767, 168 So.2d 515 (1964).

23. Young v. Board of Educ., Joint Dist. No. 10, of Village of Mukwonago, 74 Wis.2d 144, 246 N.W.2d 230 (1976).

24. Flowers v. Independent School Dist. of Tama, 235 Iowa 332, 16 N.W.2d 570 (1944).

25. People ex rel. Schuldt v. Schimanski, 130 Ill.App.2d 780, 266 N.E.2d 409 (1971).

26. Warren v. Papillion School Dist. No. 27, 199 Neb. 410, 259 N.W.2d 281 (1977).

27. West Morris Regional Bd. of Educ. v. Sills, 58 N.J. 464, 279 A.2d 609 (1971).

nonurban students only, for urban students have access to sidewalks and public transportation.[28] But definitions of city and noncity must not be discriminatory.[29]

The Supreme Court in 1988 issued its first opinion on transportation of students that did not involve religious or racial issues.[30] The specific point was the constitutionality of a North Dakota statute that authorized nonreorganized school districts to charge fees not to exceed costs for transporting children to school. The Court upheld the statute. The opinion of the Court stated flatly that "the Constitution does not require that [transportation] service be provided at all." Thus, there is no constitutional duty to provide it free of charge. The unequal protection argument that only children in nonreorganized districts may be charged was rejected because social and economic legislation can be overturned only if it is completely irrational. Here there were some reasons, such as encouraging voters to adopt plans for reorganization. As no suspect class was discriminated against by the legislation and no fundamental right was infringed, strict scrutiny was not required.

Transportation to parochial schools is treated in Chapter 2; transportation in connection with race is treated in Chapter 13.

Insurance

That local boards have implied power to insure school property seems settled. In an Alabama case it was held that a statute requiring school trustees "to care for the property" and "look after the general interests of the school" conferred such power.[31] Some legal difficulties have been encountered when districts have sought to insure school property in a so-called mutual association. This type of insurance provides for the payment of no set premium, but losses are prorated among the members of the association. Under this type the district may be subjected to a very heavy loss, the amount of which is uncertain. Furthermore, such insurance could constitute lending the credit or resources of the district to the aid of private individuals. Where the contingent liability of the district was unlimited, the purchase of insurance in such an association has been invalidated.[32] However, where the amount of the contingent liability was set at a stated maximum, it was held that the insurance was valid.[33] In so holding, the Supreme Court of Wyoming commented, however, that the mere fact that part of the liability is contingent would not be absolutely determinative of the constitutionality of the contract. It would depend on such facts as the ultimate liability in relation to the premium charged by ordinary fire insurance companies.

28. Cartwright v. Sharpe, 40 Wis.2d 494, 162 N.W.2d 5 (1968).

29. Sparrow v. Gill, 304 F.Supp. 86 (M.D.N.C.1969); Morrissette v. De Zonia, 63 Wis.2d 429, 217 N.W.2d 377 (1974).

30. Kadrmas v. Dickinson Public Schools, 487 U.S. 450, 108 S.Ct. 2481, 101 L.Ed.2d 399 (1988).

31. American Ins. Co. v. Newberry, 215 Ala. 587, 112 So. 195 (1927).

32. School Dist. No. 8 v. Twin Falls Mutual Fire Ins. Co., 30 Idaho 400, 164 P. 1174 (1917).

33. Burton v. School Dist. No. 19, 47 Wyo. 462, 38 P.2d 610 (1934).

Where a school district relied in obtaining fire insurance on a computation of the value of a building and it turned out after a fire that the replacement cost would be substantially higher than estimated by the statistical service corporation, a federal court held that the school district had a cause of action against the corporation.[34]

As regards a district's buying liability insurance under implied powers, the courts are not in agreement, but the more modern trend seems to be to permit the purchase. This matter is discussed in connection with tort liability of districts.

That local boards have the power to purchase group life, health, and disability insurance for teachers seems clear. It is highly unlikely that courts in the future would disagree with the 1921 finding of the Supreme Court of New Mexico that group insurance enabled the school board "to procure a better class of teachers" and prevented "frequent changes in the teaching force." [35] But if a statute (or city charter) creates a special agency to establish and administer "medical care" plans, a separately financed dental plan could not be provided.[36]

When a school board provides for its employees group health insurance with benefits for family members, it is likely that some employees will be afforded a more valuable benefit than will some others. A California statute authorized such insurance; another required that female employees receive the same compensation as males having equivalent certificates and performing like duties. Suit was brought to require a district providing such insurance to revise its salary schedules to give the same monetary equivalent to everyone similarly situated professionally. The court dismissed the complaint, citing administrative difficulties of determining cash equivalents for everyone and holding that whether family benefits were to be included lay within the discretion of the board.[37]

Conflicts with Business

Challenges to school enterprises which have conflicted with business interests have been substantial in number. The fact that a private enterprise suffers as the result of the school's conducting a similar operation is not determinative of whether the use of funds or property is legally permitted. The primary purpose of the school venture is the test.

There have been several cases in which it has been sought to enjoin the operation of cafeterias by boards of education. Where the cafeterias were established for the purpose of serving the welfare and convenience of pupils and the prices intended merely to cover the cost of operation and replacement of equipment, the power of boards to operate them has been uniformly sustained.

34. Independent School Dist. No. 454, Fairmont, Minnesota v. Statistical Tabulating Corp., 359 F.Supp. 1095 (N.D.Ill.1973).

35. Nohl v. Board of Educ., 27 N.M. 232, 199 P. 373 (1921).

36. City and County of San Francisco v. Cooper, 13 Cal.3d 898, 120 Cal.Rptr. 707, 534 P.2d 403 (1975).

37. Sheehan v. Eldredge, 5 Cal.App.3d 77, 84 Cal.Rptr. 894 (1970).

Legislation granting boards such authority has been considered valid as for a public purpose.[38] In a leading case on implied powers that arose in the school district of Denver the court found that operation of a cafeteria did not serve a private mercantile purpose but was conducted for the public welfare in the form of benefit for the student body and the educational welfare of the children.[39] The court quoted cases from other jurisdictions supporting health services, manual training schools, and other non-academic elements in the education process. A different court upheld a board's allowing students to run a cafeteria with profits used to finance extracurricular activities.[40] If the purpose of the cafeteria can be shown to be that of trying to destroy someone's business, however, the operation will be enjoined.[41]

In the cases dealing with provisions in schools for selling supplies to students, the question of profit has resulted in differing decisions. In Wisconsin it was judicially stated that where sales were made at cost, the schools could sell school supplies to pupils.[42] Such would be considered an aid to the efficient and successful operation of the schools. In an earlier Wisconsin case the highest court of that state had held that if a dealer could prove that the board of education permitted five school principals to conduct stores in school buildings, at which were sold school books, stationery, and supplies to students at a profit, an injunction against the practice would be granted.[43] A dealer in school supplies had brought the suit.

The year before, the Detroit school board was enjoined from purchasing and selling books to pupils, although it was shown that such could be done more conveniently and economically than through local dealers. The court found that the grant of power to local school boards to do "those things necessary to promote the interest of education" was not intended to empower the board to do everything which might advance education, but rather only such things that it could do without changing its character as a board of education, as by taking on the character of a commercial or trading corporation.[44]

In a more recent case an Illinois school board was sued for overcharging on books it was authorized to sell to students. Imposition of a 15 percent handling charge was held to be beyond the board's power.[45]

Special Equipment and Services

Special Items

Generally, and especially in more recent cases, the implied power of local boards to purchase materials and equipment reasonably necessary

38. Krueger v. Board of Educ., 310 Mo. 239, 274 S.W. 811 (1925).

39. Goodman v. School Dist. No. 1, City and County of Denver, 32 F.2d 586 (10 Cir.1929).

40. Hempel v. School Dist. No. 329 of Snohomish County, 186 Wash. 684, 59 P.2d 729 (1936).

41. Hailey v. Brooks, 191 S.W. 781 (Tex. Civ.App.1916).

42. Cook v. Chamberlain, 199 Wis. 42, 225 N.W. 141 (1929).

43. Tyre v. Krug, 159 Wis. 39, 149 N.W. 718 (1914).

44. Kuhn v. Board of Educ. of Detroit, 175 Mich. 438, 141 N.W. 574 (1913).

45. Hamer v. Board of Educ. of Tp. High School Dist. No. 113, County of Lake, 52 Ill.App.3d 531, 10 Ill.Dec. 286, 367 N.E.2d 739 (1977).

to conduct authorized curricular activities seems beyond genuine dispute.[46] The purchases without express statutes of special items to be used only for small numbers of students, however, have not been so uniformly approved by the courts over the years. A contrast between judicial approaches in Massachusetts and Pennsylvania is illustrative.

Purchase of special clothing to be worn by the basketball team in games with other schools was held beyond the power of a local board in Massachusetts.[47] The court was of the opinion that the basketball suits were not supplies under Massachusetts law. The court further noted that when subjects such as manual arts and cooking were added to the curriculum, the legislature expressly permitted the purchase and loaning to students of necessary equipment. That was not the situation when physical education was added.

In Pennsylvania a statute authorized the purchase of necessary furniture, equipment, textbooks, school supplies, and other appliances for use in the public schools. However, no statutory reference was made to athletic supplies and equipment. The Supreme Court of Pennsylvania held that this statute, together with one which authorized boards to provide gymnasiums and playgrounds, was broad enough to cover athletic supplies and equipment even though such supplies and equipment were not specifically mentioned.[48] However, the court did not sustain the unlimited authority of boards to purchase special athletic paraphernalia "for use merely by school teams playing in competitive sports." In the opinion of the court, the extent of such expenditures should be determined by school boards "in the exercise of a cautious discretion with special reference to the proportionate number of those who will receive the benefit of the supplies."

The question whether school funds could be expended for the purchase of band uniforms was raised in Oklahoma. The statute there was a broad one, permitting the board of education "to incur all expenses, within the limitations provided by law, necessary to carry out" the express powers granted the board. The highest state court upheld the board.[49] It indicated that the word "necessary" had a broad meaning beyond that of "indispensible". The board had organized a complete course in instrumental music, and the decision covered only the situation in which the pupils receiving instruction in instrumental music were furnished the uniforms.

More recently it has been held that a board may require students, faculty, and staff to carry identification cards to be presented on request

46. Commercial State Bank of Shepherd v. School Dist. No. 3 of Coe Tp., Isabella County, 225 Mich. 656, 196 N.W. 373 (1923).

47. Brine v. City of Cambridge, 265 Mass. 452, 164 N.E. 619 (1929).

48. Galloway v. School Dist. of Borough of Prospect Park, 331 Pa. 48, 200 A. 99 (1938).

49. Excise Board of Kay County v. Atchison, T. and S.F. Ry. Co., 185 Okl. 327, 91 P.2d 1087 (1939).

to school officials and may expend funds for the photographs.[50] Further, the board may select one company by proper means, here by competitive bid, to take the photographs and may grant to it exclusively the ancillary right to take and sell photographs to students on school premises. Similarly the Supreme Court of Georgia found no unlawful restraint of trade where a school board selected one band instrument company to conduct its band recruitment program.[51] Students were not required to buy or rent instruments from that company. The lack of compulsion to purchase also was material to the judicial upholding in Louisiana of a practice allowing a salesperson of a jewelry company selected by a committee of faculty and students to sell class rings on school premises.[52]

The selection of one photographer for the yearbook and designation of that party as the "official photographer" has been held by the Fourth Circuit Court of Appeals not to violate any federal laws concerning trade regulation or monopolies.[53] In the case the photographer paid to the school a portion of its profits from portrait sales. Students' purchases were optional.

Medical Services

In regard to medical services for pupils, the courts differentiate between the educational welfare of students and the welfare of children in general. A case which arose in West Virginia illustrates the point. A pupil at a public school had been severely burned. Immediately after the accident the chief local administrator called a physician to attend the child. At the request of the board of education he continued to provide service to the child. The physician presented his bill to the board for the services, it being admitted that the amount of the charge was reasonable. The superintendent of schools for the county, acting on the belief that the law did not authorize the expenditure of school funds for this purpose, refused to sign the order for payment. Under West Virginia statutes boards were expressly authorized to provide medical and dental inspection for pupils, to employ school nurses, and to take necessary action to protect pupils in the schools from infectious diseases. The Supreme Court of Appeals of West Virginia, however, held that school funds could not legally be used to provide medical services of the type and extent provided in this instance.[54] It said that the law had for its purpose the promotion of the general good of the pupils of the schools in order that they may function advantageously and that important principles of hygiene may be inculcated in the pupils. This was quite a different matter from providing medical and surgical services for a period of months for a single injured pupil. Further, the court indicated

50. LaPorte v. Escanaba Area Public Schools, 51 Mich.App. 305, 214 N.W.2d 840 (1974).

51. Ken Stanton Music, Inc. v. Board of Educ., 227 Ga. 393, 181 S.E.2d 67 (1971).

52. Givens Jewelers of Bossier, Inc. v. Rich, 313 So.2d 913 (La.App.1975).

53. Stephen Jay Photography, Ltd. v. Olan Mills, Inc., 903 F.2d 988 (4 Cir.1990).

54. Jarrett v. Goodall, 113 W.Va. 478, 168 S.E. 763 (1933).

that the authority to incur the liability involved in this case did not arise by necessary implication of the powers of boards to manage schools.

However, boards must be deemed to have implied authority to assume responsibility for first-aid services rendered to a pupil who is injured or becomes ill while engaged in school activities. Otherwise there might be serious delay in a pupil's receiving the attention which he should have, with possible serious consequences.[55] The court in the West Virginia case refused to extend the implied authority of the board beyond that which permits it to provide first aid and emergency medical attention.

The purchase of sleeping garments to be worn for extra warmth in open air classes by pupils susceptible to tuberculosis has been held not to be within the implied powers of a local board in Ohio.[56] The reasoning was similar to that in the West Virginia case.

Legal Services

The implied power of boards of education to pay for legal services has generally been sustained.[57] However, by statute in some jurisdictions, the board of education is directed to use the services of a specified governmental counsel. In such circumstances, of course, the statute is controlling. But any legal counsel to the board must engage only in activities in the public interest of the district.

A complicated New Jersey case illustrates the principle. The question was whether school funds could be used to defend an individual board member sued for libel. An allegedly libelous letter, addressed to the school superintendent, was written and sent to newspapers by the board president. When suit was brought against the president by the superintendent, the board adopted a resolution stating that the president in writing the letter was acting on behalf of the board. Then the superintendent sued the other board members because of the resolution purporting to authorize the president's letter. It was held subsequently that the resolution was not intended as a republication of the asserted libel, but rather as a legal justification for the expenditure of public funds to defend the board president. Thus, although there was no authority to so spend the funds, the resolution was adopted in the performance of their duties as board members, and the expenses of their defense for libel arising from the resolution were held properly chargeable to the board.[58] The reason that the board president could not be defended at public expense was that she had not been acting in discharge of her duties when she wrote the letter.[59]

55. See Stineman v. Fontbonne College, 664 F.2d 1082 (8 Cir.1981).

56. Board of Educ. of Cleveland v. Ferguson, 68 Ohio App. 514, 39 N.E.2d 196 (1941).

57. Arrington v. Jones, 191 S.W. 361 (Tex.Civ.App.1917).

58. Errington v. Mansfield Tp. Bd. of Educ., 100 N.J.Super. 130, 241 A.2d 271 (1968).

59. The issue of whether the letter was in fact libelous was never decided because of an out-of-court settlement.

It has been judicially recognized that it is not in the public interest to inhibit board members in the performance of their duties, and courts have been liberal in permitting reimbursements for expenses in civil litigation.[60] This liberality has not been apparent, however, in cases involving criminal charges.[61]

Boards of education generally do not have the implied power to pay attorney fees of employees who are sued as individuals rather than in their official capacities as employees. A board's paying without statutory authority would constitute a gift of public funds for a private purpose. Stating that principle, a New York appellate court declined to order a board to pay the legal fees of a teacher who had been exonerated on a criminal charge of sex abuse initiated by one of his students.[62] A statute required such payment for any civil or criminal proceeding resulting from disciplinary action taken against a student in scope of employment, but here that was not the situation. Where a sex abuse charge was connected to disciplinary action taken against a student, the court enforced the statute against a school board.[63]

A Maryland appellate court, however, held that a statute requiring furnishing of counsel by a board for a teacher acting in an authorized capacity would not be triggered in a sex abuse case because a court or reasonable jury could not conclude that teachers were " 'authorized' to sexually abuse or harass their students." [64] The Supreme Court of Rhode Island interpreted an indemnification statute covering any "claim, demand or suit" arising from employment to cover only civil proceedings.[65]

The highest court of New Jersey considered whether a consolidated school district could use its counsel to prepare a legislative bill for the purpose of deconsolidating the district. The legislature had not provided for deconsolidation, and the majority of the board wished to deconsolidate. The court found the attorney could not be paid for such an assignment.[66]

The Court of Appeals of Arizona held that public funds could not be spent for attorney fees to protect a board member's right to office.[67] There was a dispute as to whether the member's office was vacated by his moving his residence from the district.

Miscellaneous Uses of Funds

A myriad of cases treat the subject of whether local school boards have the implied power to spend money for particular purposes. As has

60. Cobb v. City of Cape May, 113 N.J.Super. 598, 274 A.2d 622 (1971).

61. Powers v. Union City Bd. of Educ., 124 N.J.Super. 590, 308 A.2d 71 (1973).

62. Lamb v. Westmoreland Central School Dist., 143 A.D.2d 535, 533 N.Y.S.2d 157 (1988).

63. Cutler v. Poughkeepsie City School Dist., 73 A.D.2d 967, 424 N.Y.S.2d 257 (1980).

64. Matta v. Board of Educ. of Prince George's County, 78 Md.App. 264, 552 A.2d 1340 (1989).

65. Monti v. Warwick School Committee, 554 A.2d 638 (R.I.1989).

66. Durgin v. Brown, 37 N.J. 189, 180 A.2d 136 (1962).

67. Campbell v. Harris, 131 Ariz. 109, 638 P.2d 1355 (App.1981).

been stated, the general rule is that the board can make expenditures to carry out expressly granted powers and powers necessarily implied to give effective meaning to the express powers.

The question of the power of boards of education to spend money for the establishment of parking facilities has been contested. The highest courts of both Pennsylvania and Ohio have approved such expenditures under broad statutes granting general powers to local boards.[68] There is divided authority, however, on the issue of whether purchase of a camp site for use by school children is an implied power of local boards.[69] Also whether local boards have implied power to build residences for staff personnel has been answered by different courts in different ways.[70] But the authority of a school board to employ architects follows from the authority of a school board to build school buildings.[71] The Appellate Court of Illinois has held that a board possesses the implied power to employ a public relations consultant to serve as liaison with the press and community.[72] The consultant arranged public meetings and otherwise assisted the board in communicating with the public.

The Supreme Judicial Court of Massachusetts considered the question of whether expenditures were authorized to cover the expenses of three board members who attended a convention of the National School Boards Association in San Francisco. The court sustained the expenditure.[73] It found that attendance at the meeting could be covered under a broad statute, for it could have resulted in "securing information" of value and could "tend to improve the service" in the school district, which purposes were specified by statute. The implied power of a board to pay the membership fee for the board in a state school boards association has also been upheld.[74]

In Ohio payment from school funds to speakers at high school commencement exercises was questioned by the state auditor. In defending the practice, the district relied on a statute which provided, "The board of education may employ competent persons to deliver lectures, or give instruction on any educational subject." The court, observing that the amounts paid were reasonable, upheld the board.[75] It took judicial notice of the fact that the auditor had approved in connection with graduation exercises such expenditures as those for renting of palms and floral decorations. The court expressed the view that the

---

68. Wayman v. Board of Educ., 5 Ohio St.2d 248, 215 N.E.2d 394 (1966); In re School Dist. of Pittsburgh, 430 Pa. 566, 244 A.2d 42 (1968). [Case No. 42]

69. Compare Wilson v. Graves County Board of Educ., 307 Ky. 203, 210 S.W.2d 350 (1948), with In re Board of Public Instr. of Alachua County, 160 Fla. 490, 35 So.2d 579 (1948).

70. Compare Taylor v. Board of Public Instr., 157 Fla. 422, 26 So.2d 180 (1946), with Denny v. Mecklenburg County, 211 N.C. 558, 191 S.E. 26 (1937).

71. People ex rel. Kiehm v. Board of Educ., 198 App.Div. 476, 190 N.Y.S. 798 (1921).

72. Ryan v. Warren Tp. High School Dist. No. 121, 155 Ill.App.3d 203, 109 Ill. Dec. 843, 510 N.E.2d 911 (1987). [Case No. 43]

73. Day v. City of Newton, 342 Mass. 568, 174 N.E.2d 426 (1961).

74. Schuerman v. State Bd. of Educ., 284 Ky. 556, 145 S.W.2d 42 (1940).

75. Fouts v. Board of Educ. of Middletown City School Dist., 175 N.E.2d 879 (Ohio Com.Pl.1960).

expenditures for speakers were equally, if not more, essential than those which the auditor had previously approved.

The practice of paying employees a sum of money and/or providing other benefits in order to settle a contract claim out of court seems to be spreading. It is obvious that abuses can occur when an employee is offered a sum of money in exchange for resigning and/or not contesting an adverse personnel decision by the board. On the other hand, with the expense of lawsuits and the turmoil they may cause in some situations, a settlement may be economically and educationally prudent. In any event, boards cannot make a payment and, if questioned, simply claim they are exercising their discretion.[76]

Usually where expenditures are held beyond a board's power to make, the legal conclusion of the matter is an injunction preventing or halting the practice. Recovery of expenditures already made under a reasonable assumption of validity of the purpose is generally not possible. However, if the expenditures were clearly unauthorized, individual board members or administrators may be liable for their replacement.[77] This is true even in the absence of an improper motive on the part of an official.[78]

Income from School Bond Issues

It has been pointed out that school districts have no authority to issue bonds or borrow money unless expressly authorized to do so by statute. As the authority to issue bonds is an extraordinary one, it may be exercised only for the express purposes set forth in the authorizing statute. The strictness with which the bonding authority is construed is understandable when it is remembered that the issuance of bonds is prospective in nature and can obligate the taxpayers in the district for long periods of time. The strict construction given to the language of the bonding statutes and the propositions as placed before the voters assures, as far as possible, that the contemplated use of bonding power and bond proceeds will be for the purposes designated.

A problem of interpretation was presented to the Supreme Court of Kansas, where bonds may be voted for "the purpose of erecting and equipping, or purchasing and equipping" schoolhouses. Bonds had been approved by the voters for the purpose of equipping a schoolhouse with necessary heating and electrical equipment and "erecting and constructing a new roof" on the building. The Supreme Court of Kansas held that these bonds were illegally voted.[79] In the opinion of the court, erecting and constructing a new roof on the building did not fall within the scope of the purpose stated above. The contemplated work, reasoned the court, consisted merely of repairing a school building presently in existence. In Wisconsin, however, a statute which authorized borrow-

76. Ingram v. Boone, 91 A.D.2d 1063, 458 N.Y.S.2d 671 (1983). [Case No. 44]

77. McGuire v. Hammond, 405 S.W.2d 191 (Ky.1966); Porter v. Tiffany, 11 Or. App. 542, 502 P.2d 1385 (1972).

78. Campbell v. Joint Dist. 28–J, 704 F.2d 501 (10 Cir.1983).

79. School Dist. No. 6, Chase County v. Robb, 150 Kan. 402, 93 P.2d 905 (1939).

ing of money to "erect or purchase" a school building was held to be sufficiently broad to cover borrowing for remodeling purposes.[80]   The supreme court of that state was of the opinion that remodeling of a building involves more than repairing it or making minor changes therein.   It expressed the view that the term "remodel" connotes a change in the building practically equivalent to constructing a new building.   The highest court of North Carolina found that "additions to the physical facilities" necessarily implied acquisition of additional land for the facilities.[81]

The question of what legally constitutes a "part of a building" arises frequently.   The Supreme Court of Wyoming considered the question whether the term "building" included its equipment.[82]   The pertinent statute contained authorization for districts to vote bonds for the "erection and enlargement" of school buildings.   The bond issue was voted to finance the enlargement of a high school and "to equip the same." Certain taxpayers sought to enjoin the issuance of the bonds on several grounds, one of them being that it appeared that they were issued in part to finance the purchase of equipment.   The court held that certain types of equipment may properly be considered parts of the building and legally paid for by the proceeds of the sale of the bonds.   Such equipment was limited to that which, when installed, became part of the building, such as the heating system, light fixtures, and laboratory desks which are firmly attached to the floor.   The court made the further very important point that even so-called "permanent" equipment should be placed in the building at the time of the construction in order to fall within the provision of the bonding statute.   Equipment placed in the building after construction is completed would be in the nature of repair and not authorized to be financed by the proceeds of bond sales.

Occasionally it is necessary for a school board to utilize bond funds in a manner which deviates somewhat from the wording of the proposition voted.   Such a situation arose in Tennessee where, after a vote on a single bond issue for several projects, it was found that estimates of costs were too low.   The board then used the money for certain of the improvements, leaving others undone.   The court held that the board could expend the funds as it judged best under the circumstances.[83]

In another Tennessee case in which improper use of bond money was alleged, a gymnasium built with proceeds of "high school" bonds was used regularly by the seventh and eighth grades of elementary school and by other grades at certain times, especially during inclement weather.   This fact did not lead the court to hold that the proceeds of the bond issue were improperly used.   The use of the facility under the

80.   Cotter v. Joint School Dist. No. 3 of Village of Plum City, 164 Wis. 13, 158 N.W. 80 (1916).

81.   Lutz v. Gaston County Bd. of Educ., 282 N.C. 208, 192 S.E.2d 463 (1972).

82.   Jewett v. School Dist. No. 25 in Fremont County, 49 Wyo. 277, 54 P.2d 546 (1936).

83.   State v. Peacock, 56 Tenn.App. 109, 405 S.W.2d 478 (1965).

circumstances was deemed by the court not to change the essential character of the building from that of a high school gymnasium.[84]

Income from School Activities

From the authority to control school activities in general, it follows that boards have the power and responsibility to control the income from such activities. Such income has been held to be classifiable as school funds, and it should be deposited, dispersed, and audited in the same manner as school funds derived from taxation or other sources.[85]

A second case, also from Pennsylvania, involved the audit of activity funds of the school. The case involved a number of accounts, such as athletics, publications, dramatics, and others. These were consolidated, and authority to make disbursements from all or any of them was placed by the board in the supervising principal. The court held that the accounts were subject to audit.[86] Pennsylvania law required that all funds belonging to or controlled by the district be audited. The test as to whether activity funds fall within this category was stated by the court to depend upon how they are produced. If they arise from the use of school property and the services of personnel employed by the district, they are district funds and must be deposited in the official account of the school treasurer, and are subject to audit.

The status of activity funds was described by the highest court of Kentucky in a case primarily concerned with a school board member's possible illegal interest in them.[87] It seems that the board member during his term of office was the principal stockholder of a bottling company that placed vending machines in various schools in the county school system and had sold soft drinks continuously to various schools. The money collected was deposited in a bank in the name of either the school or an activity fund against which checks were drawn by the principals. The principals were required to submit monthly reports to the board. The profits realized from the sales were used to pay for special equipment, such as typewriters, and class trips. The lawsuit developed because it was alleged that the board member had an illegal interest in the sale of property to the board.

The board member argued that the funds were not school funds because they were raised by children for various projects, that they belonged to various classes or school-related organizations, and that they were kept separate from tax money. Accordingly he insisted that his interest was not in any property for which school funds had been expended. The court, in holding that the board member did have an illegal interest in the funds and in vacating his membership on the

---

84. Moody v. Williamson County, 212 Tenn. 666, 371 S.W.2d 454 (1963).

85. In re German Tp. School Directors, 46 Pa. D. & C. 562 (Com.Pl.1943). [Case No. 45]

86. Petition of Auditors of Hatfield Tp. School Dist., 161 Pa.Super. 388, 54 A.2d 833 (1947).

87. Commonwealth ex rel. Breckinridge v. Collins, 379 S.W.2d 436 (Ky.1964).

board, stated that activity funds per se were school funds over which the board had full control.

It seems clear that school districts, and therefore administrators who work for them, have no authority to obtain, administer, or dispose of funds other than those which are specified in statutes. The questions then arise, can an administrator maintain a fund not under the control of the board or the public-at-large, and, if so, what accounting is necessary? A complex South Carolina case is relevant. There taxpayers sought to require an accounting by a school principal for certain funds raised over a period of four years. The funds were raised by students and teachers of the high school through extracurricular fund-raising activities. The proceeds were entrusted to the principal's care and control. The purpose of the fund was the paying of costs of some desired equipment that had not been furnished in the regular school program, such as athletic equipment and choir robes. The principal deposited the funds in a bank, and only he had authority to make withdrawals. Neither the raising nor dispersal was directed or supervised by the school board, the effort being voluntary on the part of teachers, pupils, and parents. No audit or accounting had been made during a four-year period. When the case first reached the Supreme Court of South Carolina, that court remanded it to the lower court with directions to determine whether there had been a proper accounting by the principal and whether there was in fact a shortage.[88] The court avoided the question of the legal status of the fund, since it was not shown that the fund was raised or administered directly or indirectly by the board of education.

After the lower court had made the required findings, the appellate court considered the question of whether taxpayers could recover for misappropriation of the funds. It was not shown that there was in fact any misappropriation, thus there could be no recovery. However, the court of last resort criticized the method of accounting of the principal.[89] The records were so confused that it was not possible properly to audit them. The court did specifically state that the principal had no right or authority to make "loans on salaries" to teachers from the account because no money was ever raised for that purpose. The court commented further that, although he occupied the position of a trustee of the fund, the principal's services were gratuitous, and the duties and responsibilities in connection therewith were in addition to his other duties and responsibilities as principal. Nothing in the record, said the court, could suggest that he in any manner personally profited from the fund entrusted to him, and nothing appeared from which it could be concluded that anyone had been financially damaged as the result of his manner of handling the funds.

Frequently student activity funds are used to pay for certain services. One such use in Oklahoma was to compensate football referees. In a case decided by the highest court of the state the question was whether

88. Betterson v. Stewart, 238 S.C. 574, 121 S.E.2d 102 (1961).

89. Betterson v. Stewart, 245 S.C. 296, 140 S.E.2d 482 (1965).

one so paid was included under workmen's compensation.[90] The court ruled that the source of funds was the crucial factor in deciding the question. It held that only those paid under funds appropriated by the board were covered.

Income from Gifts

In general a board of education can accept gifts to be used for any purpose within the power of the board to execute. When the gift is conveyed by will, however, the result can lead to a board's receiving funds or property designated for purposes the board is barred from carrying out by impracticality or by impossibility of circumstances including illegality. If the situation is one of pure impossibility (e.g., an award for the highest grade in a subject no longer taught) the common law of testamentary charitable trusts would provide for a court to designate another use close to the use specified by the testator. (The doctrine is known as "cy pres.")

If the situation is one of illegality (e.g., a forbidden discrimination) a court might be able to reform the trust by eliminating the offending restriction.[91] Of prime concern for the courts is to execute the intent of a testator who has expressed a general charitable purpose. If this can be done simply by changing the administrator of the will, the court could apply the doctrine of "deviation" to effect a change in the administrative terms of the trust by the appointment of a different trustee. The last situation would arise not only if a board of education was legally unable to serve as trustee but if it was unwilling to do so for policy reasons.[92] In any event, interest accruing on trust funds belongs to the beneficiary, not the trustee or the custodian of funds.[93]

Uses of School Property

Uses in General

School buildings generally are considered to be the property of the state, not of the local district. This statement is true even though buildings may have been paid for solely from funds raised on the local district level.[94] The point bears emphasis here, for the concept of the legal nature of school buildings is sometimes difficult for citizens in local school districts to comprehend. They may be inclined to look upon the buildings as "their" buildings, because they were financed with "their" money. Thus, despite the fact that the buildings are constructed for

90. Fireman's Fund Ins. Co. v. Overton, 491 P.2d 278 (Okl.1971).

91. Howard Savings Institution of Newark v. Peep, 34 N.J. 494, 170 A.2d 39 (1961).

92. Matter of Estate of Wilson, 59 N.Y.2d 461, 465 N.Y.S.2d 900, 452 N.E.2d 1228 (1983).

93. Grand Rapids Public Schools v. City of Grand Rapids, 146 Mich.App. 652, 381 N.W.2d 783 (1985).

94. Pritchett v. County Bd. of School Trustees, 5 Ill.2d 356, 125 N.E.2d 476 (1955); Moses Lake School Dist. No. 161 v. Big Bend Community College, 81 Wash.2d 551, 503 P.2d 86 (1972), app. dism. 412 U.S. 934, 93 S.Ct. 2776, 37 L.Ed.2d 393 (1973).

school purposes, various groups often seek the use of school buildings for other than school purposes. Whether and to what extent school buildings may legally be used for nonschool purposes have been widely litigated.

Determination of school building uses rests completely with the legislature except for possible constitutional restrictions. Statutes pertaining to the use of school buildings differ from state to state both in terms of number and specificity. Typically, restrictive legislation is lacking, and the management and control of school buildings are left almost exclusively to the discretion of local boards of education. In some states statutes expressly empower local boards to allow buildings to be used for certain purposes in the discretion of the board.

There have been two basic general legal objections raised when local school boards have permitted the use of school buildings for nonschool purposes. One goes to the fundamental concept that boards of education are agencies of limited powers and their authority does not extend to areas in which the legislature has not permitted them to operate. The second is that a nonschool use constitutes an expenditure of public money for a private purpose. Other objections arise over uses by special groups or for special purposes. Owners of business establishments frequently object to the use of school property for activities in possible competition with their businesses.

In the area of the use of school buildings courts across the nation have not been consistent. This is apparent even when statutory situations appear similar. Many older cases, particularly from states on the "frontier" to the West, support wide permissible use, and there has been a trend toward judicial approval of an increasingly broad range of uses.

Permissible Uses and Conditions of Use

The holding in school buildings of school-connected activities to which parents and friends are invited is clearly legally justifiable. This has been held true even where fees were charged and the general public was urged to attend through the use of advertising techniques.[95] The uncertainty arises where activities are not school-connected. But even those courts that have supported boards in allowing buildings to be so used have specified that there be no interference with the school program and no damage to the building.[96]

Except for use as polling places, relatively rarely does a statute remove from local boards discretion in the control of school buildings and require boards to open their buildings for nonschool purposes. Perhaps California has gone further than any other state in providing by statute for wide nonschool use of school buildings. State law there establishes a "civic center" at "each and every public school building and grounds within the state." It provides for the free use of these

95. Beard v. Board of Educ. of North Summit School Dist., 81 Utah 51, 16 P.2d 900 (1932).

96. Merryman v. School Dist. No. 16, 43 Wyo. 376, 5 P.2d 267 (1931).

facilities by community groups for meetings to discuss subjects which in the judgment of the group "appertain to the educational, political, economic, artistic and moral interests of the citizens." The local board is empowered to adopt "reasonable rules and regulations" to carry out the mandate, and in no event can such use interfere with the regular purposes of the schools.

Many cases have arisen under this statute. In one a local board was upheld in refusing use of the facilities to a group which intended to have as a speaker a person who, when previously he had spoken in other communities, had aroused so much organized opposition that disturbances had resulted.[97] The board had based its ruling on the fact that classes in session at the time would be disturbed. Another case involved a request made through the Civil Liberties Union for the use of a school auditorium to discuss the position of the Socialist Party on the question of peace. The request was denied by the school board on the ground that a discussion of this nature violated a rule of the board prohibiting the use of school buildings for sectarian, political or partisan purposes. The court held that the board must permit the use under the terms of the Civic Center Act.[98]

Several cases arose in the early 1960's regarding the use of buildings in California by alleged subversive organizations. Declared unconstitutional was a statute requiring those who applied for permission to use a school building to submit a statement that the organization did not advocate violent overthrow of the government and was not a Communist or Communist-front organization.[99] It was held that the right of assembly and free speech was infringed because this constituted approval of the organization, rather than of what the organization was going to do. However, the Supreme Court of California sustained two years later a board rule which required prospective users of school premises to state that they did not intend to put the property to an illegal use.[100] The court stated that although it would be improper to refuse permission to hold a parade in the public streets merely because the permitting authority was not in sympathy with the cause which the applicant espoused, it would be entirely reasonable to demand that such applicant agree in advance to comply with existing municipal ordinances dealing with use of streets, such as blocking intersections and setting off fireworks. The licensing authority has both the right and the duty, reasoned the court, to place such reasonable restrictions on the freedom of assembly.

A Kentucky school board permitted a gymnasium to be used by a local civic organization when it was not in educational use. A statute expressly permitted such arrangements. The civic organization conduct-

97. Payroll Guarantee Ass'n v. Board of Educ., 27 Cal.2d 197, 163 P.2d 433 (1945).

98. Goodman v. Board of Educ. of San Francisco, 48 Cal.App.2d 731, 120 P.2d 665 (1941).

99. American Civil Liberties Union of Southern California v. Board of Educ. of

City of Los Angeles, 55 Cal.2d 167, 10 Cal. Rptr. 647, 359 P.2d 45 (1961), cert. den. 368 U.S. 819, 82 S.Ct. 34, 7 L.Ed.2d 25 (1961).

100. American Civil Liberties Union of Southern California v. Board of Educ. of City of Los Angeles, 59 Cal.2d 203, 28 Cal. Rptr. 700, 379 P.2d 4 (1963).

ed musical programs in the gymnasium and charged admission thereto. All receipts, however, were used for civic activities and civic betterment. Suit to halt this practice was brought by one who had made a substantial expenditure in establishing and conducting a business of presenting public professional performances of country and folk music. Plaintiff's claim that the programs of the civic association were in direct competition with him and that he had lost half of his investment, with the remainder in danger of loss, was not sufficient to invalidate the lease.[101]

A North Carolina school board established an after-school program designed to alleviate problems of children who were left without supervision between the end of the school day and the time their parents came home from work. A nominal fee was charged. The school board covered costs of the facility use, and volunteers conducted the program. The program was upheld in a suit instituted by private day-care center owners.[102]

Where a school board sponsored two dances a year, a parent group wanted to sponsor additional dances at the school. Among claims in a suit against the board was one that dancing should be treated as a form of expression that was entitled to First Amendment protection. The Eighth Circuit Court of Appeals did not agree that social or recreational dancing was covered, as would be dancing before an audience as an art form.[103] Further the dancing was not to convey any particular idea, and the board was held not obliged to furnish use of school property for its conduct. In another Eighth Circuit case the board long before had adopted a rule that school premises not be used for dances.[104] A large segment of the present community opposed social dancing on religious grounds. That the board policy was congenial to the religious views of a probable majority of the community did not invalidate it in the absence of evidence that the ban was enacted to advance a religious viewpoint. No student was prohibited from engaging in or refraining from extracurricular dancing.

It should be observed that employees of the school system have no rights to hold on school premises organized meetings that are not approved by the authorities. Thus, some teachers were unsuccessful in a claim of a right to hold regularly scheduled prayer meetings only for teachers before pupils arrived at the school. The Seventh Circuit emphasized that the reason was not related to costs of electricity and maintenance nor to the content of the meetings but to the board's rightful concern that controversies and distractions could result from any meetings that were not work related.[105] Also, if some groups could meet, certain others could not be barred under the freedom of speech

101. Hall v. Shelby County Bd. of Educ., 472 S.W.2d 489 (Ky.1971).

102. Kiddie Korner Day Schools, Inc. v. Charlotte–Mecklenburg Bd. of Educ., 55 N.C.App. 134, 285 S.E.2d 110 (1981).

103. Jarman v. Williams, 753 F.2d 76 (8 Cir.1985).

104. Clayton v. Place, 884 F.2d 376 (8 Cir.1989).

105. May v. Evansville–Vanderburgh School Corp., 787 F.2d 1105 (7 Cir.1986).

clause. The court pointed out that the issue was different from that of teachers' speech in the classroom.

A Maryland statute permitted school boards to deny access to school property to those not having lawful business at the school. A Fourth Circuit decision upheld the barring of a union representative from a school parking lot.[106] Even though there was no disruption, the representative's solicitational activities were not deemed related to the education of students, and the parking lot had not become a public forum.

Courts are not in agreement as to whether boards of education have the implied power to lease school property for long-term commercial purposes. For example, different courts have responded differently when boards have been challenged on the granting of leases for production of oil or gas.[107] Also, there are inconsistent judicial answers to the question, Can public school facilities be used for conducting studies or classes for which tuition is charged and paid to those giving the instruction?[108]

Differentiating among Uses and Users

In general the power of government to regulate expression is most restricted on public properties that are "traditional public forums." These comprise parks, streets, sidewalks, and the like. In such forums a content-based exclusion can be enforced only if it is narrowly drawn to effectuate a compelling state interest. Narrowly tailored content-neutral regulations as to time, place, and manner of expression can be enforced, but only to the extent that the government interest is a significant one and alternative channels of communication are open.

A second category of public property is that which the state has opened for use by the public as a place for expressive activity. A subcategory of such a "designated public forum" is the "limited public forum" that is opened for discussion of certain subjects or to certain classes of speakers. This may be done by express policy or by substantial practice of the government unit. If there is a limited public forum the First Amendment protections provided to traditional public forums apply, but only to entities of a character similar to those the government admits to the forum. The government is not bound to retain indefinitely the open nature of a limited forum.[109]

A third category of public property is the "nonpublic forum," a place not by tradition or designation for public communication. In this setting the government can enforce regulations to reserve the forum for its intended purposes, communicative or otherwise, as long as the rules

106. Grattan v. Board of School Com'rs of Baltimore City, 805 F.2d 1160 (4th Cir. 1986).

107. Compare Herald v. Board of Educ., 65 W.Va. 765, 65 S.E. 102 (1909), with Williams v. McKenzie, 203 Ky. 376, 262 S.W. 598 (1924).

108. Compare Weir v. Day, 35 Ohio St. 143 (1878), with Appeal of Barnes, 6 R.I. 591 (1860).

109. Perry Educ. Ass'n v. Perry Local Educators' Ass'n, 460 U.S. 37, 103 S.Ct. 948, 74 L.Ed.2d 794 (1983).

are reasonable and not intended to suppress expression because public officials oppose a viewpoint.[110]

Public school property during the school day would generally be a nonpublic forum. After school hours the property could become a designated public forum, limited or not depending on policy and practice.

The preceding is based upon the freedom of speech portion of the First Amendment. An additional complication arises when the speech is of a religious nature, because the religion clauses of the First Amendment are also implicated. In 1981 the Supreme Court refused to accord to religious organizations "rights to communicate * * * superior to those of other organizations having social, political, or other ideological messages to proselytize." [111] In that case the forum was a state fair. The Court upheld, against the challenge of a religious group, the fair's general requirement that solicitations, sales of materials, and distributions of materials must be from fixed locations on the fairgrounds.

Six months later the Court addressed the opposite situation: religious speech being afforded less protection in a forum than other forms of speech. The Court found that the University of Missouri essentially had created a forum for use of its students by routinely making its facilities available to over 100 registered student organizations. Therefore, it held that the university could not bar an organization of students who wished to hold religious meetings.[112] (As amplified in Chapter 2, the Court distinguished this case from those involving public graded schools on the bases that existing here was a forum made available to many diverse groups and that university students are less impressionable than younger students.)

Many pre-1981 cases involving use of school property by outside groups upheld the barring of certain religious activities. Whether the individual cases remain valid is cloudy because often the opinions of the courts did not record some facts or respond to some arguments that have become important for the disposition of such cases in the future. For example, the Supreme Court of Pennsylvania upheld a rule that facilities must not be used "for any religious or sectarian purpose." [113] The rule was unsuccessfully attacked primarily on the grounds that the board violated the equal protection clause by permitting nonreligious uses and that the board's discretionary power to allow use of school facilities had to be exercised in full or not at all.

In the first post-1981 case a federal District Court ruled in favor of a church that was denied occasional use of school facilities for religious services.[114] The board's basic policy was that facilities were available for

110. Cornelius v. NAACP Legal Defense and Educational Fund, Inc., 473 U.S. 788, 105 S.Ct. 3439, 87 L.Ed.2d 567 (1985).

111. Heffron v. International Society for Krishna Consciousness, Inc., 452 U.S. 640, 101 S.Ct. 2559, 69 L.Ed.2d 298 (1981).

112. Widmar v. Vincent, 454 U.S. 263, 102 S.Ct. 269, 70 L.Ed.2d 440 (1981).

113. McKnight v. Board of Educ., 365 Pa. 422, 76 A.2d 207 (1950), app. dism., 341 U.S. 913, 71 S.Ct. 737, 95 L.Ed. 1349 (1951).

114. Country Hills Christian Church v. Unified School Dist. No. 512, Johnson County, State of Kansas, 560 F.Supp. 1207 (D.Kan.1983).

"recognized community organizations whose activities are of general interest to the community and whose use of the school facility is for a community purpose." There was wide use of facilities by diverse groups, and there were no guidelines to distinguish between religious and nonreligious meetings. The court held, "Having created a public forum, [the board] cannot exclude [the church group] from the forum because of the religious content of [the church group's] intended speech unless such exclusion is justified under applicable [establishment clause] case law."

A similar policy that did not allow use of school facilities "for the direct advancement of religion" was held by the First Circuit Court of Appeals not to be enforceable against a religious organization that wanted to give a free Christmas community dinner accompanied by an evangelical message.[115] The district had extended permission to such a broad spectrum of activities that it had by its actions created a public forum for speech purposes in the eyes of the court. The court commented on, but did not rule on, possible establishment clause issues and on the point that a different speech clause issue might arise if the policy was to allow activities of benefit to the school, rather than of benefit to the community.

Courts also look beyond written policies to conduct and actions in determining whether a forum is limited and if so to what subjects and/or classes of participants. Thus, when a school auditorium had been used for some fund raising activities and for at least one Christmas program, the Second Circuit required access for another religious activity.[116] It declined to rule on the question whether by an enforced rule all religious speech could be excluded from the auditorium.

In examining implications of the establishment clause for use of school facilities for religious services on a regular basis when school was not in session, a distinction between short-term and long-term use was recognized by the Supreme Court of Florida.[117] No mention of rental fees or expenses was made in the opinion of the court, which upheld a temporary arrangement. Citing this case with approval two decades later, the Supreme Court of New Jersey held that school boards were permitted to allow religious groups to use school buildings for religious purposes after school hours and on weekends where the policy was one of renting to all community non-profit groups, where fees to cover heating, cleaning, and maintenance expenses were paid, and where the period of rental was temporary.[118] Lower state courts had set a fixed one-year limit on leases and a requirement that charges should be made at fair market value. The higher court stated that these stipulations were not constitutionally nor statutorily required.[119]

115. Grace Bible Fellowship, Inc. v. Maine School Administrative Dist. No. 5, 941 F.2d 45 (1 Cir.1991).

116. Travis v. Owego–Apalachin School Dist., 927 F.2d 688 (2 Cir.1991).

117. Southside Estates Baptist Church v. Board of Trustees, Tax Dist. No. 1, 115 So.2d 697 (Fla.1959).

118. Resnick v. East Brunswick Tp. Bd. of Educ., 77 N.J. 88, 389 A.2d 944 (1978). [Case No. 46]

119. In a situation where the charging of "fair rental value" was important to the outcome, the Supreme Court of Arizona upheld the leasing of a state university stadium for a limited number of religious servic-

In 1993 the Supreme Court held that a school board which had a policy of allowing its facilities to be used when school was not in session for "social, civic, and recreational meetings and entertainments" could not bar a church group from using the facilities to show a six-part film series that dealt with family values "from the Christian perspective." [120] The Court based its decision solely on the free speech clause (not the religion clauses) of the Constitution. It reasoned that a board rule (which conformed to state law) forbidding use by any group for religious purposes had been unconstitutionally applied. (The Court expressly did not pass judgment on the constitutionality of that rule. Nor did it consider the nature of other groups that had used the facilities.) The narrow ruling was that where there was no restriction on the subject matter of the films the board could not decide to erect a bar based on the viewpoint to be expressed about that subject matter.

Although school authorities generally can close the door to all outside organizations, if they open the door to any, they must treat alike all organizations in the same category. A board can deny use if proof is presented that a clear and present danger exists that public disorder and possible damage to the building would result from a proposed use, but the board can not bar an organization simply because it, or a part of the public, might be hostile to the opinions or the program of the organization, provided the program is not unlawful per se.

The highest court in New York applied these rules where a board of education sought to bar one of a series of concerts because it was to feature as a performing artist one who was a "highly controversial figure." He had given a concert in Moscow, and some of the songs he sang were critical of American policy in Vietnam.[121] The court held that the reason asserted by the school board for cancelling the permit was unconstitutional, because it rested on the unpopularity of the singer's views, rather than the unlawfulness of the concert. It stated, "The expression of controversial and unpopular views, it is hardly necessary to observe, is precisely what is protected by both the Federal and State constitutions."

The United States Court of Appeals, Fourth Circuit, concluded that a board of education that had a policy of renting for a nominal fee a high school auditorium could not constitutionally exclude the National Socialist White People's Party. The board stated its reasons to be that this organization's use of the facility would endanger school property and that a publicly owned building could not be used by an organization that did not admit Jews or Negroes to membership.[122] The court found the first basis unsupported by evidence that there was any history of violence and damage to property when the group met. It rejected the

es. Pratt v. Arizona Bd. of Regents, 110 Ariz. 466, 520 P.2d 514 (1974).

120. Lamb's Chapel v. Center Moriches Union Free School Dist., ___ U.S. ___, 113 S.Ct. 2141, 124 L.Ed.2d 352 (1993). [Case No. 47]

121. East Meadow Community Concerts Ass'n v. Board of Educ., 18 N.Y.2d 129, 272 N.Y.S.2d 341, 219 N.E.2d 172 (1966). [Case No. 48].

122. National Socialist White People's Party v. Ringers, 473 F.2d 1010 (4 Cir. 1973).

second contention on the ground that the First Amendment protected expression of "unpopular, indeed offensive," views and that denial to an organization of the use of a public forum because of its membership policies was akin to denial because of views to be expressed.

An Oklahoma school district that routinely had been permitting use of its facilities by organizations refused a request by the local Parent Teacher Association (PTA). Subsequent to the first denial the board adopted rules for use of school property by outside organizations. The board barred "any organization that it determines to be disruptive to or unsupportive of the school board or any part of the school system." Other parts of the statement described those who would not be permitted to use school facilities as including organizations that "deal in personalities" or "engage in frequent criticisms against the school system and the school personnel in particular." The PTA sought a writ of mandamus to require the board to allow use of facilities for its meetings. After observing that the lower court record contained no evidence that the PTA actually had violated the criteria of the board, the supreme court of the state invalidated the regulations on constitutional grounds, and ordered the lower court to issue the writ.[123]

Statutes or ordinances preventing loitering on school grounds or in the vicinity of school buildings are increasingly common. As a general proposition they have been held to be constitutional provided they are not too vague as to the conduct which is prohibited nor selective as to exclusions from their force. The Supreme Court in 1972 decided two cases which illuminate the area. It held unconstitutional an ordinance that forbid picketing or demonstrating, except for peaceful labor picketing, on a public way within 150 feet of a school building while classes were in session.[124] The basis was an impermissible distinction between labor picketing and other peaceful picketing. Upheld, however, was an anti-noise ordinance that provided the noise be willfully made and that it disturb classes.[125]

On the other hand, it has been held that a state university cannot constitutionally prohibit the distribution of all handbills on a part of its campus grounds which are open to the public.[126] The University of Arizona had made a portion of its campus generally available to the public. It claimed that the complete prohibition was necessary because disputes might arise if leaflets were allowed. Citing Tinker (Case No. 114), the United States Court of Appeals, Ninth Circuit, found that the disturbance which did occur was preventable by proper action of authorities and that substantial disruption could not be so likely anticipated that freedom of speech could be curtailed.

123. Hennessey v. Independent School Dist. No. 4, Lincoln County, 552 P.2d 1141 (Okl.1976).

124. Police Dep't of City of Chicago v. Mosley, 408 U.S. 92, 92 S.Ct. 2286, 33 L.Ed.2d 212 (1972).

125. Grayned v. City of Rockford, 408 U.S. 104, 92 S.Ct. 2294, 33 L.Ed.2d 222 (1972).

126. Jones v. Board of Regents of University of Arizona, 436 F.2d 618 (9 Cir. 1970).

Whether First Amendment rights are unconstitutionally infringed by a rule which bars solicitations on school premises was decided by the United States Court of Appeals, Second Circuit.[127] A rule by the New York Board of Regents (state board of education) in effect for 47 years prohibited "soliciting funds from the pupils in the public schools." The only exception had been the Junior Red Cross. In the present case the leaflet sought to raise funds through asking a contribution or the purchase of a button to help pay for the legal defense of some political "activists" on trial in a federal court. The dissemination occurred before the school day began, there was no interference with the operation of the school, and students were not aggressively approached. The court ruled in favor of the school authorities. It found the rule to be reasonable in the education setting, and emphasized that it was not directly or indirectly intended to prevent the exercise of free speech. The Supreme Court declined to review the decision.

That school authorities may bar a display of paintings on the basis of offensiveness short of unlawful obscenity was the holding of another federal appellate court.[128] An art instructor at the University of Massachusetts had been invited by an official of the institution to exhibit paintings, unseen by the inviter, on the walls of a corridor. The paintings in fact emphasized sex in "clinical detail," and they had titles the court characterized as "cheap." Observing that the corridor was a passageway regularly used by the public, including children, the court held that the authorities were justified in ordering the paintings removed. It distinguished the case from those involving possibly unpopular speakers in that the art was not seeking to express political or social thought and the medium and subject matter of speakers were entitled to greater protection than the plaintiff's art. The same conclusion was reached in a case differing primarily in that children's use of the corridor was not present and the challenged act was to relocate, rather than remove, the art work.[129]

In an unusual situation a parent was charged with violating a statute that made guilty of a misdemeanor "any person who upbraids, abuses or insults any member of the instructional staff on school property or in the presence of the pupils at a school activity." The mother had launched what the Supreme Court of Florida characterized as a "profane verbal attack" in the presence of at least 50 students upon a teacher who apparently had corporally punished her daughter. The court reversed the conviction of the woman on the primary ground that the statute was unconstitutionally overbroad.[130] The purported prohibitions encompassed clearly protected speech and went far beyond any acceptable restraints that might be justifiable because of the setting in which the language was used.

127. Katz v. McAulay, 438 F.2d 1058 (2 Cir.1971), cert. den. 405 U.S. 933, 92 S.Ct. 930, 30 L.Ed.2d 809 (1972). [Case No. 49]

128. Close v. Lederle, 424 F.2d 988 (1 Cir.1970).

129. Piarowski v. Illinois Community College Dist. 515, 759 F.2d 625 (7 Cir.1985), cert. den. 474 U.S. 1107, 106 S.Ct. 528, 88 L.Ed.2d 460 (1985).

130. McCall v. State, 354 So.2d 869 (Fla.1978).

Freedom of expression in school settings is further treated in Chapter 12 (students) and Chapters 10 and 11 (teachers).

Disposal of Property

The implied powers of boards to utilize property do not extend to disposal of it. Usually the disposition of real estate is covered by statutes. Sometimes, however, these are not clear, as illustrated by a New York case involving disposal of an unneeded building. The intent of a statute was differently decided at each of four steps in the judicial process, ranging from the commissioner of education to the highest court of the state.[131] Where statutes do not cover the method for disposal of property, the courts will examine the circumstances of a sale, but will not interfere with board discretion unless it is manifestly abused.[132] The criterion utilized in such instances is the best interest of the school system as seen rationally by the local board.[133] General grants of authority to manage and control the public schools, however, do not imply power to sell or give away property. Furthermore, school districts cannot in effect give away real estate by leasing it for a nominal sum, even though the cause is worthy. Invalidated, for example, was an agreement whereby a school building was leased to the hospital commission for a community hospital for one dollar a year, the commission having an option to renew.[134]

Whether a school board which has authority to sell unneeded property can do so on an installment basis, rather than a cash basis, was decided affirmatively by the Court of Appeals of Michigan.[135] The court reasoned that it would be unrealistic to expect developers to mortgage vacant lands and additionally borrow for construction purposes. Thus, to compel a cash bid for land to be sold would drive down the offered price to the disadvantage of the school district. Here the district did not limit bids to installment purchase, but offered it as an alternative to cash. The district was protected in case of default on payments by the fact it would hold the legal title until all payments had been made.

The Supreme Court of Iowa emphasized the mandatory nature of statutes covering disposal of school property by voiding an attempted sale not in strict compliance with the codified law.[136] A statute permitted school boards to dispose of property valued up to a certain sum without a vote of the residents. The value depended on the size of the district. In the present case the property value in question exceeded that figure for the district involved but was less than the figure permitted larger districts. There was no issue of favoritism or fraud.

131. Ross v. Wilson, 308 N.Y. 605, 127 N.E.2d 697 (1955). [Case No. 50]

132. Merely filing a suit seeking to enjoin a school closing does not prevent a board's selling of the physical plant. Laurales v. Desha County School Dist. No. 4 of Snowlake, 632 F.2d 72 (8 Cir.1980).

133. Veal v. Smith, 221 Ga. 712, 146 S.E.2d 751 (1966).

134. Prescott Community Hospital Comm'n v. Prescott School Dist., 57 Ariz. 492, 115 P.2d 160 (1941).

135. Singer Architectural Services Co. v. Doyle, 74 Mich.App. 485, 254 N.W.2d 587 (1977).

136. Unification Church v. Clay Central School Dist., 253 N.W.2d 579 (Iowa 1977).

The city coterminous with an Alabama school district that had been operating on a segregated basis sought to lease or sell a building to a newly created private segregated school. After the trial court had indicated at a preliminary hearing that a lease would probably be invalid, the city sold the building to the private group, and the court approved. The Fifth Circuit Court of Appeals reversed, holding that the action of sale under the facts present was not taken in good faith and violated the rights to equal protection of those in the class against which the private school's admission policies discriminated.[137] The court said that it took account of the practical effect of the action rather than merely its neutral appearance on its face.

In Delaware a board of education, which had been created as one of several in connection with an areawide desegregation order, made a policy decision not to sell or lease any of its unneeded schools to private operators of kindergarten through twelfth grade programs. A religious school corporation sued to invalidate the rule as applied to its efforts to buy an unused building. The court sustained the policy as being rationally based on implementing desegregation and avoiding the encouragement of private education in the area at the time.[138] There was no unconstitutional burden on any religious rights of the plaintiffs.

Decided by the Supreme Court of North Dakota was the question, Does the discontinuance of the use of a school building for teaching purposes constitute an abandonment of the property "for school purposes," even though the building still is being used for storage of school equipment and supplies?[139] The context was that a deed conveying the property to the school district contained a reverter clause which became effective if the property were "abandoned for school purposes". The court answered in the negative.

In Texas the answer was different when most of the land to be used "for school purposes only" was leased by the school board to the city for the establishment of a recreation center. The board unsuccessfully argued that the reason for the lease was to prevent vandalism and keep the property in good repair for eventual reopening of the school on the property. The school had been closed after the students then attending were ordered to be transferred as part of a desegregation decree. The court said that the reason for breaching the provision of the deed was irrelevant.[140] So was the fact that the school district continuously used a portion of the property as a storage and maintenance facility. The pivotal and clear word in the deed was "only."

Under certain conditions one, who over a period of time continuously occupies land to which he does not have title in such a way as to indicate the property is his in all respects under circumstances where the

---

137. Wright v. City of Brighton, Alabama, 441 F.2d 447 (5 Cir.1971), cert. den. 404 U.S. 915, 92 S.Ct. 228, 30 L.Ed.2d 190 (1971).

138. Wilmington Christian School, Inc. v. Board of Educ. of Red Clay Consolidated School Dist., 545 F.Supp. 440 (D.Del.1982).

139. Ballantyne v. Nedrose Public School Dist. No. 4, Ward County, 177 N.W.2d 551 (N.D.1970).

140. Sewell v. Dallas Independent School Dist., 727 S.W.2d 586 (Tex.App. 1987).

legal owner has knowledge of the assertion of ownership, can take title to the land by what is known as adverse possession. Whether this is possible as to land held in trust for school purposes depends upon the jurisdiction.[141]

[Case No. 41] Power of Board to Suspend Transportation Service

ROSE v. NASHUA BD. OF EDUC.
United States Court of Appeals, First Circuit, 1982.
679 F.2d 279.

BREYER, CIRCUIT JUDGE. This case raises the question of the extent to which the Fourteenth Amendment imposes "due process" obligations upon a school board seeking to suspend school bus trips briefly for disciplinary purposes. After examining the facts of this case, we have concluded that the school authorities complied with whatever obligations the Constitution might impose.

I

The law of the State of New Hampshire requires school districts to provide free school bus transportation to most pupils under the age of 14. Several years ago, bus drivers began to complain about vandalism and disruptive conduct on certain bus routes in Nashua. Students were apparently throwing things about inside the buses and at passing cars; they were slashing seats; they were excessively noisy and disrespectful to the drivers. Because the drivers had to watch the road, they could not tell which specific students were responsible. The private company supplying the bus service complained to the Nashua Board of Education. After hearings and consideration of alternatives, the Board adopted a suspension policy.

The policy applied to instances of serious disruption, significant vandalism, or danger. In such cases, when other methods of dealing with the disciplinary problem failed, a school official would board the bus and tell the students that the route would be suspended if the guilty students did not come forward. If this did not work, the Board's "transportation director" would write to the parents telling them that the bus route would be suspended unless the troublemakers were identified. As a last resort, the Board could suspend the route for up to five days.

When several parents objected to this policy, the Board held hearings. It considered several alternatives, such as seat assignments, ID cards, even special police ("monitors") to ride the bus. But, believing that these alternatives were either too expensive, or not always effective, it retained its rule allowing temporary (five day) suspensions after advance notice to affected students and parents.

141. Compare Brown v. Board of Educ., Monroeville Local School Dist., 20 Ohio St.2d 68, 253 N.E.2d 767 (1969), with Boecking-Berry Equip. Co. v. Ansay, 453 P.2d 251 (Okl.1969).

According to the Board, the policy has been successful. During the first year of the policy's operation there were only 12 suspensions. Since there are 150 school bus routes and each bus makes two trips per day for 180 school days, the total number of bus trips lost could not have amounted to more than 120 out of 54,000. And, judging from the fact that the Board wishes to keep the policy, it believes that the threat of suspension has a salutary effect on discipline. Its belief is supported by the fact that only 3 or 4 routes were suspended in the policy's second year of operation.

The objecting parents, however, claim that their children are not the ones who cause the trouble. They attack the policy as unfair, for it makes their children suffer for the sins of others, and they claim it violates both state and federal law. The district court rejected their legal claims, as do we.

II

We first take up the parents' pendent state law claim. They argue that New Hampshire state law imposes a specific duty upon the school district to provide bus transportation for their children. This law, they claim, gives them a right to that transportation. They are aware that the statute specifically authorizes the school superintendent "to suspend the right of pupils from riding in a school bus when said pupils fail to conform to the reasonable rules and regulations" of the Board. But, they argue, this statute allows suspension only of the troublemakers, not those who ride the buses with them. The district court rejected this argument, holding that the statute allows the superintendent to suspend the rights of *all* the students who ride the bus.

We uphold the district court's interpretation of the statute. For one thing, we are reluctant to interfere with a reasonable construction of state law made by a district judge, sitting in the state, who is familiar with that state's law and practices. For another thing, the court's interpretation of the statute *is* reasonable. The statute specifically provides that the parents of a suspended pupil can appeal a suspension, but *in the meantime* the parents must provide transportation. Thus, the statute plainly allows suspension of those who are only *suspected* of violating the rules. In this instance, the potential rule violators include both those who slash seats, and those who don't turn the seat-slashers over to the authorities. And, since the driver does not know who on the bus has violated the rules, all are presumably suspect—or at least, so many are suspect that it is reasonable to treat the statute's reference to "pupils who fail to conform to the reasonable rules and regulations" as applying to all of them. We therefore affirm the judge's decision that, as a matter of state law, the School Board's policy is authorized.

III

Appellants' main argument is that New Hampshire law, as so interpreted, is unconstitutional. They claim that the Fourteenth Amendment, in forbidding deprivation of "property * * * without due process of law," requires a prior hearing to determine likely guilt or innocence before the Board can deprive a pupil of bus transportation—even for five days. We do not agree.

As an initial matter, we have serious doubts about whether the pupils or their parents have asserted a property interest sufficiently weighty for the Due Process Clause to apply. No one here complains about any deprivation of education, or educational opportunity. The Board asserted at oral argument, without contradiction, that as soon as it identified a pupil who could not get to school on his own (because he was handicapped) it immediately arranged for alternate transportation. Nor is anyone complaining of permanent loss of transportation. The maximum harm is the inconvenience for parents or children of a car pool, a long walk, or some other private transportation arrangement for five days in the school year. This is hardly a "grievous loss" or the deprivation of a particularly important right, privilege or opportunity. No one claims a reputational injury. And, there is no great principle at stake (as, for example, in cases dealing with voting rights, environmental issues, or public assistance) that might make the harm more important than, at first glance, it appears.

The fact that New Hampshire law guarantees free bus transportation does not seem sufficient to create a constitutionally protected interest in the *suspension-free* service that appellants seek. In deciding whether an interest in a government benefit rises to the level of protected property, the Supreme Court has us look to the reasonable expectations of those who receive the benefit. "It is a purpose of the ancient institution of property," the Court has written, "to protect those claims upon which people rely in their daily lives." While the New Hampshire statute could have created a reasonable expectation of bus service here, it could not have led the appellants to expect service *free of short suspensions*. The vagaries of weather, equipment failures, labor disputes, safety problems, and other similar occurrences, make it reasonable for riders to expect occasional interruptions in service for reasons of the sort at issue here. There thus could be no reasonable expectation, derived from the statute, of continuous service without suspensions. And since, as previously pointed out, the deprivation itself caused only inconvenience, not loss of educational opportunity or other significant injury, we believe it is a "de minimis" deprivation that does not call for constitutional "Due Process" protection.

Even if there were constitutionally protected "property" at stake, however, the appellants received the "process" they are "due." In determining whether "due process" requires a particular procedural safeguard (say, a hearing prior to deprivation), we are to take at least three factors into account: 1) the value or importance of the property interest at stake; 2) the probability of an erroneous deprivation if the safeguard is not provided; and 3) the cost of, or the burden imposed by, the safeguard.

In this case, as already pointed out, the importance of the property interest is small. The likelihood of an erroneous deprivation without a prior hearing, however, is significant. The Board's policy deprives students of bus transportation who took no part in any trouble-making activities. A prior hearing might prevent this, but at substantial cost— namely, the cost of abandoning the suspension program altogether. The program was instituted because the Board could not identify the trouble-makers in advance. To require an individual hearing is to require identification before suspension—the very thing the Board is unable to do.

The issue then comes down to the reasonableness of the suspension program itself. Appellants * * * claim that the program is inherently unreasonable, for it punishes the "innocent" along with the "guilty." We are not dealing here, however, with criminal punishments or with sending someone to prison without evidence. At issue is discipline on school buses, quite another matter, and one where the lessons drawn from criminal trials may not be totally appropriate. On the one hand, the notion of penalizing a whole class (by, say, keeping them after school or cancelling "recess") because of trouble caused by a few is (or at least used to be) fairly common in the world of school discipline. The serious risks and dangers associated with throwing objects in and outside of moving buses, on the other hand, are obvious, and warrant serious measures aimed at avoiding them. Moreover, the Board here has held full hearings on its policy, it has considered alternatives, and it has decided that its policy offers the most promising avenue to avoid vandalism, disruption, and driving hazards on school buses. We cannot find that judgment unreasonable, particularly when the Supreme Court "has repeatedly emphasized the need for affirming the comprehensive authority of the States and * * * school officials, consistent with fundamental constitutional safeguards, to prescribe and control conduct in the schools." Tinker v. Des Moines Independent Community School District.

From a constitutional perspective, then, we find no interests here at stake either sufficiently great in amount or fundamental in nature to require greater procedural protection than the Board has offered— particularly when increased protection would merely prevent the implementation of a reasonable disciplinary policy aimed at securing the safety of the children riding school buses.

For these reasons, the decision of the district court is

Affirmed.

Notes

1. The general concept of "group punishment" is at odds with the principle of individual guilt. Observe how this court responds under the facts present.

2. Parents, school authorities, and police have distinct but often intertwined roles in instances involving "vandalism and disruptive conduct" on school buses. Is a federal Court of Appeals the best place to settle such matters?

3. Is transportation to school a necessary element of a free public education, or could it be considered a privilege offered to those who do not abuse it?

4. Why did the court include the data to show that the policy could be deemed effective in curbing the problem? Under what circumstances can a

policy that is effective in its result be judicially struck down because of the means used?

[Case No. 42] Power of Board to Acquire Land for Off-Street Parking

IN RE SCHOOL DIST. OF PITTSBURGH

Supreme Court of Pennsylvania, 1968.
430 Pa. 566, 244 A.2d 42.

EAGEN, JUSTICE. * * *

On June 21, 1966, the Board of Public Education of the School District of Pittsburgh [hereinafter Board] passed a resolution authorizing the filing of declarations of taking for the involved properties [primarily to provide parking facilities at the School Administration Building]. * * * The lower court sustained the preliminary objections solely because it concluded that the Board's condemnation power does not extend to the acquisition of land for parking facilities for administrative employees.

The Board's condemnation power flows from the Act of March 10, 1949, P.L. 30, Art. VII, 24 P.S. § 7–701 et seq. Section 703, 24 P.S. § 7–703 provides:

> "In order to comply with the provisions of this act, and subject to the conditions thereof, the board of school directors of each district is hereby vested with the necessary power and authority to acquire, in the name of the district, by purchase, lease, gift, devise, agreement, condemnation, or otherwise, any and all such real estate * * * as the board of school directors may deem necessary to furnish suitable sites for proper school purposes for said district * * *."

Section 721, 24 P.S. § 7–721 provides:

> "Whenever the board of school directors of any district cannot agree on the terms of its purchase with the owner or owners of any real estate that the board has selected for school purposes, such board of school directors, after having decided upon the amount and location thereof may enter upon, take possession of, and occupy such land as it may have selected for school purposes, whether vacant or occupied, and designate and mark the boundary lines thereof, and thereafter may use the same for school purposes according to the provisions of this act * * *."

The precise issue presented here is whether the lower court correctly determined that the acquisition of land for parking facilities for employees and visitors to the School Administration Building is not a "proper school purpose" within the meaning of the Act of March 10, 1949, supra.

In interpreting the statute we must, of course, bear in mind that provisions conferring the power of eminent domain must be strictly construed. Strict construction does not require, however, that a statute be construed as narrowly as possible, or that it be construed so literally and without common sense that its obvious intent is frustrated.

A close examination of Section 703 of March 10, 1949, supra, indicates that the power and authority of the Board to acquire real estate is limited to acquisition "for proper school purposes" not only when the acquisition is by condemnation, but also when it is by "purchase, lease, gift, devise, agreement * * * or otherwise." Thus, if the Board cannot condemn real estate for the purpose of using it as a parking lot, it apparently cannot lease, purchase or otherwise acquire real estate for parking purposes. To deny the Board this power is serious not only because off street parking usually is desirable for buildings located in congested urban areas, but also because this Court has held that a school board may be compelled to comply with a zoning ordinance requiring provision for off street parking in the erection of a new building. School District of Philadelphia v. Zoning Board of Adjustment, 417 Pa. 277, 207 A.2d 864 (1965).

In approaching the question of whether or not the legislature intended to deny the Board this power, it is significant that the phrase "proper school purposes" in Section 703 of the Act of March 10, 1949, supra, replaced the phrase "school buildings and playgrounds" in Section 602 of the Act of May 18, 1911, P.L. 309. This substitution, fairly read, not only left the Board's power less precisely defined, but also broadened it somewhat. Thus the acquisition of a building to be used solely for administration undoubtedly is for a proper school purpose although an administration building may not be unquestionably within the term "schoolbuilding," which could be read to imply a school house where classes are held.

We think that the acquisition of land for off street parking for school district facilities, including an administration building, is for a "proper school purpose." With particular reference to an administration building, there are two obvious reasons why numerous automobiles are incident to its operation. First, superintendents and supervisors that have central offices in an administration building must have occasion when duty requires their presence in scattered parts of the school district. The availability and effectiveness of these professionals no doubt is greatly enhanced by their use of automobile transportation. Second, teachers, principals and other staff scattered throughout the school system must have occasion when they are required to attend meetings together in the central administration building. To do so without an excessive investment in time, they frequently will have to use automobile transportation. With reference to any school district facility, automobiles will be incident to its operation for other reasons. For instance, professionals, as well as secretarial, clerical and maintenance staff, may not accept employment unless they can commute to and from work by automobile. This might be common in areas where public transportation does not serve either the employee's home or the school district's facility. Even where public transportation is available, we must recognize that today a great part of the public is unwilling to use it because they are almost addicted to the convenience and independence provided by the automobile. Since automobiles are a necessary incident to the operation of school district facilities, off street parking is a practical necessity. The streets simply are not adequate and sometimes are not available for parking. Consequently, the acquisition of land for off street parking, which is a practical necessity to the effective and efficient operation of a school system, is certainly a "proper school purpose." To interpret the statute any more narrowly would be to frustrate its obvious intent to delegate to the Board authority to discharge the legislature's constitutional obligation to provide for an efficient public school system.

* * *

Reversed. * * *

Notes

1. In School District of Philadelphia v. Zoning Board of Adjustment, cited by the court, although the district had acquired land involved in that case by condemnation, the question of its power to do so was not before the court.

2. The court recognizes that school employees are almost "addicted to the convenience" provided by the automobile. Might this "addiction" apply also to pupils? If so, would the procurement of land for parking students' automobiles be "for a proper school purpose"? Note that in the instant case, parking space was to be provided only for school officials and employees at the administration building.

3. In Wayman v. Board of Educ., 5 Ohio St.2d 248, 215 N.E.2d 394 (1966), the Supreme Court of Ohio upheld the discretionary power of a school board to create a parking lot, but it held that if such created a nuisance, an injunction could be sought by one whose property was endangered or damaged thereby.

4. Under a statute granting the power of eminent domain to school districts for school purposes, its exercise has been upheld for an administration building for the school superintendent and his staff. Smith v. City Bd. of Educ. of Birmingham, 272 Ala. 227, 130 So.2d 29 (1961).

[Case No. 43] Power of Board to Employ Consultant—Contract Formulation

RYAN v. WARREN TP. HIGH SCHOOL DIST. NO. 121

Appellate Court of Illinois, 1987.
155 Ill.App.3d 203, 109 Ill.Dec. 843, 510 N.E.2d 911.

JUSTICE WOODWARD delivered the opinion of the court. Defendant, Warren Township High School District No. 121 (hereinafter school district), appeals from a judgment entered for the plaintiff, Keith Ryan and against the school district in the amount of $1,975. On appeal, the school district contends that it lacked the authority under the School Code (Ill.Rev.Stat.1985, ch. 122, par. 10–20.21) to contract for plaintiff's services, and that the contract was unenforceable because it violated the Election Interference Prohibition Act.

Plaintiff, the only witness in the case, testified that in September 1985, he was working as a public relations manager for Clausing and

Company. He was contacted by Dr. Paul Rundio, the superintendent of the school district, who requested a cost estimate of plaintiff's services. At that time, the school district had decided to raze Warren High School, which had been damaged by fire, and build a new school. However, community members who opposed the school district's plan instituted a lawsuit to block the destruction of the school. Dr. Rundio hired plaintiff to act as a liaison with members of the press and the community, to issue press releases, and to hold public meetings. The term of plaintiff's employment was from September to November 1985, prior to the school board elections.

Plaintiff submitted an itemized proposal and cost estimate totaling $5,000 to Dr. Rundio. Plaintiff was unaware of any public school board meeting adopting his oral contract negotiated with Dr. Rundio. The school district paid an interim bill for plaintiff's services in the amount of $3,200. On November 1, 1985, plaintiff submitted a second bill on the amount of $1,975 to the school district. When the school district refused payment, plaintiff filed this lawsuit.

* * *

The school district contends first that it did not have the authority to contract with plaintiff, so the contract is null and void.

Contracts entered into by a public body which are prohibited by an express provision of the law, or which under no circumstances could be legally entered into, are uniformly held to be *ultra vires* and void. While statutes granting powers to school boards must be strictly construed, a school board has the power expressly conferred and such powers as may be necessary to carry into effect those expressly granted. We conclude that the contract was not prohibited by an express provision of the School Code, and our interpretation of the School Code permits entering into the contract.

Implicit in the school district's power to hold regular and special meetings open to the public is the need to disseminate information to the public and receive feedback from the community. The School Code specifies that the school district should hold meetings where the members of the public are afforded an opportunity to question the board or to comment. Hiring a public relations consultant would enhance the school district's communication with the public especially where the parties described relations between them as "explosive" and "turbulent." Plaintiff arranged public meetings and tours of the old school and generally assisted the board in communicating with the public. Section 10–20.21 of the School Code contemplates the hiring of professionals and highly skilled individuals for their services, although a public relations consultant is not specifically listed. While we express no opinion regarding the board's judgment in hiring a public relations consultant, we conclude that the School Code does not prohibit entering into a contract with the plaintiff.

Defendant's reliance on *Evans v. Benjamin School District No. 25* for the proposition that the school district's actions are limited to the express provisions of the School Code is misplaced. The facts in *Evans* are distinguishable from the case at bar. At issue in *Evans* was the school board's power to grant tenure to a teacher. The teacher had not met the standards set out in section 24–11 of the Illinois School Code. The school district could not ignore the provision and grant tenure based on its own discretion. In this case, the legislature had not sought to provide specifications governing the hiring of consultants.

While the school district's actions were not void and *ultra vires,* no evidence exists establishing that the school district had voted to authorize an expenditure for plaintiff's fees. Section 10–7 of the School Code provides in relevant part:

> "On all questions involving the expenditure of money, the yeas and nays shall be taken and entered on the records of the proceedings of the board. * * *

Plaintiff testified that, to his knowledge, no meeting of the board occurred for the purpose of hiring him or approving the expenditure of his fees. By failing to call a meeting in order to authorize an expenditure for plaintiff's services, the school district irregularly contracted with the plaintiff. The parties do not dispute the trial court's finding that the board irregularly exercised its power in hiring the plaintiff.

Courts have distinguished between cases where the school district was utterly without the power to make a contract and cases in which it had the power, but exercised it in an irregular fashion. In the latter case, it is well settled that the conduct is merely voidable, and plaintiff may recover in *quantum meruit.* The rationale is as follows:

> "Contracts entered into by a municipality which are expressly prohibited by law, and which under no circumstances can be entered into, are void and ultra vires. They may not be rendered valid thereafter by estoppel or ratification of the municipality. However, there is another class of municipality contracts, distinct from the void type heretofore referred to, wherein the municipality has the power to enter into the contract, but where a portion thereof may be beyond its power, or its power may have been irregularly exercised. As to this class of contracts, a municipality may not assert its want of authority, or power, or the irregular exercise thereof, where to do so would give it an unconscionable advantage over the other party. Municipal corporations, as well as private corporations and individuals, are bound by principles of common honesty and fair dealing."

Therefore, although the contract was irregularly entered into, plaintiff is entitled to be reimbursed for his services where the school district ratified the contract by accepting the services and by making the partial payment.

* * * [P]laintiff's services continued for several months with the board's full knowledge as all the members knew of the public meetings scheduled by the plaintiff, his helping them with interviews, and his

discussion with them of ideas for various committees. In this case also, both parties agree that the hiring was done in an irregular fashion.

Defendant's final contention is that the contract is void since it violates the Election Interference Prohibition Act. Section 103 of that Act states as follows:

> "No public funds shall be used to urge any elector to vote for or against any candidate or proposition, or be appropriated for political or campaign purposes to any candidate or political organization. This provision shall not prohibit the use of public funds for dissemination of factual information relative to any proposition appearing on an election ballot * * *.

The school district alleges that the school board hired the plaintiff as a propagandist to market its decision within days of an election involving the very board members who hired the public relations consultant. Defendants, however, do not support their allegations with any specific facts. Further, even if the allegations were true, the plaintiff was only promoting the board's idea which was to build a new school rather that promoting the candidates themselves.

* * *

Affirmed.

Notes

1. Procedures for employing professionals not engaged in the education function (e.g., architects, physicians, lawyers) are generally not covered by competitive bidding statutes. The implied power of boards to engage such individuals is discussed in the text of this chapter.

2. See Chapter 8 for discussion of the general contracting power and contract liability of boards.

3. Reconcile this case with Case No. 145. (Be sure to note the specificity of the statutory bar in the Election Interference Prohibition Act.)

4. Reconcile this case with Case No. 89. (Note that here the school district made a payment to Ryan.)

[Case No. 44] Power of Board to Pay Superintendent to Resign

INGRAM v. BOONE

Supreme Court, Appellate Division [New York], 1983.
91 A.D.2d 1063, 458 N.Y.S.2d 671.

MEMORANDUM BY THE COURT. * * *

Petitioners are taxpaying residents of the Union Free School District # 1 of the Town of Hempstead. * * * They have commenced the instant proceeding to review an agreement entered into between the board of education of the school district and the district superintendent, alleging it was violative of the statutory and constitutional law of this State.

In August, 1980 Dr. Oliver Lancaster contracted with the board of education to serve as superintendent of schools for a period of four years commencing July 1, 1980. Approximately one year later, in the fall of 1981, a dispute allegedly arose between the board of education and Dr. Lancaster concerning his performance as superintendent. The board entered into negotiations with Lancaster in an effort to obtain his resignation which negotiations culminated in a resolution proposed at a public meeting of the board held on December 17, 1981 whereby Dr. Lancaster would resign effective December 31, 1981, the school district would pay him a lump sum of $65,000 and the board would continue Dr. Lancaster's insurance under several policies until the termination date of his employment contract or until he received insurance coverage from another source, whichever date occurred first. The resolution was approved by a vote of four to zero with one abstention. Thereafter, a formal stipulation was executed and general releases were signed. By order to show cause dated December 31, 1981 petitioners instituted the instant proceeding in which they challenge the lawfulness of the subject agreement.

Petitioners had standing to commence this proceeding by virtue of section 1 of article VIII of the State Constitution which forbids gifts of public funds. However, the payment of public funds as damages for breach of a contractual obligation or in settlement of a contested claim is not prohibited by this constitutional provision. On the record before us, it is impossible to determine whether the payment to Dr. Lancaster can be construed as a settlement of a legitimate claim or whether it is, in fact, a gift of public moneys. A mere claim of exercise of discretion and judgment is not enough, in the absence of competent proof, to validate the payment. Accordingly, [the trial court] properly directed that a hearing on this question be held.

Notes

1. The common law permits termination of an employee's contract where the employer can prove incompetence even if there are no provisions within the contract for termination. Here there was no information given as to the contract provisions, except for the term of four years.

2. Also, the common law permits termination of a contract by either party, subject to payment of damages if the termination constitutes a violation (breach) of the agreement.

3. Also, the common law permits termination by mutual assent, which is what occurred here. The basic issue, of course, is whether public policy is served in a situation where the taxpayers have to pay for services not rendered. Requiring proof "to validate the payment" is a judicial approach to protecting the public treasury, while not preventing a board from trying to correct what it perceives as a past error, and while not precluding an employee's willingness to forego some possible benefits in exchange for some compensation.

4. The Supreme Court of New Mexico has held that no hearing is required before a school board can suspend the superintendent with full salary for the three months remaining on his contract period. The court said this did not amount to a discharge, for which a hearing would have been required. Black v. Board of Educ. of Jemez Mountain School Dist. No. 53, 87 N.M. 45, 529 P.2d 271 (1974).

5.   The Supreme Court of Wyoming, in a decision invalidating the purchase of the remainder of a superintendent's contract on the ground that the special board meeting was not properly called, commented that there was "grave doubt about the matter" itself.   Twitchell v. Bowman, 440 P.2d 513 (Wyo.1968).

6.   "The public has a right to know the terms upon which a public employer has settled with a resigning contract employee."   So saying, the Supreme Judicial Court of Maine ordered the disclosure of the agreement between the state university and the former coach of its women's basketball team with the exception of a sentence containing medical information.   Guy Gannett Publishing Co. v. University of Maine, 555 A.2d 470 (Me.1989).

[Case No. 45] Control of School Activities and Funds by Committee of Board

IN RE GERMAN TP. SCHOOL DIRECTORS

District and County Court of Pennsylvania, 1943.
46 Pa. D. & C. 562.

[Suit was brought to remove members of the board of directors for failure to perform certain mandatory duties.   A number of derelictions were charged against the board members but only that portion of the decision dealing with the delegation of control of school activities and funds to a committee of the board will be reported here.]

DUMBAULD, P.J.   * * * Here we find a very interesting and somewhat controversial question for consideration.   Respondents, as members of the school board, have proceeded upon the theory that athletic activities, high school band organizations, and other extra-curricular activities may be entirely segregated from the supervision and control of the board as a board.   They contend that they may delegate to an appointive athletic control board all jurisdiction over the activities mentioned, and the handling of the finances incident to such management.   They insist that the purchase of equipment for athletic teams and uniforms for the high school band and the expenditure of the proceeds arising from these activities are entirely a matter for the athletic board of control without any supervisory action over the conduct of this committee by the board as a whole.   The members of the board who are not members of the athletic board of control seek to absolve themselves from their failure to exercise supervision by testifying that they are completely without knowledge of the financial transactions involved in the equipment of the athletic teams and the furnishing of uniforms for the band.   Accepting this theory, the board of control deposited the proceeds of the athletic games in a bank, not a depository, and checked out the fund in payment of bills for these departments without any attempt to comply with the provisions of the code as to the manner of authorizing and making payments by the school board.   In short, the funds arising from this form of extra-curricular activities never reach the treasury of the school board, nor is the account audited by the township auditors.

Thus we find that, on February 12, 1940, the board, as a board, authorized and drew a voucher in payment of a bill of Dice-Spalding Company, amounting to $965.30, on account of the bill of that company for athletic supplies and equipment, for use in games taken part in or played by pupils as members of the football team of the high school of the German Township School District. This bill was paid without advertisement for bids, receipt of such bids, or letting of a contract. It was paid simply because the athletic board of control or persons authorized by it had purchased equipment for the football team for the payment of which there appears not to have been sufficient money in the account of the athletic board of control at its bank.

During the school year of 1940–1941, the athletic board of control bought from D. Klein & Bros., Inc., through its agent, John Trump, uniforms for the high school band, costing $1,531.40. The check in payment of this item was drawn by the athletic board of control by O.R. Younkin, treasurer, on the Second National Bank of Masontown.

The members of the school board, not members of the athletic board of control, divorce themselves entirely from any act or responsibility in connection with this item of equipment.

* * *

* * * The members of the band, who received instructions in playing the various instruments used in such an organization, and who take part in the varied exercises that take place on the football field, particularly between the halves of the game, are as much a part of the student body as are those who specialize in intellectual achievements.

The comparatively small number of athletically inclined boys who survive the rigors of the training period and carry the colors of the school on the football field are not to be regarded as separate from the great body of pupils in the public schools who are not able, or do not choose, to participate in this line of endeavor.

If this selected few acquiring such special skill in the playing of the game of football, and the relatively small number of pupils who comprise the high school band, by their combined efforts are able to attract large crowds of spectators who are willing to pay substantial admission prices for the entertainment furnished, such students and such activities may not be regarded as a separate institution, subject only to the supervision of the athletic board of control. They constitute a unit or department of the entire school system. They receive no part of the prices of admission. They do not perform for the athletic board of control. They carry on for alma mater. The proceeds of these activities belong to the board of school directors and must be accounted for in the same manner that other funds of the school district are accounted for.

The legal status of these activities and the duty of the board of school directors with reference thereto have been clearly stated by Mr. Justice Stern, in the case of Galloway v. Prospect Park Borough School District, 331 Pa. 48, 50:

  " * * * Physical education is as much a part of the school curriculum as are subjects of intellectual study, and athletic supplies, therefore, are as 'necessary for school use' as maps, globes, and similar objects. It is not the spirit of our public school system that only children with financial means to purchase their own supplies should have the opportunity of participating in school games and athletic sports. Of course, the extent to which athletic paraphernalia should be purchased for use merely by school teams playing in competitive sports is a question to be answered by school boards in the exercise of a cautious discretion, with special reference to the proportionate number of those who will receive the benefit of such supplies."

This cautious discretion cannot be exercised by an attempt, in the form of a resolution, to delegate to an athletic board of control the entire subject of extra-curricular activities. The requirement that supplies exceeding in cost a certain amount shall be advertised for, and the contract for their furnishing let to the lowest bidder applies to all such supplies as those furnished for the football team and the band uniforms.

The provision of section 403 of the code that requires the names of the directors and the manner in which they voted to be recorded in the letting of contracts for such supplies is also applicable to the transactions mentioned. When a director testifies that he knows nothing about the transactions delegated to the athletic board of control, he admits himself negligent in the performance of his statutory duty. It is a mandatory duty that the board shall supervise, control, and comply with the statutory provisions, as to all receipts and expenditures undertaken by the athletic board of control.

* * *

The school board may hereafter continue to permit the athletic board of control to manage and direct extra-curricular activities, but all moneys received therefrom and all expenditures for equipment to be used therein, must be reported to and approved by the board of directors as a board. The board of athletic control must be considered merely as a committee, with like powers and duties as the teachers' committee, the committee on supplies, or the building committee. * * *

* * *

Notes

1. If the "entire subject of extra-curricular activities" cannot be delegated to a committee of the board, what can be delegated to it? See Chapter 14.

2. How do you react to this decision from an educational point of view?

3. Note the court's statement that when a school board member testifies that he knows nothing about transactions delegated to a committee of the board, "he admits himself negligent in the performance of his statutory duty."

4. Acting under a statute providing that it shall prescribe the accounts by which funds for school districts shall be budgeted, the state board of education has wide discretion in determining what will be current expense items and what will be capital outlay expenditures. St. Louis-San Francisco Railway v. McCurtain County, 352 P.2d 896 (Okl.1960).

[Case No. 46] Use of School Building for Religious Purposes

RESNICK v. EAST BRUNSWICK TP. BD. OF EDUC.

Supreme Court of New Jersey, 1978.
77 N.J. 88, 389 A.2d 944.

PASHMAN, J. The relationship of church and state has become one of the most sensitive areas in the law. Permitting religious observances to take place on public school property raises important and vexing constitutional issues. To some persons, use of school premises by any group necessarily carries with it the appearance of government approval of that body and its activities. Thus, whenever an issue involving the use of school property for religious purposes arises, our inquiry must be particularly searching. The specific controversy in this appeal concerns the extent to which public school facilities may be used for religious instruction and services when they are not being used for regular educational purposes.

Since 1962 defendant East Brunswick Township School Board has allowed a number of local groups to use its school facilities during non-school hours. The lessees of school premises have included various religious groups as well as other nonprofit social, civic, recreational and charitable groups. * * *

A rental is assessed which approximates the cost of janitorial services. Where a group is using the facilities for fund raising purposes or if admission is charged, a substantially higher rental is assessed in accordance with a published rental schedule. (Apparently fund raising does not include collections taken during religious services, as the higher rental for such activity was not charged the religious organizations.) * * *

Starting in 1969 the East Brunswick Baptist Church had rented an all-purpose room in an elementary school for religious services and ten classrooms for religious instruction on Sundays. The all-purpose room was also rented for Wednesday evening prayer meetings. Bibles, hymnals and a wooden pulpit with a cross were stored in a closet off the all-purpose room, along with school recreational equipment. The Church owned a five acre building site in the township and as of the trial date had retained an architect, an engineer and had applied for site plan approval to the township planning board. At the time of oral argument before this Court, the East Brunswick Baptist Church no longer used the school.

Nativity Evangelical Lutheran Church began renting facilities in an elementary school in September 1968. It used the school for religious instruction on Sundays, occupying the all-purpose room and some ten classrooms. Sunday school literature and materials were locked in a cabinet. The Church has a separate building for worship. At the time of the trial the Church had employed an architect to plan an addition to its building for purposes of having classrooms for religious education. At present, the Lutheran Church is not making use of school facilities.

Since March 1973 the Reform Temple of East Brunswick has rented most of an elementary school building for services and instruction for five hours on Sundays. It also rents the gymnasium for religious services and social gatherings on Friday evenings and five classrooms for Hebrew language instruction for children on Tuesday and Thursday evenings. A few religious artifacts were stored in the schools. The Reform Temple had an option to purchase a building site at the time of the trial and had also retained an architect. However, the building has not been completed, and use of the school continued as of the date of oral argument. (As of the date of this opinion, the Jewish Reform Temple is no longer using school premises. However, three other religious groups in East Brunswick are using public school facilities. Despite the fact that none of the original defendants is using the schools at the present time, we do not deem this case to be moot. We have determined that this is a question of public importance and thus will address the merits.)

* * *

[The court examined the statute enabling school boards to permit use of school buildings by nonschool groups for various purposes and found that it covered religious uses. Further, it found no bar to such uses in the state constitution.]

Federal Constitutional Grounds

The First Amendment requires strict governmental neutrality with respect to religion. * * * The only issue of concern to us is whether permitting religious groups to rent public school facilities at a rate reflective of the cost incurred by the school board as a result of such use runs afoul of the "establishment clause." * * *

While there is a split among jurisdictions as to whether it is constitutionally permissible for public school premises to be used for religious purposes, the only case within the last 35 years which addressed the federal constitutional issue upheld the use. In Southside Estates Bapt. Church v. Bd. of Trustees, the Supreme Court of Florida held that public schools could be used temporarily as a place of worship during non-school hours. The record did not indicate whether rent was paid by the users or expenses were incurred by the school trustees. The relevant Florida statute permitted use of school buildings during non-school hours "for any legal assembly." The court rejected the view that the public was impermissibly subsidizing religion.

> Taking note of appellant's insistence that the use of the building is something of value and that the wear and tear is an indirect contribution from the public treasury, it appears to us that we might properly apply the maxim *De minimis non curat lex.*

The court also found that no impermissible preference for one sect over another existed since four or five religious groups had been accorded the same treatment. However, the court indicated that its decision might have been different had the case involved a situation where a church contemplated permanent use of school facilities. No outer boundary was set as to how long use of the schools could continue. Instead, local boards were given reasonable discretion as to determining the use of school buildings, " * * * subject of course, to judicial review should such discretion be abused to the point that it could be construed as a contribution of public funds to a particular religious group or as the promotion or establishment of a particular religion."

In the absence of any subsequent developments in this area, we would stop here and reverse those parts of the judgment below which conflict with the analysis in Southside Estates Bapt. Church v. Bd. of Trustees, supra. However, several recent opinions by the United States Supreme Court have further refined the analysis to be applied in determining whether a given relationship between church and state is permissible.

* * *

Considering these precedents, we unequivocally find that pursuant to [the enabling statute] and under the Board's "Statement of Philosophy," there was a secular purpose in leasing the school facilities. That purpose was to enhance public use of these properties for the common benefit of the residents of East Brunswick. There was no allegation of a lack of good faith on the part of the School Board in adopting the regulations. Thus, we have no reason to doubt its stated purposes.

Many statutory schemes found to be permissible under a secular purpose test have nevertheless foundered when the Supreme Court determined that their primary effect was to advance religion. * * *

* * *

The primary intent of [the statute] is to grant school boards wide discretion in permitting use of school property when schools are not in session. The primary effect of the "Rules and Regulations Governing Use of East Brunswick School Facilities" is to benefit nonprofit community groups. While we would be naive in refusing to note the obvious advantages to young congregations in the temporary use of school premises, to hold that this scheme primarily benefits religion would be absurd. The community as a whole is benefitted when nonprofit organizations of interest to its members prosper.

Moreover, the religious groups do not have unrestrained use of valuable property * * *. They may only use the facilities when school related activities are not scheduled, and where another organization has not already claimed a given time slot. Religious groups have heretofore received evenhanded treatment in requesting facilities and we trust that this practice will continue in the future.

The regulations promulgated by the East Brunswick Board pursuant to [the statute] aid nonprofit organizations in general and religious groups only incidentally. The record shows that such groups as the Parent-Teacher Association, drama clubs, Girl Scouts, Boy Scouts, Cub Scouts, Brownies, square dancing, garden clubs, a drum and bugle corps,

St. Bartholomew's basketball team, civic associations, and Township recreation groups have used the schools. They are also used for election purposes and for Township health testing. A Chinese language school uses the facilities, too. Thus, the fact that school facilities are also used by religious groups does not render the regulations invalid as primarily advancing religion.

We also note that in Everson v. Bd. of Education, the Supreme Court upheld a New Jersey statute which provided funds for busing students to schools—including parochial schools. * * *

* * * We conclude that if actual taxpayer outlays to bus children to denominational schools are permissible, there is no question that incidental expenses of wear and tear on school property when used during non-instructional hours for religious worship and teaching as well as a myriad of other activities are not a public expense primarily for the benefit of religion.

Of further significance is Bd. of Ed. of Central School District No. 1 v. Allen, where the Court upheld a New York law authorizing the provision of secular textbooks for all children in grades 7 through 12 attending public and nonpublic schools. This, too, strikes us as being a scheme more fraught with the danger of being primarily beneficial to religion than is that at bar.

* * *

We conclude * * * that the temporary use of public school facilities by religious groups does not run afoul of the prohibition against legislation primarily benefitting religion. Where essentially no public expense is incurred as a result of a benefit received by religious groups, we do not believe that the "significantly religious" character of those groups should preclude their receipt of such a benefit on the same terms as to other groups of the same class, i.e., nonprofit organizations.

* * *

This case is not precisely analogous to any of the United States Supreme Court decisions dealing with entanglement. Those cases all involved some type of direct grant of materials or money to sectarian schools, or involved tax credits or rebates specifically directed to the aid of parents with children in such institutions. In short, there was some significant effect on the public purse. Conversely, the only conceivable public expense in the East Brunswick scheme, as we have modified it, is a degree of wear and tear on school properties. Another common factor in the federal cases was the charge that continued entanglement between government and religion would tend to verge on government sponsorship of religion.

* * *

The instant case is distinguishable. No significant administrative function is involved. The processing of an application by a clerk is hardly an act of excessive entanglement. Moreover, inasmuch as no use of school premises is made during regular school hours, there is no need of supervision to insure that no religion seeps into secular instruction. The danger of political fragmentation is miniscule, as appropriations are not involved. The mere fact that some persons in the community oppose the use of the schools by sectarian groups should not prevent these groups from enjoying the benefits of premises which the tax dollars of many of their members helped to construct.

* * * In *East Brunswick* the granting of a lease application is largely *pro forma* so long as the group involved has requested a time slot which does not conflict with school-related activities and which is not already filled by other nonprofit groups. It is more a ministerial than a discretionary determination. * * * There is no evidence in the record which so much as implies that the allocation of school facilities when the buildings are not in use for regular educational matters has caused any divisiveness in *East Brunswick*. While this Court is well advised to examine the implications of its decisions, it is not warranted in assuming, *sua sponte*, the worst conceivable state of facts for every problem it encounters.

The storage of religious artifacts and books in school closets would seem to be a minimal accommodation by the school district. * * * Of course, if it were shown that storage of these materials caused a shortage of closet space for school materials, such storage would be impermissible as an interference with public school education by religious groups. Without such a showing, or any indication that these artifacts are on prominent display while school is open, there is no constitutional infirmity in using some school closet space to store them.

Our only real concern under the entanglement test is with the lengthy use of these school premises by some of the religious groups. At some point, such continuous use will surely implicate the Board in the promotion of religion. However, notwithstanding the fact that several congregations have used school premises for a lengthy period of time, we do not intend to place a strict temporal limitation on use. In every instance, these religious groups have been diligently striving toward the procurement of their own houses of worship and instruction. However, we agree with the sentiments expressed by the Supreme Court of Florida in Southside Estates Bapt. Church v. Bd. of Trustees, that truly prolonged use of school facilities by a congregation without evidence of immediate intent to construct or purchase its own building would be impermissible. We leave it to our able trial courts to draw the line in this area, with the caveat that the continued leasing of East Brunswick school facilities from 1973 to the present by the Reform Temple is approaching the outer bounds of reasonable time and nearing the point of prohibited entanglement.

* * *

Perhaps the most important fact to remember is that contrary to the literal approach to the Establishment Clause advocated by plaintiff, in total disregard of historical reality, the Supreme Court has never required that government adopt a posture of total indifference toward religion. In fact, a more accurate assessment of the requirements of the

First Amendment is that the preferred governmental stance is one of benevolent neutrality. * * *

The East Brunswick scheme entails none of the dangers of the establishment of religion by government which the Constitution seeks to prevent. When one takes a calm look at the use of the school buildings there by religious groups, the dire predictions of sectarian sponsorship and political divisiveness conjured up by plaintiff seem rather silly.

We hold that religious groups who fully reimburse school boards for related out-of-pocket expenses may use school facilities on a temporary basis for religious services as well as educational classes. We further hold that the courts below erred in requiring these sectarian groups to pay a commercial rental rate and in placing the one-year limitation on their continued use of the school premises.

Subject to the requirement that taxpayers' funds not be expended for the benefit of religious groups, there is no reason why these organizations should not be accorded the same treatment by government as other nonprofit groups.

Reversed.

* * *

Notes

1. The federal constitutional tests applied in this case and the Supreme Court precedents referred to are covered in Chapter 2.

2. The Baptist Church "had applied for site plan approval" in 1975 at the time of the trial. It began using the school facilities in 1969. The Lutheran Church in 1975 "had employed an architect to plan an addition to its building." It began using the school facilities in 1968. The Reform Temple in 1975 "had an option to purchase a building site * * * and had also retained an architect." It began using the school facilities in 1973. Might the filing of the complaint in October of 1974, after unsuccessful public attempts to get the board to change its policy, have affected the attitude of these religious groups re obtaining their own facilities for religious purposes?

3. The court stated that the leasing of school facilities by a religious group for religious purposes for over five years at a cost covering only "out-of-pocket" expenses of the system was "nearing the point of prohibited entanglement." Might this conclusion (assuming its soundness) have been better supported by applying the "effect of aiding religion" test rather than the "excessive entanglement" test? (See Chapter 2.)

4. How do you react to the last sentence of the third full paragraph from the end of the opinion?

5. The trial court and the intermediate appellate court had read the enabling statute differently from the five-judge majority here. (Two judges dissented.)

[Case No. 47] Use of School Building for Social or Civic Purpose by Religious Group

LAMB'S CHAPEL v. CENTER MORICHES UNION FREE SCHOOL DIST.

Supreme Court of the United States, 1993.
___ U.S. ___, 113 S.Ct. 2141, 124 L.Ed.2d 352.

JUSTICE WHITE delivered the opinion of the Court.

Section 414 of the New York Education Law authorizes local school boards to adopt reasonable regulations for the use of school property for 10 specified purposes when the property is not in use for school purposes. Among the permitted uses is the holding of "social, civic and recreational meetings and entertainments, and other uses pertaining to the welfare of the community; but such meetings, entertainment and uses shall be non-exclusive and open to the general public." The list of permitted uses does not include meetings for religious purposes * * *.

Pursuant to § 414's empowerment of local school districts, the Board of Center Moriches Union Free School District (District) has issued rules and regulations with respect to the use of school property when not in use for school purposes. The rules allow only 2 of the 10 purposes authorized by § 414: social, civic, or recreational uses (Rule 10) and use by political organizations if secured in compliance with § 414 (Rule 8). Rule 7, however, consistent with the judicial interpretation of state law, provides that "[t]he school premises shall not be used by any group for religious purposes."

The issue in this case is whether, against this background of state law, it violates the Free Speech Clause of the First Amendment, made applicable to the States by the Fourteenth Amendment, to deny a church access to school premises to exhibit for public viewing and for assertedly religious purposes, a film dealing with family and child-rearing issues faced by parents today.

I

Petitioners (Church) are Lamb's Chapel, an evangelical church in the community of Center Moriches, and its pastor John Steigerwald. Twice the Church applied to the District for permission to use school facilities to show a six-part film series * * *. A brochure provided on request of the District * * * stated that the film series would discuss [a commentator's] views on the undermining influences of the media that could only be counterbalanced by returning to traditional, Christian family values instilled at an early stage. The brochure went on to describe the contents of each of the six parts of the series. The District denied the first application, saying that "[t]his film does appear to be church related and therefore your request must be refused." The second application for permission to use school premises for showing the film, which described it as a "Family oriented movie—from the Christian perspective," was denied using identical language.

[The District Court and the Court of Appeals held for the school district.]

* * *

II

There is no question that the District, like the private owner of property, may legally preserve the property under its control for the use to which it is dedicated. It is also common ground that the District need not have permitted after-hours use of its property for any of the uses permitted by § 414 of the state education law. The District, however, did open its property for 2 of the 10 uses permitted by § 414. The Church argued below that because under Rule 10 of the rules issued by the District, school property could be used for "social, civic, and recreational" purposes, the District had opened its property for such a wide variety of communicative purposes that restrictions on communicative uses of the property were subject to the same constitutional limitations as restrictions in traditional public fora such as parks and sidewalks. Hence, its view was that subject-matter or speaker exclusions on District property were required to be justified by a compelling state interest and to be narrowly drawn to achieve that end. Both the District Court and the Court of Appeals rejected this submission, which is also presented to this Court. The argument has considerable force, for the District's property is heavily used by a wide variety of private organizations, including some that presented a "close question," which the Court of Appeals resolved in the District's favor, as to whether the District had in fact already opened its property for religious uses. We need not rule on this issue, however, for even if the courts below were correct in this respect—and we shall assume for present purposes that they were—the judgment below must be reversed.

With respect to public property that is not a designated public forum open for indiscriminate public use for communicative purposes, we have said that "[c]ontrol over access to a nonpublic forum can be based on subject matter and speaker identity so long as the distinctions drawn are reasonable in light of the purpose served by the forum and are viewpoint neutral." The Court of Appeals appeared to recognize that the total ban on using District property for religious purposes could survive First Amendment challenge only if excluding this category of speech was reasonable and viewpoint neutral. The court's conclusion in this case was that Rule 7 met this test. We cannot agree with this holding, for Rule 7 was unconstitutionally applied in this case. (Although the Court of Appeals apparently held that Rule 7 was reasonable as well as viewpoint neutral, the court uttered not a word in support of its reasonableness holding. If Rule 7 were to be held unreasonable, it could be held facially invalid, that is, it might be held that the rule could in no circumstances be applied to religious speech or religious communicative conduct. In view of our disposition of this case, we need not pursue this issue.)

The Court of Appeals thought that the application of Rule 7 in this case was viewpoint neutral because it had been and would be applied in the same way to all uses of school property for religious purposes. That all religions and all uses for religious purposes are treated alike under Rule 7, however, does not answer the critical question whether it discriminates on the basis of viewpoint to permit school property to be used for the presentation of all views about family issues and child-rearing except those dealing with the subject matter from a religious standpoint.

There is no suggestion from the courts below or from the District or the State that a lecture or film about child-rearing and family values would not be a use for social or civic purposes otherwise permitted by Rule 10. That subject matter is not one that the District has placed off limits to any and all speakers. Nor is there any indication in the record before us that the application to exhibit the particular film involved here was or would have been denied for any reason other than the fact that the presentation would have been from a religious perspective. In our view, denial on that basis was plainly invalid * * * [in] that

> "[a]lthough a speaker may be excluded from a non-public forum if he wishes to address a topic not encompassed within the purpose of the forum * * * or if he is not a member of the class of speakers for whose special benefit the forum was created * * * the government violates the First Amendment when it denies access to a speaker solely to suppress the point of view he espouses on an otherwise includible subject."

The film involved here no doubt dealt with a subject otherwise permissible under Rule 10, and its exhibition was denied solely because the film dealt with the subject from a religious standpoint. The principle that has emerged from our cases "is that the First Amendment forbids the government to regulate speech in ways that favor some viewpoints or ideas at the expense of others." * * *

The District, as a respondent, would save its judgment below on the ground that to permit its property to be used for religious purposes would be an establishment of religion forbidden by the First Amendment. This Court suggested in *Widmar v. Vincent* that the interest of the State in avoiding an Establishment Clause violation "may be [a] compelling" one justifying an abridgment of free speech otherwise protected by the First Amendment; but the Court went on to hold that permitting use of University property for religious purposes under the open access policy involved there would not be incompatible with the Court's Establishment Clause cases.

We have no more trouble than did the *Widmar* Court in disposing of the claimed defense on the ground that the posited fears of an Establishment Clause violation are unfounded. The showing of this film would not have been during school hours, would not have been sponsored by the school, and would have been open to the public, not just to church members. The District property had repeatedly been used by a wide variety of private organizations. Under these circumstances, as in

Widmar, there would have been no realistic danger that the community would think that the District was endorsing religion or any particular creed, and any benefit to religion or to the Church would have been no more than incidental. As in *Widmar,* permitting District property to be used to exhibit the film involved in this case would not have been an establishment of religion under the three-part test articulated in *Lemon v. Kurtzman.* The challenged governmental action has a secular purpose, does not have the principal or primary effect of advancing or inhibiting religion, and does not foster an excessive entanglement with religion.

The District also submits that it justifiably denied use of its property to a "radical" church for the purpose of proselytizing, since to do so would lead to threats of public unrest and even violence. There is nothing in the record to support such a justification, which in any event would be difficult to defend as a reason to deny the presentation of a religious point of view about a subject the District otherwise makes open to discussion on District property.

* * *

The Attorney General also argues that there is no express finding below that the Church's application would have been granted absent the religious connection. This fact is beside the point for the purposes of this opinion, which is concerned with the validity of the stated reason for denying the Church's application, namely, that the film sought to be shown "appeared to be church related."

*   *   * *Reversed.*

Notes

1. The vote of the Justices was unanimous.

2. Observe that the Court's holding was narrow (the specific application of Rule 7). It is especially important to note precisely what the Court actually decided in this case and on what basis.

3. If the church had wanted to hold a "prayer meeting" or a "religious service," do you believe the board could have barred it?

4. Examine how the lower courts had erred in interpreting viewpoint neutrality. Also contemplate distinctions between viewpoint and subject.

[Case No. 48] Use of School Building for Performance by Controversial Singer

EAST MEADOW COMMUNITY CONCERTS ASS'N v.
BOARD OF EDUC. OF UNION FREE SCHOOL
DIST. NO. 3, COUNTY OF NASSAU

Court of Appeals of New York, 1966.
18 N.Y.2d 129, 272 N.Y.S.2d 341, 219 N.E.2d 172.

FULD, JUDGE. Involved in this litigation—which questions the right of the defendant school board to bar the folk singer, Pete Seeger, from giving a concert in one of its school buildings—are important issues of jurisdiction and constitutional law.

The plaintiff, a nonprofit educational and cultural association, has for its purpose the presentation of an annual series of musical concerts, and during the past 10 years it has been permitted by the defendant school board to present these concerts in the auditorium of a high school in East Meadow on Long Island. In June of 1965, following prior procedure, the defendant gave the plaintiff such permission for the 1965–1966 series, including a concert scheduled for March 12, 1966, which was to feature Pete Seeger as the performing artist. The concert was publicized and tickets for the series of three were sold. However, in December of 1965, the defendant withdrew the previously granted permission for the March 12 concert on the ground that, because he had given a concert in Moscow and because some of the songs he sings are critical of American policy in Viet Nam, Seeger is a "highly controversial figure" whose presence might provoke a disturbance with consequent damage to school property. Some time later that same month, the plaintiff instituted the present action in which it sought a judgment, in effect (1) declaring the defendant's action to be unconstitutional and (2) enjoining the defendant from interfering with the presentation of the scheduled concert in the school auditorium.

* * *

That the constitutional issues posed by this case are substantial and, indeed, of high public importance, there can be no doubt. The State is not under a duty to make school buildings available for public gatherings but, if it elects to do so, it is required, by constitutional provision (U.S. Const., 14th Amdt.; N.Y. Const., art. I, § 11), to grant the use of such facilities "in a reasonable and nondiscriminatory manner, equally applicable to all and administered with equality to all." The defendant has concededly allowed a number of organizations, including the very plaintiff before us, to use the school auditorium for nonacademic purposes for many years. It follows, therefore, that, in deciding who is to be permitted to use its school, the board must not unconstitutionally discriminate against the plaintiff.

Of course, this does not mean that the defendant board is prevented from barring the use of the school auditorium for an unlawful purpose, but in the case before us the justification asserted for canceling the permit is the unpopularity of Seeger's views rather than the unlawfulness of the plaintiff's concert. The expression of controversial and unpopular views, it is hardly necessary to observe, is precisely what is protected by both the Federal and State Constitutions. * * * Consequently, if there were no danger of immediate and irreparable injury to the public weal, the defendant's refusal to permit Seeger to appear at the March 12 concert would be an unlawful restriction of the constitutional right of free speech and expression.

* * *

Notes

1. What kind of evidence do you think would have to be produced in order for a school board to be able to prevent use of its facilities by a particular person or organization? The issue, of course, is that of "prior censorship."

2. Speaker bans have been declared unconstitutional in several jurisdictions, primarily on grounds of vagueness and denial of due process. See, for example, Snyder v. Board of Trustees of University of Illinois, 286 F.Supp. 927 (N.D.Ill.1968) [three-judge court], invalidating a statute regulating speakers at a state-supported university, and Brooks v. Auburn University, 412 F.2d 1171 (5 Cir.1969), enjoining a university president from barring a speaker. In the latter case the reasons given for barring the speaker had not previously been invoked, they were not in the rules and regulations of the institution, and the speaker had been approved under normal procedures before the president intervened. Under these circumstances, the speaker could be barred only if there was reason to believe he would advocate lawlessness in a way likely to incite such action.

3. Often the date of an event passes before the question of the right of the sponsors to use a public facility is judicially determined. This happened in the present case, but the court ordered another date to be set for the Seeger performance.

4. A board of education can grant access to its intra-school system mail facilities to the exclusive bargaining representative while barring use by a rival union. Perry Educ. Ass'n v. Perry Local Educators' Ass'n, 460 U.S. 37, 103 S.Ct. 948, 74 L.Ed.2d 794 (1983). (See "Restraints on Boards" in Chapter 10.)

[Case No. 49] Power of School Authorities to Bar Solicitation of Funds from Students

KATZ v. McAULAY

United States Court of Appeals, Second Circuit, 1971.
438 F.2d 1058.

ANDERSON, CIRCUIT JUDGE. The New York Board of Regents has a rule, some forty-seven years old, which prohibits "soliciting funds from the pupils in the public schools." Plaintiffs, four students at Ardsley High School, a public school in Westchester County, New York, brought this civil rights action for anticipatory relief against enforcement of that rule. Their action arose when school officials threatened plaintiffs with expulsion if they distributed on school premises leaflets soliciting funds from their fellow students.

More specifically, on February 6 and 9, 1970, plaintiffs distributed in the high school corridors a one-page leaflet entitled "Join the Conspiracy." In it they decried the prosecution of eight defendants then on trial in the District Court for the Northern District of Illinois and solicited funds for the "activists'" defense. The leaflet stated:

"More than $33,000 per month is spent on their defense. Money is desperately needed to give these people a just trial. Money is needed to pay for transcripts. PLEASE contribute and/or buy a button from Jane Katz, Carey Marvin, Greg Gottlieb or anyone else who is helping out."

The dissemination of leaflets occurred before the school day began, and the affidavits of school officials contain no evidence of a specific instance of interference by the plaintiffs with the operation of the school or of any demonstrable collision with the rights of other students to be let alone. Nonetheless, school officials warned plaintiffs that their circulation of leaflets violated the Board of Regents rule and a local Board of Education rule forbidding any "outside organization * * * to use this School * * * for the dissemination or release of information by flyers * * *" without first obtaining written approval of the Board.

Asserting the First Amendment overbreadth of both rules, plaintiffs sought a declaratory judgment declaring that "the policies, regulations and actions of the defendants * * * are unconstitutional" and preliminary and permanent injunctions restraining defendants from taking disciplinary action against students distributing this leaflet or any other leaflet soliciting funds for causes involving "matters of public interest." The court below denied plaintiffs' motion for a preliminary injunction and found that the Board of Regents' rule "was not intended to prevent the exercise of free speech" but rather set forth a reasonable regulation "to protect school children from annoyance at the hands of solicitors eager, for one cause or another, to induce them to part with their pocket money." * * *

* * *

The constitutional guarantee of free speech limits state power to regulate the personal intercommunication of secondary school pupils. Tinker v. Des Moines Independent Community School District. From this premise plaintiffs contend the distribution of leaflets which "communicat[e] thoughts between citizens, and discuss * * * public questions" is protected expression and that such expression is no less protected by virtue of the fact that solicitation of contributions is an integral part thereof.

Assuming that plaintiffs' activity was "speech" within the meaning of the First Amendment, school officials had the burden of showing governmental interests which might justify their interference with that "speech." The Supreme Court has repeatedly affirmed that such an interest lies in the implementation of "the comprehensive authority of the States and of school officials, consistent with fundamental constitutional safeguards, to prescribe and control conduct in the schools." Tinker v. Des Moines Independent Community School District; see Epperson v. Arkansas. The exercise of such authority may not, however, abridge the free expression of students in the public high schools unless that expression "materially and substantially interfere[s] with the requirements of appropriate discipline in the operation of the school." Tinker v. Des Moines Independent Community School District.

Though the skeletal evidentiary matter before the trial court disclosed minimal potential interference at most, the probability that plaintiffs' overbreadth contention would prevail at trial is so slight that the denial of preliminary relief cannot be held to have constituted an abuse of discretion. Unlike the amorphous "regulations" in Sullivan v. Houston Independent School District, 307 F.Supp. 1328 (S.D.Tex.1969), the Board of Regents' rule articulated its proscription in terms of those non-expressive features of student conduct which raise a sufficiently high probability of harm—i.e. the pressures upon students of multiple solicitations (the affidavit of the Superintendent of Schools states that some 75 to 100 requests to use school properties for solicitation of funds have been denied in the past twelve years.)—to justify the Board's interference with such communicative conduct.

Pupils are on school premises in response to the statutory requirement that they attend school for the purpose of formal education. Where outside organizations or individuals espousing various causes seek to take advantage of the required assemblage of secondary school pupils, as a captive audience, to solicit funds, either directly or through the agency of some of the pupils, for their particular project or cause, they are in effect in competition for the time, attention and interest of the pupils with those who are seeking to administer the school system. Whether it is done a few minutes before school opens or a few minutes after, its effect is not so limited in time and it is plainly harmful to the operation of the public schools. If there is no regulation against it, literally dozens of organizations and causes may importune pupils to solicit on their behalf; and it is foreseeable that pressure groups within the student body are likely to use more than polite requests to get contributions even from those who are in disagreement with the particular cause or who are, in truth, too poor to afford a donation. The Board's regulation appears to be reasonable and proper and has a rational relationship to the orderly operation of the school system.

The rule's focus upon a demonstrable harm rather than an undifferentiated fear of disturbance distinguishes plaintiffs' action from Scoville v. Board of Education, 425 F.2d 10 (7 Cir.1970). There, the complaint of students disciplined by school authorities, who were unable to prove a reasonable likelihood of substantial disruption which would follow the students' distribution of an underground newspaper, was held to state a claim for damages and declarative and injunctive relief. Though the underground newspaper was sold to students, the defendant school authorities did not act pursuant to an anti-solicitation regulation comparable to the Board of Regents' rule.

Because the Board of Regents' rule afforded a sufficient basis for the denial of preliminary relief, we do not reach the same questions with respect to the local Board of Education rule upon which defendants may also have relied.

Affirmed.

Notes

1. *Tinker* is Case No. 114; *Epperson* is Case No. 23.

2. Compare the possibility of disruption of the school by fund solicitation with that by wearing black armbands (*Tinker*).

3. If it is impossible to accept contributions to further a cause, is freedom to advocate the cause in any way impaired?

4. Note the purpose and history of the Regents' rule. Also in Case No. 115 the purpose and history of the rule was material to its validity.

5. The Court of Appeals, First Circuit, refused to permit a school board to extend a rule "obviously devised for the quite different purposes of controlling in-school advertising or promotional efforts of organizations" to cover distribu-

tion of an anti-war leaflet and a "high school bill of rights." Riseman v. School Committee of City of Quincy, 439 F.2d 148 (1 Cir.1971).

[Case No. 50] Power of Board to Dispose of School Property

ROSS v. WILSON

Court of Appeals of New York, 1955.
308 N.Y. 605, 127 N.E.2d 697.

VAN VOORHIS, JUDGE. The controversy in this proceeding concerns the sale of the schoolhouse which served common school district No. 1 of the Towns of Ellicott and Gerry, in Chautauqua County, before it was superseded by a central school district. This district had been known as the Ross Mills District. In February, 1953, the board of education of the recently formed central school district called a special meeting of the qualified voters of the former common school district to vote upon whether to close the school and sell the school property. Such procedure is required by subdivision 6 of section 1804 of the Education Law, which also provides that if the common school district schoolhouse is sold, the net proceeds be apportioned among the taxpayers of the common school district.

At the special meeting of the common school district called by the board of education in 1953, four propositions were submitted: (1) Should the school of the former common school district be closed? (2) Should the school property be sold to Ross Mills Church of God for $2,000? (3) Should the property be sold to Ross Grange No. 305 for $3,000? (4) Should the property be sold by public auction to the highest bidder? The notice stated that proposition number 1 would be voted upon, "and as many of the succeeding propositions as is necessary to dispose of the property". At the meeting, the proposal to close the school was carried. A motion was then made but declared out of order that the meeting should next ballot upon whether to sell the school property at public auction to the highest bidder. Then proposition number 2 was presented to the meeting to sell the school property to Ross Mills Church of God for $2,000. It was carried by a vote of 32 to 24. That ended the meeting.

The Commissioner of Education on appeal taken to him pursuant to section 310 of the Education Law sustained this action of the board of education. Thereupon this article 78 proceeding was instituted to review his determination, which was annulled by Special Term but reinstated by the Appellate Division upon the ground that decisions by the Commissioner of Education are final unless purely arbitrary, and that his decision could not thus be characterized in this instance inasmuch as subdivision 6 of section 1804 of the Education Law, pursuant to which this schoolhouse was sold, does not expressly state that it must be sold to the highest bidder upon the organization of a central school district.
* * *

No question was raised that Ross Grange was financially able to pay $3,000 in cash for the property. In his opinion upholding the action of the school district, the Commissioner of Education placed his decision upon the following ground: "The type and character of the purchaser of such property after centralization is often a matter of vital import to the rural communities of this State. It is my opinion that the legislature fully intended to give the voters of component districts a choice as to the type of person or organization whom they wished to have literally in their midst. If the sale were to be mandated to be made to the highest bidder, it may well be that a 'saloon', filling station or other enterprise undesirable to a specific community might be forced upon it. * * *." * * *

In the conduct of private affairs, the problem sometimes arises whether a better price can be obtained upon the sale of property at private sale or at auction. In the case of a public body, such as a school district, the object to be achieved is likewise to realize the best price for the property, although the judgment of the Legislature must be followed concerning whether that purpose is more likely to be accomplished by public auction. But if the Legislature does not require a schoolhouse to be sold at public auction, it by no means follows from that circumstance that the Legislature intended to authorize the public officials charged with the administration of school property, or even the majority of qualified electors voting at a school district meeting, to sell the property for a smaller amount than has been offered with due formality by a proper purchaser for a lawful use. * * * If, as was intimated by the Commissioner of Education, a former school site might be used for a filling station, bar and grill or other enterprise undesirable to a specific community, zoning ordinances or other lawful regulatory measures should be adopted. * * *

The amount of money involved is small, but the principle is important; the offer which was rejected was to pay 50% more for this schoolhouse than the one which was accepted. Bogert, writing on Trusts and Trustees, says (§ 745): "Whether the trustee should endeavor to sell by negotiation with possible buyers, or should put the property up at auction, depends upon the circumstances of the individual case. He should use the method which will, considering the place of sale and the type of property for sale, be apt to bring the best price." In the present situation, the Legislature has determined that it was not necessary to sell this property at auction, although that procedure would have been permissible, but the latitude allowed in the method of sale was designed to enable these public fiduciaries to adopt the method which in their judgment would bring the best price, and it was their duty to sell at the best price which it brought, not deliberately to select and to favor a buyer at a lower price than was otherwise obtainable. In the same section of Bogert it is also said: "A power to sell is not equivalent to a power to give away. If the trustee transfers for a merely nominal price or a wholly inadequate price, the sale may be set aside". * * *

* * * The direct result of what occurred is, in effect, to approve a contribution of $1,000 by the school district to the church. * * *

This contribution by a common school district to a particular church is not made in aid of any educational activity conducted by the church, but operates as an outright gift of public funds to a church for its general church purposes. Even if the facts of the case did not present the special situation of the use of public money for the support of a religious establishment, neither a common school district meeting nor the district trustees are empowered to expend the resources of the school district for other than educational objects. * * *

There is no power in either the board or the voters at a district meeting to pick and choose arbitrarily between purchasers, each desiring to use the property for lawful and proper purposes, or to transfer the funds or other property of the district in aid of one or to the disadvantage of another. In this instance, there is lack of power to use public funds to aid a church by discriminating against the grange. * * *

For the reasons mentioned, we think that there was a total lack of power in the school district to accept an offer of $2,000 from the Church of God of Ross Mills and at the same time to reject an equally bona fide offer of $3,000 from the grange. Although we respect the desire of the commissioner to uphold, if possible, the action taken by the district meeting, since the meeting lacked power to do what it did, the commissioner's confirmation was thus, in a legal sense, purely arbitrary, and thus reviewable in court. * * *

* * *

Notes

1. At each of the three appellate steps there was a reversal. This final ruling was by a vote of four-to-three.

2. In the third paragraph, the standard for judicial reversal of the commissioner's decisions is stated as "purely arbitrary." As noted in Chapter 3, the standard was relaxed to "arbitrary" in 1976. Do you think the Appellate Division and the three dissenters here would have concluded differently had the change been made before this case was heard?

3. Observe that the state commissioner of education sustained the action of the board. Is this type of question an appropriate one for decision by a chief state school officer?

4. A statute in Louisiana provided that a school board could sell or dispose of an old building and "use the proceeds thereof for procuring a new one." When a board received funds from the highway department for an expropriated building, the board decided to construct a new board office building. Taxpayers sought an injunction, citing the statute. The Court of Appeal of Louisiana declined to grant it, saying that the legislature did not intend the statute to be so restrictive as was urged by the plaintiffs. Calloway v. Ouachita Parish School Bd., 158 So.2d 360 (La.App.1963).

5. The Supreme Court of Virginia declared unconstitutional as an "unlawful delegation of power" (to the electorate) a statute requiring that boards sell property if a majority of voters favored that action in a referendum. Howard v. School Bd. of Alleghany County, 203 Va. 55, 122 S.E.2d 891 (1961).

Chapter 7

TORT LIABILITY OF SCHOOL DISTRICTS, OFFICERS, AND EMPLOYEES

A tort is a civil wrong not involving contracts. The term is applied to a variety of situations where one suffers harm or loss due to the improper (but non-criminal) conduct of another. Courts hold those who commit torts liable in damages to those injured. The most prevalent common-law tort is that of negligence. Violations of civil rights constitute a rapidly expanding area of liability imposed by statute ("Section 1983").

Doctrine of Non-Liability of Districts

It is well established in the common law that a school district is not liable for torts whether committed by the district itself or by its officers, agents, or employees. There has been increasing dissatisfaction with the principle voiced by some legal writers and some judges, and many states have modified the doctrine either legislatively or judicially. Immunity from liability is based on the theory that the state is sovereign and cannot be sued without its consent. The doctrine is made applicable to subordinate state agencies on the theory that they are arms of the state for the purpose of carrying out the functions of state government. School districts, being instrumentalities of the state through which it carries out the state function of education, fall within the category of agencies immune from liability for torts under common law.

Although immunity of school districts from liability for tort is historically derived from the concept of sovereignty, many courts have assigned grounds other than that "the King can do no wrong" to support the rule. Some deny liability because the law provides no funds for the payment of damages which might be awarded against the district. It is also said that funds raised for school purposes may not be legally diverted for the payment of tort claims against the district, the assumption being that payment of such claims is not an expenditure for school purposes. Another ground for denying liability is that in the commission of a tort the board of education is not representing the district. The reasoning is that there is never any authority in the board to commit a tort, and when it does so, the act is beyond its legal powers and cannot bind the district. District immunity for acts of employees is based on the ground that the relation of master and servant does not exist; hence, there is no application of the rule of respondeat superior (that the master is liable for the acts of his servant or agent while the latter is acting within the scope of his employment).

Unsuccessful attempts to have courts recognize a tort of "educational malpractice" are discussed in Chapter 4 under "Malpractice".

Exceptions to Doctrine of Non-Liability

In General

The doctrine of immunity is subject to certain exceptions. These are statutory or judicial. Statutory ones vary markedly from state to state. Because the doctrine of district immunity is a common law concept developed by the courts, it can be abrogated by legislative enactment or modified by the courts. Indeed, there is much controversy as to whether the legislature or the courts should change it, if it is to be changed.

It appears that since the doctrine of immunity has existed for so long in the United States and has developed so many ramifications, many courts are reluctant to abandon it in its entirety. Thus, some courts, no longer willing to support the doctrine completely, have recognized certain exceptions to it.

Proprietary Acts

One of the exceptions to the immunity doctrine recognized by some courts is that a district is liable for torts connected with "proprietary" functions, as distinguished from "governmental" ones. It is said by these courts that governmental agencies exist in a dual capacity. In one, they exercise the rights springing from sovereignty. While performing the duties pertaining thereto, their acts are political and governmental, and in the performance of such functions they are not liable. In the other, they perform functions that could be done as well by private persons, and in such acts they are not to be considered public agencies. For torts committed in the execution of such functions, they are held to legal accountability.

A detailed distinction between governmental and proprietary acts is not often attempted in the cases. The courts, while noting that there is a distinction, frequently do no more than classify particular acts involved in one category or the other. It is exceedingly difficult to predict into which category a given act will fall until a court has ruled on it. Some examples of the proprietary-governmental distinction will illustrate the problem.

The Supreme Court of Arizona considered a case in which two school districts had rented a large stadium from a third school district for a football game.[1] Because of a defect in a railing of the stadium, a spectator fell and was seriously injured. The action was brought against the school district which owned the stadium. The question was whether the district, by renting its stadium to the two districts and charging a rental therefor, had abandoned its governmental role and embarked upon a proprietary one. Under the facts the function was held to be proprietary, and recovery was granted.

----

1. Sawaya v. Tucson High School Dist., 78 Ariz. 389, 281 P.2d 105 (1955).

Two years later the Supreme Court of Michigan decided a case in which the facts surrounding an accident were substantially the same except that a bleacher seat collapsed rather than a railing.[2] One material legal fact that was different was that the teams were playing on the field of one of the school districts. The court expressly declined to follow the aforementioned Arizona decision. It stated that in leasing the stadium and receiving compensation therefor the Arizona district had exercised a proprietary function, whereas the Michigan district did not intend to make a profit from its admission fee and was merely promoting an educational activity of its own.

The Supreme Court of Appeals of Virginia considered a case in which a concert was held in a junior high school auditorium and one who paid admission was injured due to an allegedly hazardous condition.[3] The court held that there was no liability because the school board's immunity for tortious injury was based on the fact that it was a governmental agency and always acted in a governmental capacity. Since a statute authorized the school board to permit the use of property under its control, the renting of the auditorium for a concert was held to be for a governmental purpose. The court stated that the governmental-proprietary test was whether the function tended to promote the cause of education. It found that the leasing of the school auditorium for a concert was a governmental function because it "stimulates and fosters the interest of pupils and the public and promotes the efficiency of the public schools.　* * * "

Reasoning differently was the Supreme Court of Pennsylvania in a case involving an injury to a child participating in a summer recreation program.[4] That court held that conducting the summer program was a proprietary act, and imposed liability on the district. The program was open to the general public upon the payment of an admission fee. The court said that an act may be designated as proprietary if it "is one which a local government unit is not statutorily required to perform, or if it may also be carried on by private enterprise, or if it is used as a means of raising revenue." Fifteen years later the court abolished completely the common-law immunity of school districts.[5]

In Kansas, a state recognizing proprietary acts as an exception to the doctrine of non-liability of school districts for negligence, the state's highest court was asked to decide whether a school board was engaged in a governmental function when it allowed its community room to be used for a fee of $3.00 by a county agricultural extension program.[6] A member of the group participating in the program fell into an unlighted stairway and sought damages from the district. The court found that

2. Richards v. School Dist. of City of Birmingham, 348 Mich. 490, 83 N.W.2d 643 (1957).

3. Kellam v. School Bd. of the City of Norfolk, 202 Va. 252, 117 S.E.2d 96 (1960).

4. Morris v. School Dist. of Tp. of Mount Lebanon, 393 Pa. 633, 144 A.2d 737 (1958).

5. Ayala v. Philadelphia Bd. of Public Educ., 453 Pa. 584, 305 A.2d 877 (1973).

6. Smith v. Board of Educ. of Caney School Dist. No. 34, 204 Kan. 580, 464 P.2d 571 (1970).

the use of the building was governmental and, further, that the duty owed these users was only to refrain from wilfully and wantonly injuring them.

A similar conclusion was reached in a Georgia case.[7] That court held a function to be governmental even though "some incidental revenue" was received from the rental of a school auditorium for a recital by a private dance school. The court said the affair was primarily for the benefit of the public in the nature of a civic function. Thus, there was no liability of the district for plaintiff's injury because of a defective step.

The distinction between governmental and proprietary functions may be placed in the hands of the courts to decide by legislative action. In Michigan, for example, after the highest court in effect abrogated immunity from tort liability for governmental bodies, the legislature enacted a statute providing immunity "in all cases wherein the government agency is engaged in the exercise or discharge of a governmental function." The Supreme Court of Michigan has ruled that "governmental functions," undefined in the statute, is a "term of art" used to describe "those activities of government which due to their public nature should not give rise to liability at common law."[8]

Nuisances

Increasingly persons injured as a result of alleged failure of boards to maintain school premises in a safe condition are basing their suits upon an exception, recognized in some jurisdictions, which permits recovery against districts if they maintain nuisances. While there is great confusion over the specificity of conditions which can be encompassed by the word "nuisance," it has been extended by courts so inclined to forms of annoyance or inconvenience interfering with common public rights. Nuisance, in the words of the Supreme Court of Errors of Connecticut, "involves as an essential element that it can be the natural tendency of the act or thing complained of to create dangers and inflict injury upon person or property."[9] As a nuisance may have its origin in negligence, it is sometimes difficult to determine what acts will constitute a nuisance. In one situation the plaintiff was a student who was pushed by classmates in such a way as to cause an injury from a "hazardous and dangerous condition," which was not further described by the court. The court, in overruling a demurrer, said that the defense of governmental immunity does not avail against "a cause of action founded on a nuisance created by positive act" of a governmental body.[10]

Although the responsibility for maintaining a nuisance seems to be widely recognized as an exception to the general rule of non-liability, the basis for the exception is not clear. Most courts seem content to state

7. Smith v. Board of Educ. of City of Marietta, 119 Ga.App. 441, 167 S.E.2d 615 (1969).

8. Thomas v. State Highway Dep't, 398 Mich. 1, 247 N.W.2d 530 (1976).

9. Laspino v. City of New Haven, 135 Conn. 603, 67 A.2d 557 (1949).

10. Sestero v. Town of Glastonbury, 19 Conn.Sup. 156, 110 A.2d 629 (1954).

categorically that the fact that a public agency holds and manages property renders it accountable for damages which result to the property of others from mismanagement of the property of the public agency. Responsibility for careful management attaches to the owner. Some have said that one explanation for the difference between liability for nuisance and non-liability for negligence is that in most instances the district may, by judicial decree, be required to abate the nuisance without undue hardship on the district. Of course, if damages are sought against the district, the usual arguments in favor of immunity apply. Another possible factor is that a nuisance usually affects property rights, which are traditionally carefully guarded by the courts. Considerations which insure property owners the right to enjoy their property without interference from others are sufficiently strong to induce some courts to override considerations upon which non-liability is based. It has been held, for example, that discharge of sewage into a stream is a nuisance.[11] Also the maintenance of a defective privy well on school property has been found the basis for liability of a district.[12]

On the other hand, it has been decided that a school district's failing to fumigate rooms in which a teacher suffering from tuberculosis had taught, with the result that the plaintiff teacher contracted the disease, was not the maintenance of a nuisance for which the district was liable.[13] The Supreme Court of Kansas held that a washbasin located in the basement of a school building was not a nuisance even though failure to maintain it properly could cause injury to pupils.[14] The children had splashed water on the floor while using the basin and then thrown wet paper towels on the floor, rendering it slippery so that a nine-year-old girl fell and was severely injured. That court also has found no nuisance to have been created by a board's allegedly allowing students to gather on the school grounds without proper supervision.[15] In this case a student had been assaulted.

The Supreme Court of Utah held that the University of Utah was not exempt from suit for damages where construction work on the institution's property had the result of diverting surface waters and flooding with water and mud a basement on adjoining property.[16] The university had ample notice of the dangerous condition. For a previous flood the landowner had been compensated, and when she later expressed concern, the president wrote her a letter of assurance that preventive steps were being taken. The court said the university had knowingly created a private nuisance in that it invaded the interests of the adjoining landowner in the private use and enjoyment of her land.

11. Watson v. New Milford, 72 Conn. 561, 45 A. 167 (1900).

12. Briegel v. City of Philadelphia, 135 Pa. 451, 19 A. 1038 (1890).

13. Bang v. Independent School Dist. No. 27, St. Louis County, 177 Minn. 454, 225 N.W. 449 (1929).

14. Jones v. Kansas City, 176 Kan. 406, 271 P.2d 803 (1954).

15. Sly v. Board of Educ. of Kansas City, 213 Kan. 415, 516 P.2d 895 (1973).

16. Sanford v. University of Utah, 26 Utah 2d 285, 488 P.2d 741 (1971).

Liability Insurance and Immunity

The courts are not in agreement on the technical point of whether governmental immunity of school districts from liability for tort is waived when school districts purchase liability insurance. Most do not consider the procurement of insurance coverage a direct waiver of district immunity,[17] even though it may have the same effect by permitting recovery. Varied rationales are offered. One line of reasoning is that the state has permitted itself to be sued only to determine the amount of liability of the insurance carrier.[18] Another is that, since depletion of school district funds is the basic modern reason for preserving school district immunity, the reason disappears if these funds are protected through insurance policies. Thus, the doctrine is modified to the extent of permitting recovery up to the maximum of the insurance coverage.[19] It also has been held that a statute permitting a board to carry liability insurance actually is against the contingency of personal liability of board members.[20] Another judicial answer to the question of to what avail the insurance would be if there is no liability possible, has been that the insurance is intended to cover proprietary functions only.[21]

In those states in which the immunity doctrine has not been limited at all, there would appear no reason to purchase liability insurance in order to protect the district, except, perhaps, in anticipation of possible judicial abrogation of the doctrine if the doctrine exists solely in the common law of the state. Furthermore, in the absence of a statute permitting it, the purchase of insurance in such states could constitute an illegal expenditure of funds. The authority to manage a school system would not necessarily carry the implied authority to expend public funds to insure against a liability which did not exist or was unclear. A case directly in point arose in West Virginia. Under the law of that state boards had the authority to furnish school transportation, but there was no authorization to carry liability insurance on school buses. A board purchased and operated a number of buses and procured a public liability and damage policy covering them. The succeeding board, doubting the legality of the expenditure, was successful in an action against the insurance company to recover the amount of the premiums paid. The successful argument of the district was that there was nothing against which the policy of indemnification could operate, and thus the expenditure was improper.[22]

---

17. Smith v. Board of Educ. of Caney School Dist. No. 34, 204 Kan. 580, 464 P.2d 571 (1970); Barr v. Bernhard, 562 S.W.2d 844 (Tex.1978); Merrill v. Birhanzel, 310 N.W.2d 522 (S.D.1981).

18. Taylor v. Knox County Bd. of Educ., 292 Ky. 767, 167 S.W.2d 700 (1942).

19. Thomas v. Broadlands Community Consolidated School Dist., 348 Ill.App. 567, 109 N.E.2d 636 (1952).

20. Hummer v. School City of Hartford City, 124 Ind.App. 30, 112 N.E.2d 891 (1953).

21. Supler v. School Dist. of North Franklin Tp., 407 Pa. 657, 182 A.2d 535 (1962).

22. Board of Educ. of County of Raleigh v. Commercial Casualty Ins. Co., 116 W.Va. 503, 182 S.E. 87 (1935). See also Davis v. Board of County Commissioners of Carbon County, 495 P.2d 21 (Wyo.1972), and Awe v. University of Wyoming, 534 P.2d 97 (Wyo.1975).

Where statutes definitely create a liability risk it would seem clear that school districts could purchase insurance against the eventuality of liability. Although the school district could not itself abrogate its immunity, the state legislature not only could do so directly, but also indirectly by enacting statutes imposing limited liability. Further, the state could require boards to indemnify employees found guilty of negligence.

Regardless of the legal explications offered, operationally speaking it appears that where boards have purchased liability insurance most courts that have considered the question have permitted recovery up to the limits of the policy. The Supreme Court of Montana so concluded in 1991 after extensively reviewing judicial decisions based on differing legislative situations.[23]

Abrogation of Doctrine of Non-Liability

By Courts

In recent years the courts of last resort in some states have indicated that because the rule of governmental immunity from tort was created by the courts, it can be abrogated by them if the legislature remains silent. The first direct and complete repudiation of the doctrine came in 1959 from the Supreme Court of Illinois in a suit against a school district for personal injuries of a pupil sustained when the school bus in which he was riding left the road, allegedly as a result of the driver's negligence, hit a culvert, exploded, and burned.[24] The court considered at length the history of the rule and the bases upon which it rested. It concluded that the doctrine was no longer appropriate. The effect of this holding was to place school districts in Illinois in the same legal situation as are private corporations, which can be required to respond in damages for injuries caused by their negligence or that of their officers, agents, or employees.

Legislative responses to such decisions have varied. Illinois set maximums on the amounts of money to be recovered in an injury case and also later reestablished part of the immunity doctrine. Following a similar decision in Minnesota[25] the legislature in that state established a moratorium by reinstating the doctrine for a specified period of time. (See "Reestablishment of Non-Liability by Statute," infra.)

After stating that it found the doctrine of governmental immunity unacceptable, the Supreme Judicial Court of Massachusetts declined to abrogate the doctrine because "the Legislature should be afforded an opportunity to do this by a comprehensive statute."[26] After the legisla-

23. Crowell v. School Dist. No. 7 of Gallatin County, Montana, 247 Mont. 38, 805 P.2d 522 (1991).

24. Molitor v. Kaneland Community Unit School Dist. No. 302, 18 Ill.2d 11, 163 N.E.2d 89 (1959), cert. den. 362 U.S. 968, 80 S.Ct. 955, 4 L.Ed.2d 900 (1960).

25. Spanel v. Mounds View School Dist. No. 621, 264 Minn. 279, 118 N.W.2d 795 (1962).

26. Morash and Sons, Inc. v. Commonwealth, 363 Mass. 612, 296 N.E.2d 461 (1973).

ture had taken no action, the court four years later stated its intention to abrogate the doctrine in the first appropriate case decided after the conclusion of the next session of the legislature unless the legislature had "acted definitively as to the doctrine." [27]   It said it would make the abrogation retroactive to the date of the case in which it first criticized the doctrine. The Legislature then enacted a law permitting some tort claims, but excluding those based upon the exercise of discretionary functions.[28]

By Legislatures

Legislative modifications of the doctrine of non-liability have included several approaches. Some statutes have imposed liability in connection with certain types of activities. Examples are "safe place" statutes requiring owners of public buildings to construct and maintain them so as to render them safe for employees and frequenters thereof, and statutes requiring districts to purchase insurance and allowing recovery thereon in connection with negligence in the operation of school buses.

A few state legislatures have completely abrogated the common-law doctrine and placed school districts on the same basis as to liability as are individuals and private corporations. Others have abolished the general doctrine, but made exceptions that preclude liability in specific activities or classes of activities, such as those involving high degrees of discretion.

In some states, the immunity rule has been modified by indirection through the operation of what have come to be called "save harmless" statutes. Laws of this type require school districts to defend, at district expense, suits which may be brought against teachers as a result of damages caused by their allegedly tortious acts. Under such statutes districts also are required to pay any judgments which may be recovered against employees acting within the scope of their employment.

It should be emphasized that school districts and/or their employees may or may not be covered by general legislation modifying the doctrine of governmental tort immunity. A court ruling may be required to resolve the issue in a given state.

By the Supreme Court for Section 1983 Cases

In 1978 the Supreme Court, overruling a 1961 holding, declared that local governments, including school districts, are "persons" under Section 1983 [29] and may be sued directly under that provision.[30]   Some inconsistencies had developed over the years, particularly in regard to certain types of cases involving school boards, and the Court reexamined in the present case the legislative history of Section 1983, which had

---

27. Whitney v. City of Worcester, 373 Mass. 208, 366 N.E.2d 1210 (1977).

28. See Cady v. Plymouth-Carver Regional School Dist., 17 Mass.App. 211, 457 N.E.2d 294 (1983).

29. See "Federal System" in Chapter 1.

30. Monell v. Department of Social Services of City of New York, 436 U.S. 658, 98 S.Ct. 2018, 56 L.Ed.2d 611 (1978).

been added by the Civil Rights Act of 1871. It found that Congress did not intend to grant absolute immunity to local governmental bodies. The Court declined to treat the question of whether local governments could be afforded some degree of immunity short of absolute immunity. It did expressly state that a local government may not be sued for an injury "inflicted solely by its employees or agents." Liability will be present only when a government's "policy or custom" inflicted the injury of deprivation of "any rights, privileges, or immunities secured by the Constitution and laws."

Two years later the Court answered the question reserved in the previous case. It held that there could be no qualified immunity for local governments based on good faith of officers or agents in Section 1983 suits.[31] The Court reasoned that if constitutional violations committed in good faith were not subject to damage claims, the purpose of the statute would be thwarted. The Court said that it was fairer to allocate any financial burden to costs of government borne by all taxpayers than to allow the impact of violations to be felt solely by those whose rights, although newly judicially recognized, were violated. The Court observed that doctrines of tort law had changed significantly over the past century and that views of governmental responsibility should reflect that evolution.

Subsequently, the Court held that Section 1983 created a cause of action for a person whose claim of deprivation under color of state law was based on a violation of a federal statutory right. In the absence of a clear legislative history on the point, the Court elected to follow the "plain language" of the words in Section 1983: "rights, privileges, or immunities secured by the Constitution and laws."[32]

It must be emphasized, however, that liability can be imposed on a local government or a school district only if a deprivation is pursuant to a policy or custom or is the result of an act of the highest officials responsible for setting policy in that area of the local entity's business.[33]

In 1992 the United States Supreme Court answered in the affirmative the question whether a court can order monetary damages to be paid to an individual for a violation of Title IX.[34] The Court had held in 1979 that an individual could bring suit under the Act to seek its enforcement in a specific situation.[35] The Court cited the principle of old English common law that if a statute gives a right, there must be a remedy to maintain the right. In the present case a female former high school student alleged intentional discrimination through sexual harassment and abuse by a male teacher and inadequate response by school authorities.

31. Owen v. City of Independence, Missouri, 445 U.S. 622, 100 S.Ct. 1398, 63 L.Ed.2d 673 (1980).

32. Maine v. Thiboutot, 448 U.S. 1, 100 S.Ct. 2502, 65 L.Ed.2d 555 (1980).

33. City of St. Louis v. Praprotnik, 485 U.S. 112, 108 S.Ct. 915, 99 L.Ed.2d 107 (1988).

34. Franklin v. Gwinnett County Public Schools, ___ U.S. ___, 112 S.Ct. 1028, 117 L.Ed.2d 208 (1992).

35. Cannon v. University of Chicago, 441 U.S. 677, 99 S.Ct. 1946, 60 L.Ed.2d 560 (1979).

Reestablishment of Non-Liability by Statute

There has been a trend for legislatures to reestablish by statute at least portions of governmental immunity where courts have removed the doctrine from the common law. That this is within legislative power seems settled.[36] The courts then have the responsibility for construing the legislation. Although usually such legislation treats the subject directly, immunity was held by the Supreme Court of Alabama to be conferred by a statute providing that a city board of education was empowered to sue, but not mentioning that it could be sued.[37]

Some of the statutes refer to immunity of employed personnel. Although the common law doctrine of non-liability of governmental bodies does not extend to employees,[38] apparently legislatures can grant at least a measure of immunity to employees.[39] Legislatures clearly can provide for indemnification for monetary judgments entered against employees found liable, but indemnification statutes do not operate as a bar against suing employees.[40]

The Supreme Court of Illinois has had several occasions to interpret legislation that places teachers squarely in an "in loco parentis" status as regards students in the school, and provides that boards are not liable for acts of an employee unless the employee is liable. Because parents are liable to their children only in the case of "willful and wanton misconduct," the statute makes this the standard that must be met to establish liability of teachers.[41] But boards of education, according to that court, may be held liable where no "in loco parentis" relationship existed at the site of the injury, for examples, where a holder of a free pass to a football game was injured by being knocked to the ground by one of a large number of boisterous young people milling around[42] and where a board allegedly furnished an inadequate and defective football helmet.[43]

In Minnesota, statutes require school boards to attempt to purchase liability insurance up to a certain amount at a maximum cost. If this cannot be done, as certified by the state commissioner of insurance, the district is immune. If it obtains the insurance it is liable to the limits set by statute. In a case decided by the state supreme court the board had insurance, but too little to cover the claims. The court held that the

---

36. Brown v. Wichita State Univ., 219 Kan. 2, 547 P.2d 1015 (1976); English v. Newark Housing Authority, 138 N.J.Super. 425, 351 A.2d 368 (1976).

37. Enterprise City Bd. of Educ. v. Miller, 348 So.2d 782 (Ala.1977).

38. Baird v. Hosmer, 46 Ohio St.2d 273, 347 N.E.2d 533 (1976); Sansone v. Bechtel, 180 Conn. 96, 429 A.2d 820 (1980).

39. Kobylanski v. Chicago Bd. of Educ., 63 Ill.2d 165, 347 N.E.2d 705 (1976); Barr v. Bernhard, 562 S.W.2d 844 (Tex.1978).

40. Talmadge v. District School Bd. of Lake County, 355 So.2d 502 (Fla.App.1978).

41. Kobylanski v. Chicago Bd. of Educ., 63 Ill.2d 165, 347 N.E.2d 705 (1976).

42. Tanari v. School Directors of Dist. No. 502, County of Bureau, 69 Ill.2d 630, 14 Ill.Dec. 874, 373 N.E.2d 5 (1977). [Case No. 51]

43. Gerrity v. Beatty, 71 Ill.2d 47, 15 Ill.Dec. 639, 373 N.E.2d 1323 (1978).

district was liable for any uninsured loss up to the statutory limits.[44]

Liability of School Board Members

Any immunity from liability for tort enjoyed by school districts does not extend to school officers. However, it is well settled that a public official engaged in the performance of governmental duties involving the exercise of judgment and discretion may not be personally liable for mere negligence in respect to the performance of his duties. An official may be held personally liable if it is shown that his act or failure to act was corrupt or malicious, or that he acted outside of or beyond the scope of his duties. This rule is predicated upon the fact that few persons would be willing to accept positions as members of boards of education if they were required to assume the risk of personal liability were they proved to have acted negligently, even though in good faith, in the performance of their duties.

In examining the liability of school board members the distinction between discretionary responsibilities and ministerial responsibilities is crucial. The preceding statements apply to duties involving discretion. Where duties are ministerial, school board members can be held personally liable for losses suffered by other parties as a result of their nonfeasance (failure to perform a duty) or misfeasance (doing a duty improperly).

In application, the distinction between ministerial and discretionary duties in tort liability cases is not always clear. For example, individual board members in Indiana were held liable in a situation where temporary stands were constructed for spectators at a "field day exhibition" sponsored by the school board each year.[45] The board employed a carpenter to build the stands under the direction of the clerk of the board. Because of defective construction the seats fell and caused serious injury to a number of spectators. The court said that the members of the school board were exercising discretion when determining that there should be field day exercises and when determining the manner in which the exercises should be conducted. However, the duties performed "in making preparation for such field day exercises and the general management thereof" were ministerial.

In a somewhat similar case the Supreme Court of North Carolina ruled differently.[46] Here it appeared that certain repairs were being made on the school stadium. Under the direction of members of the board, cement blocks had been hauled to the stadium and stacked where the board members had directed—on a hillside adjacent to a cement wall erected around the stadium. During a game a spectator seated near the pile of blocks was killed by its falling against the cement wall and crushing it to the ground. The court found that the actions of the board

---

44. Scott v. Independent School Dist. No. 709, Duluth, 256 N.W.2d 485 (Minn. 1977).

45. Adams v. Schneider, 71 Ind.App. 249, 124 N.E. 718 (1919).

46. Smith v. Hefner, 235 N.C. 1, 68 S.E.2d 783 (1952).

members in providing for the erection of a grandstand were within the scope of the board's jurisdiction and that the situation involved the exercise of discretion. Recovery was disallowed.

The weight of authority is that school board members are not held personally liable for failure properly to perform ministerial duties placed on the board as a corporate body. The corporate body in such instances is held responsible, rather than the individual members. If, of course, district immunity prevails, there can be no recovery at all. However, where boards refuse or fail to follow specific statutory procedures, individual member liability may result. The reasoning is that no discretion is left to a board if the statutory mandate is clear. For example, the members of a school board were held individually liable as the result of their failure to procure school bus insurance as a statute required.[47] Failure to procure the insurance, coupled with district immunity, left no method of recovery for those injured in a school bus accident despite the clear legislative intent.

The Court of Appeals of Michigan was asked to determine if members of a board of education are immune from suit as individually named defendants upon a claim of tort liability based on the collective action or inaction of such board members.[48] The court held that the members would not be personally liable where the board itself was immune unless there was a specific statutory duty involved. There was no such duty in the situation where a student was beaten by students from a neighboring high school in the halls and parking lot of his school. The court also ruled that a statute, permitting governmental agencies to pay for attorney's fees when a civil action was commenced against an officer or employee for injuries allegedly caused by the negligence of that person while on duty, did not evidence an intent by the legislature to permit negligence suits against individual officers.

School board members while acting in their official capacities generally enjoy a qualified, or conditional, immunity from liability for the tort of defamation. (This tort involves the communication to third persons of statements which injure one's reputation. If in writing, the defamation is libel; if spoken, it is slander.) The immunity covers nonmalicious statements made within the scope of duty. A public board meeting would be a privileged occasion unless the defamatory utterance was not reasonably related to the purpose of the meeting.[49] Statements made at executive sessions about the professional fitness of an employee are privileged, as are resolutions of dismissal adopted in open sessions.[50] But privilege does not extend to making highly derogatory statements about an employee to the press.[51] Usually the board member must show

47. Bronaugh v. Murray, 294 Ky. 715, 172 S.W.2d 591 (1943).

48. Nichols v. Zera, 33 Mich.App. 274, 189 N.W.2d 751 (1971).

49. Frisk v. Merrihew, 42 Cal.App.3d 319, 116 Cal.Rptr. 781 (1974); Malia v. Monchak, 116 Pa.Cmwlth. 484, 543 A.2d 184 (1988).

50. Brubaker v. Board of Educ., School Dist. 149, 502 F.2d 973 (7 Cir.1974), cert. den. 421 U.S. 965, 95 S.Ct. 1953, 44 L.Ed.2d 451 (1975).

51. Lipman v. Brisbane Elementary School Dist., 55 Cal.2d 224, 11 Cal.Rptr. 97, 359 P.2d 465 (1961).

that the occasion was covered by privilege. When the board is sitting in a quasi-judicial capacity, however, board members enjoy absolute immunity.[52] (See further discussion of defamation under "Liability of Employed Personnel," infra.)

The Supreme Court has held that school board members may be sued under Section 1983.[53] The Court said that to hold school board members absolutely immune from damages claims "would deny much of the promise of Section 1983." But the Court took account of the need for school board members to exercise their "judgment independently, forcefully, and in a manner best serving the long-term interest of the school and the students." Observing that state courts over the years had recognized damages claims for bad faith or malicious acts, the Court added as a federal cause of action against board members "ignorance or disregard of settled, indisputable law." The case involved the long-term suspension of students, and the Court's holding in that context was that a board member could be required to pay damages "only if the school board member has acted with such an impermissible motivation or with such disregard of the student's clearly established constitutional rights that his action cannot reasonably be characterized as being in good faith."

The subjective "impermissible motivation" limit on qualified immunity obviously requires a trial. Its effect was that Section 1983 suits against government officials could not be disposed of by summary judgment, and courts (and defendants) were getting unduly burdened by insubstantial claims. Recognizing the problem, the Supreme Court eventually eliminated the subjective standard, leaving the objective one of "clearly established constitutional or statutory rights."[54] If such are violated by officials, they have no immunity from liability.

Another Supreme Court decision is relevant to tort liability of school board members.[55] In controversy was the question of damages in suits where claims are asserted that procedural due process rights are violated (here in connection with student suspensions). The court unanimously held that although a violation of procedural due process could trigger a suit without proof of actual damages to the victim, it would be necessary to show actual damages in order to collect more than nominal compensation where it was ultimately shown that the actions of the authorities were justified. The Court said that the common law concept of compensatory damages for violation of legal rights applied to Section 1983 cases. Damages could not be presumed in all circumstances solely predicated on a violation of due process. The Court, however, expressly recognized that mental and emotional distress could be caused by the denial of procedural due process itself. But such injury, as well as other damages, must be shown in order to recover more than the nominal damages not

52. Schulze v. Board of Educ., School Dist. No. 258, Humboldt, 221 Kan. 351, 559 P.2d 367 (1977).

53. Wood v. Strickland, 420 U.S. 308, 95 S.Ct. 992, 43 L.Ed.2d 214 (1975). [Case No. 52]

54. Harlow v. Fitzgerald, 457 U.S. 800, 102 S.Ct. 2727, 73 L.Ed.2d 396 (1982).

55. Carey v. Piphus, 435 U.S. 247, 98 S.Ct. 1042, 55 L.Ed.2d 252 (1978). [Case No. 53]

to exceed one dollar that would be awarded solely for a procedural due process violation.

Liability of Employed Personnel

In General

Because school systems operate through employed personnel, almost all cases involving torts implicate teachers or other employees directly or indirectly. Sometimes the tort claim is brought solely against the employee, sometimes it partially involves the employee, and sometimes it is against the district for not properly carrying out a corporate duty through proper use and supervision of personnel.

It should be observed that basically under the common law everyone is legally responsible for his torts. An exception is where an employer is held responsible for the torts of an employee functioning in line of duty (respondeat superior). But it should be further observed that a negligent employee may not be a competent employee, and may be disciplined for his negligence even though the employer may be required to pay the damages. As previously pointed out, the common law immunity from liability for torts cloaking school districts does not apply to employees unless state courts have so ruled.[56]

The reader is advised that the following topics are not mutually exclusive. Although each case is presented only once, many could also be classified under other of the topics.

Negligence and Adequacy of Supervision

Most of the negligence cases involving employed personnel can be viewed in the broad context of "adequacy of supervision." Theoretically, adequate supervision of pupils would prevent injuries to them from reasonably foreseeable dangers. Lack of proper supervision can be an element of negligence. All activities must be supervised, each in a fashion dependent on the activity and the participants therein. Supervisors must be sufficient in numbers and must execute their duties competently.

Negligence is a concept of the common law connoting legal fault whereby one party breaches a legal duty and becomes liable to a second party for an injury directly attributable to the unintentional conduct of the first party. Negligent conduct in its simplest definition is that conduct in which a reasonably careful person would not engage. Negligence may involve doing something that a reasonably prudent person would not do under the circumstances or not doing something that a

---

56. In a few jurisdictions courts have extended the governmental immunity to some administrators in the exercise of highly discretionary functions. See Hennessy v. Webb, 245 Ga. 329, 264 S.E.2d 878 (1980); Banks v. Sellers, 224 Va. 168, 294 S.E.2d 862 (1982). See also Cousins v. Dennis, 298 Ark. 310, 767 S.W.2d 296 (1989), for an example of judicial construction of a governmental immunity statute to encompass school district employees in their official duties.

reasonably prudent person would do under the circumstances. Circumstances play a crucial role in the determination of negligence. Public school personnel have a definite legal duty to the pupils in their schools, the duty of protecting them from reasonably foreseeable risk of harm. Educational personnel, however, are not considered insurers of pupils' safety. Undoubtedly most injuries derive from what the law calls unavoidable, or pure, accidents (accidents for which no legal fault lies, any "fault" being that of the injured or of circumstances beyond control).

An example of an unavoidable accident is found in a situation where a pupil received injuries when she was thrown from her seat in a school bus when it was driven off the highway into a ditch. The attention of the driver had been diverted momentarily from the road when a bee flew in the window and stung him on the neck. He tipped his head and tried with the left hand to extricate the bee from under his collar. In the process the bus veered onto the shoulder of the road and overturned. There was no contention that the driver had been operating the bus in a negligent manner before the bee stung him, but it was urged on behalf of the injured student that the court should determine that the driver was negligent in failing to keep the bus under control after the bee stung him. Testimony revealed that only a few seconds passed between the moment of the bee sting and the moment the driver discovered the bus had crossed the highway. He testified the sting startled him and the bee continued to buzz under his collar after it stung him. The Supreme Court of Washington sustained the lower court judgment that the bus driver was not negligent as a matter of law, and that the accident and injuries were unavoidable in the exercise of due care.[57]

A contrasting case involved an accident which occurred in the course of a lecture on safety. A teacher had taken his class out on the lawn to review a safety test. One of the boys picked up a home-made knife on the way out of the classroom, and, as the boys were seated in a semi-circle around the teacher, started flipping the knife into the ground. This action continued for quite a while until eventually the knife struck a student's drawing board, was deflected, and destroyed an eye of one of the students. The court indicated that there was sufficient evidence from which a jury might infer that the teacher knew, or should have known, that the knife throwing was going on and that he was inattentive and careless in failing to observe and stop it before the injury occurred.[58]

This point of observation and probable prevention is raised when accidents occur while a teacher is out of the room. The courts have not held that the mere absence of a teacher from a room is a basis for liability. One test is whether the presence of the teacher in the room would have been likely to prevent the accident which occurred in his absence. The length of the teacher's absence can be a critical factor. For example, the Supreme Court of Wisconsin reversed a trial court's

57. Schultz v. Cheney School Dist. No. 360, 59 Wash.2d 845, 371 P.2d 59 (1962).

58. Lilienthal v. San Leandro Unified School Dist., 139 Cal.App.2d 453, 293 P.2d 889 (1956).

summary judgment against the plaintiff and ordered a retrial in a situation where a fourteen-year-old pupil had been injured in a rough "keep away" game in the school gymnasium.[59] The game had been played for about twenty-five minutes while the teacher was out of the room, and about fifty adolescent boys were left unsupervised.

Foreseeability

Another test is whether under all the circumstances the possibility of injury while the teacher is absent is reasonably foreseeable. Under this test the Court of Appeals of Maryland held that a fourth grade teacher who had left the room for a few minutes while the class was engaged in a program of calisthenics was not liable for injuries to a girl who was struck in the mouth by a boy performing exercises in a manner contrary to instructions.[60] The fact that similar acts occurred prior to the act that caused an injury does not per se indicate foreseeability. For example, even though students previously had kicked chairs from under other students, a particular kicking was held not to be foreseeable.[61]

In a Hawaii case negligence had been found by the trial court where there was no supervision at a "light show" created by students and held during school hours. Hawaii law provided for comparative negligence judgments, a system whereby fault for an accident need not be complete in order for some liability to exist.[62] The trial court had ruled that a student injured at the show by thrown metal objects was 25 percent negligent for not leaving the lecture hall before being hit. This was reversed, the appellate court finding that the fifteen-year-old student could not have reasonably anticipated that she was in danger of physical harm when a group of students became boisterous.[63]

The question of legally sufficient supervision in situations where one student is injured by the act of another was considered by the Supreme Court of California.[64] Two boys had been "slapboxing" on the school grounds during the lunch period. The match continued for five to ten minutes, and a crowd of approximately thirty students gathered to watch. Suddenly, after being slapped, one boy fell backwards, fracturing his skull on the asphalt paving. He died that night. The responsibility for supervising the section of the campus where the incident occurred lay with the physical education department. The department head, rather than having a formal schedule, left the supervision "to the person in the gym office." The teacher in the office at the time was eating lunch and preparing for afternoon classes. The desk faced away from the windows

59. Cirillo v. City of Milwaukee, 34 Wis.2d 705, 150 N.W.2d 460 (1967).

60. Segerman v. Jones, 256 Md. 109, 259 A.2d 794 (1969).

61. Boyer v. Jablonski, 70 Ohio App.2d 141, 435 N.E.2d 436 (1980).

62. Under the common law, if the plaintiff in a negligence case acted in a manner that was unreasonable and thereby "contributed" to the injury suffered, that "contributory negligence" could bar recovery de-

spite the negligent acts of the defendant. The harshness of the rule has prompted a legislative trend toward "comparative negligence."

63. Viveiros v. State, 54 Hawaii 611, 513 P.2d 487 (1973). [Case No. 54]

64. Dailey v. Los Angeles Unified School Dist., 2 Cal.3d 741, 87 Cal.Rptr. 376, 470 P.2d 360 (1970). [Case No. 55]

and a wall obscured the view of the area where the slapboxing took place. The court concluded that there was evidence from which a jury could find negligence. It held that the mere fact another student's misconduct was the immediate precipitating cause of injury did not necessarily mean that negligent supervision was not the proximate cause.

A similar conclusion was reached by the Supreme Court of Minnesota in a case where an injury to an eighth grade pupil resulted from pebble-throwing that had continued for almost ten minutes during the morning recess.[65] The court observed that on the question of foreseeability, proof is required only that a general danger is foreseeable and that supervision likely would have prevented the accident. It is not necessary to prove that the particular accident which occurred was foreseeable.

But whether an act should be foreseen cannot be derived from speculation. If reasonable precautions are taken, and an intervening act properly not anticipated occurs, no negligence will exist. Thus when a student returned to his desk and sat on the point of a pencil placed there by another student, no liability could be placed on school authorities.[66] This ruling was made despite the fact the teacher was out of the room. She was only a few feet from the room, assisting another teacher for a brief period. The court said that under these facts a contrary conclusion would impose the standard of care akin to an insurer.

Similarly the Supreme Court of Wyoming held that no liability for the school district or a teacher aide resulted from an accident at noon recess where a seven-year-old was partially blinded by a small rock which was thrown by a fellow student and bounced off a larger rock.[67] The teacher aide had walked past a small group of boys sitting on the ground talking and laughing about thirty seconds before the incident. The court found that the aide had not acted improperly, and that even if it were to assume the district to be negligent because of the rocks lying around, the act of the rock-thrower was an intervening cause of the accident.

In New Jersey suit was brought for damages for injuries suffered when a pupil was struck by paper clips shot from an elastic band by another child before the classrooms opened. The pupil was riding his bicycle onto the school premises when the accident occurred. The principal was present. Liability of the principal was established on the grounds that he had announced no rules with respect to the congregation of students and their conduct before entering the classrooms, that he had assigned no teachers or others to assist him in supervising the pupils at that time, and that he personally was engaged in activities

---

65. Sheehan v. St. Peter's Catholic School, 291 Minn. 1, 188 N.W.2d 868 (1971).

66. Swaitkowski v. Board of Educ. of City of Buffalo, 36 A.D.2d 685, 319 N.Y.S.2d 783 (1971).

67. Fagan v. Summers, 498 P.2d 1227 (Wyo.1972).

other than overseeing the presence and activities of the pupils.[68] In a similar situation, where it was alleged that the principal was aware of students playing football before classes began (he having directed that they play only in the location where the injury to a student occurred), the Supreme Court of Idaho declined to apply a recreational use statute and held that a trial was necessary to determine whether a duty to supervise the students had been breached.[69]

Failure of a principal to take adequate measures to prevent misuse of movable stands on the school grounds was basis for a finding of negligence in a Louisiana case. There were 200 elementary school children being supervised by two teachers and the principal at the time of the injury.[70] Another Louisiana court found negligence where a school operated a breakfast program but provided only one teacher for the first half hour from the start of breakfast.[71]

While the required level of supervision is decreased before the opening of the school day and after students have been dismissed, if it is known that pupils are to be on school premises, proper precautions must be taken. For example, recovery of damages was granted against a school district where a nine-year-old girl was injured in an elementary school classroom after school hours when an upright piano fell on her.[72] Testimony indicated that the sixty-year-old piano could easily tip over backwards. At the time of the accident the keyboard side of the piano was facing toward the wall, although the piano's balance was such that it was intended to stand with its back against the wall.

The Court of Appeals of New York held that an injury from a snowball thrown on school property while the pupil was returning to school from lunch recess was not due to negligence of school authorities.[73] The school had a rule against snowball throwing, and the teacher of the injured party had warned the pupils not to throw snowballs. The court, in reversing a lower court judgment, held that the school board was not liable in the situation because there was no notice of special danger and no proof that the teacher had notice of other snowball throwing on the day that the injury had occurred. The court commented that no one grows up in New York without throwing snowballs or being hit by them, and that it would require intensive policing, almost child by child, to take all snowball throwing out of play activity. Two years later, however, the Appellate Division in New York upheld a jury verdict of negligence in another snowball case.[74] Here it was found that school authorities knew, or should have known, of hard frozen snow or ice in the school yard. Also there was evidence of inadequate supervi-

68. Titus v. Lindberg, 49 N.J. 66, 228 A.2d 65 (1967). [Case No. 56]

69. Bauer v. Minidoka School Dist. No. 331, 116 Idaho 586, 778 P.2d 336 (1989).

70. Santee v. Orleans Parish School Bd., 430 So.2d 254 (La.App.1983).

71. Laneheart v. Orleans Parish School Bd., 524 So.2d 138 (La.App.1988).

72. Kidwell v. School Dist. No. 300, Whitman County, 53 Wash.2d 672, 335 P.2d 805 (1959).

73. Lawes v. Board of Educ. of City of New York, 16 N.Y.2d 302, 266 N.Y.S.2d 364, 213 N.E.2d 667 (1965). [Case No. 57]

74. Cioffi v. Board of Educ. of City of New York, 27 A.D.2d 826, 278 N.Y.S.2d 249 (1967).

sion of the yard at the time a pupil had been injured when he became the target for iceballs thrown by a large number of boys in the school yard.

Athletics and Dangerous Activities

The more dangerous the situation, the more careful the supervision must be. The question of proper instruction before one engages in a dangerous activity is particularly important. It is not essential, however, to instruct a student about specific dangers of doing something that is clearly forbidden.[75]

In a leading case a physical education teacher permitted two husky boys untrained in the skills of boxing to fight through one round and part of another while the teacher sat in the bleachers. One of the boys was fatally injured. Suit for recovery of damages against the instructor was upheld.[76] The court pointed out that the boys had not been properly taught the principles of defense and that the teacher's being in the bleachers prevented him from giving the close supervision required.

On the other hand, the Supreme Court of Missouri has held that when one is engaged in a sport involving physical contact, such as wrestling, it is necessary to show in great detail what duty an instructor failed to observe in connection with a suit for damages because of an injury.[77] General charges of failure to properly teach or designate rules are insufficient, for it is necessary to show precisely how the omissions led to the pupil's injury or how the performance of the omitted acts would have prevented the injury. One engaging in an activity like a wrestling match is presumed to have "assumed the risks" inherent in the activity.

It is necessary, however, for teachers to see that there is proper matching in games. An example is to be found in a New York case where the state's highest court held that the evidence presented a prima facie case of negligent supervision.[78] In the playing of a game, the teacher placed some boys in facing lines seventy-five feet apart, and placed a ball midway between the lines. One boy from each line was to run toward the ball at full speed on a signal and attempt to kick it toward a goal. Although the boys in the game came from the same grade, no effort had been made to match them as to height or weight. The court noted that there was a great difference in size between two boys who competed for the ball, the smaller one being injured.

However, "mismatching" or "overmatching" must be evaluated in connection with the particular circumstances. Thus, the Supreme Court of Oregon found no negligence in the injury of one who was "uncoordinated" and not very experienced when he was injured in a scheduled

75. Payne v. North Carolina Dept. of Human Resources, 95 N.C.App. 309, 382 S.E.2d 449 (1989).

76. La Valley v. Stanford, 272 A.D. 183, 70 N.Y.S.2d 460 (1947).

77. Smith v. Consolidated School Dist. No. 2, 408 S.W.2d 50 (Mo.1966).

78. Brooks v. Board of Educ. of the City of New York, 12 N.Y.2d 971, 238 N.Y.S.2d 963, 189 N.E.2d 497 (1963).

football game by being tackled by two larger boys.[79]   The court recognized that football players vary in size even when the teams are in the same league. It found that the injury could not have been prevented by any actions of the school district or of its agents. The boy had had practice and training with competent instruction in the sport.

Where one interscholastic football team was clearly better than another, a weaker team player who had received numerous college football scholarship offers was injured after very actively participating in the game for a long time. He testified that he was fatigued, but he did not tell the coach. The coach and the department head had unsuccessfully recommended to the principal that the game not be played. The claim of negligence was based on the mismatch of the teams and the fact that the student was allowed to play without proper rest periods. Overturning two lower courts, the Court of Appeals of New York held that there was no liability because the student voluntarily was participating in an extracurricular activity for which he was fully trained by a certified coach.[80]   He was aware of the risks of fatigue and injury such as occurred. The court emphasized that its decision was not in regard to a compulsory curricular activity nor to a situation where there was direct or indirect compulsion of any sort by school personnel.

In Idaho a school custodian disregarded policy and allowed some students to enter the gymnasium and play basketball during a holiday period. One boy, a member of the basketball team of the school, was injured. The highest state court found no negligence. It held that the injury was a result of normal risks of the game, and that supervision of the game could not have prevented the collision of the two players chasing a rebounding basketball.[81]   The Supreme Court of Pennsylvania, however, found a jury question as to negligence presented where a student was injured in summer football practice.[82]   "Jungle" football, in which tackling and body-blocking were permitted, was being played without protective equipment and with the coaches engaging in the game rather than supervising. The Supreme Court of Illinois upheld a finding of negligence where a female high school student was injured in a traditional "powderpuff" football game played during half-time of the homecoming varsity football game. The girls lacked protective equipment and were only casually instructed in the rules of football.[83]

Where extracurricular activities are endorsed by the school, supervision must be provided. Perhaps one of the most dramatic cases in this area arose in South Dakota. As part of the initiation ceremony of candidates into a club, initiates were subjected to an electric shock. In one instance an initiate was killed by the shock. A suit against a teacher

---

79. Vendrell v. School Dist. No. 26C Malheur County, 233 Or. 1, 376 P.2d 406 (1962).

80. Benitez v. New York City Bd. of Educ., 73 N.Y.2d 650, 543 N.Y.S.2d 29, 541 N.E.2d 29 (1989).

81. Albers v. Independent School Dist. No. 302, 94 Idaho 342, 487 P.2d 936 (1971).

82. Rutter v. Northeastern Beaver County School Dist., 496 Pa. 590, 437 A.2d 1198 (1981).

83. Lynch v. Board of Educ. of Collinsville Community Unit Dist. No. 10, 82 Ill.2d 415, 45 Ill.Dec. 96, 412 N.E.2d 447 (1980).

was successful, and he was held personally liable. The Supreme Court of South Dakota pointed out that he had actively participated in the initiation activities, even to the point of testing the electrical appliance.[84]

The Supreme Court of Washington considered an action against a school district (which has no tort immunity in that state) for personal injuries sustained by a high school student being initiated into a club.[85] The club was a chapter of an international organization sponsored by a service group, but it was approved and faculty-supervised as an extracurricular organization. Membership was selective, being based upon scholastic and leadership ability and subject to faculty approval. Members of the club met with their faculty adviser and planned an initiation. It was determined that the event be held at the family residence of one of the members and that one act would be the disorienting of each initiate, inducing him to believe he was standing at the edge of a swimming pool, and ordering him to jump. Normally he would descend only a few inches to a level surface, and the results would be harmless. As it turned out the jump of one initiate was onto sloping ground and he was injured. The faculty adviser testified that had he been present he would not have permitted a jump to uneven ground. The board contended that the activity was not a school activity, in that it was away from school premises and beyond the scope of its proper supervisory authority and control, and that it possessed no educational or cultural value. The court, however, rejected the defense. The fact that the school administration had assumed supervisory responsibility, and thus tacitly approved the ceremony, resulted in district liability for the injury incurred. Under similar facts the Supreme Court of Florida held that a student injured in a hazing incident could bring an action against a principal and the faculty adviser of a school-sponsored club.[86] Regulations forbade hazing, but they were not enforced.

Whether school districts can require parents to sign releases from claims for negligence arising out of participation in certain school-related activities was answered in the negative by the Supreme Court of Washington.[87] That court held that the practice violated public policy. Struck down were all-inclusive releases that were an absolute precondition to participation in certain sports.

Administrative Responsibilities

In the South Dakota club-initiation case discussed in the second paragraph above, the superintendent was held not liable. He had determined that the teacher would be present at the ceremony before he permitted use of the gymnasium. Under normal circumstances a supervisor is not liable for the negligent acts of a staff member if the member

---

84. De Gooyer v. Harkness, 70 S.D. 26, 13 N.W.2d 815 (1944).

85. Chappel v. Franklin Pierce School Dist., No. 402, 71 Wash.2d 17, 426 P.2d 471 (1967).

86. Rupp v. Bryant, 417 So.2d 658 (Fla. 1982).

87. Wagenblast v. Odessa School Dist. No. 105–157–166J, 110 Wash.2d 845, 758 P.2d 968 (1988). [Case No. 58]

is qualified for the task and the supervisor establishes rules governing the situation.[88]

Some ramifications of this rule are provided in a Minnesota case in which a student was seriously injured in an eighth grade physical education class while performing a "headspring over a rolled mat." The teacher was found to be 90 percent negligent, the principal ten percent negligent, and the superintendent and the student free from negligence.[89] There was no showing that the superintendent had, or should have had, knowledge of the following events that preceded the injury. A newly certificated teacher took over the physical education instruction when the regular teacher left in March for military service. The principal gave him a copy of the state education department's curriculum bulletin, but otherwise left him on his own—not even offering "minimal guidance, such as telling him to abide by the provisions of [the bulletin] or explaining use of the bulletin's provisions." The principal took no part in the transition, simply telling the two teachers to plan classes for the rest of the year for the entire junior-senior high school. The new teacher reported to the principal what subjects he was going to teach, but did not discuss in detail activities to be included or methods for teaching gymnastics. Nine class periods into his teaching, the new teacher had the students engage in activities for which they were not properly prepared. The injury occurred during one of these activities, and the situation was aggravated by the teacher's negligent spotting of the headspring.

Failure to follow state or local regulations was a factor in two negligence cases decided by appellate courts in New York. In one a jury finding of negligence against a teacher was upheld where a student was injured while performing on rings in a gymnastics class in a situation in which the teacher was not watching the apparatus as stipulated in the state syllabus.[90] Other facts were that the students were only minimally restricted as to what they might do on the rings and stunts had not been demonstrated by the teacher. In the second it was held that a jury question was presented where there was evidence that the safety rules of the local board of education were not followed when a child died in a swimming pool.[91]

Where a statute is intended to protect a class of persons, it establishes a legal duty the violation of which may constitute negligence per se. Thus, the Supreme Court of Minnesota found negligence in a school board's failure to enforce a statute requiring the wearing of protective glasses in an industrial arts class in the case of a student who suffered an eye injury.[92] But for violation of a statute to constitute negligence

88. Cox v. Barnes, 469 S.W.2d 61 (Ky. 1971).

89. Larson v. Independent School Dist. No. 314, Braham, Minnesota, 289 N.W.2d 112 (Minn.1979).

90. Armlin v. Board of Educ. of Middleburgh Central School Dist., 36 A.D.2d 877, 320 N.Y.S.2d 402 (1971).

91. Brown v. Board of Educ. of City of New York, 37 A.D.2d 836, 326 N.Y.S.2d 9 (1971).

92. Scott v. Independent School Dist. No. 709, Duluth, 256 N.W.2d 485 (Minn. 1977).

per se the infraction must be linked to the injury. In illustration, the Court of Appeals of New York found no liability on the bus driver or the company for an injury resulting from a student's being struck by a motorist when the student emerged from between two buses on school grounds, even though the bus's warning lights were not flashing while students were boarding, as was required by state law.[93] The motorist conceded she was aware of the situation.

Failure of school personnel with special responsibilities to execute them competently has led to judgments in favor of plaintiffs in negligence actions. In one case, a counselor was requested on four occasions to supply a student's mother with a list of exercises required in physical education. The daughter had a back condition and twice in prior years had been excused from certain exercises upon the request of her doctor. She was injured in a physical education class one week after the fourth request. The doctor would have recommended she not participate in that exercise. Pointing out that one is bound by what he would have known had he been reasonably diligent, the court ruled for the plaintiffs.[94]

In a case decided by the highest court of Maryland the allegation was that two school counselors were on notice that a 13–year–old student had made several statements contemplating suicide during the week before she died.[95] The counselors did not inform the student's parents or the school administration. The lower court dismissed the suit primarily on the ground of no legally recognizable duty, but the Court of Appeals reversed the ruling and sent the case to trial. It held that "school counselors have a duty to use reasonable means to attempt to prevent a suicide when they are on notice of a child or adolescent student's suicidal intent."

In a Louisiana case, it was found to be more likely than not that had a student who suffered a heat stroke on the second day of football practice in August been given reasonably prompt medical attention he would not have died. The high school coaches who failed to summon medical assistance were held liable.[96] They had increased their culpability by not giving proper first aid treatment for heat stroke.

It was noted previously that a school district had the right and the duty to provide emergency first aid treatment for pupils injured in connection with school activities. It has been held, however, that liability for damages may result if the injuries suffered in an athletic event are aggravated by the player's being removed from the scene of the accident in a negligent fashion.[97] Yet the emergency nature of an action legally excepts certain niceties which might be required in the absence of

93. Aridas v. Caserta, 41 N.Y.2d 1059, 396 N.Y.S.2d 170, 364 N.E.2d 835 (1977).

94. Summers v. Milwaukie Union High School Dist. No. 5, 4 Or.App. 596, 481 P.2d 369 (1971).

95. Eisel v. Board of Educ. of Montgomery County, 324 Md. 376, 597 A.2d 447 (1991).

96. Mogabgab v. Orleans Parish School Bd., 239 So.2d 456 (La.App.1970).

97. Welch v. Dunsmuir Joint Union High School Dist., 326 P.2d 633 (Cal.App. 1958).

an emergency. For example, it was held that two teachers were personally liable when they attempted to administer medical treatment, and the treatment given resulted in harm to the pupil.[98] The teachers undertook to treat a ten-year-old boy by holding his infected finger under boiling water. Injuries resulted, and the teachers were required to pay damages. The court pointed out that the teachers were not school nurses, and neither of them had any medical training or experience. Furthermore, observed the court, treatment of the infected finger in the absence of an emergency was a question to be decided by the boy's parents, not the teachers.

In a similar situation, the Supreme Court of Illinois held that negligence could be found where school employees had a student's injured knee treated by untrained personnel rather than by trained medical personnel.[99] The injuries were received off school property during an activity unrelated to school, and there was no emergency. "Teachers are not privileged to do everything that a parent may do," said the court in restricting the "in loco parentis" status of teachers to activities connected to the school program.

Off Premises

Whether there is liability on school personnel and/or districts for negligence depends first on the existence of a duty of care that is somehow not properly executed. The duty to supervise students on school grounds is clear. Efforts to extend the scope of the duty beyond the premises are increasing. In this regard it is important to emphasize that the common law sets the school's duty as being coextensive with, and concomitant to, its physical custody and control over the child. Where the school undertakes to transport the child, it in effect extends its boundary via the bus to the bus stop where the child boards and leaves the bus.[100] On the homeward trip the duty extends to seeing that the child has crossed the road to the opposite side of the street if such is necessary.[101] There also may be a responsibility for establishing a reasonably safe location for the stop.[102] But once the child is safely at the bus stop, the duty of the school district and the bus driver ceases.[103]

If a child is truant the school generally is not responsible for an injury. Where, however, a job description of instructional aides at a boarding school for American Indians provided that they should supervise outside during certain hours and none were there, the Tenth Circuit Court of Appeals upheld a finding of negligence as regards some students

98. Guerrieri v. Tyson, 147 Pa.Super. 239, 24 A.2d 468 (1942).

99. O'Brien v. Township High School Dist. 214, 83 Ill.2d 462, 47 Ill.Dec. 702, 415 N.E.2d 1015 (1980).

100. Pratt v. Robinson, 39 N.Y.2d 554, 384 N.Y.S.2d 749, 349 N.E.2d 849 (1976).

101. Johnson v. Svoboda, 260 N.W.2d 530 (Iowa 1977).

102. Gleich v. Volpe, 32 N.Y.2d 517, 346 N.Y.S.2d 806, 300 N.E.2d 148 (1973).

103. Traylor v. Coburn, 597 S.W.2d 319 (Tenn.App.1980); Harrison v. Escambia County School Bd., 434 So.2d 316 (Fla. 1983).

aged seven to ten who ran away and were injured.[104] The Supreme Court of California has held that a question of fact for a jury was presented as to whether inadequate supervision had been the proximate cause of an injury to a ten-year-old student who had left school premises without permission during the school day.[105] However, after a jury had found negligence when a ten-year-old left school grounds and was abducted and slain, the Court of Appeals of Arizona held that the verdict was properly overturned, because school personnel could not reasonably have foreseen that the girl would leave after being instructed to return to her classroom.[106]

Where a student who had been suspended fatally injured another student who was on his way home from school, no liability was incurred by either the principal or the school district.[107] The court emphasized that the incident was off campus. It noted that another Florida court had upheld the sufficiency of a complaint wherein an assault and battery had occurred within the school facility.[108]

The highest court of Connecticut, where common-law governmental immunity for discretionary functions was the rule, held that the immunity prevented a suit for negligence based on a school board's policy that permitted tenth, eleventh, and twelfth grade students to leave campus during unscheduled times.[109] The court found no specific ministerial duty to supervise high school students at all times. Thus, suit for damages in connection with a student's death in an automobile accident that occurred when he left school premises in a car driven by another student was precluded.

Field trips sponsored by schools require special supervisory precautions because children are taken into unfamiliar places. An illustration is found in a case which came before the Supreme Court of Oregon.[110] Suit was brought for damages because of injuries sustained by a six-year-old child injured at a beach while on a school outing. A large log was lying on the beach. Four children climbed on the log, and the teacher posed them there for pictures. Suddenly a large wave came onto the beach causing the log to roll over. As it rolled a child fell under it on the seaward side and was injured. The trial court found the teacher negligent in failing to exercise proper supervision at the time of the accident, and this judgment was upheld on appeal. The appellate court said that whether the kind of harm was reasonably foreseeable and whether the supervision was adequate were fact questions. The court declined to hold as a matter of law that unusual wave action on the

104. Bryant v. United States, 565 F.2d 650 (10 Cir.1977).

105. Hoyem v. Manhattan Beach City School Dist., 22 Cal.3d 508, 150 Cal.Rptr. 1, 585 P.2d 851 (1978).

106. Chavez v. Tolleson Elementary School Dist. 122 Ariz. 472, 595 P.2d 1017 (App.1979).

107. Oglesby v. Seminole County Bd. of Public Instr., 328 So.2d 515 (Fla.App.1976).

108. King v. Dade County Bd. of Public Instr., 286 So.2d 256 (Fla.App.1973).

109. Heigl v. Board of Educ. of Town of New Canaan, 218 Conn. 1, 587 A.2d 423 (1991).

110. Morris v. Douglas County School Dist. No. 9, 241 Or. 23, 403 P.2d 775 (1965).

shore of the Pacific Ocean was a hazard so unforeseeable that there was no duty to guard against it. It observed that it was common knowledge that accidents substantially like the one that occurred were not uncommon on beaches along the Oregon coast.

On a field trip to a museum a student was accosted and beaten by several youths who were in the museum. About fifty students in the twelve-to-fifteen age range were accompanied by two teachers, who at the museum allowed them to view the exhibits without direct supervision. The court found no negligence.[111] It commented that the museum was not an inherently dangerous place and that to require more careful supervision would be "to ignore the realities of the situation and to make such trips impossible."

Other problems related to off campus trips are illustrated by three cases involving use of privately owned cars. In one instance a high school coach with permission of another teacher used the second teacher's car to transport members of the football team to a game in a neighboring town. An accident ensued and suit was brought against the owner of the car. The question was whether those riding in the car were classifiable as "guests," who would not have been able to recover under the circumstances. The court held that the boys were not guests within the meaning of the statute.[112] The reasoning was that they had been riding in this particular vehicle on a school-sponsored trip under instructions from the coach, and the coach was an agent of the owner of the car.

The Supreme Court of South Dakota has considered a case involving the same question.[113] There a group of girls from one school were participating in a school program in another town to raise funds for the school. The superintendent offered them the use of his automobile and provided a credit card to pay for expenses which were later reimbursed by the school. The girls who made the trip were to provide musical entertainment at a banquet. The dean of girls drove the car to the neighboring town. In the evening they decided to drive about eighty miles farther to a swimming area. On this side trip one of the girls, who had previously had very little driving experience, took over the driving. An accident occurred when the car was moving at a speed of over sixty miles an hour. The evidence was sufficient to support a finding that the driver had been negligent. The dean of girls was also found negligent in her supervision of the manner in which the automobile was being driven. The question then arose as to whether the injured passenger was a guest at the time of the accident. The court held that she was. In the court's opinion the evidence established that the side trip had been for the mutual pleasure and enjoyment of all the occupants of the automobile and had no rational relationship to the purpose of the trip to the neighboring school district. An implication of the holding is that had

111. Mancha v. Field Museum of Natural History, 5 Ill.App.3d 699, 283 N.E.2d 899 (1972).

112. Gorton v. Doty, 57 Idaho 792, 69 P.2d 136 (1937).

113. Robe v. Ager, 80 S.D. 597, 129 N.W.2d 47 (1964).

the accident occurred between the two towns while the girls were going to or from their school, they would have had passenger status and might have recovered for the injuries.

The third case was a suit against the county arising from a fatal accident involving a school's driver education car. The principal of the school, without permission of the board of education, used the car on a Sunday afternoon to drive to another community to participate in a drawing of pairings for a basketball tournament. The court held that the county was not liable because it had not authorized the use of the car.[114]

The issue of assumption and cessation of a duty on which another comes to rely was discussed in a case involving the absence of a street crossing guard who had been assigned by the police department. The department had voluntarily assumed the responsibility for supervising school crossings. There were procedures covering contingencies if a guard was ill and if the police officer assigned as substitute had to be on more urgent police business. In the instant case a mother, having observed the daily presence of a crossing guard, accepted employment two weeks after her first-grade son started school, "confident that she need not arrange for someone to provide a similar service for her child." The procedures broke down on the day her son was struck at the crossing by an automobile. The regular guard was ill. Contrary to regulations, no substitute was provided, and the principal was not notified. The Court of Appeals of New York, observing that the state had long before waived governmental immunity, applied the common law of liability to the situation and found that the duty, albeit a voluntarily assumed one, could be deemed by a jury to have been negligently performed.[115] The jury verdict in favor of the plaintiff was upheld. The Court of Appeal of Louisiana in a similar case held the school board liable for a student death when the crossing guard provided by the city was absent and school officials did nothing to remedy the situation.[116]

It must be emphasized, however, that unless school authorities assume a special obligation or express an intention to render some service to students on the way from their homes to school grounds, no duty of supervision or protection exists and, thus, negligence cannot be developed.[117]

Condition of Premises

Many cases of negligence derive from improper supervision of physical premises. If hazardous conditions are allowed to develop and reasonable steps are not taken to correct them, negligence suits are likely to succeed. If a dangerous condition exists that would have been revealed

---

114. Sumter County v. Pritchett, 125 Ga.App. 222, 186 S.E.2d 798 (1971).

115. Florence v. Goldberg, 44 N.Y.2d 189, 404 N.Y.S.2d 583, 375 N.E.2d 763 (1978).

116. Barnes v. Bott, 571 So.2d 183 (La. App.1990).

117. Honeycutt v. City of Wichita, 251 Kan. 451, 836 P.2d 1128 (1992); Brownell v. Los Angeles Unified School Dist., 4 Cal. App.4th 787, 5 Cal.Rptr.2d 756 (1992).

by proper inspections, the liability is the same as if there were actual knowledge.[118]

Where a leaking water fountain had not been repaired despite three requests over a period of six months the Supreme Court of Louisiana held that the school board was responsible for damages to a twelve-year-old student who slipped and fell on the wet asphalt.[119] The court said that the ages of children in the school and their propensity to run in the school yard required school authorities to react more expeditiously. The Supreme Court of Oklahoma held that the maintenance of the high school parking lot was a ministerial function and, therefore, suit could be brought against the school board for an injury allegedly due to faulty maintenance of a water drain grill.[120] The Supreme Court of California held that a community college district could be liable for negligence in a situation where a student was assaulted in the parking lot.[121] The district could be faulted for failing to warn students of known dangers or for failing to trim the heavy foliage around the lot that added to the danger of criminal acts.

A New York case encapsulates a number of factors. Two unsupervised youth employed as part of a summer program sponsored by a board of education stole some chemicals from an unlocked storeroom and dropped them from a window into bushes from which they intended later to retrieve them. An eight-year-old boy who lived near the school and regularly played on its grounds discovered the chemicals and believed them to be sand. As he played with the chemicals and with matches he had earlier found, the chemicals exploded and injured the boy. The Court of Appeals of New York upheld a finding of negligence.[122] It said that the school authorities had a duty to keep dangerous chemicals locked away from those whose presence on school grounds could be anticipated. The chain of events was caused by the authorities' not properly supervising their employees, as well as their failure to secure the chemicals adequately. The intervening act of the theft of the chemicals should have been anticipated, and therefore did not relieve the school district of liability.

The school district may be held responsible for injuries in connection with any equipment that it allows to be used on its premises. For example, a negligence claim was sent to trial on allegations derived from a situation in which a handicapped child was being pushed in a wheelchair by a fellow student, the chair hit a crevice, and the rider was

118. Wilkinson v. Hartford Accident and Indemnity Co., 411 So.2d 22 (La.1982) (plate glass, rather than shatterproof glass); Shetina v. Ohio University, 9 Ohio App.3d 240, 459 N.E.2d 587 (1983) (defective condition of window); Gurule v. Salt Lake City Bd. of Educ., 661 P.2d 957 (Utah 1983) (removal of ice).

119. Morris v. Orleans Parish School Bd., 553 So.2d 427 (La.1989).

120. Robinson v. City of Bartlesville Bd. of Educ., 700 P.2d 1013 (Okl.1985).

121. Peterson v. San Francisco Community College Dist., 36 Cal.3d 799, 205 Cal. Rptr. 842, 685 P.2d 1193 (1984).

122. Kush by Marszalek v. City of Buffalo, 59 N.Y.2d 26, 462 N.Y.S.2d 831, 449

injured.[123] That the wheelchair was furnished by the parents did not relieve the board of its responsibility to utilize adequate equipment.

Defamation and Other Torts

Administrators and teachers are afforded a qualified privilege as regards defamation. The general principles regarding the twin torts of slander and libel discussed under "Liability of School Board Members" also apply here. Statements supportable by evidence (but not necessarily true) made to proper parties in the line of duty are not actionable.[124] It is well established that a former employer is protected when nonmaliciously responding to an inquiry from a potential employer concerning an individual's fitness for employment.[125] It is clear that the superintendent is privileged in giving teacher evaluations to the board.[126] Likewise held not to be actionable was a letter from the state superintendent of schools to another administrator in which the higher official said a teacher was unfit because he had been under the influence of liquor.[127] Not protected, however, was a nonconfidential report by a teacher in which a student was described as "ruined by tobacco and whiskey."[128]

Suits against school personnel alleging defamation are increasing. A key ingredient of a successful suit is a showing that a significant diminution of professional reputation has occurred. Mere hurt feelings are not enough. Thus, the Court of Appeal of Louisiana has found no defamation where a principal wrote a letter to the superintendent recommending that a teacher not be re-employed and where in a conversation with her overheard by others in the teachers' lounge he referred to her as a "nut."[129]

A federal District Court in Wisconsin held that there was no defamation in a remark by an administrator, who was a member of a committee considering the promotion of an assistant professor at a state university, that the candidate was an "old biddy."[130] The comment, as part of a negative opinion of qualifications for promotion, was not made to the general community and so could not lower its estimation of the person. No professional damage was done by the remark itself. Where, however, defamatory statements are made at such a meeting with knowledge that they are false, a cause of action is stated.[131]

N.E.2d 725 (1983).

123. Bertetto v. Sparta Community Unit Dist. No. 140, 188 Ill.App.3d 954, 136 Ill.Dec. 365, 544 N.E.2d 1140 (1989).

124. Kenney v. Gurley, 208 Ala. 623, 95 So. 34 (1923); Ranous v. Hughes, 30 Wis.2d 452, 141 N.W.2d 128 (1966).

125. Neal v. Gatlin, 35 Cal.App.3d 871, 111 Cal.Rptr. 117 (1973).

126. McLaughlin v. Tilendis, 115 Ill. App.2d 148, 253 N.E.2d 85 (1969).

127. De Bolt v. McBrien, 96 Neb. 237, 147 N.W. 462 (1914).

128. Dawkins v. Billingsley, 69 Okl. 259, 172 P. 69 (1918).

129. McGowen v. Prentice, 341 So.2d 55 (La.App.1976).

130. Rubenstein v. University of Wisconsin Bd. of Regents, 422 F.Supp. 61 (E.D.Wis.1976).

131. Colson v. Stieg, 89 Ill.2d 205, 60 Ill.Dec. 449, 433 N.E.2d 246 (1982).

Because defamation is speech, some First Amendment considerations apply. In the interest of free discussion of matters of public
concern the Supreme Court has treated public officials differently from
private persons. For a public official to succeed as a plaintiff in a
defamation suit it must be shown that the communicator made a
harmful and false statement of fact that he knew was false, or that he
presented the statement with reckless disregard of its truth or falsity.[132]
Public official status would generally encompass board members and
superintendents.[133] Most courts that have considered the matter have
held that teachers are not public officials.[134] The courts are more
divided as to principals.[135]

The "public official" defamation standard also applies to a "public
figure" (one who is closely involved with specific public questions or
events in an area of concern to society at large).[136] Public figure status
is completely based on operative facts of a situation. Thus, a track coach
was considered to be a public figure in connection with an issue related
to college athletes,[137] and two professors in a public junior college were
so classified for purpose of a particular controversy.[138]

If a statement is clearly one of opinion, there would be no common
law basis for liability of the communicator. An exception would arise,
however, if the statement reasonably could be understood to be based on
defamatory underlying facts that are not disclosed.[139] The Supreme
Court, applying the First Amendment, has held that "where a statement
of 'opinion' on a matter of public concern reasonably implies false and
defamatory facts regarding public figures or officials, those individuals
[can recover damages if they] show that such statements were made with
knowledge of their false implications or with reckless disregard of their
truth." [140]

Civil liability for assault and battery can arise from situations
involving corporal punishment. (See Chapter 12.) Damages will not
generally be awarded, however, unless the punishment was actuated by
malice or inflicted in a willful and wanton manner. If the teacher did
not intend to injure or did not administer the punishment with a
reckless disregard of consequences, he generally will not be held liable.
The common law is to the effect that corporal punishment reasonable

132. New York Times v. Sullivan, 376
U.S. 254, 84 S.Ct. 710, 11 L.Ed.2d 686
(1964).

133. Kelly v. Iowa State Educ. Ass'n,
372 N.W.2d 288 (Iowa App.1985).

134. True v. Ladner, 513 A.2d 257 (Me.
1986); Johnson v. Southwestern Newspapers Corp., 855 S.W.2d 182 (Tex.App.1993)
(but holding that an athletic director and
head football coach was a public official).
For contra, see Kelley v. Bonney, 221 Conn.
549, 606 A.2d 693 (1992).

135. Compare Ellerbee v. Mills, 262 Ga.
516, 422 S.E.2d 539 (1992), cert. den. ___
U.S. ___, 113 S.Ct. 1833, 123 L.Ed.2d 460

(1993) with Palmer v. Bennington School
Dist., Inc., ___ Vt. ___, 615 A.2d 498 (1992).

136. Curtis Publishing Co. v. Butts, 388
U.S. 130, 87 S.Ct. 1975, 18 L.Ed.2d 1094
(1967).

137. Vandenburg v. Newsweek, Inc.,
507 F.2d 1024 (5 Cir.1975).

138. Johnson v. Board of Junior College
Dist. No. 508, 31 Ill.App.3d 270, 334 N.E.2d
442 (1975).

139. Baker v. Lafayette College, 516 Pa.
291, 532 A.2d 399 (1987).

140. Milkovich v. Lorain Journal Co.,
497 U.S. 1, 110 S.Ct. 2695, 111 L.Ed.2d 1
(1990).

under the circumstances does not constitute assault and battery.[141] There have, however, been cases in which infliction of excessive corporal punishment has resulted in liability.[142]

The legal authority of school personnel to discipline students is also a recognized defense to the tort of false imprisonment. This was, perhaps, first set out in an 1887 case in Indiana involving detention of a pupil after school.[143] It was accepted by the Court of Appeals of New York in 1973 in a case where, after a school bus driver stated he was driving to the police station because of damage students had done to the bus, a student tried to get out a window of the bus and was seriously injured.[144] Lower courts had erroneously excluded evidence to justify the bus driver's action. The highest New York court added that, even if false imprisonment should be found on retrial, if the student acted unreasonably for his safety in attempting to alight, recovery for bodily injuries would be barred.

Sometimes employed personnel seek to recover from school districts for injuries suffered in connection with their work. Although they may be eligible for workers compensation and for benefits of insurance arrangements, the usual rule is that they cannot hold a district liable (even where district immunity does not apply) for breach of a duty that is owed generally to persons in the school system or the public. Thus, a school district was not liable to a teacher who was injured when he sought to halt an altercation in a school hallway.[145] The teacher had sought recovery on the basis that the board of education had not properly enforced its security plan. Employees can, however, sue fellow employees or students for torts committed by them.[146]

The inchoate and elusive tort of "educational malpractice" is treated in Chapter 4 under "Malpractice." [147]

[Case No. 51]   Liability for Injury to Spectator at Athletic Event

TANARI v. SCHOOL DIRECTORS OF DIST. NO. 502, COUNTY OF BUREAU

Supreme Court of Illinois, 1977.
69 Ill.2d 630, 14 Ill.Dec. 874, 373 N.E.2d 5.

UNDERWOOD, JUSTICE: Plaintiff, Flora Tanari, brought an action * * * seeking damages for injuries she sustained when she allegedly was knocked to the ground by a group of children engaged in horseplay at a high school football game sponsored by defendant on its premises. The

---

141. People v. Ball, 58 Ill.2d 36, 317 N.E.2d 54 (1974).

142. Sansone v. Bechtel, 180 Conn. 96, 429 A.2d 820 (1980).

143. Fertich v. Michener, 111 Ind. 472, 11 N.E. 605 (1887).

144. Sindle v. New York City Transit Authority, 33 N.Y.2d 293, 352 N.Y.S.2d 183, 307 N.E.2d 245 (1973).

145. Vitale v. City of New York, 60 N.Y.2d 861, 470 N.Y.S.2d 358, 458 N.E.2d 817 (1983).

146. American States Insurance Co. v. Flynn, 102 Ill.App.3d 201, 57 Ill.Dec. 689, 429 N.E.2d 587 (1981).

147. See Hunter v. Board of Educ. of Montgomery County, 292 Md. 481, 439 A.2d 582 (1982). [Case No. 59]

complaint alleged ordinary negligence on the part of defendant in failing to provide adequate supervision and control of children at the game. At the close of the evidence, the trial court granted the defendant's motion for a directed verdict on the ground that plaintiff was a licensee on defendant's premises; that defendant therefore only owed her the duty to refrain from wilful and wanton misconduct; and that breach of such duty had neither been alleged nor proved at trial. * * *

Plaintiff, age 64, was employed as a bus driver by an individual who had a contract with the defendant school district to transport students to and from school. She had been so employed for 27 years and had attended all of the local high school football games for the last 25 years. On October 13, 1972, plaintiff attended the Hall Township High School homecoming football game with her daughter, son-in-law and grandchildren. The game was held on defendant's premises at a sports stadium under defendant's supervision and control. Plaintiff entered the stadium using a complimentary season pass issued by the defendant. As she was walking toward her seat, she noticed a crowd of boys and girls playing near the northwest end of the stadium, and the next thing she knew she had been knocked to the ground by a "big" boy who fell on top of her. The boy, who was never identified, got up, apologized and hurried away. * * *

The athletic director of Hall Township High School testified that he had hired off-duty policemen and teachers to keep order at all high school football games conducted by the defendant. * * * He responded in the affirmative when asked if he had seen boys and girls at almost every game "playing tag, or horseplaying and roughing it up" in the area in question. However, when he was later asked if there was "rowdiness and horseplaying by these kids in that area," he responded that he did not know whether it should be called rowdiness and horseplay but the children were definitely there. He further testified that on previous occasions he had tried to "correct" the children but that, as soon as he left, they were back at it again. He knew from his personal observation that a policeman was in the area of the accident on the night in question.

The trial court allowed the defendant's motion for a directed verdict on the sole ground that plaintiff was a licensee on the defendant's premises and that there was no proof whatsoever that defendant had breached its duty to refrain from wilful and wanton misconduct. On appeal, the appellate court agreed with the trial court that a verdict should be directed in favor of the defendant but stated that it preferred that such ruling be based upon the immunity granted by the Local Governmental and Governmental Employees Tort Immunity Act. * * * Considering the state of the record before us, we are unable to concur with the appellate court's conclusions regarding defendant's immunity under the above-referred-to statutes and are likewise unable to agree with the court's further determination that "irrespective of the standard of care which might have been required in this case, no verdict in favor of the plaintiff could stand as against the defendant school directors."

. The Local Governmental and Governmental Employees Tort Immunity Act (hereafter referred to as the Tort Immunity Act) provides, *inter alia,* that "a public employee serving in a position involving the determination of policy or the exercise of discretion is not liable for an injury resulting from his act or omission in determining policy when acting in the exercise of such discretion even though abused." Section 2–109 of the Act also provides that "[a] local public entity is not liable for an injury resulting from an act or omission of its employee where the employee is not liable." * * *

At the time of plaintiff's injury section 24–24 of the School Code provided in pertinent part:

> "Teachers and other certificated educational employees shall maintain discipline in the schools. In all matters relating to the discipline in and conduct of the schools and the school children, they stand in the relation of parents and guardians to the pupils. This relationship shall extend to all activities connected with the school program and may be exercised at any time for the safety and supervision of the pupils in the absence of their parents or guardians."

Since the foregoing statute specifically confers upon educators the status of parent or guardian to the students, and since a parent is not liable for injuries to his child absent wilful and wanton misconduct it therefore follows that the same standard applies as between educator and student. * * * We [have] held that section 24–24 of the School Code was intended to confer *in loco parentis* status in nondisciplinary as well as disciplinary matters, * * *.

In our view, section 24–24 of the School Code is not applicable here in view of the absence of any *in loco parentis* relationship between the injured plaintiff and the certificated employees of the defendant school district who allegedly failed to exercise proper supervision. * * * [S]ection 24–24 reflects "a legislative determination that educators should stand in the place of a parent or guardian in matters relating to discipline, the conduct of the schools and the school children. It is this status as parent or guardian which requires a plaintiff to prove wilful and wanton misconduct in order to impose liability upon educators." That status is clearly lacking here, and it seems evident that the purpose of the immunity which arises from such status would not be served by extending it to immunize school districts from liability to third parties for ordinary negligence in situations such as that now before us. We accordingly hold that section 24–24 of the School Code does not provide any basis for affirmance of the trial court's decision in this case.

It is unnecessary to dwell at length on the common law distinctions between invitees and licensees which have evolved over the years. It suffices to observe that the general definition of an invitee is a visitor who comes upon premises at the invitation of the owner in connection with the owner's business or related activity. Licensees are persons who have not been invited to enter upon the owner's premises and who come there for their own purposes and not those of the owner. However, their presence is condoned by the owner, which distinguishes them from trespassers. The trial court concluded in the case at bar that since the plaintiff had not purchased a ticket but rather had attended the football game using a complimentary season pass, there was an absence of "commercial benefit" to the defendant school district, and she must therefore be considered a licensee. For the reasons hereafter stated, we must disagree with that conclusion.

In determining whether or not a person is an invitee or a licensee in a given situation, appellate courts in this State have often looked at the surrounding circumstances to determine whether, as between the visitor and the owner, there was a "mutuality of interest in the subject to which the visitor's business relates", "a mutually beneficial interest", a "mutuality of benefit or a benefit to the owner", or whether the visitor had come to "transact business in which he and the owner have a mutual interest or to promote some real or fancied material, financial, or economic interest of the owner". Such inquiries into the purpose and nature of the visit were deemed relevant particularly in cases involving implied invitations, to ascertain whether the visitor was upon the owner's premises within the scope and purpose of the invitation or for some other reason.

That type of analysis is not necessary here. In our opinion, the complimentary pass issued to plaintiff was tantamount to an express invitation to attend Hall Township High School football games, and there can be no question about the fact that at the time of her injury, plaintiff was acting within the scope of that invitation. Unlike a person who comes upon an owner's premises for his own purposes rather than those of the owner and whose presence is merely condoned by the owner, plaintiff in this case was expressly invited and encouraged to come to the defendant's football stadium to swell the crowd in support of its team. In this type of situation, it would be entirely illogical to conclude that a person attending the game using a complimentary pass provided by the school district should be owed a lesser duty of care than a person otherwise similarly situated who had purchased a ticket. In our view, both persons should be owed the same duty of reasonable care, and we so hold.

Upon application of a reasonable care standard to the case at bar, we cannot conclude that all of the evidence, when viewed in its aspect most favorable to the plaintiff, so overwhelmingly favors the defendant that no verdict for the plaintiff could ever stand. The question of whether defendant failed to exercise reasonable care in supervising children attending the football game and whether such failure, if found to exist, was the proximate cause of plaintiff's injuries, should have been submitted to the jury.

* * *

Reversed and remanded.

* * *

Notes

1. The Tort Immunity Act was a legislative response to the decision of this court that abrogated the common law doctrine of governmental immunity from liability for torts (footnote 24).

2. The first interpretation of the relation between Section 24-24 and the Tort Immunity Act (i.e., the holding that a teacher is liable only for "wilful and wanton misconduct") was made in an action brought by a student against a school district for injuries sustained by the student in a gym class due to the alleged failure of the teacher to provide proper instruction and supervision. Kobylanski v. Chicago Bd. of Educ., 63 Ill.2d 165, 347 N.E.2d 705 (1976). The present case was the first to establish that where there is no direct teacher involvement to invoke the in loco parentis concept, an Illinois school board's liability is to be determined by the common law standards applicable to private bodies.

3. The categorization of one lawfully on another's property as invitee or licensee has proved to be so troublesome that courts in some states have abandoned the centuries-old distinction in favor of a single standard of care dependent upon the circumstances present [e.g., Basso v. Miller, 40 N.Y.2d 233, 386 N.Y.S.2d 564, 352 N.E.2d 868 (1976)]. In the present case the court retains the distinction, but transfers plaintiff from the licensee status granted by the trial court to invitee status, thereby invoking the application of a greater duty of care on the part of the board. Is the reasoning for the change persuasive to you?

[Case No. 52]   Liability for Violation of Civil Rights of Students

WOOD v. STRICKLAND

Supreme Court of the United States, 1975.
420 U.S. 308, 95 S.Ct. 992, 43 L.Ed.2d 214.

[The school board suspended three 10th grade girls for approximately three months (to the end of the semester) for "spiking" the punch at a meeting of an extracurricular school organization attended by parents and students. Suit was brought under "Section 1983" by two of the girls seeking, among other things, damages against two school administrators and the members of the school board for alleged violation of federal constitutional rights. The Supreme Court here remanded the case for a ruling on the question of a procedural due process violation. Only the part of the decision relating to liability of the school authorities is included here. The text of "Section 1983" is in Chapter 1.]

Mr. Justice White delivered the opinion of the Court.

* * *

The District Court instructed the jury that a decision for respondents had to be premised upon a finding that petitioners acted with malice in expelling them and defined "malice" as meaning "ill will against a person—a wrongful act done intentionally without just cause or excuse." In ruling for petitioners after the jury had been unable to agree, the District Court found "as a matter of law" that there was no evidence from which malice could be inferred.

The Court of Appeals, however, viewed both the instruction and the decision of the District Court as being erroneous. Specific intent to harm wrongfully, it held, was not a requirement for the recovery of damages. Instead, "[i]t need only be established that the defendants did not, in the light of all the circumstances, act in good faith. The test is an objective, rather than a subjective one."

Petitioners as members of the school board assert here, as they did below, an absolute immunity from liability under § 1983 and at the very least seek to reinstate the judgment of the District Court. If they are correct and the District Court's dismissal should be sustained, we need go no further in this case. Moreover, the immunity question involves the construction of a federal statute, and our practice is to deal with possibly dispositive statutory issues before reaching questions turning on the construction of the Constitution. We essentially sustain the position of the Court of Appeals with respect to the immunity issue.

The nature of the immunity from awards of damages under § 1983 available to school administrators and school board members is not a question which the lower federal courts have answered with a single voice. There is general agreement on the existence of a "good faith" immunity, but the courts have either emphasized different factors as elements of good faith or have not given specific content to the good-faith standard.

This Court had decided three cases dealing with the scope of the immunity protecting various types of governmental officials from liability for damages under § 1983. In Tenney v. Brandhove, 341 U.S. 367, 71 S.Ct. 783, 95 L.Ed. 1019 (1951), the question was found to be one essentially of statutory construction. Noting that the language of § 1983 is silent with respect to immunities, the Court concluded that there was no basis for believing that Congress intended to eliminate the traditional immunity of legislators from civil liability for acts done within their sphere of legislative action. That immunity, "so well grounded in history and reason * * * ", was absolute and consequently did not depend upon the motivations of the legislators. In Pierson v. Ray, 386 U.S. 547, 554, 87 S.Ct. 1213, 1218, 18 L.Ed.2d 288 (1967), finding that "[t]he legislative record gives no clear indication that Congress meant to abolish wholesale all common-law immunities" in enacting § 1983, we concluded that the common-law doctrine of absolute judicial immunity survived. Similarly, § 1983 did not preclude application of the traditional rule that a policeman, making an arrest in good faith and with probable cause, is not liable for damages, although the person arrested proves innocent. Consequently the Court said: "Although the matter is not entirely free from doubt, the same consideration would seem to require excusing him from liability for acting under a statute that he reasonably believed to be valid but that was later held unconstitutional, on its face or as applied." Finally, last Term we held that the chief executive officer of a State, the senior and subordinate officers of the State's National Guard, and the president of a state-controlled university were not absolutely immune from liability under § 1983, but instead were entitled to immunity, under prior precedent and in light of the obvious need to avoid discouraging effective official action by public officers charged with a considerable range of responsibility and discretion, only if they acted in good faith as defined by the Court:

> "[I]n varying scope, a qualified immunity is available to officers of the executive branch of Government, the variation being dependent upon the scope of discretion and responsibilities of the office and all the circumstances as they reasonably appeared at the time of the action on which liability is sought to be based. It is the existence of reasonable grounds for the belief formed at the time and in light of all the circumstances, coupled with good-faith belief, that affords a basis for qualified immunity of executive officers for acts performed in the course of official conduct."   Scheuer v. Rhodes, 416 U.S. 232, 247–248, 94 S.Ct. 1683, 1692, 40 L.Ed.2d 90 (1974).

Common-law tradition, recognized in our prior decisions, and strong public-policy reasons also lead to a construction of § 1983 extending a qualified good-faith immunity to school board members from liability for damages under that section.   Although there have been differing emphases and formulations of the common-law immunity of public school officials in cases of student expulsion or suspension, state courts have generally recognized that such officers should be protected from tort liability under state law for all good-faith, non-malicious action taken to fulfill their official duties.

As the facts of this case reveal, school board members function at different times in the nature of legislators and adjudicators in the school disciplinary process.   Each of these functions necessarily involves the exercise of discretion, the weighing of many factors, and the formulation of long-term policy.   "Like legislators and judges, these officers are entitled to rely on traditional sources for the factual information on which they decide and act."   As with executive officers faced with instances of civil disorder, school officials, confronted with student behavior causing or threatening disruption, also have an "obvious need for prompt action, and decisions must be made in reliance on factual information supplied by others."

Liability for damages for every action which is found subsequently to have been violative of a student's constitutional rights and to have caused compensable injury would unfairly impose upon the school decisionmaker the burden of mistakes made in good faith in the course of exercising his discretion within the scope of his official duties.   School board members, among other duties, must judge whether there have been violations of school regulations and, if so, the appropriate sanctions for the violations.   Denying any measure of immunity in these circumstances "would contribute not to principled and fearless decision-making but to intimidation."   The imposition of monetary costs for mistakes which were not unreasonable in the light of all the circumstances would undoubtedly deter even the most conscientious school decisionmaker from exercising his judgment independently, forcefully, and in a manner best serving the long-term interest of the school and the students. The most capable candidates for school board positions might be deterred from seeking office if heavy burdens upon their private resources from monetary liability were a likely prospect during their tenure.

These considerations have undoubtedly played a prime role in the development by state courts of a qualified immunity protecting school officials from liability for damages in lawsuits claiming improper suspensions or expulsions. But at the same time, the judgment implicit in this common-law development is that absolute immunity would not be justified since it would not sufficiently increase the ability of school officials to exercise their discretion in a forthright manner to warrant the absence of a remedy for students subjected to intentional or otherwise inexcusable deprivations.

* * * Absent legislative guidance, we now rely on those same sources in determining whether and to what extent school officials are immune from damage suits under § 1983. We think there must be a degree of immunity if the work of the schools is to go forward; and, however worded, the immunity must be such that public school officials understand that action taken in the good-faith fulfillment of their responsibilities and within the bounds of reason under all the circumstances will not be punished and that they need not exercise their discretion with undue timidity. * * *

The disagreement between the Court of Appeals and the District Court over the immunity standard in this case has been put in terms of an "objective" versus a "subjective" test of good faith. As we see it, the appropriate standard necessarily contains elements of both. The official must himself be acting sincerely and with a belief that he is doing right, but an act violating a student's constitutional rights can be no more justified by ignorance or disregard of settled, indisputable law on the part of one entrusted with supervision of students' daily lives than by the presence of actual malice. To be entitled to a special exemption from the categorical remedial language of § 1983 in a case in which his action violated a student's constitutional rights, a school board member, who has voluntarily undertaken the task of supervising the operation of the school and the activities of the students, must be held to a standard of conduct based not only on permissible intentions, but also on knowledge of the basic, unquestioned constitutional rights of his charges. Such a standard neither imposes an unfair burden upon a person assuming a responsible public office requiring a high degree of intelligence and judgment for the proper fulfillment of its duties, nor an unwarranted burden in light of the value which civil rights have in our legal system. Any lesser standard would deny much of the promise of § 1983. Therefore, in the specific context of school discipline, we hold that a school board member is not immune from liability for damages under § 1983 if he knew or reasonably should have known that the action he took within his sphere of official responsibility would violate the constitutional rights of the student affected, or if he took the action with the malicious intention to cause a deprivation of constitutional rights or other injury to the student. That is not to say that school board members are "charged with predicting the future course of constitutional law." A compensatory award will be appropriate only if the school board member has acted with such an impermissible motivation or with such disregard of the student's clearly established constitutional rights that his action cannot reasonably be characterized as being in good faith.

* * *

Notes

1. Justice Powell wrote a dissent from this part of the opinion in which he was joined by Justices Burger, Blackman, and Rehnquist. He said that the Court imposed a higher standard of care upon school authorities than "heretofore required of any other official." He expressed concern as to whether "qualified persons will continue in the desired numbers to volunteer for service in public education." Are his fears well founded in light of the circumscribed conditions under which "a compensatory award will be appropriate"?

2. The District Court said that a decision against the board must be premised on a finding of malice against the girls in the suspension. The Court of Appeals, however, said such a decision could be supported by a finding that the board did not act in good faith under the circumstances. The Supreme Court here essentially agreed with the Court of Appeals (see last paragraph of opinion).

3. Section 1983 grants rights of redress to those who have had their civil rights violated by public officials. Do you agree that sustaining the board's argument for absolute immunity would "deny much of the promise" of the statute?

4. Is any legislation needed in your state to assure conscientious board members that they will not be adversely affected by this decision?

5. On remand the Court of Appeals, Eighth Circuit, held that the students' right to procedural due process was violated and that they were entitled to have their records cleared and to try to prove their claim of damages against the individual members of the school board. The court margin was two-to-one on the last point, one judge believing the record devoid of any basis possibly to hold the board members liable. Strickland v. Inlow, 519 F.2d 744 (8 Cir.1975).

[Case No. 53] Damages When Student Is Denied Due Process before Suspension

CAREY v. PIPHUS

Supreme Court of the United States, 1978.
435 U.S. 247, 98 S.Ct. 1042, 55 L.Ed.2d 252.

MR. JUSTICE POWELL delivered the opinion of the Court.

In this case, brought under 42 U.S.C.A. § 1983, we consider the elements and prerequisites for recovery of damages by students who were suspended from public elementary and secondary schools without procedural due process. * * * We * * * hold that in the absence of proof of actual injury, the students are entitled to recover only nominal damages.

I

Respondent Jarius Piphus was a freshman at Chicago Vocational High School during the 1973–1974 school year. On January 23, 1974, during school hours, the school principal saw Piphus and another student standing outdoors on school property passing back and forth what the principal described as an irregularly shaped cigarette. The principal approached the students unnoticed and smelled what he believed was the strong odor of burning marihuana. He also saw Piphus try to pass a packet of cigarette papers to the other student. When the students became aware of the principal's presence, they threw the cigarette into a nearby hedge.

The principal took the students to the school's disciplinary office and directed the assistant principal to impose the "usual" 20-day suspension for violation of the school rule against the use of drugs. The students protested that they had not been smoking marihuana, but to no avail. Piphus was allowed to remain at school, although not in class, for the remainder of the school day while the assistant principal tried, without success, to reach his mother.

A suspension notice was sent to Piphus' mother, and a few days later two meetings were arranged among Piphus, his mother, his sister, school officials, and representatives from a Legal Aid Clinic. The purpose of the meetings was not to determine whether Piphus had been smoking marihuana, but rather to explain the reasons for the suspension. Following an unfruitful exchange of views, Piphus and his mother, as guardian *ad litem*, filed suit against petitioners in Federal District Court * * * charging that Piphus had been suspended without due process of law in violation of the Fourteenth Amendment. The complaint sought declaratory and injunctive relief, together with actual and punitive damages in the amount of $3,000. Piphus was readmitted to school under a temporary restraining order after eight days of his suspension.

Respondent Silas Brisco was in the sixth grade at Clara Barton Elementary School in Chicago during the 1973–1974 school year. On September 11, 1973, Brisco came to school wearing one small earring. The previous school year the school principal had issued a rule against the wearing of earrings by male students because he believed that this practice denoted membership in certain street gangs and increased the likelihood that gang members would terrorize other students. Brisco was reminded of this rule, but he refused to remove the earring, asserting that it was a symbol of black pride, not of gang membership.

The assistant principal talked to Brisco's mother, advising her that her son would be suspended for 20 days if he did not remove the earring. Brisco's mother supported her son's position, and a 20-day suspension was imposed. Brisco and his mother, as guardian *ad litem*, filed suit in Federal District Court * * * charging that Brisco had been suspended without due process of law in violation of the Fourteenth Amendment. The complaint sought declaratory and injunctive relief, together with actual and punitive damages in the amount of $5,000. Brisco was readmitted to school during the pendency of proceedings for a preliminary injunction after 17 days of his suspension.

* * * We granted certiorari to consider whether, in an action under § 1983 for the deprivation of procedural due process, a plaintiff must prove that he actually was injured by the deprivation before he may recover substantial "nonpunitive" damages.

II

42 U.S.C.A. § 1983, enacted as § 1 of the Civil Rights Act of 1871, 17 Stat. 13, provides:

> "Every person who, under color of any statute, ordinance, regulation, custom, or usage, of any State or Territory, subjects, or causes to be subjected, any citizen of the United States or other person within the jurisdiction thereof to the deprivation of any rights, privileges, or immunities secured by the Constitution and laws, shall be liable to the party injured in an action at law, suit in equity, or other proper proceeding for redress."

The legislative history of § 1983, demonstrates that it was intended to "create a species of tort liability" in favor of persons who are deprived of "rights, privileges, or immunities secured" to them by the Constitution.

* * *

A

Insofar as petitioners contend that the basic purpose of a § 1983 damages award should be to compensate persons for injuries caused by the deprivation of constitutional rights, they have the better of the argument. Rights, constitutional and otherwise, do not exist in a vacuum. Their purpose is to protect persons from injuries to particular interests, and their contours are shaped by the interests they protect.

Our legal system's concept of damages reflects this view of legal rights. "The cardinal principle of damages in Anglo-American law is that of *compensation* for the injury caused to plaintiff by defendant's breach of duty." The Court implicitly has recognized the applicability of this principle to actions under § 1983 by stating that damages are available under that section for actions "found * * * to have been violative of * * * constitutional rights *and to have caused compensable injury* * * *." Wood v. Strickland (emphasis supplied). * * *

The Members of the Congress that enacted § 1983 did not address directly the question of damages, but the principle that damages are designed to compensate persons for injuries caused by the deprivation of rights hardly could have been foreign to the many lawyers in Congress in 1871. Two other sections of the Civil Rights Act of 1871 appear to incorporate this principle, and no reason suggests itself for reading § 1983 differently. To the extent that Congress intended that awards under § 1983 should deter the deprivation of constitutional rights, there is no evidence that it meant to establish a deterrent more formidable than that inherent in the award of compensatory damages.

B

It is less difficult to conclude that damages awards under § 1983 should be governed by the principle of compensation than it is to apply this principle to concrete cases. But over the centuries the common law of torts has developed a set of rules to implement the principle that a person should be compensated fairly for injuries caused by the violation of his legal rights. These rules, defining the elements of damages and the prerequisites for their recovery, provide the appropriate starting point for the inquiry under § 1983 as well.

It is not clear, however, that common-law tort rules of damages will provide a complete solution to the damages issue in every § 1983 case. In some cases, the interests protected by a particular branch of the common law of torts may parallel closely the interests protected by a particular constitutional right. In such cases, it may be appropriate to apply the tort rules of damages directly to the § 1983 action. In other cases, the interests protected by a particular constitutional right may not also be protected by an analogous branch of the common law torts. In those cases, the task will be the more difficult one of adapting common-law rules of damages to provide fair compensation for injuries caused by the deprivation of a constitutional right.

Although this task of adaptation will be one of some delicacy—as this case demonstrates—it must be undertaken. The purpose of § 1983 would be defeated if injuries caused by the deprivation of constitutional rights went uncompensated simply because the common law does not recognize an analogous cause of action. In order to further the purpose of § 1983, the rules governing compensation for injuries caused by the deprivation of constitutional rights should be tailored to the interests protected by the particular right in question—just as the common-law rules of damages themselves were defined by the interests protected in the various branches of tort law. We agree with Mr. Justice Harlan that "the experience of judges in dealing with private [tort] claims supports the conclusion that courts of law are capable of making the types of judgment concerning causation and magnitude of injury necessary to accord meaningful compensation for invasion of [constitutional] rights." With these principles in mind, we now turn to the problem of compensation in the case at hand.

C

The Due Process Clause of the Fourteenth Amendment provides:

"nor shall any State deprive any person of life, liberty, or property, without due process of law; * * *."

This Clause "raises no impenetrable barrier to the taking of a person's possessions," or liberty, or life. Procedural due process rules are meant to protect persons not from the deprivation, but from the mistaken or unjustified deprivation of life, liberty, or property. Thus, in deciding what process constitutionally is due in various contexts, the Court repeatedly has emphasized that "procedural due process rules are shaped by the risk of error inherent in the truth-finding process * * *."

Such rules "minimize substantively unfair or mistaken deprivations of" life, liberty, or property by enabling persons to contest the basis upon which the State proposes to deprive them of protected interests.

* * *

The parties * * * disagree as to the * * * holding of the Court of Appeals that respondents are entitled to recover substantial—although unspecified—damages to compensate them for "the injury which is 'inherent in the nature of the wrong,'" even if their suspensions were justified and even if they fail to prove that the denial of procedural due process actually caused them some real, if intangible, injury. Respondents, elaborating on this theme, submit that the holding is correct because injury fairly may be "presumed" to flow from every denial of procedural due process. Their argument is that in addition to protecting against unjustified deprivations, the Due Process Clause also guarantees the "feeling of just treatment" by the government. They contend that the deprivation of protected interests without procedural due process, even where the premise for the deprivation is not erroneous, inevitably arouses strong feelings of mental and emotional distress in the individual who is denied this "feeling of just treatment." They analogize their case to that of defamation *per se,* in which "the plaintiff is relieved from the necessity of producing any proof whatsoever that he has been injured" in order to recover substantial compensatory damages.

Petitioners do not deny that a purpose of procedural due process is to convey to the individual a feeling that the government has dealt with him fairly, as well as to minimize the risk of mistaken deprivations of protected interests. They go so far as to concede that, in a proper case, persons in respondents' positions might well recover damages for mental and emotional distress caused by the denial of procedural due process. Petitioners' argument is the more limited one that such injury cannot be presumed to occur, and that plaintiffs at least should be put to their proof on the issue, as plaintiffs are in most tort actions.

We agree with petitioners in this respect. As we have observed in another context, the doctrine of presumed damages in the common law of defamation *per se* "is an oddity of tort law, for it allows recovery of purportedly compensatory damages without evidence of actual loss." * * * The doctrine has been defended on the grounds that those forms of defamation that are actionable *per se* are virtually certain to cause serious injury to reputation, and that this kind of injury is extremely difficult to prove. Moreover, statements that are defamatory *per se* by their very nature are likely to cause mental and emotional distress, as well as injury to reputation, so there arguably is little reason to require proof of this kind of injury either. But these considerations do not support respondents' contention that damages should be presumed to flow from every deprivation of procedural due process.

First, it is not reasonable to assume that every departure from procedural due process, no matter what the circumstances or how minor, inherently is as likely to cause distress as the publication of defamation *per se* is to cause injury to reputation and distress. Where the deprivation of a protected interest is substantively justified but procedures are deficient in some respect, there may well be those who suffer no distress over the procedural irregularities. Indeed, in contrast to the immediately distressing effect of defamation *per se,* a person may not even know that procedures *were* deficient until he enlists the aid of counsel to challenge a perceived substantive deprivation.

Moreover, where a deprivation is justified but procedures are deficient, whatever distress a person feels may be attributable to the justified deprivation rather than to deficiencies in procedure. But the injury caused by a justified deprivation, including distress, is not properly compensable under § 1983. This ambiguity in causation, which is absent in the case of defamation *per se,* provides additional need for requiring the plaintiff to convince the trier of fact that he actually suffered distress because of the denial of procedural due process itself.

Finally, we foresee no particular difficulty in producing evidence that mental and emotional distress actually was caused by the denial of procedural due process itself. Distress is a personal injury familiar to the law, customarily proved by showing the nature and circumstances of the wrong and its effect on the plaintiff. In sum, then, although mental and emotional distress caused by the denial of procedural due process itself is compensable under § 1983, we hold that neither the likelihood of such injury nor the difficulty of proving it is so great as to justify awarding compensatory damages without proof that such injury actually was caused.

* * *

III

Even if respondents' suspensions were justified, and even if they did not suffer any other actual injury, the fact remains that they were deprived of their right to procedural due process. "It is enough to invoke the procedural safeguards of the Fourteenth Amendment that a significant property interest is at stake, whatever the ultimate outcome of a hearing * * *."

Common-law courts traditionally have vindicated deprivations of certain "absolute" rights that are not shown to have caused actual injury through the award of a nominal sum of money. By making the deprivation of such rights actionable for nominal damages without proof of actual injury, the law recognizes the importance to organized society that those rights be scrupulously observed; but at the same time, it remains true to the principle that substantial damages should be awarded only to compensate actual injury or, in the case of exemplary or punitive damages, to deter or punish malicious deprivations of rights.

Because the right to procedural due process is "absolute" in the sense that it does not depend upon the merits of a claimant's substantive assertions, and because of the importance to organized society that procedural due process be observed, we believe that the denial of procedural due process should be actionable for nominal damages without proof of actual injury. We therefore hold that if, upon remand, the

District Court determines that respondents' suspensions were justified, respondents nevertheless will be entitled to recover nominal damages not to exceed one dollar from petitioners.

* * *

Notes

1. There were no dissents. Justice Blackmun took no part in the consideration or decision of the case.

2. Observe that procedural due process is considered an "absolute" right, denial of which is actionable without proof of injury, with nominal damages to be awarded regardless of whether the suspension was justified. How could one show actual damages only through a violation of procedural due process when the act of the board was legally proper?

3. Why might a case be brought on procedural due process grounds by one who was probably guilty of violating a valid rule?

4. *Wood* is Case No. 52. It was believed by some that *Wood* might have the effect of encouraging damage suits against school authorities in cases involving discipline of students or school employees. How is this case likely to affect the initiating of such suits? Bear in mind that attorney's fees are awardable if one prevails in a civil rights action.

[Case No. 54] Negligence of Student in Relation to Injury in Lecture Hall

VIVEIROS v. STATE

Supreme Court of Hawaii, 1973.
54 Hawaii 611, 513 P.2d 487.

RICHARDSON, CHIEF JUSTICE. This appeal arises out of a civil action brought by plaintiffs-appellants against the State of Hawaii under * * * the State Tort Liability Act. * * * The trial judge found that the State of Hawaii was negligent in failing to provide supervision at a program sponsored by Kailua High School during regular school hours. The trial court further found that the injuries suffered by plaintiff, Jo Ann Viveiros, were a result of the State's negligent omission. The State has not appealed these findings. General damages of $15,000.00 and special damages of $180.84 were assessed. * * * [T]he trial judge determined that defendant was 75% negligent and that plaintiff, Jo Ann Viveiros, was 25% negligent for "failing to leave the scene prior to her being injured." * * *

The facts reveal that on December 3, 1970 at about 9:30 a.m., a school sponsored "light show" created by students began in a lecture hall at Kailua High School. At this time, an educational assistant acting as a supervisor represented the only staff member present in the auditorium. Soon after the show started, this supervisor departed to observe a 15 to 20 minute coffee break. Though the show was to be supervised by three or four teachers, due to a mix-up, the hall was left in the hands of the students who were producing the light show.

At approximately 9:30 a.m. plaintiff Jo Ann Viveiros, age 15, along with two friends paid the 25¢ admission fee and entered the darkened hall to observe the performance. They could not find seating, so they stood in the aisle. Although the audience was quiet at the time plaintiff entered, a few minutes later a small group in a corner of the hall became "noisy". A student in charge of the production told the group to keep quiet or "the teachers would come in". Plaintiff was standing about thirty-five feet away from this group and did not feel any concern for her safety, although at this point she knew that no teachers were present. Shortly after the announcement, plaintiff and two other students were struck by metal objects apparently thrown by the rowdy group. Plaintiff suffered permanent damage to her left eye. * * *

We subscribe to the rule that a child is only required to use that degree of care appropriate to his age, experience and mental capacity. We must reverse the finding by the trial judge that plaintiff was 25% negligent if we find that she conformed to the above standard by remaining in the auditorium after she discovered that the event was unsupervised.

At the time the isolated group of students became boisterous, Jo Ann was standing approximately thirty-five feet in front of them. The record reveals that the group was merely vocal. There is no mention made in the record of threats being shouted or evidence that objects were being thrown during the concert. Apparently none of Jo Ann's peers felt endangered, because no one was shown to have left the program once the group became boisterous. Jo Ann did not fear for her safety possibly because she harbored the reasonable belief that she was in no imminent physical danger.

We agree with the reasoning in Ridge v. Boulder Creek Union Junior-Senior High School District, 60 Cal.App.2d 453, 460, 140 P.2d 990, 993–994 (1943). In this case, a 17 year old student was found not guilty of contributory negligence for using a power saw without its guard causing injury to himself. The court reasoned that:

> Knowledge that danger exists is not knowledge of the amount of danger necessary to charge a person with negligence in assuming the risk caused by such danger. The doing of an act with appreciation of the amount of danger in addition to mere appreciation of the danger is necessary in order to say as a matter of law that a person is negligent.

Since Jo Ann could not reasonably anticipate that she was in danger of physical harm nor appreciate the amount of danger, we must find that the trial judge erred in finding her 25% negligent. In our view, plaintiff conducted herself as a reasonable person would have under the same conditions.

* * *

Notes

1. The defendant here is the state because in Hawaii the public schools are operated directly by the state without local school boards.

2. Assess the responsibility of the principal of the school for the lack of supervision at the show.

3. One is bound to assume responsibility for harm to oneself from normal risks of an activity if one is, or should be, aware of the amount of danger involved. The rule of "assumption of risk" does not require, however, that one know of the danger of a precise type of injury.

4. Observe that the court quoted with approval from a case in another state decided thirty years before.

[Case No. 55] Liability for Death of Student during Recess

DAILEY v. LOS ANGELES UNIFIED SCHOOL DIST.

Supreme Court of California, 1970.
2 Cal.3d 741, 87 Cal.Rptr. 376, 470 P.2d 360.

SULLIVAN, JUSTICE. During the noon recess on May 12, 1965, Michael Dailey, a 16-year-old high school student, was killed on the playground of Gardena High School. His parents brought this wrongful death action against the Los Angeles Unified School District which operated Gardena High School and against two teachers employed by the district. The case was tried to a jury. Plaintiffs sought to establish that defendants' negligence in failing to provide adequate supervision was the proximate cause of Michael's death. After both sides had rested, the trial court granted a motion for a directed verdict in favor of all defendants. Plaintiffs appeal from the judgment entered on that verdict.

The sole issue in this case is whether the motion for a directed verdict was properly granted. We carefully stated the law applicable to this inquiry in Estate of Lances (1932) 216 Cal. 397, 14 P.2d 768. We there held: "A * * * directed verdict may be granted 'only when, disregarding conflicting evidence and giving to plaintiff's evidence all the value to which it is legally entitled, herein indulging in every legitimate inference which may be drawn from that evidence, the result is a determination that there is no evidence of sufficient substantiality to support a verdict in favor of the plaintiff if such a verdict were given.' [Citations.] Unless it can be said as a matter of law, that, when so considered, no other reasonable conclusion is legally deducible from the evidence, and that any other holding would be so lacking in evidentiary support that a reviewing court would be impelled to reverse it upon appeal or the trial court to set it aside as a matter of law, the trial court is not justified in taking the case from the jury. [Citation.] * * * [T]he function of the trial court on a motion for a directed verdict is analogous to * * * that of a reviewing court in determining, on appeal, whether there is evidence in the record of sufficient substance to support a verdict. Although the trial court may weigh the evidence and judge of the credibility of the witnesses on a motion for a new trial, it may not do so on a motion for a directed verdict." * * *

With these principles in mind we proceed to consider the evidence in the record which is most favorable to plaintiffs and must be accepted as true.

On the day of his death Michael and three of his friends ate lunch in an outdoor area designated for that purpose. After they finished eating, they proceeded to the boys' gymnasium where their next class was scheduled. When they reached the gym area, Michael and one of his friends began to "slap fight" or "slap box," a form of boxing employing open hands rather than clenched fists and in which the object, at least initially, is to demonstrate speed and agility rather than to inflict physical injury on the opponent. They continued boxing for 5 to 10 minutes and a crowd of approximately 30 students gathered to watch. Suddenly, after being slapped, Michael fell backwards, fracturing his skull on the asphalt paving. He died that night.

Richard Ragus, who was boys' vice principal at Gardena High School when the incident occurred, testified as to the general plan for student supervision during the noon hour. It appears that all 2,700 students ate lunch during one session. While they were actually eating, students were required to remain in either the indoor cafeteria or the enclosed outdoor area noted above. When they had finished eating, however, they were free to use any part of the 55-acre campus except the parking lot. Three administrative personnel and two teachers were assigned to supervise students during the lunch period. The area around the gymnasium, however, was the specific responsibility of the physical education department.

Defendant Raymond Maggard was the chairman of the physical education department at Gardena High School. He acknowledged that his department had supervisory responsibility for the area in which the accident occurred, but asserted that he had never been informed by the school administration that it was his duty to assign a particular teacher to supervise on a particular day. Maggard testified that there was no formal schedule assigning supervision times, and that supervision was left to the person in the gym office. Maggard himself was playing bridge in the dressing room while the slap boxing was going on.

Defendant Robert Daligney was a physical education instructor at Gardena High School. He was "the person in the gym office" during the noon hour on May 12, 1965. Like defendant Maggard, he recognized that his department had the responsibility to supervise the athletic field and the paved area immediately surrounding the gym. He conceded that there was no set procedure for determining who was to supervise on particular days or what their duties were in regard to supervision. Daligney spent the entire noon hour in the office, eating lunch and preparing for afternoon classes. The desk at which he was seated faced away from the office windows and a wall obscured the view of the area in which the slap boxing took place. He concurred with Maggard that while slap boxing was a normal activity for male high school students, it could lead to "something dangerous." He testified that initially friendly slap boxing could escalate into actual fighting and that when he observed students engaging in it he would order them to stop immediately. Daligney did not step outside the office during the noon period, did not notice a crowd, and recalled hearing no noises which would have indicated a disturbance outside the gymnasium.

* * *

Before we can decide whether or not the foregoing evidence is sufficient to support a verdict in plaintiffs' favor, we must determine what, if any, duty is owed by those in defendants' position to students on school grounds. While school districts and their employees have never been considered insurers of the physical safety of students, California law has long imposed on school authorities a duty to "supervise at all times the conduct of the children on the school grounds and to enforce those rules and regulations necessary to their protection. [Citations.]" * * * The standard of care imposed upon school personnel in carrying out this duty to supervise is identical to that required in the performance of their other duties. This uniform standard to which they are held is that degree of care "which a person of ordinary prudence, charged with [comparable] duties, would exercise under the same circumstances." * * *

The fact that Michael Dailey's injuries and death were sustained as a result of boisterous behavior engaged in by him and a fellow student does not preclude a finding of negligence. Supervision during recess and lunch periods is required, in part, so that discipline may be maintained and student conduct regulated. Such regulation is necessary precisely because of the commonly known tendency of students to engage in aggressive and impulsive behavior which exposes them and their peers to the risk of serious physical harm. High school students may appear to be generally less hyperactive and more capable of self-control than grammar school children. Consequently, less rigorous and intrusive methods of supervision may be required. Nevertheless, adolescent high school students are not adults and should not be expected to exhibit that degree of discretion, judgment, and concern for the safety of themselves and others which we associate with full maturity. * * *

We come then to the question of whether the evidence in this case was sufficient to support a finding of negligent supervision. There was evidence to the effect that Mr. Maggard, the responsible department head, had failed to develop a comprehensive schedule of supervising assignments and had neglected to instruct his subordinates as to what was expected of them while they were supervising. Instead, it appears that both the time and the manner of supervision were left to the discretion of the individual teacher. Mr. Daligney, the instructor ostensibly on duty at the time of the accident, remained inside an office during the entire lunch period, even though the area of his supervisorial responsibility was large and even though all students were outside the gymnasium. He did not station himself in the office in such a fashion as to maximize his ability to observe the students outside, but sat with his back to the window. He did not devote his full attention to supervision but ate lunch, talked on the phone, and prepared future class assignments. Neither defendant Daligney nor defendant Maggard heard or saw a 10 minute slap boxing match which attracted a crowd of approximately 30 spectators, although this took place within a few feet of the gymnasium. From this evidence a jury could reasonably conclude that those employees of the defendant school district who were charged with the responsibility of providing supervision failed to exercise due care in the performance of this duty and that their negligence was the proximate cause of the tragedy which took Michael's life.

The fact that another student's misconduct was the immediate precipitating cause of the injury does not compel a conclusion that negligent supervision was not the proximate cause of Michael's death. Neither the mere involvement of a third party nor that party's wrongful conduct is sufficient in itself to absolve the defendants of liability, once a negligent failure to provide adequate supervision is shown. Nor is this a case in which the intervening conduct of the other student is so bizarre or unpredictable as to warrant a limitation of liability through the expedient of concluding, as a matter of law, that a negligent failure to supervise was not the proximate cause of the injury.   * * *

In summary, we conclude that there was evidence of sufficient substantiality to support a verdict in favor of these plaintiffs and we are satisfied that the trial court erred in granting the motion for a directed verdict.

* * *

Notes

1.   Observe that liability was not decided here. It was decided only that a jury question was presented as to whether failure to provide adequate supervision was the proximate cause of the boy's death. In California by statute a school district is liable for injuries proximately caused by negligence of employees.

2.   The Appellate Court of Illinois has held that where a high school class uses admittedly dangerous machines, "there is a duty upon the instructor, as agent of the school, to exercise due care in instructing the students in safe and proper use of the machines and also a duty to exercise due care in proper supervision of the students in use of the machines as a part of regular school activities." Matteucci v. High School Dist. No. 208, County of Cook, 4 Ill.App.3d 710, 281 N.E.2d 383 (1972).

3.   In Kentucky, where district immunity was the law, the state's highest court held that a complaint charging the school principal, superintendent, and individual board members with gross negligence and carelessness in maintaining and supervising the playground and recreational facilities at the public school raised questions of fact and could not be summarily dismissed. Copley v. Board of Educ. of Hopkins County, 466 S.W.2d 952 (Ky.1971). A similar decision was rendered by the Supreme Court of Colorado where the allegation against the principal and superintendent was that they negligently failed to perform their duty to provide a reasonably safe passage across a street dividing school premises. Flournoy v. McComas, 175 Colo. 526, 488 P.2d 1104 (1971).

[Case No. 56] Liability for Injury to Student before Start of School Day

TITUS v. LINDBERG

Supreme Court of New Jersey, 1967.
49 N.J. 66, 228 A.2d 65.

JACOBS, J.   The Appellate Division affirmed a judgment for the plaintiffs against all three defendants, Lindberg, Smith and the Board of Education.   We granted certification on the application of Smith and the Board of Education.

On October 25, 1963 the plaintiff Robert A. Titus, who was then nine years old and a student at the Fairview School in Middletown Township, rode off from home on his bicycle to school.   He arrived at the school grounds at about 8:05 A.M., entered along the bus driveway, and headed for the bicycle rack on the west side of the school building.   As he came around a corner of the building, he was struck by a paper clip which the defendant Richard Lindberg, then thirteen years old, had shot from an elastic band.   Robert was seriously injured.

Lindberg was not then a student at Fairview but attended the Thompson School which was some distance away.   Fairview had been designated by the school system's transportation coordinator as the pickup site for three schools including Thompson, and Lindberg was one of many students who customarily boarded school buses there.   Up to two years earlier, Lindberg had attended Fairview and its records described him as "very rough" and a "bully."   On the morning of the incident he arrived early at Fairview, fooled around with an elastic band for a while, and struck a student in the back with a paper clip about 5 minutes before he shot the one which injured Robert.

Though the school doors at Fairview did not officially open until 8:15 A.M., it was customary for quite a few Fairview students to start arriving on the school grounds at about 8 A.M.   Some would arrive on their bicycles, as did Robert, and others would arrive on foot.   Oftentimes the students played the game of "keep away" before the school bell rang.   An early arrival would obtain a ball from a classroom and a team of students would try to keep it away from a second team.   The first bell rang at 8:15 A.M., the students were supposed to be in their seats by 8:30 A.M. when the late bell rang, and classes began at 8:35 A.M.

The defendant Smith had been principal of Fairview since 1960.   He testified that he "did the supervising of the arrival of the children" and that, although he had known of prior pranks and deportment problems connected with Lindberg, he was not aware of any earlier incidents involving conduct such as his shooting of paper clips.   Smith's practice was to arrive at the school grounds at 8 A.M. and he had instructed his teachers to arrive at that time and prepare for and be in their classes at 8:15 A.M. so that they could maintain order as the students filed in.   On his arrival at 8 A.M. he would supervise deliveries by the milk truck and would watch out for the safety of children in the immediate area. He would then walk from the east side of the school to the west side where the buses began to arrive at 8:15 A.M. Sometimes he would walk through a corridor within the building and at other times he would walk along the outside of the building. At the time of the incident, he was walking inside the building. As he passed one of the windows of the building, he looked out and saw a group gathered around the stricken Robert. He went to the scene to administer assistance.

There were 560 students at Fairview and approximately 70 or 80 additional students arrived at the school grounds to board the buses. There were, in addition to administrative and part-time personnel, 19 full-time classroom teachers on the Fairview staff but none of them had been assigned any responsibilities in connection with the supervision of students before their entry into the classrooms. Smith testified that he made the rules governing the conduct of students on the school grounds and that he was charged with that responsibility. Although he stated that he told the students that school arrival time was from 8:15 A.M. to 8:30 A.M., he acknowledged his awareness that students began arriving at 8 A.M. and stated flatly that he maintained "supervision outside the building on the grounds between eight and 8:30."

* * *

There is no dispute that Lindberg was soundly held liable for the injury caused by his conduct. And while there is dispute as to the liability of Smith, we are satisfied that the evidence fairly presented a jury question as to whether he had negligently failed to discharge his responsibilities with consequential injury to Robert. The duty of school personnel to exercise reasonable supervisory care for the safety of students entrusted to them, and their accountability for injuries resulting from failure to discharge that duty, are well-recognized in our State and elsewhere.

* * *

Apparently Smith does not dispute the foregoing principles although he does seem to question that his responsibilities began before 8:15 A.M. We have no doubt on that score. In the first place he assumed the responsibility for supervising the school grounds beginning at 8 A.M. and was from that point on obligated to exercise due care. In the second place, and wholly apart from the assumption, it cannot in any fair sense be said that his legal responsibility began only upon the opening of the classrooms at 8:15 A.M. Obviously the students would be expected to and could properly come to the school grounds during some short period before the classrooms actually opened. They customarily began coming at 8 A.M. and that was reasonable. Smith undoubtedly knew of their coming and of their "keep away" games. When all this is coupled with the fact that Fairview was also a pickup site for the older students, the dangers and the need for reasonable supervision from 8 A.M. on were entirely apparent. * * *

Smith contends that he was entitled to a direction on the ground that there was insufficient evidence to enable a jury to find negligence on his part. The record discloses the contrary. He had not announced any rules with respect to the congregation of his students and their conduct prior to entry into the classrooms. He had assigned none of the teachers or other personnel to assist him in supervising the students and he undertook the sole responsibility. He then failed to take any measures towards overseeing their presence and activities, except at the point of the milk delivery and by walking from east to west around or through the building. While he was walking through the building there was no semblance of supervision on the grounds outside and that was precisely when the injury to Robert occurred. Before then Lindberg had been fooling around and had struck another student while no supervisor was anywhere about. Bearing all of these circumstances in mind, it clearly cannot be said that the finding that Smith failed to take suitable supervisory precautions lacked reasonable support in the evidence.

Smith advances the further contention that, even if lack of due supervision be assumed, Lindberg's deliberate conduct rather than Smith's negligence was the "sole competent producing cause of the injury." The jury presumably found that conduct of the type engaged in by Lindberg was reasonably to be anticipated and guarded against and that Smith's failure to do so was a substantial factor in the occurrence. That being so, there was ample basis for finding proximate causation and holding Smith liable in addition to Lindberg. * * *

* * *

Notes

1. Six justices participated in this decision. All six voted for affirmance as to the liability of the principal, Smith. Two voted to reverse as to the board of education.

2. Increasingly principals are being named in tort actions for injuries suffered by pupils in school. Until the 1960's these officials usually were not included because of the common law requisite that to be liable for the tort of negligence, one's action must be the proximate, or immediate, cause of the injury. Is failure of a principal to arrange for adequate recess or lunch-time supervision a proper basis for a charge of negligence?

3. In De Gooyer v. Harkness, 70 S.D. 26, 13 N.W.2d 815 (1944), personal liability for death of a pupil was imposed on a teacher-athletic coach where a boy died as a result of an electric shock received during an initiation ceremony into a club of athletes. The teacher "actively participated in the initiation activities, * * * tested the electrical appliance, * * * and played an active role in this whole proceeding of administering the electric shock." Contributory negligence was not present, nor could it be said that the boy assumed the risk, for he had the right to assume that every proper precaution for his safety would be taken.

4. It was negligent for a first-grade teacher to have a sixth-grade student supervise the first-grade class. Schnell v. Travelers Ins. Co., 264 So.2d 346 (La.App.1972).

[Case No. 57] Liability for Injury to Student by Snowball

LAWES v. BOARD OF EDUC. OF THE CITY OF NEW YORK

Court of Appeals of New York, 1965.
16 N.Y.2d 302, 266 N.Y.S.2d 364, 213 N.E.2d 667.

BERGAN, JUDGE. Plaintiff Nuvia Alicia Lawes, a pupil at Public School No. 144 in Brooklyn, was struck by a snowball thrown by a fellow pupil while she was on her way from her home to her classroom after lunch on February 17, 1960. Plaintiff, then 11 years old, suffered a serious eye injury. A judgment for $45,000 has been rendered against the Board of Education and affirmed by a divided Appellate Division.

The snowball was thrown on school property in a yard between the street and school entrance, but this was not during a recreation period. Children were then on the property on their way into the school after having been home to lunch. The school had made a rule against snowball throwing and plaintiff's teacher had warned her pupils not to throw snowballs.

If a school is to become liable to one pupil for a snowball thrown at him by a fellow pupil, the rule governing such responsibility should be laid down clearly and be precise enough to be generally understood in the schools.

No one grows up in this climate without throwing snowballs and being hit by them. If snow is on the ground as children come to school, it would require intensive policing, almost child by child, to take all snowball throwing out of play. It is unreasonable to demand or expect such perfection in supervision from ordinary teachers or ordinary school management; and a fair test of reasonable care does not demand it.

The classic New York statement of the measure of school care for children is laid out in Judge Loughran's noted opinion in Hoose v. Drumm: "Teachers have watched over the play of their pupils time out of mind. At recess periods, not less than in the class room, a teacher owes it to his charges to exercise such care of them as a parent of ordinary prudence would observe in comparable circumstances."

A parent of ordinary prudence would not invariably stop his children from making and throwing snowballs. Indeed, he might encourage it. He would stop dangerous throwing, if he learned hard frozen snow or ice had come into play, or the pelting of one child by several others, but ordinary snowball throwing would not necessarily be stopped.

A reasonable measure of a school's responsibility for snowball throwing is to control or prevent it during recreation periods according to its best judgment of conditions, and to take energetic steps to intervene at other times if dangerous play comes to its notice while children are within its area of responsibility.

The facts in the present case do not spell out any notice of special danger. There is no proof whatever in the record that teachers had notice of any other snowball throwing on the day plaintiff was hit.

Proof that a snowball was thrown on the previous day is very thin and, even if fully credited, would not give fair notice of the kind of continued danger which should have been prevented by the active intervention of teachers.

A fellow pupil and friend of plaintiff testified that she was struck by a snowball on February 16 and that she reported this to a teacher. She did not testify that she reported that she was injured. She said: "I told her I got hit. Somebody hit me with a snowball."

The teacher denied having been told this and the Education Department records marked for identification, which the trial court refused to receive, show that this pupil reported in writing that she had been struck by a snowball, not before, but some five weeks after, plaintiff's injury.

No requirement on this kind of a record is imposed on teachers to enforce the rule against snowballs by standing outside in the cold to watch to see that children do not violate the rule as they come into the school. And it is an undue burden on the school to impose a liability because teachers did not stand outside for active intervention in the circumstances shown by this record.

A school is not liable for every thoughtless or careless act by which one pupil may injure another. Nor is liability invariably to fall on it because a school rule has been violated and an injury has been caused by another pupil.

* * *

In its result the judgment in this case imposes a greatly enlarged risk of liability on a school without showing notice of a particular danger at a particular time. A long line of decisions should cause us to proceed warily toward such an enlarged area of liability. * * *

The order should be reversed and the complaint dismissed, without costs.

Notes

1. In New York school boards may be held liable for negligence. Also, there is an indemnification statute requiring boards to pay judgments obtained against teachers for their negligence in the course of their employment.

2. Note the discussion in the text of this chapter of another snowball case subsequent to the present one in New York (footnote 67).

3. A dissenting opinion in this case was to the effect that the question of negligence should have been submitted to a jury.

4. Where a school board knew a schoolyard for years had been used as an after-school playground and where it had been requested to replace missing gates by members of the community concerned about the use of the yard by persons exploding firecrackers, it had a duty to take protective measures, and its failure to do so made it liable for an injury by an exploding firecracker. Nicholson v. Board of Educ. of City of New York, 36 N.Y.2d 798, 369 N.Y.S.2d 703, 330 N.E.2d 651 (1975).

[Case No. 58]　Power of Board to Require Releases from Claims for Negligence in Interscholastic Athletics

WAGENBLAST v. ODESSA SCHOOL DIST. NO. 105–157–166J

Supreme Court of Washington, 1988.
110 Wash.2d 845, 758 P.2d 968.

ANDERSEN, JUSTICE.

FACTS OF CASE

In these consolidated cases we consider an issue of first impression—the legality of public school districts requiring students and their parents to sign a release of all potential future claims as a condition to student participation in certain school-related activities.

The plaintiffs in these cases are public school children and their parents.

Odessa School District students Alexander and Charles Wagenblast and Ethan and Katie Herdrick all desired to participate in some form of interscholastic athletics. As a condition to such participation, the Odessa School District requires its students and their parents or guardians to sign a standardized form which releases the school district from "liability resulting from any ordinary negligence that may arise in connection with the school district's interscholastic activities programs." The releases are required by a group of small Eastern Washington school districts, including Odessa, which "pooled" together to purchase liability insurance.

The Seattle School District also requires students and their parents to sign standardized release forms as a condition to participation in interscholastic sports and cheerleading. When Richard and Paul Vulliet turned out for the Ballard High School wrestling team, they and their parents were required to sign release forms which released the Seattle School District, its employees and agents "from any liability resulting from any negligence that may arise in connection with the School District's wrestling program."

* * *

One issue is determinative of these appeals.

ISSUE

Can school districts require public school students and their parents to sign written releases which release the districts from the consequences of all future school district negligence, before the students will be allowed to engage in certain recognized school related activities, here interscholastic athletics?

DECISION

CONCLUSION. We hold that the exculpatory releases from any future school district negligence are invalid because they violate public policy.

The courts have generally recognized that, subject to certain exceptions, parties may contract that one shall not be liable for his or her own negligence to another. As Prosser and Keeton explain:

> It is quite possible for the parties expressly to agree in advance that the defendant is under no obligation of care for the benefit of the plaintiff, and shall not be liable for the consequences of conduct which would otherwise be negligent. There is in the ordinary case no public policy which prevents the parties from contracting as they see fit, as to whether the plaintiff will undertake the responsibility of looking out for himself.

In accordance with the foregoing general rule, appellate decisions in this state have upheld exculpatory agreements where the subject was a toboggan slide, a scuba diving class, mountain climbing instruction, an automobile demolition derby, and ski jumping.

As Prosser and Keeton further observe, however, there are instances where public policy reasons for preserving an obligation of care owed by one person to another outweigh our traditional regard for the freedom to contract. Courts in this century are generally agreed on several such categories of cases.

Courts, for example, are usually reluctant to allow those charged with a public duty, which includes the obligation to use reasonable care, to rid themselves of that obligation by contract. Thus, where the defendant is a common carrier, an innkeeper, a professional bailee, a public utility, or the like, an agreement discharging the defendant's performance will not ordinarily be given effect. Implicit in such decisions is the notion that the service performed is one of importance to the public, and that a certain standard of performance is therefore required.

Courts generally also hold that an employer cannot require an employee to sign a contract releasing the employer from liability for job-related injuries caused by the employer's negligence. Such decisions are grounded on the recognition that the disparity of bargaining power between employer and employee forces the employee to accept such agreements.

Consistent with these general views, this court has held that a bank which rents out safety deposit boxes cannot, by contract, exempt itself from liability for its own negligence, and that if the circumstances of a particular case suggest that a gas company has a duty to inspect the pipes and fittings belonging to the owner of the building, any contractual limitation on that duty would be against public policy.

This court has also gone beyond these usually accepted categories to hold future releases invalid in other circumstances as well. It has struck down a lease provision exculpating a public housing authority from liability for injuries caused by the authority's negligence and has also struck down a landlord's exculpatory clause relating to common areas in a multi-family dwelling complex.

In reaching these decisions, this court has focused at times on disparity of bargaining power, at times on the importance of the service provided, and at other times on other factors. In reviewing these decisions, it is apparent that the court has not always been particularly clear on what rationale it used to decide what type of release was and was not violative of "public policy". Undoubtedly, it has been much easier for courts to simply declare releases violative of public policy in a given situation than to state a principled basis for so holding.

Probably the best exposition of the test to be applied in determining whether exculpatory agreements violate public policy is that stated by the California Supreme Court. * * *

* * * We separately, then, examine each of these six characteristics as applied to the cases before us.

1. *The agreement concerns an endeavor of a type generally thought suitable for public regulation.*

Regulation of governmental entities usually means self-regulation. Thus, the Legislature has by statute granted to each school board the authority to control, supervise, and regulate the conduct of interscholastic athletics. In some situations, a school board is permitted, in turn, to delegate this authority to the Washington Interscholastic Activities Association (WIAA) or to another voluntary nonprofit entity. In the cases before us, both school boards look to the WIAA for regulation of interscholastic sports. The WIAA handbook contains an extensive constitution with rules for such athletic endeavors. These rules cover numerous topics, including student eligibility standards, athletic awards, insurance, coaches, officials, tournaments and state championships. Special regulations for each sport cover such topics as turnout schedules, regular season game or meet limitations, and various areas of regulation peculiar to the sport, including the rule book governing the sport.

Clearly then, interscholastic sports in Washington are extensively regulated, and are a fit subject for such regulation.

2. *The party seeking exculpation is engaged in performing a service of great importance to the public, which is often a matter of practical necessity for some members of the public.*

This court has held that public school students have no fundamental right to participate in interscholastic athletics. Nonetheless, the court also has observed that the justification advanced for interscholastic athletics is their educational and cultural value. * * * Given this emphasis on sports by the public and the school system, it would be unrealistic to expect students to view athletics as an activity entirely separate and apart from the remainder of their schooling.

* * *

In sum, under any rational view of the subject, interscholastic sports in public schools are a matter of public importance in this jurisdiction.

3. *Such party holds itself out as willing to perform this service for any member of the public who seeks it, or at least for any member coming within certain established standards.*

Implicit in the nature of interscholastic sports is the notion that such programs are open to all students who meet certain skill and eligibility standards. This conclusion finds direct support in the testimony of former Superintendent Nelson and the WIAA eligibility and nondiscrimination policies set forth in the WIAA handbook.

4. *Because of the essential nature of the service, in the economic setting of the transaction, the party invoking exculpation possesses a decisive advantage of bargaining strength against any member of the public who seeks the services.*

Not only have interscholastic sports become of considerable importance to students and the general public alike, but in most instances there exists no alternative program of organized competition. * * * In this regard, school districts have near-monopoly power. And, because such programs have become important to student participants, school districts possess a clear and disparate bargaining strength when they insist that students and their parents sign these releases.

5. *In exercising a superior bargaining power, the party confronts the public with a standardized adhesion contract of exculpation, and makes no provision whereby a purchaser may pay additional reasonable fees and obtain protection against negligence.*

Both school districts admit to an unwavering policy regarding these releases; no student athlete will be allowed to participate in any program without first signing the release form as written by the school district. In both of these cases, students and their parents unsuccessfully attempted to modify the forms by deleting the release language. In both cases, the school district rejected the attempted modifications. Student athletes and their parents or guardians have no alternative but to sign the standard release forms provided to them or have the student barred from the program.

6. *The person or property of members of the public seeking such services must be placed under the control of the furnisher of the services, subject to the risk of carelessness on the part of the furnisher, its employees or agents.*

A school district owes a duty to its students to employ ordinary care and to anticipate reasonably foreseeable dangers so as to take precautions for protecting the children in its custody from such dangers. This duty extends to students engaged in interscholastic sports. As a natural incident to the relationship of a student athlete and his or her coach, the student athlete is usually placed under the coach's considerable degree of control. The student is thus subject to the risk that the school district or its agent will breach this duty of care.

In sum, the attempted releases in the cases before us exhibit all six of the characteristics * * *. Because of this, and for the aforesaid reasons, we hold that the releases in these consolidated cases are invalid as against public policy.

Having decided the case on this basis, only two remaining aspects of the cases require discussion.

The first of these aspects is the relationship of this decision to the doctrine of assumption of risk. Another name for a release of the sort presented here is an express assumption of risk. If a plaintiff has released a defendant from liability for a future occurrence, the plaintiff may also be said to have assumed the risk of the occurrence. If the release is against public policy, however, it is also against public policy to say that the plaintiff has assumed that particular risk. This court has implicitly recognized that an express assumption of risk which relieves the defendant's duty to the plaintiff may violate public policy. Accordingly, to the extent that the release portions of these forms represent a consent to relieve the school districts of their duty of care, they are invalid whether they are termed releases or express assumptions of risk.

Nonetheless, risks other than that of a school district's negligence may be present in any sporting event. * * * If a student knowingly encounters one of these risks, but chooses to play on, it could be argued that the student has voluntarily encountered the risk. By our opinion today we do not rule on this question; the law of assumption of risk has developed and will continue to develop on a case-by-case basis and there are no facts before us on the basis of which we can appropriately make any decision on this.

Nor do we decide whether the listing of various risks on these forms can or will in a given case establish that the student has assumed any of the listed risks. * * * [This court has said] that in order to prove an express assumption of risk, the evidence must show that the plaintiff (1) had full subjective understanding, (2) of the presence and nature of the specific risk, and (3) voluntarily chose to encounter that risk. By their very nature, the existence of these characteristics can only be determined with reference to the facts of an actual lawsuit.

The remaining aspect of these appeals which merits discussion is the Legislature's role in deciding such matters of public policy. * * * Thus, since territorial days, the State Legislature has generally followed a policy of holding school districts accountable for their negligence. Our decision today is in general accordance with that policy.

Legislative policies may, of course, change with changing conditions. This opinion is not to be construed as precluding school districts from attempting to convince the Legislature that their problems in this area require a legislative response of one kind or another. The Legislature through its hearing processes is well suited to making such inquiries and has tools and resources adequate to the task.

* * *

Notes

1. All nine of the members of the court signed this opinion. This was the first state court of last resort to deal comprehensively with the specific "issue" presented here.

2. What corollary questions remain to be answered? See the court's discussion of express assumption of risk.

3. Observe that the court did not make its holding retroactive. That would have opened the way for negligence suits not previously brought where parents had signed releases.

4. Consider the last two paragraphs of the opinion regarding the role of the legislature now that the law of this case enunciated an aspect of public policy for the state.

[Case No. 59] Liability for "Educational Malpractice"

HUNTER v. BOARD OF EDUC. OF MONTGOMERY COUNTY

Court of Appeals of Maryland, 1982.
292 Md. 481, 439 A.2d 582.

DIGGES, JUDGE. This case primarily presents the troubling but nevertheless important question, * * * of whether an action can be successfully asserted against a school board and various individual employees for improperly evaluating, placing or teaching a student. * * *

* * * The action was instituted * * * shortly after Ross' sixteenth birthday. As best we can gather from the declaration, the parents * * * complain that the school system negligently evaluated the child's learning abilities and caused him to repeat first grade materials while being physically placed in the second grade. It is alleged that this misplacement, which continued at least through grade school, generally caused the student to feel "embarrassment," to develop "learning deficiencies," and to experience "depletion of ego strength." * * *

It is clear * * * that the gravamen of petitioners' claim in this case sounds in negligence, asserting damages for the alleged failure of the school system to properly educate young Hunter, and we first focus our attention on this aspect of it. In so doing, we note that these so-called "educational malpractice" claims have been unanimously rejected by those few jurisdictions considering the topic. * * * These decisions generally hold that a cause of action seeking damages for acts of negligence in the educational process is precluded by considerations of public policy, among them being the absence of a workable rule of care against which the defendant's conduct may be measured, the inherent uncertainty in determining the cause and nature of any damages, and the extreme burden which would be imposed on the already strained resources of the public school system to say nothing of those of the judiciary. Thus * * * where a high school graduate sought recovery in tort for a claimed inadequate education, the California court, viewing the problem as whether an actionable duty of care existed, noted that the "wrongful conduct and injuries allegedly involved in educational malfeasance" were neither comprehensible nor assessable within the judicial framework and explained as follows:

> Unlike the activity of the highway or the marketplace, classroom methodology affords no readily acceptable standards of care, or cause, or injury. The science of pedagogy itself is

fraught with different and conflicting theories of how or what a child should be taught, and any layman might—and commonly does—have his own emphatic views on the subject. The "injury" claimed here is plaintiff's inability to read and write. Substantial professional authority attests that the achievement of literacy in the schools, or its failure, is influenced by a host of factors which affect the pupil subjectively, from outside the formal teaching process, and beyond the control of its ministers. They may be physical, neurological, emotional, cultural, environmental; they may be present but not perceived, recognized but not identified.

We find in this situation no conceivable "workability of a rule of care" against which defendants' alleged conduct may be measured * * * no reasonable "degree of certainty that * * * plaintiff suffered injury" within the meaning of the law of negligence * * *, and no such perceptible "connection between the defendant's conduct and the injury suffered," as alleged, which would establish a causal link between them within the same meaning.

Although the just-articulated policy considerations alone sufficed to negate a legal duty of care * * * the court aptly identified additional, practical consequences of imposing such a duty upon the persons and agencies who administer our public educational system: * * *. * * * [T]he New York Court of Appeals addressed the identical proposition * * *, but viewed the issue as presenting solely a question of public policy * * *. The New York court concluded that the action should not be permitted because to do so would "constitute blatant interference with the responsibility for the administration of the public school system lodged by [State] Constitution and statute in school administrative agencies."

* * *

We find ourselves in substantial agreement with the reasoning employed by the [California and New York] courts, for an award of money damages, in our view, represents a singularly inappropriate remedy for asserted errors in the educational process. The misgivings expressed in these cases concerning the establishment of legal cause and the inherent immeasurability of damages that is involved in such educational negligence actions against the school systems are indeed well founded. Moreover, to allow petitioners' asserted negligence claims to proceed would in effect position the courts of this State as overseers of both the day-to-day operation of our educational process as well as the formulation of its governing policies. This responsibility we are loathe to impose on our courts. Such matters have been properly entrusted by the General Assembly to the State Department of Education and the local school boards who are invested with authority over them. * * *

* * *

Notes

1. Widespread attempts to differentiate "educational malpractice" from negligence so as to avoid the centuries-old principles of negligence law have been uniformly unsuccessful. The issues beyond the ballyhoo are addressed by this court.

2. One of the seven judges in the present case would have allowed suit against specific individuals who allegedly made the errors resulting in the alleged injuries. Two of the other judges (in a different case) joined her view insofar as a claim was made against members of a health occupation (clinical psychology) where the standard of care is objective and not dependent upon theories of how best to educate. The majority in the latter case, however, refused to permit suit against the psychologists, who were employed by the school board. Doe v. Board of Educ. of Montgomery County, 295 Md. 67, 453 A.2d 814 (1982).

3. Mistakes in classification and placement of students at various points during their school years are not susceptible to damage remedies because of difficulties in determining level of success if the mistakes had not been made. In rejecting a "malpractice" claim the Supreme Court of Alaska suggested that prompt administrative and judicial review might well correct erroneous action before harm is done. D.S.W. v. Fairbanks North Star Borough School Dist., 628 P.2d 554 (Alaska 1981).

Chapter 8

CONTRACT LIABILITY OF SCHOOL DISTRICTS AND OFFICERS

Contracts in General

The basic law related to contracts in general is applicable to contracts made by school districts. Detailed treatment of the various elements requisite to the validity of all contracts is beyond the scope of this work. A very brief overview, however, can be helpful.

In general the elements of a contract are: (1) mutual assent (that is, offer and acceptance); (2) consideration; (3) legally competent parties; (4) subject matter not prohibited by law; (5) agreement in form required by law. Mutual assent means, in effect, that there must be a "meeting of the minds." The parties must agree as to the subject covered, price, time of performance, and other details. Consideration is the price that each side pays for the promise or performance of the other. Consideration is something of value—usually money or the equivalent in merchandise or services. Promises to make gifts or to perform gratuitous services are not contracts because they are not supported by consideration. In a broader sense, a consideration is present if the promisee, in return for the promise, does anything legal which he is not required to do, or does not do something which he legally can do. Competency of parties refers to the fact that for a valid contract the parties must be authorized by law to enter into the particular relationship. The contract must be one into which the board of education has the legal power to enter, and the other party must be empowered to bind himself or his corporation. Contracts beyond the power of the board of education ("ultra vires" contracts) are not enforceable. Also, no agreement can result in a binding contract if the execution of its terms is prohibited by law. Finally, all legal requirements as to form must be followed for contractual validity.

It is to be observed that if one party modifies the other's offer, that party has in effect made a counteroffer. This counteroffer then must be accepted by the first party in order that it be binding. Also, the presentation of the counteroffer is a rejection of the original offer.[1]

When a mutual mistake has been made in a written contract, the contract may be corrected ("reformed") by a court of competent jurisdiction. Thus, where by secretarial error a one-year contract form, instead of a two-year form, had been executed for the employment of a superin-

1. Foster v. Ohio State Univ., 41 Ohio App.3d 86, 534 N.E.2d 1220 (1987). [Case No. 60]

tendent, it could not later be claimed by the board that the contract period was one year.[2] The Supreme Court of Arkansas found a two-year contract was intended, and the signatures of the parties to the wrong form did not change the intended agreement.

This chapter primarily treats contract problems other than those involving teachers. Teacher contracts are discussed in Chapter 9. Procedural requirements for school board contracting are discussed in Chapter 14.

Authority of Districts to Contract

The liability of districts on contracts is dependent upon the authority of boards of education to enter into them. Any discussion of liability, therefore, necessarily centers around the contractual authority of the board. School districts are merely instrumentalities of the state, created by it to carry out the state constitutional mandate to provide for a system of public schools, and have only such powers as are expressly granted them, and those necessarily implied to enable them to carry out their expressly granted powers. For example, the express power of boards to contract does not necessarily imply the power to include a clause for arbitration of disputes growing out of construction contracts.[3] Powers of districts to contract are granted by the state. Districts have no inherent right, merely because of their existence, to contract.

The powers of a board are set out in more or less particularity in all states. It is a well established rule of statutory construction that when a statute sets out specifically the powers of a body, or the manner in which those powers are to be exercised, all other powers or manners of exercise are precluded by implication. Thus, a California school board was barred from contracting with an outside agency for ordinary janitorial services, being required to employ and classify personnel for that purpose within its system.[4] The court stated the principle that school districts have power to contract only as provided by statute. The board had believed that the invalidated procedure would have been more economical.

Where statutes do not expressly or implicitly cover the manner in which particular board functions are to be executed, however, boards may be permitted to "contract out" certain services.[5] If the services have been performed by employed personnel, however, and if there is a collective bargaining statute, it may be necessary to bargain on the question. The Supreme Court of Wisconsin so held as regards a school

2. Hampton School Dist. No. 1 of Calhoun County v. Phillips, 251 Ark. 90, 470 S.W.2d 934 (1971).

3. W.M. Schlosser Co., Inc. v. School Bd. of Fairfax County, Va., 980 F.2d 253 (4 Cir.1992).

4. California School Employees Ass'n v. Willits Unified School Dist., 243 Cal.App.2d 776, 52 Cal.Rptr. 765 (1966); Independent School Dist. No. 88, New Ulm v. School Service Employees Union Local 284, 503 N.W.2d 104 (Minn.1993).

5. Nassau Educational Chapter of Civil Service Employees Ass'n, Inc. v. Great Neck Union Free School Dist., 57 N.Y.2d 658, 454 N.Y.S.2d 67, 439 N.E.2d 876 (1982).

district's food service program.[6] The court said that, since the same work will be done, the question was not one primarily related to "formulation or management of public policy," but was primarily related to conditions of employment. The court rejected an argument that to bargain the point would give the union undue control over the affairs of the district. It observed that the board was not obligated to accept the union's proposal. Ohio courts, which had prevented extensive contracting out before collective bargaining was required by statute for all public employment, subsequently adopted the view that "protection" of the civil service system was to be afforded "at the bargaining table."[7]

If a statute sets out the manner or form in which a board shall contract, a contract in any other manner or form is invalid. The contractual authority is circumscribed as fully by such provisions as by those designating the subject matter with reference to which the board may contract. For example, the laws of some states require that certain district contracts shall be in writing, although the same contract entered into between individuals or private corporations would be valid though oral. Under such statutes, oral contracts are held void, that is, without legal effect.[8] Certain other contracts are required to be awarded to the lowest bidder. A vote of the electors is required as a condition precedent to the making of others. Unless these provisions have been complied with, the contracts are void.

It is inevitable, of course, that boards will in good faith attempt to enter into contracts which turn out to be invalid due to failure to follow the statutory manner or form. But good faith does not validate a contract which is in violation of a statute.[9] Laws restricting the power of boards to contract are designed to protect the public, and the degree of protection afforded thereby depends upon the strictness with which the courts construe them.

A California statute required that every official action of a school board be taken by a formal vote of board members at a legally called public meeting. This has been interpreted to mean that a contract to purchase property to be used as a site for a school cannot be authorized in an executive session.[10] Since those dealing with a school district are responsible for knowing limitations on the authority of the district to contract, they may not enforce such a contract against the district.

Four days prior to commencement of the existence of a consolidated school district, the board of one of the component districts entered into a new employment contract with its superintendent. Concurrently the district filed suit seeking to set aside the reorganization. While the legal

6. Unified School Dist. No. 1 of Racine County v. Wisconsin Employment Relations Comm'n, 81 Wis.2d 89, 259 N.W.2d 724 (1977).

7. Local 4501, Communications Workers of America v. Ohio State Univ., 24 Ohio St.3d 191, 494 N.E.2d 1082 (1986).

8. Board of School Commissioners of the City of Indianapolis v. State ex rel. Wolfolk,

209 Ind. 498, 199 N.E. 569 (1936); Richard D. Kimball Co. v. City of Medford, 240 Mass. 727, 166 N.E.2d 708 (1960).

9. Conners v. City of Lowell, 246 Mass. 279, 140 N.E. 742 (1923).

10. Santa Monica School Dist. of Los Angeles County v. Persh, 5 Cal.App.3d 945, 85 Cal.Rptr. 463 (1970).

action was pending the new district refused to honor the contract. The litigation was ultimately unsuccessful, and the superintendent sought to recover his salary from the new district on the grounds he was ready, willing, and able to perform and that the new district was statutorily required to assume debts of the component districts. The Supreme Court of Colorado disagreed, holding that the contract was invalid as beyond the power of the board to make and therefore no debt could be created.[11]

Good intentions are not relevant to the validity of a contract made by a board of education. The Court of Appeals of Arizona held that a school board could not be bound by a contract to accept high school students tuition-free from another school district.[12] Twenty-seven years before, the second district had agreed, upon this condition, to "acquiesce in a school redistricting whereby certain extremely valuable taxable properties would be transferred" to the first district. The court found the contract not only legislatively unauthorized, but impliedly prohibited by a statute specifying procedures treating nonresident students.

Crucial to resolving three suits arising from the construction of a school administration center was whether it could be concluded that the board of education had authorized its president to sign the prime contract. The court refused to void the contract because it found that the jury could properly find the authorization from such evidence as the minutes of the meeting at which the board accepted the low bid of the prime contractor, testimony that he performed no work until the district's architect gave him approval, testimony from some board members who asserted he had breached the contract, testimony from some new board members that they ran on a platform to repeal the prior action of the board, and testimony that certain payments had been made under the contract.[13]

The Court of Appeals, Third Circuit, affirmed a district court decision to enforce an oral contract between a school district and a construction firm.[14] The board had agreed to allow the company to bid on three school building projects based upon the drawings, specifications, and equipment lists prepared by the company. The board subsequently withdrew the projects from bidding and the company sought reimbursement for its services, the sole consideration of the board having been to agree to hold public bidding in which the company could participate. The board's reason for changing its mind was that it found the state would not subsidize the projects. The trial court rejected the claims of the board that the agreement was not binding because it was made at a "conference" meeting rather than a "formal" meeting and that only written contracts could be enforced against boards for this type of work.

11. Achenbach v. School Dist. No. RE-2, Brush, 176 Colo. 437, 491 P.2d 57 (1971).

12. Oracle School Dist. No. 2 v. Mammoth High School Dist. No. 88, 130 Ariz. 41, 633 P.2d 450 (App.1981). [Case No.61]

13. Calvin V. Koltermann, Inc. v. Underream Piling Co., 563 S.W.2d 950 (Tex. Civ.App.1977).

14. Titan Environmental Constr. Systems, Inc. v. School Dist. of Philadelphia, 421 F.Supp. 1289 (E.D.Pa.1976), aff. 564 F.2d 90 (3 Cir.1977).

The court said that, in the absence of a statute to the contrary, the common law of contracts would prevail.

The Supreme Court of Wyoming reasoned similarly in a case involving an oral agreement to make a written contract the terms of which were mutually understood and agreed in all respects.[15] Here the board resolution approved a specific arrangement for demolishing an old school building after a time lapse to explore further alternative uses of the building. The court held that as soon as the company was informed orally of the resolution the contract became binding, with the condition precedent that no use be determined by the date specified. When that date passed the board could not revoke the contract.

In the preceding case a contract was created through a board resolution. This could not be the result if a written contract is required by statute.[16]

It should be noted here that oral contracts, like written ones, must be made by the board itself. Thus, a principal's promise of a duty-free lunch period in exchange for a promise to teach journalism classes and be the newspaper adviser was not binding on the board.[17] Neither were a superintendent's representations to students' parents even if based on conversations with individual board members.[18]

Competitive Bids

In General

There appear to be statutes in most states requiring that all or certain school contracts involving more than a specified sum shall be awarded on competitive bids. These statutes generally provide that the contracts indicated shall be let to the "lowest responsible bidder" or the "lowest and best bidder." (Under general statutes contracts for professional services are not required to be competitively bid.[19]) Obviously statutes of this type are designed to insure, as far as possible, that school districts will not become victims of wrongdoing, and that they will receive the most for their money. As the Supreme Court of Mississippi has said, these statutes were born of experience. Their object is to prevent "private and secret machinations" whereby one contractor may be favored over others at the expense of the district.[20] Courts strictly construe statutory provisions designed to safeguard public funds, and contracts that do not conform are void.[21]

15. Robert W. Anderson Housewrecking and Excavating, Inc., v. Board of Trustees, School Dist. No. 25, Fremont County, 681 P.2d 1326 (Wyo.1984).

16. Schull Construction Co. v. Board of Regents of Educ., 79 S.D. 487, 113 N.W.2d 663 (1962).

17. Wolf v. Cuyahoga Falls City School Dist. Bd. of Educ., 52 Ohio State 3d 222, 556 N.E.2d 511 (1990).

18. Walker v. Lockland City School Dist. Bd. of Educ., 69 Ohio App.2d 27, 429 N.E.2d 1179 (1980).

19. Cress v. State, 198 Ind. 323, 152 N.E. 822 (1926).

20. Beall v. Board of Supervisors, 191 Miss. 470, 3 So.2d 839 (1941).

21. Buchanan Bridge Co. v. Campbell, 60 Ohio St. 406, 54 N.E. 372 (1899).

Where there are state prequalifications for bidders on school contracts, these are generally considered mandatory, and contracts with those not prequalified are void. Obtaining the qualification between the time of submission of the bid and the time of the award of the contract has been held not to satisfy the requirement, and such a bidder must be rejected.[22]

Lowest Responsible Bidder

Much litigation has resulted from difficulties that boards have experienced in determining what constitutes the "lowest responsible bidder" or the "lowest and best bidder." The law seems clear that the bidder who submits the lowest bid does not necessarily satisfy the statute. Boards, in determining whether a bidder is responsible within the meaning of the statute, are entitled to take into account "financial standing, reputation, experience, resources, facilities, judgment, and efficiency" as a contractor.[23] It is thus seen that a bidder determined to be responsible by these criteria may well not be the lowest bidder.

Where reason existed to believe there was a connection between a bidder on a school contract and some persons suspected of, and later indicted for, perjury in connection with bid rigging on contracts with other public agencies, the board was sustained in withholding the contract, even though the party was the lowest bidder. The court said that it was not necessary to hold a hearing for the benefit of the rejected bidder before the disqualification.[24] Apparently a board may disqualify from bidding for a period a construction company which has engaged in bidding improprieties.[25] It is unconstitutional, however, to disqualify from public contracting one who has asserted the privilege against self-incrimination before a grand jury.[26] But a bidder has been held not to be a "responsible bidder" if its principal has a prior criminal conviction.[27]

The courts will, of course, examine the procedures used by a board in investigating a contractor to prevent the board from acting arbitrarily. One court-approved procedure will illustrate. A board rejected the bid of the lowest bidder on the basis of the recommendation of the school architect, its own investigation, and other evidence before it. The board had obtained information from those for whom the concern worked in the past and also had engaged an investigative agency to look into the background of the builder. The court declined to substitute its judg-

22. Donald F. Begraft, Inc. v. Borough of Franklin Bd. of Educ., 133 N.J.Super. 415, 337 A.2d 52 (1975).

23. Hibbs v. Arensberg, 276 Pa. 24, 119 A. 727 (1923). [Case No. 62]

24. Arglo Painting Corp. v. Board of Educ. of City of New York, 47 Misc.2d 618, 263 N.Y.S.2d 124 (1965).

25. Caristo Constr. Corp. v. Rubin, 10 N.Y.2d 538, 225 N.Y.S.2d 502, 180 N.E.2d 794 (1962).

26. Turley v. Lefkowitz, 342 F.Supp. 544 (W.D.N.Y.1972), aff. 414 U.S. 70, 94 S.Ct. 316, 38 L.Ed.2d 274 (1973).

27. Crescent Bus Corp. v. Board of Educ. of City of New York, 95 A.D.2d 776, 463 N.Y.S.2d 259 (1983).

ment for that of the board under the circumstances.[28]

Generally no cause of action is vested in a low bidder to contest an award to a higher bidder. The purpose of competitive bid statutes is not to grant rights to bidders, but to benefit taxpayers, and the cause of action for allegedly not observing the statutes lies with taxpayers.[29] In some states this rule has been relaxed.[30]

Conditions of Bidding

It has been held that a board may require a financial statement from bidders.[31] In that case the lowest bid had not been accepted because of failure to file the statement, and the bidder and a taxpayer sued. The bidder was held not to have standing to sue, and the taxpayer's case failed. The court found the requirement reasonable and upheld the board's position. Of twenty-six bidders, only two had not submitted the required statement with their bids.

When a non-financial item is missing from the lowest bid some courts have held that the bid may be accepted if the item is furnished before the contract is signed. In one case the lowest bidder did not submit a graphic representation of the schedule of the work with his bid, but did so before the award of the contract. The court stated that the time of submission of this item could not affect the total price bid by any of the other bidders and sustained the contract.[32] Another court has held that the failure to include a required certificate of non-collusive bidding did not render invalid the bid of the low bidder as long as there was no prejudice to other bidders and no advantage accrued to the low bidder. The board, however, could have rejected the bid.[33] Also upheld was a board's acceptance of a bid that did not contain a total bid amount, but rather a breakdown of unit prices.[34] The omission was considered to be an irregularity that the board could overlook in the best interests of the district because simple arithmetic calculations would supply the information.

Strict adherence to deadlines for filing bids can be demanded by boards. Appellate courts in New York[35] and Michigan[36] have reversed

28. Haskell-Gilroy, Inc. v. Young, 20 Misc.2d 294, 189 N.Y.S.2d 774 (1959).

29. R.S. Noonan, Inc. v. School Dist. of City of York, 400 Pa. 391, 162 A.2d 623 (1960).

30. Cardinal Glass Co. v. Board of Educ. of Mendota Community Consol. School Dist. No. 289, 113 Ill.App.3d 442, 69 Ill.Dec. 329, 447 N.E.2d 546 (1983).

31. Albert F. Ruehl Co. v. Board of Trustees of Schools for Industrial Educ., 85 N.J.Super. 4, 203 A.2d 410 (1964).

32. Gil-Bern Constr. Corp. v. City of Brockton, 353 Mass. 503, 233 N.E.2d 197 (1968).

33. Consolidated Sheet Metal Works, Inc. v. Board of Educ., 62 Misc.2d 445, 308 N.Y.S.2d 773 (1970).

34. Daniel Finley Allen & Co., Inc. v. East Williston Union Free School Dist., 143 A.D.2d 662, 533 N.Y.S.2d 19 (1988).

35. George A. Nole and Son, Inc. v. Board of Educ. of City School Dist. of Norwich, 129 A.D.2d 873, 514 N.Y.S.2d 274 (1987).

36. Great Lakes Heating, Cooling, Refrigeration and Sheet Metal Corp. v. Troy School Dist., 197 Mich.App. 312, 494 N.W.2d 863 (1992).

lower courts and upheld the decisions of boards not to consider bids submitted two or five minutes late.

Where a board had rejected a low bid, the Court of Appeals of Washington held that the bidder, who had failed to sign the bid as required by the specifications, was not entitled to a writ of mandamus to require the school board to accept the bid.[37] It said the school board could not legally accept it because the offer was not binding without the signature of the bidder. The same principle was applied by an appellate court in Louisiana.[38] There the board had improperly accepted a bid from a corporation without the specified submission of a corporate resolution authorizing the signing of the bid. The court said that the requirement of proof of the resolution was necessary to the validity of the bid.

That a board may include the statement that it reserves the right to reject all bids seems settled.[39] Probably the power to do so would be implied in the absence of a statement in the bid notice.[40] In a situation in Connecticut where there were eleven bids and all were rejected, the lowest bidder brought action against the board alleging that the rejection of his low bid along with the others was an abuse of discretion, contrary to public policy, and against the best interests of the taxpayers. His suit failed. The Supreme Court of Errors of Connecticut said that relaxation of the application of the established principle of law that local governmental units can reserve the right to reject any or all bids is only where fraud or corruption has influenced the conduct of the officials, and none was shown in the case.[41] It should be emphasized, however, that court approval of rejection of bids does not render the statute inoperative. Boards must readvertise for bids in order to get a contractor or supplier.[42]

The Supreme Court of New Mexico considered a situation in which a proposal for bids set out that school buses were to be delivered as soon as possible and that they be of the latest current production model.[43] A further specification was that the bidder guarantee all materials, equipment, and supplies for a period of one year from time of delivery. Despite the last specification, the bidder who submitted the lowest bid stated in his bid that the warranty on the body would be for one year, and on the chassis for ninety days or four thousand miles, whichever came first. His bid was rejected. The court ruled that since the bidder had not complied with a reasonable bid requirement, the board was not bound to accept the bid, even though it was substantially lower than the

37. A.A.B. Electric, Inc. v. Stevenson Public School Dist. No. 303, 5 Wash.App. 887, 491 P.2d 684 (1971).

38. Stafford Construction Co. v. Terrebonne Parish School Bd., 560 So.2d 558 (La.App.1990).

39. Metropolitan School Dist. of Martinsville v. Mason, 451 N.E.2d 349 (Ind. App.1983).

40. Conduit and Foundation Corp. v. Metropolitan Transp. Authority, 66 N.Y.2d 144, 495 N.Y.S.2d 340, 485 N.E.2d 1005 (1985).

41. Joseph Rugo, Inc. v. Henson, 148 Conn. 430, 171 A.2d 409 (1961).

42. Painting and Decorating Contractors of America, Inc. v. Ellensburg School Dist., 96 Wash.2d 806, 638 P.2d 1220 (1982).

43. New Mexico Bus Sales v. Michael, 68 N.M. 223, 360 P.2d 639 (1961).

successful bidder. The board had the right to adhere strictly to its specifications.

Where a competitive bid statute said nothing about the content of contracts, a lump-sum form has been held not required, and a board may break down the bid into separate bids if such would result in a saving.[44] A school district had advertised for separate bids on "materials, supplies, and equipment rental" and on all other work. The lowest bid was based on the sum of the two figures. The contractor was obliged to purchase for resale to the district the materials and supplies necessary to performance of the contract. It was successfully argued that the resultant contract was for "time and materials" and not a "lump-sum" contract, so that no sales tax would have to be paid on the materials by the contractor because the school district is exempt from such tax. (Under a lump-sum contract, title to the building materials would not pass to the district but become a component part of the real property, making their purchase by the contractor a retail sale subject to tax.) Since the bid estimates did not include payment of the sales tax, the beneficiary was in reality the district.

How far administrative bodies can go in placing restrictions on bidders was the basis of an Alabama case. The question was whether a state building commission could include in its contract with a builder a provision that the contractor must pay a scale of minimum wages. The commission was authorized by statute to plan, designate the location of, and construct buildings of state agencies including school districts. The Supreme Court of Alabama held that it did not have authority to make the requirement.[45] The court construed the statute as delegating authority to the commission to do such things as designating the quality and nature of the materials to be used and the quality of work to be required. But a wage requirement would, in the view of the court, be in violation of the competitive bid law of the state. A similar view was taken by a four-to-three vote of the Supreme Court of Louisiana a quarter century later.[46] There a local school board was the source of the requirement. Where, however, the legislature provided that "prevailing wages" be paid on all public construction jobs, "lowest responsible bidder" in the school code was held by the Maryland Court of Appeals to mean "lowest responsible bidder utilizing the prevailing wage rate" in the locality.[47]

The Supreme Court of Ohio has held that a bidder for a public construction contract may be required to assure nondiscrimination in employment in the entire performance of such contract by appropriate promises contained in contract provisions or related instruments.[48] The

44. Sweet Associates v. Gallman, 36 A.D.2d 95, 318 N.Y.S.2d 528 (1971).

45. Wallace v. Board of Educ. of Montgomery County, 280 Ala. 635, 197 So.2d 428 (1967).

46. Louisiana Associated General Contractors, Inc. v. Calcasieu Parish School Bd., 586 So.2d 1354 (La.1991).

47. Demory Brothers, Inc. v. Board of Public Works, 273 Md. 320, 329 A.2d 674 (1974).

48. Weiner v. Cuyahoga Community College Dist., 19 Ohio St.2d 35, 249 N.E.2d 907 (1969), cert. den. 396 U.S. 1004, 90 S.Ct. 554, 24 L.Ed.2d 495 (1970).

failure of a bidder to give such assurances when included in the specifications was a valid ground for rejection of his low bid. The de novo imposition of such a condition after bids are opened, however, has been disapproved.[49]

A distinction between the power of a state and of a local school district to institute an "affirmative action" policy was made by a federal District Court in California.[50] A policy promulgated by the San Francisco board of education required that a bidder for a general contractor job must be a minority-owned business or utilize minority-owned businesses for at least 25 percent of the base bid amount. The court said that this situation was in violation of the state statute requiring that contracts be awarded to the lowest responsible bidder. That the policy served desirable purposes was not a valid reason for changing the meaning of "responsible" in the context of the bid statute, which the Supreme Court of California had interpreted as meaning "qualified to do the particular work under consideration." The federal court said that, although only the state could authorize the challenged policy, the local board could require that bidders agree to comply with all applicable state and federal antidiscrimination laws. An injunction against the policy was affirmed.

In 1989 the United States Supreme Court addressed the constitutionality of the setting aside of a fixed percent of city government contracts for "minority business enterprises."[51] The Court held to be unconstitutional the plan of Richmond, Virginia, that required prime city contractors to subcontract at least 30 percent of the dollar amounts to one or more minority companies. The 1983–1988 plan was reviewed on the strict scrutiny standard because it was a race-based classification ("Blacks, Spanish-speaking, Orientals, Indians, Eskimos, or Aleuts"). The constitutional deficiencies included the lack of identified past discrimination in the construction industry to justify the "unyielding" racial quota as a means of remediation, the failure of the plan to be "narrowly tailored" to remedy effects of past discrimination (no geographical bounds or reason for including the specific groups to be benefitted), and improper use of statistics to demonstrate discriminatory exclusion from the industry in the Richmond market area.

A three-judge federal District Court invalidated a statutory provision in New York that on public construction projects preference must be given to citizens of the state who have been residents for a year prior to employment on the project.[52] The discrimination against resident aliens living in the state was found to violate the equal protection provision of the Fourteenth Amendment because there was no compelling reason for

49. School City of Gary v. Continental Electric Co., 149 Ind.App. 416, 273 N.E.2d 293 (1971).

50. Associated General Contractors of California v. San Francisco Unified School Dist., 431 F.Supp. 854 (N.D.Cal.1977), aff. 616 F.2d 1381 (9 Cir.1980), cert. den. 449 U.S. 1061, 101 S.Ct. 783, 66 L.Ed.2d 603 (1980).

51. City of Richmond v. J.A. Croson Company, 488 U.S. 469, 109 S.Ct. 706, 102 L.Ed.2d 854 (1989).

52. C.D.R. Enterprises, Ltd. v. Board of Educ. of City of New York, 412 F.Supp. 1164 (E.D.N.Y.1976), aff. 429 U.S. 1031, 97 S.Ct. 721, 50 L.Ed.2d 742 (1977).

treating the class of resident aliens differently from citizens. The Supreme Court affirmed the decision.

The question of preference of citizens of a state over citizens of other states, not at issue in the preceding case, was considered by the Supreme Court in 1978. The Court invalidated an Alaska statute providing that qualified state residents be given preference in employment over nonresidents in connection with developing oil and gas resources.[53] The Court did not address equal protection questions because the statute was in violation of the provision that "the citizens of each State shall be entitled to all privileges and immunities of citizens in the several States." The Court observed that Alaska's high rate of unemployment was not due to an influx of nonresidents (rather, to the fact that a substantial number of native Americans were unable to secure employment because of lack of job training or geographical remoteness from job opportunities), that highly educated residents were given the "same preferential treatment as the unskilled, habitually unemployed Arctic Eskimo enrolled in a job-training program," and that Alaska had "little or no proprietary interest in much of the activity swept within the ambit" of the statute.

In 1984 the Court held that the privileges and immunities clause applied to local laws as well as to state laws.[54] In that case the contested provision was a city ordinance requiring that at least 40 percent of employees of contractors on city projects be residents of the city. The Court said that such a provision would violate the privileges and immunities clause unless nonresidents "constitute a peculiar source of the evil at which the statute is aimed." As there had been no trial, the case was remanded for one.

In 1983 the Supreme Court had upheld, against a claim that interstate commerce was unconstitutionally burdened, a local government provision that at least half the workers on every construction project financially aided or administered by the city be city residents.[55] There the Court distinguished between the city as regulator of a market and as a participant in the market. It is only where the state or city regulates a market that the commerce clause of the Constitution is involved. "If the city is a market participant [as it was here], then the Commerce Clause establishes no barrier to conditions such as these which the city demands for its participation."

Bid laws commonly state a maximum expenditure which may be made without requiring bids. Problems often develop when a project involves separate contracts, each totaling less than the amount required for competitive bidding, but when combined exceeding the limit. Obviously, if the purpose of breaking a bid into separate contracts is to evade the competitive bid statute, the courts will not support it. Yet frequent-

---

53. Hicklin v. Orbeck, 437 U.S. 518, 98 S.Ct. 2482, 57 L.Ed.2d 397 (1978).

54. United Bldg. and Constr. Trades Council of Camden County and Vicinity v. Mayor and Council of City of Camden, 465 U.S. 208, 104 S.Ct. 1020, 79 L.Ed.2d 249 (1984).

55. White v. Massachusetts Council of Constr. Employers, Inc., 460 U.S. 204, 103 S.Ct. 1042, 75 L.Ed.2d 1 (1983).

ly the fact situations are quite complicated. For example, in Utah a school board had advertised for bids for constructing a building, not including a sprinkling system in its advertisement. Additional funds became available after the contract had been awarded. The school system then advertised for bids for the sprinkling system for materials only, and used its regularly employed maintenance personnel for installation. This process was less expensive than having the system installed. The whole procedure was challenged, but the Supreme Court of Utah sustained the school board.[56]

Unless there are statutes to the contrary, "alternative" bidding is permitted on public contracts.[57] This procedure provides for the submission of bids on alternative kinds or qualities of work or materials. The board may select one of the alternatives even though it is bid higher than another.[58] It is bound, however, to select the lowest responsible bidder in the category selected.

In situations where competitive bidding is not required by statute, it may be utilized by local boards. Unsuccessful in Montana was a professional photographer who sought to have the courts prohibit a local school board from securing bids for the taking of student photographs.[59] The state supreme court said the subject matter was within the jurisdiction of the school board and it could not interfere in the exercise of the board's discretionary power. Where competitive bidding is voluntarily utilized, the law discussed in this section would be applied by the courts.[60]

Mistaken Bids

A substantial amount of litigation involves mistaken bids. Problems usually arise in cases in which a mistaken bid has been submitted, the board has accepted or attempted to accept it, and the bidder either declines to enter into a contract on the basis of the bid or refuses to be bound by a contract entered into on the basis of it.

These situations are governed by a general rule of contract law, namely, that a mistaken bid or offer cannot be snapped up by the person or agency receiving it if the latter knew, or reasonably should have known, that a mistake had been made in it. Although it might be argued that bidders should be held to the consequences of their errors, some mistakes do not necessarily indicate carelessness. It is common practice of bidders to wait until the latest possible time before submitting their bids in order to take advantage of any last minute changes in the cost and availability of labor and materials to be used in performing

56. Utah Plumbing and Heating Contractors Ass'n v. Board of Educ., 19 Utah 2d 203, 429 P.2d 49 (1967). [Case No. 63]

57. Automatic Merchandising Corp. v. Nusbaum, 60 Wis.2d 362, 210 N.W.2d 745 (1973).

58. Trapp v. City of Newport, 115 Ky. 840, 74 S.W. 1109 (1903).

59. Knox v. School Dist. No. 1, Lewis and Clark County, 171 Mont. 521, 559 P.2d 1179 (1977).

60. Merritt Meridian Constr. Corp. v. Gallagher, 96 A.D.2d 933, 466 N.Y.S.2d 381 (1983).

the contract. Subcontractors follow the same procedure, with the result that main contractors are frequently required to compute their bids hurriedly and under extreme pressure in order that they may submit them before the deadline set for receiving bids. They often have no opportunity to check all figures before submitting them.

As illustration, a contractor, through a clerical error, bid $177,000 instead of more than $200,000, his intended bid on the job in question. The mistake was discovered after the bid had been accepted by the board. Four days later the contractor gave notice of the withdrawal of the bid and stated his refusal to be bound by the bid as he had submitted it. The Supreme Court of Nebraska held that the contractor was entitled under these circumstances to withdraw his bid even though it had been accepted by the board.[61] The court made the point that the only loss accruing to the district would be that which it sought to gain through taking undue advantage of the bidder as a result of his error. The report of the case is not clear as to whether the board actually knew of the mistake at the time it attempted to accept the mistaken bid. In any event, the bid here was so low that the board reasonably should have suspected that an error had been made and should have investigated that possibility before it sought to accept it. Absolute knowledge by the board that a mistake has been made is not necessary to the board's legal inability to accept it. It is sufficient that there appears in the bid or the circumstances surrounding it reason to suspect that a mistake has been made.

An example of a mistake that would not be judicially correctable is found in a Louisiana case. A bakery sought to escape the consequences of not performing a contract with a school board on the primary ground that the bid was mistaken. The manager of the local office had overlooked the escalating effect on cost of flour of the large sale of wheat one year by the United States to Russia. The assertion was that the school board should have been aware of the error because this company's bid for supplying bread was nine cents a loaf lower than other bids. The court held that the alleged error was in judgment, not in mathematical calculation, and that the contract was binding.[62] There was no evidence that the board had suspected an error.

The legal consequences of the requirement of a bid bond to be submitted with the bid were discussed by the Supreme Court of Ohio.[63] That court issued a ruling that, when a bid bond was in force, there could be recovery by a board against a contractor who was low bidder but who had submitted a mistaken bid. The court said that the bid bond contract is separate from the offer, but becomes effective at the time the offer is accepted. It then is in effect until a performance

61. School Dist. of Scottsbluff v. Olson Constr. Co., 153 Neb. 451, 45 N.W.2d 164 (1950). [Case No. 64]

62. Caddo Parish School Bd. v. Cotton Baking Co., Inc., 342 So.2d 1196 (La.App. 1977).

63. Board of Educ. v. Sever-Williams Co., 22 Ohio St.2d 107, 258 N.E.2d 605 (1970), cert. den. 400 U.S. 916, 91 S.Ct. 175, 27 L.Ed.2d 155 (1970).

contract is entered into. The court stated that to excuse the bidder would mean that the bid bond would be "a meaningless contract."

Withdrawal of Bids

If a bid is properly withdrawn, the bid bond would be cancelled, for the contractor would have no obligation to enter into a performance contract. That point was made in a situation where a school board was notified of a substantial clerical error in a bid on the day bids were submitted and opened.[64] The board asked for and promptly received the work sheets, which clearly showed the error in transposing a subtraction from the work sheet to the bid proposal. Three weeks later the board awarded the contract to the bidder based on the erroneous bid. The bidder's refusal to perform the contract was upheld, and recovery against him or the bid bond surety was denied.

If there is a procedure prescribed for withdrawing mistaken bids that procedure must be followed by bidders. It is obvious that if courts allowed bids too easily to be withdrawn on the ground that there were mistakes in them, manipulations would be possible and the purposes of the competitive bid statutes would be thwarted. Normally, of course, bids are merely offers, and, as with other offers, may be withdrawn prior to acceptance. However, because of the public interest involved, restrictions on the withdrawal of bids may be imposed by law. In Pennsylvania, for example, a rule by a public school building authority stated that a bidder could withdraw his bid provided that he personally appeared at the office of the authority with a written request for permission to do so prior to the time set for the opening of bids. In a complicated fact situation a bidder was not allowed by the Supreme Court of Pennsylvania to withdraw his bid even though it was substantially below others.[65] There was no attempt to withdraw except through the sending of an unverified telegram to the school building authority, which telegram did not state a reason for the withdrawal. It was shown that the bidder had been very indifferent in the matter and that his attitude was one of unconcern. The court reasoned that for the general welfare of the public such looseness in public contractual relations should not be condoned. To permit it would not only be placing a premium on negligence, but would be opening the door for fraudulent conduct between bidders or between a bidder and the public body inviting the bid. Thus, strict compliance was enforced by that court.

In Florida a bidder sought to withdraw his bid after all bids had been opened and the results announced, but before the board had the opportunity to accept the bid. Technically the contract had not been consummated because the board had not actually accepted the bid. There was no Florida statute providing that bids be irrevocable. The court, however, found there was a fundamental reason, grounded upon

---

64. City of Syracuse v. Sarkisian Bros., Inc., 87 A.D.2d 984, 451 N.Y.S.2d 945 (1982).

65. Modany v. State Public Bldg. Authority, 417 Pa. 39, 208 A.2d 276 (1965).

public policy, that mandated that the withdrawal be prohibited.[66] The court said that this was not a case in which it was sought to escape the consequence of a mistaken bid which did not arise from the negligence of the builder, nor was the case one to deny to a mistaken bidder relief from the consequences of his contract if the mistake went to the substance of the contract and the district was fully informed of the mistake promptly upon its discovery. The public body was entitled to a reasonable time after the bids were opened within which to tabulate, analyze, consider, and accept the lowest and best bid. If a bidder, after bids were opened and the results announced, could withdraw his bid without justification or cause, innumerable frauds could be perpetrated and the benefits of the procedure denied.

Changing Contracts Let on Bids

Under the general law of contracts both parties to a contract are bound, and neither may escape all or any part of his obligation under them without the consent of the other. Furthermore, the parties are at liberty to modify or amend their contract as they wish. This rule is not applicable to contracts entered into by boards and bidders pursuant to competitive bid laws. The reason for this deviation from the general law is that if boards and bidders may enter into competitive bid contracts and subsequently change them as they may desire, the benefits the competitive bid laws are designed to afford the public are circumvented and evaded. On the other hand, situations clearly may arise in which the public interest would be best served by authorizing boards and bidders to agree to limited changes in their contracts.

The rule in such cases is that a certain flexibility is permitted in changing contracts if the changes are not too extensive or so great as to amount substantially to abandoning the original contract and entering into a new one. When it appears to the courts that boards are acting in good faith in agreeing to contractual changes based on new events or data, the courts are slow to interfere with such board action.[67]

Obviously, application of this rule is difficult due to the fact that it is often impossible to determine in a particular case how substantial an agreed contractual change may be and yet fall within the rule stated. Two cases will indicate the difficulties which arise in this area. In Maryland a contract for the construction of five school buildings had been let under competitive bids for the price of $1,984,145. It developed that there was insufficient money to construct all the buildings. The board and the contractor agreed to eliminate one building and to make certain other changes which would result in reductions amounting to about $300,000. A taxpayer's suit to enjoin the board from proceeding with the revised contract was successful. The court was of the opinion that the variation in the general plan of construction was so substantial

---

66. Hotel China and Glassware Co. v. Board of Public Instr., 130 So.2d 78 (Fla. App.1961).

67. Stahelin v. Board of Educ., School Dist. No. 4, DuPage Cty., 87 Ill.App.2d 28, 230 N.E.2d 465 (1967).

as to constitute, to all intents and purposes, the formation of a new contract, which, not having been let on competitive bids, was invalid.[68]

In the second case, the Supreme Court of South Dakota construed a contractual provision which permitted the board of education to authorize changes in a building contract as the work progressed. While the building was under construction the board decided to construct a stage opening. It did not advertise for bids for the construction of the opening and none were received. However, the contractor did agree to construct the opening for about $1,700, the original contract price for the building being approximately $34,000. After the work had been completed suit was brought against the board for the full amount, including the agreed amount for the stage opening. The suit was unsuccessful. The court said that this change was not merely incidental to the complete execution of the work described in the contract, but actually constituted a supplemental contract for distinct and independent work.[69]

In Utah the low bidder on a school construction project submitted along with his bid a letter stating that he had difficulty determining the price and availability of certain material and that he stipulated a change in the price figure, higher or lower, as the information became available. The letter inadvertently was not discovered until six weeks after the contract had been signed. The state supreme court declared the contract valid.[70] It observed that the bid had been read and accepted and the contract drawn and signed, with no mention by the bidder of the contingency letter, which was found later among the papers in the bid envelope.

Recovery under Contracts

Express and Implied Contracts

Although certain contracts are void, it frequently happens that the district has received goods or services thereunder. The question then arises as to whether those who have supplied them have any remedy. In answering this question, it is necessary to distinguish among different kinds of contracts. Although much confusion arises when it is sought to classify some contracts, they all fall into one of three classifications. First, those which are express. In this type, the rights and duties are expressly stated by the parties, either orally or in writing. Second, those which are implied in fact. Under this type are found those that result from acts or conduct indicating clearly that a contract was intended, even though the parties did not expressly so agree. For example, in cases in which one accepts goods or services under conditions which show that they were not intended to be gratuitous, it will be implied that a contract was intended, and the parties will be bound by it. It is to be observed that a contract is no less binding because it is implied. The

68. Hanna v. Board of Educ., 200 Md. 49, 87 A.2d 846 (1952).

69. Seim v. Independent Dist. of Monroe, 70 S.D. 315, 17 N.W.2d 342 (1945).

70. Jaye Smith Constr. Co. v. Board of Educ., Granite School Dist., 560 P.2d 320 (Utah 1977).

difference between those express and those implied in fact is the manner in which they are formed. In the former, the contract is formed by words; in the latter, by conduct.[71] Third, those which are implied in law. This category embraces the so-called quasi-contracts.[72] A contract implied in law cannot be said to constitute a contract in the true sense of the word. It is created by law for reasons of justice and equity, and obligates a party who has received from another a benefit that would "unjustly enrich" him were he not so obligated. Recovery is permitted "as if there were a contract."

The classification is important because the measure of recovery is different in each category. In the case of the express contract, the recovery is determined by the provisions thereof. In the implied-in-fact cases, the measure of recovery is the reasonable value of the goods or services rendered. This is determined by the court or jury, and may or may not be the same as the price. In express contracts the amount stated in the contract is recoverable whether the amount be reasonable or not. If the parties have made an improvident contract, they are bound by it nevertheless. However, in the implied-in-fact cases, since there is no price set and no agreement, the law will not imply a promise to pay more than the reasonable value. In the implied-in-law cases, the measure of recovery is determined by the amount of benefit conferred upon the party receiving the property or services, and is not determined by either the price or the reasonable value. Implied-in-law contracts are imposed upon one benefited purely because the law considers it inequitable to enrich one party at the expense of another. If no benefit has been conferred, it follows that there can be no recovery regardless of the market price or reasonable value. Implied-in-fact and implied-in-law cases are frequently confused by the courts with the result that the wrong measure of recovery is sometimes applied. Indeed in many, if not in most, cases it is impossible to determine whether the courts are referring to contracts implied in fact or in law or whether they are permitting recovery on implied contracts or quasi-contracts. The terms "reasonable value" and "benefits received" seem to be used by the courts more or less indiscriminately, although the terms or the amounts of recovery are not necessarily the same. Likewise, the term "quantum meruit" is often applied to causes of action involving either type of implied contract, although historically it pertained to quasi-contracts.

Invalid Contracts in General

Statutory requirements controlling the making of school contracts are, of course, for the protection of the district and its taxpayers. For example, the requirements that certain contracts be in writing are for the purpose of avoiding misunderstandings, which so easily arise when oral contracts are relied on. The requirement of competitive bidding is

71. Ryan v. Warren Tp. High School Dist. No. 121, 155 Ill.App.3d 203, 109 Ill. Dec. 843, 510 N.E.2d 911 (1987). [Case No. 43]

72. Boyd v. Black School Tp., 123 Ind. 1, 23 N.E. 862 (1890).

to insure, as far as possible, the procuring of goods or services at as low a price as possible and to guard against collusion at the expense of the district. When, therefore, the district has received benefits under a contract which is invalid because it fails to conform to statutory requirements, the courts are faced with the necessity of relaxing the statutory protection or permitting the district to retain the benefits without compensating for them. The general rule is that if the district has the authority to enter into an express contract with reference to the subject matter, but the express contract is invalid because of some irregularity in the execution thereof, it is liable on an implied contract for the reasonable value of the goods or services, if the form or manner of letting the contract does not violate any statutory restriction upon the power to contract and is not otherwise violative of public policy. The application of the rule has caused the courts considerable difficulty, and, as is to be expected, various conclusions have been reached. The decisions seem to turn upon whether the court in a given case considers the strict enforcement of the statutory protection afforded the district or the equitable claim of the party furnishing the benefits the more sound public policy. Those which deny recovery on an implied contract do so on the ground that to allow it would open the door to glaring raids upon the school funds.[73] They point out that the protection provided by the statute is nullified to the extent of recovery permitted. Those reaching the opposite conclusion say that to allow school districts to assert the invalidity of a contract while retaining the benefits of the services thereunder can be unconscionably unfair.[74]

It is to be emphasized that there can be no implied contract if there is no authority in the district to enter into an express one.[75] The concept of an implied contract is not designed to permit a district to exceed its powers, but only to permit recovery when the board has failed to follow the statutory formalities. As has already been indicated, many courts have, through the device of the implied contract, judicially removed a measure of the protection afforded by the statutory requisites. However, the alleviation of the hardship upon those who in good faith furnish goods or services to a public school district probably justifies the sacrifice, which in most cases will be relatively slight. For example, although a statute requires the district's contract to be in writing, and some misunderstanding may result through failure to reduce it to writing, the probable loss through misunderstanding is small as compared with the hardship upon the individual which would result if he were left remediless. It is said that everyone is bound to know the limitations on the authority of a district to contract and deals with it at his peril. It is obvious, however, that as a practical matter those who deal with the district, especially if the deal be a small one, do not seek legal advice before entering into business relations with the district.

73. Oberwarth v. McCreary County Bd. of Educ., 275 Ky. 319, 121 S.W.2d 716 (1938); Goodyear v. Junior College Dist. of St. Louis, 540 S.W.2d 621 (Mo.App.1976).

74. Burk v. Livingston Parish School Bd., 190 La. 504, 182 So. 656 (1938).

75. Reams v. Cooley, 171 Cal. 150, 152 P. 293 (1915).

The implied contract concept is, it seems, a judicial device to subordinate technicalities, in a measure, to practicalities.

Ultra Vires Contracts

The weight of authority is that there can be no recovery upon quantum meruit (reasonable value of goods or services rendered or benefit conferred) if the contract is ultra vires (outside the power of the district to make). It will be apparent at once that the equitable considerations which have led a majority of the courts to permit recovery of the reasonable value of the goods or services furnished are present in cases in which the contract is ultra vires. In other words, the hardship which is suffered by one who has furnished goods or services under a contract which is ultra vires, if recovery on an implied contract is denied, is no less than it would be were recovery denied on an implied contract which the district had the authority to make. The fact that the majority of courts refuse to imply a contract if the express contract is ultra vires or would have been if made, merely indicates the limits beyond which courts refuse to go in sacrificing statutory protection of the district in order to avoid hardship upon those who have in good faith dealt with the district and conferred benefits upon it. In refusing recovery in these cases the courts reason that one dealing with the district is bound to know the limitations upon its contractual power and that the statutory provisions define the limits of that power. It is also said that one who deals with a district is a volunteer, that is, he is free to deal or not as he chooses. An examination of the ultra vires cases seems to indicate that more harmful consequences to the district are probable if recovery on an implied contract is permitted thereunder, than are probable if similar recovery is permitted under irregular contracts which the district had the power to make.

The question of which contracts are ultra vires is not free from difficulty unless something is expressly prohibited by statute [76] or there are specific conditions precedent to a board's entering into a valid contract. [77] Usually held to be ultra vires are contracts in excess of the constitutional debt limit, those let contrary to a statute requiring competitive bidding, and those let without a required vote of the district. In determining whether contracts in other cases are ultra vires, the courts sometimes merely state categorically that the contract is or is not in that classification. Statutes which determine the scope of the contractual authority of the district cannot be drawn so as to determine the specific authority in every conceivable transaction into which the district might enter. In close cases, therefore, it is impossible to determine whether the contractual authority has been exceeded until the cases have been

---

76. Board of Educ. v. Chicago Teachers Union, Local 1, American Federation of Teachers, 26 Ill.App.3d 806, 326 N.E.2d 158 (1975).

77. Cado Business Systems of Ohio, Inc. v. Board of Educ. of Cleveland City School Dist., 8 Ohio App.3d 385, 457 N.E.2d 939 (1983); Ryan v. Warren Tp. High School Dist. No. 121, 155 Ill.App.3d 203, 109 Ill. Dec. 843, 510 N.E.2d 911 (1987). [Case No. 43]

judicially determined. For example, the Supreme Court of Utah, finding no authority for a state university to invest in common stock, declared ultra vires a contract to pay commissions for handling the transactions.[78] No payments could be made to the brokers.

Not all those jurisdictions in which it is held that there can be no recovery on implied contracts if the benefits conferred upon the district are by virtue of an ultra vires contract leave those conferring the benefits remediless. If goods furnished under an ultra vires contract have not been consumed by the district and are capable of being returned without substantial injury to district property, they may be recovered. The cases are in sharp conflict as to whether, if the district has made complete or partial payment, an action may be maintained by the district to recover such payments.[79] It develops that ultra vires contracts which have been executed (performed) may not always be repudiated and the parties returned to status quo by court action. The theory sometimes advanced is that a court will not aid parties entangled in an illegal transaction. It leaves them where it finds them. In other cases the courts refuse to intervene purely on equitable grounds.

An Arizona school district entered into a contract with an architect to prepare plans for a school building. The amount to be spent was known to the architect before he drew up the plans. When bids were submitted, they were far above the amount budgeted, and the board rejected all of them. Subsequently, on revised plans and specifications, a bid close to the amount budgeted was accepted. The architect sought to collect his commission on the basis of the lowest bid on the first invitation. He relied on an express provision in his contract with the board. On the same basis he sought compensation for extra work occasioned by his having to revise the drawings after the bids to implement them were too high. The highest state court rejected his contentions.[80] It construed the pertinent statute to mean that the allowed percent was on the cost of building according to plans as finally adopted and that redrawings prior to acceptance of bids on the project were not compensable. The contractual arrangement with the local board was ultra vires because the state statute governed contracts with architects.

Where an architect proceeded with work that was provided for under a contract but that exceeded in cost the amount of money covered by the appropriation, it was held that he did so at his own risk, and it was not possible to recover even though he had proceeded in good faith.[81] In a similar situation in another state, the court reached the same result, ruling that a purported contract signed by the superintendent was void

78. First Equity Corp. of Florida v. Utah State Univ., 544 P.2d 887 (Utah 1975).

79. School Dist. No. 9 v. McLintock, 255 Mich. 197, 237 N.W. 539 (1931); Moe v. Millard County School Dist., 54 Utah 144, 179 P. 980 (1919).

80. School Dist. No. 1 of Pima County v. Hastings, 106 Ariz. 175, 472 P.2d 44 (1970).

81. Murphy v. City of Brockton, 364 Mass. 377, 305 N.E.2d 103 (1973).

because it was not in conformity with statutory requirements.[82] However, where the school board members unanimously approved entering a contract with an architect, encouraged him to begin work, and subsequently executed a written contract, it was not unlawful for the board to pay for work actually done before the written contract was executed.[83] No element of fraud was involved.

Ratification of Invalid Contracts

School districts, like other corporations and quasi-corporations, can act only through agents, and some of the general rules governing agency relationships apply to acts of agents of the board of education. One rule of agency is that even though an agent acts outside the scope of his authority, and his acts are not binding on his principal, the latter may later ratify the act and thereby bind himself as if the agent had original authority to do the act in question. This rule of ratification is applicable to acts purporting to be done in the name of the district by others than the board, or to those done by the board itself, but which for some irregularity fail to bind the district. The rule is, however, subject to the exception that there must have been power in the district to enter into the contract. There can be no ratification of an ultra vires act. Also, when others than the board act, whether the actors are legal agents can be an issue. The party alleging agency bears the burden of proof.

While it is well settled that there may be ratification of unauthorized acts, it is by no means easy to determine in all cases whether there has, in fact, been ratification. Of course, the district may ratify through a formal act, for example, correcting any informalities that may have been present in the original contract; but a formal act, by the overwhelming weight of authority, is not required. In general it may be said that an act has been ratified when the conduct of the board is such as to indicate that ratification was intended.[84] There cannot be ratification unless the board knows the facts and conducts itself in a manner inconsistent with any supposition other than that ratification was intended. Subsequent payment by the board for goods or services furnished, or the acceptance and use thereof, usually is held to constitute ratification if the board knows the circumstances surrounding the transaction. Because a board "must act through its records," some entry in board minutes could constitute ratification, and some state courts insist upon this if the board would "bear a loss because [an agent] failed to perform his duty." [85]

An Arkansas case illustrates the interplay of several factors. A superintendent signed a lease purchase agreement for $113,260 for books and materials with the understanding that federal funds could be

82. McKee v. City of Cohoes Bd. of Educ., 99 A.D.2d 923, 473 N.Y.S.2d 269 (1984).

83. Kennedy v. Ringgold School Dist., 10 Pa.Cmwlth. 191, 309 A.2d 269 (1973).

84. Frank v. Board of Educ., 90 N.J.L. 273, 100 A. 211 (1917). [Case No. 66]

85. Ramsey v. Board of Educ. of Whitley County, 789 S.W.2d 784 (Ky.App.1990). [Case No. 89]

used in payment. He was encouraged in the belief this was possible by the salesman and the assistant superintendent, even though they had been informed by state officials that federal money could not be used for payment at that time. Apparently the board of education was not aware of the situation at its inception. The materials were used for at least a year. When called upon to pay, the board refused, saying that the contract was beyond the authority of the superintendent to make. The materials were put into storage by the board and the company notified to pick them up. Finding that "neither party to the contract is without fault," the court held that there was an implied contract and applied quantum meruit.[86] The company could take back the used books or be paid $13,500.

The mere fact that the district retains benefits, even though it is cognizant of all the material facts concerning the transaction, does not constitute ratification if it is impossible for the district to reject the benefits conferred. For example, if improvements which cannot be removed have been made on school property, the use thereof by the district does not amount to ratification.[87] The reason for the rule is that if the district is obliged to refrain from using the improvements or be held to have ratified the transaction, the activities of the schools would be seriously disrupted or even rendered impossible.

In North Carolina a choral director, to whom a salesperson had been directed by the principal, signed two orders for 870 decorative oil lamps to be used in a fund-raising effort for the purchase of robes for the chorus.[88] After the choral director "ended his employment" on February 18, the principal sent two checks to the novelty company and returned unsold lamps. There was a discrepancy of about $2,500, for which the company brought suit, naming the board as a defendant. The court held that there was no contract with the board, because there was no ratification of the contract signed by the choral director. The principal's payment did not constitute a ratification by the board.

A distinctly different approach was taken by the Court of Appeal of Louisiana in a case where a teacher who was class sponsor, after conferring with the principal, signed a contract for entertainment for a prom.[89] Later he discovered that the contract was for a sound system, not a live band. The principal deemed the arrangement inappropriate, and he and the teacher informed the contractor that his services would not be needed. The present suit was for the payment called for by the contract if there was a cancellation. Referring to the general job descriptions of principal and teacher, the court decided that the principal had implied authority to bind the board and that the principal had

---

86. Responsive Environments Corp. v. Pulaski County Special School Dist., 366 F.Supp. 241 (E.D.Ark.1973). [Case No. 65]

87. Young v. Board of Educ., 54 Minn. 385, 55 N.W. 1112 (1893); Panther Oil and Grease Mfg. Co. v. Blount County Bd. of Educ., 41 Ala.App. 434, 134 So.2d 220 (1961).

88. Community Projects for Students, Inc. v. Wilder, 60 N.C.App. 182, 298 S.E.2d 434 (1982).

89. Herbert v. Livingston Parish School Bd., 438 So.2d 1141 (La.App.1983).

properly delegated it to the class sponsor. The principal's subsequent act of cancelling the contract also was held to be implicitly authorized, and, therefore, the board was held liable.

Ratification of a contract renders it as valid as if it had been made strictly in accordance with the authority given in the first instance. While there are a few cases to the contrary, it is usually held that there can be no partial ratification. The contract must be ratified as a whole or not at all. For example, if a certificated teacher begins his duties under an invalid contract and the board, knowing of such invalidity, accepts his services and pays him part of the stipulated salary, the contract for the entire employment period is ratified.[90]

In many school building projects architects are relied upon by the board to determine when performance of the contract is complete. In a Montana school district there was a problem with the gymnasium floor before completion of a new building. The contractor did more work on it, and the architect then accepted it. The board, following the architect's advice, made final payment unconditionally. There was a warranty by the contractor that he would remedy defects which appeared within a year of final payment. The school board brought legal action when the contractor subsequently refused to improve the floor. The supreme court of the state held that the board's action in issuing the final payment without conditions constituted ratification of the architect's acceptance of the floor.[91] If the floor was defective at the time of acceptance, the warranty did not apply, for it covered only defects appearing within a year. Thus, the school district was without present remedy against the contractor because it had waived its prior right not to accept the floor.

That there can be no ratification of an ultra vires contract was the basis for a court's declaring a school bus driver ineligible for retirement benefits.[92] For eleven years a woman drove a school bus with permission of the superintendent of schools and with the knowledge of the school board. However, she had no contract. Her husband had previously been legally appointed as bus driver, and when he accepted other work, she started driving the bus. No new contract was made and all checks were made payable to her husband for the period in question. Subsequently a contract was given to her. The Court of Appeal of Louisiana held that she was not legally an employee of the board during those years because the contract was with her husband. The fact that the board permitted the arrangement did not constitute ratification.

Sometimes those offering services to school boards proceed to perform apparently in the hope that irregularities in a contract will eventually be settled in their favor, or that they will at least be able to recover for reasonable value of services rendered. Such a situation ended

90. Jones v. School Dist. No. 144, 7 Kan.App. 372, 51 P. 927 (1898).

91. Grass Range High School Dist. v. Wallace Diteman, Inc., 155 Mont. 10, 465 P.2d 814 (1970).

92. Comeaux v. School Employees Retirement System, 241 So.2d 298 (La.App. 1970).

unsuccessfully for a private school in Wisconsin that had provided education to some handicapped Illinois children. The Appellate Court of Illinois refused to allow any recovery for several reasons, including some aspects of agency and the prime one that the private school had not received approval from Illinois authorities, which was statutorily required before payment could be made.[93]

A school superintendent serving under a five year contract agreed after about three and one half years to resign as superintendent and during the remainder of the term of the contract serve with no salary reduction as "research and planning administrator" under direction of the board and a new superintendent. Approximately five and a half months later the board abolished the position of research and planning director. It was held that the former superintendent could not claim the position or salary because the board was empowered to contract as to duration of employment only for specified positions, not including the new post.[94] The superintendent had voluntarily submitted his resignation according to the record. That contracts covering positions such as the one at issue became legal four months after the former superintendent became research and planning director was held to be irrelevant because the board could not ratify a contract illegal from its inception ("even assuming ratification could be inferred" by the failure of the board to repudiate the contract during the approximately month and a half from the new statute to the dismissal).

The Commonwealth Court of Pennsylvania held that where a school district business manager was given a contract approved by only four board members when the statute required five affirmative votes, there was no ratification growing out of the fact that the board president, who was absent from the meeting when the vote was taken, signed the contract.[95] Furthermore, the mere fact that some payments were made under the contract did not constitute ratification, nor did the fact that an appropriation had been made for a year's salary for that position.

Interest of Board Members in Contracts

It is fundamental that an individual may not legally represent conflicting interests. This principle as it applies to school contracts has become part of the statutory law of many states. In general these laws provide that it shall not be lawful for any person holding any office in the state to have a pecuniary interest, either directly or indirectly, in any contract in the making or letting of which the officer may be called upon to act or vote.

The most serious problems on this point involve deciding what constitutes an interest in a school contract. If a member of a board of

93. Juneau Academy v. Chicago Bd. of Educ., 122 Ill.App.3d 553, 78 Ill.Dec. 13, 461 N.E.2d 597 (1984). [Case No. 67]

94. Downey v. Lackawanna City School Dist., 51 A.D.2d 177, 379 N.Y.S.2d 557 (1976).

95. Grippo v. Dunmore School Bd., 27 Pa.Cmwlth. 507, 365 A.2d 678 (1976).

education enters into a contract with the district to furnish supplies, construct or repair a building, or furnish services, there would hardly be any doubt that his interest would be of such a nature as to fall within the prohibition. A more difficult situation develops when a corporation in which a board member has a substantial interest contracts with the district. Because a corporation is regarded as a separate entity, distinct from its stockholders, the question is whether the interest which a corporation might acquire in a school contract constitutes an interest of the board member. This question was answered in the affirmative by the Supreme Court of Wisconsin under a statute of the nature described above. A member of the board, after a contract had been let, notified the contractor that a company in which the board member held a substantial interest could furnish the necessary building materials, and a large amount was furnished. A suit by the corporation against the contractor (who had failed) for the price of the materials was successfully defended on the ground that the interest of the board member in the corporation was such that the contract was void under the statute.[96] The court said that this type of contract goes directly against the spirit of the law as well as its express provisions.

The highest court in South Dakota held that a contract to repair a school bus was ultra vires because a statute so provided where a public officer had an interest in the contract.[97] In the case a school board member was a shareholder, officer, and director of the company doing the repairs. Other sources of repair work were available within the district. Judgments requiring the board member and two other persons associated with the company to reimburse the district were affirmed.

Strict construction of a conflict of interest statute is illustrated by a Kentucky situation. The statute provided that no person could serve as board member who had an interest in any contract or claim against the board. A member who briefly continued to execute a contract to transport students and one who was the owner of a store from which purchases for the school were made were held to have violated the statute.[98] The state's highest court took judicial notice of the points that the superintendent apparently had ill will toward the board members, that there was no intention to defraud, and that the transactions were not substantial. But it commented that only a strict construction would properly serve the purpose of the statute.

A looser view of a similar statute was taken by the Supreme Court of Arkansas. A board member who was part-owner of a trucking company was charged with illegal interest in a contract with the board. After a bid had been let, he was engaged by the lowest bidder to transport some materials. The court held that, since the board member was not to receive a benefit at the time the contract with the bidder was

---

96. Bissell Lumber Co. v. Northwestern Cas. & Sur. Co., 189 Wis. 343, 207 N.W. 697 (1926).

97. Ayres v. Junek, 247 N.W.2d 488 (S.D.1976).

98. Commonwealth ex rel. Matthews v. Coatney, 396 S.W.2d 72 (Ky.1965).

executed, the contract was valid.[99] It said that the law will not presume that the parties to the contract intended an illegal act. A dissenting judge commented that the view of the majority "accomplishes nothing except to outlaw actual dishonesty if it is detected."

Ownership of a teacher employment agency and school board membership have been held not to be incompatible in Ohio.[100] It was shown that although the board member could use board information in his business, he had never done so.

The Appellate Court of Illinois has decided that the employment in a school district of spouses of board members does not per se create a prohibited conflict of interest.[101] Nevertheless, the court said a conflict may be determined to exist through examination of surrounding facts and circumstances or a statute may declare such a rule. Statutes proscribing the employment of public school personnel who have close relatives on the board, however, cannot be applied so as to remove employees already serving when the relative becomes a board member.[102]

It has been held in New Jersey that local school boards have the implied power to proscribe initial employment of persons in the immediate family of board members.[103] The highest New York court has sustained the constitutionality of a statute barring more than one member of a family from serving concurrently on a board of education.[104]

In a Mississippi case it was unsuccessfully argued that a husband boardmember who voted against employing his wife as teacher was therefore not liable for violation of a state prohibition against board members having a direct or indirect interest in any contracts made by the board. The highest state court observed that it was his interest in his wife's contract, not his vote, that was forbidden. Restitution of the wife's salary was ordered, as well as a fine for the violation.[105]

[Case No. 60]   Formation of an Employment Contract

FOSTER v. OHIO STATE UNIV.

Court of Appeals of Ohio, 1987.
41 Ohio App.3d 86, 534 N.E.2d 1220.

STRAUSBAUGH, PRESIDING JUDGE. This is an appeal by plaintiff from a summary judgment in the Court of Claims in favor of defendant and against plaintiff.

The record indicates that defendant, the Ohio State University, through Andrew Broekema, Dean of the Ohio State College of Arts, by

99. Stroud v. Pulaski County Special School Dist., 244 Ark. 161, 424 S.W.2d 141 (1968).

100. State of Ohio ex rel. Corrigan v. Hensel, 2 Ohio St.2d 96, 206 N.E.2d 563 (1965).

101. Hollister v. North, 50 Ill.App.3d 56, 8 Ill.Dec. 20, 365 N.E.2d 258 (1977).

102. Backman v. Bateman, 1 Utah 2d 153, 263 P.2d 561 (1953); Hinek v. Bow-man Public School Dist. No. 1, 232 N.W.2d 72 (N.D.1975).

103. Whateley v. Leonia Bd. of Educ., 141 N.J.Super. 476, 358 A.2d 826 (1976).

104. Rosenstock v. Scaringe, 40 N.Y.2d 563, 388 N.Y.S.2d 876, 357 N.E.2d 347 (1976).

105. Waller v. Moore ex rel. Quitman County School Dist., 604 So.2d 265 (Miss. 1992).

letter dated May 3, 1983, offered plaintiff, Philip E. Foster, an eleven-month appointment as Chairperson and Associate Professor of the Department of History of Art at the Ohio State University beginning July 1, 1983. The letter concluded: "If the terms and conditions of this letter are acceptable to you, please sign the enclosed copy and return it to my office." Subsequently, Dean Broekema notified plaintiff by express mail dated May 25, 1983: "Unless an answer to letter of offer, dated May 3, 1983, is received in my office by Thursday, June 2, 1983, offer for position of Chairperson and Associate Professor, Department of History of Art at The Ohio State University, is withdrawn." The record further indicates that, on June 2, 1983, plaintiff telephoned Dean Broekema collect and left a message with his secretary that plaintiff accepted the position effective July 15, 1983. On June 7, 1983, defendant notified plaintiff that, since he had failed to accept in writing by June 2, the offer was revoked. On June 11, plaintiff signed the May 3 letter notifying defendant of his acceptance.

The Court of Claims thereafter granted defendant's motion for summary judgment finding that plaintiff's failure to accept in writing the terms of defendant's offer by June 2 barred his later acceptance on June 11. It is from this finding and judgment that plaintiff appeals setting forth the following single assignment of error:

"The lower court erred in failing to find that appellant's telephone acceptance of appellee's letter/offer of May 3, 1983, followed by a confirmatory writing delivered in a reasonable time, met all elements of appellee's offer and created an employment contract between the parties."

In support of his assignment of error, plaintiff argues first that there is no evidence to support a finding that plaintiff had to answer by June 2 or that the answer had to be in writing and, therefore, plaintiff had a reasonable time in which to respond. Second, even if the May 25 letter required a definite answer by June 2, there is no indication that the acceptance had to be in writing alone. Third, the question of whether the acceptance had sufficiently met an offer is a question of fact and as such the evidence shows that plaintiff accepted the offer as tendered. Fourth, to the extent that the Court of Claims relied upon time being the essence of the contract, there is no indication that defendant ever believed a timely answer was critical to the appointment of the position.

The terms of defendant's offer to plaintiff were set forth in the May 3, 1983 letter and established the precise manner and place of acceptance—that a copy of the letter be signed and the copy be returned to Dean Broekema's office. Subsequently, Dean Broekema imposed an additional requirement as to time, prescribing that plaintiff's acceptance be received by June 2, 1983. The time requirement did not modify or alter any previous specifications but merely put a time limit on the duration of the offer. An offer which is unsupported by consideration is subject to revocation at any time. The offeror can wholly terminate or limit the power and mode of acceptance. When an acceptance to a contract for employment does not meet and correspond with the offer in every respect, no contract is usually formed.

Defendant's offer to plaintiff dated May 3, 1983 states that the position was to begin July 1, 1983. When plaintiff left his purported message of acceptance on June 2, 1983, he indicated July 15, 1983 as the desired date of commencement. A reply to an offer which purports to accept but is conditional on the offeror's assent to terms additional to or different from those offered is not an acceptance but is a counteroffer. Plaintiff's telephonic purported acceptance of June 2, 1983 was therefore a counteroffer and not an unconditional acceptance which was rejected by Dean Broekema in his letter of June 7, 1983 and, therefore, no contract was created. The undisputed facts indicate that plaintiff simply failed to accept the terms of the offer and therefore no contract exists. Plaintiff's single assignment of error is overruled, and the judgment of the Court of Claims is affirmed.

Notes

1. Although this type of employment situation is not infrequent, it is unusual for the matter to be carried to an appellate court. The short opinion highlights several important principles of law regarding the "mutual assent" aspect of contract formation.

2. How could the candidate have acted differently and thereby enhanced the legal chances of achieving his goals?

3. How could the dean have acted differently and thereby strengthened his legal position, possibly to the point of discouraging the candidate from filing suit?

[Case No. 61] Power of Board to Contract to Waive Tuition

ORACLE SCHOOL DIST. NO. 2 v. MAMMOTH HIGH SCHOOL DIST. NO. 88

Court of Appeals of Arizona, 1981.
130 Ariz. 41, 633 P.2d 450.

BIRDSALL, JUDGE. This is an appeal from an order granting appellees' motion to dismiss appellants' complaint. Counts One and Two of the complaint were dismissed for failure to state a claim for relief. * * *

We will assume the truth of all facts which are stated in the complaint. A motion to dismiss for failure to state a claim for relief should not be granted unless it appears that a plaintiff will not be entitled to relief under any state of facts susceptible of proof under the pleading.

According to the complaint the then acting school board for appellants and appellees agreed that if appellants would acquiesce in a school redistricting whereby certain extremely valuable taxable properties would be transferred from appellants' district into appellees', appellees would not thereafter charge tuition for high school students residing in appellants' district who attended appellees' high school.

The complaint further alleges that the redistricting was effected and from 1953 to 1975 the tuition was not charged. Since 1975, in accordance with a subsequent agreement, no tuition was charged but appellants forwarded to appellees the amount of state aid received for those high school students attending appellees' high school. In 1980, appellees requested, for the first time, tuition payments for the subject students.

The complaint further alleges that appellants justifiably relied to their detriment and that appellees' intended appellants would rely and knew that they would so rely. Further, that appellees are estopped from denying the existence or validity of the agreement and have waived the same. * * *

Count Two of the complaint alleges that the 1975 agreement created a novation separate and apart from the 1953 contract and that an implied in fact contract was created based on the parties' prior course of dealing.

The complaint sought an injunction and declaratory judgment that the agreements were binding and valid.

We believe one finding is dispositive of this appeal. The appellee school board had no power to enter into the alleged agreement which gave up the right to receive tuition for those high school students attending from without the district.

Article 11, Section 1 of the Arizona Constitution required the legislature to "enact such laws as shall provide for the establishment and maintenance of * * * common schools, high schools * * * and a university". Title 15, A.R.S., contains the legislative enactments carrying out this duty. School districts are a legislative creation having only such power as is granted to them by the legislature. A board or commission which is a creation of a statute created for a special purpose has only limited powers and it can exercise no powers which are not expressly or impliedly granted. Not only is the authority to enter into an agreement such as we have here not contained within any express or implied power granted by the legislature, the statutes impliedly prohibit such an agreement. Arizona Code Annotated § 54–908 (1939), the statute applicable at the time the parties entered into the agreement, provided in part:

> "Non-resident pupils of school age, otherwise qualified, residing in the county in which there is a high school, but in a district having no high school, nor a school wherein high school subjects are taught, shall be admitted to such high school on the same conditions as residents, upon paying a reasonable fee for each pupil to be fixed by the board in charge of the high school, not to exceed, however, such amount as would equal the average cost per pupil of the high schools of the county after deducting the amount received from the state and county, such payment to be made monthly. Said tuition shall be a legal charge against the school district in which said non-resident pupil resides, and levied and collected in the same manner as other school taxes, and shall be paid by said district out of the funds of such district upon presentation to the clerk of such district of a statement."

This requirement for the collection of tuition and that it be paid in the form of money is mandatory.   * * *

Appellee school district had no power to enter into an agreement waiving tuition or permitting it to be paid in any manner other than the payment of monies.   The agreement was unenforceable at the time of its making, is not enforceable now, and the trial court properly dismissed the complaint.

We do not agree with appellants' argument that the implied in fact contract alleged in Count Two of their complaint may be enforced regardless of whether the express contract is valid.   The school board would have no more power to bind the district by their actions than they would to enter into an express contract with the same objective and purpose.   The appellee school district has a statutory obligation to admit the high school pupils from the appellant school district.   * * *

We also find no merit in appellants' argument that appellees are estopped to deny the existence or validity of the agreement.   Generally a school district cannot be bound by estoppel when acting in its governmental capacity.   Appellants have not shown that any exception to the general rule exists here.   Even if appellees admit the agreement, it remains unenforceable since appellee had no power to make it.   Likewise, we do not believe that the illegal agreement may be upheld through the doctrine of ratification.   An agreement which is invalid by virtue of a lack of authority cannot be given legal effect in that manner.   In order to be ratified, the contract must initially be one which is in the scope of the powers of the public body.   * * *

* * *

Affirmed.

Notes

1.   General principles of contract law and powers of boards to contract are discussed in Chapters 8 and 9.

2.   Do you believe this was a situation in which one district sought "to take advantage" of the other?   If so, with which do you sympathize?

3.   The rule that estoppel (see Glossary) cannot be invoked against a public agency is well established.   Public Improvements, Inc. v. Board of Educ. of City of New York, 56 N.Y.2d 850, 453 N.Y.S.2d 170, 438 N.E.2d 876 (1982).   See Case No. 20.

[Case No. 62]   Lowest Responsible Bidder—Changing Contracts after Letting

HIBBS v. ARENSBERG

Supreme Court of Pennsylvania, 1923.
276 Pa. 24, 119 A. 727.

[Suit was brought to restrain the board from proceeding under a school contract which had been let to a bidder other than the lowest bidder.   Also it was alleged that the contract had been changed after it had been let. The lower court held for the board and the plaintiff appealed.]

KEPHART, J. * * *

It is averred, in the bill to restrain the school directors from awarding the contract to construct a badly needed school building in a school district in Fayette county, that the architect's plans and specifications do not fully state the kind, quality, and quantity of materials required. One special item reads:

"The face brick * * * to be a thoroughly vitrified, wire-cut, face brick of such color as will be selected by the architect and school board; * * * to cost not more than $34.00 per thousand."

We see no reason why an intelligent bid could not be made on this item. Vitrified, wire-cut, face brick has a definite meaning; the contract preserved the right of inspection and rejection of materials; and there was little opportunity to slight the quality. If a certain make of brick had been selected, or several makes, we can readily see a charge of a different character might be presented.

That the directors later decided to use a little more expensive brick would not condemn the letting, or cause the directors to be liable for the increased price, or avoid the purchase. There was no such departure from the general purpose as would require reletting. Unforeseen contingencies or new ideas sometimes make it necessary to change the character or quality of material or a part of a structure from the original plans. A certain flexibility in the power of officials to take care of these matters is intended to be granted, that the law relating to public letting may not become an instrument of oppression through a too rigid construction. These officers must act honestly, reasonably, and intelligently, and a new departure must not so vary from the original plan or be of such importance as to constitute a new undertaking, which the act controls, and where fairness could only be reached through competitive bidding. Courts, however, will be slow to interfere unless it appears the officers are not acting in good faith. * * *

* * * [But there were some] mistakes in the letting. The architect did not supply a sufficient number of copies of the plans and specifications for all those who expressed a wish to bid. Reputable contractors were deprived of the opportunity to submit prices. Competitive bidding could not be secured under these conditions. We cannot too strongly condemn the motives of some architects and public officials in following this practice; it opens the door to the grossest kind of fraud. A favored contractor, apprised in advance, may easily have the limited number of plans and specifications on file lifted by persons not bona fide bidders, or, through a combination none too infrequent, the favored contractor submits a price (the lowest) that is high enough to give an excessive profit and pays to other higher bidders a commission "or rake-off" as their part of the gain for participating in the combination. Of course, there are other methods. Officials must have on file enough sets of plans and specifications to supply those who demand them within a reasonable time prior to the day on which the bids are to be submitted.

The time within which a request is made should be sufficient to enable the architect to furnish additional copies if those first furnished have been exhausted. The court was in error in passing over this fact as not being of sufficient consequence to restrain the work.

At the first meeting of the board, after the bids were submitted they were all deemed too high. A week later, at an adjourned meeting, the bid of the Republic Construction Company, fourth lowest bidder, was accepted by the vote of four of the directors. Two of the board were not present, and another, though present, did not vote. * * *

The contract was awarded to the fourth lowest bidder without investigating the responsibility of the three lower bidders. This is contrary to the Act of July 10, 1919 (P.L. 889; Pa.St.1920, Sec. 4842; section 617, School Code), which directs the contract be let to the lowest responsible bidder. The term "lowest responsible bidder" does not mean the lowest bidder in dollars; nor does it mean the board may capriciously select a higher bidder regardless of responsibility or cost. What the law requires is the exercise of a sound discretion by the directors. They should call to their assistance the means of information at hand to form an intelligent judgment. They should investigate the bidders to learn their financial standing, reputation, experience, resources, facilities, judgment and efficiency as builders. This was not done. The court below censures the board for omitting this important step, but it holds, inasmuch as they had ample knowledge of the successful bidder and the merit of its work, the contract could be awarded. This might do in private affairs, but will not pass when public funds are at stake; it is not the exercise of discretion. Though the directors were not bound in law to give the contract to the lowest bidder, who might be irresponsible, they were bound to investigate, and if a bidder measured up to the law's requirement as a responsible party, the board could not capriciously award the contract to another. Giving a bond alone does not make up for responsibility; we have too many bonding companies willing to indemnify almost anything. But there should be a sufficient reason, where a bidder is lowest and responsible, why the job was not given to him. And where such reason appears, the action of the board is generally conclusive. * * *

We have indicated in this opinion where we think the court below was in error in permitting the work to go ahead. On the record presented the school board was without authority to award the contract and bind the school district.

* * *

Notes

1. In re Scranton City School Dist. Audit, 354 Pa. 225, 47 A.2d 288 (1946), the board sought to divide a project involving an expenditure of $12,673.63 into a number of contracts, each less than $300 in amount, in order to have the project completed in a short time and to save the district money. Contracts for less than $300 were not required to be let to the lowest responsible bidder in Pennsylvania. This action of the board was struck down as being in violation of the competitive bid statute.

2. After the board of education in Holyoke advertised for bids to supply milk and reserved the right to reject any bids, it accepted a bid from a firm located in Holyoke, even though it was some fifteen hundred dollars more than the lowest bid, which was from a company located elsewhere. It was held that the competitive bid statute covered only construction supplies, and thus the board action was legal. Gosselin's Dairy v. School Committee of Holyoke, 348 Mass. 793, 205 N.E.2d 221 (1965).

3. In Gil-Bern Constr. Corp. v. City of Brockton, 353 Mass. 503, 233 N.E.2d 197 (1968), the lowest bidder did not submit a graphic representation of the schedule of the work with his bid, but did so before the award of the contract. The court stated that the time of submission of this item could not affect the total price bid by any of the other bidders and sustained the contract.

[Case No. 63] Use of Regular Maintenance Personnel in School Construction

UTAH PLUMBING AND HEATING CONTRACTORS ASS'N v. BOARD OF EDUC. OF WEBER COUNTY SCHOOL DIST.

Supreme Court of Utah, 1967.
19 Utah 2d 203, 429 P.2d 49.

CROCKETT, CHIEF JUSTICE. Plaintiffs, an organization of plumbing contractors and three other trade associations, including some from Weber County, sued to enjoin defendant Weber County Board of Education from installing a sprinkling system on the Roy High School football field. Plaintiffs contend that the defendant's use of its own maintenance employees to put in the sprinkling system was a violation of Section 53–11–1, U.C.A.1953, which requires advertising for bids "[w]henever any schoolhouse is to be built" or any improvement constructed costing over $20,000.

* * *

After the contract for the school had been awarded and construction was well under way, additional funds from the State became available. It was then that the School Board decided they should install the sprinkling system on the football field at the least possible cost. By advertising for bids for the materials only, and using their regularly employed maintenance people during their free time from other duties, the job could be done for approximately $3200, about $2700 of it for materials, which they purchased from the lowest bidder.

The position essayed by plaintiffs is that the board was obliged to consider the sprinkling system as part of the "building of the schoolhouse" which cost $2,600,000, and that it should have been included in the advertisements for bids for its construction; or alternatively, even though constructed later, it still must be considered as part of the entire project and advertised for bids.

* * * The powers of the Board of Education are derived from statute and consist only of those expressly granted or those reasonably implied as necessary to carry out the duties imposed upon it. A number of sections of our code grant authority to school boards for the construction and maintenance of facilities for the operation of public school systems. Under the heading, "Further Powers of Boards of Education," Section 53–6–20, U.C.A.1953, provides:

> Every board of education shall have power * * * *to construct and erect school buildings* and to furnish the same, * * * to purchase, exchange, repair and improve high school apparatus, books, furniture, fixtures and all other school supplies. It * * * may *do all things needful for* the maintenance, prosperity and *success of the schools,* and the *promotion of education;* * * *.

The extensive discretion reposed in the school board by this section is apparent.

We are aware that in decisions construing the powers of school districts, the terms "school building" and "schoolhouse" are often given a broad meaning to encompass the entire functioning school plant, including athletic facilities. However, from this fact and the fact that under the grants of power to the board of education just referred to above, it has authority to construct and maintain athletic facilities, it does not necessarily follow that the sprinkling system in question must be regarded as coming within the language of Section 53–11–1, first referred to above, requiring bids "[w]henever any schoolhouse is to be built." Whether it does or not may depend upon the circumstances. For example, it seems quite obvious that if the schoolhouse itself has already been built, the construction of some additional facility or improvement to the school plant, such as the installation of some additional blackboards, visual aid equipment, or of a sprinkling system in the athletic field, would not be within the meaning of the phrase "building a schoolhouse." If it were so, the school administration would often be hampered in adapting school buildings and facilities to changing needs such as supplying the deficiencies listed above in this very building with which we are concerned. This would be squarely contrary to the plain intent of Section 53–6–20, above quoted which authorizes the Board to improve apparatus, books, furniture, fixtures and do all things needful for the maintenance, prosperity and success of the schools, and the promotion of education.

* * *

The principle that the School Board may not fragment a building contract into separate units to avoid the requirement of bids nor otherwise circumvent the requirements of the statutes is sound. From what we have said it should be apparent that as we view the evidence there is a reasonable basis therein to substantiate the trial court's refusal to find that the defendant Board did so. On the other hand, the evidence supports its findings to the contrary. Pertinent to this issue is the fact that the Board did request bids on the pipe and materials and bought them from the lowest bidder. This is evidence of its good faith and its desire to properly and lawfully perform its duty in administering the school system in "the most efficient and economical" manner possible.

It is our opinion that its initiative and frugality in the premises should be approved and commended, rather than censured.

* * *

Notes

1. The standing to sue of the plaintiff association led to a sharp division of the court. The justices were in agreement, however, on the merits of the case.

2. What is your opinion in general as to the desirability of the practice of using regular school employees on school repair and construction projects? If the amount of money involved exceeds that required to be let on competitive bids, is your opinion altered?

3. An Arizona school board had landscaping services performed on new school building sites without advertising for competitive bids. Plans, specifications, and actual work were executed by board employees. It was held that the competitive bid statute did apply in this situation. However, separation of landscaping from school construction was held permissible because landscaping was not an integral part of the building and because the work could be performed by regular employees at a possible lower cost. Secrist v. Diedrich, 6 Ariz.App. 102, 430 P.2d 448 (1967).

[Case No. 64] Mistaken Bids

SCHOOL DIST. OF SCOTTSBLUFF v. OLSON CONSTR. CO.

Supreme Court of Nebraska, 1950.
153 Neb. 451, 45 N.W.2d 164.

CARTER, JUSTICE. This is an action against the Olson Construction Company and its bondsman, Maryland Casualty Company, because of the failure of the former to comply with its bid and to contract for the construction of the buildings for the doing of which the bid was submitted. The trial court held against the plaintiff school district and for the defendants. The plaintiff appeals.

The school district advertised for bids for the construction of a new vocational agriculture and grandstand building and an addition to the Bryant Elementary School. The defendant Olson Construction Company was the successful bidder at $177,153.00. Pursuant to the instructions to bidders, contained in the advertisement for bids, the bid was accompanied by a bid bond in the amount of 5 percent of the bid, the defendant Maryland Casualty Company appearing as the surety thereon. The closing time for the acceptance of bids was fixed as of April 15, 1948, at 8 p.m. The bid of the Olson Construction Company was submitted on the evening of April 15, 1948, prior to 8 p.m. It was accepted and the contract awarded to the Olson Construction Company by the school board of the school district before the adjournment of the board thereafter on that day. The Olson Construction Company refused to comply with its bid and this action was brought to recover from the Olson Construction Company and its bondsman the sum of $8,857.65, the same being 5 percent of the bid, the amount the defendants obligated themselves to pay if the Olson Construction Company failed to enter into a contract to perform the work in accordance with its bid. The bid of the

Olson Construction Company was $177,153.00 which showed an itemization of $68,410.00 for the construction of the vocational agriculture and grandstand building. The only other bid was in the amount of $203,758.00 and showed an itemization of $89,905.00 on the vocational agriculture and grandstand building. The architect's estimate on the latter building was $89,340.00. The defense of the Olson Construction Company is based on a typographical error in computing the total of its bid, which resulted in a reduction of the intended bid by an amount of $23,600.

The evidence shows that on April 15, 1948, John H. Miller, the vice president and secretary of the Olson Construction Company, was in Scottsbluff for the purpose of preparing the bid in final form for submission to the school district. In preparing the bid, form estimate sheets were used. Each of these form estimate sheets listed different items such as materials, labor, unit price, bids of subcontractors, and similar items. In order to arrive at the bid to be submitted it was necessary to tabulate the various sheets and add them up to secure the total amount of the bid. This latter work was assigned to one Erma Price, an experienced employee of the company. In tabulating the amounts shown on the estimate sheets relating to the bid on the vocational agriculture and grandstand building she inadvertently dropped a figure from the amount for which the structural steel was subcontracted, so that it was listed on the adding machine as $2,689 instead of $26,289. This resulted in a total being entered upon this particular estimate sheet in the amount of $6,624.50 instead of $30,224.50, even though one of the items alone amounted to $26,289. The erroneous total of $6,624.50 was carried into the total bid and resulted in the bid of $177,153.00 instead of $200,753.00 which the bid would have been except for the error. The evidence shows that Mrs. Price checked the items back after the addition was completed and again overlooked the error made in tabulating the amounts on the adding machine. The evidence shows also that Miller and those engaged with him in preparing the bid were in a hurry because of the approaching deadline for the filing of bids. The delay in preparation is shown to have been the result of slowness on the part of sub-contractors in submitting their bids, and delays in calculating certain items due to the rising costs of labor and materials.

The evidence is that the error was not observed by anyone connected with the preparation of the bid. The sealed bid was filed with the school district by a construction superintendent who was not familiar with its contents. Miller left Scottsbluff shortly before 8 p.m. on the last day for the filing of bids. It was not until he learned on the next day of the great variance of the two bids filed that he suspected a mistake in one of them. He immediately requested that the estimate sheets be sent to him at the home office at Lincoln. They were received the following Monday and the error was immediately discovered. The architect for the school district and the school district were immediately informed of the mistake. A number of conferences were had with reference to the matter. The school district decided to insist upon compliance with the bid and upon refusal of the Olson Construction Company to do so this suit was instituted.

The record establishes that the claimed error of $23,600 in the amount of the bid was a clerical mistake in tabulating and computing the bid. It was not an error of judgment in computing the quantity or cost of materials and labor. The mistake was unilateral, there being no allegations or evidence of mutual mistake. The school district contends that under such circumstances a bidder may not be relieved of his bid except where it is shown that the party receiving the bid knew or ought to have known, because of the amount of the bid or otherwise, that the bidder had made a mistake. While we think it could be said that the difference in the bids on the vocational agriculture and grandstand building was such as to indicate to the school district that a mistake had been made and thereby bring it within the rules applicable to mutual mistake, the bidder has the right under the facts shown by the record to withdraw its bid even though it was the result of unilateral error.

The rule under such circumstances is: When the mistake is so fundamental in character that the minds of the parties have not, in fact, met, or where an unconscionable advantage has been gained by mere mistake, equity will intervene to prevent intolerable injustice where there has been no failure to exercise reasonable care on the part of the bidder and where no intervening rights have accrued. In the case before us the mistake was discovered and notice thereof given to the school district within four days after the opening of the sealed bids. It was a fundamental mistake as distinguished from an incidental one. While the bid of the Olson Construction Company had been accepted and the contract awarded to it, no contract had been entered into; it was wholly executory. Failure to use reasonable care on the part of the Olson Construction Company is not shown and rights of third persons had not intervened. The parties could have been placed in statu quo at the time of the withdrawal of the bid. The reason for the latter statement is well stated in Kutsche v. Ford, 222 Mich. 442, 192 N.W. 714, 717, wherein it is said: " 'In the instant case it may be thought that the school district cannot be said to be placed in statu quo when it is considered that the building cost nearly $6,000 more than plaintiff's bid. To place in statu quo does not mean that one shall profit out of the mistake of another. It does not appear that plaintiff's mistake has made the school building cost more than it otherwise would have cost. The school district, if placed back where it was before the bid, loses nothing except what it seeks to gain out of plaintiff's mistake. To compel plaintiff to forfeit his deposit, because of his mistake, would permit the school district to lessen the proper cost of the school building at the expense of plaintiff, and that, in equity, is no reason at all for refusing plaintiff relief. * * *' "

Numerous cases support the granting of relief to a bidder on the ground of unilateral mistake under the circumstances shown to exist in the present case. * * *

* * *

The essential conditions to relief from a unilateral mistake by rescission are: The mistake must be of so fundamental a nature that it can be said that the minds of the parties never met and that the enforcement of the contract as made would be unconscionable. The matter as to which the mistake was made must relate to the material feature of the contract. The mistake must have occurred notwithstanding the exercise of reasonable care by the party making it. Relief by way of rescission must be without undue prejudice to the other party, except for the loss of his bargain. * * *

The judgment of the trial court is supported by the law and the evidence. The judgment is affirmed.

* * *

Notes

1. Whether an error is material may depend on the margin of profit included in the bid figure as well as on the per cent of the total bid encompassed by the error. Boise Junior College Dist. v. Mattefs Constr. Co., 92 Idaho 757, 450 P.2d 604 (1969).

2. In H.R. Johnson Constr. Co. v. Board of Educ. of Painesville Tp. Local School Dist., 16 Ohio Misc. 99, 241 N.E.2d 403 (Com.Pl.1968), it was held that a school board may not entertain a bid which was filed one minute after the deadline. "Where the language is free of ambiguity there is no judicial latitude whatsoever."

3. Where a "certified check" that was required to be submitted with a bid was not signed by an official of the bank but the word "certified" with date and name of bank was stamped on the check, a school board was justified in determining plaintiff was not the "lowest responsible bidder." Menke v. Board of Educ., Independent School Dist., West Burlington, 211 N.W.2d 601 (Iowa 1973).

[Case No. 65]   Implied Contract—Quantum Meruit

RESPONSIVE ENVIRONMENTS CORP. v. PULASKI COUNTY SPECIAL SCHOOL DIST.

United States District Court, Eastern District of Arkansas, 1973.
366 F.Supp. 241.

PAUL X. WILLIAMS, DISTRICT JUDGE. On February 22, 1968 Leroy Gattin, Superintendent of the Pulaski County, Arkansas, Special School District signed a "Lease Purchase Agreement" for a quantity of school library books as itemized in the agreement.

On March 14, 1968 the authorized agent of plaintiff, Responsive Environments Corporation, signed the same instrument * * *.

* * *

There is no question but that the district received the books covered by the lease-purchase agreement, distributed them to its various schools, used the books for a year or more and never paid anything for either the books or their use.

When called upon to pay for the books as provided by the contract, the Pulaski County Special School District responded that it considered the contract to be beyond the authority of the Superintendent and to be void and unenforceable. The District caused the books to be gathered up from the various schools and stored in a suitable place and notice to be given to Responsive Environments Corporation to come get them. * * *

* * *

* * * The Court finds that neither party to the contract is without fault. The conduct of both is subject to criticism.

The plaintiff's salesman, Mr. Marder, was so anxious to sell his company's books that he oversold his merchandise and carelessly misled the purchasers by his sales pitch. He represented that he had the approval of the State Department, when in truth he and Mr. Payne both had been informed that the lease-purchase form he proposed to use did not meet the requirements of the Arkansas Law and that Title II funds could not be used for payment at that time.

On the other hand, Superintendent Gattin relying upon the advice of Mr. Payne and Mr. Cox [subordinate administrators] was willing to make the deal if federal funds were used to pay for the books. His philosophy was clearly and aptly expressed when he testified that "Federal Funds are free."

In this case we have the plaintiff seeking the pot of gold at the end of the Federal rainbow and the defendant willing to go along if the acquisition was paid for by federal funds.

Both the present plaintiff and the R.E.C. are wholly owned by Prentice-Hall. During the rainbow days, the plaintiff was acquiring and selling a large number of books—many of which were not the kind or quality desired nor needed by school libraries, but which in this case Mr. Gattin was willing to receive if payment came from the gold at the end of the rainbow.

It is elementary that the business affairs of a school district in Arkansas are by statute entrusted to its board of school directors.

In this case there is no evidence that the contract in question was ever approved or sanctioned by the school board except the action of the board authorizing the Superintendent to execute proper forms to secure federal funds.

* * *

The Court finds that this action of the board did not authorize Mr. Gattin to enter into the contract here sued on. The Court finds that Mr. Gattin did not have authority to enter into the said contract and further finds that the school board did not ratify or adopt the action taken by Mr. Gattin. On the contrary, the board expressly refused to go along with the venture and changed some of its personnel and later even the Superintendent himself.

The Court finds that the subject matter was not "ultra-vires"; the board could have ratified the contract, but deliberately chose not to do so.

* * *

* * * [T]he use of the books, in however slight degree, was beneficial to the defendant, for admittedly it needed a stronger library program and admittedly, at least a portion of the books were a desirable acquisition.

While the Court finds that both the plaintiff and the defendant are at fault and that no legal contract was made, ratified or consummated, at the same time the Court finds that the conduct of the parties was such that an implied contract arose that required the defendant school district to pay under the theory of *quantum meruit*.

* * *

"Quantum meruit refers to that class of obligations imposed by law, without regard to the intention or assent of the parties bound, for reasons dictated by reason and justice. The form of the action is contract, but they are not contracts, because the parties do not fix the terms and their intentions are disregarded. One class of such cases is those where a party wrongfully compels another to render him valuable services, and a promise to pay is implied, because on equitable grounds one ought not to be permitted to keep that which is received without compensation."

* * *

The Court finds that under the facts and circumstances in this case the plaintiff deserves the option to either have its books back or to receive in payment that sum of money which it deserves.

The next question which addresses itself to the Court is the fair amount which should be awarded to the plaintiff if it elects to take money.

* * *

After considering all factors the Court finds that plaintiff is entitled to receive $13,500.00 in full settlement for the books which the School District has received from the plaintiff. [The contract price was $113,-260.]

* * *

Notes

1. Observe that the contract here was not ultra vires. In a suit to recover payments made by a district under an ultra vires contract it was contended by the defendant that there had been no offer to return what the district had received, hence that the action could not be maintained. In overruling the contention the court said: " * * * [T]here is a void contract, hence no contract

at all. There is nothing to rescind, * * * and action may be taken for the recovery of the plaintiff's [district's] money without restoration to status quo." School Dist. No. 9 v. McLintock, 255 Mich. 197, 237 N.W. 539 (1931).

2. In Shackleford v. Thomas, 182 Ark. 797, 32 S.W.2d 810 (1930), the district sought to recover money paid under a contract not signed as required by law. The contract was for the services of an attorney. In denying recovery the court said: "The record shows that in carrying out the contract, a warrant for $50 was issued to appellant, and by him presented to the treasurer of Saline county, who paid it. This constituted an execution of the contract that far, and it is now too late to recover the money. The contract was for a purpose which was valid and would have been binding on the district having issued the warrant."

3. "The doctrine of implied contract cannot be invoked to do rough justice and fasten liability where the legal requirements specifically prohibit." Lutzken v. City of Rochester, 7 A.D.2d 498, 184 N.Y.S.2d 483 (1959).

4. What is your reaction to the conduct of the superintendent?

[Case No. 66] Invalid Contract—Ratified

FRANK v. BOARD OF EDUC. OF JERSEY CITY

Court of Errors and Appeals of New Jersey, 1917.
90 N.J.L. 273, 100 A. 211.

BLACK, J. * * * There is but a single question presented by the record in this case to be answered; viz., whether a municipal corporation is liable to pay for work done and materials furnished it by an unauthorized agent, when the municipality had the power to make a contract for such purposes. If so, whether an agency to purchase such supplies in fact can be implied from the acts and conduct of the parties and a ratification of the contract for such supplies be also implied from like acts and conduct. The application of elemental and well-recognized principles in the law of agency to the facts, as disclosed by the record in this case, leads us to answer these questions in the affirmative. * * *

The facts on which the ruling of the trial court was based are these: The above work and materials were actually furnished by the respondent to the appellant, by order of John T. Rowland, Jr., supervising architect of the appellant, except two items. He had been permitted by the appellant "for a number of years" to order labor and materials of the nature sued for in this case. His orders had been recognized by the appellant, and the amounts therefor had been paid by it. "Many previous orders of the same kind were duly paid for by the defendant," furnished by the respondent. The item of $46.70 for repairing motor generator was for labor, which was furnished by the respondent to the appellant by order of Charles C. Wilson, vice principal of the Jersey City high school, which was under appellant's control. All the items except the item of $5.00 for one pole tester were "emergency" work; i.e., they were furnished at the time the emergency existed, requiring immediate performance, and before a meeting of the appellant could be held to pass upon the necessity of doing the same and ordering it to be done.

The respondent had done other work and furnished materials of a similar character for the appellant under and by similar orders. Such work had been regularly paid for, in due course, by the appellant, when the bills for the same were presented without question as to the regularity of the requests or the authority of the said Rowland and Wilson. The work done and materials furnished, sued for in this suit, were done and furnished, relying on the fact that previous orders by Rowland and Wilson, under similar circumstances, had been paid for by the appellant. The respondent knew that this practice existed and was permitted to exist by the appellant. This practice had been so "for a number of years." The appellant knew that the work and materials had been furnished it by the respondent at or about the times they had been so furnished and it did not, until three years after the last work had been performed, deny the authority of the said Rowland and Wilson to order the work and materials. The appellant has had the use and benefit of the work so done and materials furnished. * * *

* * * [In a statute] there is express authority for the appointment of an agent, a business manager. The term is immaterial. A supervising architect or vice principal might just as well be called an agent or business manager. There is also the recognition by the legislature of the fact that the board of education probably could not act in many cases without appointing such agents, since the very necessity of some cases requires that such a board should act through agents. * * * It would be quite impracticable to require either a formal resolution for every possible small expenditure, or for the board to act by a majority in person. In the state of facts these orders under consideration are called "emergency" orders. * * *

The literature of the law of agency is rich in adjudged cases. The principles pertinent to the subject under discussion are these: An agency, as between individuals or business corporations, may be implied from prior habit, or from a course of dealings of a similar nature between the parties. The agency may be implied from the recognition or acquiescence of the alleged principal as to acts done in his behalf by the alleged agent, especially if the agent has repeatedly been permitted to perform acts like the one in question. But when it is implied, and in so far as it is implied, the power of the agent must be determined from no one fact alone but from all the facts and circumstances for which the principal is responsible. So ratification may be implied from any acts, words, or conduct on the part of the principal which reasonably tend to show an intention on the part of the principal to ratify the unauthorized acts or transactions of the alleged agent, provided the principal in doing the acts relied on as a ratification acted with knowledge of the material facts. The rule is particularly applicable where it appears that the principal has repeatedly recognized and affirmed similar acts by the agent. So a municipal corporation may ratify the unauthorized acts and contracts of its agents or officers which are within the scope of the corporate powers, but not otherwise.

* * *

We think, as the board of education had the power, under the statute, to contract for the work done and material supplied in this case, there was created by conduct an implied agency, an agency in fact, on the part of Messrs. Rowland and Wilson, and further, that by implication the contracts of these unauthorized agents have been ratified by the acts and conduct of the school board * * *.

Notes

1. In Everett v. Board of Public Instr. of Volusia County, 136 Fla. 17, 186 So. 209 (1939), the plaintiff, a janitor, sued to recover on a contract made with him by the supervising principal of the schools. The plaintiff had been recommended for the position, but the board declined to appoint him, and appointed another person. It was shown that the plaintiff rendered services under the contract, and that the board had knowledge of that fact. Furthermore, the board said and did nothing to indicate that the services were not wanted. It was held that these facts stated a cause of action, and that the plaintiff might recover in quantum meruit.

2. "School district officers cannot be permitted by the law to enter into a written contract with a teacher, none of them denying its validity for ten weeks, or half the term, but recognizing it by making payments upon it, in which payments all join, and then, after the teacher, in the utmost good faith and reliance upon the contract, has taught that length of time, discharge him without cause, and plead in bar of payment under the contract that they never met and consulted, nor took corporate action in hiring him, or made any record in a book of the execution of the contract. It appears very clearly in this case that a majority of the school board assented to this contract in the first place, as evidenced by their executing it. It was afterward ratified by all three of them. It was not necessary that there should be a direct proceeding with the express intent to ratify. It may be done indirectly, and by acts of recognition or acquiescence, or acts inconsistent with repudiation or disapproval." Crane v. Bennington School Dist., 61 Mich. 299, 28 N.W. 105 (1886).

3. In St. Paul Foundry Co. v. Burnstad School Dist. No. 31, 67 N.D. 61, 269 N.W. 738 (1936), suit was brought against the district for the contract price of steel used in a school building. The contract violated the statute requiring competitive bidding, but the steel had been used in the building. It was contended by the plaintiff that the contract had been ratified by the district. In denying recovery on the contract the court said: "It is true that a contract made by the directors on behalf of a school district, though not binding upon the district because irregularly made, may, in some instances, become binding by a subsequent ratification. * * * But this rule applies only when the contract was one into which the district might lawfully have entered at the time it was thus irregularly made and which it was within the power of the district to make at the time and in the manner of its ratification. * * * There can be no ratification unless the acts relied upon to effect it are sufficient to support the contract as an original matter." The court expressly refused to express an opinion as to whether the plaintiff might recover in quantum meruit since that question was not before it for decision.

4. In Alabama the elective county superintendent of schools was the statutory purchasing agent for the board. The board voted that no money might be spent for any improvements or purchases without the approval of the board. The superintendent ordered paint and similar supplies and charged them to the board. There was no proof that the board was aware of the purchases before they were used or that the board ratified the action of the superintendent. The

Supreme Court of the state held that the company could recover neither the purchase price nor the reasonable value of the benefits received by the schools. It said the superintendent was only the agent of the board and that a principal has the authority to restrict the authority of the agent. Panther Oil and Grease Mfg. Co. v. Blount County Bd. of Educ., 41 Ala.App. 434, 134 So.2d 220 (1961).

[Case No. 67]   Invalid Contract—Not Ratified

JUNEAU ACADEMY v. CHICAGO BD. OF EDUC.

Appellate Court of Illinois, 1984.
122 Ill.App.3d 553, 78 Ill.Dec. 13, 461 N.E.2d 597.

STAMOS, JUSTICE: Plaintiff Juneau Academy (Juneau), a special education facility, brought suit in the circuit court of Cook County against the Chicago Board of Education (CBE) and the Board of Education of High School District 108 (108) to recover the value of services rendered to students from the defendant school districts. After a bench trial, judgment was entered for defendants. Plaintiff appeals.

Juneau Academy is a residential facility for the treatment of mentally handicapped adolescent boys. It is located in Milwaukee, Wisconsin. The instant dispute arises from the placement with Juneau in late 1979 of five high school students from CBE and one from 108. Juneau, unfamiliar with Illinois procedures for the payment of tuition to private facilities for handicapped students, accepted the Illinois students into its program before it had received approval from Illinois for its rate structure. Without such approval, Juneau was ineligible under Illinois law to receive tuition payments from Illinois school boards.

The student from 108 was referred to Juneau by Michael Schack, the administrator of the Institute for Motivational Development. Schack sent a letter of referral on November 11, 1979, to Thomas O'Brien, the Assistant Director of Juneau. Upon receiving the letter, O'Brien set out to determine the student's eligibility for admission to Juneau. Schack also contacted Alex Grandt, a Supervisor of Special Education for 108, to inform him that the student was in need of residential treatment. Schack was not an agent of either Juneau or 108. The decision to place the student in a residential facility was made by 108 on December 7, 1979, with Grandt's knowledge. Juneau accepted the student on December 26, 1979, without 108's knowledge.

On January 8, 1980, Grandt wrote to O'Brien, asking that the student be considered for placement with Juneau. Upon receiving this letter, O'Brien telephoned Grandt and informed him that the student had been at Juneau since December 26. Grandt expressed satisfaction that a placement had been accomplished, but said Juneau had moved faster than he had anticipated. O'Brien informed Grandt that Juneau would soon be approved for Illinois funds, and Grandt stated that 108 would discuss payment of the tuition once approval was obtained. At this time, however, Juneau had applied only for approval of its program. It was not aware that approval of its rates by the Illinois Governor's Purchased Care Review Board was also required. Because of this misunderstanding, Juneau was not able to obtain complete approval until July 28, 1980. When the 108 student's treatment was completed in August, Juneau contacted 108 to arrange for payment of the tuition, which at that time exceeded $2,000 per month. 108 refused to pay for any treatment provided prior to Juneau's approval for Illinois funds. Juneau then filed suit, seeking recovery in contract.

The trial court found that the facts were not sufficient to prove the existence of an express or implied contract between Juneau and 108. The court found that 108 had not agreed to assume responsibility for the tuition for services provided prior to Juneau's Illinois approval.

Five students from CBE were also placed with Juneau in late 1979 and early 1980, under circumstances similar to those of the student from 108. However, the trial court found that an agreement implied in fact existed between Juneau and CBE for the period of treatment prior to Juneau's approval in Illinois. This finding was based on a statement made by James Clemons, a social worker employed by CBE, that once Juneau was approved, CBE would pay tuition retroactively to the dates of the students' placements.

The trial court went on, however, to hold that CBE was without authority to enter into such an agreement. The court cited * * * [a statute that had been interpreted by the state supreme court] as prohibiting the placement by school districts of students in nonpublic facilities which have not been approved by the Governor's Purchased Care Review Board. Because CBE was without authority to place the students with Juneau, the court held, the contract was *ultra vires* and void.

* * *

[The present court affirmed the holding as to CBE.]

Juneau next contends that the trial court erred in finding that no contract existed between Juneau and 108. Juneau argues that the finding of no contract implied in fact was error, and alternatively that the court should have allowed Juneau to recover in quasi-contract.

A contract implied in fact arises by a promissory expression which may be inferred from facts and circumstances which show an intent to be bound. * * * The trial judge in the instant case made specific findings of fact which are included in the record. These findings are supported by the evidence and the facts do not support a conclusion that a contract between Juneau and 108 can be implied in fact. The record shows that the 108 student was placed with Juneau in December 1979, without 108's knowledge. Two weeks later, when O'Brien learned that 108 hadn't been informed of the placement, he telephoned Grandt and told him that the student was already at Juneau. Grandt asked whether Juneau was approved for Illinois funding, and O'Brien told him that it was not, but that approval was forthcoming. Grandt then stated that 108 would discuss payment of the tuition once Juneau obtained approval for Illinois funds. Juneau subsequently discovered that the approval process was more involved than had been anticipated, and full approval was not in fact obtained until July 28, 1980.

When the student's treatment was completed in August 1980, Juneau contacted 108 and sought payment of the tuition. 108 agreed to pay tuition costs incurred after July 28, but refused to pay for any treatment provided prior to Juneau's Illinois approval.

The record reveals that, during the eight-month period of the 108 student's treatment, Juneau was becoming more aware, through its dealings with other Illinois boards of education, that it could not expect payment from Illinois school districts unless it obtained approval for Illinois funding. Indeed, Juneau was most likely made aware of this fact by Grandt's comment in January 1980 that 108 would discuss payment only after Juneau obtained approval. During the seven months in which Juneau provided treatment to the 108 student while it was not approved, no attempt was made by Juneau to determine whether 108 was aware of the situation or whether it intended to pay the tuition for treatment provided during the delay in approval.

It is clear that Juneau knew during this time that 108 could not pay tuition to a non-approved facility. Because Juneau believed in January that its approval was imminent, it agreed to wait until approval was obtained before billing 108. When Juneau learned that approval would be delayed, it apparently decided not to inform its Illinois customers of this, in hopes that rate approval would be granted quickly by the Governor's Purchased Care Review Board. Unfortunately, approval was not obtained until the 108 student's treatment was nearly complete, so that 108 found that the treatment of one of its students had been completed at a non-approved facility.

These facts do not establish the existence of an agreement implied in fact between Juneau and 108 for the payment of tuition for treatment provided prior to July 28, 1980. Juneau knew from the outset that approval was necessary before it could receive Illinois funds, yet when Juneau discovered that its approval would take longer than it had initially expected, it made no attempt to determine 108's position as to liability for tuition costs incurred during the delay. Consequently, 108 was aware only of what it had learned from its initial contact with Juneau in January; that Juneau was not yet approved but was expecting approval soon and would contact 108 regarding payment once the approval process was completed. Juneau knew that 108 could not pay tuition to a non-approved facility and 108 believed that Juneau's approval process would be completed immediately. The record contains no facts which suggest that 108 intended to pay tuition to a non-approved facility. Rather, the evidence shows just the opposite; that 108 believed Juneau would be approved during most of the course of the 108 student's treatment. We therefore find the trial court's finding of no contract implied in fact between Juneau and 108 to be supported by the evidence.

Juneau also contends that the evidence supports a finding that it should be permitted to recover in quasi-contract. However, the law will not imply an agreement which would be illegal if it were express. We have already held that Illinois law prohibits the placement of students in non-approved private facilities such as Juneau. Therefore, the law will not imply a contract for the placement with Juneau of a 108 student prior to Juneau's approval in Illinois.

We find that the trial court correctly held that no implied agreement existed between Juneau and 108.

* * *

Notes

1. Observe that Schack (third paragraph) was not an agent of either Juneau or 108. Therefore, there was no question of the type of ratification in Case No. 66.

2. In the CBE phase of this case, apparently the trial court considered Clemons an agent (sixth paragraph), for his statement was the basis of an agreement implied in fact, although the contract turned out to be ultra vires.

3. Do you believe the outcome was "unfair" to Juneau (1) as to CBE; (2) as to 108?

4. How do you evaluate the performance of officials of 108?

Chapter 9

CERTIFICATION, EMPLOYMENT, AND
CONTRACTS OF TEACHERS

The Teacher's Certificate

In General

To be legally competent to teach in the public schools of a state one must be certificated by that state. All states have some statutes containing provisions which govern teacher certification. These statutes vary widely both as to substantive requirements and as to procedures for certification. Differing amounts of power and discretion are vested by legislatures in state boards of education, chief state school officers, and state departments of education. Because the establishment of professional qualifications in detail is obviously beyond the practical competency of legislatures, most requirements are set by the state-level administrative agencies.

If a teacher meets all the legal requirements for a certificate, the certificating agency may not arbitrarily refuse to issue it.[1] Where discretion is placed in the designated agency, that discretion may not be exercised arbitrarily.[2] If the statute specifies the proficiency which must be shown by an applicant, the manner in which he should be examined, and other details, or if these are left to the determination of specified officers and the applicant is found qualified by the standards set, the issuance of the certificate is merely a ministerial duty which the officers may not refuse to perform. But only if refusal to issue the license is based on a ground that does not involve a proper exercise of discretion will the courts interfere. Courts may not direct that a license be issued unless there is, as a matter of law, no valid ground for its denial.

The power and control of the legislature over a license is well established.[3] A license is not a contract. The state may impose new or additional burdens on the licensee, and the certificate can be withheld or revoked for cause.[4]

In those states in which wide discretion is placed in the examining and certificating agency the courts are not inclined to interfere in the exercise of that discretion. The Court of Appeals of Maryland, for example, denied a writ of mandamus by which a candidate sought a certificate based on requirements in effect when he began training, the

1. State ex rel. Hopkins v. Wooster, 111 Kan. 830, 208 P. 656 (1922).

2. Keller v. Hewitt, 109 Cal. 146, 41 P. 871 (1895).

3. Gullett v. Sparks, 444 S.W.2d 901 (Ky.1969).

4. Hodge v. Stegall, 206 Okl. 1161, 242 P.2d 720 (1952).

473

requirements having been changed before he finished his program.[5] The court stated that the authority of the state board of education to enact bylaws and to determine the educational policies of the state permitted it to change standards for certification for those not possessing certificates at the time of the change. The complainant was denied the certificate because the board had adopted a bylaw that only graduates in the upper four-fifths of the class and having a grade of "C" or better in "practical teaching" could be issued a certificate. The court noted that the by-law made no change in the courses of study and preparation but concerned only the "diligence and ability of the student in it."

The Court of Appeals, Fifth Circuit, upheld the general power of the legislature to direct the state education agency in Texas to require as a condition for enrolling in more than six hours of professional education courses at any public institution the passing of a Pre–Professional Skills Test.[6] The court lifted a preliminary injunction that had been issued by a Federal District Court, and ordered a trial on the merits of claims that included invalidity of the test and unlawful disparate impact on Hispanic and black students when compared with white students. The court emphasized, however, that a state is "not obligated to educate or certify teachers who cannot pass a fair and valid test of basic skills necessary for professional training" and that disparate impact alone does not violate the equal protection clause.

The state board of education of North Carolina adopted a regulation providing that all teaching certificates would expire after five years and that for renewal a teacher must earn six units of credit during the five year period immediately preceding renewal. Such credit might be earned through college courses or in other prescribed ways. The regulation was contested on various grounds, including one that it was unreasonable, especially because the in-service work was required to be completed at the teacher's expense. The Supreme Court of North Carolina found that there was a reasonable basis for the belief that the quality of a teacher's classroom performance would be improved if the teacher broadened or refreshed his knowledge.[7] It was not arbitrary for the state to insist that the teachers in the public schools keep their knowledge up-to-date. It was immaterial whether, as plaintiff asserted, experience gained by continuous teaching was equally efficacious in improving quality of instruction.

On the other hand, it has been held that, in the absence of statutory authority to do so, the state superintendent of public instruction cannot fix a minimum age at which applicants may be granted certificates to teach in elementary schools.[8] It was shown in this case that the applicant had passed the necessary examinations. The court ruled that the qualification in question was one that could be imposed only by the legislature. Applying the same principle conversely, the Oklahoma

5. Metcalf v. Cook, 168 Md. 475, 178 A. 219 (1935).

6. United States v. LULAC, 793 F.2d 636 (5 Cir.1986).

7. Guthrie v. Taylor, 279 N.C. 703, 185 S.E.2d 193 (1971).

8. State ex rel. Johnson v. Matzen, 114 Neb. 795, 210 N.W. 151 (1926).

supreme court held that the state department of education could not waive a statutory requirement that principals have standard master's degrees.[9]

The legislature of Connecticut decided to replace a long standing certification pattern that had permitted teachers to receive certification valid for life and revocable only for cause. The new certificates were renewable for five-year terms upon each teacher's successful completion of professional development activities. Recognizing that under the facts holders had constitutionally protected property interests in their life-long certificates, the state supreme court proceeded to hold that the rights were not deprived without due process.[10] The legislative goal of enhancing the quality of the state's education system was an important one, and the plan was not unduly restrictive or onerous. The argument that contracts with local boards would be unconstitutionally impaired because boards could not employ uncertificated teachers also was rejected as not being an impairment drastic enough to violate the Constitution.

In Texas the legislature passed a law requiring that teachers pass a basic skills test to maintain their certificates. (Other tests were to be given, but only the basic skills test was funded.) The provision was upheld by the state's highest court against claims that it impaired contract rights, was a retroactive law, and violated due process in that there was no specific provision for a hearing or avenue of appeal.[11] The court emphasized that no contract was involved in the case of a license and that decertification was not automatic but would be governed by the statute covering revocation for cause.

A California statute provided that a teacher must verify five years of successful experience as a condition of certificate renewal. The principal of the school where a teacher was employed stated that he considered her performance unsatisfactory, whereupon renewal of the certificate was denied. Thereafter the teacher was dismissed from her position in the school system. The court held that the certificate must be renewed because successful experience was to be presumed when no charges of incompetency had been filed against the teacher who had been employed in the same school system for over ten years.[12] Four decades later, the Court of Appeals of New York reached a similar conclusion where a teacher had been employed for seven years by a district and had been granted tenure, but the board refused to make a recommendation that would have permitted the issuance of a permanent certificate without the completion of student teaching.[13] The state commissioner's decision to grant the certificate was being challenged by the board.

9. State ex rel. Thompson v. Ekberg, 613 P.2d 466 (Okl.1980). [Case No. 69]

10. Connecticut Educ. Ass'n, Inc. v. Tirozzi, 210 Conn. 286, 554 A.2d 1065 (1989).

11. State v. Project Principle, Inc., 724 S.W.2d 387 (Tex.1987).

12. Matteson v. State Bd. of Educ., 57 Cal.App.2d 991, 136 P.2d 120 (1943).

13. Bradford Central School Dist. v. Ambach, 56 N.Y.2d 158, 451 N.Y.S.2d 654, 436 N.E.2d 1256 (1982).

In order to validate a conditional certificate a teacher was required to complete certain professional courses in education by a fixed date. She was notified that her certificate would be terminated because she lacked two semester hours credit. She obtained a letter from a college professor in psychology that a course she had completed with him was really more geared to educational and teaching processes than to liberal arts and that he believed it should have been taught in the Department of Education rather than the Department of Psychology. School authorities gave no weight to the letter because of a rule that only official course descriptions in catalogs would be utilized to judge acceptability of courses. The federal district judge, observing that the teacher had received satisfactory ratings on the job and that her principal had requested her continued assignment, and concluding that she had been misled into thinking she had qualified, ordered her employment extended with the proviso she must satisfactorily complete a proper course as soon as possible. The Court of Appeals, Second Circuit, with apparent reluctance, reversed the judgment, stating that the only federal question was whether due process had been accorded and holding that it was not an unreasonable policy to rely on catalog descriptions rather than conduct time-consuming hearings on the actual content of courses.[14] Similarly, state courts in New York declined to overturn the refusal of a licensing body to accept work experience of a year and a half at a state hospital as a substitution for a college-supervised internship in clinical psychology.[15] The internship was one of several specified requirements for those seeking a school psychologist's license through a route other than that of graduation from an approved program for school psychologists.

The facts that school authorities over a period of years knowingly employed a teacher to instruct in subjects for which she was not certificated and that they "continually reassured her the non-certification was not a problem" did not prevent the authorities from eventually discharging her because of lack of legal qualifications. The Supreme Court of Wisconsin held the teacher responsible for being certificated and observed that local administrators could not waive the requirement.[16] As her reliance on their statements was not reasonable, she was not entitled to relief on principles of equity. The same view was taken by an appellate court in New York in a case in which previous to the discharge the board had sought (and obtained) permission from the state to continue the teacher in employment.[17]

Certification requirements seem subject to more careful examination by courts as federal and state antidiscrimination statutes and broadened interpretations of the Fourteenth Amendment develop. It is established

---

14. Irizarry v. Anker, 558 F.2d 1122 (2 Cir.1977).

15. Wagschal v. Board of Examiners of Bd. of Educ. of City of N.Y., 117 A.D.2d 470, 503 N.Y.S.2d 434 (1986), aff. 69 N.Y.2d 672, 511 N.Y.S.2d 836, 503 N.E.2d 1373 (1986).

16. Grams v. Melrose-Mindoro Joint School Dist. No. 1, 78 Wis.2d 569, 254 N.W.2d 730 (1977).

17. Chapman v. Board of Educ. of Yonkers City School Dist., 57 A.D.2d 835, 394 N.Y.S.2d 52 (1977).

that the right to engage in a legitimate occupation is a liberty right that can be denied under the police power of the state only by reasonable standards to protect the public health, safety, and welfare.[18] Characterization of the practice of a profession as a "privilege" does not affect the result that "a person cannot be prevented from practicing except for valid reasons."[19]

The Supreme Court has upheld the power of a state to require for certification that public school teachers be United States citizens.[20] It emphasized the important governmental role of public education "in the preparation of individuals for participation as citizens and in the preservation of the values on which our society rests." Although the citizen-alien distinction is normally irrelevant to private activity, the Court said it was crucial to government. (In the Constitution itself the distinction is made 11 times.) The Court observed that all teachers have both substantial responsibility and discretion in fulfilling a significant governmental role. Thus, a state properly may regard all teachers as having an obligation to promote civic virtues and understanding in their classes, regardless of the subject taught.

Lack of procedural due process was the basis for the Supreme Court of South Carolina's preventing the cancellation of a teaching certificate solely because the private testing agency notified the state department of education that a previously submitted score should be canceled. The court held that the regulation providing for automatic invalidation was unconstitutional.[21] A hearing had been granted at the request of the affected teacher, but the only evidence to support the action was an unamplified notification from the testing company.

The Fourth Circuit Court of Appeals has outlined the steps that must be followed to comply with the Rehabilitation Act of 1973 (and, by extension, the Americans with Disabilities Act of 1990) when an individual with disabilities cannot meet a certification requirement.[22] The hurdle missed in the case was passing the communications skills portion of the National Teacher Examination. The candidate had failed it eight times, twice after the testers provided her with several special aids and a longer time period. She had three diagnosed learning disabilities. The court said that to determine whether she was "otherwise qualified" a court must make two factual determinations: whether she can perform the "essential functions" of a school teacher, and whether the certification requirements actually measure those functions. Even if she could not now perform, a third inquiry would be needed to determine whether "reasonable" modifications could be made to allow her to teach.

18. Meyer v. Nebraska, 262 U.S. 390, 43 S.Ct. 625, 67 L.Ed. 1042 (1923). Sometimes the right is denoted as a property right. Leetham v. McGinn, 524 P.2d 323 (Utah 1974).

19. Schware v. Board of Bar Examiners of State of New Mexico, 353 U.S. 232, 77 S.Ct. 752, 1 L.Ed.2d 796 (1957).

20. Ambach v. Norwick, 441 U.S. 68, 99 S.Ct. 1589, 60 L.Ed.2d 49 (1979).

21. Brown v. South Carolina State Bd. of Educ., 301 S.C. 326, 391 S.E.2d 866 (1990). [Case No. 70]

22. Pandazides v. Virginia Board of Education, 946 F.2d 345 (4 Cir.1991). [Case No. 71]

Examinations for Certificates

Where competitive examinations are taken for licensure questions often arise as to the procedures followed. In one case an unsuccessful candidate for a license as high school department chairman asked the court to order that he be furnished model answers to the essay questions and other parts of the examination on which the denial of the license was based. The purpose claimed was to aid in an appeal of the decision on the examination evaluation. The court held that the refusal to permit the petitioner to examine the standard against which his performance was measured was unreasonable, and did substantially impair his right of appeal.[23] The result of the examination, said the court, should be so stated that the applicant can "check up the conclusions by some objective comparison."

In another case the Court of Appeals of New York refused to annul failure ratings in an interview test which was part of an examination for license as elementary school principal.[24] The case was brought by several candidates on the ground that sufficiently objective standards of rating were not utilized. The court noted that the qualities one must possess to adequately fulfill the duties of a position such as school principal are to an extent those which cannot be measured with precision. Thus, interview examination procedures are appropriate, and the one contested was legally sufficient. Several examiners were used, they made "running notes" to capture the gist of a candidate's answers to the questions and impressions of his personality and ability, after the examination they discussed the candidate's performance, and then they gave the candidate a final rating.

The same court considered the question whether eligibility lists based on competitive examinations could be avoided in appointing some elementary school principals having characteristics deemed needed in certain schools located in "black ghetto" areas.[25] In an experiment with decentralization and community involvement, the board of education created a post of "demonstration elementary school principal" and temporarily appointed persons to the post, a temporary assignment being the normal procedure. The trial court and intermediate court had found this to be a violation of the merit system in that the "special" qualifications were not set forth and tested for. The Court of Appeals reversed, ruling that the principals in question could remain in their posts pending the development of criteria and bases for assessing these criteria. The expectation that this would be accomplished soon was made explicit in the decision. (The merit system was required by the state constitution.)

The issue of discrimination through use of invalid tests is discussed under "Discriminatory Employment Practices," infra.

23. Schwartz v. Bogen, 28 A.D.2d 692, 281 N.Y.S.2d 279 (1967).

24. Nelson v. Board of Examiners of Bd. of Educ., 21 N.Y.2d 408, 288 N.Y.S.2d 454, 235 N.E.2d 433 (1968).

25. Council of Supervisory Ass'ns of Public Schools v. Board of Educ., 23 N.Y.2d 458, 297 N.Y.S.2d 547, 245 N.E.2d 204 (1969).

Revocation of Certificates

In several states there are statutory provisions making mandatory the revocation of teaching credentials upon conviction of certain crimes. The constitutionality of such statutory provisions has been upheld.[26] The Supreme Court of California has construed such a statute as meaning that criminal convictions prior to the enactment of the statute would not be considered as to those already employed.[27]

A finding by the state board of education of immoral and unprofessional conduct was challenged in California. A male teacher who had been found guilty of homosexual activity on a public beach contended that the board failed to establish any rational connection between that conduct and his fitness for service in the public schools. Among other things, he claimed that the license revocation was a double punishment for the same offense, since he had been punished under the penal code. The court, however, found "an obvious rational connection" and sustained the board.[28]

Distinguishing the facts from those in the preceding case, the Supreme Court of California held that a teacher who had engaged in homosexual conduct could not have his certificate revoked unless it was shown that the conduct indicated unfitness to teach.[29] The acts occurred about two and one-half years before the state board's hearing on the revocation. They had occurred in a private apartment of a fellow teacher, who reported them to the superintendent about a year later. The court emphasized that no evidence had been introduced to show that the teacher's conduct had in any way affected his performance as a teacher. It emphasized that it was not holding that all who perform homosexual acts must be permitted to teach, only that whatever act is committed must relate to unfitness to teach, particularly when the loss of the credential necessary to pursue the occupation is involved and the climate of the revocation is such as to seriously impair getting other employment.

Such unfitness was held to have been demonstrated in the subsequent case of a male teacher who had performed sexual acts with another male in public view in a public restroom.[30] This decision by an intermediate appellate court was cited with approval by the Supreme Court of California in an opinion upholding the revocation of the teaching credential of a female teacher who had joined a "swingers" club and engaged in sexual acts with several males in the presence of others

26. Vogulkin v. State Bd. of Educ., 194 Cal.App.2d 424, 15 Cal.Rptr. 335 (1961).

27. Di Genova v. State Bd. of Educ., 57 Cal.2d 167, 367 P.2d 865 (1962).

28. Sarac v. State Bd. of Educ., 249 Cal.App.2d 58, 57 Cal.Rptr. 69 (1967).

29. Morrison v. State Bd. of Educ., 1 Cal.3d 214, 82 Cal.Rptr. 175, 461 P.2d 375 (1969).

30. Moser v. State Bd. of Educ., 22 Cal. App.3d 988, 101 Cal.Rptr. 86 (1972).

at a party.[31]   Also, in disguise she had appeared on a television show discussing adultery and "wife swapping," and this became known.

The United States Court of Appeals, Second Circuit, upheld a state education commissioner's order to a local school board not to reemploy a tenure teacher pending a certificate revocation hearing by the commissioner.[32]   While on leave the teacher had been convicted of, and had served a prison term for, conspiring to promote bribery of public officials. The court found no legal fault with the pertinent statute and observed that the minds of elementary school students are very impressionable.

In New Mexico, where the state board of education was empowered to suspend or revoke certificates for "incompetency, immorality or for any other good and just cause," the board adopted a resolution requiring the suspension of the credential of any teacher who was elected to the state board.   The rationale was that membership on the board was incompatible with being a practicing teacher.   The rule was overturned by the supreme court of the state, which found the rule not related to fitness to teach and found no conflict in filling the two posts simultaneously.[33]

Because certificate revocation deprives one of employment in his profession in the public schools of a state, the courts also explore carefully the procedures used in making such a determination.   The considerations of required procedures before discharge from a position (discussed in Chapter 11) certainly apply here, and they are to be augmented as warranted by the more serious penalty of certificate loss. The burden is on the state body to establish cause for revocation at a proper hearing.[34]

The revocation of a teacher's certificate based upon a guilty plea to a charge of mail fraud was upheld in Pennsylvania.[35]   A statute required revocation for a crime involving moral turpitude.   It was not necessary for the secretary of education to hold a pre-revocation hearing beyond establishing that such a crime had been committed.   The court said that consideration of evidence of fitness to teach would be properly presented at a hearing upon application for reinstatement.

Evidence to justify the revocation of a certificate is not inadmissible solely upon the basis that it was improperly obtained.   Violation of a constitutional right may have different consequences depending on whether the evidence is to be used in criminal or noncriminal proceedings.   Thus, a teacher who, in an interview with a private investigator who had lied to the teacher, had admitted inappropriate sexual conduct

31. Pettit v. State Bd. of Educ., 10 Cal.3d 29, 109 Cal.Rptr. 665, 513 P.2d 889 (1973).

32. Pordum v. Board of Regents of State of New York, 491 F.2d 1281 (2 Cir.1974), cert. den. 419 U.S. 843, 95 S.Ct. 74, 42 L.Ed.2d 71 (1974).

33. Amador v. New Mexico State Bd. of Educ., 80 N.M. 336, 455 P.2d 840 (1969). [Case No. 68]

34. Huntley v. North Carolina State Bd. of Educ., 493 F.2d 1016 (4 Cir.1974); Brown v. South Carolina State Bd. of Educ., 301 S.C. 326, 391 S.E.2d 866 (1990). [Case No. 70]

35. Startzel v. Commonwealth, Dept. of Educ., 128 Pa.Cmwlth. 110, 562 A.2d 1005 (1989).

with students could not require the suppression of that evidence at a revocation hearing.[36] The purpose of the proceeding was not to punish the teacher, but to protect the welfare of children.

Certificates in Relation to Contracts

Because a teacher without a certificate is not a competent party to contract with a board of education, any agreement with a teacher not having the necessary certificate is of no legal effect. Moreover, school funds cannot be expended under it. An application of this principle is found in a Kentucky situation. A teacher began teaching at the beginning of the school year, at which time she did not have a certificate, nor was she eligible for one because she had not reached her eighteenth birthday, which was in November. It was held that she was not entitled to salary for the time before she became eighteen, although it was proper to pay her in full for the teaching she did after her birthday and concurrent receipt of the certificate.[37]

A similar holding was made by the Supreme Court of Wyoming in a situation in which a teacher suing for breach of contract and back salary was shown not to have a certificate.[38] He offered to produce one. Ten days after the trial, but before judgment had been entered, he filed a record of a back-dated certificate. Accompanying the certificate was a letter from a state official indicating that the certificate was dated back because it "should have been issued then." The teacher contended that the failure to have the certificate in his possession did not relieve the school district from liability for his salary. His suit was not successful.

The highest court in New York ruled that if a tenure teacher lacks a valid certificate, he has no claim to payment between the time he is suspended therefor and the time of a trial at which he is unsuccessful.[39] Payment to uncertificated teachers was statutorily barred.

The Commonwealth Court of Pennsylvania held that a teacher whose certificate expired and because of "bureaucratic delays" was not renewed could not be dismissed for the reason of lack of certificate.[40] Where, however, the responsibility for the lack of certificate lies with the teacher, as is more commonly the situation, the lack is fatal to the validity of an employment contract. Thus failure to register his certificate was upheld as the basis for terminating an Illinois teacher.[41] In another Illinois case, the court held that when a teacher's position is to be eliminated for bona fide reasons, and where statutes require notice 60 days before the end of the school year, that teacher must have in hand at

36. Stedronsky v. Sobol, 175 A.D.2d 373, 572 N.Y.S.2d 445 (1991).

37. Floyd County Bd. of Educ. v. Slone, 307 S.W.2d 912 (Ky.1957).

38. Sorenson v. School Dist. No. 28, 418 P.2d 1004 (Wyo.1966).

39. Meliti v. Nyquist, 41 N.Y.2d 183, 391 N.Y.S.2d 398, 359 N.E.2d 988 (1976).

40. Pointek v. Elk Lake School Dist., 26 Pa.Cmwlth. 62, 360 A.2d 804 (1976).

41. Brubaker v. Community Unit School Dist. No. 16, Sangamon and Morgan Counties, 46 Ill.App.3d 588, 4 Ill.Dec. 853, 360 N.E.2d 1228 (1977).

the time of the notice any certificates which are to be considered in determining any rights to hold other positions.[42]

A teacher in South Dakota who had taught fourth grade for eighteen years was offered a contract to teach seventh and eighth grades. She alleged a violation of the tenure law in that she was not qualified for those grades. The supreme court of the state held that as a matter of law she was qualified because her certificate covered the grades.[43] Therefore the board had the power to offer her that assignment, and if she refused it, her rights under the statute expired. The same conclusion was reached by the highest court in North Dakota in a case in which the disputed assignment was coaching girls' basketball.[44] There were no specific certification requirements covering the coaching, and the female teacher had been a major in physical education as well as English.

The general rule that one who accepts the benefits of services is legally bound to pay for them even if there is no valid contract is not applicable where a teacher with no certificate has been allowed to teach.[45] Otherwise, the law requiring that only certificated teachers can teach in the state would be defeated. Districts would be able to employ any one they chose and pay them for benefits conferred or the reasonable value of their services, thus depriving the public of competent teachers.

It must be borne in mind that certification requirements, if any, are a matter for the state legislature. Where it decided that one may teach in the public schools for a period based on passing an examination but that a regular certificate must eventually be obtained, one who did not acquire the proper certificate was remediless despite his years of service when he was summarily discharged.[46]

It is not infrequent that a contract is signed by a teacher and district before his certificate is issued, but the teacher acquires the certificate before he enters upon his duties. Whether such a contract is valid depends upon the pertinent statute and whether it contemplates possession of a certificate when the contract is signed. If the statute provides that a teacher may not enter into a contract to teach unless he has a valid certificate, the meaning is clear. Also, if in the contract itself it is specified that the teacher is holder of a valid certificate, later acquisition will not validate the contract.[47] If the law provides that an uncertificated teacher may not be employed, there is a conflict among the cases as to the meaning of the word "employed." Some cases hold that there is no actual employment until the teacher enters upon his duties as a teach-

42. Hagopian v. Board of Educ. of Tampico Community Unit School Dist. No. 4 of Whiteside and Bureau Counties, 56 Ill. App.3d 940, 14 Ill.Dec. 711, 372 N.E.2d 990 (1978).

43. Collins v. Wakonda Independent School Dist. No. 1, 252 N.W.2d 646 (S.D. 1977).

44. Enstad v. North Central of Barnes Public School Dist. No. 65, 268 N.W.2d 126 (N.D.1978).

45. Goose River Bank v. Willow Lake School Tp., 1 N.D. 26, 44 N.W. 1002 (1890).

46. Luz v. School Committee of Lowell, 366 Mass. 845, 313 N.E.2d 925 (1974).

47. Buchanan v. School Dist. No. 134, 143 Kan. 417, 54 P.2d 930 (1936).

er.[48] Others are to the effect that a teacher must have a valid certificate at the time of the making of the contract.[49]

Employment

In General

A teaching certificate attests that the holder is deemed qualified by the state to occupy the type of position specified by that license in a public school system of the state. If a certificate is required by the state, a local board may not employ for a given position any one who does not hold a valid certificate covering that post.[50] School funds may not be expended to pay a noncertificated teacher.[51]

Local boards may require qualifications in addition to those mandated by the state for certification.[52] They may add any qualification that is reasonably related to performance in the position and that is not barred by constitutional or statutory considerations. To this end they may ask applicants to supply relevant information. Forbidden by Supreme Court decision, however, because it unduly restricted freedom of association, was a requirement that all applicants for positions in a school system list all organizations to which they had belonged or had contributed during the preceding five years.[53] (See also, "Loyalty" in Chapter 10.)

In selecting individuals, boards may consider subjective factors as well as purely objective ones.[54] The courts will review only to assure that the decisions are not arbitrary or contrary to law.[55]

The Court of Appeals, Third Circuit, held on constitutional grounds that a school board could not refuse a blind person the opportunity to take the qualifying examination for teachers.[56] The court said that the right to take the examination arose under state law, and its deprivation in an arbitrary manner violated Fourteenth Amendment due process. The arbitrariness was in the creation of an irrebuttable presumption [57] that no blind person could qualify to teach. Eventually the candidate had been allowed to take the test and had passed. The District Court ordered that seniority be granted her as of the time she would have been employed but for the illegal postponement of her taking the test. This

---

48. Youmans v. Board of Educ., 13 Ohio C.C. 207 (1896).

49. McCloskey v. School Dist., 134 Mich. 235, 96 N.W. 18 (1903).

50. Seamonds v. School Dist. No. 14, Fremont County, 51 Wyo. 477, 68 P.2d 149 (1937).

51. Flanary v. Barrett, 146 Ky. 712, 143 S.W. 38 (1912).

52. Montgomery County Board of Educ. v. Messer, 257 Ky. 836, 79 S.W.2d 224 (1935).

53. Shelton v. Tucker, 364 U.S. 479, 81 S.Ct. 247, 5 L.Ed.2d 231 (1960).

54. Arnim v. Shoreline School Dist., No. 412, 23 Wash.App. 150, 594 P.2d 1380 (1979); Walter v. Independent School Dist. No. 457, Trimont, 323 N.W.2d 37 (Minn. 1982).

55. Hereford v. Huntsville Bd. of Educ., 574 F.2d 268 (5 Cir.1978).

56. Gurmankin v. Costanzo, 556 F.2d 184 (3 Cir.1977).

57. The "irrebuttable presumption" approach was utilized by the Supreme Court in Case No. 74. The present court relied on that case's exposition in regard to mandatory maternity leaves.

judgment was affirmed. (She had sought seniority from the date of her graduation from college, but she did not seek employment at once and, further, she could not have been employed until she passed the examination and was placed on the eligibility list.)

Even in the states where statutes prescribe that the board act upon nominations made by the superintendent (rather than the board's initiating candidates), the board retains the power to set qualifications. Under a Florida statute providing that the superintendent's recommendations can be rejected only for good cause, the board was sustained in refusing to appoint as administrator for finance a person with a master's degree in business administration who had no experience in school finance and had never worked in a school system.[58]

Unless prohibited directly or indirectly by the state, local boards may employ persons for special projects outside of the regular procedures, provided arrangements are made clear to employees and are not a pretext for avoidance of governing law, statutory or constitutional. Hence, the Supreme Court of Minnesota upheld the termination by expiration of contract of several teachers hired for a period of approximately six months under contracts specifically stating that employment was only until the end of the school year with no privileges accruing toward future employment.[59] The district needed the additional personnel at that particular time to reduce student-teacher ratio so as to qualify for certain federal funds. There was no evidence of any ulterior motivation of the board.

Discriminatory Employment Practices

The Supreme Court of the United States in 1971 determined that Title VII of the Civil Rights Act of 1964 (pertaining to employment opportunities)[60] proscribed not only overt discrimination, but also practices fair in form but discriminatory in operation.[61] (In 1972 the coverage of these provisions was extended to encompass public employment at all levels of government.) "If an employment practice which operates to exclude Negroes cannot be shown to be related to job performance, the practice is prohibited." Motivation of the employer is not relevant; it is the consequence of the employment practice which must bear scrutiny. The instant case involved requirements of a high school education and satisfactory performance on certain tests before one could be assigned to certain departments in a power company which had in the past practiced racial discrimination. The Court stated that Congress did not command that a person be hired simply because he was formerly the subject of discrimination or because he is a member of a minority group. Required is the removal of "artificial, arbitrary and unnecessary" barriers to employment which discriminate on the basis of

---

58. Sinclair v. School Bd. of Baker County, 354 So.2d 916 (Fla.App.1978).

59. Steiner v. Independent School Dist. No. 625, 262 N.W.2d 173 (Minn.1978).

60. See Appendix.

61. Griggs v. Duke Power Co., 401 U.S. 424, 91 S.Ct. 849, 28 L.Ed.2d 158 (1971).

"racial or other impermissible classification." Two months before, the Court had held that differential treatment of the sexes by rules not reasonably necessary to the operation of an enterprise is barred by the same federal legislation.[62]

Although disparate impact on a protected class is sufficient to sustain a prima facie case of employment discrimination under Title VII, proof of intent to discriminate is required to sustain a constitutional claim of unequal protection. Many, if not most, lower courts subsequent to Griggs (supra) had applied the legal standards of Griggs to Fifth or Fourteenth Amendment equal protection cases as well as to Title VII cases. In 1976 the Supreme Court said that the correct principle, which it had articulated in Keyes (Case No. 131) among other cases, was that only distinctions made with discriminatory purposes were forbidden by the Constitution.[63] It stated that it was not saying that disproportionate impact was irrelevant in cases involving Constitution-based claims of racial discrimination nor that invidious application of a facially neutral statute or regulation was permissible. "Disproportionate impact is not irrelevant, but it is not the sole touchstone of an invidious racial discrimination forbidden by the Constitution. Standing alone, it does not trigger the rule * * * that racial classifications are to be subjected to the strictest scrutiny and are justifiable only by the weightiest of considerations." (It should be remembered, however, that a constitutionally sound classification must be rationally related to an objective within the power of the state.)

Involved in the case was a test used to select persons to attend the training program for police officers in the District of Columbia (a Fifth Amendment case because of the federal, rather than state, jurisdiction). Admission was based on a written test of verbal skill which was alleged to discriminate against blacks, who were underrepresented on the police force. The Court commented that the mere fact that fewer blacks than whites passed the qualifying test did not invoke the constitutional necessity for a demonstration that the test was valid in terms of performance on the job. It found to be sufficient a validation study relating the test to the requirements of the training program. The Court noted the apparently successful efforts of the District of Columbia to recruit black officers as evidence of nondiscriminatory intentions regarding use of the test.

Although the distinction between constitutional rights and statutory rights is not of great practical import regarding classifications for employment purposes covered by Title VII (race, color, religion, sex, national origin) or other legislation (e.g., age, handicap), it is of great significance regarding other classifications. Of considerable impact on employment discrimination within the covered classifications, however, is the acceptance by the Supreme Court of training program validation in lieu

---

62. Phillips v. Martin Marietta Corp., 400 U.S. 542, 91 S.Ct. 496, 27 L.Ed.2d 613 (1971).

63. Washington v. Davis, 426 U.S. 229, 96 S.Ct. 2040, 48 L.Ed.2d 597 (1976).

of job performance validation. The Court said that "it seems to us the much more sensible construction of the job-relatedness requirement."

It was this form of validation which led a three-judge federal District Court to uphold the use by South Carolina of the National Teacher Examination (NTE) as a certification cut-off and as a factor in teacher salary determination, a decision the Supreme Court affirmed in 1978.[64] That examination is designed to measure academic achievement of college seniors completing four years of teacher education. An executive of Educational Testing Service (ETS), which produces and administers the test, had testified in an earlier case that the organization could not demonstrate a relationship between academic proficiency, as measured by the NTE, and effective teaching.[65] (Barred in that case was use of score on the NTE as the sole criterion for retention of teachers already employed in a Mississippi school district that was beginning to desegregate. It was known that blacks as a group did not score as high as whites as a group.) Here the issue was the validity of the test as a measure of preparation to teach, which could be judged by the training-program validity standard.

The trial court examined in detail the history of the use of the NTE in South Carolina. It found no discriminatory intent in introducing the examination in 1945 as a basis for differentiating among certificates issued; in establishing a very low cut-off point in 1957; in substantially raising the cut-off point in 1969 (thereby eliminating 41% of the graduates of predominantly black colleges and less than 1% of the graduates of predominantly white colleges, the cut-off eliminating, however, only a little over 10% of those taking the examination over the nation); nor in 1976 in calculating the minimum requirements differently and setting them by field (a procedure to be applied first to the class of 1977 so that no impact data were available at the time of trial, although plaintiffs predicted the disparate impact might be even greater).

The validation study was authorized by the State Board of Education and conducted by ETS. The referent was academic training programs in South Carolina, knowledge of the content of which the NTE is designed to measure. The design of the study was endorsed by expert witnesses. Plaintiffs claimed that the study was not properly conducted, but were unable to sustain the burden of overcoming the "reasonable showing that the study was executed in a responsible, professional manner designed to produce trustworthy results." Plaintiffs were unable to demonstrate that the results were adversely affected by some evidence of misunderstanding by some participants.

The court further observed that plaintiffs had offered only one alternative purporting to achieve the "business necessity" interest of the state in having competent teachers with less disparate impact by race— graduation from an approved teacher preparation program. Because of

64. United States v. State of South Carolina, 445 F.Supp. 1094 (D.S.C.1977), aff. 434 U.S. 1026, 98 S.Ct. 756, 54 L.Ed.2d 775 (1978). [Case No. 72]

65. Baker v. Columbus Municipal Separate School Dist., 329 F.Supp. 706 (N.D.Miss.1971), aff. 462 F.2d 1112 (5 Cir. 1972).

the nature of the process of institutional approval and the individualized achievement aspect of the test, the court found the alternative would not equally well serve the state's interest. The court, commenting that the Supreme Court had not established judicial standards for determining whether a particular practice is a business necessity (although that Court had ruled that plaintiffs in this type of case may show that other practices having less adverse effect on them would also serve the employer's interest [66]), took the position that the employer did not have to show a "compelling interest" in the procedure adopted.

The legal steps and burdens of proof pertaining in a Title VII case brought by an individual have been set forth by the Supreme Court.[67] The initial burden is on the plaintiff to establish a prima facie case of discrimination by showing the existence of five elements: (1) membership in a protected class; (2) application for the position; (3) qualification for the position; (4) rejection; (5) employer's continuing to seek applicants with plaintiff's qualifications for the position. (These elements, with appropriate adaptation, constitute a prima facie case of discrimination for any type of adverse personnel decision.) If the prima facie case is thus established, the defendant must "articulate some legitimate, nondiscriminatory reason for the employee's rejection." If this is done, a genuine issue of fact is raised. The plaintiff then must bear the burden of proving that the explanation is a pretext, the true reason for the decision being a forbidden one.

In 1993 the Supreme Court reiterated that the ultimate burden of proof in a discrimination suit lies with the plaintiff.[68] The precise issue in the case was whether a finding that the reasons offered by the employer are pretextual would require a judgment for the plaintiff. The Court held that it would not. Falsity of reason by itself is not sufficient to impose liability on the employer.

Emphasis should be redirected to the fact that although the Title VII framework would be applicable to any legislatively proscribed basis of discrimination, it is limited to those bases. In the words of one court, "Title VII is not a 'bad acts' statute." [69] If, however, an act or policy impacts disproportionately on a protected group, it may run afoul of Title VII. Such is illustrated by the holding of the Fourth Circuit Court of Appeals that word-of-mouth hiring and hiring of relatives must be restrained where the school system employees were predominantly white.[70]

Sometimes an adverse employment decision is based on several factors, one of which is illegal. In such a "mixed motive" case, after a Title VII plaintiff has proved that an illegitimate element played a part

---

66. Albemarle Paper Co. v. Moody, 422 U.S. 405, 95 S.Ct. 2362, 45 L.Ed.2d 280 (1975).

67. McDonnell Douglas Corp. v. Green, 411 U.S. 792, 93 S.Ct. 1817, 36 L.Ed.2d 668 (1973); Texas Dep't of Community Affairs v. Burdine, 450 U.S. 248, 101 S.Ct. 1089, 67 L.Ed.2d 207 (1981).

68. St. Mary's Honor Center v. Hicks, ___ U.S. ___, 113 S.Ct. 2742, 125 L.Ed.2d 407 (1993).

69. Holder v. City of Raleigh, 867 F.2d 823 (4 Cir.1989).

70. Thomas v. Washington County School Bd., 915 F.2d 922 (4 Cir.1990). [Case No. 73]

in the employment decision, the defendant can prevail against a damages claim or a request for a court order to reverse the employment action only by proving that it would have made the same decision even if the forbidden consideration had played no role in the employment determination.[71]

Many cases involve the use of statistics to show a "pattern or practice" of employment discrimination. Gross statistical disparities among groups of workers may constitute prima facie proof of a pattern or practice of discrimination. But it is clear that any comparisons must be made in the contexts of qualified persons and a proper labor market area. Plaintiffs must establish by a preponderance of the evidence that discrimination was the standard operating procedure of the employer— "the regular rather than the unusual practice".[72]

The Supreme Court in 1977 considered the relation of Title VII to racial discrimination patterns in teacher employment.[73] Suit had been brought by the Attorney General of the United States alleging violations by the school district of Hazelwood, Missouri. The District Court had ruled against the Government. The Court of Appeals reversed, relying heavily on "work force" statistics to show an unrebutted prima facie case of employment discrimination. The Supreme Court stated that the District Court had "fundamentally misconceived" the role of statistics in employment discrimination cases by its racial comparison of Hazelwood's teachers with its students. It further held that the appellate court was correct in the view that a proper comparison was between the racial composition of Hazelwood's teaching staff and the racial composition of the qualified public school teacher population in the relevant labor market. But the Court of Appeals erred in substituting its judgment for that of the District Court and holding that the Government had conclusively proved its pattern-or-practice lawsuit. Specifically that court had totally disregarded the possibility that this prima facie statistical proof in the record might at the trial court level be rebutted by statistics dealing with Hazelwood's hiring after it became subject to the Civil Rights Act. "A public employer who from that date forward made all its employment decisions in a wholly nondiscriminatory way would not violate the Act even if it had formerly maintained an all-white work force by purposefully excluding Negroes." (Actually, Hazelwood had offered virtually no evidence in response, building its case on perceived deficiencies in the government's case and its own officially promulgated policy of nondiscrimination.) Another matter to be resolved on remand by the trial court was a determination of the proper labor market area for comparison.

It merits reemphasis here that employment decisions are not required to be based solely on objective considerations. Although use of

---

71. Price Waterhouse v. Hopkins, 490 U.S. 228, 109 S.Ct. 1775, 104 L.Ed.2d 268 (1989), as modified by the Civil Rights Act of 1991. The Act provides that even if an employer demonstrates that it would have made the same decision absent the discriminatory factor, the plaintiff remains eligible for attorney's fees and costs.

72. International Brotherhood of Teamsters v. United States, 431 U.S. 324, 97 S.Ct. 1843, 52 L.Ed.2d 396 (1977).

73. Hazelwood School Dist. v. United States, 433 U.S. 299, 97 S.Ct. 2736, 53 L.Ed.2d 768 (1977).

subjective criteria and procedures may afford evidence leading to a finding of discrimination, it is not conclusive.[74] The same types of statistical analyses are applicable to results of subjective and objective methods.[75] The decision methods and their application must be defensible, though they need not be the best. But overall or "bottom-line" results will not suffice as a defense against use of discriminatory preliminary elements. "The principal focus of [Title VII] is the protection of the individual employee, rather than the protection of the minority group as a whole." [76]

An application to teachers of Section 504 of the Rehabilitation Act of 1973 was made by the Supreme Court in 1987.[77] An elementary school teacher, discharged because of reoccurrences of tuberculosis, was held to be protected by the Act as a "handicapped individual." She had been hospitalized for the condition, a fact that the Court said sufficed to establish the record of impairment required by regulations under the Act. (That contagiousness here was accompanied by physical impairment made it unnecessary for the Court to consider whether a carrier of a disease ipso facto was "handicapped" for purposes of the Act.) However, the determination whether she was "otherwise qualified" to be an elementary school teacher required an individualized inquiry, which had not been conducted by the trial court. To be examined on remand would be factors such as the severity of the teacher's condition at the time of discharge, the probability that she would transmit the disease, and whether the school board reasonably could have accommodated her.

Federal law requires that when religion or handicap discrimination is involved the employer must make a "reasonable" accommodation unless it would cause the employer "undue hardship." The test of undue hardship is met if the accommodation causes more than de minimis cost, would substantially infringe on the rights of others, or would involve violating a legal prescription.[78] If a reasonable accommodation is offered, it is not necessary that the employer show that each alternative suggested by the employee would constitute a hardship.[79]

Charges of sexual harassment can provide the basis for a Title VII claim. This is true whether the unwelcome conduct of a sexual nature is directly connected to the grant or denial of an economic quid pro quo or whether the conduct creates a hostile and offensive working environment. The latter category creates the much more difficult task for the courts. It applies to working conditions intolerable on bases of other discriminations too, but the difficulties are magnified because of the special nature of relations between the sexes.

74. McCarthney v. Griffin–Spaulding County Bd. of Educ., 791 F.2d 1549 (11 Cir.1986).

75. Watson v. Fort Worth Bank and Trust, 487 U.S. 977, 108 S.Ct. 2777, 101 L.Ed.2d 827 (1988).

76. Connecticut v. Teal, 457 U.S. 440, 102 S.Ct. 2525, 73 L.Ed.2d 130 (1982).

77. School Bd. of Nassau County, Fla. v. Arline, 480 U.S. 273, 107 S.Ct. 1123, 94 L.Ed.2d 307 (1987). See Case No. 71.

78. Trans World Airlines, Inc. v. Hardison, 432 U.S. 63, 97 S.Ct. 2264, 53 L.Ed.2d 113 (1977).

79. Ansonia Bd. of Educ. v. Philbrook, 479 U.S. 60, 107 S.Ct. 367, 93 L.Ed.2d 305 (1986).

The Supreme Court has recognized the validity under Title VII of sexual harassment suits where the acts are "sufficiently severe or pervasive 'to alter the conditions of [the victim's] employment and create an abusive working environment.' " [80] In assessing liability on employers courts must determine that "the alleged sexual advances were unwelcome, not whether [the victim's] actual participation in [them] was voluntary". If the employer knew or should have known what was transpiring or if an agent of the employer was the perpetrator, liability would be established.

In 1993 the Supreme Court elaborated on the concept of harassment through an "abusive work environment." [81] It said with no dissents that whether an environment is "hostile" or "abusive" is to be determined by examining such factors as frequency of the conduct, severity of the conduct, whether it is physically threatening or humiliating (rather than "a mere offensive utterance"), and whether it unreasonably interferes with the employee's work performance. The Court said that it was reaffirming the standard set out in the preceding case, a standard it described as taking a path between making actionable any conduct that is "merely offensive" and requiring that the conduct cause "tangible psychological injury."

Maternity Discrimination

The Supreme Court in 1974 declared unconstitutional regulations which required all pregnant teachers regardless of circumstances to absent themselves from the classroom for specified periods of several months before and after childbirth.[82] The Court stated that it had long recognized that freedom of personal choice in matters of marriage and family life is one of the liberties protected by the Fourteenth Amendment. "By acting to penalize the pregnant teacher for deciding to bear a child, overly restrictive maternity leave regulations can constitute a heavy burden on the exercise of these protected freedoms."

The explanations offered to support the rules were that firm cut-off dates are necessary to maintain continuity of instruction because a qualified substitute must be found, and that at least some teachers become physically incapable of adequately performing certain duties during the latter part of pregnancy. Recognizing continuity of instruction to be a "significant and legitimate educational goal," the Court observed that, while advance notice provisions are permissible, the absolute requirements of termination at the end of the fourth or fifth month of pregnancy are not. As regards keeping physically unfit teachers out of the classroom, the Court held that the leave rules were too broad in sweep, for they amounted to a "conclusive presumption" that

80. Meritor Savings Bank, FSB v. Vinson, 477 U.S. 57, 106 S.Ct. 2399, 91 L.Ed.2d 49 (1986).

81. Harris v. Forklift Systems, Inc., ___ U.S. ___, 114 S.Ct. 367, 126 L.Ed.2d 295 (1993).

82. Cleveland Bd. of Educ. v. LaFleur, 414 U.S. 632, 94 S.Ct. 791, 39 L.Ed.2d 52 (1974). [Case No. 74]

every pregnant teacher who reaches the fifth or sixth month of pregnancy is physically incapable of continuing. The provision that no teacher could return before a fixed period had elapsed following the birth of the child was found to suffer the same infirmity and was thus unconstitutional. The Court, however, approved a return-to-work policy that provided the teacher would be eligible to return upon submission of a medical certificate from her physician, and would be guaranteed reemployment no later than the beginning of the next school year following the eligibility determination. In a footnote the Court pointed out that it was not requiring an individualized determination of when a specific pregnant teacher is to leave the classroom. "We are not dealing in these cases with maternity leave regulations requiring a termination of employment at some firm date during the last few weeks of pregnancy."

A mandatory maternity leave beginning date for teachers set at the beginning of the ninth month of pregnancy was upheld on "business necessity" grounds by the Court of Appeals, Ninth Circuit.[83] New Jersey courts have sustained a presumptive period of disability for four weeks before expected birth and four weeks following the actual date of birth for purposes of sick leave benefits.[84] The highest court of that state was one of several which previously had held that disallowing sick leave for disability caused by pregnancy discriminated against women where it was available for disabilities due to illness or injury.[85] But, it should be noted, child-rearing is a matter quite different from child-bearing, and sick leave is only for the disabled. Thus, a nondisabled teacher would not be eligible for sick leave for child-rearing.[86] Furthermore, child-rearing leave must not be made available only to females. Such a provision in a collective bargaining agreement was declared by the Third Circuit Court of Appeals to violate Title VII.[87]

Veterans Preference

Laws benefitting veterans uniformly have been sustained by the courts in view of the overriding public interest in rewarding those who have made sacrifices to defend the country. Title VII exempts such laws from scrutiny under its mandates. A constitutional challenge to an extreme form of veterans preference in public employment failed in the Supreme Court in 1979. Upheld was a statute giving a lifetime preference in public employment to qualified veterans, even though the result was to keep from civil service positions a grossly disproportionate number of qualified women.[88]

The Court found no trace of deliberate discriminatory intent against women in the installation in 1896, or in later modifications, of the

83. deLaurier v. San Diego Unified School Dist., 588 F.2d 674 (9 Cir.1978).

84. Hynes v. Board of Educ. of Tp. of Bloomfield, Essex County, 190 N.J.Super. 36, 461 A.2d 1184 (1983).

85. Castellano v. Linden Bd. of Educ., 79 N.J. 407, 400 A.2d 1182 (1979).

86. In re Hackensack Bd. of Educ., 184 N.J.Super. 311, 446 A.2d 170 (1982).

87. Schafer v. Board of Public Educ. of School Dist. of Pittsburgh, Pa., 903 F.2d 243 (3 Cir.1990).

88. Personnel Adm'r of Massachusetts v. Feeney, 442 U.S. 256, 99 S.Ct. 2282, 60 L.Ed.2d 870 (1979).

principle of veterans preference in Massachusetts. Although female veterans always had been treated as had male veterans, when the present suit was commenced 98 percent of the veterans in Massachusetts were male. It was argued that this fact demonstrated an impact too inevitable to have been unintended, particularly when coupled with the fact that under federal military policy the status of veterans is reserved primarily to men. But the argument for such inferred intentional discrimination was internally flawed, because the female plaintiff agreed that a more limited hiring preference for veterans could be sustained. The Court observed that "invidious discrimination does not become less so because the discrimination accomplished is of a lesser magnitude." As to the place of "foreseeable consequences" in establishing "discriminatory purpose," the Court said that the latter "implies that the decisionmaker * * * selected or reaffirmed a particular course of action at least in part 'because of,' not merely 'in spite of,' its adverse effects upon an identifiable group."

The Teacher's Contract

In General

Contracts with teachers and other employed personnel must conform to all the general requirements for contracts discussed in Chapter 8. Action taken by a school board as one party to a contract must meet all the procedural requirements for valid board actions treated in Chapter 14. As statutes place the power and duty of employing teachers in the board, it follows that the board must exercise that function itself. It may not, for example, be delegated to the superintendent of schools or to individual members of the board.[89] The superintendent or individual members of the board may interview and recommend teachers to the whole board, but the final action of employment must be by the latter.[90] If, however, it is provided by statute that a board may not employ a teacher without a recommendation by the superintendent, a contract between a board and a person not recommended is unenforceable.[91]

If all the elements of the contract are contained in a number of letters, telegrams, or other written documents, the statutory requirement that the contract must be written is satisfied. In other words, it is not necessary that a single formal document be executed. Neither is it necessary that a formal contract, if one be drawn, be signed by the members of the board while the board is in session.[92] It may be signed by board members individually outside a meeting. When the district has had the benefit of the counsel of all members of the board in arriving at the terms of the contract, there is no valid reason for requiring that the purely formal act of signing be done in a board meeting.

89. Big Sandy School Dist. No. 100–J v. Carroll, 164 Colo. 173, 433 P.2d 325 (1967).

90. Justus v. Brown, 42 Ohio St.2d 53, 325 N.E.2d 884 (1975).

91. Tripp v. Martin, 210 Ga. 284, 79 S.E.2d 521 (1954).

92. Hugunin v. Madison School Tp. of Daviess County, 108 Ind.App. 573, 27 N.E.2d 926 (1940).

A teacher's persistent refusal to sign the contract document, however, was held to be a valid ground for discharge after some three months of teaching.[93] Further, signing a contract form that through clerical error contains rights which were not intended does not create such rights. A Pennsylvania court ruled that a temporary employee who signed a contract form for permanent employees did not thereby acquire the status of a permanent employee.[94]

Employees' contracts are governed by state statutes, and staff are bound to comply with statutory provisions, which are deemed automatically to be included in all contracts.[95] The same is true of locally adopted rules, whether unilaterally by the board or through collective bargaining. Whether local custom or practice gives rise to a contractual right, however, is indeterminate in the abstract.[96] It appears that most statutory contract rights are applicable only to contracts covering the regular duties of a teacher, not to extracurricular assignments carrying additional pay. Thus, continuing contract or tenure provisions generally have been held not to apply to separate contracts for extracurricular activities.[97] But wherever a statute is applicable, a contract provision in conflict is not enforceable.[98]

Problems often develop in connection with procedures used in forming contracts with staff. An example is found in a case in which the Supreme Judicial Court of Massachusetts decided whether certain actions by a board of education and subsequent events resulted in a valid three-year contract with a party to serve as head football coach.[99] It was clear that the school board, or school committee as it is called in Massachusetts, had the power to make such contracts. The board, in a regular meeting by vote of four-to-three, decided to award the contract to a certain party at a specified salary. The city solicitor was to draw up the contract for the next board meeting. However, the solicitor was in the hospital, and one of the majority members typed out a contract substantially in the form of the coach's existing contract. At the time of the next board meeting, the three minority members were in attendance and adjourned the meeting for lack of a quorum. Other board members were in the building but not at the meeting at the proper time. Later that evening the four members of the majority signed the document. The court held that no contract had been made because the offer to the coach was dependent upon the drafting and submission to the whole school board of the contract and the formal approval by the board at a regular meeting.

93. Heine v. School Dist. No. 271, 94 Idaho 85, 481 P.2d 316 (1971).

94. George v. Commonwealth, Dep't of Educ., 15 Pa.Cmwlth. 239, 325 A.2d 819 (1974).

95. Robinson v. Joint School Dist. No. 150, 100 Idaho 263, 596 P.2d 436 (1979).

96. Ramsey v. Board of Educ. of Whitley County, 789 S.W.2d 784 (Ky.App.1990). [Case No. 89]

97. Neal v. School Dist. of York, 205 Neb. 558, 288 N.W.2d 725 (1980); Stang v. Independent School Dist. 191, 256 N.W.2d 82 (Minn.1977). [Case No. 94]

98. Marvel v. Coal Hill Public School Dist., 276 Ark. 369, 635 S.W.2d 245 (1982). [Case No. 83]

99. Konovalchik v. School Committee of Salem, 352 Mass. 542, 226 N.E.2d 222 (1967). [Case No. 138]

Another illustrative case is an action by a Missouri teacher against a school district for a breach of her employment contract. There were a number of factual complications concerning the returning of a form contract to the vice president of the board when the superintendent's office was closed. The vice president took it with him to the board meeting and delivered it to the secretary, but the meeting progressed without the envelope having been opened. The superintendent said that the contract in question had been returned unsigned, and he recommended that the teacher be notified that her services would be terminated at the end of the year. At a later special meeting the superintendent told the board that in fact the plaintiff had returned the contract signed by her, but he took the position that the instrument was not a contract, primarily because it was not signed by the president of the board and attested by the clerk of the district. The court, however, disagreed.[100] It cited the facts that the plaintiff was one of a group of teachers approved by the board for reelection, she had been sent a form contract specifying a number of particulars, including salary, with a notice that she had fifteen days to return it, and she did so return it.

As with other contracts, if there is no power within the board to enter into a contract with a teacher in the first instance, such a contract may not be ratified and thus made valid. On the other hand, if there is merely the failure to comply with some formality in the formation of the contract, and the statute does not clearly indicate that it was a legislative intention that such compliance should be a condition precedent to a valid contract, the board by formal action can ratify the contract. Also, by the acceptance of the teacher's services it may be held to have ratified it. Ratification may result, for example, when the contract is entered into by individual members of the board or by the superintendent of schools, but the teacher is nevertheless permitted to teach.[101]

It should be emphasized that the doctrine of ratification may not be employed to evade provisions of the law. It is intended only to avoid injustices which would result when a contract is invalid only because of the failure of the board to observe a formality in making it. If the contract is one which the board could not enter into legally and therefore cannot ratify, the teacher cannot recover for services which he may have rendered under it.[102]

Questions frequently arise as to the interrelationships between the common law of contracts and various statutes designed to protect employed personnel against arbitrary or capricious board actions. It may be generalized that such protective statutes do not operate in situations where the employee acts voluntarily, by intent or gross neglect, to take himself out of coverage. Thus, a teacher was unsuccessful in an attempt to require the board to continue to employ him where he did not sign and return an employment contract within the time

100. Lynch v. Webb City School Dist. No. 92, 418 S.W.2d 608 (Mo.App.1967).

101. Ryan v. Humphries, 50 Okl. 343, 150 P. 1106 (1915).

102. Floyd County Bd. of Educ. v. Slone, 307 S.W.2d 912 (Ky.1957).

specified by the board.[103] The court said that there was no entitlement to the statutory due process provisions regarding nonrenewal because it is well settled that failure of the offeree to accept an offer within a specified reasonable time constitutes a rejection of the offer. No extenuating circumstances were alleged by the teacher for failure to return the signed contract.

It has also been held that employment contracts terminated by mutual consent do not come under statutory procedures. The Supreme Court of Kansas so ruled in a case where a teacher was found to have resigned voluntarily.[104] She had returned her contract unsigned and had enclosed a letter that, although it did not include the word "resignation," contained statements fairly interpretable as constituting a resignation. The board formally acted on the letter. The court held the contractual relationship between the teacher and the board to have been terminated by mutual assent, and therefore the continuing contract statute did not apply.

The same reasoning was applied by the Supreme Court of Utah in a holding that a letter of resignation from coaching duties was properly considered a letter of resignation from all duties.[105] The teacher had claimed the contract was divisible. He had been told the board disagreed, but he did not withdraw the letter. The court decided the contract was not divisible and the teacher's suit for reinstatement failed.

When an employee "resigns", it is technically an offer to dissolve the existing contract. Therefore, the resignation must be accepted to become binding on the offeror. An offer to resign, like any offer, can be withdrawn before it is accepted. (In some jurisdictions courts have held that acceptance of resignations can be delegated to an administrative officer.[106]) If the resignation is tendered orally when a statute prescribes that it be in writing, it cannot be binding even if a formal board resolution purports to accept it.[107]

Under certain circumstances a resignation might be invalidated because it was submitted under coercion or duress, that is, such illegal pressure as would have induced fear to the extent that the exercise of free will and judgment was precluded. It is to be observed, however, that for an employer merely to suggest a resignation or threaten to pursue a lawful course (such as instituting dismissal proceedings) does not constitute duress if the employee is given time and opportunity for deliberation before reaching a decision about resigning.[108]

Another way in which a resignation might be transformed into a "constructive discharge" is through the employee's showing that work-

---

103. Corcoran v. Lyle School Dist. No. 406, Klickitat County, 20 Wash.App. 621, 581 P.2d 185 (1978).

104. Brinson v. School Dist. No. 431, 223 Kan. 465, 576 P.2d 602 (1978).

105. Brown v. Board of Educ. of Morgan County School Dist., 560 P.2d 1129 (Utah 1977).

106. Kreith v. University of Colorado, 689 P.2d 718 (Colo.App.1984).

107. Petrella v. Siegel, 73 N.Y.2d 846, 537 N.Y.S.2d 124, 534 N.E.2d 41 (1988).

108. Dusanek v. Hannon, 677 F.2d 538 (7 Cir.1982), cert. den. 459 U.S. 1017, 103 S.Ct. 379, 74 L.Ed.2d 512 (1982); Parker v. Board of Regents of Tulsa Junior College, 981 F.2d 1159 (10 Cir.1992).

ing conditions were deliberately made so intolerable that it would be unreasonable to expect an employee to continue. Here, too, the employee has a heavy burden to demonstrate that specific and substantial deviations from normal operations were made intentionally for the purpose of harassment. This was found to be the situation where evidence showed that after many years of satisfactory evaluations a teacher at the top of the salary schedule had been subjected to "an intense pattern of classroom observation, criticism, and evaluation." [109]

Where a board agrees to a condition precedent to a resignation, it may not later disavow what in effect was a contractual agreement. The Supreme Court of South Carolina decided that a chief school administrator's resignation was predicated on the board's proposal of payment of six months salary.[110] The board could not subsequently accept the resignation and refuse to pay the salary. Whether the board was empowered in the first place to make the offer was not raised, but the court impliedly found the arrangement legal by its judgment enforcing the contract.

The extent to which school boards may contract for payments to employees who agree to resign is unclear. As a payment for services not rendered, it could be characterized as an illegal gift of public funds. On the other hand, it could be described as a settlement that would obviate a costly lawsuit.[111] But provisions in settlements are not immune from invalidation by courts on public policy grounds. For example, the Court of Appeals of Ohio voided a settlement agreement executed in connection with a resignation where the board had agreed not to disclose information related to pedophilia of a teacher.[112]

Rules and Regulations Included

There is no doubt that boards of education have implied, if not express, authority to adopt reasonable rules and regulations governing eligibility for employment and regulating that employment. If local policies are not contrary to state-adopted ones, or do not infringe upon federal or state constitutional or statutory rights of employees, the test of their validity is their reasonableness in terms of their purposes.

Rules that are valid in general, however, may be applied unconstitutionally in specific situations. Such seemed possible in a case ordered to trial by the Fifth Circuit Court of Appeals.[113] A teacher whose baby required breastfeeding was unable to do so while retaining her position, because one rule forbade her to leave the premises during the school day and another prohibited her from having her child on school grounds during that day.

---

109. Lee v. Rapid City Area School Dist. No. 51–4, 981 F.2d 316 (8 Cir.1992).

110. Cain v. Noel, 268 S.C. 583, 235 S.E.2d 292 (1977).

111. Ingram v. Boone, 91 A.D.2d 1063, 458 N.Y.S.2d 671 (1983). [Case No. 44]

112. Bowman v. Parma Bd. of Educ., 44 Ohio App.3d 169, 542 N.E.2d 663 (1988).

113. Dike v. School Bd. of Orange County, Florida, 650 F.2d 783 (5 Cir.1981). [Case No. 75]

The Supreme Court of the United States has made clear that, although persons have no right to work for the state on their own terms, they do have a right not to be excluded or treated differently pursuant to a provision that is arbitrary or discriminatory.[114] Stated another way, although one has no abstract right to public employment, he does have the right not to be excluded or treated differently for an unconstitutional reason. Many examples of this principle appear in this chapter and in Chapters 10 and 11.

The rules and regulations of the board, as well as the statutes, are considered part of the contract between the school district and the teacher.[115] If the teacher is not made aware of a rule by a reference in his contract or otherwise, however, the board may not be able to discipline the teacher for its violation without proof that the teacher in fact knew of the rule or should have known of it through proper diligence.[116] Also included in the teacher's contract would be the collective bargaining agreement if there is one, regardless of whether it is expressly made part of the individual contract.[117]

Problems may develop when a board of education endeavors to bind teachers by regulations adopted after the teacher has been employed. The area was explored in a decision of the Supreme Court of California.[118] After a teacher had taught for a number of years and had attained tenure status, a regulation was adopted requiring all teachers to take some graduate work or suffer a reduction in salary. The teacher involved insisted that this requirement could not be inserted into her contract after the many years the contract had been in effect. Her suit for the amount her salary had been reduced was unsuccessful. The court held that the rules and regulations of the board which were in effect at the date of the renewal of the teacher's contract were parts of it. The court stated that even though the teacher enjoyed tenure status, each yearly contract constituted a new one. It followed that the rule complained of by the teacher was really in existence at the time of the renewal, and thus the teacher was bound by it.

In a unanimous decision the Supreme Court of the United States upheld the dismissal of a tenure teacher on the ground she did not comply with a continuing education requirement.[119] For several years this teacher and a few others had not received salary increments because they had not fulfilled the local school board's requirement of completion of college courses as a prerequisite thereto. When the sanction of withholding such salary increases was withdrawn by the legislature, the board gave the recalcitrant teachers the option of taking courses or

---

114. Wieman v. Updegraff, 344 U.S. 183, 73 S.Ct. 215, 97 L.Ed. 216 (1952); Perry v. Sindermann, 408 U.S. 593, 92 S.Ct. 2694, 33 L.Ed.2d 570 (1972). [Case No. 78]

115. Fry v. Board of Educ., 17 Cal.2d 753, 112 P.2d 229 (1941).

116. Miller v. South Bend Special School Dist. No. 1, McHenry County, 124 N.W.2d 475 (N.D.1963).

117. Riley County Educ. Ass'n v. Unified School Dist. No. 378, 225 Kan. 385, 592 P.2d 87 (1979).

118. Rible v. Hughes, 24 Cal.2d 437, 150 P.2d 455 (1944).

119. Harrah Independent School Dist. v. Martin, 440 U.S. 194, 99 S.Ct. 1062, 59 L.Ed.2d 248 (1979). [Case No. 76]

facing dismissal. The plaintiff refused to take courses and was terminated. The Court found no constitutional flaw in the purpose of the requirement nor in the prospective rule establishing termination as the sanction for noncompliance. That the teacher was not given as long to complete the studies as were those who had not in the past declined to take courses did not alter the Court's view.

The Supreme Court of Indiana stated that if teachers could be bound only by rules and regulations in existence at the time the contract is formed, conditions in the district would be required to remain static for at least a year.[120] The court found no such legislative intent in the tenure law. At issue was a rule requiring an employee on tenure to take a leave of absence while campaigning for public office. More than a quarter century later, the same kind of regulation was upheld by the Supreme Court of Mississippi [121] and by a three-judge federal District Court in Wisconsin.[122]

Litigation also can develop when teachers attempt to require boards to adhere to policies they have adopted. Generally, boards must follow their rules in effect at the time. But policies enforceable against boards cannot be contrary to state-level prescriptions. Even though a local evaluation policy was incorporated into a probationary teacher's contract, the Supreme Court of Wyoming held that the district's violation of its policy did not constitute an actionable breach of contract because state law gave boards discretionary power not to renew the contracts of nontenure teachers even if the evaluations were favorable.[123]

Requiring as a contract condition that public employees become residents of the jurisdiction does not offend the federal Constitution. The Supreme Court so held in the case of a firefighter who had moved from Philadelphia, Pennsylvania, to New Jersey in contravention of a regulation.[124] Citing its dismissal of a prior challenge to such residency requirements for police "because no substantial federal question was presented,"[125] the Court said it had already held this kind of regulation "not irrational." In the Philadelphia case the Supreme Court referred with apparent approval to a decision of the Sixth Circuit Court of Appeals sustaining a residency requirement for public school teachers hired after a certain future date. In that case the Sixth Circuit, applying the rational relationship test to the requirement, found reasonable the bases offered by the board of education.[126] These included: hiring of teachers deeply committed to an urban educational system would be aided; resident teachers are more likely to support school tax levies, less

120. School City of East Chicago v. Sigler, 219 Ind. 9, 36 N.E.2d 760 (1941).

121. Chatham v. Johnson, 195 So.2d 62 (Miss.1967).

122. Wisconsin State Employees Ass'n v. Wisconsin Natural Resources Bd., 298 F.Supp. 339 (W.D.Wis.1969).

123. Leonard v. Converse County School Dist. No. 2, 788 P.2d 1119 (Wyo. 1990).

124. McCarthy v. Philadelphia Civil Service Comm'n, 424 U.S. 645, 96 S.Ct. 1154, 47 L.Ed.2d 366 (1976).

125. Detroit Police Officers Ass'n v. City of Detroit, 405 U.S. 950, 92 S.Ct. 1173, 31 L.Ed.2d 227 (1972).

126. Wardwell v. Board of Educ. of the City School Dist. of City of Cincinnati, 529 F.2d 625 (6 Cir.1976).

likely to engage in strikes, more likely to be involved in activities bringing them in contact with parents and community leaders, and more likely to gain understanding of urban problems; and the requirement is in keeping with the goal of encouraging integration in society and in the schools.[127]

The requirement that teachers become residents, however, may be barred by interpretations of state constitutions. This is the situation in New Hampshire.[128] The separate issue of preferring state or local residents over other persons for employment is discussed in Chapter 8 under "Conditions of Bidding." The Court of Appeals of Kentucky has held that a school board cannot give preference in employment to natives of the county.[129]

Statutory prohibitions against nepotism were treated in Chapter 8 under "Interest of Board Members in Contracts." If a teacher has been employed before a close relative becomes a member of the board, however, it is generally held that his contract does not automatically become void unless the statute clearly so specifies.[130] A conflict of interest would have to be shown. Related issues are presented when persons employed within a school system are closely related by birth or marriage. It is to be observed, however, that nepotism per se is not barred by common law so long as employees are qualified. If the practice leads to discrimination against a protected class, it is, of course, illegal.[131]

It has been held that a school board can enforce a policy prohibiting the employment of a husband and wife in an administrator-teacher relationship in the same building.[132] Also sustained has been the power of a school board to adopt a rule barring the employment in the system of spouses of the three highest school administrators and to apply it by not renewing the teaching contract of the superintendent's wife.[133] She was employed on a one year contract at the time of the enactment of the rule. Prior to this she had taught in the district for a three year period and had taken a three year leave of absence during which she obtained a master's degree. The court stated that it was bound to uphold decisions

---

127. Many of these reasons were offered in support of a rule prohibiting school district employees in an Alabama district from sending their children to private schools. The rule was overturned, however, the court observing that parents have constitutional rights related to educating their children and that the board failed to show that sending a child to private school interfered with a teacher's duties. Stough v. Crenshaw County Bd. of Educ. 744 F.2d 1479 (11 Cir.1984).

128. Donnelly v. City of Manchester, 111 N.H. 50, 274 A.2d 789 (1971); Angwin v. City of Manchester, 118 N.H. 336, 386 A.2d 1272 (1978).

129. Johnson v. Dixon, 501 S.W.2d 256 (Ky.1973).

130. New Mexico State Bd. of Educ. v. Board of Educ. of Alamogordo Public School Dist., 95 N.M. 588, 624 P.2d 530 (1981).

131. Thomas v. Washington County School Bd., 915 F.2d 922 (4 Cir.1990). [Case No. 73]

132. Keckeisen v. Independent School Dist. 612, 509 F.2d 1062 (8 Cir.1975), cert. den. 423 U.S. 833, 96 S.Ct. 57, 46 L.Ed.2d 51 (1975); Townshend v. Board of Educ. of County of Grant, 183 W.Va. 418, 396 S.E.2d 185 (1990).

133. Corbin v. Special School Dist. of Fort Smith, 250 Ark. 357, 465 S.W.2d 342 (1971).

of local boards within the realm of their discretionary authority unless there was a clear abuse demonstrated by convincing evidence.

The Supreme Court denied certiorari on a holding by the Court of Appeals, Seventh Circuit, that the Civil Rights Act of 1964 was not violated by an employer's rule barring the hiring of hourly employees who were married to personnel already so employed.[134] The Court of Appeals had found no sex discrimination despite disparate impact on women because there was no intent to discriminate and it was plausible that the company could believe the work environment was enhanced by the rule, which was not discriminatorily applied. Emotional involvements between spouses could create a number of problem situations.

Where a long-standing policy of a school system prohibited spouses from teaching at the same school, neither of a newly married couple would volunteer to leave the school where they had taught. The board prior to the marriage had selected the husband to be a department head. The couple took the position that the employer should choose the transferee. The male did not volunteer to relinquish his new position. The board transferred the woman, and she brought suit on a claim of sex discrimination. The suit was unsuccessful.[135]

Duties Covered by Implication

Contracts with teachers vary greatly in the extent to which the teacher's duties are set out in detail. Master collective bargaining contracts tend to include more provisions than individual contracts, but there remains the troublesome question of a teacher's implied obligation under the contract to perform duties not enumerated in it.

A detailed analysis of the legal situation was made by a New York court, substantially relying on an opinion of the state commissioner of education, in one of the first cases to deal extensively with the subject.[136] Teachers were dissatisfied with certain regulations of the board concerning the work to be required of teachers in addition to regular classroom instruction, and they brought suit to have them annulled. Although the regulations were sustained, the court established limits as to what legally could be required of teachers outside of the classroom. The court said that the board had the authority to assign teachers only duties related to their respective subject matter fields or duties inherent in the contracts of all teachers. It stated that any teacher may be expected to supervise a study hall and to conduct student conferences. English teachers may be assigned to coach school plays, physical education teachers may be required to coach intramural and interschool athletic teams, and band instructors may be expected to accompany students in

134. Yuhas v. Libby-Owens-Ford Co., 562 F.2d 496 (7 Cir.1977), cert. den. 435 U.S. 934, 98 S.Ct. 1510, 55 L.Ed.2d 531 (1978).

135. Meier v. Evansville-Vanderburgh School Corp., 416 F.Supp. 748 (S.D.Ind. 1975), aff. 539 F.2d 713 (7 Cir.1976).

136. Parrish v. Moss, 200 Misc. 375, 106 N.Y.S.2d 577 (1951), aff. 279 App.Div. 608, 107 N.Y.S.2d 580 (1951).

the band on trips. The board cannot, however, require a teacher of mathematics to coach athletic teams. No teacher may be compelled to perform services such as janitor service, traffic duty, and school bus driving. The court added that it would be legal for a board to arrange for teachers to perform duties not required of them under their contracts and to pay additional compensation for such services.

The District Court of Appeal of California extended the implied obligations of teachers under their contracts beyond the point set by the New York court.[137] Male teachers in the case were required to attend six nonclassroom activities and act in a supervisory capacity. The activities included football and basketball games under the auspices of the school, some held off school grounds. The contention of the complaining teacher was that the duties were in the nature of police work, unprofessional, foreign to his field of instruction, and posed unreasonable hours. The court, however, held that the assignments were within the duties implied in the teacher's contract. The New York case was cited by the plaintiff, but the court found that it did not support his position under the present facts. A charge of sex discrimination was not raised; nor was it in the next case.

Where male teachers were required as a condition of employment to serve as ticket-takers and to supervise conduct at high school football games, refusal twice to execute the function was held by the Fifth Circuit Court of Appeals to constitute insubordination.[138] The teacher admitted his refusals were retaliatory in nature for what he considered to be mistreatment by school officials. Coupled with an incident of violating another rule, these acts were sufficient to warrant nonrenewal of the teacher's contract by the board.

Having concluded that supervision of extracurricular activities was properly part of the duties of a teacher, a New Jersey court held that concerted resignations of teachers from these assignments constituted an illegal strike.[139]

The Appellate Court of Illinois held that teachers could be required to supervise certain extracurricular activities in the evening or on Saturday at a rate of compensation lower than their regular rate.[140] But in another case that court upheld the right of a teacher who was assigned an unreasonable number of extra duties to resign as volleyball coach while retaining her status as teacher (and retaining other extracurricular assignments).[141]

137. McGrath v. Burkhard, 131 Cal. App.2d 367, 280 P.2d 864 (1955).

138. Blair v. Robstown Independent School Dist., 556 F.2d 1331 (5 Cir.1977).

139. Board of Educ. of City of Asbury Park v. Asbury Park Educ. Ass'n, 145 N.J.Super. 495, 368 A.2d 396 (1976). On appeal, it was held that the question of whether the teachers were required to perform the duties under the collective bargaining contract should have been referred to the Public Employment Relations Commission. 155 N.J.Super. 76, 382 A.2d 392 (1977).

140. District 300 Educ. Ass'n v. Board of Educ. of Dundee Community Unit School Dist. No. 300, 31 Ill.App.3d 550, 334 N.E.2d 165 (1975).

141. Lewis v. Board of Educ. of North Clay Community Unit School Dist. No. 25, 181 Ill.App.3d 689, 130 Ill.Dec. 368, 537 N.E.2d 435 (1989).

However, the Supreme Court of Pennsylvania held that a teacher could not be required to supervise a voluntary high school boys' bowling club.[142]   The bowling sessions, each session lasting about two and a half hours, were held once a week after school hours at a privately operated bowling alley about a mile and a half from the school.   There were no bowling teams in the school, and each boy paid his own transportation to the bowling alley as well as the cost of his individual bowling.   The sponsor was not expected to teach, coach, or instruct in bowling, but simply be in attendance at the alley to maintain discipline of the boys if it became necessary.   The court found the activity not to be sufficiently related to the school program to justify the board's assigning the teacher to it.

Two "parent-conference" cases are instructive.   In one, the court sustained the dismissal of a temporary teacher who refused to attend "open house" at her school building.[143]   She had been told when interviewed and at other times that she would be expected to attend. Prior to the holding of the event, the teacher advised her administrative superior that she would not attend.   The Superior Court of Pennsylvania, reversing the trial court which had found the teacher merely "indiscreet" in her action but not guilty of "insubordination and lack of cooperation" constituting cause for dismissal, stated that the open house was a significant part of the school program in that it brought parents to the school to talk with teachers and examine their children's work.   It found that a refusal, without cause, of a teacher to participate in the program was a valid basis for dismissal.

The highest court in West Virginia, in a case in which it did not have to determine whether attendance of a teacher at a parent-teacher conference was required or optional, observed that even were it optional, a teacher would not be relieved of his "responsibility to cooperate with school administrators by informing them of his intention to attend or not attend and the reasons therefor." [144]

Teachers may be expected to help maintain discipline when special circumstances develop at the school.   Upheld by the Court of Appeals, Eighth Circuit, was the dismissal of a teacher who, when ROTC recruiters were on campus, suggested to his tenth grade class that the students could get the military personnel off the grounds if they desired.[145]   The Court of Appeals, Sixth Circuit, sustained the dismissal of a teacher who made remarks to encourage students not to obey directions from administrators to return to classes after a demonstration about removal of a teacher.[146]

142.   Pease v. Millcreek Tp. School Dist., 412 Pa. 378, 195 A.2d 104 (1963).

143.   Johnson v. United School Dist. Joint School Bd., 201 Pa.Super. 375, 191 A.2d 897 (1963).

144.   Fox v. Board of Educ. of Doddridge County, 160 W.Va. 668, 236 S.E.2d 243 (1977).

145.   Birdwell   v.   Hazelwood   School Dist., 491 F.2d 490 (8 Cir.1974).

146.   Whitsel v. Southeast Local School Dist., 484 F.2d 1222 (6 Cir.1973).

In a Vermont district, following a dispute between a teacher and the principal, rumors spread that the teacher had been or was going to be dismissed. The teacher and the principal tried to avert a student demonstration by denying the rumors over the public address system. Two teachers refused to return to their classrooms when so directed by the principal. They were dismissed on charges of failing to attend to duties and to carry out reasonable directions of their superiors. The Supreme Court of Vermont sustained the board, holding that the implied contractual obligations of cooperation and obedience to lawfully constituted school administrative authority had been violated.[147]

Assignments of direct instructional duties are covered in Chapter 10 under "Assignment and Transfer."

Nonrenewal

A key element of any contract is the time period covered. At the expiration date a contract simply dissolves unless there is some basis upon which a renewal can be required (e.g., failure of one party to perform a condition precedent to a valid termination of the contractual relationship). The parties at the end of a contract period are in the same basic positions as before the contract began. Thus, nonrenewal of a teacher's time-limited contract must be distinguished from either discharge during the term of a nontenure contract or discharge under statutory tenure provisions. In the latter two situations a hearing at which cause is demonstrated by the school board must be held. (See Chapter 11.)

The extent of the application of the due process clause of the Fourteenth Amendment to the nonrenewal of contracts of non-tenure teachers was described by the Supreme Court of the United States in 1972 when two cases involving teachers at public colleges were decided. A Seventh Circuit case from Wisconsin squarely presented the question: Does the Fourteenth Amendment require that a probationary teacher be given a statement of reasons and a hearing if his contract is not renewed?[148] In a Fifth Circuit case from Texas, the Supreme Court discussed the circumstances under which a public employee might gain the procedural rights of tenure in the absence of an express statutory or contractual provision for tenure.[149]

The Supreme Court rejected the notion that a statement of reasons and a hearing are required to protect against nonrenewal decisions improperly motivated. The Court stated that the requirements of procedural due process apply only to the deprivation of interests encompassed within the concepts of "liberty" and "property" in the Fourteenth Amendment. The "range of interests protected by procedural due process is not infinite." In the case the teacher was an assistant

147. Petitions of Davenport, 129 Vt. 546, 283 A.2d 452 (1971).

148. Board of Regents of State Colleges v. Roth, 408 U.S. 564, 92 S.Ct. 2701, 33 L.Ed.2d 548 (1972). [Case No. 77]

149. Perry v. Sindermann, 408 U.S. 593, 92 S.Ct. 2694, 33 L.Ed.2d 570 (1972). [Case No. 78]

professor whose initial contract with the college was for one year. The Court said the nature of the interest at stake was the crucial factor as to whether the interest was constitutionally protected. Being "not rehired in one job but * * * as free as before to seek another" is not a deprivation of "liberty." The state did not seriously damage his standing in his community by making a charge such as dishonesty, nor did it impose on him a stigma or disability preventing his obtaining other employment in his field, which situations would have established the right to a hearing. Regarding "property" interests, the Court stated that they do not derive from the Constitution, but are created and defined by independent sources such as state law. The specific terms of the teacher's appointment secured no interest in reemployment for the next year.

In the other case, the Court amplified the concept of "property interest for due process purposes" by stating that such an interest could derive not only from express legislative or contractual wording but from "existing rules or understandings"—"an unwritten 'common law' in a particular university that certain employees shall have the equivalent of tenure." Such a claim of "de facto tenure," which could be examined only at a hearing, must be more than "a mere subjective 'expectancy' " of reemployment. In this case the Court also restated the principle that the lack of a contractual right to reemployment was immaterial to a claim that nonrenewal was based on the exercise of a constitutional right. Such a claim requires a hearing.

A 1976 Supreme Court holding further delineated the concept of liberty interests.[150] A probationary police officer was dismissed without a hearing, although he was given the reasons privately. In addition to the common "stigma" claim, he asserted that the reasons were false. Since the communication of reasons was not made public (until a lawsuit initiated by the officer) there was no actionable stigma. The Court also held that the falsity allegation did not require a hearing because the reasons were given to the officer in private, and, therefore, his reputation was not affected by their truth or falsity. "A contrary evaluation of his contention would enable every discharged employee to assert a constitutional claim merely by alleging that his former supervisor made a mistake." The Court stated that the Constitution could not be construed to require federal judicial review of "the multitude of personnel decisions that are made daily by public agencies." As state law in this instance had been held not to grant a property right, the rejection of the liberty right left the officer with no federal remedy.

In 1977 the Supreme Court held that no stigma was imposed in the termination of a probationary police officer by the placing in his personnel file of material related to an apparent suicide attempt and the releasing, with his permission, of the file to a prospective employer.[151] The Court emphasized that the purpose of a hearing on a stigmatization claim is to afford an employee "an opportunity to refute the charge" and

---

150. Bishop v. Wood, 426 U.S. 341, 96 S.Ct. 2074, 48 L.Ed.2d 684 (1976).

151. Codd v. Velger, 429 U.S. 624, 97 S.Ct. 882, 51 L.Ed.2d 92 (1977).

"clear his name." If the truth of the charge is not contested, there is no constitutional need for a hearing. "Only if the employer creates and disseminates a false and defamatory impression about the employee in connection with his termination is such a hearing required." Any harm that may have been done the employee here was not occasioned by the lack of hearing.

It is important to observe that nonrenewed personnel generally cannot obtain a federal review of the substantive merits of their termination (i.e., the acceptability of the reasons) if a hearing is not required by the procedural due process requirements of the Fourteenth Amendment.[152] The constitutional right to substantive due process "is no greater than the right to procedural due process."[153]

As would be expected, a very large number of cases have arisen through attempts of nontenure employees to meet the criterion of "property interest" or "liberty interest" that would warrant a hearing under the Supreme Court decisions. The fact that a state may require boards to offer reasons for nonrenewal of teachers does not in itself create a federal right,[154] nor does the fact that a hearing must be held at the teacher's request where cause for nonrenewal does not have to be proved by the board.[155] State procedural rights are enforceable in state courts, which are empowered to interpret the existence and extent of a right alleged to have been created by state law.[156] Any property right granted by the state is intrinsically shaped by the procedures provided in legislation or state-constitutional interpretation for determining that right. For example, in New Jersey the supreme court granted nonrenewed teachers the right to be informed of reasons and suggested that these be communicated at an informal hearing.[157] No restrictions were placed on the board's decision itself. Therefore, nothing was added to the expectation of continued employment that could trigger a due process hearing on the reasons under the de facto tenure theory.[158]

Where, however, a statute provided that if a teacher's annual contract was not to be renewed the board must notify the teacher of a reason that the board had preestablished and afford the teacher a hearing if requested, the Supreme Court of Texas held that a property interest under the Fourteenth Amendment was created.[159] Even though

152. Excluded from this discussion are cases brought under the Civil Rights Act of 1964. In such cases it becomes necessary for federal courts to examine the reasons for nonrenewal (or any adverse personnel action) after a prima facie case of discrimination in employment has been made.

153. Jeffries v. Turkey Run Consolidated School Dist., 492 F.2d 1 (7 Cir.1974); Buhr v. Buffalo Public School Dist. No. 38, 509 F.2d 1196 (8 Cir.1974).

154. Ryan v. Aurora Bd. of Educ., 540 F.2d 222 (6 Cir.1976), cert. den. 429 U.S. 1041, 97 S.Ct. 741, 50 L.Ed.2d 753 (1977).

155. Perkins v. Board of Directors of School Administrative Dist. No. 13, 686 F.2d 49 (1 Cir.1982).

156. Sigmon v. Poe, 564 F.2d 1093 (4 Cir.1977).

157. Donaldson v. Board of Educ. of North Wildwood, 65 N.J. 236, 320 A.2d 857 (1974).

158. Mozier v. Board of Educ. of Tp. of Cherry Hill, County of Camden, 450 F.Supp. 742 (D.N.J.1977).

159. Grounds v. Tolar Independent School Dist., 856 S.W.2d 417 (Tex.1993).

local boards could establish the reasons, their discretion not to renew was considered to be sufficiently limited to create a property interest for teachers. (The court in a previous case had overturned as a matter of state law a nonrenewal for a reason not on a list of 18 adopted by a district.) [160]

Where a statewide tenure system has been established, local boards cannot change the system's allocation of powers and rights, whether by collective bargaining or otherwise. This basic principle of local board powers is amplified in Chapter 4. Thus, de facto tenure is not possible where there is a detailed de jure system.[161] In any event, a property right must develop from some affirmative government action.[162] Further, any action must be perfected by a person or body authorized to do so. Therefore, no property rights were created by an assistant superintendent's statement that he planned to recommend a teacher for tenure and that the school board rarely failed to grant it,[163] by the listing in a school district's policy manual of evaluative criteria to be used in determining contract renewal,[164] by continuous service for 11 years under a series of contracts,[165] by the board's offering to discuss a contract extension for a superintendent,[166] by the principal's having recommended the renewal of a teacher's contract,[167] or by the board's not renewing a teacher's contract without having referred parent complaints to the superintendent for an attempt at adjustment as provided for in a policy statement.[168] On the other hand, any item in the employee's contract, as discussed earlier in this chapter, does create a property right that cannot be infringed without due process. The infringement, however, has to be of some significance. Hence, a two-day suspension with pay has been held not to be a deprivation of property for constitutional purposes.[169] Neither was a transfer with no loss of rank or pay,[170] nor a change in teaching assignment or administrative duties.[171]

As for liberty interests in this context, it has become clear that it is difficult for an employee to meet the criterion of stigma if board members and administrators do not make public statements or release

160. Seifert v. Lingleville Independent School Dist., 692 S.W.2d 461 (Tex.1985).

161. Ryan v. Aurora Bd. of Educ., 540 F.2d 222 (6 Cir.1976); Willens v. University of Massachusetts, 570 F.2d 403 (1 Cir. 1978); Meyr v. Board of Educ. of Affton School Dist., 572 F.2d 1229 (8 Cir.1978). [Case No. 80]

162. Confederation of Police v. City of Chicago, 547 F.2d 375 (7 Cir.1977).

163. LaBorde v. Franklin Parish School Bd., 510 F.2d 590 (5 Cir.1975).

164. Depas v. Highland Local School Dist. Bd. of Educ., 52 Ohio St.2d 193, 370 N.E.2d 744 (1977).

165. Robertson v. Rogers, 679 F.2d 1090 (4 Cir.1982).

166. Cannon v. Beckville Independent School Dist., 709 F.2d 9 (5 Cir.1983).

167. Weathers v. West Yuma County School Dist. R–J–1, 387 F.Supp. 552 (D.Colo.1974).

168. Weathers v. West Yuma County School Dist. R–J–1, 530 F.2d 1335 (10 Cir. 1976).

169. Pitts v. Board of Educ. of U.S.D. 305, Salina, Kansas, 869 F.2d 555 (10 Cir. 1989).

170. Maples v. Martin, 858 F.2d 1546 (11 Cir.1988).

171. Dorsett v. Board of Trustees for State Colleges and Universities, 940 F.2d 121 (5 Cir.1991).

information derogatory to the employee.[172] The constitutional requirement is that the nonrenewed employee must demonstrate that he was seriously harmed in the process of nonrenewal, not merely that he was rejected and deemed to be of insufficient merit for reemployment in the district. Even where statements have gone beyond internal channels, if they describe perceived professional weakness or unsatisfactory performance in general, usually they do not rise to the constitutional level. Most cases that have found a liberty interest have involved specific and substantial charges.

Examples of characterizations not involving stigma include ineffective teaching methods,[173] tardiness and inability to maintain discipline,[174] human relations problems,[175] and an "extreme anti-establishment obsession."[176] Failure to be awarded tenure does not ipso facto create a stigma,[177] nor does the fact that no reasons for the act are given.[178] Examples of adjudicated stigmas include charges of manifest racism,[179] moral unfitness,[180] serious mental disorder,[181] a drinking problem,[182] wilful neglect of duty,[183] and responsibility for rapid deterioration of a school.[184]

The effect of the inclusion of a constitutionally protected right as a factor in a nonrenewal was set forth in a unanimous opinion of the Supreme Court in 1977.[185] In that case the trial court and the Sixth Circuit Court of Appeals had held that the inclusion of a protected activity as a substantial part of the basis for nonrenewal entitled the teacher to reinstatement with back pay.

The Supreme Court disagreed. It observed that the rule enunciated by the lower court "could place an employee in a better position as a result of the exercise of constitutionally protected conduct than he would have occupied had he done nothing. * * * The constitutional principle at stake is sufficiently vindicated if such an employee is placed in no worse a position than if he had not engaged in the conduct." Operationally this means that where a teacher shows that protected conduct—in

---

172. Hayes v. Phoenix-Talent School Dist. No. 4, 893 F.2d 235 (9 Cir.1990).

173. LaBorde v. Franklin Parish School Bd., 510 F.2d 590 (5 Cir.1975); Shirck v. Thomas, 486 F.2d 691 (7 Cir.1973).

174. Brouillette v. Board of Directors of Merged Area IX, 519 F.2d 126 (8 Cir.1975).

175. Gray v. Union County Intermediate Educ. Dist., 520 F.2d 803 (9 Cir.1975).

176. Lipp v. Board of Educ. of City of Chicago, 470 F.2d 802 (7 Cir.1972).

177. Calvin v. Rupp, 471 F.2d 1346 (8 Cir.1973); Meyr v. Board of Educ. of Affton School Dist., 572 F.2d 1229 (8 Cir.1978). [Case No. 80]

178. Cato v. Collins, 539 F.2d 656 (8 Cir.1976).

179. Wellner v. Minnesota State Junior College Bd., 487 F.2d 153 (8 Cir.1973).

180. McGhee v. Draper, 564 F.2d 902 (10 Cir.1977).

181. Lombard v. Board of Educ. of City of New York, 502 F.2d 631 (2 Cir.1974), cert. den. 420 U.S. 976, 95 S.Ct. 1400, 43 L.Ed.2d 656 (1975).

182. Dennis v. S and S Consolidated Rural High School Dist., 577 F.2d 338 (5 Cir.1978).

183. Huntley v. Community School Bd. of Brooklyn, New York School Dist. No. 14, 543 F.2d 979 (2 Cir.1976), cert.den. 430 U.S. 929, 97 S.Ct. 1547, 51 L.Ed.2d 773 (1977).

184. Staton v. Mayes, 552 F.2d 908 (10 Cir.1977), cert. den. 434 U.S. 907, 98 S.Ct. 309, 54 L.Ed.2d 195 (1977).

185. Mt. Healthy City Bd. of Educ. v. Doyle, 429 U.S. 274, 97 S.Ct. 568, 50 L.Ed.2d 471 (1977). [Case No. 79]

this case a call to a radio station about a school matter—was a "substantial factor" or a "motivating factor" in the decision not to renew, the board must be given opportunity to show, and must show by a preponderance of the evidence, that it would have reached the decision not to reemploy in the absence of the protected conduct.

[Case No. 68] Cause for Suspension of Teaching Certificate

AMADOR v. NEW MEXICO STATE BD. OF EDUC.

Supreme Court of New Mexico, 1969.
80 N.M. 336, 455 P.2d 840.

NOBLE, CHIEF JUSTICE. On November 8, 1966, Albert Amador, Jr., a certified and qualified school teacher, was elected a member of the State Board of Education. The State Board, in 1962, adopted a resolution requiring the suspension of the teaching certificate of a teacher elected to the State Board. Upon being served with an order to show cause why his teacher's certificate should not be suspended, Amador sought and was granted an injunction restraining and enjoining the State Board of Education from enforcing its resolution or suspending Amador's teaching certificate. The Board has appealed.

The State Board of Education was created by art. XII, § 6 (Supp. 1967) of the State Constitution, one member to be elected from each judicial district for terms of six years. The Constitution requires the Board to determine public school policy and to have control, management and direction of all public schools, pursuant to authority and powers provided by law. The constitutional provision respecting rules or regulations is not self-executing but the Board's power to promulgate the rule now under consideration must be found in and is limited by statute. The Board relies upon § 77–8–19(A), N.M.S.A.1953, for its authority to suspend Amador's teaching certificate. The provision reads:

"The state board may suspend or revoke a certificate held by a certified school instructor or administrator for incompetency, immorality or for any other good and just cause."

* * * [T]he Board argues that the office of member of the State Board of Education and that of a public school teacher are incompatible, and then reasons that since the statute grants authority to revoke a teacher's license for "good and just cause," the suspension of Amador's license was for "good and just cause" and is authorized by the statute.

The law requires teachers to be licensed, but it is well settled that the right to practice a profession or vocation is a property right. Legislation concerning revocation of this right is highly penal in its nature and is to be strictly construed. It is equally well established that when a statute authorizes revocation or suspension of a license entitling one to practice a profession or vocation for certain specified reasons, revocation or suspension is strictly limited to those specified. It is argued that the words "for good and just cause" grant to the Board broad discretionary authority. However, it is firmly established that statutes delegating powers to administrative agencies must clearly provide reasonable standards as a guide in the exercise of the discretionary powers.

It is likewise a fundamental principle that courts will not declare a legislative act unconstitutional if there is any reasonable basis upon which it can be upheld. In authorizing revocation or suspension of a license by reason of "incompetency or immorality" the legislature employed words having a reasonably certain meaning in the law, but then added "or for other good and just cause." These words in themselves have no reasonably defined meaning in law, and, if they are to be given the broad interpretation contended for by the Board, would seem to permit the revocation of a teacher's license for matters having no reasonable relation to the underlying purpose of the statute. * * * An examination of the Act requiring the licensing of school teachers convinces us that its purpose is to protect the public against incompetent teachers, and to insure proper educational qualifications, personal fitness and a high standard of teaching performance.

The "other good and just cause" for suspension of teachers, then, must be related to this purpose of the statutory provision. In our view, the suspension of a teacher for incompatibility with membership on the State Board of Education does not fall within the purpose of insuring a high quality of public instruction. Indeed, appellant does not argue that the supposed incompatibility detrimentally affects teaching performance.

Rather, appellant's argument goes to the ability of active teachers to effectively and fairly carry out their duties as Board members. However, the statute providing that an office becomes vacant when an officer accepts or undertakes the discharge of the duties of another incompatible office * * * has no application here. The position of school teacher is not an office within the meaning of the statute. The State Board only has jurisdiction over a school teacher in the instance where the teacher appeals to that Board from an adverse ruling by the local board of education. The fact that a teacher who is also a member of the State Board might appeal from the action of the local board presents no serious problem. The teacher would simply refrain from acting as a member of the Board in his case just as would a member of any other trade or profession who appealed to the board of which he was a member. In fact, in looking at other legislation requiring the licensing of trades or professions, in every instance to which our attention has been called, the licensing agency includes members of the trade or profession. * * *

It follows that the judgment appealed from should be affirmed.

* * *

Notes

1. Note the basis on which the court decided whether the cause for suspension of the certificate was "good and just."

2. In several states there are legislative provisions specifically excluding practicing educators from membership on state boards. Such a provision was

sustained by the Supreme Court of Illinois in Hoskins v. Walker, 57 Ill.2d 503, 315 N.E.2d 25 (1974). Can that case be reconciled with Amador?

3. Compare this court's view of "incompatibility of office" with that of the courts in cases treated under "The Teacher as Citizen" in Chapter 11. Consider the competing considerations inherent in the concepts of "incompatibility of office" and "control of professional licensure."

4. A certificate may be denied or revoked upon a showing of mental illness without a showing of improper performance of duties. Alford v. Department of Educ., 13 Cal.App.3d 884, 91 Cal.Rptr. 843 (1970).

5. The Supreme Court of Iowa has held that adultery per se was not ground for revoking a teacher's certificate. Not only was there no evidence before the state board as to any adverse effect of the teacher's conduct on teacher-student relationships, but the local school board had unanimously declined to accept the teacher's resignation, and the president of the local board testified before the state board that the teacher was highly rated, had been forgiven by his wife and the student body, and had maintained the respect of the community. Erb v. Iowa State Bd. of Public Instr., 216 N.W.2d 339 (Iowa 1974).

[Case No. 69] Contract with Uncertificated Principal

STATE EX REL. THOMPSON v. EKBERG

Supreme Court of Oklahoma, 1980.
613 P.2d 466.

SIMMS, JUSTICE: Plaintiff appeals from a defendants' judgment in a taxpayer's suit brought * * * by electors in the Vian School District of Vian, Oklahoma, to recover damages against the Vian School Board (Board) members * * * for the wrongful hiring of Moxom as principal of the Vian High School.

Moxom was hired to serve as principal for the 1974–75 school year at a salary of $11,200 per year. Moxom did not have a standard master's degree as required for his certification by 70 O.S.Supp.1972, § 3–104, subsection 9. The Board hired Moxom only after a representative of the State Department of Education, Ben Chapman, advised the Board that the degree requirement would be waived. Moxom was then working toward his master's degree, and the Board had little time in which to hire a principal before the school year began. Moxom then served as principal for the school year, acquiring his master's degree sometime thereafter.

Appellant (plaintiff below) claims that the purported waiver of the certification requirement was ineffective, and therefore the appellees are liable for double the amount of the salary for the wrongful act of hiring an uncertified principal. 70 O.S.1971, § 5–125.

The trial court found the purported "waiver" or "permission" effective and gave judgment for the defendants.

70 O.S.Supp.1972, § 3–104, in its applicable provision, reads:

"The control of the State Department of Education and the supervision of the public school system of Oklahoma shall be vested in the State Board of Education and, subject to limitations otherwise provided by law, the State Board of Education shall:

" * * *

"9. Have full and exclusive authority in all matters pertaining to standards of qualifications and the certification of persons for instructional, supervisory, and administrative positions and services in the public schools of the state, and shall formulate rules and regulations governing the issuance and revocation of certificates * * *.

" * * * Provided, further, that the requirements for a certificate for county superintendent of schools, district superintendent of schools and principal, shall include not less than a standard master's degree * * *."

Defendants claim that the State Board of Education's grant of full and exclusive authority in matters pertaining to qualifications allows it to waive the specific requirement of a master's degree for a principal, and that, in fact, this waiver is given routinely by the State Board of Education.

A plain reading of the statute shows a legislative intent that no person is to be certified to be a principal unless he or she holds a standard master's degree. This is a specific exception to the general words of grant of authority, and as a rule, general words in a statute are limited by subsequent more specific terms. To hold otherwise and allow the State Board of Education discretion to ignore the requirement, would make the requirement meaningless. This Court will not presume the legislature has done a vain and useless act. Further, statutes must be interpreted to render every word and sentence operative, rather than in a manner which would render a specific statutory provision nugatory.

Finally, the grant of authority to the State Board of Education is specifically subject to limitations otherwise provided by law. The requirement that a principal hold a standard master's degree is one such limitation.

We hold, therefore, that the State Board of Education has no authority to waive the requirement of a master's degree for a certificate for a principal, and such purported waiver is of no effect.

Plaintiffs base the liability of the defendants on 70 O.S.1971, § 5–125, providing a recovery of double the amount of money wrongfully paid, specifically including money paid on an unlawful school employment contract. This statute is penal in nature and must be strictly construed.

The policy of this statute was discussed in [a 1953 case]:

"The statutes above quoted determine the public policy of this state, which is that boards of education may not knowingly hire and pay uncertified teachers or superintendents or other employees, and if such is done, the members of such board shall be jointly liable for the return of the amount of public money thus expended."

Liability under the statute is only imposed where the Board "knowingly" hires a principal without certification. Under the facts presented, the Board could not reasonably have known that the waiver given was ineffective to satisfy the certificate requirement. We hold today that the requirement of a master's degree for a principal cannot be waived. This holding stands as notice to all school boards that any such purported waiver is of no effect, and that any money expended under such purported waiver is an unlawful expenditure that will subject the parties involved to liability under 70 O.S.1971, § 5–125.

Judgment of the trial court affirmed.

Notes

1. Whether Ben Chapman was an agent of the state department authorized to make statements on its behalf was not discussed. Do you think it was reasonable for the board to believe that he was?

2. In any event, can an agent bind his principal (the state board) to commit a violation of law? Was it clear at the time that the waiver was a violation?

3. Do you think the court properly took into account that school board members are unpaid for their services, and also that there was no evidence of intentional wrongdoing?

4. Why do you think the court added the last sentence of the last full paragraph?

[Case No. 70] Procedural Due Process in Teacher Certification Determination

BROWN v. SOUTH CAROLINA STATE BD. OF EDUC.

Supreme Court of South Carolina, 1990.
301 S.Ct. 326, 391 S.E.2d 866.

GREGORY, CHIEF JUSTICE. This appeal is from a circuit court order affirming respondent's (Board's) invalidation of appellant's teaching certificate. We reverse and remand.

Appellant took the National Teacher's Examination (NTE) for elementary school teachers which is administered by Educational Testing Service (ETS). On March 28, 1987, ETS reported to the State Department of Education (Department) that appellant had achieved a passing score. The Department then issued appellant a teaching certificate valid through June 1990.

With certificate in hand, appellant applied for a teaching position with the Dorchester County School District No. 4. The superintendent of schools who interviewed appellant noted that her NTE scores were at the 78th percentile nationally, well above the required score of 50 percent. Because of this and other qualifications, appellant was offered a position as a second grade teacher. She performed satisfactorily on the job.

On January 25, 1988, the Department received a report from ETS stating simply that appellant's March 28, 1987, NTE scores had been "canceled" and directing the Department to "delete them from your records." The Department then advised appellant that because her NTE scores had been canceled, her teaching certificate was no longer valid and she could qualify for certification only upon presentation of a valid passing NTE score. At appellant's request, a hearing was scheduled and the invalidation was suspended until that time.

A hearing was held before the Teacher Recruitment, Training, and Certification Committee of the Board. The only evidence produced at the hearing to support invalidation of appellant's teaching certificate was the notification from ETS that her NTE scores had been canceled. The Committee recommended appellant's teaching certificate be invalidated and the Board affirmed that decision. On appeal to the circuit court, the Board's decision was affirmed and this appeal followed.

Appellant contends the regulation under which her teaching certificate was invalidated is unconstitutional because it violates her right to procedural due process. Reg. 43–59 provides:

> If any testing company invalidates a test score, the State Board of Education shall accept that determination and, if a teaching certificate has been issued based upon the invalid score, shall automatically invalidate that certificate effective the date of receipt of notification of the score invalidity by the Office of Teacher Education and Certification.

The fourteenth amendment Due Process Clause requires procedural due process be afforded an individual deprived of a property or liberty interest by the State. The right to hold specific employment and the right to follow a chosen profession free from unreasonable governmental interference come within the liberty and property interests protected by the Due Process Clause. The liberty interest at stake is the individual's freedom to practice his or her chosen profession; the property interest is the specific employment. When the State seeks to revoke or deny a professional license, these interests are implicated and procedural due process requirements must be met. The State must afford notice and the opportunity for a hearing appropriate to the nature of the case.

Where important decisions turn on questions of fact, due process requires an opportunity to confront and cross-examine adverse witnesses. Procedural due process often requires confrontation and cross-examination of one whose word deprives a person of his or her livelihood. Moreover, the evidence used to prove the State's case must be disclosed to the individual so that he or she has an opportunity to show it is untrue.

We hold Reg. 43–59 unconstitutional because it does not provide for notice and an opportunity to be heard when the State deprives a teacher of his or her teaching certificate. The fact that appellant was granted a hearing as a matter of favor in this case does not save the regulation from constitutional attack under the Due Process Clause. Further, the hearing appellant was granted did not comport with procedural due process since the Board did not disclose any evidence substantiating cancellation of the NTE scores in order to allow appellant the opportunity to contest the allegations against her.

The Board contends appellant cannot complain she was deprived of due process because she failed to avail herself of ETS procedure to contest the cancellation of her scores. On the record before us, however, ETS procedure does not provide for any hearing whereby appellant could confront her accusers. The Board further contends it could not obtain information from ETS regarding cancellation of appellant's scores absent her consent which she refused to give. The record, however, reveals no attempt by the Board to obtain information regarding cancellation of appellant's test scores from ETS.

* * *

REVERSED and REMANDED.

Notes

1. Was Regulation 43–59 invalidated because of an intrinsic flaw or because of the way it was here implemented?

2. Notice how the court describes the "right" of cross-examination of adverse witnesses.

3. Consider the educational, as well as legal, ramifications of a state's accepting a testing company's unamplified notification as a condition for disqualifying a public school teacher.

4. Why might ETS not have supplied information to the state board (if indeed it had been asked)?

[Case No. 71] Relation of Disabilities Legislation to Teacher Certification Requirements

PANDAZIDES v. VIRGINIA BD. OF EDUC.

United States Court of Appeals, Fourth Circuit, 1991.
946 F.2d 345.

OPINION

ERVIN, CHIEF JUDGE: This case involves a claim of handicap discrimination under § 504 of the Rehabilitation Act of 1973 (29 U.S.C. § 794; hereinafter § 504) by plaintiff Sofia Pandazides against the defendant Virginia Board of Education ("the Board"). The issue presented is whether the district court erred in granting summary judgment to the Board on Pandazides' claim of handicap discrimination and deciding that she was not "otherwise qualified" for the position of school teacher under § 504. Holding that the district court erred, we reverse.

I.

A.

Pandazides sued the Board alleging handicap discrimination under § 504 of the Rehabilitation Act of 1973. Pandazides was an applicant for professional teacher certification in Virginia. * * *

B.

Pandazides is a teacher who suffers from several learning disabilities. * * *

The Commonwealth of Virginia requires that prospective teachers pass the NTE Core Battery and any appropriate Specialty Area test of the NTE. * * *

Between June 1987 and October 1988, Pandazides took and failed the Communications Skills portion of the NTE six times. In January 1989, and by letter dated February 10, 1989, she requested that the Board exempt her from the requirement of having to pass that part of the NTE. On August 1, 1989, Pandazides wrote to the state Superintendent of Public Instruction requesting an exemption. Dr. Thomas A. Elliot, responding on behalf of the Superintendent, stated that notwithstanding Pandazides' documentation, the office was unable to grant an exemption. Meanwhile, Pandazides persuaded the Educational Testing Service ("ETS") to some extent to alter its testing procedure by providing her with a separate room, a script for the auditory portion of the test, a cassette player that played the tape at a slower pace, and 50 percent additional time. Taking the test under these conditions, Pandazides failed it twice. Pandazides' original and ongoing request is for ETS to allow her unlimited time to complete the test, to interact with the examiner, and to write out or talk about her answers.

The handicap that prevented Pandazides from passing the required NTE, of which the Skills test was one of three sections, was described by a clinical psychologist who specialized in the diagnosis and treatment of persons with learning disabilities. According to the doctor, she possessed the intelligence for teaching. Pandazides, nevertheless has three learning disabilities which meet the clinical standard for being considered handicapped. First, she suffers from "attentional defect disorder in the auditory modality," which limits her ability to input auditory information at the normal rate for a person of her age and intelligence. Second, Pandazides has "[d]ifficulty with the rapid integration of information from auditory and visual modalities," which adversely affects her ability to read quickly as would be the case on a standardized test. Third, she suffers from "dysnomia," which limits her ability to succinctly express a word or thought upon command. According to the pscyhologist Pandazides has developed "compensatory mechanisms to neutralize the impact of [her] disabilities" and has the ability to make herself understood by using examples and paraphrasing her thoughts. * * *

II.

The grant of summary judgment to the Board was based on what we believe to be a misreading of *Southeastern Community College v. Davis*. Specifically, the trial court read the statutory term "otherwise qualified" to mean that Pandazides would have to meet all the licensure requirements. According to the trial court, her failure to meet those requirements through her inability to pass the Communication Skills section of the NTE meant she was not otherwise qualified; thus, she was not

afforded the full protection of the statute. Alexander v. Choate, 469
U.S. 287, 105 S.Ct. 712, 83 L.Ed.2d 661 (1985) and School Board of
Nassau County, Florida v. Arline, 480 U.S. 273, 107 S.Ct. 1123, 94
L.Ed.2d 307 (1987), were decided subsequent to *Davis* to explicate its
"otherwise qualified" definition, and necessitate reversal of the district
court. The reasoning of the district court opinion and the dearth of
factual findings indicate that summary judgment was improper.

The section of the Rehabilitation Act of 1973 (29 U.S.C. § 794) at
issue prohibits recipients of federal assistance from discriminating
against a person on the basis of his handicap. Section 504 states:

> No otherwise qualified individual with handicaps * * * shall,
> solely by reason of his or her handicap, be excluded from the
> participation in, be denied the benefits of, or be subjected to
> discrimination under any program or activity receiving Federal
> financial assistance * * *.

The district court read the term "otherwise qualified" in light of
Davis. The trial court held, in effect, that because Pandazides was
unable to pass the test that she was not otherwise qualified. The
holding, in light of the language of only the *Davis* case, is not altogether
unreasonable.

In *Davis*, the Supreme Court decided whether or not Southeastern
Community College violated § 504 by denying a deaf student admission
to its nursing program. The Court held the college need not admit the
deaf student and that "[a]n otherwise qualified person is one who is able
to meet all of a program's requirements in spite of his handicap." The
term's denotative meaning, indicated in the blunt holding, seems to
suggest that the court need only ask whether the plaintiff met the
requirements to determine whether he was otherwise qualified. The
factual context of the holding, however, suggests a more expansive
connotative definition and a broader inquiry as well; both suggestions
are made explicit in *Arline* and *Alexander*. Relying on the extensive
factual findings of the district court, the Court examined the relationship
between the requirement, the ability to hear, and the performance of the
duties of a nurse. The Court noted that the respondent's handicap
actually prevented her from safely performing in both the training
program and her prospective profession. Moreover, the Court noted
that the inability to hear could pose a danger to future patients. Finally,
the Court noted that accommodations necessary to allow the deaf student to attend the college, a waiver of required courses in clinical
training and individual supervision by faculty members, would represent
"a fundamental alteration" in the college's program.

Throughout the *Davis* opinion the Court's concern about the attendant social and economic costs of admitting a student to a nursing
program who was wholly unable to perform was evident. When the
statutory definition is read against this factual backdrop, "otherwise
qualified" may be understood more in terms of the job rather than an
arbitrary set of requirements. Therefore, the trial court must do more
than simply determine whether or not Pandazides meets all of the

stipulated requirements of the Board, but look to what the position she seeks actually requires.

The necessary nexus between requirements and employment is described in *Arline*. The Supreme Court considered a claim similar to the instant case, namely that a plaintiff was denied employment as a teacher because of a handicap, a contagious disease. The Court stated that in determining whether someone is otherwise qualified for employment:

> the District Court will need to conduct an individualized inquiry and make appropriate findings of fact. Such an inquiry is essential if § 504 is to achieve its goal of protecting handicapped individuals from deprivations based on prejudice, stereotypes, or unfounded fear * * *.

> Accordingly, defendants cannot merely mechanically invoke any set of requirements and pronounce the handicapped applicant or prospective employee not otherwise qualified. The district court must look behind the qualifications. To do otherwise reduces the term "otherwise qualified" and any arbitrary set of requirements to a tautology.

Arline indicates that this is particularly true in the employment context, as opposed to the education setting of *Davis*. *Arline* appears to draw a distinction between a more exclusive definition of otherwise qualified in education, and a more inclusive meaning in employment. The Court stated:

> "An otherwise qualified person is one who is able to meet all of a program's requirements in spite of his handicap." *Southeastern Community College v. Davis*. In the employment context, an otherwise qualified person is one who can perform "the essential functions" of the job in question.

Thus, in the educational arena the facts of *Davis* regarding the prospective job after nursing training suggest a necessary relationship between requirements and the position. The definition of otherwise qualified, however, in the employment area explicitly mandates this relationship. As a consequence, a determination of whether Pandazides is otherwise qualified involves two factual determinations: first, whether she can perform the "essential functions" of a school teacher; and second, whether the requirements actually measure those functions. Even if the trial court were to determine that she could not perform her duties, it would also have to determine whether or not modifications could be made to allow Pandazides to teach.

The holding of *Alexander* makes the necessity of the latter determination clear. In *Alexander* the Court held:

> *Davis* thus struck a balance between the statutory rights of the handicapped to be integrated into society and the legitimate interests of federal grantees in preserving the integrity of their programs: while a grantee need not be required to make

"fundamental" or "substantial" modifications to accommodate the handicapped, it may be required to make "reasonable" ones.

The balance struck in *Davis* requires that an otherwise qualified individual must be provided with meaningful access to the benefit the grantee offers. *The benefit itself, of course, cannot be defined in a way that effectively denies the otherwise qualified handicapped individuals the meaningful access to which they are entitled; to assure meaningful access, reasonable accommodations in the grantee's program or benefit may have to be made.* (emphasis supplied).

Alexander recognizes that a job may be defined, through a refusal to make reasonable accommodations, in a way that precludes the participation of the handicapped.

A review of the district court opinion reveals that in the wake of its conclusion that Pandazides was not otherwise qualified, no factual determinations were made as to whether the NTE requirements represented the essential functions of the job, whether she could perform the essential functions of the position, and whether a test waiver was a reasonable accommodation. Consequently, there are many material facts in dispute and unaddressed by the opinion. Therefore, the granting of summary judgment in this stage of the proceeding was improper.

* * *

Notes

1. This opinion well integrates basic Supreme Court decisions related to employment of persons with handicapping conditions under the Rehabilitation Act of 1973 (and its extension, the Americans with Disabilities Act of 1990).

2. Bear in mind that the issue before the court was essentially procedural, not substantive.

3. In Alexander v. Choate, cited in the case, the Supreme Court upheld a state's reduction in annual inpatient hospital days paid for medicaid recipients that had been challenged under the Rehabilitation Act.

4. The NTE is important also in Cases No. 70 and No. 72.

[Case No. 72] National Teacher Examination as Certification Requirement

UNITED STATES v. STATE OF SOUTH CAROLINA

United States District Court, District of South Carolina, 1977.
445 F.Supp. 1094.

Before HAYNSWORTH and RUSSELL, CIRCUIT JUDGES and SIMONS, DISTRICT JUDGE.

Order

This is a decision * * * before a three-judge court.   * * *

The United States brought this action on September 15, 1975, against the State of South Carolina, the South Carolina State Board of

Education, the South Carolina State Retirement System, the South Carolina Budget and Control Board, and three local school boards in their individual capacities and as representatives of a defendant class of all local school boards in the State. The defendants are charged with violations of the Fourteenth Amendment to the Constitution of the United States and Title VII of the Civil Rights Act of 1964 through the use of minimum score requirements on the National Teacher Examinations (hereinafter "NTE") to certify and determine the pay levels of teachers within the State.

* * *

For over thirty years the State of South Carolina and its agencies have used scores on the NTE to make decisions with respect to the certification of teachers and the amount of state aid payable to local school districts. Local school boards within the State use scores on the NTE for selection and compensation of teachers. From 1969 to 1976, a minimum score of 975 was required by the State for its certification and state aid decisions. In June, 1976, after an exhaustive validation study by Educational Testing Service (ETS), and, after a critical review and evaluation of this study by the Board of Education's Committee on Teacher Recruitment, Training and Compensation and the Department Staff, the State established new certification requirements involving different minimum scores in various areas of teaching specialization that range from 940 to 1198. * * *

* * * [B]ut there are no uniform standards with respect to test scores used by the local school boards in selecting from among the pool of certified applicants.

Plaintiffs challenge each of the uses of the NTE. They contend that more blacks than whites historically have failed to achieve the required minimum score, and that this result creates a racial classification in violation of the constitutional and statutory provisions cited in their complaints. * * *

* * *

I. Constitutional Issues

We first consider whether the use by the State and its Board of Education of a minimum score requirement on the NTE violates the equal protection clause of the Fourteenth Amendment.

* * *

* * * Plaintiffs allege that the disparate racial impact of defendants' certification and compensation systems creates a racial classification in violation of the Fourteenth Amendment. In order to sustain that allegation, the Supreme Court's decision in Washington v. Davis requires plaintiffs to prove that the State intended to create and use a racial classification. If plaintiffs fail to prove intent (or defendants adequately rebut that proof), then we must evaluate this classification under the rational relationship standard required by the Fourteenth Amendment as to all such classifications.

A. Discriminatory Intent

Because of its paramount importance under Washington v. Davis, we look first at whether the plaintiffs have proved that any of the challenged decisions of defendants were motivated by an intent to discriminate. The purpose or intent that we must assess is the purpose or intent that underlies the particular act or acts under review. In its decision in Village of Arlington Heights v. Metropolitan Housing Development Corp., the Supreme Court suggested that evidence as to several factors might have probative value in proving intent: historical background, the sequence of events leading up to the challenged decision (including substantive and procedural departures from the norm), legislative history, and testimony from officials. * * *

1. Certification

South Carolina requires persons who teach in the public schools to hold a certificate issued by the State Board of Education. From 1945 to the present the State has had four certification systems, each requiring prospective teachers to take the NTE. Candidates are able to take the NTE an unlimited number of times. (The tests are given by the State three or four times each year).

The record before us indicates that during this period, the racial composition of the South Carolina teacher force has closely paralleled the racial composition of the State's population. * * *

From 1945 through 1968, the State issued four grades of certificates: A, B, C and D. From 1945 through 1956, candidates were awarded certificates based on their relative standing with respect to test scores of all candidates in the State for the year: A certificates went to the top 25%; B certificates to the middle 50%; C certificates to the next 15%; and D certificates to the bottom 10%. Under this system, every candidate who met the other requirements was licensed.

In 1957, a new system of absolute, rather than relative, requirements was instituted. Under this system, a score of 500 or more on the Common Examinations portion of the NTE was required for an A certificate; a score of 425 to 499 for a B certificate; a score of 375 to 424 for a C certificate; and a score of 332 to 374 for a D certificate. Those with scores below 332 were not licensed. During the academic year 1967–68, that restriction eliminated less than 1% of the candidates from predominantly white colleges and approximately 3% of the candidates from predominantly black colleges. The reason for these low percentages is that the 332 minimum score, when placed on the NTE score scale of 300 to 900 points, is very near the lowest attainable score.

In 1969, the certification system was further revised by replacing the four-tiered system with two types of certificates: the professional certificate and the warrant. The minimum score requirement was set at 975 for the professional certificate, including a score of at least 450 on the Common Examinations and at least 450 on the applicable Area Examination; and 850 for the warrant, including a score of at least 400 on the Common Examinations and 400 on the applicable Area Examination. Those who attained scores below 400 were not licensed. In the academic year 1969–70, the minimum score requirement of 400 on the Common Examinations eliminated approximately 41% of the graduates of predominantly black colleges and less than 1% of the graduates of predominantly white colleges. Similar results were obtained in succeeding years, despite the fact that a score of 400 is usually below the 11th percentile nationally, and almost 90% of the candidates who take these tests get a higher score.

In 1976, the certification system was again revised, the two-tiered system being replaced with a single certificate with separate minimum score requirements in each of the 18 fields of teaching specialty replacing the single minimum score requirement. These combined scores on both Common Examinations and Area Examinations ranged from 940 in Agriculture to 1178 in Library and Media Specialties; and are set forth in detail hereinafter. There are no statistics in the record indicating the impact of the new score requirements because they will be applied first to the class of 1977; however, plaintiffs predict that, under these requirements, the disparate impact may be even greater.

* * *

The 1945 decision: In 1941, a committee was appointed by the General Assembly to review the certification and compensation of teachers. The committee recommended that a thorough study of the certification system be made and suggested that the use of an NTE score requirement be explored because of the great variation in teacher training institutions. The State Board undertook a two-year study that resulted in a four-volume report, made available in 1944. That report recommended four different teacher credentials based on relative NTE scores. On the basis of the report, the State Board adopted the four-tiered system described above under which no candidate was denied licensing. At that time, South Carolina maintained a dual public school system with segregated student bodies and faculties. After the decision to institute the new certification system, but before its effective date, the State Board tested 50% of the teachers in the State, which revealed that 90% of the white teachers, and only 27% of the black teachers, would qualify for *A* or *B* certificates (the two top grades). The remaining candidates—10% of the whites and 73% of the blacks—would receive *C* and *D* certificates. After receiving these data, the State Board did not rescind its decision to institute the new certification system.

We are unable to find any discriminatory intent from these facts. Although the historical background of segregated schools might provide some basis for the inference urged by plaintiffs, any such inference has been rebutted. The committee based its recommendation concerning the NTE in part on its conclusion that the tests "can be scored objectively and impartially and their use would not be subject to the accusation that they are used for purposes of discrimination." The Board's extensive study is viewed as an earnest effort in its time, and provided reasonable support for its decision to institute an NTE requirement. The Board's knowledge of differential impact, without more, does not support a finding of discriminatory intent.

The 1956 decision: From 1945 through 1956, the State Board received from ETS statistical summaries of the test scores of South Carolina candidates showing that blacks as a group had lower average scores than whites as a group. In 1954 and 1955, the Supreme Court handed down its historic decisions in Brown v. Board of Education, which announced the end of the "separate but equal" rationale for segregated school systems. South Carolina did not thereafter integrate its schools, but instead adopted policies which maintained its dual school system until well into the 1960's. In 1956, the School Board adopted the absolute score system without a professional study relating the scores to effective teaching or academic achievement in the teacher preparation program.

Again, we find nothing in the record to support a finding of discriminatory intent. Plaintiffs have not persuaded the court that the State's reluctance to integrate its schools infected its decisions on teacher certification. The minimum score requirement of 332 was so low as to preclude us from presuming or even inferring that this was the case. Only 3% of the candidates from black colleges (and 1% of the candidates from white colleges) were denied certificates under this system during the last year it was in effect; and its effect in earlier years was not substantially different. The State Board did not move to change the system when it discovered that very few blacks were excluded, and significantly, this system was maintained for over 11 years.

The 1969 decision: From 1957 through 1969, the State Board continued to receive from ETS statistical data indicating disparate impact by race. During this period, the State continued to maintain its essentially dual school system through a variety of administrative measures. In 1968, the State Board received a report from a committee formed in 1967 to study the certification system. The committee included black and white members who were educators, teachers, state administrators and others. The committee had before it, *inter alia,* two documents, one which was critical of the NTE as a predictor of performance in student teaching, and the other which set out the ETS position that the test scores should not be used as a sole criterion for certification if other measures were available. The committee reviewed the academic programs and admission requirements at the State's 25 teacher training institutions and determined that not all had the same resources and strengths. The committee recommended that the minimum score levels be raised to 975 for professional certificates and 850 for warrants. From the data supplied by ETS, the committee would have been able to predict the impact of its recommendations on black teacher candidates as a group and on white candidates as a group (although it is unclear that such a prediction was ever made). The State Board adopted the committee's recommendations.

We are unable to find any intent to discriminate with respect to this decision. Plaintiffs offer no direct evidence of such an intent, even though one obvious source, the black members of the committee, was apparently available to them. The State's authority to re-define minimal competence from time to time cannot reasonably be questioned.

The 1976 decision: ETS urged that the State validate its cutoff score adopted in 1969. In 1971, ETS issued Guidelines that made its position clear. In the absence of any affirmative response by the State, in 1974 ETS announced its intention to cease the reporting of scores to South Carolina. In 1975, a three-judge court issued an interim decision in the case styled United States v. North Carolina, which required objective proof by the State of a rational relationship between the minimum score requirement on the NTE and the State's objective of certifying only minimally competent teachers. Shortly thereafter, the State Board authorized an extensive validity study which was conducted by ETS over a period of three months. The results of the study are set out in a two-volume, 300-page report, which was delivered to the State Board in January, 1976. The Board adopted the study report's recommendation that there be separate minimum score requirements by teaching field, and set new higher score levels based on the data produced by the study.

The 1976 decision carries a separate importance inasmuch as a finding with respect to it is the only basis for injunctive relief. Intent with respect to prior decisions is relevant only to damages. Plaintiffs offer no additional proof with respect to the defendants' alleged intent to discriminate in establishing the new certification requirements in 1976. They apparently rely on the cumulative historical background and the imminence of litigation with regard to the prior system. Even if we had found intent to discriminate with respect to one of the State's earlier decisions, this cumulative history would be without probative value as to the 1976 decision.

While historical circumstances may illuminate the purpose of a particular State action, recent events are far more probative than distant events. With the exception of the 1969 adoption of minimum cutoff scores, the "history" relied on by plaintiffs occurred over 20 years ago. Plaintiffs' elaborate web of historical circumstances, from which the court is being asked to infer discriminatory purpose, is noticeably silent about recent events. Significantly, the cases relied on by the Supreme Court in Village of Arlington Heights v. Metropolitan Housing Development Corp. and by plaintiffs in this case (for the proposition that historical circumstances do bear upon invidious purpose) involved events occurring within four years of the state act or decision under review.

With respect to the constitutional challenge to South Carolina's use of the NTE for certification purposes, we conclude that the plaintiffs have not demonstrated the required discriminatory intent with respect to any of the specific decisions setting certification standards based on NTE scores. This is especially true in connection with the State's 1976 change in requirements where there is no indication whatsoever that the State and its officers were motivated by anything more than a desire to use an accepted and racially neutral standardized test to evaluate the teacher applicants competing for relatively few jobs in South Carolina.

The NTE are developed and administered by ETS, an independent non-profit organization of recognized professional reputation. ETS recommends that minimum score requirements not be used as a sole determinant of certification decisions where other appropriate information or criteria are available.

In this case, the plaintiffs have come forth with no other reasonably appropriate criteria upon which certification may be properly based.

Neither have plaintiffs been able to establish any defect in the NTE indicating that the examinations themselves discriminate on the basis of race. The choices as to subject matter and question format are reasonable and well-documented on the record, and although other subject matters or other examination forms might be possible or even preferable, there is no proof of any inherent discrimination. The inference that plaintiffs would have us draw from the statistics which indicate that blacks as a group have lower average scores than whites is rebutted by the evidence with respect to the construction of the tests and their content validity. Since we find that the NTE create classifications only on permissible bases (presence or absence of knowledge or skill and ability in applying knowledge), and that they are not used pursuant to any intent to discriminate, their use in making certification decisions by the State is proper and legal.

2. Pay Scales

[A similar analysis led to a similar conclusion regarding pay scales based on level of certificate.] * * *

B. Application of Rational Relationship Standard

In the absence of discriminatory intent, the classifications of teachers for both certification and pay purposes may be assessed under the "rational relationship" standard required by the Fourteenth Amendment of all classifications.

The Supreme Court has defined this standard in the following terms:

> Although no precise formula has been developed, the Court has held that the Fourteenth Amendment permits the States a wide scope of discretion in enacting laws which affect some groups of citizens differently than others. The constitutional safeguard is offended only if the classification rests on grounds wholly irrelevant to the achievement of the State's objective. State legislatures are presumed to have acted within their constitutional power despite the fact that, in practice, their laws result in some inequality. A statutory discrimination will not be set aside if any state of facts reasonably may be conceived to justify it.

McGowan v. Maryland, 366 U.S. 420, 81 S.Ct. 1101, 6 L.Ed.2d 393 (1961).

We conclude that the State's use of the NTE for both certification and pay purposes meets the "rational relationship" standard of McGowan v. Maryland, supra, and consequently does not violate the equal protection clause of the Fourteenth Amendment. No more rigorous constitutional standard need be applied to a case which does not involve express differentiation by race of other "suspect" classification, and does not involve discriminatory intent. We find however, that were an intermediate standard applied, the defendants' use of the NTE bears a "fair and substantial relationship to the achievement of an important and constitutionally permissible governmental objective."

Nevertheless, we find that the defendants have offered a legitimate and important governmental objective for their use of the NTE. The State has the right to adopt academic requirements and to use written achievement tests designed and validated to disclose the minimum amount of knowledge necessary to effective teaching. The evidence in the record supports a finding that South Carolina officials were concerned with improving the quality of public school teaching, certifying only those applicants possessed of the minimum knowledge necessary to teach effectively, utilizing an objective measure of applicants coming from widely disparate teacher training programs, and providing appropriate financial incentives for teachers to improve their academic qualifications and thereby their ability to teach. We conclude that these are entirely legitimate and clearly important governmental objectives.

In considering whether defendants' use of the NTE bears a fair and substantial relationship to these governmental objectives, we conclude that it does.

The record supports the conclusion that the NTE are professionally and carefully prepared to measure the critical mass of knowledge in academic subject matter. The NTE do not measure teaching skills, but do measure the content of the academic preparation of prospective teachers. Like the test at issue in Washington v. Davis, supra, the NTE program "is neutral on its face and rationally may be said to serve a purpose the Government is constitutionally empowered to pursue." Plaintiffs have not contended nor proved that the NTE are racially biased or otherwise deficient when measured against the applicable professional and legal standards.

Furthermore, there is ample evidence in the record of the content validity of the NTE. The NTE have been demonstrated to provide a useful measure of the extent to which prospective teachers have mastered the content of their teacher training programs. The Supreme Court has held that a substantial relationship between a test and a training program—such as is found here—is sufficient to withstand challenge on constitutional grounds. Washington v. Davis. State officials surely have the right to require graduation from approved teacher training programs as a prerequisite to being certified to teach in South Carolina. Plaintiffs have acknowledged the substantial relationship between the academic training program and the job of teaching by advocating that a requirement of graduation from an approved program *alone* is sufficient to protect the public interest.

Also, the minimum score of 975 selected by South Carolina in 1969, and the range of scores selected in 1976 were permissible exercises of judgment by the responsible officials. In fact the minimum scores adopted by the State in 1976 are for the most part substantially lower than those recommended for adoption by ETS. As in Washington v. Davis, "there is no evidence that the required passing grade was set at an arbitrarily high level." The evidence supports the conclusion that the 975 score was selected in large part because it enabled the State to deny certification to only those who scored in the lowest 10% of all candidates taking the NTE throughout the United States; and that score reflected the judgment as to minimal competence of a committee of independent responsible professionals. Such exercise of judgment, although subjective and imperfect, may nonetheless serve to support a minimum test score requirement challenged on equal protection grounds. Although we agree that a professionally designed and executed validity study is not necessarily required to demonstrate the relationship between a challenged use of a test and the governmental objective for which it is being used, we find support for our conclusions with respect to the NTE in the validity study conducted in this case and discussed below in connection with our analysis of plaintiffs' contentions under Title VII.

* * *

II.   *Title VII Issues*

* * *

A.   Certification

Plaintiffs have proved that the use of NTE scores by the State in its certification decisions disqualifies substantially disproportionate numbers of blacks. The burden of proof was thereby shifted to the defendants, and in an effort to meet this burden the State commissioned an extensive validity study by ETS. The design of this study is novel, but consistent with the basic requirements enunciated by the Supreme Court, and we accordingly hold such study sufficient to meet the burden placed on defendants under Title VII.

The study seeks to demonstrate content validity by measuring the degree to which the content of the tests matches the content of the teacher training programs in South Carolina. It also seeks to establish a minimum score requirement by estimating the amount of knowledge (measured by the ability to answer correctly test questions that have been content validated) that a minimally qualified teacher candidate in South Carolina would have.

* * *

The design of the validity study is adequate for Title VII purposes. The Supreme Court made clear once again in Washington v. Davis that a content validity study that satisfies professional standards also satisfies Title VII. The defendants called as an expert witness Dr. Robert M. Guion, the principal author of Standards for Educational and Psychological Tests published by the American Psychological Association and a nationally recognized authority in the field of testing and measurement who testified in an unqualified fashion that in his expert opinion the ETS study design met all of the requirements of the APA Standards, the Division 14 Principles, and the EEOC Guidelines. Two other experts testified similarly, and ETS sought and obtained favorable opinions on the study design, before its implementation, from another two independent experts. The ETS decision to validate against the academic training program rather than job performance is specifically endorsed in principle in *Davis* * * *.

The principal issue raised by plaintiffs in attacking the validity study is whether the execution of the design was such that the results can be trusted. Plaintiffs deposed 81 of the 456 panel members selected at random and, on the basis of those depositions, claim that the panel members did not prepare for the tasks they were asked to undertake, and did not understand or follow the instructions.

Admittedly, there is a showing from these depositions which indicates some misunderstanding did exist; however, our review of these depositions shows that the misunderstandings were much less extensive than claimed by plaintiffs. When so many people are involved some misunderstanding and failure adequately to follow instructions are inevitable.

The new cutoff scores adopted by the State which are substantially below the scores recommended by ETS after completion of its validation study provide a substantial margin of error.

* * *

We find that the results of the validity study are sufficiently trustworthy to sustain defendants' burden under Title VII. First, the possible error rate was not high. Second, the key question is not whether some of the panel members failed to understand the instructions or for other reasons failed to follow the instructions, but whether they would have reached any different result if they had understood and followed the instructions. Plaintiffs misconceive their burden once defendants have made a reasonable showing that the study was executed in a responsible, professional manner designed to produce trustworthy results. In order to rebut the presumption that trustworthy results were indeed produced, plaintiffs must not only show that the study was not executed as intended, but also that the results were adversely affected.

* * *

There remains, however, the question whether the State has satisfied the "business necessity" requirement set out in Griggs v. Duke Power Co. This "business necessity" doctrine appears neither in the explicit language nor the legislative history of Title VII. * * *

We think that *Griggs* did not import into Title VII law the concept of "compelling interest" developed as a part of the "strict scrutiny" standard for assessing certain classifications under the Fourteenth Amendment. Under this concept, the Court would balance the disparate impact on blacks against the business purpose of the employer and uphold the business practice only if it were sufficiently "compelling" to overcome the disparate impact. It is our view that the Supreme Court intended an examination of the alternatives available with respect to the legitimate employment objective identified by the employer to determine whether there is available to the employer an alternative practice that would achieve his business purpose equally well but with a lesser disparate impact by race. In examining alternatives, the risk and cost to the employer are relevant.

Here, plaintiffs have suggested only one alternative to the use of the NTE for certification purposes. Plaintiffs contend that mere graduation from an approved program should be sufficient and would have a lesser disparate impact on blacks. We cannot find that this alternative will achieve the State's purpose in certifying minimally competent persons equally well as the use of a content-validated standardized test. The record amply demonstrates that there are variations in admissions requirements, academic standards and grading practices at the various teacher training institutions within the State. The approval that the State gives to the teacher training program is to general subject matter areas covered by the program, not to the actual course content of the program, and not to the means used within the program to measure whether individual students have actually mastered the course content to which they have been exposed. The standardized test scores do reflect individual achievement with respect to specific subject matter content, which is directly relevant to (although not sufficient in itself to assure) competence to teach, and thus the use of these scores for certification purposes survives the business necessity test under Title VII.

B. Pay Scales

There remains, finally, the question whether the uses of the NTE for salary purposes are a violation of Title VII. Where the salary system was linked to the certification system, some salary benefits were available only by improving the grade of the certificate; and that, in turn, could be done only by achieving certain minimum NTE scores. That system continued in effect after March 24, 1972, when Title VII was made applicable to states, and in 1976, the distribution of teachers within the four grades of the pay scale system showed a substantial disparate impact by race. A higher proportion of whites (98%) were classified in the two higher grades (A and B) and a higher proportion of blacks (51%) were classified in the lower grades (C and D). By such showing plaintiffs have satisfied their burden of proof under Title VII to shift the burden of proof to the defendants to show a rational relationship to a legitimate employment objective and to show business necessity. The State identifies its legitimate employment objective as providing an incentive for improvement, so that teachers without adequate knowledge to teach effectively will upgrade their capability; and the State offers the same evidence of a rational relationship between its pay scales and this objective as it did with respect to the constitutional challenges. We think that evidence is sufficient to establish the relationship.

We believe that a distinction for pay purposes between those who are qualified as well as between those who are not qualified survives the business necessity test. There appears to be no alternative available to the State, within reasonable limits of risk and cost, for providing the incentive necessary to motivate thousands of persons to acquire, generally on their own time and at their own expense, the necessary additional academic training so that they will be minimally competent teachers. Having made the investment of four years in an undergraduate education, it seems reasonable to try to upgrade the talent of unqualified teachers where possible, rather than rejecting them altogether.

* * *

Ordered that judgment be entered in favor of the defendants.

Notes

1. This judgment was affirmed summarily by a five-to-two vote of the Supreme Court. 434 U.S. 1026, 98 S.Ct. 756, 54 L.Ed.2d 775 (1978). Justices Marshall and Blackmun did not participate. Justices Brennan and White dissented, stating that summary affirmance was not warranted because the lower court in their view unduly extended the Washington v. Davis holding, and because they questioned its holding that no other measure would satisfy the state's interest in obtaining qualified teachers and paying them fairly when South Carolina was one of only three states using the NTE for initial certification and the only state to use it in determining pay, and when the ETS itself advises against using it for determining pay for experienced teachers or as the sole criterion for initial certification.

2. The 1969 certification requirement eliminated 41% of the candidates from predominantly black colleges and less than 1% of the candidates from predominantly white colleges. Effective desegregation was not far underway in the state at that time. The federal government in 1966 had begun to take action to cut off federal funds because of lack of progress in desegregation. How far should presumptions of innocent intent (good faith decision-making) be indulged in light of "circumstantial evidence"? How relevant to intent is the fact that some blacks were on the committee that recommended the 1969 change?

3. Do you think it likely that the predominantly black teacher education institutions had been "equal" while they were separate from the predominantly white ones? Do you think it likely they were "equal" at the time of the validation study?

4. If a state other than South Carolina instituted a certification plan like that approved here, would there be any basis to challenge it?

5. In 1992 the United States Supreme Court observed that one reason the state-operated universities in Mississippi remained predominantly identified by race was that they had different automatic-admission requirements based on scores achieved on the American College Testing Program examinations (ACT), which tests had a demonstrated disparate impact on blacks. Requiring higher scores for admission to historically white institutions restricted the range of choice of black students and was not justifiable on educational grounds. Indeed the testing agency discouraged use of the test as sole admission criterion. The Court emphasized that use of the tests had originally been for a discriminatory purpose in 1963. United States v. Fordice, ___ U.S. ___, 112 S.Ct. 2727, 120 L.Ed.2d 575 (1992).

[Case No. 73]   Discriminatory Initial Employment Practices

THOMAS v. WASHINGTON COUNTY SCHOOL BD.

United States Court of Appeals, Fourth Circuit, 1990.
915 F.2d 922.

BUTZNER, SENIOR CIRCUIT JUDGE: Patricia A. Thomas appeals a judgment of the district court that dismissed her action against the Washington County School Board, alleging racial discrimination in violation of Title VII of the Civil Rights Act of 1964. In her complaint Thomas sought remedies for two alleged violations of the Act: first, a teaching position and monetary relief for the Board's denial of employment and, second, injunctive relief to restrain the Board from continuing its hiring practices. We affirm the district court's dismissal of the hiring claim, vacate the judgment with respect to the omission of injunctive relief, and remand for further proceedings.

I

Thomas is a black woman who was raised and educated in Washington County, Virginia. She graduated *cum laude* from Emory & Henry College and shortly thereafter was certified by the Commonwealth of Virginia to teach social studies in secondary schools. In 1982, while in her final year of college, she applied for a teaching position in Washington County. Although she kept her application current, the Board failed to notify her of job openings on three separate occasions over a two year period. Those jobs were filled by white teachers.

One position was filled by someone more qualified than Thomas and another position was filled by someone transferring from another school within the county. It does not appear that there was any discrimination against Thomas in those instances. A third position, however, was filled by Mary Sue Smith, one of two white applicants interviewed for the position. Smith also graduated from Emory & Henry College with excellent grades, although not *cum laude*. She was the wife of a Washington County school teacher. She heard of the opening through word-of-mouth and was hired after having only one interview—the norm was three. Thomas heard of the vacancies after the Board filled them. She filed a complaint with the Equal Employment Opportunity Commission (EEOC) alleging racial discrimination. The EEOC issued a right to sue letter and this action followed.

The Board's evidence disclosed that Thomas's application was overlooked because the cover sheet indicated she had not yet been certified to teach. There was information within Thomas's file to indicate that she was certified, but apparently the file was not opened.

The district court found that the Board's failure to consider Thomas for the vacancies was a mistake rather than an act of intentional discrimination. This was a factual finding and is subject to review under a clearly erroneous standard. The court's finding of mistake was based largely on credibility determinations and is supported by the evidence. Consequently, it is binding upon us.

II

The district court did not grant Thomas's request for an injunction to require the Board to change its discriminatory hiring procedure. Instead the court admonished the Board:

> As a practical matter, however, the defendant should seriously consider plaintiff's application the next time a position in her field becomes vacant. The defendant was successful in this case primarily because it showed that it was ignorant of plaintiff's credentials and qualifications. Defendant now knows that plaintiff is a qualified teacher and cannot plead ignorance again. The defendant should remember that it is still subject to Title VII and act accordingly.

Although Thomas is presently teaching in nearby Tennessee, she is, as the district court recognized, a prospective applicant for a teaching position in Washington County. Consequently, she is entitled to hiring practices that conform to the requirements of Title VII.

The legal premise for Thomas's claim is sound. Congress enacted Title VII "to achieve equality of employment opportunities" through the removal of "artificial, arbitrary, and unnecessary barriers to employment when the barriers operate invidiously to discriminate on the basis of racial or other impermissible classification." *Griggs v. Duke Power Co.* *Griggs* held that a plaintiff need not prove intentional discrimination, for Title VII also proscribes "practices that are fair in form, but discriminatory in operation." "The necessary premise of the disparate impact approach is that some employment practices, adopted without a deliberately discriminatory motive, may in operation be functionally equivalent to intentional discrimination." *Watson v. Fort Worth Bank & Trust.*

The factual basis of Thomas's claim is disclosed by evidence that establishes that the Board has erected barriers that invidiously discriminate on the basis of race. The Washington County school system was desegregated in 1963. At that time there were six black elementary teachers. There remained six black elementary teachers and no black high school teachers until 1981 when Dennis Hill, following an EEOC complaint, was hired as a physical education teacher and coach for one of the high schools. He remained the only black high school teacher in the county schools. Apart from Hill, no black teacher was hired from 1975 until 1988, after this action was filed. In 1988, the superintendent, having learned that an elderly black teacher was retiring, requested Hill to recruit another black teacher. Wittingly or unwittingly, the Board has limited black teachers over the years to a rather rigid quota.

Between 1981 and 1988, at least 46 relatives of school employees were hired, including Smith. Notices of teaching vacancies are generally not advertised; they are posted in each school in the Washington County school system. Several black applicants testified that they learned of vacancies only after they had been filled. These policies and practices amount to nepotism and word-of-mouth hiring, which, in the context of a predominantly white work force, serve to freeze the effects of past discrimination.

Courts generally agree that, whatever the benefits of nepotism and word-of-mouth hiring, those benefits are outweighed by the goal of providing everyone with equal opportunities for employment. * * * Nepotism and word-of-mouth hiring constitute badges of discrimination in the context of a predominantly white work force.

Nepotism is not per se violative of Title VII. Given an already integrated work force, nepotism might have no impact on the racial composition of that work force. In such cases, nepotism, word-of-mouth hiring, and similar practices might simply amount to "bad acts" which discriminate against all outsiders without having any disparate impact on racial or religious minorities. "Title VII is not a 'bad acts' statute" and does not proscribe that type of discrimination. However, when the work force is predominantly white, nepotism and similar practices which operate to exclude outsiders may discriminate against minorities as effectively as any intentionally discriminatory policy.

Thomas proved the existence of "artificial, arbitrary, and unnecessary barriers to employment [that] operate invidiously to discriminate on the basis of racial * * * classifications." *Griggs.* Two of the Board's practices bear a causal relationship to her unsuccessful efforts to secure employment. They are the Board's practice of nepotism and the general practice of posting notice of vacancies only in the schools. Thomas did not learn of the vacancies until after they were filled. She is therefore entitled to injunctive relief to remedy these unlawful practices.

The district court's admonition, while well intentioned, fell short of affording the relief Title VII contemplates. * * * "The trial judge in a Title VII case bears a special responsibility in the public interest to resolve the employment dispute, for once the judicial machinery has been set in train, the proceeding takes on a public character in which remedies are devised to vindicate the policies of the Act, not merely to afford private relief to the employee." * * *

The district court quite properly found that Thomas did not offer sufficient statistical evidence to prove discrimination under the disparate impact theory by the means of statistics. The county's population is 98.2% white and 1.8% black. Black teachers constitute only .5% of the secondary schools' faculties. The Board's policy of generally limiting its pool of applicants to county residents, coupled with the lack of proof of the number of qualified applicants living in the county, other than Thomas, made the data base inadequate for statistical purposes. However, although disparate impact cases usually focus on statistics, they are neither the exclusive nor a necessary means of proof. The paucity of statistics is no bar to the prospective injunctive relief Thomas seeks, for Thomas has proved by other means that the Board's hiring practices have a disparate impact on minorities and violate Title VII. She produced evidence of at least 46 cases of nepotism, a stipulation from the Board which revealed a practice of posting vacancies in schools and offices with public notice only in exceptional circumstances, and testimony from other black applicants which indicated they were not being given an opportunity to compete for teaching jobs, largely because the Board's practices of nepotism and word-of-mouth hiring kept them unaware of job openings.

III

We affirm the district court's judgment insofar as it denies Thomas's claim that the Board intentionally discriminated against her when it failed to hire her.

Thomas has shown that as a prospective applicant she is entitled to injunctive relief to conform the Board's hiring policies to Title VII. We vacate the district court's judgment insofar as it dismisses her complaint and remand the case for further proceedings.

The district court is directed to fashion an injunction requiring the Board to publicly advertise vacancies and fill them by a selection process that is not influenced by race. The district court should also prohibit the Board from giving preference to relatives of employees. The court should prescribe any other conditions that it deems proper to achieve equality of employment opportunities without regard to race for all qualified applicants certified by the state. The court may limit the injunction to a reasonable number of years.

* * *

Notes

1. Contemplate that in this case the plaintiff was the catalyst for a substantial legal change in the practices of the school district (and probably in other districts also), yet she received no personalized tangible benefit. (See note 5 below.)

2. The appellate court's requirement that an injunction be issued would put teeth into the general "admonition" of the trial judge. An injunction would mandate specifics and be enforceable in court.

3. Is there professional support for the hiring policies practiced here? The courts cannot intervene unless the result of "bad acts" conflicts with constitutional or statutory mandates.

4. The last two paragraphs of Part I are of critical import. Observe the procedural points. In 1985 the Supreme Court had emphasized them for the federal courts. Anderson v. Bessemer City, 470 U.S. 564, 105 S.Ct. 1504, 84 L.Ed.2d 518 (1985).

5. The Civil Rights Act of 1991 authorized courts to award damages, both compensatory and punitive, to persons discriminated against in violation of Title VII. Title VII had previously provided only remedies of injunctions and lost pay to correct unlawful actions. Do you think Thomas could have demonstrated damages due to, say, emotional distress as a result of the board's actions, or that the board could have been subject to punitive damages for its actions?

[Case No. 74]   Constitutionality of Maternity Leave Provisions

CLEVELAND BD. OF EDUC. v. LAFLEUR

COHEN v. CHESTERFIELD COUNTY SCHOOL BD.

Supreme Court of the United States, 1974.
414 U.S. 632, 94 S.Ct. 791, 39 L.Ed.2d 52.

Mr. Justice Stewart delivered the opinion of the Court.

The respondents in [Cleveland Board of Education] and the petitioner in [Cohen] are female public school teachers. During the 1970–71 school year, each informed her local school board that she was pregnant; each was compelled by a mandatory maternity leave rule to quit her job without pay several months before the expected birth of her child. These cases call upon us to decide the constitutionality of the school boards' rules.

I

* * *

We granted certiorari in both cases in order to resolve the conflict between the Courts of Appeals regarding the constitutionality of such mandatory maternity leave rules for public school teachers.

II

This Court has long recognized that freedom of personal choice in matters of marriage and family life is one of the liberties protected by the Due Process Clause of the Fourteenth Amendment. * * * [T]here is a right "to be free from unwarranted governmental intrusion into matters so fundamentally affecting a person as the decision whether to bear or beget a child."

By acting to penalize the pregnant teacher for deciding to bear a child, overly restrictive maternity leave regulations can constitute a heavy burden on the exercise of these protected freedoms. Because public school maternity leave rules directly affect "one of the basic civil rights of man," the Due Process Clause of the Fourteenth Amendment requires that such rules must not needlessly, arbitrarily, or capriciously impinge upon this vital area of a teacher's constitutional liberty. The question before us in these cases is whether the interests advanced in support of the rules of the Cleveland and Chesterfield County School Boards can justify the particular procedures they have adopted.

The school boards in these cases have offered two essentially overlapping explanations for their mandatory maternity leave rules. First, they contend that the firm cut-off dates are necessary to maintain continuity of classroom instruction, since advance knowledge of when a pregnant teacher must leave facilitates the finding and hiring of a qualified substitute. Secondly, the school boards seek to justify their maternity rules by arguing that at least some teachers become physically incapable of adequately performing certain of their duties during the latter part of pregnancy. By keeping the pregnant teacher out of the classroom during these final months, the maternity leave rules are said to protect the health of the teacher and her unborn child, while at the same time assuring that students have a physically capable instructor in the classroom at all times.

It cannot be denied that continuity of instruction is a significant and legitimate educational goal. Regulations requiring pregnant teachers to provide early notice of their condition to school authorities undoubtedly facilitate administrative planning toward the important objective of continuity. But, * * *:

> "Where a pregnant teacher provides the Board with a date certain for commencement of leave * * * that value [continuity] is preserved; * * *." * * *

Thus, while the advance notice provisions in the Cleveland and Chesterfield County rules are wholly rational and may well be necessary to serve the objective of continuity of instruction, the absolute requirements of termination at the end of the fourth or fifth month of pregnancy are not. Were continuity the only goal, cut-off dates much later during pregnancy would serve as well or better than the challenged rules, providing that ample advance notice requirements were retained. Indeed, continuity would seem just as well attained if the teacher herself were allowed to choose the date upon which to commence her leave, at least so long as the decision were required to be made and notice given of it well in advance of the date selected.

In fact, since the fifth or sixth months of pregnancy will obviously begin at different times in the school year for different teachers, the present Cleveland and Chesterfield County rules may serve to hinder attainment of the very continuity objectives that they are purportedly designed to promote. For example, the beginning of the fifth month of pregnancy for both Mrs. LaFleur and Mrs. Nelson [another Cleveland teacher] occurred during March of 1971. Both were thus required to leave work with only a few months left in the school year, even though both were fully willing to serve through the end of the term. Similarly, if continuity were the only goal, it seems ironic that the Chesterfield County rule forced Mrs. Cohen to leave work in mid-December 1970 rather than at the end of the semester in January, as she requested.

We thus conclude that the arbitrary cut-off dates embodied in the mandatory leave rules before us have no rational relationship to the valid state interest of preserving continuity of instruction. As long as the teacher is required to give substantial advance notice of her condition, the choice of firm dates later in pregnancy would serve the boards' objectives just as well, while imposing a far lesser burden on the women's exercise of constitutionally protected freedom.

The question remains as to whether the fifth and sixth month cut-off dates can be justified on the other ground advanced by the school boards—the necessity of keeping physically unfit teachers out of the classroom. There can be no doubt that such an objective is perfectly legitimate, both on educational and safety grounds. And, despite the plethora of conflicting medical testimony in these cases, we can assume *arguendo* that at least some teachers become physically disabled from effectively performing their duties during the latter stages of pregnancy.

The mandatory termination provisions of the Cleveland and Chesterfield County rules surely operate to insulate the classroom from the presence of potentially incapacitated pregnant teachers. But the question is whether the rules sweep too broadly. That question must be answered in the affirmative, for the provisions amount to a conclusive presumption that every pregnant teacher who reaches the fifth or sixth month of pregnancy is physically incapable of continuing. There is no individualized determination by the teacher's doctor—or the school board's—as to any particular teacher's ability to continue at her job. The rules contain an irrebuttable presumption of physical incompetency, and that presumption applies even when the medical evidence as to an individual woman's physical status might be wholly to the contrary.

As the Court noted last Term in Vlandis v. Kline, "permanent irrebuttable presumptions have long been disfavored under the Due Process Clause of the Fifth and Fourteenth Amendments." * * *

* * *

* * * While the medical experts in these cases differed on many points, they unanimously agreed on one—the ability of any particular pregnant woman to continue at work past any fixed time in her pregnancy is very much an individual matter. Even assuming *arguendo* that there are some women who would be physically unable to work past the particular cut-off dates embodied in the challenged rules, it is evident that there are large numbers of teachers who are fully capable of continuing work for longer than the Cleveland and Chesterfield County regulations will allow. Thus, the conclusive presumption embodied in these rules * * * is neither "necessarily nor universally true," and is violative of the Due Process Clause.

The school boards have argued that the mandatory termination dates serve the interest of administrative convenience, since there are many instances of teacher pregnancy, and the rules obviate the necessity for case-by-case determinations. Certainly, the boards have an interest in devising prompt and efficient procedures to achieve their legitimate objectives in this area. But, * * *:

"[T]he Constitution recognizes higher values than speed and efficiency. * * *."

While it might be easier for the school boards to conclusively presume that all pregnant women are unfit to teach past the fourth or fifth month or even the first month, of pregnancy, administrative convenience alone is insufficient to make valid what otherwise is a violation of due process of law. (This is not to say that the only means for providing appropriate protection for the rights of pregnant teachers is an individualized determination in each case and in every circumstance. We are not dealing in these cases with maternity leave regulations requiring a termination of employment at some firm date during the last few weeks of pregnancy. We therefore have no occasion to decide whether such regulations might be justified by considerations not presented in these records—for example, widespread medical consensus about the "disabling" effect of pregnancy on a teacher's job performance during these latter days, or evidence showing that such firm cutoffs were the only reasonable method of avoiding the possibility of labor beginning while some teacher was in the classroom, or proof that adequate substitutes could not be procured without at least some minimal lead time and certainty as to the dates upon which their employment was to begin.) The Fourteenth Amendment requires the school boards to employ alternative administrative means, which do not so broadly infringe upon basic constitutional liberty, in support of their legitimate goals.

We conclude, therefore, that neither the necessity for continuity of instruction nor the state interest in keeping physically unfit teachers out of the classroom can justify the sweeping mandatory leave regulations that the Cleveland and Chesterfield County School Boards have adopted. While the regulations no doubt represent a good-faith attempt to achieve a laudable goal, they cannot pass muster under the Due Process Clause of the Fourteenth Amendment, because they employ irrebuttable presumptions that unduly penalize a female teacher for deciding to bear a child.

III

In addition to the mandatory termination provisions, both the Cleveland and Chesterfield County rules contain limitations upon a teacher's eligibility to return to work after giving birth. Again, the school boards offer two justifications for the return rules—continuity of instruction and the desire to be certain that the teacher is physically competent when she returns to work. As is the case with the leave provisions, the question is not whether the school board's goals are legitimate, but rather whether the particular means chosen to achieve those objectives unduly infringe upon the teachers' constitutional liberty.

Under the Cleveland rule, the teacher is not eligible to return to work until the beginning of the next regular school semester following the time when her child attains the age of three months. A doctor's certificate attesting to the teacher's health is required before return; an additional physical examination may be required at the option of the school board.

The respondents in [Cleveland Board of Education] do not seriously challenge either the medical requirements of the Cleveland rule or the policy of limiting eligibility to return to the next semester following birth. The provisions concerning a medical certificate or supplemental physical examination are narrowly drawn methods of protecting the school board's interest in teacher fitness; these requirements allow an individualized decision as to the teacher's condition, and thus avoid the pitfalls of the presumptions inherent in the leave rules. Similarly, the provision limiting eligibility to return to the semester following delivery is a precisely drawn means of serving the school board's interest in avoiding unnecessary changes in classroom personnel during any one school term.

The Cleveland rule, however, does not simply contain these reasonable medical and next-semester eligibility provisions. In addition, the school board requires the mother to wait until her child reaches the age of three months before the return rules begin to operate. The school boards have offered no reasonable justification for this supplemental limitation, and we can perceive none. To the extent that the three-month provision reflects the school board's thinking that no mother is fit to return until that point in time, it suffers from the same constitutional deficiencies that plague the irrebuttable presumption in the termination rules. The presumption, moreover, is patently unnecessary, since the requirement of a physician's certificate or a medical examination fully protects the school's interests in this regard. And finally, the three-month provision simply has nothing to do with continuity of instruction, since the precise point at which the child will reach the relevant age will obviously occur at a different point throughout the school year for each teacher.

Thus, we conclude that the Cleveland return rule, insofar as it embodies the three-month age provision, is wholly arbitrary and irrational, and hence violates the Due Process Clause of the Fourteenth Amendment. The age limitation serves no legitimate state interest, and unnecessarily penalizes the female teacher for asserting her right to bear children.

We perceive no such constitutional infirmities in the Chesterfield County rule. In that school system, the teacher becomes eligible for reemployment upon submission of a medical certificate from her physician; return to work is guaranteed no later than the beginning of the next school year following the eligibility determination. The medical certificate is both a reasonable and narrow method of protecting the school board's interest in teacher fitness, while the possible deferring of return until the next school year serves the goal of preserving continuity of instruction. In short, the Chesterfield County rule manages to serve the legitimate state interests here without employing unnecessary presumptions that broadly burden the exercise of protected constitutional liberty.

IV

For the reasons stated, we hold that the mandatory termination provisions of the Cleveland and Chesterfield County maternity regulations violate the Due Process Clause of the Fourteenth Amendment, because of their use of unwarranted conclusive presumptions that seriously burden the exercise of protected constitutional liberty. For similar reasons, we hold the three-month provision of the Cleveland return rule unconstitutional.

* * *

Notes

1. Justices Burger and Rehnquist dissented.

2. "Old" cases in state courts had uniformly sustained such provisions as were here invalidated. In the early 1970's there had been conflict among Courts of Appeals on maternity leave problems. What problems remain for resolution in future cases in the subject area?

3. Note that the Court did not accept as the constitutional standard that time of beginning and ending leave is completely up to the teacher and her physician.

4. To what extent is this decision a reflection of women's rights; of changing mores; of students being more sophisticated?

5. See the Appendix for the Pregnancy Discrimination Act of 1978. This was an amendment to Title VII of the Civil Rights Act of 1964.

[Case No. 75]   Right of Teacher to Breastfeed Baby during Duty-Free Period

DIKE v. SCHOOL BD. OF ORANGE COUNTY, FLORIDA

United States Court of Appeals, Fifth Circuit, 1981.
650 F.2d 783.

GODBOLD, CHIEF JUDGE: Janice Dike, a teacher in the Orange County (Florida) School System, sued the school board and the superintendent of schools under 42 U.S.C. § 1983, challenging the board's refusal to permit her to breastfeed her child during her duty-free lunch period. Dike alleged that she could breastfeed the child in privacy without any disruption of school activities. She also alleged that breastfeeding was necessary to her child's health. She sought to characterize breastfeeding as a constitutional right with which the school board had unduly interfered. The district court dismissed the complaint * * *. We reverse the dismissal * * *.

I. BACKGROUND

For the purpose of assessing the dismissal of the complaint for failure to state a claim, we regard the plaintiff's allegations as true. Our discussion of the case is therefore based on her assertions.

Dike is employed by the school board as a kindergarten teacher at an elementary school. After giving birth to her child she returned to her teaching post. Having chosen to breastfeed her child, Dike wished to feed the child in this manner at all feedings, including the one feeding necessary during the school day. She sought a means of doing so that would not disrupt the education of children attending the school or interfere with her discharge of work responsibilities.

Dike therefore arranged for her husband or her babysitter to bring the child to school during her lunch period, when she was free from any duties. Dike would then nurse the child in privacy in a locked room into which other persons could not see. On occasions when the school asked Dike to perform duties during her lunch period she would hand the infant to her husband or babysitter. She was thus always available for work even during her duty-free hour. She alleges that this routine did not disrupt the educational process at the school or her work performance.

After three months of this routine without disruption or incident the school principal directed Dike to stop nursing her child on campus, citing a school board directive prohibiting teachers from bringing their children to work with them for any reason. The rule's stated rationale is to avoid possible disruptions by the children of teachers and to avoid the possibility of the children having an accident and subjecting the school board to litigation. The principal threatened disciplinary action should Dike continue to nurse the child at school.

Dike heeded these warnings and stopped nursing her child during the school day. But because the child developed an allergic reaction to formula milk, Dike had to artificially extract milk with a breast pump and leave it for the child's mid-day feeding. Dike asserts this new routine caused the child to develop observable psychological changes that also affected her own emotional well-being. She requested permission to resume her earlier procedure, alternatively requesting permission to nurse the child off campus during her non-duty time or to nurse the child in her camper van in the school parking lot. The school board denied these requests, apparently relying on another policy prohibiting teachers from leaving school premises during the school day.

A short time later the infant began refusing to nurse from a bottle. Dike thus had no choice but to breastfeed the child. Because the school board denied her permission to breastfeed on campus or off, Dike was compelled to take an unpaid leave of absence for the remainder of the school term.

* * *

II. ANALYSIS

Our evaluation of plaintiff's claim proceeds in two steps. First, we consider whether her interest in nurturing her child by breastfeeding is entitled in some circumstances to constitutional protection against state infringement. We hold that it is. But a second inquiry, equally critical, concerns the justifications that the school board may have for restricting its employees' exercise of such a right during the work day. We recognize that the school board has legitimate interests in, for example, preventing disruption of the educational process and preventing interference with teachers' efficient performance of their duties.

We conclude that the complaint should not have been dismissed because Dike's interest in breastfeeding during her non-duty time and the school board's interests can only be properly evaluated after factfinding.

1. Nature of the Plaintiff's Interest

The Constitution protects from undue state interference citizens' freedom of personal choice in some areas of marriage and family life.

These protected interests have been described as rights of personal privacy or as "fundamental" personal liberties. While the opinions of the Court have linked these rights to various constitutional provisions, their existence is now an established part of our constitutional jurisprudence.

Among these protected liberties are individual decisions respecting marriage, procreation, contraception, abortion, and family relationships. The Supreme Court has long recognized that parents' interest in nurturing and rearing their children deserves special protection against state interference. * * *

Breastfeeding is the most elemental form of parental care. It is a communion between mother and child that, like marriage, is "intimate to the degree of being sacred." Nourishment is necessary to maintain the child's life, and the parent may choose to believe that breastfeeding will enhance the child's psychological as well as physical health. In light of the spectrum of interests that the Supreme Court has held specially protected we conclude that the Constitution protects from excessive state interference a woman's decision respecting breastfeeding her child.

   2. Justifications for the Regulations

Our conclusion that Dike's interest in breastfeeding is a protected liberty interest, however, is the beginning rather than the end of the constitutional inquiry. We reverse because a complaint should not be dismissed for failure to state a claim unless it appears beyond doubt that the plaintiff can prove no set of facts in support of her claim that would entitle her to relief, and because the district court's dismissal rests on the erroneous premise that no specially protected interest is involved. But this does not mean that the school board's restrictions on the exercise of this liberty in the employment context are necessarily constitutionally invalid. The Constitution does not prohibit all restrictions of protected liberties, and the school board may establish by appropriate pleading and proof that its regulations prohibiting teachers from leaving campus or bringing children to school, as applied to teachers who wish to breastfeed their children during non-duty time, further sufficiently important state interests and are closely tailored to effectuate only those interests. * * * The school board's interests in avoiding disruption of the educational process, in ensuring that teachers perform their duties without distraction, and in avoiding potential liability for accidents are presumably legitimate. Whether these or other interests are strong enough to justify the school board's regulations, and whether the regulations are sufficiently narrowly drawn, must be determined at trial.

* * *

Reversed.

Notes

   1. Bear in mind that the question before the Court of Appeals was whether the District Court properly prevented the case from proceeding to trial. The

truth of the allegations was assumed, and the weighing of the competing interests (the merits) was not reached.

2. On their faces, do you find each of the two board rules invoked to be rational? Does your answer change if the rules are viewed as a pair? (It was through the pair of rules that Janice Dike was boxed in.)

3. Do you believe the school authorities administered the rules (1) as they were intended; (2) with wisdom; (3) with compassion?

4. Do you believe the case would have been decided the same way if there were no medical considerations and breastfeeding was only a preference of Janice Dike?

[Case No. 76] Constitutionality of Professional Growth Requirement for Teachers

HARRAH INDEPENDENT SCHOOL DIST. v. MARTIN

Supreme Court of the United States, 1979.
440 U.S. 194, 99 S.Ct. 1062, 59 L.Ed.2d 248.

PER CURIAM. Respondent Martin was employed as a teacher by petitioner School District under a contract that incorporated by reference the School Board's rules and regulations. Because respondent was tenured, Oklahoma law required the School Board to renew her contract annually unless she was guilty of, among other things, "wilful neglect of duty." The same Oklahoma statute provided for hearing and appeal procedures in the event of nonrenewal. One of the regulations incorporated into respondent's contract required teachers holding only a bachelor's degree to earn five semester hours of college credit every three years. Under the terms of the regulation, noncompliance with the continuing-education requirement was sanctioned by withholding salary increases.

Respondent, hired in 1969, persistently refused to comply with the continuing-education requirement and consequently forfeited the increases in salary to which she would have otherwise been entitled during the 1972–1974 school years. After her contract had been renewed for the 1973–1974 school term, however, the Oklahoma Legislature enacted a law mandating certain salary raises for teachers regardless of the compliance with the continuing-education policy. The School Board, thus deprived of the sanction which it had previously employed to enforce the provision, notified respondent that her contract would not be renewed for the 1974–1975 school year unless she completed five semester hours by April 10, 1974. Respondent nonetheless declined even to enroll in the necessary courses and, appearing before the Board in January 1974, indicated that she had no intention of complying with the requirement in her contract. Finding her persistent noncompliance with the continuing-education requirement "wilful neglect of duty," the Board voted at its April 1974 meeting not to renew her contract for the following school year. * * *

* * *

The School District has conceded at all times that respondent was a "tenured" teacher under Oklahoma law, and therefore could be dismissed only for specified reasons. She was accorded the usual elements of procedural due process. * * *

* * * [R]espondent's claim is simply that she, as a tenured teacher, cannot be discharged under the School Board's purely prospective rule establishing contract nonrenewal as the sanction for violations of the continuing-education requirement incorporated into her contract.

The School Board's rule is endowed with a presumption of legislative validity, and the burden is on respondent to show that there is no rational connection between the Board's action and its conceded interest in providing its students with competent, well-trained teachers. Respondent's claim that the Board acted arbitrarily in imposing a new penalty for noncompliance with the continuing-education requirement simply does not square with the facts. By making pay raises mandatory, the state legislature deprived the Board of the sanction that it had earlier used to enforce its teachers' contractual obligation to earn continuing-education credits. The Board thus turned to contract nonrenewal, but applied this sanction purely prospectively so that those who might have relied on its past practice would nonetheless have an opportunity to bring themselves into compliance with the terms of the contracts. * * *

* * *

The School District's concern with the educational qualifications of its teachers cannot under any reasoned analysis be described as impermissible, and respondent does not contend that the Board's continuing-education requirement bears no rational relationship to that legitimate governmental concern. Rather, respondent contests "the permissibility of the classification by which [she] and three other teachers were required to achieve [by April 1974] the number of continuing education credits that all other teachers were given three years to achieve."

The Board's objective in sanctioning violations of the continuing-education requirement was, obviously, to encourage future compliance with the requirement. Admittedly, imposition of a penalty for noncompliance placed respondent and three other teachers in a "class" different from those teachers who had complied with their contractual obligations in the past. But any sanction designed to enforce compliance with a valid rule, whatever its source, falls only on those who break the rule. Respondent and those in her "class" were the only teachers immediately affected by the Board's action because they were the only teachers who had previously broken their contractual obligation. * * *

That the Board was forced by the state legislature in 1974 to penalize noncompliance differently than it had in the past in no way alters the equal protection analysis of respondent's claim. Like all teachers employed in the School District, respondent was given three years to earn five continuing-education credits. Unlike most of her colleagues, however, respondent refused to comply with the requirement, thus forfeiting her right to routine pay raises. Had the legislature not mandated salary increases in 1974, the Board presumably would have penalized respondent's continued refusal to comply with the terms of her contract by denying her an increase in salary for yet another year. The Board, having been deprived by the legislature of the sanction previously employed to enforce the continuing-education requirement, merely substituted in its place another, albeit more onerous, sanction. The classification created by both sanctions, however, was between those who had acquired five continuing-education credits within the allotted time and those who had not.

At bottom, respondent's position is that she is willing to forgo routine pay raises, but she is not willing to comply with the continuing-education requirement or to give up her job. The constitutional permissibility of a sanction imposed to enforce a valid governmental rule, however, is not tested by the willingness of those governed by the rule to accept the consequences of noncompliance. The sanction of contract nonrenewal is quite rationally related to the Board's objective of enforcing the continuing education obligation of its teachers. Respondent was not, therefore, deprived of equal protection of the laws.

The petition for certiorari is granted, and the judgment of the Court of Appeals is

Reversed.

Notes

1. This was a unanimous reversal of the Tenth Circuit Court of Appeals. In parts of the opinion not included here, the Supreme Court was critical of the lower court's reasoning, which it described as being based on "an amalgam" of constitutional guarantees.

2. Do you think Martin should have been given more time to meet the requirement that she had "persistently" flaunted? Observe that that point was argued in her behalf. Also observe that the Court notes that she "declined even to enroll" in courses, and in January said she did not intend to comply.

3. It had long been regarded as settled that reasonable inservice requirements could be made conditions of employment for teachers [e.g., Last v. Board of Educ. of Community Unit School Dist. No. 321, 37 Ill.App.2d 159, 185 N.E.2d 282 (1962)], and professional associations had long advocated increased training for teachers. Do you think the cause of education was advanced by the National Education Association's legal support of Martin's position?

4. An inability to adapt to current instructional procedures was held to be a cause for discharging a tenure teacher with twenty years of service. The school system was eliminating self-contained classrooms in a curriculum revision. Jennings v. Caddo Parish School Bd., 276 So.2d 386 (La.App.1973).

[Case No. 77] Procedural Due Process for Nontenure Teachers Who Are Not Reappointed, I

BOARD OF REGENTS OF STATE COLLEGES v. ROTH

Supreme Court of the United States, 1972.
408 U.S. 564, 92 S.Ct. 2701, 33 L.Ed.2d 548.

MR. JUSTICE STEWART delivered the opinion of the Court.

In 1968 the respondent, David Roth, was hired for his first teaching job as assistant professor of political science at Wisconsin State University-Oshkosh. He was hired for a fixed term of one academic year. The notice of his faculty appointment specified that his employment would begin on September 1, 1968, and would end on June 30, 1969. The respondent completed that term. But he was informed that he would not be rehired for the next academic year.

The respondent had no tenure rights to continued employment. * * * There are no statutory or administrative standards defining eligibility for re-employment. State law thus clearly leaves the decision whether to rehire a nontenured teacher for another year to the unfettered discretion of University officials.

* * *

The respondent * * * brought this action in a federal district court alleging that the decision not to rehire him for the next year infringed his Fourteenth Amendment rights. He attacked the decision both in substance and procedure. First, he alleged that the true reason for the decision was to punish him for certain statements critical of the University administration, and that it therefore violated his right to freedom of speech. Second, he alleged that the failure of University officials to give him notice of any reason for nonretention and an opportunity for a hearing violated his right to procedural due process of law.

* * * The only question presented to us at this stage in the case is whether the respondent had a constitutional right to a statement of reasons and a hearing on the University's decision not to rehire him for another year. We hold that he did not.

I

The requirements of procedural due process apply only to the deprivation of interests encompassed within the Fourteenth Amendment's protection of liberty and property. When protected interests are implicated the right to some kind of prior hearing is paramount. But the range of interests protected by procedural due process is not infinite.

* * * [T]o determine whether due process requirements apply in the first place, we must look not to the "weight" but to the *nature* of the interest at stake. We must look to see if the interest is within the Fourteenth Amendment's protection of liberty and property.

* * *

Yet, while the Court has eschewed rigid or formalistic limitations on the protection of procedural due process, it has at the same time observed certain boundaries. For the words "liberty" and "property" in the Due Process Clause of the Fourteenth Amendment must be given some meaning.

II

"While this Court has not attempted to define with exactness the liberty * * * guaranteed [by the Fourteenth Amendment] the term has received much consideration, and some of the included things have been definitely stated. Without doubt, it denotes not merely freedom from bodily restraint but also the right of the individual to contract, to engage in any of the common occupations of life, to acquire useful knowledge, to marry, establish a home and bring up children, to worship God according to the dictates of his own conscience, and generally to enjoy those privileges long recognized * * * as essential to the orderly pursuit of happiness by free men." In a Constitution for a free people, there can be no doubt that the meaning of "liberty" must be broad indeed.

There might be cases in which a State refused to re-employ a person under such circumstances that interests in liberty would be implicated. But this is not such a case.

The State, in declining to rehire the respondent, did not make any charge against him that might seriously damage his standing and associations in his community. It did not base the nonrenewal of his contract on a charge, for example, that he had been guilty of dishonesty, or immorality. Had it done so, this would be a different case. For "[w]here a person's good name, reputation, honor or integrity is at stake because of what the government is doing to him, notice and an opportunity to be heard are essential." In such a case, due process would accord an opportunity to refute the charge before University officials. (The purpose of such notice and hearing is to provide the person an opportunity to clear his name. Once a person has cleared his name at a hearing, his employer, of course, may remain free to deny him future employment for other reasons.) In the present case, however there is no suggestion whatever that the respondent's interest in his "good name, reputation, honor or integrity" is at stake.

Similarly, there is no suggestion that the State, in declining to re-employ the respondent, imposed on him a stigma or other disability that foreclosed his freedom to take advantage of other employment opportunities. The State, for example, did not invoke any regulations to bar the respondent from all other public employment in State universities. Had it done so, this, again, would be a different case. For "[t]o be deprived not only of present government employment but of future opportunity for it is no small injury * * *." The Court has held, for example, that a State, in regulating eligibility for a type of professional employment, cannot foreclose a range of opportunities "in a manner * * * that contravene[s] * * * due process," and, specifically, in a manner that denies the right to a full prior hearing. In the present case, however, this principle does not come into play.

To be sure, the respondent has alleged that the nonrenewal of his contract was based on his exercise of his right to freedom of speech. But this allegation is not now before us. The District Court stayed proceedings on this issue, and the respondent has yet to prove that the decision not to rehire him was, in fact, based on his free speech activities.

Hence, on the record before us, all that clearly appears is that the respondent was not rehired for one year at one University. It stretches the concept too far to suggest that a person is deprived of "liberty" when he simply is not rehired in one job but remains as free as before to seek another.

III

The Fourteenth Amendment's procedural protection of property is a safeguard of the security of interests that a person has already acquired in specific benefits. These interests—property interests—may take many forms.

Thus the Court has held that a person receiving welfare benefits under statutory and administrative standards defining eligibility for them has an interest in continued receipt of those benefits that is safeguarded by procedural due process. * * *. Similarly, in the area of public employment, the Court has held that a public college professor dismissed from an office held under tenure provisions, Slochower v. Board of Education, and college professors and staff members dismissed during the terms of their contracts, Wieman v. Updegraff, have interests in continued employment that are safeguarded by due process. Only last year, the Court held that this principle "proscribing summary dismissal from public employment without a hearing or inquiry required by due process" also applied to a teacher recently hired without tenure or a formal contract but nonetheless with a clearly implied promise of continued employment. Connell v. Higginbotham.

Certain attributes of "property" interests protected by procedural due process emerge from these decisions. To have a property interest in a benefit, a person clearly must have more than an abstract need or desire for it. He must have more than a unilateral expectation of it. He must, instead, have a legitimate claim of entitlement to it. It is a purpose of the ancient institution of property to protect those claims upon which people rely in their daily lives, reliance that must not be arbitrarily undermined. It is a purpose of the constitutional right to a hearing to provide an opportunity for a person to vindicate those claims.

Property interests, of course, are not created by the Constitution. Rather, they are created and their dimensions are defined by existing rules or understandings that stem from an independent source such as state law—rules or understandings that secure certain benefits and that support claims of entitlement to those benefits. Thus the welfare recipients * * * had a claim of entitlement to welfare payments that was grounded in the statute defining eligibility for them. The recipients had not yet shown that they were, in fact, within the statutory terms of eligibility. But we held that they had a right to a hearing at which they might attempt to do so.

Just as the welfare recipients' "property" interest in welfare payments was created and defined by statutory terms, so the respondent's "property" interest in employment at the Wisconsin State University-Oshkosh was created and defined by the terms of his appointment. Those terms secured his interest in employment up to June 30, 1969. But the important fact in this case is that they specifically provided that the respondent's employment was to terminate on June 30. They did not provide for contract renewal absent "sufficient cause." Indeed, they made no provision for renewal whatsoever.

Thus the terms of the respondent's appointment secured absolutely no interest in re-employment for the next year. They supported absolutely no possible claim to entitlement to re-employment. Nor, significantly, was there any state statute or University rule or policy that secured his interest in re-employment or that created any legitimate claim to it. In these circumstances, the respondent surely had an abstract concern in being rehired, but he did not have a *property* interest sufficient to require the University authorities to give him a hearing when they declined to renew his contract of employment.

IV

Our analysis of the respondent's constitutional rights in this case in no way indicates a view that an opportunity for a hearing or a statement of reasons for nonretention would, or would not, be appropriate or wise in public colleges and universities. For it is a written Constitution that we apply. Our role is confined to interpretation of that Constitution.

* * *

[Case No. 78] Procedural Due Process for Nontenure Teachers Who Are Not Reappointed, II

PERRY v. SINDERMANN

Supreme Court of the United States, 1972.
408 U.S. 593, 92 S.Ct. 2694, 33 L.Ed.2d 570.

Mr. Justice Stewart delivered the opinion of the Court.

From 1959 to 1969 the respondent, Robert Sindermann, was a teacher in the state college system of the State of Texas. After teaching for two years at the University of Texas and for four years at San Antonio Junior College, he became a professor of Government and Social Science at Odessa Junior College in 1965. He was employed at the college for four successive years, under a series of one-year contracts. He was successful enough to be appointed, for a time, the cochairman of his department.

During the 1968–1969 academic year, however, controversy arose between the respondent and the college administration. The respondent was elected president of the Texas Junior College Teachers Association.

In this capacity, he left his teaching duties on several occasions to testify before committees of the Texas Legislature, and he became involved in public disagreements with the policies of the college's Board of Regents. In particular, he aligned himself with a group advocating the elevation of the college to four-year status—a change opposed by the Regents. And, on one occasion, a newspaper advertisement appeared over his name that was highly critical of the Regents.

Finally, in May 1969, the respondent's one-year employment contract terminated and the Board of Regents voted not to offer him a new contract for the next academic year. The Regents issued a press release setting forth allegations of the respondent's insubordination. But they provided him no official statement of the reasons for the nonrenewal of his contract. And they allowed him no opportunity for a hearing to challenge the basis of the nonrenewal.

* * *

I

The first question presented is whether the respondent's lack of a contractual or tenure right to re-employment, taken alone, defeats his claim that the nonrenewal of his contract violated the First and Fourteenth Amendments. We hold that it does not.

For at least a quarter century, this Court has made clear that even though a person has no "right" to a valuable governmental benefit and even though the government may deny him the benefit for any number of reasons, there are some reasons upon which the government may not act. It may not deny a benefit to a person on a basis that infringes his constitutionally protected interests—especially his interest in freedom of speech. For if the government could deny a benefit to a person because of his constitutionally protected speech or associations, his exercise of those freedoms would in effect be penalized and inhibited. This would allow the government to "produce a result which [it] could not command directly." Such interference with constitutional rights is impermissible.

* * *

In this case, of course, the respondent has yet to show that the decision not to renew his contract was, in fact, made in retaliation for his exercise of the constitutional right of free speech. * * *

* * * The respondent has alleged that his nonretention was based on his testimony before legislative committees and his other public statements critical of the Regents' policies. And he has alleged that this public criticism was within the First and Fourteenth Amendment's protection of freedom of speech. Plainly, these allegations present a *bona fide* constitutional claim. For this Court has held that a teacher's public criticism of his superiors on matters of public concern may be constitutionally protected and may, therefore, be an impermissible basis for termination of his employment.

* * *

II

The respondent's lack of formal contractual or tenure security in continued employment at Odessa Junior College, though irrelevant to his free speech claim, is highly relevant to his procedural due process claim. But it may not be entirely dispositive.

We have held today in Board of Regents v. Roth that the Constitution does not require opportunity for a hearing before the nonrenewal of a nontenured teacher's contract, unless he can show that the decision not to rehire him somehow deprived him of an interest in "liberty" or that he had a "property" interest in continued employment, despite the lack of tenure or a formal contract. In *Roth* the teacher had not made a showing on either point to justify summary judgment in his favor.

Similarly, the respondent here has yet to show that he has been deprived of an interest that could invoke procedural due process protection. As in *Roth*, the mere showing that he was not rehired in one particular job, without more, did not amount to a showing of a loss of liberty. Nor did it amount to a showing of a loss of property.

But the respondent's allegations—which we must construe most favorably to the respondent at this stage of the litigation—do raise a genuine issue as to his interest in continued employment at Odessa Junior College. He alleged that this interest, though not secured by a formal contractual tenure provision, was secured by a no less binding understanding fostered by the college administration. In particular, the respondent alleged that the college had a *de facto* tenure program, and that he had tenure under that program. He claimed that he and others legitimately relied upon an unusual provision that had been in the college's official Faculty Guide for many years:

> "*Teacher Tenure:* Odessa College has no tenure system. The Administration of the College wishes the faculty member to feel that he has permanent tenure as long as his teaching services are satisfactory and as long as he displays a cooperative attitude toward his co-workers and his superiors, and as long as he is happy in his work."

Moreover, the respondent claimed legitimate reliance upon guidelines promulgated by the Coordinating Board of the Texas College and University System that provided that a person, like himself, who had been employed as a teacher in the state college and university system for seven years or more has some form of job tenure. Thus the respondent offered to prove that a teacher, with his long period of service, at this particular State College had no less a "property" interest in continued employment than a formally tenured teacher at other colleges, and had no less a procedural due process right to a statement of reasons and a hearing before college officials upon their decision not to retain him.

We have made clear in *Roth* that "property" interests subject to procedural due process protection are not limited by a few rigid, technical forms. Rather, "property" denotes a broad range of interests that are secured by "existing rules or understandings." A person's interest in a benefit is a "property" interest for due process purposes if there are such rules or mutually explicit understandings that support his claim of entitlement to the benefit and that he may invoke at a hearing.

A written contract with an explicit tenure provision clearly is evidence of a formal understanding that supports a teacher's claim of entitlement to continued employment unless sufficient "cause" is shown. Yet absence of such an explicit contractual provision may not always foreclose the possibility that a teacher has a "property" interest in re-employment. For example, the law of contracts in most, if not all, jurisdictions long has employed a process by which agreements, though not formalized in writing, may be "implied." Explicit contractual provisions may be supplemented by other agreements implied from "the promisor's words and conduct in the light of the surrounding circumstances." And, "[t]he meaning of [the promisor's] words and acts is found by relating them to the usage of the past."

A teacher, like the respondent, who has held his position for a number of years, might be able to show from the circumstances of this service—and from other relevant facts—that he has a legitimate claim of entitlement to job tenure. Just as this Court has found there to be a "common law of a particular industry or of a particular plant" that may supplement a collective-bargaining agreement, so there may be an unwritten "common law" in a particular university that certain employees shall have the equivalent of tenure. This is particularly likely in a college or university, like Odessa Junior College, that has no explicit tenure system even for senior members of its faculty, but that nonetheless may have created such a system in practice.

In this case, the respondent has alleged the existence of rules and understandings, promulgated and fostered by state officials, that may justify his legitimate claim of entitlement to continued employment absent "sufficient cause." We disagree with the Court of Appeals insofar as it held that a mere subjective "expectancy" is protected by procedural due process, but we agree that the respondent must be given an opportunity to prove the legitimacy of his claim of such entitlement in light of "the policies and practices of the institution." Proof of such a property interest would not, of course, entitle him to reinstatement. But such proof would obligate college officials to grant a hearing at his request, where he could be informed of the grounds for his nonretention and challenge their sufficiency.

* * *

Notes

1. Justices Douglas, Brennan, and Marshall dissented; Justice Powell did not participate. Justice Douglas said, "Without a statement of the reasons for the discharge and an opportunity to rebut these reasons * * * there is no means short of a lawsuit to safeguard the right not to be discharged for the exercise of First Amendment guarantees." Justice Marshall said, "In my view, every citizen who applies for a government job is entitled to it unless the government can establish some reason for denying the employment."

2. Only a relatively few courts had gone beyond the bounds of these opinions in regard to constitutional rights of nontenure teachers. The publicity given the exceptions, particularly the *Roth* case in the lower courts, tended to obscure that fact.

3. Specific charges and a hearing before removal constitute the heart of tenure protection. Had the Supreme Court upheld the lower courts in *Roth*, would any practical differences have remained between tenure and nontenure status?

4. *Roth* is an exceptionally important constitutional case because of its scope. Any public employee whose employment is not continued beyond the term of a contract may seek to come under its umbrella by alleging impairment of a liberty interest or a property interest, as defined in the opinion. In some circumstances the hearing (or the quest for it) may, in practical terms, be almost tantamount to a just cause proceeding.

5. How may the *Perry* holding benefit teachers in those states having no tenure statutes?

6. Would a board of education be legally well advised to state publicly no reason for nonrenewal of a probationary teacher? Suppose only the teacher was told the reason privately. Would this reconcile some professional and ethical concerns with legal realities, or would it be legally perilous? Would your answer differ depending on what in fact the reason was?

[Case No. 79] Nonreappointment of Teacher—Partially Based on Unconstitutional Reason

MT. HEALTHY CITY SCHOOL DIST. BD. OF EDUC. v. DOYLE

Supreme Court of the United States, 1977.
429 U.S. 274, 97 S.Ct. 568, 50 L.Ed.2d 471.

Mr. Justice Rehnquist delivered the opinion of the Court.

Respondent Doyle sued petitioner Mt. Healthy Board of Education in the United States District Court for the Southern District of Ohio. Doyle claimed that the Board's refusal to renew his contract in 1971 violated his rights under the First and Fourteenth Amendments to the United States Constitution. After a bench trial the District Court held that Doyle was entitled to reinstatement with back pay. The Court of Appeals for the Sixth Circuit affirmed the judgment * * *.

* * *

Doyle was first employed by the Board in 1966. He worked under one-year contracts for the first three years, and under a two-year contract from 1969 to 1971. In 1969 he was elected president of the Teachers' Association, in which position he worked to expand the subjects of direct negotiation between the Association and the Board of Education. During Doyle's one-year term as president of the Association, and during the succeeding year when he served on its executive committee, there was apparently some tension in relations between the Board and the Association.

Beginning early in 1970, Doyle was involved in several incidents not directly connected with his role in the Teachers' Association. In one instance, he engaged in an argument with another teacher which culminated in the other teacher's slapping him. Doyle subsequently refused to accept an apology and insisted upon some punishment for the other teacher. His persistence in the matter resulted in the suspension of both teachers for one day, which was followed by a walkout by a number of other teachers, which in turn resulted in the lifting of the suspensions.

On other occasions, Doyle got into an argument with employees of the school cafeteria over the amount of spaghetti which had been served him; referred to students, in connection with a disciplinary complaint, as "sons of bitches"; and made an obscene gesture to two girls in connection with their failure to obey commands made in his capacity as cafeteria supervisor. Chronologically the last in the series of incidents which respondent was involved in during his employment by the Board was a telephone call by him to a local radio station. It was the Board's consideration of this incident which the court below found to be a violation of the First and Fourteenth Amendments.

In February of 1971, the principal circulated to various teachers a memorandum relating to teacher dress and appearance, which was apparently prompted by the view of some in the administration that there was a relationship between teacher appearance and public support for bond issues. Doyle's response to the receipt of the memorandum—on a subject which he apparently understood was to be settled by joint teacher-administration action—was to convey the substance of the memorandum to a disc jockey at WSAI, a Cincinnati radio station, who promptly announced the adoption of the dress code as a news item. Doyle subsequently apologized to the principal, conceding that he should have made some prior communication of his criticism to the school administration.

Approximately one month later the superintendent made his customary annual recommendations to the Board as to the rehiring of nontenured teachers. He recommended that Doyle not be rehired. The same recommendation was made with respect to nine other teachers in the district, and in all instances, including Doyle's, the recommendation was adopted by the Board. Shortly after being notified of this decision, respondent requested a statement of reasons for the Board's actions. He received a statement citing "a notable lack of tact in handling professional matters which leaves much doubt as to your sincerity in establishing good school relationships." That general statement was followed by references to the radio station incident and to the obscene gesture incident.

The District Court found that all of these incidents had in fact occurred. It concluded that respondent Doyle's telephone call to the radio station was "clearly protected by the First Amendment," and that because it had played a "substantial part" in the decision of the Board not to renew Doyle's employment, he was entitled to reinstatement with back pay. The District Court did not expressly state what test it was applying in determining that the incident in question involved conduct protected by the First Amendment, but simply held that the communication to the radio station was such conduct. The Court of Appeals affirmed in a brief *per curiam* opinion.

Doyle's claims under the First and Fourteenth Amendments are not defeated by the fact that he did not have tenure. Even though he could have been discharged for no reason whatever, and had no constitutional right to a hearing prior to the decision not to rehire him, Board of Regents v. Roth, he may nonetheless establish a claim to reinstatement if the decision not to rehire him was made by reason of his exercise of constitutionally protected First Amendment freedoms. Perry v. Sindermann.

That question of whether speech of a government employee is constitutionally protected expression necessarily entails striking "a balance between the interests of the teacher, as a citizen, in commenting upon matters of public concern and the interest of the State as an employer, in promoting the efficiency of the public services it performs through its employees." Pickering v. Board of Education. There is no suggestion by the Board that Doyle violated any established policy, or that its reaction to his communication to the radio station was anything more than an *ad hoc* response to Doyle's action in making the memorandum public. We therefore accept the District Court's finding that the communication was protected by the First and Fourteenth Amendments. We are not, however, entirely in agreement with that court's manner of reasoning from this finding to the conclusion that Doyle is entitled to reinstatement with back pay.

The District Court made the following "conclusions" on this aspect of the case:

"(1) If a non-permissible reason, e.g., exercise of First Amendment rights, played a substantial part in the decision not to renew—even in the face of other permissible grounds—the decision may not stand (citations omitted).

"(2) A non-permissible reason did play a substantial part. That is clear from the letter of the Superintendent immediately following the Board's decision, which stated two reasons—the one, the conversation with the radio station clearly protected by the First Amendment. A court may not engage in any limitation of First Amendment rights based on 'tact'—that is not to say that 'tactfulness' is irrelevant to other issues in this case."

At the same time, though, it stated that "in fact, as this Court sees it and finds, both the Board and the Superintendent were faced with a situation in which there did exist in fact reason * * * independent of any First Amendment rights or exercise thereof, to not extend tenure."

Since respondent Doyle had no tenure, and there was therefore not even a state law requirement of "cause" or "reason" before a decision could be made not to renew his employment, it is not clear what the District Court meant by this latter statement. Clearly the Board legally *could* have dismissed respondent had the radio station incident never come to its attention. One plausible meaning of the court's statement is that the Board and the Superintendent not only could, but in fact *would* have reached that decision had not the constitutionally protected incident of the telephone call to the radio station occurred. We are thus brought to the issue whether, even if that were the case, the fact that the protected conduct played a "substantial part" in the actual decision not to renew would necessarily amount to a constitutional violation justifying remedial action. We think that it would not.

A rule of causation which focuses solely on whether protected conduct played a part, "substantial" or otherwise, in a decision not to rehire, could place an employee in a better position as a result of the exercise of constitutionally protected conduct than he would have occupied had he done nothing. The difficulty with the rule enunciated by the District Court is that it would require reinstatement in cases where a dramatic and perhaps abrasive incident is inevitably on the minds of those responsible for the decision to rehire, and does indeed play a part in that decision—even if the same decision would have been reached had the incident not occurred. The constitutional principle at stake is sufficiently vindicated if such an employee is placed in no worse a position than if he had not engaged in the conduct. A borderline or marginal candidate should not have the employment question resolved against him because of constitutionally protected conduct. But that same candidate ought not to be able, by engaging in such conduct, to prevent his employer from assessing his performance record and reaching a decision not to rehire on the basis of that record, simply because the protected conduct makes the employer more certain of the correctness of its decision.

This is especially true where, as the District Court observed was the case here, the current decision to rehire will accord "tenure." The long term consequences of an award of tenure are of great moment both to the employee and to the employer. They are too significant for us to hold that the Board in this case would be precluded, because it considered constitutionally protected conduct in deciding not to rehire Doyle, from attempting to prove to a trier of fact that quite apart from such conduct Doyle's record was such that he would not have been rehired in any event.

* * *

Initially, in this case, the burden was properly placed upon respondent to show that his conduct was constitutionally protected, and that this conduct was a "substantial factor"—or to put it in other words, that it was a "motivating factor" in the Board's decision not to rehire him. Respondent having carried that burden, however, the District Court should have gone on to determine whether the Board had shown by a preponderance of the evidence that it would have reached the same decision as to respondent's reemployment even in the absence of the protected conduct.

We cannot tell from the District Court opinion and conclusions, nor from the opinion of the Court of Appeals affirming the judgment of the

would he have been terminated anyway?

District Court, what conclusion those courts would have reached had they applied this test. The judgment of the Court of Appeals is therefore vacated, and the case remanded for further proceedings consistent with this opinion.

Notes

1. This decision was unanimous. Most, but not all, lower federal courts had been following the procedure and reasoning set forth by the Supreme Court. The courts here reversed were following a minority view.

2. Consider the consequences of having to retain a teacher who was unsatisfactory simply because a First Amendment claim was successfully injected into the teacher's defense. Observe that the Court was aware of this problem.

3. Would teachers be protected by the First Amendment from disciplinary action for any and all calls to radio stations? Explain your answer.

4. In the next to last paragraph, note that the auxiliary verb is "would." How, if at all, would the rule established be different if the auxiliary were "could"?

5. On remand it was held that Doyle would not have been renewed even if he had not called the radio station. Doyle v. Mt. Healthy City School Dist. Bd. of Educ., 670 F.2d 59 (6 Cir.1982).

[Case No. 80] Nonreappointment of Teacher—Various Claims

MEYR v. BOARD OF EDUC. OF AFFTON SCHOOL DIST.

United States Court of Appeals, Eighth Circuit, 1978.
572 F.2d 1229.

Van Oosterhout, Senior Circuit Judge. This is a timely appeal from the final judgment of the district court dismissing plaintiff's complaint * * *.

For a reversal the plaintiff [whose probationary contract was not renewed] urges that the trial court erred in the following respects:

I. Holding plaintiff had no property interest in continued employment.

II. Holding that plaintiff's liberty interests had not been infringed by the defendants.

III. Holding that termination was not based, even partially, upon plaintiff's exercise of her first amendment free speech rights.

We affirm for the reasons hereinafter set out.

* * *

I

The court committed no error in determining plaintiff had no property right in continued employment. * * *

* * * [T]he record reflects that the plaintiff had not acquired tenure at the time notice of non-renewal was served.

Plaintiff urges that the Board is required to provide the benefits conferred by Board Policy No. 4118 III D, which reads:

If the Board determines that a teacher is not doing satisfactory work, the Board through its administrative representative shall give the teacher a written statement definitely setting forth his alleged incompetency and specifying the nature thereof. * * *

and by Board Policy No. 4119 which reads:

Teachers not considered satisfactory shall be notified by their supervisor and be given such reasonable time to improve as the Board of Education may determine.

Board Policy No. 4118 III D is substantially identical to Mo.Ann. Stat. § 168.126 (Vernon Supp.1977), which the Missouri Court of Appeals in White v. Scott County School District, 503 S.W.2d 35 (Mo.App. 1973) holds to be applicable only to termination within the contract period and not to a failure to renew an existing contract of a probationary teacher.

We find nothing in Policy No. 4119 which indicates that it is applicable to probationary teachers whose contracts are not renewed. As a probationary teacher under Missouri law plaintiff has no property interest in continued employment. * * *

The record clearly reflects that the school had suffered a substantial decrease in enrollment, that it was economically necessary to substantially reduce the teaching staff and that the policy of the Board was to limit acquisition of tenure to exceptionally qualified teachers. Such policy was reasonable under the circumstances to protect the rights of teachers who had attained tenure. Many probationary contracts were not renewed in pursuance of this policy.

The Board's minutes reflect a clear intention not to renew plaintiff's contract for the school year commencing in the fall of 1976. The Board had a right to do so without a finding of incompetency and without assigning any other reason for its action. Plaintiff continued to serve under her existing contract until its expiration.

II

Plaintiff has not in her affidavit or otherwise set out any material facts as distinguished from legal conclusions to support her contention that her liberty interests have been violated by the Board's failure to renew her teaching contract.

The failure to receive tenure does not constitute the deprivation of a liberty interest protected by the fourteenth amendment.

Plaintiff has failed to show that she has any evidence to support her claim that she was stigmatized by any action of the defendants in refusing to renew her probationary contract.

The record reflects that when the President and President-elect of the Affton school teachers acting as a grievance committee, at the request of the plaintiff, went to the superintendent to investigate the

non-renewal of plaintiff's contract, they were told that many probationary teachers were not re-employed by reason of the economic necessity of
reducing the teaching staff, and that Mrs. Meyr was not re-employed for
the additional reason that she was not considered a satisfactory teacher
because of excessive absences and tardiness and poor staff relations.
Nevertheless, economic necessity for reduction of the teaching staff
remained the prime reason for not renewing plaintiff's contract. The
Board's minutes above quoted do not set forth the additional factors as a
basis for not rehiring, and as heretofore emphasized the Board's action
was not to renew and was not termination of the plaintiff's existing
contract prior to expiration. Such does not constitute the publication by
defendants of stigmatizing information. The posting of the vacancy in
the position held by Mrs. Meyr does not, standing alone, support stigmatization. Mrs. Meyr herself told many people she had not been re-
employed.

In any event, the burden is on Mrs. Meyr to prove the charges made
by the superintendent were false. Plaintiff admits that she had a
substantial number of absences and tardiness and has set out no facts in
her affidavits to disprove such charges. Plaintiff has not shown that she
has any evidence to establish the falsity of any charges made against her.
Plaintiff has not indicated that she has any evidence that stigmatizing
information was given to school districts in which she applied for
employment. She admits in her deposition the fact that she had too
many years of experience, which resulted in entitlement to a higher
salary and was a substantial factor in her failure to obtain a teaching
contract. She admits that she was employed as a substitute teacher by
several school districts.

* * *

III

The trial court committed no error in determining that plaintiff's
exercise of her right of free speech was not a substantial factor in the
non-renewal of her contract. In Mt. Healthy City Board of Education v.
Doyle, the Court holds:

> Initially, in this case, the burden was properly placed upon
> respondent to show that his conduct was constitutionally pro-
> tected, and that this conduct was a "substantial factor"—or, to
> put it in other words, that it was a "motivating factor" in the
> Board's decision not to rehire him.

Judged by such standard, we are satisfied that the plaintiff by affidavit
or otherwise has failed to establish that her exercise of free speech was a
substantial or motivating factor in the Board's decision not to renew.

Plaintiff in a speech to the mothers' club in January 1976 criticized
the Board for not supplying equipment the plaintiff deemed essential for
her physical education classes. Board member Lemp was present at this
meeting and was upset by such remarks and reported the incident to
Superintendent Onkle. Plaintiff under the first amendment had a right
to make such remark. School boards and other public boards are as a

matter of public knowledge frequently subjected to public criticism for making or failing to make appropriations for various projects or for failure to grant salary increases. The statement made by the plaintiff is not the kind of statement that could be reasonably supposed to upset the school board officials.

The power to determine whether a contract should be renewed is in the school board. The superintendent can make recommendations which the board can accept or reject.

Each of the board members serving at the time here material, except Mrs. Lemp, filed affidavits stating that they had no knowledge of plaintiff's statement at the time they voted not to renew plaintiff's contract and that no consideration was given to such statement. Mrs. Lemp in her affidavit states plaintiff's speech was not a factor in her vote not to renew, and Superintendent Onkle filed a similar affidavit.

Plaintiff in her affidavit has merely claimed by way of conclusion that the speech was a substantial factor in inducing the Board's action. She points to no evidence available to her to disprove the sworn statements made by the Board members, and we consequently see no reasonable possibility that plaintiff could meet the burden of refuting these statements. * * *

The judgment is affirmed.

Notes

1. Notice that the board had a policy of limiting new tenure appointments only to "exceptionally qualified" teachers. Was the existence of such policy important to the disposition of the case?

2. Observe the emphasis placed by the court on the point of lack of evidence to support the claims of plaintiff as to stigmatization and as to infringement of free speech rights. What kinds of evidence might have supported plaintiff's claims?

3. Was it sound administrative procedure for the superintendent to discuss plaintiff's nonreappointment with the teachers association officials? Did any legal consequences flow from that discussion?

4. If board member Lemp had discussed the "mothers' club" incident with other board members prior to the board's vote not to renew plaintiff's contract, would the outcome of this case have been affected?

Chapter 10

TERMS AND CONDITIONS
OF EMPLOYMENT OF
TEACHERS

State-level statutes and regulations relative to terms and conditions of employment of teachers have been increasing in numbers. Some acts have wide impact, the broadest probably being those in the area of collective negotiations. The processes established for achieving bilateral agreement affect many personnel policies, more in some states than in others. Compensation programs, however, always are included where there is any form of collective bargaining. Details, of course, ultimately must be determined locally.

Some state-level provisions are narrowly focused. For example, Oklahoma enacted a statute, applying only to public school teachers, that forbade the commission of specified homosexual acts in public and also the advocacy or encouragement of public or private homosexual activity. The United States Court of Appeals, Tenth Circuit, declared the second part of the statute unconstitutional on its face because the First Amendment "does not permit someone to be punished for advocating [even] illegal conduct at some indefinite future time." [1] The first part, however, the court upheld.

A 1990 Kentucky statute enacted as part of a broad education reform thrust prohibited any employee of a school district from taking part in the "management or activities of any political campaign for school board" and barred a school board candidate from accepting any political "contribution or service" from a district employee. Criminal sanctions were prescribed. The word "activities" was held to be unconstitutionally vague and overbroad by the state's highest court.[2] The remainder of the statute was upheld.

A statutory duty of school personnel to report promptly cases of suspected child abuse was accepted by the Seventh Circuit Court of Appeals as within the power of the legislature to require. That a school psychologist who had delayed his report did so because he had promised confidentiality to the student was held not to be a basis for invalidating a five-day payless suspension and a reassignment by the local school board.[3] The circumstances involved the boy's having a sexual relation-

1. National Gay Task Force v. Board of Educ. of City of Oklahoma City, 729 F.2d 1270 (10 Cir.1984), aff. 470 U.S. 903, 105 S.Ct. 1858, 84 L.Ed.2d 776 (1985). [Case No. 81]

2. State Bd. for Elementary and Secondary Educ. v. Howard, 834 S.W.2d 657 (Ky. 1992).

3. Pesce v. J. Sterling Morton High School Dist. 201, 830 F.2d 789 (7 Cir.1987).

ship with a male teacher at the school and displaying possible suicidal tendencies.

Items denotable as conditions of employment also can be found in Chapters 9 and 11.

Salaries

In General

Implied in the power of local boards of education to employ teachers is the authority to set their salaries. In the absence of statutes limiting this power, it is plenary. Increasingly, however, states are enacting legislation directly or indirectly related to teachers' salaries and thus narrowing the scope of local-level discretion. The virtually universal use of salary schedules for teachers by local districts raises no basic legal question if there is reasonableness of classifications and uniformity of treatment of those performing similar services and having like training and experience. Differentiations among individual teachers or classes of teachers must be based on differences germane to the education function or having a reasonable relation to the work assigned.

Placement on Salary Schedules

When teachers new to a school system are placed on a salary schedule, it is not necessary that a local board grant credit for experience outside the system.[4] If, however, it does grant credit, it is possible to do so on the basis of an examination of each individual case, according to fixed rules, or by a combination of the two methods. Once it has a policy in place, that policy must not be administered arbitrarily or discriminatorily, as by making a new rule retroactive to the disadvantage of those already employed.[5] A board may credit other than teaching experience. Military service, for example, may be credited at the discretion of the board. A policy of such credit, however, may be prospectively rescinded.[6]

Where qualifications and performance are the same, teachers must be treated the same.[7] However, position titles alone are not controlling. For example, the Supreme Court of Minnesota sustained a determination by a local board that teachers in a special vocational-technical school be a class treated differently from teachers of vocational subjects in the regular secondary schools because their qualifications differed.[8] Also, the highest court of Massachusetts has held that not all persons holding

---

4. Fry v. Board of Educ., 17 Cal.2d 753, 112 P.2d 229 (1941).

5. Aebli v. Board of Educ., 62 Cal. App.2d 706, 145 P.2d 601 (1944); Board of Educ. of Katonah-Lewisboro Union Free School Dist. v. Ambach, 77 A.D.2d 108, 432 N.Y.S.2d 661 (1980).

6. Mukilteo Educ. Ass'n v. Mukilteo School Dist. No. 6, 11 Wash.App. 675, 524 P.2d 441 (1974).

7. Vittal v. Long Beach Unified School Dist., 8 Cal.App.3d 112, 87 Cal.Rptr. 319 (1970).

8. Frisk v. Board of Educ. of Duluth, 246 Minn. 366, 75 N.W.2d 504 (1956).

the rank of "supervisor" need be paid similarly.[9] A supervisor of arithmetic was unsuccessful in claiming that she should be paid the same salary as a supervisor of manual training. The court indicated that supervision was the only common element of the work, and that supervising manual training differed substantially from supervising the teaching of arithmetic. It has also been held that the workyears of different categories of positions may differ. Thus a principal could be required to work one month more than teachers without receiving an additional payment of one-ninth of his annual salary.[10]

A teacher brought suit to be placed on a school district's salary schedule for holders of master's degrees when a seminary he had attended changed the nomenclature of the degree he had been awarded from Bachelor of Divinity to Master of Divinity. The Southern Association of Colleges and Schools accredited the seminary. The school board refused to honor the request under the wording in its schedule, which was "approved degree." A state minimum salary statute used the term "recognized institution of higher learning." The Appellate Court of Illinois held that in certification statutes and in the one regarding salary the word "recognized" meant teacher training institutions that met certain criteria established by the state education agency, and that the word "approved" in the local schedule meant the same.[11] Thus, the board was justified in refusing to recognize for salary purposes the degree that had changed in name only.

A similar result was reached in a case in which the holder of a Juris Doctor degree sought to be placed on the schedule in the Ph.D.–Ed.D. category.[12] The court upheld the power of the board to restrict entry to that salary classification. Further, it found irrelevant the fact the word "doctorate" appeared in the collective bargaining agreement rather than the full description which appeared in the board rules and which had been consistently enforced for over 15 years.

Bases of Salary Classification

It may now be said with confidence that there is no power in school boards to differentiate salaries on bases of race, sex, or marital status. Those old cases to the contrary have been expressly or impliedly overruled. Some individuals, however, may be incidentally benefitted or disadvantaged by some valid general policies legitimately aimed at attracting and retaining highly qualified teachers under prevailing conditions. One illustration has already been given in Chapter 6: that some health insurance programs benefitting some teachers more than others are a proper expenditure of school funds.[13]

9. Murphy v. School Committee of Lawrence, 321 Mass. 478, 73 N.E.2d 835 (1947).

10. Taggart v. Board of Directors of Canon-McMillan Joint School System, 409 Pa. 33, 185 A.2d 332 (1962).

11. Loyd v. Board of Educ. of Meridian Community Unit School Dist. No. 223, Ogle County, 49 Ill.App.3d 996, 7 Ill.Dec. 686, 364 N.E.2d 977 (1977).

12. Sullivan v. Hannon, 58 Ill.App.3d 572, 16 Ill.Dec. 136, 374 N.E.2d 911 (1978).

13. Sheehan v. Eldredge, 5 Cal.App.3d 77, 84 Cal.Rptr. 894 (1970).

In apparently the only reported decision on the point, the Supreme Judicial Court of Massachusetts upheld a "dependency allowance" plan for any teacher who was the sole support of spouse or children.[14] At the time teachers were in very short supply. The court indicated that it was not to be assumed that it would support "further or different incursions" into the field of "domestic economy." In New York a school board had provided that children of nonresident teachers employed in the district could attend the district's schools free of tuition. When the board decided unilaterally to abandon the practice, the teachers association sought arbitration on a claim that the collective bargaining contract would be violated. The board took the position that the matter was not arbitrable because the practice was unconstitutional on equal protection grounds. The highest state court rejected the argument.[15]

Women coaches of female basketball teams brought suit on the ground of alleged sex discrimination because coaches of male teams were paid a higher stipend. The suit failed because all coaches of female basketball (four men and four women) were paid the same, and there was no allegation that the women were denied coaching positions for male basketball teams.[16]

Contested in California was a board rule that a teacher must be on duty seventy-five percent of the school year in order to receive an annual increment. The Court of Appeal sustained the rule.[17] That exceptions were made for those on military or sabbatical leave was held not to constitute a denial of equal protection to the plaintiff, who had been on sick leave. There is a strong public policy in favor of granting credit to those on military leave, and sabbatical leave activities of teachers are intended to benefit the district.

The Fifth Circuit Court of Appeals upheld a classification whereby a board of education supplemented the state-paid minimum base salaries of teachers of academic subjects but not those of teachers of vocational education.[18] The court accepted as reasonable the board's action in utilizing limited funds because the post-secondary vocational programs also served students from other districts and the base salaries of vocational teachers in the district's secondary schools were higher than those for academic teachers.

The highest court of Massachusetts decided that it was within the power of a local school board to enter into a collective bargaining agreement which provided for a salary increase for a teacher's final year of service before retirement based on the number of days over 170 he has

14. Cotter v. City of Chelsea, 329 Mass. 314, 108 N.E.2d 47 (1952).

15. Board of Educ. of New Paltz Central School Dist. v. New Paltz United Teachers, 44 N.Y.2d 890, 407 N.Y.S.2d 632, 379 N.E.2d 160 (1978).

16. Jackson v. Armstrong School Dist., 430 F.Supp. 1050 (W.D.Pa.1977). See also Erickson v. Board of Educ., Proviso Tp.

High School Dist. No. 209, 120 Ill.App.3d 264, 75 Ill.Dec. 916, 458 N.E.2d 84 (1983), cert. den., 469 U.S. 823, 105 S.Ct. 98, 83 L.Ed.2d 44 (1984).

17. Hunt v. Alum Rock Union Elementary School Dist., 7 Cal.App.3d 612, 86 Cal. Rptr. 663 (1970).

18. Harper v. Wood, 560 F.2d 202 (5 Cir.1977).

attended in each year of service.[19]   The court said that this item was part of the overall package of services and benefits worked out by the parties pursuant to state-required collective bargaining. Moreover, as the board had power to set salaries and to provide for sick leaves, it could regard the arrangement as having the effect of discouraging frivolous use of sick leave and rewarding lengthy continuing service by teachers. As only ten days over 170 may be worked in a year, no open-ended financial liability would ensue. A provision for a terminal year increase based on years of service in the district was approved by the Court of Appeals of New York in a four-to-three decision.[20]   The dissenters considered the arrangement an unconstitutional gift of public funds. New Jersey courts have disapproved any salary arrangements that may substantially affect retirement age, because of possible effects on the actuarial base of the retirement system.[21]

Classifications including a quality of performance or merit factor have been involved in a number of cases. The rewarding of capability and of efficiency can take the form of additional increases or the withholding of normally scheduled increments.

That annual increments in a locally adopted salary schedule can be predicated upon favorable reports from supervisors on performance of teachers seems legally settled.[22]   The requirement of "professional growth" as a condition for advancement on the salary schedule was considered by the Supreme Court of Illinois in a declaratory judgment action by a regular teacher on tenure with eleven years service.[23]   The teacher had not received a salary increase because he did not comply with the local board of education's professional growth requirement, which was three semester hours of college work or the equivalent during a seven year period. The teacher held an M.A. degree in mathematics and a life high school teaching certificate. The court found that the life teaching certificate entitled one to eligibility to teach, not to a particular place on the salary schedule. Also, it found no violation of the tenure law, for the plaintiff's job was not threatened nor his salary reduced.

Perhaps the most subjective classification found to have been upheld by an appellate court was in a California situation where the regulations of the board provided for periodic salary increases to all teachers except those found to be unsatisfactory.[24]   Whether a teacher was unsatisfactory was decided by the board acting upon the recommendation of a committee consisting of the principal, two vice-principals, and the head of the teacher's department. The committee evaluated the teacher's

19. Fitchburg Teachers Ass'n v. School Committee, 360 Mass. 105, 271 N.E.2d 646 (1971).

20. Board of Educ. v. Associated Teachers of Huntington, 30 N.Y.2d 122, 331 N.Y.S.2d 17, 282 N.E.2d 109 (1972).

21. Miller v. Board of Trustees of Teachers' Pension and Annuity Fund, 179 N.J.Super. 473, 432 A.2d 560 (1981).

22. Kopera v. Board of Educ. of Town of West Orange, Essex County, 60 N.J.Super.

288, 158 A.2d 842 (1960); Wheeler v. Board of Educ. of Cleveland Heights, 30 Ohio App.2d 136, 283 N.E.2d 652 (1972).

23. Richards v. Board of Educ. of Tp. High School Dist. No. 201, 21 Ill.2d 104, 171 N.E.2d 37 (1960).

24. Heinlein v. Anaheim Union High School Dist., 96 Cal.App.2d 19, 214 P.2d 536 (1950).

effectiveness by measuring his performance against a number of factors including personality, skill as an instructor, scholarship, ability to discipline, power of expression, influence on pupils, initiative, and personal appearance.

Even though differentiations in salary based on subjective judgments have generally been sustained, criteria for evaluation must be reasonably specific and relevant. The purported application of subjective standards cannot be asserted to justify discriminatory action against a teacher for other reasons.[25] Federal jurisdiction does not arise, however, from claims that the superintendent failed to follow committee recommendations for a merit increase, that other teachers no more qualified than the plaintiff received the increase, and that no written reasons for denying the increase were given.[26]

Tying of certain salary increases to scores on the National Teacher Examination has been upheld.[27] (See Case No. 72 as to validation of this examination.) So has the predication of the right to a longevity increase on the provisions of a collective bargaining contract. Thus, where a provision was dropped from a new contract, there was no claim for those who completed the performance which would have entitled them to the increase under the old contract.[28]

Changes in Salary Classification

In general, changes can be made after the expiration of a contract, before entering into a new one. In the absence of specific legislation, for example, a board could legally offer a teacher or classification of teachers for a given year a salary less than that of a previous year. If, however, the salary was substantially lower, it could constitute a "failure to renew," with whatever legal machinery applicable thereto being invoked.[29] Even where there is apparent mutual consent, however, state statutes must be observed. Thus, provisions related to salary cannot be avoided by clauses in contracts. It has been held in Washington, Tennessee, and Arkansas that a teacher may sue to recover the full salary to which he is entitled under a state minimum salary law even if he has signed a contract to teach at a lower salary.[30] Likewise a black teacher who was under contract could challenge the practice of paying white teachers on a higher scale.[31] In New York where a statute required boards of education to grant salary increases to principals

25. Kacsur v. Board of Trustees, 18 Cal.2d 586, 116 P.2d 593 (1941).

26. Kanter v. Community Consolidated School Dist. 65, 558 F.Supp. 890 (N.D.Ill. 1982).

27. Newman v. Crews, 651 F.2d 222 (4 Cir.1981).

28. Rouse v. Anchorage School Dist., 613 P.2d 263 (Alaska 1980).

29. Barnes v. Seattle School Dist. No. 1, 88 Wash.2d 483, 563 P.2d 199 (1977);

Quarles v. McKenzie Public School Dist. No. 34, 325 N.W.2d 662 (N.D.1982).

30. Malcolm v. Yakima County Consolidated School Dist. 90, 23 Wash.2d 80, 159 P.2d 394 (1945); McMinn County Bd. of Educ. v. Anderson, 200 Tenn. 333, 292 S.W.2d 198 (1956); Marvel v. Coal Hill School Dist., 276 Ark. 369, 635 S.W.2d 245 (1982). [Case No. 83]

31. Alston v. School Bd. of Norfolk, 112 F.2d 992 (4 Cir.1940), cert. den. 311 U.S. 693, 61 S.Ct. 75, 85 L.Ed. 448 (1940).

whenever an increase was granted to teachers on the maximum of the teachers' salary schedule, a board of education granted salary increases to teachers on all steps of the salary schedule except the top step. No increase was given the principal. A court found this action to be an evasion of the statute and ordered that the contract with the principal include an increase.[32]

It is well established that salary schedules cannot be reduced by a board during a school year.[33] Whether the general rule applies to extra pay provisions for extra work was decided in the affirmative by the California Court of Appeal.[34] At issue was the attempted withdrawal by the board of a special stipend for continuation teachers who were required to make calls on absentee students. This had been regarded as extra work, and the board here claimed it was simply terminating an extra duty assignment, which it could do at any time according to a statute. The court found that there was no material change in duties, and that the board was in effect reducing pay for the work, which was not permissible. Attorney's fees had been awarded the teachers by the trial court, which had found the board's conduct to be arbitrary and capricious. This finding was upheld. That the district's legal counsel had advised the district it could proceed as it did was not relevant where neither counsel nor board "relied upon the authority of an appellate opinion."

Changes in classifications of teachers on salary schedules can lead to legal complications. For example, in San Diego, teachers in the highest class were required to have a doctor's degree or seventy-two hours of graduate study. A new schedule added a step limited to those with an earned doctorate or ninety graduate units. Some teachers with seventy-two graduate credits claimed that they had been downgraded by this change in schedule, for they were not getting as much money on the new schedule as they would have without the change in graduate point equivalency. The court, however, rejected their contention, stating that the board had the right to adjust its classifications, and that it had not abused its discretion.[35] It had not downgraded the teachers with seventy-two credits, but had upgraded those having a doctorate.

In a similar situation a Massachusetts school board reclassified teachers for salary purposes. For many years the local salary schedules had differentiated between teachers with bachelor's degrees and those with master's, and subsequently the doctor's degree was recognized. The action that instigated the lawsuit was a board determination that the salary schedule pertaining to master's and doctor's degrees should apply only to those who obtained degrees from accredited institutions. Some teachers who had post-graduate degrees from unaccredited schools

32. Petition of Hickey, 49 Misc.2d 930, 268 N.Y.S.2d 914 (1966).

33. Abraham v. Sims, 2 Cal.2d 698, 42 P.2d 1029 (1935).

34. A.B.C. Federation of Teachers v. A.B.C. Unified School Dist., 75 Cal.App.3d 332, 142 Cal.Rptr. 111 (1977).

35. San Diego Federation of Teachers, Local 1278, AFL–CIO v. Board of Educ. of San Diego, 216 Cal.App.2d 758, 31 Cal.Rptr. 146 (1963).

contended that the board's reclassification impaired the obligation of contracts. The highest state court disagreed, saying that as long as the reclassification was part of a general salary revision equally affecting all teachers of the same salary grade it was permissible.[36] The new classification that increased salaries for persons with degrees from accredited schools was deemed reasonable.

The New York legislature enacted an "excellence in teaching" program and provided funds to local districts to improve salaries for teachers. The state commissioner of education defined teacher to include administrators and supervisors who did some teaching and who belonged to the teachers bargaining unit. The latter criterion was held to be a denial of equal protection to administrators who taught but did not come under the collective bargaining contract in their districts.[37] The commissioner then replaced the criterion with that of being paid on the teachers salary schedule (possibly with an administrative supplement, but not on a separate schedule for administrators). This arrangement was upheld.[38]

It is an accepted principle that one who receives a benefit through error is generally not entitled to continue to enjoy the benefit after the error is discovered.[39] If the benefit is overpayment of salary, it has been held that a school board can unilaterally deduct overpayments from subsequent payments when the amounts of money are not substantial, no great hardship results, and there is no violation of an express contract condition.[40] Any deprivation by the reductions was deemed to be inconsequential in the case decided.

However, once one has been evaluated for public employment, he cannot be arbitrarily reclassified. The foundation of a complicated fact situation was that a teacher with advanced graduate training in a foreign institution was placed in a particular column on the salary schedule. Later, an attempt by school authorities to reevaluate and revoke his placement was declared illegal.[41] The court found that the board originally had properly exercised its discretion in placing the teacher on the schedule in the Ph.D.-Ed.D. category based on equivalency of the foreign degree. The board was empowered, in the court's view, to interpret its own rules liberally to allow degrees equivalent to the Ph.D. and Ed.D. for that placement. But when subsequently it decided to reevaluate the teacher's background and remove him from that level, it could not legally do so because his original placement was not due to fraud, duress, or mistake. The court further noted that there was evidence that some other teachers without the specific degrees of Ed.D.

36. A'Hearne v. City of Chelsea, 351 Mass. 105, 217 N.E.2d 767 (1966).

37. Schneider v. Ambach, 135 A.D.2d 284, 526 N.Y.S.2d 857 (1988).

38. Schneider v. Sobol, 76 N.Y.2d 309, 559 N.Y.S.2d 221, 558 N.E.2d 23 (1990).

39. Shoban v. Board of Trustees of Desert Center Unified School Dist., 276 Cal. App.2d 534, 81 Cal.Rptr. 112 (1969).

40. Green Local Teachers Ass'n v. Blevins, 43 Ohio App.3d 71, 539 N.E.2d 653 (1987).

41. People ex rel. Cinquino v. Board of Educ. of City of Chicago, 86 Ill.App.2d 298, 230 N.E.2d 85 (1967).

or Ph.D. were left on the schedule from which the petitioner was removed.

The Supreme Court of the United States decided a case in which it was contended that teachers' salaries could not be reduced by a local school board acting under a permissive statute because of a conflict with the statewide tenure law, which it was maintained prohibited any reductions of salary without following tenure procedures.[42] The Court, however, held that the tenure law was a statement of legislative policy, not a contract, and that the reduction of salaries for all teachers in a nondiscriminatory way was constitutional. The court noted that under the plan teachers were divided into classes for the application of a percent reduction, and all in a given class were treated alike. It did not consider significant the fact that in the operation of the plan incidental individual inequalities resulted in a few instances.

State legislative action occasioned by a fiscal emergency was held constitutional by the Court of Appeals of New York even though it precluded payment of wage increases provided for in an existing collective bargaining agreement.[43] The reality of the financial crisis found by the legislature to confront New York City was accepted by the plaintiff union of public employees "without intimation of doubt." The wage-freeze legislation was found by the court to be "reasonable and necessary" and not in violation of the constitutional bar against impairing obligations of contracts. The court differentiated contracts that had been performed from those that were executory.

However, it has been held that the concept of deferred-salary or lag-payroll (amounts of an employee's salary are withheld for a period of time) can constitute a violation of the contracts clause of the Constitution.[44] Simply declaring and presenting evidence of financial crisis by state or local authorities cannot support a postponement of due dates for salary; neither can plausible explanations as why a plan is minimally painful.

Personnel Files

Obviously school districts must keep records on employed personnel. Content of such files and accessibility to data therein have been subjects of litigation. Sometimes the two aspects are intertwined.

As to content, a major concern is whether a teacher has the right to challenge the placement in the file of uncomplimentary material. The Court of Appeals of New York has ruled that letters critical of performance or conduct can be placed in the file without any hearing thereon.[45] The court regarded them as evaluations that supervisors have a

---

42. Phelps v. Board of Educ., 300 U.S. 319, 57 S.Ct. 483, 81 L.Ed. 674 (1937). [Case No. 82]

43. Subway-Surface Supervisors Ass'n v. New York City Transit Authority, 44 N.Y.2d 101, 404 N.Y.S.2d 323, 375 N.E.2d 384 (1978).

44. Condell v. Bress, 983 F.2d 415 (2 Cir.1993).

45. Holt v. Board of Educ. of Webutuck Central School Dist., 52 N.Y.2d 625, 439 N.Y.2d 839, 422 N.E.2d 499 (1981).

right and a duty to make unless they constitute formal reprimands having serious repercussions or contain grave charges of misconduct. An admonition of a teacher for a comment made in class and an instruction not to comment on items that would reflect negatively on individual members of the student body was held by the Tenth Circuit to have been legitimately placed in a teacher's file even though the teacher disputed some facts.[46] He had said in class that one of several signs of deterioration of the quality of the school was the rumored sexual intercourse of two students on the tennis court. The board also had put him on paid administrative leave for four days while the incident was investigated. The court saw no violation of academic freedom and declined to focus on the alleged vague language of the written reproach.

The Sixth Circuit, however, ordered expunged from his personnel file a letter of censure for a teacher who as education association representative had engaged in alleged unprofessional conduct at a meeting with the school librarian and the principal.[47] The court found that retaliation for zealous union activity had violated the teacher's First Amendment rights.

A teacher also has a constitutional right to challenge the correctness of an item in the file that is stigmatizing or a barrier to future employment if it is placed there in connection with a termination and is likely to be disclosed to future employers.[48] The liberty right is to a name-clearing hearing. Also, there may be a defamation claim under state tort law if false information is released. However, there is no federal constitutional claim based solely on injury to reputation occasioned by release of derogatory information not in the context of discharge or nonrenewal.[49]

Whether confidential information must be divulged is generally decided by courts on a case-by-case basis weighing competing considerations.[50] The United States Supreme Court has held that a professor's tenure files are subject to subpoena by the Equal Employment Opportunity Commission when it is investigating a discrimination claim against a university.[51]

Whether certain data pertaining to individual teachers must be made public was discussed by the Court of Appeals, Fifth Circuit, in a case in which the issue involved disclosure of a teacher's college transcript.[52] The Family Educational Rights and Privacy Act of 1974[53] was held not to apply because the coverage therein of educational records

---

46. Miles v. Denver Public Schools, 944 F.2d 773 (10 Cir.1991).

47. Columbus Educ. Ass'n v. Columbus City School Dist., 623 F.2d 1155 (6 Cir. 1980).

48. Brandt v. Board of Cooperative Educational Services, 820 F.2d 41 (2 Cir.1987). [Case No. 85]

49. Siegert v. Gilley, 500 U.S. 226, 111 S.Ct. 1789, 114 L.Ed.2d 277 (1991).

50. Berst v. Chipman, 232 Kan. 180, 653 P.2d 107 (1982).

51. University of Pennsylvania v. Equal Employment Opportunity Commission, 493 U.S. 182, 110 S.Ct. 577, 107 L.Ed.2d 571 (1990).

52. Klein Independent School Dist. v. Mattox, 830 F.2d 576 (5 Cir.1987), cert. den. 485 U.S. 1008, 108 S.Ct. 1473, 99 L.Ed.2d 702 (1988). [Case No. 84]

53. See Appendix.

applies only to records of students, and the teacher's record here was that of an employee. As to protected privacy, the court said that, even assuming the teacher had a recognizable privacy interest in her college transcript, the interest was outweighed by the public's interest in evaluating the competence of its teachers.

Where "personnel and medical files" were excluded from coverage as public records, it was held that written evaluations by students of university faculty were not subject to compulsory disclosure.[54] That some faculty members released their evaluations and that at one time the University of Massachusetts contemplated making summaries of the evaluations available to students did not vitiate the general policy of the university.

Accessibility of personnel records is further discussed in Chapter 14 under "Records."

Misrepresentations or falsifications on application materials may be the basis for termination of employees when deliberately misleading information in the files is discovered. Satisfactory performance in a position does not negate the principle, especially if the information likely would have prevented hiring. The very act of misrepresenting may render the person unfit. For example, a teacher, who falsely stated in his application that he was a citizen of the United States and repeated the statement later in a loyalty oath, could be discharged despite his having acquired tenure status because the falsification of his records constituted a "continuing deception." [55]

It should be further noted that under some circumstances the purposeful withholding of material facts can form a basis for nonrenewal [56] or render a contract null from its beginning [57] if the suppression was designed to induce school authorities to enter into it. That a specific question was not asked does not always permit an applicant to "remain silent" on an important point.

Leaves

Although there is no right to paid sick leave for teachers, its legal validity is well established.[58] Abuse of sick leave clearly constitutes cause for disciplinary action against an employee.[59] Evidence that an employee is in fact ill or disabled may be required, either as a matter of

---

54. Connolly v. Bromery, 15 Mass.App. 661, 447 N.E.2d 1265 (1983).

55. Negrich v. Dade County Bd. of Public Instruction, 143 So.2d 498 (Fla.App. 1962).

56. Acanfora v. Board of Educ. of Montgomery County, 491 F.2d 498 (4 Cir.1974), cert. den. 419 U.S. 836, 95 S.Ct. 64, 42 L.Ed.2d 63 (1974).

57. Ostrolenk v. Louise S. McGehee School, 402 So.2d 237 (La.App.1981).

58. Averell v. Newburyport, 241 Mass. 333, 135 N.E. 463 (1922).

59. Reddick v. Leon County School Bd., 405 So.2d 757 (Fla.App.1981); Board of Educ. of Laurel County v. McCollum, 721 S.W.2d 703 (Ky.1986).

general policy[60] or in an instance where there is a question.[61] Conversely, evidence of physical fitness to return to duty may be required of those who have been on leave for reasons of health.[62] Requiring two medical opinions is not unreasonable.[63]

Details of sick leave policy are generally negotiable under collective bargaining statutes, so long as an agreement does not violate any state statute on the subject.[64] Where a school board is authorized to incorporate a benefit in an employee's compensation package, it also may withdraw it. Thus, the Supreme Court of Iowa, while holding that payment for accrued sick leave upon retirement was legally permissible, ruled that teachers who retired after the benefit had been withdrawn in subsequent bargaining had no claim to such payment.[65]

It is the responsibility of the person alleging that the act of an agent of a school board was authorized to establish that fact. Hence, although superintendents over a period of years had allowed unlimited accumulation of sick leave for use covering illnesses, it was held that when the board began to allow payment for unused sick leave upon a teacher's retirement the board was not obliged to honor the number of days listed in the superintendents' records.[66] No statute or board resolution bound the board. The Court of Appeals of Kentucky ruled that no contract with teachers had been formed, and it noted that the new policy regarding unused sick leave payments upon retirement was reasonable.

Where state statutes provide for leaves, questions arise as to the power of local boards to establish supplementary rules. Upheld by the Court of Appeal of Louisiana was a board rule specifying that a state-authorized sabbatical leave would not be granted a teacher who was going to work in full-time regular employment as a teacher in another state even though he would be taking graduate courses there.[67] The Supreme Court of Delaware held that a statute providing that each teacher may be absent with pay for one day a year for personal reasons did not cover absences for the reason of committing an unlawful act, here participating in an unlawful strike.[68]

Local boards must, however, make reasonable accommodations for leaves for teachers for religious reasons.[69] It is not constitutionally

60. Crowston v. Jamestown Public School Dist. No. 1, 335 N.W.2d 775 (N.D. 1983).

61. Compton College Federation of Teachers v. Compton Community College Dist., Bd. of Trustees, 132 Cal.App.3d 704, 183 Cal.Rptr. 341 (1982).

62. Strong v. Board of Educ. of Uniondale Union Free School Dist., 902 F.2d 208 (2 Cir.1990). [Case No. 22]

63. Scheideman v. West Des Moines Community School Dist., 989 F.2d 286 (8 Cir.1993).

64. Jefferson Classroom Teachers Ass'n v. Jefferson Elementary School Dist., 137 Cal.App.3d 993, 187 Cal.Rptr. 542 (1982).

65. Bettendorf Educ. Ass'n v. Bettendorf Community School Dist., 262 N.W.2d 550 (Iowa 1978).

66. Ramsey v. Board of Educ. of Whitley County, 789 S.W.2d 784 (Ky.App.1990). [Case No. 89]

67. Shaw v. Caddo Parish School Bd., 347 So.2d 39 (La.App.1977).

68. Board of Educ. of Marshallton-McKean School Dist. v. Sinclair, 373 A.2d 572 (Del.1977).

69. Rankins v. Commission on Professional Competence of Ducor Union School Dist., 24 Cal.3d 167, 154 Cal.Rptr. 907, 593 P.2d 852 (1979); Wangsness v. Watertown School Dist., 541 F.Supp. 332 (D.S.D.1982).

required, however, that those observing religious holidays when schools are in session be paid on a special basis for those days merely because schools are closed on the Christian holiday of Christmas and may be closed on Good Friday. A Jewish teacher unsuccessfully argued that his free exercise of religion was unconstitutionally burdened by his having to use paid personal leave days or take unpaid leave to observe Yom Kippur and Rosh Hashanah. The Court of Appeals, Tenth Circuit, found no violation of either the Constitution or of Title VII.[70]

The Supreme Court considered a Title VII challenge to a leave policy in a Connecticut school district.[71] The collectively bargained policy allowed specified numbers of days for certain personal purposes such as death in the immediate family, attendance at a wedding, and observance of mandatory religious holidays. Three days' annual leave was allowed for the last category. Also, three days' accumulated leave could be used for "necessary personal business" exclusive of that covered by the specific categories.

A member of the Worldwide Church of God was required by his faith to be absent during approximately six school days each year. Rather than lose pay for the days beyond the three for religious holidays, he proposed either that he be allowed to use his "necessary personal business" days or, if this were not approved, to receive his pay minus the cost of a substitute. The board, adhering to the written policy, declined the alternatives to leave without pay for the excess days.

The Court held that the requirement in Title VII that employers not discriminate based on an employee's religious tenets means that the employer must offer a reasonable accommodation. The employer is not required to demonstrate undue hardship in relation to alternatives suggested by the employee. The Court said the policy at issue "would generally be a reasonable one." However, the Court remanded the case because the record in the lower courts was not sufficiently clear as to whether in fact the personal business leave policy was being administered in a fashion discriminatory to religion by allowing paid leave for all but religious purposes. (On remand, the evidence did not show any animus toward religious activities in the granting of leaves for "necessary personal business." [72])

Where local boards provide for various leaves under general authorizations of power, the legal issues that arise are primarily those of contract interpretation. For sabbatical leaves, there are the troublesome factors of determining eligibility and what position the teacher will get upon return from leave. The board has general discretion as to the former.[73] As to the latter, the courts seem to view the matter according

70. Pinsker v. Joint Dist. No. 28J of Adams and Arapahoe Counties, 735 F.2d 388 (10 Cir.1984). [Case No. 88]

71. Ansonia Bd. of Educ. v. Philbrook, 479 U.S. 60, 107 S.Ct. 367, 93 L.Ed.2d 305 (1986).

72. Philbrook v. Ansonia Bd. of Educ., 925 F.2d 47 (2 Cir.1991), cert. den. ___ U.S. ___, 111 S.Ct. 2828, 115 L.Ed.2d 998 (1991).

73. Board of Educ. of Three Village Central Schools of Towns of Brookhaven and Smithtown v. Three Village Teachers' Ass'n, Inc., 71 A.D.2d 870, 419 N.Y.S.2d 665 (1979).

to the principles discussed under "Assignment and Transfer," infra. Thus, "the same position" was held not to mean teaching the same academic subject matter.[74] If the sabbatical contract is breached, either the teacher [75] or the board [76] can sue.

Maternity leaves are discussed in Chapter 9 under "Maternity Discrimination."

Assignment and Transfer

Assignment of teachers to individual school buildings lies within the discretion of the local school board. Teachers have no common law rights to specific building assignments.[77] Normally state statutes do not treat transfers that do not involve a change in status or salary. Local boards of education, however, frequently adopt rules governing transfers. When this is done, they are bound to follow their own rules, or transfers will be set aside by courts.[78]

Assignments within the scope of a teacher's certificate may be made at the discretion of the school board.[79] The point is amplified in Chapter 9 under "Duties Covered by Implication." If a separate certificate is not required for a position, any teacher can be assigned to it. Further, one holding a position with a locally designated title, other than that recognized by a certificate, does not acquire a vested right to the position. The Court of Appeals of Ohio decided a case which illustrates the point.[80] A teacher had been employed in a school system for eleven years and had a continuing contract. During three years she received the regular notices appointing her to the position of teacher at a certain salary, and each of the notices contained a further stipulation that she would receive a supplemental salary in a stated amount for additional duties as a guidance counselor. For the next two years she received and approved the same notices, but during these years she devoted full-time to her duties as counselor. Then she was notified by the superintendent that she was being reassigned to classroom teaching duties. The precise issue before the court was whether the teacher had acquired a status which could not be altered without reason. There was no question regarding salary. The court examined the certification procedure in Ohio and found that guidance counselors were "teachers," the certificates issued to them being "teaching certificates." The teacher's rights

74. Scott v. Dennis, 392 So.2d 169 (La. App.1980).

75. Cahill v. Board of Educ. of City of Stamford, 187 Conn. 94, 444 A.2d 907 (1982).

76. Trumansburg Central School Dist. v. Chalone, 87 A.D.2d 921, 449 N.Y.S.2d 92 (1982).

77. Matthews v. Board of Educ., 198 Cal.App.2d 748, 18 Cal.Rptr. 101 (1962); Maupin v. Independent School Dist. No. 26, 632 P.2d 396 (Okl.1981).

78. Rockey v. School Dist. No. 11, in El Paso County, 32 Colo.App. 203, 508 P.2d

796 (1973); Pasadena Unified School Dist. v. Commission on Professional Competence, 20 Cal.3d 309, 142 Cal.Rptr. 439, 572 P.2d 53 (1977).

79. Leithliter v. Board of Trustees of Lancaster School Dist., 12 Cal.App.3d 1095, 91 Cal.Rptr. 215 (1970); Quarles v. McKenzie Public School Dist. No. 34, 325 N.W.2d 662 (N.D.1982).

80. State ex rel. Fox v. Board of Educ., City of Springfield, 11 Ohio App.2d 214, 229 N.E.2d 663 (1966).

were based exclusively on her position as a teacher, rather than her assignment as a counselor, and, thus, the reassignment was upheld.

Whether a teacher's voluntary withdrawal of a subject area from her certificate (in effect when she obtained tenure status in a school system) would entitle her to refuse a reassignment to that area during a reduction-in-force was decided in the negative by the Missouri Court of Appeals.[81] The court said that the teacher's act was tantamount to a unilateral modification of her contractual obligations. Thus, refusal to teach in the area would be ground for termination. In this case the teacher acted two days before being officially informed of her new assignment.

In a California case a tenure teacher upon return from a sabbatical leave was assigned to teach a fifth-sixth grade in a school. She claimed the right to be restored to her previous position. Her suit failed. The court stated that, since her certification covered all elementary grades, her permanent employment was within the scope of the certificate under which tenure was acquired.[82] "Tenure does not bestow on the school teacher a vested right to a specific school or to a specific class level of students within any school."

Teachers must accept teaching assignments in their areas of competence. Unsuccessful in court was a physical education teacher who, when he was relieved of his post as football coach, refused to continue to coach basketball and was dismissed for his refusal. The court held the assignment to be proper, and his declining to accept it was ground for discharge.[83] Likewise held subject to discipline was a teacher who was a source of friction because of his strong opinions against the use of federal funds in public schools, and who refused to attend a school workshop using federally financed materials.[84] He unsuccessfully contested a forced transfer.

In addition to the absence of a constitutionally protected property right in a transfer situation, there is absence of a liberty interest of constitutional magnitude. Thus, no due process hearing is required before an employee can be transferred to a similar position.[85] This is true even if coaching responsibilities are eliminated in the reassignment.[86]

Involuntary transfers are subject to heightened judicial examination if a factor in the transfer decision relates to the teacher's exercise of First Amendment rights. A case decided by the Court of Appeals, Ninth Circuit, involved the transfer of a counselor of Mexican-American ances-

81. McLaughlin v. Board of Educ., 659 S.W.2d 249 (Mo.App.1983).

82. Adelt v. Richmond School Dist., 250 Cal.App.2d 149, 58 Cal.Rptr. 151 (1967).

83. Appeal of Ganaposki, 332 Pa. 550, 2 A.2d 742 (1938).

84. Brough v. Board of Educ. of Millard County School Dist., 23 Utah 2d 353, 463 P.2d 567 (1970), cert. den. 398 U.S. 928, 90 S.Ct. 1818, 26 L.Ed.2d 90 (1970).

85. Thomas v. Smith, 897 F.2d 154 (5 Cir.1989).

86. Jett v. Dallas Independent School Dist., 798 F.2d 748 (5 Cir.1986), aff. in part, remanded in part 491 U.S. 701, 109 S.Ct. 2702, 105 L.Ed.2d 598 (1989).

try who had been critical of school district policies related to classification of Mexican-American children on the basis of tests given in the medium of English.[87] Also she had advised certain parents to consult the local legal aid society. The teacher was trained in bilingual psychometry and originally assigned as counselor in a school enrolling many Mexican-Americans. Her transfer was to a school attended primarily by "well-to-do Anglo students." The trial court had found that the transfer was partially based upon retaliation for the exercise of First Amendment rights, but had denied relief because the transfer involved no loss of pay or status. The appellate court concluded that the teacher deserved a remedy and remanded the case for the trial judge to fashion an appropriate one under the "somewhat unusual circumstances." The court emphasized that the counselor had engaged in no harassment of officials and had not been insubordinate. Similarly, the Supreme Court of California invalidated the transfer of a teacher who had been critical of school policies, but who had obeyed them.[88]

In a Wyoming school district a provision in a collective bargaining contract specified that the "ultimate decision" with respect to voluntary transfers "may rest with the superintendent." The superintendent selected one of two candidates for a vacancy that each had sought. The board, however, at the highest level of grievance-resolution decided the other person should receive the transfer. The state supreme court upheld the board's decision, stating that "may" was permissive, and, more important, that in any event it was not legally possible for the board to delegate final authority over transfers by collective bargaining or otherwise.[89]

Those holding administrative posts may be reassigned to other administrative posts,[90] including those lower in the administrative hierarchy,[91] or to teaching posts [92] unless there are statutory or contractual provisions to the contrary. No hearing need be provided before such transfers may be effectuated.[93] Also, appropriate professional duties may be assigned to administrators, even if the duties were not traditionally associated with specific administrative positions.[94]

Assignments involving considerations of race are discussed in Chapter 13 under "Teacher Desegregation." Important to note here is that courts accept as a legitimate factor in teacher assignment the provision

87. Bernasconi v. Tempe Elementary School Dist. No. 3, 548 F.2d 857 (9 Cir. 1977), cert. den. 434 U.S. 825, 98 S.Ct. 72, 54 L.Ed.2d 82 (1977).

88. Adcock v. Board of Educ. of San Diego Unified School Dist., 10 Cal.3d 60, 109 Cal.Rptr. 676, 513 P.2d 900 (1973).

89. Diefenderfer v. Budd, 563 P.2d 1355 (Wyo.1977).

90. McCoy v. McConnell, 224 Tenn. 677, 461 S.W.2d 948 (1970).

91. Scottsdale School Dist. v. Clark, 20 Ariz.App. 321, 512 P.2d 853 (1973).

92. Holbrook v. Board of Educ. of Palo Alto Unified School Dist., 37 Cal.2d 316, 231 P.2d 853 (1951); Odegaard v. Everett School Dist. No. 2, 115 Wash.2d 323, 797 P.2d 1152 (1990).

93. McCoy v. Lincoln Intermediate Unit No. 12, 38 Pa.Cmwlth. 29, 391 A.2d 1119 (1978), cert. den. 441 U.S. 923, 99 S.Ct. 2033, 60 L.Ed.2d 397 (1979).

94. Gere v. Council Bluffs Community School Dist., 334 N.W.2d 307 (Iowa 1983).

of integrated staffs in all schools of a district.[95]

Loyalty

Loyalty Oaths

During the period following World War II loyalty oaths for teachers proliferated. The provisions of the oaths became increasingly more extensive, and focused more on what acts the teacher was prohibited from doing than on what he was required to do. Certain types of statements and associations outside the school setting were frequently barred. Also, some of the oaths contained stipulations that during a period prior to employment the party had not engaged in proscribed activities. Frequently criminal penalties for false swearing were included, in addition to the disqualification for a teaching position of one refusing to take the oath or swearing falsely.

In 1925 the Supreme Court of the United States observed that a state could require its teachers to be "of patriotic disposition" and that anything "manifestly inimical to the public welfare" could be barred.[96] But as legislatures and local boards of education became more zealous in carrying out their duty and responsibility to keep true subversives out of the schools, serious problems arose which eventually found their way into the courts. In 1952 the Supreme Court decided its first case regarding loyalty oaths.[97] Unanimously it declared unconstitutional an Oklahoma oath law. The primary basis for invalidating it was the fact that disqualification was based on membership during the preceding five years in an organization determined to be subversive, regardless of whether the person knew the character of the organization at the time of membership. The court said that "membership may be innocent" and that "a state servant may have joined a proscribed organization unaware of its activities and purposes."

In 1961, again unanimously, the Court found a specific provision in a Florida loyalty oath to be unconstitutionally vague.[98] That provision barred the lending of "aid, support, advice, counsel or influence to the Communist Party." The Court said it did not question the power of the state to safeguard the public service from disloyalty, but ruled that the state must describe proscribed conduct in "terms susceptible of objective measurement."

Subsequently, by increasingly divided votes, the Court struck down other oaths. In 1966, by a five-to-four vote, it introduced a new criterion to be met by loyalty legislation: no penalties could accrue unless the individual member of an organization could be shown to have joined with specific intent to further the unlawful purposes of the organization

95. Jacobson v. Cincinnati Bd. of Educ., 961 F.2d 100 (6 Cir.1992), cert. den. ___ U.S. ___, 113 S.Ct. 94, 121 L.Ed.2d 55 (1992). [Case No. 90]

96. Pierce v. Society of the Sisters of the Holy Names of Jesus and Mary, 268 U.S. 510, 45 S.Ct. 571, 69 L.Ed. 1070 (1925).

97. Wieman v. Updegraff, 344 U.S. 183, 73 S.Ct. 215, 97 L.Ed. 216 (1952).

98. Cramp v. Board of Public Instr. of Orange County, Florida, 368 U.S. 278, 82 S.Ct. 275, 7 L.Ed.2d 285 (1961).

or to have participated in them.[99] Teachers might be inhibited from participating in certain activities under certain sponsorship if the new criterion were not added, according to the majority. The Court held that to presume that a member shares the unlawful aims of an organization to which he belongs is an unconstitutional inference.

In 1967, however, the Supreme Court affirmed a lower court decision upholding the constitutionality of the following oath:

> "I do solemnly swear (or affirm) that I will support the constitution of the United States of America and the constitution of the State of New York, and that I will faithfully discharge, according to the best of my ability, the duties of the position of _____, to which I am now assigned."[100]

Citing Knight as the leading case, the Supreme Court in 1971 unanimously upheld a similar Florida requirement.[101] The Court said, "The validity of this section of the oath would appear settled." All Justices also agreed that the state could not summarily dismiss those who refused to pledge that they "do not believe in the overthrow of the government * * * by force or violence."

The New York oath upheld in Knight subsequently was attacked unsuccessfully on the ground of religious objection. A three-judge federal District Court held that the state had a compelling interest in a teacher's affirming her support of federal and state constitutions and that she would do her best as a teacher.[102] No hearing as to her reasons was necessary. She had adequate opportunity to make the oath or affirmation and thus retain her position. The Supreme Court affirmed.

In 1972 the Supreme Court split four-to-three in holding constitutional the inclusion in a required oath of the clause "oppose the overthrow of the government of the United States of America or of this Commonwealth [Massachusetts] by force, violence or by any illegal or unconstitutional method." [103] All seven participating Justices found the other clause of the oath ("uphold and defend" federal and state constitutions) to be constitutional. The majority stated that the second clause did not expand the obligation of the first, but rather made an application of the first clause to a particular issue. It said that such repetition, whether for emphasis or cadence, is common in oaths and that the Court "is not charged with correcting grammar but with enforcing a constitution."

The New York "Feinberg Law"

New York in 1949 enacted a statute known as the "Feinberg Law," which, while not prescribing an oath, was designed to implement and

---

99. Elfbrandt v. Russell, 384 U.S. 11, 86 S.Ct. 1238, 16 L.Ed.2d 321 (1966).

100. Knight v. Board of Regents of University of State of New York, 269 F.Supp. 339 (S.D.N.Y.1967), aff. 390 U.S. 36, 88 S.Ct. 816, 19 L.Ed.2d 812 (1968). [Case No. 86]

101. Connell v. Higginbotham, 403 U.S. 207, 91 S.Ct. 1772, 29 L.Ed.2d 418 (1971).

102. Biklen v. Board of Educ., 333 F.Supp. 902 (N.D.N.Y.1971), aff. 406 U.S. 951, 92 S.Ct. 2060, 32 L.Ed.2d 340 (1972).

103. Cole v. Richardson, 405 U.S. 676, 92 S.Ct. 1332, 31 L.Ed.2d 593 (1972).

enforce statutes enacted in 1917 and 1939. It made membership in a "subversive" organization prima facie evidence of disqualification for appointment or retention in the public schools of the state. It further required the state board of education (Board of Regents) to take certain measures and local boards to file reports on the loyalty of all teachers. In 1952 the Supreme Court of the United States by a vote of six-to-three, with one of the dissents being essentially on procedural grounds, upheld the constitutionality of the statute on its face.[104] The court found that if an organization was declared subversive, and if an employee was notified, he would have a freedom of choice between membership in the organization and employment in the school system, which was not considered at that time an encroachment upon his freedom of speech or assembly.

A 1953 amendment extended the application of the Feinberg Law to personnel of public colleges. Over the years many complex administrative procedures were developed. In 1967 the Supreme Court was asked to declare unconstitutional the system the state had adopted to keep out subversive employees. Involved were the Feinberg Law, its administrative regulations, and the two older statutes the Feinberg Law had been enacted to implement. A five-Justice majority of the Court found all of them unconstitutional.[105] "The regulatory maze created by New York is wholly lacking in 'terms susceptible of objective measurement,'" concluded the Court. It pointed out that the 1952 case had been a declaratory judgment suit, and that the Court had not considered any charge of unconstitutional vagueness because such had not been made in the pleadings or in the proceedings of the lower courts. However, in the 1967 opinion it stated that "to the extent that [the 1952 opinion] sustained the provision of the Feinberg Law constituting membership in an organization advocating forceful overthrow of government a ground for disqualification, pertinent constitutional doctrines have since rejected the premises upon which that conclusion rested."

The Fifth Amendment

Investigating committees of Congress and of state legislatures were frequent in the early 1950's. One congressional committee investigating communist activities attempted to question a teacher at a publicly supported college in New York City. He refused to answer, pleading the Fifth Amendment's provision against self-incrimination. A section of the charter of the city provided that whenever an employee utilized the privilege against self-incrimination to avoid answering a question regarding his official conduct, his employment was terminated automatically. This action was taken, and the teacher sued to annul his dismissal and for reinstatement in his position. The case was carried to the Supreme Court, which held, five-to-four, that the teacher's dismissal was violative

104. Adler v. Board of Educ. 342 U.S. 485, 72 S.Ct. 380, 96 L.Ed. 517 (1952).

589, 87 S.Ct. 675, 17 L.Ed.2d 629 (1967). [Case No. 87]

105. Keyishian v. Board of Regents of University of State of New York, 385 U.S.

of due process.[106] The Court emphasized that it was not saying that the teacher had a constitutional right to teach in the public college, or that proper inquiry might not show dismissal warranted. It was summary dismissal with no hearing that violated due process.

Two years later a second "refusal to answer" case came to the Supreme Court. A teacher was informed that the superintendent had information reflecting on his loyalty. The superintendent inquired whether the teacher had been, eight years previously, an officer of the Communist Political Association. The teacher told the superintendent he would not answer that question or others of that type or questions about his political or religious beliefs. The board of education then discharged him on the ground of "incompetency." The board avoided any issue of the teacher's loyalty. His discharge was based solely on his refusal to answer the superintendent's questions.

In a five-to-four decision the Court sustained the discharge. It found the teacher insubordinate and lacking in frankness and candor.[107] The approved dismissal was based upon the teacher's refusal to answer any inquiry about his relevant activities—not upon those activities themselves. The Court stated that a teacher's classroom conduct is not the sole basis for determining fitness to teach. Fitness depends upon a broad range of factors.

Thus, school authorities may inquire into areas relevant to the teacher's position, and the teacher must answer. What action, if any, is taken based on the answers raises entirely different issues, namely, those associated with disciplinary actions against teachers.

Collective Negotiations

In General

The extent to which public employers in general, and local school boards in particular, may engage in the process of collective bargaining with employees varies from state to state. It is completely clear that public employees may legally maintain memberships in associations organized on occupational lines. Most states have enacted statutes specifically establishing some rights of employees in public schools to negotiate with boards of education following certain procedures. Even in the absence of such statutes, no law would prevent boards of education from discussing working conditions with representatives of teachers associations, and in a majority of jurisdictions there would be an implied power of local boards to enter into limited collective bargaining contracts.

The principal judicial issues in the area cluster around three main points: the limits within which school boards can legally "bargain" or "negotiate" with teachers organizations, the pressures school employees

---

106. Slochower v. Board of Higher Educ. of New York City, 350 U.S. 551, 76 S.Ct. 637, 100 L.Ed. 692 (1956).

107. Beilan v. Board of Educ., School Dist. of Philadelphia, 357 U.S. 399, 78 S.Ct. 1317, 2 L.Ed.2d 1414 (1958).

can bring upon boards of education to persuade them to subscribe to the association's point of view, and the role that can be assigned to arbitrators. There are also, of course, myriad procedural details, such as recognition, unit determination, and impasse arrangements.

Regarding the first point, local boards of education cannot divest themselves of their discretionary authority by agreeing to be bound by agreements reached through other than legally sanctioned processes or incorporating items not permitted by the legislature. It becomes obvious that there is some nicety to the determination of when a board is divesting itself of its statutory duties, and when it is merely being persuaded by the logic of the employees' position to adopt a policy and record it in a master contract. There seems no question that the state can permit or require boards of education to develop personnel policies with participation of the employees, the limits of the participation being decided by the state. No constitutional right to have collective bargaining exists. The voluntary entry into collective bargaining by a board does not preclude the board's ceasing to continue the process at the end of the contract period. Also, use of collective bargaining only with some classifications of employees does not create constitutional equal protection rights for other categories.

As to the second point, it seems clear that the state has the power to permit teachers to engage in certain concerted actions designed to bring about changes in employment conditions. Absent affirmative state action, employees still have certain rights. The United States Constitution not only guarantees to employees freedom of speech and of association, but also restricts the conditions which can be placed upon public employees. That public employees have the right to join organizations of their choosing is settled, and they cannot be disciplined for organizational activity per se.

Concerning the third point, there is no doubt that the state can go far in allowing decisions about school board-employee relations to be made by parties other than those directly involved. This power is almost beyond question as to the interpretation of collective bargaining contracts. It is not so free of doubt in the matter of determining what elements will go into a master contract. The former in essence establishes a tribunal other than the courts to decide contract-meaning disputes. The latter implicates fundamental concepts of our constitutional system of government.

Emphasis should be given here to the fact that collective bargaining describes a general process for determining policies. It has nothing to do with the legality of a given policy or with the interpretation of the wording of the policy. Thus, discussions of the legal aspects of policies in other sections of this book are not dependent on how the policies were derived. An illegal policy does not become legal because it was collectively negotiated. Nor does the doctrine of precedents diminish where courts interpret elements in collective agreements. (Interpretations by arbitrators are discussed under "Arbitration", infra.).

Negotiable Items

What, if anything, is negotiable (i.e., a proper subject to treat through the process of collective bargaining) lies within the power of the legislature to determine. Among those states having legislation wide variations exist as regards degree of specificity. Some statutes state only "terms and conditions of employment," but even where the statutes are more specific, there are broad gray areas requiring eventual judicial interpretation. On this topic there is no consistency among the courts, and, since no federal question is involved, it is necessary to examine the rulings in a given state to determine the law in that jurisdiction.

It is important to distinguish between what *may* be negotiated by boards and what *must* be negotiated. One generalization from judicial interpretations is that anything within a board's power to decide *may* be negotiated if the board elects to do so *except* those matters directly or indirectly excluded by legislation and those matters in which it must maintain an instant discretion in order to fulfil its duties and responsibilities. Obviously this principle can be given a broad or narrow interpretation by a court. Another generalization is that a board *must* negotiate only those matters specifically required to be negotiated by express legislation or implied from that legislation. What is implied, of course, is for the courts ultimately to decide.

One example of a matter that was held not to be bargainable arose from a board of education's desire to act to correct a situation where a gross imbalance existed between percent of black students and percent of black administrators. A collective bargaining contract provided for selection of administrators from promotional lists. The lists, however, contained only a few blacks. State and federal appellate courts held the board not to be bound by the provision, for the circumstances constituted "a real threat or obstacle" to the proper functioning of the school system.[108] Other specific matters found to be beyond a board's implied power to bargain include the determination to consolidate two department chairmanships,[109] the "control" of assignments and transfers,[110] the granting of tenure,[111] the withholding of a salary increment,[112] the frequency of grade cards,[113] the appointment of a principal,[114] and the

---

108. Porcelli v. Titus, 108 N.J.Super. 301, 261 A.2d 364 (1969). See Porcelli v. Titus, 431 F.2d 1254 (3 Cir.1970), cert. den. 402 U.S. 944, 91 S.Ct. 1612, 29 L.Ed.2d 112 (1971).

109. Dunellen Bd. of Educ. v. Dunellen Educ. Ass'n, 64 N.J. 17, 311 A.2d 737 (1973).

110. School Dist. of Seward Educ. Ass'n v. School Dist., 188 Neb. 772, 199 N.W.2d 752 (1972).

111. Cohoes City School Dist. v. Cohoes Teachers Ass'n, 40 N.Y.2d 774, 390 N.Y.S.2d 53, 358 N.E.2d 878 (1976); School

Committee of Danvers v. Tyman, 372 Mass. 106, 360 N.E.2d 877 (1977).

112. Board of Educ. of Tp. of Bernards v. Bernards Tp. Educ. Ass'n, 79 N.J. 311, 399 A.2d 620 (1979).

113. Chee-Craw Teachers Ass'n v. Unified School Dist. No. 247, Crawford County, 225 Kan. 561, 593 P.2d 406 (1979).

114. Berkshire Hills Regional School Dist. Committee v. Berkshire Hills Educ. Ass'n, 375 Mass. 522, 377 N.E.2d 940 (1978).

appointment of a department head.[115]

Where a subject is not excluded from negotiation, the question arises whether a board must negotiate it. Although the initial decision may be made by an administrative agency established in connection with the collective bargaining legislation, the ultimate determination is judicial.[116] The complexity of the issue may be illustrated by noting two common specifics on which courts have differed even though enabling legislation was similar: class size [117] and school calendar.[118]

Some courts, rather than simply proclaiming a matter subject or not subject to mandatory negotiation, have attempted to offer guides beyond restatements of "condition of employment," "managerial prerogative," "basic policy issue," and other conclusory expressions. The Supreme Court of Kansas has stated the "key" to be "how direct the impact of an issue is on the well-being of the individual teacher, as opposed to its effect on the operation of the school system as a whole." [119] The Supreme Court of Pennsylvania has set the test as "whether the impact of the issue on the interest of the employee in wages, hours and terms and conditions of employment outweighs its probable effect on the basic policy of the system as a whole." [120] Both courts emphasized, however, the need for a case by case approach. The Pennsylvania court warned that experiences in the private sector might not be entirely applicable, a caution voiced by other courts.

The Supreme Court of Alaska, stating that "logically and semantically it is nearly impossible to assign specific items" beyond salaries, fringe benefits, number of hours worked, and amount of leave time to either the category of negotiable or that of nonnegotiable, and strongly suggesting that more specific guidance from the legislature would be helpful, categorized some fifty items which had been raised in three cases it had consolidated for decision.[121] The nonnegotiable nine included "relief from nonprofessional chores," class size and teacher load, evaluation of administrators, teacher aides, and calendar.

Within the area of transfer policies the Supreme Court of Minnesota delineated some distinctions.[122] The decision to transfer a number of teachers is managerial and not required to be negotiated. But the

---

115. Maine School Administrative Dist. No. 61 Bd. of Directors v. Lake Region Teachers Ass'n, 567 A.2d 77 (Me.1989).

116. Jefferson County Bd. of Supervisors v. New York State Public Employment Relations Bd., 36 N.Y.2d 534, 369 N.Y.S.2d 662, 330 N.E.2d 621 (1975); Westbrook School Committee v. Westbrook Teachers Ass'n, 404 A.2d 204 (Me.1979).

117. Compare West Irondequoit Teachers Ass'n v. Helsby, 35 N.Y.2d 46, 358 N.Y.S.2d 720, 315 N.E.2d 775 (1974) with West Hartford Educ. Ass'n v. DeCourcy, 162 Conn. 566, 295 A.2d 526 (1972).

118. Compare City of Biddeford v. Biddeford Teachers Ass'n, 304 A.2d 387 (Me.1973) with Joint School Dist. No. 8 v.

Wisconsin Employment Relations Bd., 37 Wis.2d 483, 155 N.W.2d 78 (1967).

119. National Educ. Ass'n of Shawnee Mission v. Board of Educ. of Shawnee Mission Unified School Dist. No. 512, 212 Kan. 741, 512 P.2d 426 (1973).

120. Pennsylvania Labor Relations Bd. v. State College Area School Dist., 461 Pa. 494, 337 A.2d 262 (1975).

121. Kenai Peninsula Borough School Dist. v. Kenai Peninsula Educ. Ass'n, 572 P.2d 416 (Alaska 1977).

122. Minneapolis Federation of Teachers, Local 59 v. Minneapolis Special School Dist. No. 1, 258 N.W.2d 802 (Minn.1977).

criteria for determining which teachers are to be transferred involve a teacher's welfare and are mandatorily negotiable. Each individual transfer is subject to grievance arbitration to insure conformity to the negotiated contract. By contrast, the Supreme Court of New Jersey has excluded the whole subject of transfers from the scope of negotiable items.[123]

The difference between substance and procedures arises frequently in connection with teacher evaluation. Although who is to evaluate and what is to be evaluated are usually considered policy decisions, procedures are generally subject to mandatory bargaining.[124] Violations of the bargained procedures, however, generally do not result in one's acquiring tenure so long as state statutory procedures have been observed.[125] Reemployment for a period during which compliance with the negotiated procedures can be effectuated is a remedy that has been approved judicially.[126]

The Court of Appeals of New York considered the issues "whether a public employer is free to bargain voluntarily about job security and also free, under the collective agreement's provisions, to submit to arbitration disputes about job security."[127] The court held in the affirmative on both matters. Citing its often repeated view that any item may be voluntarily bargained by a public employer unless it is prohibited by statute or controlling decisional law or is contrary to public policy, the court held that "severe financial stringency" was not a basis for abrogating a contract provision specifically preventing termination for "budgetary reasons or abolition of programs." The court observed that the contract was of "relatively brief duration" (three years), that the provisions were not negotiated "in a time of financial emergency between parties of unequal bargaining power," and that arbitrators may consider financial conditions in their resolution of the dispute. Expressly disagreeing with this case, the Supreme Judicial Court of Massachusetts held that a job security clause in a multiyear contract was not enforceable beyond the first year of the agreement.[128]

Although monetary fringe benefits are clearly connected to compensation, the question of whether a school board possesses the power to spend funds for certain purposes sometimes arises. The Supreme Court of Iowa decided two cases where the key issue was authority of school boards to agree to finance certain expenditures through collective bar-

123. Ridgefield Park Educ. Ass'n v. Ridgefield Park Bd. of Educ., 78 N.J. 144, 393 A.2d 278 (1978).

124. City of Beloit by Beloit City School Bd. v. Wisconsin Employment Relations Comm'n, 73 Wis.2d 43, 242 N.W.2d 231 (1976); Central Point School Dist. No. 6 v. Employment Relations Bd., 27 Or.App. 285, 555 P.2d 1269 (1976); Milberry v. Board of Educ. of School Dist. of Philadelphia, 467 Pa. 79, 354 A.2d 559 (1976).

125. Illinois Educ. Ass'n Local Community High School Dist. 218 v. Board of Educ.

of School Dist. 218, Cook County, 62 Ill.2d 127, 340 N.E.2d 7 (1975).

126. Cohoes City School Dist. v. Cohoes Teachers Ass'n, 40 N.Y.2d 774, 390 N.Y.S.2d 53, 358 N.E.2d 878 (1976).

127. Board of Educ. of Yonkers City School Dist. v. Yonkers Federation of Teachers, 40 N.Y.2d 268, 386 N.Y.S.2d 657, 353 N.E.2d 569 (1976).

128. Boston Teachers Union, Local 66 v. School Committee of Boston, 386 Mass. 197, 434 N.E.2d 1258 (1982).

gaining agreements. In one the contested point was reimbursement of teachers for tuition expense for approved graduate studies [129] and in the other it was payment of a lump-sum upon retirement for unused sick leave.[130] Both provisions were upheld. Implied financial powers of boards are treated in Chapter 6.

When legislatures establish special programs for recognition of quality of teaching they can exclude the provisions from the sphere of mandatory collective bargaining. That local boards are given an option to participate [131] and that the economic incentive is awarded directly to the teacher [132] have withstood legal challenges. In the first case the court reversed the public employment relations board, which had ruled that whether to apply must be bargained. In the later situation a collective bargaining right in the state constitution was held not to be violated.

Strikes

Attention to some ramifications of collective action by public employees was given by the Supreme Court of Errors of Connecticut in a declaratory judgment suit involving a teachers' association in 1951.[133] In that leading case the court found strikes by school employees to be illegal. It stated that such a "drastic remedy * * * to enforce the demands of unions of governmental employees is in direct contravention" of the principle that "the government is established by and run for all the people, not for the benefit of any person or group." The court further observed that "the profit motive, inherent in the principle of free enterprise, is absent." The court, however, upheld the right of teachers to organize and the implied power of the board to negotiate so long as it does not "negotiate a contract which involves the surrender of the board's legal discretion, is contrary to law or is otherwise ultra vires."

The Supreme Court of Florida reviewed judicial holdings on strikes and concluded that "a strike against the government [is one] which all authorities agree cannot be tolerated in the absence of expressed consent by the government."[134] It considered a situation in which teachers refused to start work in the fall, but concurrently laid claim to their positions, saying they were still negotiating for terms more acceptable to them. The court rejected a claim of "involuntary servitude," saying that they could resign, but they could not strike and bargain for a return to work while retaining their rights as teachers in the system.

129. Barnett v. Durant Community School Dist., 249 N.W.2d 626 (Iowa 1977).

130. Bettendorf Educ. Ass'n v. Bettendorf Community School Dist., 262 N.W.2d 550 (Iowa 1978).

131. City School Dist. of City of Elmira v. New York State Public Employment Relations Bd., 74 N.Y.2d 395, 547 N.Y.S.2d 820, 547 N.E.2d 75 (1989).

132. United Teachers of Dade FEA/United AFT, Local 1974, AFL–CIO v. Dade County School Bd., 500 So.2d 508 (Fla.1986).

133. Norwalk Teachers' Ass'n v. Board of Educ., 138 Conn. 269, 83 A.2d 482 (1951).

134. Pinellas County Classroom Teachers Ass'n v. Board of Public Instr. of Pinellas County, 214 So.2d 34 (Fla.1968).

A New York court has determined that the tactic of "mass resignations" was in essence a strike.[135] It found that the executed resignations were delivered to the union at its request as part of its plan for compelling the board of education to accede to its demands.

Some states have passed statutes expressly forbidding strikes of public employees. The constitutionality of such statutes has been sustained.[136] That the legislature is free to provide by statute that public employees may enforce their right to collective bargaining by the strike has been suggested by several courts which have ruled strikes illegal in the absence of legislation.[137] However, the Supreme Court of New Jersey commented that, although the legislature could find strikes by public employees tolerable within certain limits, it "could not legislate the branches of government into idleness."[138]

Legislative authorization of strikes as part of a comprehensive plan for conducting collective bargaining in Pennsylvania was attacked as being in violation of the state constitutional requirement of a thorough and efficient system of public education. The state's top court disagreed.[139] It said that arguments about the effectiveness of the state plan should be directed to the legislature. The fact that there were arguments on both sides of the issue supported the power of the legislature to act as it had.

Although the common law barrier against strikes by teachers remains firm, the courts are not unaware of the fact that collective bargaining statutes may be hollow benefits for teachers if boards can flaunt the intent of such statutes as regards procedures for resolving impasses as to contract terms. Thus, while holding that the absence of an express prohibition against strikes in a collective bargaining statute did not inferentially grant a right to strike, the Supreme Court of Idaho ruled that accompanying the injunctive relief against a teacher strike should be an order to the board to engage in the statutorily prescribed procedure for resolving bargaining impasses.[140]

Teachers on a statewide basis in Delaware engaged in a one-day "job action" after the legislature failed to enact pay raises. As had been suggested by leaders of the association, many attempted to count the day as one of "personal leave." The state's highest court held that the action amounted to an illegal strike and that school boards were justified in not granting the leave and in withholding a day's pay.[141] In another case the same court considered an appeal from a fine levied against a

135. Board of Educ. of the City of New York v. Shanker, 54 Misc.2d 641, 283 N.Y.S.2d 432 (1967).

136. City of New York v. De Lury, 23 N.Y.2d 175, 295 N.Y.S.2d 901, 243 N.E.2d 128 (1968), app. dism. 394 U.S. 455, 89 S.Ct. 1223, 22 L.Ed.2d 414 (1969).

137. City of Manchester v. Manchester Teachers Guild, 100 N.H. 507, 131 A.2d 59 (1957).

138. Board of Educ., Borough of Union Beach v. New Jersey Educ. Ass'n, 53 N.J. 29, 247 A.2d 867 (1968).

139. Reichley v. North Penn School Dist., 533 Pa. 519, 626 A.2d 123 (1993).

140. School Dist. No. 351 Oneida County v. Oneida Educ. Ass'n, 98 Idaho 486, 567 P.2d 830 (1977).

141. Board of Educ. of Marshallton-McKean School Dist. v. Sinclair, 373 A.2d 572 (Del.1977).

teachers union and its officers for civil contempt for violating an injunction against a strike.[142] The claim presented was that the lower court lacked jurisdiction in the matter because the decision to seek the injunction had been made by the school board in executive session in violation of the open meetings statute. Without deciding whether the open meetings statute was in fact violated, the court upheld the validity of the decision of the board to seek the injunction and, therefore, the jurisdiction of the trial court to impose contempt sanctions.

When teachers threaten a strike, the board of education may apply for a court injunction against it. Generally, upon a proper showing, such injunction will be granted. What constitutes a proper showing, however, may vary among jurisdictions. The Supreme Court of Michigan in 1968 was the first to apply restraints on issuance of injunctions.[143] It required a showing of "violence, irreparable injury, or breach of the peace," because injunctions in "labor disputes" on other grounds are "basically contrary to public policy" in that state. The Supreme Court of New Hampshire, while acknowledging its prior holding that strikes of public employees were illegal, nevertheless followed the Michigan court and decided that an injunction should not automatically be issued, but that consideration should also be given to operational factors, such as, whether negotiations were conducted in good faith and whether recognized methods of settlement had failed.[144]

Violations of court orders issued to end strikes may be punished in contempt of court proceedings. Fines may be imposed on unions.[145] Also, forfeiture of the dues checkoff privilege has been upheld as an acceptable sanction.[146] Punishment, by fine and imprisonment for contempt, of the president of a local teachers' organization and of a representative of the national union has been sustained where there was no anti-strike legislation.[147] Both had been very vocal in their defiance of a court order issued to restrain a strike. In affirming the penalty, the Supreme Court of New Jersey held that teachers could not strike. The Court of Appeals of New York has held that it is not necessary for the legislature to provide for jury trials in contempt proceedings growing out of public employees' strikes.[148]

The Supreme Court decided a case where the question was whether a school board could discharge teachers for striking when the strike developed from a stalemate in collective bargaining.[149] The Court answered in the affirmative. It said that the due process clause of the

---

142. Wilmington Federation of Teachers v. Howell, 374 A.2d 832 (Del.1977).

143. School Dist. for City of Holland v. Holland Educ. Ass'n, 380 Mich. 314, 157 N.W.2d 206 (1968).

144. Timberlane Regional School Dist. v. Timberlane Regional Educ. Ass'n, 114 N.H. 245, 317 A.2d 555 (1974). [Case No. 91]

145. Labor Relations Comm'n v. Fall River Educators' Ass'n, 382 Mass. 465, 416 N.E.2d 1340 (1981).

146. Buffalo Teachers Federation, Inc. v. Helsby, 676 F.2d 28 (2 Cir.1982).

147. In re Block, 50 N.J. 494, 236 A.2d 589 (1967).

148. Rankin v. Shanker, 23 N.Y.2d 111, 295 N.Y.S.2d 625, 242 N.E.2d 802 (1968).

149. Hortonville Joint School Dist. No. 1 v. Hortonville Educ. Ass'n, 426 U.S. 482, 96 S.Ct. 2308, 49 L.Ed.2d 1 (1976).

Fourteenth Amendment did not guarantee striking teachers that the decision to terminate their employment would be made or reviewed by a body other than the school board. The Court found that in the instant case the teachers who had been dismissed for striking "failed to demonstrate that the decision [by the board] to terminate their employment was infected by the sort of bias that we have held to disqualify other decisionmakers as a matter of federal due process." The record showed neither a personal or financial stake of board members in the decision that might create a conflict of interest nor any personal animosity. The teachers had admitted they were engaged in a work stoppage; therefore there was no possibility of factual error on "this critical threshold issue."

The Court viewed the issue of discharge as a policy question rather than an adjudicative decision: "What choice among the alternative responses to the teachers' strike will best serve the interests of the school system, the interests of the parents and children who depend on the system, and the interests of the citizens whose taxes support it?" The Court said that state law gave the board the power to employ and dismiss teachers "as a part of the balance it has struck in the area of municipal labor relations."

A long standing statute provided that employees of the federal government must not assert the right to strike. Taking an oath to this effect was a condition of employment. A three-judge federal District Court found this to be an unconstitutional restraint on freedom of speech.[150] The government did not appeal.

Another clause in the employment affidavit specified that one would not "participate" in a strike while employed by the federal government. This clause was sustained by a three-judge District Court in a decision affirmed by the Supreme Court.[151] "Participate" was held not to be unconstitutionally vague, and Congress was held to have the power to expressly prohibit strikes.

In New York the "Taylor Law," covering collective bargaining in the public sector, requires an organization of public employees seeking exclusive bargaining recognition to file an affirmation that it does not assert the right to strike. This was held constitutional by the highest state court, and the appeal was dismissed by the Supreme Court for "want of a substantial federal question."[152] The case differed from National Association of Letter Carriers (supra) in that here the issue was not individual job acquisition or retention, but rather certification of an organization to be benefitted by the provisions of the Taylor Law.

Another provision of the Taylor Law provides that an employee be notified by the chief executive officer of his division that he has been

---

150. National Ass'n of Letter Carriers v. Blount, 305 F.Supp. 546 (D.D.C.1969), app. dism. under Rule 60 [at request of appellant], 400 U.S. 801, 91 S.Ct. 7, 27 L.Ed.2d 33 (1970).

151. United Federation of Postal Clerks v. Blount, 325 F.Supp. 879 (D.D.C.1971),

aff. 404 U.S. 802, 92 S.Ct. 80, 30 L.Ed.2d 38 (1971).

152. Rogoff v. Anderson, 28 N.Y.2d 880, 322 N.Y.S.2d 718, 271 N.E.2d 553 (1971), app. dism. 404 U.S. 805, 92 S.Ct. 108, 30 L.Ed.2d 37 (1971).

found to have violated the law by engaging in a strike. If the employee wishes to contest the finding, he may have an administrative review by that officer if he submits within twenty days an affidavit with evidence to the contrary. Following this review, he may go to court. It was held that this system of review by objection is adequate as regards due process, and, further, that a failure to seek such review foreclosed judicial examination of any issues.[153] The Supreme Court dismissed the appeal for "want of a substantial federal question."

Other "Job Actions"

The use of "sanctions," as an alternative to the strike, was considered by the Supreme Court of New Jersey.[154] A local board of education declined to reemploy three nontenure teachers, one of whom happened to be the president of the local teachers association. At a meeting attended by representatives of the state education association, it was urged that the teachers resign en masse. Thirty-one of forty-seven teachers submitted resignations early in April to be effective two weeks before the end of the school term. The local and the state associations "imposed sanctions," which included sending notices to all members, to teacher preparation institutions in New Jersey and neighboring states, and to all state education associations. Conditions in the school district were criticized, and there were statements that teachers who accepted employment in the district were in violation of "the professional code of ethics," which could lead to censure, expulsion, or denial of membership in the state association. The court held that the action to support the withholding of services a school district might need to discharge its public duty was as illegal as "the usual concerted refusal to work."

If picketing is employed solely to induce a breach of contract,[155] or obstruct a government function,[156] it can be restrained. The fact that the picketing is peaceful does not validate its use, nor does it become legal upon the offer to perform certain "essential" services. Thus, picketing could be enjoined when it was engaged in by custodial employees striking against a board of education's rejection of a proposed collective bargaining agreement.[157] Picket lines were established around school buildings and were found to be disruptive of normal school operations.

The Supreme Court of Illinois, extending the last mentioned case, held that a court could issue a temporary restraining order without notice or hearing when striking and picketing by public school teachers

---

153. Lawson v. Board of Educ. of Vestal Central School Dist. No. 1, 35 A.D.2d 878, 315 N.Y.S.2d 877 (1970), app. dism. 404 U.S. 907, 92 S.Ct. 230, 30 L.Ed.2d 180 (1971).

154. Board of Educ., Borough of Union Beach v. New Jersey Educ. Ass'n, 53 N.J. 29, 247 A.2d 867 (1968).

155. Board of Educ. of Martins Ferry City School Dist. v. Ohio Educ. Ass'n, 13 Ohio Misc. 308, 235 N.E.2d 538 (1967).

156. State v. Heath, 177 N.W.2d 751 (N.D.1970).

157. Board of Educ. v. Redding, 32 Ill.2d 567, 207 N.E.2d 427 (1965). See also City of Pana v. Crowe, 57 Ill.2d 547, 316 N.E.2d 513 (1974).

were underway.[158] The Constitution does not afford the same kind of freedom to those who communicate ideas by picketing as it affords those who communicate ideas by pure speech. But informational picketing cannot be enjoined unless it is shown that the picketing likely will cause disruption.[159]

When a strike was imminent in Newark, New Jersey, a broad restraining order was served on the union, its officers, and those acting in concert with them in connection with specified acts concomitant to a strike. At the union's mass meeting the president told the audience that the union had been served with the order but would strike anyway as the only means of redress of its grievances. She and 184 others were subsequently adjudged in contempt and sentenced. The appellate court was satisfied that the evidence supported the conclusion that the teachers were not summarily found guilty of contempt for absence from the classroom per se as an act of disobedience of the order.[160] There was proof of prohibited picketing by most of those held in contempt. Also there was absence from the classroom coupled with failure to comply with a school regulation requiring the explaining of the absences. Statements that one intends to violate an injunction against a strike, however, are not an acceptable basis for a finding of contempt of court.[161]

A public employee has the right to voice a point of view or express a grievance as long as doing so does not interfere with the performance of his duties. But absence en masse of teachers to go to the state capital to consult with legislative members about changes in conditions of employment and other matters was held to constitute a strike under a New York statute.[162] The court, however, commended to the legislature the view that approved leaves of absence for specific individuals to represent teachers before the legislature or other appropriate bodies would be a desirable amendment to the statute.

Organizational activities, however, that interfere with an individual's effectiveness or disrupt school operations can be prohibited by boards. Absence unrelated to one's teaching duties where no substitute teacher was available has been held cause for dismissal.[163] In that case the teacher, an association officer, was told he could not absent himself to attend a meeting of a state school problems commission and a national teachers' association meeting. His wilful violation of instructions with consequent loss to the students was proper cause for discharge.

158. Board of Educ. v. Kankakee Federation of Teachers Local No. 886, 46 Ill.2d 439, 264 N.E.2d 18 (1970), cert. den. 403 U.S. 904, 91 S.Ct. 2203, 29 L.Ed.2d 679 (1971).

159. Board of Educ. of Danville Community Consolidated School Dist. No. 118 v. Danville Educ. Ass'n, 59 Ill.App.3d 726, 17 Ill.Dec. 431, 376 N.E.2d 430 (1978).

160. Board of Educ. v. Newark Teachers Union, Local No. 481, 114 N.J.Super. 306, 276 A.2d 175 (1971), cert. den. 404 U.S. 950, 92 S.Ct. 275, 30 L.Ed.2d 267 (1971).

161. Board of Educ. of Brunswick City School Dist. v. Brunswick Educ. Ass'n, 61 Ohio St.2d 290, 401 N.E.2d 440 (1980).

162. Pruzan v. Board of Educ. of City of New York, 25 Misc.2d 945, 209 N.Y.S.2d 966 (1960).

163. Yuen v. Board of Educ. of School Dist. No. U–46, 77 Ill.App.2d 353, 222 N.E.2d 570 (1966).

Restraints on Boards

Some states have statutes expressly forbidding collective bargaining contracts between units of government and unions of employees. Their constitutionality has been sustained.[164] The legislature can establish such procedures covering school board-teacher relations as it deems appropriate. A substantial majority of states have enacted collective negotiations legislation applicable to teachers. Some of these statutes cover all public employees including teachers, and others treat teachers separately from employees of state government and local municipal government. That teachers constitute a sufficiently distinct classification to warrant separate treatment was decided by the supreme courts of Minnesota and Alaska.[165] At issue was the exclusion of teachers from coverage under certain legislation for other public employees.

The Supreme Court of Minnesota also upheld a provision that striking public employees could not later be reimbursed for pay lost while they were striking and that their salaries could not be increased for one year after the strike.[166] Thus, board resolutions to the contrary, adopted as part of a strike settlement, were void. The Supreme Court of Illinois vacated as repugnant to public policy an arbitration award that benefited those who had illegally struck over others.[167]

It is judicially well settled that boards may not dismiss or fail to rehire a teacher solely because of union activity.[168] Such activity is a constitutionally protected right. Furthermore, statements critical of the administration's posture in negotiating sessions are not cause for nonrenewal of a teacher's contract.[169]

Likewise, a board of education cannot require that teachers join a union as a condition of employment [170] or as a basis for a benefit such as a salary increase.[171] This raises the issues of "free riders" and of financial support for the union's cost of negotiating the collective contract. One way to balance equities is to adopt an "agency fee" arrangement, whereby one who is not a member of the recognized union must pay the union a fee to cover his share of services rendered by the union in negotiating and administering policies governing his employment.

The Supreme Court has held that there is no federal constitutional bar against an agency fee provision in a collective bargaining contract

---

164. Winston-Salem/Forsyth County Unit, North Carolina Ass'n of Educators v. Phillips, 381 F.Supp. 644 (M.D.N.C.1974).

165. Minneapolis Federation of Teachers Local No. 59 v. Obermeyer, 275 Minn. 347, 147 N.W.2d 358 (1966); Anchorage Educ. Ass'n v. Anchorage School Dist., 648 P.2d 993 (Alaska 1982).

166. Head v. Special School Dist. No. 1, 288 Minn. 496, 182 N.W.2d 887 (1970), cert. den. 404 U.S. 886, 92 S.Ct. 196, 30 L.Ed.2d 168 (1971).

167. Board of Trustees of Community College Dist. No. 508 v. Cook County College Teachers Union, 74 Ill.2d 412, 24 Ill. Dec. 843, 386 N.E.2d 47 (1979).

168. McLaughlin v. Tilendis, 398 F.2d 287 (7 Cir.1968). See also Muskego-Norway Consolidated Schools Joint Dist. No. 9 v. Wisconsin Employment Relations Bd., 35 Wis.2d 540, 151 N.W.2d 617 (1967).

169. Roberts v. Lake Central School Corp., 317 F.Supp. 63 (N.D.Ind.1970).

170. Shelton v. Tucker, 364 U.S. 479, 81 S.Ct. 247, 5 L.Ed.2d 231 (1960).

171. Benson v. School Dist. No. 1 of Silver Bow County, 136 Mont. 77, 344 P.2d 117 (1959).

provided a public employee's fee is not used to support those ideological activities by the union that are opposed by the member and are not related to the collective bargaining function of the union.[172] The employee, however, must notify the union of his objection to such use. This is to be done in general terms so that the employee does not have to reveal his position on particular matters.

In 1984 the Court dealt with some specifics of uses of agency fees.[173] It upheld their use for conventions, business meetings and occasional social activities, and publications that communicate about nonpolitical activities. Forbidden, however, was use of agency fees for organizing activities and for litigation not connected to the bargaining unit. Also, the Court disapproved of the "rebate" way of handling the fees, even if interest were paid. It approved advance reduction of fees for nonmembers.

In 1986 the Court examined some procedures established to effectuate the preceding decisions.[174] It disapproved a rebate system (because it does not avoid the risk that funds of nonunion members may be used temporarily for an improper purpose), a system whereby inadequate information is offered by the union to justify the agency percent (because potential objectors cannot gauge the propriety of the union's fee), and a system which does not afford a reasonably prompt decision regarding expenditures and fees by an impartial decisionmaker.

The Court in a 1991 case involving a faculty union in a public college derived from previous cases three guidelines for determining which activities a union constitutionally may charge to nonmembers.[175] Chargeable items "must (1) be 'germane' to collective bargaining activity; (2) be justified by the government's vital policy interest in labor peace and avoiding 'free riders'; and (3) not significantly add to the burdening of free speech that is inherent in the allowance of an agency or union shop." Specifics upheld included costs associated with otherwise chargeable activities of the local union's state and national affiliates even when those activities were not performed for the direct benefit of the local (e.g., charges for publications dealing not only with collective bargaining but with teaching and education generally, professional development, employment opportunities, and miscellaneous matters "neither political nor public" in nature; participation by delegates in state and national conventions). Disapprovals included lobbying and general public relations activities.

In 1983 the Supreme Court considered the question "whether the First Amendment * * * is violated when a union that has been elected by public school teachers as their exclusive bargaining representative is granted access to certain means of communication while such access is

---

172. Abood v. Detroit Bd. of Educ., 431 U.S. 209, 97 S.Ct. 1782, 52 L.Ed.2d 261 (1977).

173. Ellis v. Brotherhood of Ry., Airline and Steamship Clerks, Freight Handlers, Express and Station Employees, 466 U.S. 435, 104 S.Ct. 1883, 80 L.Ed.2d 428 (1984).

174. Chicago Teachers Union, Local No. 1, AFT, AFL–CIO v. Hudson, 475 U.S. 292, 106 S.Ct. 1066, 89 L.Ed.2d 232 (1986).

175. Lehnert v. Ferris Faculty Ass'n, 500 U.S. 507, 111 S.Ct. 1950, 114 L.Ed.2d 572 (1991).

denied to a rival union." The answer, by a five-to-four vote, was "no." [176]

The Court found that the privilege of exclusive access to intra-school system mail facilities was properly characterized as an appropriate restriction on use of public property that is not, by designation or in fact, a general public forum or a limited public forum.[177] Even if the mailing system was considered to be a limited public forum by virtue of its occasional use by groups such as Cub Scouts and YMCAs, the Constitution would require only that similar groups be granted access. The rival union would not fall into that category. Because the representative union has a unique function in the collective bargaining process, it is rational in the interests of labor peace and effective relationships for the board to agree to limit access solely to that organization within the class of associations concerned with terms and conditions of teacher employment. The rival union is excluded not because of its views, but because of its status in relation to the school system. Alternative channels for communication (bulletin boards, meeting rooms, the United States mail) were available, and during election periods there was equal access to mailboxes. (It should be noted here that some specific mail delivery practices within school systems may be barred by federal statutes and regulations governing the Postal Service.[178])

Another element of exclusive privilege was decided by the Supreme Court of Wisconsin.[179] The court invalidated a provision in a collective bargaining contract that granted teachers in the majority organization the right to go to the state convention of that organization's parent group with pay. No equivalent right was granted other teachers. The court said this provision had the effect of discouraging membership in a minority group by affecting adversely the terms and conditions of employment of minority group members.

The Supreme Court decision upholding the right of a nonunion teacher to speak at an open, public board meeting on a matter under negotiation is covered in Chapter 11 under "The Teacher as Citizen." [180]

Problems arise from the situation where a collective contract has expired and no agreement has been reached on a new one. The highest court in New York held that after the expiration of an agreement there is no duty on the employer to pay salary increments to teachers during negotiations for a new contract.[181] The court said that the principle of maintaining the status quo during negotiations is not served by what is a

176. Perry Educ. Ass'n v. Perry Local Educators' Ass'n, 460 U.S. 37, 103 S.Ct. 948, 74 L.Ed.2d 794 (1983).

177. See Chapter 6, "Differentiating Among Uses and Users."

178. Fort Wayne Community Schools v. Fort Wayne Educ. Ass'n, 977 F.2d 358 (7 Cir.1992), cert. den. ___ U.S. ___, 114 S.Ct. 90, 126 L.Ed.2d 57 (1993).

179. Board of Educ. of Unified School Dist. No. 1 v. Wisconsin Employment Rela-

tions Comm'n, 52 Wis.2d 625, 191 N.W.2d 242 (1971).

180. City of Madison, Joint School Dist. No. 8 v. Wisconsin Employment Relations Comm'n, 429 U.S. 167, 97 S.Ct. 421, 50 L.Ed.2d 376 (1976).

181. Board of Cooperative Educational Services of Rockland County v. New York State Public Employment Relations Bd., 41 N.Y.2d 753, 395 N.Y.S.2d 439, 363 N.E.2d 1174 (1977). (This opinion was superseded by subsequent legislation.)

change in a negotiable item of working conditions, namely, salary increases. The same court, however, upheld a contract provision to keep the contract in effect until changed by mutual agreement in subsequent negotiations.[182] The Supreme Court of Indiana held that the statutory requirement of maintenance of the status quo during bargaining was met only if the salary increases for experience and training that were part of the old contract were granted during the period of negotiations for a new contract.[183]

A right of taxpayers and students to challenge directly in court (rather than initially in the Pennsylvania Labor Relations Board) provisions in a collective bargaining contract alleged to violate state law was upheld by the highest state court.[184]

Arbitration

The term "arbitration" is properly used to denote a process whereby the parties to a dispute agree to be bound by the decision of a third party selected by the disputants. Arbitration is an alternative to use of the judicial system to decide controversies. It is not to be confused with "mediation," "conciliation," "fact-finding," "advisory arbitration," or other forms of conflict resolution that do not culminate in legally binding determinations. Also, in relation to collective bargaining, an important distinction exists between arbitration of interests (determination of the terms of an agreement) and arbitration of rights (determination of the application of a provision in an existing agreement). The latter, referred to as grievance arbitration, is prevalent in the public sector as well as in the private sector. The former is virtually unused in the private sector, but constitutes one way to resolve impasses in the public sector when work stoppages, whether or not legally sanctioned, pose a serious danger to the public welfare.

Questions of lawful delegation of governmental power arise in connection with use of arbitration, especially arbitration of interests. Courts have not been in agreement as to whether authority ultimately to prescribe the provisions of a contract with a public body can be reposed in the hands of a separate body created to resolve impasses.[185] Where interest arbitration has been approved, the courts have emphasized the necessity for the enabling statutes to contain standards and parameters circumscribing the focus and scope of the process.[186]

182. Niagara Wheatfield Administrators Ass'n v. Niagara Wheatfield Central School Dist., 44 N.Y.2d 68, 404 N.Y.S.2d 82, 375 N.E.2d 37 (1978).

183. Indiana Educ. Employment Relations Bd. v. Mill Creek Classroom Teachers Ass'n, 456 N.E.2d 709 (Ind.1983), [Case No. 92]

184. Parents Union for Public Schools in Philadelphia v. Board of Educ. of School Dist. of Philadelphia, 480 Pa. 194, 389 A.2d 577 (1978).

185. Compare City of Biddeford v. Biddeford Teachers Ass'n, 304 A.2d 387 (Me.1973) and City of Amsterdam v. Helsby, 37 N.Y.2d 19, 371 N.Y.S.2d 404, 332 N.E.2d 290 (1975) with Greeley Police Union v. City Council of Greeley, 191 Colo. 419, 553 P.2d 790 (1976) and Xenia City Bd. of Educ. v. Xenia Educ. Ass'n, 52 Ohio App.2d 373, 370 N.E.2d 756 (1977).

186. City of Amsterdam v. Helsby, 37 N.Y.2d 19, 371 N.Y.S.2d 404, 332 N.E.2d 290 (1975).

As to grievance arbitration, most, but not all,[187] courts have followed the lead of the highest court of Connecticut, which in 1951 upheld the power of a local board to enter into a contract with a teachers association to arbitrate certain grievances.[188] Boards, of course, must agree to arbitrate grievances only if there is a statute to that effect. If, however, a board voluntarily agrees to a grievance arbitration provision in a collective bargaining contract in a state that does not forbid the arrangement, the board generally will be held to the agreement (unless a particular matter is beyond the power of the board to delegate). Courts are becoming increasingly reluctant to allow boards to escape the consequences of what they may have improvidently agreed to in collective bargaining. Thus, the Court of Appeals of New York enforced an arbitration clause in a dispute concerning disciplinary action taken against teachers.[189] The court said that use of an arbitrator is simply a possible alternative to appeal to the state commissioner of education or to the courts. It added, however, that under such a provision, a teacher could utilize only one forum.

In New York there was a statute requiring collective bargaining. In Ohio, where there was no statute, the highest court ruled that a board has discretionary authority to enter into such a contract, and if the contract has a binding grievance arbitration clause, the clause must be honored by the board.[190]

The inclusion of grievance arbitration clauses in public education collective bargaining contracts has spawned a very large amount of litigation. Because the process of arbitration was developed in the private sector as a substitute for use of the regular judicial process, and as it is entered into voluntarily by the contracting parties, the courts over the years have been reluctant to intervene in labor disputes that arguably are subject to arbitration. Thus, in the absence of contract language to the contrary, in construing labor contracts in the private sector the presumption has been that the parties have agreed to arbitrate a dispute, with doubts to be resolved in favor of coverage.[191] Some state courts have transferred this view to the public sector.[192]

The first court of last resort in a state that mandates public sector collective bargaining to take a contrary view was the Court of Appeals of New York. In 1977 it held that thereafter the courts in that state in

187. See School Bd. of City of Richmond v. Parham, 218 Va. 950, 243 S.E.2d 468 (1978).

188. Norwalk Teachers' Ass'n v. Board of Educ., 138 Conn. 269, 83 A.2d 482 (1951).

189. Board of Educ. of Union Free School Dist. No. 3 of Town of Huntington v. Associated Teachers of Huntington, Inc., 30 N.Y.2d 122, 331 N.Y.S.2d 17, 282 N.E.2d 109 (1972).

190. Dayton Classroom Teachers Ass'n v. Dayton Bd. of Educ., 41 Ohio St.2d 127, 323 N.E.2d 714 (1975).

191. United Steelworkers of America v. Warrior and Gulf Navigation Co., 363 U.S. 574, 80 S.Ct. 1347, 4 L.Ed.2d 1409 (1960).

192. Kaleva-Norman-Dickson School Dist. No. 6 v. Kaleva-Norman-Dickson Teachers' Ass'n, 393 Mich. 583, 227 N.W.2d 500 (1975); West Fargo Public School Dist. v. West Fargo Educ. Ass'n, 259 N.W.2d 612 (N.D.1977); Joint School Dist. No. 10, City of Jefferson v. Jefferson Educ. Ass'n, 78 Wis.2d 94, 253 N.W.2d 536 (1977).

public sector labor cases would be governed by a rule to the effect that it was up to the courts to determine whether a particular dispute is arbitrable [193] and that in such a proceeding the courts would not be bound by any presumption of arbitrability.[194] The court said that "it must be taken, in the absence of clear, unequivocal agreement to the contrary, that the board of education did *not* intend to refer differences which might arise to the arbitration forum." The court here was referring to matters that survived the initial test of being within the subject matter categories permissible for collective bargaining (i.e., negotiable items). It based its deviation from the private sector labor rules primarily on nondelegability considerations.

In practice, however, the court has broadly construed general arbitration clauses in collective bargaining contracts, granting stays of arbitration under unrestricted arbitration clauses only where statutes have vested a power solely in the board or where arbitration would violate "public policy" as defined by explicit court decisions.[195] It has held that, although provisions interfering with the function of granting tenure are unenforceable through arbitration, disputes involving procedures preliminary to the actual determination of whether to grant or to deny tenure can be arbitrated (provided the arbitrator does not award tenure as a remedy for a violation).[196] This position also has been taken by the highest court of Massachusetts.[197]

In regard to discharge or nonrenewal of nontenure teachers, it has been held that arbitration may be used to determine whether termination has been for "just cause" if there is a "just cause" provision in the contract and if no statute prohibits the arrangement.[198] The arbitrator can review terminations to see that procedural due process was followed and that a basis for the adverse action was presented. Where a statute provided that the board's decision was final as to nonrenewals, the Supreme Court of Oklahoma, after reviewing decisions from several states, concluded that the merits of a school board's decision could not be made subject to arbitration.[199]

There is disagreement among courts as to whether this type of contract provision can be enforced as to dismissal of tenure teachers.[200]

---

193. In the private sector the parties can agree to have the arbitrator determine the question of arbitrability. United Steelworkers of America v. Warrior and Gulf Navigation Co., 363 U.S. 574, 80 S.Ct. 1347, 4 L.Ed.2d 1409 (1960).

194. Acting Superintendent of Schools of Liverpool Central School Dist. v. United Liverpool Faculty Ass'n, 42 N.Y.2d 509, 399 N.Y.S.2d 189, 369 N.E.2d 746 (1977). [Case No. 93]

195. Board of Educ., West Babylon Union Free School Dist. v. West Babylon Teachers Ass'n, 52 N.Y.2d 1002, 438 N.Y.S.2d 291, 420 N.E.2d 89 (1981).

196. Candor Central School Dist. v. Candor Teachers Ass'n, 42 N.Y.2d 266, 397 N.Y.S.2d 737, 366 N.Ed.2d 826 (1977).

197. School Committee of West Bridgewater v. West Bridgewater Teachers' Ass'n, 372 Mass. 121, 360 N.E.2d 886 (1977).

198. Danville Bd. of School Directors v. Fifield, 132 Vt. 271, 315 A.2d 473 (1974); Board of Educ. of School Dist. of Philadelphia v. Philadelphia Federation of Teachers Local No. 3, AFT, AFL-CIO, 464 Pa. 92, 346 A.2d 35 (1975).

199. Mindemann v. Independent School Dist. No. 6 of Caddo County, 771 P.2d 996 (Okl.1989).

200. Compare Neshaminy Federation of Teachers v. Neshaminy School Dist., 501

But where layoffs are due to lack of work or funds, the determination of financial necessity is usually deemed not an arbitrable issue,[201] although an arbitrator may be authorized to determine whether a board of education has in fact acted because of economic necessity or for some other reason.[202]

It is important to emphasize that when arbitration is used, the role of the courts is severely curtailed. Because the parties have bargained for the interpretation of the arbitrator, the courts will not deal with the merits of a dispute. If the subject matter of a grievance arguably is covered by the contract, whether the petitioner is right or wrong is a question for the arbitrator.[203] Ambiguities as to coverage are not justiciable in the courts. Nor are an arbitrator's alleged errors of interpretation of law or of fact (if not utterly irrational[204] or based on fraud, collusion, or bad faith). The courts will review an arbitrator's award only to assure that it "draws its essence" [205] from the collective bargaining agreement (as distinguished from the arbitrator's "own brand" of justice) and that any remedy is not contrary to law or public policy (such as ordering a school board to make a payment beyond its powers). The need for the arbitrator to have flexibility in determining remedies is deemed integral to the theory underlying the use of arbitration to resolve disputes in the wide variety of situations that may develop in an ongoing relationship between organized employees and management.[206] Restrictions as to remedies may, of course, be placed in the contract.

It should be observed that the issue of nondelegability of board power cannot be raised to stay arbitration where there is a broad arbitration clause in the collective bargaining contract and the arbitrator might fashion a remedy adequately narrow so as to encompass only procedural guarantees. Thus, while ultimate determination of class composition may be in the board's discretion, arbitration was allowed to proceed on a contention that the contract was violated because the board summarily acceded to the requests of some parents and reassigned students without complying with a provision that principals shall arrange for appointments between teacher and parent upon receipt of a

Pa. 534, 462 A.2d 629 (1983) with Cape Elizabeth School Bd. v. Cape Elizabeth Teachers Ass'n, 459 A.2d 166 (Me.1983).

201. Arrowhead Public Service Union v. City of Duluth, 336 N.W.2d 68 (Minn.1983).

202. Board of Educ. of Bremen Community High School Dist. No. 228 v. Bremen Dist. No. 228 Joint Faculty Ass'n, 101 Ill.2d 115, 77 Ill.Dec. 783, 461 N.E.2d 406 (1984).

203. United Steelworkers of America v. American Mfg. Co., 363 U.S. 564, 80 S.Ct. 1343, 4 L.Ed.2d 1403 (1960).

204. "An arbitrator's interpretation [must] be upheld if it can, in *any rational way*, be derived from the language and con-

text of the agreement. * * * [R]eversal is not warranted even if a court believes that the decision, though rational, is incorrect." Greater Johnstown Area Vocational-Technical School v. Greater Johnstown Area Vocational-Technical Educ. Ass'n, 520 Pa. 197, 553 A.2d 913 (1989).

205. United Steelworkers of America v. Enterprise Wheel and Car Corp., 363 U.S. 593, 80 S.Ct. 1358, 4 L.Ed.2d 1424 (1960).

206. See United Steelworkers of America v. Warrior and Gulf Navigation Co., 363 U.S. 574, 80 S.Ct. 1347, 4 L.Ed.2d 1409 (1960).

parental complaint.[207]

Some courts have expressed concern about the traditional role of the public in the formulation and application of policy if too many matters are decided by collective bargaining and applications determined largely by arbitrators. "There would be little room for community involvement if agreements concerning educational policy matters could be negotiated behind closed doors and disputes concerning that agreement settled by an arbitrator who lacks public accountability," stated the Supreme Court of New Jersey in a decision restricting the scope of matters that in public education are negotiable and/or arbitrable.[208]

[Case No. 81] Constitutionality of Statute Barring Public Homosexual Activity by Teachers

NATIONAL GAY TASK FORCE v. BOARD OF EDUC. OF CITY OF OKLAHOMA CITY

United States Court of Appeals, Tenth Circuit, 1984.
729 F.2d 1270.

LOGAN, CIRCUIT JUDGE. The National Gay Task Force (NGTF), whose membership includes teachers in the Oklahoma public school system, filed this action in the district court challenging the facial constitutional validity of Okla.Stat. tit. 70, § 6–103.15. The district court held that the statute was constitutionally valid.   * * *

* * *

I

We see no constitutional problem in the statute's permitting a teacher to be fired for engaging in "public homosexual activity." Section 6–103.15 defines "public homosexual activity" as the commission of an act defined in Okla.Stat. tit. 21, § 886, that is committed with a person of the same sex and is indiscreet and not practiced in private. * * * Section 6–103.15 does not punish acts performed in private. Thus, the right of privacy, whatever its scope in regard to homosexual acts, is not implicated.

* * *

Plaintiff also argues that the statute violates its members' right to equal protection of the law. We cannot find that a classification based on the choice of sexual partners is suspect, especially since only four members of the Supreme Court have viewed gender as a suspect classification. Thus something less than a strict scrutiny test should be applied here. Surely a school may fire a teacher for engaging in an indiscreet public act of oral or anal intercourse. * * *

207. Babylon Union Free School Dist. v. Babylon Teachers Ass'n, 79 N.Y.2d 773, 579 N.Y.S.2d 629, 587 N.E.2d 267 (1991).

208. Ridgefield Park Educ. Ass'n v. Ridgefield Park Bd. of Educ., 78 N.J. 144, 393 A.2d 278 (1978).

II

The part of § 6–103.15 that allows punishment of teachers for "public homosexual conduct" does present constitutional problems. To be sure, this is a facial challenge, and facial challenges based on First Amendment overbreadth are "strong medicine" and should be used "sparingly and only as a last resort." Nonetheless, invalidation is an appropriate remedy in the instant case because this portion of § 6–103.15 is overbroad, is "not readily subject to a narrowing construction by the state courts," and "its deterrent effect on legitimate expression is both real and substantial." Also, we must be especially willing to invalidate a statute for facial overbreadth when, as here, the statute regulates "pure speech."

Section 6–103.15 allows punishment of teachers for "public homosexual conduct," which is defined as "advocating, soliciting, imposing, encouraging or promoting public or private homosexual activity in a manner that creates a substantial risk that such conduct will come to the attention of school children or school employees." The First Amendment protects "advocacy" even of illegal conduct except when "advocacy" is "directed to inciting or producing imminent lawless action and is likely to incite or produce such action." The First Amendment does not permit someone to be punished for advocating illegal conduct at some indefinite future time.

"Encouraging" and "promoting," like "advocating," do not necessarily imply incitement to imminent action. * * * [S]tatements, which are aimed at legal and social change, are at the core of First Amendment protections. * * * Finally, the deterrent effect of § 6–103.15 is both real and substantial. It applies to all teachers, substitute teachers, and teachers aides in Oklahoma. To protect their jobs they must restrict their expression. Thus, the § 6–103.15 proscription of advocating, encouraging, or promoting homosexual activity is unconstitutionally overbroad.

We recognize that a state has interests in regulating the speech of teachers that differ from its interests in regulating the speech of the general citizenry. Pickering v. Board of Education. But a state's interests outweigh a teacher's interests only when the expression results in a material or substantial interference or disruption in the normal activities of the school. See Tinker v. Des Moines Independent Community School District. This Court has held that a teacher's First Amendment rights may be restricted only if "the employer shows that some restriction is necessary to prevent the disruption of official functions or to insure effective performance by the employee." Defendant has made no such showing.

The statute declares that a teacher may be fired under § 6–103.15 only if there is a finding of "unfitness" and lists factors that are to be considered in determining "unfitness" * * *. * * * The statute does not require that the teacher's public utterance occur in the classroom. Any public statement that would come to the attention of school children, their parents, or school employees that might lead someone to object to the teacher's social and political views would seem to justify a finding that the statement "may adversely affect" students or school employees. * * * A statute is saved from a challenge to its overbreadth only if it is "readily subject" to a narrowing construction. It is not within this Court's power to construe and narrow state statutes. The unfitness requirement does not save § 6–103.15 from its unconstitutional overbreadth.

III

The parts of § 6–103.15 that deal with "public homosexual conduct" can be severed from the rest of the statute without creating a result that the legislature did not intend or contemplate. We reverse the judgment of the district court, holding that the statute, insofar as it punishes "homosexual conduct," as that phrase is defined in the statute to include "advocating * * * encouraging or promoting public or private homosexual activity" is unconstitutional. We also hold that the unconstitutional portion is severable from the part of the statute that proscribes "homosexual activity," and we find that portion constitutional.

Reversed.

Notes

1. The third judge on the panel agreed with the trial judge and would have upheld both portions of the statute.

2. As to facial challenges on freedom of speech grounds, see "Loyalty" in this Chapter. The distinction between "advocacy" and "action" can be critical to constitutionality. Note, however, what this court says about advocacy "even of illegal conduct."

3. If state courts interpret a state statute as being enforceable only under certain conditions, that construction becomes part of the statute. Oklahoma courts had not interpreted the challenged statute. Note that the federal court says that it is not empowered to construe and narrow state statutes.

4. The Supreme Court of Florida held that a parent who had made a "profane verbal attack upon the instructor [that] took place in the presence of at least 50 students" could not be punished under a statute specifying that a misdemeanor was committed by "any person who upbraids, abuses or insults any member of the instructional staff on school property or in the presence of the pupils at a school activity * * *." McCall v. State, 354 So.2d 869 (Fla.1978).

5. The Supreme Court "affirmed [the judgment] by an equally divided Court." 470 U.S. 903, 105 S.Ct. 1858, 84 L.Ed.2d 776 (1985). Justice Powell was temporarily off the bench for health reasons. When there is a "tie", the votes of the individual Justices are not revealed. The effect of the affirmance is to uphold the outcome but not necessarily endorse all of the reasoning.

[Case No. 82] Salary Reduction—Legislation Impairing Obligation of Contract

PHELPS v. BOARD OF EDUC.

Supreme Court of the United States, 1937.
300 U.S. 319, 57 S.Ct. 483, 81 L.Ed. 674.

MR. JUSTICE ROBERTS delivered the opinion of the Court.

The people of New Jersey have ordained by their Constitution that the Legislature "shall provide for the maintenance and support of a thorough and efficient system of free public schools." In fulfillment of this command a comprehensive school law was adopted in 1903 by which boards of education were set up for cities, towns, and school districts throughout the state. * * * This general school law was amended by the Act of April 21, 1909, section 1 of which provided: "The service of all teachers, principals, supervising principals of the public schools in any school district of this state shall be during good behavior and efficiency, after the expiration of a period of employment of three consecutive years in that district, unless a shorter period is fixed by the employing board. * * * No principal or teacher shall be dismissed or subjected to reduction of salary in said school district except for inefficiency, incapacity, conduct unbecoming a teacher or other just cause, and after a written charge of the cause or causes shall have been preferred against him or her, * * * and after the charge shall have been examined into and found true in fact by said board of education, upon reasonable notice to the person charged, who may be represented by counsel at the hearing."

An Act of February 4, 1933, premising that existing economic conditions require that boards of education be enabled to fix and determine the amount of salary to be paid to persons holding positions in the respective school districts, authorizes each board to fix and determine salaries to be paid officers and employees for the period July 1, 1933, to July 1, 1934, "notwithstanding any such person be under tenure"; prohibits increase of salaries within the period named; forbids discrimination between individuals in the same class of service in the fixing of salaries or compensation; and sets a minimum beyond which boards may not go in the reduction of salaries. On June 23, 1933, the board adopted a resolution reducing salaries for the school year July 1, 1933, to July 1, 1934, by a percentage of the existing salaries graded upward in steps as the salaries increased in amount, except with respect to clerks, the compensation of each of whom was reduced to a named amount.

* * *

The position of the appellants is that by virtue of the Act of 1909 three years of service under contract confer upon an employee of a school district a contractual status indefinite in duration which the legislature is powerless to alter or to authorize the board of education to alter. The Supreme Court holds that the Act of 1909 "established a legislative status for teachers, but we fail to see that it established a contractual one that the Legislature may not modify. * * * The status of tenure teachers, while in one sense perhaps contractual, is in essence dependent on a statute, like that of the incumbent of a statutory office, which the Legislature at will may abolish, or whose emoluments it may change."

This court is not bound by the decision of a state court as to the existence and terms of a contract, the obligation of which is asserted to be impaired, but where a statute is claimed to create a contractual right we give weight to the construction of the statute by the courts of the state. Here those courts have concurred in holding that the act of 1909 did not amount to a legislative contract with the teachers of the state and did not become a term of the contracts entered into with employees by boards of education. Unless these views are palpably erroneous we should accept them.

It appears from a stipulation of facts submitted in view of evidence that after a teacher has served in a school district under yearly contracts for three years it has not been customary to enter into further formal contracts with such teacher. From time to time, however, promotions were granted and salary raised for the ensuing year by action of the board. In the case of many of the appellants there have been several such increases in salary.

Although after the expiration of the first three years of service the employee continued in his then position and at his then compensation unless and until promoted or given an increase in salary for a succeeding year, we find nothing in the record to indicate that the board was bound by contract with the teacher for more than the current year. The employee assumed no binding obligation to remain in service beyond that term. Although the act of 1909 prohibited the board, a creature of the state, from reducing the teacher's salary or discharging him without cause, we agree with the courts below that this was but a regulation of the conduct of the board and not a term of a continuing contract of indefinite duration with the individual teacher.

The resolution of June 23, 1933, grouped the existing salaries paid by the board into six classes the lowest of which comprised salaries between $1200 and $1999; and the highest included salaries ranging between $4000 and $5600. The reduction in the lowest class for the coming year was 10 per cent; that in highest class 15 per cent. Salaries in the intermediate classes were reduced 11, 12, 13, and 14 per cent. It resulted that in some instances a teacher receiving the lowest salary in a given bracket would have his compensation reduced to a figure lower than the reduced compensation of one receiving the highest salary in the next lower bracket. From this circumstance it is argued that the board's action arbitrarily discriminated between the employees and so denied them the equal protection of the laws guaranteed by the Fourteenth Amendment.

We think it was reasonable and proper that the teachers employed by the board should be divided into classes for the application of the percentage reduction. All in a given class were treated alike. Incidental individual inequality resulting in some instances from the operation of the plan does not condemn it as an unreasonable or arbitrary method of dealing with the problem of general salary reductions or deny the equality guaranteed by the Fourteenth Amendment.

* * *

Notes

1. Observe the Court's statement that although it is not bound by the decision of a state court as to the existence and terms of a contract, it gives weight to the construction by a state court of a statute claimed to create a contractual right. In the year following this decision, the Supreme Court held that contractual rights were created by a tenure statute in Indiana. The word "contract" had appeared many times in the statute, and earlier decisions in Indiana under that statute had construed it as creating contract rights. State ex rel. Anderson v. Brand, 303 U.S. 95, 58 S.Ct. 443, 82 L.Ed. 685 (1938).

2. If a legislature can change the tenure status and retirement allowances of a teacher at will, the teacher's rights would appear flimsy. Are individual teachers or groups of teachers seriously threatened by precipitous legislative action in these areas? Consider the history of such legislation, the influence of teachers on political bodies, and public attitudes toward teachers.

3. A board of education has implied power to establish regulations which impose salary sanctions for substandard teaching performance. It is not necessary that the board adopt either of the alternatives of accepting such performance or instituting dismissal proceedings. Sawin v. Town of Winslow, 253 A.2d 694 (Me.1969).

[Case No. 83] Right of Teacher to Minimum Salary

MARVEL v. COAL HILL PUBLIC SCHOOL DIST.

Supreme Court of Arkansas, 1982.
276 Ark. 369, 635 S.W.2d 245.

HICKMAN, JUSTICE. The question in this case is whether a full-time school teacher can be denied the minimum salary due to teachers because of a written contract for a lesser amount. The trial court found such a contract enforceable. We disagree and reverse.

Deborah Marvel had been a part-time librarian and teacher for the Coal Hill Public School District when her contract was negotiated for the 1979–1980 school year. She said that Mr. Nolan Williams, the superintendent of schools, told her she would serve as part-time librarian and part-time teacher but would receive the same salary that full-time teachers did. (She had been paid in the past as an aide, but was now to be paid as a teacher.) Williams refuted that. But the contract only provided for a salary of $9,800.00 and the minimum a full-time teacher with her experience would receive is $11,450.00. She accepted the position and signed the contract but chose to sue for the difference, which was $1,650.00, plus interest.

The parties disagreed as to whether Miss Marvel signed the contract under protest but that is irrelevant. It is not disputed that she was a "teacher" within the meaning of Ark.Stat.Ann. § 80–1326 (Repl.1980), and performed all the duties of a full-time teacher. She performed the ancillary duties of all teachers such as hall monitor, attending ball games and faculty meetings. She kept grade, class planning and attendance records. In order to qualify as full-time, she was required to work six periods a day. She acted as a teacher five periods a day and as a librarian two periods. It is also undisputed that the school district filed with the State Department of Education a salary schedule, as required by Ark.Stats.Ann. §§ 80–1324 and 80–850.7 (Repl.1980), and that her salary as a full-time teacher would have been $11,450.00.

The superintendent said the reason Miss Marvel was not paid the minimum salary is because the part of her salary for teaching remedial reading was Title I money (federal money) and the grant did not allow her to be paid more.

The trial court held that the contract did not violate Arkansas law which requires that school districts promulgate minimum salary schedules, * * *. The court found that since she was paid fairly for librarian duties from general funds that the district complied with the law, and found further that Miss Marvel knowingly and freely entered into a binding agreement.

The trial court was wrong in its interpretation of the law. Miss Marvel was a full-time teacher and the district could not receive her services and refuse to pay her the minimum salary it paid other full-time teachers. Title I provisions cannot be used to avoid Ark.Stats.Ann. §§ 80–1327 and 80–850.7, which require each school district to set a schedule of minimum salaries and abide by it.

If the district's position were to prevail, then no teacher could be sure of equal treatment when he or she was hired or retained—at least to the extent that a minimum salary would apply to all hired for full-time duties. The school district received the benefit of the services of a full-time teacher and it should not be allowed to manipulate the law to avoid its legal responsibility.

The judgment is reversed * * *.

* * *

Notes

1. Accepting as true the superintendent's statements about use of Title I money, still there was no prohibition against supplementing those salary funds with state (or local) money.

2. Is a teacher who is seeking employment on an equal footing with a school district in the process of determining contract terms? State legislation such as that involved here is said to help equalize bargaining power and to prevent exploitation of teachers. What, if any, state controls on local salaries do you favor?

3. Why did the court not need to resolve the disagreement as to whether Miss Marvel signed the contract under protest?

4. A school board has the implied power to establish criteria for local salary supplements, and where the criteria appear in the "Teacher's Handbook", they

are part of each teacher's contract. Moreover, courts cannot intervene to modify signed contracts upon allegations that there was a misinterpretation of school board minutes and calculation of salaries for some teachers was incorrect. Weatherford v. Martin, 418 So.2d 777 (Miss.1982).

[Case No. 84] Right of Public to See Teacher's College Transcript

KLEIN INDEPENDENT SCHOOL DIST. v. MATTOX
United States Court of Appeals, Fifth Circuit, 1987.
830 F.2d 576.

GARZA, CIRCUIT JUDGE:

* * *

I. Facts and Proceedings

During the months of October and November of 1985, Dr. Donald Collins, the Superintendent of the Klein Independent School District, received two letters requesting copies of the "personnel file and other related public records" of Rebecca J. Holt. Ms. Holt is a public school-teacher employed by the school district. The requests were made pursuant to the Texas Open Records Act. Dr. Collins asked the Attorney General's Office for the State of Texas whether the contents of Ms. Holt's personnel file, particularly her college transcript, were public records subject to disclosure under state law. An Assistant Attorney General sent an opinion to Dr. Collins informing him that, in addition to the other documents, Ms. Holt's college transcript must be released according to the Texas Open Records Act. Moreover, such disclosure was not proscribed by the Family Educational Rights and Privacy Act of 1974 (FERPA). * * *

On July 14, 1986, Ms. Holt and the school district brought suit against Jim Mattox, the Attorney General for the State of Texas, alleging that he issued an opinion which, if followed, would cause the school district to act in violation of Ms. Holt's rights secured under FERPA and the First Amendment to the United States Constitution. * * *

* * *

On November 21, 1986, the district court granted the defendant's motion for summary judgment, and entered a final order dismissing the case. * * *

II. Discussion

* * * The appellants present two issues to this Court. The first issue is whether the lower court erred in ruling that they are not entitled to maintain this action pursuant to FERPA * * *. The second issue is whether the court erred in finding that Ms. Holt's interest in maintaining the confidentiality of her academic record did not outweigh the public's interest in learning whether she is qualified to teach.

A. *FERPA*

* * *

FERPA was designed to regulate the release of student records. A student's or parent's consent is required where personally identifiable information from the education records of a student is to be disclosed. The Secretary of Education is empowered to enforce the various provisions of FERPA. An educational agency or institution that unlawfully releases a student's record may lose federal funding. This is the only express remedy provided in the statute. FERPA neither explicitly provides for a private cause of action, nor does its legislative history indicate that its drafters intended one.

Naturally, we are alerted to the problem that Ms. Holt is employed by the school district, and is not a student and never has been a student of the subject school district. It is fundamental from a reading of FERPA that a "student" is a "person with respect to whom an educational agency or institution maintains education records or personally identifiable information, but does not include a person who has not been in attendance at such agency or institution." * * *

It cannot be disputed that the statute was enacted to prevent an educational agency or institution from releasing the record of one of its own students. Excluded from FERPA's protections are records relating to an individual who is employed by an educational agency or institution. Because Ms. Holt has not attended any school within the Klein Independent School District, the agency which has been directed to release her transcript, she cannot be considered a "student" under the FERPA definition. Rather, Ms. Holt's capacity with the school district is that of an employee. Because she is an employee and not a student of the institution requested to disclose her transcript, she does not fall within that class of people for whose benefit FERPA was created. Ms. Holt is not a "student" and her college transcript is not an "education record" protected from disclosure pursuant to FERPA's provisions.

* * *

B. *Balancing the Interests*

The district court found that Ms. Holt had a privacy interest in her college transcript. The Supreme Court has written that there are two different kinds of privacy interests. "One is the individual interest in avoiding disclosure of personal matters, and another is the interest in independence in making certain kinds of important decisions."

Under the autonomy branch of privacy, constitutional protection has been limited to intimate personal relationships or activities, and freedoms to make fundamental choices involving oneself, one's family, and one's relationships with others. The appellants seek constitutional protection from an action quite dissimilar from that which has been held to be protected. Their claim is based not upon a challenge to the state's ability to restrict her freedom of action in a private matter, but rather on a claim that the state directed a college record to be released. Obviously, this is not a question concerning the autonomy branch of the right to privacy.

Regarding the interest in confidentiality, the Supreme Court has defined this branch as "the individual interest in avoiding disclosure of personal matters." * * * Without engaging in an inquiry into whether Ms. Holt has a recognizable privacy interest in her college transcript, we believe that, under the balancing test, even if she did have an interest it is significantly outweighed by the public's interest in evaluating the competence of its schoolteachers.

The district court * * * [stated] that Ms. Holt has a constitutional right to avoid disclosure of personal matters. The court then balanced Ms. Holt's privacy interest against the public's interest in knowing about her educational background. Although her file may contain "embarrassing or confidential information," the court noted, the public interest in learning whether those who teach young children are qualified clearly outweighs her limited right to disclosural privacy.

The appellants contend that the public's interest can be vindicated through less intrusive means than presented in this case. The appellants propose that since her teaching certificate represents the informed judgment of the Texas Board of Education that she is qualified to teach, disclosure of the certificate itself fully serves the public's interest in being assured that those who teach are qualified. Therefore, the certificate and not a college transcript suffices, and to require disclosure of the transcript operates to invade Ms. Holt's interest in maintaining the confidentiality of her academic career.

The public's interest in disclosure of a schoolteacher's transcript is set forth in section 1 of the Texas Open Records Act.

> Pursuant to the fundamental philosophy of the American constitutional form of representative government which holds to the principle that government is the servant of the people, and not the master of them, it is hereby declared to be the public policy of the State of Texas that all persons are, unless otherwise expressly provided by law, at all times entitled to full and complete information regarding the affairs of government and the official acts of those who represent them as public officials and employees. The people, in delegating authority, do not give their public servants the right to decide what is good for the people to know and what is not good for them to know. The people insist on remaining informed so that they may retain control over the instruments they have created. To that end, the provisions of this Act shall be liberally construed with the view of carrying out the above declaration of public policy.

The Open Records Act, however, does make provision for safeguarding the personal privacy of the individual. Section 3(a)(2) of the statute exempts from public disclosure "information in personnel files, the disclosure of which would constitute a clearly unwarranted invasion of personal privacy[.]" We do not find that the disclosure of a schoolteacher's college transcript rises to the level of that information which constitutes an unwarranted invasion of personal privacy, as provided in section 3(a)(2). * * *

We agree with the district court in tipping the balance in favor of the right of the public to know the academic records of the schoolteachers of their children. The appellants' reasoning concerning the regulations imposed by the Texas Legislature and the screening procedures of the Texas Board of Education is unavailing. Recently, there has been grave concern in Texas about the quality of public education, notwithstanding the state's regulations. Many teachers who had been certified and were teaching in Texas classrooms could not pass a basic test of minimal competency. In light of this apparent lack of competency prevalent in the state, the public must have full and complete information concerning the teachers who serve the public in educating their children.

III.   Conclusion

Finding no merit in the appellants' claims and agreeing with the district court that the defendant was entitled to judgment as a matter of law, we AFFIRM the court's decision to grant summary judgment in this case.

Notes

1. The Supreme Court without dissent denied certiorari. 485 U.S. 1008, 108 S.Ct. 1473, 99 L.Ed.2d 702 (1988).

2. Even if Holt once had been a student in the district, only records related to those days would come under FERPA protection.

3. What do you believe was the reason that the district joined Holt in her appeal?

4. Observe that the court did not directly rule on the point of whether a student has a constitutionally protected privacy interest in educational records. It ruled, however, that even if Holt did, the interest could not prevail over the public interest involved here.

5. The Supreme Court of North Dakota, citing the present case with approval, has held that under that state's open records law the personnel file maintained by a school district for a teacher is a public record and must be available for inspection. The court commented that there were strong arguments for an exception but "such policy considerations are for the legislature and the courts must apply the law as it exists." Hovet v. Hebron Public School Dist., 419 N.W.2d 189 (N.D.1988).

[Case No. 85] Right of Teacher to Hearing on Stigmatizing Information in File

BRANDT v. BOARD OF CO–OP. EDUCATIONAL SERVICES

United States Court of Appeals, Second Circuit, 1987.
820 F.2d 41.

FEINBERG, CHIEF JUDGE.   This appeal concerns whether appellant Wayne Brandt, after his dismissal as a public school teacher, was entitled to a name-clearing hearing pursuant to 42 U.S.C. § 1983 based on the presence of allegedly false and defamatory charges in his personnel file. In October 1980, the Board of Cooperative Educational Services, Third Supervisory District, Suffolk County, New York (the Board), appointed Brandt as a substitute teacher of autistic children * * *. In a series of meetings held in March and April 1981, appellees * * * charged Brandt with various acts of sexual misconduct involving his students. Despite pressure from appellees, Brandt refused to resign. His demand for a hearing to clear himself of the charges was denied. He was discharged in April 1981, in the middle of his term.

* * *

In February 1984 [following some state court proceedings] Brandt sought relief in federal court pursuant to 42 U.S.C. § 1983, claiming that appellees had violated his right to liberty under the Fourteenth Amendment. * * *

* * *

A government employee's liberty interest is implicated where the government dismisses him based on charges "that might seriously damage his standing and associations in his community" or that might impose "on him a stigma or other disability that foreclose[s] his freedom to take advantage of other employment opportunities." *Board of Regents of State Colleges v. Roth.* In addition, the charges against the employee must be made "public" by the government employer, *Bishop v. Wood,* and the employee must allege that the charges are false, *Codd v. Velger.* Where the employee's liberty interest is implicated, he is entitled under the due process clause to notice and an opportunity to be heard.

The issue before us is whether the district court properly granted summary judgment to appellees based on its ruling that Brandt must prove that appellees had actually disclosed false allegations of sexual misconduct. As a preliminary matter, it is not clear whether the district court ruled that Brandt had to prove the falsity of the charges in order to establish his right to a name-clearing hearing or only in order to establish damages. While we do not take issue with the latter proposition, we have no doubt that the former is erroneous. The Supreme Court has required only that a plaintiff raise the issue of falsity regarding the stigmatizing charges—not prove it—in order to establish a right to a name-clearing hearing. Here, Brandt satisfied that requirement by alleging in his complaint that the charges were false. The truth or falsity of the charges would then be determined at the hearing itself. If Brandt had to prove the falsity of the charges *before* he could obtain a hearing, there would be no need for the hearing.

Appellees do not contest that point but they argue that under *Bishop* no liberty interest is implicated where there has been no public disclosure of the reasons for the discharge. Brandt has conceded that appellees have disclosed the charges against him only to those involved in the investigation. Brandt argues, however, that the presence of the charges in his personnel file satisfies the "public disclosure" requirement because there is a likelihood that these charges may be disclosed in the future. He claims that prospective employers will want to know about his qualifications as a teacher, will gain access to the file and "will most certainly not hire him" when they learn of the charges.

It is important to emphasize that we are reviewing a grant of summary judgment. If there was any genuine issue of material fact before the district court, then the grant of summary judgment was improper. * * * [In the district court] the Board did not stipulate that it would never disclose the charges to Brandt's prospective employers. The Board's counsel stated that he believed the Board's policy was to not disclose but Brandt vigorously contested this representation. Thus, there was a genuine issue of fact regarding the likelihood of disclosure to Brandt's prospective employers. The question now is whether the likelihood of such disclosure is material to Brandt's claim, and we conclude that it is.

The Supreme Court set forth the "public disclosure" requirement in *Bishop.* In that case, the reasons for the employee's termination were communicated orally to the employee in private, and prior to litigation, the reasons had not been made public. With respect to the impact on the discharged employee's future employment opportunities, the Court concluded that despite termination, the employee "remain[ed] as free as before to seek another" job where there had been no public disclosure of the reasons for the discharge. The Court also concluded that because the communication was not made public, "it cannot properly form the basis for a claim that [the employee's] interest in his 'good name, reputation, honor, or integrity' was thereby impaired."

* * *

Thus, where the reasons for an employee's termination are kept private, it is clear that the "public disclosure" requirement has not been met and there has been no violation of the employee's liberty interest. The purpose of the requirement is to limit a constitutional claim to those instances where the stigmatizing charges made in the course of discharge have been or are likely to be disseminated widely enough to damage the discharged employee's standing in the community or foreclose future job opportunities. In determining the degree of dissemination that satisfies the "public disclosure" requirement, we must look to the potential effect of dissemination on the employee's standing in the community and the foreclosure of job opportunities. As a result, what is sufficient to constitute "public disclosure" will vary with the circumstances of each case.

In this case, we consider the effect on Brandt's future job opportunities since that is the harm he contends will result from dissemination of the reasons for his discharge. If Brandt is able to show that prospective employers are likely to gain access to his personnel file and decide not to hire him, then the presence of the charges in his file has a damaging effect on his future job opportunities. Brandt need not wait until he actually loses some job opportunities because the presence of the charges in his personnel file coupled with a likelihood of harmful disclosure already place him "between the devil and the deep blue sea." In applying for jobs, if Brandt authorizes the release of his personnel file, the potential employer would find out about the allegations of sexual misconduct and probably not hire him. If he refuses to grant authorization, that, too, would hurt his chances for employment. Thus, Brandt, unlike the employee in *Bishop,* would not be "as free as before to seek another" job.

* * *

* * * The stigmatizing charges of sexual misconduct were made against Brandt during the course of his termination and apparently were placed in his personnel file at that time. Brandt has alleged that the charges are false, and has raised a genuine issue of fact concerning the likelihood of future disclosure. Any disclosure of the charges to prospective employers would inevitably deprive Brandt of job opportunities. We therefore * * * hold that Brandt must have an opportunity to prove that his liberty interest has been implicated.

We reverse the grant of summary judgment to appellees and remand to the district court. On remand, Brandt must be given the opportunity to substantiate his contention that appellees are likely to make his personnel file available to prospective employers. Only if he is able to prove a likelihood of future disclosure will he be entitled to relief under § 1983. * * *

Notes

1. Bear in mind that mere presence of false information in a confidential personnel file does not amount to a violation of one's liberty interests. Burris v. Willis Independent School Dist., Inc., 713 F.2d 1087 ((5 Cir.1983). Further, state law that may create a right to damages for defamation does not by itself trigger federal constitutional protections.

2. Subsequent to this opinion the defendants removed the stigmatizing allegations from the file, and staff were instructed not to reveal them to prospective employers. In addition it was uncontroverted that the information in Brandt's file had never been publicly disclosed. Under these facts on remand, summary judgment was granted the defendants. Brandt v. Board of Cooperative Educational Services, 845 F.2d 416 (2 Cir.1988).

3. A head football coach won in state court a breach of contract claim for damages for his removal as coach (but not as teacher) based on his making an alleged racial slur. The Sixth Circuit held that he could not bring a federal suit based on the stigmatizing nature of the charges because he had been afforded a name-clearing hearing in connection with the state court action. Holthaus v. Board of Educ., Cincinnati Public Schools, 986 F.2d 1044 (6 Cir.1993).

[Case No. 86] Constitutionality of Teachers' Oath

KNIGHT v. BOARD OF REGENTS OF UNIVERSITY OF STATE OF NEW YORK

United States District Court, Southern District of New York, 1967.
269 F.Supp. 339.

TYLER, DISTRICT JUDGE. Plaintiffs are twenty-seven faculty members at Adelphi University, a private, non-profit institution of higher learning located in Garden City, New York and tax exempt under Section 420 of the New York Real Property Tax Law, McKinney's Consol.Laws, c. 50–A.

Section 3002 of the New York Education Law, McKinney's Consol.Laws, c. 16, requires every citizen teacher, instructor or professor in any public school or in any private school the real property of which is in whole or in part exempt from taxation to execute an oath. In pertinent part, Section 3002 reads as follows:

"Oath to support federal and state constitutions. It shall be unlawful for any citizen of the United States to serve as teacher, instructor or professor in any school or institution in the public school system of the state or in any school, college, university or other educational institution in this state, whose real property, in whole or in part, is exempt from taxation under section four of the tax law unless and until he or she shall have taken and subscribed the following oath or affirmation: 'I do solemnly swear (or affirm) that I will support the constitution of the United States of America and the constitution of the State of New York, and that I will faithfully discharge, according to the best of my ability, the duties of the position of * * * (title of position and name or designation of school, college, university or institution to be here inserted), to which I am now assigned.' "

Although this statutory requirement dates back to 1934, through inadvertence Adelphi had not previously requested that its faculty members execute the oath. In October, 1966, however, upon being made aware of the statute, the administrative offices of Adelphi asked all the members of its teaching staff to sign and return the oath. Plaintiffs have refused to do so, instead bringing this action to enjoin the enforcement of the oath provision. * * *

* * *

So far as we can determine, the precise question of whether an oath such as that provided for by Section 3002 may constitutionally be required of teachers has not been ruled upon by the Supreme Court. That Court, however, has recently stated that Georgia's requirement that her legislators take a similar oath in no way impinges upon the First Amendment's protection of free speech. Bond v. Floyd, 385 U.S. 116, at 132, 87 S.Ct. 339, 17 L.Ed.2d 235 (1966). Moreover, the Court, in striking down so called "negative loyalty oath" requirements of the states, has never suggested that the First Amendment proscribes any form of oath or affirmation required of teachers.

Plaintiffs rely heavily upon West Virginia State Board of Education v. Barnette, in which the Supreme Court held unconstitutional a state statute requiring school children to salute and pledge allegiance to the American flag. The pledge of allegiance there involved, however, was far more elaborate than the affirmation required by New York of teachers in public and tax supported educational institutions. Furthermore, the decision in *Barnette* was based on the First Amendment's guarantee of religious freedom. The plaintiffs there were members of a religious group who claimed that the requirement of the oath and accompanying salute violated their religious beliefs. No such claim or allegation is made here. * * *

Plaintiffs also urge that section 3002 suffers the vice of vagueness. In support of this theory, they rely upon the line of Supreme Court cases striking down "negative loyalty oaths" or "non-Communist oaths". As plaintiffs' counsel candidly conceded at oral argument, however, such oaths, which typically require an affiant to state that he is not now and has never been a member of certain organizations, present a very different problem.

The language of Section 3002 is simple and clear in its import. It requires no more than that the subscriber affirm that he will support the constitutions of the United States and the State of New York and that he will be a dedicated teacher. The statutory language of support of the constitutional governments can be substantially equated to that allegiance which, by the common law, every citizen was understood to owe his sovereign. * * * In our view, a state can reasonably ask teachers in public or tax exempted institutions to subscribe to professional competence and dedication.

Plaintiffs, conceding that it is constitutionally permissible to demand from public officials, federal and state, an oath or affirmation substantially the same as that set forth in Section 3002, suggest that different considerations apply to teachers. In sum, it is said that teachers' speech must be totally "free of interference". But, as may be implied from what has already been said, we interpret the statute to impose no restrictions upon political or philosophical expressions by teachers in the State of New York. A state does not interfere with its teachers by requiring them to support the governmental systems which shelter and nourish the institutions in which they teach, nor does it restrict its teachers by encouraging them to uphold the highest standards of their chosen profession. Indeed, it is plain that a state has a clear interest in assuring " * * * careful and discriminating selection of teachers" by its publicly supported educational institutions.

* * *

Notes

1. The decision of this three-judge court was summarily affirmed by the Supreme Court, 390 U.S. 36, 88 S.Ct. 816, 19 L.Ed.2d 812 (1968). Note the date

of this decision in relation to the chronology of "loyalty" cases discussed in the text of this chapter.

2. What was the legal basis for making the oath applicable to the faculty of private schools?

3. Is this oath a threat to academic freedom?

4. Note the argument of the teachers that they should be classified differently from other public employees as regards oaths. What is your reaction to their argument?

[Case No. 87] Constitutionality of State Program to Remove Subversive Teachers

KEYISHIAN v. BOARD OF REGENTS OF UNIVERSITY OF STATE OF NEW YORK

Supreme Court of the United States, 1967.
385 U.S. 589, 87 S.Ct. 675, 17 L.Ed.2d 629.

MR. JUSTICE BRENNAN delivered the opinion of the Court.

Appellants were members of the faculty of the privately owned and operated University of Buffalo, and became state employees when the University was merged in 1962 into the State University of New York, an institution of higher education owned and operated by the State of New York. As faculty members of the State University their continued employment was conditioned upon their compliance with a New York plan, formulated partly in statutes and partly in administrative regulations, which the State utilizes to prevent the appointment or retention of "subversive" persons in state employment.

Appellants Hochfield and Maud were Assistant Professors of English, appellant Keyishian, an instructor in English, and appellant Garver, a lecturer in philosophy. Each of them refused to sign, as regulations then in effect required, a certificate that he was not a Communist, and that if he had ever been a Communist, he had communicated that fact to the President of the State University of New York. Each was notified that his failure to sign the certificate would require his dismissal. Keyishian's one-year-term contract was not renewed because of his failure to sign the certificate. * * *

* * *

I.

We considered some aspects of the constitutionality of the New York plan 15 years ago in Adler v. Board of Education. That litigation arose after New York passed the Feinberg Law which added § 3022 to the Education Law, McKinney's Consol.Laws, c. 16. The Feinberg Law was enacted to implement and enforce two earlier statutes. The first was a 1917 law, now § 3021 of the Education Law, under which "the utterance of any treasonable or seditious word or words or the doing of any treasonable or seditious act" is a ground for dismissal from the public school system. The second was a 1939 law which was § 12–a of the Civil

Service Law when *Adler* was decided and, as amended, is now § 105 of that law, McKinney's Consol.Laws, c. 7. This law disqualifies from the civil service and from employment in the educational system any person who advocates the overthrow of government by force, violence, or any unlawful means, or publishes material advocating such overthrow or organizes or joins any society or group of persons advocating such doctrine.

The Feinberg Law charged the State Board of Regents with the duty of promulgating rules and regulations providing procedures for the disqualification or removal of persons in the public school system who violate the 1917 law or who are ineligible for appointment to or retention in the public school system under the 1939 law. The Board of Regents was further directed to make a list, after notice and hearing, of "subversive" organizations, defined as organizations which advocate the doctrine of overthrow of government by force, violence, or any unlawful means. Finally, the Board was directed to provide in its rules and regulations that membership in any listed organization should constitute prima facie evidence of disqualification for appointment to or retention in any office or position in the public schools of the State.

The Board of Regents thereupon promulgated rules and regulations containing procedures to be followed by appointing authorities to discover persons ineligible for appointment or retention under the 1939 law, or because of violation of the 1917 law. The Board also announced its intention to list "subversive" organizations after requisite notice and hearing, and provided that membership in a listed organization after the date of its listing should be regarded as constituting prima facie evidence of disqualification, and that membership prior to listing should be presumptive evidence that membership has continued, in the absence of a showing that such membership was terminated in good faith. Under the regulations, an appointing official is forbidden to make an appointment until after he has first inquired of an applicant's former employers and other persons to ascertain whether the applicant is disqualified or ineligible for appointment. In addition, an annual inquiry must be made to determine whether an appointed employee has ceased to be qualified for retention, and a report of findings must be filed.

Adler was a declaratory judgment suit in which the Court held, in effect, that there was no constitutional infirmity in former § 12–a or in the Feinberg Law on their faces and that they were capable of constitutional application. But the contention urged in this case that both § 3021 and § 105 are unconstitutionally vague was not heard or decided. Section 3021 of the Education Law was challenged in *Adler* as unconstitutionally vague, but because the challenge had not been made in the pleadings or in the proceedings in the lower courts, this Court refused to consider it. * * * Appellants in this case timely asserted below the unconstitutionality of all these sections on grounds of vagueness and that question is now properly before us for decision. Moreover, to the extent that *Adler* sustained the provision of the Feinberg Law constituting membership in an organization advocating forceful overthrow of government a ground for disqualification, pertinent constitutional doctrines have since rejected the premises upon which that conclusion rested. *Adler* is therefore not dispositive of the constitutional issues we must decide in this case.

II.

A 1953 amendment extended the application of the Feinberg Law to personnel of any college or other institution of higher education owned and operated by the State or its subdivisions. In the same year, the Board of Regents, after notice and hearing, listed the Communist Party of the United States and of the State of New York as "subversive organizations." In 1956 each applicant for an appointment or the renewal of an appointment was required to sign the so-called "Feinberg Certificate" declaring that he had read the Regents Rules and understood that the Rules and the statutes constituted terms of employment, and declaring further that he was not a member of the Communist Party, and that if he had ever been a member he had communicated that fact to the President of the State University. This was the certificate that appellants Hochfield, Maud, Keyishian, and Garver refused to sign.

In June 1965, shortly before the trial of this case, the Feinberg Certificate was rescinded and it was announced that no person then employed would be deemed ineligible for continued employment "solely" because he refused to sign the certificate. In lieu of the certificate, it was provided that each applicant be informed before assuming his duties that the statutes, §§ 3021 and 3022 of the Education Law and § 105 of the Civil Service Law, constituted part of his contract. He was particularly to be informed of the disqualification which flowed from membership in a listed "subversive" organization. The 1965 announcement further provides: "Should any question arise in the course of such inquiry such candidate may request * * * a personal interview. Refusal of a candidate to answer any question relevant to such inquiry by such officer shall be sufficient ground to refuse to make or recommend appointment." A brochure is also given new applicants. It outlines and explains briefly the legal effect of the statutes and invites any applicant who may have any question about possible disqualification to request an interview. The covering announcement concludes that "a prospective appointee who does not believe himself disqualified need take no affirmative action. No disclaimer oath is required."

The change in procedure in no wise moots appellants' constitutional questions raised in the context of their refusal to sign the now abandoned Feinberg Certificate. The substance of the statutory and regulatory complex remains and from the outset appellants' basic claim has been that they are aggrieved by its application.

III.

Section 3021 requires removal for "treasonable or seditious" utterances or acts. * * *

* * *

* * * We cannot gainsay the potential effect of this obscure wording on "those with a conscientious and scrupulous regard for such undertakings." * * * The teacher cannot know the extent, if any, to which a "seditious" utterance must transcend mere statement about abstract doctrine, the extent to which it must be intended to and tend to indoctrinate or incite to action in furtherance of the defined doctrine. The crucial consideration is that no teacher can know just where the line is drawn between "seditious" and nonseditious utterances and acts.

Other provisions of § 105 also have the same defect of vagueness. Subdivision 1(a) of § 105 bars employment of any person who "by word of mouth or writing wilfully and deliberately advocates, advises or teaches the doctrine" of forceful overthrow of government. This provision is plainly susceptible of sweeping and improper application. It may well prohibit the employment of one who merely advocates the doctrine in the abstract without any attempt to indoctrinate others, or incite others to action in furtherance of unlawful aims. And in prohibiting "advising" the "doctrine" of unlawful overthrow does the statute prohibit mere "advising" of the existence of the doctrine, or advising another to support the doctrine? Since "advocacy" of the doctrine of forceful overthrow is separately prohibited, need the person "teaching" or "advising" this doctrine himself "advocate" it? Does the teacher who informs his class about the precepts of Marxism or the Declaration of Independence violate the prohibition?

Similar uncertainty arises as to the application of subdivision 1(b) of § 105. That subsection requires the disqualification of an employee involved with the distribution of written material "containing or advocating, advising or teaching the doctrine" of forceful overthrow, and who himself "advocates, advises, teaches, or embraces the duty, necessity or propriety of adopting the doctrine contained therein." Here again, mere advocacy of abstract doctrine is apparently included. And does the prohibition of distribution of matter "containing" the doctrine bar histories of the evolution of Marxist doctrine or tracing the background of the French, American, or Russian revolutions? The additional requirement, that the person participating in distribution of the material be one who "advocates, advises, teaches, or embraces the duty, necessity or propriety of adopting the doctrine" of forceful overthrow, does not alleviate the uncertainty in the scope of the section, but exacerbates it. Like the language of § 105, subd. 1(a), this language may reasonably be construed to cover mere expression of belief. For example, does the university librarian who recommends the reading of such materials thereby "advocate * * * the propriety of adopting the doctrine contained therein"?

We do not have the benefit of a judicial gloss by the New York courts enlightening us as to the scope of this complicated plan. In light of the intricate administrative machinery for its enforcement, this is not surprising. The very intricacy of the plan and the uncertainty as to the scope of its proscriptions make it a highly efficient *in terrorem* mechanism. It would be a bold teacher who would not stay as far as possible from utterances or acts which might jeopardize his living by enmeshing him in this intricate machinery. The uncertainty as to the utterances and acts proscribed increases that caution in "those who believe the written law means what it says." The result must be to stifle "that free play of the spirit which all teachers ought especially to cultivate and practice * * *." That probability is enhanced by the provisions requiring an annual review of every teacher to determine whether any utterance or act of his, inside the classroom or out, came within the sanctions of the laws. * * *

There can be no doubt of the legitimacy of New York's interest in protecting its education system from subversion. But "even though the governmental purpose be legitimate and substantial, that purpose cannot be pursued by means that broadly stifle fundamental personal liberties when the end can be more narrowly achieved." The principle is not inapplicable because the legislation is aimed at keeping subversives out of the teaching ranks. * * *

Our Nation is deeply committed to safeguarding academic freedom, which is of transcendent value to all of us and not merely to the teachers concerned. That freedom is therefore a special concern of the First Amendment, which does not tolerate laws that cast a pall of orthodoxy over the classroom. "The vigilant protection of constitutional freedoms is nowhere more vital than in the community of American schools." The classroom is peculiarly the "marketplace of ideas." The Nation's future depends upon leaders trained through wide exposure to that robust exchange of ideas which discovers truth "out of a multitude of tongues, [rather] than through any kind of authoritative selection." * * *

* * *

The regulatory maze created by New York is wholly lacking in "terms acceptable of objective measurement." * * * Vagueness of wording is aggravated by prolixity and profusion of statutes, regulations, and administrative machinery, and by manifold cross-references to interrelated enactments and rules.

We therefore hold that § 3021 of the Education Law and subdivisions 1(a), 1(b) and 3 of § 105 of the Civil Service Law as implemented by the machinery created pursuant to § 3022 of the Education Law are unconstitutional.

IV.

Appellants have also challenged the constitutionality of the discrete provisions of subdivision 1(c) of § 105 and subdivision 2 of the Feinberg Law, which make Communist Party membership, as such, prima facie evidence of disqualification. The provision was added to subdivision 1(c) of § 105 in 1958 after the Board of Regents, following notice and hearing, listed the Communist Party of the United States and the Communist Party of the State of New York as "subversive" organizations. Subdivision 2 of the Feinberg Law was, however, before the Court in *Adler* and its constitutionality was sustained. But constitutional doctrine which has emerged since that decision has rejected its major premise. That premise was that public employment, including academic employment, may be conditioned upon the surrender of constitutional rights which could not be abridged by direct government action.   * * *

* * *

We proceed then to the question of the validity of the provisions of subdivision 1 of § 105 and subdivision 2 of § 3022, barring employment to members of listed organizations. Here again constitutional doctrine has developed since *Adler*. Mere knowing membership without a specific intent to further the unlawful aims of an organization is not a constitutionally adequate basis for exclusion from such positions as those held by appellants.

In Elfbrandt v. Russell, we said, "Those who join an organization but do not share its unlawful purposes and who do not participate in its unlawful activities surely pose no threat, either as citizens or as public employees." We there struck down a statutorily required oath binding the state employee not to become a member of the Communist Party with knowledge of its unlawful purpose, on threat of discharge and perjury prosecution if the oath were violated. We found that "[a]ny lingering doubt that proscription of mere knowing membership, without any showing of 'specific intent,' would run afoul of the Constitution was set at rest by our decision in Aptheker v. Secretary of State, 378 U.S. 500, 84 S.Ct. 1659, 12 L.Ed.2d 992 (1964)." * * *

These limitations clearly apply to a provision, like § 105, subd. 1(c), which blankets all state employees, regardless of the "sensitivity" of their positions. But even the Feinberg Law provision, applicable primarily to activities of teachers, who have captive audiences of young minds, are subject to these limitations in favor of freedom of expression and association; the stifling effect on the academic mind from curtailing freedom of association in such manner is manifest, and has been documented in recent studies. *Elfbrandt* and *Aptheker* state the governing standard: legislation which sanctions membership unaccompanied by specific intent to further the unlawful goals of the organization or which is not active membership violates constitutional limitations.

* * *

We therefore hold that Civil Service Law § 105, subd. 1(c), and Education Law § 3022, subd. 2, are invalid insofar as they proscribe mere knowing membership without any showing of specific intent to further the unlawful aims of the Communist Party of the United States or of the State of New York.

* * *

Notes

1. This case marked the ultimate demise of most efforts by states affirmatively to check on teacher loyalty.

2. While not expressly repudiating all of its 1952 opinion in *Adler,* the Court does here strike down the Feinberg Law as implemented. Can you think of other examples where "constitutional doctrines" have "evolved" so as to lead

to new conclusions far different from prior ones? Precisely what formerly valid doctrines were rejected by the Court in the present case?

3. Justice Clark wrote a strongly-worded dissent, which was joined by Justices Harlan, Stewart, and White. He said that the majority had "swept away one of our most precious rights, namely, the right of self-preservation."

4. At what point does the "legitimacy of New York's interest in protecting its education system" end and the "personal liberties" of teachers begin?

[Case No. 88] Right of Teacher to Paid Leave on Religious Holidays

PINSKER v. JOINT DIST. NO. 28J OF ADAMS AND ARAPAHOE COUNTIES

United States Court of Appeals, Tenth Circuit, 1984.
735 F.2d 388.

Logan, Circuit Judge.   * * *

Pinsker is a teacher in the Aurora, Colorado, public schools. He claims that the defendant school district's school schedule and leave policy discriminate against him and other Jewish teachers on the basis of religion and unconstitutionally burden his right to free exercise of religion. The basis of his claim is that the school year in the district is arranged so that Christmas is not a school day, and in most school years there has been no school on Good Friday or Good Friday afternoon; thus, Christian teachers need not use their personal leave time or take unpaid leave to observe religious holidays. Pinsker does not work on three Jewish holidays: one day for Yom Kippur and two days for Rosh Hashanah. In some years all three of those holidays fall on school days.

The leave policy in the defendant district is a product of collective bargaining. A teacher has a pool of twelve days of paid leave, all of which the teacher may use for sick leave and parts of which the teacher may use for other specified purposes. A teacher may use a maximum of two days from the pool for "special leave." Teachers have been allowed to use special leave to observe Jewish holidays.   * * *

* * *

I

* * * Pinsker still works for defendant, and the terms and conditions of his employment are identical to those of other teachers similarly situated. However, [a section of Title VII] provides:

> "The term 'religion' includes all aspects of religious observance and practice, as well as belief, unless an employer demonstrates that he is unable to reasonably accommodate to an employee's or prospective employee's religious observance or practice without undue hardship on the conduct of the employer's business."

The Supreme Court has held that the intent and effect of this definition of "religion" is to make it a violation of [Title VII] for an employer not to make reasonable accommodations, short of undue hardship, for the religious practices of employees and prospective employees. Simply put, Title VII requires reasonable accommodation or a showing that reasonable accommodation would be an undue hardship on the employer. * * *

Pinsker does not suggest that he should receive more paid leave or other special treatment. Rather, he argues that Title VII requires the defendant to institute a generally applicable policy that is less burdensome to his religious practices than its present policy. At trial plaintiffs showed that other school districts have leave policies under which Pinsker would not have to take unpaid leave in a year when Yom Kippur and both days of Rosh Hashanah fell on school days. * * *

Title VII requires reasonable accommodation. It does not require employers to accommodate the religious practices of an employee in exactly the way the employee would like to be accommodated. Nor does Title VII require employers to accommodate an employee's religious practices in a way that spares the employee any cost whatsoever. Defendant's policy and practices jeopardized neither Pinsker's job nor his observation of religious holidays. Because teachers are likely to have not only different religions but also different degrees of devotion to their religions, a school district cannot be expected to negotiate leave policies broad enough to suit every employee's religious needs perfectly. Defendant's policy, although it may require teachers to take occasional unpaid leave, is not an unreasonable accommodation of teachers' religious practices. * * *

II

Plaintiffs also claim that defendant's leave policy unconstitutionally burdens Pinsker's First Amendment right to free exercise of religion. The trial court correctly characterized the issue as whether the economic impact of losing a day's wages in order to attend a religious service is a denial of freedom of religion.

In Thomas v. Review Board of the Indiana Employment Security Division, 450 U.S. 707, 101 S.Ct. 1425, 67 L.Ed.2d 624 (1981), the Supreme Court considered whether the First Amendment permits a state to deny unemployment benefits to a man who quit his job because it required him to engage in behavior that violated his religious beliefs. The Court set out the following standard:

> "Where the state conditions receipt of an important benefit upon conduct proscribed by a religious faith, or where it denies such a benefit because of conduct mandated by religious belief, thereby putting substantial pressure on an adherent to modify his behavior and to violate his beliefs, a burden upon religion exists."

Loss of a day's pay for time not worked does not constitute substantial pressure on a teacher to modify his or her behavior. * * *

Affirmed.

Notes

1. The Supreme Court in Thomas v. Review Bd. of the Indiana Employment Security Division (cited in case) held that a Jehovah's Witness could not be denied unemployment compensation when he "quit due to his religious convictions" against producing weapons of war.

2. Evidence was presented that leave policies in some other Colorado school districts would have spared Pinsker the loss of a day's pay. Is this the basis of an unequal protection claim? Why?

3. The Supreme Court of California, by a vote of four-to-three, concluded that under the state constitution a tenure teacher was entitled to be absent on holidays of his religion when the total of his religious absences would approximate only the mandatory number of paid leave days for the state's teachers. Rankins v. Commission on Professional Competence of Ducor Union School Dist., 24 Cal.3d 167, 154 Cal.Rptr. 907, 593 P.2d 852 (1979).

4. See text accompanying footnote 71 for a relevant Supreme Court case.

[Case No. 89] Administration of Sick Leave Policy

RAMSEY v. BOARD OF EDUC.

Court of Appeals of Kentucky, 1990.
789 S.W.2d 784.

CLAYTON, JUDGE. This appeal arises from a dispute as to the number of sick leave days to which Ramsey is entitled. The Board effected a reduction in the number of sick days to which Ramsey had previously been credited. She filed suit, and the Whitley Circuit Court, on cross-motions for summary judgment, granted summary judgment to the Board. We now affirm.

Ramsey was employed as a teacher by the Board from 1956 through 1985–86, at which time she was eligible for full retirement. Prior to April 11, 1985, the minutes of the Board reflect that no policy regarding sick leave had been adopted. Nonetheless, the Board's records of individual teacher's accumulated sick leave demonstrated that an unlimited amount had been allowed to accumulate. Ramsey had accumulated 142 days.

The accumulation was allowed in an apparent disregard of the sick leave statute, KRS 161.155. The statute has been amended several times. A summary of those changes is provided.

In 1948, KRS 161.155 provided that the Board shall allow a teacher not less than ten (10) days of sick leave during each school year without deduction of salary with accumulation in subsequent school years not to exceed twenty (20) days, unless a greater number was authorized by the local School Board.

It was amended in 1970 to provide for the increase of the maximum accumulated days of sick leave to not more than sixty (60) days, unless a greater number authorized by the local Board, and further provided the ten (10) days granted each school year shall be in addition to the accumulated days.

Then, in 1974, KRS 161.155 was amended to provide the same as the 1970 amendment, and further provided: "days of sick leave not taken by teacher during any school year shall accumulate without limitations and be credited to that teacher. Accumulated sick leave may be taken in any school year."

Finally, KRS 161.155 was amended, effective July 1, 1981, to state: "After July 1, 1981, a District Board of Education may compensate, at the time of retirement, a teacher for each unused sick leave day. The rate of compensation for each unused sick leave day shall be based on a percentage of the teacher's last annual salary, not to exceed thirty (30) percent. Payment for unused sick leave days shall be incorporated into the annual salary of the final year of service. The accumulation of such days includes unused sick leave days held by the teacher at the time of the implementation of such a program."

On April 11, 1985, the Board adopted a sick leave policy. That policy was to go back and correct each teacher's sick leave record to conform to the statute. Additionally, the Board decided to pay teachers, pursuant to the 1981 amendment, for unused sick leave days as a retirement benefit. Specifically, twenty-five (25%) percent of the teacher's salary was allowed for the first 79 days of accumulated sick leave, and thirty (30%) percent for any additional days.

Pursuant to the Board's decision, Ramsey's accumulated sick leave days were reduced to twenty-nine (29). She filed suit challenging the loss of 113 days.

In challenging the reduction, Ramsey argues that the unlimited accumulation of sick leave became part of her contract. Specifically, she asserts that based upon the failure of the Board to object to the administrative procedure allowing unlimited accumulation her contract included the sick leave days accumulated in excess of the statutory cap even though the inclusion was not part of her written contract.

The difficulty with the argument, which would undoubtedly be upheld in an ordinary contract situation, is that her contract is with the Board, which is a public agency. Public agencies cannot become liable under implied contracts. To be bound, a public agency must act through its records. Consequently, the Board could only be bound through its minutes. In this matter, it is admitted that the Board did not adopt any policy regarding sick leave before 1985. As a result, the Board did not initiate any contract with Ramsey regarding the accumulation of sick leave days beyond the statutory cap.

The Board could become bound, however, if it ratified the contract. Ratification involves an after-the-fact validation by the Board in the same manner and form prescribed in initially making the contract. In fact, even where a public agency has accepted the benefit of the contract, it will not be bound by its act (or inaction) unless the contract was formally ratified. Consequently, we must hold that the Board did not make a contract with Ramsey regarding accumulating sick leave either initially or by ratification.

In an effort to avoid the result reached above, Ramsey cites us to Martin v. Board of Education of Bath County, 284 Ky. 818, 146 S.W.2d 12 (1940), and Knox County Board of Education v. Willis, Ky., 405 S.W.2d 952 (1966). We find both cases distinguishable.

In *Martin,* the Court upheld the inclusion of a proviso from the resolution of the school board authorizing the hiring of a principal even though it was not included in the written contract actually signed.

As a result, we find it unpersuasive in the present matter where there was no resolution or other action of the Board entered in the minutes to be included in the contract Ramsey signed.

The *Knox County Board of Education* case held that a school board was not required to adopt formal procedural rules for hearings regarding dismissal of teacher for cause under KRS 161.690, since the statute itself provided adequate due process procedures. It does not follow that failure of the Board in the present matter to adopt a sick leave policy allowing unlimited accumulation of excess days resulted in Ramsey having a right thereto. At most, it would require a finding in her favor if KRS 161.155 by itself allowed it. Instead, there is no dispute but that the statute requires affirmative action by the Board to allow accumulation above the statutory caps. We are, therefore, not persuaded to hold other than as previously indicated that Ramsey has no contract right to the excess sick leave days.

Ramsey next argues that the Board became bound by the acts of its agent, the superintendent. In support of her argument, she relies upon several cases which hold principals bound by acts of their agents, where the agent had implied or apparent authority. For purposes of this opinion, we will accept Ramsey's allegation that if general principal and agency principles were applied the Board would be bound by the superintendent's allowance of unlimited accumulation of sick leave.

We do not find, however, that the general principle applies. A public agency will not be permitted to bear a loss because an officer failed to perform his duty. As a result, the Board will not be held accountable for the failure of its superintendents to properly apply the statute regarding sick leave. We also note that a school board will not be bound by the individual or separate acts of its members. Thus, a member of a school board could not make a contract for the board. We do not think that a superintendent acting individually (i.e. without proper authority from the board) should be treated any differently.

It has also been held that parties contracting with a school board are charged with the knowledge that agents of the board have only limited authority and must look to the board's records to determine the agent's authority. Thus, Ramsey is charged with the knowledge that the administrative failure to properly apply the statutory limit on sick leave was not authorized by the Board. In sum, the Board is not bound by the allowance of unlimited accumulation of sick leave days by its agent. As a result, Ramsey's excess accumulated sick leave days are not part of her contract.

Ramsey's final argument is that the Board's actions are arbitrary under Section Two of our Constitution. The Board has the responsibility of determining whether to allow retirement pay for accumulated sick leave, and how to implement that decision. They are under no compulsion to do so, and Ramsey had no contractual right to any compensation for any sick leave days prior to the Board's decision to allow it. In other words, the policy question of retirement pay for sick leave days is committed to the Board's discretion. We are directed not to substitute our judgment on policy in their place.

The Board's discretion is not, however, without limit. It cannot act arbitrarily or unreasonably. Arbitrariness has been defined as a clearly erroneous decision, which is a failure to have a decision supported by substantial evidence. Unreasonableness has been explained as when under the evidence presented there is no room for a difference of opinion among reasonable minds. In the present matter, the Board decided to grant a retirement pay benefit at a certain level near the statutory maximum for the sick leave days which were accumulated when the statute was applied. We do not find the Board's decision to be arbitrary or capricious under the facts presented.

Ramsey asserts that City of Frankfort v. Triplett, Ky., 365 S.W.2d 328 (1963), compels a different result. We disagree. The Court in *Triplett* held that a city council's discretion did not extend to allow it to indirectly abolish a statutorily created position by providing only a *de minimis* salary. Ramsey, however, had no right to retirement pay for sick leave until the Board acted. Consequently, there was nothing for the Board to take away either directly or indirectly. As noted, the determination of the extent of the right to retirement pay is committed to the Board's discretion within the statutory parameters of KRS 161.-155. It did so. We will not substitute our judgment therefor. As a result, we do not find that *Triplett*, requires a different result.

* * *

[Affirmed.]

Notes

1. The claim of Ramsey previously had been rejected on jurisdictional grounds by the Sixth Circuit, which held that the claim was a common-law one for breach of an employment contract actionable under state law rather than Section 1983. Ramsey v. Board of Educ. of Whitley County, Kentucky, 844 F.2d 1268 (6 Cir.1988).

2. Observe that the superintendent had been acting solely on his own with no affirmative board action, that until the 1981 amendment state sick leave provisions covered only absences due to sickness and were not connected with deferred compensation payable on retirement, and that the board's newly adopted plan was not unreasonable.

3. Kentucky courts are among those that generally deny claims against public bodies on implied contracts and are strict as regards informal ratifications. (See Chapter 8). All state courts, however, examine closely implied-contract arguments because of the potential for abuse in the public sector.

4. Note how the present court distinguishes the facts in this case from those in cases submitted on behalf of Ramsey (Martin v. Board of Educ. of Bath County, Knox County Bd. of Educ. v. Willis [Case No. 103], and City of Frankfort v. Triplett).

[Case No. 90]   Constitutionality of Race–Based Teacher Transfer Plan

JACOBSON v. CINCINNATI BD. OF EDUC.

United States Court of Appeals, Sixth Circuit, 1992.
961 F.2d 100.

ALAN E. NORRIS, CIRCUIT JUDGE. Eight Cincinnati public school teachers and the Cincinnati Federation of Teachers ("CFT"), the union that represents them, brought suit in the district court challenging the teacher transfer policy adopted by the Cincinnati Board of Education ("Board") to ensure that the faculty of its schools reflects system-wide racial balance. After an evidentiary hearing, the district court concluded that the policy did not violate either plaintiffs' Fourteenth Amendment right to equal protection or the terms of the collective bargaining agreement ("CBA") negotiated by the CFT and the Board. Accordingly, the district court denied plaintiffs' request to enjoin the transfer policy. For the reasons outlined below, we affirm the judgment of the district court.

This dispute has its genesis in the 1970s, when concerted efforts to eradicate indicia of racial segregation within the Cincinnati public school system began. On January 14, 1974, the Board adopted a policy designed to ensure that the teaching staff of a given school approximated the racial balance of the teaching staff of the system as a whole. Shortly thereafter, the Board issued a statement indicating how this general policy would be implemented. Among other things, the statement provided that the percentage of black teachers in any school should not be five percent greater or less than the percentage of black teachers throughout the system. In order to implement this racial balance, the policy restricts the ability of some teachers to voluntarily transfer to other school buildings, and requires the reassignment of others. It is this portion of the policy which plaintiffs challenge.

In the same year that these efforts to balance the racial composition of the faculty were initiated, a group of school children and their parents filed a lawsuit against the Board, contending that the school system was unlawfully segregated. That suit was ultimately settled by the parties, and the district court adopted the settlement agreement as a consent decree. Paragraph 5 of the settlement agreement reads as follows:

> The Cincinnati Board of Education currently has in force a policy which requires that the staff in each of its schools has a racial composition which is within 5% of the racial composition of the staff in the district as a whole. The Board shall maintain that policy in effect and take steps necessary to assure that it is enforced.

The CFT actively participated in the resolution of [the settled suit] and did not object to the maintenance of the staff racial balance policy. The position of the CFT is reflected in the CBA negotiated with the Board. Section 250, paragraph 1, of the CBA contains the following provision regarding teacher transfers: "Teacher requests for transfer will be honored if positions are available and the teacher is qualified for a particular vacancy, provided that the transfer is consistent with the racial balance of the staff."

We begin by noting that school authorities have broad discretion to implement educational policy. *Swann v. Charlotte–Mecklenburg Bd. of Educ.* This authority includes the power to prescribe a ratio of white to minority students that reflects the composition of the overall school district, particularly when such a policy is implemented in order to prepare students for life in a pluralistic society. And we believe that this discretionary authority includes the power to assign faculty to achieve a racial ratio reflecting the racial composition of the system's teachers. The Supreme Court has recognized that the attainment of an integrated teaching staff is a legitimate concern in achieving a school system free of racial discrimination. *United States v. Montgomery County Bd. of Educ.*

Here, the district court found that the policy adopted by the Board is race conscious in the sense that it allows the Board to determine the schools at which a teacher may teach solely on the basis of his or her race. However, the court went on to find that the policy is "specific race neutral in that there is no disparate impact as to race in its application. It is applied equally to both black and white teachers. In some instances, it will benefit or harm white teachers; in others, it will benefit or harm black teachers." We agree with that characterization. We are therefore unable to agree with plaintiffs' contention that the policy establishes preferences based on race that require us to examine the policy with strict scrutiny to determine whether it conflicts with guarantees afforded them under the Constitution.

Under analogous circumstances, the Court of Appeals for the Third Circuit offered these observations concerning the appropriate level of scrutiny to which such a policy should be subjected:

> No case has suggested that the mere utilization of race as a factor, together with seniority, school need, and subject qualification, is prohibited. Since the classification is not preferential, it might most appropriately be reviewed for its rational relationship to a legitimate government objective, under which standard it would be patently valid. At most, since there is some element of racial classification, albeit not of preference, the appropriate level of scrutiny would be the intermediate level suggested by four members of the Court in *Bakke,* in which the classification was indeed preferential.

> The appropriate question under that standard is whether the classification "serve[s] important governmental objectives" and is "substantially related to achievement of those objectives."

Kromnick v. School Dist. (citing *Regents of the Univ. of Cal. v. Bakke*).

In our view, this intermediate level of scrutiny is the proper one, since the Cincinnati teacher transfer policy, like the policy challenged in *Kromnick,* does not prefer one race over another. Accordingly, we must determine whether the policy is substantially related to an important governmental objective. We believe the policy at issue meets that test. It was implemented to achieve a racially integrated faculty throughout the Cincinnati public school system. Not only is this a legitimate objective, it has been endorsed in the past by the CFT. In fact, section 250 of the CBA, which appellants mistakenly contend has been violated by the Board, expressly allows for the accommodation of such a transfer policy.

We therefore hold that plaintiffs have failed to demonstrate how their interest in selecting the schools to which they are assigned outweighs the Board's interest in fostering an integrated, pluralistic school system.

The judgment of the district court is affirmed.

Notes

1. The Supreme Court without dissent denied certiorari. ___ U.S. ___, 113 S.Ct. 94, 121 L.Ed.2d 55 (1992).

2. In an equal protection case, such as this, the court first must determine the level of scrutiny to apply to the classification. Observe how the court decided on the level, and note what that level requires in order to meet the constitutional standard.

3. What is your impression of the role of the teachers union in pursuit of the claim of unconstitutionality in this case?

4. Would this case serve as a precedent for deciding a case where a factor in an involuntary transfer is (1) the sex of the teacher, (2) the years of experience of the teacher, (3) the religion of the teacher? Why?

[Case No. 91] Injunction against Teachers' Strike

TIMBERLANE REGIONAL SCHOOL DIST. v. TIMBERLANE REGIONAL EDUC. ASS'N

Supreme Court of New Hampshire, 1974.
114 N.H. 245, 317 A.2d 555.

KENISON, CHIEF JUSTICE. The major issue in this case is whether the presiding justice properly denied the plaintiff's petition to enjoin the defendants from engaging in or aiding and abetting a strike. * * *

The Timberlane Regional Education Association (hereinafter TREA) is the collective bargaining agent for some, if not all, of the teachers in the Timberlane Regional School District and is affiliated with the New Hampshire Education Association, whose membership consists of school teachers employed throughout the State. The TREA and the Timberlane Regional School Board (hereinafter board) agreed to meet during the spring and summer of 1973 for the purpose of negotiating a contract for the 1974–75 school year.

The board proceeded to hire a professional negotiator and delayed meeting with the TREA until July 31, 1973. The parties met throughout the fall and early winter and, by January 14, 1974, had reached a tentative agreement on approximately one-quarter of the items submitted for negotiation by the TREA. The majority of the remaining items, which included salary schedules, sick and emergency leave, teacher rights and responsibilities, teacher evaluation, academic freedom and grievance procedures, had been declared non-negotiable by the board. It became apparent that an impasse was developing in regard to these items, and the members of the TREA voted to submit their differences with the board to a mediator for resolution. The TREA contacted the Federal Mediation Service which agreed to undertake mediation if both parties so requested. The board, however, declined to accept this offer, and several other attempts to find a mutually agreeable mediator came to naught.

The parties resumed negotiations on February 15, 1974, and met again on February 18, 20 and 23. These meetings resulted in a tentative agreement on several of the remaining items, but their differences with respect to great majority of these items were unresolved. During the course of negotiations on February 23, 1974, the TREA discovered for the first time that on February 16, 1974, the board had submitted salary proposals to the budget committee, despite the fact that an agreement had not been worked out between the parties on this matter. The board then stated at the end of this session that it would go no further and declined to negotiate on the evening of February 23, or at any time on February 24, and 25, 1974.

The members of the TREA met on February 25, 1974, and voted to call for mediation because of an impasse in negotiations and to refuse to teach until mediation began. Last minute efforts to achieve compromise between the positions of the parties came to no avail, and the strike commenced on February 26, 1974. Approximately two-thirds of the teaching staff in the district did not report to work, and pickets were set up in the vicinity of the schools. The board was initially able to keep all of the schools in the district open by hiring substitute teachers, and student attendance did not drop appreciably. The board, however, was ultimately forced to shut down the Timberlane Regional High and Junior High Schools.

"[P]ublic employer collective bargaining is now an established fact at the federal level and in the majority of state and local governments. The transition from uniform disapproval to majority acceptance of public employer collective bargaining began in 1955, when New Hampshire adopted legislation authorizing town governments to engage in collective bargaining with public employee unions." Nevertheless, in most jurisdictions, a strike by public employees is prohibited either by statute or by judicial decision. New Hampshire is no exception to this rule, for this court held in Manchester v. Manchester Teachers Guild, 100 N.H. 507, 510, 131 A.2d 59, 63 (1957), that such strikes are illegal under the common law of this State and characterized this prohibition as a matter of public policy solely within the province of the legislature.

We are aware of the general dissatisfaction with the effect of this prohibition on labor negotiations between government and public employees. In the private sector, the right to strike is viewed as an integral part of the collective bargaining process. * * * In the public sector, however, the denial of the right to strike has the effect of heavily weighing the collective bargaining process in favor of the government. Without legislation providing alternative methods for resolving impasses in negotiation, there is no ultimate sanction available to the public employees for compelling the good faith of the government, and as a consequence, the only recourse available to them, if they are being treated unfairly, is to terminate their employment or to engage in an illegal strike.

It is not a proper judicial function to make policy judgments as to the merits of providing public employees with the right to strike or of developing alternative processes such as compulsory mediation or arbitration to resolve government labor disputes. This decision must be made by the legislature.

However, in the absence of legislation, the courts are necessarily compelled to consider the problems inherent in labor relations between the government and public employees when called upon to issue an injunction to prevent an illegal strike. The injunction is an extraordinary remedy which is only granted under circumstances where a plaintiff has no adequate remedy at law and is likely to suffer irreparable harm unless the conduct of the defendant is enjoined. The availability of injunctive relief is a matter within the sound discretion of the court exercised on a consideration of all the circumstances of each case and controlled by established principles of equity.

In view of the nature of this remedy, a growing number of jurisdictions have applied equitable principles to deny the government the use of an injunction against illegal strikes by teachers unless there is a showing of irreparable harm to the public. One of the first cases in formulating this new approach was School Dist. for Holland v. Holland Educ. Ass'n, 380 Mich. 314, 157 N.W.2d 206 (1968) in which the Michigan Supreme Court indicated that the refusal of the government to bargain in good faith would be a factor of importance in the determination of whether or not to issue an injunction. This position was embraced by the Rhode Island Supreme Court in School Committee of Westerly v. Westerly Teachers Ass'n, R.I., 299 A.2d 441, 445 (1973) which held that an injunction would not issue "unless it clearly appears from specific facts * * * that irreparable harm will result. * * * *"

We are persuaded by these recent developments that it would be detrimental to the smooth operation of the collective bargaining process to declare that an injunction should automatically issue where public teachers have gone on strike. The essence of the collective bargaining process is that the employer and the employees should work together in resolving problems relating to the employment. The courts should intervene in this process only where it is evident the parties are incapable of settling their disputes by negotiation or by alternative methods such as arbitration and mediation. Judicial interference at any earlier stage could make the courts "an unwitting third party at the bargaining table and a potential coercive force in the collective bargaining processes." Accordingly, it is our view that in deciding to withhold an injunction the trial court may properly consider among other factors whether recognized methods of settlement have failed, whether negotiations have been conducted in good faith, and whether the public health, safety and welfare will be substantially harmed if the strike is allowed to continue.

We have reviewed the * * * record and are satisfied that the trial court took these matters into account in denying the injunction for the present. We agree * * * that the parties had not yet exhausted the possibilities of finding compromise in the collective bargaining process at the time the injunction was refused.

* * *

Notes

1. What are the pros and cons of granting teachers in public schools the right to strike? Are the arguments equally valid for (1) public transportation workers, (2) public sanitation workers, (3) police?

2. Can teachers bargain effectively if they have no right to use the weapon of the strike? Can boards of education bargain effectively if they cannot use the weapon of the lock-out or close-down?

3. Do you agree with this court's view as to the proper role of courts in connection with collective bargaining disputes involving public employees?

4. How can this case be squared with this court's holding in Manchester v. Manchester Teachers Guild, 100 N.H. 507, 131 A.2d 59 (1957) [cited in paragraph 6]? How may the prohibition against strikes be enforced other than by court injunctions?

5. In a case related to the instant case the same court held that striking teachers, as citizens, had a right to the disclosure of the names and addresses of the substitute teachers who were replacing them during the strike. Timberlane Regional Educ. Ass'n v. Crompton, 114 N.H. 315, 319 A.2d 632 (1974).

6. When teachers engage in an illegal strike there is no requirement that the school board continue to treat them as employees and accord them the rights of tenure teachers. National Educ. Ass'n v. Lee County Bd. of Instr., 467 F.2d 447 (5 Cir.1972). See the section "Strikes" in this chapter.

[Case No. 92] Maintenance of Status Quo of Expired Collective Bargaining Contract

INDIANA EDUC. EMPLOYMENT RELATIONS BD. v. MILL CREEK CLASSROOM TEACHERS ASS'N

Supreme Court of Indiana, 1983.
456 N.E.2d 709.

HUNTER, JUSTICE, * * *.

* * *

The primary issue in this case which was resolved by the trial court in favor of the Teachers is whether the School Board violated the statutory provision requiring a maintenance of the status quo by with-holding salary increases provided under a prior contract pending agree-ment on a new contract. We agree with appellees that although this issue is moot with respect to the parties in the instant case, it is an issue which does recur whenever negotiation on a new contract continues after the start of a new school year and also recurs in many school districts throughout the state. Appellees have introduced evidence to show that salary increments have been denied to teachers during the status quo period in at least twelve school corporations during the last two years.

It also is an issue of great public interest since violations of the statute governing collective bargaining between school corporations and their certified employees would necessarily undermine the bargaining relationship between school corporations and teachers and have a detri-mental effect upon the overall educational environment. * * *

The law in Indiana is well settled that although a specific issue may be moot, the fact that it recurs year after year and is of great public interest is sufficient to allow the issue to be considered on its merits. * * *

Turning to the merits of the issue, we must determine precisely what is the status quo within the meaning of the statute. While the term is not defined in the statute, the following is the generally accepted legal definition: "STATUS QUO: The existing state of things at any given date. * * * the last actual, peaceable, uncontested status which preceded the pending controversy." Black's Law Dictionary.

In this case, it is apparent that the experience-based salary increases and lane change adjustments were part of the last uncontested contract of 1977–78. In order to maintain the status quo of that contract, the school board was required to maintain the status quo both as to the salary schedule and the increments which were a part of that schedule.

Furthermore, it is clear that one of the major factors in determining the status quo is the expectation of employees in the continuance of existing terms and conditions of their employment. Where the school corporation has consistently paid incremental wage increases based merely upon years of service or the attainment of an additional degree, employees still reasonably expect their accrued wage increases even though negotiations for a new agreement are pending. If school corpora-tions are not required to pay the increments, they are free to use the increments as a bargaining tool.

For instance, an employer may be encouraged to prolong negotia-tions past the expiration of the existing agreement to gain bargaining leverage. In effect, this tactic would exact a penalty on the employees and their bargaining agent for exercising their rights under an existing agreement. The employees would be deprived of the present use of the increments to their salary even though they may later recover these increments as part of a new contract. Maintenance of the status quo after expiration of a contract and during negotiations for a new contract is important because it serves to continue the balance in the bargaining power of the parties as well as provide the flexibility necessary to reach agreement in the give and take inherent in the collective bargaining process.

Other jurisdictions have found that school corporations are legally required to pay wage increments which are part of an existing contract in order to maintain the status quo pending negotiation of a new contract. * * *

Our statute clearly provides the school corporation "may not unilaterally change the terms or conditions of employment that are issues in dispute" during the status quo period. Since the salary increments were part of the existing wage structure, they were part of the status quo. The trial court properly found that the denial of the scheduled increases was a failure to maintain the status quo and that the school corporation had committed an unfair labor practice.

* * *

Notes

1. The Indiana Education Employment Relations Board, set up to administer the collective bargaining statute, had supported the position of the school board [corporation]. The trial court had reversed that ruling.

2. As a matter of policy, do you agree with the reasoning of this court regarding "status quo"? The legislature had failed to cover the critical point. Here the Supreme Court of Indiana filled the gap, even though it was not necessary to do so because during the period of the litigation a contract had been signed that provided for full payment of all incremental and lane change raises that had been withheld during the negotiation period.

3. The present court refers to "other jurisdictions" that agree with its view, and cites three administrative and two judicial rulings. It makes no reference to a contrary holding by the Court of Appeals of New York in Board of Cooperative Educational Services of Rockland County v. New York State Public Employment Relations Bd., 41 N.Y.2d 753, 395 N.Y.S.2d 439, 363 N.E.2d 1174 (1977). In that case, the administrative agency, which took the Indiana view, was overruled by the court. (Subsequently, the New York legislature provided that automatic salary increments must be paid.)

[Case No. 93] Arbitration in Public Sector Labor Contracts

ACTING SUPERINTENDENT OF SCHOOLS OF LIVERPOOL CENTRAL SCHOOL DIST. v. UNITED LIVERPOOL FACULTY ASS'N

Court of Appeals of New York, 1977.
42 N.Y.2d 509, 399 N.Y.S.2d 189, 369 N.E.2d 746.

JONES, JUDGE. We hold that in arbitrations which proceed under the authority of the Taylor Law [the New York statute covering public sector collective bargaining], the scope of the particular arbitration clause, and thus whether the question sought to be submitted to arbitration is within or without the ambit of that clause, is to be determined by the courts. In making such determinations the courts are to be guided by the principle that the agreement to arbitrate must be express, direct and unequivocal as to the issues or disputes to be submitted to arbitration; anything less will lead to a denial of arbitration.

In this case Liverpool Central School District and the United Liverpool Faculty Association entered into a collective bargaining agreement which provided a grievance procedure, the fourth and final step of which called for submission of an unresolved grievance to arbitration. * * * [T]he school district and the faculty association defined a grievance as follows: "*Grievance* shall mean any claimed violation, misinterpretation, or inequitable application of the existing laws, rules, procedures, regulations, administrative orders or work rules of the District, which relates to or involves Teachers' health or safety, physical facilities, materials or equipment furnished to teachers or supervision of Teachers; provided, however, that such term shall not include any matter involving a Teacher's rate of compensation, retirement benefits, disciplinary proceeding or any matter which is otherwise reviewable pursuant to law or any rule or regulation having the force and effect of law."

In November, 1974, Mrs. Lorraine Gargiul, an elementary school teacher, was obliged to take sick leave due to illness. In February, 1975 she notified the school district that she would be able to return to her teaching duties the following month. On February 26 she was advised that pursuant to the provisions of section 913 of the Education Law she would be required to submit to a complete medical examination by the school district physician, Dr. Paul Day, before being permitted to return to the classroom. The teacher took the position that she would participate only in an examination by a female physician. Following further correspondence of similar tenor, on March 17, 1975 the board of education passed a resolution directing her to be examined by Dr. Day before returning to her teaching responsibilities, if, after reviewing her health history, he determined that such examination was necessary. On the same day, based on the teacher's refusal to be examined by Dr. Day, she was placed on leave of absence without pay until the matter was resolved.

On April 10, 1975 the faculty association instituted grievance procedures on behalf of Mrs. Gargiul. When the issue was not resolved, the faculty association demanded arbitration in accordance with the provisions of the collective bargaining agreement. The school district promptly applied for a stay of arbitration which was granted at Special Term. The Appellate Division reversed. We now reverse the determination of that court and reinstate the disposition of Special Term.

It will be useful to place this case, and indeed all arbitration under the Taylor Law, in a broader context. Generally speaking, as the law of arbitration between private parties has developed and progressed, a difference in perspective and approach has evolved between arbitration in commercial matters and arbitration in labor relations. In the former it is the rule that the parties will not be held to have chosen arbitration as the forum for the resolution of their disputes in the absence of an express, unequivocal agreement to that effect; absent such an explicit commitment neither party may be compelled to arbitrate. In the field of labor relations, by contrast, the general rule is the converse. Because of the recognition that arbitration has been demonstrated to be a salutary method of resolving labor disputes, because of the public policy (principally expressed in the Federal cases) which favors arbitration as a means of resolving such disputes, and because of the associated available inference that the parties to a collective bargaining agreement probably intended to resolve their differences by arbitration, the courts have held that controversies arising between the parties to such an agreement fall within the scope of the arbitration clause unless the parties have employed language which clearly manifests an intent to exclude a particular subject matter.

Arbitration agreements that derive their vitality from the Taylor Law are sufficiently different that they cannot properly be categorized under either of these headings. Initially we observe that our court has never held that boards of education, unless authorized by specific legislation, are free to delegate to arbitrators the resolution of issues for which the boards have official responsibility. The enactment of the Taylor Law, establishing authority for the use of voluntary arbitration, confirmed rather than vitiated the principle of the nondelegable responsibility of elected representatives in the public sector. Hence, we approach consideration of the scope of arbitration clauses in public employment from this perspective.

When challenge is raised to the submission to arbitration of a dispute between employer and employee in the public sector the threshold consideration by the courts as to whether there is a valid agreement to arbitrate must proceed in sequence on two levels. Initially it must be determined whether arbitration claims with respect to the particular subject matter are authorized by the terms of the Taylor Law. The permissible scope of arbitration under that law is variously limited. If, of course, the subject matter of the dispute between the parties falls outside the permissible scope of the Taylor Law, there is no occasion further to consider the language or the reach of the particular arbitration clause.

If it is concluded, however, that reference to arbitration is authorized under the Taylor Law, inquiry then turns at a second level to a determination of whether such authority was in fact exercised and whether the parties did agree by the terms of their particular arbitration clause to refer their differences in this specific area to arbitration. In the field of public employment, as distinguished from labor relations in the private sector, the public policy favoring arbitration—of recent origin—does not yet carry the same historical or general acceptance, nor, as evidenced in part by some of the litigation in our court, has there so far been a similar demonstration of the efficacy of arbitration as a means for resolving controversies in governmental employment. Accordingly, it cannot be inferred as a practical matter that the parties to collective bargaining agreements in the public sector always intend to adopt the broadest permissible arbitration clauses. Indeed, inasmuch as the responsibilities of the elected representatives of the tax-paying public are overarching and fundamentally nondelegable, it must be taken, in the absence of clear, unequivocal agreement to the contrary, that the board of education did *not* intend to refer differences which might arise to the arbitration forum. Such reference is not to be based on implication.

We turn then to the appeal now before us to make the necessary judicial determinations both with respect to Taylor Law authorization and as to the scope of this arbitration clause, i.e., whether Mrs. Gargiul's present complaint falls within the contract definition of grievance. We have no difficulty at the first level in concluding that there is nothing in statute, decisional law or public policy which would preclude the board of education, acting in behalf of the district, and the association, should they agree to do so, from referring disputes of the present nature to arbitration.

At the second level, we address the particular language employed by the parties for the articulation of their agreement to arbitrate. Surely their definition of grievances does not approach the breadth of provisions which in other contexts are referred to as "broad arbitration clauses". This clause is explicitly a limited one. Indeed in form it expresses two separate agreements. First, the parties agree that certain disputes * * * shall be submitted to arbitration. In the same paragraph they then agree that other disputes shall not be referred to arbitration * * *. Thus, the question is not to determine the outer boundaries of a single definition; the problem is rather to determine into which of two different classifications the present dispute falls, or more precisely in this instance, how it shall be treated when it may reasonably be included within both groups.

As is evident from the arguments pressed by the parties, * * * the present controversy could be classified both in surface description and substantive context in either category. On the one hand, although contending principally that the issue of arbitrability is for the arbitrator and not for the courts, the faculty association has labeled the board's action a claimed violation or inequitable application of existing laws and rules relating to the teacher's health, thus in the included category. On the other hand, the school district classifies the dispute as a matter involving disciplinary proceedings, in the excluded category. The labels attached by the parties, each evidently for its own advantage, can never be determinative. A very reasonable assertion can be made that this particular controversy falls within both the included and the excluded categories.

In this circumstance, we cannot conclude that the present dispute falls clearly and unequivocally within the class of claims agreed to be referred to arbitration. Accordingly, the application of the school district for a stay of arbitration was properly granted.

* * *

Notes

1. This was the first highest state court expressly to repudiate for public sector bargaining the "presumption of arbitrability" doctrine entrenched in private sector bargaining. The principle of nondelegability is discussed in Chapter 3 (state level) and Chapter 4 (local level).

2. Some people believe that the fact an arbitrator is employed for resolving a given grievance only if accepted by both teacher and board places some pressure on him to try not to become typed as "pro-" or "anti-" teacher over a

series of decisions. Would possible pressure be eliminated if arbitrators were salaried by the public (as are judges) rather than paid ad hoc by the parties?

3. Three of the seven judges, in a concurring opinion, agreed completely with the analysis of Taylor Law arbitration, but stated the belief that a more compelling reason for denying arbitration in this case was that the dispute arose more from a disciplinary matter than from a matter related to the teacher's health. They said the teacher was suspended for "simply ignor[ing]" an apparently valid directive. She had not challenged its validity by filing a grievance.

4. It should be observed that, in practice since this decision, this court has broadly construed coverage of general arbitration clauses. New York school boards that agree to contracts containing general arbitration clauses are, practically speaking, in a situation little different from that of boards in states where courts expressly follow the pattern of the private sector (i.e., a matter not barred by law is arbitrable unless it is clearly precluded).

Chapter 11

DISCHARGE AND RETIREMENT
OF TEACHERS

Discharge

In General

Under the common law the right to employ includes the right to discharge except as restricted by contractual or constitutional considerations. Even if there is no express contractual provision indicating the grounds upon which a teacher may be discharged, the common law permits dismissals for sufficient cause. What constitutes sufficient cause is a question of fact to be determined by the court in each case.

The mere fact that a statute gives the board of education the right to employ teachers does not confer upon it the right arbitrarily to discharge them at any time. If a teacher complies with all express and implied conditions in his contract, he has the right to remain in his position until the end of the contract period or be remunerated in damages if the board refuses to retain him. A critical distinction is that between failure to renew a contract which has expired, and discharge of an employee during the period of a contract or under a tenure law. Failure to renew a contract under the common law is legally related to failure to enter into a contract initially. That topic is discussed in Chapter 9. This chapter primarily treats dismissals during the term of the contract, including both contracts for a fixed term and so-called tenure contracts. Some "Section 1983" cases are included, as are some cases arising in situations requiring boards to justify nonrenewals.

Tenure Statutes

In most states today there is legislation granting most, or all, teachers tenure protection upon their having satisfactorily served a probationary period. The constitutionality of such statutes has been uniformly sustained.[1]

Tenure statutes provide that a teacher's contract continues without any need for express renewal. Specified procedures must be followed to terminate it. Although these procedures vary widely in detail from state to state, they involve three elements: timely notice that dismissal is being contemplated, specification of charges against the teacher, and a hearing at which the charges are examined and a decision made regarding the teacher's retention. Most of the statutes include provisions for

---

1. Teachers' Tenure Act Cases, 329 Pa. 213, 197 A. 344 (1938); State ex rel. Bishop v. Board of Education, 139 Ohio St. 427, 40 N.E.2d 913 (1942).

appeal of decisions to dismiss a teacher, and a large number of them cover matters such as salary reductions and demotions.

The general rule is that only those positions enumerated in the tenure statute are encompassed by its provisions.[2] Thus locally-created positions with titles not set out in the statute are not covered. Which positions are to be covered is within the prerogative of the legislature. The judicial approach of strict construction for tenure statutes is evident in the courts' not extending tenure protection to supplementary positions such as coach. Coaches generally may be relieved of their special assignments without following tenure procedures as long as their regular full-time teaching positions are not impaired.[3] The Supreme Court of Wyoming has held that the tenure statute covering teachers does not cover the position of principal.[4] Tenure as a teacher, however, once achieved is not lost there by reassignment as a principal.

The power of the legislature to change tenure provisions has been upheld in most cases, the courts reasoning that the legislature cannot permanently bind itself to particular employment practices.[5] However, the language of the statute, the effect on the employee, the method of the change, and the desirability or necessity of change for purposes of public policy are crucial in determining whether tenure protection for an already tenured teacher may be subsequently withdrawn. In 1990 the tenure status of all principals in Chicago was eliminated by the state legislature as part of a reorganization of that school system. The state's highest court upheld the action.[6] A federal court in Maryland ruled likewise in a reorganization involving the state's takeover of a financially troubled public community college.[7]

The United States Supreme Court has held that a state may make tenure for a teacher contractual, as distinguished from a legislative status.[8] The case involved an unusually worded tenure statute in Indiana, which was repealed subsequent to a teacher's acquiring tenure under it. When she was not rehired by the local school board, the teacher sued, claiming she could not be dismissed without following the tenure procedure. The Supreme Court noted that the word "contract" appeared many times in the statute and that, although in the present case the Supreme Court of Indiana had ruled otherwise, earlier decisions in Indiana had construed the statute as creating contract rights. The

2. Lascari v. Board of Educ. of Lodi, 36 N.J.Super. 426, 116 A.2d 209 (1955); Thrash v. Board of Educ., School Dist. 189, 106 Ill.App.3d 182, 62 Ill.Dec. 68, 435 N.E.2d 866 (1982).

3. Stang v. Independent School Dist. No. 191, 256 N.W.2d 82 (Minn.1977). [Case No. 94] Smith v. Board of Educ. of Urbana School Dist. No. 116 of Champaign County, Illinois, 708 F.2d 258 (7 Cir.1983).

4. Spurlock v Board of Trustees, Carbon County School Dist. No. 1, 699 P.2d 270 (Wyo.1985).

5. Morgan v. Potter, 238 Wis. 246, 298 N.W. 763 (1941). See also Phelps v. Board of Educ., 300 U.S. 319, 57 S.Ct. 483, 81 L.Ed. 674 (1937). [Case No. 82].

6. Fumarolo v. Chicago Bd. of Educ., 142 Ill.2d 54, 153 Ill.Dec. 177, 566 N.E.2d 1283 (1990).

7. Gardiner v. Tschechtelin, 765 F.Supp. 279 (D.Md.1991).

8. State ex rel. Anderson v. Brand, 303 U.S. 95, 58 S.Ct. 443, 82 L.Ed. 685 (1938).

Court denied the state's right to repudiate the tenure protection of the teacher. The legislature, of course, could change the statute for prospective employees, but it could not do so for those who came under the original provisions.

Because tenure statutes are in derogation of the common law (for the protection of teachers), they are strictly construed by the courts. An example is found in an Arizona case in which a teacher was tendered a contract for a school year at an annual salary less than that in his prior contract. Upon being relieved of his previously assigned duties, his working year would be two weeks less, and his salary was reduced accordingly. The teacher was given an annual increment which offset all but $56 of the reduction. The reassignment was from counseling duties to teaching duties. The court ruled that the tenure law barred a teacher's salary being reduced without following the tenure procedure, except in accordance with a general salary reduction in the whole district.[9] In this instance, because the teacher was not notified of the reduction prior to March 15, he was entitled by statute to automatic renewal of his contract with the same salary as for the prior year.

In Pennsylvania the highest state court ordered that permanent professional status be granted two school nurses who were certified and had served the appropriate probationary period.[10] A section of the tenure statute provided that temporary professional employees shall be rated twice a year and not be dismissed unless rated unsatisfactory. One nurse received no ratings during the probationary period and the other only one, which was excellent. The court held that the absence of ratings indicated satisfactory performance. To hold otherwise it said would permit a superintendent to bring about unlawful termination of a temporary professional employee by wilfully not complying with the statutory rating requirement.

Many tenure statutes are not clear as to meaning at certain vital points of the process. The Supreme Court of Michigan in 1971 reversed its 1970 decision on one such point, namely, whether the board's failure to comply with a specific of the statute placed a teacher on tenure.[11] The statute required notice to the teacher during the probationary period as to whether or not his work has been satisfactory. The board's letter, which was sent well before the sixty day deadline, stated only that a tenure contract would not be offered at the end of the period of probation. The original decision was by a four-to-three vote. Two of the four judges were replaced during the ensuing year by judges who disagreed with the decision, and a third changed his vote, with the result that by a six-to-one vote it was ultimately held that failure to notify a

9. Board of Educ., Tucson High School Dist. No. 1 v. Williams, 1 Ariz.App. 389, 403 P.2d 324 (1965).

10. Elias v. Board of School Directors of the Windber Area, 421 Pa. 260, 218 A.2d 738 (1966).

11. Munro v. Elk Rapids Schools, 385 Mich. 618, 189 N.W.2d 224 (1971), rev'g 383 Mich. 661, 178 N.W.2d 450 (1970).

teacher in writing that his work is unsatisfactory entitles him to tenure status upon completion of the probationary period. The highest court of Massachusetts held that a teacher had acquired tenure because the statutory notice of nonreemployment was defective in that the board had not voted not to rehire the teacher at the time the superintendent notified the teacher that she was not to receive tenure.[12]

In the preceding three cases school authorities failed to take some appropriate steps during the probationary period, and their lack of timely action was not allowed to work to the disadvantage of the professional employee. In each case the probationary period had expired before school officials acted. In New Jersey a board acted before the end of the probationary period, but not prior to the date for cancellation of a term contract which was to run beyond the statutory period of probation. A teacher, who would have completed the probationary period a few days hence, received a letter purporting to dismiss her. Her contract contained a sixty-day cancellation clause. The letter stated that the board was terminating the contract effective immediately and giving her two months pay. In her suit to be declared a tenure teacher she reasoned that the term contract could not be terminated without the notice and that therefore she had acquired tenure. The Supreme Court of New Jersey, reversing the state commissioner, state board of education, and a lower court, held that tenure was a statutory status, arising only by passage of the time fixed by the statute, and the discharge of the employee before the passage of the required time barred tenure.[13] This would be the rule even if the discharge were in breach of an employment contract, which issue was not before the court. Using similar reasoning, the Supreme Court of Ohio held that a teacher would not automatically gain tenure by virtue of serving under a limited contract that carried beyond the statutory probationary period.[14]

It is doubtful that failure of a school board to comply with a procedural provision in a collective bargaining contract (as distinguished from a statutory provision) can have the effect of granting tenure to a teacher. Most courts have taken the view that failure of school authorities to meet terms of the agreement covering kinds and numbers of evaluations do not confer any rights with regard to tenure on a teacher.[15] However, such infractions by the board may warrant reinstatement of a terminated probationary teacher for a reasonable period of time during which the board would comply with the evaluation procedures enumerated in the contract.[16]

12. Farrington v. School Committee of Cambridge, 382 Mass. 324, 415 N.E.2d 211 (1981).

13. Canfield v. Board of Educ. of Borough of Pine Hill, 51 N.J. 400, 241 A.2d 233 (1968).

14. State ex rel. Paul v. Board of Education of Van Buren Local School Dist., 44 Ohio St.2d 5, 335 N.E.2d 703 (1975).

15. Board of Trustees of Junior College Dist. No. 508, County of Cook v. Cook County College Teachers Union, Local 1600, 62 Ill.2d 470, 343 N.E.2d 473 (1976).

16. Board of Educ., Bellmore-Merrick Central High School Dist. v. Bellmore-Merrick United Secondary Teachers, Inc., 39 N.Y.2d 167, 383 N.Y.S.2d 242, 347 N.E.2d 603 (1976).

In an unusual fact situation the Court of Appeals of New York held that a tenure appointment could be offered prior to the end of the probationary period and, once accepted, could not be rescinded.[17] The facts were that a teacher in the spring of the last year of probation was offered and accepted an appointment to tenure. Later, but still within the statutory sixty-day-notice period, the board notified the teacher that it had changed its mind and sought to rescind the appointment. The court refused to permit such action.

Unless tenure statutes so provide, the recommendation of the superintendent is not relevant to decisions thereunder made by the school board. That the superintendent allegedly withdrew his recommendation that a principal and a teacher be terminated was held to be irrelevant where all statutory provisions were observed before the discharge.[18] In another case a board attempted to rescind its action placing a teacher on tenure for the upcoming year after it learned that expected funding would not be forthcoming from the state. The superintendent and the board unsuccessfully contended that the appointment was conditional on the superintendent's recommendation, which he had not given.[19]

Where, however, the recommendation of the superintendent is statutorily required, courts have consistently held the act of the board without the recommendation to be without effect. In a case stating this point, a federal District Court held that a board could not avoid the requirement by abolishing a position rather than removing a person, here an assistant to the superintendent.[20]

There seems to be general agreement that short-term substitute service cannot be counted toward fulfillment of probationary service for the acquisition of tenure.[21] Service as a substitute in many different schools for a total of about two-thirds of each of three consecutive years was not accepted by the Supreme Court of Colorado as meeting the requirement to serve "continuously and without interruption for three full years." [22] The place of part-time teaching is less settled. Some courts will not credit it.[23] Others consider some part-time teaching assignments to meet fully probationary requirements. The Supreme Court of Alaska, for example, decided that appointment on a half-time basis fulfilled the probationary period requirement when a teacher's duties were regular and substantial enough to afford intelligent evalua-

17. Weinbrown v. Board of Educ. of Union Free School Dist. No. 15, 28 N.Y.2d 474, 322 N.Y.S.2d 714, 271 N.E.2d 549 (1971).

18. Bell v. Board of Educ. of Harlan Independent School Dist., 557 S.W.2d 433 (Ky.App.1977).

19. Sanders v. Vinson, 558 S.W.2d 838 (Tenn.1977).

20. Armstrong v. Board of Educ. of City of Birmingham, Ala., 430 F.Supp. 595 (N.D.Ala.1977).

21. Biancardi v. Waldwick Board of Educ., 139 N.J.Super. 175, 353 A.2d 123 (1976); Hudson v. Independent School Dist. No. 77, 258 N.W.2d 594 (Minn.1977).

22. Tyler v. School Dist. No. 1, City and County of Denver, 177 Colo. 188, 493 P.2d 22 (1972).

23. Johnson v. Board of Educ. of Decatur School Dist. No. 61, 85 Ill.2d 338, 53 Ill.Dec. 234, 423 N.E.2d 903 (1981); Ceparano v. Ambach, 53 N.Y.2d 873, 440 N.Y.S.2d 615, 423 N.E.2d 38 (1981) (holding commissioner's rejection of it not arbitrary, but noting that the matter could be put in a collective bargaining contract because there is no statute on it and public policy does not prohibit crediting part-time service).

tion.[24] The Supreme Court of Ohio ruled likewise in a case where the teacher had never taught less than the state-prescribed number of hours for a student's school day.[25]

A point to be noted is that mere performance in a position does not serve as a predicate for acquiring tenure in it. Where a person was designated acting principal for some 11 years but had not passed the examination required for appointment as principal, it was held that no tenure had been acquired.[26] Further, there must be an appointment by the board, an assignment to duties by an administrator not being sufficient to establish a period of probationary service.[27]

Many legislatures have enacted statutes giving protections to non-tenure teachers. The phrase "for cause" as a criterion of discharge of nontenure teachers is particularly troublesome. If it is equated to a requirement for a complete adversary procedure, the situation becomes indistinguishable from tenure; that is, "instant" tenure protection is provided—an arrangement contrary to good personnel theory and also contrary to the judicial canon that when separate provisions apply to separate sets of closely allied circumstances the enacting body is presumed to have intended a distinction. Thus, courts, in general, have construed procedural protections for nontenure teachers in states having applicable tenure statutes less broadly in favor of teachers than traditionally they have construed the tenure statutes. For example, the Supreme Court of California has interpreted a "just cause" provision for probationary teachers to mean that "arbitrary and oppressive" action is forbidden, not that the board must prove cause by a preponderance of the evidence.[28] Problems related to "just cause" provisions in collective bargaining contracts are discussed in Chapter 10 under "Arbitration".

School boards have the implied power to suspend for short periods without pay school employees as a form of sanction.[29] The power to make and enforce rules for managing schools would be "an empty power without the ability to discipline misconduct in a flexible manner," said an appellate Indiana court that also upheld the sanction of making the teacher pay $146 for damage to science textbooks from which he removed the glossary.[30]

Causes for Discharge in General

In many states statutes provide that teachers may be dismissed only upon stated grounds. It is generally held that where there is a specifica-

24. State v. Redman, 491 P.2d 157 (Alaska 1971).

25. State ex rel. Rodgers v. Hubbard Local School Dist. Bd. of Educ., 10 Ohio St.3d 136, 461 N.E.2d 1308 (1984).

26. Board of Educ. of City of New York v. Nyquist, 31 N.Y.2d 468, 341 N.Y.S.2d 441, 293 N.E.2d 819 (1973).

27. Markon v. Ambach, 58 A.D.2d 666, 395 N.Y.S.2d 529 (1977).

28. Turner v. Board of Trustees, Calexico Unified School Dist., 16 Cal.3d 818, 129 Cal.Rptr. 443, 548 P.2d 1115 (1976).

29. Rike v. Commonwealth Secretary of Educ., 508 Pa. 190, 494 A.2d 1388 (1985).

30. Board of Trustees of Hamilton Heights School Corp. v. Landry, 560 N.E.2d 102 (Ind.App.1990).

tion of grounds, other grounds are precluded by implication unless there is a phrase such as "other just cause." The legislature has the power to determine the grounds upon which teachers may be discharged. Local boards may not, by the weight of authority, append other grounds to those stated in applicable statutes. From a practical point of view, however, most courts give a broad interpretation to such words as "incompetency," "immorality," and "conduct unbecoming a teacher."

Incompetency is a valid ground for dismissal in common law [31] as well as under the statutes of most states. Abstractly, incompetency is a relative term without precise meaning. It has been given a wide variety of meanings extending far beyond those related to subject matter, teaching methods, or maintenance of discipline. There exists a legal presumption of competence on the part of a properly certificated teacher. It is further accepted that if a teacher has served for a period of time without being rated incompetent, the presumption is that the service was satisfactory. In any event, during a contract term the burden of proof of unfitness is upon those who assert that a teacher has fallen short of his obligations.

It has been pointed out that a teacher may not be disciplined for exercise of a constitutional right. Most often cited are First Amendment guarantees of freedom of expression and association. That a teacher also has been involved in constitutionally protected activities, however, does not preclude dismissal on grounds independent of those activities. Usually charges against a teacher involve more than a single act, and the court must decide whether at least one charge or a combination of charges justifies the board action, even though some of the charges might not.

Some tenure statutes provide for warnings before serious disciplinary action may be taken against teachers for remediable weaknesses. Also such provisions may be locally adopted by collective bargaining or board policy. In the absence of such provisions there is no absolute requirement that warnings and opportunity to remediate must be given. [32]

The issue as to whether a possible cause is remediable has been dealt with extensively by Illinois courts. They have determined that a teacher's conduct is irremediable "if it (1) has caused significant damage to students, the faculty, or the school and (2) could not have been corrected even if superiors had given the teacher the statutorily prescribed warning." [33] Criminal conduct has been held irremediable per se. [34]

31. City of Crawfordsville v. Hays, 42 Ind. 200 (1873).

32. Roberts v. Lincoln County School Dist. No. One, 676 P.2d 577 (Wyo.1984).

33. Board of Educ. of City of Chicago v. Harris, 218 Ill.App.3d 1017, 161 Ill.Dec. 598, 578 N.E.2d 1244 (1991).

34. McBroom v. Board of Educ., Dist. No. 205, 144 Ill.App.3d 463, 98 Ill.Dec. 864, 494 N.E.2d 1191 (1986).

The Teacher as Professional

Noncompliance with legitimate orders of superiors or with valid rules and regulations is a settled basis for disciplinary action, sometimes denoted "insubordination." Thus, termination has been judicially sustained where the teacher had difficulties in carrying out school policies because of substantial and continuing disagreements with administrators and supervisors;[35] where the teacher lacked self-direction and was uncooperative in relation to extracurricular duties; [36] where the teacher left her class unattended on frequent occasions, failed to perform corridor duty adequately, and made offensive references to sex in class;[37] where the teacher persisted in acting independently of the wishes and policies of a superior, including leaving in a funding-request to the state department of education some items he directed be removed;[38] where the teacher failed to follow rules regarding classroom methodology and also refused to stop teaching politics in a course in economics;[39] where the teacher, after a request in midyear for a leave to work full-time for the American Federation of Teachers was denied, abandoned his position with the school system and took the union position;[40] where the teacher was late to class, failed to prepare outlines, and did not properly supervise his classes;[41] where the teacher refused to stop criticizing in class the school authorities and discussing in class personal experiences with prostitutes;[42] where the teacher refused to teach in a separate school for part of the day;[43] where the teacher would not attend an enrichment program;[44] where the teacher refused to sign a supplement to her contract containing excerpts of board policies;[45] where a teacher failed to follow directives to make timely reports on lost books and to retain final examinations;[46] where a guidance counselor did not comply with guidelines regarding registration of students and contacting of parents;[47] where a journalism teacher disobeyed several directives including submitting for approval certain articles to appear in the school newspaper;[48] and where a teacher refused to accept a particular student into her class.[49]

35. Albaum v. Carey, 310 F.Supp. 594 (E.D.N.Y.1969).

36. Simcox v. Board of Educ. of Lockport Tp. High School, Dist. No. 205, 443 F.2d 40 (7 Cir.1971).

37. Robbins v. Board of Educ. of Argo Community High School Dist., 313 F.Supp. 642 (N.D.Ill.1970).

38. Long v. Board of Educ. of City of St. Louis, 456 F.2d 1058 (8 Cir.1972).

39. Ahern v. Board of Educ. of School Dist. of Grand Island, 456 F.2d 399 (8 Cir. 1972).

40. Miller v. Board of Educ. of Jefferson County, Kentucky, 452 F.2d 894 (6 Cir. 1971).

41. Simard v. Board of Educ. of Town of Groton, 473 F.2d 988 (2 Cir.1973).

42. Moore v. School Bd. of Gulf County, Florida, 364 F.Supp. 355 (N.D.Fla.1973).

43. Board of Trustees of School Dist. No. 4, Big Horn County v. Colwell, 611 P.2d 427 (Wyo.1980).

44. Howell v. Alabama State Tenure Comm'n, 402 So.2d 1041 (Ala.Civ.App. 1981).

45. Sims v. Board of Trustees, Holly Springs Municipal Separate School Dist., 414 So.2d 431 (Miss.1982).

46. Moffitt v. Batesville School Dist., 278 Ark. 77, 643 S.W.2d 557 (1982).

47. Bickford v. Board of Educ. of School Dist. No. 82 of Hall County, 214 Neb. 642, 336 N.W.2d 73 (1983).

48. Nicholson v. Board of Educ. Torrance Unified School Dist., 682 F.2d 858 (9 Cir.1982).

49. Hatton v. Wicks, 744 F.2d 501 (5 Cir.1984). [Case No. 95]

There is general judicial consensus that insubordination as a cause for discharge must be intentional. The Supreme Court of Tennessee, for example, ruled that a teacher could not be discharged for failure to return to duty when directed by the superintendent in a situation where she was medically unable to work due to stress, fear, and intimidation caused by events surrounding her having failed a star basketball player.[50] The Court of Appeals of Indiana overturned a dismissal based upon a charge of insubordination because it found ambiguous an order purportedly requiring attendance at a convocation.[51] There is some disagreement among the courts as to whether there must be more than one incident of noncompliance with a valid directive in order to support a discharge for insubordination.[52]

Failure to maintain proper student discipline is frequently offered as a cause for teacher termination. It has been held serious enough, without more, to warrant an unsatisfactory rating for a teacher,[53] or even dismissal during the school year.[54] Moreover, in maintaining classroom decorum teachers must follow school rules regarding methods of punishment. Even though state criminal law may permit teachers to resort to physical force to discipline students, such a statute "does not set the standard to which teachers may be held in the performance of their professional duties in a non-criminal context." [55] So speaking, the Court of Appeals of New York sustained the dismissal of a tenure teacher on grounds of physical abuse of students and insubordination primarily involving failure to adhere to instructions regarding corporal punishment. Corporal punishment infractions are involved in a great number of cases involving dismissal or other discipline of teachers. Excessive corporal punishment, improper corporal punishment, and failure to observe procedural rules for administering corporal punishment are three aspects of the area, in addition to the use of such punishment when it is expressly forbidden.

A statutory ground for dismissal of tenure teachers in Illinois is "cruelty." Upheld under this cause was the termination of a sixth-grade teacher for using an electric cattle prod as a disciplinary tool.[56] Unacceptable disciplinary practices that included the kicking of a student's chair so that he fell backward were the prime consideration in a

---

50. McGhee v. Miller, 753 S.W.2d 354 (Tenn.1988).

51. Werblo v. Board of School Trustees of Hamilton Heights School Corp., 519 N.E.2d 185 (Ind.App.1988), aff. on this point, 537 N.E.2d 499 (Ind.1989).

52. Compare Sims v. Board of Trustees, Holly Springs Municipal Separate School Dist., 414 So.2d 431 (Miss.1982) with Ware v. Morgan County School Dist. No. RE–3, 748 P.2d 1295 (Colo.1988).

53. Steffen v. Board of Directors of South Middletown Tp. School Dist., 32 Pa. Cmwlth. 187, 377 A.2d 1381 (1977).

54. McWhirter v. Cherokee County School Dist. No. 1, 274 S.C. 66, 261 S.E.2d 157 (1979).

55. Bott v. Board of Educ., Deposit Central School Dist., 41 N.Y.2d 265, 392 N.Y.S.2d 274, 360 N.E.2d 952 (1977). [Case No. 102]

56. Rolando v. School Directors of Dist. No. 125, LaSalle County, 44 Ill.App.3d 658,

judicially approved discharge of a Washington teacher.[57]   A Louisiana appellate court supported a teacher's dismissal during a contract period because he brandished a starter pistol to gain control of a situation in which several students had become hostile.[58]   An Alabama appellate court upheld the dismissal of a teacher-principal who fired into the floor as a scare tactic to break up a fight where a specific board policy forbade staff members to bring firearms onto school property.[59]   However, where a Louisiana teacher was seriously threatened by a student armed with a large board, his discharge for getting a gun from his car when the student pursued him was overturned.[60]

Some incidents with sexual overtones involving spanking teenage girls were sufficient to justify dismissal of a male teacher in Pennsylvania.[61]   The teacher also had discussed matters of an explicitly sexual nature with the students.   Insertion into the classroom of sexually suggestive statements,[62] materials,[63] or actions [64] is not judicially approved.   Such generally could not be justified by legitimate professional purposes.   Often, however, the manner and circumstances of the presentation are as crucial to its acceptability as its substance.[65]

The last statement also applies to the introduction of ideas or language that is offensive to many persons.   Two cases decided by the United States Court of Appeals, First Circuit, are illustrative.   In one the question was whether a teacher could, for educational purposes, assign and discuss in class an article containing a term, highly offensive to many, for an incestuous son.[66]   The article was written by a psychiatrist and appeared in "a publication of high reputation."   The teacher discussed the word's origin and context and the reasons the author included it.   Any student who felt the assignment to be personally distasteful was permitted an alternative one.   The teacher would not agree never again to use the word in the classroom.   While stating that some regulation of classroom speech is proper, the court found the present restriction to be unenforceable.   It observed that the word in question appeared in at least five books in the library, but did not rest its holding on this ground.

In the second case the teacher had discussed the meaning of "taboo" words by use of a word, highly offensive to many, for sexual intercourse.

3 Ill.Dec. 402, 358 N.E.2d 945 (1976).

57.   Sargent v. Selah School Dist. No. 119, 23 Wash.App. 916, 599 P.2d 25 (1979).

58.   Myres v. Orleans Parish School Bd., 423 So.2d 1303 (La.App.1982).

59.   Burton v. Alabama State Tenure Com'n, 601 So.2d 113 (Ala.Civ.App.1992).

60.   Landry v. Ascension Parish School Bd., 415 So.2d 473 (La.App.1982).

61.   Penn-Delco School Dist. v. Urso, 33 Pa.Cmwlth. 501, 382 A.2d 162 (1978).

62.   Simon v. Jefferson Davis Parish School Bd., 289 So.2d 511 (La.App.1974); Pryse v. Yakima School Dist. No. 7, 30 Wash.App. 16, 632 P.2d 60 (1981).

63.   Shurgin v. Ambach, 56 N.Y.2d 700, 451 N.Y.S.2d 722, 436 N.E.2d 1324 (1982).

64.   Ricci v. Davis, 627 P.2d 1111 (Colo. 1981); Potter v. Kalama Public School Dist. No. 402, 31 Wash.App. 838, 644 P.2d 1229 (1982).

65.   State ex rel. Wasilewski v. Board of School Directors of City of Milwaukee, 14 Wis.2d 243, 111 N.W.2d 198 (1961); Oakland Unified School Dist. v. Olicker, 25 Cal. App.3d 1098, 102 Cal.Rptr. 421 (1972); De-Vito v. Board of Educ., County of Marion, 169 W.Va. 53, 285 S.E.2d 411 (1981).

66.   Keefe v. Geanakos, 418 F.2d 359 (1 Cir.1969).   [Case No. 96]

This time the First Circuit reaffirmed the preceding holding, but reemphasized that teachers did not have a license to say or write in class whatever they choose.[67] It said it could see no substitute for a case-by-case inquiry into whether the legitimate interests of school authorities are sufficient to circumscribe a teacher's speech. The judges stated they were not in agreement as to whether the First Amendment protected the teacher's act, but held for the teacher on grounds of due process because officials had invoked a vague rule after the incident had occurred.

Held not to be the basis for terminating a teacher was his reading in class a story he had written which contained language objectionable to school authorities.[68] The Supreme Court of California observed that the reading was only a single incident and that it was done in good faith as a teaching technique that was not barred by any school rule. On the other hand, the Court of Appeals, Seventh Circuit, found to be sufficient cause for removal of a teacher the distribution to eighth grade students of brochures referring to pleasures of using marijuana and encouraging children to free themselves of the moral environment of their homelife and experience a new sense of love and community.[69] The Court of Appeals, Fifth Circuit, upheld the termination of a college teacher on the ground of persistent use of profane language in class.[70]

Introduction by a teacher of materials or methods that are controversial in that they are disapproved by some persons outside the school system is protected as long as the technique in contention is pedagogically supportable. Citizen and parent objections were found not acceptable as the heart of the basis for termination of a teacher for not ceasing to "discuss controversial issues" in a high school civics class,[71] or of a teacher in a different district for continuing to "discuss Blacks in American history" in a history class.[72] Nor could a school board adopt a policy of banning "all political speakers" when (after a Democrat, a Republican, and a member of the John Birch Society had already appeared in connection with a high school political science class) a Communist was invited.[73] The court found the only apparent reason for the policy was to "placate angry residents and taxpayers."

It must not be assumed, however, that teachers are not subject to reasonable restrictions on their teaching techniques. If there is in effect a directive that is not unreasonable, teachers must conform to it, even though they prefer different methods or a different philosophy accept-

67. Mailloux v. Kiley, 448 F.2d 1242 (1 Cir.1971).

68. Lindros v. Governing Bd. of Torrance Unified School Dist., 9 Cal.3d 524, 108 Cal.Rptr. 185, 510 P.2d 361 (1973), cert. den. 414 U.S. 1112, 94 S.Ct. 842, 38 L.Ed.2d 739 (1973).

69. Brubaker v. Board of Educ., School Dist. 149, Cook County, Illinois, 502 F.2d 973 (7 Cir. 1974), cert. den. 421 U.S. 965, 95 S.Ct. 1953, 44 L.Ed.2d 451 (1975).

70. Martin v. Parrish, 805 F.2d 583 (5 Cir.1986).

71. Sterzing v. Fort Bend Independent School Dist., 376 F.Supp. 657 (S.D.Tex. 1972), vac. on remedy grounds 496 F.2d 92 (5 Cir.1974).

72. Kingsville Independent School Dist. v. Cooper, 611 F.2d 1109 (5 Cir.1980). [Case No. 97]

73. Wilson v. Chancellor, 418 F.Supp. 1358 (D.Or.1976).

able in the abstract.[74] The burden of a teacher's showing that a pedagogical rule established by the administration or the school board is not enforceable is an extremely heavy one. Overseeing the education process is not a judicial prerogative. This matter is further explored in Chapter 4 under "Curriculum."

Certain classroom conduct is so clearly improper for a teacher to engage in that no rules need exist to support disciplinary action. Showing a violent and sexually suggestive movie, the content of which the teacher never discussed, could not be defended as protected by academic freedom.[75] No proper educational purpose was present. The teacher had shown the film as a "treat" for students 14 to 17 years old on a noninstructional day while she attended to clerical matters.

Upheld has been the dismissal of a tenure teacher for proselytization for a religious organization.[76] The classroom was used to encourage students to accept beliefs, attend meetings, and disregard parent wishes about involvement with the religious group. Beginning the school day with an audible extemporaneous prayer (no request to students to participate) and the reading of a Bible story (no comments except to explain the meaning of a word or phrase) was held to be cause for discharging a fourth grade teacher in Pennsylvania.[77] Dismissal of a college teacher for starting classes with a reading from the Bible was judicially supported in Indiana.[78] There was no right of either teacher to continue the practice after warning to cease. The Seventh Circuit has sustained a school board's prohibiting the teaching of a nonevolutionary theory of creation to junior high school students during the school day.[79] The Eleventh Circuit has upheld the authority of the University of Alabama to bar "extra" or "optional" meetings connected with a class in exercise physiology where the meetings were oriented toward a religious view of the creation of mankind.[80]

Misuse of the classroom to vent a teacher's personal feelings against the police, following an automobile accident in which she was involved, was found to be a proper basis for a written reprimand.[81] Sufficient for discharge without a specific prohibition was a teacher's offering higher

74. Clark v. Holmes, 474 F.2d 928 (7 Cir.1972), cert. den. 411 U.S. 972, 93 S.Ct. 2148, 36 L.Ed.2d 695 (1973); Hetrick v. Martin, 480 F.2d 705 (6 Cir.1973), cert. den. 414 U.S. 1075, 94 S.Ct. 592, 38 L.Ed.2d 482 (1973); Adams v. Campbell County School Dist., Campbell County, Wyoming, 511 F.2d 1242 (10 Cir.1975); Millikan v. Board of Directors of Everette School Dist. No. 2, 93 Wash.2d 522, 611 P.2d 414 (1980); Kirkland v. Northside Independent School Dist., 890 F.2d 794 (5 Cir.1989).

75. Fowler v. Board of Educ. of Lincoln County, Ky., 819 F.2d 657 (6 Cir.1987), cert. den. 484 U.S. 986, 108 S.Ct. 502, 98 L.Ed.2d 501 (1987).

76. La Rocca v. Board of Educ. of Rye City School Dist., 63 A.D.2d 1019, 406 N.Y.S.2d 348 (1978).

77. Fink v. Board of Educ. of Warren County School Dist., 65 Pa.Cmwlth. 320, 442 A.2d 837 (1982), app. dism. 460 U.S. 1048, 103 S.Ct. 1493, 75 L.Ed.2d 927 (1983).

78. Lynch v. Indiana State Univ. Bd. of Trustees, 177 Ind.App. 172, 378 N.E.2d 900 (1978), cert. den. 441 U.S. 946, 99 S.Ct. 2166, 60 L.Ed.2d 1048 (1979).

79. Webster v. New Lenox School Dist. No. 122, 917 F.2d 1004 (7 Cir.1990).

80. Bishop v. Aronov, 926 F.2d 1066 (11 Cir.1991), cert. den. ___ U.S. ___, 112 S.Ct. 3026, 120 L.Ed.2d 897 (1992).

81. Petrie v. Forest Hills School Dist. Bd. of Educ., 5 Ohio App.3d 115, 449 N.E.2d 786 (1982).

grades to students who purchased raffle tickets.[82] Likewise inherently unprofessional conduct was demonstrated by a teacher's improperly disclosing to her students words on a standard achievement test which they were to take[83] and by a teacher's reneging on a promise not to have his students read a certain novel.[84]

Sometimes teachers defend certain actions on the basis of religious rights. That claim by a probationary kindergarten teacher, who was a member of the Jehovah's Witnesses religion, was rejected as a basis for her refusing to teach any subject having to do with love of country, the flag, or other patriotic matters.[85] The court distinguished the issue from that of requiring the teacher to participate in flag salute ceremonies, which could not be done. (See footnotes 184 and 185, infra.)

Continued failure to file advance lesson plans covering two-week periods was upheld as cause for dismissal of a highly regarded high school English department chairman.[86] His academic freedom claims were to no avail. In another case in which termination was judicially sustained, a teacher who had failed to submit lesson plans began to comply by filing plans in a form that was illegible.[87] Withholding of a merit increase was not improper for disobedience of the University of Colorado's requirement that teacher evaluation forms be distributed to all students.[88] An education professor unsuccessfully contended that use of standardized forms undermined her teaching students that such forms were useless as a measure of performance.

It seems obvious that policies on student assessment and grading are integral to the functioning of an educational institution and also that the substance of grade determination is professional. Individual teachers assign the grades, but that power is subject to some restrictions. The courts seem agreed that a teacher can be required to conform to reasonable rules and be evaluated on this aspect of the teaching function.[89] Forcing a teacher to change a grade, however, involves First Amendment protections of speech and cannot be accomplished.[90] Nevertheless, a grade can be changed administratively without violating any constitutional rights of the teacher.[91] Also, an administrator's merely

82. Gatewood v. Little Rock Public Schools, 2 Ark.App. 102, 616 S.W.2d 784 (1981).

83. Altsheler v. Board of Educ. of Great Neck Union Free School Dist., 62 N.Y.2d 656, 476 N.Y.S.2d 281, 464 N.E.2d 979 (1984).

84. Harris v. Mechanicville Central School Dist., 45 N.Y.2d 279, 408 N.Y.S.2d 384, 380 N.E.2d 213 (1978).

85. Palmer v. Board of Educ. of City of Chicago, 603 F.2d 1271 (7 Cir.1979), cert. den. 444 U.S. 1026, 100 S.Ct. 689, 62 L.Ed.2d 659 (1980). [Case No. 98]

86. Worley v. Allen, 12 A.D.2d 411, 212 N.Y.S.2d 236 (1961).

87. Clarke v. Board of Educ. of Vestal Central School Dist., 105 A.D.2d 893, 482 N.Y.S.2d 80 (1984).

88. Wirsing v. Board of Regents of Univ. of Colorado, 739 F.Supp. 551 (D.Colo.1990), aff. 945 F.2d 412 (10 Cir.1991), cert. den. ___ U.S. ___, 112 S.Ct. 1264, 117 L.Ed.2d 492 (1992).

89. Levi v. University of Texas at San Antonio, 840 F.2d 277 (5 Cir.1988); Brown v. Wood County Bd. of Educ., 184 W.Va. 205, 400 S.E.2d 213 (1990).

90. Parate v. Isibor, 868 F.2d 821 (6 Cir.1989).

91. Hillis v. Stephen F. Austin State Univ., 665 F.2d 547 (5 Cir.1982), cert. den.

asking a teacher to reevaluate a student's grade does not raise any constitutional issue.[92] Penalizing a teacher for expressing an opinion concerning grading policy would, of course, implicate the First Amendment.[93]

An academic freedom claim was not successful in warding off the discharge of a mathematics teacher for inefficiency in teaching and insubordination. Students were not learning properly, as reflected in a large number of failures. The teacher was given specific directions (such as providing worksheets rather than having students copy problems from the blackboard), but he refused to change his basic methods. The court, however, expressed strong disapproval of a directive to the teacher that his grade distribution not deviate by more than two percent from distributions in other similar classes.[94]

A Colorado teacher unsuccessfully defended against a charge of insubordination for refusing to perform the duty of supervising a hall by asserting that such would nullify his teaching precepts and would force him to espouse beliefs he did not hold.[95] As a psychology teacher he said he was committed to teaching that students were responsible for their own behavior. The court said that the protected speech interest of a public employee was in commenting on matters of public concern and that the hall duty was tied purely to matters of the individual's employment.

As has already been indicated, evaluations of classroom performance are connected to many lawsuits. The general rule regarding the substance of an evaluation is that, if it is made on arguably professional criteria by arguably competent evaluators, it is not subject to judicial review unless there is a claim that low ratings are influenced by, or in retaliation for, exercise by the teacher of a constitutional right. Evaluations leading to termination of employment may be based on results of achievement tests of students [96] or on other measures of pupil progress.[97] Conversely, where such data existed, the failure of the hearing officer for a board of education to admit it into evidence in a case of a teacher charged with incompetency was sufficient to annul the finding thereof.[98]

The standard to be applied in assessing evidence regarding incompetency was enunciated by the Supreme Court of Nebraska as being, not that "of perfection," but that of performance required of others execut-

457 U.S. 1106, 102 S.Ct. 2906, 73 L.Ed.2d 1315 (1982).

92. Meckley v. Kanawha County Bd. of Educ., 181 W.Va. 657, 383 S.E.2d 839 (1989).

93. Lovelace v. Southeastern Massachusetts Univ., 793 F.2d 419 (1 Cir.1986).

94. In re Proposed Termination of James E. Johnson's Teaching Contract with Independent School Dist. No. 709, 451 N.W.2d 343 (Minn.App.1990).

95. Lockhart v. Board of Educ. of Arapahoe County School Dist. No. 6, 735 P.2d 913 (Colo.App.1986).

96. Scheelhaase v. Woodbury Central Community School Dist., 488 F.2d 237 (8 Cir.1973), cert. den. 417 U.S. 969, 94 S.Ct. 3173, 41 L.Ed.2d 1140 (1974).

97. Whaley v. Anoka-Hennepin Independent School Dist. No. 11, 325 N.W.2d 128 (Minn.1982).

98. McCrum v. Board of Educ. of New

ing the same or similar duties.[99]   In a later case, the same court said that the "just cause" provision of the tenure statute was intended "to grant to tenured teachers some protection from either disgruntled parents or angry school boards."[100]   In that case the court found insufficient evidence to support the discharge of a teacher who, it said, "might do herself a favor by being less rigid."   The Supreme Court of Michigan, however, reversed the state's intermediate appellate court and upheld the discharge of a teacher whose classroom was frequently unruly, despite the fact her students were at least equal in achievement level to those in other classes.[101]   The lower court had considered the basis of the discharge to be a disagreement in teaching philosophy; the court of last resort said there was "no question of academic freedom involved."

The use of videotapes in the evaluation process has been held not to invade any privacy or other rights of a teacher.[102]   That the teacher was given access to the tapes, though not in edited form, sufficed as notice of evidence to be considered when discharge proceedings were instituted. In the case there was no claim that the composite videotape inaccurately presented the teacher's performance.

An evaluation of a teacher turned into an evaluation of a principal in Illinois.   The principal, who had been closely connected with the evaluation of a tenure teacher and had found her performance to be inadequate, suddenly three days before the hearing regarding discharge denied any knowledge of some 30 observations of the teacher that he had made.   He insisted his notes did not refresh his memory.   The charges against the teacher had to be dropped.   The principal was then given a hearing and suspended for 24 school days.   The court upheld the action.[103]

The Teacher as Exemplar

"[A] teacher serves as a role model for his students, exerting a subtle but important influence over their perceptions and values."[104] The courts over the years have been in agreement with this 1979 statement of the Supreme Court, and have expected a teacher's character and conduct to be above those of the average person not working in so sensitive a relationship as that of teacher and student.   Nevertheless, there has been a discernible trend toward according teachers more freedom in their personal lives than was true in the more distant past. Obviously the line is difficult to draw between the rights of teachers as

York City School Dist., 58 A.D.2d 864, 396 N.Y.S.2d 691 (1977).

99. Sanders v. Board of Educ. of South Sioux City Community School Dist. No. 11, 200 Neb. 282, 263 N.W.2d 461 (1978).

100. Schulz v. Board of Educ. of School Dist. of Fremont, 210 Neb. 513, 315 N.W.2d 633 (1982).

101. Beebee v. Haslett Public Schools, 406 Mich. 224, 278 N.W.2d 37 (1979).

102. Roberts v. Houston Independent School Dist., 788 S.W.2d 107 (Tex.App. 1990). [Case No. 99]

103. Stutzman v. Board of Educ. of City of Chicago, 171 Ill.App.3d 670, 121 Ill.Dec. 596, 525 N.E.2d 903 (1988).

104. Ambach v. Norwick, 441 U.S. 68, 99 S.Ct. 1589, 60 L.Ed.2d 49 (1979).

citizens, and the obligations imposed by the necessity for effective instructors of youth to be more than subject-matter and teaching-method specialists.

If a teacher is to be disciplined for an act, that act must somehow reduce the teacher's occupational effectiveness. Stated another way, there must be a connection ("nexus") between the act and the role of effective teacher, the latter being impaired or destroyed as a consequence of the former. The deleterious result may be direct or derivative, inherent in the act or requiring proof under the circumstances. The standard of proof of adverse effect varies widely depending on the act and the circumstances.

Some factors relevant to determining whether a teacher's act indicates unfitness to teach were set out in a leading case by the Supreme Court of California.[105] The court listed "the likelihood that the conduct may have adversely affected students or fellow teachers, the degree of such adversity anticipated, the proximity or remoteness in time of the conduct, the type of teaching certificate held by the party involved, the extenuating or aggravating circumstances, if any, surrounding the conduct, the praiseworthiness or blameworthiness of the motives resulting in the conduct, the likelihood of the recurrence of the questioned conduct, and the extent to which disciplinary action may inflict an adverse impact or chilling effect upon the constitutional rights of the teacher involved or other teachers." A dozen years later the Supreme Court of Washington found the list, with the addition of "the age and maturity of the students," to be an appropriate checklist to be used by a trial court in determining whether a teacher could be dismissed for having purchased a stolen motorcycle.[106]

It should be emphasized that these factors were set out in contexts of conduct outside of the professional sphere and were designed especially to ensure that such conduct was sufficiently related to the teaching function and duties as to constitute cause for dismissal. Classroom deficiencies and acts on school premises generally are connected sufficiently to the duties of a teacher as to meet the "nexus" criterion as a matter of law (that is, without need for proof of connection). The factors remain important to the determination of the reasonableness of the sanction placed on the teacher.[107]

Even if there are circumstances that may reduce the personally controllable reasons for inappropriate conduct, the role model criterion is not diminished. Thus, dismissals have been upheld for drug dependency derived from an effort to combat obesity [108] and for shoplifting possibly a

105. Morrison v. State Bd. of Educ., 1 Cal.3d 214, 82 Cal.Rptr. 175, 461 P.2d 375 (1969). See Chapter 9, "Revocation of Certificates."

106. Hoagland v. Mount Vernon School Dist. No. 320, Skagit County, 95 Wash.2d 424, 623 P.2d 1156 (1981).

107. Mott v. Endicott School Dist., No. 308, 105 Wash.2d 199, 713 P.2d 98 (1986).

108. Martin v. Guillot, 875 F.2d 839 (11

result of temporary mental instability.[109]

Increasing through the years have been judicial rulings on whether specific conduct constitutes "immorality" for purposes of dismissal under pertinent statutes. The term, as with incompetency, is basically one of art, its meaning shaped by contemporary concepts of improper personal conduct of a teacher. Thus, immorality as a cause for termination is not unconstitutionally vague.[110]

One of the most quoted definitions of the term was set out in 1939 by the Supreme Court of Pennsylvania: "a course of conduct as offends the morals of the community and is a bad example to the youth whose ideals a teacher is supposed to foster and to elevate." [111] Subsequent Pennsylvania decisions have noted that this definition excludes conduct simply incurring disapproval of the board;[112] but it does not require (as the chief state school officer had stated in a quasi-judicial proceeding) that the conduct be a "grievous assault" on community mores.[113]

Being an unwed mother does not per se constitute immorality. The Fifth Circuit invalidated a rule proscribing the employment or retention of unwed mothers.[114] The fatal flaw was the irrebuttable presumption that a disqualifying degree of immorality was involved in the cases of all unwed mothers. The Supreme Court of New Mexico overturned the dismissal of an unwed pregnant teacher where there was no showing of adverse effect on students and where five other unwed mothers were retained.[115] An Alabama school board that dismissed a teacher who had conceived out of wedlock attempted to rely on the additional charge of violation by the teacher of a rule requiring notification to the superintendent of pregnancy no later than the fourth month thereof. The teacher had told the principal some six weeks before the expected delivery date. The Court of Appeals, Eleventh Circuit, held that the discharge was constitutionally flawed.[116] The Constitution protects out of wedlock pregnancy, and, therefore, the burden was on the board to show that the teacher would have been discharged irrespective of the circumstances of her pregnancy. There was no evidence that a married teacher who had violated the rule would have been dismissed.

The Court of Appeal of California upheld the dismissal of a teacher who had executed an affidavit recounting her long and beneficial use of

Cir.1989).

109. Board of Directors of Lawton–Bronson Community School Dist. v. Davies, 489 N.W.2d 19 (Iowa 1992).

110. Sullivan v. Meade Independent School Dist. No. 101, 530 F.2d 799 (8 Cir. 1976); Weissman v. Board of Educ. of Jefferson County School Dist. No. R–1, 190 Colo. 414, 547 P.2d 1267 (1976); Ross v. Robb, 662 S.W.2d 257 (Mo.1983).

111. Horosko v. Mount Pleasant Tp. School Dist., 335 Pa. 369, 6 A.2d 866 (1939), cert. den. 308 U.S. 553, 60 S.Ct. 101, 84 L.Ed. 465 (1939).

112. Baker v. School Dist. of City of Allentown, 29 Pa.Cmwlth. 453, 371 A.2d 1028 (1977).

113. Penn-Delco School Dist. v. Urso, 33 Pa.Cmwlth. 501, 382 A.2d 162 (1978).

114. Andrews v. Drew Municipal Separate School Dist., 507 F.2d 611 (5 Cir.1975).

115. New Mexico State Bd. of Educ. v. Stoudt, 91 N.M. 183, 571 P.2d 1186 (1977).

116. Avery v. Homewood City Bd. of Educ., 674 F.2d 337 (5 Cir.1982), cert. den. 461 U.S. 943, 103 S.Ct. 2119, 77 L.Ed.2d 1300 (1983).

marijuana.[117] She took the action to support another person's motion for an arrest of judgment. The other party had been convicted of possession of marijuana and related offenses. The affidavit attracted national publicity, though it was not her intention that this occur. Although no evidence of actual effect of the incident on the teacher's students was presented (she was promptly suspended), there was what the court considered competent evidence on the likely deleterious effect, both in terms of student use of marijuana and in terms of breaking a law one disagrees with. The court said the affidavit per se was not the basis of the charge, but it was evidence as to competence to teach because of what it revealed. The court stated that a person can advocate changing a law without violating it, and such advocacy would be protected. In fact, another teacher had filed an affidavit in the same criminal case and no action was taken by the board.

In a subsequent case the court discussed penalizing by dismissal or certificate revocation teachers who had been convicted of possession of marijuana.[118] The court stated that the mere fact of arrest and conviction for this offense would not support punitive action in absence of some evidence relative to fitness to teach or effects on the school system. Acceptable evidence, however, could be testimony to indicate "a potential for adverse school relationships in the future" or "such notoriety as to impair" present relationships. The widespread publicity about proved involvement with raising marijuana was a key element in the decision of a Florida court to uphold a certificate revocation.[119]

In Arizona a male teacher and a female companion visited a bar. During the evening two men had annoyed the female. In the parking lot the teacher had an altercation with the men during which weapons were drawn. The teacher entered a plea of guilty to disturbing the peace, being under the influence of intoxicants, attempting to fight, and displaying a gun. The teacher, who was on tenure, was given a hearing by the board and then dismissed. The discharge was upheld.[120]

An Illinois teacher had been on the public streets many times in an intoxicated condition. She had been arrested several times. This conduct received publicity and was a subject of talk in the community among parents, pupils, and teachers. The court sustained her dismissal, noting that it was not simply for consuming intoxicants, but for the results of the excessiveness thereof.[121] Twenty-seven years later this case was cited as a precedent for upholding the dismissal of a teacher who pleaded guilty to stealing a check from a student's unlocked locker,

117. Governing Bd. of Nicasio School Dist. of Marin County v. Brennan, 18 Cal. App.3d 396, 95 Cal.Rptr. 712 (1971).

118. Comings v. State Bd. of Educ., 23 Cal.App.3d 94, 100 Cal.Rptr. 73 (1972).

119. Adams v. State Professional Practices Council, 406 So.2d 1170 (Fla.App. 1981).

120. Williams v. School Dist. No. 40 of Gila County, 4 Ariz.App. 5, 417 P.2d 376 (1966).

121. Scott v. Board of Educ. of Alton

a widely publicized incident.[122]

The fact that a teacher becomes the focus of a community controversy has been held not ground for dismissal. A trial judge, not making any findings on specific charges against the teacher herself or her teaching abilities, found as the cause of dismissal that she had become a "center of controversy," which cause he considered sufficient for removal. This decision was reversed by the Supreme Court of Arizona, which held that the teacher could not have her contract terminated simply because she became the center of a controversy not of her own seeking.[123] There had been several incidents involving pupils, the handling of which divided the community, some for and some against the teacher. Her own conduct, however, was not such as to warrant discharge.

Similar reasoning has been applied in a case where letters written by a teacher to a former pupil fell into the hands of his mother.[124] She turned them over to the police, and subsequently local newspapers wrote stories about the letters, which, in the words of the court, contained "language which many adults would find gross, vulgar and offensive and which some 18-year-old males would find unsurprising and fairly routine." The board's attempt to dismiss the teacher failed. The court examined the teacher's excellent record, and also noted that the writing of the letters did not adversely affect the welfare of the school community until the public disclosures, which were not the result of any misconduct on the teacher's part.

The First Circuit Court of Appeals upheld the dismissal of a teacher who had engaged in deviant conduct with a mannequin, which conduct had become widely known in the town.[125] The act took place on the teacher's property, but in full view of the public. The court rejected contentions of right of privacy, lack of effect on classroom performance, and vagueness of the criterion "conduct unbecoming a teacher."

Even though records indicated that his in-class teaching performance had been satisfactory over nine years of employment, the highest court of Kentucky upheld the discharge of a teacher for an incident of smoking marijuana in his apartment with others, including two 15-year-old students, during the summer months when school was not in session.[126] The court found the conduct to be of an immoral and criminal nature and to be directly related to the teacher's work because students were involved.

The courts, however, will not sustain dismissals of teachers merely for actions disapproved by certain segments of the community. For example, the Eighth Circuit Court of Appeals ruled in favor of a teacher

Community Unit School Dist. No. 11, 20 Ill.App.2d 292, 156 N.E.2d 1 (1959).

122. McBroom v. Board of Educ., Dist. No. 205, 144 Ill.App.3d 463, 98 Ill.Dec. 864, 494 N.E.2d 1191 (1986).

123. Kersey v. Maine Consolidated School Dist. No. 10, 96 Ariz. 266, 394 P.2d 201 (1964).

124. Jarvella v. Willoughby-Eastlake City School Dist. Board of Educ., 12 Ohio Misc. 288, 233 N.E.2d 143 (Com.Pl.1967).

125. Wishart v. McDonald, 500 F.2d 1110 (1 Cir.1974).

126. Board of Educ. of Hopkins County v. Wood, 717 S.W.2d 837 (Ky.1986).

who was charged with unbecoming conduct for having on several occasions allowed men not related to her to stay overnight in her apartment.[127] The setting was a small town where hotel accommodations were sparse, and the guests were friends of her son, who lived in a neighboring town. The same court, however, sustained a school board's termination of an unmarried woman teacher in a small community who insisted on living out-of-wedlock with an unmarried man in a dwelling within the community.[128]

The Supreme Court of California has held that evidence of unfitness to teach must be examined even in cases in which there has been a conviction for a public sexual offense under the criminal code. Convictions cannot be accepted as conclusive proof of unfitness.[129] The court here found that the risk of students' imitating his conduct was insubstantial where a teacher's act of homosexual solicitation was unknown to his students and testimony was to the effect that he would not repeat such conduct. A similar ruling was made in a case in which a community college teaching credential was found improperly to have been summarily withheld from a male convicted seven years before of lewd conduct in a public place, the conduct having been observed by a police officer peering through a grating two feet from the floor.[130]

The Supreme Court of Montana decided that a tenure teacher could not be dismissed for the traffic violations of driving while under the influence of intoxicating liquor and driving without a driver's license in the absence of a showing that the person's performance as a teacher was adversely affected.[131] The Supreme Court of Ohio reinstated a teacher who had been dismissed after an incident in which he left the scene of a minor accident with a parked car and falsely denied that his car was involved.[132] There was also a charge that his classroom work was inefficient, but the court found the evidence regarding that matter to be inadequate and to have been generated after the incident.

Courts in Pennsylvania and West Virginia reached different conclusions as to whether an incident of shoplifting rendered a teacher unfit.[133] Several such incidents known to the community were ruled to be sufficient cause for termination of a guidance counselor in New York[134] and an elementary school teacher in Iowa.[135]

127. Fisher v. Snyder, 476 F.2d 375 (8 Cir.1973).

128. Sullivan v. Meade Independent School Dist. No. 101, 530 F.2d 799 (8 Cir. 1976).

129. Board of Educ. of Long Beach Unified School Dist. of Los Angeles County v. Jack M., 19 Cal.3d 691, 139 Cal.Rptr. 700, 566 P.2d 602 (1977).

130. Newland v. Board of Governors of California Community Colleges, 19 Cal.3d 705, 139 Cal.Rptr. 620, 566 P.2d 254 (1977).

131. Lindgren v. Board of Trustees, High School Dist. No. 1, 171 Mont. 360, 558 P.2d 468 (1976).

132. Hale v. Board of Educ., 13 Ohio St.2d 92, 234 N.E.2d 583 (1968).

133. Lesley v. Oxford Area School Dist., 54 Pa.Cmwlth. 120, 420 A.2d 764 (1980); Golden v. Board of Educ., County of Harrison, 169 W.Va. 63, 285 S.E.2d 665 (1981).

134. Caravello v. Board of Educ., Norwich City School Dist., 48 A.D.2d 967, 369 N.Y.S.2d 829 (1975).

135. Board of Directors of Lawton–Bronson Community School Dist. v. Davies, 489 N.W.2d 19 (Iowa 1992). See footnote 109, supra.

Nexus to performance of professional work of an assistant superintendent who was involved in an "amorous relationship" with a married woman was held to be satisfactorily shown by his unexplained absences from his office and from sessions at conventions.[136] The court said that neglect of duty as a cause for dismissal need not be spelled out by express declaration.

The Supreme Court of Washington has upheld the dismissal of a homosexual teacher.[137] The court noted that in a conference with a student, which had been arranged by a homosexual friend of the teacher, he had revealed that he was homosexual and had been "deeply involved" for about a month with the other male (whose advertisement in a newspaper he had answered); that the matter became known and was objected to by some persons; that some administrators testified that his presence on the faculty would create problems; that the psychiatrist who was the teacher's expert witness said on cross-examination that the teacher's homosexuality was an acquired, not inborn, orientation; and that the teacher at the trial had not taken the opportunity possibly "to explain that he was not an overt homosexual and did not engage in the conduct the [trial] court ascribed to him which the court found immoral and illegal." (See footnote 1 in Chapter 10).

Although there are some older cases to the contrary, the weight of authority, particularly more recent authority, is that merely being arrested and charged with a criminal act is not a basis for dismissal of a teacher.[138] It may, however, be a basis for suspension of a teacher if the act is one that would justify dismissal upon conviction. For examples, the Appeals Court of Massachusetts has upheld suspensions upon indictment for possession with intent to distribute cocaine [139] and for welfare fraud.[140]

It already has been observed that conviction in a criminal court is not necessarily a basis for discharge, the offense and the nexus to the teaching function being crucial factors. Conversely, a school board is not bound to retain a teacher who has been found not guilty of charges related to those that the board considers to support discharge. The board may conduct its own hearing independent of the criminal proceeding and base a discharge thereon.[141]

---

136. Sedule v. Capital School Dist., 425 F.Supp. 552 (D.Del.1976), aff. 565 F.2d 153 (3 Cir.1977), cert. den. 434 U.S. 1039, 98 S.Ct. 780, 54 L.Ed.2d 789 (1978).

137. Gaylord v. Tacoma School Dist. No. 10, 88 Wash.2d 286, 559 P.2d 1340 (1977), cert. den. 434 U.S. 879, 98 S.Ct. 234, 54 L.Ed.2d 160 (1977).

138. Johnson v. Board of Educ. for Phoenix High School Dist., 101 Ariz. 268, 419 P.2d 52 (1966).

139. Dupree v. School Committee of Boston, 15 Mass.App. 535, 446 N.E.2d 1099 (1983).

140. Perryman v. School Committee of Boston, 17 Mass.App. 346, 458 N.E.2d 748 (1983).

141. Yang v. Special Charter School Dist. No. 150, Peoria County, 11 Ill.App.3d 239, 296 N.E.2d 74 (1973); Board of Educ. of El Monte School Dist. of Los Angeles County v. Calderon, 35 Cal.App.3d 490, 110 Cal.Rptr. 916 (1973), cert. den. 414 U.S. 807, 95 S.Ct. 19, 42 L.Ed.2d 33 (1974); Lakeside School v. Harrington, 8 Ark.App. 205, 649 S.W.2d 847 (1983).

The teacher-as-example theme also appears in connection with in-school situations. Courts have upheld dismissals of teachers not only for sexual or vulgar remarks to students, as previously noted, but for racial slurs uttered to, or about, students.[142] However, isolated remarks that are considered to be disrespectful of students may not be sufficient to justify termination of a teacher. Calling a student a "slob" for not paying attention and being slumped in her seat was held by the Supreme Court of Montana not to be cause for dismissal.[143]

At the heart of a dismissal case decided by the Court of Appeal of Louisiana was a vulgar remark made by a teacher to the school principal.[144] Although there were other factors in the case, the decision was on the question whether the school board had acted in an arbitrary manner in dismissing the teacher based on this incident. He was the high school band director and had become involved in an argument with the principal over his having permitted students to take band uniforms home in violation of previous instructions she had given him. The vulgar statement had been made in a loud and angry voice and was overheard by others, including several pupils. The dismissal was upheld, the court observing that a teacher is obliged to display proper respect for the principal.

The Second Circuit Court of Appeals upheld a dress code for teachers against various claims of First Amendment rights, academic freedom, and need to establish rapport with students.[145] The code generally prescribed dress "to reflect the professional position of the employee" and specified "in most circumstances" a tie for men. It was administered with exceptions, as for the plaintiff teacher in his filmmaking class, but he sought an injunction against being required to wear a tie while teaching English. The court in an eight-to-two en banc decision found the rule not to be unreasonable and the claim of gaining rapport with students to be simply "an assertion that one teaching technique is to be preferred over another" and unrelated to the First Amendment.

Extension to teachers of a student dress code's prohibition against wearing beards has been upheld by the Fifth Circuit,[146] as has been by the First Circuit a school board's barring female teachers from wearing short skirts even though such were worn at the time by some "young, respectable professional women." [147] The latter court said it was not foreclosing judicial intervention in extreme circumstances, but that "in employee-employer relationships the constitutional area is, and should be, small."

142. Resetar v. State Bd. of Educ., 284 Md. 537, 399 A.2d 225 (1979), cert. den. 444 U.S. 838, 100 S.Ct. 74, 62 L.Ed.2d 49 (1979); Clarke v. Board of Educ. of School Dist. of Omaha, 215 Neb. 250, 338 N.W.2d 272 (1983).

143. Trustees of Lincoln County School Dist. No. 13, Eureka v. Holden, 231 Mont. 491, 754 P.2d 506 (1988).

144. Moffett v. Calcasieu Parish School Bd., 179 So.2d 537 (La.App.1965).

145. East Hartford Educ. Ass'n v. Board of Educ. of Town of East Hartford, 562 F.2d 838 (2 Cir.1977).

146. Domico v. Rapides Parish School Bd., 675 F.2d 100 (5 Cir.1982).

147. Tardif v. Quinn, 545 F.2d 761 (1 Cir.1976).

Religious garb of teachers is discussed in Chapter 2 under "Other Religious Influences."

The Teacher as Citizen

The Supreme Court of the United States in 1968 rendered its first opinion in a case involving teacher conduct not connected with alleged subversive activities.[148] The basis for dismissal of a teacher was a letter the teacher had written to a newspaper attacking the school board's handling of a bond issue and its subsequent allocation of financial resources between the school's educational and athletic programs. A further statement was that the superintendent attempted to prevent teachers in the district from opposing or criticizing the proposed bond issue. Although it did not "deem it either appropriate or feasible to attempt to lay down a general standard against which all such statements may be judged," the Court discussed the conflicting claims of First Amendment protection and the need for orderly school administration.

The board contended that the letter was detrimental to the best interests of the schools. It also objected to certain statements which were not accurate. The Court noted that the criticisms were in no way directed to any person with whom the teacher would normally be in contact in the course of his daily work as a teacher. Observing that the interests of the board members were not synonymous with the interests of the schools, the Court found no evidence that any actual harm to the schools or interference with their operation had resulted. The inaccuracies contained in the statements were not considered serious, nor knowingly or recklessly made. The court noted that the public interest in having free and unhindered debate on matters of public importance was crucial, and that "teachers are, as a class, the members of a community most likely to have informed and definite opinions as to how funds allotted to the operation of the schools should be spent." Thus it was essential that they be able to speak freely on such a question. The "balance between the interests of the teacher, as a citizen, in commenting upon matters of public concern and the interest of the State, as an employer, in promoting the efficiency of the public services it performs through its employees" was here definitely in favor of the teacher's right.

In 1979 the Supreme Court for the first time expressly held that the First Amendment's protection of a public employee's speech includes private, as well as public, communication.[149] The occasion was a case in which a teacher had been terminated for, among other reasons, allegedly making "petty and unreasonable demands" of the principal in a manner variously described by the principal as "insulting," "hostile," "loud," and "arrogant." The subject of the black teacher's comments was racial

148. Pickering v. Board of Educ. of Tp. High School Dist. 205, 391 U.S. 563, 88 S.Ct. 1731, 20 L.Ed.2d 811 (1968). [Case No. 100]

149. Givhan v. Western Line Consol. School Dist., 439 U.S. 410, 99 S.Ct. 693, 58 L.Ed.2d 619 (1979).

discrimination in employment policies and practices in the school system, which was under a court-ordered desegregation plan. There were some gaps in the record, and the Supreme Court did not order the teacher reinstated. It held that the Court of Appeals had erred in finding the removal justified by the teacher's communicative acts, but it suggested that under Mt. Healthy City School Dist. (Case No. 79) there may have been sufficient cause on other grounds. This determination would require further proceedings. The Court stated that under the preceding case of Pickering a court must consider working relationships of personnel as well as content of communication in determining whether private communication by a public employee has gone beyond the protection of the Constitution as regards position retention.

In 1983 in a case of an assistant district attorney dismissed for vigorously opposing a transfer by the district attorney, the Court emphasized the point that for the First Amendment speech clause to be operative, a public employee's speech must be on a matter of public concern, not a matter of private interest.[150] This determination is made by examining the content, form, and context of a given statement.

Examples of subjects that have met the criterion of public concern are corporal punishment by a coach,[151] school district's medication policy,[152] school's delay in implementing federally mandated programs for handicapped students,[153] tenure for a school principal,[154] and grade fraud.[155] It must be emphasized here, however, that speech's being of public interest is only the threshold and does not bar discipline of the speaker after the "Pickering balance" is applied. But if that balance tips in favor of the employee (and the speech was a substantial or motivating factor in a detrimental employment decision), the board can prevail only by showing that it would have made the decision in the absence of the protected speech. (See last three paragraphs of Chapter 9.)

Examples of subjects of speech found not to qualify as being of public concern for First Amendment purposes are sharing a position with another teacher,[156] receiving an unfavorable evaluation rating,[157] delay in administration's handling of problems of disciplining a teacher,[158] permitting students to choose subjects and teachers,[159] and general-

---

150. Connick v. Myers, 461 U.S. 138, 103 S.Ct. 1684, 75 L.Ed.2d 708 (1983).

151. Bowman v. Pulaski County Special School Dist., 723 F.2d 640 (8 Cir.1983).

152. Johnsen v. Independent School Dist. No. 3 of Tulsa County, 891 F.2d 1485 (10 Cir.1989).

153. Southside Public Schools v. Hill, 827 F.2d 270 (8 Cir.1987).

154. Piver v. Pender County Bd. of Educ., 835 F.2d 1076 (4 Cir.1987), cert. den. 487 U.S. 1206, 108 S.Ct. 2847, 101 L.Ed.2d 885 (1988).

155. Powell v. Gallentine, 992 F.2d 1088 (10 Cir.1993).

156. Renfroe v. Kirkpatrick, 722 F.2d 714 (11 Cir.1984), cert. den. 469 U.S. 823, 105 S.Ct. 98, 83 L.Ed.2d 44 (1984).

157. Day v. South Park Independent School Dist. 768 F.2d 696 (5 Cir.1985), cert. den. 474 U.S. 1101, 106 S.Ct. 883, 88 L.Ed.2d 918 (1986).

158. Alinovi v. Worcester School Committee, 777 F.2d 776 (1 Cir.1985), cert. den. 479 U.S. 816, 107 S.Ct. 72, 93 L.Ed.2d 29 (1986).

159. Ferrara v. Mills, 781 F.2d 1508 (11 Cir.1986).

ized faculty morale concerns.[160]

Time, place, and nature of a teacher's criticism of school authorities are material as to whether the teacher is immune from discipline for his acts. Protected was a teacher who in reporting to his association was alleged to have made intentional misrepresentations of the administration's position in regard to financing salary increases for teachers. The court found there was no deliberate attempt to undermine the administration or to disrupt the district's operations.[161] In contrast, it was held that a teacher could be terminated who consistently denounced school officials personally to teachers and other school employees in abusive language.[162] Also unsuccessful in contesting her dismissal was the president of a local teachers association who, on the occasion of an orientation meeting for new teachers conducted by the school administration, delivered a scathing attack on school board members and the superintendent.[163] She poked fun at the names of some officials, analogized their acts to those of evil persons, called the school system a "snakepit," and advised the new teachers to say "yes, sir" to everyone and "hide" during their probationary periods.

When teachers become involved in situations with political connotations, problems frequently arise. Teachers have the right to engage in normal political activities that are conducted off school premises and do not interfere with the teacher's work.[164] Successfully challenged was a board rule that any teacher who actively participated in certain elections would not be eligible for appointment. A teacher who had engaged in the canvass and election of a subdistrict trustee brought suit to compel her appointment. Under applicable law teachers were appointed by the county board of education upon the recommendation of subdistrict trustees, and the teacher was so recommended. It was held that the board had no legal power to adopt such a rule, and the action to compel the appointment was successful.[165] The court said that the teacher had done nothing except that which any good citizen had a right to do in support of a candidate.

By contrast, it was held that a teacher was guilty of unprofessional conduct and legally discharged for using the following language before his class during a political campaign: "Many of you know Mr. Golway [a candidate for election as county superintendent of schools], what a fine man he is, and that his hopes are to be elected soon. I think he would be more helpful to our department than a lady, and we need more men in our schools. Sometimes your parents do not know one candidate from

160. Sanguigni v. Pittsburgh Bd. of Public Educ., 968 F.2d 393 (3 Cir.1992).

161. Gieringer v. Center School Dist. No. 58, 477 F.2d 1164 (8 Cir.1973), cert. den. 414 U.S. 832, 94 S.Ct. 165, 38 L.Ed.2d 66 (1973).

162. Amburgey v. Cassady, 507 F.2d 728 (6 Cir.1974).

163. Pietrunti v. Board of Educ. of Brick Tp., 128 N.J.Super. 149, 319 A.2d 262

(1974), cert. den. 419 U.S. 1057, 95 S.Ct. 640, 42 L.Ed.2d 654 (1974).

164. The Supreme Court, however, in 1973 upheld the right of a state to restrict certain partisan political activities of its employees. Broadrick v. Oklahoma, 413 U.S. 601, 93 S.Ct. 2908, 37 L.Ed.2d 830 (1973).

165. Board of Educ. for Logan County v. Akers, 243 Ky. 177, 47 S.W.2d 1046 (1932).

another; so they might be glad to be informed. Of course, if any of you have relatives or friends trying for the same office, be sure and vote for them."[166]

A board cannot, however, enforce a rule prohibiting all types of political activities on school premises. A board attempted to invoke the rule to halt the circulation by a teachers' organization of a petition addressed to state and local authorities protesting a threatened cutback in expenditures for education. The Supreme Court of California stated that such activity could be prevented only upon a showing of a "clear and substantial threat to order and efficiency" in the schools.[167]

The United States Supreme Court summarily affirmed a judgment that had invalidated on First Amendment grounds school board policies that prohibited teachers from discussing during school hours (including nonclass hours) matters relating to any teacher organization and that prevented use of school media facilities (otherwise open for personal use) for mention of such organizations.[168] Also affirmed was the judgment upholding the board's power to prohibit visitation to the premises and use of school media by outside employee organization representatives during school hours. The Fifth Circuit had distinguished employees from visitors, holding that the former could be restricted in private communication only if there was material disruption; the latter had no rights to be in the schools during the school day.

Attempts to punish individual personnel for their political activities clearly are not permissible. Thus Kentucky courts have invalidated demotions [169] and transfers,[170] and federal District Courts in West Virginia and Texas have invalidated nonrenewals on such grounds.[171] A federal District Court in Illinois held that a wife's constitutional rights of marital association would be infringed if her contract had not been renewed because of her husband's activities in connection with a state education association.[172] The case was ordered to trial on the woman's allegations.

Whether teachers can hold political office while continuing to teach depends on the facts. That one may not hold incompatible public positions is well established. Offices are incompatible when their duties may come into conflict or where one post is subordinate to the other. In addition, many states have statutes specifically classifying certain offices as being incompatible. For example, a charter provision prohibiting a member of the city council from holding another public office or employ-

166. Goldsmith v. Board of Educ. of Sacramento City High School Dist., 66 Cal. App. 157, 225 P. 783 (1924).

167. Los Angeles Teachers Union v. Los Angeles Bd. of Educ., 71 Cal.2d 551, 78 Cal.Rptr. 723, 455 P.2d 827 (1969).

168. Texas State Teachers Ass'n v. Garland Independent School Dist., 777 F.2d 1046 (5 Cir.1985), aff. 479 U.S. 801, 107 S.Ct. 41, 93 L.Ed.2d 4 (1986).

169. Harlan County Bd. of Educ. v. Stagnolia, 555 S.W.2d 828 (Ky.App.1977).

170. Calhoun v. Cassady, 534 S.W.2d 806 (Ky.1976).

171. Miller v. Board of Educ. of County of Lincoln, 450 F.Supp. 106 (S.D.W.Va. 1978); Guerra v. Roma Independent School Dist., 444 F.Supp. 812 (S.D.Tex.1977).

172. Newborn v. Morrison, 440 F.Supp. 623 (S.D.Ill.1977).

ment was unsuccessfully challenged by a teacher in Ohio.[173] The teacher had been elected to the council, but was denied a seat thereon under the charter provision.

In the absence of specific legislation, questions of incompatibility of offices are often closely drawn. In Oregon it was held that a teacher cannot serve in the legislature because such would be a violation of the principle of separation of powers as embodied in the state constitution (which was later amended specifically to permit the practice).[174] A constitutional provision in Oklahoma barring legislators from having an interest in any public contract was construed to mean that a teacher's contract would be invalid if it depended on state aid for its validity.[175] An Alaska constitutional provision that no legislator may hold another position of profit under the state was interpreted to bar employment in those schools that were directly administered by the state.[176] The court expressly did not answer the question as to the effect of the provision on employees of local school districts.

The courts are in agreement as to the incompatibility of position between employee and member of the school board in the same district.[177] "Intolerable potential conflicts of interest" could be the result, said a New Jersey appellate court.[178] Under common law a teacher can serve as board member in a district where he does not teach.[179] The legislature, however, can disqualify all public school employees from serving on any local school board in the state.[180]

The generally followed common-law rule is that formal acceptance or assumption of duties of an incompatible position automatically vacates the first position.[181] When a choice is feasible a court may allow the person to make the choice of position, as did the Supreme Court of North Dakota in a teacher-board member situation.[182]

The right of a teacher to wear a black armband in class as an expression of protest against the Vietnam War has been upheld by the Court of Appeals, Second Circuit.[183] The teacher wore the armband on the day designated as a "moratorium" day by opponents of the War. He refused to remove the symbol and was summarily ordered to leave school at once. The next day he was reinstated by letter with "the understanding that [he] engage in no political activities while in the school." On the second "moratorium" day he again wore the symbol. He was

173. State ex rel. Platz v. Mucci, 10 Ohio St.2d 60, 225 N.E.2d 238 (1967).

174. Monaghan v. School Dist. No. 1, 211 Or. 360, 315 P.2d 797 (1957).

175. State ex rel. Settles v. Board of Educ. of Dependent School Dist. No. D–38, 389 P.2d 356 (Okl.1964).

176. Begich v. Jefferson, 441 P.2d 27 (Alaska 1968).

177. Haskins v. State ex rel. Harrington, 516 P.2d 1171 (Wyo.1973).

178. Visotcky v. City Council of City of Garfield, 113 N.J.Super. 263, 273 A.2d 597 (1971).

179. Jones v. Kolbeck, 119 N.J.Super. 299, 291 A.2d 378 (1972).

180. Culpepper v. Veal, 246 Ga. 563, 272 S.E.2d 253 (1980).

181. De Feo v. Smith, 17 N.J. 183, 110 A.2d 553 (1955).

182. Tarpo v. Bowman Public School Dist. No. 1, 232 N.W.2d 67 (N.D.1975).

183. James v. Board of Educ. of Central School Dist. No. 1, Addison, 461 F.2d 566 (2 Cir.1972), cert. den. 409 U.S. 1042, 93 S.Ct. 529, 34 L.Ed.2d 491 (1972). [Case No. 101]

suspended and subsequently discharged. In invalidating the dismissal the court stated that where First Amendment rights are involved school authorities must demonstrate a reasonable basis for concluding that the teacher's conduct threatens to impair their legitimate interests in regulating school operations. In this case there was no evidence of disruption, the teacher made no attempt to proselytize his eleventh-grade students, and there was inconsistency in enforcement on the part of school authorities, no action having been taken against a teacher who displayed prominently in his room the slogan "Peace with Honor." The court cautioned, however, that its opinion should not be interpreted as condoning "partisan political activities in the public schools which reasonably may be expected to interfere with the educational process."

Subsequently the same court upheld the right of a teacher not to participate in the flag salute ceremony. She could not be terminated solely on the ground she stood silently at attention during the recitation.[184] Requiring teachers to lead the class in the Pledge of Allegiance violated First Amendment rights of teachers, said the highest court of Massachusetts.[185] (See, however, Case No. 98.)

After several years of service a teacher who was elected chair of the local chapter of the American Civil Liberties Union began to challenge long accepted practices at the high school as violative of church-state separation. A letter on the subject he wrote to a newspaper sparked a public controversy. Later, another letter defending ACLU's position favoring legalization of marijuana provoked intense, largely critical comment. Then it was brought to public attention that he had made available to his students a pamphlet entitled "The Student as Nigger," which in unrestrained language analogized the student-teacher relationship to a system of slavery. Criticisms of his teaching by school authorities increased with the public clamor, and he was dismissed allegedly on grounds of professional inadequacy. The Ninth Circuit Court of Appeals held that the dismissal could not stand.[186]

Freedom of speech rights of teachers in another context were set out when the Supreme Court unanimously answered in the negative the following question: May a state "require that an elected Board of Education prohibit teachers, other than union representatives, to speak at open meetings, at which public participation is permitted, if such speech is addressed to the subject of pending collective-bargaining negotiations?"[187]

One of the bargaining issues was whether the contract should include an agency shop provision (called "fair share" clause in Wiscon-

184. Russo v. Central School Dist. No. 1, Towns of Rush et al., 469 F.2d 623 (2 Cir.1972), cert. den. 411 U.S. 932, 93 S.Ct. 1899, 36 L.Ed.2d 391 (1973).

185. Opinions of the Justices to the Governor, 372 Mass. 874, 363 N.E.2d 251 (1977).

186. Wagle v. Murray, 560 F.2d 401 (9 Cir.1977), cert. den. 434 U.S. 1014, 98 S.Ct.

729, 54 L.Ed.2d 758 (1978). More facts are given in an earlier opinion, 546 F.2d 1329 (9 Cir.1976).

187. City of Madison, Joint School Dist. No. 8 v. Wisconsin Employment Relations Comm'n, 429 U.S. 167, 97 S.Ct. 421, 50 L.Ed.2d 376 (1976).

sin). Because of a stalemate in the negotiations the teachers union arranged to have pickets present at a public board meeting and to have some 350 teachers in attendance to support the union's position. During the portion of the meeting provided for comments by the public, the president of the union spoke on the teachers' position and presented a petition signed by some 1,350 teachers. Then a teacher, who, although part of the bargaining unit, was not a member of the union, said that he desired to inform the board, as he had the union, that an informal survey he had conducted concerning the "fair share" clause revealed much confusion about the meaning of the proposal. He stated that a large number of teachers had already signed a petition taking no stand on the proposal but urging that all alternatives be presented clearly to the teachers and the general public before action was taken. The statement was two and one-half minutes in length, and the only board response was a question by the president asking if the petition would be presented to the board (the teacher answered affirmatively). Later that evening the board met in executive session and voted to accept all of the union's demands except the "fair share" proposal. The next day the union negotiators accepted the board's proposal and a contract was subsequently signed.

A few weeks later the union filed a prohibited-labor-practices complaint with the Wisconsin Employment Relations Commission against the board for permitting the teacher to speak. The claim was that this constituted negotiations with a member of the bargaining unit other than the exclusive representative. The commission agreed and ordered the school board not to permit employees other than representatives of the union to appear and speak at board meetings on matters subject to collective bargaining.

In reversing the order, which had been upheld by the Supreme Court of Wisconsin, the Supreme Court of the United States emphasized that the First Amendment requires that "the participation in public discussion of public business [not] be confined to one category of interested individuals. * * * Whatever its duties as an employer, when the board sits in public meetings to conduct public business and hear the views of citizens, it may not be required to discriminate between speakers on the basis of their employment, or the content of their speech."

Procedural Due Process in Discharge

The Fourteenth Amendment requires procedural due process before a person may be deprived of property, and holding a teaching position clearly qualifies as a property right if the teacher has an unexpired contract or is on tenure. In Chapter 9 it was pointed out that nonrenewals may qualify for constitutional due process under certain circumstances. In addition, within a given state various statutes may establish procedures relative to termination of teachers. Such statutory due process is strictly enforced by the courts, and if a provision is not observed by the school board the discharge will probably be held invalid.[188] Constitutional due process, on the other hand, is not so precise as to requirements. In effect it is a question of "fair play," and the concept encompasses different rules in accordance with different factual contexts and different types of proceedings.[189]

The Supreme Court has said that "identification of the specific dictates of due process generally requires consideration of three distinct factors: First, the private interest that will be affected by the official action; second, the risk of an erroneous deprivation of such interest through the procedures used, and the probable value, if any, of additional or substitute procedural safeguards; and finally, the Government's interest, including the function involved and the fiscal and administrative burdens that the additional or substitute procedural requirement would entail."[190]

The core of procedural due process is the hearing, at which the teacher must have an opportunity to refute the charges or to establish that they do not constitute grounds for termination. In most jurisdictions the initial hearing is held by the local school board or an administrative agency of the state. The hearing need not conform to the strict procedures used in courts, nor must technical rules of evidence be observed.[191] Although written procedural rules are not constitutionally necessary, there must be order to the proceedings.[192] Also the hearing must be fair and complete, which is ultimately a judicial determination.

Boards must not consider charges beyond those of which the employee has been properly informed before the hearing.[193] All evidence relied upon by the board for its decision must be presented at the hearing so that the person charged may respond to it.[194] Events are not excluded from consideration in separation proceedings simply because they occurred during previous school years. To be inadmissible as evidence there would be a need to show that passage of time somehow created prejudice to the teacher's defense, such as unavailability of witnesses or fuzziness of memory.[195] The notice, however, must apprise the teacher of the time span involved.[196]

Following the hearing, it is necessary for the board to make specific findings of fact on the basis of evidence introduced at the hearing. The evidence must be relevant and have probative value. The record of the hearing must indicate what evidence was relied upon to establish the

188. Irwin v. Board of Educ. of School Dist. No. 25 of Holt County, 215 Neb. 794, 340 N.W.2d 877 (1983).

189. Morrissey v. Brewer, 408 U.S. 471, 92 S.Ct. 2593, 33 L.Ed.2d 484 (1972).

190. Mathews v. Eldridge, 424 U.S. 319, 96 S.Ct. 893, 47 L.Ed.2d 18 (1976).

191. Knox County Bd. of Educ. v. Willis, 405 S.W.2d 952 (Ky.1966). [Case No. 103]; Baxter v. Poe, 42 N.C.App. 404, 257 S.E.2d 71 (1979); Cope v. Board of Educ. of Town of West Hartford, 4 Conn.App. 464, 495 A.2d 718 (1985).

192. Adams v. Professional Practices Comm'n, 524 P.2d 932 (Okl.1974).

193. Turk v. Franklin Special School Dist., 640 S.W.2d 218 (Tenn.1982).

194. Haddock v. Board of Educ., Unified School Dist. No. 462, Crowley County, 233 Kan. 66, 661 P.2d 368 (1983).

195. Tomczik v. State Tenure Com'n, 175 Mich.App. 495, 438 N.W.2d 642 (1989).

196. Allen v. Texarkana Public Schools, 303 Ark. 59, 794 S.W.2d 138 (1990).

findings.[197] Although, in general, courts will uphold findings of administrative bodies unless they are contrary to the manifest weight of evidence, there is an increasing tendency for courts to examine the evidence. For example, where there were inadequate factual findings based on proper evidence, the board hearing was nullified by the Supreme Court of Minnesota, and the board was given the option of holding a new hearing or dropping the charges against a teacher.[198]

At issue in many cases is the adequacy of the notice that sets forth the charges on which a teacher is to be tried at the hearing. The charges must be specific enough for the teacher to be able to prepare a response. A charge of "inability to establish rapport with students" is too vague.[199] A charge of incompetency must be accompanied by "names, dates, occurrences, or other data" upon which school authorities relied in reaching their recommendation for discharge.[200] If the charge involves a pattern of conduct, the time period covered, as well as the specifics, must be included in the notice.[201]

If statutes or board rules prescribe details for conducting the hearing, they must be strictly followed or the hearing will be a nullity and any action based on it void. As examples, an appellate court in Arizona invalidated a hearing held shortly after a statutory deadline,[202] and one in New York ruled likewise where the notice of the hearing did not tell the teacher of her rights as required by a board bylaw.[203]

If a teacher fails to avail himself of certain procedural rights he cannot later claim his dismissal was invalid because of lack thereof. Thus, where a teacher resigned and declined to exercise an option for a hearing, the community college was excused from further due process requirements.[204] The teacher knowingly had chosen to waive his right to a hearing in order to improve the possibility of obtaining other employment. Where a tenure teacher willfully left a hearing before evidence against him was presented, the board was not required to proceed with the hearing in order to discharge the teacher.[205]

Under state statutory or judicial provision [206] when a hearing is held before a hearing officer rather than the board, the teacher may be entitled to see the report of the officer and have a chance to respond

197. Kinsella v. Board of Educ. of Central School Dist. No. 7, Erie County, 378 F.Supp. 54 (W.D.N.Y.1974); Ross v. Springfield School Dist. No. 19, 294 Or. 357, 657 P.2d 188 (1982).

198. Morey v. School Bd. of Independent School Dist. No. 492, 276 Minn. 48, 148 N.W.2d 370 (1967).

199. Powell v. Board of Trustees of Crook County School Dist. No. 1, 550 P.2d 1112 (Wyo.1976).

200. Blackburn v. Board of Educ. of Breckinridge County, 564 S.W.2d 35 (Ky. App.1978).

201. Allen v. Texarkana Public Schools, 303 Ark. 59, 794 S.W.2d 138 (1990).

202. Flowing Wells School Dist. v. Stewart, 18 Ariz.App. 19, 499 P.2d 750 (1972).

203. Ambrose v. Community School Bd. No. 30, 48 A.D.2d 654, 367 N.Y.S.2d 550 (1975).

204. Stewart v. Bailey, 556 F.2d 281 (5 Cir.1977).

205. Ferguson v. Board of Trustees of Bonner County School Dist. No. 82, 98 Idaho 359, 564 P.2d 971 (1977).

206. Winston v. Board of Educ. of Borough of South Plainfield, 125 N.J.Super. 131, 309 A.2d 89 (1973), aff. 64 N.J. 582, 319 A.2d 226 (1974); Powell v. Brown, 160 W.Va. 723, 238 S.E.2d 220 (1977).

before the meeting at which the board is to act. That this does not occur does not per se constitutionally invalidate a proceeding, however, according to the Second Circuit Court of Appeals.[207] In the case neither the teacher nor her attorney had asked to see the report at any time. The board gave the teacher a week's notice of the fact her case would be considered at an upcoming public meeting of the board. She did not attend the meeting, where, according to the record, she could have responded to the trial examiner's report. The court refused to annul the discharge, saying that under the facts due process had not been violated by failure to send her the report in advance of the meeting.

It has been held that a teacher has no absolute due process right to directly address a school board orally or in writing before it acts on the question of his termination.[208] If there has been an evidentiary hearing on the merits of the case before an impartial officer or panel, the board may act on the full factual report of that hearing, subject to judicial review as to whether the board's decision was supported by the evidence adduced at the hearing.

That the motivation of school authorities in not following procedures is benign may be of little legal consequence (except to defend a possible case where bad faith is an issue). Where a notice of unsatisfactory work was to be written, advising the teacher in a private conference because the administration chose not "to hurt the feelings" of the teacher was not compliance with the statute, and the teacher was awarded tenure by the Court of Appeals of Michigan.[209] Where, however, there was no tenure statute the Court of Civil Appeals of Texas ruled in favor of a board that had delayed final action on a teacher's nonrenewal beyond the date established in board policies so that the teacher might have more time to establish her competence.[210] She was fully aware of the situation, and the court held that there was no implied renewal by this "accommodation" to the teacher.

The Supreme Court of South Carolina, stating that allegations of incompetency are often broad based and require close examination, found the task "simplified" where it was "apparent" from letters in evidence that the teacher did not possess "even a rudimentary competence in English." [211] The fact the board allowed him to serve out the year despite the surfacing of the inadequacies gave no rights to the teacher.

Generally where a hearing before termination is required by statute, contract, or otherwise, it must precede removal from the payroll of the

207. Buck v. Board of Educ. of City of New York, 553 F.2d 315 (2 Cir.1977), cert. den. 438 U.S. 904, 98 S.Ct. 3122, 57 L.Ed.2d 1147 (1978).

208. Jones v. Morris, 541 F.Supp. 11 (S.D.Ohio 1981), aff. 455 U.S. 1009, 102 S.Ct. 1699, 72 L.Ed.2d 127 (1982).

209. Amato v. Oxford Area Community School Dist. No. 7, 70 Mich.App. 305, 245 N.W.2d 728 (1976). The Supreme Court of Michigan reversed the award of tenure on

the ground that the intermediate appellate court had applied the wrong statute to the situation. 402 Mich. 521, 266 N.W.2d 445 (1978).

210. Carl v. South San Antonio Independent School Dist., 561 S.W.2d 560 (Tex. Civ.App.1978).

211. Adams v. Clarendon County School Dist. No. 2, 270 S.C. 266, 241 S.E.2d 897 (1978).

employee.[212] The absence of a full adversarial pretermination hearing, however, does not per se invalidate the board action under the federal constitution. The Supreme Court in 1985 clarified the minimum requirements of constitutional due process that must be afforded before one having a property right to a position may be terminated.[213] "Some kind of hearing" must be conducted prior to the discharge. The pretermination hearing need not be "elaborate," for a post-termination hearing would follow. However, a "tenured public employee is entitled to oral or written notice of the charges against him, an explanation of the employer's evidence, and an opportunity to present his side of the story."

That the board has had some prior involvement in the matter does not per se bar it as decisionmaker at an otherwise full and fair hearing. The Supreme Court has discussed the question of impartiality of a school board in relation to a board decision dismissing striking teachers.[214] The Court drew on prior decisions to add emphasis to its statement that mere familiarity with the facts of a case gained in the performance of one's statutory role does not disqualify a decisionmaker. Nor does the simple fact that one has taken a position, even in public, on an issue related to a dispute that is to be decided. To disqualify a decisionmaker it would have to be shown that he is not capable of judging fairly a particular controversy under existing circumstances.

The Court of Appeals of Kentucky found no bias because some school board members had discussed the charges against a teacher with some of those who signed affidavits in support of the charges.[215] Each board member had stated under oath that he could and would decide the issue solely upon the evidence at the hearing, and the trial court found nothing to suggest that they did otherwise. However, where the board initiated charges against a teacher and where there were no witnesses (making it necessary for the board members to call on their personal knowledge) the Supreme Court of Iowa overturned the decision to dismiss the teacher on the ground the board was not an impartial decisionmaker.[216]

In some states statutes provide that the dismissal of a teacher can be reviewed by a trial de novo in court. This type of statute gives the court original, rather than appellate, jurisdiction, and the adequacy of the administrative hearing is not directly involved. Other statutes provide that, although review by the courts is to be on the record, they are empowered to make additional inquiries or take additional testimony in their discretion. The Supreme Court of Kansas has held that the

212. Vanelli v. Reynolds School Dist. No. 7, 667 F.2d 773 (9 Cir.1982). [Case No. 104]

213. Cleveland Bd. of Educ. v. Loudermill, 470 U.S. 532, 105 S.Ct. 1487, 84 L.Ed.2d 494 (1985). [Case No. 105]

214. Hortonville Joint School Dist. No. 1 v. Hortonville Educ. Ass'n, 426 U.S. 482, 96 S.Ct. 2308, 49 L.Ed.2d 1 (1976).

215. Burkett v. Board of Educ. of Pulaski County, 558 S.W.2d 626 (Ky.App.1977).

216. Keith v. Community School Dist. of Wilton in the Counties of Cedar and Muscatine, 262 N.W.2d 249 (Iowa 1978).

legislature may provide that an external hearing committee, rather than the local board, will make the final decision as to whether a tenure teacher is to be terminated.[217] The court said that as long as the board can appeal the committee's decision to a court, the board's general power to operate the school system is not unconstitutionally impaired.

The Supreme Court of California considered a case where a teacher had been dismissed after a hearing.[218] The board at the hearing stated and supported adequate cause for dismissal. The teacher, however, presented evidence that, notwithstanding this cause, the dismissal resulted from official dissatisfaction with his exercise of constitutional rights. The board made a finding that the real reason was not what the teacher claimed. The court held that under these circumstances the teacher was entitled to have an independent judicial determination of why he was dismissed, rather than only a review to see if the administrative determination was supported by adequate evidence. The court stated that it could neither permit school authorities to mask an unconstitutional dismissal behind a statement of valid causes nor permit a teacher genuinely dismissed for valid cause to be reinstated because school authorities were also displeased with his exercise of constitutional rights.

Abolition and Creation of Positions

Abolition of a teaching or other educational position occurs in two basic forms: the elimination of a particular position or job classification for reasons of lack of students, economy, or internal reorganization; and reduction in the total number of positions needed for one of those reasons or following a consolidation of school districts.

In the first situation the basic legal question is whether the abolition of the position was bona fide, or whether the purported discontinuance of the post was really intended to remove an incumbent without breaching his contract or following the tenure procedure. The general rule is that a teacher has no right to a position no longer deemed necessary for proper reasons, such as those listed above. In a leading case a teacher whose department was discontinued maintained that she could not be dismissed under the tenure statute because abolition of position was not one of the grounds set out in the statute for discharge. The Supreme Court of Pennsylvania, however, held that it was not the intention of the legislature by the tenure act to confer the right upon professional employees to be retained permanently in their positions regardless of circumstances.[219] But the court emphasized that a department could not be abolished to accomplish a dismissal by subterfuge. A half century

217. Unified School Dist. No. 380, Marshall County v. McMillen, 252 Kan. 451, 845 P.2d 676 (1993).

218. Bekiaris v. Board of Educ. of City of Modesto, 6 Cal.3d 575, 100 Cal.Rptr. 16, 493 P.2d 480 (1972).

219. Ehret v. Kulpmont School Dist., 333 Pa. 518, 5 A.2d 188 (1939).

later the Supreme Court of Ohio cited this and other cases when it overturned the suspension of a teacher's contract on the asserted ground of declining enrollment and held that this cause could be valid only when an actual and current decline is shown to exist at the time of a reduction in the number of teachers.[220]   Further, such a decline must not be caused by actions of the board (such as rearranging curriculum or departments) even if the board's intent is benign.[221]

Although there seems no doubt as to the power of a school board to abolish a position,[222] it is essential that the position be abolished in fact. In an illustrative case, the position of district principal, a title at the time given to chief school administrators in small districts in New Jersey, was allegedly abolished in the interests of economy. Concurrently another position of "teaching principal" was established. The basic duties of the district principalship were transferred to the new position. The court found that in substance the position had not been abolished, and ordered the district principal reinstated.[223]   There was no bad faith allegation in this case. Where bad faith is present, of course, courts will not sustain the abolition of a position.[224]

A New York teacher was dismissed when the school district terminated driver education as a regular course. It instituted "after hours" instruction and employed part-time personnel to do the teaching. The new instruction was accredited. The Court of Appeals found this situation not to be a bona fide abolition of position and ordered the teacher reinstated.[225]   That court, however, sustained the power of a local school board to abolish the position of attendance teacher and divide the duties among principals and assistant principals.[226]

The Supreme Judicial Court of Massachusetts held that a school board could not through collective bargaining divest itself of the authority to abolish a supervisory position after the expiration of the contract.[227] In another case that court extended the prohibition, and held that a board could not agree to retain a supervisory position beyond a given school year even though the collective bargaining contract was still in effect.[228]   In neither case was there any evidence that the abolitions were

220. Phillips v. South Range Local School Dist. Bd. of Educ., 45 Ohio St.3d 66, 543 N.E.2d 492 (1989).

221. Freiberg v. Board of Educ. of Big Bay De Noc School Dist., 91 Mich.App. 462, 283 N.W.2d 775 (1979).

222. Kaplan v. School Committee of Melrose, 363 Mass. 332, 294 N.E.2d 209 (1973); Williams v. Seattle School Dist. No. 1, 97 Wash.2d 215, 643 P.2d 426 (1982); Gross v. Board of Educ. of Elmsford Union Free School Dist., 78 N.Y.2d 13, 571 N.Y.S.2d 200, 574 N.E.2d 438 (1991).

223. Viemeister v. Board of Educ. of Borough of Prospect Park, 5 N.J.Super. 215, 68 A.2d 768 (1949). [Case No. 106]

224. Paradis v. School Administrative Dist. No. 33 School Bd., 462 A.2d 474 (Me. 1983); Clairborne Country Bd. of Educ. v. Martin, 500 So.2d 981 (Miss.1986).

225. Baron v. Mackreth, 26 N.Y.2d 1039, 311 N.Y.S.2d 925, 260 N.E.2d 554 (1970).

226. Young v. Board of Educ. of Central School Dist. No. 6, 35 N.Y.2d 31, 358 N.Y.S.2d 709, 315 N.E.2d 768 (1974).

227. School Committee of Hanover v. Curry, 369 Mass. 683, 343 N.E.2d 144 (1976).

228. School Committee of Braintree v. Raymond, 369 Mass. 686, 343 N.E.2d 145 (1976).

pretextual. The court held in the second case, however, that the director of music who was reassigned as a teacher could be awarded the difference in salary by an arbitrator.

The term reduction-in-force (RIF) is given generally to a broader-based diminution of staff. How such a transition is to be effectuated and the rights of employees to "bump" others and to be recalled after layoffs are matters of state law. The states vary widely not only as to operational details, but as to sources of effective law (statute, state education agency rule, local board policy, collective bargaining contract, judicial pronouncement). Some generalizations and examples follow.

Generally there is no requirement that an individual teacher be given notice and hearing before termination of employment in a RIF situation.[229] The cause is not personal to a teacher and, therefore, there is no charge of inadequacy to be proved against the teacher.

Where teachers or other employees on tenure status are terminated on the ground of financial exigency, the courts will examine relevant financial data to determine if the reductions are so necessary as to supersede rights of employees. In such instances the board generally must show that there is a financial exigency and that a uniform and rational set of procedures is being applied to effectuate the reduction.[230] The board may not decline to articulate its staff reduction policy, for this would preclude judicial review of whether the termination decisions were based on impermissible grounds.[231] Having adopted a policy, the board must follow it.[232]

In Yonkers, New York, a collective bargaining contract contained a "job security" clause, that is, a provision preventing any lay-offs during the period of the contract. When the fiscally dependent board received sharp cuts in its budget, it attempted to terminate some teachers, and the union filed a grievance. The state's highest court refused to stay the arbitration.[233] It observed that the matter of job security was a permissible subject of bargaining, that the contract was of only three years duration, that the contract explicitly protected teachers from abolition of their positions "due to budgetary reasons or abolition of programs," and that the contract had been negotiated before the so-called emergency arose.

The Supreme Judicial Court of Massachusetts expressly disagreed with this reasoning and held that a job security clause was unenforceable because ability to determine size of teaching staff in light of available

229. Martin v. School Committee of Natick, 393 Mass. 430, 472 N.E.2d 231 (1984), cert. den. 471 U.S. 1077, 105 S.Ct. 2157, 85 L.Ed.2d 512 (1985).

230. Bignall v. North Idaho College, 538 F.2d 243 (9 Cir.1976); Hartman v. Board of Educ. of Jefferson County, 562 S.W.2d 674 (Ky.App.1978).

231. Matter of Waterloo Community School Dist., 338 N.W.2d 153 (Iowa 1983).

A deviation from this principle appears in Reed v. Edgeley Public School Dist. No. 3, 313 N.W.2d 775 (N.D.1981).

232. Ward v. Viborg School Dist. No. 60–5, 319 N.W.2d 502 (S.D.1982).

233. Board of Educ. of Yonkers City School Dist. v. Yonkers Federation of Teachers, 40 N.Y.2d 268, 386 N.Y.S.2d 657, 353 N.E.2d 569 (1976).

funds was nondelegable.[234]　That court indicated in a different case that means of implementing a reduction in force decision and the impact of the decision on terms and conditions of employment were mandatory subjects of bargaining.[235]

Where a position occupied by a tenure teacher is abolished, generally nontenure teachers cannot be retained in similar positions.[236]　Nor can the overall RIF policy and procedures operate so as to give nontenure teachers the status of tenure faculty in any aspect.[237]　For example, a music teacher with tenure had been dismissed because of decreased enrollment in instrumental music.　The enrollment did decline in that branch of music, but the total enrollment in the school had increased, and the teacher was certified to teach in several continued branches of music.　A nontenure teacher had been retained by the board as director of music.　Even though the tenure law permitted dismissal of teachers because of decreased enrollment, the Supreme Court of Delaware held that since the teacher had tenure he could not be discharged while a nontenure teacher continued in employment, even though the latter was called director of music.[238]

Where tenure teachers must be "riffed" in order of seniority when positions are abolished determination of seniority can lead to litigation if the method is not specified by statute.　Generally the first common-law criterion is actual full-time service rendered by one properly appointed.[239]　Beyond that, the board's method must be a reasonable one not foreclosed by statute.　Where a statute provided that the discontinued teacher be the one "having the least seniority in the system within the tenure of the position abolished," a collectively bargained arrangement for teachers who voluntarily changed tenure areas to apply accrued seniority in the district to the new tenure area was held to be unenforceable.[240]

The Supreme Court of Pennsylvania has held that the statutory prescription of seniority in RIF situations applies to positions as they exist.[241]　Thus, the incumbent of an eliminated position is entitled to a retained position (for which he is certificated) that is held by a less senior person.　There is no requirement that the district consider all the certifications of its staff and carry out a realignment that furloughs the

234. Boston Teachers Union, Local 66 v. School Committee of Boston, 386 Mass. 197, 434 N.E.2d 1258 (1982).

235. School Committee of Newton v. Labor Relations Comm'n, 388 Mass. 557, 447 N.E.2d 1201 (1983).

236. Watson v. Burnett, 216 Ind. 216, 23 N.E.2d 420 (1939); State ex rel. Marolt v. Independent School Dist. 695, 299 Minn. 134, 217 N.W.2d 212 (1974).　An exception is found in Paradis v. School Administrative Dist. No. 33 School Bd., 446 A.2d 46 (Me. 1982).

237. Babb v. Independent School Dist. No. I–5 of Rogers County, Okl., 829 P.2d 973 (Okl.1992).

238. Board of School Trustees of Gunning Bedford Junior School Dist. No. 53 v. O'Brien, 56 Del. 79, 190 A.2d 23 (1963).

239. Schoenfeld v. Board of Cooperative Educational Services of Nassau County, 98 A.D.2d 723, 469 N.Y.S.2d 133 (1983).

240. Szumigala v. Hicksville Union Free School Dist. Bd. of Educ., 148 A.D.2d 621, 539 N.Y.S.2d 83 (1989).

241. Duncan v. Rochester Area School Bd., 524 Pa. 254, 571 A.2d 365 (1990); Dallap v. Sharon City School Dist., 524 Pa. 260, 571 A.2d 368 (1990).

least senior employee possible. Where circumstances permit more than one realignment the district may consider educational impact.

A school nurse was employed by a school district before state certification requirements were imposed. (The certificate made one eligible for all rights of teachers.) Under the certification statute she could continue to be employed without becoming certificated, although eventually she obtained a certificate. Before she did so another school nurse, who had received certification earlier, was employed by the district. It was held that the second nurse had seniority under the tenure statute when one nursing position was to be reduced to part-time.[242]

Seniority rights are not derived from common law. Any such rights must be based on a statute or a contract.[243] The Supreme Court of Nebraska upheld a school board's decision to retain a tenure business education teacher with three years experience rather than one with six years experience because of the greater contribution of the former to the extracurricular activities program.[244] On the other hand, courts can construe tenure statutes broadly to include seniority rights within the category of probationary teachers, as the highest court of New York has done.[245]

In the same case the court also made the point that merely abolishing the position of a professional employee is not equivalent to discharging him. It is necessary to see if other positions for which he is qualified are open to him under applicable statutes. Generally the board of education has the burden of showing the absence of such a position.[246] The board, however, is not obliged under normal circumstances to interchange a large number of courses among established positions to create a position that a riffed teacher would be qualified to fill.[247]

It is the responsibility of an employee facing RIF to assure the board that certifications for other positions are valid at the time the board must make its decisions about "bumping" and reassignments. To be eligible for a certificate is not the same as having the certificate. Thus, a teacher who eventually received a certain certificate (there being a question as to whether the state department would accept certain courses) was not entitled to bump a less senior teacher who was qualified at the proper time.[248] Where a not-fully-qualified nontenure profession-

242. Verdeyen v. Board of Educ. of Batavia Public School Dist. No. 101, Kane County, 150 Ill.App.3d 915, 103 Ill.Dec. 620, 501 N.E.2d 937 (1986).

243. Fivehouse v. Passaic Valley Water Comm'n, 127 N.J.Super. 451, 317 A.2d 755 (1974).

244. Dykeman v. Board of Educ. of School Dist. of Coleridge, Cedar County, 210 Neb. 596, 316 N.W.2d 69 (1982). [Case No. 108]

245. Lezette v. Board of Educ., Hudson City School Dist., 35 N.Y.2d 272, 360 N.Y.S.2d 869, 319 N.E.2d 189 (1974).

246. Penasco Independent School Dist. No. 4 v. Lucero, 86 N.M. 683, 526 P.2d 825

(1974). [Case No. 107] Bauer v. Board of Educ., Unified School Dist. No. 452, Johnson, 244 Kan. 6, 765 P.2d 1129 (1988).

247. Peters v. Board of Educ. of Rantoul Twp. High School Dist. No. 193 of Champaign County, 97 Ill.2d 166, 73 Ill. Dec. 450, 454 N.E.2d 310 (1983); Butler v. Board of Educ., Unified School Dist. No. 440, Harvey County, 244 Kan. 458, 769 P.2d 651 (1989).

248. Hancon v. Board of Educ. of Barrington Community Unit School Dist. No. 220, 130 Ill.App.3d 224, 85 Ill.Dec. 679, 474 N.E.2d 407 (1985).

al was retained over a not-fully-qualified tenure professional because she was closer to attaining a needed second certificate for a new position category, the Supreme Court of Indiana sustained the school board.[249] Tenure bumping rights were held applicable only to those qualified for a position.

When school districts are consolidated, the question arises as to the continuation of tenure status acquired in the former separate districts. The inquiry is whether the new district is a continuation of the old districts, or a new entity, insofar as tenure is concerned. The Supreme Court of New Mexico held that for tenure purposes the consolidated district was a continuation of the former districts comprising it;[250] the Supreme Judicial Court of Maine held to the contrary.[251] The New Mexico case developed when a tenure teacher in one of the former districts, after teaching one year in the consolidated district, was notified of nonrenewal the following year due to a reduction in staff size. The teacher's request for a hearing had been denied by the board because she was considered a probationary teacher, having served the consolidated district for only one year. The court required that tenure rights be afforded the teacher, noting that reduction in force was insufficient reason for the dismissal of a tenure teacher when teachers without tenure were retained in the system. The Maine court said that, in the absence of "clear legislative language to that effect," the court would not deprive the school board of the consolidated district of its "discretion in the initial staffing of the new high school."

The Appellate Court of Illinois held that any reduction in the number of full-time equivalent teachers triggered the statutory procedures covering dismissals.[252] A board had reduced a tenure teacher to a one-half time teaching position, so that the total of full-time teachers was decreased. This, said the court, activated the "bumping" privileges for tenure teachers.

When schools are reorganized and new principalships created, complications can occur under tenure statutes. For example, in Massachusetts a new and enlarged grammar school had been constructed in a school district to replace two small schools, which were closed and abandoned. The principal of one of the closed schools insisted that she had the legal right to the principalship of the new school because she had attained tenure as a principal. The school board had named a principal from another system for the new school, and had assigned the principal in question to teach the eighth grade in the new school with no reduction in salary. The board's action was sustained on the ground that the school in which the plaintiff had served as principal had ceased

---

249. Stewart v. Fort Wayne Community Schools, 564 N.E.2d 274 (Ind.1990), cert. den. ___ U.S. ___, 112 S.Ct. 169, 116 L.Ed.2d 133 (1991).

250. Hensley v. State Bd. of Educ., 71 N.M. 182, 376 P.2d 968 (1962).

251. Beckett v. Roderick, 251 A.2d 427 (Me.1969).

252. Caviness v. Board of Educ. of Ludlow Community Consolidated School Dist. No. 142 of Champaign County, 59 Ill. App.3d 28, 16 Ill.Dec. 526, 375 N.E.2d 157 (1978).

to exist.[253]   There was no obligation upon the board to employ her as principal in the new school. Similar reasoning led a Louisiana court to uphold a school board's assigning the tenure principal of the former six-year high school to the principalship of the newly formed junior high school, rather than to the principalship of the senior high school.[254]

In a New York situation a six-year secondary school was reorganized with a junior and a senior high school. Several years later the junior high school principalship was abolished and the responsibilities transferred to the senior high school principalship. The displaced principal, holder of a secondary school principal's certificate, had acquired tenure and had greater seniority than the senior high school principal. He claimed he was entitled to the position of principal of the senior high school because the positions were similar and within the same tenure classification. The board of education urged the view that, although all principalships involve the performance of some common duties, the principalship of the senior high school was sufficiently different to warrant a different classification. The highest state court agreed with the petitioner, and ordered that he be appointed to the six-year high school principalship.[255]

In an internal reorganization of a school system the person who held the position of supervisor of elementary education was moved one step lower in the table of organization. His salary was not reduced (in fact he received an increase) and his title was not changed. He claimed, however, that he should be placed in the position which was as close to the top of the hierarchy as he previously had been. That position paid more salary. He maintained that the applicable tenure law protected him against a salary reduction except after a hearing and that it was applicable to the facts at hand. As his salary had in fact not been reduced, the Supreme Court of Tennessee found the tenure provision inapplicable and ruled for the board.[256]

Discharge of Superintendents

Tenure statutes vary in their coverages of other than classroom teachers. Some grant tenure protection to those in selected administrative positions. Some cover the administrative assignments per se, and others afford tenure only as teachers.

The weight of authority is that the superintendent is not covered by tenure in that post unless the statute specifically includes him. Attempts to include superintendents under general language usually have failed. For example, in Minnesota the tenure law stated that a teacher was "a person regularly employed as a principal, or to give instruction in a classroom, or to superintend or supervise classroom instruction." A

253. Jantzen v. School Committee of Chelmsford, 332 Mass. 175, 124 N.E.2d 534 (1955).

254. Verret v. Calcasieu Parish School Bd., 103 So.2d 560 (La.App.1958).

255. Jadick v. Board of Educ. of City School Dist. of Beacon, 15 N.Y.2d 652, 255 N.Y.S.2d 870, 204 N.E.2d 202 (1964).

256. State ex rel. Underwood v. Adams, 225 Tenn. 553, 473 S.W.2d 188 (1971).

superintendent argued that he was entitled to the protection of the law due to the fact that he supervised classroom instruction. The state's highest court disagreed.[257] It held that the superintendent was not a teacher because his supervision of instruction comprised only a small part of his duties and responsibilities. The Supreme Court of North Dakota ruled that the fact a superintendent taught one class did not make him a teacher in the context of contract renewal.[258]

In Missouri, however, where there was no tenure law but where a teacher's contract could be annulled only by the revocation of his certificate by proper authority, it was held that a superintendent could be discharged during the period of his contract only in the same fashion.[259] In Illinois an appellate court ruled that, although the superintendency is not a position in which tenure can be achieved, service as superintendent is teaching service. Thus, one who served as superintendent cannot be discharged from the system without use of the tenure procedures, but he can be reassigned as teacher at the salary for the latter post.[260]

Where a statute provided that written notice of a school board's intention not to renew contracts of administrators must be given by the board of education before a certain date, a letter well before that date from the superintendent stating that he intended to recommend nonrenewal for an assistant superintendent was held not to suffice in meeting the notice requirement.[261] The vote of the board took place after the prescribed date, and, therefore, the contract had been renewed by operation of law.

Removal procedures for public officers differ from those for public employees. Chief administrators of local school districts, however, almost universally are considered in this context to be employees, rather than officers. This status is not affected merely by the semantics of an isolated statute. For example, in California it was unsuccessfully maintained that a superintendent was an officer because a statute used the word "elected" instead of "employed." [262] It was held that the word "elected" in the statute meant "selected" and was synonymous with the word "appointed." Therefore, the superintendent could be discharged following the procedures applicable to an employee.

As public employees, chief administrators enjoy the same protections against discharges for unconstitutional reasons as do teachers. Thus, even though the contract may specify employment at the pleasure of the board, the superintendent cannot be removed from his position sum-

257. Eelkema v. Board of Educ. of City of Duluth, 215 Minn. 590, 11 N.W.2d 76 (1943).

258. Storbeck v. Oriska School Dist. No. 13, 277 N.W.2d 130 (N.D.1979).

259. Lemasters v. Willman, 281 S.W.2d 580 (Mo.App.1955).

260. Lester v. Board of Educ. of School Dist. No. 119, 87 Ill.App.2d 269, 230 N.E.2d 893 (1967).

261. State ex rel. Luckey v. Etheridge, 62 Ohio St.3d 404, 583 N.E.2d 960 (1992).

262. Main v. Claremont Unified School Dist., 161 Cal.App.2d 189, 326 P.2d 573 (1958).

marily for exercise of First Amendment rights of expression.[263]   If the contract prescribes nonprohibited termination procedures, naturally these are binding on the board.[264]

The Supreme Court of California found that an associate superintendent had no right to reinstatement to his position despite the fact that a four-year contract had been entered into a year before it was "rescinded" (because he failed to carry out certain duties, follow certain directives, properly let bids, and prevent improper use of district property).[265]   The plaintiff sought reinstatement to the position on the ground he was not afforded the procedural benefits of notice or reasons before the recision.   The court examined the statutes and construed them not to cover demotion or reassignment of administrators.   (Reinstatement as a teacher was apparently available, but was not sought.)   The court held that no constitutional right had been violated and therefore no constitutional due process was required.

The Court of Appeals, Tenth Circuit, held invalid a finding of incompetency and willful neglect of duty against a superintendent made by a school board some of the members of which had made public statements against the superintendent and had campaigned on a platform of getting a new superintendent.[266]   The court said that the extent of the remarks cast a shadow on the impartiality of the board members as fact finders where the superintendent had a property interest in his contract, which had not expired, and a liberty interest in his reputation, which had been damaged.

When, however, the political speech and activity of a superintendent led to a serious conflict as to how the school system should be operated, the Court of Appeals, Fifth Circuit, with an en banc vote of thirteen-to-two upheld the board's relieving the superintendent of his duties (but with full pay and benefits).[267]   The superintendent clearly had aligned himself with one faction of the board, and through "numerous conversations" with citizens in the small community he had expressed strong support for one slate of candidates for school board membership and concerns about the other slate.   Shortly after those he opposed won election and the board majority changed, he was relieved.   The court emphasized the need for harmony between board and superintendent, which need here superseded the individual right of the superintendent to remain in his position as executive to carry out board policies.

It will be recalled that in cases involving liberty rights upon nonrenewal of contracts the purpose of the constitutionally required hearing is

263.   Hostrop v. Board of Junior College Dist. No. 515, Cook and Will Counties, 471 F.2d 488 (7 Cir.1972), cert. den. 411 U.S. 967, 93 S.Ct. 2150, 36 L.Ed.2d 688 (1973).

264.   Averback v. Board of Educ. of New Paltz Central School Dist., 147 A.D.2d 152, 541 N.Y.S.2d 655 (1989).

265.   Barthuli v. Board of Trustees of Jefferson Elementary School Dist., 19 Cal.3d 717, 139 Cal.Rptr. 627, 566 P.2d 261

(1977), cert. den. 434 U.S. 1040, 98 S.Ct. 782, 54 L.Ed.2d 790 (1978).

266.   Staton v. Mayes, 552 F.2d 908 (10 Cir.1977), cert. den. 434 U.S. 907, 98 S.Ct. 309, 54 L.Ed.2d 195 (1977).

267.   Kinsey v. Salado Independent School Dist., 950 F.2d 988 (5 Cir.1992), cert. den. ___ U.S. ___, 112 S.Ct. 2275, 119 L.Ed.2d 201 (1992).

to give the employee a chance to clear his reputation. The Court of Appeals, Fourth Circuit, reviewed the termination of the superintendent of schools in Baltimore, Maryland, following a lengthy hearing.[268] It concluded that the board had afforded "far more process than was constitutionally due" and that "the victim here is not the fired superintendent" but rather "the uncompensated public-interest-motivated school board member subjected to hours and hours, days and days, lost weekend after weekend, of interminable administrative hearings."

Termination during the period of his contract of a superintendent was upheld by the Court of Appeals, Eighth Circuit, where the evidence showed that, although there may have been some flaws in procedures and inadequacy of evidence regarding some of the charges, the superintendent's relationships with principals and with faculty were "destroyed." [269] The court said that "here, if ever, the Board members were fully warranted" in terminating the contract.

As superintendents typically serve under term contracts, rather than under any tenure provisions, their property rights expire at contract's end. It has been held that the property right is to be fully compensated, not to function in the office.[270] Thus, there is no constitutional due process issue as to possible violation of a property right if the superintendent is paid for the period of the contract extending beyond his being relieved of duties. If he is to be removed from the payroll, the situation would be as previously described for teachers. Any liberty interests requiring constitutional due process also would be no different from those of teachers. For example, a public statement that the superintendent was being relieved because of "ineffective leadership" and "lack of communication with personnel" was held not to be stigmatizing.[271]

Remedies for Wrongful Discharge

If a teacher is wrongfully dismissed, he is entitled to whatever damages he has sustained, just as in the case of the breach of any other contract. The theory of contractual recovery is that the one against whom the breach operates shall be entitled to an amount which will place him in the same position he would have occupied had the contract not been broken. If the teacher is unable to procure another position, the amount of recovery is the full amount of salary he would have received had he not been discharged. However, the teacher must make reasonable effort to secure other employment in order that the amount of damages the board may be obliged to pay shall be reduced.[272] This requirement is based on the theory that there is a duty by one entitled to

268. Patterson v. Ramsey, 552 F.2d 117 (4 Cir.1977).

269. Miller v. Dean, 552 F.2d 266 (8 Cir.1977).

270. Royster v. Board of Trustees of Anderson County School Dist. No. 5, 774 F.2d 618 (4 Cir.1985).

271. Bristol Virginia School Bd. v. Quarles, 235 Va. 108, 366 S.E.2d 82 (1988).

272. Farrell v. School Dist. No. 2 of Rubicon Tp., 98 Mich. 43, 56 N.W. 1053 (1893); Williams v. Albemarle City Bd. of Educ., 485 F.2d 232 (4 Cir.1973).

damages for breach of contract to "mitigate the damages" in every reasonable way. There may be no recovery in some instances. If a teacher immediately upon being dismissed is successful in being offered or obtaining another position at the same or a higher salary, he has suffered no damages. He is not, however, legally bound to accept any position which may be offered him in order to mitigate the damages. The rule, as usually stated, is that he is obliged to accept only employment of the same general character as that for which he contracted.[273] Nor is he bound to accept work in a different part of the state or country even if the offered position is as good or better than the one from which he was discharged.[274] One is not legally bound to sacrifice in order to mitigate damages. What is reasonably necessary is a question of fact in each case. The burden of proof is on the board to show that a teacher has not made enough effort to mitigate the damages.[275]

Money earned by a wrongfully discharged employee can be either substitute or supplemental. It is the former if it could not have been earned while retaining the position. It is supplemental if it was earnable while concurrently performing the breached contract. Only substitute income must be deducted from lost salary, but regardless of the source no substitute earned income is exempt. If, however, statutes provide for suspension with pay, there is no duty to mitigate while on suspension.[276]

Under tenure statutes one may sue to be reinstated to his position. These statutes constitute a legislative exception to the common law rule precluding specific performance as a remedy in cases of wrongful discharge under a personal services contract.

"Section 1983" provides a basis for the seeking of damages by a discharged public employee for alleged deprivations of civil rights in connection with the dismissal. (See "Section 1983" in Index.) The Civil Rights Attorney's Fees Awards Act of 1976[277] provides for the granting of attorney's fees to prevailing parties in civil rights suits, making "Section 1983" cases more attractive as vehicles for redress of wrongful discharges that can be linked to deprivations of rights "secured by the Constitution and laws."

Retirement

In General

All states have legislation covering teacher retirement. Most cases that have been decided by the courts pertain to specific legislative

---

273. Zeller v. Prior Lake Public Schools, 259 Minn. 487, 108 N.W.2d 602 (1961); Selland v. Fargo Public School Dist. No. 1, 302 N.W.2d 391 (N.D.1981).

274. Kenaston v. School Administrative Dist. No. 40, 317 A.2d 7 (Me. 1974); Board of School Trustees of Baugo Community Schools v. Indiana Educ. Employment Relations Bd., 412 N.E.2d 807 (Ind.App.1980).

275. Crosby v. Plummer, 111 Me. 355, 89 A. 145 (1913); University of Alaska v. Chauvin, 521 P.2d 1234 (Alaska 1974); Assad v. Berlin-Boylston Regional School Committee, 406 Mass. 649, 550 N.E.2d 357 (1990).

276. Matter of South Orangetown Central School Dist., 106 A.D.2d 642, 483 N.Y.S.2d 434 (1984).

277. 42 U.S.C.A. § 1988.

provisions and narrow fact situations not relevant beyond the jurisdictions involved. Also, many of the legal issues crucial in the early days of the concept of teacher retirement have been long settled.

The constitutionality of statutes providing for teacher retirement is beyond doubt. The charges of unconstitutionality judicially rejected have included: retirement statutes are unconstitutional class legislation; they provide compensation to public employees beyond their contracted salaries and thus make a gift of public money; they provide for money to be spent for a private purpose because there is no public benefit; the deductions constitute a taking of the teacher's property without due process of law.

Retirement plans for teachers, as they exist virtually universally throughout the country, comprise two elements. One is a financial amount derived from the contributions of the employee, the other, from the contributions of the employer. The former is known technically as an annuity, the latter as a pension. The typical retirement system mandates deductions from the employee's salary, and the state contributes the remainder necessary to provide the retirement allowance. Details of the systems generally are extremely complicated.

Specific Provisions

Retirement legislation includes many detailed stipulations covering eligibility and amounts of money to be received after retirement. Also frequently included are provisions for death benefits and other related matters. Except for changes in existing retirement provisions, or where constitutional provisions may intrude, the legislature has plenary power to establish plans as it sees fit. Historically, local retirement systems preceded state-level ones in many jurisdictions. But because many of these local ones were not actuarially sound, and because the states have more economic ability to finance retirement plans than do local districts, most states have dissolved the local systems except for some in very large school districts. Legal problems involved in making such changes are discussed in the next section.

Local districts cannot adopt any rules which are in contravention of state laws related to retirement. If certain eligibility requirements are established by the state as part of the retirement program, a local district cannot deviate from them.[278] Nor can local authorities institute incentive plans for early retirement if those plans might threaten the actuarial soundness of the state system.[279]

The state teacher retirement board or its equivalent is bound to follow the letter of the retirement law. For example, a teacher moving into Ohio purchased prior service credit under a statute which stated that such service shall be treated by the retirement board as if it were prior service in the state of Ohio. When the teacher reached retirement

278. Herzig v. Board of Educ. of the Town of West Hartford, 152 Conn. 144, 204 A.2d 827 (1964).

279. Fair Lawn Educ. Ass'n v. Fair Lawn Bd. of Educ., 79 N.J. 574, 401 A.2d 681 (1979). [Case No. 21]

age, the board computed his Ohio-teaching allowance by one formula and gave him an additional allowance, calculated separately, for his six years of out-of-state service. The retirement board contended that the purchase by the teacher was only for an annuity, and that there was no vested right to a pension before it was granted. The Supreme Court of Ohio ruled that the six years should be credited exactly as if they had been served in Ohio.[280] It reasoned that because he had voluntarily paid the amount specified when he entered Ohio, this constituted an acceptance of the state's offer, which the retirement board was obligated to honor. The court stated that although the teacher did not acquire a vested right to a specific sum of money when he purchased the out-of-state service credit, he did acquire a contractual right to have it treated as if it were Ohio credit.

The question of precisely what service will be credited within the state has led to judicial determinations adverse to teachers who have held other educational positions. One case decided by the Supreme Court of Iowa turned on the point of whether particular posts were those of school officers or those of school employees.[281] In controversy was whether the plaintiff had met the requirements of having been an employee for at least 25 years. The state retirement plan covered only employees. She had taught for over fifteen years, and had been a local district superintendent of schools for two years, a county superintendent for four, a state inspector of rural schools for two, and the state superintendent of education for four years. The court ruled against the educator on the ground that while she was acting as county superintendent and as state superintendent she was an officer rather than an employee. Each of these posts was created by statute, had duties prescribed by statute, was elective for a fixed term, and was performed without control by a superior officer. These are characteristics of an office.

No violation of equal protection was found by a state's not permitting the purchase of service credit in its retirement system for teaching in a school operated by a foreign country.[282] The fact that the provision excluding such teaching service credit was adopted after the plaintiff became a member of the system was not relevant. He could have purchased the credit before the revision, but did not do so.

Over the years there have been many lawsuits attacking the constitutionality of mandatory retirement ages for public employees. The concept has withstood both equal protection and due process challenges.[283] The Supreme Court has held that the constitutional test for examining a mandatory retirement provision is the usual one of whether

280. Cook v. State Teachers Retirement Bd., 176 Ohio St. 117, 198 N.E.2d 49 (1964).

281. Francis v. Iowa Employment Security Comm'n, 250 Iowa 1300, 98 N.W.2d 733 (1959).

282. Morton v. State Teachers Retirement Bd., 70 Ohio App.2d 114, 434 N.E.2d 1101 (1980).

283. Palmer v. Ticcione, 576 F.2d 459 (2 Cir.1978), cert. den. 440 U.S. 945, 99 S.Ct. 1421, 59 L.Ed.2d 633 (1979).

there is a rational relationship to a permissible state objective.[284]   It stated that a right to governmental employment could not be classified as fundamental in the constitutional sense, and therefore a strict scrutiny analysis was not required.   The case involved a challenge to a provision for mandatory retirement of uniformed state police officers at age fifty.   The Court said that because physical ability declines with age it could not find the particular age selected for this occupational group to be irrational.   It added that whether the policy was wise, was the best to accomplish the purpose of having qualified police, or was the most humane was not in the province of judicial review.

The federal Age Discrimination in Employment Act (ADEA) now provides that adverse personnel employment decisions must not be made on the basis of age for persons who are at least 40 years old.[285]   This act parallels Title VII in its application, operation, and "business necessity" exception.   It is not tied to receipt of federal funds.   (See "Discriminatory Employment Practices" in Chapter 9.)   Its constitutionality has been upheld by the Supreme Court as it applies to public employment.[286]

Changes in Provisions

The legality of a change in a retirement plan depends on whether the arrangement to be changed is considered contractual between the state and teachers affected.   The general rule is that legislation does not create contract rights unless such is clearly indicated as the legislative intent.   It follows that retirement statutes in general have been regarded as expressions of legislative policy, subject to future change if circumstances warrant.   The substantial weight of authority, however, is against permitting the allowances of those already retired to be changed to their disadvantage.   The only major exception is a dire financial crisis in the retirement system.   When a "substantial substitute" is provided by a change, courts have readily approved it.[287]

The more common view is illustrated by a case decided by the Supreme Court of Utah.   That court declared unconstitutional a change which would eventually have cut off the allowance of a retired teacher.[288]   However, the court suggested that it would have approved legislation making changes for the purpose of strengthening retirement plans.   The legislature had not directly repealed any retirement legislation, but had indirectly done so by enacting legislation permitting the members of local retirement associations to dissolve them by a vote of the members and distribute the assets.   The court agreed with those holding that if the state or one of its agencies encourages employees to enter and remain in service with the expectation of an allowance if they contribute

284. Massachusetts Bd. of Retirement v. Murgia, 427 U.S. 307, 96 S.Ct. 2562, 49 L.Ed.2d 520 (1976).

285. 29 U.S.C.A. § 623. (See Appendix.)

286. E.E.O.C. v. Wyoming, 460 U.S. 226, 103 S.Ct. 1054, 75 L.Ed.2d 18 (1983).

287. Nelson v. Board of Directors of Independent School Dist. of Sioux City, 246 Iowa 1079, 70 N.W.2d 555 (1955).

288. Newcomb v. Ogden City Public School Teachers' Retirement Comm'n, 121 Utah 503, 243 P.2d 941 (1952).

to a retirement fund, when an employee has met all the conditions thereof, the state or agency is bound to perform the contract. The court expressed no opinion as to the constitutionality of the dissolution of the retirement association as it pertained to persons not already retired.

The Supreme Court of the United States decided a case in this area in 1937. The legislature of Illinois had enacted legislation providing for a stated allowance to be paid to retired teachers entirely from tax funds. A later legislative act reduced the allowance for all teachers, both those who had retired and those who would retire subsequently. Certain teachers contended that the original act created a contract between them and the state which could not be impaired. The Supreme Court of Illinois had ruled there was no contract. The United States Supreme Court agreed that the payments were gratuities involving no agreement of the parties and that thus no vested rights accrued.[289]

In more recent years many courts have adopted an attitude toward retirement benefits different from that of most of their predecessors. These courts view them as an inducement to enter and remain in public service, and as such they may be classified as property rights.[290] The Supreme Judicial Court of Massachusetts has discussed the matter and pointed out that ordinary contract law never has been a truly feasible framework for dealing with retirement benefits, even when there was mutual assent in that membership in the plans was voluntary, a situation now almost nonexistent.[291] Considering the benefits as a right of expectancy of employees, the courts will examine any diminutions with reference to the state's need for involving the police power to effectuate them. In the instant case the court approved for prospective members of the retirement system, but not for present members, an increased rate of deduction from compensation.

State constitutional problems can develop when the legislature proposes to increase retirement benefits. An attempt to use the constitutional provision of a state debt limit as a bar to increasing retirement allowances was unsuccessful in Washington. The challenged legislation increased the benefits of all teachers retiring after the effective date of the enactment and made succeeding sessions of the legislature responsible for funding the increases from the state's general fund for fifty years. The highest state court was asked to consider whether this enactment put the state in debt beyond the constitutional limit. Parties agreed that the statute would incur a contingent liability in excess of the limit and that no part of this liability was the result of the issuance of bonds. Because future appropriations would be needed to fund this liability, the taxpayer argued that the debt limit would in effect be exceeded. The opposing contention was that the liability was not a debt in the constitutional sense because the constitutional provision was intended to refer to liabilities created by borrowing money through bonds. The court agreed

289. Dodge v. Board of Educ., 302 U.S. 74, 58 S.Ct. 98, 82 L.Ed. 57 (1937).

290. Olson v. Cory, 27 Cal.3d 203, 164 Cal.Rptr. 217, 609 P.2d 991 (1980).

291. Opinion of the Justices, 364 Mass. 847, 303 N.E.2d 320 (1973).

with the latter view and held the statute constitutional.[292] It stated that the retirement allowance was not a gratuity, but a form of deferred compensation for services performed.

This view of the nature of retirement payments also is relied on to reconcile increases in such allowances with the general principle, written into some constitutions, that additional payments from public funds for services already rendered and compensated for are not legal. The fact that periods of rapid inflation can place retired personnel in a very poor economic condition beyond their control has caused a relaxation of the prohibition against expenditures to raise retirement allowances in some states. In one situation, for example, the Supreme Court of Wisconsin distinguished "moral obligation" from gratuity, the former being "an obligation which, though lacking in any foundation cognizable in law, springs from a sense of justice and equity, * * * but not from a mere sense of doing benevolence or charity." [293] Because the statute in question authorized the additional payments to be made from the funds of the local district, the court held that such payment did not fall within the specific constitutional inhibition, which was held to apply only to the state treasury.

In New York a constitutional provision made retirement benefits contractual and beyond the power of the legislature to diminish. There the state retirement board adopted new mortality tables to take into account increases in life expectancy. If these were applied to members in the system prior to the adoption of the new tables, some of them would have their anticipated monthly allowances based on a fixed contribution reduced. To apply the tables only to those who joined after the tables were adopted would, according to administrators of the retirement system, bankrupt the system. A suit to bar the reductions prevailed.[294] The highest state court held that the attempted reduction was in violation of the state constitution. If the system were threatened with bankruptcy, it would be necessary for the legislature to provide the funds needed for the allowances of those already members of the system. The same court held to be unconstitutional a statute requiring that certain funds of the retirement system be invested in municipal bonds floated as part of a plan to alleviate a severe fiscal emergency in New York City.[295] This could interfere with the integrity and security of the sources from which the protected benefits were to be paid. However, health insurance benefits were held not to be covered by the state constitutional provision. A statute permitted local boards to pay part or all of premiums for such benefits to retirees, and a local board that had decided to do so was challenged when it sought to reduce its percent of

292. State ex rel. Wittler v. Yelle, 65 Wash.2d 660, 399 P.2d 319 (1965).

293. State ex rel. Holmes v. Krueger, 271 Wis. 129, 72 N.W.2d 734 (1955).

294. Birnbaum v. New York State Teachers' Retirement System, 5 N.Y.2d 1,

176 N.Y.S.2d 984, 152 N.E.2d 241 (1958). [Case No. 109]

295. Sgaglione v. Levitt, 37 N.Y.2d 507, 375 N.Y.S.2d 79, 337 N.E.2d 592 (1975).

the costs. The court held that the no-reduction-in-benefits clause applied only to changes directly related to the basic retirement benefit.[296]

A similar provision in the Illinois constitution was construed by the highest court of that state in a case brought to invalidate the governor's item reduction of some appropriations to the retirement funds.[297] The suit failed, the court holding that the constitutional provision did not require a specific level of current funding. A different judicial view was taken in Washington, where the governor attempted to reduce the allocation of general funds appropriated to the retirement fund for the biennium on the ground that general funds were insufficient for state operation. He proposed transfers of money from the pension fund reserve to cover current pension payments. The state supreme court, however, ordered that this not be done because it would have been contrary to legislative intent over the years to keep the retirement system actuarially sound.[298] The court said further that where the legislature had expressed for so long a deep concern for actuarial soundness and had adopted a systematic method of funding to attain the desired soundness, the principle of systematic funding became one of the vested contractual rights of participants, subject only to modifications to keep the retirement apparatus flexible and to maintain its integrity.

Gender-Based Retirement Rates

The general practice of treating women differently from men regarding financial aspects of retirement, in recognition of the fact that women as a group outlive men as a group, was declared unconstitutional by the Supreme Court in 1978.[299] The Court decided that Title VII of the Civil Rights Act of 1964 barred plans requiring women to contribute more than men for equal benefits. It reasoned that Title VII prohibited different treatment of individuals, and that class characteristics were not a suitable basis for comparison. The court added that neither Title VII nor its opinion was intended to "revolutionize" the insurance and pension industries. It said that nothing in the holding should be taken to imply either that it would be unlawful for an employer to set aside equal retirement contributions for each employee and have the retiree purchase a benefit in the open market, or that insurance companies would be prevented from considering the composition of the employer's work force in determining the cost of a retirement or death benefit plan.

In that case the retirement plan was operated by the public employer. In 1983 the Supreme Court held that Title VII also prohibited an employer from offering its employees the option of receiving retirement benefits from one of several companies selected by the employer, all of

296. Lippman v. Board of Educ. of Sewanhaka Central High School Dist., 66 N.Y.2d 313, 496 N.Y.S.2d 987, 487 N.E.2d 897 (1985).

297. People ex rel. Illinois Federation of Teachers v. Lindberg, 60 Ill.2d 266, 326 N.E.2d 749 (1975).

298. Weaver v. Evans, 80 Wash.2d 461, 495 P.2d 639 (1972).

299. City of Los Angeles, Dep't of Water and Power v. Manhart, 435 U.S. 702, 98 S.Ct. 1370, 55 L.Ed.2d 657 (1978).

which pay a woman lower monthly benefits than a man who has made the same contributions.[300]

[Case No. 94] Application of Tenure Statute to Coach

STANG v. INDEPENDENT SCHOOL DIST. NO. 191

Supreme Court of Minnesota, 1977.
256 N.W.2d 82.

SCOTT, JUSTICE. * * *

Appellant, Donald Stang, is a certified, continuing-contract mathematics teacher in District 191 (Burnsville). From the 1966–67 school year through the 1974–75 school year he was also employed as head secondary basketball coach at Burnsville Senior High School. For the 1974–75 school year he received $1,650 as compensation for this position. Stang received the following memorandum on April 25, 1975, from Dr. Harold Bergquist, assistant superintendent for secondary education:

"This communication should serve to inform you that you will not receive a Letter of Assignment (P.S. 4120.1) for the role of Head Basketball Coach at Burnsville Senior High School for the 1975–76 school year.

"This action will not change your position as a classroom instructional staff member in the Burnsville High School District."

Stang immediately filed suit in district court under the teacher tenure act, Minn.St. 125.12. Specifically, Stang alleged that he was a "teacher" within the meaning of subdivision 1, in that certification was required of all head coaches in secondary schools under Rule 345 of the State Board of Education. He further alleged that he had not been given written notice and a hearing as required by § 125.12, subd. 8, of the tenure act. * * *

The question is: Under the facts of this case, does the appellant have a right to notice and hearing under the teacher tenure act?

* * *

Stang * * * contends that his termination as a coach is * * * a "discharge" governed by the tenure act. Minn.St. 125.12, subd. 1, which is applicable here, reads:

"A superintendent, principal, supervisor, and classroom teacher and any other professional employee required to hold a license from the state department shall be deemed to be a 'teacher' within the meaning of this section."

If Stang were protected by this statute, he would be entitled to written notice and an adversary hearing * * *.

---

300. Arizona Governing Committee for Tax Deferred Annuity and Deferred Comp. Plans v. Norris, 463 U.S. 1073, 103 S.Ct. 3492, 77 L.Ed.2d 1236 (1983).

This court decided a case virtually identical to the present one adversely to Stang's position. In Chiodo v. Board of Educ. of Special School Dist. No. 1, 298 Minn. 380, 215 N.W.2d 806 (1974), a head basketball coach of 10 years' standing was informed he would not be reassigned, as is the case here. He brought suit under Minn.St. 125.17 for a declaratory judgment entitling him to written notice and hearing pursuant to that statute. We held that the coach did not qualify as a "teacher" for purposes of Minn.St. 125.17, subd. 1, applying only to cities of the first class, which reads in part as follows:

> "(a) Teachers. The term 'teacher' includes every person regularly employed, as a principal, or to give instruction in a classroom, or to superintend or supervise classroom instruction, or as placement teacher and visiting teacher. Persons regularly employed as counselors and school librarians shall be covered by these sections as teachers if licensed as teachers or as school librarians."

The opinion notes that while "instruction" and "classroom" could be broadly interpreted to encompass the function of a coach, the overall setting of the statutory language indicates that coaches were not meant to be included. The opinion further points out that the legislature could have specifically included coaches within the definition, but did not, and concludes by noting:

> "There is no case law in Minnesota governing the issue presented by this appeal but several decisions from other state courts are brought to the court's attention by defendants and by amicus curiae. While all these decisions can be distinguished on their facts, or on differences in the tenure acts or certification requirements, they are significant in their unanimity in denying tenure to coaches and other similar positions."

The present case is different from *Chiodo* only in the statutory definition of "teacher." Minn.St. 125.12, applicable to school districts not within cities of the first class, includes an additional category of protected persons defined as "any other professional employee required to hold a license from the state department." * * *

The language of the *Chiodo* case indicates the result should be the same here, despite the variation in statutory language, and it is therefore consistent that we so hold. It was also stated in *Chiodo* that the court was "not impressed by the contention that certification as a coach confers tenure upon the coaching position." Stang had like certification. We therefore reiterate that coaches do not acquire tenure rights to their coaching positions under this factual setting. The legislature could have explicitly included coaches in the definition of "teacher," and we feel that such a revolutionary step should only be considered by that body.

* * *

Notes

1. Note the distinction made in the last paragraph between certification and tenure.

2. Observe that here the court relied heavily on one of its prior decisions, which had given substantial weight to decisions of courts in other states.

3. Do you think the legislature should change the statute so as to grant tenure for part-time positions such as coach?

4. Suppose that there had been no extra pay for the coaching position, but that it had been part of the teacher's regular load, which would be replaced with an additional class. Would this be a legally significant difference?

5. For some 25 years a school system had offered to about 20 percent of the staff 11–month contracts obligating a teacher to render 220 (rather than 200) professional duty days "at such assignment as [is] directed by the district." The longer contracts were used as an attraction and incentive. The present court held that the Stang case did not control because the 11–month contracts were "single annual employment" contracts specifying only one salary figure for the period of service; no "extra duties" were involved. The board could not reduce the "period of service of a teacher's general assignment" without following the procedures of the tenure statute. Rochester Educ. Ass'n v. Independent School Dist. No. 535, 271 N.W.2d 311 (Minn.1978).

[Case No. 95] Right of Teacher to Refuse to Accept Student

HATTON v. WICKS

United States Court of Appeals, Fifth Circuit, 1984.
744 F.2d 501.

JERRE S. WILLIAMS, CIRCUIT JUDGE. This is an unusual case in which an established sixth grade teacher, under contract and who had taught sixth grade at the same school for ten years, was discharged for refusing to accept into her class a thirteen year old "disciplinary problem student" who chose her as his teacher in what the discharged teacher calls a "lineup" of the available teachers. The use of the word "lineup" to describe what actually occurred is, to some extent at least, a stigmatizing overstatement. Appellant Ethel Hatton was an established and qualified school teacher under contract to teach in the Columbus Municipal Separate School District, Columbus, Mississippi. She was called into the office of the principal of her school, appellee Marshall Wicks, together with two other available sixth grade teachers. Also present in the office was the thirteen year old male student and that student's mother. The principal asked the student which of the three teachers he would like to have as his sixth grade teacher, and he chose the appellant. The principal then stated that it was settled and the student would be in appellant's class. When the mother presented the thirteen year old boy for enrollment in appellant's class the next Monday, appellant refused to enroll him.

In the afternoon of the same day, appellant was summoned to appellee's office for a conference. When appellee told her at the conference that she was under an obligation to accept the student in her class, she indicated she would not do so and walked out of the meeting without further discussion.

Appellee later wrote her a letter granting her a conference with him, setting a date ten days later. She failed to appear at this conference. In the meantime the child had been assigned to another teacher.

Appellant was discharged for these two instances of what the principal and other school authorities call "insubordination". She was afforded hearings before the Superintendent of Schools, and the entire School Board, and then a review by the Department of Education of the State of Mississippi. All three of these tribunals upheld her discharge.

Five years later appellant brought this suit in the United States District Court under 42 U.S.C. § 1983 claiming substantive due process of law violations on the ground that the public school authorities did not have the constitutional right under the Fourteenth Amendment to discharge her under the facts outlined above. After a full trial, the district court held that there had been no constitutional violation in her discharge. We affirm.

There is no procedural due process of law challenge in this case. Appellant does not challenge the adequacy of the administrative hearings which she was given in accordance with Mississippi law. She challenges only the result of those hearings which upheld her discharge.

Appellant raises the question of whether there was "substantial evidence" in the administrative proceedings and in the district court to establish the existence of a constitutional due process violation. The issue is not one of "substantial evidence", however. The critical and controlling facts in this case are not in dispute at all. They are as reported above. The sole question which is before us, then, is whether the existence of these facts and these events constitutes a violation of appellant Hatton's civil rights under the due process of law clause of the Fourteenth Amendment. That question obviously is a question of law, a question of the interpretation and application of the Constitution. As such we are not bound to a clearly erroneous standard of review of the findings and conclusions of the district court.

No issue was raised concerning the motive for appellant's discharge. The finding, not disputed, is that appellant was discharged for insubordination for twice failing to accept the pupil in her class when ordered to do so by the principal. Thus we do not have the typical mixed motive case so we need not inquire whether or not she would have been discharged absent these circumstances. Neither party challenges the finding of the district court that the discharge was for the overt circumstances shown in this case.

Appellant takes the position that she could not be fired for "insubordination" because under Mississippi law insubordination requires "a constant or continuing intentional refusal to obey a direct or implied order, reasonable in nature and given by or with proper authority." Sims v. Bd. of Trustees, Holly Springs Municipal Separate School Dist., 414 So.2d 431 (Miss.1982). Whether or not her actions constituted insubordination under the Mississippi law does not control this case. Mississippi cannot by defining "insubordination" or other grounds for discharge of teachers create or eliminate federal constitutional rights. The federal rights are independent of the state law. It is not amiss, however, to point out that her two refusals to accept this pupil into her class may constitute insubordination under the Mississippi definition.

Whether or not appellant was insubordinate under Mississippi law, the issue before this Court is whether she has established that her discharge under the admitted facts and circumstances of this case constituted a violation of her substantive due process right under the Fourteenth Amendment. The district court concluded that she had not established a violation of such a constitutional right, and we agree.

The action of the principal may have been somewhat unusual in giving this particular pupil the opportunity to choose which teacher he wished to have in the sixth grade. It should be pointed out, however, that such choice was under the supervision of the principal, who had ruled out two other teachers who otherwise would have been available because their classes were housed in temporary buildings outside the main school building, and the principal felt that this particular pupil might create less problems if he remained in the main school building. Further, while no one disputes appellant's claim that this particular pupil was a "disciplinary problem", he did not constitute such a serious problem that he could not attend regular school classes with other students. After appellant's refusal to accept this student, the student was assigned to another sixth grade class as a regular pupil in that class. Finally, the record reveals that the pupil had rational and sensible reasons for choosing the class of this particular teacher rather than the other two sixth grade teachers who accompanied appellant to the principal's office.

The record reveals that this particular student was being given an opportunity that students generally did not have. But we cannot quarrel with a conclusion of a school administrator that treating a particular student with such care might be to the advantage not only of the pupil but also of the other students in the school as well.

This discussion of the circumstances yields the constitutional answer. This Court would be intruding in the details of the administration of the school if it found a constitutional violation in this case. Appellant was not placed in a lineup. She and two other teachers were simply brought into the principal's room to enable this pupil to decide which class he wanted to go into for the sixth grade. The principal then directed that his choice be implemented, and appellant refused. Later when he attempted to talk to her about it again, she again refused and walked out on him. She makes no showing that she is entitled to any privilege over any other teacher who might have this pupil assigned to her or his classroom. There was not the slightest hint of racial, religious, or gender discrimination, or interference with her free speech or other personal rights. She was simply assigned a pupil for her class who had the right to be assigned to such a class. She refused the assignment twice and was discharged. It must be recognized that under these circumstances a teacher who refuses to carry out her or his obligations in this manner is "interfering with the regular operation of the schools," *Pickering v. Board of Education,* and is engaged in conduct which "materially and substantially impedes the operation or effectiveness of the educational program." Appellant's asserted section 1983 claim must fail.

AFFIRMED.

Notes

1. Why do you believe Hatton went to federal court under Section 1983 rather than appealing to the courts of Mississippi after losing before the state department of education? Notice precisely what this federal court was deciding.

2. The definition of insubordination enunciated by the Supreme Court of Mississippi in Sims v. Board of Trustees, Holly Springs Municipal Separate School Dist., cited in the case, was taken directly from the Supreme Court of Minnesota in Ray v. Minneapolis Bd. of Educ., 295 Minn. 13, 202 N.W.2d 375 (1972). Bear in mind that the definition is offered in connection with a dismissal.

3. A single act has been held to constitute cause for dismissal for insubordination in some jurisdictions. Ware v. Morgan County School Dist. No. RE–3, 748 P.2d 1295 (Colo.1988); Gaylord v. Board of Educ., Unified School Dist. No. 218, Morton County, 14 Kan.App.2d 462, 794 P.2d 307 (1990).

4. Should there be any conditions under which a teacher can refuse to instruct a student? Consider the last paragraph of the opinion.

[Case No. 96] Right of Teacher to Use "Dirty Word" in Class Instruction

KEEFE v. GEANAKOS

United States Court of Appeals, First Circuit, 1969.
418 F.2d 359.

ALDRICH, CHIEF JUDGE. * * *

The plaintiff is the head of the English department and coordinator for grades 7 through 12 for the Ipswich (Massachusetts) Public School System, with part-time duties as a teacher of English. He has tenure, pursuant to Mass.G.L. c. 71, § 41. The defendants are the members of the Ipswich School Committee. Briefly, after some preliminaries, five charges were furnished the plaintiff as grounds for dismissal, and a hearing was scheduled thereon, which plaintiff seeks to enjoin as violating his civil rights. * * *

Reduced to fundamentals, the substance of plaintiff's position is that as a matter of law his conduct which forms the basis of the charge did not warrant discipline. Accordingly, he argues, there is no ground for any hearing. He divides this position into two parts. The principal one is that his conduct was within his competence as a teacher, as a matter of academic freedom, whether the defendants approved of it or not. The second is that he had been given inadequate prior warning by such regulations as were in force, particularly in the light of the totality of the circumstances known to him, that his actions would be considered improper, so that an ex post facto ruling would, itself, unsettle academic freedom. The defendants, essentially, deny plaintiff's contentions. They accept the existence of a principle of academic freedom to teach, but state that it is limited to proper classroom materials as reasonably determined by the school committee in the light of pertinent conditions, of which they cite in particular the age of the students. Asked by the court whether a teacher has a right to say to the school committee that it is wrong if, in fact, its decision was arbitrary, counsel candidly and commendably (and correctly) responded in the affirmative. This we consider to be the present issue.   * * *

On the opening day of school in September 1969 the plaintiff gave to each member of his senior English class a copy of the September 1969 Atlantic Monthly magazine, a publication of high reputation, and stated that the reading assignment for that night was the first article therein. ("The Young and the Old," by Robert J. Lifton, a psychiatrist and professor at a noted medical school.) September was the educational number, so called, of the Atlantic, and some 75 copies had been supplied by the school department. Plaintiff discussed the article, and a particular word that was used therein, and explained the word's origin and context, and the reasons the author had included it. The word, admittedly highly offensive, is a vulgar term for an incestuous son. Plaintiff stated that any student who felt the assignment personally distasteful could have an alternative one.

The next evening the plaintiff was called to a meeting of the school committee and asked to defend his use of the offending word. Following his explanation, a majority of the members of the committee asked him informally if he would agree not to use it again in the classroom. Plaintiff replied that he could not, in good conscience, agree. His counsel states, however, without contradiction, that in point of fact plaintiff has not used it again. No formal action was taken at this meeting. Thereafter plaintiff was suspended, as a matter of discipline, and it is now proposed that he should be discharged.

The Lifton article, which we have read in its entirety, has been described as a valuable discussion of "dissent, protest, radicalism and revolt." It is in no sense pornographic. We need no supporting affidavits to find it scholarly, thoughtful and thought-provoking. The single offending word, although repeated a number of times, is not artificially introduced, but, on the contrary, is important to the development of the thesis and the conclusions of the author. Indeed, we would find it difficult to disagree with plaintiff's assertion that no proper study of the article could avoid consideration of this word. It is not possible to read the article, either in whole or in part, as an incitement to libidinous conduct, or even thoughts. If it raised the concept of incest, it was not to suggest it, but to condemn it; the word was used, by the persons described, as a superlative of opprobrium. We believe not only that the article negatived any other concept, but that an understanding of it would reject, rather than suggest, the word's use.

With regard to the word itself, we cannot think that it is unknown to many students in the last year of high school, and we might well take judicial notice of its use by young radicals and protesters from coast to coast. No doubt its use genuinely offends the parents of some of the students—therein, in part, lay its relevancy to the article.

Hence the question in this case is whether a teacher may, for demonstrated educational purposes, quote a "dirty" word currently used in order to give special offense, or whether the shock is too great for high school seniors to stand. If the answer were that the students must be protected from such exposure, we would fear for their future. We do not question the good faith of the defendants in believing that some parents have been offended. With the greatest of respect to such parents, their sensibilities are not the full measure of what is proper education.

We of course agree with defendants that what is to be said or read to students is not to be determined by obscenity standards for adult consumption. At the same time, the issue must be one of degree. A high school senior is not devoid of all discrimination or resistance. Furthermore, as in all other instances, the offensiveness of language and the particular propriety or impropriety is dependent on the circumstances of the utterance.

* * * We accept the conclusion of the court below that "some measure of public regulation of classroom speech is inherent in every provision of public education." But when we consider the facts at bar as we have elaborated them, we find it difficult not to think that its application to the present case demeans any proper concept of education. The general chilling effect of permitting such rigorous censorship is even more serious.

We believe it equally probable that the plaintiff will prevail on the issue of lack of any notice that a discussion of this article with the senior class was forbidden conduct. The school regulation upon which defendants rely, although unquestionably worthy, is not apposite. It does not follow that a teacher may not be on notice of impropriety from the circumstances of a case without the necessity of a regulation. In the present case, however, the circumstances would have disclosed that no less than five books, by as many authors, containing the word in question were to be found in the school library. It is hard to think that any student could walk into the library and receive a book, but that his teacher could not subject the content to serious discussion in class.

Such inconsistency on the part of the school has been regarded as fatal. We, too, would probably so regard it. At the same time, we prefer not to place our decision on this ground alone, lest our doing so diminish our principal holding, or lead to a bowdlerization of the school library.

Finally, we are not persuaded by the district court's conclusion that no irreparable injury is involved because the plaintiff, if successful, may recover money damages. Academic freedom is not preserved by compulsory retirement, even at full pay.

* * *

Notes

1. The teacher stated that any student "who felt the assignment personally distasteful" could have an alternative one. Is this approach educationally sound? How, if at all, does the problem presented here differ from the problem of offering instruction in sex education (see Case No. 14)?

2. How do you react to the court's view of (1) the "issue" as stated at the end of the second paragraph; (2) the "question" as stated at the beginning of the seventh paragraph?

3. Suppose the board of education (school committee) banned the article and/or the word and subsequently Keefe repeated his actions. Would he be protected under this case?

4. This court was less sure of the bounds of "academic freedom" as regards "dirty words" when it subsequently considered the case of Mailloux v. Kiley, 448 F.2d 1242 (1 Cir.1971). (See text.)

5. In Presidents Council, Dist. 25 v. Community School Bd. Number 25, 457 F.2d 289 (2 Cir.1972), cert. den. 409 U.S. 998, 93 S.Ct. 308, 34 L.Ed.2d 260 (1972), the court held that the First Amendment was not violated by a school board's making a book about a youth's life in "Spanish Harlem" available to junior high school students only on request of their parents.

[Case No. 97] Right of Teacher to Use Controversial Teaching Technique

KINGSVILLE INDEPENDENT SCHOOL DIST. v. COOPER

United States Court of Appeals, Fifth Circuit, 1980.
611 F.2d 1109.

GODBOLD, CIRCUIT JUDGE. * * *

* * *

I. The facts

Cooper was hired as an American history teacher in 1967. The District has no formal system of tenure, and all teachers are employed under annual teaching contracts. Renewal decisions are made each spring for the following academic year. Despite the fact that some complaints were received about Cooper's teaching, her contract was renewed each year until 1972. The number of complaints received was about average for a Kingsville teacher, and most were neither investigated nor discussed with Cooper.

In the fall of 1971, Cooper employed a technique known as "Sunshine simulation" to teach American history of the post-Civil War Reconstruction period. The technique involved role-playing by students in order to recreate the period of history. It evoked strong student feelings on racial issues. Parental complaints about Cooper increased significantly as a result of the Sunshine project. Cooper was twice called before the principal to discuss the project. The District's personnel director was present at the second meeting, and he told Cooper "not to discuss Blacks in American history" and that "nothing controversial should be discussed in the classroom." However, no District official ever prohibited her from completing the project, and she did complete it.

Despite the controversy engendered by the Sunshine project, both the principal and the superintendent recommended that Cooper's contract be renewed for the 1972–73 academic year. The Board of Trustees disagreed, however, and declined to renew her contract. Board members testified at trial and by deposition that they disapproved of the Sunshine project and that the volume of complaints received diminished Cooper's effectiveness as a teacher. Although vague references were made to other complaints, Board members, when pressed, could remember few complaints other than those about the Sunshine project. The district court found that the nonrenewal was "precipitated" by Cooper's use of the Sunshine technique and that other complaints were "minimal in effect."

* * *

[*Section II discussed procedural matters.*]

III. Constitutional violations

* * *

The findings that the Sunshine project precipitated the nonrenewal and that other complaints about Cooper were minimal in effect are not clearly erroneous. We reach this conclusion on the basis of the evidence considered by the district court. Both the principal and the superintendent, to whom Cooper was directly responsible, and who were best able to observe her performance, recommended that her contract be renewed. In his final evaluation of her the principal rated her as "outstanding" or as "thoroughly satisfactory" on each category of her teaching performance. Until the Sunshine controversy arose most complaints about Cooper were neither investigated nor discussed with her, and the Board voted to renew her contract despite these complaints. Several Board members stated in depositions that they thought the Sunshine technique and subject matter inappropriate for a high school history class. Board members who testified that the volume and not the substance of complaints influenced their decisions placed primary emphasis on the Sunshine complaints. One Board member testified that complaints about the Sunshine project were the sole reason for her vote. Finally, the difference between the handling of earlier complaints and the handling of complaints about Sunshine—the latter included two conferences with the principal and several reports to the Board—suggests that all concerned considered the earlier complaints routine and insignificant when compared with the Sunshine project.

The District's argument that the Sunshine project was unprotected by the First Amendment because it was private expression must fail in light of Givhan v. Western Line Consolidated School District, which holds that private expression by a public employee is protected speech. We thus join the First and Sixth Circuits in holding that classroom discussion is protected activity. Minarcini v. Strongsville City School District; Keefe v. Geanakos.

It follows that Cooper's discharge for discussions conducted in the classroom cannot be upheld unless the discussions "clearly * * * overbalance [her] usefulness as an instructor * * *." The district court found that such a condition was not present, and the District does not contest this finding. Thus, the district court's finding that Cooper sustained her prima facie burden of showing a violation of her constitutional rights must be upheld.

The District also argues, however, that it should have been given, and was denied, a chance to rebut this finding by demonstrating that it would have made the decision to discharge Janet Cooper even had it not considered the Sunshine project, citing Mt. Healthy City School District v. Doyle. The district court's findings that the Sunshine project precipitated the nonrenewal and that other complaints were minimal in effect together satisfy the requirement of Mt. Healthy * * *. The district court did not explicitly find that Cooper would have been rehired but for the Sunshine project. However, that court's findings of fact adequately support such an inference. This case is therefore unlike that before the Supreme Court in *Mt. Healthy,* where the district court found only that the protected activity played a "substantial part" in the discharge * * *.

* * *

Notes

1. Observe that no direct order was given to Cooper to change her methodology. If she had been told by the school administrators to change and she did not comply, would the outcome of this case likely have been different? Why?

2. Cooper did not have tenure. Keefe (in Case No. 96) did. Both won "academic freedom" cases. How did the tenure statute make Keefe's path easier?

3. "Academic freedom" re teaching methods did not prevent the discharge of a fifth-grade tenure teacher who required two female students to write a vulgar word 1,000 times after they had said the word aloud. Celestine v. Lafayette Parish School Bd., 284 So.2d 650 (La.App.1973). Nor did it invalidate a demotion based on a teacher's reading to her fifth-grade class a note she had confiscated which contained "vulgar colloquialisms." She explained them to the class and repeated the procedure in another class. Frison v. Franklin County Bd. of Educ., 596 F.2d 1192 (4 Cir.1979). However, where a teacher expressed his disapproval of sexual slang words he had heard used on the playground, the fact that he asked his sixth-grade class to write and define them was held not to be grounds for termination. Central York School Dist. v. Ehrhart, 36 Pa. Cmwlth. 278, 387 A.2d 1006 (1978).

[Case No. 98] Duty of Teacher to Follow Curriculum

PALMER v. BOARD OF EDUC. OF CITY OF CHICAGO

United States Court of Appeals, Seventh Circuit, 1979.
603 F.2d 1271.

HARLINGTON WOOD, JR., CIRCUIT JUDGE. Plaintiff states the issue to be whether or not a public school teacher in her classes has the right to refuse to participate in the Pledge of Allegiance, the singing of patriotic songs, and the celebration of certain national holidays when to do so is claimed to violate her religious principles. The issue is more correctly stated to be whether or not a public school teacher is free to disregard the prescribed curriculum concerning patriotic matters when to conform to the curriculum she claims would conflict with her religious principles.

Plaintiff also claims her ultimate discharge denied her due process of law.

Plaintiff, a member of the Jehovah's Witnesses religion, was a probationary kindergarten teacher in the Chicago public schools. After her appointment, but prior to the commencement of classes, plaintiff informed her principal that because of her religion she would be unable to teach any subjects having to do with love of country, the flag or other patriotic matters in the prescribed curriculum. Extraordinary efforts were made to accommodate plaintiff's religious beliefs at her particular school and elsewhere in the system, but it could not reasonably be accomplished.

The trial court allowed defendants' motion for summary judgment. * * *

In Epperson v. Arkansas, the Court held invalid as offending the First Amendment an Arkansas statute prohibiting the teaching of a particular doctrine of evolution considered contrary to the religious views of most citizens. The Court recognized, however, that the states possess an undoubted right so long as not restrictive of constitutional guarantees to prescribe the curriculum for their public schools. Plaintiff would have us fashion for her an exception to that general curriculum rule. The issue is narrow.

Our decision in Clark v. Holmes is of some guidance. In that case the complaint about a university teacher was that he ignored the prescribed course content and engaged in unauthorized student counseling. We held that the First Amendment was not a teacher license for uncontrolled expression at variance with established curricular content. The individual teacher was found to have no constitutional prerogative to override the judgment of superiors as to the proper content for the course to be taught. In Ahern v. Board of Education the court upheld a teacher dismissal for insubordination on the basis that the Constitution bestowed no right on the teacher to disregard the valid dictates of her superiors by teaching politics in a course on economics. In Adams v. Campbell County School District the court stated that the Board and the principal had a right to insist that a more orthodox teaching approach be used by a teacher who was found to have no unlimited authority as to the structure and content of courses.

Plaintiff relies on a cross-section of First Amendment cases, but they are of little assistance with the specific issue in this case. Plaintiff argues that the defendants are trying to determine and limit the extent of her religious freedoms. The facts do not justify that legal perspective. * * * Plaintiff also cites Russo v. Central School District No. 1 as squarely considering the present issue, but it does not. The court held that a high school art teacher could not be dismissed for her silent refusal to participate in her school's daily flag ceremonies. She would only stand silently and respectfully at attention while the senior instructor led the program. Her job was not to teach patriotic matters to children, but to teach art. The court carefully indicated that through its holding it did not mean to limit the traditionally broad discretion that has always rested with local school authorities to prescribe curriculum.

The curriculum which plaintiff complains about is not spelled out in specific detail, but can be found in the Board of Education policy and the directives of plaintiff's principal and superiors. There is after all nothing innovative or unique in this phase of the curriculum. It is traditional. There was no misunderstanding about what was expected to be taught.

Plaintiff in seeking to conduct herself in accordance with her religious beliefs neglects to consider the impact on her students who are not members of her faith. Because of her religious beliefs, plaintiff would deprive her students of an elementary knowledge and appreciation of our national heritage. She considers it to be promoting idolatry, it was explained during oral argument, to teach, for instance, about President Lincoln and why we observe his birthday. However, it would apparently not offend her religious views to teach about some of our past leaders less proudly regarded. There would only be provided a distorted and unbalanced view of our country's history. Parents have a vital interest in what their children are taught. Their representatives have in general prescribed a curriculum. There is a compelling state interest in the choice and adherence to a suitable curriculum for the benefit of our young citizens and society. It cannot be left to individual teachers to teach what they please. Plaintiff's right to her own religious views and practices remains unfettered, but she has no constitutional right to require others to submit to her views and to forego a portion of their education they would otherwise be entitled to enjoy. In this unsettled world, although we hope it will not come to pass, some of the students may be called upon in some way to defend and protect our democratic system and Constitutional rights, including plaintiff's religious freedom. That will demand a bit of patriotism.

There remains the plaintiff's claim that plaintiff's right to due process was violated by her discharge. It is conceded that as an untenured teacher plaintiff had no property interest in the teaching position. It is plaintiff's claim that her right to freedom of religion is a liberty interest which can only be extinguished by due process. Due process, it is argued, required that plaintiff be afforded an adversary hearing prior to dismissal. The statement of this issue is likewise contorted. Plaintiff's religious freedom is not being extinguished. The Fourteenth Amendment does not create a protected interest, but if one is found to exist by reason of some independent source, the Fourteenth Amendment protects it. * * *

Affirmed.

Notes

1. The Supreme Court denied certiorari, 444 U.S. 1026, 100 S.Ct. 689, 62 L.Ed.2d 659 (1980).

2. Do you think Palmer's religion-based claim was weakened by (1) inconsistencies in her applications (e.g., re different "past leaders"); (2) by expecting too much accommodation of her religion?

3. Observe how this case is distinguished by the court from Russo v. Central School Dist. No. 1 (sixth paragraph). Russo's reason was not religion-based; she thought "liberty and justice for all" was hypocritical in light of contemporary affairs.

4. Notice the case of Clark v. Holmes (fifth paragraph). Even a college teacher has no constitutional right to teach as he pleases.

5. In Millikan v. Board of Directors of Everett School Dist. No. 2, 93 Wash.2d 522, 611 P.2d 414 (1980), it was held that a school board decision to discontinue a team-teaching arrangement developed by two teachers was not an infringement on any rights of the teachers to choose teaching methods. "While teachers should have some measure of freedom in teaching techniques employed, they may not ignore or omit essential course material or disregard the course calendar." In Bradley v. Pittsburgh Bd. of Educ., 913 F.2d 1064 (3 Cir.1990), the court differentiated between a teacher's right to advocate the use of a method of instruction and the lack of a right to employ the method where school authorities expressly disapproved.

[Case No. 99] Discharge of Teacher—Evaluation Procedure

ROBERTS v. HOUSTON INDEPENDENT SCHOOL DIST.

Court of Appeals of Texas, 1990.
788 S.W.2d 107.

EVANS, CHIEF JUSTICE. This is an appeal from a judgment upholding a school district's administrative decision to terminate appellant's employment for inefficiency or incompetency in the performance of duties. The cause was submitted to the trial court on an agreed stipulation of facts and exhibits, and on appeal, only a question of law is presented for review.

The stipulation of facts shows that appellant, Verna Roberts, had a continuing teacher's contract with the Houston Independent School District (school district). On numerous occasions during school years 1982–1983 and 1983–1984, the school district's assessment team, composed of an associate superintendent and an instructional supervisor, evaluated appellant's teaching performance. These evaluations included both written assessments and videotaping of appellant's classroom performance. The evaluation team used videotapes so that the teacher could more easily follow and understand the evaluation team's observations and criticisms. Appellant objected to the use of videotaping in her classroom.

Both the written evaluations and videotapes revealed problems with appellant's teaching performance. Appellant was told of these problems, but according to the assessment team, she did not correct or improve her performance. Based on appellant's classroom performance, the assessment team recommended that the school district terminate her employment at the end of the 1983–84 school year. (Appellant's contract allowed for termination for inefficiency or incompetence in the performance of duties.) The deputy superintendent accepted this recommendation and, in turn, recommended termination to the general superintendent. The deputy superintendent and three members of the assessment team met with appellant and notified her of the recommendation and the reason for their recommendation. On March 9, 1984, the board of education authorized the general superintendent to notify appellant that it had proposed her employment be terminated at the end of the 1983–84 school year * * *.

Appellant then notified the school district of her desire to contest the proposed termination and asked for a public hearing, which was scheduled for June 2, 1984. About 45 days before the hearing, appellant and her attorney were notified of the date, time, place, and procedures to be used at the termination proceedings. Appellant and her attorney were later given a witness list, a description of the testimony to be provided at the hearing, and a copy of the exhibits to be used. Appellant was not, however, given a copy of the videotape exhibits. Appellant asked for copies of all videotapes made of her classroom performance, but the school district refused. The school district did make the tapes available for appellant's review and inspection at its administrative offices.

On June 2, 1984, the school board heard testimony from appellant's supervisors, and it reviewed approximately 100 documents offered as evidence of appellant's classroom performance. The school board also viewed a 30–minute videotape, which included excerpts from the five separate videotapes made of appellant's classroom performance. The five tapes were all used by the assessment team in its evaluation of appellant's classroom performance.

Appellant chose not to testify at the hearing, and she did not present any witnesses or evidence on her own behalf. She limited her presentation to the cross-examination of appellee's witnesses. The hearing lasted approximately six hours, and at the end of the hearing, the school board voted unanimously to terminate appellant's employment at the end of the 1983–84 school year.

In her first point of error, appellant claims the trial court's judgment is flawed, as a matter of law, because she was denied both procedural and substantive due process in the termination proceedings.

I. *Procedural Due Process*

Appellant, as the holder of a continuing contract with the school district, possessed a property interest in her continued employment. The state may not deprive a person of a property interest without due process of law. At the very least, the law requires that a public employee with a protected right in continued employment be given notice and an opportunity to reply prior to termination.

The record reflects that appellant did receive notice and had an opportunity to respond before the termination of her employment.

On February 29, 1984, the deputy superintendent and members of the assessment team met with appellant, and explained their recommendation that the school district terminate her employment at the end of the 1983–84 school year. On March 12, 1984, the general superintendent wrote to appellant, notifying her of the proposed termination of her employment. In that letter, the general superintendent discussed the sections of appellant's contract upon which the school district was basing the proposed termination, and he enumerated specific complaints about her teaching performance. The superintendent stated that appellant had 10 days after receipt of the letter to notify him of her desire to contest the proposed termination, and that she could obtain copies of the evaluation reports and memoranda "touching or concerning" her "fitness or conduct as a teacher."

Appellant also received notice of the time, date, and place of the termination hearing. The school district notified appellant of the witnesses and testimony it would be offering, and gave appellant an opportunity to cross-examine each school district witness and produce evidence on her own behalf.

Appellant's principal contention is that she did not have notice of the contents of the edited videotape. We reject this contention. Appellant was told she could view the unedited videotapes at the school district's offices during regular business hours at any time between May 17, 1984, and June 2, 1984. This was about 10 days before the hearing. Appellant had also previously reviewed the tapes with the members of her assessment team after each evaluation. Although appellant was not given an opportunity, before the hearing, to view the composite tape that had been edited from the five evaluation tapes, she was given ample opportunity to view the five videotapes from which the composite was made. She simply chose not to do so.

II. *Substantive Due Process*

Appellant argues that the administrative hearing, which resulted in her termination, violated her right of due process because "of the nature of the evidence presented and the resulting inability of (appellant) to defend against the evidence as presented."

In evaluating a substantive due process claim, based on allegedly arbitrary state action in academic matters, a reviewing court must ascertain whether the state's action was "such a substantial departure from accepted academic norms as to demonstrate that the person or committee responsible did not actually exercise professional judgment." *Regents of the Univ. of Michigan v. Ewing.* In a suit challenging an academic dismissal, the reviewing court must determine from the record whether there was "some rational academic basis for the decision." If there was a rational academic basis for the decision, the court may not override the state's action, even though the evidence may indicate such action was arbitrarily made.

Here, the school board listened to six hours of testimony and other evidence before deciding to terminate appellant's employment. The board reviewed appellant's teaching evaluations, listened to testimony of appellant's supervisors, and viewed a 30–minute composite videotape of appellant's teaching. Appellant was represented by her attorney during the hearing, she was given an opportunity to testify and to present witnesses on her own behalf, and she was allowed to cross-examine the witnesses called by the school district. Appellant could have even shown portions of the unedited videotapes, had she chosen to do so.

We conclude that the school board did not act arbitrarily or deviate from accepted academic norms in reaching its judgment to terminate appellant's employment.

Appellant further complains that the board saw the composite videotape without any showing that the tape was authentic, and that the tape was not made available to her for copying before the hearing.

Although an administrative proceeding must meet minimum requirements of due process, strict rules applicable to courts of law do not apply to such proceedings. In the absence of some showing that the school district acted arbitrarily in considering the composite videotape, or that the videotape falsely or inaccurately presented appellant's teaching performance, we can only conclude that the administrative proceedings complied with applicable substantive due process requirements.

We overrule appellant's first point of error.

In her second point of error, appellant contends that the trial court erred in granting a judgment for the school district because the termination proceedings violated her right of privacy. Under this point, appellant argues that she had an expectation of privacy in her classroom to be free from intrusion by videotaping, and that by videotaping her performance, over her objection, the school district violated her right of privacy as well as its own policy.

* * *

Appellant has not cited any authority, and we have found none, relating to her claim of "involuntary videotaping" of her performance as a teacher. Based on the record before us, we conclude that appellant has not demonstrated that she had a "reasonable expectation of privacy" in her public classroom. The record shows that appellant was videotaped in a public classroom, in full view of her students, faculty members, and administrators. At no point, did the school district attempt to record appellant's private affairs.

The activity of teaching in a public classroom does not fall within the expected zone of privacy. To fall within the "zone of privacy," the activity must be one about which the individual possesses a reasonable expectation of privacy in the activity.

The right of privacy has been defined as the right of an individual to be left alone, to live a life of seclusion, to be free from unwarranted publicity. There is no invasion of the right of privacy when one's movements are exposed to public views generally.

The second point of error is overruled.

Appellant contends, in her third point of error, that the school district violated its own policy against involuntary videotaping. Under this point, she refers to the school district's Administrative Procedure Guide, section 572.720, which provides:

No mechanical or electronic device shall be utilized to listen to or record the procedures unless requested or permitted by the teacher.

The school district responds to this argument by suggesting that a newer administrative procedure manual has repealed section 572.720, and that the new manual provides:

The Teacher Quality Assurance Program was adopted by the Board of Education on October 7, 1982, and amended on August 4, 1983. The adoption and amendment supercede all prior policies and procedures on teacher evaluation in effect and will repeal and replace any policies or procedures in conflict.

* * *

If videotaping is used * * *, the principal is to make arrangements for the videotaping. The taping session period should be a minimum of one hour/class session with the teacher. Videotaping can provide the teacher with an opportunity to see herself as the assessment team does.

Appellant contends these two sections are not in conflict, and that the section first quoted effectively prohibits videotaping "unless requested or permitted by the teacher."

We agree with the school district's interpretation of its own administrative procedures. The language in the new section expressly authorizes the principal to make arrangements for videotaping, and the quoted section does not require that the teacher must request or give consent to the videotaping. We accordingly conclude that the videotaping of appellant did not violate any of the school district's policies or procedures.

The third point of error is overruled.

* * *

The judgment of the trial court is affirmed.

Notes

1. Observe that Roberts did not take advantage of the opportunity to view (again) the videotapes before the hearing. Also she did not choose to testify at the hearing or present witnesses or evidence on her behalf. In assessing this strategy bear in mind that the standard of proof in a civil case is preponderance of the evidence.

2. The court relied substantially on Regents of the Univ. of Michigan v. Ewing, which involved an academic decision involving evaluation of students. Is a school board reviewing a teacher's performance essentially the same as a medical faculty evaluating a student?

3. No First Amendment rights of teachers or students were violated by the act of placing at the request of school officials an undercover policewoman in two classes to try to obtain evidence of drug sales. Gordon v. Warren Consolidated Bd. of Educ., 706 F.2d 778 (6 Cir.1983).

[Case No. 100] Right of Teacher to Write Public Letter Critical of Board

PICKERING v. BOARD OF EDUC. OF TP. HIGH SCHOOL DIST. 205

Supreme Court of the United States, 1968.
391 U.S. 563, 88 S.Ct. 1731, 20 L.Ed.2d 811.

Mr. Justice Marshall delivered the opinion of the Court.

Appellant Marvin L. Pickering, a teacher in Township High School District 205, Will County, Illinois, was dismissed from his position by the appellee Board of Education for sending a letter to a local newspaper in connection with a recently proposed tax increase that was critical of the way in which the Board and the district superintendent of schools had handled past proposals to raise new revenue for the schools. Appellant's dismissal resulted from a determination by the Board, after a full hearing, that the publication of the letter was "detrimental to the efficient operation and administration of the schools of the district" and hence, under the relevant Illinois statute, that "interests of the schools require[d] [his dismissal]."

* * *

The letter constituted, basically, an attack on the school board's handling of the 1961 bond issue proposals and its subsequent allocation of financial resources between the schools' educational and athletic programs. It also charged the superintendent of schools with attempting to prevent teachers in the district from opposing or criticizing the proposed bond issue.

The Board dismissed Pickering for writing and publishing the letter. Pursuant to Illinois law, the Board was then required to hold a hearing on the dismissal. At the hearing the Board charged that numerous statements in the letter were false and that the publication of the statements unjustifiably impugned the "motives, honesty, integrity, truthfulness, responsibility and competence" of both the Board and the school administration. The Board also charged that the false statements damaged the professional reputations of its members and of the school administrators, would be disruptive of faculty discipline, and would tend to foment "controversy, conflict and dissension" among teachers, administrators, the Board of Education, and the residents of the district. * * *

* * *

To the extent that the Illinois Supreme Court's opinion may be read to suggest that teachers may constitutionally be compelled to relinquish the First Amendment rights they would otherwise enjoy as citizens to comment on matters of public interest in connection with the operation of the public schools in which they work, it proceeds on a premise that has been unequivocally rejected in numerous prior decisions of this Court. * * * At the same time it cannot be gainsaid that the State has interests as an employer in regulating the speech of its employees that differ significantly from those it possesses in connection with regulation of the speech of the citizenry in general. The problem in any case is to arrive at a balance between the interests of the teacher, as a citizen, in commenting upon matters of public concern and the interest of the State, as an employer, in promoting the efficiency of the public services it performs through its employees.

* * * Because of the enormous variety of fact situations in which critical statements by teachers and other public employees may be thought by their superiors, against whom the statements are directed, to furnish grounds for dismissal, we do not deem it either appropriate or feasible to attempt to lay down a general standard against which all such statements may be judged. However, in the course of evaluating the conflicting claims of First Amendment protection and the need for orderly school administration in the context of this case, we shall indicate some of the general lines along which an analysis of the controlling interests should run.

An examination of the statements in appellant's letter objected to by the Board reveals that they, like the letter as a whole, consist essentially of criticism of the Board's allocation of school funds between educational and athletic programs, and of both the Board's and the superintendent's methods of informing, or preventing the informing of, the district's taxpayers of the real reasons why additional tax revenues were being sought for the schools. The statements are in no way directed towards any person with whom appellant would normally be in contact in the course of his daily work as a teacher. Thus no question of maintaining either discipline by immediate superiors or harmony among coworkers is presented here. Appellant's employment relationships with the Board and, to a somewhat lesser extent, with the superintendent are not the kind of close working relationships for which it can persuasively be claimed that personal loyalty and confidence are necessary to their proper functioning. * * *

We next consider the statements in appellant's letter which we agree to be false. The Board's original charges included allegations that the publication of the letter damaged the professional reputations of the Board and the superintendent and would foment controversy and conflict among the Board, teachers, administrators, and the residents of the district. However, no evidence to support these allegations was introduced at the hearing. So far as the record reveals, Pickering's letter was greeted by everyone but its main target, the Board, with massive apathy and total disbelief. The Board must, therefore, have decided, perhaps by analogy with the law of libel, that the statements were *per se* harmful to the operation of the schools.

However, the only way in which the Board could conclude, absent any evidence of the actual effect of the letter, that the statements contained therein were *per se* detrimental to the interest of the schools was to equate the Board members' own interests with that of the schools. Certainly an accusation that too much money is being spent on athletics by the administrators of the school system (which is precisely the import of that portion of appellant's letter containing the statements that we have found to be false) cannot reasonably be regarded as *per se* detrimental to the district's schools. Such an accusation reflects rather a difference of opinion between Pickering and the Board as to the preferable manner of operating the school system, a difference of opinion that clearly concerns an issue of general public interest.

In addition, the fact that particular illustrations of the Board's claimed undesirable emphasis on athletic programs are false would not normally have any necessary impact on the actual operation of the schools, beyond its tendency to anger the Board. For example, Pickering's letter was written after the defeat at the polls of the second proposed tax increase. It could, therefore, have had no effect on the ability of the school district to raise necessary revenue, since there was no showing that there was any proposal to increase taxes pending when the letter was written.

More importantly, the question whether a school system requires additional funds is a matter of legitimate public concern on which the judgment of the school administration, including the School Board, cannot, in a society that leaves such questions to popular vote, be taken as conclusive. On such a question free and open debate is vital to informed decision-making by the electorate. Teachers are, as a class, the members of a community most likely to have informed and definite opinions as to how funds allotted to the operation of the schools should be spent. Accordingly, it is essential that they be able to speak out freely on such questions without fear of retaliatory dismissal.

In addition, the amounts expended on athletics which Pickering reported erroneously were matters of public record on which his position as a teacher in the district did not qualify him to speak with any greater authority than any other taxpayer. The Board could easily have rebutted appellant's errors by publishing the accurate figures itself, either via a letter to the same newspaper or otherwise. We are thus not presented with a situation in which a teacher has carelessly made false statements about matters so closely related to the day-to-day operations of the schools that any harmful impact on the public would be difficult to counter because of the teacher's presumed greater access to the real facts. Accordingly, we have no occasion to consider at this time whether under such circumstances a school board could reasonably require that a teacher make substantial efforts to verify the accuracy of his charges before publishing them.

What we do have before us is a case in which a teacher has made erroneous public statements upon issues then currently the subject of public attention, which are critical of his ultimate employer but which are neither shown nor can be presumed to have in any way either impeded the teacher's proper performance of his daily duties in the classroom or to have interfered with the regular operation of the schools generally. In these circumstances we conclude that the interest of the school administration in limiting teachers' opportunities to contribute to public debate is not significantly greater than its interest in limiting a similar contribution by any member of the general public.

* * *

In sum, we hold that, in a case such as this, absent proof of false statements knowingly or recklessly made by him, a teacher's exercise of his right to speak on issues of public importance may not furnish the basis for his dismissal from public employment.   * * *

* * *

Notes

1. At what point is a teacher "ethically" free to criticize the school authorities in his district through the public press? How, if at all, do the teacher's responsibilities differ from those of any citizen in regard to criticisms of educational practices in the system in which the teacher is employed?

2. The court declined to "lay down a general standard against which all such [critical] statements may be judged," because of the "enormous variety of fact situations" which may arise. What are some changes in fact that could lead to an opposite holding?

3. Judgments upholding dismissals of teachers for actions related to criticism of school authorities were vacated by the Supreme Court and the cases remanded to the highest courts of New York and Alaska for reconsideration in light of *Pickering*. The Court of Appeals of New York held for the teacher by a vote of four-to-two. Puentes v. Board of Educ. of Union Free School Dist. No. 21 of Town of Bethpage, 24 N.Y.2d 996, 302 N.Y.S.2d 824, 250 N.E.2d 232 (1969). The Supreme Court of Alaska reinstated its original judgment by a vote of two-to-one. Watts v. Seward School Bd., 454 P.2d 732 (Alaska 1969), cert. den. 397 U.S. 921, 90 S.Ct. 899, 25 L.Ed.2d 101 (1970).

4. A cause of action was stated by a complaint alleging that an acting principal had been reassigned as a teacher because he gave an interview to a newspaper reporter which led to an article critical of the superintendent and board of education. Washington v. Board of Educ., School Dist. 89, Cook County, Illinois, 498 F.2d 11 (7 Cir.1974).

[Case No. 101] Right of Teacher to Wear Black Armband in Class

JAMES v. BOARD OF EDUC. OF CENTRAL
SCHOOL DIST. NO. 1, ADDISON

United States Court of Appeals, Second Circuit, 1972.
461 F.2d 566.

Irving R. Kaufman, Circuit Judge. * * *

* * * We are asked to decide whether a Board of Education, without transgressing the first amendment, may discharge an 11th grade English teacher who did no more than wear a black armband in class in symbolic protest against the Vietnam War, although it is agreed that the armband did not disrupt classroom activities, and as far as we know did not have any influence on any students and did not engender protest from any student, teacher or parent. We hold that the Board may not take such action.

The facts essential to a resolution of the conflicting interests are undisputed. On June 7, 1969, Charles James was employed as an 11th grade English teacher at Addison High School, located near Elmira, New York. He previously had taught in the New York City public schools. After moving to the Elmira area, James, a practicing Quaker, joined the Elmira Meeting of the Religious Society of Friends.

When November 14 and December 12, 1969, were designated as "moratorium" days by the opponents of the Vietnam War, the Elmira Meeting determined to observe the two days by wearing black armbands. On November 14 James affixed one of the armbands, which had been prepared by the Meeting, to the sleeve of his jacket. He since has stated that he "resolved to wear one of the black armbands as an expression of [his] religious aversion to war in any form and as a sign of [his] regret over the loss of life in Vietnam."

Shortly after school began that day, Carl Pillard, the Principal, entered James's homeroom, noticed the armband, but made no comment. Pillard waited until midway through the second period when James was teaching poetry, apparently without any incident or discussion whatsoever relating to Vietnam or the armband, to summon James to his office and to request him to remove the armband. When James refused to remove it, Pillard sent him to the District Principal, Edward J. Brown. Brown ordered James to remove the armband or risk suspension or dismissal because the armband would tend to be disruptive and would possibly encourage pupils to engage in disruptive demonstrations." When James again refused to remove the armband, Brown summarily suspended him and ordered James to leave the school at once.

The following day James received a letter from the Board of Education of Central District No. 1, reinstating him on "the understanding that [he] engage in no political activities while in the school." James resumed his teaching duties, but, steadfastly abiding by his principles, whether religious (Quakers are doctrinally opposed to war) or political in nature, he came to school wearing an armband on December 12, the second moratorium day. He was summarily suspended as soon as Brown learned that James again had worn an armband. Here, too, the record is barren of a scintilla of evidence indicating that there were any incidents or threats to school discipline, that any students or teachers had complained of or were offended by James's first or second symbolic protest, or that the armband constituted more than a silent expression of James's own feelings. On January 13, however, without affording James a hearing, the Board of Education of Central District No. 1 discharged him from his teaching position in accordance with [a statute covering probationary teachers]. * * *

We come now to the crucial issue we must decide—did the Board of Education infringe James's first amendment right to freedom of speech?

Any meaningful discussion of a teacher's first amendment right to wear a black armband in a classroom as a symbolic protest against this nation's involvement in the Vietnam War must begin with a close examination of the case which dealt with this question as it applied to a

student. Tinker v. Des Moines Independent Community School District,
* * *.

With respect to both teacher and student, the responsibility of
school authorities to maintain order and discipline in the schools remains the same. The ultimate goal of school officials is to insure that
the discipline necessary to the proper functioning of the school is
maintained among both teachers and students. Any limitation on the
exercise of constitutional rights can be justified only by a conclusion,
based upon reasonable inferences flowing from concrete facts and not
abstractions, that the interests of discipline or sound education are
materially and substantially jeopardized, whether the danger stems
initially from the conduct of students or teachers. Although it is not
unreasonable to assume that the views of a teacher occupying a position
of authority may carry more influence with a student than would those
of students *inter sese,* that assumption merely weighs upon the inferences which may be drawn. It does not relieve the school of the necessity to
show a reasonable basis for its regulatory policies. As the Court has
instructed in discussing the state's power to dismiss a teacher for
engaging in conduct ordinarily protected by the first amendment: "The
problem in any case is to arrive at a balance between the interest of the
teacher, as a citizen, in commenting upon matters of public concern and
the interest of the State, as an employer, in promoting the efficiency of
the public services it performs through its employees." Pickering v.
Board of Education.

It is to be noted that in this case, the Board of Education has made
no showing whatsoever at any stage of the proceedings that Charles
James, by wearing a black armband, threatened to disrupt classroom
activities or created any disruption in the school. Nor does the record
demonstrate any facts "which might reasonably have led school authorities to forecast substantial disruption of or material interference with
school activities * * *." Tinker v. Des Moines Independent Community
School District. All we can learn from the record is that in the opinion
of Edward Brown, the District Principal, "wearing the armband would
tend to be disruptive and would possibly encourage pupils to engage in
disruptive demonstrations." "But," the Supreme Court warned in
Tinker, "in our system, undifferentiated fear or apprehension of disturbance is not enough to overcome the right to freedom of expression."

* * *

That does not end our inquiry, however. The interest of the state in
promoting the efficient operation of its schools extends beyond merely
securing an orderly classroom. Although the pros and cons of progressive education are debated heatedly, a principal function of all elementary and secondary education is indoctrinative—whether it be to teach the
ABC's or multiplication tables or to transmit the basic values of the
community. "[S]ome measure of public regulation is inherent in the
very provision of public education." Accordingly, courts consistently
have affirmed that curriculum controls belong to the political process
and local school authorities. * * *

Appellees argue that this broad power extends to controlling a teacher's speech in public schools, that "assumptions of the 'free marketplace of ideas' on which freedom of speech rests do not apply to school-aged children, especially in the classroom where the word of the teacher may carry great authority." Certainly there must be some restraints because the students are a "captive" group. But to state the proposition without qualification is to uncover its fallacy. More than a decade of Supreme Court precedent leaves no doubt that we cannot countenance school authorities arbitrarily censoring a teacher's speech merely because they do not agree with the teacher's political philosophies or leanings. This is particularly so when that speech does not interfere in any way with the teacher's obligations to teach, is not coercive and does not arbitrarily inculcate doctrinaire views in the minds of the students.

As we have indicated, there is merit to appellees' argument that *Tinker* does not control this case, because a teacher may have a far more pervasive influence over a student than would one student over another. Although sound discussions of ideas are the beams and buttresses of the first amendment, teachers cannot be allowed to patrol the precincts of radical thought with the unrelenting goal of indoctrination, a goal compatible with totalitarianism and not democracy. When a teacher is only content if he persuades his students that his values and only his values ought to be their values, then it is not unreasonable to expect the state to protect impressionable children from such dogmatism. But, just as clearly, those charged with overseeing the day-to-day interchange between teacher and student must exercise that degree of restraint necessary to protect first amendment rights. The question we must ask in every first amendment case is whether the regulatory policy is drawn as narrowly as possible to achieve the social interests that justify it, or whether it exceeds permissible bounds by unduly restricting protected speech to an extent "greater than is essential to the furtherance of" those interests. Thus, when a teacher presents a colorable claim that school authorities have infringed on his first amendment rights and arbitrarily transgressed on these transcendent values, school authorities must demonstrate a reasonable basis for concluding that the teacher's conduct threatens to impair their legitimate interests in regulating the school curriculum. What we require, then, is only that rules formulated by school officials be reasonably related to the needs of the educational process and that any disciplinary action taken pursuant to those rules have a basis in fact.

Several factors present here compel the conclusion that the Board of Education arbitrarily and unjustifiably discharged James for wearing the black armband. Clearly, there was no attempt by James to proselytize his students. It does not appear from the record that any student believed the armband to be anything more than a benign symbolic expression of the teacher's personal views. Moreover, we cannot ignore the fact that James was teaching 11th grade (high school) English. His students were approximately 16 or 17 years of age, thus more mature than those junior high school students in *Tinker*.

* * *

Finally, James was first removed from class while he was teaching poetry. There is no suggestion whatsoever that his armband interfered with his teaching functions, or, for that matter, that his teaching ever had been deficient in any respect.

We emphasize that we do not question the broad discretion of local school authorities in setting classroom standards, nor do we question their expertise in evaluating the effects of classroom conduct in light of the special characteristics of the school environment. The federal courts, however, cannot allow unfettered discretion to violate fundamental constitutional rights.   * * *

The dangers of unrestrained discretion are readily apparent. Under the guise of beneficent concern for the welfare of school children, school authorities, albeit unwittingly, might permit prejudices of the community to prevail. It is in such a situation that the will of the transient majority can prove devastating to freedom of expression. Indeed, James has alleged in his complaint that another teacher, "without incurring any disciplinary sanction, prominently displayed the slogan 'Peace with Honor' on a bulletin board in his classroom." This slogan has been associated with our foreign policy. If the allegation is true, and we must assume that it is in light of the summary dismissal of the complaint, it exemplifies the concern we have expressed. The Board's actions under such circumstances would indicate that its regulation against political activity in the classroom may be no more than the fulcrum to censor only that expression with which it disagrees. By requiring the Board of Education to justify its actions when there is a colorable claim of deprivation of first amendment rights, we establish a prophylactic procedure that automatically tempers abuse of properly vested discretion.

* * *

It is appropriate, however, lest our decision today (which is based on the total absence of any facts justifying the Board of Education's actions) be misunderstood, that we disclaim any intent to condone partisan political activities in the public schools which reasonably may be expected to interfere with the educational process.

* * *

Notes

1. The present court relied heavily on *Tinker* (Case No. 114). Are there situations where teachers should not possess as much freedom of action as students?

2. Note that the court did not base its decision on the religious basis of the teacher's act, although he stated the armband was an expression of his "religious aversion" to war. Why, then, was the subject of his Quaker persuasion introduced?

3. *Pickering* (Case No. 100) involved an exercise of freedom of expression by a teacher outside of school. Are there actions which teachers should be permitted outside of school but not inside the classroom?

4. Suppose James had worn a button saying "Elect Robert Roe to get us out of Vietnam." Do you think the court would have ruled the same way?

5. Following this decision and the denial of certiorari by the Supreme Court, 409 U.S. 1042, 93 S.Ct. 529, 34 L.Ed.2d 491 (1972), the school board asserted that the wearing of the armband had caused disruption and that therefore James could be discharged. In a trial on this point the District Court ruled against the board. James v. Board of Educ. of Central School Dist. No. 1, 385 F.Supp. 209 (W.D.N.Y.1974).

[Case No. 102] Discipline of Teacher—Cause and Penalty

BOTT v. BOARD OF EDUC., DEPOSIT CENTRAL SCHOOL DIST.

Court of Appeals of New York, 1977.
41 N.Y.2d 265, 392 N.Y.S.2d 274, 360 N.E.2d 952.

FUCHSBERG, JUDGE. * * * [T]he Board of Education of Deposit Central School District appeals from a judgment which, while confirming so much of the determination of the board as sustained a charge of incompetence and professional misconduct lodged against the petitioner, a tenured teacher, annulled so much of it as sustained two charges relating to physical abuse of his students. The Appellate Division also reduced the penalty from dismissal as of the date of filing of the charges to three months' suspension without pay.

The principal issue is whether the excessive use of force against schoolchildren by a teacher may form the basis for the disciplining of the teacher where the force employed is not sufficient to constitute a crime. We hold that it may.

The two charges with which we are primarily concerned here are one for physical abuse and one for insubordination, the latter stemming in the main from a failure to adhere to regulations and instructions regarding corporal punishment. The board sustained both of these charges after a full hearing at which there was ample opportunity for the teacher to present his defense. The parties concede that, while State law does not forbid teachers from administering corporal punishment, State educational policy delegates its permissibility and control to local school authorities and that, when permitted, corporal punishment must be "reasonable in manner and moderate in degree". Our review of the record here discloses that there was substantial evidence to support the factual determinations of the board. There was proof that the teacher had engaged in repeated acts of physical abuse, some in the face of prior admonitions to the teacher by school authorities, and that he had ignored binding guidelines with respect to corporal punishment contained in the district's teaching manuals and in supplementary instructions communicated to him by the school principal. The board's findings should therefore have been upheld on appeal.

But that does not end the matter.   The teacher * * * takes the categorical position that the two charges must be dismissed because of lack of proof that petitioner's acts of corporal punishment constituted a crime.

* * * [T]he Penal Law grants a defense of justification to parents, guardians, teachers and other persons entrusted with the care of minors who "reasonably" resort to physical force to discipline their charges. However, the statute does not set the standard to which teachers may be held in the performance of their professional duties in a noncriminal context.

Thus, a school district may conclude that the use of corporal punishment is improper when administered in particular circumstances or in a particular manner, irrespective of whether it is or is not a crime. Put another way, disciplinary charges against teachers are not criminal proceedings.   Indeed, their primary function is not punitive, but rather the determination of the fitness of the teachers against whom they may be brought to continue to carry on their professional responsibilities. Moreover, the proof necessary to sustain such charges is not the same as that required to disprove the justification defense provided by the Penal Law.

Nor does the fact that the statute under which the proceedings here were brought does not, in so many words, expressly refer to physical abuse of pupils as a ground on which tenured teachers may be removed mean that the conduct here was not within the embrace of that statute. Although the statute, as relevant to this case, lists only "(a) insubordination, immoral character or conduct unbecoming a teacher [and] (b) inefficiency, incompetency * * * or neglect of duty" as causes for removal, * * * the Commissioner of Education has long held that excessive or otherwise improper use of physical force against pupils comes within the scope of the statute.

It is interesting too that even in [a prior Appellate Division case], assuming that case was correctly decided, while the charges of excessive force were rejected because they were not supported by substantial evidence, the court indicated that, had they been so supported, they could have served to "establish the charges" of insubordination and conduct unbecoming a teacher.

Having concluded that the determination of the board should have been upheld as to all three charges, we also find that the punishment imposed by the board is not so disproportionate as to warrant judicial correction.

We do, however, agree with the Appellate Division that petitioner was entitled to be paid his salary up to December 16, 1974, the date of his termination. Section 3020–a of the Education Law does not authorize the withholding of pay during a period of suspension pending determination of disciplinary charges. The proscription against such withholding may not be circumvented indirectly by fixing the effective date of punishment retroactively.

Accordingly, the judgment of the Appellate Division should be modified as indicated in this opinion.

* * *

Notes

1. The court here succinctly discusses the relationships between criminal
law and civil law as regards a given offense. The principles are not confined to
matters of teacher discipline.

2. Observe that the court disapproved the Appellate Division's reducing the
penalty determined by the board. Under what circumstances, if any, could the
court reduce a penalty placed on a "guilty" teacher by a board of education?

3. Observe the disposition of the pay question. Could the relevant statute
be amended to provide for suspension without pay (payment to be made, of
course, if the teacher eventually was found not guilty of the charges)? See Case
No. 105.

4. Other representative cases upholding terminations for improper use of
corporal punishment include Mavis v. Board of Educ. of Owensboro Independent
School Dist., 563 S.W.2d 738 (Ky.App.1977); Rowley v. Board of Educ. of
Duchesne County School Dist., 576 P.2d 865 (Utah 1978); McLaughlin v.
Machias School Committee, 385 A.2d 53 (Me.1978); Mott v. Endicott School
Dist. No. 308, 105 Wash.2d 199, 713 P.2d 98 (1986); Burton v. Kirby, 775 S.W.2d
834 (Tex.App.1989).

5. That a teacher who allegedly struck a fifteen-year-old student several
times in the face, while ordering students back to their seats at a football game,
could have used unreasonable force was a matter properly in the hands of the
trial court. That court had found the teacher guilty of violating a city ordinance
prohibiting fighting. City of Macomb v. Gould, 104 Ill.App.2d 361, 244 N.E.2d
634 (1969).

[Case No. 103] Discharge of Teacher—Classroom Performance; Board Procedures

KNOX COUNTY BD. OF EDUC. v. WILLIS

Court of Appeals of Kentucky, 1966.
405 S.W.2d 952.

CLAY, COMMISSIONER. Appellant, Knox County Board of Education,
terminated appellee's teaching contract after a hearing upon charges
brought under KRS 161.790. On appeal to the circuit court the action of
the Board was reversed, from which judgment the Board appeals to this
court.

The charges against appellee were for "inefficiency, incompetency
and neglect of duty". The notice of charges with which appellee was
served made specific reference to and included a copy of a "supervisor's
report". This report criticized appellee's conduct of classes, her lack of
control and discipline over her students, and the destruction of classroom furniture. At the hearing substantial evidence was introduced
concerning the inadequacy of records kept by appellee, although this
deficiency did not appear in the charges. The Board found that appellee
(1) failed and refused to keep proper order in her classes; (2) allowed the

children to damage and destroy furniture and to use improper language, and failed to take appropriate corrective and disciplinary measures; and (3) failed to keep proper records. On the basis of these findings, the Board terminated her contract.

The circuit court on appeal found these proceedings arbitrary in almost every respect.

The first ground of alleged arbitrariness was the failure of the Board to furnish appellee with rules and regulations governing procedure in the conduct of the hearing. Apparently the Board did not have such rules and regulations, as the trial court found. Our first question is whether, as appellee insists, the Board is without power to conduct, or acts arbitrarily in conducting, a hearing such as this without written rules of procedure.

We find nothing in the statutes which *requires* a board of education to adopt formal procedural rules for the conduct of a hearing. While KRS 160.290(2) provides that each board "shall make and adopt * * * rules, regulations and by-laws" for the regulation and management of schools and the transaction of its business, we must construe this language sensibly to require such rules and regulations as are necessary and proper. Otherwise a school board could not legally perform *any* act without a pre-established written rule specifically pertaining to it. If we adopt appellee's theory, it would require each board to draft a comprehensive code of procedure for hearings on the termination of teachers' contracts, and if such code failed to cover a single phase of procedure sought to be invoked, the board could not proceed. We simply cannot construe this statute so unrealistically. The average school board would certainly lack the competency to draft such a code.

We believe that KRS 161.790(2), (3) adequately outlines the procedure required for such a hearing, although a board could adopt consistent supplementary rules. As pointed out in Board of Education v. Chattin, Ky., 376 S.W.2d 693, 697, a proper hearing of this nature simply requires "orderly procedure" and "fundamental fairness" and not "the esoteric formalities of a medieval jousting match". Within the scope of "fundamental fairness" we must recognize the necessity for procedural flexibility, particularly since these proceedings ordinarily must be conducted by laymen. As suggested in that case, under proper circumstances resort may be had to our Rules of Civil Procedure.

Appellee's plea for the requirement of technical rules of procedure is really an academic one. She makes no claim that the hearing was not a fair one, that she was denied any right to be fully heard, or that she was prejudiced by the manner in which the hearing was conducted. We find nothing illegal or arbitrary in the conduct of this hearing without written rules of procedure.

The trial court correctly found that the Board acted arbitrarily in sustaining the charges against appellee for failure to keep proper records. She was given no fair notice of this charge, as required by KRS 161.790(2). However, the Board sustained two other charges against her. If she was given adequate notice of these other charges and there was substantial evidence to support them, the Board's action may be upheld even though the charge of failing to keep records was not properly prosecuted.

The trial court found the Board acted arbitrarily in sustaining the charges against appellee which involved the failure to keep proper order in her classroom and the failure to take appropriate corrective and disciplinary measures against students who were guilty of flagrant misconduct. The basis of this determination was that the charges against appellee were not sufficiently specific, and the evidence did not support the findings.

The charges against appellee were for "inefficiency, incompetency and neglect of duty". We agree that these charges, appearing in the "Notice of Termination of Contract", were not sufficiently specific under KRS 161.790(2). However, the notice incorporates a "supervisor's report" wherein certain details are set forth. It is apparently appellee's contention that the details must appear in the formal charges and that an interoffice communication does not have sufficient formal dignity to constitute adequate charges. It is also contended by appellee, and the trial court found, that the "supervisor's report" was not sufficiently detailed.

It is our opinion that the formal charges against appellee, coupled with the facts stated in the "supervisor's report", gave appellee fair notice that the charges of inefficiency, incompetency and neglect were based upon the manner in which she conducted her classes, with particular emphasis upon her failure to maintain any sort of discipline. We cannot go along with appellee's argument that the "supervisor's report" cannot be considered as part and parcel of the charges. This report was incorporated in the formal notice just as an exhibit to a pleading. The informality of the report has no bearing on the adequacy of the charges since we are seeking fair notice to the teacher.

We are also disinclined to agree with the trial court that the "supervisor's report" did not contain sufficient detail. We are convinced that it did give appellee fair notice that the charges were based upon the method of conducting her classes, which resulted in the specified abnormal conditions.

There was ample evidence of intolerable conduct on the part of students in her classroom, and there was ample evidence of a neglect upon her part in controlling her classes and students. Such being the case, we cannot find that the Board acted arbitrarily in upholding these grounds as justification for terminating appellee's contract. It may be noted in passing that there is no claim that this proceeding was politically or otherwise motivated except in the interest of efficient school administration.

* * *

The judgment is reversed, with directions to enter a judgment sustaining the action of the Knox County Board of Education.

Notes

1. In Tichenor v. Orleans Parish School Bd., 144 So.2d 603 (La.App.1962), the Court of Appeal of Louisiana held that a teacher who refused supervision may be discharged on the ground of incompetency and wilful neglect of duty. The court said that "incompetency" is a relative term meaning "disqualification, inability or incapacity."

2. The Supreme Court of Colorado found insufficient as cause for discharge a female teacher's slapping a girl pupil "who wouldn't keep quiet." There was a question as to whether the board had a rule on corporal punishment. The court said that there must be "proof of the school board rule" and also that the teacher "deliberately violated" it to sustain a charge of insubordination. Nordstrom v. Hansford, 164 Colo. 398, 435 P.2d 397 (1967).

3. Proof of incompetency due to mental disability more than a year prior to the teacher's discharge was not sufficient to support discharge when it was not shown that such disability existed at the date of the trial. Board of Trustees of Placerville Union High School Dist. v. Porini, 263 Cal.App.2d 784, 70 Cal.Rptr. 73 (1968).

4. The Supreme Court of Nebraska annulled the discharge of a teacher because of inadequate notice of the charges where he had received a "vague and conclusory" letter, even though he had been granted access to his personnel file. Irwin v. Board of Educ. of School Dist. No. 25 of Holt County, 215 Neb. 794, 340 N.W.2d 877 (1983).

[Case No. 104] Discharge of Teacher—Immoral Conduct; Board Procedures

VANELLI v. REYNOLDS SCHOOL DIST. NO. 7

United States Court of Appeals, Ninth Circuit, 1982.
667 F.2d 773.

KENNEDY, CIRCUIT JUDGE: In this case we examine again the procedural protections afforded by the due process clause when a public employee is dismissed. * * *

* * *

Appellant, George Vanelli, was hired by the school district to teach sophomore English at Reynolds High School during the 1975–76 school year under a probationary contract which ran for one academic year, and which reserved the school board's right to discharge the teacher "for any cause deemed in good faith sufficient by the Board." Midway through the year, some female students complained of offensive conduct by Vanelli. An assistant principal called him to discuss the matter and when Vanelli arrived he was given a letter notifying him of suspension. The meeting lasted a few minutes and Vanelli did not attempt to present his side of the case, though he did request to appear at the school board meeting on March 11, 1976, to respond to the charges leveled against him. He was told not to attend and that he would be given an opportunity to respond at a later date. Vanelli made no attempt to present a written rebuttal to the board, apparently because he was under the reasonable impression the board would not consider it.

The school board met for approximately 45 minutes on Sunday, March 11, and, after the school administrators had presented the case against Vanelli, the board voted to terminate his contract without giving him an opportunity to respond to the charges either in person or in writing. Another school board meeting was scheduled for April 7, 1976, to review the termination decision. At that hearing, Vanelli was represented by an attorney and was permitted to cross-examine the witnesses, all of whom testified under oath. Four of the five girls who filed the complaints were present (the fifth was ill), and the hearing was tape recorded.

Despite certain objections to the procedures at the hearing, the board upheld the earlier dismissal. Soon thereafter, Vanelli sought employment at other high schools, but found difficulty in securing a permanent position due to the circumstances surrounding his dismissal from Reynolds.

The fourteenth amendment's guarantee of procedural due process applies when a constitutionally protected liberty or property interest is at stake. Board of Regents v. Roth. * * * It is well established that an employee dismissed during the term of a one-year contract and in breach of its provisions has a legitimate claim of entitlement and a property interest in continued employment. * * * Accordingly, we hold appellant's midyear dismissal implicated a property interest protectible under the due process clause.

Appellant's interest in liberty is similarly implicated if a charge impairs his reputation for honesty or morality. The procedural protections of due process apply if the accuracy of the charge is contested, there is some public disclosure of the charge, and it is made in connection with the termination of employment or the alteration of some right or status recognized by state law. Under these principles, appellant's midyear dismissal implicated a protectible liberty interest.

We must decide next whether the timing and procedures of the hearing provided by the school district adequately protected appellant's property and liberty interests. We are met at the outset with the school district's contention that a post-termination hearing is sufficient compliance with the due process clause. Under the circumstances of this case, however, we cannot agree.

There is a strong presumption that a public employee is entitled to some form of notice and opportunity to be heard before being deprived of a property or liberty interest. Apart from this general presumption, a court should analyze whether the timing of a hearing comports with due process, given the exigencies and circumstances of any particular case, according to the three part balancing test outlined in Mathews v. Eldridge. The factors to consider include the private interest that will be affected, the risk of an erroneous deprivation of that interest through the procedures used, and the fiscal and administrative burdens that any additional procedural requirements would entail.

Application of this balancing test necessarily compels our determination that under these circumstances a pre-termination hearing is constitutionally required. The weight of the private interest affected is apparent. Teaching had been Vanelli's livelihood for over sixteen years, and the stigma arising from a midyear dismissal on the grounds here asserted would seriously impair opportunities for future employment. The interest of the school district in dismissing, rather than merely suspending, Vanelli without affording him a hearing is less clear. The lower court found no emergency situation requiring immediate dismissal, and on this record we cannot say the finding was clearly erroneous. The risk of an erroneous deprivation was substantial, since appellant was dismissed without an opportunity to confront the evidence and was denied the opportunity to respond to the charges at the school board meeting. The administrative burdens of permitting appellant to appear at the March 11 school board meeting and rebut the charges made against him or present a written rebuttal were minimal. In denying appellant's request to attend the March 11 meeting and thereby proceeding to dismiss him without any opportunity to be heard in person or in writing, the board deprived him of property and liberty interests without due process.

Appellant characterizes the April 7 hearing as a mere review of the March 11 termination decision and, accordingly, claims his right to a de novo trial was violated. Under the circumstances of this case, however, we cannot agree that the April 7 hearing was unconstitutionally infirm because of the board's participation in the prior termination decision. Irrespective of whether the April 7 hearing is labeled a review of a prior hearing or a de novo hearing, the critical inquiry is whether it comported with due process. The key component of due process, when a decisionmaker is acquainted with the facts, is the assurance of a central fairness at the hearing. Essential fairness is a flexible notion, but at a minimum one must be given notice and an opportunity to be heard "at a meaningful time and in a meaningful manner." An individual must have an opportunity to confront all the evidence adduced against him, in particular that evidence with which the decisionmaker is familiar.

The April 7 post-termination hearing met the standards of fairness required by the due process clause. Appellant's counsel was present, he was permitted to cross-examine all the witnesses (except for one who was ill), and was given ample opportunity to rebut all evidence which the school board had heard on March 11. No issues were raised at the prior meeting which were not thoroughly examined at the subsequent hearing. The board members did not have any personal or financial stake in the action, nor was any personal animosity alleged. For these reasons, we uphold the validity of the subsequent dismissal action.

* * *

Judgment vacated and case remanded for redetermination of damages and attorneys' fees. * * *

Notes

1. Four female students complained that Vanelli (in the summary words of the court) "stared at their physical attributes and made statements with sexual overtones. More specific incidents were detailed by the girls, but most seemed

innocuous or susceptible to differing interpretations." Vanelli contacted a teachers organization to represent him at a conference called by the superintendent to discuss the complaints. The day before the scheduled meeting, "a fifth complaint by a female student surfaced," and the purpose of the meeting with the superintendent (on March 9) was changed so as "to discuss his immediate dismissal rather than the complaints."

2. On the point of remand for damages, the court referred to the standards of Carey v. Piphus (Case No. 43), covering situations where due process is violated but the deprivation itself is justified.

3. This case represents a not uncommon occurrence. The school board's decision was ultimately found to be correct, but its overreaction was costly.

4. Justice Kennedy was confirmed as Associate Justice of the United States Supreme Court in 1988.

[Case No. 105] Procedural Due Process before Removal from Payroll of Employee Dischargeable Only for Cause

CLEVELAND BD. OF EDUC. v. LOUDERMILL

PARMA BD. OF EDUC. v. DONNELLY

Supreme Court of the United States, 1985.
470 U.S. 532, 105 S.Ct. 1487, 84 L.Ed.2d 494.

Ohio Civil rights statute

JUSTICE WHITE delivered the opinion of the Court.

In these cases we consider what pretermination process must be accorded a public employee who can be discharged only for cause.

I

In 1979 the Cleveland Board of Education * * * hired respondent James Loudermill as a security guard. On his job application, Loudermill stated that he had never been convicted of a felony. Eleven months later, as part of a routine examination of his employment records, the Board discovered that in fact Loudermill had been convicted of grand larceny in 1968. By letter dated November 3, 1980, the Board's Business Manager informed Loudermill that he had been dismissed because of his dishonesty in filling out the employment application. Loudermill was not afforded an opportunity to respond to the charge of dishonesty or to challenge his dismissal. On November 13, the Board adopted a resolution officially approving the discharge.

Under Ohio law, Loudermill was a "classified civil servant." Ohio Rev.Code Ann. § 124.11. Such employees can be terminated only for cause, and may obtain administrative review if discharged. § 124.34. Pursuant to this provision, Loudermill filed an appeal with the Cleveland Civil Service Commission on November 12. The Commission appointed a referee, who held a hearing on January 29, 1981. Loudermill argued that he had thought that his 1968 larceny conviction was for a misdemeanor rather than a felony. The referee recommended reinstatement. On July 20, 1981, the full Commission heard argument and orally announced that it would uphold the dismissal. * * *

Although the Commission's decision was subject to judicial review in the state courts, Loudermill instead brought the present suit in the Federal District Court for the Northern District of Ohio. The complaint alleged that § 124.34 was unconstitutional on its face because it did not provide the employee an opportunity to respond to the charges against him prior to removal. As a result, discharged employees were deprived of liberty and property without due process. * * *

* * *

The other case before us arises on similar facts and followed a similar course. Respondent Richard Donnelly was a bus mechanic for the Parma Board of Education. In August 1977, Donnelly was fired because he had failed an eye examination. He was offered a chance to retake the examination but did not do so. Like Loudermill, Donnelly appealed to the Civil Service Commission. After a year of wrangling about the timeliness of his appeal, the Commission heard the case. It ordered Donnelly reinstated, though without backpay. In a complaint essentially identical to Loudermill's, Donnelly challenged the constitutionality of the dismissal procedures. * * *

* * *

II

Respondents' federal constitutional claim depends on their having had a property right in continued employment. *Board of Regents v. Roth.* If they did, the State could not deprive them of this property without due process.

Property interests are not created by the Constitution, "they are created and their dimensions are defined by existing rules or understandings that stem from an independent source such as state law * * *." *Board of Regents v. Roth.* The Ohio statute plainly creates such an interest. Respondents were "classified civil service employees," entitled to retain their positions "during good behavior and efficient service," who could not be dismissed "except * * * for * * * misfeasance, malfeasance, or nonfeasance in office." The statute plainly supports the conclusion * * * that respondents possessed property rights in continued employment. * * *

The Parma Board argues, however, that the property right is defined by, and conditioned on, the legislature's choice of procedures for its deprivation. The Board stresses that in addition to specifying the grounds for termination, the statute sets out procedures by which termination may take place. The procedures were adhered to in these cases. According to petitioner, "[t]o require additional procedures would in effect expand the scope of the property interest itself."

* * *

* * * More recently, however, the Court has clearly rejected [this argument]. In Vitek v. Jones, 445 U.S. 480, 491, 100 S.Ct. 1254, 1263, 63 L.Ed.2d 552 (1980), we pointed out that "minimum [procedural]

requirements [are] a matter of federal law, they are not diminished by the fact that the State may have specified its own procedures that it may deem adequate for determining the preconditions to adverse official action." This conclusion was reiterated in Logan v. Zimmerman Brush Co., 455 U.S. 422, 432, 102 S.Ct. 1148, 1155, 71 L.Ed.2d 265 (1982), where we reversed the lower court's holding that because the entitlement arose from a state statute, the legislature had the prerogative to define the procedures to be followed to protect that entitlement.

In light of these holdings, it is settled that the "bitter with the sweet" approach misconceives the constitutional guarantee. If a clearer holding is needed, we provide it today. The point is straightforward: the Due Process Clause provides that certain substantive rights—life, liberty, and property—cannot be deprived except pursuant to constitutionally adequate procedures. The categories of substance and procedure are distinct. Were the rule otherwise, the Clause would be reduced to a mere tautology. "Property" cannot be defined by the procedures provided for its deprivation any more than can life or liberty. The right to due process "is conferred, not by legislative grace, but by constitutional guarantee. While the legislature may elect not to confer a property interest in [public] employment, it may not constitutionally authorize the deprivation of such an interest, once conferred, without appropriate procedural safeguards."

In short, once it is determined that the Due Process Clause applies, "the question remains what process is due." The answer to that question is not to be found in the Ohio statute.

III

An essential principle of due process is that a deprivation of life, liberty, or property "be preceded by notice and opportunity for hearing appropriate to the nature of the case." * * * We have described "the root requirement" of the Due Process Clause as being "that an individual be given an opportunity for a hearing *before* he is deprived of any significant property interest." This principle requires "some kind of a hearing" prior to the discharge of an employee who has a constitutionally protected property interest in his employment. *Board of Regents v. Roth, Perry v. Sindermann.* * * * [T]his rule has been settled for some time now. Even decisions finding no constitutional violation in termination procedures have relied on the existence of some pretermination opportunity to respond. * * *

The need for some form of pretermination hearing, recognized in these cases, is evident from a balancing of the competing interests at stake. These are the private interests in retaining employment, the governmental interest in the expeditious removal of unsatisfactory employees and the avoidance of administrative burdens, and the risk of an erroneous termination. See *Mathews v. Eldridge.*

First, the significance of the private interest in retaining employment cannot be gainsaid. We have frequently recognized the severity of depriving a person of the means of livelihood. While a fired worker may find employment elsewhere, doing so will take some time and is likely to be burdened by the questionable circumstances under which he left his previous job.

Second, some opportunity for the employee to present his side of the case is recurringly of obvious value in reaching an accurate decision. Dismissals for cause will often involve factual disputes. Even where the facts are clear, the appropriateness or necessity of the discharge may not be; in such cases, the only meaningful opportunity to invoke the discretion of the decisionmaker is likely to be before the termination takes effect. (This is not to say that where state conduct is entirely discretionary the Due Process Clause is brought into play. Nor is it to say that a person can insist on a hearing in order to argue that the decisionmaker should be lenient and depart from legal requirements. The point is that where there is an entitlement, a prior hearing facilitates the consideration of whether a permissible course of action is also an appropriate one.)

The cases before us illustrate these considerations. Both respondents had plausible arguments to make that might have prevented their discharge. The fact that the Commission saw fit to reinstate Donnelly suggests that an error might have been avoided had he been provided an opportunity to make his case to the Board. As for Loudermill, given the Commission's ruling we cannot say that the discharge was mistaken. Nonetheless, in light of the referee's recommendation, neither can we say that a fully informed decisionmaker might not have exercised its discretion and decided not to dismiss him, notwithstanding its authority to do so. In any event, the termination involved arguable issues (Loudermill's dismissal turned not on the objective fact that he was an exfelon or the inaccuracy of his statement to the contrary, but on the subjective question whether he had lied on his application form. His explanation for the false statement is plausible in light of the fact that he received only a suspended 6–month sentence and a fine on the grand larceny conviction.), and the right to a hearing does not depend on a demonstration of certain success.

The governmental interest in immediate termination does not outweigh these interests. As we shall explain, affording the employee an opportunity to respond prior to termination would impose neither a significant administrative burden nor intolerable delays. Furthermore, the employer shares the employee's interest in avoiding disruption and erroneous decisions; and until the matter is settled, the employer would continue to receive the benefit of the employee's labors. It is preferable to keep a qualified employee on than to train a new one. A governmental employer also has an interest in keeping citizens usefully employed rather than taking the possibly erroneous and counterproductive step of forcing its employees onto the welfare rolls. Finally, in those situations where the employer perceives a significant hazard in keeping the employee on the job, it can avoid the problem by suspending with pay.

IV

The foregoing considerations indicate that the pretermination "hearing," though necessary, need not be elaborate. We have pointed out that "[t]he formality and procedural requisites for the hearing can vary, depending upon the importance of the interests involved and the nature of the subsequent proceedings." In general, "something less" than a full evidentiary hearing is sufficient prior to adverse administrative action. Under state law, respondents were later entitled to a full administrative hearing and judicial review. The only question is what steps were required before the termination took effect.

* * * Here, the pretermination hearing need not definitively resolve the propriety of the discharge. It should be an initial check against mistaken decisions—essentially, a determination of whether there are reasonable grounds to believe that the charges against the employee are true and support the proposed action.

The essential requirements of due process * * * are notice and an opportunity to respond. The opportunity to present reasons, either in person or in writing, why proposed action should not be taken is a fundamental due process requirement. The tenured public employee is entitled to oral or written notice of the charges against him, an explanation of the employer's evidence, and an opportunity to present his side of the story. To require more than this prior to termination would intrude to an unwarranted extent on the government's interest in quickly removing an unsatisfactory employee.

V

Our holding rests in part on the provisions in Ohio law for a full post-termination hearing. * * *

VI

We conclude that all the process that is due is provided by a pretermination opportunity to respond, coupled with post-termination administrative procedures as provided by the Ohio statute. Because respondents allege in their complaints that they had no chance to respond, * * * the case is remanded for further proceedings consistent with this opinion.

Notes

1. Compare the minimum requirements of constitutional procedural due process that must precede the termination of a public employee where a property interest exists with those that must precede the short-term suspension of a student where a property interest (found in state compulsory education statutes) exists. See Goss v. Lopez, Case No. 127.

2. Bear in mind that: a property right is an individualized benefit that can be withdrawn only for cause; a showing of proper cause by a government body must be accomplished through due process of law; constitutional due process, enunciated by the Supreme Court, is not affected by provisions of state law.

3. How do you react to the Court's reasoning as to the balancing of the interests of the employer and those of the employee before withdrawal of financial benefits can be made? Note the last sentence under III.

4. Would extensive post-termination procedures (and remedies including reinstatement, back pay, and lawyer's fees) suffice to correct pretermination constitutional due process deficiencies? In the present posture of this case, the

Supreme Court did not give attention to post-termination procedures beyond noting their existence as an integral part of Loudermill's property right.

[Case No. 106] Discharge of Administrator—Abolition of Position

VIEMEISTER v. BOARD OF EDUC. OF BOROUGH OF PROSPECT PARK

Superior Court of New Jersey, Appellate Division, 1949.
5 N.J.Super. 215, 68 A.2d 768.

Jacobs, S.J.A.D. This is an appeal from a decision of the State Board of Education which affirmed the action of the Commissioner of Education in directing the appellant Board of Education to reinstate respondent Edmund H. Viemeister as principal in the school district of Prospect Park.

The respondent was employed as principal in 1937 and thereafter duly acquired tenure within the contemplation of R.S. 18:13–16, N.J.S.A. The respondent performed no teaching duties. There were seventeen teachers employed including Miss Amelia Berdan, an eighth grade teacher under tenure, who, in addition to her teaching duties, acted as vice principal. In May, 1948, the appellant adopted a resolution which stated that, in the interests of economy, the position of principal was abolished and the services of respondent terminated, and further resolutions which provided that the position of "teaching principal" be established and that Amelia Berdan be appointed thereto. No charges were ever made against the respondent who questioned the appellant's action and tendered his services at the opening of the school term in September, 1948. This tender was refused; the respondent appealed to the Commissioner of Education who directed his reinstatement; and, on appeal, the State Board of Education sustained the Commissioner's action.

The position of principal is recognized throughout the school laws and the regulations of the State Board of Education. The tenure of office provisions of the school laws expressly designate when "teachers, principals and supervising principals" shall attain tenure and be subject to dismissal only for cause after charges and hearing. R.S. 18:13–16, 17 N.J.S.A. To attain tenure a principal must be qualified to teach (R.S. 18:13–16, N.J.S.A.); but, as Mr. Justice Parker held in Davis v. Overpeck (Sup.Ct.1913), School Law Decisions (1938) p. 470 (not officially reported), having attained tenure he may not, without charges and hearing, be reduced to the rank of teacher and replaced by another as principal. The appellant suggests that the Davis case goes further and would prohibit a Board of Education from assigning, to a principal, teaching functions in addition to his duties as principal. Mr. Justice Parker's opinion does not in anywise support this contention and we find nothing in our statutes or decisions which would deny to a Board of Education the right, which it ought have and presumably has, to assign, in good faith and in the interests of economy, teaching duties to a principal, not in conflict with his duties as principal.

The appellant has contended that it has, in fact, abolished the position of principal and relies upon the cases which hold generally that tenure acts "are not designed to prevent the abolition of an office and the transfer of its duties to another official." In overruling this contention the Commissioner of Education expressed the view (1) that the "position of principal cannot be abolished as long as the school continues", and (2) that the "position of principal in the School District of Prospect Park was not abolished in fact". Without expressing any opinion as to his first finding, we are in complete accord with his second. As we interpret the facts stipulated by the parties, the position of principal continues, as heretofore, and its functions are assigned to Miss Berdan to be performed by her in addition to her duties as eighth grade teacher. The fact that the formal resolutions adopted by the Board speak in terms of abolition of the position of principal and creation of a new position of "teaching principal", which finds no recognition in the tenure statutes, does not appear to be significant. We look to the substance rather than the form and, in substance, the principalship was continued but transferred to Miss Berdan.

The tenure provisions in our school laws were designed to aid in the establishment of a competent and efficient school system by affording to principals and teachers a measure of security in the ranks they hold after years of service. They represent important expressions of legislative policy which should be given liberal support, consistent, however, with legitimate demands for governmental economy. It seems to us that if the appellant had assigned teaching duties to the principal and had reduced the regular teaching staff, with due regard to pertinent considerations such as tenure status, seniority and competence, it would have fairly approached its desired result without impairing the purposes underlying the tenure provisions of the school laws. On the other hand, if the procedure it adopted were to be sustained the tenure of principals generally would rest on frail reeds; nothing would remain as a barrier to the removal of a principal, no matter how long and efficient his service, by the simple expedient of transferring his duties to a member of the teaching staff.

The decision of the State Board of Education is affirmed.

Notes

1. Viemeister was chief executive officer of the school district. In small districts in New Jersey at the time of the case the title of superintendent was not used.

2. In only a very few jurisdictions are chief executives covered by tenure in that post. If the chief executive is on tenure, to what avail is changing the membership of the board?

3. It has been held that a board may abolish a department of physical training and create a new position combining physical training and other teaching and dismiss a tenure teacher holding the former position when the teacher was qualified to teach only physical training. Weider v. Board of Educ. of Borough of High Bridge, 112 N.J.L. 289, 170 A. 631 (1934). This case was cited with approval by the Supreme Court of Minnesota in Jordahl v. Independent School Dist. No. 129, 302 Minn. 286, 225 N.W.2d 224 (1974). There the

court held that there may be discontinuance of a teacher's position even though the functions he performed are spread among other teachers.

4. Where a six-year high school was divided into a junior high school and a senior high school, the Court of Appeal of Louisiana stated that one of the new principalships was lower in "rank, status, position, and prestige" than the six-year principalship and that the other new principalship was higher. Verret v. Calcasieu Parish School Bd., 103 So.2d 560 (La.App.1958).

[Case No. 107] Discharge of Teacher—Abolition of Position

PENASCO INDEPENDENT SCHOOL DIST. NO. 4 v. LUCERO

Court of Appeals of New Mexico, 1974.
86 N.M. 683, 526 P.2d 825.

HENDLEY, JUDGE. After working eight consecutive years for the Penasco School District and becoming a tenure teacher, appellee Lucero was refused re-employment for the 1973–74 year. During 1972–73 he worked as an elementary school counselor. Before that he taught various subjects in the high school. At a termination hearing, the local school board found cause for refusal to reemploy Lucero in that: (1) funding for his position as elementary school counselor was unavailable in 1973–74, and (2) no other position was available for which he was qualified. The State Board of Education reversed the local board's decision. The local board appeals, claiming there was substantial evidence to support its two findings. Lucero and the state board do not argue the substantiality of the evidence supporting the finding that funds were unavailable for the elementary school counselor's position. They argue solely that there was insubstantial evidence that no other position was available for which he was qualified. Our review is limited to this issue. We agree with Lucero and the state board and affirm.

* * * We review the state board's determination to assure it is not "arbitrary, unlawful, unreasonable or capricious."

The controlling rule on the local board's power to terminate a tenure teacher was stated in Swisher v. Darden, 59 N.M. 511, 287 P.2d 73 (1955):

"* * * Absent grounds personal to the teacher, to terminate her services it * * * [is] necessary to show affirmatively that there * * * [is] no position available which she * * * [is] qualified to teach. * * *"

The Penasco board asserted no grounds personal to the teacher in this case. It was therefore up to them to prove the negative—that no position was available for which Lucero was qualified. They fail to do this.

The evidence establishes that Jose Rodriguez was a non-tenure teacher. He was to teach only "Resource Room—Special Education" at the high school in 1973–74. At the time of the local board hearing, he was not certified to teach special education. He was, however, enrolled in summer courses that would give him the requisite education for certification in the area. He was also certified to teach biology and general science.

Alonzo Lucero is a tenure teacher and had taught at the high school level prior to his year as counselor. He was not certified to teach special education at the time of the local board hearing. However, he repeatedly expressed a desire to take the same courses Rodriguez had enrolled in, become certified and teach special education. He was certified to teach biology and general science like Rodriguez. In addition he had certification in chemistry, social science, American history and world history. As to qualification for teaching special education measured by certification, he was in the same position as Rodriguez. There is nothing in the record to indicate he was educationally less qualified than Rodriguez to teach special education. The only mention of relative qualification to teach special education came from Superintendent Duran. The board's lawyer asked him: "In your opinion are you able to determine whether or not Jose Rodriguez would be a more effective resource person than Mr. Lucero?" Duran answered: "I am not able to determine as far as next year in the resource room. * * *" The school district had, by hiring Rodriguez, found him to be qualified to teach special education, provided he took the summer courses. Since Lucero's qualifications on the record are as good or better than those of Rodriguez, and since Lucero is willing to attend the courses for which Rodriguez is enrolled, Lucero must also be considered qualified. Further, since Lucero has more additional certifications than Rodriguez, hiring him would if anything, expand the curriculum possibilities of the school.

The school district counters by contending that since Lucero did not teach any courses in the high school in the prior year, but was a counselor in the elementary school, the high school need not include him in its curriculum. The school district, however, does not assert that Lucero lost his tenure by working as elementary school counselor. Indeed, [the tenure statute] requires only that a certified school instructor be "* * * employed by a school district * * *." It does not limit that employment to teaching positions or to employment in a single school within that district. Although administrators [are excepted] from the tenure statute, a counselor is not an administrator. Any argument to that effect is without merit.

We affirm the decision of the state board. Appellee Alonzo Lucero must be reinstated.

* * *

Notes

1. Note that the "controlling rule on the local board's power to terminate a tenure teacher" was established by the Supreme Court of New Mexico nineteen years before, not by the legislature. In 1988 the Supreme Court of New Mexico, while expressly reaffirming both that case and this case, approved the termination of a tenure teacher and the retention of a nontenure teacher "as an alternative to a staff realignment which would seriously affect the [school] program." New Mexico State Bd. of Educ. v. Abetya, 107 N.M. 1, 751 P.2d 685 (1988).

2.   Consider the various reasons for its act asserted by the board.   Are they convincing educationally?

3.   Many cases involving reductions in school staffing for economic reasons can be prevented by giving legislative attention to details in tenure laws.   Where legislation on a subject contains gaps, the courts must fill them in when presented with proper cases.   Analyze the pertinent statutes in your state and decide what, if any, legislative action is called for.

4.   While a bona fide economic reason will support abolition of a position and termination or reassignment of the incumbent, courts will invalidate dismissals where the economic reason is a subterfuge.   Walker v. Wildwood Bd. of Educ., 120 N.J.L. 408, 199 A. 392 (1938).

5.   A teacher under tenure in Pennsylvania who had been teaching a ninth grade class was reassigned to teach a sixth grade class.   She sued to require tenure procedure to be followed, maintaining that this was a demotion because the sixth grade was in elementary school and the ninth grade in secondary.   Her suit was not successful.   Appeal of Santee, 397 Pa. 601, 156 A.2d 830 (1959).   A high school assistant principal in Massachusetts, however, successfully claimed that assignment as middle school assistant principal was a demotion.   Powers v. Freetown-Lakeville Regional School Dist. Committee, 392 Mass. 656, 467 N.E.2d 203 (1984).

[Case No. 108] Reduction in Force—Selection of Teacher

DYKEMAN v. BOARD OF EDUC. OF SCHOOL DIST. OF COLERIDGE, CEDAR COUNTY

Supreme Court of Nebraska, 1982.
210 Neb. 596, 316 N.W.2d 69.

BOSLAUGH, JUSTICE.   This is an appeal * * * to review an order of the Board of Education of the School District of Coleridge, Cedar County, Nebraska, terminating the contract of the plaintiff pursuant to a reduction in force.   The District Court found that the action of the Board was not arbitrary or capricious * * *.

The plaintiff had been employed by the district for 6 years as a business education teacher.   In 1980 the Board determined that it was necessary to reduce its staff for the next school year and that a teacher in the business education department of the high school should be dropped from the staff.   There were two teachers employed to teach business education, both of whom were tenured, and whose teaching certificates contained identical endorsements.

In deciding which teacher should be dropped from the staff, the Board considered the contribution that each made to the activities program.   The plaintiff was co-sponsor of the annual staff [sic] and sponsor of the sophomore class.   For her duties in connection with the activities program, the plaintiff was paid an additional $228, amounting to 2.5 percent of her annual base salary.   The other teacher, who had been employed for 3 years and was retained, was the assistant volleyball coach, head girls' basketball coach, and co-sponsor of the "C" Club.   For these duties he was paid an additional $1,592.50, which amounted to 17.5 percent of his annual base salary.

The reduction in force policy which the Board had adopted pursuant to Neb.Rev.Stat. § 79–1254.05 (Cum.Supp.1980) provided in part: "Within the separate category of tenured teachers, the process of selecting personnel for termination will involve consideration of (listed in order of priority):

"1. Certification and area(s) of endorsement.

"2. Program to be offered.

"3. Contribution to the activity program.

"4. Length of uninterrupted service.

"5. Special qualifications that may require specific training and/or experience. Part-time employees shall have lowest priority for retention."

The plaintiff contends that a school board may not consider the contribution teachers make to an activities program in making a reduction in force. * * *

* * *

Although § 79–1254.05 does not specifically authorize consideration of a teacher's contribution to an activities program as a criterion to be used in making a reduction in force, neither does it prohibit its use as a criterion. Certainly, extracurricular activities such as athletics are generally considered to be important parts of any educational program. It has been held that a school board may impose extracurricular activity duties upon a teacher as a condition to continued employment in the system.

It is generally held that the selection of a teacher to be eliminated from the staff through a reduction in force is an executive or administrative function as distinguished from quasi-judicial action.

In the absence of statutory or contractual restrictions, the decision of a school board in such a matter is generally subject to but a limited review. School boards should have broad discretionary powers in such matters free from judicial interference in the absence of a finding that their actions were arbitrary and capricious.

In making a selection of the teacher to be dismissed pursuant to a reduction in force, the school board may exercise its discretion and consider noneducational factors as well as educational ones.

The board of education is given the general authority to manage and direct the schools within the district. This includes the power to conduct nonteaching and extracurricular duties as a part of the educational program. It follows that the board may consider a teacher's contribution to the activities program when deciding upon a reduction in force.

The judgment of the District Court is affirmed.

Notes

1. Nebraska required local districts to articulate the criteria to be used in reduction-in-force situations. Do you approve of the ones adopted by this district?

2. The teacher attempted to buttress her basic claim by noting that the present court had held that the tenure law did not apply to coaching duties. Neal v. School Dist. of York, 205 Neb. 558, 288 N.W.2d 725 (1980). The court found the case inapposite.

3. Why did the court include data as to amounts of extra pay for extra duties earned by the two business education teachers?

4. Where notice-of-termination requirements are part of a teacher's contract, they will be enforced in cases of reduction in staff. Zimmerman v. Minot State College, 198 N.W.2d 108 (N.D.1972).

5. Seniority generally is viewed by the courts to be a rational criterion to be considered in making personnel decisions. There is no common-law requirement that it be used or be given particular weight if it is used. Board of Educ. of County of Wood v. Enoch, 186 W.Va. 712, 414 S.E.2d 630 (1992).

[Case No. 109] Constitutional Designation of Membership in Retirement System as Contractual

BIRNBAUM v. NEW YORK STATE TEACHERS RETIREMENT SYSTEM

Court of Appeals of New York, 1958.
5 N.Y.2d 1, 176 N.Y.S.2d 984, 152 N.E.2d 241.

CONWAY, CHIEF JUDGE. * * *

This is an action for a declaratory judgment brought by plaintiffs on behalf of themselves and all other school teachers in the State of New York similarly situated. They challenge the validity of the action of the defendant, the New York State Teachers Retirement System, in adopting on or about January 9, 1946, an actuarial table for computing the annuity benefits of the members of the defendant pursuant to subdivisions 4 and 5 of section 508 of the Education Law of the State of New York. Their contention is that the action of the defendant constitutes a breach of the contractual relationship established by section 7 of article V of the Constitution of the State of New York, as to members of the retirement system prior to the effective date (July 1, 1940) of the constitutional provision.

The complaint alleges, and the answer admits, that since 1920 the Education Law has established a retirement system for public school-teachers within the State whereby the teachers make regular contributions to a retirement fund and receive in return upon their retirement an annuity; that the plaintiffs have made the required contributions, the plaintiff Birnbaum since 1935 and the plaintiff Cate since 1922; that they are eligible to retire after having completed 25 years of service and having attained the age of 60 years or over; and that the mortality table adopted on January 9, 1946, reduces by approximately 5% the amount to be paid to the plaintiffs pursuant to the table in use on July 1, 1940, when section 7 of article V of the Constitution went into effect.

The answer pleads two affirmative defenses. The first is that the plaintiffs have no present interest in the subject matter of the action and will have none until and when, if ever, they seek retirement and apply for their retirement benefits. The second is that subdivision 4 of section 508 of the Education Law mandates the periodical adjustment of annuity benefits payable upon retirement according to mortality and actuarial tables adopted pursuant to subdivisions 4 and 5 of section 508 of the Education Law, and that such section constitutes and forms part of the contract between each member of the retirement system and the New York State Teachers Retirement System.

* * *

* * * The Education Law provides that the "annuity * * * shall be the actuarial equivalent of his accumulated contributions at the time of his [the member's] retirement".

The term "actuarial equivalent" has reference to the mathematical formula for computing annuity payments according to the mortality table calculated and adopted pursuant to the provisions of subdivisions 4 and 5 of section 508 of the Education Law.

The issue in this case relates solely to the use of new mortality tables to compute the "annuity" which is payable upon retirement from funds contributed by the member. When the Teachers Retirement System adopted new mortality tables in 1946, the new tables were made applicable to the computation of all annuities of all members who had not previously retired. The new tables, as mentioned earlier, have the effect of reducing the annuities of all members of the system by approximately 5%.

As a practical matter, the controversy here comes to this: Plaintiffs argue that the contractual arrangement which the Constitution envisaged was the usual annuity policy whereby an insurance company, on the day the policy is issued, agrees that it will pay periodically a fixed and stated amount commencing on a certain date and that, viewed in that light, it was intended that a teacher who was a member of the Retirement System on July 1, 1940, after making the required contributions to the Retirement System over the required period of time, should receive an annuity computed from mortality tables in use on July 1, 1940 (the date the constitutional amendment became effective). The defendant Retirement System, on the other hand, maintains that it was intended that the Retirement System should determine, at the time of retirement, the amount of annuity which the member's contributions will purchase at the time of retirement, employing the mortality table in effect at the time of making such calculation.

* * *

* * * [T]his court [has] held that where the statutory conditions for retirement from the civil service have been met "and the award of the pension or benefit has been made, or as of right should have been made * * * the interest becomes vested and takes on the attributes of a contract, which, in the absence of statutory reservations, may not legally be diminished or otherwise adversely affected by subsequent legislation". We pointed out, however, that "[w]here the statutory scheme creates a fund wholly or largely out of public moneys, the interest of the member down to the point where there has been compliance with all precedent conditions and the award has been or as of right should have been made can hardly be deemed contractual" and that "whatever its legal nature may be, there seems to be no doubt that it is subject to change or even to revocation at the will of the Legislature." Thereafter, in 1938, section 7 of article V of the New York State Constitution was adopted by the Constitutional Convention and approved by the people. It reads: "After July first, nineteen hundred forty, membership in any pension or retirement system of the state or of a civil division thereof shall be a contractual relationship, the benefits of which shall not be diminished or impaired."

It seems clear that the foregoing constitutional provision was designed to overcome the dictum in the Roddy case, supra, to the effect that *prior to retirement,* pension and retirement systems of the State or of a civil division thereof, created wholly or largely out of public moneys, were subject to the will of the Legislature. By the constitutional amendment the people determined to confer contractual protection upon the benefits of pension and retirement system of the State and of the civil divisions thereof, and to prohibit their diminution or impairment *prior to retirement.* * * *

* * *

While it is clear that section 508 contemplates a periodic review of the mortality tables to be used in determining the amounts of annuities to be allowed on the basis of the contributions of members, the section nowhere declares that mortality tables adopted after a person has become a member of the system are to be employed in determining the annuity benefits to which such person is entitled upon retirement. Nor do we see that we should read such an intention into the statute. The constitutional amendment, as demonstrated above, prohibits official action during a public employment membership in a retirement system which adversely affects the amount of the retirement benefits payable to the members on retirement under laws and conditions existing at the time of his entrance into retirement system membership. If we are to construe section 508 of the Education Law as authorizing that which the Constitution prohibits, then, the statute must be held to have been superseded by the constitutional amendment. It seems to us that there is no necessity for so holding since it is reasonable to construe the Education Law as authorizing (1) a periodic review by the State Teachers Retirement System of the mortality tables being used to compute annuities, (2) the adoption of new mortality tables, and (3) the use of the new mortality tables in the computation of the annuities *of only such persons as enter the system thereafter.*

Defendant argues that if this court holds that new mortality tables adopted by the Retirement System are applicable only to those persons who joined the system subsequent to the date of such adoption, the system will be plunged into bankruptcy. The answer to that argument must be that if the people intended to decree, by the constitutional amendment, that mortality tables adopted by the system after one has become a member are not to be applied in the computation of the annuity of such person, we are not at liberty to hold otherwise simply because the system may become bankrupt as a result. * * * If bankruptcy now threatens to overtake the Teachers Retirement System, the system must turn to the Legislature for financial assistance. It may not ask us to ignore the will of the people as expressed in their Constitution.

* * *

Notes

1. Constitutionally protected retirement allowances exist in only a few states. What are the pros and cons of designating retirement rights as contractual in nature?

2. In 1937 the Supreme Court of the United States held that Illinois could reduce the allowances of teachers who had already retired as well as those to be retired subsequently because the retirement allowances were paid wholly from tax funds. The Court said, "The presumption is that such a law is not intended to create private contractual or vested rights, but merely declares a policy to be pursued until the Legislature shall ordain otherwise. * * * If, upon a construction of the statute, it is found that the payments are gratuities, involving no agreement of the parties, the grant of them creates no vested right." Dodge v. Board of Educ., 302 U.S. 74, 58 S.Ct. 98, 82 L.Ed. 57 (1937).

3. In *Dodge,* supra Note 2, the Court rejected the argument that because the statute in question used the word "annuity," rather than "pension," contract rights accrued. The Court found that the words "pension," "benefit," and "annuity" had been used interchangeably as having the same connotation by the Illinois legislature.

4. In 1984 the Court of Appeals of New York again construed the state constitutional provision. It invalidated a 1983 statute that barred refunds before age 62 (or death) for employees who left the retirement system before vesting of benefits. Previously such refunds had been made upon termination of employment. The court said that the change could be made effective for new members, but not for those already employed. Public Employees Federation, AFL–CIO v. Cuomo, 62 N.Y.2d 450, 478 N.Y.S.2d 588, 467 N.E.2d 236 (1984).

Chapter 12

STUDENT PERSONNEL[1]

Compulsory Education

In General

Statutes requiring compulsory education of children within certain ages have long formed the backbone of the American educational system. These statutes have uniformly been sustained against various charges that individual liberties guaranteed by the Constitution are unreasonably infringed.[2] The courts have found that the enactment of compulsory attendance laws is a valid exercise of the police power of the state. The welfare of the state is served by the creation of an enlightened citizenry. These statutes make it the duty of parents or guardians to see that their children are educated and provide penalties for noncompliance. Also the statutes grant a right to children of specified ages to attend the public schools. Usually criteria for exceptions, such as mental or physical disability, are covered in the laws. In the enforcement of compulsory education legislation the aim is to strike a reasonable balance between the rights of the individual and those of the state. The individual is obliged to sacrifice a measure of freedom of action for the good of the state. There exists, however, a point beyond which the state may not go without violating basic rights guaranteed by the Constitution. That point cannot be determined abstractly, since the inquiry concerns the reasonableness of the restrictions sought to be imposed in each case. As personal rights cherished by both parents and students are involved, it is not surprising that the number of cases decided by courts in this area is large.

There is a basic constitutional limitation placed on compulsory education statutes. It is that attendance at a public school is not the sole way to satisfy the requirement. Since the fundamental purpose of the statutes is to require that one obtain a minimum level of education, it follows that the education itself, rather than the place of the education, is at the heart of the matter. The Supreme Court expressed the constitutional principle in invalidating an Oregon law requiring normal children between the ages of eight and sixteen to attend public schools.[3] Although the action was brought by private school operators seeking to avoid being forced out of business and basing their claim on property rights, the issue of parents' rights was raised and considered by the

1. Other aspects of the basic legal status of students are presented in Chapter 4.

2. Parr v. State, 117 Ohio St. 23, 157 N.E. 555 (1927); Concerned Citizens for Neighborhood Schools, Inc. v. Board of

Educ. of Chattanooga, 379 F.Supp. 1233 (E.D.Tenn.1974).

3. Pierce v. Society of the Sisters of the Holy Names of Jesus and Mary, 268 U.S. 510, 45 S.Ct. 571, 69 L.Ed. 1070 (1925).

Court. The balance struck in that decision was that parents had the right to direct the upbringing of their children and could send them to private schools, but that the state could establish certain minimum standards of education for the schools. The state has the power, said the Court, "reasonably to regulate all schools, to inspect, supervise, and examine them, their teachers and pupils."

In 1972 the Supreme Court held that the free exercise of religion clause of the First Amendment prevented a state from requiring Amish children to submit to compulsory formal education requirements beyond the eighth grade.[4] The Court said that the Amish had made a convincing showing that for almost three hundred years their sustained faith had pervaded and regulated their whole mode of life, and this would be gravely endangered if not destroyed by enforcement of the requirement of compulsory formal education beyond the eighth grade. The Court stated that there was no doubt as to the power of a state to impose reasonable regulations for the control and duration of basic education. But in the balancing process of weighing competing interests, weight must be given to the First Amendment and to the "traditional interest" of parents with respect to the religious upbringing of their children. Only those interests of the highest order and not otherwise served can overbalance legitimate claims to the free exercise of religion. The Court noted that Wisconsin statutes required only two years more education than the Amish would accept. It observed that compulsory education age limits historically were related to child labor laws, and that the latter historically permitted earlier school-leaving ages for those entering agricultural employment, which in effect was what the Amish children were doing after eighth grade. The Court said it could not overemphasize that the Amish were not a group claiming to have "recently discovered some 'progressive' or more enlightened process for rearing children for modern life." It cautioned that courts must move with great care in performing the sensitive and delicate task of evaluating religious claims for exemptions from generally applicable educational requirements. Moreover, it was not ruling out the power of the state to promulgate reasonable standards for continuing agricultural education under parental or church guidance so long as there was no impairment of the free exercise of religion. A partial dissent by Justice Douglas was predicated on a right of the child separate from that of the parent. He was wary of the possibility of a child's "being harnessed" to the Amish way of life without an opportunity to express personal preferences. The opinion of the Court expressly responded to the point by stating that the issue was not in the case, having not been introduced by either party.

It becomes clear that few, if any, other religions can meet the test set by the preceding case for avoiding compulsory education requirements. Except for the Amish, appellate courts have been uniform in denying religion-based applications for exceptions to substantial or mate-

---

4. Wisconsin v. Yoder, 406 U.S. 205, 92 S.Ct. 1526, 32 L.Ed.2d 15 (1972). [Case No. 110]

rial parts of the compulsory education requirement.[5] Excuses from specific curricular elements are discussed in Chapter 4. Where the health or safety of a child is imminently threatened, the parent may withdraw the child temporarily, but the facts must establish a clear and present threat.[6]

Equivalent Instruction

One electing not to attend public school must obtain equivalent instruction elsewhere. Attempts to meet this obligation have been made through instruction at private schools or home instruction. Actually the two can become merged in litigation, as it is sometimes claimed that instruction in a family group constitutes a private school. Some states have statutes which provide that instruction shall be had only in a public or approved private school. Such provisions generally have been sustained by the courts.[7]

In a complicated case decided by the Supreme Court of Washington it was found that home instruction did not satisfy the law covering attendance at a private school.[8] The court described the character of a school as being that of a regularly organized and existing institution making a business of instructing children of school age in the required studies for the full time required by the laws of the state. There are, according to the court, three essential elements of a school: the teacher, the pupil or pupils, and the place or institution. In this case the court found that the arrangement did not meet the requirements because there was no qualified teacher. The parent who was doing the teaching did not hold a teaching certificate. That attendance at the public school conflicted with the religious beliefs of the family was not accepted as a basis for not complying with the compulsory education law. The tenets of the family's religion barred being present where meat, fish, or fowl was served or where music was played.

Statutes and state-level regulations establishing requirements for equivalent instruction (such as qualifications of teachers, subjects taught, and time devoted to study) generally have been upheld.[9] An exception was the finding by the Supreme Court of Ohio that the minimum standards in that state were "so pervasive and all-encompass-

---

5. Rice v. Commonwealth, 188 Va. 224, 49 S.E.2d 342 (1948); Duro v. District Attorney, Second Judicial Dist. of North Carolina, 712 F.2d 96 (4 Cir.1983), cert. den. 465 U.S. 1006, 104 S.Ct. 998, 79 L.Ed.2d 230 (1984).

6. Zebra v. School Dist. of City of Pittsburgh, 449 Pa. 432, 296 A.2d 748 (1972); Commonwealth ex rel. School Dist. of Pittsburgh v. Ross, 17 Pa.Cmwlth. 105, 330 A.2d 290 (1975).

7. State v. Hoyt, 84 N.H. 38, 146 A. 170 (1929); State v. Edgington, 99 N.M. 715, 663 P.2d 374 (App.1983), cert. den. 464 U.S. 940, 104 S.Ct. 354, 78 L.Ed.2d 318 (1983).

8. State ex rel. Shoreline School Dist. No. 412 v. Superior Court, 55 Wash.2d 177, 346 P.2d 999 (1959).

9. State v. Shaver, 294 N.W.2d 883 (N.D.1980); State ex rel. Douglas v. Faith Baptist Church of Louisville, 207 Neb. 802, 301 N.W.2d 571 (1981), app. dism. 454 U.S. 803, 102 S.Ct. 75, 70 L.Ed.2d 72 (1981); New Life Baptist Church Academy v. Town of East Longmeadow, 885 F.2d 940 (1 Cir. 1989), cert. den. 494 U.S. 1066, 110 S.Ct. 1782, 108 L.Ed.2d 784 (1990).

ing" that total compliance by a nonpublic school would "effectively eradicate the distinction" between public and nonpublic education.[10]

Where, however, the compulsory education statutes or state-level regulations do not define with sufficient clarity the standards for private schools, they are unenforceable. The supreme courts of Wisconsin and Georgia have held such statutes unconstitutional because they provided for penalties to parents without sufficient guidance as to what is required.[11] Also, leaving definitions to local authorities without guidelines is an improper delegation of state power to local officials.

The Court of Appeal of California, noting the state requirement of a competent teacher as evidenced by a teaching credential, found that children who were studying at home through enrollment in a correspondence school were not receiving equivalent instruction.[12] Rejection of correspondence courses has also been upheld by the highest court of West Virginia.[13] However, the Supreme Court of Illinois held that there was no violation of the compulsory attendance law in a case of instruction at home by a mother who had "two years of college and some training in pedagogy and educational psychology."[14] There were regular hours of study, the proper subjects were taught, and the children were progressing satisfactorily. The court ruled that under the circumstances the home instruction constituted a "private school" within the meaning of the law, which provided that the only alternative to public school was a private school.

A few courts, principally in New Jersey, have strongly suggested that lack of free association with other children denied equivalency in education to those children instructed at home.[15] However, another New Jersey court has expressly rejected the inclusion of social development in determining whether instruction is equivalent.[16] It found the prior interpretation to be untenable in face of the language of the statute. The statute stated that the requirement of compulsory education could be fulfilled if the child received "equivalent instruction elsewhere than at school." The court reasoned that to develop socially, group education would be needed. But a group would constitute a de facto school. Thus, the only reason for the phrasing of the statute would be to permit individual education which was to be judged on the basis of academic equivalency. In the case before it the court found the education equivalent, based on an examination of evidence which included the materials used by the parents, a report by an independent testing

10. State v. Whisner, 47 Ohio St.2d 181, 351 N.E.2d 750 (1976). See also State ex rel. Nagle v. Olin, 64 Ohio St.2d 341, 415 N.E.2d 279 (1980).

11. State v. Popanz, 112 Wis.2d 166, 332 N.W.2d 750 (1983) [Case No. 111]; Roemhild v. State, 251 Ga. 569, 308 S.E.2d 154 (1983).

12. In re Shinn, 195 Cal.App.2d 683, 16 Cal.Rptr. 165 (1961).

13. State v. Riddle, 168 W.Va. 429, 285 S.E.2d 359 (1981).

14. People v. Levisen, 404 Ill. 574, 90 N.E.2d 213 (1950).

15. Stephens v. Bongart, 15 N.J.Misc. 80, 189 A. 131 (1937); Knox v. O'Brien, 7 N.J.Super. 608, 72 A.2d 389 (1950).

16. State v. Massa, 95 N.J.Super. 382, 231 A.2d 252 (1967). [Case No. 112]

service of the girl's scores, and the organization of the program the mother used.

It should be emphasized that compulsory education is dependent on the statutes establishing it. It does not exist at common law. Equivalencies can be specified in the statutes, or established by judicial construction of the statutes. Thus, home instruction per se is not precluded by common law as a possible substitute for instruction in a school.[17]

Parents have no general right, however, to require that states permit home instruction [18] or measure its equivalence by use of standardized tests.[19] Tests are "after the fact," often cumbersome to administer, and may not cover legitimate curriculum objectives. States can require prior approval of home programs.[20] Also they can require annual tests of those schooled at home even if they do not have that mandate for students in private schools.[21] Annual reports not unreasonably cumbersome to prepare can be required covering directory information and curriculum of children involved.[22] That home teachers meet reasonable certification requirements is a generally permissible way for states to assure teacher quality.[23] Assessing individually a parent's competence to teach might be required if the objection to a requirement raises a significant free exercise of religion point and the children are fulfilling the academic and socialization goals of compulsory education.[24]

The Supreme Judicial Court of Massachusetts issued an extensive opinion upholding the basic power of the state reasonably to regulate education in home schools.[25] The court suggested guidelines for approval of home education plans that would accommodate competing interests. Prior approval may be required, but parents must have an opportunity to explain their plan and present witnesses on their behalf. The burden is on parents to show that their proposal is equivalent. If rejected, detailed reasons must be given by the board, and parents must be given a chance to remedy inadequacies. If, however, the parents commence home education in the face of school board refusal to approve, the burden shifts to the board to prove that the education is not equivalent. Factors to be considered include number of hours in the various subjects, competency of the parents (though regular certification would not be required), materials used, and standardized test results.

Residence for School Purposes

Eligibility to attend tuition-free the schools of a district is generally extended by statute to those school-age youth who are residents of the

---

17. People v. Turner, 277 App.Div. 317, 98 N.Y.S.2d 886 (1950).

18. See footnote 7.

19. Fellowship Baptist Church v. Benton, 815 F.2d 485 (8 Cir.1987).

20. Blount v. Department of Educational and Cultural Services, 551 A.2d 1377 (Me.1988).

21. Murphy v. State of Arkansas, 852 F.2d 1039 (8 Cir.1988).

22. State v. Rivera, 497 N.W.2d 878 (Iowa 1993).

23. State v. Anderson, 427 N.W.2d 316 (N.D.1988).

24. People v. DeJonge, 442 Mich. 266, 501 N.W.2d 127 (1993).

25. Care and Protection of Charles, 399 Mass. 324, 504 N.E.2d 592 (1987).

district. The greater weight of authority is that residence for school purposes does not necessarily mean that the child must have his legal domicile there.[26] Domicile is a place where one intends to remain indefinitely. Each person may have only one domicile. The common-law rule has been that the legal domicile of a minor child is that of the father. He is legally incapable of establishing another in the absence of special circumstances, such as, death of the father, separation of the parents when the mother is given custody of the child, or being in legal charge of other persons. Residence, by contrast, is a factual place of abode, where one is physically living. It is possible to have several residences. When a child is actually living in a district, generally he is entitled to enter the school there. There always has been a major exception, however: purpose for living in the district being to gain entrance to the school.[27]

In 1983 the Supreme Court rejected a constitutional challenge to a statute that denied tuition-free admission to public schools to minors living apart from parents or guardians if their presence in the school district was for the primary purpose of attending free public schools.[28] The exclusion was found neither to violate the Fourteenth Amendment nor to interfere with the constitutional right of interstate travel. Anyone could establish residence and gain the benefit.

Illustrative of the kinds of problems that arise is one decided by the Supreme Court of New Hampshire.[29] It was called upon to decide residence for school purposes of a boy living during the school year with his divorced father, although his custody had been given to the mother in the divorce decree. He did not live with the father during the summer. The major reason the boy was living with his father during the winter, however, was one of health. The factor of where he went to school was not related to his choice of home during the school year. The mother lived and worked in a location where the humidity affected adversely the boy's asthma. The court considered him to be a bona fide resident of the district for school purposes.

Children living in orphanages or other charitable homes, in the absence of contrary legislative provisions, are generally considered to be children residing within the district for school purposes.[30] If a court appoints a guardian with whom a child lives in the district, the school system must accept the child tuition-free.[31] A state, however, can enforce a statute providing that those children residing at a child-care institution whose maintenance expenses are paid for in whole or part by another state are not entitled to tuition-free attendance in local public

26. State ex rel. Doe v. Kingery, 157 W.Va. 667, 203 S.E.2d 358 (1974).

27. Fangman v. Moyers, 90 Colo. 308, 8 P.2d 762 (1932); Turner v. Board of Educ., North Chicago Community High School Dist. 123, 54 Ill.2d 68, 294 N.E.2d 264 (1973).

28. Martinez v. Bynum, 461 U.S. 321, 103 S.Ct. 1838, 75 L.Ed.2d 879 (1983). [Case No. 113]

29. Luoma v. Union School Dist. of Keene, 106 N.H. 488, 214 A.2d 120 (1965).

30. State ex rel. Board of Christian Service of Lutheran Minnesota Conference v. School Bd. of Consolidated School Dist. No. 3, 206 Minn. 63, 287 N.W. 625 (1939).

31. University Center, Inc. v. Ann Arbor Public Schools, 386 Mich. 210, 191 N.W.2d 302 (1971).

schools. A three-judge federal District Court found a rational relationship between the statute and the state's legitimate objectives of preserving the financial integrity of school districts and not burdening taxpayers of the state with the expense of educating children who were wards of other states.[32]

The Supreme Court in 1982 answered in the negative the question "whether, consistent with the Equal Protection Clause of the Fourteenth Amendment, Texas may deny to undocumented school-age children the free public education that it provides to children who are citizens of the United States or legally admitted aliens." [33] Challenged successfully was a provision that withheld from local school districts any state funds for the education of children not "legally admitted" into the United States, and authorized local school districts to refuse to enroll such children in the public schools.

The Court, after holding that the equal protection clause applies to undocumented aliens, said that the constitutionality of the classification at issue depended on "whether it may fairly be viewed as furthering a substantial interest of the State." The view of the Court was that the uniqueness of education distinguishes it from general forms of social welfare and triggers the necessity for a state to support withholding it by more substantial justification than that required by the usual rational relationship criterion. The state's reasons for the statute failed to meet this test. Further, although the children were innocent of the unlawful conduct of their parents, the impact of the law was to severely punish the children while they were in this country. (Any illegal entrants can, of course, be deported under federal law.)

The conditions under which students living in one district may be transferred to another district depend upon the statutes, as does any right of a child to attend school in a district other than that in which he resides. The weight of authority is that school districts may accept pupils from other districts upon payment of tuition unless this is barred by statute.[34] If a parent prefers to enroll a child in the schools of a district in which the child does not reside, the parent must pay the tuition.[35] This is true even if the parent operates a business and pays taxes in the district.[36]

If statutes specify reasons that may constitute bases for tuition-free attendance in a district other than that of residence, they are strictly construed. Where a lower court had ordered to be granted a transfer application for reason of "basic inconsistency," predicated on the fact that one child was permitted to transfer and a sibling in a different grade was not, the Supreme Court of Oklahoma reversed because that

32. East Texas Guidance and Achievement Center, Inc. v. Brockette, 431 F.Supp. 231 (E.D.Tex.1977).

33. Plyler v. Doe, 457 U.S. 202, 102 S.Ct. 2382, 72 L.Ed.2d 786 (1982).

34. Union Free High School Dist. No. 1, Town of Iron River v. Joint School Dist. No. 1 of Town of Maple, 17 Wis.2d 409, 117 N.W.2d 273 (1962).

35. Logan City School Dist. v. Kowallis, 94 Utah 342, 77 P.2d 348 (1938).

36. Cape Girardeau School Dist. v. Frye, 225 S.W.2d 484 (Mo.App.1949).

reason was not one specified by the applicable statute.[37]　Where a statute required approval of the board of education of the district of residence before students could attend school in another district, the Supreme Court of Arkansas held that neither payment of tuition nor the appointment of "school guardianships" would empower another district to enroll such students.[38]

Vaccination

Requirements related to vaccination of children as a condition of school attendance have been a subject of much judicial consideration.　It is settled that the legislature may delegate to local agencies power to make regulations for the protection of public health.　But conflict arises as to whether a requirement of vaccination is necessarily such a regulation.　Although more cases arose in days when inoculations were less generally accepted as effective protection against disease than is the situation today, they still recur.　Challenges are based on charges of invasion of personal rights, especially religious beliefs.

The Supreme Court has decided two relevant cases.　A statute empowering local authorities to require everyone to be vaccinated was held not in violation of the United States Constitution in 1905.[39]　In 1922 the Supreme Court ruled that a parent did not have a constitutional right to have his child attend school without being vaccinated.[40]　State statutes requiring or authorizing local authorities to adopt vaccination policies have been uniformly sustained.[41]

Most of the early cases dealt with smallpox and diphtheria vaccinations.　More recently, the cases involve immunization against other diseases.　The courts have shown no tendency to alter their views.[42]

Where children are not vaccinated by direction of their parents and are barred from school, the remedy against the parents is normally a fine and possibly imprisonment.　In extreme situations, removal from the parents to the guardianship of a welfare agency can be ordered by the courts.[43]　The parent's refusal to act cannot be allowed to prevent a child from getting the education it is his right to obtain.

Many statutes provide for certain exceptions to the compulsory vaccination requirements.　These may lead to litigation.　For example, a

37. Board of Educ. of Independent School Dist. Number One of Tulsa County v. Beasley, 554 P.2d 12 (Okl.1976).

38. Delta Special School Dist. No. 5 v. McGehee Special School Dist. No. 17, 280 Ark. 489, 659 S.W.2d 508 (1983).

39. Jacobson v. Commonwealth of Massachusetts, 197 U.S. 11, 25 S.Ct. 358, 49 L.Ed. 643 (1905).

40. Zucht v. King, 260 U.S. 174, 43 S.Ct. 24, 67 L.Ed. 194 (1922).

41. Board of Educ. of Mt. Lakes v. Maas, 56 N.J.Super. 245, 152 A.2d 394 (1959).　Where no such authority existed and where there was no epidemic immi-

nent, courts in old cases have disagreed as to an implied power of local boards to establish such requirements.

42. McCartney v. Austin, 31 A.D.2d 370, 298 N.Y.S.2d 26 (1969); Itz v. Penick, 493 S.W.2d 506 (Tex.1973), app. dism. 412 U.S. 925, 93 S.Ct. 2754, 37 L.Ed.2d 152 (1973); Syska v. Montgomery County Bd. of Educ., 45 Md.App. 626, 415 A.2d 301 (1980), app. dism. 450 U.S. 961, 101 S.Ct. 1475, 67 L.Ed.2d 610 (1981).

43. Cude v. State of Arkansas, 237 Ark. 927, 377 S.W.2d 816 (1964).

three-judge federal District Court declared unconstitutionally vague a provision that a child may be excused "for religious reasons at the discretion of the local school board." [44] The court cited the lack of criteria governing such decisions.

The Massachusetts vaccination statute provided exemption from the general immunization requirement for school admission of those presenting an affidavit from a church official that vaccination conflicts with the "tenets and practices of a recognized church or religious denomination" and the parent is a member in good standing. One who was not a member of a church was thus unable to get an exemption. The Supreme Judicial Court of Massachusetts ruled the provision to be unconstitutional because it favored those who belonged to "recognized" churches over those who sincerely held religious beliefs but did not belong to churches.[45] The same conclusion on a similar statute was reached by the highest court of Maryland.[46]

One who was "philosophically" opposed to immunization was held not to be entitled to an exception for his children under a Kentucky immunization statute which provided an exemption for "members of a nationally recognized and established church or religious denomination, the teachings of which are opposed to medical immunization against disease." [47] The case was decided by a three-judge federal District Court that based its decision on the ground that the First Amendment's establishment of religion clause was not violated by the fact religious reasons were accepted for an exemption and nonreligious reasons were not. Curiously the court did not address the constitutionally questionable formulation in the statute of what constituted a religious reason (apparently because plaintiffs did not attack it.) Three years later, with no reference to this case, the Supreme Court of Mississippi held that no religious exemption could be permitted where there was a compulsory immunization statute, because such would constitute unequal protection.[48]

An unusual aspect of the problem arose in Arkansas. When their children were legally barred from the public school for not being vaccinated against smallpox, members of a church group organized and conducted their own school. Vaccination was not a condition for entrance. The compulsory education statute required children to attend a "public, private, or parochial school." The state health regulation requiring vaccination specified only children attending a "public or private school." The parents asserted that their school was "parochial," thereby satisfying the compulsory education requirement, but not coming under the health rule. Their argument did not prevail. The Supreme Court of Arkansas held that a parochial school was also a

44. Avard v. Dupuis, 376 F.Supp. 479 (D.N.H.1974).

45. Dalli v. Board of Educ., 358 Mass. 753, 267 N.E.2d 219 (1971).

46. Davis v. State, 294 Md. 370, 451 A.2d 107 (1982).

47. Kleid v. Board of Educ. of Fulton, Kentucky, Independent School Dist., 406 F.Supp. 902 (W.D.Ky.1976).

48. Brown v. Stone, 378 So.2d 218 (Miss.1979), cert. den. 449 U.S. 887, 101 S.Ct. 242, 66 L.Ed.2d 112 (1980).

private school within the meaning of the health regulation, since it was managed and supported by a private organization.[49] It thus followed that children enrolled there had to be vaccinated.

Rules of Student Conduct

In General

The power of local school authorities to adopt reasonable rules and regulations covering student conduct is essential to the efficient functioning of the schools. However, reasonableness of rules usually cannot be decided in the abstract, but only in the context of application. Whether a rule may legally be enforced depends upon the fact situation, but any enforceable rule must be connected with the welfare of the schools. School boards can prohibit that conduct which can be shown to be detrimental to the operation of the schools.

In general, the validity of a board rule is legally presumed, and the burden of showing unreasonableness is on the complaining party. This should not be misunderstood, however, to imply that courts will not examine the basis of a conduct rule. The closer a rule encroaches on a constitutional right of students, the greater the need for justification by school authorities. If the rule actually infringes a fundamental constitutional right, the burden of proof shifts to school officials to show a compelling need for the rule. Also, courts examine rules more closely if a severe punishment has been, or could be, imposed.

Clearly a compelling interest of the state is the maintenance in its schools of a proper atmosphere for learning. But many rules ostensibly so aimed have been invalidated by courts because they are not rationally connected with the purported objective, or they are too vague as to what conduct is proscribed by them, or they are overbroad in that they encompass constitutionally protected activities along with those which may be restricted in the school setting.

Whether or not the rule is written is immaterial if the offense would clearly be punishable under general norms of behavior. The courts recognize that written rules cannot govern every specific offense that may be committed by youth. Generally, however, before being subject to punishment for an infraction, a student must be informed as to expectations of conduct through a written statement, oral instruction, or observance of general custom.

While students have a right to know what is prohibited, it is well settled that discipline rules need not meet the stringent criteria judicially required for acceptability of criminal statutes.[50] Thus, although "mis-

---

49. Mannis v. State of Arkansas ex rel. Dewitt School Dist., 240 Ark. 42, 398 S.W.2d 206 (1966).

50. Esteban v. Central Missouri State College, 415 F.2d 1077 (8 Cir.1969), cert. den. 398 U.S. 965, 90 S.Ct. 2169, 26 L.Ed.2d 548 (1970); Soglin v. Kauffman,

418 F.2d 163 (7 Cir.1969); Sword v. Fox, 446 F.2d 1091 (4 Cir.1971); Murray v. West Baton Rouge Parish School Bd., 472 F.2d 438 (5 Cir.1973); Black Coalition v. Portland School Dist. No. 1, 484 F.2d 1040 (9 Cir.1973).

conduct"[51] and "conduct inimical to the best interests of the school"[52] standing alone have been declared unconstitutionally vague, "dangerous drug,"[53] "loitering in the areas of heavy traffic"[54] and action that "unreasonably interferes with * * * the right of access to [school facilities]"[55] have survived the challenge of vagueness. The less clearly conduct is disruptive to the educational environment, the more detail is required in a rule designed to prohibit it.

Although the rule and its enforcement are different matters, frequently they are intertwined, and it is not always necessary in issuing an injunction against the enforcement of a rule for a court to distinguish between them. In drawing implications from decided cases, therefore, it is extremely important to differentiate among the rule, the punishment, and the process of determining the punishment.

Political Expression

It is obvious that any actual disruption of the school may be quelled by school authorities. Problems arise, however, when it is sought to prevent an expressive activity because it might lead to a disturbance.

Some clarification of how the courts view the area can be found by examining two cases decided the same day in 1966 by the same panel of judges of the Court of Appeals, Fifth Circuit. Both cases involved students in all-black high schools in Mississippi who were wearing buttons which depicted political positions. Students who refused to remove the buttons were suspended in each case. The constitutional issue raised was the right of freedom of expression versus the right of school authorities to establish reasonable rules for governing the school.

In one case a number of students appeared wearing buttons containing the words "One Man, One Vote" around the perimeter with "SNCC" inscribed in the center. The principal informed the student body that wearing such buttons was not permitted in school because the buttons did not "have any bearing" on the students' education and "would cause commotion." Some students, who continued to display the buttons, were given the choice of removing them or being sent home. Most chose to go home and the principal thereupon suspended them for a period of one week. The Court of Appeals invalidated this rule, noting that on prior occasions students had worn other types of buttons and that these had not been forbidden.[56] The court held that the school children had a right silently to communicate an idea and to encourage the members of their community to exercise their civil rights. The pupils had been suspended not for causing a disruption, but for violating the school regulation.

51. Soglin v. Kauffman, 418 F.2d 163 (7 Cir.1969).

52. Mitchell v. King, 169 Conn. 140, 363 A.2d 68 (1975). [Case No. 15]

53. Fisher v. Burkburnett Independent School Dist., 419 F.Supp. 1200 (N.D.Tex. 1976).

54. Alex v. Allen, 409 F.Supp. 379 (W.D.Pa.1976).

55. Sill v. Pennsylvania State Univ., 462 F.2d 463 (3 Cir.1972).

56. Burnside v. Byars, 363 F.2d 744 (5 Cir.1966).

In the second case, school authorities were sustained in banning buttons following a disturbance by students noisily talking in the corridor when they should have been in class. Subsequently, almost 200 pupils came to the school wearing buttons. These students distributed the buttons in the corridors of the building and pinned buttons on some other students, even though the latter did not want them. Such activity created a state of confusion, disrupted class instruction, and resulted in a general breakdown of discipline. The principal called the students to the cafeteria and informed them they were forbidden to wear the buttons. At this session several students conducted themselves discourteously and displayed an attitude of hostility. The next day students wearing buttons were again told that if they returned to school once more with the buttons, they would be suspended. They ignored the directive, and as the suspended students were leaving, they created a general disturbance by urging other students to leave with them. The court found the rule and suspensions valid, there being a disturbance which the school authorities had a right, if not a duty, to control.[57]

In 1969 the Supreme Court of the United States decided its first case on a matter directly related to public school student discipline.[58] By a vote of seven-to-two it invalidated a rule preventing students from wearing in school black armbands signifying an objection to the hostilities in Vietnam and support for a truce. Its opinion accepted the position of the Court of Appeals, Fifth Circuit, described above. The prohibition of wearing of symbols can be sustained only if the wearing would "materially and substantially interfere with the requirements of appropriate discipline in the operation of the school." The Court pointed out that the problems presented involved "direct, primary First Amendment rights akin to 'pure speech.'" It did not concern "speech or action that intrudes upon the work of the school or the rights of other students." Also, the Court observed that the case did not relate to "regulation of the length of skirts or the type of clothing, to hair style, or deportment."

The Court took notice of the fact that other kinds of insignia previously had been permitted, and that the present rule was drawn after school officials knew that certain students were going to wear the armbands. To justify a prohibition of a particular expression of opinion, said the Court, school officials must be able to show that their action was caused by "something more than a mere desire to avoid the discomfort and unpleasantness that always accompany an unpopular viewpoint." There must be "facts which might reasonably [lead] school authorities to forecast substantial disruption of or material interference with school activities."

Subsequently, many courts have considered bans on symbols with differing results based primarily on differing facts. The first to be carried to an appellate court arose in Ohio. A school in which there had

57. Blackwell v. Issaquena County Bd. of Educ., 363 F.2d 749 (5 Cir.1966).

58. Tinker v. Des Moines Independent Community School Dist., 393 U.S. 503, 89 S.Ct. 733, 21 L.Ed.2d 731 (1969). [Case No. 114]

been severe racial tensions had a forty-year-old rule against emblems and other insignia not related to school activities. It was sought to prevent enforcement of the rule, which originally was intended to reduce undesirable divisions created within the student body by fraternities and sororities. Evidence was produced that in recent years students increasingly had attempted to wear buttons and badges expressing messages of an inflammatory racial nature. Some disorders occasioned by the buttons had broken out. The United States Court of Appeals, Sixth Circuit, supported the school authorities and the Supreme Court declined to review the holding.[59] The court stated that the rule was "relatively nonoppressive" and that it would serve the goal of meaningful integration in the schools. It commented that classrooms would lose their usefulness as places for education if pupils wear the "badges of their respective disagreements, and provoke confrontations with their fellows and their teachers."

In another Court of Appeals case, the Fifth Circuit found that alleged disruptions and threats of disruption by wearers of black armbands were not sufficient to justify exclusion of the wearers.[60] Here the superintendent decided it was against long-standing school policy for students to wear black armbands in school in connection with the "Vietnam Moratorium of October 15, 1969." He attempted to prevent students from so doing by sending directions to that effect to the principals. The court found the cited regulation to be inapplicable and suggested the armband policy was "improvised ad hoc for the occasion." It observed that other "peace symbols" previously had been allowed, and that on the moratorium day the principals of different schools apparently received the instruction at different times. The mere expectation of disruption, said the court, does not by itself justify suspending the exercise of constitutional rights. The court stated that where a board finds the existence of circumstances allowing no practical alternative to a ban, the board will be supported if its conclusion is within the range where reasonable minds may differ. However, school officials must make some inquiry and establish substantial basis for a ban.

In an Oregon school district where the teachers commenced a lawful strike and the board hired replacement teachers, two students were suspended for the rest of the day because they wore buttons and stickers with such expressions as "I'm not listening, scab." The next scheduled school day they displayed slogans such as "We want our real teachers back" and more expressions using the word "scab." They complied with an instruction from an administrator to remove all references containing the word "scab" and filed a lawsuit. The Court of Appeals, Ninth Circuit, held that the students were protected in wearing the buttons because the buttons were not vulgar and no disruption occurred or could be reasonably forecast.[61]

59. Guzick v. Drebus, 431 F.2d 594 (6 Cir.1970), cert. den. 401 U.S. 948, 91 S.Ct. 941, 28 L.Ed.2d 231 (1971). [Case No. 115]

60. Butts v. Dallas Independent School Dist., 436 F.2d 728 (5 Cir.1971).

61. Chandler v. McMinnville School Dist., 978 F.2d 524 (9 Cir.1992).

Whether a "quiet procession" of 29 black students from a pep rally when the song "Dixie" was played qualified as protected symbolic speech was decided in the negative by the Court of Appeals, Eighth Circuit.[62] A school rule expressly forbade disturbances in assemblies. The rally had been scheduled in advance, and it was known that "Dixie" was to be played. Those who did not wish to attend the rally in the gymnasium were instructed to report to the auditorium, and some 25 black students and five white students did so. The black students, whose short-term suspensions of three to five days were being challenged, went to the gymnasium and when "Dixie" was played, as the fourth number, they arose and left the pep assembly. The court supported the position of school authorities that this was a disruption, and thus a violation of a reasonable rule, rather than a constitutionally protected dissent. The court reviewed at length the history of the song "Dixie", and concluded that it was not racially abusive per se, nor was it being used in a racially offensive fashion, which would warrant its prohibition by the judiciary.

The Court of Appeals, Ninth Circuit, made an important distinction in a case involving a student who was a leader in a demonstration against the school board's not renewing a teacher's contract.[63] The holding was that the student was protected by the First Amendment in his right to have and distribute signs, but he had no right to refuse to surrender the signs when requested by the vice-principal after tensions mounted. As the student did acquiesce to a second request, he could not be disciplined for the sign incident because no substantial disruption properly could be forecast after he relinquished the signs. But where a reasonable forecast of serious disturbance could be made, and a student refused to halt his symbolic expression (wearing a Confederate flag as a sleeve patch in a racially-tense, newly-integrated Tennessee school), the Sixth Circuit Court of Appeals upheld the suspension of the student.[64] When the symbol ("Johnny Reb") was that of the school itself and was objected to by some black students and parents, the decision of the principal to remove it was held not to violate any free speech rights.[65]

Limits of the definition of "speech" were discussed by the Court of Appeals of Oregon in a case involving a protest by college students against the inclusion on the menu of dining halls of products being boycotted by supporters of a farm workers group. The court upheld the rights to distribute leaflets, speak to passers-by, and collect signatures on petitions, but it sustained a conviction of criminal trespass growing out of the erection on the lawn of a tent-like structure that was intended to symbolize the plight of farm workers.[66] The contention that the structure was symbolic speech entitled to First Amendment protection was rejected.

62. Tate v. Board of Educ. of Jonesboro, Arkansas, Special School Dist., 453 F.2d 975 (8 Cir.1972). [Case No. 116]

63. Karp v. Becken, 477 F.2d 171 (9 Cir.1973).

64. Melton v. Young, 465 F.2d 1332 (6 Cir.1972), cert. den. 411 U.S. 951, 93 S.Ct. 1926, 36 L.Ed.2d 414 (1973).

65. Crosby v. Holsinger, 852 F.2d 801 (4 Cir.1988).

66. State v. Ybarra, 25 Or.App. 633, 550 P.2d 763 (1976).

The United States Supreme Court has identified two factors to be considered in determining whether speech connected with conduct qualifies as symbolic speech for constitutional protection: whether the expression is intended to convey a particularized message and whether the message will be understood by recipients.[67] In another "shanty erection" case the Fourth Circuit accepted the structure as symbolic speech against segregation policies in South Africa, but approved its being banned from the historic and architecturally recognized lawn area directly in front of the Rotunda of the University of Virginia because of the unique status of the area and because other parts of the campus close-by were available.[68] Esthetics and prevention of damage can be governmental interests in connection with property use for communicative conduct.

Reasonable restrictions may be placed on the time, place, and manner of any form of speech, including demonstrations. The Supreme Court (in upholding an antinoise ordinance prohibiting a person while on grounds adjacent to a building in which a school is in session from willfully making a noise that disturbs the peace of the school session) said, "The crucial question [in determining whether regulations concerning time, place, and manner of speech are reasonable] is whether the manner of expression is basically incompatible with the normal activity of a particular place at a particular time."[69] Such regulations, if they are not deceptively used as a guise for suppression of content of speech, are judicially recognized as inherently necessary for a proper educational atmosphere.[70] Existence of alternatives for the activity restricted is often an important consideration.

Distributions of printed material are treated under "Publications" in this chapter and "Differentiating among Uses and Users" in Chapter 6.

Educationally Inappropriate Expression

The Supreme Court answered in the negative the question, in its words, "whether the First Amendment prevents a school district from disciplining a high school student for giving a lewd speech at a school assembly."[71] The setting was an assembly attended by some 600 students of both sexes of ages 14 and up. The students were required to attend the assembly or report to the study hall. The assembly was part of a school-sponsored educational program in self-government. The speech was a nominating one in which the speaker's candidate was referred to "in terms of an elaborate, graphic, and explicit sexual metaphor." The school had a rule prohibiting disruptive conduct "in-

---

67. Spence v. Washington, 418 U.S. 405, 94 S.Ct. 2727, 41 L.Ed.2d 842 (1974).

68. Students Against Apartheid Coalition v. O'Neil, 838 F.2d 735 (4 Cir.1988).

69. Grayned v. City of Rockford, 408 U.S. 104, 92 S.Ct. 2294, 33 L.Ed.2d 222 (1972).

70. Shanley v. Northeast Independent School Dist., Bexar County, Texas, 462 F.2d 960 (5 Cir.1972).

71. Bethel School Dist. No. 403 v. Fraser, 478 U.S. 675, 106 S.Ct. 3159, 92 L.Ed.2d 549 (1986). [Case No. 117]

cluding the use of obscene, profane language or gestures." Two teachers with whom the student discussed the speech in advance obliquely warned him of possible repercussions.

By a vote of seven-to-two the Court upheld the power of the school authorities to discipline the student. The Court distinguished this speech from that in Tinker (Case No. 114). The armbands were a passive, nondisruptive expression of a political position, rather than a use of "lewd and obscene" speech to make a point in a student election. The assembly constituted a captive audience that included 14–year–olds. The schools have an obligation to inculcate habits and manners of civility and teach students the boundaries of socially appropriate behavior. The discipline here, unlike in Tinker, was unrelated to any political viewpoint. "The determination of what manner of speech in the classroom or in school assembly is inappropriate properly rests with the school board."

It hardly needs observing here that oral speech disrespectful of school authorities or disruptive of instructional activities can form a basis for disciplinary action against a student. The fact that "discourteous and rude" remarks were made by a candidate for student council president at an election assembly did not render them protected by the First Amendment, and the punishment of disqualification was upheld in an Eighth Circuit case.[72]

Educationally inappropriate speech is involved in many of the cases discussed elsewhere in this chapter, especially under "Publications."

Dress and Appearance

That schools may enact some regulations concerning dress and appearance of students is self-evident. The extent to which they may control such matters of personal preference depends on the facts and on "the tenor of the times." A leading case was decided by the Supreme Court of Arkansas in 1923.[73] Upheld was a board rule prohibiting the "wearing of transparent hosiery, low-necked dresses, or any style of clothing tending toward immodesty in dress, or the use of face paint or cosmetics." In sustaining the rule the court stated that it would not annul a rule adopted by a locally elected board of education unless it could be demonstrated that the rule was not "reasonably calculated to effect * * * promoting discipline in the school." (This case was cited by the Supreme Court in the Tinker armband case. The Court stated that Tinker was not a case involving this type of regulation.) Similar reasoning was used by the Supreme Court of North Dakota in upholding a prohibition against wearing metal heel plates.[74] Here the court sustained the rule because of damage to school floors and disturbance from the noise created.

72. Poling v. Murphy, 872 F.2d 757 (6 Cir.1989), cert. den. 493 U.S. 1021, 110 S.Ct. 723, 107 L.Ed.2d 742 (1990).

73. Pugsley v. Sellmeyer, 158 Ark. 247, 250 S.W. 538 (1923).

74. Stromberg v. French, 60 N.D. 750, 236 N.W. 477 (1931).

But a rule mandating the wearing of cap and gown for commencement exercises has been voided as a basis for withholding a diploma.[75] In that case, however, refusal to allow the female to participate in the public ceremonies without cap and gown was judicially approved. Over half a century later, a requirement that males wear "dress pants as opposed to jeans" was upheld as a condition for participation in the graduation ceremony.[76] Courts considering elements of student "dress codes" have differed on the question of enforceability of bans against specific items of clothing, for example, girls' jeans.[77] Immodest or suggestive clothing, of course, clearly may be prohibited.[78]

Well in excess of 150 cases involving male head and face hairstyles in public schools have been decided by appellate state courts or federal courts. A substantial majority of these have been decided in federal courts, with Circuit Courts of Appeals having handed down decisions in one or more cases in all circuits except the Second and the District of Columbia. Many of the cases were not decided on the ultimate merits, but on the issue of whether a preliminary injunction would be warranted. It appears that virtually every conceivable argument has been made by counsel for plaintiffs or defendants in one or more of the cases which brought challenges to rules or applications of rules pertaining to dress and appearance of students. The permutations of arguments and fact situations constitute a staggering mass of material. No reliable trend in decisions for the board or for the student is discernible, nor is the reasoning consistent even among courts reaching basically the same conclusions. The circuits that have ruled are split six-to-four on the question in the absence of unusual facts. The Third, Fifth, Sixth, Ninth, Tenth, and Eleventh support in general the validity of such rules; the First, Fourth, Seventh, and Eighth do not.[79] Several of the key circuit decisions were by votes of two-to-one. The Supreme Court has consistently denied certiorari on the cases, thereby adding another unusual twist to the area. Included in this volume as Case No. 118 is a Fourth Circuit decision that quotes widely from the opinions of the other circuits, and through the majority and minority opinions summarizes the unclear status of the law.[80]

75. Valentine v. Independent School Dist., 191 Iowa 1100, 183 N.W. 434 (1921).

76. Fowler v. Williamson, 448 F.Supp. 497 (W.D.N.C. 1978); Fowler v. Williamson, 39 N.C.App. 715, 251 S.E.2d 889 (1979).

77. Compare Murphy v. Pocatello School Dist. No. 25, 94 Idaho 32, 480 P.2d 878 (1971) [overturning a ban] with Dunkerson v. Russell, 502 S.W.2d 64 (Ky.1973) [sustaining a ban].

78. Wallace v. Ford, 346 F.Supp. 156 (E.D.Ark.1972); Graber v. Kniola, 52 Mich. App. 269, 216 N.W.2d 925 (1974).

79. The leading cases are: (supporting the regulations) Zeller v. Donegal School Dist. Bd. of Educ., 517 F.2d 600 (3 Cir. 1975); Ferrell v. Dallas Independent School Dist., 392 F.2d 697 (5 Cir.1968); Jackson v. Dorrier, 424 F.2d 213 (6 Cir.1970); King v. Saddleback Junior College Dist., 445 F.2d 932 (9 Cir.1971); Freeman v. Flake, 448 F.2d 258 (10 Cir.1971); (striking down the regulations) Richards v. Thurston, 424 F.2d 1281 (1 Cir.1970); Massie v. Henry, 455 F.2d 779 (4 Cir.1972); Breen v. Kahl, 419 F.2d 1034 (7 Cir.1969); Bishop v. Colaw, 450 F.2d 1069 (8 Cir.1971). The Eleventh Circuit follows Fifth Circuit decisions rendered before its creation in 1981. See footnote 85.

80. Massie v. Henry, 455 F.2d 779 (4 Cir.1972). [Case No. 118]

Where the rules on dress and appearance are more narrowly drawn to cover specific activities some, but not all, of the judicial disagreement dissolves. Upheld have been a rule applied to participation in a voluntary postgraduation "diploma ceremony",[81] one applied to participation in the band,[82] and one applied to a vocational school where "image" presented to prospective employers was deemed important in terms of encouraging prospective employers to recruit on campus.[83] On the question of hairstyle rules for athletes not for purposes of safety, the courts are not in agreement.[84] However, the Eleventh Circuit Court of Appeals, in its first hairstyle case, upheld a policy that basketball and football players must be "clean shaven." [85] Plaintiffs tried to distinguish the case from the Fifth Circuit precedents by arguing that if the policy applied only to these teams, the board would have to prove a link between athletic performance and being shaved. The court pointed out, however, that the policy was rationally aimed at presenting the school in a favorable light, not at improving performance.

Where the item of dress signifies an affiliation that is clearly detrimental to the interests of the school the object can be banned. For example, the authority of a school board to forbid male students to wear earrings connected with gang membership has been upheld.[86] That females were allowed to wear earrings did not create an invalid discrimination. Also, when the wearing of berets (originally to express a perceived need to improve treatment of Mexican–Americans) became a symbol of defiance of school authority, the berets could be prohibited.[87]

Secret Societies

Problems related to control by school authorities of membership of students in secret societies have been frequently litigated. In general, state statutes and local board regulations designed to control membership in such bodies are constitutional. The Supreme Court in 1915 upheld a Mississippi statute requiring state university students to refrain from fraternity membership.[88] The Court also has affirmed a lower court decision upholding the authority of a school board to suspend or expel pupils under a statute giving local boards the power to control membership in secret societies.[89]

81. Christmas v. El Reno Bd. of Educ., 313 F.Supp. 618 (W.D.Okl.1970), aff. 449 F.2d 153 (10 Cir.1971).

82. Corley v. Daunhauer, 312 F.Supp. 811 (E.D.Ark.1970). But see Dostert v. Berthold Public School Dist. No. 54, 391 F.Supp. 876 (D.N.D.1975).

83. Farrell v. Smith, 310 F.Supp. 732 (D.Me.1970); Bishop v. Cermenaro, 355 F.Supp. 1269 (D.Mass.1973).

84. Compare Neuhaus v. Torrey, 310 F.Supp. 192 (N.D.Cal.1970) with Dunham v. Pulsifer, 312 F.Supp. 411 (D. Vt.1970).

85. Davenport by Davenport v. Randolph County Bd. of Educ., 730 F.2d 1395 (11 Cir.1984).

86. Olesen v. Board of Educ. of School Dist. No. 228, 676 F.Supp. 820 (N.D.Ill. 1987).

87. Hernandez v. School Dist. No. 1, Denver, Colo., 315 F.Supp. 289 (D.Colo. 1970).

88. Waugh v. Board of Trustees of the University of Mississippi, 237 U.S. 589, 35 S.Ct. 720, 59 L.Ed. 1131 (1915).

89. Hughes v. Caddo Parish School Bd., 57 F.Supp. 508 (W.D. La.1944), aff. 323 U.S. 685, 65 S.Ct. 562, 89 L.Ed. 554 (1945).

In upholding the reasonableness of anti-fraternity rules, courts have pointed out that secret societies can have a detrimental influence on the schools by tending to destroy good order, discipline, and scholarship. They may be considered anti-democratic in their exclusiveness and out of place in a public school open to all on equal terms. Various formulations of the themes of individual rights of parents and students have not prevailed. In the only appellate case found where a rule was not upheld, the evidence that fraternity membership was a detriment to the efficient operation of the school was not sufficient for the court to sustain the rule.[90] In that situation there was no state statute on the matter. In one other case a court, which approved the power of the board to control fraternities, stated that the controls could not be extended into vacation periods.[91]

In Oregon challenge was made to a rule which specified that any school-affiliated organization could enroll only students from one high school. Graduates or students who had dropped from school were not permitted to retain membership. The highest court of the state found that constitutional rights were not violated by the rule.[92] The court pointed out that youth could, outside of the schools, associate in any manner they or their parents desired.

Acting under a Texas statute barring secret societies in public schools, the board of education of Fort Worth adopted a regulation requiring parents of students in junior and senior high schools to sign an application for enrollment which included a certification that the student was not a member and would not become a member of a secret society. The test contained in the statute for what constitutes a secret society was that additional members from the pupils in the school were selected by decision of the membership, rather than by free choice of any pupil who was qualified by the rules of the school to fill the special aims of the organization. Both the statute and the rule were challenged as applied to a certain type of organization, locally called "charity clubs," members of which were chosen by boards of sponsors consisting in part of mothers of active members. The suit was unsuccessful.[93] Neither rights of association of students nor rights of parents to control their children were infringed.

Marriage and/or Parenthood

It has long been established that one within the age limits of statutorily permitted school attendance may not be barred for reason of marriage. In a leading case a girl, who had given birth to a child conceived out of wedlock but born in wedlock, and whose husband had

90. Wright v. Board of Educ. of St. Louis, 295 Mo. 466, 246 S.W. 43 (1922).

91. Wilson v. Abilene Independent School Dist., 190 S.W.2d 406 (Tex.Civ.App. 1945).

92. Burkitt v. School Dist. No. 1, Multnomah County, 195 Or. 471, 246 P.2d 566 (1952).

93. Passel v. Fort Worth Independent School Dist., 453 S.W.2d 888 (Tex.Civ.App. 1970), cert. den. 402 U.S. 968, 91 S.Ct. 1667, 29 L.Ed.2d 133 (1971).

deserted her, sought to return to school. The Supreme Court of Kansas, although recognizing that the schools could bar one who was "of a licentious or immoral character," found that the girl was not of such character, for the only proved adverse fact was that her child was conceived out of wedlock.[94]

The Supreme Court of Mississippi, in that same year of 1929, invalidated a school board resolution prohibiting married persons from attending public schools. The board argued that the marriage relation "brings about views of life which should not be known to unmarried children." The court, in ordering the student admitted, commented that marriage is a domestic relation "highly favored by law" and is "refining and elevating, rather than demoralizing."[95]

In more recent years courts have invalidated rules for differentiated treatment of unwed mothers. Not only may they not be barred from school solely on that ground,[96] but they may not be isolated from contact with other students within the school setting.[97]

Until 1972 state courts had been in agreement that boards had the power to limit the participation of married students in extracurricular activities. Since then, however, the opposite view has prevailed. The first three federal District Courts to rule on the issue held in rapid succession, and without citing each other, that eligibility for various school sponsored activities could not be made dependent on marital status.[98] Other federal and state courts followed the lead.[99]

The Colorado Court of Appeals reviewed the cases related to exclusion of married students from extracurricular activities and decided to follow the post-1972 ones rather than the older cases.[100] Although the case had become moot because the student had been graduated, the court addressed the issue and held that because marriage is a fundamental right the board's rationale of requiring married students to focus on their basic education and their family responsibilities did not suffice as justification for exclusion from extracurricular opportunities. If discipline problems should develop the authorities could deal with them when they arose. Discouragement of early marriages was held to contravene the state's general policy of promoting and fostering the marriage institution and its specific statutes regarding eligibility to marry.

94. Nutt v. Board of Educ. of City of Goodland, 128 Kan. 507, 278 P. 1065 (1929).

95. McLeod v. State ex rel. Colmer, 154 Miss. 468, 122 So. 737 (1929).

96. Shull v. Columbus Municipal Separate School Dist., 338 F.Supp. 1376 (N.D.Miss.1972).

97. Ordway v. Hargraves, 323 F.Supp. 1155 (D.Mass.1971).

98. Holt v. Shelton, 341 F.Supp. 821 (M.D.Tenn.1972); Davis v. Meek, 344 F.Supp. 298 (N.D.Ohio 1972); Moran v. School Dist. No. 7, Yellowstone County, 350 F.Supp. 1180 (D.Mont.1972).

99. Hollon v. Mathis Independent School Dist., 358 F.Supp. 1269 (S.D.Tex. 1973); Bell v. Lone Oak Independent School Dist., 507 S.W.2d 636 (Tex.Civ.App. 1974); Indiana High School Athletic Ass'n v. Raike, 329 N.E.2d 66 (Ind.App.1975).

100. Beeson v. Kiowa County School Dist. RE–1, 39 Colo.App. 174, 567 P.2d 801 (1977).

Publications

The guidelines of Tinker (Case No. 114) have been applied to cases involving student publications. That they are a form of expression entitled to First Amendment protection is incontrovertibly clear from the Tinker holding, if it may not have been before. Thus, their content is not subject to the unrestricted will or opinions of school officials. This does not mean, however, that school authorities must permit all printed material to be distributed in any manner at any time and place on school premises.

The first modern federal case involving the disciplining of high school students for remarks in a publication centered on an editorial criticizing a school pamphlet sent to parents and urging "all students in the future to either refuse to accept or destroy upon acceptance all propaganda that Central's administration publishes," and a comment "imputing a 'sick mind' to the dean." The Court of Appeals, Seventh Circuit, held there was no basis to justify a "forecast of disruption" from the aforementioned remarks, which were characterized by the court as reflecting a "disrespectful and tasteless attitude toward authority."[101]

Another type of control of student publications was invalidated by a federal District Court in New York.[102] Some students sought to publish in the school paper a paid advertisement opposing the Vietnam policy of the United States and saying "we can stop it; we must stop it." The principal prevented the publication, saying the policy was that only purely commercial advertising was acceptable, and news items and editorials were restricted to high school activities. The court examined back issues of the paper and observed that, as was proper for teaching journalism, the paper was being used to communicate about controversial topics, such as the draft, drugs, and political candidates. There had been an article on student opinion about the participation of the United States in the war. The court concluded that there was no logical reason to permit news stories on the subject and to preclude student advertising on it.

Where the restriction on a publication is based on extreme vulgarity in content the attitude of the courts is different from when political views or criticism of school authorities is the basis for control. Vulgarity, to be subject to prohibition, however, must go well beyond being offensive to some.[103] The vulgar manner in which views were expressed was the basis for court-approved discipline in a case which was distinguished from the case in the preceding paragraph.[104] Two students had published off school premises a paper critical of both school authorities and national Vietnam policy. No action was taken, however, until the

101. Scoville v. Board of Educ. of Joliet Tp. High School Dist. 204, 425 F.2d 10 (7 Cir.1970), cert. den. 400 U.S. 826, 91 S.Ct. 51, 27 L.Ed.2d 55 (1970).

102. Zucker v. Panitz, 299 F.Supp. 102 (S.D.N.Y.1969).

103. Sullivan v. Houston Independent School Dist., 333 F.Supp. 1149 (S.D.Tex.

1971); Jacobs v. Board of School Comm'rs, 490 F.2d 601 (7 Cir.1973), vac. as moot, 420 U.S. 128, 95 S.Ct. 848, 43 L.Ed.2d 74 (1975).

104. Baker v. Downey Bd. of Educ., 307 F.Supp. 517 (C.D.Cal.1969).

"vulgar" issue was distributed on the perimeter of the school grounds. But where production and distribution of a paper containing vulgar satire about the school community were accomplished essentially off campus, the Second Circuit Court of Appeals held that the students could not be punished.[105] Nevertheless, the court accepted the principles that "in at least some circumstances, school officials can * * * deem specific publications unsuitable" and that "in some circumstances, expression that is suitable for adults can be suppressed because of its potential effect on children." An example of the latter situation lies in the Eighth Circuit's approval of discipline of students for circulating an unofficial newspaper containing vulgar and indecent language and indirectly encouraging violence against teachers.[106]

The extent to which school officials can exercise "prior restraint" on a publication to be distributed on school grounds was discussed by the United States Court of Appeals, Second Circuit.[107] The decision modified and affirmed a District Court decision which had disapproved on its face a school board rule that literature to be distributed shall have prior approval by the school administration. The trial court had enjoined not only the board's policy, but any requirement that students obtain prior approval before publishing or distributing literature in the schools. The Court of Appeals, however, did not agree with the District Court that regulations requiring prior submission of material for approval would in all circumstances be an unconstitutional "prior restraint." The court said that to be valid a regulation requiring prior submission of material to be distributed must prescribe a definite brief period within which the review of the material will be completed. It must specify to whom and how the material is to be submitted for clearance. It must precisely specify what materials are covered. It must clearly define "distribute." Unless and until such a screening procedure is in operation, no rule on prior approval can be enforced. As to the policy statement, the court strongly suggested more specificity concerning what was forbidden so as to "reduce the likelihood of future litigation."

With the added point that there must be provision for a prompt appeal from any adverse administrative decision, this case has been followed in other circuits.[108] In the Seventh Circuit, however, although students may be punished for publishing certain items, they may not be prevented from doing so at their peril.[109] The Ninth Circuit, expressing doubts that a constitutionally sound predistribution policy could be effectively established, struck down a policy that required approval for

---

105. Thomas v. Board of Educ., Granville Central School Dist., 607 F.2d 1043 (2 Cir.1979), cert. den. 444 U.S. 1081, 100 S.Ct. 1034, 62 L.Ed.2d 765 (1980).

106. Bystrom v. Fridley High School, 686 F.Supp. 1387 (D.Minn.1987), aff. 855 F.2d 855 (8 Cir.1988).

107. Eisner v. Stamford Bd. of Educ., 440 F.2d 803 (2 Cir.1971). [Case No. 119]

108. Baughman v. Freienmuth, 478 F.2d 1345 (4 Cir.1973); Shanley v. Northeast Independent School Dist., Bexar County, Texas, 462 F.2d 960 (5 Cir.1972); Bystrom v. Fridley High School, Independent School Dist. No. 14, 822 F.2d 747 (8 Cir. 1987).

109. Fujishima v. Board of Educ., 460 F.2d 1355 (7 Cir.1972).

all non-school-sponsored materials.[110] The court said that the policy violated the First Amendment because of its content overbreadth.

In a Virginia school district that had adopted a policy specifically forbidding instruction in birth control, the student newspaper staff sought to publish an article entitled "Sexually Active Students Fail to Use Contraception," which included some information on contraceptives. The school board barred the publication of the article (unless some portions were excised) on the grounds that the paper was not a public forum entitled to First Amendment protection, that the students were a captive audience, and that the article violated the curricular policy of the board regarding birth control. The Court of Appeals, Fourth Circuit, rejected all three contentions.[111] It found that the publication, as described in board rules and as revealed through review of articles previously published, was in fact not an "in-house" organ of the school system, but was a medium of expression entitled to First Amendment protection against content restrictions. The students were not a captive audience in that they were not required to read the paper; indeed, they had to act affirmatively to pick it up. The publication was not to be regarded as an integral part of the curriculum, which properly was controlled by the board, because of the finding that it was a vehicle for expression. It was like an item in the library, and under the facts it could not be barred.

Important to note is that the "substantial disruption" criterion of Tinker is not the sole basis acceptable for restricting what can be disseminated on school premises. For example, the Fourth Circuit Court of Appeals approved a prior restraint on a publication containing an advertisement for drug paraphernalia.[112] A rule prohibiting distribution of publications that encourage actions which endanger the health or safety of students was invoked by the principal.

As basis for an article a high school newspaper staff sought to distribute a questionnaire to students on the subject of sex attitudes and habits. The school officials forbade it on the ground that it might do emotional harm to some students. The trial court upheld the ban for ninth and tenth grade students, but enjoined the board from preventing the distribution to eleventh and twelfth grade students. The Court of Appeals, Second Circuit, upheld the ban for all grades.[113] Although testimony of experts had varied as to the extent of the risk of harm, the court said that the established fact that some children could suffer serious emotional harm was sufficient to support the board's position. The court emphasized that the issue was not the banning of distribution of sex-related information, nor was it an attempt to restrict expression of views. The court stated that First Amendment rights of expression did not include the "right to importune others to respond to questions when

110. Burch v. Barker, 861 F.2d 1149 (9 Cir.1988).

111. Gambino v. Fairfax County School Bd., 564 F.2d 157 (4 Cir.1977).

112. Williams v. Spencer, 622 F.2d 1200 (4 Cir.1980).

113. Trachtman v. Anker, 563 F.2d 512 (2 Cir.1977), cert. den. 435 U.S. 925, 98 S.Ct. 1491, 55 L.Ed.2d 519 (1978). [Case No. 120]

there is reason to believe that such importuning may result in harmful consequences."

The Supreme Court decided its first secondary-school newspaper case in 1988.[114] The case arose when a principal deleted an article describing experiences of some students with pregnancy and an article on the impact of divorce on students at the school from a newspaper produced by the journalism class. By a vote of five-to-three the Court held that the First Amendment speech rights of students were not violated. That the paper was written and edited by members of the journalism class as part of the established curriculum indicated that it was not an open forum by policy, and it had not become one by any past practice. As a supervised learning experience for journalism students, the content could be regulated in any reasonable manner. The Court found that the principal had acted reasonably based on factors such as possible identification of unnamed pregnant students in the first article, references to sex activity and birth control that were inappropriate for some of the younger students, and unilateral criticism of her father by a named student in the second article (her name was subsequently deleted, but the principal was unaware of that fact when he acted).

The Court differentiated the case from Tinker (Case No. 114) in that here the issue was not the right of students to speak on a particular matter but rather the right of school authorities not to promote particular student speech. The latter area concerns educators' authority over school-sponsored publications, theatrical productions, and other expressive activities that could reasonably be perceived to bear the imprimatur of the school. These are properly considered to be part of the curriculum and can be reasonably controlled by school authorities based on "legitimate pedagogical concerns." The Court noted that this case did not cover censorship of publications not sponsored by the school.

It is important to bear in mind that a "school publication" could be a public forum, with or without limits, by designation or by practice. Mere connection to a journalism class does not resolve that issue. Nor does the sole fact that a publication is financially aided by the school give the authorities either the duty [115] or the right [116] to determine content per se.

Whether a particular school-sponsored publication is a forum for expression by students and/or the public, or whether it bears the imprimatur of the school so that access may be more limited, is a crucial fact question. When it arose in the context of advertising, the Ninth Circuit in an en banc decision of eleven judges held with a seven-to-four vote that, if a school newspaper was produced in a manner similar to that in the preceding Supreme Court case and if advertising was accepted, it was permissible to bar an advertisement by a chapter of Planned

114. Hazelwood School Dist. v. Kuhlmeier, 484 U.S. 260, 108 S.Ct. 562, 98 L.Ed.2d 592 (1988). [Case No. 121]

115. Panarella v. Birenbaum, 32 N.Y.2d 108, 343 N.Y.S.2d 333, 296 N.E.2d 238 (1973).

116. Antonelli v. Hammond, 308 F.Supp. 1329 (D.Mass.1970); Stanley v. McGrath, 719 F.2d 279 (8 Cir.1983).

Parenthood.[117]   The advertisement gave the organization's address for "routine gynecological exams; birth control methods; pregnancy testing and verification; pregnancy counseling and referral."   The court said that control of advertising was part of the control of the publication and that it would not second-guess educators' determinations as to access to what was here a nonpublic forum unless determinations were not viewpoint neutral.   The school board's reasons were to avoid any perception of non-neutrality regarding family planning, avoid being required to open school publications to organizations with competing views, and avoid conflicts with the sex education curriculum.

Conduct off Premises

The extent of the authority of school officials in relation to off-campus conduct of those enrolled as students has been the subject of a substantial amount of litigation.   As emphasized in the preceding sections, school boards can govern that conduct which can be shown to be detrimental to the operation of the schools.   The effect on the schools, rather than where an incident occurs, is controlling.   It is, of course, legally more difficult to enforce a rule of conduct outside of school than inside because of more potential conflicts with the rights of parents and attenuated connections between acts of students and the education process.

In a much-quoted case the Supreme Court of Errors of Connecticut stated that an examination of the authorities clearly revealed the true test of the teacher's right to punish for offenses off school property to be "not the time or place of the offense, but its effect upon the morale and efficiency of the school."[118]   In that case a boy pupil had been punished for annoying small girls on their way home from school.   The boy was on his mother's property at the time of the offense, but the court found that this did not affect the power of the school authorities to punish him because the conduct was detrimental to the interests of the school.   Over a half century later the Supreme Court of Wyoming upheld the punishment of a student for harassing with his vehicle a school bus en route to school with student riders.[119]   An Arizona appellate court has ruled that if students from one school precipitate a fight on the campus of another school, school authorities can punish them.[120]   Where the conduct off school grounds was a continuation of improper conduct on school premises and occurred shortly after the school day, the school board was held by the highest Massachusetts court to be justified in punishing a student who assaulted another student.[121]

117. Planned Parenthood of Southern Nevada, Inc. v. Clark County School Dist., 941 F.2d 817 (9 Cir.1991).

118. O'Rourke v. Walker, 102 Conn. 130, 128 A. 25 (1925).

119. Clements v. Board of Trustees of Sheridan County School Dist. No. 2, in Sheridan County, 585 P.2d 197 (Wyo.1978).

120. Tucson Public Schools, Dist. No. 1 of Pima County v. Green, 17 Ariz.App. 91, 495 P.2d 861 (1972).

121. Nicholas B. v. School Committee of Worcester, 412 Mass. 20, 587 N.E.2d 211 (1992).

Regulations preventing use of drugs and alcohol on or off campus by student <u>athletes</u> can be enforced on the basis of health and safety concerns.[122] The penalty of suspension or dismissal from the team is the usual penalty. That parents may approve the acts of the students is not relevant here. Of course, the rules cannot be too broad, such as one forbidding an athlete from being in a car where beer is being transported.[123] But presence at an event where alcohol is being consumed by others can be made the basis for an <u>athlete's</u> disqualification.[124]

Activities of students off campus that would clearly threaten the health or safety of students on campus can be the basis for punishment, including long-term exclusions. Thus, drug sales [125] or aggravated assaults [126] off premises have been upheld as reasons for expulsion. The Fourth Circuit Court of Appeals has upheld the validity of a rule providing for disciplinary action against public college students for unlawful use or possession of drugs on or off campus.[127]

Perhaps the oldest appellate case involving discipline for off premises acts was decided in 1859. A high school student, in the presence of other students but after he had returned home following school, called his teacher "old Jack Seaver." The Supreme Court of Vermont upheld punishment for this offense, which had "a direct and immediate tendency to injure the school and bring the master's authority into contempt." [128] The court added that "misbehavior generally, * * * even towards the master in matters in no ways connected with or affecting the school," would not be punishable. In 1976 a United States District Court sustained the disciplining of a high school student for loudly making a vulgar remark in the presence of others about a teacher (who was there to hear it) in a shopping center.[129] In 1986 a United States District Court enjoined punishment of a student who off campus had made a vulgar gesture to a teacher as he passed by the teacher's parked car.[130]

Searches

The Fourth Amendment to the Constitution provides: "The right of the people to be secure in their persons, houses, papers, and effects, against unreasonable searches and seizures, shall not be violated. * * *" This clause and the one following it, which pertains to issuance

122. Braesch v. DePasquale, 200 Neb. 726, 265 N.W.2d 842 (1978), cert. den. 439 U.S. 1068, 99 S.Ct. 836, 59 L.Ed.2d 34 (1979). [Case No. 122]

123. Bunger v. Iowa High School Athletic Ass'n, 197 N.W.2d 555 (Iowa 1972).

124. Clements v. Board of Educ. of Decatur Public School Dist. No. 61, 133 Ill. App.3d 531, 88 Ill.Dec. 601, 478 N.E.2d 1209 (1985); Bush v. Dassel–Cokato Bd. of Educ., 745 F.Supp. 562 (D.Minn.1990).

125. Howard v. Colonial School Dist., 621 A.2d 362 (Del.Super.1992).

126. Pollnow v. Glennon, 594 F.Supp. 220 (S.D.N.Y.1984), aff. 757 F.2d 496 (2 Cir.1985).

127. Krasnow v. Virginia Polytechnic Institute and State Univ., 551 F.2d 591 (4 Cir.1977).

128. Lander v. Seaver, 32 Vt. 114 (1859).

129. Fenton v. Stear, 423 F.Supp. 767 (W.D.Pa.1976).

130. Klein v. Smith, 635 F.Supp. 1440 (D.Me.1986).

of warrants for searches, have been invoked in almost innumerable criminal cases, for if evidence is obtained in violation of the amendment it may not be used against a defendant. Most of the cases involving searches in schools have arisen in connection with the admissibility in court of evidence seized, and thus are not of direct concern to internal school discipline. However, regardless of criminal considerations, it is very possible that acts of school authorities may violate the civil rights of students and create liabilities for school authorities.[131]

N J v TLO   In 1985 the Supreme Court issued an opinion in which it adopted as the standard for searches in the school setting that of "reasonableness under all the circumstances." [132]   Reasonableness was said to involve two elements: whether circumstances justified the action at its inception and whether the scope of the search was reasonable in relation to the situation. The first criterion is met when a "teacher or other school official" has "reasonable grounds for suspecting that the search will turn up evidence that the student has violated or is violating either the law or the rules of the school." The scope is permissible when the measures are reasonably related to the objectives of the search and not excessively intrusive in relation to the age and sex of the student and nature of the infraction.

The instant case involved a search by the assistant principal of the purse of a student who had denied a teacher's report of smoking in the lavatory and said that she did not smoke at all. Found in the purse, in addition to cigarettes, was drug paraphernalia and evidence that the student had sold drugs. The Court upheld the constitutionality of the search.

Legitimate searches by school authorities must be predicated on their duty to provide a safe atmosphere conducive to learning. Although school personnel are government employees, they are not charged with law enforcement. In assessing sufficiency of cause to conduct a school search, courts consider such factors as the source of the information prompting the search, the child's record, the seriousness and prevalence of the problem being addressed by the search, and the urgency of making the search without delay. Information supplied to school authorities by reliable students can suffice to initiate a search.[133] So can observations of teachers or other employees.[134] An odor emanating from a locker has been held to be adequate cause,[135] as has an unusual metallic thud when a student's bookbag was placed on a cabinet.[136]

That which is searched can range from a student's desk or locker, through pockets, purse, or packages, to underclothes or body. Acceptable cause for a search must meet increasingly higher standards as the continuum is traversed.

---

131. See Chapter 7.

132. New Jersey v. T.L.O., 469 U.S. 325, 105 S.Ct. 733, 83 L.Ed.2d 720 (1985). [Case No. 123]

133. Commonwealth v. Snyder, 413 Mass. 521, 597 N.E.2d 1363 (1992).

134. Cornfield v. Consolidated High School Dist. No. 230, 991 F.2d 1316 (7 Cir.1993).

135. People v. Lanthier, 5 Cal.3d 751, 97 Cal.Rptr. 297, 488 P.2d 625 (1971).

136. Matter of Gregory M., 82 N.Y.2d 588, 606 N.Y.S.2d 579, 627 N.E.2d 500 (1993).

Blanket searches of lockers on a regular basis for routine administrative purposes connected with the general welfare of the school are generally permissible, more clearly so if students are notified of the practice at the time lockers are assigned.[137] Using dogs trained to detect contraband to sniff lockers, desks, or cars does not violate the Fourth Amendment, but allowing the dogs to sniff students' persons is constitutional only upon "individualized reasonable suspicion."[138]

Individualized suspicion was also held to be a necessary precondition for a strip search of the students in a class when a small sum of money was reported missing.[139] Where there was individualized suspicion regarding a missing $100 (and the money was eventually found in the student's underwear) the highest court of West Virginia found the search to have been unjustified because of its intrusiveness, although the court said a less intrusive search could have met constitutional standards.[140] Strip searches conducted by school personnel are not, however, unconstitutional per se. They do require more basis because of their scope.[141]

Punishments

In General

When children are under the jurisdiction of the school, teachers are said to stand "in loco parentis" (in the place of the parent) to the students.[142] In order properly to carry out the functions of the school it is necessary for the teacher to have authority to direct the pupil and to punish for infractions, much as a parent would. This relationship of the teacher to the child is an essential element in establishing the standard of reasonableness in regard to punishment: Under similar circumstances, would it be reasonable for a parent to inflict the punishment?[143]

The punishment must be in proportion to the gravity of the offense. It must be reasonably defensible in terms of its purpose, to deter improper conduct. Although courts can invalidate punishments they find to be arbitrary, unreasonable, capricious, or oppressive, some deference to expertise of school authorities is shown, especially if the school's rationale is clearly explainable. Also crucial to the legality of a penalty is the ability of the child to bear it. Thus, sex, age, size, and mental,

137. Zamora v. Pomeroy, 639 F.2d 662 (10 Cir.1981); Commonwealth v. Carey, 407 Mass. 528, 554 N.E.2d 1199 (1990); In Interest of Isiah B., 176 Wis.2d 639, 500 N.W.2d 637 (1993).

138. Horton v. Goose Creek Independent School Dist., 690 F.2d 470 (5 Cir. 1982), cert. den. 463 U.S. 1207, 103 S.Ct. 3536, 77 L.Ed.2d 138 (1983).

139. Bellnier v. Lund, 438 F.Supp. 47 (N.D.N.Y.1977).

140. State ex rel. Galford v. Mark Anthony B., 189 W.Va. 538, 433 S.E.2d 41 (1993).

141. Williams v. Ellington, 936 F.2d 881 (6 Cir.1991); Cornfield v. Consolidated High School Dist. No. 230, 991 F.2d 1316 (7 Cir.1993). In both cases strip searches were upheld.

142. State ex rel. Burpee v. Burton, 45 Wis. 150 (1878).

143. Indiana State Personnel Bd. v. Jackson, 244 Ind. 321, 192 N.E.2d 740 (1963).

emotional, and physical condition of the student are to be considered.[144] Punishment must not be meted in such manner as to be considered cruel or excessive.[145] The teacher is granted very wide discretion in administering punishments, and the many cases on the point indicate that a clear instance of malice or obviously unreasonable punishment must be established before it will be held that a teacher has transcended his authority. The authority, of course, can be limited by valid state or local regulations.

Specific Punishments

Withholding of privileges is a punishment generally judicially accepted. However, an activity from which a pupil is barred because of conduct must be one in the category of a privilege rather than a right of the student. If that which is to be denied the student is an integral part of the curriculum, the ban could conflict with his right to participate in all elements of the curriculum under reasonable rules relevant to the subject. The courts recognize two categories of school activities: those to which the pupil has a right—the basic curriculum—and those which are "extracurricular." It is apparent that the question of categorizing certain activities is a very close one.[146] Furthermore, even an extracurricular activity may not be denied arbitrarily.[147]

The most serious penalty is exclusion from school. Although usage is not consistent, "suspension" generally connotes a temporary exclusion for a specified period or until something is done by student or parent, and "expulsion" connotes permanent separation. As will be amplified in the next section, the minimal elements of procedural due process depend to a substantial extent on the length of the exclusion being considered. Most states have statutes related to expulsion, covering causes and sometimes procedures. This penalty may be imposed only by the school board on evidence it has itself considered.[148] Sometimes, however, permanent exclusion in effect may be brought about by a suspension until a rule is complied with. Many of the decided cases challenging school rules involve such circumstances.

The inclusion of specific punishments in policies relating to discipline, is often attacked on due process grounds, either for being too inflexible by not permitting adequate consideration of extenuating circumstances, or for being too vague regarding which offenses may result in which penalties. *Generally such claims are rejected by the courts. There was no constitutional violation where a school board, after a hearing on why a policy excluding for the balance of the trimester students who used drugs in school should not be applied, imposed that

144. Berry v. Arnold School Dist., 199 Ark. 1118, 137 S.W.2d 256 (1940).

145. Bramlet v. Wilson, 495 F.2d 714 (8 Cir.1974).

146. Palmer v. Merluzzi, 868 F.2d 90 (3 Cir.1989).

147. See Chapter 4 and "Marriage and/or Parenthood" in this chapter.

148. Lee v. Macon County Bd. of Educ., 490 F.2d 458 (5 Cir.1974).

penalty on a girl who had overdosed on a drug while at school.[149] The court commented that in the criminal area "most recent jurisprudence has urged less rather than more discretion in the imposition of punishment." The Fifth Circuit Court of Appeals cited this case when it approved rules providing for mandatory exclusion in situations involving carrying of weapons in school, as long as a rule did not impose a "grossly disproportionate punishment" for the offense.[150] A different court found no constitutional flaw in regulations that for drug related offenses did not differentiate between those warranting a suspension and those from which expulsion might flow. It commented that this situation was "not improper or undesirable, much less a violation of due process." [151]

The Supreme Court of Mississippi, while upholding the implementation of a mandatory suspension-to-end-of-semester rule covering deliberate damage to school property, emphasized that a rule worded in mandatory language does not absolutely prevent school authorities from administering the rule with flexibility and leniency.[152] "The school board may choose not to exercise its power of leniency. In doing so, however, it may not hide behind the notion that the law prohibits leniency for there is no such law." The court observed that individualized punishment is a "hallmark of our criminal justice system" so long as decisions are not arbitrarily or discriminatorily made.

A very large number of cases involving some form of corporal punishment have reached the courts. Under the common law the teacher has the right to administer reasonable corporal punishment, which category includes not only paddling but also any other infliction of discomfort to the student's body. Some states have statutes expressly giving the use of that form of punishment legislative approval under specified conditions. Such a statute is constitutional on its face.[153] So is a local board rule authorizing corporal punishment.[154] Many local school boards have rules either forbidding it or establishing conditions under which it may be administered. If not contrary to any state-level provisions, such regulations are controlling in general,[155] although it is not clear how far local boards can reduce the teacher's authority to administer corporal punishment (as defined supra) in certain circumstances.[156] The criteria of reasonableness for punishments in general would apply to

149. Fisher v. Burkburnett Independent School Dist., 419 F.Supp. 1200 (N.D.Tex. 1976).

150. Mitchell v. Board of Trustees of Oxford Municipal Separate School Dist., 625 F.2d 660 (5 Cir.1980).

151. M. v. Board of Educ. Ball-Chatham Community Unit School Dist. No. 5, Chatham, Illinois, 429 F.Supp. 288 (S.D.Ill. 1977).

152. Clinton Municipal Separate School Dist. v. Byrd, 477 So.2d 237 (Miss.1985).

153. Baker v. Owen, 395 F.Supp. 294 (M.D.N.C.1975), aff. 423 U.S. 907, 96 S.Ct. 210, 46 L.Ed.2d 137 (1975). A parent's

disapproval of corporal punishment did not preclude its being used on her child.

154. Ware v. Estes, 328 F.Supp. 657 (N.D.Tex.1971), aff. 458 F.2d 1360 (5 Cir. 1972), cert. den. 409 U.S. 1027, 93 S.Ct. 463, 34 L.Ed.2d 321 (1972).

155. Bott v. Board of Educ., Deposit Central School Dist., 41 N.Y.2d 265, 392 N.Y.S.2d 274, 360 N.E.2d 952 (1977) [Case No. 102]; McKinney v. Greene, 379 So.2d 69 (La.App.1979).

156. Andreozzi v. Rubano, 145 Conn. 280, 141 A.2d 639 (1958); Simms v. School Dist. No. 1, Multnomah County, 13 Or.App. 119, 508 P.2d 236 (1973); Streeter v. Hundley, 580 S.W.2d 283 (Mo.1979).

this form of chastisement.[157] Unreasonable corporal punishment is basis
for a civil and/or criminal charge of assault and battery. Also it can be
cause for teacher discharge.

The Supreme Court in 1977 held that corporal punishment of
students per se was not constitutionally prohibited.[158] The Court said
that the Eighth Amendment's bar of "cruel and unusual punishments"
was designed to protect those guilty of crimes and does not apply to "the
paddling of children as a means of maintaining discipline in public
schools." The Court observed that "at common law a single principle
has governed the use of corporal punishment since before the American
Revolution: teachers may impose reasonable but not excessive force to
discipline a child." It said that of 23 states addressing the problem
legislatively, 21 authorized the moderate use of corporal punishment. It
noted that professional and public opinion is sharply divided on the
practice, and has been for more than a century. The Court refused to
accept an analogy between school children and prisoners. It said that
not only does the "openness of the public school and its supervision by
the community" afford safeguards against the kinds of abuses from
which the Eighth Amendment protects prisoners, but the common law
restricts school personnel in infliction of corporal punishment. Subsequent to this case, the Fourth Circuit Court of Appeals recognized that a
substantive due process claim was still possible if, in its words, the
punishment was "so brutal, demeaning, and harmful as literally to shock
the conscience of a court." [159] The Tenth Circuit has agreed with this
view.[160] The Fifth has not, reasoning that state statutory and common
law provisions offer redress in the way of damages and possible criminal
liability.[161]

Most corporal punishment cases brought by parents to appellate
courts have been decided in favor of the teacher. There is a presumption of correctness of the teacher's actions, which must be refuted by a
complaining pupil or parent. The burden is a heavy one, but an example
will illustrate how it has been met. A boy who had not participated in a
physical education class in conformity with the instructions of the
teacher was ordered to the sideline. Three times he attempted to re-
enter the class activity against the instructions of the teacher. Finally it
became necessary to discipline the boy. There was conflicting testimony
as to precisely what happened, but the boy struck the floor and broke his
arm. He claimed that the teacher lifted him from the floor, shook him,
and released him so suddenly that he fell. The teacher testified that the
boy had tried to strike him when he was escorting the boy out of the
gymnasium, and that he was only attempting to restrain the boy. The
Court of Appeal of Louisiana said that its credulity was taxed to believe

157. Suits v. Glover, 260 Ala. 449, 71
So.2d 49 (1954).

158. Ingraham v. Wright, 430 U.S. 651,
97 S.Ct. 1401, 51 L.Ed.2d 711 (1977).
[Case No. 124]

159. Hall v. Tawney, 621 F.2d 607 (4
Cir.1980).

160. Garcia v. Meira, 817 F.2d 650 (10
Cir.1987), cert. den. 485 U.S. 959, 108 S.Ct.
1220, 99 L.Ed.2d 421 (1988).

161. Cunningham v. Beavers, 858 F.2d
269 (5 Cir.1988), cert. den. 489 U.S. 1067,
109 S.Ct. 1343, 103 L.Ed.2d 812 (1989).

that the teacher, who was almost a foot taller than the pupil and weighed more than twice as much, could actually believe that his safety was endangered by a blow from the boy, but, in any event, the teacher's actions were clearly in excess of the physical force necessary either to discipline the pupil or to protect himself.[162]

The Appellate Court of Illinois has upheld the right of teachers to verbally chastise pupils.[163] Suit had been brought against a teacher and the school board for damages allegedly arising from severe emotional distress resulting from a student's being scolded by the teacher. The court, analogizing the situation to one involving corporal punishment, held that disparaging comments about a pupil are not actionable unless made maliciously or wantonly.

Generally, courts are not empowered to supervise the enforcement of student conduct rules with the scrutiny they apply to criminal laws. The Supreme Court has said, in reference to a school board rule on "alcoholic beverages," that federal courts are not to "supplant the interpretation of [a] regulation of those officers who adopted it and are entrusted with its enforcement."[164] It added that "Section 1983 does not extend the right to relitigate in federal court evidentiary questions arising in school disciplinary proceedings or the proper construction of school regulations." The Court, in a brief opinion, repeated the point in 1982 in reinstating suspensions for students found intoxicated on school grounds.[165]

Citing these cases, the highest court of Ohio in 1989 upheld a rule authorizing suspensions of students for being "under the influence" of alcohol while attending a school activity.[166] Some indicators of influence were stated. A student had drunk two beers while attending a school-approved "college visitation day." At wrestling practice in the late afternoon alcohol was smelled on his breath by the coach. The court said that the rule was enforceable in this situation because one of the indicators was "odor of chemicals" and the student admitted his drinking.

The fact that the pills a student intended to give to other students did not contain a controlled substance was held not to prevent a school board from punishing the student under a rule banning "unauthorized drugs."[167] The caffeine and ephedrine in the pills (for dieting) could cause harm to some students and, further, the distribution of any form of pills in the school could be thought to contribute to the creation of a drug oriented atmosphere.

1983

162. Frank v. Orleans Parish School Bd., 195 So.2d 451 (La.App.1967).

163. Wexell v. Scott, 2 Ill.App.3d 646, 276 N.E.2d 735 (1971).

164. Wood v. Strickland, 420 U.S. 308, 95 S.Ct. 992, 43 L.Ed.2d 214 (1975). [Case No. 52]

165. Board of Educ. of Rogers, Arkansas v. McCluskey, 458 U.S. 966, 102 S.Ct. 3469, 73 L.Ed.2d 1273 (1982).

166. In re Suspension of Huffer, 47 Ohio St.3d 12, 546 N.E.2d 1308 (1989).

167. Wilson v. Collinsville Community Unit School Dist. No. 10, 116 Ill.App.3d 557, 71 Ill.Dec. 785, 451 N.E.2d 939 (1983).

The Supreme Court in the 1982 case recognized, however, the possibility that "a school board's interpretation of its rules [may be] so extreme as to be a violation of due process." The District Court of Appeal of Florida found this type of situation to exist where a school board excluded a 13-year-old girl for a year, under a mandatory expulsion rule covering weapons, for bringing to school a boxed commemorative knife from her father intended as a Christmas gift to her boyfriend.[168] The Court of Appeals of Kentucky overturned a penalty of exclusion from school for one semester and exclusion from extracurricular activities for one academic year, because the board had considered only whether the students had consumed alcoholic beverages on a school band trip.[169] The court found it arbitrary not to have considered before imposing the penalty such factors as general conduct record, academic standing, probability of recurrence of the violation, and alternative punishments.

The Appellate Court of Illinois overturned the penalty of exclusion from January 7 to the end of the school year in a case of a relatively minor fight off school grounds involving some first-year high school girls.[170] The court articulated some considerations for a court's review of a board action for possible abuse of discretion: the egregiousness of the student's conduct, the history or record of the student's past conduct, the likelihood that such conduct will affect the delivery of educational services to other children, the severity of the punishment, and the interest of the child.

Some peculiar problems exist in connection with the disciplining of handicapped students. The Education for All Handicapped Children Act grants a right to a special type of due process hearing before the school system can change the "educational placement" of a handicapped child. It has been held that a long term exclusion represents a "change in placement." [171] Thus, a handicapped child cannot be expelled in the manner of a nonhandicapped student; detailed procedures, different at points from those discussed in the next section, must be followed. Furthermore, if the conduct of the child eventually is found to justify long-term exclusion, the school system must continue to provide educational services, according to a Fifth Circuit Court of Appeals decision.[172] That a short term suspension was not a "change in placement" was held by a United States District Court, which overturned a decision

---

168. C.J. v. School Bd. of Broward County, 438 So.2d 87 (Fla.App.1983). [Case No. 125]

169. Clark County Bd. of Educ. v. Jones, 625 S.W.2d 586 (Ky.App.1981).

170. Robinson v. Oak Park and River Forest High School, 213 Ill.App.3d 77, 156 Ill.Dec. 951, 571 N.E.2d 931 (1991). [Case No. 126]

171. The first case was Stuart v. Nappi, 443 F.Supp. 1235 (D.Conn.1978). That

there must be a causal relationship between the handicapping condition and the disruptive behavior before the limitation on expulsion applies, was added by Doe v. Koger, 480 F.Supp. 225 (N.D.Ind.1979).

172. S–1 v. Turlington, 635 F.2d 342 (5 Cir.1981), cert. den. 454 U.S. 1030, 102 S.Ct. 566, 70 L.Ed.2d 473 (1981). See also Metropolitan School Dist. of Wayne Tp., Marion County, Ind. v. Davila, 969 F.2d 485 (7 Cir.1992), cert. den. ___ U.S. ___, 113 S.Ct. 1360, 122 L.Ed.2d 740 (1993).

to the contrary by the state board of education in Illinois.[173]   (The hearing officer had found that the misconduct was not due to the handicap.)   This distinction between suspensions and expulsions of handicapped students was endorsed in dicta by the Sixth Circuit Court of Appeals.[174]

In 1988 the Supreme Court held that the "stay-put" provision of the Education of the Handicapped Act forbids state or local school authorities unilaterally to exclude handicapped children from the classroom for more than 10 days for dangerous or disruptive conduct growing out of their disabilities during the pendency of the statutory review proceedings.[175]   The Court rejected as clearly contrary to Congressional intent an exception from the general pattern for students who were dangerous to themselves or others.   It said that normal procedures for dealing with dangerous students (study carrels, detention, etc.) could be utilized, and if those and the maximum exclusion of 10 days did not suffice, court intervention could be sought.   The statute provides for a change in placement of a handicapped student only with parental or court approval, and the Supreme Court is not free to alter the wording.

Process of Determining Punishments

It is possible that a rule covering pupil conduct could be reasonable and the penalty for breaking it also reasonable, but the procedure for determining whether the individual had broken the rule and warranted the penalty could be unreasonable.   Involved here is the critical, but necessarily imprecise, concept of procedural "due process."   The elements essential to due process depend upon the circumstances, and literally thousands of cases have dealt with the question in innumerable types of fact situations in various fields of human endeavor.[176]

A remarkably large number of student discipline cases have been decided against school authorities not on their merits, but on the ground that procedural due process was inadequate.   The "hearing" element is perhaps the most crucial in public school discipline cases: Did the student have sufficient opportunity to respond to specific charges of misconduct and to have his side of the matter impartially considered before a decision to punish him in a particular way was made?   That due process in disciplinary cases does not require all safeguards afforded in a criminal proceeding is settled, as is the point that essential elements depend on the circumstances and on the gravity of the possible punishment.

In 1975 the Supreme Court set out the minimum constitutional requirements in cases involving suspensions of ten or fewer days.[177]   The

173. Board of Educ. of City of Peoria, School Dist. 150 v. Illinois State Bd. of Educ., 531 F.Supp. 148 (C.D.Ill.1982).

174. Kaelin v. Grubbs, 682 F.2d 595 (6 Cir.1982).

175. Honig v. Doe, 484 U.S. 305, 108 S.Ct. 592, 98 L.Ed.2d 686 (1988).

176. See "Procedural Due Process in Discharge" in Chapter 11.

177. Goss v. Lopez, 419 U.S. 565, 95 Ct. 729, 42 L.Ed.2d 725 (1975). [Case No. 127]

Court said due process requires that the student be given "oral or written notice of the charges against him and, if he denies them, an explanation of the evidence the authorities have and an opportunity to present his side of the story." It further said that there "need be no delay between the time 'notice' is given and the time of the hearing. In the great majority of cases the disciplinarian may informally discuss the alleged misconduct with the student minutes after it has occurred." Where, however, a student's presence constitutes a threat of disruption he may be removed immediately, with the due process requirements to be fulfilled as soon as practicable. The Court expressly rejected requirements for allowing representation by counsel, for presenting witnesses, and for confronting and cross-examining adverse witnesses. But it emphasized the facts before it, and stated that "longer suspensions or expulsions for the remainder of the school term, or permanently, may require more formal procedures."

The procedural requirements of Goss have been held to apply to transfers between schools of students for disciplinary reasons [178] and to suspensions for three days.[179] In each case the federal District Court concluded that property interests of students were involved and that the interests were of sufficient magnitude to qualify for the minimal constitutional due process protections. The court that ruled on transfers emphasized that its holding applied only to disciplinary transfers, because students have no general right to choose schools. Such a transfer may have an adverse impact on a student's education and, further, it connotes punishment. The requirements of due process for in-school suspensions depend on the degree of exclusion from the regular activities of the school.[180]

No constitutionally protected property right of a student to attend the graduation ceremony was found to exist by the Commonwealth Court of Pennsylvania, which said that the ceremony was only symbolic of the educational result, not an essential component of it.[181] Thus, federal due process did not apply regarding a suspension that overlapped graduation day. The student in this case did receive the diploma. Where a student who had completed all requirements for graduation was expelled on graduation day for sale of drugs, the court ordered the diploma issued.[182]

The argument that more extensive process is required when the disciplinary penalty indirectly leads to academic disadvantages is not necessarily persuasive. That examinations missed due to a three-day suspension led to a grade reduction was held not ground for court

---

178. Everett v. Marcase, 426 F.Supp. 397 (E.D.Pa.1977).

179. Hillman v. Elliott, 436 F.Supp. 812 (W.D.Va.1977).

180. Cole v. Newton Special Municipal Separate School Dist., 676 F.Supp. 749 (S.D.Miss.1987), aff. 853 F.2d 924 (5 Cir. 1988); Wise v. Pea Ridge School Dist., 855 F.2d 560 (8 Cir.1988).

181. Mifflin County School Dist. v. Stewart, 94 Pa.Cmwlth 313, 503 A.2d 1012 (1986).

182. Shuman v. Cumberland Valley School Dist. Bd. of Directors, 113 Pa. Cmwlth. 63, 536 A.2d 490 (1988).

intervention where the timing of the suspension was not intended to make it a more onerous penalty.[183] The Seventh Circuit Court of Appeals ruled similarly where the effect of a three-day suspension was to delay a student's graduation.[184]

The courts are not in agreement as to the precise demands of constitutional procedural due process in connection with possible penalties more severe than the ten day suspension involved in Goss. The lodestar is the elusive criterion of fairness in given circumstances. The more severe the punishment, the more carefully scrutinized are the procedures. But the technical demands of criminal law as to evidence and procedures are not imposed on education authorities in their conduct of a discipline hearing.

Perhaps the earliest set of guidelines as to the nature of the notice and hearing required prior to a long term exclusion from an educational institution was offered by the Fifth Circuit Court of Appeals in a case involving expulsion from a public college for nonacademic reasons.[185] The court said that "the notice should contain a statement of the specific charges and grounds which, if proven, would justify expulsion under the regulations of the Board of Education." Because assessing misconduct depends on collecting facts easily colored by the witnesses, the deciding body must hear both sides "in considerable detail." In the education setting, "the rudiments of an adversary proceeding" would require that "the student should be given the names of the witnesses against him and an oral or written report on the facts to which each witness testifies. He should also be given the opportunity to present * * * his own defense against the charges and to produce either oral testimony or written affidavits of witnesses in his behalf." The court expressly rejected any requirement of "a full-dress judicial hearing, with the right to cross-examine witnesses."

These criteria were later applied in the Fifth Circuit to a 30-day suspension on the public school level.[186] The Seventh Circuit Court of Appeals, however, has held that a student in such a situation is not entitled to the names of witnesses and information about their testimony.[187] Where expulsion was at issue, the Ninth Circuit Court of Appeals has required production and cross-examination of witnesses.[188] Such was not required by the Second Circuit Court of Appeals where credibility was not involved.[189] Over the years the weight of authority is

183. Donaldson v. Board of Educ., Danville School Dist. No. 118, 98 Ill.App.3d 438, 53 Ill.Dec. 946, 424 N.E.2d 737 (1981).

184. Lamb v. Panhandle Community Unit School Dist. No. 2, 826 F.2d 526 (7 Cir.1987).

185. Dixon v. Alabama State Bd. of Educ., 294 F.2d 150 (5 Cir.1961), cert. den. 368 U.S. 930, 82 S.Ct. 368, 7 L.Ed.2d 193 (1961).

186. Williams v. Dade County School Bd., 441 F.2d 299 (5 Cir.1971).

187. Linwood v. Board of Educ., City of Peoria, School Dist. No. 150, Illinois, 463 F.2d 763 (7 Cir.1972), cert. den. 409 U.S. 1027, 93 S.Ct. 475, 34 L.Ed.2d 320 (1972).

188. Black Coalition v. Portland School Dist. No. 1, 484 F.2d 1040 (9 Cir.1973).

189. Winnick v. Manning, 460 F.2d 545 (2 Cir.1972).

definitely that so long as basic fairness is preserved there is no require-ment for cross-examination of witnesses in student discipline cases.[190]

The Supreme Court of New Jersey invalidated an expulsion based on incidents reported by fellow students who told school authorities they were fearful of physical reprisal by the accused if they appeared at the hearing.[191] The court said that where the decision of a governmental agency which has power to compel attendance of witnesses turns on questions of fact, the party charged must be given the opportunity to confront and cross-examine adverse witnesses. Where there is clear and serious danger to student witnesses, however, it may not always be necessary to identify or produce them.[192] The balance between any right of confrontation and danger to accusers is a fine one in some school situations. The Sixth Circuit Court of Appeals has concluded that generally the necessity of protecting student witnesses from reprisal and ostracism outweighs the value to the truth-determining process of allow-ing the accused student to cross-examine the accusers.[193]

Cross-examination of the administrators who investigated the inci-dents leading to expulsion is not a general requirement for meeting due process standards.[194] Confronting a teacher, however, was necessary where a student's expulsion was based solely on a report by the teacher, who accused him of a defiant attitude when he remarked, "What a drag," after the teacher told him to stop kissing a girl in the hallway.[195]

Due process in discipline hearings on long term suspensions or expulsions does not, according to a three-judge federal District Court in Illinois, require a stenographic or mechanical recording of the proceed-ings.[196] Agreeing with this point, and adding that an open hearing is not essential, a federal District Court in Massachusetts upheld expulsion of a student with a long history of misconduct.[197] If, however, the student requests that testimony given at a closed hearing be recorded electroni-cally, the request must be honored, according to the highest court of that state.[198]

Right to counsel at an expulsion hearing for a public school student

190. Nash v. Auburn University, 812 F.2d 655 (11 Cir.1987); Gorman v. University of Rhode Island, 837 F.2d 7 (1 Cir. 1988); Newsome v. Batavia Local School Dist., 842 F.2d 920 (6 Cir.1988).

191. Tibbs v. Board of Educ. of Tp. of Franklin, 59 N.J. 506, 284 A.2d 179 (1971), aff'g 114 N.J.Super. 287, 276 A.2d 165 (1971).

192. Graham v. Knutzen, 362 F.Supp. 881 (D.Neb.1973); Dillon v. Pulaski County Special School Dist., 468 F.Supp. 54 (E.D.Ark.1978); John A. v. San Bernardino City Unified School Dist., 33 Cal.3d 301, 187 Cal.Rptr. 472, 654 P.2d 242 (1982).

193. Newsome v. Batavia Local School Dist., 842 F.2d 920 (6 Cir.1988).

194. Boykins v. Fairfield Bd. of Educ., 492 F.2d 697 (5 Cir.1974), cert. den. 420 U.S. 962, 95 S.Ct. 1350, 43 L.Ed.2d 438 (1975); Newsome v. Batavia Local School Dist., 842 F.2d 920 (6 Cir.1988).

195. Dillon v. Pulaski County Special School Dist., 594 F.2d 699 (8 Cir.1979).

196. Whitfield v. Simpson, 312 F.Supp. 889 (E.D.Ill.1970).

197. Pierce v. School Committee of New Bedford, 322 F.Supp. 957 (D.Mass.1971).

198. Nicholas B. v. School Committee of Worcester, 412 Mass. 20, 587 N.E.2d 211 (1992).

seems settled.[199] But that right does not extend to all hearings affecting students. The question of right to be represented by counsel at a "guidance conference" conducted within a school system was considered by the Court of Appeals, Second Circuit.[200] The purpose of the guidance conference was to provide opportunity for parents, teachers, counselors, supervisors, and others to plan educationally for the benefit of the child. It was instituted because a child was temporarily suspended for behavioral problems. Aside from changing the school of attendance, no final decision could be made at the conference. The appellate court, reversing a lower court, held that there was no requirement under constitutional due process for counsel to be present. It pointed out that the penalty was not grave, that it was not a criminal proceeding, and that the purpose of the conference was to help the pupil, rather than to make a quasi-judicial finding about him. The introduction of adversary proceedings involving counsel could be destructive of the purpose of the conference, reasoned the court.

In its decision upholding the constitutionality of corporal punishment, the Supreme Court addressed the question of procedural due process.[201] It concluded that, although corporal punishment in a public school implicates a constitutionally protected liberty interest, "traditional common law remedies are fully adequate to afford due process." Florida (the state of origin of the case) by statute required that both teacher and principal decide on the reasonable need for corporal punishment, and the Dade County school board policy contained explicit directions and limitations. The Supreme Court found no constitutional requirement of advance procedural safeguards, citing impracticability and cost as factors outweighing any "incremental benefit." It pointed out that, unlike the situation in Goss, corporal punishment did not deprive the student of any property right because his education would not be interrupted. State courts, of course, can set procedural, as well as substantive, restrictions on corporal punishment.[202]

Many challenges are brought against disciplinary actions where procedures specified by statute or board rule have not been strictly followed. If the infractions are minor and have not in fact prejudiced a student's rights, the courts tend not to overturn the punishments (as they probably would in the criminal area). Thus, where a student received no written notice as specified, but knew of the rules and the charges, the Supreme Court of Vermont refused to invalidate his expulsion;[203] where the student admitted he had brought a switchblade knife to school in violation of a rule, it was held not necessary that all

199. Givens v. Poe, 346 F.Supp. 202 (W.D.N.C.1972).

200. Madera v. Board of Educ. of City of New York, 386 F.2d 778 (2 Cir.1967), cert. den. 390 U.S. 1028, 88 S.Ct. 1416, 20 L.Ed.2d 284 (1968).

201. Ingraham v. Wright, 430 U.S. 651, 97 S.Ct. 1401, 51 L.Ed.2d 711 (1977). [Case No. 124]

202. Smith v. West Virginia State Bd. of Educ., 170 W.Va. 593, 295 S.E.2d 680 (1982).

203. Rutz v. Essex Junction Prudential Committee, 142 Vt. 400, 457 A.2d 1368 (1983).

witnesses and their testimony be identified before the hearing; [204] where hearsay evidence was admitted in an expulsion hearing, the court declined to overturn the decision based on that error; [205] and where a precise basis for a contemplated three-day suspension may not have been given but where the substantive evidence against the student was so overwhelming that a second hearing would not have altered the resultant suspension, no due process violation was found.[206] Where, however, a state board of education regulation required that no long term suspension be imposed without trying other punishments first, a 64-day suspension for one incident of drinking champagne was set aside.[207]

[Case No. 110] Applicability of Compulsory Education Statute to Children of Amish Parents

WISCONSIN v. YODER

Supreme Court of the United States, 1972.
406 U.S. 205, 92 S.Ct. 1526, 32 L.Ed.2d 15.

Mr. Chief Justice Burger delivered the opinion of the Court.

* * *

Respondents Jonas Yoder and Adin Yutzy are members of the Old Order Amish Religion, and respondent Wallace Miller is a member of the Conservative Amish Mennonite Church. They and their families are residents of Green County, Wisconsin. Wisconsin's compulsory school attendance law required them to cause their children to attend public or private school until reaching age 16 but the respondents declined to send their children, ages 14 and 15, to public school after completing the eighth grade. The children were not enrolled in any private school, or within any recognized exception to the compulsory attendance law, and they are conceded to be subject to the Wisconsin statute.

On complaint of the school district administrator for the public schools, respondents were charged, tried, and convicted of violating the compulsory attendance law in Green County Court and were fined the sum of $5 each. * * *

In support of their position, respondents presented as expert witnesses scholars on religion and education whose testimony is uncontradicted. They expressed their opinions on the relationship of the Amish belief concerning school attendance to the more general tenets of their religion, and described the impact that compulsory high school attendance could have on the continued survival of Amish communities as they exist in the United States today. * * *

204. McClain v. Lafayette County Bd. of Educ., 687 F.2d 121 (5 Cir.1982).

205. Racine Unified School Dist. v. Thompson, 107 Wis.2d 657, 321 N.W.2d 334 (App.1982).

206. Bystrom v. Fridley High School, 686 F.Supp. 1387 (D.Minn.1987), aff. 855 F.2d 855 (1988).

207. Quinlan v. University Place School Dist. 83, 34 Wash.App. 260, 660 P.2d 329 (1983).

A related feature of Old Order Amish communities is their devotion to a life in harmony with nature and the soil, as exemplified by the simple life of the early Christian era which continued in America during much of our early national life. Amish beliefs require members of the community to make their living by farming or closely related activities. Broadly speaking, the Old Order Amish religion pervades and determines the entire mode of life of its adherents. * * *

Amish objection to formal education beyond the eighth grade is firmly grounded in these central religious concepts. They object to the high school and higher education generally because the values it teaches are in marked variance with Amish values and the Amish way of life; they view secondary school education as an impermissible exposure of their children to a "worldly" influence in conflict with their beliefs. The high school tends to emphasize intellectual and scientific accomplishments, self-distinction, competitiveness, worldly success, and social life with other students. Amish society emphasizes informal learning-through-doing, a life of "goodness," rather than a life of intellect, wisdom, rather than technical knowledge, community welfare rather than competition, and separation, rather than integration with contemporary worldly society.

* * *

I

There is no doubt as to the power of a State, having a high responsibility for education of its citizens, to impose reasonable regulations for the control and duration of basic education. See, e.g., Pierce v. Society of Sisters. Providing public schools ranks at the very apex of the function of a State. Yet even this paramount responsibility was, in *Pierce,* made to yield to the right of parents to provide an equivalent education in a privately operated system. There the Court held that Oregon's statute compelling attendance in a public school from age eight to age 16 unreasonably interfered with the interest of parents in directing the rearing of their offspring including their education in church-operated schools. As that case suggests, the values of parental direction of the religious upbringing and education of their children in their early and formative years have a high place in our society. Thus, a State's interest in universal education, however highly we rank it, is not totally free from a balancing process when it impinges on other fundamental rights and interests, such as those specifically protected by the Free Exercise Clause of the First Amendment and the traditional interest of parents with respect to the religious upbringing of their children so long as they, in the words of *Pierce,* "prepare [them] for additional obligations."

It follows that in order for Wisconsin to compel school attendance beyond the eighth grade against a claim that such attendance interferes with the practice of a legitimate religious belief, it must appear either that the State does not deny the free exercise of religious belief by its requirement, or that there is a state interest of sufficient magnitude to override the interest claiming protection under the Free Exercise Clause. Long before there was general acknowledgment of the need for universal formal education, the Religion Clauses had specifically and firmly fixed the right to free exercise of religious beliefs, and buttressing this fundamental right was an equally firm, even if less explicit, prohibition against the establishment of any religion by government. The values underlying these two provisions relating to religion have been zealously protected, sometimes even at the expense of other interests of admittedly high social importance. The invalidation of financial aid to parochial schools by government grants for a salary subsidy for teachers is but one example of the extent to which courts have gone in this regard, notwithstanding that such aid programs were legislatively determined to be in the public interest and the service of sound educational policy by States and by Congress. Lemon v. Kurtzman; * * *.

The essence of all that has been said and written on the subject is that only those interests of the highest order and those not otherwise served can overbalance legitimate claims to the free exercise of religion. We can accept it as settled, therefore, that however strong the State's interest in universal compulsory education, it is by no means absolute to the exclusion or subordination of all other interests.

II

We come then to the quality of the claims of the respondents concerning the alleged encroachment of Wisconsin's compulsory school attendance statute on their rights and the rights of their children to the free exercise of the religious beliefs they and their forbears have adhered to for almost three centuries. In evaluating those claims we must be careful to determine whether the Amish religious faith and their mode of life are, as they claim, inseparable and interdependent. A way of life, however virtuous and admirable, may not be interposed as a barrier to reasonable state regulation of education if it is based on purely secular considerations; to have the protection of the Religion Clauses, the claims must be rooted in religious belief. Although a determination of what is a "religious" belief or practice entitled to constitutional protection may present a most delicate question, the very concept of ordered liberty precludes allowing every person to make his own standards on matters of conduct in which society as a whole has important interests. Thus, if the Amish asserted their claims because of their subjective evaluation and rejection of the contemporary secular values accepted by the majority, much as Thoreau rejected the social values of his time and isolated himself at Walden Pond, their claim would not rest on a religious basis. Thoreau's choice was philosophical and personal rather than religious, and such belief does not rise to the demands of the Religion Clause.

Giving no weight to such secular considerations, however, we see that the record in this case abundantly supports the claim that the traditional way of life of the Amish is not merely a matter of personal preference, but one of deep religious conviction, shared by an organized group, and intimately related to daily living. * * *

* * *

In sum, the unchallenged testimony of acknowledged experts in education and religious history, almost 300 years of consistent practice, and strong evidence of a sustained faith pervading and regulating respondents' entire mode of life support the claim that enforcement of the State's requirement of compulsory formal education after the eighth grade would gravely endanger if not destroy the free exercise of respondents' religious beliefs.

III

* * *

The State advances two primary arguments in support of its system of compulsory education. It notes, as Thomas Jefferson pointed out early in our history, that some degree of education is necessary to prepare citizens to participate effectively and intelligently in our open political system if we are to preserve freedom and independence. Further, education prepares individuals to be self-reliant and self-sufficient participants in society. We accept these propositions.

However, the evidence adduced by the Amish in this case is persuasively to the effect that an additional one or two years of formal high school for Amish children in place of their long established program of informal vocational education would do little to serve those interests. Respondents' experts testified at trial, without challenge, that the value of all education must be assessed in terms of its capacity to prepare the child for life. It is one thing to say that compulsory education for a year or two beyond the eighth grade may be necessary when its goal is the preparation of the child for life in modern society as the majority live, but it is quite another if the goal of education be viewed as the preparation of the child for life in the separated agrarian community that is the keystone of the Amish faith.

The State attacks respondents' position as one fostering "ignorance" from which the child must be protected by the State. No one can question the State's duty to protect children from ignorance but this argument does not square with the facts disclosed in the record. Whatever their idiosyncrasies as seen by the majority, this record strongly shows that the Amish community has been a highly successful social unit within our society even if apart from the conventional "mainstream." Its members are productive and very law-abiding members of society; they reject public welfare in any of its usual modern forms. The Congress itself recognized their self-sufficiency by authorizing exemption of such groups as the Amish from the obligation to pay social security taxes.

* * *

The State, however, supports its interest in providing an additional one or two years of compulsory high school education to Amish children because of the possibility that some such children will choose to leave the Amish community, and that if this occurs they will be ill-equipped for life. The State argues that if Amish children leave their church they should not be in the position of making their way in the world without the education available in the one or two additional years the State requires. However, on this record, that argument is highly speculative. There is no specific evidence of the loss of Amish adherents by attrition, nor is there any showing that upon leaving the Amish community Amish children, with their practical agricultural training and habits of industry and self-reliance, would become burdens on society because of educational shortcomings. Indeed, this argument of the State appears to rest primarily on the State's mistaken assumption, already noted, that the Amish do not provide any education for their children beyond the eighth grade, but allow them to grow in "ignorance." To the contrary, not only do the Amish accept the necessity for formal schooling through the eighth grade level, but continue to provide what has been characterized by the undisputed testimony of expert educators as an "ideal" vocational education for their children in the adolescent years.

* * *

The requirement for compulsory education beyond the eighth grade is a relatively recent development in our history. Less than 60 years ago, the educational requirements of almost all of the States were satisfied by completion of the elementary grades, at least where the child was regularly and lawfully employed. The independence and successful social functioning of the Amish community for a period approaching almost three centuries and more than 200 years in this country is strong evidence that there is at best a speculative gain, in terms of meeting the duties of citizenship, from an additional one or two years of compulsory formal education. Against this background it would require a more particularized showing from the State on this point to justify the severe interference with religious freedom such additional compulsory attendance would entail.

We should also note that compulsory education and child labor laws find their historical origin in common humanitarian instincts, and that the age limits of both laws have been coordinated to achieve their related objectives. * * *

* * *

IV

* * *

Contrary to the suggestion of the dissenting opinion of Mr. Justice Douglas, our holding today in no degree depends on the assertion of the religious interest of the child as contrasted with that of the parents. It is the parents who are subject to prosecution here for failing to cause their children to attend school, and it is their right of free exercise, not that of their children, that must determine Wisconsin's power to impose criminal penalties on the parent. The dissent argues that a child who expresses a desire to attend public high school in conflict with the wishes of his parent should not be prevented from doing so. There is no reason for the Court to consider that point since it is not an issue in the case.

The children are not parties to this litigation. The State has at no point tried this case on the theory that respondents were preventing their children from attending school against their expressed desires, and indeed the record is to the contrary. The State's position from the outset has been that it is empowered to apply its compulsory attendance law to Amish parents in the same manner as to other parents—that is, without regard to the wishes of the child. That is the claim we reject today.

* * *

V

For the reasons stated we hold, with the Supreme Court of Wisconsin, that the First and Fourteenth Amendments prevent the State from compelling respondents to cause their children to attend formal high school to age 16. Our disposition of this case, however, in no way alters our recognition of the obvious fact that courts are not school boards or legislatures, and are ill-equipped to determine the "necessity" of discrete aspects of a State's program of compulsory education. This should suggest that courts must move with great circumspection in performing the sensitive and delicate task of weighing a State's legitimate social concern when faced with religious claims for exemption from generally applicable educational requirements. It cannot be over-emphasized that we are not dealing with a way of life and mode of education by a group claiming to have recently discovered some "progressive" or more enlightened process for rearing children for modern life.

Aided by a history of three centuries as an identifiable religious sect and a long history as a successful and self-sufficient segment of American society, the Amish in this case have convincingly demonstrated the sincerity of their religious beliefs, the interrelationship of belief with their mode of life, the vital role which belief and daily conduct play in the continued survival of Old Order Amish communities and their religious organization, and the hazards presented by the State's enforcement of a statute generally valid as to others. Beyond this, they have carried the even more difficult burden of demonstrating the adequacy of their alternative mode of continuing informal vocational education in terms of precisely those overall interests that the State advances in support of its program of compulsory high school education. In light of this convincing showing, one which probably few other religious groups or sects could make, and weighing the minimal difference between what the State would require and what the Amish already accept, it was incumbent on the State to show with more particularity how its admittedly strong interest in compulsory education would be adversely affected by granting an exemption to the Amish.

Nothing we hold is intended to undermine the general applicability of the State's compulsory school attendance statutes or to limit the power of the State to promulgate reasonable standards that, while not impairing the free exercise of religion, provide for continuing agricultural vocational education under parental and church guidance by the Old Order Amish or others similarly situated. The States have had a long history of amicable and effective relationships with church-sponsored schools, and there is no basis for assuming that, in this related context, reasonable standards cannot be established concerning the content of the continuing vocational education of Amish children under parental guidance, provided always that state regulations are not inconsistent with what we have said in this opinion.

Affirmed.

* * *

Notes

1. Justices Powell and Rehnquist did not participate in deciding this case. Justice White wrote a concurring opinion in which Justices Brennan and Stewart joined. The concurring opinion emphasized "the legitimacy of the State's concern for enforcing minimal educational standards" and expressly rejected "the contention that parents may replace state educational requirements with their own idiosyncratic views of what knowledge a child needs to be a productive and happy member of society."

2. Justice Douglas dissented in part, disagreeing with "the Court's conclusion that the matter [of high school education] is within the dispensation of parents alone. * * * If the parents in this case are allowed a religious exemption, the inevitable effect is to impose the parents' notions of religious duty upon their children. * * * As the child has no other effective forum, it is in this litigation that his rights should be considered. And, if an Amish child desires to attend high school, and is mature enough to have that desire respected, the State may well be able to override the parents' religiously motivated objections." To what extent, if any, do you agree with this reasoning?

3. Amish religion "pervades and determines the entire mode of life of its adherents." "Its members are productive and very law-abiding members of society." Consider whether the result might have been different had the religion been less pervasive and/or if its members created problems for society.

4. Under federal law certain religious groups may be exempted from the payment of social security taxes if they waive the benefits of social security legislation and make provision for dependent members. 26 U.S.C. § 1402(h). Consider whether such exemption should apply to other than religious groups under the same conditions.

5. Is the power of the state over education of its citizens in any manner weakened by this decision? Are parents' rights or students' rights in any manner strengthened by this decision?

6. Less than five years earlier the Supreme Court had declined to review a Kansas holding against the Amish [State v. Garber, 197 Kan. 567, 419 P.2d 896 (1966), cert. den. 389 U.S. 51, 88 S.Ct. 236, 19 L.Ed.2d 50 (1967)]. In 1968 the Kansas legislature provided an exemption from the compulsory education statute for the Amish.

[Case No. 111] Constitutionality of Compulsory Education Statute

STATE v. POPANZ

Supreme Court of Wisconsin, 1983.
112 Wis.2d 166, 332 N.W.2d 750.

ABRAHAMSON, JUSTICE. This is an appeal from a judgment of conviction of * * * Lawrence C. Popanz on two counts of violating Wisconsin's compulsory school attendance law, sec. 118.15(1)(a), Stats.1981–82. Sec. 118.15(1)(a), requires a person having control of a child who is between the ages of 6 and 18 years to cause the child to attend public or private school regularly. * * *

The issue presented on certification is whether the phrase "private school" as used in sec. 118.15(1)(a) is impermissibly vague and sec. 118.15(1)(a) as applied to prosecutions involving "private schools" violates the fourteenth amendment to the United States Constitution and art. I, sec. 8, of the Wisconsin constitution. * * *

* * *

There is no simple litmus-paper test to determine whether a criminal statute is void for vagueness. The principles underlying the void for vagueness doctrine * * * stem from concepts of procedural due process. Due process requires that the law set forth fair notice of the conduct prohibited or required and proper standards for enforcement of the law and adjudication. * * *

A criminal statute must be sufficiently definite to give a person of ordinary intelligence who seeks to avoid its penalties fair notice of conduct required or prohibited. "Vague laws may trap the innocent by not providing fair warning."

A criminal statute must also provide standards for those who enforce the laws and those who adjudicate guilt. A statute should be sufficiently definite to allow law enforcement officers, judges, and juries to apply the terms of the law objectively to a defendant's conduct in order to determine guilt without having to create or apply their own standards. The danger posed by a vague law is that officials charged with enforcing the law may apply it arbitrarily or the law may be so unclear that a trial court cannot properly instruct the jury as to the applicable law. * * *

* * *

Like this defendant, we have searched the statutes, administrative rules and regulations and official Department of Public Instruction writings for a definition of "private school" or criteria which an entity must meet to be classified as a "private school" for purposes of sec. 118.15(1)(a). We have found neither a definition nor prescribed criteria. Nor does the phrase "private school" have a well-settled meaning in common parlance or in decisions of this court which could be used for purposes of applying sec. 118.15(1)(a). We therefore decline to adopt the definition of "private school" proposed by the court of appeals [in a prior decision, State v. White, 109 Wis.2d 64, 325 N.W.2d 76 (App.1982)] or by the State Superintendent of Public Instruction in an amicus brief.

* * *

We are not convinced that these definitions are the only ones a citizen, an administrator, or a court using dictionary definitions, court decisions and the statutes could deduce. In any event the legislature or its delegated agent should define the phrase "private school"; citizens or the courts should not have to guess at its meaning.

Since there is no definition of "private school," as that term is used in sec. 118.15(1)(a), the determination of what constitutes a "private school" apparently rests solely in the discretion of the school attendance officer of the district. * * * The record shows that in this school district a person seeking to comply with sec. 118.15(1)(a) apparently must consult the district school administrator to find out what that administrator considers a "private school" and must comply with the procedure set forth by that particular administrator to have a school classified as a private school. * * *

The lack of definition of "private school" delegates the basic policy matter, the determination of whether or not children are attending a private school, to local school officials whose decisions may rest on *ad hoc* and subjective standards. Sec. 118.15(1)(a) thus poses the danger of arbitrary and discriminatory enforcement, contrary to the basic values underlying the principles of due process.

The persons who must obey the law should not have to guess at what the phrase "private school" means. They should have some objective standards to guide them in their attempts to "steer between lawful and unlawful conduct." Furthermore, standards cannot lie only in the minds of persons whose duty it is to enforce the laws. We must conclude that the statute fails to provide fair notice to those who would seek to obey it and also lacks sufficient standards for proper enforcement.

The Department of Public Instruction, recognizing that there are no standards for determining what constitutes a "private school" under sec. 118.15(1)(a), suggests that the school attendance officer file a charge under that section if he or she "felt the attendance was not at a 'private school,'" leaving the final determination of what constitutes a "private school" to the courts. * * * We do not think that sec. 118.15(1)(a) or any other statutes or any rules equip the courts to define "private school" or to instruct a jury on what constitutes a private school. Defining the contours of laws subjecting a violator to criminal penalty is a legislative, not a judicial, function. The legislature, not the courts, should clarify sec. 118.15(1)(a).

We hold that sec. 118.15(1)(a) is void for vagueness insofar as it fails to define "private school." The court of appeals' decision in State v. White * * * is hereby overruled. * * *

Judgment of the circuit court reversed; cause remanded with directions to dismiss the complaint.

Notes

1. Wisconsin is the only state without a state board of education. (The State Superintendent of Public Instruction is popularly elected.) Might the problem here have been recognized and dealt with long ago by a state board responsible for education?

2. Certification is a process for having a higher court answer a question at the request of a lower court. Here the Court of Appeals of Wisconsin certified the question in the second paragraph because two panels of that court had differed on the answer.

3. Keep in mind that violation of a compulsory education statute is a criminal offense, and thus clarity requirements are much more stringent than in the area of civil law.

4. Observe that the court refused to approve a definition of "private school" despite both the request of the state department of education in an amicus brief and the effort of the Court of Appeals to do so. Was the court exercising appropriate judicial restraint or failing to exercise appropriate judicial leadership?

5. The United States Supreme Court has held that the Civil Rights Act of 1866 (see "Section 1981" in Appendix) "prohibits private, commercially operated, nonsectarian schools from denying admission to prospective students because they are Negroes." Runyon v. McCrary, 427 U.S. 160, 96 S.Ct. 2586, 49 L.Ed.2d 415 (1976).

[Case No. 112] Compulsory Education Statute—Satisfied by Home Instruction

STATE v. MASSA

Morris County Court of New Jersey, 1967.
95 N.J.Super. 382, 231 A.2d 252.

COLLINS, J.C.C. This is a trial *de novo* on appeal from the Pequannock Township Municipal Court. Defendants were charged and convicted with failing to cause their daughter Barbara, age 12, regularly to attend the public schools of the district and further for failing to either send Barbara to a private school or provide an equivalent education elsewhere than at school, contrary to the provisions of N.J.S.A. 18:14–14. The municipal magistrate imposed a fine of $2490 for both defendants.

* * *

The State presented two witnesses who testified that Barbara had been registered in the Pequannock Township School but failed to attend the 6th grade class from April 25, 1966 to June 1966 and the following school year from September 8, 1966 to November 16, 1966—a total consecutive absence of 84 days.

Mrs. Massa testified that she had taught Barbara at home for two years before September 1965. Barbara returned to school in September 1965, but began receiving her education at home again on April 25, 1966.

Mrs. Massa said her motive was that she desired the pleasure of seeing her daughter's mind develop. She felt she wanted to be with her child when the child would be more alive and fresh. She also maintained that in school much time was wasted and that at home a student can make better use of her time.

Mrs. Massa is a high school graduate. Her husband is an interior decorator. Neither holds a teacher's certificate. However, the State stipulated that a child may be taught at home and also that Mr. or Mrs. Massa need not be certified by the State of New Jersey to so teach. The sole issue in this case is one of equivalency. Have defendants provided their daughter with an education equivalent to that provided by the Pequannock Township School System?

Mrs. Massa introduced into evidence 19 exhibits. Five of these exhibits, in booklet form, are condensations of basic subjects, are concise and seem to contain all the basic subject material for the respective subjects. Mrs. Massa also introduced textbooks which are used as supplements to her own compilations as well as for test material and written problems.

Mrs. Massa introduced English, spelling and mathematics tests taken by her daughter at the Pequannock School after she had been taught for two years at home. The lowest mark on these tests was a B.

Other exhibits included one of over 100 geography booklets prepared by Mrs. Massa from National Geographic Magazine, each containing articles and maps concerning the topography and societies of a particular part of the world; a 1' wide and 30' long scroll depicting the evolution of life on earth commencing five billion years ago and continuing to the present, which appears to be a good visual aid not merely for children but adults as well; a series of 27 maps for study and memorization; textbooks used to supplement defendant's material; examples of books used as either references or historical reading, and photographs to show that the Massa family lives a normal, active, wholesome life. The family consists of the parents, three sons, (Marshall, age 16 and Michael, age 15, both attend high school; and William, age 6) and daughter Barbara.

There is also a report by an independent testing service of Barbara's scores on standard achievement tests. They show that she is considerably higher than the national median except in arithmetic.

Mrs. Massa satisfied this court that she has an established program of teaching and studying. There are definite times each day for the various subjects and recreation. She evaluates Barbara's progress through testing. If Barbara has not learned something which has been taught, Mrs. Massa then reviews that particular area.

Barbara takes violin lessons and attends dancing school. She also is taught art by her father, who has taught this subject in various schools.

Mrs. Massa called Margaret Cordasco as a witness. She had been Barbara's teacher from September 1965 to April 1966. She testified basically that Barbara was bright, well behaved and not different from the average child her age except for some trouble adjusting socially.

The State called as a witness David MacMurray, the Assistant Superintendent of Pequannock Schools. He testified that the defendants were not giving Barbara an equivalent education. Most of his testimony dealt with Mrs. Massa's lack of certification and background for teaching and the lack of social development of Barbara because she is being taught alone.

He outlined procedures which Pequannock teachers perform, such as evaluation sheets, lesson plans and use of visual aids. He also stressed specialization since Pequannock schools have qualified teachers for certain specialized subjects. He did not think the defendants had the specialization necessary to teach all basic subjects. He also testified about extra-curricular activity, which is available but not required.

The State placed six exhibits in evidence. These included a more recent mathematics book than is being used by defendants, a sample of teacher evaluation, a list of visual aids, sample schedules for the day and lesson plans, and an achievement testing program.

Leslie Rear, the Morris County Superintendent of Schools, then testified for the State. His testimony, like that of MacMurray, dealt primarily with social development of the child and Mrs. Massa's qualifications. He felt that Barbara was not participating in the learning process since she had not participated in the development of the material. Mrs. Massa, however, testified that these materials were used as an outline from which she taught her daughter and as a reference for her daughter to use in review—not as a substitute for all source material.

N.J.S.A. 18:14–14 provides:

"Every parent, guardian or other person having custody and control of a child between the ages of 6 and 16 years shall cause such child regularly to attend the public schools of the district or a day school in which there is given instruction equivalent to that provided in the public schools for children of similar grades and attainments *or to receive equivalent instruction elsewhere than at school.*" (Emphasis added)

* * *

This case presents two questions on the issue of equivalency for determination. What does the word "equivalent" mean in the context of N.J.S.A. 18:14–14? And, has the State carried the required burden of proof to convict defendants?

In Knox v. O'Brien, 7 N.J.Super. 608, 72 A.2d 389 (1950), the County Court interpreted the word "equivalent" to include not only academic equivalency but also the equivalency of social development. This interpretation appears untenable in the face of the language of our own statute and also the decisions in other jurisdictions.

If the interpretation in *Knox,* were followed, it would not be possible to have children educated outside of school. Under the *Knox* rationale, in order for children to develop socially it would be necessary for them to be educated in a group. A group of students being educated in the same manner and place would constitute a *de facto* school. Our statute provides that children may receive an equivalent education elsewhere than at school. What could have been intended by the Legislature by adding this alternative?

The Legislature must have contemplated that a child could be educated alone provided the education was equivalent to the public schools. Conditions in today's society illustrate that such situations exist. Examples are the child prodigy whose education is accelerated by private tutoring, or the infant performer whose education is provided by private tutoring. If group education is required by our statute, then these examples as well as all education at home would have to be eliminated.

* * *

Perhaps the New Jersey Legislature intended the word "equivalent" to mean taught by a certified teacher elsewhere than at school. However, I believe there are teachers today teaching in various schools in New Jersey who are not certified. The prosecutor stipulated, as stated above, that the State's position is that a child may be taught at home and that a person teaching at home is not required to be certified as a teacher by the State for the purpose of teaching his own children. Had the Legislature intended such a requirement, it would have so provided.

* * *

Faced with exiguous precedent in New Jersey and having reviewed * * * cases in other states, this court holds that the language of the New Jersey statute providing for "equivalent education elsewhere than at school," requires only a showing of academic equivalence. As stated above, to hold that the statute requires equivalent social contact and development as well would emasculate this alternative and allow only group education, thereby eliminating private tutoring or home education. A statute is to be interpreted to uphold its validity in its entirety if possible. This is the only reasonable interpretation available in this case which would accomplish this end.

Having determined the intent of the Legislature as requiring only equivalent academic instruction, the only remaining question is whether the defendants provided their daughter with an education equivalent to that available in the public schools. After reviewing the evidence presented by both the State and the defendants, this court finds that the State has not shown beyond a reasonable doubt that defendants failed to provide their daughter with an equivalent education.

The majority of testimony of the State's witnesses dealt with the lack of social development.

The other point pressed by the State was Mrs. Massa's lack of teaching ability and techniques based upon her limited education and experience. However, this court finds this testimony to be inapposite to the actual issue of equivalency under the New Jersey statute and the stipulations of the State. In any case, from my observation of her while testifying and during oral argument, I am satisfied that Mrs. Massa is self-educated and well qualified to teach her daughter the basic subjects from grades one through eight.

The remainder of the testimony of the State's witnesses dealt primarily with the child's deficiency in mathematics. This alone, however, does not establish an educational program unequivalent to that in the public schools in the face of the evidence presented by defendants.

Defendants presented a great deal of evidence to support their position, not the least of which was their daughter's test papers taken in the Pequannock school after having been taught at home for two years. The results speak for themselves. The evidence of the State which was actually directed toward the issue of equivalency in this case fell short of the required burden of proof.

The Massa family, all of whom were present at each of the hearings, appeared to be a normal, well-adjusted family. The behavior of the four Massa children in the courtroom evidenced an exemplary upbringing.

It is the opinion of this court that defendants' daughter has received and is receiving an education equivalent to that available in the Pequannock public schools. There is no indication of bad faith or improper motive on defendants' part. Under a more definite statute with sufficient guidelines or a lesser burden of proof, this might not necessarily be the case. However, within the framework of the existing law and the nature of the stipulations by the State, this court finds the defendants not guilty and reverses the municipal court conviction.

* * *

Notes

1. In Prince v. Commonwealth of Massachusetts, 321 U.S. 158, 64 S.Ct. 438, 88 L.Ed. 645 (1944), the Supreme Court said, "Acting to guard the general interest in youth's well being, the state as *parens patriae* may restrict the parent's control by requiring school attendance, regulating or prohibiting the child's labor, and in many other ways." In that case a Jehovah's Witness sent her minor child "to preach the gospel" by selling religious pamphlets on the public highways and was convicted of a violation of a child labor law.

2. Observe that this was a criminal case, where the standard of proof by the state is "beyond reasonable doubt."

3. Note the reason offered by the parent for her actions. If a parent is dissatisfied with the local public school, should he be required to pay for enrolling his child in a private school rather than teaching him at home? Would there be a difference between a parent's doing the teaching and a tutor's teaching at the parent's home?

4. Why do you think the court included the next to the last paragraph above?

5. "The parent cannot assert an absolute freedom to remove his child from all schooling, or to send him to a school where the curriculum includes not only mathematics but also the desirability and techniques of immediate violent overthrow of the government." Green v. Connally, 330 F.Supp. 1150 (D.D.C. 1971), aff. 404 U.S. 997, 92 S.Ct. 564, 30 L.Ed.2d 550 (1971).

[Case No. 113] Constitutionality of Residence Requirement for Tuition-Free Admission to Public Schools

MARTINEZ v. BYNUM

Supreme Court of the United States, 1983.
461 U.S. 321, 103 S.Ct. 1838, 75 L.Ed.2d 879.

JUSTICE POWELL delivered the opinion of the Court.

This case involves a facial challenge to the constitutionality of the Texas residency requirement governing minors who wish to attend public free schools while living apart from their parents or guardians.

I

Roberto Morales was born in 1969 in McAllen, Texas, and is thus a United States citizen by birth. His parents are Mexican citizens who reside in Reynosa, Mexico. He left Reynosa in 1977 and returned to McAllen to live with his sister, petitioner Oralia Martinez, for the primary purpose of attending school in the McAllen Independent School District. Although Martinez is now Morales's custodian, she is not—and does not desire to become—his guardian. As a result, Morales is not entitled to tuition-free admission to the McAllen schools. * * *

* * *

II

This Court frequently has considered constitutional challenges to residence requirements. On several occasions the Court has invalidated requirements that condition receipt of a benefit on a minimum period of residence within a jurisdiction, but it always has been careful to distinguish such durational residence requirements from bona fide residence requirements. In Shapiro v. Thompson, 394 U.S. 618, 89 S.Ct. 1322, 22 L.Ed.2d 600 (1969), for example, the Court invalidated one-year durational residence requirements that applicants for public assistance benefits were required to satisfy despite the fact that they otherwise had "met the test for residence in their jurisdictions." * * *

We specifically have approved bona fide residence requirements in the field of public education. The Connecticut statute before us in Vlandis v. Kline, 412 U.S. 441, 93 S.Ct. 2230, 37 L.Ed.2d 63 (1973), for example, was unconstitutional because it created an irrebuttable presumption of nonresidency for state university students whose legal addresses were outside of the State before they applied for admission. The statute violated the Due Process Clause because it in effect classified some bona fide state residents as nonresidents for tuition purposes. * * *

A bona fide residence requirement, appropriately defined and uniformly applied, furthers the substantial state interest in assuring that services provided for its residents are enjoyed only by residents. Such a requirement with respect to attendance in public free schools does not violate the Equal Protection Clause of the Fourteenth Amendment. It does not burden or penalize the constitutional right of interstate travel, for any person is free to move to a State and to establish residence there. A bona fide residence requirement simply requires that the person does establish residence before demanding the services that are restricted to residents.

There is a further, independent justification for local residence requirements in the public-school context. * * * The provision of primary and secondary education, of course, is one of the most important functions of local government. Absent residence requirements, there can be little doubt that the proper planning and operation of the schools would suffer significantly. The State thus has a substantial interest in imposing bona fide residence requirements to maintain the quality of local public schools.

III

The central question we must decide here is whether § 21.031(d) is a bona fide residence requirement. Although the meaning may vary according to context, "residence" generally requires both physical presence and an intention to remain. * * * This classic two-part definition of residence has been recognized as a minimum standard in a wide range of contexts time and time again.

* * *

Section 21.031 is far more generous than this traditional standard. It compels a school district to permit a child such as Morales to attend school without paying tuition if he has a bona fide intention to remain in the school district indefinitely, for he then would have a reason for being there other than his desire to attend school: his intention to make his home in the district. Thus § 21.031 grants the benefits of residency to all who satisfy the traditional requirements. The statute goes further and extends these benefits to many children even if they (or their families) do not intend to remain in the district indefinitely. As long as the child is not living in the district for the sole purpose of attending school, he satisfies the statutory test. For example, if a person comes to Texas to work for a year, his children will be eligible for tuition-free admission to the public schools. * * * In short, § 21.031 grants the benefits of residency to everyone who satisfies the traditional residence definition and to some who legitimately could be classified as nonresidents. Since there is no indication that this extension of the traditional definition has any impermissible basis, we certainly cannot say that § 21.031(d) violates the Constitution.

IV

The Constitution permits a State to restrict eligibility for tuition-free education to its bona fide residents. We hold that § 21.031 is a bona fide residence requirement that satisfies constitutional standards. The judgment of the Court of Appeals accordingly is affirmed.

Notes

1. The vote here was eight-to-one.

2. The Texas statute parallels the general common-law view (see "Residence for School Purposes" in this Chapter).

3. In Vlandis v. Klein (cited in case) the Supreme Court held that the constitutional flaw in the Connecticut arrangement was that one could not become a resident for purposes of tuition benefits after being admitted to the state university system. (Once admitted as a nonresident, that classification was permanent for tuition purposes.) That nonresidents could be charged a higher rate than residents was upheld.

4. As education is a state function, why should a child who resides in the state not be able to attend tuition-free any public school in the state? Should school districts be permitted to enroll out-of-district students upon payment of tuition by their parents?

[Case No. 114]   Constitutionality of Rule Forbidding Students to Wear Black Armbands

TINKER v. DES MOINES INDEPENDENT COMMUNITY SCHOOL DIST.

Supreme Court of the United States, 1969.
393 U.S. 503, 89 S.Ct. 733, 21 L.Ed.2d 731.

MR. JUSTICE FORTAS delivered the opinion of the Court.

Petitioner John F. Tinker, 15 years old, and petitioner Christopher Eckhardt, 16 years old, attended high schools in Des Moines. Petitioner Mary Beth Tinker, John's sister, was a 13-year-old student in junior high school.

In December 1965, a group of adults and students in Des Moines, Iowa, held a meeting at the Eckhardt home. The group determined to publicize their objections to the hostilities in Vietnam and their support for a truce by wearing black armbands during the holiday season and by fasting on December 16 and New Year's Eve. Petitioners and their parents had previously engaged in similar activities, and they decided to participate in the program.

The principals of the Des Moines schools became aware of the plan to wear armbands. On December 14, 1965, they met and adopted a policy that any student wearing an armband to school would be asked to remove it, and if he refused he would be suspended until he returned without the armband. Petitioners were aware of the regulation that the school authorities adopted.

On December 16, Mary Beth and Christopher wore black armbands to their schools. John Tinker wore his armband the next day. They were all sent home and suspended from school until they would come back without their armbands. They did not return to school until after the planned period for wearing armbands had expired—that is, until after New Year's Day.

* * *

✗ ⟨⟨First Amendment rights, applied in light of the special characteristics of the school environment, are available to teachers and students. It can hardly be argued that either students or teachers shed their constitutional rights to freedom of speech or expression at the schoolhouse gate. ⟩⟩This has been the unmistakable holding of this Court for almost 50 years.   * * *

* * * On the other hand, the Court has repeatedly emphasized the need for affirming the comprehensive authority of the States and of school officials, consistent with fundamental constitutional safeguards, to prescribe and control conduct in the schools.   * * *

The problem presented by the present case does not relate to regulation of the length of skirts or the type of clothing, to hair style or deportment.   Compare Ferrell v. Dallas Independent School District; Pugsley v. Sellmeyer.   It does not concern aggressive, disruptive action or even group demonstrations. ⟨Our problem involves direct, primary First Amendment rights akin to "pure speech."⟩

The school officials banned and sought to punish petitioners for a silent, passive, expression of opinion, unaccompanied by any disorder or disturbance on the part of petitioners.   There is here no evidence whatever of petitioners' interference, actual or nascent, with the school's work or of collision with the rights of other students to be secure and to be let alone.   Accordingly, this case does not concern speech or action that intrudes upon the work of the school or the rights of other students.

Only a few of the 18,000 students in the school system wore the black armbands.   Only five students were suspended for wearing them. There is no indication that the work of the school or any class was disrupted.   Outside the classrooms, a few students made hostile remarks to the children wearing armbands, but there were no threats or acts of violence on school premises.

The District Court concluded that the action of the school authorities was reasonable because it was based upon their ⟨fear of a disturbance⟩ from the wearing of the armbands.   But, in our system, undifferentiated fear or apprehension of disturbance is not enough to overcome the right to freedom of expression.   Any departure from absolute regimentation may cause trouble.   Any variation from the majority's opinion may inspire fear.   Any word spoken, in class, in the lunchroom or on the campus, that deviates from the views of another person, may start an argument or cause a disturbance.   But our Constitution says we must take this risk; and our history says that it is this sort of hazardous freedom—this kind of openness—that is the basis of our national strength and of the independence and vigor of Americans who grow up and live in this relatively permissive, often disputatious society.

In order for the State in the person of school officials to justify prohibition of a particular expression of opinion, it must be able to show that its action was caused by something more than a mere desire to avoid the discomfort and unpleasantness that always accompany an unpopular viewpoint.   Certainly where there is no finding and no showing that the exercise of the forbidden right would "materially and substantially interfere with the requirements of appropriate discipline in the operation of the school," the prohibition cannot be sustained. Burnside v. Byars.

In the present case, the District Court made no such finding, and our independent examination of the record fails to yield evidence that the school authorities had reason to anticipate that the wearing of the armbands would substantially interfere with the work of the school or impinge upon the rights of other students. Even an official memorandum prepared after the suspension that listed the reasons for the ban on wearing the armbands made no reference to the anticipation of such disruption.

On the contrary, the action of the school authorities appears to have been based upon an urgent wish to avoid the controversy which might result from the expression, even by the silent symbol of armbands, of opposition to this Nation's part in the conflagration in Vietnam. It is revealing, in this respect, that the meeting at which the school principals decided to issue the contested regulation was called in response to a student's statement to the journalism teacher in one of the schools that he wanted to write an article on Vietnam and have it published in the school paper. (The student was dissuaded.)

It is also relevant that the school authorities did not purport to prohibit the wearing of all symbols of political or controversial significance. The record shows that students in some of the schools wore buttons relating to national political campaigns, and some even wore the Iron Cross, traditionally a symbol of nazism. The order prohibiting the wearing of armbands did not extend to these. Instead, a particular symbol—black armbands worn to exhibit opposition to this Nation's involvement in Vietnam—was singled out for prohibition. Clearly, the prohibition of expression of one particular opinion, at least without evidence that it is necessary to avoid material and substantial interference with school work or discipline, is not constitutionally permissible.

* * *

* * * The principal use to which the schools are dedicated is to accommodate students during prescribed hours for the purpose of certain types of activities. Among those activities is personal intercommunication among the students. This is not only an inevitable part of the process of attending school. It is also an important part of the educational process. A student's rights therefore, do not embrace merely the classroom hours. When he is in the cafeteria, or on the playing field, or on the campus during the authorized hours, he may express his opinions, even on controversial subjects like the conflict in Vietnam, if he does so "[without] materially and substantially interfering with * * * appropriate discipline in the operation of the school" and without colliding with the rights of others. Burnside v. Byars. But conduct by the student, in class or out of it, which for any reason—whether it stems from time, place, or type of behavior—materially disrupts classwork or involves substantial disorder or invasion of the rights of others is, of course, not immunized by the constitutional guaranty of freedom of speech. Cf. Blackwell v. Issaquena County Board of Education.

Under our Constitution, free speech is not a right that is given only to be so circumscribed that it exists in principle but not in fact. Freedom of expression would not truly exist if the right could be exercised only in an area that a benevolent government has provided as a safe haven for crackpots. The Constitution says that Congress (and the States) may not abridge the right to free speech. This provision means what it says. We properly read it to permit reasonable regulation of speech-connected activities in carefully restricted circumstances. But we do not confine the permissible exercise of First Amendment rights to a telephone booth or the four corners of a pamphlet, or to supervised and ordained discussion in a school classroom.

If a regulation were adopted by school officials forbidding discussion of the Vietnam conflict, or the expression by any student of opposition to it anywhere on school property except as part of a prescribed classroom exercise, it would be obvious that the regulation would violate the constitutional rights of students, at least if it could not be justified by a showing that the students' activities would materially and substantially disrupt the work and discipline of the school. * * * In the circumstances of the present case, the prohibition of the silent passive "witness of the armbands," as one of the children called it, is no less offensive to the constitution's guaranties.

As we have discussed the record does not demonstrate any facts which might reasonably have led school authorities to forecast substantial disruption of or material interference with school activities, and no disturbances or disorders on the school premises in fact occurred. * * *

* * *

Reversed and remanded.

* * *

Notes

1. Justices Black and Harlan dissented. Justice Stewart added a concurring opinion in which he said that he did not believe that, "school discipline aside, the First Amendment rights of children are co-extensive with those of adults." Justice White added a concurrence to emphasize the "distinction between communicating by words and communicating by acts or conduct which sufficiently impinge on some valid state interest."

2. The case is cited almost ritualistically in student discipline cases, by school authorities as well as student plaintiffs. It establishes general guidelines applicable to myriad situations. It was the first Supreme Court decision with opinion in the area of student discipline in general.

3. The court said that the wearing of armbands in the circumstances of this case was "entirely divorced from actually or potentially disruptive conduct." Justice Black said that wearing the bands was designed to and did divert the students' minds from their studies to the highly emotional subject of the Vietnam war. To what extent is either view capable of proof?

4. Observe that the burden of showing that the wearing of armbands "might reasonably have led school authorities to forecast substantial disruption" of school activities is placed upon the board. To what extent should a board be permitted to adopt preventive rules and when should it be required to wait "until the horse is stolen" before "locking the door"?

5. Notice that the court points out what types of school rules the case does not involve. *Ferrell* was the first student hairstyle case to be decided by a United States Court of Appeals. (It was decided in favor of school authorities). *Pugsley* is discussed in this chapter.

6. Two weeks after the *Tinker* decision, the Supreme Court, with only Justice Douglas believing to the contrary, denied certiorari in a case involving the suspension of some college students for disruptive activities. Justice Fortas added the following statement:

"I agree that certiorari should be denied. The petitioners were suspended from college *not* for expressing their opinions on a matter of substance, but for violent and destructive interference with the rights of others. An adequate hearing was afforded them on the issue of suspension. The petitioners contend that their conduct was protected by the First Amendment, but the findings of the District Court, which were accepted by the Court of Appeals, establish that the petitioners here engaged in an aggressive and violent demonstration, and not in peaceful nondisruptive expression, such as was involved in [*Tinker*]. The petitioners' conduct was therefore clearly not protected by the First and Fourteenth Amendments." Barker v. Hardway, 394 U.S. 905, 89 S.Ct. 1009, 22 L.Ed.2d 217 (1969).

[Case No. 115] Constitutionality of Rule Forbidding Students to Wear Buttons

GUZICK v. DREBUS

United States Court of Appeals, Sixth Circuit, 1970.
431 F.2d 594.

O'SULLIVAN, SENIOR CIRCUIT JUDGE. Plaintiff-Appellant, Thomas Guzick, Jr.,—prosecuting this action by his father and next friend, Thomas Guzick—appeals from dismissal of his complaint in the United States District Court for the Northern District of Ohio, Eastern Division. Plaintiff's complaint sought an injunction and other relief against defendant Drebus, the principal of Shaw High School in East Cleveland, Ohio, as well as against the Superintendent and Board of Education for the schools of said city. Plaintiff also asked for declaratory relief and damages.

The complaint charged that Thomas Guzick, Jr., a seventeen year old, eleventh grade student at Shaw High School, had been denied the right of free speech guaranteed to him by the United States Constitution's First Amendment. He asserted that this right had been denied him when he was suspended for refusing to remove, while in the classrooms and the school premises, a button which solicited participation in an anti-war demonstration that was to take place in Chicago on April 5. The legend of the button was:

"April 5 Chicago

GI—Civilian

Anti-War

Demonstration

Student Mobilization Committee"

* * *

On March 11, 1969, young Guzick and another student Havens, appeared at the office of defendant Drebus, principal of the high school, bringing with them a supply of pamphlets which advocated attendance at the same planned Chicago anti-war demonstration as was identified by the button. The boys were denied permission to distribute the pamphlets, and were also told to remove the buttons which both were then wearing. Guzick said that his lawyer, counsel for him in this litigation, told him that a United States Supreme Court decision entitled him to wear the button in school. Principal Drebus directed that he remove it and desist from wearing it in the school. Being told by Guzick that he would not obey, the principal suspended him and advised that such suspension would continue until Guzick obeyed. The other young man complied, and returned to school. Guzick did not, and has made no effort to return to school. This lawsuit promptly followed on March 17.

* * *

The District Judge denied plaintiff's application for a preliminary injunction, and after a plenary evidentiary hearing, which was concluded on March 26, 1969, the complaint was dismissed. * * *

We affirm.

Plaintiff insists that the facts of this case bring it within the rule of Tinker v. Des Moines Independent Community School District. We are at once aware that unless *Tinker* can be distinguished, reversal is required. We consider that the facts of this case clearly provide such distinction.

The rule applied to appellant Guzick was of long standing—forbidding all wearing of buttons, badges, scarves and other means whereby the wearers identify themselves as supporters of a cause or bearing messages unrelated to their education. Such things as support the high school athletic teams or advertise a school play are not forbidden. The rule had its genesis in the days when fraternities were competing for the favor of the students and it has been uniformly enforced. The rule has continued as one of universal application and usefulness. While controversial buttons appeared from time to time, they were required to be removed as soon as the school authorities could get to them.

* * *

From the total evidence, including that of educators, school administrators and others having special relevant qualifications, the District Judge concluded that abrogation of the rule would inevitably result in collisions and disruptions which would seriously subvert Shaw High School as a place of education for its students, black and white.

1. The Rule of *Tinker*.

Contrasting with the admitted long standing and uniform enforcement of Shaw's no symbol rule, the majority opinion in *Tinker* was careful to point out,

> "It is also relevant that the school authorities [in *Tinker*] did not purport to prohibit the wearing of all symbols of political or controversial significance. * * * "

The armband demonstration in *Tinker* was a one time affair, with a date for its ending fixed in its original plan. Plaintiff here argues that Shaw's no symbol rule should be abrogated to accommodate his wish to be relieved from obeying it. * * *

Further distinguishing *Tinker* from our case are their respective settings. No potential racial collisions were background to *Tinker,* whereas here the changing racial composition of Shaw High from all white to 70% black, made the no symbol rule of even greater good than had characterized its original adoption. In our view, school authorities should not be faulted for adhering to a relatively non-oppressive rule that will indeed serve our ultimate goal of meaningful integration of our public schools. * * *

2. Shaw High School's need for its Rule.

In *Tinker* the Court concluded that a regulation forbidding expressions opposing the Vietnam conflict anywhere on school property would violate the students' constitutional rights,

> "at least *if it could not be justified* by a showing that the students' activities would materially and substantially disrupt the work and discipline of the school." (Emphasis supplied.)

* * *

The District Judge was of the view that the situation at Shaw was "incendiary." The evidence justified such a view.

> "The Court has concluded that if all buttons were permitted at Shaw High, many students would seek to wear buttons conveying an inflammatory or provocative message or which would be considered as an insult or affront to certain of the other students. Such buttons have been worn at Shaw High School in the past. One button of this nature, for example, contained the message 'Happy Easter, Dr. King.' This button caused a fight last year in the school cafeteria at Shaw. Other buttons, such as 'Black Power,' 'Say it loud, Black and Proud,' and buttons depicting a black mailed fist have been worn at Shaw and would likely be worn again, if permitted. These buttons would add to the already incendiary situation and would undoubtedly provoke further fighting among the students and lead

to a material and substantial disruption of the educational process at Shaw High."

Further distinction from *Tinker* is provided by the long standing and *universal application* of Shaw's rule. * * *

The District Judge here points out that for school authorities to allow some buttons and not others would create an unbearable burden of selection and enforcement. * * *

In our view, the potentiality and the imminence of the admitted rebelliousness in the Shaw students support the wisdom of the no-symbol rule. Surely those charged with providing a place and atmosphere for educating young Americans should not have to fashion their disciplinary rules only after good order has been at least once demolished.

3. Conclusion.

We will not attempt extensive review of the many great decisions which have forbidden abridgment of free speech. We have been thrilled by their beautiful and impassioned language. They are part of our American heritage. None of these masterpieces, however, were composed or uttered to support the wearing of buttons in high school classrooms. We are not persuaded that enforcement of such a rule as Shaw High School's no-symbol proscription would have excited like judicial classics. Denying Shaw High School the right to enforce this small disciplinary rule could, and most likely would, impair the rights of its students to an education and the rights of its teachers to fulfill their responsibilities.

* * *

Notes

1. The Supreme Court denied certiorari with only Justice Douglas in dissent. 401 U.S. 948, 91 S.Ct. 941, 28 L.Ed.2d 231 (1971). What are the distinctions between this case and *Tinker* (Case No. 114)?

2. Consider whether *Tinker* might have been decided differently if all symbols of controversial significance had been prohibited rather than only black armbands. How does the concept of invalidity for overbreadth square with the holding in this case?

3. Two cases involving symbolic expression by students of Mexican descent resulted in different outcomes in federal District Courts. Brown armbands were held to be constitutionally protected when they symbolized the view that certain educational policies should be changed. Aguirre v. Tahoka Independent School Dist., 311 F.Supp. 664 (N.D.Tex.1970). Black berets were held not protected where the wearers used the symbol to indicate their power to disrupt the conduct of the school and to exercise control over the student body. Hernandez v. School Dist. No. 1, Denver, Colorado, 315 F.Supp. 289 (D.Colo.1970).

[Case No. 116] Power of Board to Suspend Students for Disrupting Pep Rally

TATE v. BOARD OF EDUC. OF JONESBORO, ARKANSAS, SPECIAL SCHOOL DIST.

United States Court of Appeals, Eighth Circuit, 1972.
453 F.2d 975.

MEHAFFY, CIRCUIT JUDGE. The sole issue before us is whether or not plaintiffs, the parents of two Negro students attending Jonesboro High School and others similarly situated, have been denied their constitutional rights of freedom of speech, due process and equal protection by their suspension from school for a five-day period (later reduced to three days) for violating the school rules by deliberately attending a regularly scheduled pep rally where they knew that the tune "Dixie" would be played and demonstrating by getting up and walking out in violation of the rules of the school. All students had been notified in advance that the tune would be played in the gymnasium and that those not desirous of attending the rally did not have to do so but could report instead to the auditorium. Despite their forewarned notice and option, the offending students deliberately violated established school rules and thereafter they failed and refused to discuss their suspension with school authorities and offered no evidence in justification at their trial, as will be more detailed hereafter. The case was tried to the district court on a stipulation of facts. The court held that there was no federal question involved and the complaint was dismissed. We affirm the judgment of the district court.

Factual Background. Jonesboro High School voluntarily commenced operating a unitary school system in 1966. The school had thus operated as a completely integrated school without any abnormal problems for the first two years of total integration. For many years the playing of the song "Dixie" at pep assemblies had been permitted. For these first two years, black and white students participated in curricular and extracurricular activities together.

At a faculty meeting on September 26, 1968 one of the members stated that a few individual requests had been made to omit the playing of "Dixie" at pep assemblies as the song allegedly was offensive to some Negro students. The school authorities concluded to experiment with the discontinuance of the playing of "Dixie" at pep assemblies but without any notice or publicity. This was done for approximately a month during which time there were complaints from white students and parents about discontinuing playing "Dixie" as it had been on the program for many years. On October 25, 1968 the committee decided to submit the matter to a vote to determine how many students were in favor of the continued use and how many were opposed. The vote being favorable to the playing of the tune, it was announced that thereafter attendance at the pep assemblies would be optional and anyone who did not want to attend could report to the auditorium instead of the gymnasium while pep assemblies were being held.

On November 1, 1968 some twenty-five black students and five white students chose not to attend the scheduled pep rally and reported to the auditorium as instructed. Others went to the gymnasium where the assembly was being held and when "Dixie" was played as the fourth number on the program twenty-nine black students "got up and left the pep assembly in protest of the playing of 'Dixie'." These dissenters did not destroy any property en route to the auditorium. The principal handed them a piece of paper and asked that all who had left the pep assembly sign their names on it. After consulting with other school officials, the superintendent advised the students that the walkout action was deemed disruptive of the school program and they were being suspended for a period of five days for such action. The superintendent and principal then offered to answer any questions which they might have but the suspended students became so loud and unruly that the meeting was terminated.

On November 4, 1968 the parents were advised that the suspension would be reduced to three days for those who would promise the principal privately that when they returned to school they would come to get an education and do something to make the school a better one.

* * *

Defendant school officials denied that the complainants or any members of their class had been intimidated, harassed or unreasonably punished, and asserted that during the 1968 school year friction between the white and black students had noticeably increased. They also alleged that the playing of "Dixie" by the pep rally band and the school band at pep rallies and regularly scheduled athletic events at Jonesboro High School had been a time honored practice, that after discontinuance of playing "Dixie" participation at pep rallies and enthusiasm diminished with resultant loss of student morale and that the experiment they had adopted to eliminate its playing was a failure. They pleaded affirmatively that they had made an honest, sincere and conscientious effort to operate a completely integrated high school in such a manner as to give all students equal opportunity to receive the best possible education and that the policies, rules and regulations promulgated by them are reasonable and necessary and have been administered in a fair and impartial manner without regard to race, creed or color.

* * *

Plaintiffs argue first that their departure from the pep rally was symbolic action guarded from suppression by the Free Speech Clause of the First Amendment to the Federal Constitution. For purposes of this opinion, we accept the argument that plaintiffs' actions constituted speech although the problem is somewhat different from Tinker v. Des Moines Independent Community School District, 393 U.S. 503, 89 S.Ct. 733, 21 L.Ed.2d 731 (1969), where the Supreme Court was dealing with "direct, primary First Amendment rights akin to 'pure speech' " and not with "aggressive, disruptive action or even group demonstrations." First Amendment rights may be infringed upon by reasonable regulations necessary for keeping orderly conduct during school sessions. A reasonable regulation has been defined as one "which is 'essential in maintaining order and discipline on school property' and 'which measurably contributes to the maintenance of order and decorum within the educational system.'" The school regulation involved here provided: "It is strictly against the rules to create a disturbance in assembly." Plaintiffs attack the rule as applied to the facts of this case but do not otherwise attack the rule itself. They argue that a "quiet procession" from a pep rally to another authorized place, done as a protest, cannot be prohibited since this conduct is not disruptive. The school officials found that the walkout was disruptive. Inasmuch as the walkout took place during the fourth number on the program and involved twenty-nine students we cannot find that no disruption of school "order and decorum" occurred or that this conduct was a constitutionally protected form of dissent. It is not necessary for school officials to refrain from taking any action until there is a complete breakdown in school discipline. They have inherent authority to maintain order and hence have latitude and discretion in formulating rules and regulations and general standards of conduct. The school officials here were dealing with growing student unrest which had already resulted in a scheduled assembly being cancelled. * * *

We cannot say that the district court's finding was clearly erroneous.

Plaintiffs argue that the district court erred in holding that the suspension did not violate due process. We will assume arguendo that due process applies when a publicly financed educational institution imposes a mild, as well as a severe, penalty upon a student.

"The 'differing rules of fair play' encompassed by the concept of due process '[vary] according to specific factual contexts * * * and differing types of proceedings.'" Madera v. Board of Education of the City of New York. In these school discipline cases the nature of the sanction affects the validity of the procedure used in imposing it. Here, the students were suspended for five days which was reduced to three days for any student who would state privately to the principal that on his return he would come to get an education and "do something to make it a better school." A suspension carries with it a grade reduction of two points of the student's average daily score for each day suspended. However, if this reduction should result in lowering a student's grade as much as two letter grades or cause him to make a failing grade, then the student may do extra work to remove the penalty. There is no contention that any student who failed was refused an opportunity to make up the work or that any suspension caused any failure or otherwise adversely affected the student's over-all grades. When the students were notified of the suspension and the cause for the suspension, they were also offered a question and answer period. Because of the loudness and unruliness of the suspended students the question and answer period was terminated.

We apply the standard of reasonableness in determining whether or not a student has been deprived of his constitutional rights. We do not regard those cases involving expulsion or suspension for a substantial interval as controlling here. Under the circumstances of the case before us, where there was no question as to what acts were involved or what individuals were involved, where notice was given and an opportunity for an informal hearing was given, and where the penalty was mild, there was no violation of due process shown and the district court's holding was not clearly erroneous.

Finally plaintiffs argue that the lower court's decision denied them equal protection of the laws within the meaning of the Fourteenth Amendment by refusing to enjoin the playing of "Dixie" at the school assemblies.

Plaintiffs' allegation in support of the requested injunction is that the tune is racially abusive and its playing constitutes officially sanctioned racial abuse; hence the playing of the offensive song forces them not to attend the pep rallies and denies them equal protection of the law. Plaintiffs argue that the First Amendment does not protect the rights of defendants since we "cannot countenance in our public schools officially-sponsored expression of sentiment which defies the law of the Nation." They also urge that "the right to free speech does not give rise to the right to publicly insult or defame. * * *"

At the outset we note that the tune is not shown to be offensive to all blacks even at Jonesboro High School. We reject the idea that the words or the tune of "Dixie" are within that "well-defined and narrowly limited classes of speech, the prevention and punishment of which have never been thought to raise any Constitutional problem. These include the lewd and obscene, the profane, the libelous, and the insulting or 'fighting' words—those which by their very utterance inflict injury or tend to incite an immediate breach of the peace." It is therefore necessary to look at the history of the song to determine whether the song is racially abusive.

"Dixie." There is many a myth about "Dixie" as well as claims of authorship and there have been many variations of its lyrics by various people. There seems to be little doubt, however, that the song was written prior to the Civil War by Daniel Decatur Emmett, a native of Ohio, as a "walk-around" for a minstrel show. It is best described as a "typical American song with a gay and catchy tune." See *Sampler of American Songs,* a Copyright 1969, by Maymie R. Krythe, a book narrating the "background and lore connected with 18 of our most famous and beloved American songs." At page 100, the author states:

> "Over a century ago (1859) Daniel Decatur Emmett, an American minstrel performer and composer, wrote both the words and music for 'Dixie,' a typical American song with a gay and catchy tune. Although he was a Northerner, his song won immediate popularity.

* * *

"At the beginning of the Civil War, 'Dixie' was taken over by the Southerners as their Confederate battle song. But today all sections of our great country sing 'Dixie,' termed one of 'the most rollicking of our national songs,' known and loved throughout the world."

Referring to "Dixie" as "Emmett's masterpiece," the author noted that it has been given much praise by various writers. She also states that Louis C. Elson, in *The National Music of America,* emphasized that " 'Dixie' was a great favorite of the Civil War President, Abraham Lincoln, as well as of the Northern soldiers, pointing out that 'it was one of the most characteristic melodies that sprang from the epoch of the war, although written as a picture of peace and happiness' " and that "[t]he contagious nature of its melody helped to bring about its rapid spread and popularity." Lincoln had used the tune prior to the War as one of his campaign songs, and after the War was over he asked the Marine Band to play it at the White House.

* * *

On this record we cannot say that the tune "Dixie" constitutes a badge of slavery or that the playing of the tune under the facts as presented constituted officially sanctioned racial abuse. Such a ruling would lead to the prohibition of the playing of many of our most famous tunes.

The atmosphere on the campus had been so tense as to cause the school principal in an address to the student body on October 21, 1968 to say, "presently on our campus there are cries of 'Black Power,' I suppose 'White Power,' * * *" and warn the students against such declarations under pain of being dealt with as disrupting the school. The action taken by the school authorities obviously averted serious trouble and was not only practical but clearly and properly within the rights of the school officials if we are to have any discipline in our public schools. Court intervention could in such situations only serve to fan the embers of unrest. The court should never interfere except where there is a clear case of constitutional infringement. This is not such a case.

Accordingly, the judgment is affirmed.

Notes

✗ 1. There was evidence of intention to disrupt the rally. Compare this situation with that in *Tinker* (Case No. 114) and that in *Guzick* (Case No. 115).

2. In Gebert v. Hoffman, 336 F.Supp. 694 (E.D.Pa.1972), it was held that students could be temporarily suspended after they disrupted the school by engaging in a sit-in, did not attend classes, forced removal of some classes from their scheduled locations, and moved noisily through the halls.

3. In Smith v. St. Tammany Parish School Bd., 448 F.2d 414 (5 Cir.1971), it was held that symbols or indicia expressing desire of the school board or its employees to maintain segregated schools must be removed. The Confederate flag was one such symbol. Where there had not been de jure racial segregation, however, the Seventh Circuit declined to require changing the school flag that

resembled the Confederate flag and the name of the glee club from "Southern Aires." Banks v. Muncie Community Schools, 433 F.2d 292 (7 Cir.1970).

4. In upholding the inherent power of school authorities to discipline students involved in a "walkout" connected with a dispute over the racial composition of the school's cheerleader squad, the Fifth Circuit Court of Appeals stated that "no student needs a regulation to be told he is expected and required to attend classes." Dunn v. Tyler Independent School Dist., 460 F.2d 137 (5 Cir.1972).

[Case No. 117]   Power of Board to Discipline Student for Vulgar Speech

BETHEL SCHOOL DIST. NO. 403 v. FRASER

Supreme Court of the United States, 1986.
478 U.S. 675, 106 S.Ct. 3159, 92 L.Ed.2d 549.

CHIEF JUSTICE BURGER delivered the opinion of the Court.

We granted certiorari to decide whether the First Amendment prevents a school district from disciplining a high school student for giving a lewd speech at a school assembly.

I

A

On April 26, 1983, respondent Matthew N. Fraser, a student at Bethel High School in Bethel, Washington, delivered a speech nominating a fellow student for student elective office. Approximately 600 high school students, many of whom were 14–year–olds, attended the assembly. Students were required to attend the assembly or to report to the study hall. The assembly was part of a school-sponsored educational program in self-government. Students who elected not to attend the assembly were required to report to study hall. During the entire speech, Fraser referred to his candidate in terms of an elaborate, graphic, and explicit sexual metaphor.

Two of Fraser's teachers, with whom he discussed the contents of his speech in advance, informed him that the speech was "inappropriate and that he probably should not deliver it" and that his delivery of the speech might have "severe consequences."

During Fraser's delivery of the speech, a school counselor observed the reaction of students to the speech. Some students hooted and yelled; some by gestures graphically simulated the sexual activities pointedly alluded to in respondent's speech. Other students appeared to be bewildered and embarrassed by the speech. One teacher reported that on the day following the speech, she found it necessary to forgo a portion of the scheduled class lesson in order to discuss the speech with the class.

A Bethel High School disciplinary rule prohibiting the use of obscene language in the school provides:

"Conduct which materially and substantially interferes with the educational process is prohibited, including the use of obscene, profane language or gestures."

The morning after the assembly, the Assistant Principal called Fraser into her office and notified him that the school considered his speech to have been a violation of this rule. Fraser was presented with copies of five letters submitted by teachers, describing his conduct at the assembly; he was given a chance to explain his conduct, and he admitted to having given the speech described and that he deliberately used sexual innuendo in the speech. Fraser was then informed that he would be suspended for three days, and that his name would be removed from the list of candidates for graduation speaker at the school's commencement exercises.

Fraser sought review of this disciplinary action through the School District's grievance procedures. The hearing officer determined that the speech given by respondent was "indecent, lewd, and offensive to the modesty and decency of many of the students and faculty in attendance at the assembly." The examiner determined that the speech fell within the ordinary meaning of "obscene," as used in the disruptive-conduct rule, and affirmed the discipline in its entirety. Fraser served two days of his suspension, and was allowed to return to school on the third day.

B

* * * Respondent alleged a violation of his First Amendment right to freedom of speech and sought both injunctive relief and monetary damages under 42 U.S.C. § 1983. * * * The District Court awarded respondent $278 in damages, $12,750 in litigation costs and attorney's fees, and enjoined the School District from preventing respondent from speaking at the commencement ceremonies. Respondent, who had been elected graduation speaker by a write-in vote of his classmates, delivered a speech at the commencement ceremonies on June 8, 1983.

The Court of Appeals for the Ninth Circuit affirmed the judgment of the District Court * * *. * * *

* * * We reverse.

II

This Court acknowledged in *Tinker v. Des Moines Independent Community School Dist.,* that students do not "shed their constitutional rights to freedom of speech or expression at the schoolhouse gate." The Court of Appeals read that case as precluding any discipline of Fraser for indecent speech and lewd conduct in the school assembly. That court appears to have proceeded on the theory that the use of lewd and obscene speech in order to make what the speaker considered to be a point in a nominating speech for a fellow student was essentially the same as the wearing of an armband in *Tinker* as a form of protest or the expression of a political position.

The marked distinction between the political "message" of the armbands in *Tinker* and the sexual content of respondent's speech in this case seems to have been given little weight by the Court of Appeals. In upholding the students' right to engage in a nondisruptive, passive expression of a political viewpoint in *Tinker,* this Court was careful to note that the case did "not concern speech or action that intrudes upon the work of the schools or the rights of other students."

It is against this background that we turn to consider the level of First Amendment protection accorded to Fraser's utterances and actions before an official high school assembly attended by 600 students.

III

The role and purpose of the American public school system was well described by two historians, saying "public education must prepare pupils for citizenship in the Republic * * *. It must inculcate the habits and manners of civility as values in themselves conducive to happiness and as indispensable to the practice of self-government in the community and the nation." In *Ambach v. Norwick* we echoed the essence of this statement of the objectives of public education as the "inculcat[ion of] fundamental values necessary to the maintenance of a democratic political system."

These fundamental values of "habits and manners of civility" essential to a democratic society must, of course, include tolerance of divergent political and religious views, even when the views expressed may be unpopular. But these "fundamental values" must also take into account consideration of the sensibilities of others, and, in the case of a school, the sensibilities of fellow students. The undoubted freedom to advocate unpopular and controversial views in schools and classrooms must be balanced against the society's countervailing interest in teaching students the boundaries of socially appropriate behaviour. Even the most heated political discourse in a democratic society requires consideration for the personal sensibilities of the other participants and audiences.

In our Nation's legislative halls, where some of the most vigorous political debates in our society are carried on, there are rules prohibiting the use of expressions offensive to other participants in the debate. * * * Can it be that what is proscribed in the halls of Congress is beyond the reach of school officials to regulate?

The First Amendment guarantees wide freedom in matters of adult public discourse. A sharply divided Court upheld the right to express an antidraft viewpoint in a public place, albeit in terms highly offensive to most citizens. It does not follow, however, that simply because the use of an offensive form of expression may not be prohibited to adults making what the speaker considers a political point, that the same latitude must be permitted to children in a public school. In *New Jersey v. T.L.O.* we reaffirmed that the constitutional rights of students in public school are not automatically coextensive with the rights of adults in other settings. * * *

Surely it is a highly appropriate function of public school education to prohibit the use of vulgar and offensive terms in public discourse.

Indeed, the "fundamental values necessary to the maintenance of a democratic political system" disfavor the use of terms of debate highly offensive or highly threatening to others. Nothing in the Constitution prohibits the states from insisting that certain modes of expression are inappropriate and subject to sanctions. The inculcation of these values is truly the "work of the schools." The determination of what manner of speech in the classroom or in school assembly is inappropriate properly rests with the school board.

The process of educating our youth for citizenship in public schools is not confined to books, the curriculum, and the civics class; schools must teach by example the shared values of a civilized social order. Consciously or otherwise, teachers—and indeed the older students—demonstrate the appropriate form of civil discourse and political expression by their conduct and deportment in and out of class. Inescapably, like parents, they are role models. The schools, as instruments of the state, may determine that the essential lessons of civil, mature conduct cannot be conveyed in a school that tolerates lewd, indecent, or offensive speech and conduct such as that indulged in by this confused boy.

The pervasive sexual innuendo in Fraser's speech was plainly offensive to both teachers and students—indeed to any mature person. By glorifying male sexuality, and in its verbal content, the speech was acutely insulting to teenage girl students. The speech could well be seriously damaging to its less mature audience, many of whom were only 14 years old and on the threshold of awareness of human sexuality. Some students were reported as bewildered by the speech and the reaction of mimicry it provoked.

This Court's First Amendment jurisprudence has acknowledged limitations on the otherwise absolute interest of the speaker in reaching an unlimited audience where the speech is sexually explicit and the audience may include children. In *Ginsberg v. New York*, 390 U.S. 629, 88 S.Ct. 1274, 20 L.Ed.2d 195 (1968), this Court upheld a New York statute banning the sale of sexually oriented material to minors, even though the material in question was entitled to First Amendment protection with respect to adults. And in addressing the question whether the First Amendment places any limit on the authority of public schools to remove books from a public school library, all Members of the Court, otherwise sharply divided, acknowledged that the school board has the authority to remove books that are vulgar. *Board of Education v. Pico.* These cases recognize the obvious concern on the part of parents, and school authorities acting *in loco parentis* to protect children—especially in a captive audience—from exposure to sexually explicit, indecent, or lewd speech.

We have also recognized an interest in protecting minors from exposure to vulgar and offensive spoken language. * * *

We hold that petitioner School District acted entirely within its permissible authority in imposing sanctions upon Fraser in response to his offensively lewd and indecent speech. Unlike the sanctions imposed on the students wearing armbands in *Tinker,* the penalties imposed in

this case were unrelated to any political viewpoint. The First Amendment does not prevent the school officials from determining that to permit a vulgar and lewd speech such as respondent's would undermine the school's basic educational mission. A high school assembly or classroom is no place for a sexually explicit monologue directed towards an unsuspecting audience of teenage students. Accordingly, it was perfectly appropriate for the school to disassociate itself to make the point to the pupils that vulgar speech and lewd conduct is wholly inconsistent with the "fundamental values" of public school education.
* * *

IV

Respondent contends that the circumstances of his suspension violated due process because he had no way of knowing that the delivery of the speech in question would subject him to disciplinary sanctions. This argument is wholly without merit. We have recognized that "maintaining security and order in the schools requires a certain degree of flexibility in school disciplinary procedures, and we have respected the value of preserving the informality of the student-teacher relationship." Given the school's need to be able to impose disciplinary sanctions for a wide range of unanticipated conduct disruptive of the educational process, the school disciplinary rules need not be as detailed as a criminal code which imposes criminal sanctions. Two days' suspension from school does not rise to the level of a penal sanction calling for the full panoply of procedural due process protections applicable to a criminal prosecution. The school disciplinary rule proscribing "obscene" language and the prespeech admonitions of teachers gave adequate warning to Fraser that his lewd speech could subject him to sanctions.

The judgment of the Court of Appeals for the Ninth Circuit is
Reversed.

Notes

1. The vote was seven-to-two. Justice Brennan concurred in the judgment, but wrote "separately to express my understanding of the breadth of the Court's holding," which he placed in the framework of some prior Supreme Court opinions. Justice Blackmun simply concurred "in the result." Justices Marshall and Stevens dissented. This opinion was one of the last three written by Chief Justice Burger before his retirement.

2. *Tinker* is Case No. 114. *New Jersey* is Case No. 123.

3. Consider the broad implications of Part IV of the opinion.

4. Observe the Court's use of the expression "in loco parentis" (third paragraph before section IV).

5. Compare this case with *Tinker* (Case No. 114). In the intervening 27 years courts were surfeited with public school discipline cases involving student expression, but no cases were accepted for decision by the Supreme Court. Do you agree with the observation: "Taken alone, *Tinker* could be read to exaggerate rights of students; taken alone, *Bethel* could be read to exaggerate powers of school authorities"?

[Case No. 118] Constitutionality of Rule Governing Length of Students' Hair

MASSIE v. HENRY

United States Court of Appeals, Fourth Circuit, 1972.
455 F.2d 779.

WINTER, CIRCUIT JUDGE. The minor plaintiffs, male students at the Tuscola Senior High School, Haywood County, North Carolina, were suspended from school for their deliberate refusal to conform to a "guide line," recommended by a student-faculty-parent committee and adopted by the high school principal, regulating the length of hair and side burns. Plaintiffs wore their hair at a length extending below their collars and below and covering their ears; and at least two of the plaintiffs wore their side burns below their ear lobes, all in violation of the regulation. Their suit for declaratory and injunctive relief under 42 U.S.C.A. § 1983 followed. The district court, finding the regulation justified, and finding that none of plaintiffs' constitutional rights had been denied them, dismissed the action. We reverse.

I

The operative facts proved at the trial and found by the district court are as stated. Additionally, the district court found that establishment of the regulation had been requested by the President of the Student Body following an incident in which a student with long hair was called a "hippie" and a fight ensued.

There was also evidence before the district court that the length of plaintiffs' hair evoked considerable jest, disgust and amusement rendering the restoration and preservation of order in the classrooms difficult. Two "long hair" students reported that they had been threatened with being beaten up. One teacher said that plaintiffs had difficulty in writing on the black board because their hair fell into their eyes. A welding instructor stated that he would not permit a student with long hair to take his course or even enter his classroom because of the danger of fire and injury from flying sparks and molten metal particles.

There was no claim that plaintiffs' hair was unhygienic. Indeed, plaintiffs testified that they washed it daily, and the district judge said that it appeared clean and well-groomed when plaintiffs were in court.

II

Whether the right of a male to wear long hair and to have long or fulsome side burns is a constitutionally protected right is a question which has given birth to a rash of recent litigation resulting in conflicting adjudications. And if the right is recognized as a constitutionally protected one, there is a similar lack of agreement as to its precise nature, that is, the chapter and verse of the Constitution which protects it. Unquestionably, the issue is current because there is abroad a trend for the male to dress himself more extravagantly both in the nature, cut and color of his clothing and the quantity and mode of his facial and tonsorial adornment. The shift in fashion has been more warmly embraced by the young, but even some of the members of this court, our male law clerks and counsel who appear before us have not been impervious to it. With respect to hair, this is no more than a harkening back to the fashion of earlier years. For example, many of the founding fathers, as well as General Grant and General Lee, wore their hair (either real or false) in a style comparable to that adopted by plaintiffs. Although there exists no depiction of Jesus Christ, either reputedly or historically accurate, He has always been shown with hair at least the length of that of plaintiffs. If the validity and enforcement of the regulation in issue is sustained, it follows that none of these persons would have been permitted to attend Tuscola Senior High School.

III

If we limit ourselves only to decisions of United States Courts of Appeals, we find that the Fifth Circuit, in Ferrell v. Dallas Independent School District, 392 F.2d 697 (5 Cir.1968), cert. den., 393 U.S. 856, 89 S.Ct. 98, 21 L.Ed.2d 125 (1968), upheld the validity and enforcement of a school regulation which excluded male students having a "Beatle type haircut" upon the mere showing that their presence in the schools might be disruptive. Circuit Judge Tuttle dissented, expressing the view that equal protection had been denied, and that the majority was overly prone to limit the exercise of constitutional rights because of the possibility that disorder, resistance or violence might ensue. Although *Ferrell* implicitly and explicitly assumed a constitutional right to select the length of one's hair, later Fifth Circuit decisions appear to proceed on the basis that the right to select the length of one's hair is too insubstantial to warrant federal court consideration. Wood v. Alamo Heights Independent School District, 433 F.2d 355 (5 Cir.1970); Stevenson v. Board of Ed. of Wheeler County, Georgia, 426 F.2d 1154 (5 Cir.1970), cert. den., 400 U.S. 957, 91 S.Ct. 355, 27 L.Ed.2d 265 (1970); Griffin v. Tatum, 425 F.2d 201 (5 Cir.1970); Davis v. Firment, 408 F.2d 1085 (5 Cir.1969).

The Sixth Circuit in Jackson v. Dorrier, 424 F.2d 213 (6 Cir.1970), cert. den., 400 U.S. 850, 91 S.Ct. 55, 27 L.Ed.2d 88 (1970), followed the Fifth Circuit's decision in *Ferrell*. The Sixth Circuit held, upon evidence that the wearing of excessively long hair caused classroom disruption and constituted a distraction from the educational process, that there was no violation of a First Amendment right (the evidence was that the "long hair" students adopted that style to further a musical group of which they were members), that there was no denial of substantive or procedural due process, that there was no denial of equal protection (the district court had found that the regulation banning long hair had a real and reasonable connection with successful operation of the educational system and the maintenance of discipline) and that there had been no violation of the right of privacy. Accordingly, it sustained enforcement of a regulation which was applied to prohibit the wearing of excessively long hair and suspension of students who violated it.

More recently, the Ninth Circuit has held that a suit by male students who objected to compliance with a school regulation limiting the length of their hair failed to establish "the existence of any substantial constitutional right * * * being infringed," King v. Saddleback Junior College District, 445 F.2d 932, 940 (9 Cir.1971); and the Tenth Circuit has followed the lead of the Fifth Circuit in treating the problem as one too insubstantial to justify cognizance of it in the federal courts. Freeman v. Flake, 448 F.2d 258 (10 Cir.1971).

In contrast, the First, Seventh and Eighth Circuits have found regulations limiting the length of hair invalid, at least in the absence of persuasive reason and persuasive proof to support their promulgation and enforcement. Their approach to these issues is quite different from that of the other circuits. See note, 84 Harv.L.Rev. 1702 (1971). See also, the opinion of Mr. Justice Douglas dissenting with regard to the denial of certiorari in Olff v. East Side Union High School District, 404 U.S. 1042, 92 S.Ct. 703, 30 L.Ed.2d 736 (1972). In Breen v. Kahl, 419 F.2d 1034 (7 Cir.1969), cert. den. 398 U.S. 937, 90 S.Ct. 1836, 26 L.Ed.2d 268 (1970), it was held that the right to select the length of one's hair was a due process right, falling within the penumbras of the First Amendment or within the rights guaranteed by the Ninth Amendment, and one which could be limited only upon a showing of substantial countervailing state interests. In *Breen,* the regulation was invalidated and the expulsion and threatened expulsions were nullified. The court rejected the state justification that long hair *may* distract short haired students from their school work, that students whose appearance conforms to community standards perform better in school, and that, in any event, the power of a school board to discipline must be upheld.

Factually, *Breen* is distinguishable from the case at bar and the decision in *Ferrell* but Crews v. Cloncs, 432 F.2d 1259 (7 Cir.1970), which followed, is more in point. In *Crews,* a male student with long hair was denied readmission to high school because of the length of his hair. In holding that the student was entitled to an injunction to require his readmission, the court reiterated its holding in *Breen* that the right to select the length of one's hair was a personal freedom protected by the Constitution and then considered whether the substantial burden of justification to limit the right had been shown. The court rejected, as sufficient grounds of justification, evidence that other students were distracted and preoccupied in observing the plaintiff, and evidence that short hair was required for health and safety reasons when engaging in athletics or laboratory work around Bunsen burners. As to the former, the court invoked the principle that it is absurd to punish a person because his neighbors lack self-control and cannot refrain from violence; and, as to the latter, the court concluded that the objectives of health and safety could be achieved by use of hair nets or other protective devices.

Richards v. Thurston, 424 F.2d 1281 (1 Cir.1970), was decided on the sparse facts that the male student, whose hair fell loosely about his shoulders, was suspended from school because of an unwritten policy (treated as a regulation) prohibiting "unusually long hair." An injunction to require his reinstatement was affirmed, the court holding that the right to select the length and style of one's hair was a personal right of liberty protected by the due process clause and that that right could be limited only by an outweighing state interest justifying the intrusion. Because the record was so bare, the court had no occasion to discuss specific evidence, but it elaborated on the outweighing state interest by saying:

> Once the personal liberty is shown, the countervailing interest must either be self-evident or be affirmatively shown. We see no inherent reason why decency, decorum, or good conduct requires a boy to wear his hair short. Certainly eccentric hair styling is no longer a reliable signal of perverse behavior. We do not believe that mere unattractiveness in the eyes of some parents, teachers, or students, short of uncleanliness, can justify the proscription. Nor, finally, does such compelled conformity to conventional standards of appearance seem a justifiable part of the educational process.

Id., 424 F.2d at 1286.

Finally, Bishop v. Colaw, 450 F.2d 1069 (8 Cir.1971), the latest expression on the subject, held invalid and unenforceable a dress regulation which, *inter alia,* required male students to wear their hair at a length shorter than their collar and above their ears. The Court considered thoroughly prior court of appeals, as well as district court, decisions on the subject. It rejected the claim that the plaintiff (Stephen) was deprived of any First Amendment right for lack of any "evidence suggesting that Stephen's hairstyle represented a symbolic expression of any kind," 450 F.2d at 1074; and while it noted the possibility of a claim of denial of equal protection (discrimination between males with differing hair lengths), it declined to pass on this issue. It also rejected the argument that the regulation violated Stephen's parents' rights because the record showed that they supported but did not select Stephen's hairstyle. It did hold, however, that Stephen had a due process right to govern his own personal appearance, declining in the process to choose a label as to whether the right was "fundamental," "substantial," "basic," or simply a "right," but that the right was not absolute and must yield when its exercise infringed upon the rights of others. The court then examined the purported justifications for the regulation, i.e., disruption in the classroom, sanitation problem in the swimming pool, safety problem in shop classes, and asserted correlation of long hair with poor grades, and, finding them insufficient to demonstrate the necessity for the regulation, invalidated it.

IV

We find *Breen, Crews, Richards* and *Bishop,* and their decisional approaches, more persuasive than *Ferrell* and its progeny, and we have concluded to follow the former.

Perhaps the length of one's hair may be symbolic speech which under some circumstances is entitled to the protection of the First

Amendment. But the record before us does not establish that the minor plaintiffs selected the length of their hair for any reasons other than personal preference. For that reason, we prefer in this case to treat their right to wear their hair as they wish as an aspect of the right to be secure in one's person guaranteed by the due process clause, Union Pacific Railway Co. v. Botsford, 141 U.S. 250, 251, 11 S.Ct. 1000, 35 L.Ed. 734 (1891); Bishop v. Colaw, 450 F.2d at 1075; Clews v. Cloncs, supra, 432 F.2d at 1263–1264; Richards v. Thurston, supra, 424 F.2d at 1284–1285, but having overlapping equal protection clause considerations since the purported limitation of the right was by a state public school official. But, our inquiry is not ended by this conclusion, because, as said in Bishop v. Colaw, 450 F.2d at 1075, "[p]ersonal freedoms are not absolute; they must yield when they intrude upon the freedoms of others. Our task, therefore, is to weigh the competing interests asserted here. In doing so, we proceed from the premise that the school administration carries the burden of establishing the necessity of infringing upon Stephen's freedom in order to carry out the educational mission of the * * * High School."

So, too, we turn to the sufficiency of proof of state interest and violation of the rights of others in this case which may constitute justification for the regulation. There was no evidence that consideration of health entered into the picture; the only claimed justifications were the need for discipline and considerations of safety. We think the proof of the disruptive effect of some students having long hair was insufficient to justify the regulation and its enforcement. Proof that jest, disgust and amusement were evoked, rendering restoration and preservation of order difficult, and that there were threats of violence was insufficient. Moreover, there was no proof of the ineffectiveness of discipline of disrupters or a showing of any concerted effort to convey the salutary teaching that there is little merit in conformity for the sake of conformity and that one may exercise a personal right in the manner that he chooses so long as he does not run afoul of considerations of safety, cleanliness and decency. In short, we are inclined to think that faculty leadership in promoting and enforcing an attitude of tolerance rather than one of suppression or derision would obviate the relatively minor disruptions which have occurred.

The asserted considerations of safety need not detain us long. Unrestrained or unprotected long hair is undoubtedly a safety hazard in a welding shop or in a laboratory where Bunsen burners or other fire are present, but it is manifest that hairbands, hairnets or protective caps provide a complete solution, short of shearing one's locks. Requiring restraint or protection is, we think, the manner in which the state interest should be asserted.

Since the regulation lacks justification outweighing the minor plaintiffs' rights, the district court should declare it invalid and enjoin its enforcement in the particulars alleged.

Reversed and remanded.

BOREMAN, SENIOR CIRCUIT JUDGE (dissenting):

dissenting opinion

The operation of public schools and the safeguarding of public education have traditionally been the responsibility of the several states. As the Supreme Court recently declared in Epperson v. Arkansas, 393 U.S. 97, 104, 89 S.Ct. 266, 270, 21 L.Ed.2d 228 (1968):

> By and large, public education in our Nation is committed to the control of state and local authorities. Courts do not and cannot intervene in the resolution of conflicts which arise in the daily operation of school systems and which do not *directly and sharply* implicate basic constitutional values. (Emphasis added.)

The issue herein, as I see it, is whether a conflict arising over the length of a schoolboy's hair and the possible effects thereof on educational environment "directly and sharply" implicates a basic constitutional value. I reach the opinion that it does not and that therefore the resolution of the conflict should be entirely within the control of the local authorities.

The majority concludes that the constitutional right involved here is "an aspect of the right to be secure in one's person guaranteed by the due process clause," with "overlapping equal protection clause considerations." It is difficult to understand how such a general and imprecise statement would support a direct and sharp implication of "basic constitutional values." (The general confusion, noted by the majority, as to precisely which constitutional right, if any, is involved when a student is prohibited from letting his hair grow to a desired length, perhaps is, in itself, indicative that there is *none*. Such confusion surely indicates to me that a specific constitutional right is not "directly and sharply" implicated.) I respectfully disagree with the implied determination of the majority that a male student's interest in maintaining a personally preferred hair style so "directly and sharply" implicates these constitutional values as to give federal courts the power and obligation to review a regulation promulgated by local school authorities such as the one here involved.

There is no hint here of an improper motivation or arbitrary procedure by the school officials in establishing the regulation or an uneven application thereof. Further, there is no specific clause in the Constitution which may be said to expressly prohibit regulation of a male student's hair length by local school authorities. Thus the invalidation of the regulation on due process grounds would appear to be no more than a substitution of the majority's judgment concerning the reasonableness of the regulation for that of the local officials. Simply stated, the school authorities, who must deal with such problems on a daily basis, say that the regulation is reasonable and necessary for reasons of safety and the maintenance of order; my colleagues say that it is not. Facts giving rise to nothing more than such differences of personal opinion and which do not clearly fall under a specific constitutional prohibition cannot, in my view, be said to "directly and sharply" implicate basic constitutional values.

Indeed, the majority decision might be criticized on the merits as representing a return to the day when courts regularly struck down state legislation as violative of the due process clause if the legislation was thought to be "unreasonable," a long since discarded test of constitutionality discussed fully in the dissenting opinion of the late Mr. Justice Black in Tinker v. Des Moines School Dist., 393 U.S. 503, 518–523, 89 S.Ct. 733, 21 L.Ed.2d 731 (1969). I find it unnecessary to reach this question, however, in view of my conclusion that the matter is simply not a proper one for litigation in the federal courts.

Perhaps the fallacy inherent in the majority's reliance on the due process clause is best seen by contrasting this case with the decision of the Supreme Court in Tinker v. Des Moines School Dist., 393 U.S. 503, 89 S.Ct. 733, 21 L.Ed.2d 731 (1969). In that case the Court held unconstitutional a policy adopted by Des Moines school principals which would suspend any student who wore and refused to remove a black armband to publicize his objections to the war in Vietnam. That decision was based on the determination that the wearing of an armband was a symbolic act within the free speech clause of the First Amendment. As such, it was an act which "directly and sharply" implicated a constitutional right of precise nature. The Court expressly noted, 393 U.S. at 507–508, 89 S.Ct. at 737:

> [T]he Court has repeatedly emphasized the need for affirming the comprehensive authority of the States and of school officials, consistent with fundamental constitutional safeguards, to prescribe and control conduct in the schools. See Epperson v. Arkansas * * *. Our problem lies in the area where students in the exercise of First Amendment rights collide with the rules of the school authorities.

* * *

> The problem posed by the present case does not relate to regulation of the length of skirts or the type of clothing, to hair style, or deportment. * * * Our problem involves direct, primary First Amendment rights akin to "pure speech."

The general rule against judicial interference with public education as expressed in Epperson v. Arkansas, supra, and the concerns of the late Mr. Justice Black as expressed in his dissent in *Tinker* relating to the limitations of the due process clause, seem clearly applicable where, as here, the nature of the "constitutional value" asserted is nebulous and the facts only inferentially are within its protection.

It is unclear from the majority opinion as to exactly how or in what manner the equal protection clause is here implicated. The majority's holding that the issue has "overlapping equal protection clause considerations since the purported limitation of the right was by a state public school official" appears susceptible to at least three interpretations. If, as the majority's language at first blush would seem to indicate, it is meant that there is discrimination as between students and nonstudents, I would counter it is patently arguable, if not manifest, that the need for disciplinary rules designed to provide an orderly educational environment for students is present and that the resulting discrimination against them could in no way be considered invidious. If it is meant that there is discrimination as between boy students and girl students, the answer is simply that long hair for girls has long been accepted as a matter of social custom and therefore constitutes no threat to an orderly educational system. If it is meant that there is discrimination as between long-haired male students and short-haired male students with respect to the equal right to obtain an education, I would submit that the right of an individual to an education in the public schools is not protected and assured in the face of his demonstrated unwillingness to obey rules of conduct designed to further the educational opportunities of all. I conclude that application of the equal protection clause, if implicated at all, is not "directly and sharply" brought into question by the facts of this case.

My colleagues' determination that there was no sufficient showing by the defendants of disruption attributable to plaintiffs' long hair poses an additional problem for me. I agree with the position of Senior Judge Duffy as expressed in his dissenting opinion in Breen v. Kahl, 419 F.2d 1034, 1039 (7 Cir.1969), cert. denied, 398 U.S. 937, 90 S.Ct. 1836, 26 L.Ed.2d 268 (1970):

> A point emphasized by the District Court and apparently approved by my colleagues, is that there was no sufficient proof that the long hair worn by Breen was a disruptive influence. However, if Breen had gone to his classes carrying a sign which stated "I am defying school regulations as to required hair length," the effect would not be different. Why is formal proof necessary for something that is so obvious? All of the students were aware of the rule forbidding the boys wearing long hair and every time Breen appeared with his flowing locks, he was showing his defiance of and his contempt for the school authorities and the regulations as to hair length.

A somewhat similar position was adopted by the court in King v. Saddleback Junior College District, 445 F.2d 932 (9 Cir.1971), cert. denied, 404 U.S. 979, 92 S.Ct. 342, 30 L.Ed.2d 294 (1972), and its companion case, Olff v. East Side Union High School District, Id. The Court there stated, 445 F.2d at 940:

> Much emphasis was placed upon the fact that no disruption had occurred in either school even though some of the male students wore long hair. Disruption, of course, if related, would be significant. Its absence, however, does not establish that long-haired males cannot be a distracting influence which would interfere with the educative process the same as any extreme in appearance, dress, or deportment.

In *King* and *Olff,* cases which involved regulations pertaining to hair styling very similar to the one at issue in the instant case, the court concluded, 445 F.2d at 940:

This is not a question of preference for or against certain male hair styles or the length to which persons desire to wear their hair. This court could not care less. It is a question of the right of school authorities to develop a code of dress and conduct best conducive to the fulfillment of their responsibility to educate, and to do it without unconstitutionally infringing upon the rights of those who must live under it. We do not believe that the plaintiffs have established the existence of any substantial constitutional right which is in these two instances being infringed. We are satisfied that the school authorities have acted with consideration for the rights and feelings of their students and have enacted their codes, including the ones in question here, in the best interests of the educational process. A court might disagree with their professional judgment, but it should not take over the operation of their schools.

The general rule against federal judicial interference in the public schools is supported by sound policy considerations. Primary among these is the proper allocation of power within a federal republic as influenced by the need for the expertise which comes only with first-hand knowledge and experience as to the requirements of a particular school or locality. With respect to rules of conduct and discipline as established by local officials, additional factors must be recognized. The very fact of such judicial interference, for example, must in and of itself tend to contribute to a breakdown of order and discipline. A student who successfully challenges a school policy or regulation would be encouraged to disregard other regulations and other students might well be similarly tempted.

The instant case illustrates another problem which arises when courts are willing to interfere with the control of students' conduct. As the district court below found:

> The testimony discloses that the plaintiffs have not been involved in any prior disciplinary proceeding at this school and that all four of them would be classified as below average in academic achievement. Their attendance records have been poor and they appear to have very little interest in school. All of them are failing some of their work and the plaintiff Massie is failing more than half of his subjects.

> The testimony indicates without doubt that the plaintiffs are intelligent young men who are not performing in school anywhere near their capacity. All of them scored more than average on the college entrance examinations. It is apparent that they have allowed their quarrel with the School Board and the high school authorities to interfere with their school work. Their attendance record prior to suspension was poor indeed. *They deliberately and intentionally allowed their hair to grow longer than permitted by the dress code and requested their favorite teacher to report them as being in violation. This was*

Excellent Points

apparently done for the purpose of being suspended to test the
guidelines in federal court. (Emphasis added.)

To me these findings indicate that plaintiffs, admittedly bright and
intelligent but apparently not too ambitious or successful as students,
are seeking to use the federal courts as a diversion from the boredom of
their school work and as a means of seeking a measure of recognition
and notoriety among their fellow students. The majority decision would
seem to insure the success of their tactics as well as to foster the creation
of similar future problems for the school authorities.

Fully aware of the existence of numerous decisions in which the
courts are in conflict I favor the approach of the court in Freeman v.
Flake, 448 F.2d 258 (10 Cir.1971). The court there stated, 448 F.2d at
259, 262:

> We are convinced that the United States Constitution and
> statutes do not impose on the federal courts the duty and
> responsibility of supervising the length of a student's hair. The
> problem, if it exists, is one for the states and should be handled
> through state procedures.

* * *

> Complaints which are based on nothing more than school regu-
> lations of the length of a male student's hair do not "directly
> and sharply implicate basic constitutional values" and are not
> cognizable in federal courts. * * *

My position may best be summarized by quoting from the opinion of
Mr. Justice Black, sitting as an Individual Justice assigned to the Fifth
Circuit, in Karr v. Schmidt, 401 U.S. 1201, 91 S.Ct. 592, 27 L.Ed.2d 797
(1971). School authorities in El Paso, Texas, adopted a rule providing
that schoolboys' hair must not "hang over the ears or the top of the
collar of a standard dress shirt and must not obstruct vision." The
district court enjoined the enforcement of this rule as violative of the
Due Process and Equal Protection Clauses. The Court of Appeals for
the Fifth Circuit stayed and suspended the district court's injunction and
the students presented to Justice Black an "Emergency Motion to Vacate
Stay of Injunction Pending Appeal." In denying this motion Mr. Justice
Black stated:

> I refuse to hold for myself that the federal courts have
> constitutional power to interfere in this way with the public
> school system operated by the States. And I furthermore refuse
> to predict that our Court will hold they have such power. * * *

> * * * The records of the federal courts, including ours,
> show a heavy burden of litigation in connection with cases of
> great importance—the kind of litigation our courts must be able
> to handle if they are to perform their responsibility to our
> society. Moreover, our Constitution has sought to distribute
> the powers of government in this Nation between the United
> States and the States. Surely the federal judiciary can perform
> no greater service to the Nation than to leave the States

unhampered in the performance of their purely local affairs. Surely few policies can be thought of that States are more capable of deciding than the length of the hair of schoolboys. There can, of course, be honest differences of opinion as to whether any government, state or federal, should as a matter of public policy regulate the length of haircuts, but it would be difficult to prove by reason, logic, or common sense that the federal judiciary is more competent to deal with hair length than are the local school authorities and state legislatures of all our 50 States. Perhaps if the courts will leave the States free to perform their own constitutional duties they will at least be able successfully to regulate the length of hair their public school students can wear.

I respectfully dissent.

Notes

1. The majority and dissenting opinions here constitute an excellent summary of the conflict among the Circuit Courts of Appeals on the "hairstyle controversy." Those keenly interested in the problem area will want to read for themselves the decisions cited in the two opinions here. The Supreme Court has consistently denied certiorari on the cases.

2. Usually, the Supreme Court fairly promptly resolves divisions among the circuits. Why has it not done so in the hairstyle cases?

3. Why have hairstyle cases been so numerous? Why have the cases, with only a very few exceptions, involved males rather than females or both males and females? To what extent are hairstyles in a special category as regards dress and appearance of students?

4. Where it was stipulated that the purpose of the student's long hair was to express a sincerely held political viewpoint, a clear *Tinker*-type fact situation was presented, and school authorities could not discipline the student for violating the dress code. Church v. Board of Educ. of Saline Area School Dist., Michigan, 339 F.Supp. 538 (E.D.Mich.1972). But where there was conflicting testimony regarding the significance of braided hair as an essential part of the religious and cultural tradition of the Pawnees, the school's hairstyle regulation was upheld. New Rider v. Board of Educ. of Independent School Dist. No. 1, Oklahoma, 480 F.2d 693 (10 Cir.1973), cert. den. 414 U.S. 1097, 94 S.Ct. 733, 38 L.Ed.2d 556 (1973).

5. In 1972 the Fifth Circuit Court of Appeals in an en banc decision by a vote of eight-to-seven held: "Where a complaint merely alleges the constitutional invalidity of a high school hair and grooming regulation, the district courts are directed to grant an immediate motion to dismiss for failure to state a claim for which relief can be granted." Karr v. Schmidt, 460 F.2d 609 (5 Cir.1972), cert. den. 409 U.S. 989, 93 S.Ct. 307, 34 L.Ed.2d 256 (1972).

6. In 1975 the Third Circuit Court of Appeals in an en banc decision by a vote of five-to-four dismissed the complaint of a student who had been excluded from a soccer team because of his hairstyle. Zeller v. Donegal School Dist. Bd. of Educ., 517 F.2d 600 (3 Cir.1975).

[Case No. 119] Power of Board to Prohibit Distribution of Printed Material by Students

EISNER v. STAMFORD BD. OF EDUC.

United States Court of Appeals, Second Circuit, 1971.
440 F.2d 803.

IRVING R. KAUFMAN, CIRCUIT JUDGE. The deceptively simple facts in this case generate legal problems which summon up many centuries of political and social thought and action concerning the relation between the rights and powers of men, women, and children, and their government. To resolve this problem we are required to consider principles and concepts which courts have fashioned over several decades of this century, giving concrete effect to the proscription of the first amendment against any law abridging freedom of expression, and apply them to the unique social structure prevailing in a public system of secondary schools.

The Board of Education of the City of Stamford, Connecticut, on November 18, 1969, adopted the following "policy":

"Distribution of Printed or Written Matter

"The Board of Education desires to encourage freedom of expression and creativity by its students subject to the following limitations:

"No person shall distribute any printed or written matter on the grounds of any school or in any school building unless the distribution of such material shall have prior approval by the school administration.

"In granting or denying approval, the following guidelines shall apply.

"No material shall be distributed which, either by its content or by the manner of distribution itself, will interfere with the proper and orderly operation and discipline of the school, will cause violence or disorder, or will constitute an invasion of the rights of others."

Plaintiffs are students at Rippowam High School in Stamford. They wish to distribute free of the restraint imposed by the quoted policy, or of any other similar restraint, a mimeographed newspaper of their own creation and other printed and written literature.　* * *

* * *

I.

Consideration of the judicial interpretations enunciated over the years in this highly complex free speech-press area are a necessary backdrop to our discussion. In Near v. Minnesota, 283 U.S. 697, 51 S.Ct. 625, 75 L.Ed. 1357 (1931), the Supreme Court struck down a statute which if analogized to the instant case would place a prior restraint upon distribution of literature by any student who had in the past regularly distributed material deemed by school authorities to be obscene, lewd, and lascivious, or malicious, scandalous, and defamatory. The law held unconstitutional in *Near* permitted such a broad restraint to be imposed by county courts upon publishers of newspapers and periodicals in the state of Minnesota. The Court considered such a scheme to be "of the essence of censorship" and in strong terms, gave expression to the enmity reflected in the first amendment toward "previous restraints upon publication." The Court's particular concern was directed at that aspect of the law under which crusading newspaper publishers would hazard not only libel actions, but the utter abatement of their publications and consequently the squelching of their campaigns, if they should attempt systematically to expose the derelictions of public officials. But Chief Justice Hughes made it clear that his opinion was not to be read as invalidating all "previous restraints." He took pains to catalogue several varieties of "exceptional cases" which would justify a "previous restraint." Thus, it was well established then as it is now that "[t]he constitutional guaranty of free speech does not 'protect a man from an injunction against uttering words that may have all the effect of force'." Nor did it question that "the primary requirements of decency may be enforced against obscene publications." * * *

The sensitive analysis of the constitutional validity of previous restraints of speech * * * requires that we address ourselves to the following questions. First, is the Board's policy justified as included within one or more of the categories of exceptional cases to which previous restraints are permissible? Second, is the policy as narrowly drawn as may reasonably be expected so as to advance the social interests that justify it or, to the contrary, does it unduly restrict protected speech, to an extent "greater than is essential to the furtherance of" those interests? In light of Freedman v. Maryland, 380 U.S. 51, 85 S.Ct. 734, 13 L.Ed.2d 649 (1965), the latter question might usefully be addressed, alternatively, to the substantive and to the procedural aspects of the policy—that is, first to the criteria by which school officials are permitted to bar literature from the school and second to the means by which the bar is to be effected.

II.

* * *

Moreover, we cannot ignore the oft-stressed and carefully worded dictum in the leading precedent, Tinker v. Des Moines School District, that protected speech in public secondary schools may be forbidden if school authorities reasonably "forecast substantial disruption of or material interference with school activities." In an apparent reformulation of that dictum, the *Tinker* Court dissociated its holding that school authorities may not prohibit entirely non-disruptive student speech from cases involving "speech or action that intrudes upon the work of the schools or the rights of other students."

Many cases, following in the choppy waters left by *Tinker,* have applied the quoted language either to validate or to restrain a school's attempt to prevent students from engaging in constitutionally protected activity. Nor need we search far for a theoretical underpinning for the authority of school officials to control disruptive speech, in view of the unassailable power of the state to suppress "words * * * which by their very utterance inflict injury or tend to incite an immediate breach of the peace." These phrases have a venerable ancestry, descending from the principle at least as old and as formidable as Schenck v. United States, 249 U.S. 47, 52, 39 S.Ct. 247, 249, 63 L.Ed. 470 (1919), that "[t]he question in every case is whether the words are used in such circumstances and are of such a nature as to create a clear and present danger that they will bring about the substantive evils that Congress has a right to prevent."

The potential "evil," the School Board urges, is the disruption of the effort by the state of Connecticut through its system of public schooling, to give its children "opportunities for growth into free and independent well-developed men and citizens." * * *

III.

The policy criteria by which school authorities may prevent students from distributing literature on school property departs in no significant respect from the similarly very general and broad instruction of *Tinker* itself. Although the policy does not specify that the foreseeable disruption be either "material" or "substantial" as *Tinker* requires, we assume that the Board would never contemplate the futile as well as unconstitutional suppression of matter that would create only an *im*material disturbance. Thus, the regulation tracks the present state of the authoritative constitutional law, and while we realize this does not end the matter it does save the regulation from the charge that it is on its face fatally overbroad, since the policy statement does not purport to authorize suppression of a significant class of protected activity.

Absence of overbreadth, of course, does not in itself absolve the policy statement of the plaintiff's charge that it is also unduly vague. The phrase "invasion of the rights of others" is not a model of clarity or preciseness. But several factors present here lessen or remove the familiar dangers to first amendment freedoms often associated with vague statutes. Thus, the statement does not attempt to authorize *punishment* of students who publish literature that under the policy may be censored by school officials. If it did, students would be left to guess at their peril the thrust of the policy in a specific case and the resultant chill on first amendment activity might be intolerable. Also, because any ban that school authorities may impose would apply only to students *on school property,* the policy statement does not threaten to foreclose, e.g., from the publisher of a newspaper, a significant market or block of potential buyers should the publisher guess wrongly as to the kind of literature that a school principal will tolerate under particular circumstances. The policy does not in any way interfere with students' freedom to disseminate and to receive material outside of school property; nor does it threaten to interfere with the predominate responsibility of *parents* for their children's welfare. The statement is, therefore, in many ways narrowly drawn to achieve its permissible purposes, and indeed may fairly be characterized as a regulation of speech, rather than a blanket prior restraint.

In sum, we believe that the Board's policy statement is neither overbroad nor unconstitutionally vague, so far as it prescribes *criteria* by which school officials may prevent the distribution on secondary school property of written or printed matter.

IV.

Since, however, the policy statement is in other ways constitutionally deficient, it would not be remiss for us to observe that greater specificity in the statement would be highly desirable. The Board would in no way shackle school administrators if it attempted to confront and resolve in some fashion, prior to court intervention, some of the difficult constitutional issues that will almost inevitably be raised when so broad a rule is applied to particular cases. For example, to what extent and under what circumstances does the Board intend to permit school authorities to suppress criticism of their own actions and policies? Similarly, does the Board anticipate that school officials will take reasonable measures to minimize or forestall potential disorder and disruption that might otherwise be generated in reaction to the distribution of controversial or unpopular opinions, before they resort to banishing the ideas from school grounds? The Board might also undertake to describe the kinds of disruptions and distractions, and their degree, that it contemplates would typically justify censorship, as well as other distractions or disorders that it would consider do not justify suppression of students' attempts to distribute literature. At the same time it would be wise for the Board to consider the areas of school property where it would be appropriate to distribute approved material.

Refinements of the sort we mention would lessen the possibility that the policy statement under attack here because of its tendency to overgeneralization, will be administered arbitrarily, erratically, or unfairly. By grappling with some of the difficult issues suggested, the Board might also succeed in demonstrating its conscientious intent to formulate policy not only within the outer limits of constitutional permissibility, but also with a sensitivity to some of the teaching reflected in relevant constitutional doctrine and to the dangers lurking in improper and unconstitutional administration of a broad and general standard.

Finally, greater specificity might reduce the likelihood of future litigation and thus forestall the possibility that federal courts will be called upon again to intervene in the operation of Stamford's public schools. It is to everyone's advantage that decisions with respect to the operation of local schools be made by local officials. The greater the generosity of the Board in fostering—not merely tolerating—students' free exercise of their constitutional rights, the less likely it will be that local officials will find their rulings subjected to unwieldy constitutional litigation.

V.

Although the Board's regulation passes muster as authorizing prior restraints, we believe it is constitutionally defective in its lack of procedure for prior *submission* by students for school administration approval, of written material before "distribution."   * * *

For the reasons we have already set forth, we do not regard the Board's policy as imposing nearly so onerous a "prior restraint" as was involved in *Freedman*. Also, we believe that it would be highly disruptive to the educational process if a secondary school principal were required to take a school newspaper editor to court every time the principal reasonably anticipated disruption and sought to restrain its cause. Thus, we will not require school officials to seek a judicial decree before they may enforce the Board's policy. As for the burden of proof, *Tinker* as well as other federal cases establish that, if students choose to litigate, school authorities must demonstrate a reasonable basis for interference with student speech, and that courts will not rest content with officials' bare allegation that such a basis existed. We believe that this burden is sufficient to satisfy the intent of *Freedman* in the special context of a public secondary school. Of course, this standard is a matter for courts to enforce and need not be reflected in the policy statement.

We see no good reason, however, why the Board should not comply with *Freedman* to the extent of ensuring an expeditious review procedure. The policy as presently written is wholly deficient in this respect for it prescribes no period of time in which school officials must decide whether or not to permit distribution. To be valid, the regulation must prescribe a definite brief period within which review of submitted material will be completed.

The policy is also deficient in failing to specify to whom and how material may be submitted for clearance. Absent such specifications, students are unreasonably proscribed by the terms of the policy statement from distributing *any* written material on school property, since the statement leaves them ignorant of clearance procedures. Nor does it provide that the prohibition against distribution without prior approval is to be inoperative until each school has established a screening procedure.

Finally, we believe that the proscription against "distributing" written or printed material without prior consent is unconstitutionally vague. We assume that by "distributing" the Board intends something more than one student passing to a fellow student his copy of a general newspaper or magazine. Indeed, this assumption underpins most of our discussion concerning the constitutional validity of the policy statement, apart from the deficiencies we describe here. If students are to be required to secure prior approval before they may pass notes to each other in the hallways or exchange Time, Newsweek or other periodicals among themselves, then the resultant burden on speech might very likely outweigh the very remote possibility that such activities would ever cause disruption. We assume, therefore, that the Board contemplates that it will require prior submission only when there is to be a *substantial* distribution of written material, so that it can reasonably be anticipated that in a significant number of instances there would be a likelihood that the distribution would disrupt school operations. If the Board chooses to redraft its policy in light of what we have said in this opinion, it must make its intentions in this respect clear. Once it does, courts may better evaluate the potential "chill" of the policy on speech. The Board would be wise to be mindful of this danger zone.

* * *

Notes

1. The court refers to the "choppy waters" left by *Tinker* (Case No. 114). To what is the choppiness due?

2. On similar facts the same conclusion regarding "prior restraints" upon publications distributed on school premises during school hours was reached by the Fourth Circuit in Quarterman v. Byrd, 453 F.2d 54 (4 Cir. 1971), and by the Fifth Circuit in Shanley v. Northeast Independent School Dist., Bexar County, Texas, 462 F.2d 960 (5 Cir. 1972).

3. The Seventh Circuit in Fujishima v. Board of Educ., 460 F.2d 1355 (7 Cir. 1972), declared unconstitutional a rule of the Chicago Board of Education prohibiting any distribution on school premises of any publication "unless the same shall have been approved by the General Superintendent of Schools." In its discussion the court criticized the reasoning in *Eisner* and *Quarterman* as to possible criteria and procedural safeguards, and stated that prior restraint of publications must be based on a "prediction by school officials that existing conduct * * * if allowed to continue will probably interfere with school discipline." Time, place, and manner regulations will be permitted, and post-publication penalties are not absolutely forbidden.

4. Might there be any justifiable educational differences between restraints applied to materials produced with school funds and those not? That a publication is supported by public funds does not ipso facto give rights to administrators or boards to control editorial content, according to several college-level cases, e.g., Antonelli v. Hammond, 308 F.Supp. 1329 (D.Mass.1970), Stanley v. Magrath, 719 F.2d 279 (8 Cir. 1983).

5. Other cases relevant to the problem area of this case are discussed in "Differentiating among Uses and Users [of School Property]" in Chapter 6.

[Case No. 120] Power of Board to Prohibit Distribution of Questionnaire Developed by School Newspaper Staff

TRACHTMAN v. ANKER

United States Court of Appeals, Second Circuit, 1977.
563 F.2d 512.

LUMBARD, CIRCUIT JUDGE. These are cross appeals from a judgment * * * which enjoined defendants from restraining plaintiffs' attempts to distribute a sex questionnaire to eleventh and twelfth-grade students at Stuyvesant High School in New York City and to publish the results in the student publication, "The Stuyvesant Voice." * * * We conclude that defendants' actions in prohibiting the proposed sexual survey did not violate any constitutional right of the plaintiffs * * *.

* * *

* * * Trachtman and Marks submitted for review a questionnaire consisting of twenty-five questions, which, they advised, was to be used as a means for obtaining information for an article on "Sexuality in Stuyvesant" to appear in the "Voice." The questions, which the district court described as "requiring rather personal and frank information about the student's sexual attitudes, preferences, knowledge and experience," covered such topics as pre-marital sex, contraception, homosexuality, masturbation and the extent of students' "sexual experience." The questionnaire included a proposed cover letter which described the nature and purpose of the survey; it stressed the importance of honest and open answers but advised the student that, "[y]ou are not required to answer any of the questions and if you feel particularly uncomfortable—don't push yourself."

The students sought permission to distribute the questionnaire on school grounds on a random basis. The answers were to be returned anonymously and were to be kept "confidential." The students were to tabulate the results and publish them in an article in the "Voice," which would also attempt to interpret the results.

* * *

[Permission was denied.]

On appeal both parties agree that the defendants' restraint of the students' efforts to collect and disseminate information and ideas involves rights protected by the First Amendment. See Tinker v. Des Moines Independent Community School District. Essentially, resolution of the issues here turns upon a narrow question: What was it necessary for the defendants to prove to justify the prohibition of the distribution of the questionnaire and did the defendants meet this burden of proof?

* * *

Essentially, the defendants' position is that the students here seek not only to communicate an idea but to utilize school facilities to solicit a response that will invade the rights of other students by subjecting them to psychological pressures which may engender significant emotional harm. Plaintiffs do not question defendants' authority to protect the physical and psychological well being of students while they are on school grounds, rather, they contend that defendants have not made a sufficient showing to justify infringement of the students' rights to speech and expression.

In interpreting the standard laid down in *Tinker,* this court has held that in order to justify restraints on secondary school publications, which are to be distributed within the confines of school property, school officials must bear the burden of demonstrating "a reasonable basis for interference with student speech, and * * * courts will not rest content with officials' bare allegation that such a basis existed." Eisner v. Stamford Board of Education. At the same time, it is clear that school authorities need not wait for a potential harm to occur before taking protective action. Although this case involves a situation where the potential disruption is psychological rather than physical, *Tinker* and its progeny hold that the burden is on the school officials to demonstrate that there was reasonable cause to believe that distribution of the questionnaire would have caused significant psychological harm to some of the Stuyvesant students.

In support of their argument that students confronted with the questionnaire could suffer serious emotional harm, defendants submitted affidavits from four experts in the fields of psychology and psychiatry. Florence Halpern, professor of psychology at the New York University School of Medicine, stated that many adolescents are anxious about the "whole area of sex" and that attempts to answer the questionnaire by such students "would be very likely" to create anxiety and feelings of self-doubt; further, she stated that there were almost certainly some students with a "brittle" sexual adjustment and that for "such adolescents, the questionnaire might well be the force that pushes them into a panic state or even a psychosis." She concluded that distribution of the questionnaire was a "potentially dangerous" act that was "likely to result in serious injury to at least some of the students."

The record shows that the curriculum at Stuyvesant includes various courses on sex and sexuality and that professionally supervised peer-group discussions are sponsored by the school. The defendants have consistently treated the topic of sexuality as an important part of students' lives, which requires special treatment because of its sensitive nature. Thus, the school system has provided several courses on the physical and emotional aspects of sex; such courses are taught by teachers with special qualifications and administrative materials emphasize the sensitive nature of the topic. Further, the Board has consistently taken the position that even professional researchers may not conduct "sexual surveys" of students without meeting certain specific requirements.

Plaintiffs offered statements from five experts, including Gilbert Trachtman, who is a professor of educational psychology at New York University. Plaintiffs' experts questioned the possibility that any emotional harm could be caused by students' attempts to answer the questionnaire, pointed out that the survey might be of substantial benefit to many students, and expressed the opinion that "squelching" the survey could have deleterious effects. They indicated that the topics covered in the questionnaire are of normal interest to adolescents and are common subjects of conversation; further, some of these experts emphasized that students in Manhattan are bombarded with sexually explicit materials and that it was highly unlikely that any student could be harmed by answering the questionnaire. It is noteworthy, however, that at least two of plaintiffs' experts, one of whom was Gilbert Trachtman, recognized that there was some possibility that some students would suffer emotional damage as a result of answering the questionnaire.

* * *

In determining the constitutionality of restrictions on student expression such as are involved here, it is not the function of the courts to reevaluate the wisdom of the actions of state officials charged with protecting the health and welfare of public school students. The inquiry of the district court should have been limited to determining whether defendants had demonstrated a substantial basis for their conclusion that distribution of the questionnaire would result in significant harm to some Stuyvesant students. * * *

We believe that the school authorities did not act unreasonably in deciding that the proposed questionnaire should not be distributed because of the probability that it would result in psychological harm to some students. The district court found this to be so with respect to ninth and tenth-grade students. We see no reason why the conclusion of the defendants that this was also true of eleventh and twelfth-grade students was not within their competence. Although psychological diagnoses of the type involved here are by their nature difficult of precision, * * * we do not think defendants' inability to predict with certainty that a certain number of students in all grades would be harmed should mean that defendants are without power to protect students against a foreseen harm. We believe that the school authorities are sufficiently experienced and knowledgeable concerning these matters, which have been entrusted to them by the community; a federal court ought not impose its own views in such matters where there is a rational basis for the decisions and actions of the school authorities. Their action here is not so much a curtailment of any First Amendment rights; it is principally a measure to protect the students committed to their care, who are compelled by law to attend the school, from peer contacts and pressures which may result in emotional disturbance to some of those students whose responses are sought. The First Amendment right to express one's views does not include the right to importune others to respond to questions when there is reason to believe that such importuning may result in harmful consequences. Consequently where school authorities have reason to believe that harmful consequences might result to students, while they are on the school premises, from solicitation of answers to questions, then prohibition of such solicitation is not a violation of any constitutional rights of those who seek to solicit.

In sum, we conclude that the record established a substantial basis for defendants' belief that distribution of the questionnaire would result in significant emotional harm to a number of students throughout the Stuyvesant population. * * *

Notes

1. Certiorari was denied by the Supreme Court without dissent. 435 U.S. 925, 98 S.Ct. 1491, 55 L.Ed.2d 519 (1978).

2. The District Judge in the case had upheld the ban on the questionnaire for ninth and tenth graders, but had enjoined its application to eleventh and twelfth graders. She had concluded that the potential benefits of permitting the distribution to the older students outweighed the potential harmful effects. Is this the type of distinction to be made by a judge? Both sides brought appeals from that ruling.

3. Why did the court include the paragraph dealing with curricular treatment of "sex and sexuality" at the school?

4. Suppose the questionnaire had been distributed off school grounds. Could the results then be published?

5. *Tinker* is Case No. 114; *Eisner* is Case No. 119.

[Case No. 121] Power of School Authorities to Control Newspaper Produced by Journalism Class

HAZELWOOD SCHOOL DIST. v. KUHLMEIER

Supreme Court of the United States, 1988.
484 U.S. 260, 108 S.Ct. 562, 98 L.Ed.2d 592.

JUSTICE WHITE delivered the opinion of the Court.

This case concerns the extent to which educators may exercise editorial control over the contents of a high school newspaper produced as part of the school's journalism curriculum.

I

Petitioners are the Hazelwood School District in St. Louis County, Missouri; various school officials; Robert Eugene Reynolds, the principal of Hazelwood East High School, and Howard Emerson, a teacher in the school district. Respondents are three former Hazelwood East students who were staff members of Spectrum, the school newspaper. They contend that school officials violated their First Amendment rights by deleting two pages of articles from the May 13, 1983, issue of Spectrum.

Spectrum was written and edited by the Journalism II class at Hazelwood East. The newspaper was published every three weeks or so during the 1982–1983 school year. More than 4,500 copies of the newspaper were distributed during that year to students, school personnel, and members of the community.

The Board of Education allocated funds from its annual budget for the printing of Spectrum. These funds were supplemented by proceeds from sales of the newspaper. The printing expenses during the 1982–1983 school year totaled $4,668.50; revenue from sales was $1,166.84. The other costs associated with the newspaper—such as supplies, textbooks, and a portion of the journalism teacher's salary—were borne entirely by the Board.

The Journalism II course was taught by Robert Stergos for most of the 1982–1983 academic year. Stergos left Hazelwood East to take a job in private industry on April 29, 1983, when the May 13 edition of Spectrum was nearing completion, and petitioner Emerson took his place as newspaper adviser for the remaining weeks of the term.

The practice at Hazelwood East during the spring 1983 semester was for the journalism teacher to submit page proofs of each Spectrum issue to Principal Reynolds for his review prior to publication. On May 10, Emerson delivered the proofs of the May 13 edition to Reynolds, who objected to two of the articles scheduled to appear in that edition. One of the stories described three Hazelwood East students' experiences with pregnancy; the other discussed the impact of divorce on students at the school.

Reynolds was concerned that, although the pregnancy story used false names "to keep the identity of these girls a secret," the pregnant students still might be identifiable from the text. He also believed that the article's references to sexual activity and birth control were inappropriate for some of the younger students at the school. In addition, Reynolds was concerned that a student identified by name in the divorce story had complained that her father "wasn't spending enough time with my mom, my sister and I" prior to the divorce, "was always out of town on business or out late playing cards with the guys," and "always argued about everything" with her mother. Reynolds believed that the student's parents should have been given an opportunity to respond to these remarks or to consent to their publication. He was unaware that Emerson had deleted the student's name from the final version of the article.

Reynolds believed that there was no time to make the necessary changes in the stories before the scheduled press run and that the newspaper would not appear before the end of the school year if printing were delayed to any significant extent. He concluded that his only options under the circumstances were to publish a four-page newspaper instead of the planned six-page newspaper, eliminating the two pages on which the offending stories appeared, or to publish no newspaper at all. Accordingly, he directed Emerson to withhold from publication the two pages containing the stories on pregnancy and divorce.[1] He informed his superiors of the decision, and they concurred.

Respondents subsequently commenced this action * * *.

II

Students in the public schools do not "shed their constitutional rights to freedom of speech or expression at the schoolhouse gate." They cannot be punished merely for expressing their personal views on the school premises—whether "in the cafeteria, or on the playing field, or on the campus during the authorized hours"—unless school authorities have reason to believe that such expression will "substantially interfere with the work of the school or impinge upon the rights of other students."

We have nonetheless recognized that the First Amendment rights of students in the public schools "are not automatically coextensive with the rights of adults in other settings," and must be "applied in light of the special characteristics of the school environment." A school need not tolerate student speech that is inconsistent with its "basic education-

---

1. The two pages deleted from the newspaper also contained articles on teenage marriage, runaways, and juvenile delinquents, as well as a general article on teenage pregnancy. Reynolds testified that he had no objection to these articles and that they were deleted only because they appeared on the same pages as the two objectionable articles.

al mission," even though the government could not censor similar speech outside the school. Accordingly, we held in *Bethel School District No. 403 v. Fraser* that a student could be disciplined for having delivered a speech that was "sexually explicit" but not legally obscene at an official school assembly, because the school was entitled to "disassociate itself" from the speech in a manner that would demonstrate to others that such vulgarity is "wholly inconsistent with the 'fundamental values' of public school education." We thus recognized that "[t]he determination of what manner of speech in the classroom or in school assembly is inappropriate properly rests with the school board," rather than with the federal courts. It is in this context that respondents' First Amendment claims must be considered.

A

We deal first with the question whether Spectrum may appropriately be characterized as a forum for public expression. The public schools do not possess all of the attributes of streets, parks, and other traditional public forums that "time out of mind, have been used for purposes of assembly, communicating thoughts between citizens, and discussing public questions." Hence, school facilities may be deemed to be public forums only if school authorities have "by policy or by practice" opened those facilities "for indiscriminate use by the general public," or by some segment of the public, such as student organizations. If the facilities have instead been reserved for other intended purposes, "communicative or otherwise," then no public forum has been created, and school officials may impose reasonable restrictions on the speech of students, teachers, and other members of the school community. "The government does not create a public forum by inaction or by permitting limited discourse, but only by intentionally opening a nontraditional forum for public discourse."

The policy of school officials toward Spectrum was reflected in Hazelwood School Board Policy 348.51 and the Hazelwood East Curriculum Guide. Board Policy 348.51 provided that "[s]chool sponsored publications are developed within the adopted curriculum and its educational implications in regular classroom activities." The Hazelwood East Curriculum Guide described the Journalism II course as a "laboratory situation in which the students publish the school newspaper applying skills they have learned in Journalism I." The lessons that were to be learned from the Journalism II course, according to the Curriculum Guide, included development of journalistic skills under deadline pressure, "the legal, moral, and ethical restrictions imposed upon journalists within the school community," and "responsibility and acceptance of criticism for articles of opinion." Journalism II was taught by a faculty member during regular class hours. Students received grades and academic credit for their performance in the course.

School officials did not deviate in practice from their policy that production of Spectrum was to be part of the educational curriculum and a "regular classroom activit[y]." The District Court found that Robert Stergos, the journalism teacher during most of the 1982–1983 school year, "both had the authority to exercise and in fact exercised a great deal of control over *Spectrum*." For example, Stergos selected the editors of the newspaper, scheduled publication dates, decided the number of pages for each issue, assigned story ideas to class members, advised students on the development of their stories, reviewed the use of quotations, edited stories, selected and edited the letters to the editor, and dealt with the printing company. Many of these decisions were made without consultation with the Journalism II students. The District Court thus found it "clear that Mr. Stergos was the final authority with respect to almost every aspect of the production and publication of *Spectrum*, including its content." Moreover, after each Spectrum issue had been finally approved by Stergos or his successor, the issue still had to be reviewed by Principal Reynolds prior to publication. Respondents' assertion that they had believed that they could publish "practically anything" in Spectrum was therefore dismissed by the District Court as simply "not credible." These factual findings are amply supported by the record, and were not rejected as clearly erroneous by the Court of Appeals.

* * * School officials did not evince either "by policy or by practice" any intent to open the pages of Spectrum to "indiscriminate use" by its student reporters and editors, or by the student body generally. Instead, they "reserve[d] the forum for its intended purpos[e]" as a supervised learning experience for journalism students. Accordingly, school officials were entitled to regulate the contents of Spectrum in any reasonable manner. It is this standard, rather than our decision in *Tinker v. Des Moines Independent Community School Dist.*, that governs this case.

B

The question whether the First Amendment requires a school to tolerate particular student speech—the question that we addressed in *Tinker*—is different from the question whether the First Amendment requires a school affirmatively to promote particular student speech. The former question addresses educators' ability to silence a student's personal expression that happens to occur on the school premises. The latter question concerns educators' authority over school-sponsored publications, theatrical productions, and other expressive activities that students, parents, and members of the public might reasonably perceive to bear the imprimatur of the school. These activities may fairly be characterized as part of the school curriculum, whether or not they occur in a traditional classroom setting, so long as they are supervised by faculty members and designed to impart particular knowledge or skills to student participants and audiences.

Educators are entitled to exercise greater control over this second form of student expression to assure that participants learn whatever lessons the activity is designed to teach, that readers or listeners are not exposed to material that may be inappropriate for their level of maturity, and that the views of the individual speaker are not erroneously attributed to the school. Hence, a school may in its capacity as publisher of a school newspaper or producer of a school play "disassociate itself" not only from speech that would "substantially interfere with [its] work * * * or impinge upon the rights of other students," but also from speech that is, for example, ungrammatical, poorly written, inadequately researched, biased or prejudiced, vulgar or profane, or unsuitable for immature audiences. A school must be able to set high standards for the student speech that is disseminated under its auspices—standards that may be higher than those demanded by some newspaper publishers or theatrical producers in the "real" world—and may refuse to disseminate student speech that does not meet those standards. In addition, a school must be able to take into account the emotional maturity of the intended audience in determining whether to disseminate student speech on potentially sensitive topics, which might range from the existence of Santa Clause in an elementary school setting to the particulars of teenage sexual activity in a high school setting. A school must also retain the authority to refuse to sponsor student speech that might reasonably be perceived to advocate drug or alcohol use, irresponsible sex, or conduct otherwise inconsistent with "the shared values of a civilized social order," or to associate the school with any position other than neutrality on matters of political controversy. Otherwise, the schools would be unduly constrained from fulfilling their role as "a principal instrument in awakening the child to cultural values, in preparing him for later professional training, and in helping him to adjust normally to his environment."

Accordingly, we conclude that the standard articulated in *Tinker* for determining when a school may punish student expression need not also be the standard for determining when a school may refuse to lend its name and resources to the dissemination of student expression. Instead, we hold that educators do not offend the First Amendment by exercising editorial control over the style and content of student speech in school-sponsored expressive activities so long as their actions are reasonably related to legitimate pedagogical concerns.

This standard is consistent with our oft-expressed view that the education of the Nation's youth is primarily the responsibility of parents, teachers, and state and local school officials, and not of federal judges. It is only when the decision to censor a school-sponsored publication, theatrical production, or other vehicle of student expression has no valid educational purpose that the First Amendment is so "directly and sharply implicate[d]" as to require judicial intervention to protect students' constitutional rights.

III

We also conclude that Principal Reynolds acted reasonably in requiring the deletion from the May 13 issue of Spectrum of the pregnancy article, the divorce article, and the remaining articles that were to appear on the same pages of the newspaper.

The initial paragraph of the pregnancy article declared that "[a]ll names have been changed to keep the identity of these girls a secret." The principal concluded that the students' anonymity was not adequately protected, however, given the other identifying information in the article and the small number of pregnant students at the school. Indeed, a teacher at the school credibly testified that she could positively identify at least one of the girls and possibly all three. It is likely that many students at Hazelwood East would have been at least as successful in identifying the girls. Reynolds therefore could reasonably have feared that the article violated whatever pledge of anonymity had been given to the pregnant students. In addition, he could reasonably have been concerned that the article was not sufficiently sensitive to the privacy interests of the students' boyfriends and parents, who were discussed in the article but who were given no opportunity to consent to its publication or to offer a response. The article did not contain graphic accounts of sexual activity. The girls did comment in the article, however, concerning their sexual histories and their use or nonuse of birth control. It was not unreasonable for the principal to have concluded that such frank talk was inappropriate in a school-sponsored publication distributed to 14–year–old freshmen and presumably taken home to be read by students' even younger brothers and sisters.

The student who was quoted by name in the version of the divorce article seen by Principal Reynolds made comments sharply critical of her father. The principal could reasonably have concluded that an individual publicly identified as an inattentive parent—indeed, as one who chose "playing cards with the guys" over home and family—was entitled to an opportunity to defend himself as a matter of journalistic fairness. These concerns were shared by both of Spectrum's faculty advisers for the 1982–1983 school year, who testified that they would not have allowed the article to be printed without deletion of the student's name.

Principal Reynolds testified credibly at trial that, at the time that he reviewed the proofs of the May 13 issue during an extended telephone conversation with Emerson, he believed that there was no time to make any changes in the articles, and that the newspaper had to be printed immediately or not at all. It is true that Reynolds did not verify whether the necessary modifications could still have been made in the articles, and that Emerson did not volunteer the information that printing could be delayed until the changes were made. We nonetheless agree with the District Court that the decision to excise the two pages containing the problematic articles was reasonable given the particular circumstances of this case. These circumstances included the very recent replacement of Stergos by Emerson, who may not have been entirely familiar with Spectrum editorial and production procedures, and the pressure felt by Reynolds to make an immediate decision so that students would not be deprived of the newspaper altogether.

In sum, we cannot reject as unreasonable Principal Reynolds' conclusion that neither the pregnancy article nor the divorce article was suitable for publication in Spectrum. Reynolds could reasonably have concluded that the students who had written and edited these articles had not sufficiently mastered those portions of the Journalism II curriculum that pertained to the treatment of controversial issues and personal attacks, the need to protect the privacy of individuals whose most intimate concerns are to be revealed in the newspaper, and "the legal, moral, and ethical restrictions imposed upon journalists within [a] school community" that includes adolescent subjects and readers. Finally, we conclude that the principal's decision to delete two pages of Spectrum, rather than to delete only the offending articles or to require that they be modified, was reasonable under the circumstances as he understood them. Accordingly, no violation of First Amendment rights occurred.

    * * *

Notes

1. The vote was five-to-three.

2. Compare this case with Case No. 24.

3. Why do you think the Court so emphasized the number of restrictions placed on production of the newspaper and the fact that there had been no deviation in practice from the policy of tight control by school officials?

4. In a footnote the Court said that it was not necessary to have specific written regulations covering prepublication controls over school-sponsored publications because "to require such regulations in the context of a curricular activity could unduly constrain the ability of educators to educate."

5. From an educational viewpoint, how would you rate the journalism program as conducted in Hazelwood?

[Case No. 122] Power of Board to Establish Discipline Rules for Interscholastic Athletics—Penalties

BRAESCH v. DePASQUALE

Supreme Court of Nebraska, 1978.
200 Neb. 726, 265 N.W.2d 842.

McCown, Justice. The plaintiffs brought this proceeding * * * to enjoin the defendant school officials from enforcing any rules of conduct that would prevent full participation by the plaintiffs in the interscholastic basketball program of the Arlington Public Schools. * * *

The plaintiffs in this action were all minors under the age of 19 and represented by their respective parents. All five plaintiffs were senior members of either the boys or the girls interscholastic basketball teams of Arlington High School. Rules of conduct for boys and girls basketball teams were distributed at the beginning of the 1976–77 basketball season. Participants in the basketball program were required to sign them and obtain one parent's signature on a copy of the rules. The rule involved here was: "DRINKING, SMOKING OR DRUGS: Do not come out for basketball if you plan on using any of the above. Any use of them will result in the immediate expulsion from the squad." Each of the plaintiffs and one or more of their parents had signed the rule.

On Saturday evening, January 8, 1977, a party was held at the home of one of the plaintiffs. The other plaintiffs, along with other seniors who were not members of the interscholastic basketball teams, attended the party. A few days later, Robert Krempke, the coach of the boys basketball team, overheard conversations at school about the party and learned that a senior boy not on the basketball team had been arrested on the evening of the party on a charge of minor in possession. On January 12, 1977, the coach approached the plaintiff who had been the host for the party and questioned him about the party. The plaintiff host admitted that there had been beer at the party and that he and other members of the basketball team were "involved." After consulting with the school principal, the basketball coach talked with each of the plaintiff members of the boys basketball team. Each admitted being at the party and drinking. The coach told them to leave basketball practice, and told them that he would arrange a meeting with them and their parents, and the principal, the following morning. The following morning, January 13, 1977, Daniel DePasquale, the principal of the high school, and Mr. Krempke, the coach, met with two of the boys involved, and on the next morning with the third. Each boy was accompanied by a parent or adult member of his family. At these brief meetings the coach told the persons present that the rules required expulsion from the basketball team, and the principal supported the coach. The principal testified that at the conclusion of these meetings he considered the boys suspended from the team and told them the decision would be confirmed by mail.

On January 13, 1977, Eloise Hiemke, the girls basketball coach, learned about the drinking party from one of the girls involved and from an assistant coach. On the morning of January 14, 1977, the girls coach met with the two girls involved, asked each of them if they had been at the party, and if they had had any alcoholic beverages to drink. Each of the girls admitted she had. The principal and the girls basketball coach met with the girls and their parents on the afternoon of January 14, 1977. The principal and the girls coach advised the girls and their parents that they felt the girls should be expelled from the team, and that an official letter would be mailed to them advising them of the decision and telling them what could be done to appeal the decision. The principal opinion expressed by the parents at the various meetings was that the penalty was too severe.

By letter dated January 18, 1977, the principal notified all the plaintiffs and their parents that each of the plaintiffs had been suspended from the basketball team until January 31, 1977, and then expelled from the team for the remainder of the season. The letter also informed them that they had 5 days in which to give written notice of their desire to appeal to the board of education, and that at the hearing they would each have the right to present their side of the issue, present any documents or statements, and cross-examine witnesses and be represented by counsel. By letters dated January 20, 1977, each of the plaintiffs requested a hearing.

On January 21, 1977, the plaintiffs filed this action in the District Court for Washington County, and obtained a temporary order restraining the defendant school officials from enforcing any rules that would prevent full participation by the plaintiffs in the interscholastic basketball program. Hearing on a temporary injunction was set for January 28, 1977.

On January 24, 1977, the plaintiffs were advised by the principal that they were entitled to a hearing before a hearing examiner. The hearing examiner advised the plaintiffs that hearing would be held at 4:30 p.m., on January 26, 1977, at the school. The plaintiffs declined to participate in the appeals procedures established by the school board.

On January 28, 1977, following a hearing, the District Court granted a temporary injunction enjoining the defendants from preventing the plaintiffs from full participation on the interscholastic basketball teams. Trial on the permanent injunction was later set for and held on February 18, 1977. * * * The District Court entered a permanent injunction * * *. The defendants have appealed.

The plaintiffs filed a motion to dismiss the appeal in this court on the ground that the matter is moot. All the plaintiffs have now graduated from high school. * * *

* * * As a general rule, appellate courts do not sit to give opinions on moot questions on abstract propositions, and an appeal will ordinarily be dismissed where no actual controversy exists between parties at the time of the hearing. * * * "This general rule, however, is subject to some exceptions, as where the question involved is a matter of public interest; * * *." In the context of disciplinary action in the field of interscholastic athletic competition, almost no case could reach this court for decision before it became moot if we refused to decide all cases where no actual controversy still exists between the parties at the time of appellate hearing and decision. The motion to dismiss is not well taken.

There is some disagreement between the parties as to whether participation in high school athletics is a constitutional right or is a privilege not protected by any constitutional principle. * * * [T]he Supreme Court of the United States has abandoned much of the former dichotomy between rights and privileges in constitutional classifications. The Fourteenth Amendment's protection of property extends to benefits to which, under state law or practice, a person has a claim or entitlement. Bd. of Regents v. Roth. The Supreme Court of the United States has also held that temporary suspension from public school infringes upon property or liberty interests protected by the due process clause of the Fourteenth Amendment. Goss v. Lopez.

The State of Nebraska, as a part of its program for public education, has provided athletic opportunities to all public school students. Participation in interscholastic athletics ordinarily has significantly less important constitutional dimensions than does participation in traditional academic education. A student's interest in participation in high school athletics is nevertheless a significant one. Brenden v. Independent School Dist. In the light of these constitutional principles, the question is whether the due process clause limits the power of the defendants to exclude the plaintiffs from participation in the interscholastic athletic program of Arlington High School.

Assuming that the application of the rule of conduct involved here implicates a property or liberty interest which is protected by the Fourteenth Amendment, the question becomes one of what process was due the plaintiffs under the circumstances of this case. Due process is not a technical fixed concept to be applied in all conditions, but must be flexible. It calls for such procedural protection as may be appropriate to meet the particular situation. * * *

There can be no doubt that each of the plaintiffs here had specific advance notice of the rule of conduct involved, and notice of the date, time, and place of the violation charged. Each of the plaintiffs admitted his or her violation of the rule. Courts that have considered the issue have generally concluded that when the acts which are the basis for disciplinary action are admitted, the requirements of due process are far less stringent, and that due process requirements with respect to the "guilt" finding process have been met by the admissions. * * *

In the case before us the plaintiffs do not dispute that there was a specific rule of conduct for interscholastic basketball participants; that each of them and their parents had actual notice of the rule in advance; and that each of the plaintiffs violated the rule. The plaintiffs' position is simply that the rule was arbitrary and unreasonable or that the penalty was too great.

Rules prohibiting use of alcoholic liquor or drugs by participants in interscholastic athletics are clearly appropriate. * * * "The wisdom or expediency of a rule adopted by a school board and the motive prompting it are not open to judicial inquiry, where it is within the administrative power of that body." Rules governing the conduct of participants in interscholastic athletics duly and regularly adopted by school authorities ought to be valid and enforceable unless they are clearly arbitrary and unreasonable and serve no legitimate end of educational athletic policy.

The rule involved in this case, even though the penalty of expulsion for the season might be deemed severe by some persons, clearly serves a legitimate rational interest and directly affects the discipline of student athletes. It cannot be said that the prescribed penalty was an arbitrary and unreasonable means to attain the legitimate end of deterrence of the use of alcoholic liquor by student athletes.

Although due process may also contemplate an opportunity to be heard on the question of the penalty to be imposed where the penalty is discretionary rather than prescribed, that opportunity was also provided here. In addition to the informal procedures and meetings, which met all rudimentary requirements of due process, the plaintiffs here were also given the right to appear at a formal hearing with a right to present evidence, cross-examine witnesses, and be represented by counsel. A hearing examiner was appointed and a date set for hearing but the plaintiffs declined to participate in any of the appeals procedures established by the school board. Instead, they commenced this injunction action 1 day after they had requested the appeals procedures offered by defendants, and the temporary injunction was obtained in the District Court 2 days after the date set for the school hearing which plaintiffs had already refused. Under such circumstances courts should be reluctant to interfere prior to completion of prompt and reasonable procedures for obtaining a final order of the school board. A few days suspension from interscholastic athletic competition can hardly be said to constitute such irreparable harm as to justify judicial interference with orderly and prompt school board procedures.

* * * It is the general rule that administrative action which is not final cannot be attacked in an injunction proceeding, the reason being that in the absence of a final order or decision, power has not been fully and finally exercised and there can usually be no irreparable harm. On the evidence in this case, a few days delay could not constitute irreparable harm in a constitutional sense or otherwise.

It is clear in this case that the school board had the power to change or reduce the penalty if it were determined to be arbitrary and unreasonable. The plaintiffs refused to exhaust that remedy or to pursue it to the point of finality at which it might be ripe for judicial review. Where a board of education has provided effective, reasonable, and prompt procedures for notice, hearing, and review of an order of expulsion from participation in interscholastic athletics, and the athlete neglects or refuses to follow or comply with such procedures and exhaust such remedies, such neglect or refusal ordinarily constitutes a waiver of any right to subsequent injunctive relief.

The action of the District Court in granting the injunction here was erroneous and is therefore reversed.

Reversed.

Notes

1. The Supreme Court without dissent denied certiorari on this case. 439 U.S. 1068, 99 S.Ct. 836, 59 L.Ed.2d 34 (1979).

2. Observe the reasons the court decided the case even though it was moot. Other examples of cases decided after they were moot are Cases No. 48, 92, and 145.

3. Whether participation in interscholastic athletics is a constitutional right or a privilege has tended to become one of rhetoric rather than substance. Different constitutional considerations come into play in various ways as various rules are attacked on various grounds. See "Interscholastic Activities" in Chapter 4 and Cases No. 31, 32 and 33.

4. The court discusses the proper relationship between the judiciary as protector of rights of students and the school authorities as those governmentally charged with operating the schools. Those dissatisfied with actions of subordinate school authorities frequently "jump the gun" in taking the matter to court—and sometimes succeed in achieving their substantive goal through lower court error (as here).

[Case No. 123] Constitutionality of Searches of Students

NEW JERSEY v. T.L.O.

Supreme Court of the United States, 1985.
469 U.S. 325, 105 S.Ct. 733, 83 L.Ed.2d 720.

JUSTICE WHITE delivered the opinion of the Court.

* * * [W]e here address only the questions of the proper standard for assessing the legality of searches conducted by public school officials and the application of that standard to the facts of this case.

I

On March 7, 1980, a teacher at Piscataway High School in Middlesex County, N.J., discovered two girls smoking in a lavatory. One of the two girls was the respondent T.L.O., who at that time was a 14–year–old high school freshman. Because smoking in the lavatory was a violation of a school rule, the teacher took the two girls to the Principal's office, where they met with Assistant Vice Principal Theodore Choplick. In response to questioning by Mr. Choplick, T.L.O.'s companion admitted that she had violated the rule. T.L.O., however, denied that she had been smoking in the lavatory and claimed that she did not smoke at all.

Mr. Choplick asked T.L.O. to come into his private office and demanded to see her purse. Opening the purse, he found a pack of cigarettes, which he removed from the purse and held before T.L.O. as he accused her of having lied to him. As he reached into the purse for the cigarettes, Mr. Choplick also noticed a package of cigarette rolling papers. In his experience, possession of rolling papers by high school students was closely associated with the use of marihuana. Suspecting that a closer examination of the purse might yield further evidence of drug use, Mr. Choplick proceeded to search the purse thoroughly. The search revealed a small amount of marihuana, a pipe, a number of empty plastic bags, a substantial quantity of money in one-dollar bills, an index card that appeared to be a list of students who owed T.L.O. money, and two letters that implicated T.L.O. in marihuana dealing.

Mr. Choplick notified T.L.O.'s mother and the police, and turned the evidence of drug dealing over to the police. At the request of the police, T.L.O.'s mother took her daughter to police headquarters, where T.L.O. confessed that she had been selling marihuana at the high school. On the basis of the confession and the evidence seized by Mr. Choplick, the State brought delinquency charges against T.L.O. * * * Contending that Mr. Choplick's search of her purse violated the Fourth Amendment, T.L.O. moved to suppress the evidence found in her purse as well her confession, which, she argued, was tainted by the allegedly unlawful search. * * *

* * *

II

In determining whether the search at issue in this case violated the Fourth Amendment, we are faced initially with the question whether that Amendment's prohibition on unreasonable searches and seizures applies to searches conducted by public school officials. We hold that it does.

It is now beyond dispute that "the Federal Constitution, by virtue of the Fourteenth Amendment, prohibits unreasonable searches and seizures by state officers." Equally indisputable is the proposition that the Fourteenth Amendment protects the rights of students against encroachment by public school officials * * *.

* * *

* * * We have held school officials subject to the commands of the First Amendment, see *Tinker v. Des Moines Independent Community School District,* and the Due Process Clause of the Fourteenth Amendment, see *Goss v. Lopez.* * * * More generally, the Court has recognized that "the concept of parental delegation" as a source of school authority is not entirely "consonant with compulsory education laws." *Ingraham v. Wright.* Today's public school officials do not merely exercise authority voluntarily conferred on them by individual parents; rather, they act in furtherance of publicly mandated educational and disciplinary policies. In carrying out searches and other disciplinary functions pursuant to such policies, school officials act as representatives of the State, not merely as surrogates for the parents, and they cannot claim the parents' immunity from the strictures of the Fourth Amendment.

III

To hold that the Fourth Amendment applies to searches conducted by school authorities is only to begin the inquiry into the standards governing such searches. Although the underlying command of the Fourth Amendment is always that searches and seizures be reasonable, what is reasonable depends on the context within which a search takes place. The determination of the standard of reasonableness governing any specific class of searches requires "balancing the need to search against the invasion which the search entails." On one side of the balance are arrayed the individual's legitimate expectations of privacy and personal security; on the other, the government's need for effective methods to deal with breaches of public order.

We have recognized that even a limited search of the person is a substantial invasion of privacy. We have also recognized that searches of closed items of personal luggage are intrusions on protected privacy interests, for "the Fourth Amendment provides protection to the owner of every container that conceals its contents from plain view." A search of a child's person or of a closed purse or other bag carried on her person, no less than a similar search carried out on an adult, is undoubtedly a severe violation of subjective expectations of privacy.

Of course, the Fourth Amendment does not protect subjective expectations of privacy that are unreasonable or otherwise "illegitimate." To receive the protection of the Fourth Amendment, an expectation of privacy must be one that society is "prepared to recognize as legitimate." * * *

* * *

* * * In short, schoolchildren may find it necessary to carry with them a variety of legitimate, noncontraband items, and there is no reason to conclude that they have necessarily waived all rights to privacy in such items merely by bringing them onto school grounds.

Against the child's interest in privacy must be set the substantial interest of teachers and administrators in maintaining discipline in the classroom and on school grounds. * * *

How, then, should we strike the balance between the schoolchild's legitimate expectations of privacy and the school's equally legitimate need to maintain an environment in which learning can take place? It is evident that the school setting requires some easing of the restrictions to which searches by public authorities are ordinarily subject. The warrant requirement, in particular, is unsuited to the school environment: requiring a teacher to obtain a warrant before searching a child suspected of an infraction of school rules (or of the criminal law) would unduly interfere with the maintenance of the swift and informal disciplinary procedures needed in the schools. * * * [W]e hold today that school officials need not obtain a warrant before searching a student who is under their authority.

The school setting also requires some modification of the level of suspicion of illicit activity needed to justify a search. Ordinarily, a search—even one that may permissibly be carried out without a warrant—must be based upon "probable cause" to believe that a violation of the law has occurred. However, "probable cause" is not an irreducible requirement of a valid search. The fundamental command of the Fourth Amendment is that searches and seizures be reasonable * * *.

We join the majority of courts that have examined this issue in concluding that the accommodation of the privacy interests of schoolchildren with the substantial need of teachers and administrators for freedom to maintain order in the schools does not require strict adherence to the requirement that searches be based on probable cause to believe that the subject of the search has violated or is violating the law. Rather, the legality of a search of a student should depend simply on the reasonableness, under all the circumstances, of the search. Determining the reasonableness of any search involves a twofold inquiry: first, one must consider "whether the * * * action was justified at its inception"; second, one must determine whether the search as actually conducted "was reasonably related in scope to the circumstances which justified the interference in the first place." Under ordinary circumstances, a search of a student by a teacher or other school official will be "justified at its inception" when there are reasonable grounds for suspecting that the search will turn up evidence that the student has violated or is violating either the law or the rules of the school. Such a search will be permissible in its scope when the measures adopted are reasonably related to the objectives of the search and not excessively intrusive in light of the age and sex of the student and the nature of the infraction.

This standard will, we trust, neither unduly burden the efforts of school authorities to maintain order in their schools nor authorize unrestrained intrusions upon the privacy of schoolchildren. By focusing attention on the question of reasonableness, the standard will spare teachers and school administrators the necessity of schooling themselves in the niceties of probable cause and permit them to regulate their conduct according to the dictates of reason and common sense. At the same time, the reasonableness standard should ensure that the interests of students will be invaded no more than is necessary to achieve the legitimate end of preserving order in the schools.

IV

There remains the question of the legality of the search in this case. * * * Our review of the facts surrounding the search leads us to conclude that the search was in no sense unreasonable for Fourth Amendment purposes.

The incident that gave rise to this case actually involved two separate searches, with the first—the search for cigarettes—providing the suspicion that gave rise to the second—the search for marihuana. Although it is the fruits of the second search that are at issue here, the validity of the search for marihuana must depend on the reasonableness of the initial search for cigarettes, as there would have been no reason to suspect that T.L.O. possessed marihuana had the first search not taken place. Accordingly, it is to the search for cigarettes that we first turn our attention.

* * *

* * * T.L.O. had been accused of smoking, and had denied the accusation in the strongest possible terms when she stated that she did not smoke at all. Surely it cannot be said that under these circumstances, T.L.O.'s possession of cigarettes would be irrelevant to the charges against her or to her response to those charges. T.L.O.'s possession of cigarettes, once it was discovered, would both corroborate the report that she had been smoking and undermine the credibility of her defense to the charge of smoking. To be sure, the discovery of the cigarettes would not prove that T.L.O. had been smoking in the lavatory; nor would it, strictly speaking, necessarily be inconsistent with her claim that she did not smoke at all. But it is universally recognized that evidence, to be relevant to an inquiry, need not conclusively prove the ultimate fact in issue, but only have "any tendency to make the existence of any fact that is of consequence to the determination of the action more probable or less probable than it would be without the evidence." The relevance of T.L.O.'s possession of cigarettes to the question whether she had been smoking and to the credibility of her denial that she smoked supplied the necessary "nexus" between the item searched for and the infraction under investigation. * * *

* * *

Our conclusion that Mr. Choplick's decision to open T.L.O.'s purse was reasonable brings us to the question of the further search for marihuana once the pack of cigarettes was located. The suspicion upon which the search for marihuana was founded was provided when Mr. Choplick observed a package of rolling papers in the purse as he removed the pack of cigarettes. * * * The discovery of the rolling papers concededly gave rise to a reasonable suspicion that T.L.O. was carrying marihuana as well as cigarettes in her purse. This suspicion justified further exploration of T.L.O.'s purse, which turned up more evidence of drug-related activities: a pipe, a number of plastic bags of the type commonly used to store marihuana, a small quantity of marihuana, and a fairly substantial amount of money. Under these circumstances, it was not unreasonable to extend the search to a separate zippered compartment of the purse; and when a search of that compartment revealed an index card containing a list of "people who owe me money" as well as two letters, the inference that T.L.O. was involved in marihuana trafficking was substantial enough to justify Mr. Choplick in examining the letters to determine whether they contained any further evidence. In short, we cannot conclude that the search for marihuana was unreasonable in any respect.

* * *

Notes

1. *Tinker* is Case No. 114. *Goss* is Case No. 127. *Ingraham* is Case No. 124.

2. Evidence uncovered by the government in violation of the Fourth Amendment is not admissible in a criminal proceeding. The legal genesis of this case was the state's bringing charges of delinquency against T.L.O. based primarily on the evidence discovered by Mr. Choplick's search, which evidence T.L.O. sought to suppress. This was not a case of school discipline being based on the evidence, nor was it a civil rights suit brought by a student against school authorities.

3. A substantial majority of courts prior to this decision had adopted the standard of "reasonable suspicion," rather than the strict "probable cause" standard, for searches by school authorities.

4. In a footnote the Court stated that it was not here addressing "whether a schoolchild has a legitimate expectation of privacy in lockers, desks, or other school property provided for the storage of school supplies."

5. In another footnote the Court said that it was not here deciding "whether individualized suspicion is an essential element of the reasonableness standard" adopted for searches by school authorities.

[Case No. 124] Constitutional Rights of Students regarding Corporal Punishment

INGRAHAM v. WRIGHT

Supreme Court of the United States, 1977.
430 U.S. 651, 97 S.Ct. 1401, 51 L.Ed.2d 711.

MR. JUSTICE POWELL delivered the opinion of the Court.

This case presents questions concerning the use of corporal punishment in public schools: first, whether the paddling of students as a means of maintaining school discipline constitutes cruel and unusual punishment in violation of the Eighth Amendment; and second, to the extent that paddling is constitutionally permissible, whether the Due Process Clause of the Fourteenth Amendment requires prior notice and an opportunity to be heard.

I

* * *

Petitioners' evidence may be summarized briefly. In the 1970–1971 school year many of the 237 schools in Dade County used corporal punishment as a means of maintaining discipline pursuant to Florida legislation and a local school board regulation. The statute then in effect authorized limited corporal punishment by negative inference, proscribing punishment which was "degrading or unduly severe" or which was inflicted without prior consultation with the principal or the teacher in charge of the school. The regulation * * * contained explicit directions and limitations.   * * *

Petitioners focused on Drew Junior High School, the school in which both Ingraham and Andrews were enrolled in the fall of 1970. In an apparent reference to Drew, the District Court found that "[t]he instances of punishment which could be characterized as severe, accepting the students' testimony as credible, took place in one junior high school." * * *

The District Court made no findings on the credibility of the students' testimony. Rather, assuming their testimony to be credible, the court found no constitutional basis for relief.   * * *

A panel of the Court of Appeals voted to reverse.   * * * Upon rehearing, the en banc court rejected these conclusions and affirmed the judgment of the District Court.   * * *

* * *

II

In addressing the scope of the Eighth Amendment's prohibition on cruel and unusual punishment this Court has found it useful to refer to "[t]raditional common law concepts," and to the "attitude[s] which our society has traditionally taken." So too, in defining the requirements of procedural due process under the Fifth and Fourteenth Amendments, the Court has been attuned to what "has always been the law of the land," and to "traditional ideas of fair procedure." We therefore begin by examining the way in which our traditions and our laws have responded to the use of corporal punishment in public schools.

The use of corporal punishment in this country as a means of disciplining school children dates back to the colonial period. It has survived the transformation of primary and secondary education from the colonials' reliance on optional private arrangements to our present system of compulsory education and dependence on public schools. Despite the general abandonment of corporal punishment as a means of punishing criminal offenders, the practice continues to play a role in the public education of school children in most parts of the country. Professional and public opinion is sharply divided on the practice, and has been for more than a century. Yet we can discern no trend toward its elimination.

At common law a single principle has governed the use of corporal punishment since before the American Revolution: teachers may impose reasonable but not excessive force to discipline a child.   * * * The basic doctrine has not changed. The prevalent rule in this country today privileges such force as a teacher or administrator "reasonably believes to be necessary for [the child's] proper control, training, or education." * * * To the extent that the force is excessive or unreasonable, the educator in virtually all States is subject to possible civil and criminal liability.

Although the early cases viewed the authority of the teacher as deriving from the parents, the concept of parental delegation has been replaced by the view—more consonant with compulsory education laws—that the State itself may impose such corporal punishment as is reasonably necessary "for the proper education of the child and for the maintenance of group discipline." * * * All of the circumstances are to be taken into account in determining whether the punishment is reasonable in a particular case. Among the most important considerations are the seriousness of the offense, the attitude and past behavior of the child, the nature and severity of the punishment, the age and strength of the child, and the availability of less severe but equally effective means of discipline. * * *

Of the 23 States that have addressed the problem through legislation, 21 have authorized the moderate use of corporal punishment in public schools. Of these States only a few have elaborated on the common law test of reasonableness, typically providing for approval or notification of the child's parent, or for infliction of punishment only by the principal or in the presence of an adult witness. Only two States, Massachusetts and New Jersey, have prohibited all corporal punishment in their public schools. Where the legislatures have not acted, the state courts have uniformly preserved the common law rule permitting teachers to use reasonable force in disciplining children in their charge.

Against this background of historical and contemporary approval of reasonable corporal punishment, we turn to the constitutional questions before us.

III

The Eighth Amendment provides, "Excessive bail shall not be required, nor excessive fines imposed, nor cruel and unusual punishments inflicted." Bail, fines and punishment traditionally have been associated with the criminal process, and by subjecting the three to parallel limitations the text of the Amendment suggests an intention to limit the power of those entrusted with the criminal law function of government. An examination of the history of the Amendment and the decisions of this Court construing the proscription against cruel and unusual punishment confirms that it was designed to protect those convicted of crimes. We adhere to this longstanding limitation and hold that the Eighth Amendment does not apply to the paddling of children as a means of maintaining discipline in public schools.

A

The history of the Eighth Amendment is well known. The text was taken, almost verbatim, from a provision of the Virginia Declaration of Rights of 1776, which in turn derived from the English Bill of Rights of 1689. The English version, adopted after the accession of William and

Mary, was intended to curb the excesses of English judges under the reign of James II. * * *

At the time of its ratification, the original Constitution was criticized in the Massachusetts and Virginia Conventions for its failure to provide any protection for persons convicted of crimes. * * * This criticism provided the impetus for inclusion of the Eighth Amendment in the Bill of Rights. * * *

B

In light of this history, it is not surprising to find that every decision of this Court considering whether a punishment is "cruel and unusual" within the meaning of the Eighth and Fourteenth Amendments has dealt with a criminal punishment. * * *

In the few cases where the Court has had occasion to confront claims that impositions outside the criminal process constituted cruel and unusual punishment, it has had no difficulty finding the Eighth Amendment inapplicable. * * *

C

Petitioners acknowledge that the original design of the Cruel and Unusual Punishments Clause was to limit criminal punishments, but urge nonetheless that the prohibition should be extended to ban the paddling of school children. Observing that the Framers of the Eighth Amendment could not have envisioned our present system of public and compulsory education, with its opportunities for noncriminal punishments, petitioners contend that extension of the prohibition against cruel punishments is necessary lest we afford greater protection to criminals than to schoolchildren. It would be anomalous, they say, if schoolchildren could be beaten without constitutional redress, while hardened criminals suffering the same beatings at the hands of their jailors might have a valid claim under the Eighth Amendment. Whatever force this logic may have in other settings, we find it an inadequate basis for wrenching the Eighth Amendment from its historical context and extending it to traditional disciplinary practices in the public schools.

The prisoner and the schoolchild stand in wholly different circumstances, separated by the harsh facts of criminal conviction and incarceration. * * *

The schoolchild has little need for the protection of the Eighth Amendment. Though attendance may not always be voluntary, the public school remains an open institution. Except perhaps when very young, the child is not physically restrained from leaving school during school hours; and at the end of the school day, the child is invariably free to return home. Even while at school, the child brings with him the support of family and friends and is rarely apart from teachers and other pupils who may witness and protest any instances of mistreatment.

The openness of the public school and its supervision by the community afford significant safeguards against the kinds of abuses from which the Eighth Amendment protects the prisoner. In virtually every community where corporal punishment is permitted in the schools, these safeguards are reinforced by the legal constraints of the common law. Public school teachers and administrators are privileged at common law to inflict only such corporal punishment as is reasonably necessary for the proper education and discipline of the child; any punishment going beyond the privilege may result in both civil and criminal liability. * * * As long as the schools are open to public scrutiny, there is no reason to believe that the common law constraints will not effectively remedy and deter excesses such as those alleged in this case.

We conclude that when public school teachers or administrators impose disciplinary corporal punishment, the Eighth Amendment is inapplicable. The pertinent constitutional question is whether the imposition is consonant with the requirements of due process.

IV

The Fourteenth Amendment prohibits any State deprivation of life, liberty or property without due process of law. Application of this prohibition requires the familiar two-stage analysis: we must first ask whether the asserted individual interests are encompassed within the Fourteenth Amendment's protection of "life, liberty or property"; if protected interests are implicated, we then must decide what procedures constitute "due process of law." Following that analysis here, we find that corporal punishment in public school implicates a constitutionally protected liberty interest, but we hold that the traditional common law remedies are fully adequate to afford due process.

A

"[T]he range of interests protected by procedural due process is not infinite." * * *

* * * Among the historic liberties * * * protected was a right to be free from, and to obtain judicial relief for, unjustified intrusions on personal security.

While the contours of this historic liberty interest in the context of our federal system of government have not been defined precisely, they always have been thought to encompass freedom from bodily restraint and punishment. It is fundamental that the state cannot hold and physically punish an individual except in accordance with due process of law.

This constitutionally protected liberty interest is at stake in this case. There is, of course a *de minimis* level of imposition with which the Constitution is not concerned. But at least where school authorities, acting under color of state law, deliberately decide to punish a child for misconduct by restraining the child and inflicting appreciable physical pain, we hold that Fourteenth Amendment liberty interests are implicated.

B

" [T]he question remains what process is due." Were it not for the common law privilege permitting teachers, to inflict reasonable corporal punishment on children in their care, and the availability of the traditional remedies for abuse, the case for requiring advance procedural safeguards would be strong indeed. But here we deal with a punishment—paddling—within that tradition, and the question is whether the common law remedies are adequate to afford due process.

* * * Whether in this case the common law remedies for excessive corporal punishment constitute due process of law must turn on an analysis of the competing interests at stake, viewed against the background of "history, reason, [and] the past course of decisions." The analysis requires consideration of three distinct factors: "first, the private interest that will be affected * * *; second, the risk of an erroneous deprivation of such interest * * * and the probable value, if any, of additional or substitute procedural safeguards; and, finally, the [state] interest, including the function involved and the fiscal and administrative burdens that the additional or substitute procedural requirement would entail."

1

Because it is rooted in history, the child's liberty interest in avoiding corporal punishment while in the care of public school authorities is subject to historical limitations. * * *

The concept that reasonable corporal punishment in school is justifiable continues to be recognized in the laws of most States. * * * It represents "the balance struck by this country," between the child's interest in personal security and the traditional view that some limited corporal punishment may be necessary in the course of a child's education. Under that longstanding accommodation of interests, there can be no deprivation of substantive rights as long as disciplinary corporal punishment is within the limits of the common law privilege.

This is not to say that the child's interest in procedural safeguards is insubstantial. The school disciplinary process is not "a totally accurate, unerring process, never mistaken and never unfair. * * *" In any deliberate infliction of corporal punishment on a child who is restrained for that purpose, there is some risk that the intrusion on the child's liberty will be unjustified and therefore unlawful. In these circumstances the child has a strong interest in procedural safeguards that minimize the risk of wrongful punishment and provide for the resolution of disputed questions of justification.

We turn now to a consideration of the safeguards that are available under applicable Florida law.

2

Florida has continued to recognize, and indeed has strengthened by statute, the common law right of a child not to be subjected to excessive corporal punishment in school. Under Florida law the teacher and principal of the school decide in the first instance whether corporal punishment is reasonably necessary under the circumstances in order to discipline a child who has misbehaved. But they must exercise prudence and restraint. For Florida has preserved the traditional judicial proceedings for determining whether the punishment was justified. If the punishment inflicted is later found to have been excessive—not reasonably believed at the time to be necessary for the child's discipline or training—the school authorities inflicting it may be held liable in damages to the child and, if malice is shown, they may be subject to criminal penalties.

Although students have testified in this case to specific instances of abuse, there is every reason to believe that such mistreatment is an aberration. The uncontradicted evidence suggests that corporal punishment in the Dade County schools was, " [w]ith the exception of a few cases, * * * unremarkable in physical severity." Moreover, because paddlings are usually inflicted in response to conduct directly observed by teachers in their presence, the risk that a child will be paddled without cause is typically insignificant. In the ordinary case, a disciplinary paddling neither threatens seriously to violate any substantive rights nor condemns the child "to suffer grievous loss of any kind."

In those cases where severe punishment is contemplated, the available civil and criminal sanctions for abuse—considered in light of the openness of the school environment—afford significant protection against unjustified corporal punishment. Teachers and school authorities are unlikely to inflict corporal punishment unnecessarily or excessively when a possible consequence of doing so is the institution of civil or criminal proceedings against them.

* * *

3

But even if the need for advance procedural safeguards were clear, the question would remain whether the incremental benefit could justify the cost. Acceptance of petitioners' claims would work a transformation in the law governing corporal punishment in Florida and most other States. Given the impracticability of formulating a rule of procedural due process that varies with the severity of the particular imposition, the prior hearing petitioners seek would have to precede *any* paddling, however moderate or trivial.

Such a universal constitutional requirement would significantly burden the use of corporal punishment as a disciplinary measure. Hearings—even informal hearings—require time, personnel, and a diversion of attention from normal school pursuits. * * *

Elimination or curtailment of corporal punishment would be welcomed by many as a societal advance. But when such a policy choice may result from this Court's determination of an asserted right to due process, rather than from the normal processes of community debate and legislative action, the societal costs cannot be dismissed as insubstantial. * * *

* * * In view of the low incidence of abuse, the openness of our schools, and the common law safeguards that already exist, the risk of error that may result in violation of a schoolchild's substantive rights can only be regarded as minimal. Imposing additional administrative safeguards as a constitutional requirement might reduce that risk marginally, but would also entail a significant intrusion into an area of primary educational responsibility. We conclude that the Due Process Clause does not require notice and a hearing prior to the imposition of corporal punishment in the public schools, as that practice is authorized and limited by the common law.

* * *

Notes

1. The Court divided five-to-four on the decision. The dissenting Justices were of the opinion the Eighth Amendment was applicable to *some* cases of corporal punishment and that the rudimentary due process requirements of *Goss* (Case No. 127) should apply.

2. Board regulations included requirements that (1) the principal should determine the necessity of the punishment, (2) the pupil should understand the reason for the punishment, and (3) it should be administered in the presence of another adult under circumstances not calculated to hold the student up to shame or ridicule. What effect, if any, will the requirement that this "checklist" be followed have upon the decision whether to administer corporal punishment and upon its nature and severity?

3. Notice that the original doctrine of parental delegation of authority to teachers has been replaced by the view that the state itself has the right to administer corporal punishment reasonably necessary "for the proper education of the child and for the maintenance of group discipline."

4. The efficacy of corporal punishment of students has been contested since long before there were public schools. To what extent is this issue properly a legislative, rather than judicial, concern? To what extent is it an educational, rather than legal, concern?

5. California statutes permit corporal punishment only if a parent or guardian approves in writing. A "fundamental school" established by a school board had as an admission requirement that the child's parent agree that corporal punishment may be used. The Court of Appeal of California held that such a requirement could not be enforced. Burton v. Pasadena City Bd. of Educ., 71 Cal.App.3d 52, 139 Cal.Rptr. 383 (1977).

[Case No. 125] Misapplication of Policy Barring Weapons in School

C.J. v. SCHOOL BD. OF BROWARD COUNTY

District Court of Appeal of Florida, 1983.
438 So.2d 87.

GLICKSTEIN, JUDGE. At issue is whether an order of expulsion by the School Board of Broward County of a thirteen-year-old girl from public school for the 1982 summer session and both semesters of the following school year can be affirmed under the facts of this case. We conclude that such order is not supported by substantial, competent evidence; therefore, we reverse and remand.

Although a number of issues have been raised by the parties, we have not dealt with all of them because of our opinion that one controls the disposition of the case. For the purpose of argument, we accept the proposition that the mandatory policy that existed here is enforceable; namely, automatic expulsion for possession of a weapon. We do so, again for the sake of argument, for the reasons contained in Mitchell v. Board of Trustees of Oxford Municipal Separate School District, 625 F.2d 660 (5th Cir.1980). However, we are very sensitive to the principle that entitlement to an education has been recognized as a property interest protected by the due process clause of the fourteenth amendment, in Goss v. Lopez. Further, we share the concern of Judge Godbold in Lee v. Macon County Board of Education, 490 F.2d 458, 460 (5th Cir.1974) wherein he said:

> But a sentence of banishment from the local educational system is, insofar as the institution has power to act, the extreme penalty, the ultimate punishment. In our increasingly technological society getting at least a high school education is almost necessary for survival. Stripping a child of access to educational opportunity is a life sentence to second-rate citizenship, unless the child has the financial ability to migrate to another school system or enter private school.

Because of our sensitivity and concern, we intend that school boards turn square corners, dot all of their "i's" and cross all of their "t's," if they intend to enforce such a rigid, mandatory rule. In this case, the school board did not pass muster.

The uncontradicted facts establish that Cynthia Jones, a thirteen-year-old girl, had received a commemorative knife from her father to give to her boyfriend as a Christmas gift. This was a bone-handled knife with a plate thereon for initials or other inscription. It had no switch mechanism and had to be opened as whittlers have done for generations. The child had a girlfriend who was moving away from the city, lived too far to come to Cynthia's home, but wanted to see the knife. To accommodate her girlfriend, Cynthia brought the knife to the school bus stop to show it to her, with the intention of taking the knife home before the school bus arrived. However, the bus approached; and Cynthia, reluctant to face the consequences at home for missing the bus, elected to take the knife with her to school. The knife was in a pouch, packed in the gift box with paper, and she could not open it if she wanted to for a practical reason—she was a nail biter.

Life being a matter of timing—good or bad—for most of us, Cynthia was in the bathroom at school when an older student, not with her, commenced smoking a cigarette in the bathroom. An administrative assistant discovered the smoking and in due course the purses of all of the girls in the bathroom were searched. The knife was found and Cynthia's school life metamorphosed into a chapter of *Les Miserables*.

The bases for Cynthia's expulsion were two school board policies—5006 and 2304. Rule 26(1) of the former provides for mandatory expulsion in the event of the following:

> The possession, use or transmittal of a weapon or use of any article as a weapon or use in a manner reasonably calculated to threaten any person. Weapons are defined in Board Policy 2304.

The latter in pertinent part defines weapons as follows:

> 2. Knives—switchblade, hunting or any knife used to intimidate.

In our view, the commemorative, boxed knife in this case did not fit any of the three descriptive requirements in the Board's policy. It was not a switchblade, nor a hunting knife, nor any knife used to intimidate.

We have no misgiving about requiring the School Board to toe the mark in their choice of language in light of the irreplaceability of education and of the Board's position at oral argument that if a student with a knife asked a second student to take the knife to the principal's office and en route the second student was stopped by an official, the second student would be expelled. We are as mindful as every member of the School Board of the absolute necessity of preventing violence in school. Every day we must deal with evidence of man's inhumanity to his fellows; and we are as cognizant as all public officials of the necessity for strict disciplinary requirements in the schools. But the School Board cannot have it both ways. If it is going to urge the validity of a mandatory rule of such gravity, then it had better use in its rule making all of the punctiliousness that Seurat did in his painting. Here, it failed to do so by not meeting its definition of knives as weapons.

Notes

1. In Mitchell v. Board of Trustees of Oxford Municipal Separate School Dist. (cited in case), the court upheld a policy of automatic expulsion for the balance of the semester for bringing weapons (knives) to school. It said that the absence of the possibility of a lesser penalty simply meant that the board had favored consistency of punishment over tailoring the punishment to the child, a decision it could constitutionally make.

2. Was the present court being overly technical in interpreting the three descriptive requirements in the board policy defining "knives"? Were school authorities being overly technical in following the letter of their mandatory expulsion policy? On educational grounds, do you support the conclusion of the court or of the school authorities?

3. Suppose the board rule also had barred penknives (and thus the commemorative knife would have been covered). Would the court likely have upheld C.J.'s exclusion? Why?

4. Stating at three points that it might have acted differently from the school board, the Missouri Court of Appeals upheld the 78–day suspension of an eighth-grader who had an "excellent school record" but who had brought a "butterfly knife" to school. The board operated under a uniform policy of suspension for possession of knives at school. Consolidated School Dist. No. 2 v. King, 786 S.W.2d 217 (Mo.App.1990).

[Case No. 126] Power of Board to Determine Punishment of Student—Abuse of Discretion

ROBINSON v. OAK PARK AND RIVER FOREST HIGH SCHOOL

Appellate Court of Illinois, 1991.

213 Ill.App.3d 77, 156 Ill.Dec. 951, 571 N.E.2d 931.

JUSTICE GREIMAN delivered the opinion of the Court. The appeal [is] from the entry of a temporary injunction restraining the Board from expelling plaintiffs, Tamika Robinson and Nicole Jenkins, freshmen students enrolled at the high school for the balance of the 1990–91 academic year.

* * *

Plaintiffs were apparently involved in a fight or altercation on December 10, 1990, a school day, between 4:00 PM and 4:30 PM near the school operated by the Board. Plaintiffs, two other students who have been similarly expelled and two non-students were involved with a fifth person, Tameko Warren, a student who was apparently the focal point of the attack.

Approximately thirteen witnesses gave testimony at the hearing conducted by the Board's hearing officer and the record indicates that the facts are seriously in dispute among the various participants. One of the young women, not a plaintiff, Wanda Shelby, acknowledged that there had been bad words between Tameko Warren and her on a previous day and that some of the antagonism resulted from some competition for a boyfriend at a gospel sing in Wisconsin. Ms. Shelby admits that she began the altercation by first pushing Tameko Warren, this being corroborated by the statements of others who were present. There is testimony that plaintiff, Tamika Robinson, struck Ms. Warren in the melee although Ms. Robinson testifies that Ms. Warren had taken the first swing and that her action was limited to self-defense.

Another of the non-plaintiff students apparently picked up a stick to protect herself from a man who intervened in an attempt to stop the battle. She admitted striking Ms. Warren, but stated that she also did not strike the first blow.

Finally, Nicole Jenkins, according to all of the witnesses, had no previous problems or difficulties with Ms. Warren and, in fact, attempted to break up the incident. She testified that she did not strike Ms. Warren and Ms. Warren did not recall her being struck by Ms. Jenkins.

Apparently, no injuries were sustained by the combatants since none were noted by the various witnesses.

On the day following the incident, school personnel became deeply involved in the investigation of the occurrence * * *.

On December 12, 1990, the plaintiffs were suspended and the hearing * * * was held on December 19, 1990. On January 7, 1991, the Board, meeting *in camera,* voted to impose the harshest available punishment on plaintiffs and expelled them for the remainder of the 1990–91 school year.

Sec. 10–22.6 of the School Code (Ill.Rev.Stat. ch. 122, par. 10–22.6) empowers a school board to " * * * expel pupils guilty of gross disobedience or misconduct * * * " without incurring any liability provided that the proper procedures set out in the statute have been observed.

In this regard, the Board has adopted certain Board policies and Board Policy 5115 provides:

> "gross disobedience or misconduct, which may lead to suspension or expulsion of a student pursuant to the provisions of Section 10–22.6 of the School Code shall include any activity or behavior which might reasonably lead school authorities to forecast substantial disruption or material interference with school activities or which in fact is a substantial disruption or material interference with school activities and shall also include but is not limited to the following types of activities of behavior:

> * * *

> 7. fighting or assaulting any person

> * * *

> Action to suspend or expel may be taken whether the gross disobedience or misconduct occurs on school property, on a school bus, on the way to or from school, or at a school-related function."

Similar language appears in a document entitled "Student Expulsion Procedures" issued by the Oak Park and River Forest High School although indicating Board Policy 5114 rather than 5115.

The Board's written policies have significantly varied the scope of "gross disobedience or misconduct" as set out in the statute. Article 10 of the School Code (Ill.Rev.Stat. ch. 122, par. 10–22 et seq.) does not provide the Board with rule making power or the power to enact interstitial legislation. However, in any event, the definition provided by the Board would appear to limit its right to expel in the case at bar. Nothing in the record indicates that school authorities are able to forecast that these plaintiffs would substantially disrupt or materially interfere with school activities or that they, in fact, did substantially disrupt or materially interfere with school activities. They engaged in an altercation on the way home from school in the fourth month of their freshman year. No prior misconduct would have been the basis for such a forecast into the future. If a school board limits its powers granted by the statute, the Board should be held to the limitations which it has imposed upon itself, such as the adoption of policy number 5115 (or 5114). However, we do not rely on this issue in affirming the trial court.

The maximum penalty that the Board may impose upon plaintiffs appears to be expulsion for the remainder of the school year. Under the Act, a board is not authorized to expel a pupil for more than the remainder of the school year. Accordingly, the Board here has elected to impose upon these young women the harshest penalty available. Plaintiffs assert, and the trial court below agreed, that the imposition of such a penalty is arbitrary, unreasonable and an abuse of the Board's discretion.

School discipline is an area in which school officials have broad discretion. Illinois courts have been reluctant to overturn decisions to suspend or expel students.

Defendant Board relies on the language of Donaldson v. Board of Educ., Danville School Dist. No. 118:

> "School discipline is an area which courts enter with great hesitation and reluctance and rightly so. School officials are trained and paid to determine what form of punishment best addresses a particular student's transgression. They are in a far better position than is a black robed judge to decide what to do with a disobedient child at school."

While school officials may be better trained and more experienced in handling disciplinary matters concerning students, they are not infallible.

The record here discloses that the Board consists of a theatrical director, a hospital administrator, an accountant, a businessman, a doctor and two lawyers. While the courts are reluctant to involve themselves with a board's exercise of discretion, they have been willing to closely examine the facts of each case to determine the propriety of the court's review of board action.

Donaldson dealt with a three-day expulsion of a seventh grader for fighting while the case before us deals with a January through June expulsion. The impact of a semester expulsion on two students cannot be compared with the three-day suspension, albeit at final week, meted out in *Donaldson*.

In Clements v. Board of Education (1985), 133 Ill.App.3d 531, 88 Ill.Dec. 601, 478 N.E.2d 1209, suspension of a student from participation on a school athletic team after attendance at a beer party was an appropriate exercise of the Board's power. Similarly, expulsion from school for the balance of the school year was appropriate for a student who carried a loaded .357 Magnum pistol into the school cafeteria (Lusk v. Triad Community Unit No. 2 (1990), 194 Ill.App.3d 426, 141 Ill.Dec. 473, 551 N.E.2d 660) or possessed look-alike caffeine pills (Wilson v. Collinsville Community Unit School District No. 10 (1983), 116 Ill. App.3d 557, 71 Ill.Dec. 785, 451 N.E.2d 939).

It is ludicrous to imagine that the conduct of Nicole Jenkins and Tamika Robinson rises to the level of gun toting as in *Lusk* or carrying pills as in *Wilson*. Nor, as we have previously noted, can their six month expulsion be compared to the three-day suspension in *Donaldson*.

The record reveals that Jenkins' only involvement in the events of December 10, 1990 was to attempt to bring peace. Apparently, in Oak Park and River Forest High School, the peacemaker is not blessed. As to this student, there is nothing in the record upon which the Board based its decision except that she was in the wrong place at the wrong time. This is hardly a basis for drastic interruption of her academic career.

Even the testimony with respect to Tamika Robinson was confusing and conflicting. The evidence against her indicates that she did strike the victim, but did so in self-defense. Even though self-defense may not be an appropriate response or may be disbelieved by the Board, the imposition of the maximum penalty available would seem to be oppressive and unreasonable and an abuse of discretion where the evidence does not disclose gross misconduct and is likely to have an extreme and unfortunate impact upon this young woman. The record discloses that Tamika Robinson is a poor student and at the time of the disciplinary hearing had been "working hard to bring up her grades" and showing improvement. What will be the impact of the Board's punishment on this young struggling student?

If the Memoranda of Opinion [issued by the lower court] has any fault, it is the notion that the punishment is too harsh because the facts are in conflict and difficult to determine. Once the trier of fact has made its determination as to the facts, the penalty or judgment should not be affected because of the original difficulties of the fact finder.

The affidavit of Bunny Carey, the president of the Board of Education of Oak Park and River Forest High School reveals a good deal about the reasons for the imposition of this harsh penalty. President Carey states that Board members take a strong stand with respect to disciplinary problems and that at the meeting "Board members expressed their concern over the rising incidents of gang related activities and situations where a group would attack a lone individual."

Nothing in the record indicates that these are gang related activities. Instead, they appear to be a random incident of young people resolving an imagined injustice by resorting to violence.

Although officials have broad discretion in the area of student discipline and a strong interest in discouraging packs of students or the organization of gangs, the Board's discretion has limits. In reviewing the Board's action to determine whether it has abused its discretion, the court must consider (1) the egregiousness of the student's conduct; (2) the history or record of the student's past conduct; (3) the likelihood that such conduct will affect the delivery of educational services to other children; (4) severity of the punishment; and (5) the interest of the child.

Considering all of these elements, the Board of Education of Oak Park and River Forest High School, District 200, has abused its discretion and the order providing for a temporary injunction restraining defendant Board from expelling the plaintiffs for the 1990–91 academic year is hereby affirmed.

Notes

1. Notice how the court differentiates this case from those cited by the board in an effort to justify its action legally. The discussion regarding Donaldson v. Board of Educ., Danville School Dist. No. 118 is particularly instructive.

2. Do you think the board's position was sound from an educational viewpoint?

3. Reflect on the court's comments regarding the interplay of state statute and board rule.

4. Bear in mind that the challenged decision focused on discipline, not on an academic matter.

[Case No. 127] Procedural Due Process before Short-Term Suspension of Students

GOSS v. LOPEZ

Supreme Court of the United States, 1975.
419 U.S. 565, 95 S.Ct. 729, 42 L.Ed.2d 725.

MR. JUSTICE WHITE delivered the opinion of the Court.

This appeal by various administrators of the Columbus, Ohio, Public School System ("CPSS") challenges the judgment of a three-judge federal court, declaring that appellees—various high school students in the CPSS—were denied due process of law contrary to the command of the Fourteenth Amendment in that they were temporarily suspended from their high schools without a hearing either prior to suspension or within a reasonable time thereafter, and enjoining the administrators to remove all references to such suspensions from the students' records.

I

Ohio Law, Rev.Code § 3313.64, provides for free education to all children between the ages of six and 21. Section 3313.66 of the Code empowers the principal of an Ohio public school to suspend a pupil for misconduct for up to 10 days or to expel him. In either case, he must notify the student's parents within 24 hours and state the reasons for his action. A pupil who is expelled, or his parents, may appeal the decision to the Board of Education and in connection therewith shall be permitted to be heard at the board meeting. The board may reinstate the pupil following the hearing. No similar procedure is provided in § 3313.66 or any other provision of state law for a suspended student. Aside from a regulation tracking the statute, at the time of the imposition of the suspensions in this case the CPSS had not itself issued any written procedure applicable to suspensions. Nor, so far as the record reflects, had any of the individual high schools involved in this case. Each, however, had formally or informally described the conduct for which suspension could be imposed.

* * *

II

At the outset, appellants contend that because there is no constitutional right to an education at public expense, the Due Process Clause does not protect against expulsions from the public school system. This position misconceives the nature of the issue and is refuted by prior decisions. The Fourteenth Amendment forbids the State to deprive any person of life, liberty or property without due process of law. Protected interests in property are normally "not created by the Constitution. Rather, they are created and their dimensions are defined" by an independent source such as state statutes or rules entitling the citizen to certain benefits. Board of Regents v. Roth.

Accordingly, a state employee who under state law, or rules promulgated by state officials, has a legitimate claim of entitlement to continued employment absent sufficient cause for discharge may demand the procedural protections of due process. So may welfare recipients who have statutory rights to welfare as long as they maintain the specified qualifications. * * *

Here, on the basis of state law, appellees plainly had legitimate claims of entitlement to a public education. Ohio Rev.Code §§ 3313.48 and 3313.64 direct local authorities to provide a free education to all residents between six and 21 years of age, and a compulsory attendance law requires attendance for a school year of not less than 32 weeks. Ohio Rev.Code § 3321.04. It is true that § 3313.66 of the code permits school principals to suspend students for up to two weeks; but suspensions may not be imposed without any grounds whatsoever. All of the schools had their own rules specifying the grounds for expulsion or suspension. Having chosen to extend the right to an education to people of appellees' class generally, Ohio may not withdraw that right on grounds of misconduct absent fundamentally fair procedures to determine whether the misconduct has occurred.

Although Ohio may not be constitutionally obligated to establish and maintain a public school system, it has nevertheless done so and has required its children to attend. Those young people do not "shed their constitutional rights" at the schoolhouse door. Tinker v. Des Moines Community School District. "The Fourteenth Amendment, as now applied to the States, protects the citizen against the State itself and all of its creatures—Boards of Education not excepted." West Virginia v. Barnette. The authority possessed by the State to prescribe and enforce standards of conduct in its schools, although concededly very broad, must be exercised consistently with constitutional safeguards. Among other things, the State is constrained to recognize a student's legitimate entitlement to a public education as a property interest which is protected by the Due Process Clause and which may not be taken away for misconduct without adherence to the minimum procedures required by that clause.

The Due Process Clause also forbids arbitrary deprivations of liberty. "Where a person's good name, reputation, honor, or integrity is at stake because of what the government is doing to him," the minimal requirements of the clause must be satisfied. School authorities here suspended appellees from school for periods of up to 10 days based on charges of misconduct. If sustained and recorded, those charges could seriously damage the students' standing with their fellow pupils and their teachers as well as interfere with later opportunities for higher education and employment. It is apparent that the claimed right of the State to determine unilaterally and without process whether that misconduct has occurred immediately collides with the requirements of the Constitution.

Appellants proceed to argue that even if there is a right to a public education protected by the Due Process Clause generally, the clause comes into play only when the State subjects a student to a "severe detriment or grievous loss." The loss of 10 days, it is said, is neither severe nor grievous and the Due Process Clause is therefore of no relevance. Appellee's argument is again refuted by our prior decisions; for in determining "whether due process requirements apply in the first place, we must look not to the 'weight' but to the *nature* of the interest at stake." Board of Regents v. Roth. The Court's view has been that as long as a property deprivation is not *de minimis,* its gravity is irrelevant to the question whether account must be taken of the Due Process Clause. A 10-day suspension from school is not *de minimis* in our view and may not be imposed in complete disregard of the Due Process Clause.

* * * Neither the property interest in educational benefits temporarily denied nor the liberty interest in reputation, which is also implicated, is so insubstantial that suspensions may constitutionally be imposed by any procedure the school chooses, no matter how arbitrary.

III

"Once it is determined that due process applies, the question remains what process is due." * * *

There are certain bench marks to guide us, * * *. Mullane v. Central Hanover Trust Co., 339 U.S. 306, 70 S.Ct. 652, 94 L.Ed. 865 (1950), a case often invoked by later opinions, said that "[m]any controversies have raged about the cryptic and abstract words of the Due Process Clause but there can be no doubt that at a minimum they require that deprivation of life, liberty or property by adjudication be preceded by notice and opportunity for hearing appropriate to the nature of the case." * * * "The fundamental requisite of due process of law is the opportunity to be heard," a right that "has little reality or worth unless one is informed that the matter is pending and can choose for himself whether to * * * contest." At the very minimum, therefore, students facing suspension and the consequent interference with a protected property interest must be given *some* kind of notice and afforded *some* kind of hearing. * * *

It also appears from our cases that the timing and content of the notice and the nature of the hearing will depend on appropriate accommodation of the competing interests involved. The student's interest is to avoid unfair or mistaken exclusion from the educational process, with all of its unfortunate consequences. The Due Process Clause will not shield him from suspensions properly imposed, but it disserves both his interest and the interest of the State if his suspension is in fact unwarranted. The concern would be mostly academic if the disciplinary process were a totally accurate, unerring process, never mistaken and never unfair. Unfortunately, that is not the case, and no one suggests that it is. Disciplinarians, although proceeding in utmost good faith, frequently act on the reports and advice of others; and the controlling facts and the nature of the conduct under challenge are often disputed. The risk of error is not at all trivial, and it should be guarded against if that may be done without prohibitive cost or interference with the educational process.

The difficulty is that our schools are vast and complex. Some modicum of discipline and order is essential if the educational function is to be performed. Events calling for discipline are frequent occurrences and sometimes require immediate, effective action. Suspension is considered not only to be a necessary tool to maintain order but a valuable educational device. The prospect of imposing elaborate hearing requirements in every suspension case is viewed with great concern, and many school authorities may well prefer the untrammeled power to act unilaterally, unhampered by rules about notice and hearing. But it would be a strange disciplinary system in an educational institution if no communication was sought by the disciplinarian with the student in an effort to inform him of his defalcation and to let him tell his side of the story in order to make sure that an injustice is not done.   * * *

We do not believe that school authorities must be totally free from notice and hearing requirements if their schools are to operate with acceptable efficiency. Students facing temporary suspension have interests qualifying for protection of the Due Process Clause, and due process requires, in connection with a suspension of 10 days or less, that the student be given oral or written notice of the charges against him and, if he denies them, an explanation of the evidence the authorities have and an opportunity to present his side of the story. The clause requires at least these rudimentary precautions against unfair or mistaken findings of misconduct and arbitrary exclusion from school.

There need be no delay between the time "notice" is given and the time of the hearing. In the great majority of cases the disciplinarian may informally discuss the alleged misconduct with the student minutes after it has occurred. We hold only that, in being given an opportunity to explain his version of the facts at this discussion, the student first be told what he is accused of doing and what the basis of the accusation is. Lower courts which have addressed the question of the *nature* of the procedures required in short suspension cases have reached the same conclusion. Since the hearing may occur almost immediately following the misconduct, it follows that as a general rule notice and hearing should precede removal of the student from school. We agree with the District Court, however, that there are recurring situations in which prior notice and hearing cannot be insisted upon. Students whose presence poses a continuing danger to persons or property or an ongoing threat of disrupting the academic process may be immediately removed from school. In such cases, the necessary notice and rudimentary hearing should follow as soon as practicable, as the District Court indicated.

* * *

We stop short of construing the Due Process Clause to require, countrywide, that hearings in connection with short suspensions must afford the student the opportunity to secure counsel, to confront and cross-examine witnesses supporting the charge or to call his own witnesses to verify his version of the incident. Brief disciplinary suspensions are almost countless. To impose in each such case even truncated trial type procedures might well overwhelm administrative facilities in many places and, by diverting resources, cost more than it would save in educational effectiveness. Moreover, further formalizing the suspension process and escalating its formality and adversary nature may not only make it too costly as a regular disciplinary tool but also destroy its effectiveness as part of the teaching process.

On the other hand, requiring effective notice and informal hearing permitting the student to give his version of the events will provide a meaningful hedge against erroneous action. At least the disciplinarian will be alerted to the existence of disputes about facts and arguments about cause and effect. He may then determine himself to summon the accuser, permit cross-examination and allow the student to present his own witnesses. In more difficult cases, he may permit counsel. In any event, his discretion will be more informed and we think the risk of error substantially reduced.

Requiring that there be at least an informal give-and-take between student and disciplinarian, preferably prior to the suspension, will add little to the factfinding function where the disciplinarian has himself witnessed the conduct forming the basis for the charge. But things are not always as they seem to be, and the student will at least have the opportunity to characterize his conduct and put it in what he deems the proper context.

We should also make it clear that we have addressed ourselves solely to the short suspension, not exceeding 10 days. Longer suspensions or expulsions for the remainder of the school term, or permanently, may require more formal procedures. Nor do we put aside the possibility that in unusual situations, although involving only a short suspension, something more than the rudimentary procedures will be required.

IV

The District Court found each of the suspensions involved here to have occurred without a hearing, either before or after the suspension, and that each suspension was therefore invalid and the statute unconstitutional insofar as it permits such suspensions without notice or hearing. Accordingly, the judgment is affirmed.

* * *

Notes

1. Note that this decision relates only to suspensions of up to ten days. Consider the possible consequences to a student of being suspended for ten days and having the suspension put on his permanent record.

2. Particular attention should be given to Section III of the opinion. It sets out in detail guidelines of the nature and extent of the hearing required.

3. Justice Powell, writing a dissent in which Justices Burger, Blackmun, and Rehnquist joined, said that the majority decision opens avenues for judicial intervention in school operation which might adversely affect the quality of education. Consider situations, if any, in which this might be true.

4. Observe that under this decision suspension without a hearing may be had in certain extreme cases, if followed reasonably soon by a hearing. Consider whether this places an undue burden on a disciplinarian of deciding what cases are "extreme." Why not conduct a hearing in all cases, extreme or otherwise? Does the nature of the hearing affect your answer?

Chapter 13

RACE[1]–STATE–EDUCATION
RELATIONSHIPS

The 1954–55 Supreme Court Decisions

"Does segregation of children in public schools solely on the basis of race, even though the physical facilities and other 'tangible' factors may be equal, deprive the children of the minority group of equal educational opportunities?" In 1954 the Supreme Court of the United States unanimously declared that the answer was "Yes."[2]

Challenged was the point of law, existing in seventeen states and the District of Columbia on a mandatory basis and in four states on a local option basis, that children were to be assigned to public schools on the factor of race. The Court concluded that "in the field of public education the doctrine of 'separate but equal' has no place. Separate educational facilities are inherently unequal." Plaintiffs and others similarly situated were deprived by segregation of equal protection of the laws guaranteed by the Fourteenth Amendment. Repudiated was the doctrine of "separate but equal" which had been generally accepted since 1896, when it was first enunciated in a case dealing with separation of the races in railroad coaches in Louisiana.[3] The Supreme Court, although it had indirectly inferred that the doctrine was acceptable there,[4] had never applied it directly in a public school case. Not until 1954 had it been squarely faced with the question of its applicability to public schools, and it decided the case in light of modern psychological knowledge.

Because the cases consolidated for this decision were class actions, because of the wide applicability of the decision, and because of the great variety of local conditions, the Court postponed for a year the issuance of a decree to enforce its holding. Further argument was requested by the Court on certain procedural questions. One year later, the Court issued its order that admissions to public schools on a racially non-discriminatory basis must proceed "with all deliberate speed."[5] Lower courts were instructed to require that there be "a prompt and reasonable start toward full compliance." While recognizing that additional time might

1. Racial or ethnic groups frequently are designated by the terms used in the judicial opinions being treated.

2. Brown v. Board of Educ. of Topeka, 347 U.S. 483, 74 S.Ct. 686, 98 L.Ed. 873 (1954). [Case No. 128]

3. Plessy v. Ferguson, 163 U.S. 537, 16 S.Ct. 1138, 41 L.Ed. 256 (1896).

4. Cumming v. Board of Educ. of Richmond County, 175 U.S. 528, 20 S.Ct. 197, 44 L.Ed. 262 (1899); Gong Lum v. Rice, 275 U.S. 78, 48 S.Ct. 91, 72 L.Ed. 172 (1927).

5. Brown v. Board of Educ. of Topeka, 349 U.S. 294, 75 S.Ct. 753, 99 L.Ed. 1083 (1955). [Case No. 129]

be necessary to bring about the change, the Court placed the burden of proving the need for such time on the school boards acting in the public interest and consistent with good faith compliance as soon as practicable. School authorities were given the primary responsibility for taking initial action. Lower courts were ordered to retain jurisdiction of the cases and to decide whether the board actions constituted good faith implementation of the governing principles.

Delineation of the Constitutional Mandate

The specific applications of the principles aforementioned were the subject of many hundreds of cases in lower federal courts. Meanwhile the Supreme Court made clear that a state governor and legislature could not defeat the implementation of the desegregation decree. One year after the President of the United States dispatched federal troops to Little Rock, Arkansas, to enforce the desegregation order of the federal District Court there, the local board asked that the effective date of its plan be postponed because of turmoil and hostilities in the area, a situation encouraged by actions of state officials. The Court indicated some sympathy with the position of the board, but regardless of the good faith request for the postponement, it was not granted because constitutional rights "are not to be sacrificed or yielded to the violence and disorder which have followed upon the actions of the Governor and Legislature." [6]

The Supreme Court decided no cases on specific implementation plans until 1963. In that year it accepted a case involving a local procedure used in Knoxville, Tennessee.[7] It invalidated a transfer provision whereby a student upon request would be permitted to transfer from a school where, after a rezoning, he would be in a racial minority, back to his former school. In the former school his race would be in the majority because of the prior segregation policy. Since the transfer plan was based solely on racial factors which "inevitably" would lead back toward segregation of the students by race, it was held unconstitutional.

In 1964 the Supreme Court said that "the time for mere 'deliberate speed' has run out." [8] The statement was in connection with the Court's holding that the closing of the public schools in Prince Edward County, Virginia, while the state contributed to the support of private segregated white schools that took their place, denied black students equal protection of the law. In 1965 the Court, showing increasing impatience with desegregation delays, held that certain black students were entitled to immediate relief.[9] They were high school students who were still assigned to school on the basis of their race. The one-grade-a-year plan adopted in 1957 had not yet reached the high school in Fort

---

6. Cooper v. Aaron, 358 U.S. 1, 78 S.Ct. 1401, 3 L.Ed.2d 5 (1958).

7. Goss v. Board of Educ., 373 U.S. 683, 83 S.Ct. 1405, 10 L.Ed.2d 632 (1963).

8. Griffin v. County School Bd. of Prince Edward County, 377 U.S. 218, 84 S.Ct. 1226, 12 L.Ed.2d 256 (1964).

9. Rogers v. Paul, 382 U.S. 198, 86 S.Ct. 358, 15 L.Ed.2d 265 (1965).

Smith, Arkansas. Also they were prevented from taking certain courses offered only in another high school limited to whites.

The question of constitutionality of a freedom-of-choice plan was decided by the Supreme Court in 1968.[10] Little progress in breaking down the dual system in New Kent County, Virginia, had been made over the thirteen years since the original desegregation decision. Nothing had been done until 1965, when a freedom-of-choice plan was adopted. The Court concluded that "the burden on a school board today is to come forward with a plan that promises realistically to work, and promises realistically to work *now*." The Court expressly did not hold that a freedom-of-choice plan was unconstitutional per se. But "if there are reasonably available other ways, such for illustration as zoning, promising speedier and more effective conversion to a unitary, nonracial school system, 'freedom of choice' must be held unacceptable."

In 1969 the Supreme Court discarded the "all deliberate speed" criterion for evaluating progress in school desegregation. It stated, in reversing lower court decisions granting a further extension of time to some Mississippi school districts, that dual systems must immediately give way to unitary, and that objections and amendments to court-ordered plans could be heard only after a system was "being operated as a unitary system." In the words of the Court: "The question presented is one of paramount importance, involving as it does the denial of fundamental rights to many thousands of school children, who are presently attending Mississippi schools under segregated conditions contrary to the applicable decisions of this Court. Against this background the Court of Appeals should have denied all motions for additional time because continued operation of segregated schools under a standard of allowing 'all deliberate speed' for desegregation is no longer constitutionally permissible. Under explicit holdings of this Court the obligation of every school district is to terminate dual school systems at once and to operate now and hereafter only unitary schools." [11]

Remedies for De Jure Segregation

The Alexander decision, saying, in effect, "integrate now and litigate later," had as an immediate result the issuing of hundreds of orders by lower federal courts for desegregating dual systems that had moved slowly, if at all, to correct unlawful discrimination against black students. Many types of arrangements were ordered, and inconsistencies appeared in regard to precisely what was constitutionally required and by what techniques it could constitutionally be achieved. The Court addressed itself to these problems in 1971, when it delineated "with more particularity the responsibilities of school authorities in desegregating a state-enforced dual school system in light of the Equal Protec-

10. Green v. County School Bd. of New Kent County, 391 U.S. 430, 88 S.Ct. 1689, 20 L.Ed.2d 716 (1968).

11. Alexander v. Holmes County Bd. of Educ., 396 U.S. 19, 90 S.Ct. 29, 24 L.Ed.2d 19 (1969).

tion Clause." [12]

On the specific point of busing, the Court said that bus transportation has been an integral part of public education systems for a long time and that in 1969–1970 thirty-nine percent of all public school children were transported to school. It observed that busing had been extensively used in Charlotte and that the "new" busing plan compared favorably with the existing one so far as numbers of students and time spent on buses were concerned. It stated, "In these circumstances, we find no basis for holding that the local school authorities may not be required to employ bus transportation as one tool of school desegregation. Desegregation plans cannot be limited to the walk-in school."

The Court discussed several other matters which had not been extensively treated in prior decisions. In reference to school construction, the Court stated, "In devising remedies where legally imposed segregation has been established, it is the responsibility of local authorities and district courts to see to it that future school construction and abandonment is not used and does not serve to perpetuate or re-establish the dual system." As to "one-race" schools, the Court said, "Where the school authority's proposed plan for conversion from a dual to a unitary system contemplates the continued existence of some schools that are all or predominately of one race, they have the burden of showing that such school assignments are genuinely nondiscriminatory. The court should scrutinize such schools, and the burden upon the school authorities will be to satisfy the court that their racial composition is not the result of present or past discriminatory action on their part." Although it is not constitutionally required that every school in a district reflect the racial composition of the system as a whole, a district court may utilize a racial ratio or quota as a starting point in shaping a remedy. "Racially neutral" assignment plans are not sufficient to counteract the continuing effects of past segregation. Looking to the future, the Court said that there was no constitutional requirement "to make year-by-year adjustments of the racial composition of student bodies once the affirmative duty to desegregate has been accomplished and racial discrimination through official action is eliminated from the system." The Court expressly indicated it was not presented with, and therefore it did not decide, the question "whether a showing that school segregation is a consequence of other types of state action, without any discriminatory action by the school authorities, is a constitutional violation requiring remedial action by a school desegregation decree."

In 1972 the Supreme Court held in two cases that school district boundary changes could not be made in areas where de jure segregation had not yet been remedied.[13] In Scotland Neck, North Carolina, the change, which would have removed a disproportionate number of whites from the county, was permitted by special legislation found by the Court

---

12. Swann v. Charlotte-Mecklenburg Bd. of Educ., 402 U.S. 1, 91 S.Ct. 1267, 28 L.Ed.2d 554 (1971). [Case No. 130]

13. United States v. Scotland Neck City Bd. of Educ., 407 U.S. 484, 92 S.Ct. 2214, 33 L.Ed.2d 75 (1972); Wright v. Council of the City of Emporia, 407 U.S. 451, 92 S.Ct. 2196, 33 L.Ed.2d 51 (1972).

to have been prompted by the likelihood of desegregation in the county. In Virginia the municipality of Emporia had changed its political status and had become a separate political jurisdiction independent of the county. Communities of the status it acquired were entitled to establish their own school systems. In the North Carolina case the unanimity of the Court in school desegregation cases was preserved, but in the Virginia case there was a dissent by four Justices. The dissenters stated that the purpose of the change in Virginia was not to preclude meaningful desegregation, and that the immediate effect of Emporia's withdrawal on percentages of white and black students in the county was slight. The majority saw the effect differently and stated that "the existence of a permissible purpose cannot sustain an action that has an impermissible effect."

In 1973 the Court by a divided vote [14] established some new principles to guide courts in handling desegregation cases outside of the "South." [15] It upheld lower court findings of de jure segregation in one section of Denver, Colorado, caused by acts of the board over the period 1960–1969, the acts involving the establishment of some school sites and attendance zones which created and maintained some schools as segregated. It further ruled that "a finding of intentionally segregative school board actions in a meaningful portion of a school system, as in this case, creates a presumption that other segregated schooling within the system is not adventitious." The impact of "racially inspired school board actions" goes beyond the particular schools that are the subjects of those actions. Unless a substantial pocket of segregation is a "separate, identifiable and unrelated" unit of the school district (due to geographical structure or natural boundaries), the whole system must be desegregated. If the pocket is not substantial, and if other segregated schools exist in the district, the burden is placed on the board to show that the segregation in the other segregated schools is not the result of intentional board action. The Court also stated that in defining a segregated school "Negroes" and "Hispanos" must be considered together because "in Denver [they] suffer identical discrimination in treatment when compared with the treatment afforded Anglo students." [16]

In 1974 the Court considered the question: If a de jure segregated district contains at the time of adjudication such a high percent of blacks that meaningful racial mixing cannot take place because of the small percent of whites attending the district's schools, does the federal Constitution require that adjacent districts heavily populated by whites participate in remedying the situation? In what has come to be known

---

14. See Note 1 on Case No. 131.

15. Keyes v. School Dist. No. 1, Denver, Colorado, 413 U.S. 189, 93 S.Ct. 2686, 37 L.Ed.2d 548 (1973). [Case No. 131]

16. The rationale of Brown and its progeny has been applied to Mexican-American students [Cisneros v. Corpus Christi Independent School Dist., 467 F.2d 142 (5 Cir. 1972), cert. den. 413 U.S. 922, 93 S.Ct. 3052, 37 L.Ed.2d 1044 (1973); Arvizu v.

Waco Independent School Dist., 495 F.2d 499 (5 Cir.1974); Morales v. Shannon, 516 F.2d 411 (5 Cir.1975), cert. den. 423 U.S. 1034, 96 S.Ct. 566, 46 L.Ed.2d 408 (1975)] and to American Indian students [Natonabah v. Board of Educ. of Gallup-McKinley County School Dist., 355 F.Supp. 716 (D.N.M.1973); Geraud v. Schrader, 531 P.2d 872 (Wyo.1975)].

as the "Detroit case" it answered, in effect, "not unless the state or those surrounding districts were involved in discriminatory acts."[17]

The Court, by a five-to-four vote, held that "it must be shown that racially discriminatory acts of the state or local school districts, or of a single school district have been a substantial cause of inter-district segregation." An inter-district remedy "might be in order where the racially discriminatory acts of one or more school districts caused racial segregation in an adjacent district, or where district lines have been deliberately drawn on the basis of race."

That there was de jure segregation in Detroit was affirmed, and the lower courts were instructed to promptly formulate a decree to eliminate it within the district. But the Court rejected the lower courts' statement that "school district lines are no more than arbitrary lines on a map 'drawn for political convenience.' " The Court said that although boundary lines may be bridged where there has been a constitutional violation calling for inter-district relief, "the notion that school district lines may be casually ignored or treated as a mere administrative convenience is contrary to the history of public education in our country." The Court expressed concern about problems that would develop if the fifty-four independent school districts included in the possible metropolitan plan were, in effect, consolidated. It further observed that in resolving the problems the District Court would first take on a legislative function and then an administrative one.

Emphasis was placed on the fact that evidence of de jure segregated conditions was presented only for Detroit schools. The Court stated that "the constitutional right of the Negro respondents residing in Detroit is to attend a unitary school system in that district." Except for one relatively minor instance, there was no evidence that any acts of any other district may have affected the de jure condition in Detroit. Subsequent to this decision some fact situations have been found to warrant inter-district remedies, and they have been ordered.[18]

In 1976 the Supreme Court, by a vote of six-to-two, invalidated that aspect of a desegregation order of a district judge to the effect that there must be "no majority of any minority" in any school in Pasadena, California.[19] Compliance with the order would have meant periodic readjustments in the student assignment patterns to reflect demographic changes in population after the initial assignment pattern for desegregation was implemented. The Court majority said that annual readjustments for population changes for which the board was not responsible

17. Milliken v. Bradley, 418 U.S. 717, 94 S.Ct. 3112, 41 L.Ed.2d 1069 (1974). [Case No. 132]

18. Newburg Area Council, Inc. v. Board of Educ. of Jefferson County, Kentucky, 510 F.2d 1358 (6 Cir.1974), cert. den. 421 U.S. 931, 95 S.Ct. 1658, 44 L.Ed.2d 88 (1975); United States v. Board of School Commissioners of City of Indianapolis, 503 F.2d 68 (7 Cir.1974), cert. den. 421 U.S. 929, 95 S.Ct. 1655, 44 L.Ed.2d 86 (1975);

Evans v. Buchanan, 555 F.2d 373 (3 Cir. 1977), cert. den. 434 U.S. 880, 98 S.Ct. 235, 54 L.Ed.2d 160 (1977); Hoots v. Commonwealth of Pennsylvania, 672 F.2d 1107 (3 Cir.1982), cert. den. 459 U.S. 824, 103 S.Ct. 55, 74 L.Ed.2d 60 (1982).

19. Pasadena City Bd. of Educ. v. Spangler, 427 U.S. 424, 96 S.Ct. 2697, 49 L.Ed.2d 599 (1976).

were not constitutionally mandated. The minority believed that the order was valid until the school system was found to be unitary.

The Detroit case was before the Supreme Court again in 1977. This time the Court unanimously answered two questions heretofore not expressly treated by it.[20] Both pertained to remedies available to federal courts for correction of de jure segregation.

Upheld as within the power of the lower courts to order were elements of a remedial program designed to help eradicate the vestiges of the de jure segregation. "In a word, discriminatory student assignment policies can themselves manifest and breed other inequalities built into a dual system founded on racial discrimination. Federal courts need not, and cannot, close their eyes to inequalities, shown by the record, which flow from a long-standing segregated system." The Court observed that lower courts on many occasions had ordered relief beyond changes of assignments of students (and teachers). Specifically ordered in this case had been a remedial reading and communications skills program, in-service training of teachers, a new nondiscriminatory testing program, and expanded counseling and career guidance.

The Court also upheld the order that the state should pay one-half the additional costs attributable to the four educational components noted above. Allocating the costs of a desegregation plan was properly part of the remedial power of the federal courts. (In the Indianapolis, Indiana, area the entire burden of paying for the inter-district remedy was placed on the state because it was found to be solely responsible for the inter-district violations.[21])

Also in 1977 the Court delivered another unanimous decision concerning remedies for correcting de jure segregation.[22] The case essentially involved questions of proof and of functions of federal District Courts and Courts of Appeals. The District Court (after two reversals by the Sixth Circuit Court of Appeals largely because of inadequate remedy) had ordered an extensive systemwide busing plan for Dayton, Ohio, which was affirmed by the circuit court. While expressly reaffirming Keyes (Case No. 131), the Supreme Court found the remedy to be "entirely out of proportion to the constitutional violations found by the District Court," as recorded in that court's opinion. The Supreme Court therefore remanded the case "for the making of more specific findings and, if necessary, the taking of additional evidence." Nevertheless, the Supreme Court left the plan in effect for the upcoming year, it having been in effect for the year ending at the time of the decision "without creating serious problems." The District Court then held that there was no constitutional violation and dismissed the suit. Again the Court of Appeals reversed, and it reinstated the systemwide plan for desegrega-

20. Milliken v. Bradley, 433 U.S. 267, 97 S.Ct. 2749, 53 L.Ed.2d 745 (1977). [Case No. 133]

21. United States v. Board of School Comm'rs of City of Indianapolis, 677 F.2d 1185 (7 Cir.1982), cert. den. 459 U.S. 1086, 103 S.Ct. 568, 74 L.Ed.2d 931 (1982). See also [for the St. Louis area] Liddell v. State of Missouri, 731 F.2d 1294 (8 Cir. 1984), cert. den. 469 U.S. 816, 105 S.Ct. 82, 83 L.Ed.2d 30 (1984).

22. Dayton Bd. of Educ. v. Brinkman, 433 U.S. 406, 97 S.Ct. 2766, 53 L.Ed.2d 851 (1977).

tion. That judgment was affirmed by a five-to-four vote of the Supreme Court.[23]

Decided at the same time as the Dayton case was another Ohio case, this one from Columbus. The cases were similar in allegations, but here a different District Court had found a constitutional violation and had ordered a systemwide remedy, which the Sixth Circuit Court of Appeals had affirmed. The Supreme Court upheld the findings that intentional segregation by local school board actions had existed in 1954 (the time of *Brown*) and that subsequently as the "direct result of cognitive acts or omissions" there was maintained "an enclave of separate black schools." [24] The extent of the segregation was deemed sufficient to support the order for a systemwide desegregation plan to bring each school in the system roughly within proportionate racial balance. In the years since 1954 the intentional segregative acts included assigning black teachers only to schools with predominantly black student bodies, manipulation of attendance zones, and site selections for new schools that had the "foreseeable and anticipated effect of maintaining the racial separation of the schools." The Court observed that there was more evidence of intent in certain actions than merely the existence of foreseeable disparate impacts, but that such foreseeability was a relevant element of evidence to support a conclusion of forbidden purposes. The vote was seven-to-two.

The issue of the financing of desegregation plans reached the Supreme Court again in 1990. A court-ordered plan for remedying segregation in Kansas City, Missouri, was to be financed jointly by the school district and the state. The local board, however, could not raise its share of the money without violating several provisions of state law related to property assessments, rates of levy, and percents of voters who must approve certain increases. Here the Supreme Court by a five-to-four vote held that, although a federal court cannot impose a tax increase (a point made unanimously), it can require the board of education to levy property taxes at a rate adequate to fund the desegregation plan.[25] Further, it can enjoin the operation of statutes that would prevent the board from complying with the order. Four Justices found this approach constitutionally unacceptable primarily because taxation is a legislative function. The majority relied on the need to enforce the equal protection clause of the Fourteenth Amendment and the precedent of Griffin (footnote 8) where the Court unanimously stated that if public schools were closed in one county to avoid desegregation the courts could require the county legislative body to levy taxes to maintain a desegregated system.

The Supreme Court in 1991 treated for the first time the question of when has a formerly de jure segregated school system corrected the

23. Dayton Bd. of Educ. v. Brinkman, 443 U.S. 526, 99 S.Ct. 2971, 61 L.Ed.2d 720 (1979).

24. Columbus Bd. of Educ. v. Penick, 443 U.S. 449, 99 S.Ct. 2941, 61 L.Ed.2d 666 (1979).

25. Missouri v. Jenkins, 495 U.S. 33, 110 S.Ct. 1651, 109 L.Ed.2d 31 (1990).

constitutional violation.[26]   Oklahoma City schools had adopted under court order in 1972 an extensive busing plan as a remedy for its de jure segregation. In 1977 the federal District Court held that the system had achieved unitary status and terminated the case. In 1984 the school board established a student reassignment plan with reduced busing, a plan under which a number of previously desegregated schools would return to substantially one-race status. The reason for the change, said the board, was that there were increasing burdens brought on young black children because of demographic (residential) changes.

Jurisdictional and procedural issues arose when there was an effort to revive the case. The important substantive point, however, involved the tests that were to be applied before federal court supervision of a desegregation process could (or must) cease. Five of the eight Justices deciding the case accepted the view that in determining whether the "vestiges of de jure segregation had been eliminated as far as practicable", the District Court should examine policies and practices in six areas: students, faculty, staff, transportation, extracurricular activities, and facilities. These areas were first noted by the Court in 1968 in Green (footnote 10).

The next year the Supreme Court decided a case in which the District Court had used the Green factors as a basis for determining that the school district of DeKalb County, Georgia, had complied with most, but not all, of the constitutional mandates for desegregating the system.[27]   The District Court then returned control of some facets of operation to the school board, concurrently ordering more to be done in the other areas. This incremental approach (which was rejected by the Eleventh Circuit Court of Appeals) was approved by the Supreme Court. The Court reasoned that equity principles dictated the adjustment of remedies in a feasible and practical way so as to correct the constitutional violation and return the control of the system to regular governmental authorities. If one aspect of the violation had been corrected, and that aspect did not impinge on other conditions, it was proper to relinquish judicial supervision thereof. The Court emphasized that the most important facet of compliance with a school desegregation decree is the current degree of racial imbalance of students in the system and the reasons for it. It found credible the District Court's conclusion that demographic factors beyond the board's control had led to present imbalances in student school attendance patterns. In remanding the case for further proceedings the Court recognized that the Green areas were not necessarily mutually exclusive or necessarily all-inclusive. It set out some factors for courts to consider in connection with partial withdrawal, including whether the district "has demonstrated, to the public and to the parents and students of the once disfavored race, its good faith commitment to the whole of the court's decree and to those

---

26. Board of Educ. of Oklahoma City Public Schools v. Dowell, 498 U.S. 237, 111 S.Ct. 630, 112 L.Ed.2d 715 (1991).

27. Freeman v. Pitts, ___ U.S. ___, 112 S.Ct. 1430, 118 L.Ed.2d 108 (1992). [Case No. 137]

provisions of the law and the Constitution that were the predicate for judicial intervention in the first instance."

The Civil Rights Act and HEW Guidelines

In 1964 Congress passed the Civil Rights Act. Title VI forbade discrimination on the basis of race or color in programs receiving federal funds.[28] Thus, federal financial aid to schools became linked to the elimination of segregated schools. The Department of Health, Education, and Welfare (Department of Education since 1980) issued guidelines to be utilized in determining whether formerly segregated school districts were making sufficient progress in eliminating separate schools for blacks. Failure to comply with the "HEW Guidelines" was made the basis for halting federal funds. School districts in the South were required to file compliance plans with the United States Office of Education unless they were under court-ordered desegregation plans. Enforcement lay with the Department of Health, Education, and Welfare.

The Department of Justice was the agency to enforce other pertinent sections of the Civil Rights Act. The Attorney General was empowered to institute suits to effectuate desegregation of schools and also to intervene in private suits where persons had alleged denial of equal protection rights and the case was of "general public importance."

The courts, mindful of the principle of separation of powers among the branches of government, but also mindful of the expertise available in the executive branch, gave "great weight" to the HEW Guidelines in assessing the adequacy of proposed desegregation plans.[29] They made clear, however, that they were not bound by them, for constitutional rights are uniquely in the sphere of the judiciary and are unaffected by legislative and executive actions.

Extensive treatment was given to the interrelationships of the three branches of government in the context of desegregation by the United States Court of Appeals, Fifth Circuit.[30] Consolidating several cases from Alabama and Louisiana, the court issued a very comprehensive decree covering all aspects of desegregation and relying heavily on the HEW Guidelines. Because of its significance, the matter was reheard by the circuit court en banc. The original opinion and decree were adopted with slight adjustments by a vote of eight-to-four.[31] One very important statement in the en banc opinion was that any prior decisions which made a legal distinction between "integration" and "desegregation" were overruled.

28. See Appendix.

29. Singleton v. Jackson Municipal Separate School Dist., 348 F.2d 729 (5 Cir. 1965).

30. United States v. Jefferson County Bd. of Educ., 372 F.2d 836 (5 Cir.1966).

31. United States v. Jefferson County Bd. of Educ., 380 F.2d 385 (5 Cir.1967), cert. den. 389 U.S. 840, 88 S.Ct. 67, 19 L.Ed.2d 103 (1967).

In Swann (Case No. 130, Part III), the Supreme Court expressly rejected the contention that the Civil Rights Act of 1964 limited the powers of federal District Courts. The Court said that, as regards public education, the Act was not intended to limit, but to define, the role of the federal government in the implementation of the desegregation decisions. It stated that the provision defining "desegregation" as not meaning "the assignment of students to public schools in order to overcome racial imbalance" was intended to apply to de facto segregation only. So, too, was the provision that an order for transportation to achieve "racial balance" was not authorized by the Act. The Court said there was "nothing in the Act which provides us material assistance in answering the question of remedy for state-imposed segregation."

Teacher Desegregation

It was not until late 1965 that the question of faculty desegregation reached the United States Supreme Court. Race of teachers had not been raised in the original desegregation cases. Lower courts had not been requiring plans for faculty desegregation to be included in court-approved plans for pupil desegregation. The plan for desegregation of Richmond, Virginia, accepted by the District Court, did not contain a provision regarding the assignment of faculty personnel. The United States Court of Appeals, Fourth Circuit, held that omission from the plan of any provision regarding the assignment of faculty personnel was not sufficient cause to require the rejection of the plan. It stated that after all direct discrimination in the assignment of pupils was eliminated, the effect of assignment of teachers could be examined. The Supreme Court ruled that the case should have been remanded for hearings regarding the contention that racial assignments of staff affected the rights of pupils.[32] "There is no merit to the suggestion that the relation between faculty allocation on an alleged racial basis and the adequacy of the desegregation plans is entirely speculative." The Court could perceive no reason for postponing the hearings. It noted that "more than a decade has passed since we directed desegregation of public school facilities 'with all deliberate speed.' "

Progress in faculty desegregation was even slower than that of pupil desegregation. The absence of a test to be applied made it cumbersome for District Courts and Courts of Appeals to formulate specific decrees required to prevent unconstitutional delay. In 1969 one concrete plan ordered by a lower court was sustained by the United States Supreme Court.[33] The goal for faculty desegregation was that each school in the district would have assigned to it approximately the same ratio of black and white teachers as was the ratio existing in the school system as a whole.

---

32. Bradley v. School Bd., City of Richmond, 382 U.S. 103, 86 S.Ct. 224, 15 L.Ed.2d 187 (1965).

33. United States v. Montgomery County Bd. of Educ., 395 U.S. 225, 89 S.Ct. 1670, 23 L.Ed.2d 263 (1969).

The next year the Fifth Circuit Court of Appeals adopted this ratio concept as a guide for integrating teaching staffs throughout the circuit.[34] In 1978 it stated that, as of the date of its 1970 decision, District Courts should have been insisting on immediate steps to assure that "the faculty of each school reflect[s] the systemwide racial ratio of faculty members and that teachers accept reassignment as a condition of continued employment." [35] The District Court in the case at bar had accepted a slow pace of faculty change predicated on the school board's assertion that a more rapid pace would result in "white flight among the faculty." The Court of Appeals said that the fear of faculty resistance to desegregation measures, like the fear of community resistance, cannot be the basis of not moving into the plan most likely to achieve a unitary school system.

Other legal problems affecting teachers in the process of desegregation arose in connection with nonretention of large numbers of black teachers. Where no tenure laws existed, an effective legal remedy was sought in the courts. Eventually, courts, taking into account the long history of racial discrimination, and the failure of many public school systems to desegregate in compliance with the Supreme Court's 1954 mandate until forced to do so by litigation, examined carefully situations where there was a sudden disproportionate reduction in the ranks of the black teachers. This was held to raise an inference of discrimination which placed upon a school board the burden of justifying its conduct with clear evidence. School boards were required to set up objective standards for the employment and retention of teachers and to apply them to all teachers—black and white—in like manner. In the North Carolina case in which the Fourth Circuit Court of Appeals first stated this principle, every formerly employed white teacher who indicated a desire to be retained had been reemployed, and fourteen inexperienced white teachers were employed.[36] But sixteen out of twenty-four black teachers employed the previous year were not offered reemployment. Subsequently it was held by the same court that black teachers not needed in their former posts, because of a reduction of black enrollment in their buildings, were entitled to preference for reemployment in the system over new candidates when this was the arrangement for white teachers.[37]

These holdings were followed in the other circuits that included states where de jure segregation had existed. The Fifth Circuit Court of Appeals ruled that the "objective and reasonable non-discriminatory standards" which must be applied in cases of dismissal or demotion were to be developed prior to the time of a reduction in staff.[38] Further, it prescribed that no staff vacancy may be filled through "recruitment of a

34. Singleton v. Jackson Municipal Separate School Dist., 419 F.2d 1211 (5 Cir. 1969), cert. den. 396 U.S. 1032, 90 S.Ct. 612, 24 L.Ed.2d 530 (1970).

35. United States v. DeSoto Parish School Bd., 574 F.2d 804 (5 Cir.1978).

36. Chambers v. Hendersonville City Bd. of Educ., 364 F.2d 189 (4 Cir.1966).

37. North Carolina Teachers Ass'n v. Asheboro City Bd. of Educ., 393 F.2d 736 (4 Cir.1968).

38. Singleton v. Jackson Municipal Separate School Dist., 419 F.2d 1211 (5 Cir. 1969), cert. den. 396 U.S. 1032, 90 S.Ct. 612, 24 L.Ed.2d 530 (1970).

person of a race, color, or national origin different from that of the individual dismissed or demoted, until each displaced staff member who is qualified" has rejected an offer to fill the vacancy.

That court also has held, however, that these Singleton criteria, applicable to dismissal or demotion during a time of staff reduction due to desegregation, are not applicable to such personnel actions occurring when there is no reduction, even though the school system is still in the desegregation process.[39] Also, any reduction invoking the Singleton criteria must be related to desegregation.[40] The reduction may be measured by appropriate subclasses (e.g., high school teachers, principals) rather than by overall figures.[41] Regarding demotions, responsibility is the "central value protected." [42] Thus, one may be considered to have been demoted even if he received an increase in salary.[43] In another case a principal who was made an administrative assistant to the superintendent of schools was held not to have been demoted despite the change of title.[44] Where a demotion is at issue, the burden is on the plaintiff to show that there was in fact a demotion.[45]

Although a black professional employee who suffers an adverse personnel action after he has been reassigned in accordance with a plan to transform a dual school system into a unitary one is no longer protected by the Singleton criteria, he is protected against invidious discrimination by the equal protection clause of the Fourteenth Amendment and the Civil Rights Act of 1964.[46] An immediate past history of segregation in the school district would establish a prima facie case of violation of equal protection in a demotion or a discharge situation, placing the burden on the school district to justify its actions by "clear and convincing evidence." [47]

Cases involving nonretention of individual black teachers have led to some important judicial holdings. In North Carolina a local school board failed to rehire a black teacher who had taught for thirteen years in the school system. She held bachelor's and master's degrees, and the black principal of the all-black school where she had taught recommended her for reemployment. Shortly thereafter, the principal was notified by the superintendent that the allocation of teachers for his school had been reduced for the next year, because under a newly instituted freedom-of-choice plan some black pupils had transferred to formerly all-white schools. The principal received no instructions as to how to reduce the number of his teachers. When the teacher in

---

39. Wright v. Houston Independent School Dist., 569 F.2d 1383 (5 Cir.1978).

40. Hardy v. Porter, 546 F.2d 1165 (5 Cir.1977).

41. Pickens v. Okolona Municipal Separate School Dist., 527 F.2d 358 (5 Cir.1976).

42. Lee v. Russell County Bd. of Educ., 563 F.2d 1159 (5 Cir.1977).

43. Lee v. Macon County Bd. of Educ., 453 F.2d 1104 (5 Cir.1971).

44. Lee v. Macon County Bd. of Educ., 470 F.2d 958 (5 Cir.1972).

45. Lee v. Pickens County School System, 563 F.2d 143 (5 Cir.1977).

46. See "Discriminatory Employment Practices" in Chapter 9.

47. Barnes v. Jones County School Dist., 544 F.2d 804 (5 Cir.1977). [In this case the school board met the burden. Barnes v. Jones County School Dist., 575 F.2d 490 (5 Cir.1978).]

question was notified that she was the one not to be reemployed in her former school, the superintendent merely suggested that she apply at other schools in the county to the individual principals. None employed her. The principal later stated that he considered her a "trouble maker" and had had some difficulties with her. The superintendent made no independent evaluation of her fitness, nor had he or the board compared her qualifications, or the gravity of her alleged faults, with those of other teachers in the system. The superintendent said he believed the principal had "properly evaluated her largely as the result of his faith in the judgment" of the principal. The District Court upheld the board's decision not to reemploy without affording the teacher a hearing. In the absence of a tenure law, it said, the lack of hearing "would not be a denial of due process of law in itself, even though the procedure used was not, as an eminent educator testified, in accordance with the preferable norms of personnel administration." [48] This reasoning was unanimously rejected by the Fourth Circuit en banc, which held that the teacher was entitled to the opportunity of being objectively considered for reemployment, with the burden of justifying a failure to rehire placed on the board.[49] In addition to this judgment that a form of constitutional due process was required under the circumstances, the court awarded damages for the losses suffered by the teacher. The principles enunciated in this case became firmly established in ensuing years.

It should be observed that desegregating the teaching staff is an essential element in correcting de jure segregation of students. Thus, court orders to this effect are premised on the rights of the students and are not confined to actions necessary to vindicate rights of black teachers. This point was made by the Court of Appeals, First Circuit, in upholding a District Court order to the school district of Boston, Massachusetts, in which de jure segregation had been found.[50] The Court of Appeals, Third Circuit, agreed in principle when it rejected a suit by four white teachers to invalidate a racial ratio for staff assignments in Philadelphia, Pennsylvania, after the Department of Education had released the school district from that requirement, which had been imposed as a condition of eligibility for federal funds to aid school districts to desegregate. The school district had retained the system "so that public school pupils will have the opportunity to be taught by an integrated faculty." [51] The court held that neither the Constitution nor Title VII of the Civil Rights Act of 1964 was violated.

In 1992 the Sixth Circuit Court of Appeals upheld the continuation of a similar teacher assignment policy in Cincinnati, Ohio.[52] The policy,

48. Wall v. Stanly County Bd. of Educ., 259 F.Supp. 238 (M.D.N.C. 1966).

49. Wall v. Stanly County Bd. of Educ., 378 F.2d 275 (4 Cir.1967).

50. Morgan v. Kerrigan, 509 F.2d 599 (1 Cir.1975). See also Morgan v. Kerrigan, 509 F.2d 580 (1 Cir.1974), cert. den. 421 U.S. 963, 95 S.Ct. 1950, 44 L.Ed.2d 449 (1975).

51. Kromnick v. School District of Philadelphia, 739 F.2d 894 (3 Cir.1984), cert. den. 469 U.S. 1107, 105 S.Ct. 782, 83 L.Ed.2d 777 (1985).

52. Jacobson v. Cincinnati Bd. of Educ., 961 F.2d 100 (6 Cir.1992), cert. den. __ U.S. __, 113 S.Ct. 94, 121 L.Ed.2d 55 (1992). [Case No. 90]

first adopted in 1974 and made a part of a consent decree settling a desegregation suit in 1984, was here attacked on the grounds of unequal protection and of conflict with the collective bargaining contract. The court found that the plan was substantially related to an important governmental objective (racially integrated faculty throughout the system) and did not in fact conflict with the contract. Furthermore, the involuntary transfers and denials of requests for voluntary transfers were race-neutral as to impact on the races, with "benefit" or "harm" not unbalanced.

In 1984 the Supreme Court denied certiorari on a case involving a plan approved by the Second Circuit Court of Appeals for both preserving elements of a teacher desegregation program that had required hiring of minority teachers, and considering seniority rights of majority teachers in a period of layoffs due to fiscal problems and declining enrollments.[53] The circuit court rejected arguments that state law or collective bargaining contracts could prevail over the constitutional mandate to eliminate from the schools of Buffalo, New York, vestiges of de jure segregation that were being perpetuated in the teaching staff. It upheld a "percentage layoff" plan, but found one aspect of the plan to be "needlessly harsh" in its treatment of recall rights of laid-off probationary and permanent teachers vis-a-vis employment of new teachers. (The Supreme Court action came after its decision a few days earlier that a bona fide seniority plan for layoffs of firefighters could not be superseded by a judicial order modifying a consent decree that applied to hiring and did not mention layoffs.[54] In that case the result of the lower court's modification of the decree had been that senior white employees were laid off instead of more recently employed black firefighters who themselves had not been direct victims of discriminatory hiring practices.)

The Supreme Court found to be unconstitutional a plan in Jackson, Michigan, that had been collectively bargained to cover teacher layoffs.[55] There had been no judicial finding of discrimination prior to institution of the plan. The provision was that the seniority basis for layoffs would be adjusted so that at no time would there be a greater percent of minority personnel terminated than the current percent of minority personnel employed at the time of the reduction in force. This arrangement led to layoffs of some white teachers who were senior to some retained black teachers.

By a vote of five-to-four with no opinion supported by a majority of Justices, the Court invalidated the plan as violative of the equal protection clause. The plurality opinion observed that layoffs place the entire burden of achieving racial equality on particular individuals, whereas hiring goals are a "less intrusive means of accomplishing similar pur-

53. Arthur v. Nyquist, 712 F.2d 816 (2 Cir.1983), cert. den. 467 U.S. 1259, 104 S.Ct. 3555, 82 L.Ed.2d 856 (1984). [Case No. 134]

54. Firefighters Local Union No. 1784 v. Stotts, 467 U.S. 561, 104 S.Ct. 2576, 81 L.Ed.2d 483 (1984).

55. Wygant v. Jackson Bd. of Educ., 476 U.S. 267, 106 S.Ct. 1842, 90 L.Ed.2d 260 (1986).

poses" because "the burden to be borne by innocent individuals is diffused to a considerable extent among society generally."

In 1993 the Court of Appeals, Second Circuit, applied the preceding decision to disapprove a teacher layoff plan in Bridgeport, Connecticut, that would have removed only white teachers.[56] Citing also its decision of a decade before regarding this problem (Arthur v. Nyquist, Case No. 134), the court emphasized that a RIF plan must be "narrowly tailored." It said, however, that a proportional layoff scheme could be developed here, where there was a consent decree fourteen years before that had not treated layoffs. The collective bargaining agreement spoke in terms of "preserving gains made." The court concluded that "exclusive layoffs of one race, in an effort to rectify past injustices, is an impermissible means to a legitimate end." The lower court was also instructed that before crafting any remedy it must determine whether there was a strong basis for concluding that hiring practices had contributed to making a segregated school system. (A consent decree is not a judicial finding of de jure segregation.)

In 1987 by a vote of six-to-three the Court upheld the selection for a promotional position of a female employee over a male with a higher score on a test under an affirmative action program that had been voluntarily adopted by a county transportation agency.[57] At the time none of 238 positions in the job classification was filled by a woman—a "manifest imbalance" in a "traditionally segregated job category." The purpose of Title VII was to eliminate the effects of employment discrimination. Thus, a voluntary affirmative action program could be adopted provided that it did not unduly infringe the interests of employees not benefitting from the plan. Here the plan was flexible (no fixed quotas) and temporary (subject to annual reassessments). The decision to promote the woman was not made solely on the basis of sex. (She was one of several who were deemed eligible for the selection to be made by the administration. The male's test score, however, was a little higher, and he was the one recommended by a second interview panel. The female was recommended by the agency's Affirmative Action Coordinator.) The Court emphasized the need for a case-by-case approach in this sensitive area.

The impact of Title VII of the Civil Rights Act of 1964 is treated in Chapter 9 under "Discriminatory Employment Practices."

De Facto Segregation

Definition and Scope

De facto segregation is a situation in which a very substantial majority of students in a school are of a racial or ethnic minority, and where the situation developed through no governmental action intended to require or encourage it. The decision of the Supreme Court in Brown

---

56. Crumpton v. Bridgeport Educ. Ass'n, 993 F.2d 1023 (2 Cir.1993).

57. Johnson v. Transportation Agency, Santa Clara County, Cal., 480 U.S. 616, 107 S.Ct. 1442, 94 L.Ed.2d 615 (1987).

ruled out only de jure segregation in public schools, that is, segregation resulting from intentional governmental action.

In parts of the country outside of the South some local school officials had gerrymandered school attendance areas, or taken other actions that contributed to large concentrations of blacks being assigned to certain schools of a school district. Correction of such actions comes under the direct mandate of Brown, for it is segregation which has developed, not fortuitously, but by governmental action. Although often called de facto segregation, it is really "covert de jure" segregation.

The leading case of such "false de facto" segregation came from New Rochelle, New York. It was found that the board of education had realigned certain school attendance boundaries in the past, and had, prior to about ten years before the case, permitted transfers of white pupils, but not of black pupils, living within the area of the school in controversy. Over ninety percent of the student body of that school were black. "The purpose and effect" of the school districting was to produce a substantially segregated school, said the Court of Appeals, Second Circuit.[58] Such conduct clearly violated the Fourteenth Amendment and the Brown holding, for it was de jure segregation.

In an increasing number of jurisdictions courts have ruled that "false de facto" segregation must be corrected. For example, a federal District Court found that the Pasadena, California, pattern of racial imbalance at all levels involving both students and staff was a result of certain board actions and inactions.[59] The board had redrawn certain attendance zone lines from time to time while adhering to a neighborhood school policy and a policy against forced cross-town busing. Staff assignment policies had resulted in racial imbalances in faculties in various schools. When ordered to submit a plan for correcting the situation the board complied, rather than appealing the decision. Some parents, however, dissatisfied with the decree and the fact the board was not going to appeal, sought to intervene in the case in order to press an appeal. They were unsuccessful.[60] A few years later the board sought to be relieved from implementing the plan because of changed circumstances, one of which was alleged "white flight" from the district. The Court of Appeals, Ninth Circuit, denied relief.[61]

A similar set of facts led to a finding that school authorities in Pontiac, Michigan, over a long period of years had purposefully segregated black students.[62] Some steps recently taken to alleviate racial imbalance were found to be "inadequate to cure the effects of years of

58. Taylor v. Board of Educ. of City School Dist. of New Rochelle, 294 F.2d 36 (2 Cir.1961), cert. den. 368 U.S. 940, 82 S.Ct. 382, 7 L.Ed.2d 339 (1961).

59. Spangler v. Pasadena City Bd. of Educ., 311 F.Supp. 501 (C.D.Cal.1970).

60. Spangler v. Pasadena City Bd. of Educ., 427 F.2d 1352 (9 Cir.1970), cert. den. 402 U.S. 943, 91 S.Ct. 1607, 29 L.Ed.2d 111 (1971).

61. Spangler v. Pasadena City Bd. of Educ., 519 F.2d 430 (9 Cir.1975). See footnote 19 for a Supreme Court decision on desegregating Pasadena.

62. Davis v. School Dist. of City of Pontiac, Inc., 443 F.2d 573 (6 Cir.1971), cert. den. 404 U.S. 913, 92 S.Ct. 233, 30 L.Ed.2d 186 (1971).

purposeful segregation." The board was ordered to present a plan for desegregation, which the lower court ordered into effect. Then, on appeal, the board argued that the plan would require the expenditure of large sums of money which might not be available. The alternative offered to the Court of Appeals was, in that court's words, "no more than the reaffirmation of existing policies." The lower court order was affirmed.

The order in the preceding case included the use of busing to correct what was de jure segregation. The first case outside of the South in which a court required busing to correct segregation was the first brought by the United States Attorney General to desegregate a northern school district.[63] The past discrimination was in policies of school zoning, student transfers, and transportation.

Duty to Correct

A basic legal question relevant to "true de facto" segregation is: *Must* school authorities take action to correct racial imbalances which have developed in the schools of a district through housing patterns and the uniform application of school zoning and pupil transfer policies? The answer is "No."

Holdings to this effect have been made by United States Courts of Appeals in several circuits.[64] This does not mean, however, that unequal facilities, unequal programs, or unequal staffs will be permitted in schools which are predominantly minority in population. Certain tangible deficiencies of such schools may necessitate positive corrective action by school boards, not on the ground of racial balance per se, but on the ground of general equality of educational opportunity. The disposition of the courts regarding de facto segregation seems to be to order corrected material and reasonably correctable educational inequalities, but not to require racial mixing per se.[65]

In a Washington, D.C., case, extensive changes related to race in the school system were court ordered.[66] The court found a school zoning pattern and teacher segregation to be de jure segregation and, therefore, unconstitutional. It found many inequalities not to be rationally explainable. The "track" system of ability grouping was specifically invalidated, based primarily on the facts that students were placed in programs of study by questionable testing procedures early in their

63. United States v. School Dist. 151 of Cook County, Illinois, 432 F.2d 1147 (7 Cir.1970), cert. den. 402 U.S. 943, 91 S.Ct. 1610, 29 L.Ed.2d 111 (1971).

64. The leading cases in the circuits are: Bell v. School City of Gary, Indiana, 324 F.2d 209 (7 Cir.1963), cert. den. 377 U.S. 924, 84 S.Ct. 1223, 12 L.Ed.2d 216 (1964); Downs v. Board of Educ., 336 F.2d 988 (10 Cir.1964), cert. den. 380 U.S. 914, 85 S.Ct. 898, 13 L.Ed.2d 800 (1965); Springfield School Committee v. Barksdale, 348 F.2d 261 (1 Cir.1965); Offerman v. Nitkowski, 378 F.2d 22 (2 Cir.1967); Deal v. Cincinnati Bd. of Educ., 369 F.2d 55 (6 Cir.1966), cert. den. 389 U.S. 847, 88 S.Ct. 39, 19 L.Ed.2d 114 (1967). [Case No. 135]

65. Deal v. Cincinnati Bd. of Educ., 369 F.2d 55 (6 Cir.1966), cert. den. 389 U.S. 847, 88 S.Ct. 39, 19 L.Ed.2d 114 (1967). [Case No. 135]

66. Hobson v. Hansen, 269 F.Supp. 401 (D.D.C.1967).

schooling, and it was exceedingly difficult to change tracks later. The board of education declined to appeal the decision and refused to allow the superintendent to appeal. He then resigned, and, joined by a member of the board, appealed. The detailed decree was attacked as being a judicial interference in the administration of the educational system. The Court of Appeals, District of Columbia Circuit, upheld the lower court on most substantive points, including abolition of the track system.[67] However, instead of affirmance of the extensive decree, a remand was ordered so that a newly elected board of education, replacing the former appointed board, would not be unduly restricted in evolving new programs and patterns.

The Supreme Court of New Jersey has determined that the state commissioner of education has broad powers to deal with de facto segregation, which is contrary to state policy.[68] The court found that he had a duty to act in a situation in which there would be an increase in such segregation if he did nothing. A three-judge federal District Court, however, has ruled that the "degeneration" of New Jersey's unitary system of public education to "extreme racial imbalance in some school districts" is not susceptible to federal judicial intervention. This holding was affirmed by the Supreme Court without opinion.[69]

The Supreme Court of California held that "California school boards bear a [state] constitutional obligation to take reasonably feasible steps to alleviate school segregation, whether such segregation is de jure or de facto in nature." [70] The court said that the function of the judiciary is to ascertain if a school board has "initiated a course of action to alleviate the effects of segregation in its schools and has made reasonable progress toward that goal." If such is not the situation, the court must intervene to "protect the constitutional rights of minority children." The court stated that there is no requirement that each school in a district reflect the racial composition of the district as a whole. The duty is to eliminate those schools in which the minority enrollment is so disproportionate as to isolate those students from "an integrated educational experience."

Subsequently the voters of the state approved an amendment to the state constitution to prohibit state courts from ordering "mandatory pupil assignment or transportation unless a federal court would do so to remedy a [federal constitutional] violation." The amendment was attacked as a violation of the equal protection clause. However, by an eight-to-one vote, the Supreme Court of the United States rejected the contention that once a state chose to do more than the Fourteenth Amendment requires, it may never recede.[71] The Court said that the

67. Smuck v. Hobson, 408 F.2d 175 (D.C.Cir.1969).

68. Jenkins v. Township of Morris School Dist., 58 N.J. 483, 279 A.2d 619 (1971). See footnotes 83 and 84 in Chapter 3.

69. Spencer v. Kugler, 326 F.Supp. 1235 (D.N.J.1971), aff. 404 U.S. 1027, 92 S.Ct. 707, 30 L.Ed.2d 723 (1972).

70. Crawford v. Board of Educ. of City of Los Angeles, 17 Cal.3d 280, 130 Cal.Rptr. 724, 551 P.2d 28 (1976).

71. Crawford v. Board of Educ. of City of Los Angeles, 458 U.S. 527, 102 S.Ct. 3211, 73 L.Ed.2d 948 (1982).

amendment did not embody a racial classification, and neither said nor implied that persons be treated differently on account of their race. It only forbade state courts to order pupil school assignment or transportation in the absence of a Fourteenth Amendment violation. "The benefit it seeks to confer—neighborhood schooling—is made available regardless of race in the discretion of school boards." The Court added that discriminatory motive could not be imputed to the almost sixty-nine percent of the electorate that voted for the amendment.

Rejected by the Seventh Circuit Court of Appeals as basis for a federal constitutional claim was the argument that failure to eliminate de facto segregation as required by Illinois state law created a conclusive presumption of segregative intent.[72] The court said that failure to act to correct de facto segregation was not per se sufficient to establish segregative intent by local boards, especially so where the statute invoked provided that a school board under certain conditions could conclude that existing attendance unit boundaries should not be revised.

Power to Correct

Another basic question is: *May* school authorities take action to correct racial imbalances which have developed in the schools of a district through housing patterns and the uniform application of school zoning and pupil transfer policies? The answer is "Yes."

This position has been taken by both state and federal courts. The Supreme Court included dicta to this effect in Swann, and endorsed it in "the Seattle case" of 1982.[73] The main challenges came from those who maintained that race cannot be considered for any purpose, that "the Constitution is colorblind" for all purposes. This contention has now been thoroughly rejected in its absolute form. Constitutionality is dependent upon the purpose of looking at the factor of race. What the Constitution prevents, according to the courts, is invidious use of race to the disadvantage of a person or racial group. Obviously, to ignore race would make dismantlement of dual school systems virtually impossible, and would defeat the mandate of Brown. Also, it would preclude any attempts to prevent or correct de facto segregation.

Courts generally have accepted the views of educators that the public school in a democracy serves its purpose better where the pupil population is not homogeneous, that certain learning takes place better in situations which reflect broad community composition, and that de facto segregation has an undesirable effect on attitudes related to successful learning. The reasoning of most courts is that these are basically educational determinations, and thus they can neither substitute their judgments for those of the educational authorities nor deeply probe the social and psychological bases of the educational conclusions.[74]

---

72. Coates v. Illinois State Board of Educ., 559 F.2d 445 (7 Cir.1977).

73. See footnote 92.

74. Van Blerkom v. Donovan, 15 N.Y.2d 399, 259 N.Y.S.2d 825, 207 N.E.2d 503 (1965); Booker v. Board of Educ. of the

State legislation requiring local school boards to take race into account in pupil assignment policies has been sustained.[75] The courts have supported state-level educational authorities in initiating steps to correct racial imbalances in the schools of the state.[76] Local board actions for this purpose also have been supported.[77]

The Supreme Court of Washington has discussed at length many of the arguments advanced against busing to achieve better racial balance in schools that have been de facto segregated.[78] A corporation had been formed by some Seattle, Washington, citizens for the purpose of opposing mandatory busing. They were successful in getting a lower court to enjoin for one year the implementation of a plan adopted by the board. The higher court, however, dissolved the injunction. It observed that a system of voluntary transfers of students had not accomplished the altogether proper objective of providing for desegregated education. It commented that the board had developed the plan with the help of experts and laymen and had held hearings where all were urged to express opinions. (Plaintiffs, who here sought the delay to study the board's final plan, had not submitted a plan.) The contention that a referendum should be held on the issue was not sustained. The court rejected the notion that students have a right to attend the school closest to their homes. It pointed out that in a city of the size of Seattle, the confines of a neighborhood were not much observed in day to day life. That some parents thought their children would suffer a disadvantage in attending a school outside the neighborhood was not a basis for invalidating the board's overall plan for equalizing educational opportunity. The court also rejected the theory that parents had a right to select the public school for their children. (The United States Supreme Court decision on "the Seattle case" is discussed in the next section.)

Most lawsuits against local school board policies intended to correct racial imbalance have been brought by white parents. Some legal actions, however, have been brought by blacks contending that they were being forced to absorb all or most of the inconveniences of reassignment. A federal District Court declared unconstitutional the Pittsburg, California, school board's plan for "the closing of an apparently suitable negro school and transfer of its pupils back and forth to white schools without similar arrangements for white pupils."[79] The court found the plan "not absolutely or reasonably necessary under the particular circumstances" and said that consideration must be given to the "fairly obvious fact" that the plan placed the burden of desegregation entirely upon one racial group.

City of Plainfield, 45 N.J. 161, 212 A.2d 1 (1965).

75. School Committee of Boston v. Board of Educ., 352 Mass. 693, 227 N.E.2d 729 (1967), app. dism. 389 U.S. 572, 88 S.Ct. 692, 19 L.Ed.2d 778 (1968); Tometz v. Board of Educ., 39 Ill.2d 593, 237 N.E.2d 498 (1968).

76. Vetere v. Allen, 15 N.Y.2d 259, 258 N.Y.S.2d 77, 206 N.E.2d 174 (1965); Jen-

kins v. Township of Morris School Dist., 58 N.J. 483, 279 A.2d 619 (1971).

77. Balaban v. Rubin, 14 N.Y.2d 193, 250 N.Y.S.2d 281, 199 N.E.2d 375 (1964).

78. Citizens Against Mandatory Bussing v. Palmason, 80 Wash.2d 445, 495 P.2d 657 (1972). See footnote 92 for later developments.

79. Brice v. Landis, 314 F.Supp. 974 (N.D.Cal.1969).

The Second Circuit Court of Appeals, however, has ruled that the Norwalk, Connecticut, board of education did not deny black and Puerto Rican children equal protection of law by busing them to white neighborhood schools without concurrently maintaining black neighborhood schools and cross-busing white children to them.[80] Norwalk had voluntarily undertaken the plan without a history of de jure segregation. There was therefore no duty on the board to do anything. Its good faith attempt to improve education of children in some neighborhoods by transferring them to other schools did not infringe any rights. Not all neighborhoods must be treated the same unless the distinctions are for an improper purpose.

State-level commissions have been created by the legislatures of many states to deal with problems of discrimination and human relations. Their power to order corrective action to be taken in situations of de facto segregation in school systems depends upon the enabling statutes. For example, it was found by the Supreme Court of Pennsylvania that such a commission in that state could, upon proper findings, order a local school district to halt certain discriminatory practices and also to draw up plans for eliminating de facto segregation in some schools.[81] The court held that for the commission to invoke its authority it was not necessary to find that the school district had intentionally fostered and maintained segregation, only necessary to find there was in fact an imbalance. The court agreed with the observation that a "neighborhood school, which encompasses a homogeneous racial and socio-economic grouping, * * * is the very antithesis of the common school heritage." Subsequently the court ruled that the commission had the power to adopt a mathematical definition of de facto segregation.[82] On the other hand a commission in Kansas was held not empowered to order a local school board to take steps to reassign already employed teachers so as to effect a better racial balance in the teaching staff of the district.[83]

In 1978 the Supreme Court decided its first case involving the question whether a benefit can be offered only to members of defined minority groups when the public institution conferring the benefit has no history of de jure segregative policies or other discrimination against members of those groups.[84] In the widely publicized Bakke case the operative facts were that a campus of the University of California had set aside 16 of 100 seats in its entering medical school class specifically for "Blacks," "Chicanos," "Asians," and "American Indians." There was a separate admissions program for these groups, characterized as "disadvantaged" one year (with no formal definition of the term) and as "minority groups" the next. Bakke was a white applicant who, after he was not admitted on either occasion, sued under the equal protection

80. Norwalk Core v. Norwalk Bd. of Educ., 423 F.2d 121 (2 Cir.1970); Moss v. Stamford Bd. of Educ., 356 F.Supp. 675 (D.Conn.1973).

81. Pennsylvania Human Relations Comm'n v. Chester School Dist., 427 Pa. 157, 233 A.2d 290 (1967).

82. Pennsylvania Human Relations Comm'n v. Uniontown Area School Dist., 455 Pa. 52, 313 A.2d 156 (1973).

83. Londerholm v. Unified School Dist. No. 500, 199 Kan. 312, 430 P.2d 188 (1967).

84. Regents of Univ. of California v. Bakke, 438 U.S. 265, 98 S.Ct. 2733, 57 L.Ed.2d 750 (1978).

clause of the Fourteenth Amendment on a claim of racial discrimination. The Supreme Court of California found the program to be unconstitutional because it considered race, and ordered Bakke admitted (after the University conceded it could not prove that Bakke would not have been admitted in the absence of the special program).

The Supreme Court of the United States held that the specific program was illegal and that Bakke must be admitted, but that consideration of race per se was not constitutionally forbidden in such a situation. These conclusions were not supported in a single opinion of the Court. Four Justices found that Bakke was unlawfully excluded in violation of Title VI of the Civil Rights Act of 1964. They believed that the constitutional question need not and should not be reached. Justice Powell, who cast the fifth vote for Bakke's admission, said that there also was a constitutional infirmity in the California plan—namely the fact that members of the specified minorities could compete for the whole 100 seats whereas whites could compete for only 84 seats. Justice Powell stated, however, that there was no constitutional bar to considering race or ethnic origin as one of a number of factors to be considered in an admissions program, because a university's quest for a diverse student body can be considered of paramount importance in the fulfillment of its mission. On the latter point he was joined by the other four Justices, who believed that the California plan was completely constitutional. The first bloc of four Justices said nothing about "race as *one* factor," taking the position that the case did not call for a discussion of that matter because race was the *only* factor in selecting those for the 16 "minority seats."

Power to Prevent Correction

State legislation aimed at preventing correction of de facto segregation had been struck down by federal courts in cases from New York and Michigan (and given an innocuous meaning to preserve its constitutionality by the Supreme Court of California) prior to the Supreme Court's doing so in 1982. A 1969 New York statute prohibited assignment of students for balancing purposes except by an elected school board. The act was held to be unconstitutional by a three-judge federal District Court.[85] Because it created a single exception to the broad supervisory powers the state commissioner of education exercised over local public education, the basis for the exception was carefully examined. As the statute established a purely racial classification by treating educational matters involving racial criteria differently from other educational matters, and as it made dealing with racial imbalances in the public schools more difficult, it could not stand.

In Michigan the Detroit board of education had voluntarily adopted a plan designed to provide a better balance between black and white students in twelve high schools. In attempting to counteract this, the

---

85. Lee v. Nyquist, 318 F.Supp. 710 (W.D.N.Y.1970), aff. 402 U.S. 935, 91 S.Ct. 1618, 29 L.Ed.2d 105 (1971).

legislature mandated an open-enrollment policy with preference to be given to students living near each school. The legislation applied to "first class school districts," of which Detroit was the only one. The United States Court of Appeals, Sixth Circuit, declared the act unconstitutional because it obstructed steps lawfully taken for the purpose of protecting Fourteenth Amendment rights.[86] It said it was expressing no opinion "as to whether it was the constitutional obligation of the School Board to adopt all or any part" of its plan. The court distinguished this case from Deal,[87] decided in the same circuit, in that here the school board had decided to take action, whereas in Deal the plaintiffs sought to force the board to take action.

A 1970 California statute provided that no school board could require a student to be transported "for any purpose or for any reason without the written permission of the parent or guardian." This was interpreted by that state's highest court as not interfering with the school board's power to assign pupils to schools for the purpose of improving racial balance.[88] The statute was given the literal meaning that pupils were not required to use any school transportation offered. Any other interpretation would render the statute unconstitutional, said the court, for it could not be upheld "to the extent that it lends governmental support to such [de facto] segregation."

After the board of education of Lansing, Michigan, adopted a plan to correct de facto segregation, a recall election removed all members of the board who had voted for the plan. At the first meeting of the "new" board, it was decided to rescind the plan at the end of the school year. This action was not permitted by the Court of Appeals, Sixth Circuit, because its effect would be to reassign many students to their previously segregated schools.[89]

Subsequent to the unsuccessful attempts to block plans for correction of de facto segregation in Seattle by busing,[90] the voters of Washington passed by referendum a measure that prevented local boards of education from requiring students to attend schools other than one of the two closest to their residences that offered a specific curriculum, and from utilizing any of a number of methods of assignment, such as redefining attendance zones and pairing of schools. Expressly accepting the analytical approach of the three-judge federal District Court in Lee,[91] the Supreme Court by a vote of five-to-four concluded that the constitutionally fatal flaw was that the voter-approved initiative removed "the authority to address a racial problem—and only a racial problem—from the existing decision-making body, in such a way as to burden minority interests."[92] Authority over all other student assignment decisions

86. Bradley v. Milliken, 433 F.2d 897 (6 Cir.1970).

87. See footnote 65.

88. San Francisco Unified School Dist. v. Johnson, 3 Cal.3d 937, 92 Cal.Rptr. 309, 479 P.2d 669 (1971).

89. National Ass'n for the Advancement of Colored People, Lansing Branch v. Lansing Bd. of Educ., 485 F.2d 569 (6 Cir.1973).

90. See footnote 78.

91. See footnote 85.

92. Washington v. Seattle School Dist. No. 1, 458 U.S. 457, 102 S.Ct. 3187, 73 L.Ed.2d 896 (1982). [Case No. 136]

remained on the local level, but "those favoring the elimination of de facto school segregation * * * [would be required to] seek relief from the state legislature, or from the statewide electorate. * * * The community's political mechanisms are modified to place effective decisionmaking authority over a racial issue at a different level of government." The Court said that although the state could have decided to make all student assignments from the state-level, it could not delegate the matter to local boards with the race-conscious strings attached.

Proof of Intent to Discriminate

Whether a particular governmental action that results in a disproportionately adverse effect on blacks (singly or as a class) was racially motivated is the crux of constitutional litigation, for on the answer depends whether the courts will apply the law of de jure segregation or the law of de facto segregation. In the South in 1954 the segregation was based on codified state law and was districtwide in all school districts. Thus, the question of intent was academic, and courts examined districtwide remedies for the de jure segregation. Outside of those states it was necessary to prove segregative intent before federal courts could order correction, the extent of the correction depending on the extent of the violation.

Some examples of judicially-found segregative intent in the field of education have been given in preceding sections. The basic Supreme Court opinion is in the Denver case.[93] In cases in other fields, however, the Supreme Court has presented guidelines as to what evidence may be probative as to discriminatory intent. The most extensive elaboration was in a case involving zoning for low-cost housing.[94] Although stating that they are not exhaustive, the Court addressed six factors for assessment of discriminatory intent in an official action. In essence, they are (1) impact of the action, (2) historical background, (3) sequence of events leading up to the action, (4) departures from normal procedural sequence, (5) departures from the weighting usually given operative factors, and (6) legislative or administrative history.

The standard of responsibility for the foreseeable consequences of a governmental action increasingly is being accepted by the courts as a predicate for finding sufficient discriminatory intent to warrant a court ordered remedy for segregation. The Second, Fifth, Sixth, and Eighth Circuit Courts of Appeals, within 14 months after the Arlington Heights housing decision of the Supreme Court, specifically held that it did not preclude this approach, which is well established in the common law of torts. In the post-Arlington Heights cases, the Second Circuit found discriminatory intent in the Buffalo, New York, board of education's policies on student assignments and transfers, its siting of a school, its actions "to thwart" directives of state-level authorities to correct the

93. See footnote 15.

94. Village of Arlington Heights v. Metropolitan Housing Development Corp., 429 U.S. 252, 97 S.Ct. 555, 50 L.Ed.2d 450 (1977). The zoning ordinance here was held to be constitutional.

segregation, and its staff assignment policies;[95] the Fifth Circuit found intent to discriminate against Mexican-Americans in the Austin, Texas, board of education's method of grade-level desegregation, its school siting and capacity policies, and its staff assignment policies;[96] the Sixth Circuit found discriminatory intent in the Lansing, Michigan, board of education's policies of busing for desegregation black children but not white children, using mobile units at some schools, and granting special transfers;[97] the Eighth Circuit found discriminatory intent in the Omaha, Nebraska, board of education's policies for faculty assignment, student transfers, optional attendance zones, and school construction.[98]

If a prima facie case of purposeful discrimination has been established by such factors as those enunciated in the Arlington Heights case, the board has the opportunity to rebut the presumption by offering evidence that its actions or inactions were consistent with racially neutral policies reasonably associated with acceptable educational practice. It must be emphasized that to support a finding of a constitutional violation, more than mere disparate impact of a policy must be shown. There must be evidence, in the words of the Supreme Court, that the decisionmaker "selected or reaffirmed a particular course of action at least in part 'because of,' not merely 'in spite of,' its adverse effects."[99] The Court added to that statement a footnote that included the comment, "This is not to say that the inevitability or foreseeability of consequences of a neutral rule has no bearing upon the existence of discriminatory intent."

[Case No. 128] Constitutionality of Racial Segregation in Public Schools

BROWN v. BOARD OF EDUC. OF TOPEKA (I)

Supreme Court of the United States, 1954.
347 U.S. 483, 74 S.Ct. 686, 98 L.Ed. 873.

Mr. Chief Justice Warren delivered the opinion of the Court.

These cases come to us from the States of Kansas, South Carolina, Virginia, and Delaware. They are premised on different facts and different local conditions, but a common legal question justifies their consideration together in this consolidated opinion.

In each of the cases, minors of the Negro race, through their legal representatives, seek the aid of the courts in obtaining admission to the public schools of their community on a nonsegregated basis. In each instance, they have been denied admission to schools attended by white

---

95. Arthur v. Nyquist, 573 F.2d 134 (2 Cir.1978), cert. den. 439 U.S. 860, 99 S.Ct. 179, 58 L.Ed.2d 169 (1978).

96. United States v. Texas Educ. Agency, 564 F.2d 162 (5 Cir.1977).

97. National Ass'n for the Advancement of Colored People v. Lansing Board of Educ., 559 F.2d 1042 (6 Cir.1977), cert. den.

434 U.S. 997, 98 S.Ct. 635, 54 L.Ed.2d 491 (1977).

98. United States v. School Dist. of Omaha, 565 F.2d 127 (8 Cir.1977).

99. Personnel Adm'r of Massachusetts v. Feeney, 442 U.S. 256, 99 S.Ct. 2282, 60 L.Ed.2d 870 (1979).

children under laws requiring or permitting segregation according to race. This segregation was alleged to deprive the plaintiffs of the equal protection of the laws under the Fourteenth Amendment. In each of the cases other than the Delaware case, a three-judge federal district court denied relief to the plaintiffs on the so-called "separate but equal" doctrine announced by this Court in Plessy v. Ferguson. Under that doctrine, equality of treatment is accorded when the races are provided substantially equal facilities, even though these facilities be separate. In the Delaware case, the Supreme Court of Delaware adhered to that doctrine, but ordered that the plaintiffs be admitted to the white schools because of their superiority to the Negro schools.

The plaintiffs contend that segregated public schools are not "equal" and cannot be made "equal," and that hence they are deprived of the equal protection of the laws. Because of the obvious importance of the question presented, the Court took jurisdiction. Argument was heard in the 1952 Term, and reargument was heard this Term on certain questions propounded by the Court.

* * *

In the first cases in this Court constructing the Fourteenth Amendment, decided shortly after its adoption, the Court interpreted it as proscribing all state-imposed discriminations against the Negro race. The doctrine of "separate but equal" did not make its appearance in this Court until 1896 in the case of Plessy v. Ferguson, supra, involving not education but transportation. American courts have since labored with the doctrine for over half a century. In this Court, there have been six cases involving the "separate but equal" doctrine in the field of public education. In Cumming v. Board of Education of Richmond County, 175 U.S. 528, 20 S.Ct. 197, 44 L.Ed. 262, and Gong Lum v. Rice, 275 U.S. 78, 48 S.Ct. 91, 72 L.Ed. 172, the validity of the doctrine itself was not challenged. In more recent cases, all on the graduate school level, inequality was found in that specific benefits enjoyed by white students were denied to Negro students of the same educational qualifications. State of Missouri ex rel. Gaines v. Canada, 305 U.S. 337, 59 S.Ct. 232, 83 L.Ed. 208; Sipuel v. Board of Regents of University of Oklahoma, 332 U.S. 631, 68 S.Ct. 299, 92 L.Ed. 247; Sweatt v. Painter, 339 U.S. 629, 70 S.Ct. 848, 94 L.Ed. 1114; McLaurin v. Oklahoma State Regents, 339 U.S. 637, 70 S.Ct. 851, 94 L.Ed. 1149. In none of these cases was it necessary to re-examine the doctrine to grant relief to the Negro plaintiff. And in Sweatt v. Painter, supra, the Court expressly reserved decision on the question whether Plessy v. Ferguson should be held inapplicable to public education.

In the instant cases, that question is directly presented. Here, unlike Sweatt v. Painter, there are findings below that the Negro and white schools involved have been equalized, or are being equalized, with respect to buildings, curricula, qualifications and salaries of teachers, and other "tangible" factors. Our decision, therefore, cannot turn on merely a comparison of these tangible factors in the Negro and white schools involved in each of the cases. We must look instead to the effect of segregation itself on public education.

In approaching this problem, we cannot turn the clock back to 1868 when the Amendment was adopted, or even to 1896 when Plessy v. Ferguson was written. We must consider public education in the light of its full development and its present place in American life throughout the Nation. Only in this way can it be determined if segregation in public schools deprives these plaintiffs of the equal protection of the laws.

Today, education is perhaps the most important function of state and local governments. Compulsory school attendance laws and the great expenditures for education both demonstrate our recognition of the importance of education to our democratic society. It is required in the performance of our most basic public responsibilities, even service in the armed forces. It is the very foundation of good citizenship. Today it is a principal instrument in awakening the child to cultural values, in preparing him for later professional training, and in helping him to adjust normally to his environment. In these days, it is doubtful that any child may reasonably be expected to succeed in life if he is denied the opportunity of an education. Such an opportunity, where the state has undertaken to provide it, is a right which must be made available to all on equal terms.

We come then to the question presented: Does segregation of children in public schools solely on the basis of race, even though the physical facilities and other "tangible" factors may be equal, deprive the children of the minority group of equal educational opportunities? We believe that it does.

In Sweatt v. Painter, in finding that a segregated law school for Negroes could not provide them equal educational opportunities, this Court relied in large part on "those qualities which are incapable of objective measurement but which make for greatness in a law school." In McLaurin v. Oklahoma State Regents, the Court, in requiring that a Negro admitted to a white graduate school be treated like all other students, again resorted to intangible considerations: " * * * his ability to study, to engage in discussions and exchange views with other students, and, in general, to learn his profession." Such considerations apply with added force to children in grade and high schools. To separate them from others of similar age and qualifications solely because of their race generates a feeling of inferiority as to their status in the community that may affect their hearts and minds in a way unlikely ever to be undone. The effect of this separation on their educational opportunities was well stated by a finding in the Kansas case by a court which nevertheless felt compelled to rule against the Negro plaintiffs:

> "Segregation of white and colored children in public schools has a detrimental effect upon the colored children. The impact is greater when it has the sanction of the law; for the policy of separating the races is usually interpreted as denoting the inferiority of the Negro group. A sense of inferiority affects the

motivation of a child to learn. Segregation with the sanction of law, therefore, has a tendency to [retard] the educational and mental development of Negro children and to deprive them of some of the benefits they would receive in a racial[ly] integrated school system."

Whatever may have been the extent of psychological knowledge at the time of Plessy v. Ferguson, this finding is amply supported by modern authority. Any language in Plessy v. Ferguson contrary to this finding is rejected.

We conclude that in the field of public education the doctrine of "separate but equal" has no place. Separate educational facilities are inherently unequal. Therefore, we hold that the plaintiffs and others similarly situated for whom the actions have been brought are, by reason of the segregation complained of, deprived of the equal protection of the laws guaranteed by the Fourteenth Amendment. This disposition makes unnecessary any discussion whether such segregation also violates the Due Process Clause of the Fourteenth Amendment.

Because these are class actions, because of the wide applicability of this decision, and because of the great variety of local conditions, the formulation of decrees in these cases presents problems of considerable complexity. On reargument, the consideration of appropriate relief was necessarily subordinated to the primary question—the constitutionality of segregation in public education. We have now announced that such segregation is a denial of the equal protection of the laws. In order that we may have the full assistance of the parties in formulating decrees, the cases will be restored to the docket, and the parties are requested to present further argument on Questions 4 and 5 previously propounded by the Court for the reargument this Term. The Attorney General of the United States is again invited to participate. The Attorneys General of the states requiring or permitting segregation in public education will also be permitted to appear as *amici curiae* upon request to do so by September 15, 1954, and submission of briefs by October 1, 1954.

It is so ordered.

Notes

1. In Cumming v. Board of Educ. of Richmond County (1899), cited in the case, the Court refused to enjoin a school board from maintaining a high school for white children when lack of funds was given as the reason for not having a high school for Negro children. To grant the relief sought would disadvantage the white children, without providing any advantage to the Negro children. The opinion was written by Justice Harlan, the sole dissenter in the Plessy case three years before.

2. In Gong Lum v. Rice (1927), cited in the case, mandamus was sought to compel the admission of Martha Lum to the white school, she having been assigned to the Negro school. The Supreme Court concluded that she was not being deprived of equal protection because there was a Negro school which she could attend.

3. The Court for the first time in 1950 in Sweatt v. Painter and McLaurin v. Oklahoma State Regents, cited in the case, emphasized the importance of

"intangible factors" in connection with equal educational opportunity. But purely psychological considerations were not emphasized until the present case.

4. Consider the rarity of a unanimous decision with no concurring opinions on any significant matter of social policy. Clearly the Justices were aware of the importance of a single statement in this situation.

[Case No. 129]   Implementation of the Desegregation Decree

BROWN v. BOARD OF EDUC. OF TOPEKA (II)

Supreme Court of the United States, 1955.
349 U.S. 294, 75 S.Ct. 753, 99 L.Ed. 1083.

MR. CHIEF JUSTICE WARREN delivered the opinion of the Court.

These cases were decided on May 17, 1954. The opinions of that date, declaring the fundamental principle that racial discrimination in public education is unconstitutional, are incorporated herein by reference. All provisions of federal, state, or local law requiring or permitting such discrimination must yield to this principle. There remains for consideration the manner in which relief is to be accorded.

Because these cases arose under different local conditions and their disposition will involve a variety of local problems, we requested further argument on the question of relief. In view of the nationwide importance of the decision, we invited the Attorney General of the United States and the Attorneys General of all states requiring or permitting racial discrimination in public education to present their views on that question. The parties, the United States, and the States of Florida, North Carolina, Arkansas, Oklahoma, Maryland, and Texas filed briefs and participated in the oral argument.

These presentations were informative and helpful to the Court in its consideration of the complexities arising from the transition to a system of public education freed of racial discrimination. The presentations also demonstrated that substantial steps to eliminate racial discrimination in public schools have already been taken, not only in some of the communities in which these cases arose, but in some of the states appearing as *amici curiae,* and in other states as well. Substantial progress has been made in the District of Columbia, and in the communities in Kansas and Delaware involved in this litigation. The defendants in the cases coming to us from South Carolina and Virginia are awaiting the decision of this Court concerning relief.

Full implementation of these constitutional principles may require solution of varied local school problems. School authorities have the primary responsibility for elucidating, assessing, and solving these problems; courts will have to consider whether the action of school authorities constitutes good faith implementation of the governing constitutional principles. Because of their proximity to local conditions and the possible need for further hearings, the courts which originally heard these cases can best perform this judicial appraisal. Accordingly, we believe it appropriate to remand the cases to those courts.

In fashioning and effectuating the decrees, the courts will be guided by equitable principles. Traditionally, equity has been characterized by a practical flexibility in shaping its remedies and by a facility for adjusting and reconciling public and private needs. These cases call for the exercise of these traditional attributes of equity power. At stake is the personal interest of the plaintiffs in admission to public schools as soon as practicable on a nondiscriminatory basis. To effectuate this interest may call for elimination of a variety of obstacles in making the transition to school systems operated in accordance with the constitutional principles set forth in our May 17, 1954, decision. Courts of equity may properly take into account the public interest in the elimination of such obstacles in a systematic and effective manner. But it should go without saying that the vitality of these constitutional principles cannot be allowed to yield simply because of disagreement with them.

While giving weight to these public and private considerations, the courts will require that the defendants make a prompt and reasonable start toward full compliance with our May 17, 1954, ruling. Once such a start has been made, the courts may find that additional time is necessary to carry out the ruling in an effective manner. The burden rests upon the defendants to establish that such time is necessary in the public interest and is consistent with good faith compliance at the earliest practicable date. To that end, the courts may consider problems related to administration, arising from the physical condition of the school plant, the school transportation system, personnel, revision of school districts and attendance areas into compact units to achieve a system of determining admission to the public schools on a nonracial basis, and revision of local laws and regulations which may be necessary in solving the foregoing problems. They will also consider the adequacy of any plans the defendants may propose to meet these problems and to effectuate a transition to a racially nondiscriminatory school system. During this period of transition, the courts will retain jurisdiction of these cases.

The judgments below, except that in the Delaware case, are accordingly reversed and remanded to the District Courts to take such proceedings and enter such orders and decrees consistent with this opinion as are necessary and proper to admit to public schools on a racially nondiscriminatory basis with all deliberate speed the parties to these cases. The judgment in the Delaware case—ordering the immediate admission of the plaintiffs to schools previously attended only by white children—is affirmed on the basis of the principles stated in our May 17, 1954, opinion, but the case is remanded to the Supreme Court of Delaware for such further proceedings as that court may deem necessary in the light of this opinion.

It is so ordered.

Notes

1. In 1968 Justice Black suggested in a television interview that the inclusion of the phrase "with all deliberate speed" was a mistake. Do you agree?

Considering the realities of the situation existing in the South in 1955, what alternatives were available to the Court?

2. Was it realistic for the court to believe that locally elected school boards would be effective in eliminating racial segregation?

3. Observe that the burden of establishing a time frame for compliance was placed primarily on each local board operating under the supervision of the courts. Education being a "state" function, why do you believe no responsibilities were expressly placed on the states?

4. It was not until after the Civil Rights Act of 1964 that either the Department of Health, Education, and Welfare or the Department of Justice became very active in regard to desegregation. Would not the *Brown* decisions have afforded the authority, if not the duty, for these departments of the executive branch to act to expedite desegregation of schools?

[Case No. 130] Constitutional Guidelines for Eliminating Racial Segregation

SWANN v. CHARLOTTE–MECKLENBURG BD. OF EDUC.

Supreme Court of the United States, 1971.
402 U.S. 1, 91 S.Ct. 1267, 28 L.Ed.2d 554.

MR. CHIEF JUSTICE BURGER delivered the opinion of the Court.

We granted certiorari in this case to review important issues as to the duties of school authorities and the scope of powers of federal courts under this Court's mandates to eliminate racially separate public schools established and maintained by state action. Brown v. Board of Education (*Brown I*).

This case and those argued with it arose in states having a long history of maintaining two sets of schools in a single school system deliberately operated to carry out a governmental policy to separate pupils in schools solely on the basis of race. That was what Brown v. Board of Education was all about. These cases present us with the problem of defining in more precise terms than heretofore the scope of the duty of school authorities and district courts in implementing *Brown I* and the mandate to eliminate dual systems and establish unitary systems at once. * * *

I

The Charlotte-Mecklenburg school system, the 43d largest in the Nation, encompasses the city of Charlotte and surrounding Mecklenburg County, North Carolina. The area is large—550 square miles—spanning roughly 22 miles east-west and 36 miles north-south. During the 1968–1969 school year the system served more than 84,000 pupils in 107 schools. Approximately 71% of the pupils were found to be white and 29% Negro. As of June 1969 there were approximately 24,000 Negro students in the system, of whom 21,000 attended schools within the city of Charlotte. Two-thirds of those 21,000—approximately 14,000 Negro students—attended 21 schools which were either totally Negro or more than 99% Negro.

* * *

II

Nearly 17 years ago this Court held, in explicit terms, that state-imposed segregation by race in public schools denies equal protection of the laws. At no time has the Court deviated in the slightest degree from that holding or its constitutional underpinnings. * * *

* * *

Over the 16 years since *Brown II,* many difficulties were encountered in implementation of the basic constitutional requirement that the State not discriminate between public school children on the basis of their race. Nothing in our national experience prior to 1955 prepared anyone for dealing with changes and adjustments of the magnitude and complexity encountered since then. Deliberate resistance of some to the Court's mandates has impeded the good-faith efforts of others to bring school systems into compliance. The detail and nature of these dilatory tactics have been noted frequently by this Court and other courts.

By the time the Court considered Green v. County School Board in 1968, very little progress had been made in many areas where dual school systems had historically been maintained by operation of state laws. In *Green,* the Court was confronted with a record of a freedom-of-choice program that the District Court had found to operate in fact to preserve a dual system more than a decade after *Brown II.* While acknowledging that a freedom-of-choice concept could be a valid remedial measure in some circumstances, its failure to be effective in *Green* required that

> "The burden on a school board today is to come forward with a plan that promises realistically to work *now* * * * until it is clear that state-imposed segregation has been completely removed."

This was plain language, yet the 1969 Term of Court brought fresh evidence of the dilatory tactics of many school authorities. Alexander v. Holmes County Bd. of Educ. restated the basic obligation asserted in Griffin v. County School Board and *Green,* that the remedy must be implemented *forthwith.*

The problems encountered by the district courts and courts of appeals make plain that we should now try to amplify guidelines, however incomplete and imperfect, for the assistance of school authorities and courts. The failure of local authorities to meet their constitutional obligations aggravated the massive problem of converting from the state-enforced discrimination of racially separate school systems. * * *

III

The objective today remains to eliminate from the public schools all vestiges of state-imposed segregation. * * *

If school authorities fail in their affirmative obligations under these holdings, judicial authority may be invoked. Once a right and a violation have been shown, the scope of a district court's equitable powers to remedy past wrongs is broad, for breadth and flexibility are inherent in equitable remedies.   * * *

* * *

School authorities are traditionally charged with broad power to formulate and implement educational policy and might well conclude, for example, that in order to prepare students to live in a pluralistic society each school should have a prescribed ratio of Negro to white students reflecting the proportion for the district as a whole. To do this as an educational policy is within the broad discretionary powers of school authorities; absent a finding of a constitutional violation, however, that would not be within the authority of a federal court. As with any equity case, the nature of the violation determines the scope of the remedy. In default by the school authorities of their obligation to proffer acceptable remedies, a district court has broad power to fashion a remedy that will assure a unitary school system.

The school authorities argue that the equity powers of federal district courts have been limited by Title IV of the Civil Rights Act of 1964, 42 U.S.C. § 2000c et seq. The language and the history of Title IV shows that it was not enacted to limit but to define the role of the Federal Government in the implementation of the *Brown I* decision. It authorizes the Commissioner of Education to provide technical assistance to local boards in the preparation of desegregation plans, to arrange "training institutes" for school personnel involved in desegregation efforts, and to make grants directly to schools to ease the transition to unitary systems. It also authorizes the Attorney General, in specified circumstances, to initiate federal desegregation suits. Section 2000c(b) defines "desegregation" as it is used in Title IV:

" 'Desegregation' means the assignment of students to public schools and within such schools without regard to their race, color, religion, or national origin, but 'desegregation' shall not mean the assignment of students to public schools in order to overcome racial imbalance."

Section 2000c–6, authorizing the Attorney General to institute federal suits, contains the following proviso:

"nothing herein shall empower any official or court of the United States to issue any order seeking to achieve a racial balance in any school by requiring the transportation of pupils or students from one school to another or one school district to another in order to achieve such racial balance, or otherwise enlarge the existing power of the court to insure compliance with constitutional standards."

On their face, the sections quoted support only to insure that the provisions of Title IV of the Civil Rights Act of 1964 will not be read as granting new powers. The proviso in § 2000c–6 is in terms designed to foreclose any interpretation of the Act as expanding the *existing* powers of federal courts to enforce the Equal Protection Clause. There is no suggestion of an intention to restrict those powers or withdraw from courts their historic equitable remedial powers. The legislative history of Title IV indicates that Congress was concerned that the Act might be read as creating a right of action under the Fourteenth Amendment in the situation of so-called "de facto segregation," where racial imbalance exists in the schools but with no showing that this was brought about by discriminatory action of state authorities. In short, there is nothing in the Act which provides us material assistance in answering the question of remedy for state-imposed segregation in violation of *Brown I.* The basis of our decision must be the prohibition of the Fourteenth Amendment that no State shall "deny to any person within its jurisdiction the equal protection of the laws."

IV

We turn now to the problem of defining with more particularity the responsibilities of school authorities in desegregating a state-enforced dual school system in light of the Equal Protection Clause. Although the several related cases before us are primarily concerned with problems of student assignment, it may be helpful to begin with a brief discussion of other aspects of the process.

In *Green,* we pointed out that existing policy and practice with regard to faculty, staff, transportation, extracurricular activities, and facilities were among the most important indicia of a segregated system. Independent of student assignment, where it is possible to identify a "white school" or a "Negro school" simply by reference to the racial composition of teachers and staff, the quality of school buildings and equipment, or the organization of sports activities, a *prima facie* case of violation of substantive constitutional rights under the Equal Protection Clause is shown.

When a system has been dual in these respects, the first remedial responsibility of school authorities is to eliminate invidious racial distinctions. With respect to such matters as transportation, supporting personnel, and extracurricular activities, no more than this may be necessary. Similar corrective action must be taken with regard to the maintenance of buildings and the distribution of equipment. In these areas, normal administrative practice should produce schools of like quality, facilities, and staffs. Something more must be said, however, as to faculty assignment and new school construction.

In the companion *Davis* case, the Mobile school board has argued that the Constitution requires that teachers be assigned on a "color blind" basis. It also argues that the Constitution prohibits district courts from using their equity power to order assignment of teachers to achieve a particular degree of faculty desegregation. We reject that contention.

* * *

The construction of new schools and the closing of old ones is one of the most important functions of local school authorities and also one of the most complex. They must decide questions of location and capacity in light of population growth, finances, land values, site availability, through an almost endless list of factors to be considered. The result of this will be a decision which when combined with one technique or another of student assignment, will determine the racial composition of the student body in each school in the system. Over the long run, the consequences of the choices will be far reaching. People gravitate toward school facilities, just as schools are located in response to the needs of people. The location of schools may thus influence the patterns of residential development of a metropolitan area and have important impact on composition of inner city neighborhoods.

In the past, choices in this respect have been used as a potent weapon for creating or maintaining a state-segregated school system. In addition to the classic pattern of building schools specifically intended for Negro or white students, school authorities have sometimes, since *Brown,* closed schools which appeared likely to become racially mixed through changes in neighborhood residential patterns. This was sometimes accompanied by building new schools in the areas of white suburban expansion farthest from Negro population centers in order to maintain the separation of the races with a minimum departure from the formal principles of "neighborhood zoning." Such a policy does more than simply influence the short-run composition of the student body of a new school. It may well promote segregated residential patterns which, when combined with "neighborhood zoning," further lock the school system into the mold of separation of the races. Upon a proper showing a district court may consider this in fashioning a remedy.

* * *

V

The central issue in this case is that of student assignment, and there are essentially four problem areas:

(1) to what extent racial balance or racial quotas may be used as an implement in a remedial order to correct a previously segregated system;

(2) whether every all-Negro and all-white school must be eliminated as an indispensable part of a remedial process of desegregation;

(3) what are the limits, if any, on the rearrangement of school districts and attendance zones, as a remedial measure; and

(4) what are the limits, if any, on the use of transportation facilities to correct state-enforced racial school segregation.

(1) Racial Balances or Racial Quotas.

* * *

We are concerned in these cases with the elimination of the discrimination inherent in the dual school systems, not with myriad factors of human existence which can cause discrimination in a multitude of ways on racial, religious, or ethnic grounds. The target of the cases from

Brown I to the present was the dual school system. The elimination of racial discrimination in public schools is a large task and one that should not be retarded by efforts to achieve broader purposes lying beyond the jurisdiction of school authorities. One vehicle can carry only a limited amount of baggage. It would not serve the important objective of *Brown I* to seek to use school desegregation cases for purposes beyond their scope, although desegregation of schools ultimately will have impact on other forms of discrimination. We do not reach in this case the question whether a showing that school segregation is a consequence of other types of state action, without any discriminatory action by the school authorities, is a constitutional violation requiring remedial action by a school desegregation decree. This case does not present that question and we therefore do not decide it.

Our objective in dealing with the issues presented by these cases is to see that school authorities exclude no pupil of a racial minority from any school, directly or indirectly, on account of race; it does not and cannot embrace all the problems of racial prejudice, even when those problems contribute to disproportionate racial concentrations in some schools.

* * *

* * * If we were to read the holding of the District Court to require, as a matter of substantive constitutional right, any particular degree of racial balance or mixing, that approach would be disapproved and we would be obliged to reverse. The constitutional command to desegregate schools does not mean that every school in every community must always reflect the racial composition of the school system as a whole.

* * *

We see therefore that the use made of mathematical ratios was no more than a starting point in the process of shaping a remedy, rather than an inflexible requirement. From that starting point the District Court proceeded to frame a decree that was within its discretionary powers, an equitable remedy for the particular circumstances. As we said in *Green,* a school authority's remedial plan or a district court's remedial decree is to be judged by its effectiveness. Awareness of the racial composition of the whole school system is likely to be a useful starting point in shaping a remedy to correct past constitutional violations. In sum, the very limited use made of mathematical ratios was within the equitable remedial discretion of the District Court.

(2) One-Race Schools.

The record in this case reveals the familiar phenomenon that in metropolitan areas minority groups are often found concentrated in one part of the city. In some circumstances certain schools may remain all or largely of one race until new schools can be provided or neighborhood patterns change. Schools all or predominantly of one race in a district of mixed population will require close scrutiny to determine that school assignments are not part of state-enforced segregation.

In light of the above, it should be clear that the existence of some small number of one-race, or virtually one-race, schools within a district is not in and of itself the mark of a system which still practices segregation by law. The district judge or school authorities should make every effort to achieve the greatest possible degree of actual desegregation and will thus necessarily be concerned with the elimination of one-race schools. No *per se* rule can adequately embrace all the difficulties of reconciling the competing interests involved; but in a system with a history of segregation the need for remedial criteria of sufficient specificity to assure a school authority's compliance with its constitutional duty warrants a presumption against schools that are substantially disproportionate in their racial composition. Where the school authority's proposed plan for conversion from a dual to a unitary system contemplates the continued existence of some schools that are all or predominately of one race, they have the burden of showing that such school assignments are genuinely nondiscriminatory. The court should scrutinize such schools, and the burden upon the school authorities will be to satisfy the court that their racial composition is not the result of present or past discriminatory action on their part.

* * *

(3) Remedial Altering of Attendance Zones.

The maps submitted in these cases graphically demonstrate that one of the principal tools employed by school planners and by courts to break up the dual school system has been a frank—and sometimes drastic—gerrymandering of school districts and attendance zones. An additional step was pairing, "clustering," or "grouping" of schools with attendance assignments made deliberately to accomplish the transfer of Negro students out of formerly segregated Negro schools and transfer of white students to formerly all-Negro schools. More often than not, these zones are neither compact nor contiguous; indeed they may be on opposite ends of the city. As an interim corrective measure, this cannot be said to be beyond the broad remedial powers of a court.

* * *

No fixed or even substantially fixed guidelines can be established as to how far a court can go, but it must be recognized that there are limits. The objective is to dismantle the dual school system. "Racially neutral" assignment plans proposed by school authorities to a district court may be inadequate; such plans may fail to counteract the continuing effects of past school segregation resulting from discriminatory location of school sites or distortion of school size in order to achieve or maintain an artificial racial separation. When school authorities present a district court with a "loaded game board," affirmative action in the form of remedial altering of attendance zones is proper to achieve truly nondiscriminatory assignments. In short, an assignment plan is not acceptable simply because it appears to be neutral.

In this area, we must of necessity rely to a large extent, as this Court has for more than 16 years, on the informed judgment of the district courts in the first instance and on courts of appeals.

We hold that the pairing and grouping of non-contiguous school zones is a permissible tool and such action is to be considered in light of the objectives sought.   * * *

(4) Transportation of Students.

The scope of permissible transportation of students as an implement of a remedial decree has never been defined by this Court and by the very nature of the problem it cannot be defined with precision. No rigid guidelines as to student transportation can be given for application to the infinite variety of problems presented in thousands of situations. Bus transportation has been an integral part of the public education system for years, and was perhaps the single most important factor in the transition from the one-room schoolhouse to the consolidated school. Eighteen million of the nation's public school children, approximately 39% were transported to their schools by bus in 1969–1970 in all parts of the country.

The importance of bus transportation as a normal and accepted tool of educational policy is readily discernible in this and the companion case. The Charlotte school authorities did not purport to assign students on the basis of geographically drawn zones until 1965 and then they allowed almost unlimited transfer privileges. The District Court's conclusion that assignment of children to the school nearest their home serving their grade would not produce an effective dismantling of the dual system is supported by the record.

Thus the remedial techniques used in the District Court's order were within that court's power to provide equitable relief; implementation of the decree is well within the capacity of the school authority.

The decree provided that the buses used to implement the plan would operate on direct routes. Students would be picked up at schools near their homes and transported to the schools they were to attend. The trips for elementary school pupils average about seven miles and the District Court found that they would take "not over 35 minutes at the most." This system compares favorably with the transportation plan previously operated in Charlotte under which each day 23,600 students on all grade levels were transported an average of 15 miles one way for an average trip requiring over an hour. In these circumstances, we find no basis for holding that the local school authorities may not be required to employ bus transportation as one tool of school desegregation. Desegregation plans cannot be limited to the walk-in school.

An objection to transportation of students may have validity when the time or distance of travel is so great as to risk either the health of the children or significantly impinge on the educational process.   * * *

VI

The Court of Appeals, searching for a term to define the equitable remedial power of the district courts, used the term "reasonableness." In *Green,* supra, this Court used the term "feasible" and by implication, "workable," "effective," and "realistic" in the mandate to develop "a plan that promises realistically to work, and * * * to work *now.*" On the facts of this case, we are unable to conclude that the order of the District Court is not reasonable, feasible and workable. However, in seeking to define the scope of remedial power or the limits on remedial power of courts in an area as sensitive as we deal with here, words are poor instruments to convey the sense of basic fairness inherent in equity. Substance, not semantics, must govern, and we have sought to suggest the nature of limitations without frustrating the appropriate scope of equity.

At some point, these school authorities and others like them should have achieved full compliance with this Court's decision in *Brown I.* The systems will then be "unitary" in the sense required by our decisions in *Green* and *Alexander.*

It does not follow that the communities served by such systems will remain demographically stable, for in a growing, mobile society, few will do so. Neither school authorities nor district courts are constitutionally required to make year-by-year adjustments of the racial composition of student bodies once the affirmative duty to desegregate has been accomplished and racial discrimination through official action is eliminated from the system. This does not mean that federal courts are without power to deal with future problems; but in the absence of a showing that either the school authorities or some other agency of the State has deliberately attempted to fix or alter demographic patterns to affect the racial composition of the schools, further intervention by a district court should not be necessary.

* * *

Notes

1. The Court said, "Nothing in our national experience prior to 1955 prepared anyone for dealing with changes and adjustments of the magnitude and complexity encountered since then." Consider the extent to which the same may be said for other areas in education (such as aid to church-related schools, religion in the public schools, student rights, teacher rights, financing of schools) and in society (such as rights of accused criminals, reapportionment, women's rights).

2. In connection with presidential and congressional attempts to restrict "court-ordered busing" consider the last two paragraphs of section III of the opinion.

3. Study the Court's discussion of "racial quotas" and the possibility, desirability, and/or necessity of their use by federal courts in fashioning remedies to correct de jure segregation.

4. In one of the companion cases decided the same day, the Supreme Court referred to the paragraphs in Note 2 in reversing a holding by the Supreme Court of Georgia which had erroneously interpreted the provisions about busing

in the Civil Rights Act of 1964.   McDaniel v. Barresi, 402 U.S. 39, 91 S.Ct. 1287, 28 L.Ed.2d 582 (1971).   In another case the Court reversed part of a federal court judgment because "inadequate consideration was given to the possible use of bus transportation and split zoning" to correct segregation in Mobile County, Alabama.   Davis v. Board of School Commissioners of Mobile County, 402 U.S. 33, 91 S.Ct. 1289, 28 L.Ed.2d 577 (1971).

   5.   The Fourth and Fifth Circuits have held that a school district as part of a desegregation plan must provide free busing for students assigned to schools beyond normal walking distance from their homes.   Brewer v. Norfolk School Bd., 456 F.2d 943 (4 Cir.1972), cert. den. 406 U.S. 933, 92 S.Ct. 1778, 32 L.Ed.2d 136 (1972);   United States v. Greenwood Municipal Separate School Dist., 460 F.2d 1205 (5 Cir.1972).

[Case No. 131] Constitutional Standards Applicable to De Jure Segregation Not Imposed by Statute

KEYES v. SCHOOL DIST. NO. 1, DENVER, COLORADO

Supreme Court of the United States, 1973.
413 U.S. 189, 93 S.Ct. 2686, 37 L.Ed.2d 548.

MR. JUSTICE BRENNAN delivered the opinion of the Court.

This school desegregation case concerns the Denver, Colorado, school system.   That system has never been operated under a constitutional or statutory provision that mandated or permitted racial segregation in public education.   Rather, the gravamen of this action * * * is that respondent School Board alone, by use of various techniques such as the manipulation of student attendance zones, schoolsite selection and a neighborhood school policy, created or maintained racially or ethnically (or both racially and ethnically) segregated schools throughout the school district, entitling petitioners to a decree directing desegregation of the entire school district.

* * *

I

Before turning to the primary question we decide today, a word must be said about the * * * method of defining a "segregated" school. Denver is a tri-ethnic, as distinguished from a bi-racial, community. The over-all racial and ethnic composition of the Denver public schools is 66% Anglo, 14% Negro, and 20% Hispano.   * * * What is or is not a segregated school will necessarily depend on the facts of each particular case.   In addition to the racial and ethnic composition of a school's student body, other factors, such as the racial and ethnic composition of faculty and staff and the community and administration attitudes toward the school must be taken into consideration.   * * *

* * * [T]hough of different origins Negroes and Hispanos in Denver suffer identical discrimination in treatment when compared with the treatment afforded Anglo students.   In that circumstance, we think petitioners are entitled to have schools with a combined predominance of Negroes and Hispanos included in the category of "segregated" schools.

II

* * *

* * * Petitioners proved that for almost a decade after 1960 respondent School Board had engaged in an unconstitutional policy of deliberate racial segregation in the Park Hill schools. Indeed, the District Court found that "[b]etween 1960 and 1969 the Board's policies with respect to these northeast Denver schools show an undeviating purpose to isolate Negro students" in segregated schools "while preserving the Anglo character of [other] schools." This finding did not relate to an insubstantial or trivial fragment of the school system. On the contrary, respondent School Board was found guilty of following a deliberate segregation policy at schools attended, in 1969, by 37.69% of Denver's total Negro school population, including one-fourth of the Negro elementary pupils, over two-thirds of the Negro junior high pupils, and over two-fifths of the Negro high school pupils. In addition, there was uncontroverted evidence that teachers and staff had for years been assigned on the basis of a minority teacher to a minority school throughout the school system. Respondent argues, however, that a finding of state-imposed segregation as to a substantial portion of the school system can be viewed in isolation from the rest of the district, and that even if state-imposed segregation does exist in a substantial part of the Denver school system, it does not follow that the District Court could predicate on that fact a finding that the entire school system is a dual system. We do not agree. We have never suggested that plaintiffs in school desegregation cases must bear the burden of proving the elements of *de jure* segregation as to each and every school or each and every student within the school system. Rather, we have held that where plaintiffs prove that a current condition of segregated schooling exists within a school district where a dual system was compelled or authorized by statute at the time of our decision in *Brown I,* the State automatically assumes an affirmative duty "to effectuate a transition to a racially nondiscriminatory school system," that is, to eliminate from the public schools within their school system "all vestiges of state-imposed segregation."

This is not a case, however, where a statutory dual system has ever existed. Nevertheless, where plaintiffs prove that the school authorities have carried out a systematic program of segregation affecting a substantial portion of the students, schools, teachers, and facilities within the school system, it is only common sense to conclude that there exists a predicate for a finding of the existence of a dual school system. Several considerations support this conclusion. First, it is obvious that a practice of concentrating Negroes in certain schools by structuring attendance zones or designating "feeder" schools on the basis of race has the reciprocal effect of keeping other nearby schools predominantly white. Similarly, the practice of building a school—such as the Barrett Elementary School in this case—to a certain size and in a certain location, "with conscious knowledge that it would be a segregated school," has a substantial reciprocal effect on the racial composition of other nearby schools. So also, the use of mobile classrooms, the drafting of student transfer policies, the transportation of students, and the assignment of faculty and staff, on racially identifiable bases, have the clear effect of earmarking schools according to their racial composition, and this, in turn, together with the elements of student assignment and school construction, may have a profound reciprocal effect on the racial composition of residential neighborhoods within a metropolitan area, thereby causing further racial concentration within the schools. * * *

In short, common sense dictates the conclusion that racially inspired school board actions have an impact beyond the particular schools that are the subjects of those actions. This is not to say, of course, that there can never be a case in which the geographical structure of, or the natural boundaries within, a school district may have the effect of dividing the district into separate, identifiable and unrelated units. Such a determination is essentially a question of fact to be resolved by the trial court in the first instance, but such cases must be rare. In the absence of such a determination, proof of state-imposed segregation in a substantial portion of the district will suffice to support a finding by the trial court of the existence of a dual system. Of course, where that finding is made, as in cases involving statutory dual systems, the school authorities have an affirmative duty "to effectuate a transition to a racially nondiscriminatory school system."

III

* * *

On the question of segregative intent, petitioners presented evidence tending to show that the Board, through its actions over a period of years, intentionally created and maintained the segregated character of the core city schools. Respondents countered this evidence by arguing that the segregation in these schools is the result of a racially neutral "neighborhood school policy" and that the acts of which petitioners complain are explicable within the bounds of that policy. * * *

* * * Plainly, a finding of intentional segregation as to a portion of a school system is not devoid of probative value in assessing the school authorities' intent with respect to other parts of the same school system. On the contrary where, as here, the case involves one school board, a finding of intentional segregation on its part in one portion of a school system is highly relevant to the issue of the board's intent with respect to the other segregated schools in the system. This is merely an application of the well-settled evidentiary principle that "the prior doing of other similar acts, whether clearly a part of a scheme or not, is useful as reducing the possibility that the act in question was done with innocent intent." * * *

* * * [W]e hold that a finding of intentionally segregative school board actions in a meaningful portion of a school system, as in this case, creates a presumption that other segregated schooling within the system is not adventitious. It establishes, in other words, a prima facie case of unlawful segregative design on the part of school authorities, and shifts

to those authorities the burden of proving that other segregated schools within the system are not also the result of intentionally segregative actions. This is true even if it is determined that different areas of the school district should be viewed independently of each other because, even in that situation, there is high probability that where school authorities have effectuated an intentionally segregative policy in a meaningful portion of the school system, similar impermissible consider-ations have motivated their actions in other areas of the system. We emphasize that the differentiating factor between *de jure* segregation and so-called *de facto* segregation * * * is *purpose* or *intent* to segregate. Where school authorities have been found to have practiced purposeful segregation in part of a school system, they may be expected to oppose system-wide desegregation, as did the respondents in this case, on the ground that their purposefully segregative actions were isolated and individual events, thus leaving plaintiffs with the burden of proving otherwise. But at that point where an intentionally segregative policy is practiced in a meaningful or significant segment of a school system, as in this case, the school authorities cannot be heard to argue that plaintiffs have proved only "isolated and individual" unlawfully segregative ac-tions. In that circumstance, it is both fair and reasonable to require that the school authorities bear the burden of showing that their actions as to other segregated schools within the system were not also motivated by segregative intent.

* * *

Thus, respondent School Board having been found to have practiced deliberate racial segregation in schools attended by over one-third of the Negro school population, that crucial finding establishes a prima facie case of intentional segregation in the core city schools. In such case, respondent's neighborhood school policy is not to be determinative "simply because it appears to be neutral."

IV

In summary, the District Court on remand, *first,* will afford respon-dent School Board the opportunity to prove its contention that the Park Hill area is a separate, identifiable and unrelated section of the school district that should be treated as isolated from the rest of the district. If respondent School Board fails to prove that contention, the District Court, *second,* will determine whether respondent School Board's con-duct over almost a decade after 1960 in carrying out a policy of deliberate racial segregation in the Park Hill schools constitutes the entire school system a dual school system. If the District Court deter-mines that the Denver school system is a dual school system, respondent School Board has the affirmative duty to desegregate the entire system "root and branch." If the District Court determines, however, that the Denver school system is not a dual school system by reason of the Board's actions in Park Hill, the court, *third,* will afford respondent School Board the opportunity to rebut petitioners' prima facie case of intentional segregation in the core city schools raised by the finding of intentional segregation in the Park Hill schools. There, the Board's burden is to show that its policies and practices with respect to school-site location, school size, school renovations and additions, student-attendance zones, student assignment and transfer options, mobile class-room units, transportation of students, assignment of faculty and staff, etc., considered together and premised on the Board's so-called "neigh-borhood school" concept, either were not taken in effectuation of a policy to create or maintain segregation in the core city schools, or, if unsuc-cessful in that effort, were not factors in causing the existing condition of segregation in these schools. Considerations of "fairness" and "poli-cy" demand no less in light of the Board's intentionally segregative actions. If respondent Board fails to rebut petitioners' prima facie case, the District Court must, as in the case of Park Hill, decree all-out desegregation of the core city schools.

* * *

Notes

1. The vote was seven-to-one. Four Justices (Brennan, Stewart, Marshall, and Blackmun) expressly endorsed the view that there still was a substantial *constitutional* difference between de facto and de jure segregation. Justice Powell agreed with the disposition of the case but wrote an opinion in which he disagreed with the reasoning that perpetuated the de jure/de facto distinction. Justice Douglas joined the opinion of the Court, but agreed with Justice Powell that the time had come to drop the distinction "for each is the product of state actions or policies." Chief Justice Burger simply "concurred in the result." Justice Rehnquist wrote a dissenting opinion. Justice White did not participate.

2. Note the indicia for determining what is a "segregated" school (last paragraph).

3. Observe that the Court made no reference to constitutional duties of school boards in regard to de facto segregation. Its ruling extended the defini-tion of de jure segregation to cover the facts presented by the case.

4. On remand the District Court held that the evidence established Denver to be a dual school system. "Under the [Supreme] Court's definition it cannot be argued that within a unified school district such as that at bar there can exist conscious and knowing segregation in one area and innocent segregation in another." Keyes v. School Dist. No. 1, Denver, Colorado, 368 F.Supp. 207 (D.Colo.1973). This finding was affirmed, 521 F.2d 465 (10 Cir.1975).

5. Consider that the documented acts of de jure segregation did not begin until six years after *Brown I* was decided.

[Case No. 132] Constitutionality of Federally-Ordered Desegre-gation of Single District through Multidistrict Arrangements

MILLIKEN v. BRADLEY (I)

Supreme Court of the United States, 1974.
418 U.S. 717, 94 S.Ct. 3112, 41 L.Ed.2d 1069.

Mr. Chief Justice Burger delivered the opinion of the Court.

We granted certiorari in these consolidated cases to determine whether a federal court may impose a multidistrict, areawide remedy to a single district *de jure* segregation problem absent any finding that the other included school districts have failed to operate unitary school systems within their districts, absent any claim or finding that the boundary lines of any affected school district were established with the purpose of fostering racial segregation in public schools, absent any finding that the included districts committed acts which effected segregation within the other districts, and absent a meaningful opportunity for the included neighboring school districts to present evidence or be heard on the propriety of a multidistrict remedy or on the question of constitutional violations by those neighboring districts.

I

* * *

The District Court found that the Detroit Board of Education created and maintained optional attendance zones within Detroit neighborhoods undergoing racial transition and between high school attendance areas of opposite predominant racial compositions. These zones, the court found, had the "natural, probable, foreseeable and actual effect" of allowing White pupils to escape identifiably Negro schools. Similarly, the District Court found that Detroit school attendance zones had been drawn along north-south boundary lines despite the Detroit Board's awareness that drawing boundary lines in an east-west direction would result in significantly greater desegregation. * * *

The District Court found that in the operation of its school transportation program, which was designed to relieve overcrowding, the Detroit Board had admittedly bused Negro Detroit pupils to predominantly Negro schools which were beyond or away from closer White schools with available space. This practice was found to have continued in recent years despite the Detroit Board's avowed policy, adopted in 1967, of utilizing transportation to increase desegregation. * * *

With respect to the Detroit Board of Education's practices in school construction, the District Court found that Detroit school construction generally tended to have segregative effect with the great majority of schools being built in either overwhelmingly all-Negro or all-white neighborhoods so that the new schools opened as predominantly one race schools. * * *

The District Court also found that the State of Michigan had committed several constitutional violations with respect to the exercise of its general responsibility for, and supervision of, public education. The State, for example, was found to have failed, until the 1971 Session of the Michigan Legislature, to provide authorization or funds for the transportation of pupils within Detroit regardless of their poverty or distance from the school to which they were assigned; during this same period the State provided many neighboring, mostly White, suburban districts the full range of state supported transportation.

* * *

Turning to the question of an appropriate remedy for these several constitutional violations, the District Court * * * proceeded to order the

Detroit Board of Education to submit desegregation plans limited to the segregation problems found to be existing within the city of Detroit. At the same time, however, the state defendants were directed to submit desegregation plans encompassing the three-county metropolitan area despite the fact that the school districts of these three counties were not parties to the action and despite the fact that there had been no claim that these outlying counties, encompassing some 85 separate school districts, had committed constitutional violations. * * *

* * *

* * * [Eventually] the court designated 53 of the 85 suburban school districts plus Detroit as the "desegregation area" and appointed a panel to prepare and submit "an effective desegregation plan" for the Detroit schools [276,000 students] that would encompass the entire desegregation area [503,000 additional students]. * * *

* * *

The Court of Appeals * * * agreed with the District Court that "any less comprehensive a solution than a metropolitan area plan would result in an all black school system immediately surrounded by practically all white suburban school systems, with an overwhelming white majority population in the total metropolitan area." The court went on to state that it could "[not] see how such segregation can be any less harmful to the minority students than if the same result were accomplished within one school district."

Accordingly, the Court of Appeals concluded that "the only feasible desegregation plan involves the crossing of the boundary lines between the Detroit School District and adjacent or nearby school districts for the limited purpose of providing an effective desegregation plan." It reasoned that such a plan would be appropriate because of the State's violations, and could be implemented because of the State's authority to control local school districts. * * *

* * *

II

* * *

Proceeding from these basic principles [from prior desegregation cases], we first note that in the District Court the complainants sought a remedy aimed at the *condition* alleged to offend the Constitution—the segregation within the Detroit City School District. * * * Thereafter, however, the District Court abruptly rejected the proposed Detroit-only plans on the ground that "while it would provide a racial mix more in keeping with the Black-White proportions of the student population, [it] would accentuate the racial identifiability of the [Detroit] district as a Black school system, and would not accomplish desegregation." * * * Consequently, the court reasoned, it was imperative to "look beyond the limits of the Detroit school district for a solution to the problem of segregation in the Detroit schools * * *" since "[s]chool district lines are simply matters of political convenience and may not be used to deny constitutional rights." Accordingly, the District Court proceeded to redefine the relevant area to include areas of predominantly White pupil population in order to ensure that "upon implementation, no school, grade or classroom [would be] substantially disproportionate to the overall racial composition" of the entire metropolitan area.

* * *

Viewing the record as a whole, it seems clear that the District Court and the Court of Appeals shifted the primary focus from a Detroit remedy to the metropolitan area only because of their conclusion that total desegregation of Detroit would not produce the racial balance which they perceived as desirable. Both courts proceeded on an assumption that the Detroit schools could not be truly desegregated—in their view of what constituted desegregation—unless the racial composition of the student body of each school substantially reflected the racial composition of the population of the metropolitan area as a whole. The metropolitan area was then defined as Detroit plus 53 of the outlying school districts. * * *

* * *

Here the District Court's approach to what constituted "actual desegregation" raises the fundamental question * * * as to the circumstances in which a federal court may order desegregation relief that embraces more than a single school district. The court's analytical starting point was its conclusion that school district lines are no more than arbitrary lines on a map "drawn for political convenience." Boundary lines may be bridged where there has been a constitutional violation calling for interdistrict relief, but, the notion that school district lines may be casually ignored or treated as a mere administrative convenience is contrary to the history of public education in our country. No single tradition in public education is more deeply rooted than local control over the operation of schools; local autonomy has long been thought essential both to the maintenance of community concern and support for public schools and to quality of the educational process. * * *

The Michigan educational structure involved in this case, in common with most States, provides for a large measure of local control and a review of the scope and character of these local powers indicates the extent to which the inter-district remedy approved by the two courts could disrupt and alter the structure of public education in Michigan. The metropolitan remedy would require, in effect, consolidation of 54 independent school districts historically administered as separate units into a vast new super school district. * * * Entirely apart from the logistical and other serious problems attending large-scale transportation of students, the consolidation would give rise to an array of other problems in financing and operating this new school system. Some of the more obvious questions would be: What would be the status and authority of the present popularly elected school boards? Would the children of Detroit be within the jurisdiction and operating control of a school board elected by the parents and residents of other districts? What board or boards would levy taxes for school operations in these 54 districts constituting the consolidated metropolitan area? What provisions could be made for assuring substantial equality in tax levies among the 54 districts, if this were deemed requisite? What provisions would be made for financing? Would the validity of long-term bonds be jeopardized unless approved by all of the component districts as well as the State? What body would determine that portion of the curricula now left to the discretion of local school boards? Who would establish attendance zones, purchase school equipment, locate and construct new schools, and indeed attend to all the myriad day-to-day decisions that are necessary to school operations affecting potentially more than three quarters of a million pupils? * * *

It may be suggested that all of these vital operational problems are yet to be resolved by the District Court * * *. But it is obvious from the scope of the inter-district remedy itself that absent a complete restructuring of the laws of Michigan relating to school districts the District Court will become first, a *de facto* "legislative authority" to resolve these complex questions, and then the "school superintendent" for the entire area. This is a task which few, if any, judges are qualified to perform and one which would deprive the people of control of schools through their elected representatives.

Of course, no state law is above the Constitution. School district lines and the present laws with respect to local control, are not sacrosanct and if they conflict with the Fourteenth Amendment federal courts have a duty to prescribe appropriate remedies. * * * But our prior holdings have been confined to violations and remedies within a single school district. We therefore turn to address, for the first time, the validity of a remedy mandating cross-district or inter-district consolidation to remedy a condition of segregation found to exist in only one district.

The controlling principle consistently expounded in our holdings is that the scope of the remedy is determined by the nature and extent of the constitutional violation. Before the boundaries of separate and autonomous school districts may be set aside by consolidating the separate units for remedial purposes or by imposing a cross-district remedy, it must first be shown that there has been a constitutional violation within one district that produces a significant segregative effect in another district. Specifically it must be shown that racially discriminatory acts of the state or local school districts, or of a single school district have been a substantial cause of inter-district segregation. Thus an inter-district remedy might be in order where the racially discriminatory acts of one or more school districts caused racial segregation in an adjacent district, or where district lines have been deliberately drawn on the basis of race. In such circumstances an inter-district remedy would be appropriate to eliminate the inter-district segregation directly caused by the constitutional violation. Conversely, without an inter-district violation and inter-district effect, there is no constitutional wrong calling for an inter-district remedy.

The record before us, voluminous as it is, contains evidence of *de jure* segregated conditions only in the Detroit schools; indeed, that was the theory on which the litigation was initially based and on which the District Court took evidence. * * *

* * *

The constitutional right of the Negro respondents residing in Detroit is to attend a unitary school system in that district. Unless petitioners drew the district lines in a discriminatory fashion, or arranged for White students residing in the Detroit district to attend schools in Oakland and Macomb Counties, they were under no constitutional duty to make provisions for Negro students to do so. * * *

III

We recognize that the six-volume record presently under consideration contains language and some specific incidental findings thought by the District Court to afford a basis for interdistrict relief. However, these comparatively isolated findings and brief comments concern only one possible inter-district violation and are found in the context of a proceeding that, as the District Court conceded, included no proofs of segregation practiced by any of the 85 suburban school districts surrounding Detroit. * * *

* * *

IV

* * *

We conclude that the relief ordered by the District Court and affirmed by the Court of Appeals was based upon an erroneous standard and was unsupported by record evidence that acts of the outlying districts affected the discrimination found to exist in the schools of Detroit. Accordingly, the judgment of the Court of Appeals is reversed and the case is remanded for further proceedings consistent with this opinion leading to prompt formulation of a decree directed to eliminating the segregation found to exist in Detroit city schools, a remedy which has been delayed since 1970.

* * *

Notes

1. Justices Douglas, Brennan, White, and Marshall dissented. Justice Stewart wrote a concurring opinion in which he emphasized, "in view of some of the extravagant language of the dissenting opinions," that the present decision did not preclude an inter-district remedy in some other factual situation. As referenced in the textual part of this chapter, some such remedies have been ordered subsequent to this decision.

2. In Haney v. County Bd. of Educ. of Sevier County [Arkansas], 429 F.2d 364 (8 Cir.1970), the court ordered consolidation of uniracial school districts that

had been continued in existence following *Brown*. Would this order stand under the present decision?

3. Observe the emphasis of the Court on "local control" of education. The dissenters believed that, since the state is responsible for education, the state could be ordered to correct the segregation with all the resources of the state regardless of where it occurred and which officials caused it. What, if any, is the relationship between control of the schools and segregation?

4. How do you react to the emphases of the Court on the lack of evidence of segregation outside of Detroit and on the fact the other districts were not allowed to be heard on the "propriety of a multidistrict remedy?"

5. Notice how the Court defined "the constitutional right of the Negro respondents residing in Detroit." See Case No. 133 regarding the remedy ordered for desegregation of Detroit schools.

[Case No. 133] Power of Federal Courts to Correct De Jure Segregation—Specific Remedies

MILLIKEN v. BRADLEY (II)

Supreme Court of the United States, 1977.
433 U.S. 267, 97 S.Ct. 2749, 53 L.Ed.2d 745.

Mr. Chief Justice Burger delivered the opinion of the Court.

We granted certiorari in this case to consider two questions concerning the remedial powers of federal district courts in school desegregation cases, namely, whether a District Court can, as part of a desegregation decree, order compensatory or remedial educational programs for schoolchildren who have been subjected to past acts of *de jure* segregation, and whether, consistent with the Eleventh Amendment, a federal court can require state officials found responsible for constitutional violations to bear part of the costs of those programs.

[The Court reviewed its 1974 decision in this case (Case No. 132).]

Due to the intervening death of Judge Stephen J. Roth, who had presided over the litigation from the outset, the case on remand was reassigned to Judge Robert E. DeMascio. Judge DeMascio promptly ordered respondent Bradley and the Detroit Board to submit desegregation plans limited to the Detroit school system. On April 1, 1975, both parties submitted their proposed plans. * * *

In addition to student reassignments, the Board's plan called for implementation of 13 remedial or compensatory programs, referred to in the record as "educational components." These compensatory programs, which were proposed in addition to the plan's provisions for magnet schools and vocational high schools, included three of the four components at issue in this case—in-service training for teachers and administrators, guidance and counseling programs, and revised testing procedures. Pursuant to the District Court's direction, the State Department of Education on April 21, 1975, submitted a critique of the Detroit Board's desegregation plan; in its report, the Department opined that, although "[i]t is possible that none of the thirteen 'quality education' components is essential * * * to correct the constitutional violation * * * ", eight of the 13 proposed programs nonetheless deserved special consideration in the desegregation setting. Of particular relevance here, the State Board said:

"Within the context of effectuating a pupil desegregation plan, the in-service training [and] guidance and counseling * * * components appear to deserve special emphasis."

After receiving the State Board's critique, the District Court conducted extensive hearings on the two plans over a two-month period. Substantial testimony was adduced with respect to the proposed educational components, including testimony by petitioners' expert witnesses. Based on this evidence and on reports of court-appointed experts, the District Court on August 11, 1975, approved, in principle, the Detroit Board's inclusion of remedial and compensatory educational components in the desegregation plan. * * *

The District Court expressly found that the two components of testing and counseling, as then administered in Detroit's schools, were infected with the discriminatory bias of a segregated school system. * * * The District Court also found that, to make desegregation work, it was necessary to include remedial reading programs and in-service training for teachers and administrators * * *.

Having established these general principles, the District Court formulated several "remedial guidelines" to govern the Detroit Board's development of a final plan. Declining "to substitute its authority for the authority of elected state and local officials to decide which educational components are beneficial to the school community," the District Judge laid down the following guidelines with respect to each of the four educational components at issue here:

(a) *Reading.* Concluding that "[t]here is no educational component more directly associated with the process of desegregation than reading," the District Court directed the General Superintendent of Detroit's schools to institute a remedial reading and communications skills program "[t]o eradicate the effects of past discrimination * * *." The content of the required program was not prescribed by the court; rather, formulation and implementation of the program was left to the Superintendent and to a committee to be selected by him.

(b) *In-Service Training.* The court also directed the Detroit Board to formulate a comprehensive in-service teacher training program, an element "essential to a system undergoing desegregation." In the District Court's view, an in-service training program for teachers and administrators, to train professional and instructional personnel to cope with the desegregation process in Detroit, would tend to ensure that all students in a desegregated system would be treated equally by teachers and administrators able, by virtue of special training, to cope with special problems presented by desegregation, and thereby facilitate Detroit's conversion to a unitary system.

(c) *Testing.* Because it found, based on record evidence, that Negro children "are especially affected by biased testing procedures," the

District Court determined that, frequently, minority students in Detroit were adversely affected by discriminatory testing procedures. Unless the school system's tests were administered in a way "free from racial, ethnic and cultural bias," the District Court concluded that Negro children in Detroit might thereafter be impeded in their educational growth. Accordingly, the court directed the Detroit Board and the State Department of Education to institute a testing program along the lines proposed by the local school board in its original desegregation plan.

(d) *Counseling and Career Guidance.* Finally, the District Court addressed what expert witnesses had described as psychological pressures on Detroit's students in a system undergoing desegregation. Counselors were required, the court concluded, both to deal with the numerous problems and tensions arising in the change from Detroit's dual system, and, more concretely, to counsel students concerning the new vocational and technical school programs available under the plan through the cooperation of state and local officials.

Nine months later, on May 11, 1976, the District Court entered its final order. Emphasizing that it had "been careful to order only what is essential for a school district undergoing desegregation," the court ordered the Detroit Board and the state defendants to institute comprehensive programs as to the four educational components by the start of the September 1976 school term. The cost of these four programs, the court concluded, was to be equally borne by the Detroit School Board and the State. To carry out this cost-sharing, the court directed the local board to calculate its highest budget allocation in any prior year for the several educational programs and, from that base, any excess cost attributable to the desegregation plan was to be paid equally by the two groups of defendants responsible for prior constitutional violations, i.e., the Detroit Board and the state defendants.

* * *

This Court has not previously addressed directly the question whether federal courts can order remedial education programs as part of a school desegregation decree. However, the general principles governing our resolution of this issue are well settled by the prior decisions of this Court. In the first case concerning federal courts' remedial powers in eliminating *de jure* school segregation, the Court laid down the basic rule which governs to this day: "In fashioning and effectuating the [desegregation] decrees, the courts will be guided by equitable principles." Brown v. Board of Education (II).

Application of those "equitable principles," we have held, requires federal courts to focus upon three factors. In the first place, like other equitable remedies, the nature of the desegregation remedy is to be determined by the nature and scope of the constitutional violation. Swann v. Charlotte-Mecklenburg Board of Education. The remedy must therefore be related to "the *condition* alleged to offend the Constitution * * *." *Milliken I.* Second, the decree must indeed be *remedial* in nature, that is, it must be designed as nearly as possible "to restore the victims of discriminatory conduct to the position they would have occupied in the absence of such conduct." Third, the federal courts in devising a remedy must take into account the interests of state and local authorities in managing their own affairs, consistent with the Constitution. In *Brown II* the Court squarely held that "[s]chool authorities have the *primary* responsibility for elucidating, assessing, and solving these problems * * *." If, however, "school authorities fail in their affirmative obligations * * * judicial authority may be invoked." *Swann.* Once invoked, "the scope of a district court's equitable powers to remedy past wrongs is broad, for breadth and flexibility are inherent in equitable remedies." *Swann.*

In challenging the order before us, petitioners do not specifically question that the District Court's mandated programs are designed, as nearly as practicable, to restore the schoolchildren of Detroit to a position they would have enjoyed absent constitutional violations by state and local officials. And, petitioners do not contend, nor could they, that the prerogatives of the Detroit School Board have been abrogated by the decree, since of course the Detroit School Board itself proposed incorporation of these programs in the first place. Petitioners' sole contention is that, under *Swann,* the District Court's order exceeds the scope of the constitutional violation. Invoking our holding in *Milliken I* petitioners claim that, since the constitutional violation found by the District Court was the unlawful segregation of students on the basis of race, the court's decree must be limited to remedying unlawful pupil assignments. This contention misconceives the principle petitioners seek to invoke, and we reject their argument.

The well-settled principle that the nature and scope of the remedy are to be determined by the violation means simply that federal court decrees must directly address and relate to the constitutional violation itself. Because of this inherent limitation upon federal judicial authority, federal court decrees exceed appropriate limits if they are aimed at eliminating a condition that does not violate the Constitution or does not flow from such a violation, or if they are imposed upon governmental units that were neither involved in nor affected by the constitutional violation, as in *Milliken I,* supra. But where, as here, a constitutional violation has been found, the remedy does not "exceed" the violation if the remedy is tailored to cure the "*condition* that offends the Constitution." *Milliken I.*

The "condition" offending the Constitution is Detroit's *de jure* segregated school system, which was so pervasively and persistently segregated that the District Court found that the need for the educational components flowed directly from constitutional violations by both state and local officials. These specific educational remedies, although normally left to the discretion of the elected school board and professional educators, were deemed necessary to restore the victims of discriminatory conduct to the position they would have enjoyed in terms of education had these four components been provided in a nondiscriminatory manner in a school system free from pervasive *de jure* racial segregation.

In the first case invalidating a *de jure* system, a unanimous Court, speaking through Chief Justice Warren, held in *Brown I:* "Separate educational facilities are inherently unequal." And in United States v. Montgomery County Board of Education, the Court concerned itself not with pupil assignment, but with the desegregation of faculty and staff as part of the process of dismantling a dual system. In doing so, the Court, there speaking through Mr. Justice Black, focused on the reason for judicial concerns going beyond pupil assignment: "The dispute * * * deals with faculty and staff desegregation, a goal that we have recognized to be an important aspect of *the basic task of achieving a public school system wholly free from racial discrimination.*"

Montgomery County therefore stands firmly for the proposition that matters other than pupil assignment must on occasion be addressed by federal courts to eliminate the effects of prior segregation. Similarly, in *Swann* we reaffirmed the principle that "existing policy and practice with regard to faculty, staff, transportation, extracurricular activities, and facilities were among the most important indicia of a segregated system." In a word, discriminatory student assignment policies can themselves manifest and breed other inequalities built into a dual system founded on racial discrimination. Federal courts need not, and cannot, close their eyes to inequalities, shown by the record, which flow from a longstanding segregated system.

In light of the mandate of *Brown I* and *Brown II,* federal courts have, over the years, often required the inclusion of remedial programs in desegregation plans to overcome the inequalities inherent in dual school systems.   * * *

* * *

* * * On this record * * * we are bound to conclude that the decree before us was aptly tailored to remedy the consequences of the constitutional violation. Children who have been thus educationally and culturally set apart from the larger community will inevitably acquire habits of speech, conduct, and attitudes reflecting their cultural isolation. They are likely to acquire speech habits, for example, which vary from the environment in which they must ultimately function and compete, if they are to enter and be a part of that community. This is not peculiar to race; in this setting, it can affect any children who, as a group, are isolated by force of law from the mainstream.

Pupil assignment alone does not automatically remedy the impact of previous, unlawful educational isolation; the consequences linger and can be dealt with only by independent measures.   * * *

Petitioners also contend that the District Court's order, even if otherwise proper, violates the Eleventh Amendment.   * * *

The decree to share the future costs of educational components in this case fits squarely within the prospective-compliance exception * * *. That exception * * * permits federal courts to enjoin state officials to conform their conduct to requirements of federal law, notwithstanding a direct and substantial impact on the state treasury. The order challenged here does no more than that. The decree requires state officials, held responsible for unconstitutional conduct, in findings which are not challenged, to eliminate a *de jure* segregated school system. More precisely, the burden of state officials is that set forth in *Swann*— to take the necessary steps "to eliminate from the public schools all vestiges of state-imposed segregation." The educational components, which the District Court ordered into effect *prospectively,* are plainly designed to wipe out continuing conditions of inequality produced by the inherently unequal dual school system long maintained by Detroit.

* * * We * * * hold that such prospective relief is not barred by the Eleventh Amendment.

* * *

Notes

1. This was a unanimous decision. The former decision in this litigation is Case No. 132. See also footnote 86 in this chapter.

2. Lower federal courts frequently have ordered specific remedies other than busing or other pupil assignment techniques to correct the effects of de jure segregation. This was the first time the Supreme Court in an opinion considered remedies other than pupil or teacher reassignments. Also this was the first time the Court dealt with the subject of payment by the state itself for services mandatorily added to correct de jure segregation in a school district.

3. Increasingly in complicated technical cases trial courts will appoint "experts" (and/or referees or masters who take testimony and recommend actions to the court) to assist the court in interpreting technical evidence. Notice that the District Court in this case did so.

4. Do you agree with the guidelines laid down by the District Court? To what extent, if at all, did the District Court, despite its disclaimer, substitute its authority for that of the state and local education officials in deciding which programs were beneficial to the school community? Was there likely to be effective desegregation without the remedies here contested?

[Case No. 134]   Layoffs during Efforts to Correct Faculty Segregation

ARTHUR v. NYQUIST

United States Court of Appeals, Second Circuit, 1983.
712 F.2d 816.

NEWMAN, CIRCUIT JUDGE: This appeal concerns primarily the degree to which a district court can impair the seniority rights of teachers in order to eliminate the vestiges of racial segregation within the faculty of a public school system and to vindicate the school children's right to a desegregated education. The Buffalo Teachers Federation (Federation) challenges a remedial plan * * *. As part of that plan, the [District] Court approved an elaborate remedy designed to achieve a goal of twenty-one percent minority teachers in all teaching areas through a race-conscious system for hiring and laying off teachers. Although we find the District Court's plan to be basically sound, we conclude that in one respect the Court's remedy is unnecessarily harsh. We therefore affirm in part, reverse in part, and remand for the entry of a modified order.

I.

In April 1976, the District Court found the Buffalo Board of Education responsible for intentionally causing and maintaining a segregated school system. Among the Board's discriminatory policies was a purposeful program "that has segregated, and was intended to segregate, the teacher and administrative staffs in the Buffalo public schools." Between 1967 and 1973, minority employees had held roughly ten to twelve percent of all staff positions, even though the minority population of Buffalo was twenty-one percent, according to the 1970 Census. Moreover, a disproportionate share of the minority staff was assigned to schools with predominantly minority student bodies.

* * *

The District Court's remedial plan affects the contractual and statutory rights of the Federation's majority members in numerous ways. First, the plan denies some long-term "temporary" teachers their contractual right to be offered yearly appointments on the basis of their years of experience within the school system. Second, the plan abridges the rights of applicants on the current eligibility lists by limiting the number of available probationary positions and yearly temporary positions to which they have statutory and contractual claims. Finally and most seriously, the plan undercuts the job security of majority probationary and permanent teachers. Under the plan, these tenure-track teachers were more likely to be laid off during force reductions because the plan overrode the "last-in, first-out" seniority system created by statute. In addition, once a majority tenure-track teacher is laid off, the plan makes it more difficult for that teacher to be rehired. Under statute and contract, excessed teachers on preferred eligibility lists are entitled to whatever temporary or tenure-track positions become available based on seniority. Under the plan, however, all appointments to temporary and permanent positions are to be made under the one-to-one formula. Consequently, under the plan, an excessed tenured majority member of the faculty, already laid off in contravention of seniority, might be denied reemployment in favor of a minority applicant with no experience.

II.

During the liability portion of this case, the District Court found that the Board of Education had consistently hired a disproportionately small percentage of minority staff members, and had intentionally assigned these minorities to schools with large minority student bodies. Such discriminatory policies are important indicia of a segregated school system, and the Supreme Court has repeatedly encouraged district courts presiding over school desegregation cases to remedy the effects of these practices. The question raised by this appeal is whether the District Court exceeded its equitable powers by the means chosen to desegregate the faculty of the Buffalo school system.

The Federation argues that the District Court's remedial plan is invalid simply because it infringes upon statutory and contractual rights of majority teachers who played no role in the Board's past practices of segregation. We reject this argument. In Milliken v. Bradley (*Milliken I*), the Supreme Court ruled that state laws cannot stand in the way of full remedies for constitutional violations. Here, the fact that the Federation has a seniority system should not be allowed to prevent or inordinately delay the achievement of a fully desegregated school system for the children of Buffalo.

Nor was the District Court's authority impaired, as the Federation contends, by the Supreme Court's decisions in [cases brought under Title VII]. In those Title VII cases, the Supreme Court ruled that bona fide seniority systems must be honored unless there has been a finding of actual intent to discriminate. Here, however, the suit was brought to remedy violations of the Constitution rather than Title VII, and the District Court made a finding of intentional discrimination in the Board's maintenance of a segregated school system. We therefore agree with the District Court that it had the authority to curtail the seniority rights of the Federation's membership in order to vindicate the constitutional rights of the minority children in the Buffalo school system. * * * Once a local board of education has been found to have employed staff hiring practices that contribute to a racially segregated school system, the District Court has the power to remedy those practices and to override seniority systems that perpetuate those practices.

However, a district court should not exercise this power excessively. It must balance "individual and collective interests." Moreover, "a federal court is required to tailor 'the scope of the remedy' to fit 'the nature and extent of the constitutional violation.'" In particular, when a district court is shaping relief that will infringe upon seniority rights, the court must take care that the relief is necessary to correct constitutional violations.

Applying these standards, we find the District Court's remedial plan to be largely acceptable. Certainly the District Court's imposition of "one-to-one" hiring goals was permissible. The Court set these goals only after the Board failed to increase significantly the number of minority teachers in the system. Indisputably, these goals have the effect of delaying the appointment of some majority candidates on the eligibility lists and preventing certain long-term "temporary" teachers from being rehired. But the District Court was aware of these effects, and nevertheless concluded that the plaintiffs' interests in having a fully desegregated faculty in the foreseeable future justified the hardship to the teachers. We agree with the District Court that the expectations of the temporary teachers and the candidates on the eligibility lists were not so strong as to preclude the use of "one-to-one" hiring.

* * *

A closer question is raised by the District Court's decision to order that future layoffs be made on a percentage basis to guarantee maintenance of the existing ratio of minority to majority teachers. Strong interests lie on both sides. Probationary and permanent teachers have a statutorily established expectation that layoffs will be based on seniority. However, the effect of such layoffs would constitute a serious setback for desegregation of the school system. Between 1976 and 1981, the percentage of minority teachers in the Buffalo system increased from eight percent to fourteen percent. Seniority based layoffs would erode much of this progress and put the system even further away from the District Court's twenty-one percent target. Faced with this conflict, the District Court concluded that percentage layoffs presented an equitable solution. Although some majority teachers who would otherwise have retained their jobs might be fired under the Court's plan, minority teachers would also bear some burden during cutbacks, and no tenured faculty members—either majority or minority—would be released until all probationary employees in the particular area were fired. In this way, the children in the school district would enjoy the benefits of a significantly, if not wholly, integrated faculty.

Considering the intractability of the problem before the District Court, we find its use of percentage layoffs acceptable. We agree with the First Circuit that percentage layoffs present a permissible means of achieving constitutionally mandated objectives despite contractually or statutorily established seniority systems during periods of staff reduction. See Morgan v. O'Bryant, 671 F.2d 23 (1 Cir. 1982), cert. den. 459 U.S. 827, 103 S.Ct. 62, 74 L.Ed.2d 64 (1982). Although we sympathize with the individual teachers who suffered because of percentage layoffs, theirs is a burden that must be borne if we are to "eliminate root and branch" the segregated school system that once existed in Buffalo.

The District Court's plan, however, does seem needlessly harsh in its treatment of laid-off probationary and permanent teachers. Under statute and collective bargaining agreement, these excessed teachers should be placed on preferred eligibility lists and given first chance, according to their seniority, at whatever temporary or permanent positions become available. However, under the District Court's scheme, these excessed teachers would be entitled to these positions only within the constraints of the Court's "one-to-one" hiring goals. While we can appreciate the District Court's desire to continue to make progress toward the twenty-one percent target even while majority excessed teachers remain on the preferred eligibility lists, we nevertheless find this aspect of the remedial plan unjustified.

Although the District Court found the lack of minority teachers to be a serious problem deserving a prompt remedy, the Court did not determine that relief could or should be instantaneous. For example, there is no reason to think that, in the absence of layoffs, the District Court would have ordered the Board to fire tenured majority teachers and replace them with minority candidates. We do not believe that the Court was justified in using firings precipitated by fiscal crises to achieve the same result. Without an explicit finding of demonstrable necessity, the District Court should not have impaired the rehiring rights of excessed probationary and tenured teachers.

On remand, the District Court should modify its remedial plan along the following lines. Layoffs may still be conducted on a percentage basis for each tenure area, but the laid-off teachers should be placed on preferred eligibility lists as they are laid off. Excessed teachers on preferred eligibility lists should then enjoy the same rights to new temporary and permanent positions that they are guaranteed by statute and collective bargaining agreement. This modification should eventually establish percentage rehiring equivalent to the percentage layoffs established in the District Court's plan, although majority excessed teachers with more seniority than minority excessed teachers will more quickly be rehired. We trust that the parties will assist the District Court in making these modifications.

* * *

Notes

1. The Supreme Court denied certiorari on this case, 467 U.S. 1259, 104 S.Ct. 3555, 82 L.Ed.2d 856 (1984).

2. Observe that it is the constitutional right of children to a desegregated education that forms the cornerstone for the remedial order. Title VII's recognition of bona fide seniority plans is irrelevant here, for this is a constitutional case.

3. The concept of constructive seniority (the seniority one would have if he had not been discriminated against) can be helpful in individual instances when one can establish a fixed point at which he suffered the discriminatory action. Remedying discrimination against a class whose membership changes is exceedingly difficult.

4. How do you react to the modifications ordered by this court?

5. In Offermann v. Nitkowski, 378 F.2d 22 (2 Cir.1967), the Court of Appeals, Second Circuit, had held that actions by Buffalo school authorities "to undo" de facto segregation were not unconstitutional because race was considered in drawing attendance zones and assigning students. This was before it was proved that the segregation was in reality de jure.

[Case No. 135] Duty of Board to Correct De Facto Segregation

DEAL v. CINCINNATI BD. OF EDUC.

United States Court of Appeals, Sixth Circuit, 1966.
369 F.2d 55.

WEICK, CHIEF JUDGE. The suit in the District Court was a class action against the Board of Education of the City of Cincinnati, brought by the parents and next friends of Negro pupils enrolled in the public schools of the city, to enjoin the operation of allegedly racially segregated public schools, to enjoin the construction of new schools on sites which would increase and harden alleged existing patterns of racial segregation, and for declaratory and other relief.

The Board denied that it created, operated or maintained racially segregated schools, and alleged that the only genuine issue in the case was whether it violated the constitutional rights of the plaintiffs by refusing to adopt and enforce an affirmative policy of balancing the races in the Cincinnati Public School System. * * *

Was There A Constitutional Duty On The Part Of The Board To Balance The Races In The Cincinnati Public Schools Where The Imbalance Was Not Caused By Any Act Of Discrimination On Its Part?

At the outset it should be pointed out that the State of Ohio abolished segregation in the public schools on February 22, 1887, * * *.

The so-called neighborhood plan for the location of public schools is authorized by statute under which Ohio School Boards are required to—

" * * * provide for the free education of the youth of school age within the district under its jurisdiction, at such places as will be convenient for the attendance of the largest number thereof."

We think the legislature had the power to enact this statute. The Cincinnati Board of Education has complied with it.

Appellants contend that the maintenance of a public school system in which racial imbalance exists is a violation of their constitutional right to the equal protection of the law. They assert that because the Negro student population is not spread uniformly throughout the Cincinnati school system, without a showing of deliberate discrimination or even racial classification, there is a duty of constitutional dimensions imposed on the school officials to eliminate the imbalance. Appellants claim that it is harmful to Negro children to attend a racially imbalanced school and this fact alone deprives them of equal educational opportunity.

The essence of the *Brown* decision was that the Fourteenth Amendment does not allow the state to classify its citizens differently solely because of their race. While the detrimental impact of compulsory segregation on the children of the minority race was referred to by the Court, it was not indispensable to the decision. Rather, the Court held that segregation of the races was an arbitrary exercise of governmental power inconsistent with the requirements of the Constitution.

A finding of educational or other harm is not essential to strike down enforced segregation. This is shown by many subsequent cases nullifying separate facilities of all kinds with no evidence of harm.

* * *

The principle thus established in our law is that the state may not erect irrelevant barriers to restrict the full play of individual choice in any sector of society. Since it is freedom of choice that is to be protected, it is not necessary that any particular harm be established if it is shown that the range of individual options had been constricted without the high degree of justification which the Constitution requires. It is harm enough that a citizen is arbitrarily denied choices open to his fellows.

Conversely, a showing of harm alone is not enough to invoke the remedial powers of the law. If the state or any of its agencies has not adopted impermissible racial criteria in its treatment of individuals, then there is no violation of the Constitution. If factors outside the schools operate to deprive some children of some of the existing choices, the school board is certainly not responsible therefor.

Appellants, however, argue that the state must take affirmative steps to balance the schools to counteract the variety of private pressures that now operate to restrict the range of choices presented to each school child. Such a theory of constitutional duty would destroy the well-settled principle that the Fourteenth Amendment governs only state action. Under such a theory, all action would be state action, either because the state itself had moved directly, or because some private person had acted and thereby created the supposed duty of the state to counteract any consequences.

The standard to be applied is "equal educational opportunity". The Court in *Brown* cast its decision thus because it recognized that it was both unnecessary and impossible to require that each child come through the complex process of modern education with the same end result. This approach grants due respect for the unavoidable consequences of variations in individual ability, home environment, economic circumstances, and occupational aspirations. Equal opportunity requires that each child start the race without arbitrary official handicaps; it does not require that each shall finish in the same time.

Appellants, however, pose the question of whether the neighborhood system of pupil placement, fairly administered without racial bias, comports with the requirements of equal opportunity if it nevertheless results in the creation of schools with predominantly or even exclusively Negro pupils. The neighborhood system is in wide use throughout the nation and has been for many years the basis of school administration. This is so because it is acknowledged to have several valuable aspects which are an aid to education, such as minimization of safety hazards to children in reaching school, economy of cost in reducing transportation needs, ease of pupil placement and administration through the use of neutral, easily determined standards, and better home-school communication. * * *

Because of factors in the private housing market, disparities in job opportunities, and other outside influences, (as well as positive free choice by some Negroes), the imposition of the neighborhood concept on existing residential patterns in Cincinnati creates some schools which are predominantly or wholly of one race or another. Appellants insist that this situation, which they concede is not the case in every school in Cincinnati, presents the same separation and hence the same constitutional violation condemned in *Brown*. We do not accept this contention. The element of inequality in *Brown* was the unnecessary restriction on freedom of choice for the individual, based on the fortuitous, uncontrollable, arbitrary factor of his race. The evil inherent in such a classification is that it fails to recognize the high value which our society places on individual worth and personal achievement. Instead a racial characterization treats men in the mass and is unrelated to legitimate governmental considerations. It fails to recognize each man as a unique member of society.

In the present case, the only limit on individual choice in education imposed by state action is the use of the neighborhood school plan. Can it be said that this limitation shares the arbitrary, invidious characteristics of a racially restrictive system? We think not. In this situation, while a particular child may be attending a school composed exclusively of Negro pupils, he and his parents know that he has the choice of attending a mixed school if they so desire, and they can move into the neighborhood district of such a school. This situation is far removed from *Brown,* where the Negro was condemned to separation, no matter what he as an individual might be or do. Here, if there are obstacles or restrictions imposed on the ability of a Negro to take advantage of all the choices offered by the school system, they stem from his individual economic plight, or result from private, not school, prejudice. We read *Brown* as prohibiting only enforced segregation.

The School Board, in the operation of the public schools, acts in much the same manner as an administrative agency exercising its accumulated technical expertise in formulating policy after balancing all legitimate conflicting interests. If that policy is one conceived without bias and administered uniformly to all who fall within its jurisdiction, the courts should be extremely wary of imposing their own judgment on those who have the technical knowledge and operating responsibility for the educational system. * * *

We hold that there is no constitutional duty on the part of the Board to bus Negro or white children out of their neighborhoods or to transfer classes for the sole purpose of alleviating racial imbalance that it did not cause, nor is there a like duty to select new school sites solely in furtherance of such a purpose.

* * *

If the separation in imbalanced schools is the result of racial discrimination, the officials must take steps to remedy the situation. However, the Constitution does not prescribe any single particular cure, and the mere fact of imbalance alone is not a deprivation of equality in the absence of discrimination.

Two other Circuits have considered this question and have come to the same conclusion.

* * *

Did The Board Of Education Intentionally Cause Racial Imbalance In The Cincinnati Public Schools, Deprive Negro Children Of Equal Educational Opportunities, And Discriminate Against Negroes In The Hiring And Assignment Of Teachers?

* * *

Appellants, through extensive use of discovery techniques, adduced vast quantities of information concerning matters such as alleged discrimination in school attendance zoning, transportation policies, teacher selection and assignment, comparative test results, and policies on transfers and overcrowding of students. Some of their contentions with respect thereto are answered by appellees on appeal here, but some are not. This is due partly to the truncated status of the case at the time of the District Court's decision on the motion to dismiss, and partly because the Court considered only appellants', and not the School Board's, evidence in ruling on the motion.

An example of such unanswered and unaccounted for situations is the districting of the Sawyer Junior High School where the enrollment is mostly Negro. The fact is that its boundaries exclude children who live across the street from it in a largely white neighborhood. The School Board in its brief offered no explanation for this situation or for the selection of the Sawyer site so close to the existing Withrow Junior High School.

We have stated above that a showing of impairment of a Negro student's capacity to learn, arising from his school's racial imbalance, does not, standing alone, make out a case of constitutional deprivation. Evidence of such harm, however, may indeed be relevant to the issues of the case before us. Appellants offered expert evidence on this subject. The School Board offered no opposing expert testimony, no doubt because the Court granted the Board's motion to dismiss, made at the close of plaintiffs' proofs. Our review would be helped by a finding as to whether the District Judge considered plaintiffs' expert testimony of such relevance, weight or probative value as to make an issue calling for rebuttal proof by defendant.

No findings were made on these disputed issues. Without findings we are unable to determine whether discrimination existed with respect to specific schools and programs.

* * *

The judgment of the District Court is affirmed on the issue of racial imbalance not intentionally caused by the Board, and the case is remanded for further findings on the issues of claimed discrimination in specific schools and programs and claimed harm to Negro students, allegedly caused by racially imbalanced schools, and for the taking of such additional relevant evidence as either party may offer.

Notes

1. The "neighborhood school" plan until recently was the almost universal basis for assignment of pupils to school buildings. The Supreme Court of Pennsylvania, in Pennsylvania Human Relations Comm'n v. Chester School Dist., 426 Pa. 360, 233 A.2d 290 (1967), stated that the historical rationale for the neighborhood school was lost if the school encompassed a homogeneous racial and socio-economic grouping. "Rather than neighborhood schools, we have all too frequently developed a system of ghetto schools." Consider the advantages and disadvantages of the neighborhood school. Is the issue basically educational, administrative, political, or legal?

2. The leading case in the line of judicial holdings that there is no affirmative duty on school boards to correct de facto segregation is Bell v. School City of Gary, 324 F.2d 209 (7 Cir.1963), cert. den. 377 U.S. 924, 84 S.Ct. 1223, 12 L.Ed.2d 216 (1964). In the instant case the Sixth Circuit concurred with the Seventh, Tenth, and First. The Second Circuit later expressly accepted the view. (Citations are in footnote 64 of this chapter.)

3. The Supreme Court denied certiorari, 389 U.S. 847, 88 S.Ct. 39, 19 L.Ed.2d 114 (1967). On the remand for further findings, the lower court found that no actions of the school authorities had been intended to promote or perpetuate segregation. It further found no probative evidence that children in the predominantly black schools were receiving an inferior education. The Court of Appeals affirmed, restating its position that there was no constitutional duty to take affirmative action to correct de facto segregation. Deal v. Cincinnati Bd. of Educ., 419 F.2d 1387 (6 Cir.1969), cert. den. 402 U.S. 692, 91 S.Ct. 1630, 29 L.Ed.2d 128 (1971).

[Case No. 136] Constitutionality of Initiative-Statute Blocking Correction of De Facto Segregation

WASHINGTON v. SEATTLE SCHOOL DIST. NO. 1

Supreme Court of the United States, 1982.
458 U.S. 457, 102 S.Ct. 3187, 73 L.Ed.2d 896.

JUSTICE BLACKMUN delivered the opinion of the Court.

We are presented here with an extraordinary question: whether an elected local school board may use the Fourteenth Amendment to *defend* its program of busing for integration from attack by the State.

I

A

Seattle School District No. 1 (District), which is largely coterminous with the city of Seattle, Wash., is charged by state law with administering 112 schools and educating approximately 54,000 public school students. About 37% of these children are of Negro, Asian, American Indian, or Hispanic ancestry. Because segregated housing patterns in Seattle have created racially imbalanced schools, the District historically has taken steps to alleviate the isolation of minority students; since 1963, it has permitted students to transfer from their neighborhood schools to help cure the District's racial imbalance.

Despite these efforts, the District in 1977 came under increasing pressure to accelerate its program of desegregation. In response, the District's Board of Directors (School Board) enacted a resolution defining "racial imbalance" as "the situation that exists when the combined minority student enrollment in a school exceeds the districtwide combined average by 20 percentage points, provided that the single minority enrollment * * * of no school will exceed 50 percent of the student body." The District resolved to eliminate all such imbalance from the Seattle public schools by the beginning of the 1979–1980 academic year. (The District Court found that the actions of the School Board were prompted by its members' "desire to ward off threatened litigation, their desire to prevent the threatened loss of federal funds, their desire to relieve the black students of the disproportionate burden which they had borne in the voluntary efforts to balance the schools racially and their perception that racial balance in the schools promotes the attainment of equal educational opportunity and is beneficial in the preparation of all students for democratic citizenship regardless of their race.")

In September 1977, the District implemented a "magnet" program, designed to alleviate racial isolation by enhancing educational offerings at certain schools, thereby encouraging voluntary student transfers. A "disproportionate amount of the overall movement" inspired by the program was undertaken by Negro students, however, and racial imbalance in the Seattle schools was found to have actually increased between the 1970–1971 and 1977–1978 academic years. The District therefore concluded that mandatory reassignment of students was necessary if racial isolation in its schools was to be eliminated. Accordingly, in March 1978, the School Board enacted the so-called "Seattle Plan" for desegregation. The plan, which makes extensive use of busing and mandatory reassignments, desegregates elementary schools by "pairing" and "triading" predominantly minority with predominantly white attendance areas, and by basing student assignments on attendance zones rather than on race. The racial makeup of secondary schools is moderated by "feeding" them from the desegregated elementary schools. The District represents that the plan results in the reassignment of roughly equal numbers of white and minority students, and allows most students to spend roughly half of their academic careers attending a school near their homes.

The desegregation program, implemented in the 1978–1979 academic year, apparently was effective: the District Court found that the Seattle Plan "has substantially reduced the number of racially imbalanced schools in the district and has substantially reduced the percentage of minority students in those schools which remain racially imbalanced."

B

In late 1977, shortly before the Seattle Plan was formally adopted by the District, a number of Seattle residents who opposed the desegregation strategies being discussed by the School Board formed an organization called the Citizens for Voluntary Integration Committee (CiVIC). This organization, which the District Court found "was formed because of its founders' opposition to The Seattle Plan," attempted to enjoin implementation of the Board's mandatory desegregation program though litigation in state court; when these efforts failed, CiVIC drafted a statewide initiative designed to terminate the use of mandatory busing for purposes of racial integration. This proposal, known as Initiative 350, provided that "no school board * * * shall directly or indirectly require any student to attend a school other than the school which is geographically nearest or next nearest the student's place of residence * * * and which offers the course of study pursued by such student * * *." The initiative then set out, however, a number of broad exceptions to this requirement: a student may be assigned beyond his neighborhood school if he "requires special education, care or guidance," or if "there are health or safety hazards, either natural or man made, or physical barriers or obstacles * * * between the student's place of residence and the nearest or next nearest school," or if "the school nearest or next nearest to his place of residence is unfit or inadequate because of overcrowding, unsafe conditions or lack of physical facilities." Initiative 350 also specifically proscribed use of seven enumerated methods of "indirec[t]" student assignment—among them the redefinition of attendance zones, the pairing of schools, and the use of "feeder" schools—that are a part of the Seattle Plan. * * *

* * *

On November 8, 1978, two months after the Seattle Plan went into effect, Initiative 350 passed by a substantial margin, drawing almost 66% of the vote statewide. The initiative failed to attract majority support in two state legislative districts, both in Seattle. In the city as a whole, however, the initiative passed with some 61% of the vote. * * *

* * *

II

The Equal Protection Clause of the Fourteenth Amendment guarantees racial minorities the right to full participation in the political life of the community. * * * [T]he Fourteenth Amendment also reaches "a political structure that treats all individuals as equals," yet more subtly distorts governmental processes in such a way as to place special burdens on the ability of minority groups to achieve beneficial legislation.

This principle received its clearest expression in Hunter v. Erickson, 393 U.S. 385, 89 S.Ct. 557, 21 L.Ed.2d 616 (1969), a case that involved attempts to overturn antidiscrimination legislation in Akron, Ohio. The Akron city council, pursuant to its ordinary legislative processes, had enacted a fair housing ordinance. In response, the local citizenry, using an established referendum procedure, amended the city charter to provide that ordinances regulating real estate transactions "on the basis of race, color, religion, national origin or ancestry must first be approved by a majority of the electors voting on the question at a regular or general election before said ordinance shall be effective." This action "not only suspended the operation of the existing ordinance forbidding housing discrimination, but also required the approval of the electors before any future [fair housing] ordinance could take effect." In essence, the amendment changed the requirements for the adoption of one type of local legislation * * *.

* * * In effect, * * * the charter amendment served as an "explicitly racial classification treating racial housing matters differently from other racial and housing matters." * * *.

Lee v. Nyquist, 318 F.Supp. 710 (WDNY 1970) (three-judge court), offers an application of the *Hunter* doctrine in a setting strikingly similar to the one now before us. That case involved the New York education system, which made use of both elected and appointed school boards and which conferred extensive authority on state education officials. In an effort to eliminate *de facto* segregation in New York's schools, those officials had directed the city of Buffalo—a municipality with an appointed school board—to implement an integration plan. While these developments were proceeding, however, the New York Legislature enacted a statute barring state education officials and appointed—though not elected—school boards from "assign[ing] or compell[ing] [students] to attend any school on account of race * * * or for the purpose of achieving [racial] equality in attendance * * * at any school."

Applying *Hunter,* the three-judge District Court invalidated the statute, noting that under the provision "[t]he Commissioner [of Education] and local appointed officials are prohibited from acting in [student assignment] matters only where racial criteria are involved." In the court's view, the statute therefore "place[d] *burdens* on the implementation of educational policies designed to deal with race on the local level" by "treating educational matters involving racial criteria differently from other educational matters and making it more difficult to deal with racial imbalance in the public schools." This drew an impermissible distinction "between the treatment of problems involving racial matters and that afforded other problems in the same area." This Court affirmed the District Court's judgment without opinion.

* * *

III

We * * * find the principle of those cases dispositive of the issue here. In our view, Initiative 350 must fall because it does "not attemp[t] to allocate governmental power on the basis of any general principle." Instead, it uses the racial nature of an issue to define the governmental decisionmaking structure, and thus imposes substantial and unique burdens on racial minorities.

A

Noting that Initiative 350 nowhere mentions "race" or "integration," appellants suggest that the legislation has no racial overtones * * *. * * * Initiative 350 in fact allows school districts to bus their students "for most, if not all," of the non-integrative purposes required by their educational policies. The Washington electorate surely was aware of this, for it was "assured" by CiVIC officials that " '99% of the school districts in the state' "—those that lacked mandatory integration programs—"would not be affected by the passage of 350." It is beyond reasonable dispute, then, that the initiative was enacted " 'because of,' not merely 'in spite of,' its adverse effects upon" busing for integration. Personnel Administrator of Massachusetts v. Feeney.

Even accepting the view that Initiative 350 was enacted for such a purpose, the United States—which has changed its position during the course of this litigation, and now supports the State—maintains that busing for integration, unlike the fair housing ordinance involved in *Hunter,* is not a peculiarly "racial" issue at all. Again, we are not persuaded.   * * *

* * *

B

We are also satisfied that the practical effect of Initiative 350 is to work a reallocation of power of the kind condemned in *Hunter.* The initiative removes the authority to address a racial problem—and only a racial problem—from the existing decisionmaking body, in such a way as to burden minority interests. Those favoring the elimination of *de facto* school segregation now must seek relief from the state legislature, or from the statewide electorate. Yet authority over all other student assignment decisions, as well as over most other areas of educational policy, remains vested in the local school board. Indeed, by specifically exempting from Initiative 350's proscriptions most non-racial reasons for assigning students away from their neighborhood schools, the initiative expressly requires those championing school integration to surmount a considerably higher hurdle than persons seeking comparable legislative action. As in *Hunter,* then, the community's political mechanisms are modified to place effective decisionmaking authority over a racial issue at a different level of government.   * * *

* * *

V

* * * [W]e do not undervalue the magnitude of the State's interest in its system of education. Washington could have reserved to state officials the right to make all decisions in the areas of education and student assignment. It has chosen, however, to use a more elaborate system; having done so, the State is obligated to operate that system within the confines of the Fourteenth Amendment. That, we believe, it has failed to do.

Accordingly, the judgment of the Court of Appeals is affirmed.

Notes

1. The vote was five-to-four.

2. Justice Blackmun called the question here "extraordinary." The case also was extraordinary in that "the United States" (federal government) changed its legal position on the meaning of the Constitution in midstream—arguing before the Ninth Circuit Court of Appeals that the statute was unconstitutional and here arguing the opposite. In the interim President Reagan succeeded President Carter.

3. Notice the reasons for the board's actions to integrate (third paragraph). Evaluate them.

4. Would the outcome have been different (1) if the legislature had passed the measure, rather than its being an initiative-statute; (2) if the measure had been an amendment to the Washington constitution?

5. Could the school board of Seattle return to a neighborhood school pattern?

[Case No. 137] Termination of Court Supervision of Desegregation Plans

FREEMAN v. PITTS

Supreme Court of the United States, 1992.
___ U.S. ___, 112 S.Ct. 1430, 118 L.Ed.2d 108.

JUSTICE KENNEDY delivered the opinion of the Court.

DeKalb County, Georgia, is a major suburban area of Atlanta. This case involves a court-ordered desegregation decree for the DeKalb County School System (DCSS). DCSS now serves some 73,000 students in kindergarten through high school and is the 32nd largest elementary and secondary school system in the Nation.

DCSS has been subject to the supervision and jurisdiction of the United States District Court for the Northern District of Georgia since 1969, when it was ordered to dismantle its dual school system. In 1986, petitioners filed a motion for final dismissal. * * * We now [hold] that a district court is permitted to withdraw judicial supervision with respect to discrete categories in which the school district has achieved compliance with a court-ordered desegregation plan. A district court need not retain active control over every aspect of school administration until a school district has demonstrated unitary status in all facets of its system.

I

A

For decades before our decision in *Brown v. Board of Education* (*Brown I*) and our mandate in *Brown v. Board of Education* (*Brown II*), which ordered school districts to desegregate with "all deliberate speed," DCSS was segregated by law. DCSS's initial response to the mandate of *Brown II* was an all too familiar one. Interpreting "all deliberate speed" as giving latitude to delay steps to desegregate, DCSS took no positive action toward desegregation until the 1966–1967 school year, when it did nothing more than adopt a freedom of choice transfer plan. Some black students chose to attend former *de jure* white schools, but the plan had no significant effect on the former *de jure* black schools.

In 1968 we decided *Green v. New Kent County School Bd.* We held that adoption of a freedom of choice plan does not, by itself, satisfy a school district's mandatory responsibility to eliminate all vestiges of a dual system. *Green* was a turning point in our law in a further respect. * * * We said that the obligation of school districts once segregated by law was to come forward with a plan that "promises realistically to work, and promises realistically to work *now.* " The case before us requires an understanding and assessment of how DCSS responded to the directives set forth in *Green.*

Within two months of our ruling in *Green,* respondents, who are black school children and their parents, instituted this class action in the United States District Court for the Northern District of Georgia. After the suit was filed, DCSS voluntarily began working with the Department of Health, Education and Welfare to devise a comprehensive and final plan of desegregation. The District Court in June 1969 entered a consent order approving the proposed plan, which was to be implemented in the 1969–1970 school year. The order abolished the freedom of choice plan and adopted a neighborhood school attendance plan that had been proposed by the DCSS and accepted by the Department of Health, Education and Welfare subject to a minor modification. Under the plan all of the former *de jure* black schools were closed and their students were reassigned among the remaining neighborhood schools. The District Court retained jurisdiction.

Between 1969 and 1986 respondents sought only infrequent and limited judicial intervention into the affairs of DCSS. * * *

In 1986 petitioners filed a motion for final dismissal of the litigation. They sought a declaration that DCSS had satisfied its duty to eliminate the dual education system, that is to say a declaration that the school system had achieved unitary status. The District Court approached the question whether DCSS had achieved unitary status by asking whether DCSS was unitary with respect to each of the factors identified in *Green.* [See Note 2 at end of case.] The court considered an additional factor that is not named in *Green:* the quality of education being offered to the white and black student populations.

The District Court found DCSS to be "an innovative school system that has travelled the often long road to unitary status almost to its end," noting that "the court has continually been impressed by the successes of the DCSS and its dedication to providing a quality education for all students within that system." It found that DCSS is a unitary system with regard to student assignments, transportation, physical facilities, and extracurricular activities, and ruled that it would order no further relief in those areas. The District Court stopped short of dismissing the case, however, because it found that DCSS was not unitary in every respect. The court said that vestiges of the dual system remain in the areas of teacher and principal assignments, resource allocation, and quality of education. DCSS was ordered to take measures to address the remaining problems.

B

Proper resolution of any desegregation case turns on a careful assessment of its facts. Here, as in most cases where the issue is the degree of compliance with a school desegregation decree, a critical beginning point is the degree of racial imbalance in the school district, that is to say a comparison of the proportion of majority to minority students in individual schools with the proportions of the races in the district as a whole. This inquiry is fundamental, for under the former *de jure* regimes racial exclusion was both the means and the end of a policy motivated by disparagement of or hostility towards the disfavored race. In accord with this principle, the District Court began its analysis with an assessment of the current racial mix in the schools throughout DCSS and the explanation for the racial imbalance it found.   * * *

In the extensive record that comprises this case, one fact predominates: remarkable changes in the racial composition of the county presented DCSS and the District Court with a student population in 1986 far different from the one they set out to integrate in 1969. Between 1950 and 1985, DeKalb County grew from 70,000 to 450,000 in total population, but most of the gross increase in student enrollment had occurred by 1969, the relevant starting date for our purposes. Although the public school population experienced only modest changes between 1969 and 1986 (remaining in the low 70,000's), a striking change occurred in the racial proportions of the student population. The school system that the District Court ordered desegregated in 1969 had 5.6% black students; by 1986 the percentage of black students was 47%.

To compound the difficulty of working with these radical demographic changes, the northern and southern parts of the county experienced much different growth patterns. The District Court found that "[a]s the result of these demographic shifts, the population of the northern half of DeKalb County is now predominantly white and the southern half of DeKalb County is predominantly black." In 1970, there were 7,615 nonwhites living in the northern part of DeKalb County and 11,508 nonwhites in the southern part of the county. By 1980, there were 15,365 nonwhites living in the northern part of the county, and 87,583 nonwhites in the southern part. Most of the growth in the nonwhite population in the southern portion of the county was due to the migration of black persons from the city of Atlanta. Between 1975 and 1980 alone, approximately 64,000 black citizens moved into southern DeKalb County, most of them coming from Atlanta. During the same period, approximately 37,000 white citizens moved out of southern DeKalb County to the surrounding counties.

* * *

The demographic changes that occurred during the course of the desegregation order are an essential foundation for the District Court's analysis of the current racial mix of DCSS. As the District Court observed, the demographic shifts have had "an immense effect on the racial compositions of the DeKalb County schools." From 1976 to 1986, enrollment in elementary schools declined overall by 15%, while black enrollment in elementary schools increased by 86%. During the same period, overall high school enrollment declined by 16%, while black enrollment in high school increased by 119%. These effects were even more pronounced in the southern portion of DeKalb County.

* * *

Respondents argued in the District Court that this racial imbalance in student assignment was a vestige of the dual system, rather than a product of independent demographic forces. In addition to the statistical evidence that the ratio of black students to white students in individual schools varied to a significant degree from the system-wide average, respondents contended that DCSS had not used all available desegregative tools in order to achieve racial balancing. * * *

Although the District Court found that DCSS was desegregated for at least a short period under the court-ordered plan of 1969, it did not base its finding that DCSS had achieved unitary status with respect to student assignment on that circumstance alone. Recognizing that "[t]he achievement of unitary status in the area of student assignment cannot be hedged on the attainment of such status for a brief moment," the District Court examined the interaction between DCSS policy and demographic shifts in DeKalb County.

The District Court noted that DCSS had taken specific steps to combat the effects of demographics on the racial mix of the schools. Under the 1969 order, a biracial committee had reviewed all proposed changes in the boundary lines of school attendance zones. Since the original desegregation order, there had been about 170 such changes. It was found that only three had a partial segregative effect. * * *

The District Court also noted that DCSS, on its own initiative, * * * [had taken some steps to promote more balanced student assignments].

* * *

Having found no constitutional violation with respect to student assignment, the District Court next considered the other *Green* factors, beginning with faculty and staff assignments. * * * [It ordered more to be done to integrate teachers and to disperse black administrators throughout the system.]

* * *

Addressing the more ineffable category of quality of education, the District Court rejected most of respondents' contentions that there was racial disparity in the provision of certain educational resources (e.g., teachers with advanced degrees, teachers with more experience, library books), contentions made to show that black students were not being given equal educational opportunity. The District Court went further, however, and examined the evidence concerning achievement of black students in DCSS. It cited expert testimony praising the overall educational program in the district, as well as objective evidence of black achievement * * *. * * *

Despite its finding that there was no intentional violation, the District Court found that DCSS had not achieved unitary status with respect to quality of education because teachers in schools with disproportionately high percentages of white students tended to be better educated and have more experience than their counterparts in schools with disproportionately high percentages of black students, and because per pupil expenditures in majority white schools exceeded per pupil expenditures in majority black schools. From these findings, the District Court ordered DCSS to equalize spending and remedy the other problems.

The final *Green* factors considered by the District Court were: (1) physical facilities, (2) transportation, and (3) extracurricular activities. * * *

In accordance with its factfinding, the District Court held that it would order no further relief in the areas of student assignment, transportation, physical facilities and extracurricular activities. The District Court, however, did order DCSS to establish a system to balance teacher and principal assignments and to equalize per pupil expenditures throughout DCSS. Having found that blacks were represented on the school board and throughout DCSS administration, the District Court abolished the biracial committee as no longer necessary.

Both parties appealed to the United States Court of Appeals for the Eleventh Circuit. * * * [The Court of Appeals held that the board must satisfy all six *Green* factors at the same time over a period of several years in order to achieve unitary status. As this had not been done, the board must do more to correct racial imbalances in student assignments.]

II

Two principal questions are presented. The first is whether a district court may relinquish its supervision and control over those aspects of a school system in which there has been compliance with a desegregation decree if other aspects of the system remain in noncompliance. As we answer this question in the affirmative, the second question is whether the Court of Appeals erred in reversing the District Court's order providing for incremental withdrawal of supervision in all the circumstances of this case.

A

The duty and responsibility of a school district once segregated by law is to take all steps necessary to eliminate the vestiges of the unconstitutional *de jure* system. This is required in order to insure that the principal wrong of the *de jure* system, the injuries and stigma inflicted upon the race disfavored by the violation, is no longer present. * * *

* * *

The concept of unitariness has been a helpful one in defining the scope of the district courts' authority, for it conveys the central idea that a school district that was once a dual system must be examined in all of its facets, both when a remedy is ordered and in the later phases of desegregation when the question is whether the district courts' remedial control ought to be modified, lessened, or withdrawn. But, as we explained last term in *Board of Education of Oklahoma City v. Dowell*, the term "unitary" is not a precise concept:

> "[I]t is a mistake to treat words such as 'dual' and 'unitary' as if they were actually found in the Constitution * * *. Courts have used the term 'dual' to denote a school system which has engaged in intentional segregation of students by race, and 'unitary' to describe a school system which has been brought into compliance with the command of the Constitution. We are not sure how useful it is to define these terms more precisely, or to create subclasses within them."

It follows that we must be cautious not to attribute to the term a utility it does not have. The term "unitary" does not confine the discretion and authority of the District Court in a way that departs from traditional equitable principles.

That the term "unitary" does not have fixed meaning or content is not inconsistent with the principles that control the exercise of equitable power. The essence of a court's equity power lies in its inherent capacity to adjust remedies in a feasible and practical way to eliminate the conditions or redress the injuries caused by unlawful action. Equitable remedies must be flexible if these underlying principles are to be enforced with fairness and precision. * * *

* * *

* * * A federal court in a school desegregation case has the discretion to order an incremental or partial withdrawal of its supervision and control. This discretion derives both from the constitutional authority which justified its intervention in the first instance and its ultimate objectives in formulating the decree. The authority of the court is invoked at the outset to remedy particular constitutional violations. In construing the remedial authority of the district courts, we have been guided by the principles that "judicial powers may be exercised only on the basis of a constitutional violation," and that "the nature of the violation determines the scope of the remedy." A remedy is justifiable only insofar as it advances the ultimate objective of alleviating the initial constitutional violation.

We have said that the court's end purpose must be to remedy the violation and in addition to restore state and local authorities to the control of a school system that is operating in compliance with the Constitution. * * * Partial relinquishment of judicial control, where justified by the facts of the case, can be an important and significant step in fulfilling the district court's duty to return the operations and control of schools to local authorities. * * *

* * *

We hold that, in the course of supervising desegregation plans, federal courts have the authority to relinquish supervision and control of school districts in incremental stages, before full compliance has been achieved in every area of school operations. While retaining jurisdiction over the case, the court may determine that it will not order further remedies in areas where the school district is in compliance with the decree. That is to say, upon a finding that a school system subject to a court-supervised desegregation plan is in compliance in some but not all areas, the court in appropriate cases may return control to the school system in those areas where compliance has been achieved, limiting further judicial supervision to operations that are not yet in full compliance with the court decree. In particular, the district court may determine that it will not order further remedies in the area of student assignments where racial imbalance is not traceable, in a proximate way, to constitutional violations.

A court's discretion to order the incremental withdrawal of its supervision in a school desegregation case must be exercised in a manner consistent with the purposes and objectives of its equitable power. Among the factors which must inform the sound discretion of the court in ordering partial withdrawal are the following: whether there has been full and satisfactory compliance with the decree in those aspects of the system where supervision is to be withdrawn; whether retention of judicial control is necessary or practicable to achieve compliance with the decree in other facets of the school system; and whether the school district has demonstrated, to the public and to the parents and students of the once disfavored race, its good faith commitment to the whole of the court's decree and to those provisions of the law and the Constitution that were the predicate for judicial intervention in the first instance.

In considering these factors a court should give particular attention to the school system's record of compliance. A school system is better positioned to demonstrate its good-faith commitment to a constitutional course of action when its policies form a consistent pattern of lawful conduct directed to eliminating earlier violations.   * * *

* * *

B

We reach now the question whether the Court of Appeals erred in prohibiting the District Court from returning to DCSS partial control over some of its affairs. We decide that the Court of Appeals did err in holding that, as a matter of law, the District Court had no discretion to permit DCSS to regain control over student assignment, transportation, physical facilities, and extracurricular activities, while retaining court supervision over the areas of faculty and administrative assignments and the quality of education, where full compliance had not been demonstrated.

It was an appropriate exercise of its discretion for the District Court to address the elements of a unitary system discussed in *Green,* to inquire whether other elements ought to be identified, and to determine whether minority students were being disadvantaged in ways that required the formulation of new and further remedies to insure full compliance with the court's decree. Both parties agreed that quality of education was a legitimate inquiry in determining DCSS' compliance with the desegregation decree, and the trial court found it workable to consider the point in connection with its findings on resource allocation. * * * The District Court's approach illustrates that the *Green* factors need not be a rigid framework.   * * *

* * *

That there was racial imbalance in student attendance zones was not tantamount to a showing that the school district was in noncompliance with the decree or with its duties under the law. Racial balance is not to be achieved for its own sake. It is to be pursued when racial imbalance has been caused by a constitutional violation. Once the racial imbalance due to the *de jure* violation has been remedied, the school district is under no duty to remedy imbalance that is caused by demographic factors. * * * If the unlawful *de jure* policy of a school system has been the cause of the racial imbalance in student attendance, that condition must be remedied. The school district bears the burden of showing that any current imbalance is not traceable, in a proximate way, to the prior violation.

The findings of the District Court that the population changes which occurred in DeKalb County were not caused by the policies of the school district, but rather by independent factors, are consistent with the mobility that is a distinct characteristic of our society. * * *

* * *

The requirement that the school district show its good faith commitment to the entirety of a desegregation plan so that parents, students and the public have assurance against further injuries or stigma also should be a subject for more specific findings. We stated in [*Board of Educ. of Oklahoma City v.*] *Dowell* that the good faith compliance of the district with the court order over a reasonable period of time is a factor to be considered in deciding whether or not jurisdiction could be relinquished. A history of good-faith compliance is evidence that any current racial imbalance is not the product of a new *de jure* violation, and enables the district court to accept the school board's representation that it has accepted the principle of racial equality and will not suffer intentional discrimination in the future. * * *

* * *

Notes

1. The vote here was eight-to-zero. (Justice Marshall had retired and Justice Thomas had not taken office at the time the case was argued.)

2. In Green v. New Kent County School Bd. the Court said that vestiges of de jure segregation must be eliminated not only from student assignment (the focus of the 1968 case) but from "every facet of school operations—faculty, staff, transportation, extracurricular activities, and facilities." The expression was not amplified. Board of Educ. of Oklahoma City v. Dowell in 1991 gave the list enhanced significance by instructing lower courts to examine the areas when determining whether de jure segregation has been corrected.

3. Consider the Court's emphasis in the first paragraph under IB. Also observe its repeated emphasis on the element of good-faith compliance.

4. Notice that the Court places on the school board the burden of showing that any current imbalance in student attendance patterns is not the result of the de jure segregation that previously had been found.

5. Review the factors a court must consider if it is partially to withdraw from supervising a desegregation process (next to last paragraph in IIA).

Chapter 14

SCHOOL BOARD PROCEDURES
AND SCHOOL ELECTIONS

Board Procedures

In General

As a local board of education is considered to be a legal entity only as a whole, it follows that individual members have no legal authority as individuals to act for the district.[1] Further, in order that any action taken by a board shall be legal and binding on the district, there must be a legal meeting of the board. Even if members of a board individually have signed a document, it is not a valid contract if later repudiated by the board at a meeting.[2] Some relevant cases are presented in Chapters 8 and 9 in connection with contracts.

The state can set qualifications for school board membership. It cannot, of course, adopt an unconstitutional criterion. The Supreme Court has rejected ownership of real property in the district as a qualification.[3] Where no minimum age was specified an appellate court in New Jersey held it to be implied that candidates be old enough to vote.[4]

In a Massachusetts school district a collective bargaining agreement provided that if the board and the teachers association agreed to abide by the decision of an arbitrator, that method would be followed in resolving grievances. When a grievance arose regarding the payment of teachers for certain extracurricular activities, the chairman of the board of education and the officers of the educational association signed an agreement to submit the controversy to arbitration. Following the arbitration the board declined to accede to the arbitrator's award on the ground the president of the board had no authority to commit the board. The Supreme Judicial Court of Massachusetts agreed, holding that neither the collective bargaining agreement nor the application signed by the board chairman constituted an assent by the school board to submit the controversy to arbitration.[5] That could be done only by a majority vote of the board as a whole.

1. Bender v. Williamsport Area School Dist., 475 U.S. 534, 106 S.Ct. 1326, 89 L.Ed.2d 501 (1986).

2. State ex rel. Steinbeck v. Treasurer of Liberty Tp., 22 Ohio St. 144 (1871).

3. Turner v. Fouche, 396 U.S. 346, 90 S.Ct. 532, 24 L.Ed.2d 567 (1970).

4. Vittoria v. West Orange Bd. of Educ., 122 N.J.Super. 340, 300 A.2d 356 (1973).

5. Sheahan v. School Committee of Worcester, 359 Mass. 702, 270 N.E.2d 912 (1971).

In the absence of statutes to the contrary, school boards have the authority to formulate and adopt rules of procedure for their meetings. If neither the board nor the legislature has established rules of procedure for boards, the rules of parliamentary procedure, which flow from general principles of common law, govern board meetings.[6] In some states the legislatures have required boards to adopt rules and bylaws for their operations. The Court of Appeals of Kentucky has held that a statute of this sort clothes rules and regulations adopted by the board with the effect and force of the statutory provision authorizing them, and an action taken contrary to the procedures adopted is void.[7] Even though boards generally can change their rules of procedure, they may be bound by their rules in situations where variation from them may lead to a violation of some right of another party who has reasonably relied upon them.

Procedures for quasi-judicial hearings involving possible disciplinary action against teachers or students are discussed in Chapters 11 and 12.

The question whether a school board can reconsider a prior determination not to terminate a probationary school secretary was raised in the Court of Appeals of New York. A resolution to dismiss the employee, which had not received at one meeting the majority vote of the board members required for passage, was reintroduced at the next meeting and was adopted. The employee sought to invalidate the action on the ground that the first vote had made the matter res judicata. The court sustained the board, stating that the doctrine of res judicata applied to judicial determinations rather than administrative ones.[8] Only when an administrative body engages in an adjudicatory activity may res judicata be invoked. In the latter type of situation the doctrine prevents reversals of decisions by decisionmaking bodies once a matter has been adjudicated by them.[9]

Notice of Meetings

School boards may take official action only at a legal meeting of the board. In order for a board meeting to be legal the common law requires that notice be given to all members of the board unless the meetings are regular ones, the dates of which have been set by law.[10] In the case of regular meetings all persons and officials are charged with notice of the dates on which such meetings will be held. The purpose of the notice requirement for special meetings is to insure that all board members have the opportunity to attend. If board meetings could be held by part of the board without notice to the remaining members, it is

---

6. McCormick v. Board of Educ., 58 N.M. 648, 274 P.2d 299 (1954).

7. Montenegro-Riehm Music Co. v. Board of Educ., 147 Ky. 720, 145 S.W. 740 (1912).

8. Venes v. Community School Bd. of Dist. 26, 43 N.Y.2d 520, 402 N.Y.S.2d 807, 373 N.E.2d 987 (1978).

9. Murdock v. Perkins, 219 Ga. 756, 135 S.E.2d 869 (1964).

10. Twitchell v. Bowman, 440 P.2d 513 (Wyo.1968).

clear that the public might thereby be deprived of part of its representation at board meetings. Of course, the presence of all board members is not essential to the legality of the board meeting. Only a legal quorum need be present. The notice requirement is to afford as far as possible each board member the opportunity to be present.

The courts construe these notice requirements quite strictly. Not only does the public have a right to have all board members made aware of a meeting, but individual board members have a right to be so notified.[11] Where there are statutes indicating requirements for special meetings, these, of course, must be followed. However, even in the absence of any statutory requirement for notice of a special meeting of a board of education, it is consistently held that no authority exists in the board in the absence of any members of the group unless all have had reasonable notice and opportunity to be present. A reasonable time before such meeting within which notice of the meeting must be given means sufficient time for the party notified for preparation and attendance at the time and place of the meeting.[12]

Circumstances may arise which render it unnecessary to give notice to all board members. An Iowa case illustrates the point. Here the board of education had employed a superintendent of schools at a contested meeting. It appeared that one member of the board had not been given notice of the meeting at which the employment occurred. Later the board, upon which there had been some changes of personnel, sought to annul the superintendent's contract on the ground that he had been employed at an illegal board meeting. The evidence showed that the absent member was in California on the day of the meeting and had been there for several months. Since he would have been unable to attend had notice of the meeting been given him, the legality of the meeting and the appointment of the superintendent were sustained.[13]

If, despite a lack of notice, all members of the board actually attend and participate in the meeting, actions taken cannot be invalidated on the basis of lack of notice.[14] Applied is a common sense rule that if all members are present the purpose of the notice requirement is met. It should be observed, however, that even when all board members are present at a special meeting held without proper notice thereof, if any of the board members refuse to act at that meeting, actions taken will have no effect.[15]

Local board members cannot by private agreement waive the right to receive notice. Thus, even though there is agreement that two members of a three member board can act in the absence of the third and without prior notice to him, an action taken at such a meeting is

11. Elsemore v. Inhabitants of Town of Hancock, 137 Me. 243, 18 A.2d 692 (1941).

12. Green v. Jones, 144 W.Va. 276, 108 S.E.2d 1 (1959).

13. Consolidated School Dist. of Glidden v. Griffin, 201 Iowa 63, 206 N.W. 86 (1925).

14. Hanna v. Wright, 116 Iowa 275, 89 N.W. 1108 (1902).

15. Johnson v. Dye, 142 Mo.App. 424, 127 S.W. 413 (1910). See also Knickerbocker v. Redlands High School Dist., 49 Cal.App.2d 722, 122 P.2d 289 (1942).

invalid.[16] When a regular meeting is postponed to a subsequent date, it is necessary under the common law to notify only those who were absent from the meeting at which the date of the next meeting was established.[17] When a meeting is continued on another day, however, it is not necessary to send notice of the continuance to an absent board member.[18]

Voting

For a legal board meeting there must be present a quorum of members.[19] Under the common law, a quorum is a simple majority. For an action to be considered legally approved by the board, in the absence of a statute specifying differently, a majority vote of a quorum is required.[20] The legislature may specify different numerical votes to transact specific items of business.[21] (See infra re abstentions).

Unless a statute prescribes a form of voting, board members may vote in any manner they wish (e.g., raising the hand, secret ballot, or voice vote). Indeed the board may adopt one form of voting on some propositions and another form of voting on others at the same meeting. For example, it might be desirable in the opinion of the board to vote by secret ballot on some questions and by voice vote on others. Nothing in the common law forbids this procedure. The absence of a statute in the area gives the board free range regarding voting methods, subject only to the general proscription that it cannot operate arbitrarily or fraudulently. Under the statutes of some states, board action can legally be taken only by roll call vote. Usually, though not universally, this requirement has been held to be mandatory, and action taken by any other form of vote would not be legally binding.[22]

A Colorado statute required that before an administrator on tenure could be transferred to a teaching position, he must be "deemed" unsatisfactory in his administrative capacity. Another statute required that voting by boards of education be on a roll call basis. A principal's performance was discussed at board meetings, board members testified that they had reached the conclusion he was unsatisfactory, and the superintendent had written the principal telling him the board considered him to be unsatisfactory. Nevertheless, because a roll call vote had not been taken, the Court of Appeals of Colorado held the reassignment to be invalid.[23]

---

16. School Dist. No. 22 v. Castell, 105 Ark. 106, 150 S.W. 407 (1912).

17. Keyes v. Class "B" School Dist. No. 421 of Valley County, 74 Idaho 314, 261 P.2d 811 (1953).

18. Barnhart Independent School Dist. v. Mertzon Independent School Dist., 464 S.W.2d 197 (Tex.Civ.App.1971).

19. Konovalchik v. School Committee of Salem, 352 Mass. 542, 226 N.E.2d 222 (1967). [Case No. 138]

20. State ex rel. Mason v. Mayor and Aldermen of the City of Paterson, 35 N.J.L. 190 (1871); Federal Trade Comm'n v. Flotill Products, Inc., 389 U.S. 179, 88 S.Ct. 401, 19 L.Ed.2d 398 (1967).

21. Board of School Trustees of South Vermillion School Corp. v. Benetti, 492 N.E.2d 1098 (Ind.App.1986).

22. Ready v. Board of Educ., 297 Ill. App. 342, 17 N.E.2d 635 (1938).

23. Robb v. School Dist. No. RE 50(J), 28 Colo.App. 453, 475 P.2d 30 (1970).

The Supreme Court of Pennsylvania, however, overruled prior decisions and held that the statutory requirement of a recorded roll call vote for appointment of teachers was not mandatory, but directory (that is, failure to follow the statute would not automatically invalidate the contract).[24] The new ruling was made in a case where a board sought to repudiate a contract with a teacher on the ground it was unenforceable because of the absence of the recorded vote. The teacher had served for over a year with good ratings. The highest state court said that, under the facts present in the case, to permit the avoidance of an otherwise valid contract would be unconscionable. Boards could fail to record the necessary item and then remove teachers at their whim. The court commented that the force of the statute would not be impaired, for where the vote was not recorded evidence would have to be presented that the board members did in fact approve the appointment.

That an illegal voting procedure is well intentioned and of long standing does not validate it, as was demonstrated by an Arkansas case. In a three-school district it was the custom for the chief administrator to get the approval of the board members living in the area of each school in regard to employment and discharge of teachers assigned to that school. The whole board did not consider these actions. The Supreme Court of Arkansas found the discharge of a teacher to be a nullity under these conditions and ordered her salary paid to the end of the contract period.[25]

Many questions arise regarding the legal effects of a board member's refraining from voting on an issue properly before the board. A member of the board who is present at a meeting at which there is a quorum has the legal duty to vote on matters that come before the board. If he refrains from voting, he is regarded as acquiescing in the action of those members of the board who voted.[26] Abstentions are not counted in determining whether a majority has voted for a motion. Thus, if seven members are present, three vote in favor, two vote against, and two do not vote, the resolution is considered passed if there is no statutory requirement of an affirmative vote of a majority of all present or of a majority of the full membership of the board.[27]

Although these rules are firmly established in the common law, cases develop as to their application. For example, a Missouri suit involved the legality of a meeting at which action was taken to call a certain election. Two members of the three-member board had attended the meeting. The third member declined to attend, saying that he was opposed to calling the election. The president of the board, who was in favor of calling the election, presented the petition to the other member who was present. This member refused to vote either for or against the proposition. The president then cast his vote in favor of the proposition

24. Mullen v. Board of School Directors of DuBois Area School Dist., 436 Pa. 211, 259 A.2d 877 (1969).

25. Farris v. Stone County School Dist. No. 1, 248 Ark. 19, 450 S.W.2d 279 (1970).

26. Payne v. Petrie, 419 S.W.2d 761 (Ky.1967).

27. Bunsen v. County Bd. of School Trustees, 48 Ill.App.2d 291, 198 N.E.2d 735 (1964).

and called the election. In a suit to contest the validity of the action, the court sustained its legality.[28] The fact that only one member, the president of the board, actually voted to call the election did not render it invalid. The court stated that when a member sits silently by during a call for a vote, in law he is regarded as acquiescing in, rather than opposing, the measure in question. If one not wishing to vote on a measure actually withdraws from the meeting, thereby leaving no quorum, action cannot be taken under normal circumstances.[29] However, the withdrawal must be genuine. Where three board members during a vote stepped from the part of the room occupied by the board to a place among the bystanders, the court held that they could not change from trustees to mere spectators when they still had an opportunity to act and vote with the others.[30] Thus their intended procedural maneuver was thwarted, and the action of the three voting members was ruled to be valid (in effect, by a vote of three-to-none with three abstentions).

In a situation in Minnesota the highest court of that state was called upon to decide whether a three-member board had approved a particular action.[31] One member of the board had favored so doing and made a motion to that effect. A second opposed the doing and made a motion to that effect. The third member supported neither at that time and subsequently became incapacitated. In this dilemma the Supreme Court of Minnesota ruled that it was the duty of the third member to take sides and vote, and that if he had desired to reject the proposition he should have done so. This is in line with the general holding that main motions are voted on in the order they are made. The first motion, in effect, passed by a vote of one-to-none with two abstentions.

In some states the statutes require on certain questions an affirmative vote of a fixed percent of all members or of all members present. In this type of situation a blank ballot or a refusal to vote is not considered an acquiescence in the will of the majority.[32]

Local boards cannot change the common law on basic procedures for voting without legislative permission. Formally adopted rules to that effect are generally invalid, and customary procedure of boards is irrelevant to the issue. Local bodies cannot make rules in derogation of the "law of the land, whether common law or statutory" regarding how ballots are counted and a majority determined.[33] Similarly it has been held by the Supreme Court of Wisconsin that a local board has no authority to change the common law rule regarding a quorum, even though a statute authorizes it to establish its own rules of procedure.[34] The court ruled that where the legislature confers a power upon a board to be exercised by it without the legislature's providing the number of

---

28. Mullins v. Eveland, 234 S.W.2d 639 (Mo.App.1950).

29. Levisa Oil Corp. v. Quigley, 217 Va. 898, 234 S.E.2d 257 (1977).

30. State ex rel. Walden v. Vanosdal, 131 Ind. 388, 31 N.E. 79 (1892).

31. Edwards v. Mettler, 268 Minn. 472, 129 N.W.2d 805 (1964).

32. Forbis v. Fremont County School Dist. No. 38, 842 P.2d 1063 (Wyo. 1992).

33. Murdoch v. Strange, 99 Md. 89, 57 A. 628 (1904).

34. Endeavor-Oxford Union Free High School Dist. v. Walters, 270 Wis. 561, 72 N.W.2d 535 (1955).

members necessary to act in concert to exercise the power, the common law rule prevails, and a majority of a board quorum may lawfully act. While noting that the legislature itself could change the rule or could empower a local board to do so, it said also that, in the absence of a controlling provision, the common law rule that a majority of a whole body is necessary to constitute a quorum applies. In the instant situation the board had required for approval of a petition a greater vote than was provided by the common law.

Rejected in New Jersey was a claim that a board was bound by its by-law that specified a two-thirds vote of its full membership to close and sell a school building.[35] A state statute required only "a recorded roll call majority vote of its full membership." (In the present case the board vote was by a majority of the full membership, but not by two-thirds.) However, the sale was blocked by another by-law that required two public meetings for adoption of such a policy. The court explained that the second by-law was not in direct or indirect conflict with state legislation or the common law.

Sometimes it develops after a board action has been taken that a member of the board was ineligible to hold the seat. Also, during challenges to the election of a person or to the continued eligibility of one already on the board, the board cannot suspend operations pending a judicial determination. Under such circumstances questions arise as to the validity of board actions taken. Board members whose eligibility is subsequently rejected are considered "de facto members" as regards actions taken during the pendency of an ultimately successful challenge. The issue was raised in a case in which a board appointed the superintendent to a new term commencing some seven months later when his current contract expired and also to the post of secretary of the board. The vote of a de facto member was necessary for the second action to be approved. The Court of Appeals of Kentucky stated the general rule to be that a contract made by a board pending ouster proceedings against a member would normally not be retroactively invalidated if it had depended on the vote of a member ultimately removed.[36] But here there was a special circumstance leading to the opposite conclusion: there had been no necessity to act on the superintendent's renewal nor on his appointment as secretary so far in advance of the expiration of his two contracts "except to avoid the possible outcome of the challenge." The court declared that the vote of the de facto member could not be counted. That vote had not been a necessary one on the appointment as superintendent, but had been necessary for the appointment as secretary.

In Wyoming one ground advanced for contesting a personnel action by a school board was that there was no record of the votes of individual members of the board. The highest state court found no statutory requirement for such, and stated that the common law does not require

35. Matawan Regional Teachers Ass'n v. Matawan–Aberdeen Regional School Dist. Bd. of Educ., 223 N.J.Super. 504, 538 A.2d 1331 (1988). [Case No. 139]

36. Board of Educ. of McCreary County v. Nevels, 551 S.W.2d 15 (Ky.App.1977).

that individual votes be recorded as long as the totals are made a matter of record.[37]

Public Nature of Meetings

Under the statutes of most states school board meetings are required to be public meetings. Often, however, it is not a simple matter to determine abstractly whether a particular meeting was public in terms of the statute. There are two particularly troublesome legal aspects: that the public is permitted to be present, and that records of the meeting are made available to the public. It may be said that the term "public" is relative, rather than absolute, when it describes a meeting. The Court of Appeal of California construed a statute of that state on the point.[38] The facts were that a board had met briefly in open session, adjourned for an hour or so, reconvened in executive session, and finally met again in open session. Certain teachers whose contracts were terminated at this meeting questioned the legality of the meeting on the ground that it did not meet the statutory requirement that the meeting be public. The court held the meeting to be a legal one despite the fact that the board had met in executive session from which the public was excluded. According to the court, the board was permitted to convene in executive session for the purpose of discussing matters affecting teachers' contracts, provided the final action was taken in open session.

Generally it is not required that all discussions of the board be open to the public. The meetings at which decisions are made, however, generally must be open.[39] In one case the Supreme Court of Minnesota construed the pertinent statute of that state and held that it was essential that meetings be held in a public place located within the territorial confines of the school district involved.[40] The board members of a school district had convened in a private office at the county seat, some twenty miles from the district. At this meeting a resolution which initiated consolidation proceedings was passed. The court found the consolidation fatally defective because it had been adopted at an improperly constituted meeting. Even without a specific statute, the Supreme Court of Utah has commented that "unless matters were of such a delicate nature or of the type where public policy dictates nondissemination, the meeting itself should be open to the public and press." [41]

A statute in Michigan required that although a school board was permitted to hold executive sessions, no "final action" could be taken in such a meeting. A teacher asserted that he was entitled to continued employment based on a charge of invalid board action in terminating his

37. Diefenderfer v. Budd, 563 P.2d 1355 (Wyo.1977).

38. Alva v. Sequoia Union High Dist., 98 Cal.App.2d 656, 220 P.2d 788 (1950).

39. Jewell v. Board of Educ., DuQuoin Community Unit Schools, Dist. No. 300, 19 Ill.App.3d 1091, 312 N.E.2d 659 (1974).

40. Quast v. Knudson, 276 Minn. 340, 150 N.W.2d 199 (1967).

41. Conover v. Board of Educ. of Nebo School Dist., 1 Utah 2d 375, 267 P.2d 768 (1954). [Case No. 140]

employment because no announcement was made of the decision and reasons therefor at a public meeting. The board, after discussing the matter in executive session, had passed with no discussion in a public meeting a resolution that the teacher be released at the end of the school year. Thereafter the teacher was notified of the action and reasons were given him. The state supreme court found no legal flaw in the board's action.[42]

A large number of statutes have been enacted in recent years limiting the use of closed or executive sessions by public bodies including school boards. The "open meeting" statutes vary widely in details, especially as regards exceptions to the general premise that government business should be conducted in public view. Exceptions may be on a basis of subject matter treated or character of the session. On the latter point the Supreme Court of Louisiana has forbidden any closed session of a school board for which there is an advance call, an agenda, a polling of members' views, and a recording of what transpired, except as it is a recess of a legal meeting.[43] Similarly the Supreme Court of Colorado has barred closed gatherings of school board members at which matters are discussed prior to their being voted on without discussion in a public meeting.[44] The Supreme Court of Minnesota (commenting that "there is a way to illegally circumvent any rule the court might fashion, and therefore it is important that the rule not be so restrictive as to lose the public benefit of personal discussion between public officials while gaining little assurance of openness") held that the open meeting law covered gatherings of a quorum or more members of the board at which they discussed, decided, or received information as a group on issues related to the official business of the board.[45]

Where the statute does not so specify, the courts are not agreed whether an action taken in violation of open meeting legislation is void.[46] (This issue is separate from that of sanctions against violators.)

An interesting resolution of one situation was made by the highest court of Massachusetts. A school board that had advertised for applicants for the position of superintendent received more than 90 candidates. A screening committee selected 16. The board considered them at a public meeting, not by names but by assigned numbers. Five finalists were selected. The names of these five persons were released, and the board interviewed each at a public meeting. The board refused, however, to disclose the names of any other candidates. The court determined that the open meeting statute required that the names of the 16 finalists considered at the meeting be released and that the minutes

42. Dryden v. Marcellus Community Schools, 401 Mich. 76, 257 N.W.2d 79 (1977).

43. Reeves v. Orleans Parish School Bd., 281 So.2d 719 (La.1973).

44. Bagby v. School Dist. No. 1, Denver, 186 Colo. 428, 528 P.2d 1299 (1974).

45. Moberg v. Independent School Dist. No. 281, 336 N.W.2d 510 (Minn.1983).

46. Compare Toyah Independent School Dist. v. Pecos-Barstow Independent School Dist., 466 S.W.2d 377 (Tex.Civ.App.1971), with Anti-Administration Ass'n v. North Fayette County Community School Dist., 206 N.W.2d 723 (Iowa 1973).

of the meeting where they were considered contain the names.[47]   The court recognized the possibility that disclosure of a particular candidate's name might invade privacy, but said that no showing had been made for any of the 16, who at that point in the selection process would expect public discussion of their qualifications. It said that the question of disclosure's reducing the effectiveness of hiring procedures should be addressed to the legislature.   The court approved the trial judge's arrangement for handling the list of names, which list came under the public records statute: the circumstances of those candidates who would not consent for their names to be disclosed would be considered on an individual basis by the judge in chambers.

It should be observed that under the common law there is no necessity that an agenda be published in advance of a properly noticed meeting. Generally, any matter that could be considered at a regular meeting may be acted on at a special meeting.[48] If a board decides to issue an agenda in advance, it does not thereby waive its right to amend the agenda at the meeting.[49] If a statute requires a prior agenda, however, transaction of other business at the meeting will not be permitted.[50]

Records

Official minutes of board meetings fall into the category of records that the public has a right to examine. However, not every document or writing of a public body is a public document. A practical aspect of the issue was raised in Utah. The basic question was whether the notes that the clerk of the board took at a board meeting were a "public writing." A statute extended to all citizens the right to inspect "public writings." On the day following a certain board meeting a number of individuals unsuccessfully sought to examine and copy the notes of the clerk. The Supreme Court of Utah discussed the matter at length.[51] The court stated that the statutes and cases related to public writings were "divergent as the shading of the spectrum. However, between two extremes, not necessarily midway, there is a point where reason shows brightest, dimming as the point shifts in one direction or the other." In the case before it, the court was of the opinion that the notes which the clerk took fell outside the category of public writings, whereas the transcribed minutes, in final form awaiting only approval and placement in the journal, were classifiable as such and therefore subject to public inspection.

The method of copying public school board records led to a case in Illinois where the question was whether the records could be photo-

47. Attorney General v. School Committee of Northampton, 375 Mass. 127, 375 N.E.2d 1188 (1978).

48. Moore v. City Council of City of Perry, 119 Iowa 423, 93 N.W. 510 (1903).

49. Crifasi v. Governing Body of Oakland, 156 N.J.Super. 182, 383 A.2d 736 (1978); Unified School Dist. No. 407 by

Boatwright v. Fisk, 232 Kan. 820, 660 P.2d 533 (1983).

50. Santa Barbara School Dist. v. Superior Court, 13 Cal.3d 315, 118 Cal.Rptr. 637, 530 P.2d 605 (1975).

51. Conover v. Board of Educ. of Nebo School Dist., 1 Utah 2d 375, 267 P.2d 768 (1954). [Case No. 140]

graphed. The school officials had conceded the right to inspect the records and make written copies thereof. The court held that photographing must be permitted.[52] A professional photographer had been brought along to photograph the records. Thus, there was no danger of damage to the documents.

Tape recording of public board meetings also has been upheld.[53] The right to videotape such meetings was approved by a New Jersey appellate court.[54] However, tape recording of an executive session of a board by a member of the board could be prevented by a board rule, according to the Court of Appeal of Louisiana.[55]

Attempts to keep records from the public are often defended by a concern for privacy. School boards, however, not only are acting for the public, but are spending public money. The inquiry under the common law, augmented by widespread freedom-of-information statutes, is whether the materials sought would in fact invade personal privacy and, if so, whether the privacy interest would outweigh the public interest served by disclosure. Presumptions favor disclosure.[56] The courts seem in complete agreement that salary data must be disclosed.[57] The highest court of Massachusetts has held that the public records statute requires disclosure of absentee records of individual teachers when the records show only the dates and generic classifications of the absences.[58] The Fifth Circuit Court of Appeals has found no constitutional privacy interest of teachers to prevent public disclosure of college transcripts.[59] Also, it has been held that board minutes must identify by name, rather than student number, those students who have been suspended.[60]

A school board cannot adopt a policy in conflict with a state law regarding open records. In Oregon a board had promised confidentiality of names and addresses to teachers employed during any strikes. The Supreme Court of Oregon held that such a blanket policy thwarted the legislative intent to have records of public bodies open to the public unless there was an individualized reason not to do so.[61] Similarly the Supreme Court of Georgia held that records of candidates for the state

52. People ex rel. Gibson v. Peller, 34 Ill.App.2d 372, 181 N.E.2d 376 (1962). [Case No. 141]

53. Belcher v. Mansi, 569 F.Supp. 379 (D.R.I.1983); Mitchell v. Board of Educ. of Garden City Union Free School Dist., 113 A.D.2d 924, 493 N.Y.S.2d 826 (1985).

54. Maurice River Tp. Bd. of Educ. v. Maurice River Tp. Teachers Ass'n, 193 N.J.Super. 488, 475 A.2d 59 (1984).

55. Dean v. Guste, 414 So.2d 862 (La. App.1982).

56. See footnote 47. See also "Personnel Files" in Chapter 10.

57. Mans v. Lebanon School Bd., 112 N.H. 160, 290 A.2d 866 (1972); Hastings

and Sons Pub. Co. v. City Treasurer of Lynn, 374 Mass. 812, 375 N.E.2d 299 (1978).

58. Brogan v. School Committee of Westport, 401 Mass. 306, 516 N.E.2d 159 (1987).

59. Klein Independent School Dist. v. Mattox, 830 F.2d 576 (5 Cir.1987), cert. den. 485 U.S. 1008, 108 S.Ct. 1473, 99 L.Ed.2d 702 (1988). [Case No. 84]

60. Palladium Pub. Co. v. River Val. School Dist., 115 Mich.App. 490, 321 N.W.2d 705 (1982).

61. Guard Pub. Co. v. Lane County School Dist. No. 4J, 310 Or. 32, 791 P.2d 854 (1990).

university presidency must be made public.[62] It stated that it could not consider the concern of the regents that the law hampered obtaining good candidates because the law was clear and only the legislature could change the policy of full openness.

The adequacy of records of board actions has been a prolific source for litigation. The courts have not been in complete agreement on whether failure to keep a record will invalidate an action which should have been recorded. Much depends upon the nature of the action taken. Courts are aware of the fact that it would not be salutary to hold that no action may be upheld unless it is completely recorded in the official minute book. The Supreme Court of Iowa, for example, has held that a statute requiring an official record of board proceedings in connection with designating students whose tuition should be paid in another district was directory only, and that the board's action, even though it did not keep a record, could be upheld where there was other evidence which would substantiate the board's action.[63]

Where records must be kept, it is not always required by the courts that the record give all details. The minimum requirement for a record is that it show that an action was taken. The Supreme Court of Oregon has stated that a board's action would not be vulnerable to attack if it had in fact made required findings but simply failed to record them in detail.[64] In that case, however, no record at all was kept, and the board's action was invalidated. Where enough information was contained for full understanding, even though more details would have been desirable, the Supreme Court of Montana declined to invalidate a bond sale.[65] Although the exact contents of the resolution had not been recorded in the minute book, the court found no Montana statute requiring this nor any abstract basis for the interpretation that absence of exact wording would be justification for voiding a bond issue. If no action is taken at an executive session of a board, there is apparently no need for minutes.[66] The minutes of the regular meeting presumably would record the fact of the closed session, its length, and the general subject.

The official record of a school board or any public body is prima facie evidence of the action taken by the body. Oral testimony cannot be used to enlarge or restrict that which is in the records.[67] Oral evidence may be used, however, to supply omissions or to clarify the record if it is not clear on its face.[68] When, as occasionally happens, it is discovered that a record is incorrect, a board may amend its record to make it convey

62. Board of Regents of University System of Georgia v. The Atlanta Journal, 259 Ga. 214, 378 S.E.2d 305 (1989).

63. School Dist. of Soldier Tp. v. Moeller, 247 Iowa 239, 73 N.W.2d 43 (1955).

64. Union High School Dist. No. 1 v. Linn Dist. Boundary Bd., 244 Or. 207, 416 P.2d 656 (1966).

65. Elliot v. School Dist. No. 64–JT, 149 Mont. 299, 425 P.2d 826 (1967).

66. State ex rel. Zinngrabe v. School Dist. of Sevastopol, 146 Wis.2d 629, 431 N.W.2d 734 (App.1988).

67. Lewis v. Board of Educ. of Johnson County, 348 S.W.2d 921 (Ky.1961); Tuscaloosa City Bd. of Educ. v. Roberts, 440 So.2d 1058 (Ala.1983).

68. Spann v. Joint Boards of School Directors, 381 Pa. 338, 113 A.2d 281 (1955); Knutsen v. Frushour, 92 Idaho 37, 436 P.2d 521 (1968).

events accurately.[69] The legal remedy to require correction of minutes is the writ of mandamus. Records may not be attacked collaterally.

Ohio statutes provided that, when the regular clerk of the board was not present, the board was to choose one of its number to serve in his place. This was not done at a session in which the recommendation of the superintendent not to reemploy a teacher was acted upon. The Court of Appeals of Ohio declined to declare the meeting a nullity.[70] There was no claim of error in the minutes; the claim was that only the clerk or one selected to take his place in accordance with the statute had authority to record the minutes. The court said that its concern was with what happened, not with who transcribed the minutes.

Use of Committees

Just as board members have no power as individuals to act for the board, committees of boards have no power to act for the board. The reason for this general principle is that all board decisions are to be considered and determined by the board as a whole. Obviously it is sometimes necessary or desirable to have fact-finding and preliminary work done by small groups of board members. These committees, however, must report back to the board as a whole, for only the board as a whole can take legal action.

It is sometimes charged that the recommendation of a board committee is passed on perfunctorily by the whole board without proper deliberation by the total membership. This was the situation in a New Jersey case where it was alleged that a committee had made a recommendation regarding the purchase of desks and that approval of the proposal was made by the board without proper consideration. In an action to invalidate the award of the contract the plaintiffs were unsuccessful.[71] The Supreme Court of New Jersey stated that where corporate action was necessary the board must act as a whole. The fact, however, that negotiation had been conducted by a committee for that purpose did not invalidate the contract. But the result of such negotiation had to be reported to the board, and discussed and considered by it, before final action. It becomes apparent that it is very difficult to prove lack of proper consideration by a board approving a committee recommendation.

A board can delegate to one or more members the performance of purely ministerial functions, for example, procuring and recording a deed to property that the board had decided to purchase for a fixed price.[72] Discretionary functions cannot be delegated, even to the board presi-

69. State v. Board of Educ. of Bath-Richfield Local School Dist., 7 Ohio St.2d 49, 218 N.E.2d 616 (1966).

70. Crabtree v. Board of Educ., Wellston City School Dist., 26 Ohio App.2d 237, 270 N.E.2d 668 (1970), cert. den. 408 U.S. 943, 92 S.Ct. 2847, 33 L.Ed.2d 766 (1972).

71. State v. Board of Educ., 67 N.J.L. 512, 51 A. 483 (1902).

72. Looney v. Consolidated Independent School Dist., 201 Iowa 436, 205 N.W. 328 (1925).

dent.[73]

A board committee cannot legally be allowed to make final decisions on matters which must be considered by the entire board. Thus, a committee could not be charged with selecting a building site and contracting to have the school built,[74] nor could a committee act to rescind a contract with a consultant.[75]

Whether the entire board must participate in all phases of an activity is not always clear. Failure of all members to be present at all points in a proceeding is frequently challenged. Generally, in absence of a statute to the contrary, a quorum may act for the board as a whole. However, where the adjective "full" preceded "board" in a Rhode Island statute related to a type of hearing for nontenure teachers, the highest court of the state ruled that all members must be present.[76] The District of Columbia Court of Appeals held in a situation in which there was no indication that all members of a university disciplinary board must attend a hearing that, "consistent with the usual rule of law," a quorum could act.[77] The Commonwealth Court of Pennsylvania upheld the use by the state board of education of a panel to hear a case involving school district reorganization where the record was reviewed by the whole board before the board took action.[78]

Whether there is an implied power for a board of education to utilize a hearing examiner to conduct hearings with no board members present was decided affirmatively by the Supreme Court of Minnesota.[79] The examiner heard the evidence, summarized the facts for the board, and gave his conclusions. He did not render a decision on the merits, made no recommendation with respect to how the matter should be resolved, and took no part in the decision-making of the board.

Actions Extending beyond the Term of the Board

The authority of a school board to enter into contracts or to take other action which extends beyond the term of the board has been frequently called into question on legal grounds. Technically, the board is a legal entity as a board, and the fact that the personnel of the board may change does not change the board as such. If this concept were carried to its logical conclusion, it would be entirely possible for the members constituting the board at a given moment to deprive boards as subsequently constituted of a large part of their powers. Recognizing the dangers inherent in such possibilities, the courts consistently hold

73. Maasjo v. McLaughlin School Dist. No. 15–2, 489 N.W.2d 618 (S.D.1992).

74. Kinney v. Howard, 133 Iowa 94, 110 N.W. 282 (1907).

75. School Dist. No. 1 of Silver Bow County v. Driscoll, 176 Mont. 555, 568 P.2d 149 (1977).

76. Jacob v. Board of Regents for Educ., 117 R.I. 164, 365 A.2d 430 (1976).

77. Pride v. Howard Univ., 384 A.2d 31 (D.C.App.1978).

78. Independent School Dist. Comprised of Western Portions of Hamlin and Sargeant Tps., McKean County v. Commonwealth, State Bd. of Educ., 53 Pa.Cmwlth. 38, 417 A.2d 269 (1980).

79. Whalen v. Minneapolis Special School Dist. No. 1, 309 Minn. 292, 245 N.W.2d 440 (1976).

that a board does not have unlimited powers to bind its successors in office. On the other hand, if new board members could repudiate actions of the board as formerly constituted, the uncertainty and instability would lead to chaos. The courts examine very carefully the fact situations surrounding circumstances where it appears that either of the aforementioned extremes has occurred.

Two contract cases can be cited as illustrations of actions beyond the power of boards. One was decided by the Court of Appeals of Kentucky.[80] Here a board of education attempted to employ a superintendent for an additional four-year term commencing one year before the end of the term for which he was currently employed. The outgoing members of the board apparently were interested in extending the term of the current superintendent. At least they participated in a decision with which their successors on the board did not concur. Under the facts the court concluded that the board was without power to create a new term before the end of the previous term. The court noted that any other conclusion would make it possible for a superintendent to secure the votes of the majority of board members, splice terms, and perpetuate himself in office indefinitely, thereby defeating the right of the people to indirectly select this important officer.

In a similar situation in New Jersey, a board of education, which had employed a superintendent for a two-year probationary term, attempted, after eight and a half months to give him a three-year contract, which would include tenure under New Jersey statutes. The court examined carefully the proceedings and determined that there had been an illegal modus operandi.[81] The court found merit in the suggestion that the real reason for the change was that the members of the majority block, mindful of the coming election, decided to give the superintendent tenure while they could, even though it meant shortening his probationary period by almost two-thirds. Although the court recognized that the action was taken at a regular public board meeting and that the members of the majority block could well have acted in the honest belief that it was in the best interests of the educational system to grant the superintendent tenure at that point, it took judicial notice of the fact that the change was effected by a majority block of five members, three of whom were serving terms which were to expire within a few months, and that the matter had been privately discussed and planned in advance but the notice withheld from the other board members and the public. Of course, ordinary transition of an employee to tenure status would create a contract binding on all succeeding boards.

The general rule appears to be that, in the absence of express or implied statutory limitation on authority to do so, or unless there is fraud or collusion, a board can enter into a contract which extends for a reasonable period beyond the term of the board entering into it. This result is especially likely if the contract begins during the term of the incumbent board. It is less certain where such is not the situation. It

80. Board of Educ. of Pendleton County v. Gulick, 398 S.W.2d 483 (Ky.1966).

81. Thomas v. Board of Educ. of Morris Tp., 89 N.J.Super. 327, 215 A.2d 35 (1965).

has been held, for instance, that if the period for which a contract is made lies totally within the term of a succeeding board, the contract is invalid.[82] Under other facts courts have construed statutes to empower a board, because it was a continuing body, to bind its successors even though the services under the contract would be performed wholly within the term of a new board.[83] A common law test for a board not to be able to bind its successor boards is that the discretionary decision by the board, presumably for the welfare of the schools, has a high probability of being tainted with improper considerations. A party wishing to obtain a ruling that an action is not binding may be required to show that the agreement extending beyond the term of the contracting board is not reasonably necessary or has no definable advantage to the board.[84] State statutes relevant to this area vary markedly, as do court interpretations thereof.[85]

School Elections

In General

One way in which the public can participate directly in the operation of the schools is through elections. These may be on whatever matters the legislature chooses, and the procedures specified by the legislature for conducting them are subject only to restrictions of the state and federal constitutions. Elections for school board members may differ from those on bond issues or those for other purposes, and special elections may be subject to restrictions not placed on regular elections. Elections may be held only by virtue of legislative authority. If one is held without such authority, or contrary to material provisions of the law, it is a nullity.

Petitions for Elections

Election procedures in special elections are usually set in motion by the filing of a petition in the form provided by law. Also, candidates for office often are required to file petitions in order to have their names placed on the ballot. Statutes usually provide that a petition shall contain the signatures of a specified number or a certain percentage of electors of the district. The petition must be presented to the designated officer or board that is required or authorized to call the election. Whether the calling of the election upon receiving the petition is ministerial or discretionary depends upon the statute on the point. Even where it is discretionary, the courts may order the election held if it finds the

82. Independent School Dist. v. Pennington, 181 Iowa 933, 165 N.W. 209 (1917).

83. King Union High School Dist. v. Waibel, 2 Cal.App.2d 65, 37 P.2d 861 (1934).

84. Michie v. Board of Trustees of Carbon County School Dist. No. 1, 847 P.2d 1006 (Wyo.1993). [Case No. 20]

85. See last full paragraph of Case No. 40.

discretion abused.[86]

The officials designated to act on these petitions have the responsibility for determining whether the signers are in fact legal electors, and whether the signatures are genuine. It has been held that a recital in the petition itself that its signers are legal electors is no evidence of that fact.[87] In some states, the officer or agency designated to act upon a petition may rely upon the affidavits of those who circulated the petitions that the signatures are genuine and the persons signing are electors. Such a verification must be made before the filing deadline.[88] Where there is no statutory requirement that signatures be compared, the failure to do so is no basis for striking names from petitions.[89] However, the principal saving circumstance that protects districts from having elections invalidated because of inadequate petitions is the rule that the validity of signatures thereon may not be attacked for the first time after an election has been held, or after action on the petition has been taken. This rule was applied by the Supreme Court of Nebraska in a case in which it was sought to enjoin one district from asserting dominion and control over certain territory. Those who brought the action alleged that one person who signed was not a qualified voter, and that if his name were struck from the petition it would not bear the requisite number of signatures. The court dismissed the suit without hearing evidence on this point.[90] Since the validity of the petition was attacked collaterally in a suit brought for another purpose, the validity of the election was sustained.

The sufficiency of a petition in Michigan was challenged on the grounds that a number of the signers had signed on Sunday, in some instances the petition was not signed in the presence of the circulator, and in some cases persons had signed for others. The election involved the consolidation of certain school districts, and a number of those who opposed the consolidation based their challenge to the validity of the election on the irregularity of the signing of the petition for the election. The election was sustained.[91] The court referred to the rule that before an election is held, it is mandatory to follow the exact provisions of the statute if direct proceedings are brought to enforce them; however, if the action to contest the election is brought after it is held, the statutory requirements will be held to be directory only unless a noncompliance with their terms is expressly declared by the statute to be fatal or will change or render doubtful the result.

The legality of one person's signing for another has been challenged in a number of states. The most frequent instance is when one spouse signs the petition in behalf of the other. The question is whether the

---

86. Gibson v. Winterset Community School Dist., 258 Iowa 440, 138 N.W.2d 112 (1965).

87. People ex rel. Anderson v. Community Unit School Dist. No. 201, 7 Ill.App.2d 32, 129 N.E.2d 28 (1955).

88. Burns v. Kurtenbach, 327 N.W.2d 636 (S.D.1982).

89. Johnson v. Maehling, 123 Ariz. 15, 597 P.2d 1 (1979).

90. Cacek v. Munson, 160 Neb. 187, 69 N.W.2d 692 (1955).

91. Richey v. Board of Educ. of Monroe County, 346 Mich. 156, 77 N.W.2d 361 (1956).

general rule of signature ratification or adoption is applicable to signatures on school petitions. The general rule is that a person is bound on a legal instrument if he ratifies, or adopts as his own, a signature placed thereon in his behalf by another person. The Supreme Court of Missouri applied this rule where evidence showed that the husband had authorized his wife to sign his name to the petition in question.[92] Generally, no particular mode or form of authorization is necessary to authorize one person to sign another's name to a legal document. Oral authority is sufficient unless the statute requires the authority to be in writing. No such statute appeared in this case.

Assuming a petition has been validly signed, the question frequently arises as to the right of signers to withdraw their names from the petition. Obviously there must be a cutoff point beyond which signatures may not be withdrawn. Otherwise, the petition procedure could not operate. The common law rule is that a signer of a petition always may withdraw his name before it has been presented to the agency or officer designated by statute to receive and act upon it. Some courts have held that names may not be withdrawn from a petition after it has been filed with the proper agency or officer, even though no action has yet been taken on it.[93] Other courts have held that signers may legally withdraw their names at any time before the petition has been acted upon. For example, the Supreme Court of Nebraska did not feel justified in placing any restrictions upon the free action of a citizen to withdraw his name from a petition when the statutes had not done so, and when no consideration seemed to require such restrictions.[94] It stated that permitting withdrawal of names from petitions before action has been taken upon them is calculated to discourage hasty presentation of a petition without a full disclosure of the merits of the question. This rule, in the opinion of the court, is also more likely to result in a more thoroughly considered and mature judgment of the voters. The Appellate Court of Illinois held that withdrawal of names from a petition after action on it has begun, but before final disposition of the matter has been made, is permissible, and terminates the proceedings if an insufficient number of names remain on the petition.[95]

The Supreme Court of North Dakota refused to allow withdrawal of names from a petition respecting opening a closed school after the petition had been filed.[96] The court said the petition at the time of filing was either sufficient or not, and the school board was not empowered to permit withdrawals. There was no statutory provision for a hearing on such petitions, and thus the filing was equivalent to the board's taking action because the statute required school reopenings if petitioned for by a specified percent of electors.

92. State ex rel. Kugler v. Tillatson, 312 S.W.2d 753 (Mo.1958).

93. Zilske v. Albers, 238 Iowa 1050, 29 N.W.2d 189 (1947).

94. State ex rel. Larson v. Morrison, 155 Neb. 309, 51 N.W.2d 626 (1952).

95. Konald v. Board of Educ. of Community Unit School Dist. 220, 114 Ill. App.3d 512, 69 Ill.Dec. 837, 448 N.E.2d 555 (1983).

96. Judson PTO v. New Salem School Bd., 262 N.W.2d 502 (N.D.1978).

A few states have statutory provisions that prevent removal of signatures once affixed except under unusual circumstances, such as having signed because of duress or misrepresentation. Where such statutes exist, they are governing.[97] Even after jurisdiction has attached to the petition, names may be withdrawn if it can be shown that the signers had been induced to sign by fraud, misrepresentation, or misapprehension as to the true facts involved. Usually, withdrawal under these circumstances may be made only by leave of the court or other body having jurisdiction of the proceedings.[98]

The Supreme Court of Nebraska has held that rules for withdrawing names from petitions also apply to adding them.[99] Thus, even though the deadline for signing had passed, names could be added before the petition was filed.

The Supreme Court of Ohio has answered two questions about petitions under the statutes of that state. In one the question was whether the addition of a name to a petition after the petition had been declared valid by a board of elections would invalidate the petition under the statutory proscription against altering, correcting, or adding to a petition after it has been filed.[100] The court answered in the negative, stating that fraud, deception, or undue influence in the petitioning process was not alleged, and that the purpose of the prohibition was to prevent alterations between the time of filing and the consideration of the petition by the board of elections.

In the other case, the question was whether noncompliance with a statute prohibiting the signing of another's name on an election petition with the knowledge and permission of the circulator invalidated the signature only or the entire petition paper. The statute specified the latter result, but it was claimed that the import of the wording was to infer fraudulent intent, which in this case was absent. The court disagreed, saying that in the absence of evidence indicating the word "knowingly" in the statute meant more than its ordinary meaning, it was that common meaning which would be enforced.[101]

Notice of Elections

Notice of elections is ordinarily required to be given. Statutes vary widely as to the nature and extent of notice required. Among the common specifications are the publication of notice for a stated number of days or weeks prior to the date of the election and the posting of notices in "public places." Notices are required to inform the voters on such matters as the purpose of the election, the date and place at which it will be held, and when the polls will open and close.

97. State ex rel. Muter v. Mercer County Bd. of Educ., 112 Ohio App. 66, 175 N.E.2d 305 (1959).

98. In re Mercerburg Independent School Dist., 237 Pa. 368, 85 A. 467 (1912).

99. Retzlaff v. Synovec, 178 Neb. 147, 132 N.W.2d 314 (1965).

100. State ex rel. Dennis v. Miller, 28 Ohio St.2d 1, 274 N.E.2d 459 (1971).

101. State ex rel. Carson v. Jones, 24 Ohio St.2d 70, 263 N.E.2d 567 (1970).

The adequacy of the notice has frequently been challenged on the ground that there were omissions or errors in it. The entire matter of the proper wording of election notices is one of considerable nicety. This is particularly true of notices of bond elections. The terminology of the notice should be sufficiently detailed to enable voters to understand the nature of the proposition involved in the election, yet sufficiently broad to avoid unduly restricting the board in the use of the proceeds of the bond sale.

The effect of an error in a notice is illustrated by a situation which arose in Ohio. The law of that state required that bond election notices state the amount of the proposed issue, the purpose of the issue, the maximum term of the bonds, and the estimated additional tax rate, expressed in dollars and cents for each one hundred dollars of valuation as well as in mills for each dollar of valuation. However, through error, the notice omitted to state the amount of the annual tax levy in mills for each one dollar of valuation, omitted to state a portion of the purpose of the issue, and the amount of the annual tax levy in cents for each one hundred dollars of valuation was stated as being 3.2 instead of .32, the proper rate. The legality of the election was attacked on the ground that these errors in the notice invalidated it.

However, despite the numerous errors in the notice, the validity of the election was sustained.[102] There was evidence that the election had received wide publicity within the district. Numerous articles describing the needs of the schools, the amount of the bond issue, and the uses to which the proceeds would be put appeared in several issues of the local newspapers. Drawings of the proposed school building also had appeared in the newspapers. The court held that the purpose of the notice of election had been accomplished adequately through other media.

Inadequacy of notice was urged in a Missouri case as the basis for invalidating an election. It was contended that three of five notices were not in public places because they were on school property and "inaccessible to individuals of the public who must become trespassers to read the notices." The supreme court of the state found no merit in the contention that people on school property for the purpose of reading the notice were trespassers, because trespass is an unauthorized entry.[103] Also, it was insisted that having the three notices back from the street rendered them improper. The court rejected this argument too, saying that a "public place" need not be near a street. There was abundant evidence that wide publicity had been given the election through newspapers and a brochure mailed to electors.

Alleged misadvice to electors through notices can be the basis of litigation. For example, a school board issued a brochure explaining a bond election and its purpose. Parts were printed in newspapers "in conjunction with," but not as a part of, the statutory notice. After the election, due to underestimates of costs, the board sought to use relative-

---

102. State ex rel. Bd. of Educ. of the Plain Local School Dist. v. McGlynn, 100 Ohio App. 57, 135 N.E.2d 632 (1955).

103. Montgomery v. Reorganized School Dist. No. 1, 339 S.W.2d 831 (Mo.1960).

ly more of the funds for one school project, and thus not allocate the funds for all of the projects specified in the brochure. Suit was brought to enjoin the readjusted building program. The Supreme Court of Utah stated the usual rule to be that it is the notice published by the board pursuant to statute that binds the board, and that collateral statements or explanatory materials do not.[104] The decision did not turn on the brochure's status, however. The court sustained the board's power reasonably to reallocate bond money after an election where no deceit, fraud, or corruption was shown.

Courts tend to construe election laws to preserve, if possible, the choice of the people as expressed at the election.[105] Mere irregularity in giving notice, or the failure to give notice for the full time prescribed in the statute, is generally not fatal to the validity of the election if knowledge of the approach of the election and the question to be passed upon is general throughout the district, if a comparatively full vote is cast, and if the irregularity in the notice did not mislead any elector to his disadvantage. In the great majority of cases the courts have construed notice requirements as directory, rather than mandatory, unless the statute indicates clearly the legislative intention that the election shall be invalid if the statutory requirements are not fulfilled or unless there is a gross irregularity in the notice.[106]

An example of the latter is found in an election in New Mexico. The resolution calling a bond election stated that a specified sum of money was to be voted "for school purposes." The state supreme court held that this wording was not sufficiently precise so as to advise the electorate of the actual purpose of the proposed bond issue.[107] The notice was not required to include details of proposed uses of the money, but was required to be less broad than was the wording used.

Ballots

Assuming an election is legally called, certain officials are charged with the responsibility of preparing the ballot for use in the election. The usual requirement that the ballot be secret is ordinarily applicable to school elections. When, by accident or design, the election is conducted in such a manner as to destroy the secrecy of the ballot, the election is usually invalidated.[108]

Despite the strong public interest in the secrecy of the ballot and the right of a voter to decline to reveal how he voted, there are exceptions to the exercise of this right. If investigation establishes that one who has voted in an election was not legally eligible to do so, and if it appears

104. Ricker v. Board of Educ. of Millard County School Dist., 16 Utah 2d 106, 396 P.2d 416 (1964). [Case No. 39]

105. Abts v. Board of Educ. of School Dist. RE–1 Valley in Logan County, 622 P.2d 518 (Colo.1980).

106. Eustace v. Speckhart, 14 Or.App. 485, 514 P.2d 65 (1973); Wright v. Board of Trustees of Tatum Independent School Dist., 520 S.W.2d 787 (Tex.Civ.App.1975).

107. Board of Educ. of City of Aztec v. Hartley, 74 N.M. 469, 394 P.2d 985 (1964).

108. Corn v. Blackwell, 191 S.C. 183, 4 S.E.2d 254 (1939).

that the result of the election could have been changed by his vote, he may be required to disclose how he voted. This requirement is for the purpose of purging the election of the illegal votes. The right to a secret ballot may, in such a situation, have to give way to the public interest in having all voters qualified.[109]

Requirements aimed at insuring the integrity of the election process usually are considered to be mandatory. Thus, failure of election officials to follow provisions covering duplicate ballots when originals are damaged has been held to invalidate the ballots, even if thereby the voters who cast the ballots were disenfranchised.[110] In that case there was no allegation of impropriety, and defendants had claimed that the damaged ballots and the duplicates could be matched.

Many elections have been challenged because the ballots were not worded so as to provide the voters with a clear choice between alternative propositions. A large number of cases have involved charges that the ballots contained more than one proposition. It is the rule that the language of the ballot must be plain, understandable, and subject to only one interpretation. From many cases there has evolved what is referred to as the "single proposition" rule. This rule is designed to prevent the including of two or more unrelated propositions on one ballot, thereby compelling the voters to accept an undesirable proposition in order to obtain a desirable one. In order to constitute a single proposition or question there must exist a natural relationship between the objects covered by the ballot so that they form but one rounded whole or single plan.

The Supreme Court of Minnesota has said that to constitute duplicity of subject matter, in violation of the single proposition requirement in the Minnesota constitution, the ballot must embrace "two or more dissimilar and discordant subjects which cannot reasonably be said to have any legitimate connection." [111] In that case the court approved, as conforming with the single proposition rule, a bond issue for "the purpose of the acquisition and betterment of schoolhouses of the district." The Supreme Court of Illinois has ruled that "constructing" and "equipping" school buildings can be treated as a single purpose.[112] These two items "are not unrelated so as to require separate propositions upon the ballot."

A case in which the single proposition rule was held violated arose in Minnesota.[113] A ballot in the following language was declared illegal:

Shall the Independent Consolidated School District No. 1 of Stevens County issue bonds in the sum of $400,000 for the

---

109. Wehrung v. Ideal School Dist. No. 10, 78 N.W.2d 68 (N.D.1956). [Case No. 142]. See also Note 4 on the case.

110. Larson v. Board of Educ. of Bement Community School Dist. No. 5, in Piatt and Champaign Counties, 118 Ill. App.3d 1015, 74 Ill.Dec. 437, 455 N.E.2d 866 (1983).

111. Buhl v. Joint Independent School Dist., 249 Minn. 480, 82 N.W.2d 836 (1957).

112. Carstens v. Board of Educ. of East Alton-Wood River Community High School Dist., 27 Ill.2d 88, 187 N.E.2d 682 (1963).

113. Green v. Independent Consolidated School Dist. No. 1, 243 Minn. 519, 68 N.W.2d 493 (1955).

erection of a new schoolhouse and/or expansion, improvement, and equipment of its schoolhouses?

The court pointed out that this single question contained three alternative proposals: (1) erection of a new school building, (2) improvement, equipment, and expansion of existing school buildings, or (3) a combination of new construction and improvements. It stated that the vice of this ballot was that the three-part question made it impossible to ascertain whether a majority of the voters was obtained to authorize any of the three proposals. Voters could not approve their choice without also voting for its alternatives. Furthermore, if the proposition carried, after the election the board could decide which of the three plans it would adopt.

When elections are completed, the propositions as worded on the ballots are binding. The full text of a proposition need not be on the ballot, but what is printed on the ballot must clearly identify the matter and its chief features in words of plain meaning.[114] "Agreements" not part of the resolutions voted are generally not enforceable. An Oregon case is an example. The supreme court of the state was asked to decide whether an agreement signed by all school board members of all districts involved in a consolidation was binding on a new district voted into existence with some voters having the understanding that the agreement would be incorporated in the reorganization plan. The agreement was that no school would be changed, moved, or consolidated without approval of electors in the attendance area served by the school. Five years later the voters of the new district passed a bond issue for one high school for the entire district. The court held that the agreement was not in fact incorporated in the plan, and that the alleged misadvice would not serve to invalidate the election and its binding effect on the entire district.[115]

Qualifications for Voting

One who meets all qualifications set for those casting ballots in an election is known technically as an elector. If he actually casts the ballot, he is a voter. Although the terms are often used synonymously, the difference can be important. For example, some statutes require certain percents of "electors" to approve certain items. In the absence of such express provisions, measures are carried by a majority of those voting.

Constitutional and statutory provisions prescribing the eligibility of voters exist in all states. These requirements vary, but a common one is that of residence. Generally, statutes cover both residence per se and residence for a specified minimum period before an election. Whether a particular voter is a resident at the time he seeks to vote, or has been a resident of the district a sufficient period of time to entitle him to vote, is

114. Wright v. Board of Trustees of Tatum Independent School Dist., 520 S.W.2d 787 (Tex.Civ.App.1975).

115. Grant v. School Dist. No. 61, Baker County, 244 Or. 131, 415 P.2d 165 (1966). [Case No. 143]

not always a simple matter to determine. The mere fact that a person may be physically present in the district does not necessarily constitute him a resident thereof for voting purposes. By the same token, neither is the absence of a voter from the district, even for a substantial period of time, necessarily determinative of his ineligibility to vote. Whether one is a resident depends upon a wide variety of circumstances. Some courts equate residence for voting purposes with "domicile," or permanent place of abode, only one of which a person may legally have.

It has been held that one does not lose residence for voting purposes merely because he moves his family from the district, enters his children in schools outside it, and accepts a position in another district. If it is the intention of the voter to return to the first district, and the evidence shows that he had been living only temporarily in the second district, his voting residence remains in the first district.[116]

Statutes requiring that a person reside in a district for a period of time before becoming eligible to vote are subject to strict scrutiny by the courts. The Supreme Court in 1972 held that bona fide residents of a jurisdiction could not be required to reside there for three months before voting.[117] The Court suggested that a period of 30 days appeared ample to complete administrative tasks related to checking on residence and preventing voting fraud. The 30-day period has been adopted by some state courts as the rule for their states.[118] The Supreme Court, however, has upheld as reasonable a 50-day requirement.[119]

In some states there are special qualifications required for participation in school elections. Whether these are valid depends on whether they constitute classifications inconsistent, under strict scrutiny, with the equal protection clause of the Fourteenth Amendment. The Supreme Court in 1969 ruled unconstitutional a New York provision that to vote in certain school elections, one or one's spouse must own or rent real property, or be a parent of a child in public school.[120] The Court said that the classification could not be justified by a belief that parents of children in the schools and payers of property taxes were the most intimately interested in the schools.

One Person-One Vote Principle

The principle of one person-one vote also has been considered in connection with other types of situations in school board elections. The Supreme Court has ruled that the principle did not apply to county

116. Wehrung v. Ideal School Dist. No. 10, 78 N.W.2d 68 (N.D.1956). [Case No. 142]

117. Dunn v. Blumstein, 405 U.S. 330, 92 S.Ct. 995, 31 L.Ed.2d 274 (1972).

118. Torres v. Laramie County School Dist. No. 1, 506 P.2d 817 (Wyo.1973), cert. den. 414 U.S. 990, 94 S.Ct. 342, 38 L.Ed.2d 229 (1973).

119. Marston v. Lewis, 410 U.S. 679, 93 S.Ct. 1211, 35 L.Ed.2d 627 (1973).

120. Kramer v. Union Free School Dist. No. 15, 395 U.S. 621, 89 S.Ct. 1886, 23

school boards in Michigan.[121]　County boards there were chosen by delegates from local boards.　The election of the latter was not contested.　Challenged was the fact that each local board had one delegate, regardless of the size of the population of the school district.　The Court held that the system was basically appointive, rather than elective, and that county boards performed essentially administrative, and not legislative, functions.　Since the choice of members of the county board was based on appointment and not election, and since no election was required for nonlegislative officers, the principle of one person-one vote had no relevancy.

Emphasizing its holding in the preceding case as regards the dichotomy between appointive and elective boards, the Supreme Court later held that, when members of an elected body are chosen from separate districts, the arrangement must be such that, to the extent practicable, equal numbers of voters can vote for proportionally equal numbers of officials.[122]　Found unconstitutional was a Missouri statute that provided for establishment of consolidated junior college districts by component public school districts.

Some states require more than a simple majority vote to pass bond referenda.　Such an arrangement mathematically gives more weight to negative votes.　That it does not violate the Fourteenth Amendment was determined by the Supreme Court in 1971.[123]　The Court observed that the Constitution itself requires more than majority votes on certain matters.　Bonded indebtedness is a matter of import to future generations, who may have to pay.　As long as voting provisions do not discriminate against any class identifiable by an extraneous condition such as race or wealth, they do not violate the equal protection clause.

In 1990 the Supreme Court of Illinois nullified a decentralization arrangement for governance of the Chicago public schools.[124]　The state legislature had provided for the establishment of a school council for each school and granted substantial governmental powers to the councils.　Each council was to comprise ten elected members: six parents elected by parents, two residents of the school area elected by residents, and two teachers elected by the school staff.　That six members of each council were to be elected solely by parents could not be justified on the ground that parents had a greater interest in the school than qualified voters without children in attendance (see Kramer, footnote 120, supra) or on the ground that they had any special competence to choose council members of quality.　The court emphasized that the councils had broad powers.

L.Ed.2d 583 (1969).　See Notes 3 and 4, Case No. 144.

U.S. 50, 90 S.Ct. 791, 25 L.Ed.2d 45 (1970). [Case No. 144]

121.　Sailors v. Board of Educ. of the County of Kent, 387 U.S. 105, 87 S.Ct. 1549, 18 L.Ed.2d 650 (1967).

122.　Hadley v. Junior College Dist. of Metropolitan Kansas City, Missouri, 397

123.　Gordon v. Lance, 403 U.S. 1, 91 S.Ct. 1889, 29 L.Ed. 273 (1971).

124.　Fumarolo v. Chicago Bd. of Educ., 142 Ill.2d 54, 153 Ill.Dec. 177, 566 N.E.2d 1283 (1990).

Use of School Funds in Relation to Elections

At best, election notices can contain only brief statements of the purpose for which the election is to be held. Intelligent judgment by the voters depends upon the completeness of their knowledge and understanding of the proposition to be voted upon. Local boards have the implied power, if not the duty, to disseminate relevant information about such propositions. Reasonable expenditures to this end are clearly proper. (See Case No. 43.)

Quite a different issue is presented, however, when the board of education seeks to use school monies to advocate its views. It has been held that when a board abandons its function of providing information on both sides of a proposition, and uses school funds for the purpose of advocating a favorable vote on one side or the other, it is exceeding its authority.[125] In reaching this conclusion in a case involving a brochure which contained an exhortation to "vote yes," the Supreme Court of New Jersey stated that it did not mean to imply that the board was restrained from advocating adoption of its plan in any ways other than those involving expenditures of public funds. Also it stated that public forums and radio or television broadcasts might be financed, provided views pro and con could be freely expressed.

The Supreme Court of California has said that neutrality of the government in election contests is a "fundamental precept of this nation's democratic electoral process," and that lobbying to promote one position is a prohibited use of public funds.[126] The Court of Appeals, Tenth Circuit, has held that a city and a school district improperly made expenditures to help defeat a proposed amendment to the Colorado constitution that would have mandated voter approval of all acts resulting in tax increases.[127] The court decided that a statute permitting contributions to "campaigns involving only issues in which [political subdivisions of the state] have an official concern" did not provide authorization.

Overruling the state commissioner of education and the intermediate appellate court, New York's highest court held that "vote yes" to "help protect our school facilities and the quality of education in our District" went beyond what was reasonably necessary to educate the public about budget and bond issue proposals.[128] The Supreme Court of Mississippi held personally liable board members who voted affirmatively for extravagant expenditures in support of a school bond referendum.[129]

125. Citizens to Protect Public Funds v. Board of Educ. of Parsippany-Troy Hills Tp., 13 N.J. 172, 98 A.2d 673 (1953). [Case No. 145]

126. Stanson v. Mott, 17 Cal.3d 206, 130 Cal.Rptr. 697, 551 P.2d 1 (1976).

127. Campbell v. Joint Dist. 28–J, 704 F.2d 501 (10 Cir.1983).

128. Phillips v. Maurer, 67 N.Y.2d 672, 499 N.Y.S.2d 675, 490 N.E.2d 542 (1986).

129. Smith v. Dorsey, 599 So.2d 529 (Miss.1992).

[Case No. 138] Board Procedures in Contracting

KONOVALCHIK v. SCHOOL COMMITTEE OF SALEM

Supreme Judicial Court of Massachusetts, 1967.
352 Mass. 542, 226 N.E.2d 222.

WHITTEMORE, JUSTICE. The issue on this appeal in a proceeding under G.L. c. 231A is whether, as the judge in the Superior Court ruled, certain votes of the defendant school committee on December 13, 1965, and subsequent events resulted in a three year contract with the plaintiff as head coach of football. The evidence is reported.

Most of the facts are not in dispute. We state others as the judge could have found them. The committee has power to make such a contract. G.L. c. 71, § 47A.

The school committee on December 13, 1965, by a vote of four in favor to three opposed voted to award to the plaintiff a contract as football coach for three years from December 31, 1965, at a salary of $3,000 for the first year and $3,500 for the two succeeding years. Motions to reconsider failed of passage. In another vote the city solicitor was requested to draw up a contract and have it at the December 27, 1965, meeting. The city solicitor was in the hospital from December 21, 1965, to January 15, 1966. Charles Geary, a member of the majority, typed out a contract substantially in the form of the plaintiff's existing contract that was to expire August 31, 1966, except for the term, the compensation, and one omission, and had the plaintiff sign it. The December 27 meeting was convened at the stated hour with the three dissenters in attendance. They adjourned the meeting at 8:20 P.M. for lack of a quorum with knowledge that at least some of the majority were then in the building but had not responded promptly to the mayor's notice that the meeting was in session. They knew that Geary was there and had the draft contract with him. About 8:20 P.M. the four members of the majority signed the contract form in the secretary's office "where we sign most contracts." One copy of the contract was given to the plaintiff, one went to the office of the superintendent of schools and one to the city hall records. There was newspaper notice of the purported contract "sometime after the meeting of December 27."

We hold that no contract was made. The engagement was dependent upon the drafting and submission to the committee, and its approval, of a formal contract. The December 13 votes were not in themselves an offer which the plaintiff could accept.

Geary and his associates of the December 13 majority were without authority to determine for the committee the contract terms or to submit any document or offer of contract to the plaintiff. It may not be inferred that counsel would have recommended or the committee would have approved Geary's draft, or a contract like the existing contract.

We recognize that parliamentary tactics have operated to defeat the basic intention of the committee, at least as constituted in December, 1965. That circumstance cannot, however, operate to change rules of law.

The final decree is reversed. A decree is to enter in accordance with this opinion.

So ordered.

Notes

1. Do you believe that the cause of education was served by this ruling?

2. Do you consider the actions of the dissenters unethical, or were they simply "playing by the rules of the game?"

3. A written document may be necessary to the validity of a contract, or it may be only a memorandum of a previously formed contract. Apparently the court considered this case to fall within the first category. Might the court have held that a contract was actually formed at the December 13 meeting? Review pertinent sections on contracts in Chapters 8 and 9.

[Case No. 139] Voting Procedures of Boards

MATAWAN REGIONAL TEACHERS ASS'N v. MATAWAN–ABERDEEN REGIONAL SCHOOL DIST. BD. OF EDUC.

Superior Court of New Jersey, Appellate Division, 1988.
223 N.J.Super. 504, 538 A.2d 1331.

BRODY, J.A.D. The issue in this appeal is whether a local school board may lawfully adopt a plan, which includes the closing and sale of a school building, by a majority vote of its full membership after consideration at a single public meeting even though its bylaws require adoption by a ⅔ vote of its full membership after consideration at two public meetings. We hold that the board is not bound by the bylaw that limits the authority of the majority, but is bound by the bylaw that requires two public meetings for adoption of the plan.

The dispute arose when the nine members of the Matawan–Aberdeen Regional School District Board of Education (the board) voted 5 to 4 to reorganize the school district by adopting "Plan C" (the plan). The cornerstone of the plan is the closing and sale of a school and an administration building in the Borough of Matawan. Closing the school requires relocating students and changing the range of classes in the remaining schools. Adoption of the plan is a matter of substantial local public interest. Petitioners are the union that represents board employees, and 92 resident-taxpayers of the district.

An administrative law judge (ALJ) summarily dismissed the claim that the bylaws barred adoption of the plan. The Commissioner of Education and the State Board of Education affirmed the ALJ's summary dismissal for the reasons he had expressed.

The relevant bylaws provide the following:

> No policy shall be adopted by the Board until it has received a ⅔ vote of the full Board at two public meetings.

* * *

Bylaws shall be adopted, amended or repealed by a ⅔ vote of the full Board.

Local boards of education "may exercise only those powers granted to them by the Legislature—either expressly or by necessary or fair implication." Fair Lawn Ed. Assn. v. Fair Lawn Bd. of Education. Boards derive the authority to adopt bylaws from N.J.S.A. 18A:11–1c, which provides that a local board shall

> Make, amend and repeal rules, not inconsistent with this title or with the rules of the state board, for its own government and the transaction of its business and for the government and management of the public schools and public school property of the district and for the employment, regulation of conduct and discharge of its employees * * *.

Boards derive the authority to govern and manage the district from N.J.S.A. 18A:11–1d, which provides that a local board shall

> Perform all acts and do all things, consistent with law and the rules of the state board, necessary for the lawful and proper conduct, equipment and maintenance of the public schools of the district.

N.J.S.A. 18A:11–1 is silent with respect to the number of votes necessary to adopt rules and to govern and manage the district. It must be assumed that by its silence the Legislature intended the common-law rule to apply, i.e., a majority vote of the members of the board constituting a quorum shall be sufficient. At common law, a majority of a public body constitutes a quorum. Thus the Legislature has empowered a majority of the majority of a local board to adopt bylaws and conduct the board's business.

We reject the argument that the Legislature has merely established a minimum number of affirmative votes necessary for local board action, which the board may increase in its bylaws to assure a broader consensus. Depriving the majority of its authority and responsibility to govern in favor of a broader consensus carries the risk of inaction where action is warranted. There may be actions which should be taken with the affirmative votes of an enhanced majority because of their overwhelming importance or because they constitute a departure from the norm. The Legislature has provided for such particular instances by requiring the vote of an enhanced majority. A relevant example is the statute that prohibits a local board from selling school lands except "by a recorded roll call majority vote of its full membership." N.J.S.A. 18A:20–5. That requirement was met here.

We conclude that the Legislature has preempted a local board's authority to strike the balance between requiring a broad consensus for action and the attendant risk of inaction. We arrive at this conclusion because striking that delicate balance is a matter of major governmental importance calling for uniform treatment throughout the State and is a subject on which the Legislature has acted in many specific instances by requiring an enhanced majority.

Our holding conforms to long-standing precedent in this State. In Barnert v. Paterson, 48 N.J.L. 395, 400, 6 A. 15 (Sup.Ct.1886), the court held:

> When the charter of a municipal corporation or a general law of the state does not provide to the contrary, a majority of the board of aldermen constitute a quorum, and the vote of a majority of those present, there being a quorum, is all that is required for the adoption or passage of a motion or the doing of any other act the board has power to do.

> Under the twenty-third section of the charter, the board is given power "to establish its own rules of procedure." But I do not think that under this power it was designed to confer upon this board the adoption of a rule changing either the general law or any special provision in the charter. Power to make such rules and by-laws was inherent in the corporation without this provision. Such by-laws must be in accordance with the charter or the general rules of law. The charter is silent and the general law requires a majority vote.

* * *

By contrast, the bylaw requiring that action on non-emergent matters of policy be considered at two public meetings does not conflict directly or indirectly with any statute. Its purpose is not to remove the responsibility and authority to act from those members of a local board who are authorized by state law to act. Rather, its purpose is to assure that those having that responsibility and authority act only upon due deliberation after notice to the public and interested third parties. Our courts have long compelled public bodies to adhere to such bylaws.

In Eggers v. Newark, 77 N.J.L. 198, 71 A. 665 (Sup.Ct.1908), a Board of Street and Water Commissioners adopted an ordinance during the meeting at which it was introduced despite a bylaw that required publication between the first and second readings. The commissioners purported to suspend the bylaw by unanimous consent. The court held that the bylaws had been duly adopted pursuant to statute and therefore "constituted the working regulations governing [the Board's] action so far as not regulated by higher authority of the statute." In upholding the bylaws and setting aside the ordinance the court said,

> [I]t is evident that if they can be rendered nugatory by the suspension of a mere rule of order, the by-laws are little more than a suggestion instead of being, as they should be, a set of regulations for the transaction of public business by a public body, on which regulations the public itself has a right to rely. The more radical proposition is also advanced that, as the vote was unanimous to suspend the by-law and pass the ordinance, no one can be heard to complain. But this likewise loses sight of the right of the public to expect that ordinances, involving as they do the interests of the public, shall be enacted in due form as provided by law, and that part of that law is the regulations

adopted and promulgated by the legislative body. The ordinance in question was one in which the public were vitally interested.

In Hicks v. Long Branch Commission, 69 N.J.L. 300, 55 A. 250 (E. & A.1903), the Court set aside a special appropriation because, in violation of the Commission's bylaws, each commissioner's vote was not recorded. The Court said,

> The standing rules, adopted by ordinance under the express authority of the charter, as before stated, provide that "on every vote relating to any special appropriation the yeas and nays shall be taken and recorded." This rule was as binding upon the commission and its members as any statute or other law of the commonwealth. Its importance is manifest. It is designed to secure, in matters relating to the public funds, deliberate action on the part of each commissioner, and immediate as well as permanent public evidence thereof, readily accessible to the voters of the municipality, on which their representatives may be held responsible.

The binding effect of bylaws designed to give the public notice before official action is taken was reaffirmed by the Court in Erie R.R. Co. v. Paterson, 79 N.J.L. 512, 76 A. 1065 (E. & A.1910), where a Board of Public Works adopted an ordinance at a meeting held on a date not scheduled in its bylaws. In setting aside the ordinance the Court cited the language in *Eggers* with approval.

In the absence of any statute to the contrary, the board's bylaw requiring two public meetings to adopt the plan is binding. We must therefore set aside the resolution that purported to adopt the plan at a single meeting. Our determination renders moot the other issues that have been raised in this appeal.

Reversed.

Notes

1. Fair Lawn Educ. Ass'n v. Fair Lawn Bd. of Educ. (cited in the case) is Case No. 21.

2. The court in Barnert v. Paterson (quoted in the case) used the expression "general rules of law" to denote what is more usually called "the common law".

3. Very important is the distinction illustrated in this case between those procedural rules that can be enacted and then must be followed by lower government bodies and those that cannot be enacted in the absence of state legislation. The administrative law judge, the commissioner of education, and the state board of education erred as to the distinction.

4. Contemplate the rationale expressed in Eggers v. Newark and Hicks v. Long Branch Commission (quoted in the case) that served as basis of the decision in this case. How does it serve the long-range interests of democratic government?

[Case No. 140] Public Nature of Board Meetings and Records

CONOVER v. BOARD OF EDUC. OF NEBO SCHOOL DIST.

Supreme Court of Utah, 1954.
1 Utah 2d 375, 267 P.2d 768.

HENRIOD, JUSTICE. Appeal from a judgment holding that the minutes of a local board of education meeting, transcribed by its Clerk, were not a public writing subject to inspection under Titles 78–26–1, 2, U.C.A. 1953. Reversed, no costs awarded.

This appears to be a friendly suit to determine applicability of our statutes on public writings to the facts of this case, and there is nothing here indicating any disposition to withhold information on the part of anyone. It is here on the pleadings, which reflect the following circumstances: On Feb. 16, 1953, in answer to the Clerk's inquiry, the State Superintendent of Public Instr., legal adviser to boards under the terms of an unusual statute, where one not an attorney may act in that capacity, advised the Clerk that minutes of local board meetings were not official until approved by the board, which body should determine its own policy with reference to releasing such minutes to persons other than board members. On Feb. 18, the board held a meeting which was open to the public. The Clerk took notes of what transpired, and transcribed them into minutes for board approval and placement in his Journal. On Feb. 19 the plaintiffs asked permission to examine and copy the minutes so transcribed, but the Clerk, partly because of the Superintendent's letter, advised that they would not be available for inspection until the board approved them at its next meeting. The minutes, as transcribed, later were approved by the board unchanged, and were placed in the Journal which, by statute, the Clerk must keep. What was in the minutes, unfortunately, was not presented to us, so we cannot determine what, if any, action was taken that might have been of such public concern as to require immediate publication, or whether it was so inconsequential that immediate publication would serve no useful purpose.

Plaintiffs urge that the notes of the Clerk, or at least the transcribed minutes, prepared for Journal entry, subject only to board approval, were a public writing under our statute and should have been open to inspection immediately after preparation, and that preparation immediately should have followed the meeting. Defendants say this might lead to public misinformation and embarrassment to board members because of possible inaccuracies in what they claim were tentative minutes, unofficial until approved and placed in the Journal.

The statutes and cases relating to public writings are divergent as the shading of the spectrum. There appears to be no formula for determining what is or is not a public writing, except by defining the terms, looking at the facts, and relying on court decisions for determination and settlement. The contentions of opposing counsel, however, point up what frequently is true, that between two extremes, not necessarily midway, there is a point where reason shows brightest, dimming as the point shifts in one direction or the other. To hold that a public writing includes the unexpurgated scribbled notes of a Clerk, legible, perhaps, to him alone, would be unreasonable, we think, and even might deify doodling. It would be unreasonable also to hold that any record made by the Clerk short of approval by a board and placement in a Journal, is not a public writing. Such conclusion might deify dawdling. We hold, therefore, that the Clerk's untranscribed notes reasonably are not classifiable as a public writing under the statute, whereas the transcribed minutes, in final form, but awaiting only approval and placement in the Journal, are a public writing in contemplation of the statute. In so holding, we are aware of those authorities stating that not every memorandum of a public officer is a public record. We believe, however, that the more pertinent cases are found in a long line holding that whenever a written record of a transaction of a public officer in his office is a *convenient* and *appropriate* mode of discharging the duties of his office, and is kept by him as such, whether required by express provision of law or not, such a record is a public record. To hold that the minutes in this case were not, but the Journal was, a public writing, would attach a magic significance to the word "journal," and might repose in boards a power to act on matters of great public moment without opportunity for public scrutiny.

Here the Clerk did everything he intended to do by way of recording the meeting. Under the statute he could have placed the minutes in the Journal as soon as prepared. The board's policy of having him refrain from doing so until approval was had cannot justify circumvention of a statute requiring him to prepare the minutes, nor the withholding of information from the public for an unreasonable length of time. It is no answer to our conclusions to say that the meeting was open to the public. We cannot blind ourselves to the facts that many such meetings go unattended by the public, that no newspaper can have its agents at all of such meetings, and that no country editor can be in two towns or counties at once.

The parties here have requested that we address ourselves also to the matter of *when* the minutes should be available for public inspection. We cannot determine here *when* the Clerk reasonably should have had his minutes available to the public, since nobody has told us what was in them. We believe that what is a reasonable time to prepare a record of a public board meeting depends entirely on the facts of each case. If the board action called for the purchase of textbooks advocating communism, the record reasonably should be prepared for public release at once after the meeting, while a resolution to dismiss school on Washington's Birthday perhaps need never be documented,—at least so far as one very important segment of the public is concerned,—the children. It seems to us that the reasonable time when the record of such meetings should be made available to the public, may vary with the exigencies of the particular case, and the time for preparation and dissemination would be directly proportional to the importance of the action taken.

Both sides concede that the public is entitled to know what happened at school board meetings within a reasonable time. Competent authority supports this proposition. We believe further, that a reasonable time after the meeting for making available the record of actions taken there would be some time *before* any important action was to take place. If available only *after* action was taken, such information would have little or no news value, except as it might be the basis for criticism of injudicious action. The people would be precluded from indulging their traditionally democratic practice and privilege of complaining of or approving the actions of their elected servants.

There is the further problem as to when *information* of what transpired at the meeting should be made available to the public, quite apart from documentation in a public writing. It would seem that, unless matters were of such a delicate nature or of the type where public policy dictates nondissemination, the meeting itself should be open to the public and press, and information concerning what transpired there should be made available, at least in a general way, to both at any time thereafter, by him whose duties require its recordation. There is nothing unreasonable in that under our free and democratic way of life. The truth about the official acts of public servants always should be displayed in the public market place, subject to public appraisal. Any attempt to withhold information after a meeting, itself should be a subject for a wide publicity, irrespective of the fact that withholding it might prevent someone's embarrassment because of inaccuracy. Such inaccuracy may be reason enough to replace him responsible therefor, but most certainly is no reason for withholding information to which the public is entitled; nor to prevent the embarrassment of anyone; nor to perpetuate anyone in public office. We believe and hold that although the Clerk's action in refusing permission to inspect his minutes, was reasonable for the purpose of obtaining an adjudication of correlative rights and duties, it would be unreasonable in preventing the public and press from obtaining information as to what happened at the meeting.

* * *

Notes

1. What problems may arise from having citizens or the press gain information about a meeting through the words of the board clerk before they have been approved by the board? Is possible misinformation a risk well-taken in the interest of prompt public access to the records?

2. Do you agree with the court's view that a reasonable time after the meeting for making available the record of actions taken there would be some time *before* any important action was to take place?

3. Board minutes may be amended at any time to conform to what in fact occurred at a meeting. Jewell v. Board of Educ., DuQuoin Community Unit Schools, Dist. No. 300, 19 Ill.App.3d 1091, 312 N.E.2d 659 (1974).

[Case No. 141] Right of Taxpayer to Photograph Board Records

PEOPLE EX REL. GIBSON v. PELLER

Appellate Court of Illinois, 1962.

34 Ill.App.2d 372, 181 N.E.2d 376.

BURKE, JUSTICE. Plaintiffs are residents and taxpayers of the area comprising School District 89 and have children who attend a school of the district. Defendants are members of the Board of Education of the district and govern and administer the schools within the district. On April 4, 1960, at a designated time and place previously consented to by the defendants for the inspection of the financial records of the Board of Education of the district for the years 1955 through 1960, the plaintiffs were refused the right to make photographic reproduction thereof. They had brought a professional photographer with them to enable them to photographically reproduce the records. In their pleadings plaintiffs allege the right to photograph the records under the common law as well as pursuant to the State Records Act, Sec. 43.7, Ch. 116, Ill.Rev.Stat. 1959. The pleadings present the issue whether relators have the right to photograph the records. From the judgment that a writ of mandamus issue commanding the defendants to permit relators to examine and reproduce by photographic means the financial records of expenditures and receipts of the Board for the years 1955 to 1960, inclusive, the defendants appeal.

Defendants insist that the State Records Act does not apply to them. They concede the right of relators to inspect the records and take copies thereof when necessary to the attainment of justice. They deny the right of relators to photograph the records for the period mentioned. We are of the opinion that the State Records Act applies to members of a Board of Education and to the public records in custody of the members and the Board. A Board of Education is an agency of the state government. As an agency of the state government the nature and status of the Board of Education is administrative. The Board of Education executes and administers the law promulgated by the Legislature. The Board of Education is an executive administrative agency of the state. Inasmuch as it is an agency of the state government and its members public officers of the state government, Sec. 43.7 of the State Records Act applies to permit the relators to photograph the records of the Board of Education.

The right of relators to reproduce the public records is not solely dependent upon statutory authority. There exists at common law the right to reproduce, copy and photograph public records as an incident to the common law right to inspect and use public records. Good public policy requires liberality in the right to examine public records. In 76 C.J.S. Records § 35, p. 133, the author states: "The right of access to, and inspection of, public records is not entirely a matter of statute. The right exists at common law, and, in the absence of a controlling statute, such right is still governed by the common law. * * * All authorities are agreed that at common law a person may inspect public records * * * or make copies or memoranda thereof." In Clay v. Ballard, 87 Va. 787, 790, 13 S.E. 262, 263, the court said that at common law the right to inspect includes the right to copy.

Defendants say that relators have the right to look, examine and inspect with the naked eye the public records and copy by hand these public records, but that they have no right to photograph the records. This argument cannot be sustained by logic or common knowledge. Modern photography is accurate, harmless, noiseless and time saving. It does nothing more than capture that which is seen with the naked eye. Neither defendants nor the public can be harmed by the reproduction of the records exactly as they exist. The fact that more modern methods of copying are devised should not lessen the basic right given under the common law. The State Records Act declares the public policy relating to public records in the State of Illinois. It does not abrogate the common law.

* * *

Notes

1. Are there any valid reasons for not allowing the use of photographic equipment with official documents? Note that in this case a professional photographer accompanied the taxpayers.

2. An appellate court in New Jersey has held that records may be copied with portable photographic equipment that would not impair records and is used within business hours without interfering with office routine. Moore v. Board of Freeholders of Mercer County, 76 N.J.Super. 396, 184 A.2d 748 (1962), mod. 39 N.J. 26, 186 A.2d 676 (1962).

3. The Court of Appeals of Michigan found no affirmative duty on a school board to furnish copies of board minutes by mail to the teachers association even if the association paid the cost. Ravenna Educ. Ass'n v. Ravenna Public Schools, 70 Mich.App. 196, 245 N.W.2d 562 (1976), remanded [on technical grounds], Ravenna Educ. Ass'n v. Ravenna Public Schools, 399 Mich. 854, 251 N.W.2d 564 (1977).

[Case No. 142] Residence for Voting Purposes—Disqualified Voters

WEHRUNG v. IDEAL SCHOOL DIST. NO. 10

Supreme Court of North Dakota, 1956.
78 N.W.2d 68.

GRIMSON, JUDGE. On the 14th day of October 1955, the Ideal School District No. 10, of McKenzie County, North Dakota, held an election to determine whether to issue negotiable bonds in the amount not exceeding $120,000. A notice of said election was duly published and at said election 480 votes were cast in favor of issuance of the bonds and 237 were cast against it. The vote in favor was more than the required 66⅔ rds percent of the voters who had voted. As a result the proposition of issuing the bonds was declared carried. In due time seven taxpayers of Ideal School District No. 10 commenced a contest of the election alleging that the election had been conducted illegally and that many illegal votes were cast. They prayed that the officers of the district be enjoined from proceeding further and that the election be declared null and void. The contestees deny the illegality of the election. A hearing was duly had in district court and judgment entered sustaining the election. The contestants appealed to this court and ask for a trial de novo.

There are several issues but appellants summarize them under three points as follows:

"1. Permitting, or requiring, an unqualified voter to disclose how he voted.

"2. Permitting people, not qualified voters of the district, to vote.

"3. Permitting the voters of the First Addition to the Wold Addition in the townsite of Watford City to vote claiming that that Addition was not legally annexed to the Ideal School District."

As to the first point the contestants and appellants presented 12 witnesses who were examined as to their legal qualifications to vote at that election. When the witnesses were examined as to how they voted at this election the court informed those whom it found to be qualified voters that they did not need to disclose that fact unless they wished to do so. In Torkelson v. Byrne, 68 N.D. 13, 276 N.W. 134, 113 A.L.R. 1213, this court held the qualified elector cannot be compelled to disclose for whom he voted. However, this privilege of secrecy is entirely a personal one and the voter himself may waive his privilege and testify for whom he voted.

Two voters were found to be disqualified to vote in this election. As to those two voters the court ruled they would have to disclose how they voted. In Hanson v. Village of Adrian, 126 Minn. 298, 148 N.W. 276, the court held:

"Having proven that the contestees voted without right, it is proper by competent evidence to ascertain how they voted, so as to purge the election of the illegal vote."

The court was clearly right in requiring the disqualified voters to disclose how they voted and to deduct their votes from the total. As it happened one voted for and the other against the bonds so that the result was not changed, and more than 66⅔rds percent remained in favor of bonds.

On the next point the contestants and appellants object to the ruling of the court holding several of the challenged voters were qualified to vote. They especially question the votes of Earl Quale and his wife. Mr. Quale testified that he had a home in Watford City located in Ideal School District No. 10; that for more than a year while he had no work in Watford City he had been living temporarily in Arnegard, renting his home in Watford City because he needed the income from the rent to save his home from foreclosure; that even though his children went to school at Arnegard during that time he always intended to come back to make Watford City his permanent home; that he now has work there and is waiting until his tenant finds another place to move into, so that he can bring his family back to his home; that he never voted in Arnegard. Other witnesses were cross-examined as to their residence and disclosed that even though they temporarily worked on a farm or other places, they had a home in Watford City and always intended to return there and never voted anywhere else.

Residence is the place where one lives when not called elsewhere for labor or other special purposes and to which on such occasions he returns. There can be only one residence and it cannot be lost until another is gained. It can be changed only by union of act and intent. The testimony of the witnesses whose residence in Watford City was questioned was that they had homes in Watford City and intended to return there and did return when occasion arrived. They had no intent of obtaining a residence anywhere else. Residence is a question of fact in which the intention of the party enters as an important element. Under the testimony those witnesses had a residence in Watford City of sufficient length of time to become qualified electors. The district court so found and the evidence supports such finding.

* * *

Notes

1. Do you agree with the rationale for the rule that a qualified voter cannot be compelled to disclose for whom he voted, but a disqualified voter can be so compelled?

2. Compare the legal concept of residence for purpose of voting with that of residence for tuition-free attendance in the public schools of a district. For the latter, see "Residence for School Purposes" in Chapter 12.

3. In Corn v. Blackwell, 191 S.C. 183, 4 S.E.2d 254 (1939), the ballots were printed and numbered consecutively from one up to hundreds. They were voted in such a manner as to render it easy to determine how each person voted. The situation arose purely by inadvertence. It was held that this destroyed the secrecy of the ballot and invalidated the election.

4. Reversing lower courts, not attempting to distinguish contrary prior Michigan cases or the many contrary cases in other jurisdictions, and not supporting its judgment with any cases or with a rationale, the Supreme Court of Michigan held that only upon a showing that the voter acted fraudulently could he be required to reveal to a court how he voted. In the case at bar 17 voters were mistakenly registered in Ann Arbor and "apparently in good faith" had voted in an election for mayor that had been decided by one vote out of 21,319 votes cast. Belcher v. Mayor of City of Ann Arbor, 402 Mich. 132, 262 N.W.2d 1 (1978).

[Case No. 143] Misadvice to Electors in School Election

GRANT v. SCHOOL DIST. NO. 61, BAKER COUNTY

Supreme Court of Oregon, 1966.
244 Or. 131, 415 P.2d 165.

DENECKE, JUSTICE. This is a declaratory judgment proceeding brought because of a controversy concerning the formation of an Administrative School District and the acts of such District.

Under the provisions of what is now ORS 330.505 et seq., the Baker County School Reorganization Committee proposed an Administrative School District, in effect consolidating several school districts in the northeastern part of the county. The residents of Eagle Valley, the area of one of the school districts, were apprehensive that the proposed district would cause them to lose their high school and that one high school, to serve the entire district, would be built in the more populous Pine Valley. At a public hearing on the proposed new district, called pursuant to the school reorganization statute, a document was referred to which commenced, "To Whomsoever It May Concern." It was signed by the directors and clerks of all the districts proposed to be in the new Administrative District. It provided, among other things, as follows: "That no school be changed, moved or consolidated without the approval of the patrons in the attendance area which that school serves."

The complaint filed by plaintiffs as representatives of the residents of Eagle Valley alleges that the Eagle Valley residents "were advised that said agreement [the above-quoted statement] would be incorporated in the school district reorganization plan." The "said agreement" was not in fact incorporated in the school reorganization plan. Plaintiffs further allege that because of their belief that they would continue to have their own high school until they approved a change, they voted in favor of the new Administrative District.

About five years after the new Administrative District was formed, a majority of the voters of the new district passed a bond issue for one high school for the entire district, to be built in Pine Valley.

The plaintiffs sought a declaration that the defendant Administrative District had no right to move the school without obtaining the consent of the Eagle Valley voters.

The trial court held against the plaintiffs and we affirm its ruling.

Art. VIII, § 3, of the Oregon Constitution, vests the state legislature with the responsibility for public education.

The legislature has provided that a bond issue is passed and binding upon the entire district if it is approved by a majority of the voters in the entire district. ORS 328.230.

That legislative command is binding upon the new district. The alleged misadvice to the Eagle Valley voters cannot change or limit that legislative command. See West Missouri Power Co. v. City of Washington, 80 F.2d 420, 422 (10th Cir.1935), and Anselmi v. City of Rock Springs, 53 Wyo. 223, 239, 80 P.2d 419, 425, 116 A.L.R. 1250 (1938), holding that misrepresentations made during a campaign by public officials will not vitiate an election.

Affirmed.

Notes

1. Compare this case with Ricker v. Board of Education [Case No. 39] in which alleged misinformation was included in a widely circulated brochure.

2. In common business transactions, misrepresentations relied upon by another to his detriment are grounds for invalidating the transactions. Should a different rule apply to misadvice in election cases?

3. Consider the possible effect upon the sale of school bonds if their validity might be destroyed because of misadvice to voters. If this case had not involved a bond issue which was passed, but rather some other action by the board of education, do you think the decision might have been different?

4. The Supreme Court of Arizona, reversing the state Court of Appeals, held that an election to rescind a bond issue approved at a prior election could be compelled upon proper petition as long as no bonds had been sold. The court acknowledged that other courts were divided on the question. Members of Bd. of Educ. of Pearce Union High School Dist. v. Leslie, 112 Ariz. 463, 543 P.2d 775 (1975).

5. The election was invalidated where, contrary to statute, a school board candidate was not designated as an incumbent. Other incumbents were properly designated. The error was unintentional. Rizzo v. Board of Election Com'rs of Revere, 403 Mass. 20, 525 N.E.2d 409 (1988).

[Case No. 144] Applicability of One Person-One Vote to School Boards

HADLEY v. JUNIOR COLLEGE DIST. OF METROPOLITAN KANSAS CITY, MISSOURI

Supreme Court of the United States, 1970.
397 U.S. 50, 90 S.Ct. 791, 25 L.Ed.2d 45.

Mr. Justice Black delivered the opinion of the Court.

This case involves the extent to which the Fourteenth Amendment and the "one man, one vote" principle apply in the election of local governmental officials. Appellants are residents and taxpayers of the Kansas City School District, one of eight separate school districts that have combined to form the Junior College District of Metropolitan Kansas City. Under Missouri law separate school districts may vote by referendum to establish a consolidated junior college district and elect six trustees to conduct and manage the necessary affairs of that district. The state law also provides that these trustees shall be apportioned among the separate school districts on the basis of "school enumeration," defined as the number of persons between the ages of six and 20 years, who reside in each district. In the case of the Kansas City School District this apportionment plan results in the election of three trustees, or 50% of the total number from that district. Since that district contains approximately 60% of the total school enumeration in the junior college district, appellants brought suit claiming that their right to vote for trustees was being unconstitutionally diluted in violation of the Equal Protection Clause of the Fourteenth Amendment. The Missouri Supreme Court upheld the trial court's dismissal of the suit, stating that the "one man, one vote" principle was not applicable in this case. * * * [F]or the reasons set forth below we reverse and hold that the Fourteenth Amendment requires that the trustees of this junior college district be apportioned in a manner that does not deprive any voter of his right to have his own vote given as much weight, as far as is practicable, as that of any other voter in the junior college district.

* * *

This Court has consistently held in a long series of cases, that in situations involving elections, the States are required to insure that each person's vote counts as much, insofar as it is practicable, as any other person's. We have applied this principle in congressional elections, state legislative elections, and local elections. The consistent theme of those decisions is that the right to vote in an election is protected by the United States Constitution against dilution or debasement. While the particular offices involved in these cases have varied, in each case a constant factor is the decision of the government to have citizens participate individually by ballot in the selection of certain people who carry out governmental functions. Thus in the case now before us, while the office of junior college trustee differs in certain respects from those offices considered in prior cases, it is exactly the same in the one crucial factor—these officials are elected by popular vote.

When a court is asked to decide whether a State is required by the Constitution to give each qualified voter the same power in an election open to all, there is no discernible, valid reason why constitutional distinctions should be drawn on the basis of the purpose of the election. If one person's vote is given less weight through unequal apportionment, his right to equal voting participation is impaired just as much when he votes for a school board member as when he votes for a state legislator. While there are differences in the powers of different officials, the crucial consideration is the right of each qualified voter to participate on an equal footing in the election process. It should be remembered that in cases like this one we are asked by voters to insure that they are given equal treatment, and from their perspective the harm from unequal treatment is the same in any election, regardless of the officials selected.

* * *

It has also been urged that we distinguish for apportionment purposes between elections for "legislative" officials and those for "administrative" officers. Such a suggestion would leave courts with an * * * unmanageable principle since governmental activities "cannot easily be classified in the neat categories favored by civics texts," and it must also be rejected. We therefore hold today that as a general rule, whenever a state or local government decides to select persons by popular election to perform governmental functions, the Equal Protection Clause of the Fourteenth Amendment requires that each qualified voter must be given an equal opportunity to participate in that election, and when members of an elected body are chosen from separate districts, each district must be established on a basis that will insure, as far as is practicable, that equal numbers of voters can vote for proportionally equal numbers of officials. * * *

* * *

Although the statutory scheme reflects to some extent a principle of equal voting power, it does so in a way that does not comport with constitutional requirements. This is so because the Act necessarily results in a systematic discrimination against voters in the more populous school districts. This discrimination occurs because whenever a large district's percentage of the total enumeration falls within a certain percentage range it is always allocated the number of trustees corresponding to the bottom of that range. Unless a particular large district has exactly 33⅓%, 50%, or 66⅔% of the total enumeration it will always have proportionally fewer trustees than the small districts. As has been pointed out, in the case of the Kansas City School District approximately 60% of the total enumeration entitles that district to only 50% of the trustees. Thus while voters in large school districts may frequently have less effective voting power than residents of small districts, they can never have more. Such built-in discrimination against voters in large districts cannot be sustained as a sufficient compliance with the constitutional mandate that each person's vote count as much as another's, as far as practicable. Consequently Missouri cannot allocate the junior college trustees according to the statutory formula employed in this case. We would be faced with a different question if the deviation from equal apportionment presented in this case resulted from a plan that did not contain a built-in bias in favor of small districts, but rather from the inherent mathematical complications in equally apportioning a small number of trustees among a limited number of component districts. We have said before that mathematical exactitude is not required; but a plan that does not automatically discriminate in favor of certain districts is.

In holding that the guarantee of equal voting strength for each voter applies in all elections of governmental officials, we do not feel that the States will be inhibited in finding ways to insure that legitimate political goals of representation are achieved. We have previously upheld against constitutional challenge an election scheme that required that candidates be residents of certain districts that did not contain equal numbers of people. Since all the officials in that case were elected at large, the right of each voter was given equal treatment. We have also held that where a State chooses to select members of an official body by appointment rather than election, and that choice does not itself offend the Constitution, the fact that each official does not "represent" the same number of people does not deny those people equal protection of the laws. And a State may, in certain cases, limit the right to vote to a particular group or class of people. * * * But once a State has decided to use the process of popular election and "once the class of voters is chosen and their qualifications specified, we see no constitutional way by which equality of voting power may be evaded."

* * *

Notes

1. The vote was six-to-three.

2. Do you see any disadvantages that might accrue to education if legislatures, in order to avoid the instant interpretation, would make more education offices appointive?

3. In Kramer v. Union Free School Dist. No. 15, 395 U.S. 621, 89 S.Ct. 1886, 23 L.Ed.2d 583 (1969), the Supreme Court by a five-to-three margin declared unconstitutional a New York statute restricting voting in school elections in some districts essentially to parents of children enrolled in the public schools and owners or lessees of taxable real property and their spouses. " * * * [T]he issue is not whether the legislative judgments are rational. A more exacting standard obtains. The issue is whether the [statutory] requirements do in fact sufficiently further a compelling state interest to justify denying the franchise" to a bachelor living with his parents. The statutory requirements were "not sufficiently tailored to limiting the franchise to those 'primarily interested' in school affairs to justify the denial of the franchise to appellant and members of his class."

4. On the day it announced the *Kramer* decision (preceding Note), the Court unanimously invalidated a Louisiana statute allowing only "property taxpayers" to vote in an election called to approve the issuance of public utility bonds. Cipriano v. City of Houma, 395 U.S. 701, 89 S.Ct. 1897, 23 L.Ed.2d 647 (1969). Justices Black and Stewart, who had dissented in *Kramer*, here concurred because "this case involves a voting classification 'wholly irrelevant to achievement' of the State's objective."

5. The power to levy taxes is not absolutely requisite for a school board to be subject to the one person-one vote rule. Baker v. Regional High School Dist. No. 5, 520 F.2d 799 (2 Cir.1975), cert. den. 423 U.S. 995, 96 S.Ct. 422, 46 L.Ed.2d 369 (1975).

[Case No. 145] Power of Board to Expend Funds to Advocate Favorable Vote

CITIZENS TO PROTECT PUBLIC FUNDS v. BOARD OF EDUC. OF PARSIPPANY-TROY HILLS TP.

Supreme Court of New Jersey, 1953.
13 N.J. 172, 98 A.2d 673.

WILLIAM J. BRENNAN, JR., J. * * * Defendant proposed a program for enlarging several school buildings and to issue bonds in the amount of $560,000 to finance the first half of the program. There being existing debt limitations, approval of the proposal, as required by R.S. 18:5–86, as amended, N.J.S.A., was first obtained from the State Commissioner of Education and the Local Government Board before the proposal was submitted, as is also required by that statute and as was in any event required by R.S. 18:7–73, N.J.S.A., to a referendum vote at an election held December 2, 1952 when the proposal was adopted by a vote of 875 to 542. However, the defendant board did not prior to that election submit the proposed building expansion plans to the local planning board for approval as to "location, character and extent thereof," according to R.S. 40:55–7, as amended by L.1948, c. 464, and L.1949, c. 157, N.J.S.A.

When the building program was authorized by resolution adopted August 27, 1952, the 1952–1953 school budget included an appropriation

captioned "Current expenses, administrative, architecture fees, preliminary." Some $358.85 of this appropriation was spent by defendant for
"printing, artist's work and postage" to print and circulate an 18-page
booklet entitled "Read the Facts Behind the Parsippany-Troy Hills
School Building Program." All but one page of the booklet depicts in
graphic form, effectively illustrated to arrest the reader's attention, such
facts as the growth of the grade school population (from 1945, doubled,
and by 1956 to be tripled), the inadequacies of existing facilities, the
proposed immediate additions, with architectural sketches, to two
schools, other expansions planned to be deferred until 1955, the aggregate and annual costs, principal and interest, of the immediate program
and the effect upon taxes of such cost. However, there also appears on
the cover and on two of the pages "Vote Yes," and "Vote Yes—December
2, 1952," and an entire page which, except for an accompanying sketch,
we reproduce:

"What Will Happen if You Don't Vote Yes?"

"Double Sessions!!!"

"This will automatically Cheat your child of $\frac{1}{3}$ of his education
(4 hours instead of 6).

"Yearly school changing and hour long Bus rides will continue
for many children.

"Morning Session (8:30–12:30) Children will leave home $\frac{1}{2}$
hour earlier.

"Afternoon Session (12:30–4:30) Children will return home 1$\frac{1}{2}$
hours later (many after dark).

"Children in some families would be attending different sessions (depending upon grade).

"Transportation costs will increase (could double) with 2 sets of
bus routes per day.

"Temporary room rentals will continue ($4,000 per year).

"Double use of equipment will necessitate more rapid replacement.

"Note: Operating expenses will continue to rise as the enrollment increases (more teachers, more supplies and equipment
for children. This Will Be So Whether We Build Or Not.)"

On December 1, the day before the referendum election, radio
station WMTR broadcast a 15-minute panel discussion of the proposed
building program as one of the station's "public interest" programs.
The panel was composed of a member of the defendant board of
education and two members of a citizens advisory committee which
assisted the board in the formulation of the building program. The
superintendent of schools, with the approval of the board's president,
advised the principals of the several schools equipped with public address
systems or radios that school children in grades four to eight might be
permitted to hear the broadcast. According to the numerous affidavits
of teachers offered to support defendant's motion for dismissal, some

turned on the program and others did not, the reception was unsatisfactory in many instances and the broadcast for that reason was not heard, many children paid no attention to it, and the reaction of at least one class was why "do we have to listen to this sort of thing." And it appears without contradiction that the panel discussion was purely informative as to the scope of the building program and that there was no exhortation to vote affirmatively for the proposed bond issue at the referendum election the next day. * * *

The contention that there was error in the denial of a declaratory judgment as to the legality of the expenditures for the printing and distribution of the booklet, and the exposure of school children to the radio broadcast is premised solely upon the assertion that the same things may be done or attempted by the defendant board in connection with the balance of the building program upon its submission to the electorate for adoption. It was conceded on the oral argument that the actions under attack, if improper, would not suffice to invalidate the election already held. But the actions taken, it is admitted, had particular relation only to the proposal before the electorate on December 2, 1952, and for aught that appears they seem to have spent their force. The booklet on its face shows that it is not intended for use in connection with future plans for completing the balance of the expansion program. Plainly, then, any issues as to both the booklet and the radio broadcast are moot and the resolution of new, or even similar, issues as to other actions attempted by the defendant for a similar purpose in the future must await the event.

* * *

There is no express statutory provision authorizing the expenditure by boards of education of public funds in the manner done by the defendant board for the printing and distribution of the booklet. The power, however, within the limits hereafter stated, is to be found by necessary or fair implication in the powers expressly conferred by R.S. 18:7–77.1, N.J.S.A., which enumerates the permissible items which may be included in the annual budget, and more particularly as incident to "(b) the building, enlarging, repairing or furnishing of a schoolhouse or schoolhouses."

The power so implicit plainly embraces the making of reasonable expenditures for the purpose of giving voters relevant facts to aid them in reaching an informed judgment when voting upon the proposal. In these days of high costs, projects of this type invariably run into very substantial outlays. This has tended to sharpen the interest of every taxpayer and family man in such projects. Adequate and proper school facilities are an imperative necessity, but the large additional tax burden their cost often entails concerns taxpayers that they be obtained with the maximum economy of cost. At the same time the complexities of today's problems make more difficult the task of every citizen in reaching an intelligent judgment upon the accommodation of endurable financial cost with the acknowledged need for adequate education. The need for full disclosure of all relevant facts is obvious, and the board of education is well qualified to supply the facts. But a fair presentation of the facts will necessarily include all consequences, good and bad, of the proposal, not only the anticipated improvement in educational opportunities, but also the increased tax rate and such other less desirable consequences as may be foreseen. If the presentation is fair in that sense, the power to make reasonable expenditure for the purpose may fairly be implied as within the purview of the power, indeed duty, of the board of education to formulate the construction program in the first instance. And the choice of the media of communication to give such facts, whether by the use of a booklet, as in this case, radio broadcast, newspaper advertising, or other means, is within the discretion, reasonably exercised, of the board of education. The booklet under attack here, in 17 of its 18 pages, fairly presents the facts as to need and the advantages and disadvantages of the program, including the tax effect of its cost, and if it stopped there, none could fairly complain that the reasonable expenditure made for its preparation and distribution was without the scope of the implied power.

But the defendant board was not content simply to present the facts. The exhortation "Vote Yes" is repeated on three pages, and the dire consequences of the failure so to do are over-dramatized on the page reproduced above. In that manner the board made use of public funds to advocate one side only of the controversial question without affording the dissenters the opportunity by means of that financed medium to present their side, and thus imperilled the propriety of the entire expenditure. The public funds entrusted to the board belong equally to the proponents and opponents of the proposition, and the use of the funds to finance not the presentation of facts merely but also arguments to persuade the voters that only one side has merit, gives the dissenters just cause for complaint. The expenditure is then not within the implied power and is not lawful in the absence of express authority from the Legislature. In Mines v. DelValle, 201 Cal. 273, 257 P. 530, 537 (Cal.Sup.Ct.1927), it was said:

> "It must be conceded that the electors of said city opposing said bond issue had an equal right to and interest in the funds in said power fund as those who favored said bonds. To use said public funds to advocate the adoption of a proposition which was opposed by a large number of said electors would be manifestly unfair and unjust to the rights of said last-named electors, and the action of the board of public service commissioners in so doing cannot be sustained, unless the power to do is given to said board in clear and unmistakable language."

And in Elsenau v. City of Chicago, 334 Ill. 78, 165 N.E. 129, 131 (Ill.Sup.Ct.1929), appears the following:

> "The conduct of a campaign, before an election, for the purpose of exerting an influence upon the voters, is not the exercise of an authorized municipal function and hence is not a corporate purpose of the municipality."

We do not mean that the public body formulating the program is otherwise restrained from advocating and espousing its adoption by the voters. Indeed, as in the instant case, when the program represents the body's judgment of what is required in the effective discharge of its responsibility, it is not only the right but perhaps the duty of the body to endeavor to secure the assent of the voters thereto. The question we are considering is simply the extent to and manner in which the funds may with justice to the rights of dissenters be expended for espousal of the voters' approval of the body's judgment. Even this the body may do within fair limits. The reasonable expense, for example, of the conduct of a public forum at which all may appear and freely express their views pro and con would not be improper. The same may be said of reasonable expenses incurred for radio or television broadcasts taking the form of debates between proponents of the differing sides of the proposition. It is the expenditure of public funds in support of one side only in a manner which gives the dissenters no opportunity to present their side which is outside the pale.

We acknowledge that the limits here pronounced are not suggested in the decision of the former Court of Errors and Appeals in City Affairs Committee of Jersey City v. Board of Com'rs of Jersey City, 134 N.J.L. 180, 46 A.2d 425 (1945). We are persuaded, however, that simple fairness and justice to the rights of dissenters require that the use by public bodies of public funds for advocacy be restrained within those limits in the absence of a legislative grant in express terms of the broader power.

* * *

Notes

1. Justice Brennan was confirmed as Associate Justice of the United States Supreme Court in 1957.

2. Observe that the court relies more on holdings from Illinois and California than on prior New Jersey holdings.

3. A school board appropriated $100 toward the cost of a one-day workshop conducted by a public relations consulting firm on the subject of promoting a bond issue. It was held that this was not ground for invalidating the election. The court did not have before it the legality of the expenditure, but it commented that "if this expenditure was illegal, the board members may be liable to repay the amount spent." Eustace v. Speckhart, 14 Or.App. 485, 514 P.2d 65 (1973).

4. School funds may be spent for school employees to draw up building plans, and in most jurisdictions funds may be expended for educational and architectural consultants. Examine the logic that no funds may be spent to urge acceptance of the result.

5. If school authorities have worked diligently with community participation to develop a proposal for school improvement, is strict neutrality as regards its acceptance clearly in the public interest? How can board members work for its acceptance within the bounds of this decision?

6. In 1992 the Supreme Court of Mississippi cited this case as "unquestionably, the most thorough discussion of permissible expenditures by public bodies." That court held personally liable for flagrantly unauthorized expenditures (including campaign workers and a fish fry) in support of a school bond referendum those board members who voted affirmatively on the matter. Smith v. Dorsey, 599 So.2d 529 (Miss.1992).

APPENDIX

PRINCIPAL PROVISIONS OF THE UNITED STATES CONSTITUTION

Article I, Section 10

No State shall * * * pass any * * * law impairing the obligation of contracts * * *.

after 14th – State & municipal too!

Amendment 1

Congress shall make no law respecting an establishment of religion, or prohibiting the free exercise thereof; or abridging the freedom of speech, or of the press; or the right of the people peaceably to assemble, and to petition the Government for a redress of grievances.

Amendment 4

The right of the people to be secure in their persons, houses, papers, and effects, against unreasonable searches and seizures, shall not be violated, and no warrants shall issue, but upon probable cause, supported by oath or affirmation, and particularly describing the place to be searched, and the persons or things to be seized.

Amendment 5

No person * * * shall be compelled in any criminal case to be a witness against himself, nor be deprived of life, liberty, or property, without due process of law; nor shall private property be taken for public use, without just compensation.

Amendment 8

Excessive bail shall not be required, nor excessive fines imposed, nor cruel and unusual punishments inflicted.

Amendment 10

The powers not delegated to the United States by the Constitution, nor prohibited by it to the States, are reserved to the States respectively, or to the people.

Amendment 11

The judicial power of the United States shall not be construed to extend to any suit in law or equity, commenced or prosecuted against one of the United States by citizens of another State, or by citizens or subjects of any foreign State.

Amendment 14

All persons born or naturalized in the United States, and subject to the jurisdiction thereof, are citizens of the United States and of the State wherein they reside. No State shall make or enforce any law which shall abridge the privileges or immunities of citizens of the United States; nor shall any State deprive any person of life, liberty, or property, without due process of law; nor deny to any person within its jurisdiction the equal protection of the laws.

* * *

PRINCIPAL FEDERAL STATUTORY PROVISIONS

Title VI of Civil Rights Act of 1964

[42 U.S.C. § 2000d]

No person in the United States shall, on the ground of race, color or national origin, be excluded from participation in, be denied the benefits of, or be subjected to discrimination under any program or activity receiving Federal financial assistance. [See Civil Rights Restoration Act of 1987.]

Title VII of Civil Rights Act of 1964

[42 U.S.C. § 2000e-2(a)]

It shall be an unlawful employment practice for an employer (1) to fail or refuse to hire or to discharge any individual, or otherwise to discriminate against any individual with respect to his compensation, terms, conditions, or privileges of employment, because of such individual's race, color, religion, sex, or national origin; or (2) to limit, segregate, or classify his employees or applicants for employment in any way which would deprive or tend to deprive any individual of employment opportunities or otherwise adversely affect his status as an employee, because of such individual's race, color, religion, sex, or national origin.

Age Discrimination in Employment Act of 1967

[29 U.S.C. § 623a]

It shall be unlawful for an employer (1) to fail or refuse to hire or to discharge any individual or otherwise discriminate against any individual with respect to his compensation, terms, conditions, or privileges of employment, because of such individual's age; (2) to limit, segregate, or classify his employees in any way which would deprive or tend to deprive any individual of employment opportunities or otherwise adversely affect his status as an employee, because of such individual's age; or (3) to reduce the wage rate of any employee in order to comply with this chapter.

The prohibitions in this Chapter shall be limited to individuals who are at least 40 years of age. 29 U.S.C. § 631(a). [Originally (1967) an upper age of 65 was established. Amendment in 1978 raised the upper age to 70. Amendment in 1986 removed it completely.]

Title IX of Education Amendments of 1972

[20 U.S.C. § 1681]

No person in the United States shall, on the basis of sex, be excluded from participation in, be denied the benefits of, or be subjected to discrimination under any education program or activity receiving Federal financial assistance. [See Civil Rights Restoration Act of 1987.]

Section 504 of Rehabilitation Act of 1973

[29 U.S.C. § 794]

No otherwise qualified handicapped individual in the United States * * * shall, solely by reason of his handicap, be excluded from the participation in, or be denied the benefits of, or be subjected to discrimination under any program or activity receiving Federal financial assistance * * *. [See Civil Rights Restoration Act of 1987.]

Family Educational Rights and Privacy Act of 1974

[20 U.S.C. § 1232g]

[Applies to educational records maintained by institutions receiving federal funds. Records of individual students must be accessible to their parents and not be released to third parties without parental knowledge or consent. A parent has the right to a hearing to challenge the accuracy of a record and the right to place with the record a statement of disagreement.]

Education for All Handicapped Children Act of 1975

Individuals with Disabilities Education Act (as of 1990)

[20 U.S.C. § 1401]

[States receiving federal financial assistance must identify handicapped children and provide a "free appropriate public education which emphasizes special education and related services designed to meet their unique needs." Parents must be involved in helping school authorities develop an "individualized education program" for each student. "Related services" include "developmental, corrective, and other supportive services * * * as may be required to assist a handicapped child to benefit from special education * * *." Extensive "procedural safeguards" are afforded parents.]

Pregnancy Discrimination Act of 1978

[42 U.S.C. § 2000e (k)]

The terms "because of sex" or "on the basis of sex" include, but are not limited to, because of or on the basis of pregnancy, childbirth, or related medical conditions; and women affected by pregnancy, childbirth, or related medical conditions shall be treated the same for all employment-related purposes, including receipt of benefits under fringe benefit programs, as other persons not so affected but similar in their ability or inability to work * * *.

Equal Access Act of 1984

[20 U.S.C. § 4071]

[Provides that if a public secondary school receiving financial assistance "grants an offering to or opportunity for one or more noncurriculum related student groups to meet on school premises during noninstructional time" it must not "deny equal access or a fair opportunity to, or discriminate against, any students who wish to conduct a meeting * * * on the basis of the religious, political, philosophical, or other content of the speech at such meetings."]

Civil Rights Restoration Act of 1987

[20 U.S.C. § 1687]

[If "any part" of an educational entity receives federal funds, "all of the operations" of the entity must comply with "Title VI," "Title IX," and "Section 504."]

Americans with Disabilities Act of 1990

[42 U.S.C. § 12101]

[Prohibits discrimination in employment (and other situations) against any "qualified individual with a disability." Essentially it amplifies and extends prohibitions of Section 504 of the Rehabilitation Act of 1973. Coverage is not dependent on involvement of federal funds. A "reasonable accommodation" that would permit a qualified individual with a disability to perform the "essential functions" of a position must be provided.]

Civil Rights Act of 1991

[P.L. 102–166, 105 Stat. 1071]

[Treats several technical, procedural, and remedial matters related to discrimination-in-employment cases. It authorizes jury trials and affords new remedies including compensatory and punitive damages for intentional discrimination (disparate treatment). The former could include future pecuniary loss and emotional pain, and the latter could be awarded if the defendant acted with malice or reckless indifference to the rights of the plaintiff. Also, see footnote 71 in Chapter 9.]

Section 1981 (Civil Rights Act of 1866)

[42 U.S.C. § 1981]

All persons within the jurisdiction of the United States shall have the same right in every State and Territory to make and enforce contracts * * * as is enjoyed by white citizens * * *.

Section 1983 (Civil Rights Act of 1871)

[42 U.S.C. § 1983]

Every person who, under color of any statute, ordinance, regulation, custom, or usage, of any State or Territory, subjects, or causes to be subjected, any citizen of the United States or other person within the jurisdiction thereof to the deprivation of any rights, privileges, or immunities secured by the Constitution and laws, shall be liable to the party injured in an action at law, suit in equity, or other proper proceeding for redress.

GLOSSARY

[See also Index]

Abatement. Termination of a lawsuit.

Action. Lawsuit.

Ad litem. For the purposes of a particular lawsuit.

Affidavit. A written statement made under oath.

Agent. One authorized to act in behalf of another.

Amicus curiae. Friend of the court, applied to a brief submitted by one not a party to the suit.

Appellant. Party who brings an action in a higher court.

Appellee. Party against whom an action is brought in a higher court.

Arguendo. For the sake of argument something is assumed to be true.

Assault. A threat or attempt to inflict bodily injury where the victim has reason to believe the injury may be inflicted.

Battery. Wrongful physical touching of a person.

Bequest. Gift of personal property by a will.

Bona fide. In good faith.

Case at bar. The case presently being decided by the court.

Caveat. Let him or her beware; a warning.

Certiorari. Proceeding in which a higher court reviews a decision of an inferior court.

Class action. A lawsuit brought by one or more persons on behalf of all persons similarly situated as to complaint and remedy sought.

Collateral. Indirect; not directly connected to the matter at hand.

Color of law. Appearance of legal right, but actually contrary to law.

Complainant. One initiating a lawsuit; plaintiff.

Consent decree. A judgment that is agreed upon by the parties to a suit and approved by a court. It is not the result of a judicial determination, but is subject to continued judicial supervision.

Cy pres. As near as possible. Doctrine can be invoked by a court when the purpose of a charitable trust cannot be literally fulfilled.

Damages. Monetary award to a party who has been injured by the wrongful act of another party. Damages usually are "compensatory" (actually demonstrated or reasonably estimated) to redress the wrong. Under very special circumstances they can be "punitive" or "exemplary" to punish the wrongdoer and serve as a deterrent.

993

Declaratory judgment. A judgment establishing the rights of the parties or deciding a point of law without an order for any action.

De facto. In fact; in reality.

Defendant. Party against whom an action is brought.

De jure. By action of law.

De minimis. Something so insignificant as to be unworthy of judicial attention.

Demurrer. Allegation to the effect that, even if facts asserted by plaintiff are true, there is no cause of action.

De novo. New; a proceeding at which all that transpired at prior proceedings is ignored.

Deposition. Statement of a witness under oath (obtained before trial) in question and answer format with cross-examination (as if it were given in court).

Devise. Gift of real estate by a will.

Dicta. Statements in a judicial opinion not necessary to the decision of the case.

Directory. Involving no invalidating consequence if disregarded.

Duress. Unlawful pressure to do what one ordinarily would not do.

Ejusdem generis. Rule that if a listing of specifics is followed by general words, the general words are considered to apply only to items of the same kind or nature as the specifics.

En banc. By all judges of the court.

Enjoin. Command to maintain the status quo either by doing or refraining from doing a specific act; the writ is called an injunction.

Equity. Concept of fairness or justice whereby a court is empowered to remedy a situation where rights are being violated but existing law does not cover the situation.

Estoppel. A bar precluding one from making an assertion because of his prior act.

Et al. And others.

Et seq. And those following.

Executory. Not completed; dependent on the occurrence of some future act.

Ex officio. By authority of the office held.

Express. Directly set forth in words.

Expunge. Obliterate; physically remove, as from a record.

Ex rel. On the information supplied by.

Face. What the words alone mean, without amplification or specific application.

Haec verba. The same words; identical.

Holding. A ruling by the court; court's decision on a question properly raised in a case.

Inclusio unius est exclusio alterius. Rule that the inclusion of certain items constitutes an exclusion of others.

Infra. Below; following.

Injunction. See "enjoin."

In loco parentis. In place of the parent, having some of the rights and duties of a parent.

Instant case. The case presently being decided by the court.

Inter alia. Among other things.

Ipso facto. In and of itself.

Judgment. Final determination by the court of the rights of parties of a case.

Laches. Unreasonable delay in bringing a legal action to assert a right, which delay may result in prejudice to an adverse party.

Liable. Legally responsible.

Malfeasance. Doing of an act that is unlawful.

Malice. Improper motive; intentionally committing a wrongful act without justification or excuse.

Mandamus. Writ ordering the execution of a non-discretionary duty by one charged with responsibility therefor.

Mandatory. Involving an invalidating consequence if violated.

Material. Important.

Merits. The factual issues raised, as distinguished from procedural issues; substance of a case, rather than technicalities.

Ministerial. Not involving discretion as to whether or how an act is to be performed; administrative rather than policy-making.

Misfeasance. Doing improperly an act that is lawful.

Mitigation. Diminution of a penalty imposed by law, as with damages for breach of contract which are reduced in amount by circumstances not barring the cause of action but affecting only the extent of the injury.

Modus operandi. Method of accomplishing an act.

Moot case. A case in which the factual controversy no longer exists and in which a judgment would be abstract with no practical effect.

Nexus. Connection.

Nolens volens. With or without consent.

Nonfeasance. Failing to perform a duty.

Novation. Substitution of a new obligation for an old one.

Nunc pro tunc. Acts permitted to be done after the time that they should have been done and given retroactive effect.

Opinion. Reasoning that explains the conclusion reached by a judge. The "opinion of the court" is that reasoning accepted by a majority of the participating judges; it authoritatively enunciates the law of the case. Views of individual judges who agree with the court's judgment may appear in "concurring opinions"; of judges who disagree, in "dissenting opinions".

Parens patriae. Concept of the state's guardianship over persons unable to direct their own affairs, e.g., minors.

Pari materia. On the same subject matter.

Pendent jurisdiction. Doctrine whereby federal courts under limited conditions can decide matters of state law as well as federal matters involved in a single lawsuit.

Per curiam. By the court; an opinion with no identification of the author.

Per se. In and of itself.

Petitioner. Party bringing a case before a court; the appellant in a case appealed.

Plaintiff. Party instituting a legal action.

Police power. The inherent power of government to impose restrictions in order to provide for health, safety, and welfare of its constituents.

Preempt. Take control of; preclude actions by others.

Prima facie. On its face; evidence supporting a conclusion unless it is rebutted.

Pro forma. As a matter of form; not carefully considered.

Quantum meruit. As much as was deserved; reasonable value of goods furnished or services rendered.

Quasi. As if; almost.

Quid pro quo. Something done in exchange for an act of another.

Quo warranto. By what authority, writ to test claim to a public office.

Ratio decidendi. Reasoning applied by a court to crucial facts of a case in process of determining the judgment.

Reductio ad absurdum. Interpretation which would lead to results clearly illogical or not intended.

Remand. Send back a case to the court from which it was appealed for further action by the lower court.

Res judicata. A matter finally decided by the highest court of competent jurisdiction.

Respondent. Party against whom a legal action is brought; the appellee in a case appealed.

Reverter. A provision whereby one who transfers property retains the right to reclaim the property under specific conditions.

Scienter. Knowledge of a set of facts.

Stare decisis. Doctrine of precedents whereby prior decisions of courts are followed under similar facts.

Status quo. Positions and relationships existing at a particular point in time.

Sua sponte. Voluntarily; without necessity or prompting.

Sub judice. Being considered by a court.

Summary. Immediate; without a full proceeding.

Supra. Above; preceding.

Tort. A civil wrong not involving contracts.

Ultra vires. Outside the legal power of an individual or body.

Vacate. Annul.

Vel non. Or not.

Vested. Fixed; accrued; not subject to any contingency.

Void. Having no legal force or effect.

Waiver. Voluntary and intentional relinquishment of a known right.

*

INDEX

References are to Pages

TRANSPORTATION—Cont'd
Use for desegregation, 185–186, 866, 869–870, 879–880, 881–884, 886–887, 902–903.
Use of funds for, 303–308.
Use of privately owned automobiles, 388–389.
Withdrawal of, 306.
Withholding state funds, 129.

TRUANCY
See Compulsory Education.

ULTRA VIRES CONTRACTS
See Contracts.

UNIONS
See Collective Negotiations.

UNWED MOTHERS
Students, 754–755.
Teachers, 653.

VACCINATION
Prerequisite to school attendance, 743–745.

VACCINATION—Cont'd
Requirement for all persons, 743.

VETERANS PREFERENCE
In employment, 491–492.

VOTER QUALIFICATIONS
In general, 962–963.
One person-one vote principle, 963–964.
Special qualifications for school elections, 963, 982.

VOTING
At board meetings, see Board Voting.
On school propositions, see Elections.
Qualifications of voters, see Voter Qualifications.

WARRANTS
Issued by school districts, 264, 466.

WORKERS COMPENSATION
Coverage, 319–320, 393.

ZONING CODE
Application to schools, 199–200.

†